# Springer International Handbooks of Education

The *Springer International Handbooks of Education* series aims to provide easily accessible, practical, yet scholarly, sources of information about a broad range of topics and issues in education. Each *Handbook* follows the same pattern of examining in depth a field of educational theory, practice and applied scholarship, its scale and scope for its substantive contribution to our understanding of education and, in so doing, indicating the direction of future developments. The volumes in this series form a coherent whole due to an insistence on the synthesis of theory and good practice. The accessible style and the consistent illumination of theory by practice make the series very valuable to a broad spectrum of users. The volume editors represent the world's leading educationalists. Their task has been to identify the key areas in their field that are internationally generalizable and, in times of rapid change, of permanent interest to the scholar and practitioner.

Joerg Zumbach • Douglas A. Bernstein •
Susanne Narciss • Giuseppina Marsico
Editors

# International Handbook of Psychology Learning and Teaching

Volume 2

With 64 Figures and 92 Tables

*Editors*
Joerg Zumbach
Department of Educational Research
University of Salzburg
Salzburg, Austria

Douglas A. Bernstein
Department of Psychology
University of South Florida
Tampa, FL, USA

Susanne Narciss
School of Science -
Faculty of Psychology, Psychology
of Learning and Instruction
Technische Universitaet Dresden
Dresden, Sachsen, Germany

Giuseppina Marsico
Department of Human, Philosophical and
Educational Sciences (DISUFF)
University of Salerno
Fisciano, Italy

ISSN 2197-1951  ISSN 2197-196X (electronic)
Springer International Handbooks of Education
ISBN 978-3-030-28744-3  ISBN 978-3-030-28745-0 (eBook)
https://doi.org/10.1007/978-3-030-28745-0

© Springer Nature Switzerland AG 2023
This work is subject to copyright. All rights are reserved by the Publisher, whether the whole or part of the material is concerned, specifically the rights of translation, reprinting, reuse of illustrations, recitation, broadcasting, reproduction on microfilms or in any other physical way, and transmission or information storage and retrieval, electronic adaptation, computer software, or by similar or dissimilar methodology now known or hereafter developed.
The use of general descriptive names, registered names, trademarks, service marks, etc. in this publication does not imply, even in the absence of a specific statement, that such names are exempt from the relevant protective laws and regulations and therefore free for general use.
The publisher, the authors, and the editors are safe to assume that the advice and information in this book are believed to be true and accurate at the date of publication. Neither the publisher nor the authors or the editors give a warranty, expressed or implied, with respect to the material contained herein or for any errors or omissions that may have been made. The publisher remains neutral with regard to jurisdictional claims in published maps and institutional affiliations.

This Springer imprint is published by the registered company Springer Nature Switzerland AG.
The registered company address is: Gewerbestrasse 11, 6330 Cham, Switzerland

# Preface

As reflected in its title, this *International Handbook of Psychology Learning and Teaching* was designed to be a comprehensive reference text devoted to presenting ideas for how to improve the learning and teaching of psychology worldwide. Its chapters are aimed at a broad audience, including psychology teacher trainees and new faculty members who are interested in the basics of how and what to teach, as well as more experienced professors who are interested in training psychology teachers or in evaluating and improving the effectiveness of their own teaching.

We were motivated to create the handbook partly because, although teaching and learning can be designed and evaluated from a general educational perspective, psychology, like all other academic disciplines, has its own traditions, course content, and approaches to teaching and learning, a phenomenon sometimes referred to as *pedagogical content knowledge* (cf. Koehler & Mishra, 2008). We wanted to showcase that knowledge by providing a comprehensive description of psychology's core goals, contents, and topics, as well as the methods, approaches, and resources available for teaching psychology in psychology programs and elsewhere.

We hope the handbook will also inspire psychology teachers to engage in research in the scholarship of teaching and learning (SoTL; e.g., Felten, 2013). SoTL has been defined as "the systematic study of teaching and learning, using established or validated criteria of scholarship, to understand how teaching (beliefs, behaviors, attitudes, and values) can maximize learning, and/or develop a more accurate understanding of learning, resulting in products that are publicly shared for critique and use by an appropriate community" (Potter & Kustra, 2011, p. 2).

In psychology, that community is growing dramatically as the role of pedagogical content knowledge in our discipline has received more and more attention in recent years from psychology teachers who conduct, share, and discuss research on psychology learning and teaching (Dunn et al., 2010). Their ideas and results are being published in such US journals as *Teaching of Psychology* and *The Scholarship of Teaching and Learning in Psychology*, as well as in *Psychology Learning and Teaching*, the journal of the European Society of Psychology Learning and Teaching (ESPLAT), and elsewhere. Their work is also being presented at numerous national and international teaching conferences (e.g., ESPLAT and the U.S.'s National Institute on the Teaching of Psychology) as well as in teaching strands at research-oriented international conferences such as those of the American Psychological Association, the

Association for Psychological Science, and the International Congress of Psychology. We hope that this handbook will contribute to, expand, and inspire further the discussion among members of this community.

The handbook's chapters were written by expert psychology teachers from all over the world and cover topics germane to the teaching of all core courses in psychology, whether taught in psychology programs or as part of curricula in other disciplines. Each chapter includes an introduction to its topic, provides some historical context, a review of relevant literature, a summary of theory- and evidence-based approaches to teaching course content, including in various educational and cultural contexts, and advice on best practices in those contexts. Some chapters also provide guidelines and checklists designed to support psychology teachers in their daily work.

The handbook includes three major sections, each of which contains several chapters. The first section, "Teaching Psychology as Main Discipline in Undergraduate and Graduate Programs," focuses on psychology teaching and learning as a main discipline in undergraduate and graduate psychology programs. The chapters in this section address each of the major psychological sub-disciplines and offers evidence-based advice on how best to teach the courses within those sub-disciplines. The second section, "Psychology Learning and Teaching for All Audiences," focuses on several target audiences within and outside tertiary education. The third section includes several chapters on "General Educational and Instructional Approaches to Psychology Learning and Teaching."

Because it covers all central fields of Psychology, all major target groups, and all major relevant educational and instructional approaches, we hope that this handbook will provide a solid base for psychology teachers worldwide, serving as a stimulus for SoTL research in psychology, as an introductory text for new teachers, and as a guide for those involved in the development of teacher training programs, course and curriculum design, syllabus writing, assessment of teacher and student performance, and the like.

December 2022

Joerg Zumbach
Douglas A. Bernstein
Susanne Narciss
Giuseppina Marsico

**References**

Dunn, D. S., Beins, B. B., McCarthy, M.A., & Hill, G. W. (Eds.). (2010). *Best practices for teaching beginnings and endings in the psychology major: Research, cases, and recommendations*. Oxford: University Press.

Felten, P. (2013). Principles of good practice in SoTL. *Teaching and Learning Inquiry, 1*(1), 121–125.

Koehler, M., & Mishra, P. (2009). What is technological pedagogical content knowledge (TPACK)? *Contemporary Issues in Technology and Teacher Education, 9*(1), 60–70.

Potter, M. K., & Kustra, E. (2011). The relationship between scholarly teaching and SoTL: Models, distinctions, and clarifications. *International Journal for the Scholarship of Teaching and Learning, 5*(1). http://www.georgiasouthern.edu/ijsotl

# Contents

## Volume 1

**Part I  Teaching Psychology as Main Discipline in Undergraduate and Graduate Programs** ........................................ 1

1 **Teaching Introductory Psychology** .......................... 3
   Melissa J. Beers and Bridgette Martin Hard

2 **Learning and Teaching in Clinical Psychology** ............... 25
   Susanne Knappe

3 **Mapping Normality: Teaching Abnormal Psychology** .......... 49
   Brian L. Burke and Megan C. Wrona

4 **Sensation and Perception** .................................. 75
   Robert Gaschler, Mariam Katsarava, and Veit Kubik

5 **Teaching the Psychology of Learning** ...................... 101
   Stephanie A. Jesseau

6 **Teaching of General Psychology: Problem Solving** ........... 131
   David Gibson, Dirk Ifenthaler, and Samuel Greiff

7 **General Psychology Motivation** ........................... 151
   Maria Tulis and J. Lukas Thürmer

8 **Topics, Methods, and Research-Based Strategies for Teaching Cognition** ................................................. 177
   Maya M. Khanna and Michael J. Cortese

9 **How to Design and Teach Courses on Volition and Cognitive Control** ................................................... 201
   Thomas Goschke and Annette Bolte

10 **Developmental Psychology** ................................ 239
    Moritz M. Daum and Mirella Manfredi

| 11 | Developmental Psychology: Moving Beyond the East–West Divide | 273 |
|---|---|---|
| | Nandita Chaudhary, Mila Tuli, and Ayesha Raees | |
| 12 | Teaching Physiological Psychology | 301 |
| | Jane A. Foster | |
| 13 | Teaching Social Psychology Effectively | 313 |
| | Scott Plous, David G. Myers, Mary E. Kite, and Dana S. Dunn | |
| 14 | Teaching Health Psychology Here, There, and Everywhere | 339 |
| | Arianna M. Stone and Regan A. R. Gurung | |
| 15 | Educational Psychology: Learning and Instruction | 357 |
| | Neil H. Schwartz, Kevin Click, and Anna N. Bartel | |
| 16 | Neuroscience in the Psychology Curriculum | 391 |
| | Jennifer Parada and Leighann R. Chaffee | |
| 17 | Teaching the Foundations of Psychological Science | 421 |
| | Regan A. R. Gurung and Andrew Christopher | |
| 18 | The Methodology Cycle as the Basis for Knowledge | 437 |
| | Jaan Valsiner and Angela Uchoa Branco | |
| 19 | Qualitative Methodology | 453 |
| | Günter Mey | |
| 20 | Psychological Assessment and Testing | 479 |
| | Leslie A. Miller and Ruby A. Daniels | |
| 21 | Individual Differences and Personality | 513 |
| | Manfred Schmitt | |
| 22 | Teaching of Work and Organizational Psychology in Higher Education | 539 |
| | Niclas Schaper | |
| 23 | Teaching Engineering Psychology | 567 |
| | Sebastian Pannasch, Martin Baumann, Lewis L. Chuang, and Juergen Sauer | |
| 24 | Cultural Psychology | 589 |
| | Luca Tateo, Giuseppina Marsico, and Jaan Valsiner | |
| 25 | Teaching Media Psychology | 609 |
| | Christopher J. Ferguson | |
| 26 | Unfurling the Potential of the Counselor | 629 |
| | Sujata Sriram and Swarnima Bhargava | |

| 27 | Gender Studies | 659 |

Tissy Mariam Thomas and U. Arathi Sarma

| 28 | Teaching School Psychology to Psychologists | 699 |

M. Beatrice Ligorio, Stefano Cacciamani, and Emanuela Confalonieri

| 29 | Community Psychology and Psychological Distress | 725 |

Paul Rhodes

| 30 | Indigenous Psychology | 741 |

Danilo Silva Guimarães

| 31 | Teaching Psychopharmacology for Undergraduates | 763 |

Jennifer M. J. McGee

## Volume 2

**Part II  Psychology Learning and Teaching for All Audiences** .... **789**

| 32 | Psychology in Social Science and Education | 791 |

Monica Mollo and Ruggero Andrisano Ruggieri

| 33 | Psychology in Teacher Education | 807 |

Susanne Narciss and Joerg Zumbach

| 34 | Teaching Psychology in Secondary Education | 847 |

Rob McEntarffer and Kristin Whitlock

| 35 | Psychology in Work and Organizational Education | 865 |

Pedro F. Bendassolli, Sonia Gondim, and Fellipe Coelho-Lima

| 36 | Psychological Literacy and Learning for Life | 881 |

Julie A. Hulme and Jacquelyn Cranney

| 37 | Psychology in Professional Education and Training | 911 |

Christoph Steinebach

| 38 | Teaching Sport and Exercise Psychology | 943 |

Robert Weinberg and Joanne Butt

| 39 | Family Therapy | 965 |

Maria Elisa Molina, Pablo Fossa, and Viviana Hojman

| 40 | Medical Education | 979 |

Ricardo Gorayeb and M. Cristina Miyazaki

| 41 | Psychology of Art | 993 |

Lia da Rocha Lordelo

42  Psychology and Social Work Through Critical Lens  ........... 1011
    Maria Cláudia Santos Lopes de Oliveira and Tatiana Yokoy

43  Learning and Teaching Geropsychology  .................... 1041
    Thomas Boll

44  Psychology of Special Needs and Inclusion  ................. 1077
    Mirella Zanobini, Paola Viterbori, and Maria Carmen Usai

45  Teaching the Psychology of Religion and Spirituality  ......... 1097
    Timothy A. Sisemore

46  Epistemology of Psychology  .............................. 1117
    Gordana Jovanović

47  Psychology in Health Science  ............................ 1143
    Giulia Savarese, Luna Carpinelli, and Tiziana Marinaci

**Part III  General Educational and Instructional Approaches to Psychology Learning and Teaching** ........................ **1169**

48  Basic Principles and Procedures for Effective Teaching
    in Psychology  ......................................... 1171
    Douglas A. Bernstein

49  First Principles of Instruction Revisited  .................... 1201
    M. David Merrill

50  Problem-Based Learning and Case-Based Learning  ........... 1235
    Joerg Zumbach and Claudia Prescher

51  Inquiry-Based Learning in Psychology  ..................... 1255
    Marie Lippmann

52  Small Group Learning  .................................. 1285
    Ingo Kollar and Martin Greisel

53  Service Learning  ...................................... 1305
    Robert G. Bringle, Roger N. Reeb, Luzelle Naudé, Ana I. Ruiz, and
    Faith Ong

54  Assessment of Learning in Psychology  ..................... 1331
    Lisa Durrance Blalock, Vanessa R. Rainey, and Jane S. Halonen

55  Formative Assessment and Feedback Strategies  .............. 1359
    Susanne Narciss and Joerg Zumbach

56  Technology-Enhanced Psychology Learning and Teaching  ...... 1387
    Helmut Niegemann

| | | |
|---|---|---|
| **57** | **A Blended Model for Higher Education** ..................... 1407 <br> M. Beatrice Ligorio, Francesca Amenduni, and Katherine McLay | |
| **58** | **Learning and Instruction in Higher Education Classrooms** ..... 1431 <br> Neil H. Schwartz and Anna N. Bartel | |
| **Index** | ............................................................ | 1457 |

# About the Editors

**Joerg Zumbach** received his Diploma in Psychology in 1999 from Ruprecht-Karls-University Heidelberg, Germany. He got his Dr. phil. in Educational Psychology 2003 from Ruprecht-Karls-University Heidelberg, Germany. Since 2006 he is Full Professor for Science Teaching and Learning Research and e-Learning at the Paris-Lodron University Salzburg, Austria. He served there as head of department and co-director of the School of Education. He also was and is in different editorial boards (e.g., *Journal of Educational Multimedia and Hypermedia*, *International Journal of Learning Technologies*, *Journal of Interactive Learning Research*, *Computers in Human Behavior*, *Psychology Teaching and Learning*). He authored and co-authored various research articles and textbooks in the areas of Multimedia and Hypermedia Learning, Higher Education, Problem-Based Learning, and Violent Media and Aggression among others.

**Doug A. Bernstein** received his bachelor's degree in psychology at the University of Pittsburgh in 1964 and his master's and Ph.D. degrees in clinical psychology at Northwestern University in 1966 and 1968, respectively. From 1968 to 1998, he was on the psychology faculty at the University of Illinois at Urbana-Champaign where he served as Associate Department Head and Director of Introductory Psychology. He is currently Professor Emeritus at Illinois and Courtesy Professor of Psychology at the University of South Florida. In 2013, he stepped down after 30 years as chairman of the National Institute on the Teaching of Psychology, and in 2018 he founded the Biennial International Seminar on the Teaching of Psychological Science in Paris. He has written or co-authored a book on the teaching of psychology, as well as textbooks on introductory, clinical, and abnormal psychology and on criminal behavior and progressive relaxation training.

**Susanne Narciss** is full professor and head of the research team "Psychology of Learning and Instruction (PsyLI)" at the Technische Universitaet Dresden. Her current interests include research on (a) promoting self-regulated learning, (b) the role of motivation and metacognition in instructional contexts, (c) conditions and effects of interactive learning tasks, and (d) conditions and effects of informative tutoring feedback strategies. Her work on feedback strategies was considered cutting-edge by the American Association on Educational Communication and Technology (AECT) and was awarded the prestigious AECT Distinguished Development Award 2007. Susanne Narciss is not only a productive scholar but also dedicates her expertise, time, and effort to improve the teaching and learning of psychology. She has been member of the founding executive board of the European Society for Psychology Teaching and Learning (ESPLAT) and was elected ESPLAT's President in September 2021.

## About the Editors

**Giuseppina Marsico** is Associate Professor of Development and Educational Psychology at the University of Salerno (Italy) and Visiting Professor at Ph.D. Programme in Psychology, Federal University of Bahia (Brazil). She is President Elect of the American Psychological Association – Division 52 International Psychology and President Elect of the European Society of Psychology Learning and Teaching (ESPLAT). She has 20 years of experience as a researcher, with a proven international research network. She is Editor-in-Chief of the Book Series Cultural Psychology of Education (Springer), Latin American Voices – Integrative Psychology and Humanities (Springer), co-editor of SpringerBriefs Psychology and Cultural Developmental Sciences (together with Jaan Valsiner), and Annals of Cultural Psychology: Exploring the Frontiers of Mind and Society (InfoAge Publishing, N.C., USA, together with Carlos Cornejo e Jaan Valsiner). She is also co-editor of *Human Arenas: An Interdisciplinary Journal of Psychology, Culture and Meaning* (Springer), and of *Trends in Psychology* (Springer); Associate Editor of *Cultural & Psychology Journal* (Sage) and *Social Psychology of Education* (Springer); and member of the editorial board of several international academic journals (i.e., IPBS – *Integrative Psychological & Behavioural Science*, Springer). Her academic tracks and list of publications include two complementary lines of investigations: (1) an educational-focused research activity where Giuseppina Marsico is the leading figure of the new field of Cultural Psychology of Education and (2) a cultural-oriented interdisciplinary perspective based on both theoretical and empirical investigation, focusing on the borders as a new ontogenetic perspective in psychology and other social sciences. Giuseppina Marsico has established a new research field called Developmental Mereotopology.

# Contributors

**Francesca Amenduni**  University of Rome 3, Rome, Italy

**Ruggero Andrisano Ruggieri**  University of Salerno, Fisciano, Italy

**Anna N. Bartel**  Department of Psychology, University of Wisconsin, Madison, WI, USA

**Martin Baumann**  Department of Human Factors, Ulm University, Ulm, Germany

**Melissa J. Beers**  The Ohio State University, Columbus, OH, USA

**Pedro F. Bendassolli**  Universidade Federal do Rio Grande do Norte, Natal, Brazil

**Douglas A. Bernstein**  Department of Psychology, University of South Florida, Tampa, FL, USA

**Swarnima Bhargava**  School of Human Ecology, Tata Institute of Social Sciences, Mumbai, India

**Lisa Durrance Blalock**  Department of Psychology, University of West Florida, Pensacola, FL, USA

**Thomas Boll**  Department of Cognitive, and Behavioural Sciences, Institute for Lifespan Development, Family, and Culture, University of Luxembourg, Esch-sur-Alzette, Luxembourg

**Annette Bolte**  Faculty of Psychology, Technische Universität Dresden, Dresden, Germany

**Angela Uchoa Branco**  Department of Psychology, University of Brasilia, Brasilia DF, Brazil

**Robert G. Bringle**  Indiana University Purdue University Indianapolis, Indianapolis, IN, USA

**Brian L. Burke**  Psychology, Fort Lewis College, Durango, CO, USA

**Joanne Butt**  School of Sport & Exercise Sciences, Liverpool John Moores University, Liverpool, UK

**Stefano Cacciamani** University of Valle D'Aosta, Aosta, Italy

**Luna Carpinelli** Department of Medicine, Surgery, and Dentistry 'Scuola Medica Salernitana', University of Salerno (Italy), Fisciano/Baronissi, Italy

**Leighann R. Chaffee** University of Washington, Tacoma, Tacoma, WA, USA

**Nandita Chaudhary** Department of Human Development and Childhood Studies, Lady Irwin College, University of Delhi, Delhi, India

**Andrew Christopher** Albion College, Albion, MI, USA

**Lewis L. Chuang** Institute for Informatics, Ludwig-Maximilians-Universität München, München, Germany

IfADo – Leibniz Research Centre for Working Environment and Human Factors, Dortmund, Germany

**Kevin Click** Department of Psychology, California State University, Chico, CA, USA

**Fellipe Coelho-Lima** Universidade Federal do Rio Grande do Norte, Natal, Brazil

**Emanuela Confalonieri** Catholic University of the Sacred Heart of Milan, Milan, Italy

**Michael J. Cortese** Department of Psychology, University of Nebraska at Omaha, Omaha, NE, USA

**Jacquelyn Cranney** Psychology, University of New South Wales, Sydney, NSW, Australia

**Ruby A. Daniels** Texas A&M University - San Antonio, San Antonio, TX, USA

**Moritz M. Daum** Department of Psychology, Developmental Psychology: Infancy and Childhood, University of Zurich, Zurich, Switzerland

Jacobs Center for Productive Youth Development, University of Zurich, Zurich, Switzerland

**Maria Cláudia Santos Lopes de Oliveira** Institute of Psychology, University of Brasília, Brasília, Brazil

**Dana S. Dunn** Moravian University, Bethlehem, PA, USA

**Christopher J. Ferguson** Stetson University, DeLand, FL, USA

**Pablo Fossa** Universidad del Desarrollo de Chile, Santiago, Chile

**Jane A. Foster** Department of Psychiatry and Behavioural Neurosciences, McMaster University, Hamilton, ON, Canada

**Robert Gaschler** Department of Psychology, FernUniversität in Hagen, Hagen, Germany

**David Gibson** Curtin University, Perth, Australia

**Sonia Gondim** Universidade Federal da Bahia, Salvador, Brazil

**Ricardo Gorayeb** School of Medicine, São Paulo University, Ribeirão Preto, Brazil

**Thomas Goschke** Faculty of Psychology, Technische Universität Dresden, Dresden, Germany

**Samuel Greiff** University of Luxembourg, Esch-sur-Alzette, Luxembourg

**Martin Greisel** Lehrstuhl für Psychologie m.b.B.d. Pädagogischen Psychologie, University of Augsburg, Augsburg, Germany

**Regan A. R. Gurung** Psychological Science, Oregon State University, Corvallis, OR, USA

**Jane S. Halonen** Department of Psychology, University of West Florida, Pensacola, FL, USA

**Bridgette Martin Hard** Duke University, Durham, NC, USA

**Viviana Hojman** Universidad del Desarrollo de Chile, Santiago, Chile

**Julie A. Hulme** School of Psychology, Keele University, Keele, Staffordshire, UK

**Dirk Ifenthaler** Curtin University, Perth, Australia
University of Mannheim, Mannheim, Germany

**Stephanie A. Jesseau** University of Nebraska-Omaha, Omaha, NE, USA

**Gordana Jovanović** Belgrade, Serbia

**Mariam Katsarava** Department of Psychology, FernUniversität in Hagen, Hagen, Germany

**Maya M. Khanna** Department of Psychological Science, Creighton University, Omaha, NE, USA

**Mary E. Kite** Ball State University, Muncie, IN, USA

**Susanne Knappe** Institute of Clinical Psychology and Psychotherapy, Technische Universität Dresden, Dresden, Germany
Evangelische Hochschule Dresden (ehs), University of Applied Sciences for Social Work, Education and Nursing, Dresden, Germany

**Ingo Kollar** Lehrstuhl für Psychologie m.b.B.d. Pädagogischen Psychologie, University of Augsburg, Augsburg, Germany

**Veit Kubik** Department of Psychology, Universität Bielefeld, Bielefeld, Germany

**M. Beatrice Ligorio** University of Bari, Bari, Italy

**Marie Lippmann** California State University, Chico, CA, USA

**Mirella Manfredi** Department of Psychology, Developmental Psychology: Infancy and Childhood, University of Zurich, Zurich, Switzerland

**Tiziana Marinaci** Department of Medicine, Surgery, and Dentistry 'Scuola Medica Salernitana', University of Salerno (Italy), Fisciano/Baronissi, Italy

**Giuseppina Marsico** Department of Human, Philosophical and Educational Sciences (DISUFF), University of Salerno, Fisciano, Italy

**Rob McEntarffer** Lincoln Public Schools, Lincoln, NE, USA

**Jennifer M. J. McGee** Department of Psychology, Oxford College of Emory University, Atlanta, GA, USA

**Katherine McLay** University of Queensland (AU), Brisbane, Australia

**M. David Merrill** Utah State University, St. George, UT, USA

**Günter Mey** University of Applied Sciences Magdeburg-Stendal, Stendal, Germany

**Leslie A. Miller** LanneM TM, LLC and Rollins College, Winter Park, FL, USA

**M. Cristina Miyazaki** School of Medicine, FAMERP, São José do Rio Preto, Brazil

**Maria Elisa Molina** Universidad del Desarrollo de Chile, Santiago, Chile

**Monica Mollo** University of Salerno, Fisciano, Italy

**David G. Myers** Hope College, Holland, MI, USA

**Susanne Narciss** School of Science - Faculty of Psychology, Psychology of Learning and Instruction, Technische Universitaet Dresden, Dresden, Sachsen, Germany

**Luzelle Naudé** University of the Free State, Bloemfontein, South Africa

**Helmut Niegemann** Saarland University, Educational Technology, Saarbrücken, Germany

**Faith Ong** Ngee Ann Polytechnic, Singapore, Singapore

**Sebastian Pannasch** Faculty of Psychology, Technische Universität Dresden, Dresden, Germany

**Jennifer Parada** Bellevue College, Bellevue, WA, USA

**Scott Plous** Wesleyan University, Middletown, CT, USA

**Claudia Prescher** Technische Universität Dresden, Dresden, Germany

**Ayesha Raees** Department of Human Development and Childhood Studies, Institute of Home Economics, University of Delhi, Delhi, India

**Vanessa R. Rainey** Department of Psychology, University of West Florida, Pensacola, FL, USA

**Roger N. Reeb**  University of Dayton, Dayton, OH, USA

**Paul Rhodes**  Clinical Psychology Unit, University of Sydney, Sydney, Australia

**Lia da Rocha Lordelo**  Federal University of Recôncavo of Bahia, Santo Amaro da Purificação, Brazil

**Ana I. Ruiz**  Alvernia University, Reading, PA, USA

**U. Arathi Sarma**  Department of Psychology, University of Kerala, Thiruvananthapuram, Kerala, India

**Juergen Sauer**  Department of Psychology, University of Fribourg, Fribourg, Switzerland

**Giulia Savarese**  Department of Medicine, Surgery, and Dentistry 'Scuola Medica Salernitana', University of Salerno (Italy), Fisciano/Baronissi, Italy

**Niclas Schaper**  Psychology, University of Paderborn, Paderborn, Germany

**Manfred Schmitt**  Department of Psychology, University of Koblenz-Landau, Landau, Germany

**Neil H. Schwartz**  Department of Psychology, California State University, Chico, CA, USA

**Danilo Silva Guimarães**  Universidade de São Paulo, São Paulo, Brasil

**Timothy A. Sisemore**  St. Louis Behavioral Medicine Institute, St. Louis, MO, USA

**Sujata Sriram**  School of Human Ecology, Tata Institute of Social Sciences, Mumbai, India

**Christoph Steinebach**  ZHAW Zurich University of Applied Sciences, School of Applied Psychology, Zürich, Switzerland

**Arianna M. Stone**  Oregon State University, Corvallis, OR, USA

**Luca Tateo**  University of Oslo, Oslo, Norway

**Tissy Mariam Thomas**  Department of Psychology, University of Kerala, Thiruvananthapuram, Kerala, India

**J. Lukas Thürmer**  Department of Psychology, University of Salzburg, Salzburg, Austria

**Mila Tuli**  Department of Human Development and Childhood Studies, Institute of Home Economics, University of Delhi, Delhi, India

**Maria Tulis**  Department of Psychology, University of Salzburg, Salzburg, Austria

**Maria Carmen Usai**  Department of Educational Sciences, University of Genova, Genova, Italy

**Jaan Valsiner** Centre of Cultural Psychology, Department of Communication and Psychology, Aalborg University, Aalborg, Denmark

Sigmund Freud Privatuniversität, Vienna, Austria

**Paola Viterbori** Department of Educational Sciences, University of Genova, Genova, Italy

**Robert Weinberg** Department of Sport Leadership and Management, Miami University, Oxford, OH, USA

**Kristin Whitlock** Davis High School, Kaysville, UT, USA

**Megan C. Wrona** Fort Lewis College, Durango, CO, USA

**Tatiana Yokoy** School of Education, University of Brasília, Brasília, Brazil

**Mirella Zanobini** Department of Educational Sciences, University of Genova, Genova, Italy

**Joerg Zumbach** Department of Educational Research, University of Salzburg, Salzburg, Austria

# Part II

# Psychology Learning and Teaching for All Audiences

# Psychology in Social Science and Education

## 32

Monica Mollo and Ruggero Andrisano Ruggieri

## Contents

| | |
|---|---|
| Introduction | 792 |
| Mind and Context: What Is the Relationship? | 793 |
| From Lewin to Bronfenbrenner: Environment and Person | 795 |
| Context in Cultural-Historical Perspective and the Theory of Activity | 799 |
| From Bruner to Music: The Mind as a Generator of Sense and Meaning Within a Cultural Dynamic | 800 |
| An Example of Using the Dependent Context of the Mind in Psychology Teacher Training | 802 |
| Some Concluding Remarks | 803 |
| References | 804 |

### Abstract

The objective of this chapter is to provide skills in the analysis of the relationship between individual, social, and educational contexts. To do this, some of the theories of context in the literature are examined, which propose different interpretative models useful to understanding the relationship between context and human action. In this chapter, the concept of context is understood in terms of a complex cultural construct and represents the theoretical-conceptual background of this chapter. Following socio-constructivist theories, it is shown how the mind is influenced by context. Moreover, we provide theoretical-methodological tools that are necessary, in our opinion, to analyze the individual-mind-context relationship.

### Keywords

Mind · Context · Culture · Psychology intervention · School psychology

M. Mollo (✉) · R. Andrisano Ruggieri
University of Salerno, Fisciano, Italy
e-mail: mmollo@unisa.it; rruggeri@unisa.it

## Introduction

The purpose of this chapter is to provide the theoretical and methodological foundations for the study of social and educational psychology, as applied in social and educational settings. The ability to fruitfully analyze the network of meaning and significance present in interpersonal activities, in our opinion, allows stakeholders in the fields of education and social science to be able to enact a change in those same activities in terms of development. This is made possible when we understand the role that contexts play in the lives of individuals, how they influence their worldviews, and how they help generate meaning and significance in their actions.

In recent decades, the concept of context has been defined in multiple senses and widely used by human sciences on theoretical and operational levels. The construct has been used to understand and interpret the collective dimension of activities that human beings perform within community structures or groups.

The explicit intent of this chapter is to provide skills in analyzing the relationship between the individual and social and educational contexts. For this reason, we present some context theories that are most useful for analysis.

Empirical research on the role that social interaction plays on cognitive activity, conducted within the socio-constructivist genetic approach (Grossen & Perret-Clermont, 1984; Schubauer-Leoni, Bell, Grossen, & Perret-Clermont, 1989), has led to the re- examination of the notion of context itself, abandoning the idea of context as a mere moderator or an element external to cognitive activity. Research has empirically demonstrated how context is an integral part of cognitive activity. This notion of context has allowed research to be oriented toward more specific characteristics of social interaction, referring to the organizational factors of the setting such as norms, rules, scripts, or scenarios. Research in this direction has shown how implicit and explicit systems of rules, present within each type of social context, orient the processes of interaction and communication, creating specific spaces of activity (Iannaccone & Zittoun, 2014; Perret-Clermont, 2004).

From another point of view, the concept of context, understood in terms of social and cultural place, refers first to a general cultural theory of education (Andrisano Ruggieri, Pozzi, & Ripamonti, 2014; Bruner, 1990; Cole, 1996; Mollo, 2021; Salvatore & Scotto di Carlo, 2005; Vygotsky, 1934), which is heir to a well-established tradition of thought that has marked, with varying incisiveness, humanistic studies and particularly the search for specific interpretative models of human activity. In this way, it has been shown how individuals construct knowledge of reality by attributing meaning to it. Learning and thinking are always situated in a sociocultural context and always depend on the use of cultural resources; in this sense, the context conditions positively and/or negatively affect both the activity and the relationships and the codes of meaning and significance present (Bruner, 1996; Carli & Paniccia, 2004).

From here emerges a definition of in-text context as the place of psychic interconnection between individuals (cum *text* = text put together, written together), in which the activities of individuals, the processes through which the mind generates systems of knowledge and thought, and relationships come to be configured as inseparable from interpretive processes and the constant search for meaning within specific cultural frameworks (Bruner, 1990; Cole, 1996; Perret-Clermont, 2004; Vygotsky, 1934).

Adopting this last perspective and following a socio-constructivist approach, we intend to show in this work both how the mind is influenced by context and how the mind forms the context in connection with other minds, based on the recognition of an inter- and intra- subjective model of mental functioning. At the same time, we provide the tools necessary to analyze the individual-mind-context relationship and develop skills in this regard. In addition, the chapter examines the practical-operational implications of the proposed theoretical-methodological framework, with the example of a teacher education case.

In summary, the learning objective of this chapter is to provide theoretical-methodological tools for analyzing the relationship between the individual and context, both social and educational.

## Mind and Context: What Is the Relationship?

As mentioned above, the point of this work is to show how the main processes through which the mind generates systems of knowledge, thought, and action can be analyzed from theoretical/practical perspectives that consider the contextual, psychosocial, and cultural dimensions of human activity. Although numerous empirical studies over the years have helped to break down the individualist conception of the mind and its products, even today and particularly in collective and shared representations, this conception persists, supported by the undue generalization of the biological isolation of the human body from the environment. When we find ourselves in front of a "behavior" that we consider *strange*, i.e., not conforming/conventional, the explanation that we give is usually anchored to the individual dimension and rarely to the relational/contextual one. However, the mind, from our point of view, cannot be considered as Leibniz's monad, as a sophisticated apparatus isolated from social reality and, therefore, external to it. Vygotsky (1934) already showed how cognitive processes evolve into higher processes, thanks to the cultural dimension present in the external context and interpersonal interactions. According to Vygotsky, it is through relationships with others, mediated by cultural artifacts, that we become exponents of the human race (and ourselves). Being born part of the human species is not enough to account for the greatest creation of humanity: culture.

Even Wundt, in his famous masterpiece, *Völkerpsychologie* (Wundt devoted the last 20 years of his life to deepening the study of *Völkerpsychologie* to the point of mentioning it in his will), written in ten volumes between 1900 and 1920, stressed the importance of studying the relationship between the mind and context and, in particular, the influence that the language and customs of a given culture have on thought. Wundt's (1900) psychology analyzes consciousness, understood both in terms of individual consciousness and collective consciousness. Collective consciousness, according to Wundt, is connected to the unions between individuals and limited to certain aspects of psychic life. According to Wundt (1900), the subordinate concepts of collective consciousness, national consciousness, and others can be distinguished in the general concept of consciousness. Individual consciousness is the basis of all these further forms of consciousness. In Wundt, we find two parallel orientations: the first analyzing the individual mind, its structures, and functions, with a rigorously experimental method, and the second, interested in the mind that relates to other minds, in a historical and cultural context. According to Wundt, a further task of psychology is to explain the relationships from which the products of collective consciousness, collective will, and their properties arise.

The effort to understand the problem of the relationship between the individual mind and collective consciousness, as posed by Wundt, was taken up by George Herbert Mead, whose symbolic interactionism approach, traditionally recognized as socio-constructivist, assumes that both mind and self are constituted in social interaction. According to Mead (1934), it is through others that we become objects to ourselves; awareness of the existence of others is at the origin of awareness of ourselves. Mead theorized a constructive movement from mind to society, at the center of which is the self. In this way, he attempted to resolve the Wundtian antimony of the relationship between mind and collective consciousness, in relation to society. Mead attached considerable importance to the social act, understood as a communicative act that, according to Mead, is transformed during phylogeny, evolving from conversation to gestures to communication. Mead starts from an evolutionary perspective and takes gestures, typical of the animal species, as the key to fully understanding the construction of the mind at the level of individual development. This should be considered as part of an action completed by others; the meaning and sense are given by the response that it arouses in the person to whom the act is addressed.

For Mead, the existence of mind or intelligence is possible only in terms of gestures that are understood as meaningful symbols, because only in this way can thought take place. Thinking is an internalized or implicit conversation of the individual within the individual that takes place through such gestures, as gestures have the same meanings for all members of the society or social group. If this were not so, the individual could not internalize them or be aware of their meanings. Internalizing the external conversations of gestures that we carry on with other individuals is the essence of thought (Mead, 1934). It follows that the mind is nothing more than the internalization by the individual of the social process of communication consisting of symbols, the meaning of which is attributed during interaction.

The social act and communicative interaction are the basis of self-awareness, and from that awareness, according to Mead, emerges the self, defined as the self-aware mind. The self is divided into me and I (ego). The me is the generalized other, the internalization by the individual of the attitudes of the social group of reference. The ego, on the contrary, is the spontaneous part of the self; it is the individual who knows him/herself as an object to him/herself (Mead, 1934).

## From Lewin to Bronfenbrenner: Environment and Person

Within a processual and dynamic perspective, Kurt Lewin (1935) analyzed the psychological influence of the environment on behavior, affirming that all aspects of child behavior (instinctive activity, play, emotion, language, and expression) are co-determined by the environment. Lewin (1935) conceived of the environment as both a momentary situation and a *milieu*, that is, the main characteristics of a situation considered as something permanent. Behavior depends on individual characteristics and the structure of the situation at a given time, meaning that it is generally impossible to separate what is attributable to the individual and what is attributable to the environment. The reference to a specific environment and a set of specific environments is indispensable to the concept of predisposition. According to Lewin, a predisposition or characteristic of an individual person ($Pa$) can be defined by a set of forms of behavior ($Ba$, $B^i$...) that different environmental situations arouse ($E1$, $E2$) at that particular time. In the presence of the same individual characteristics, variations in behavior may also occur ($Ba$, $B^i$...). For example, a child may appear shy in one situation, negativistic in another, and yet at ease in another (Lewin, 1935). The genetic conditional nature of Lewin's theory focuses attention on the relationship between the occurrence of certain forms of behavior and the presence of certain environmental situations.

This brings us to Lewin's field theory (Lewin et al., 1972), which can be defined as a method of analyzing the causal relationships between events, a scientific construct aimed at providing a scientific understanding of social facts. The basic assumption of the theory is that any behavior or change within a psychological field depends on the particular configuration of the field at that given moment (in the *hic et nunc*, the here and now). The field, a dynamic system defined by Lewin as the totality of facts coexisting in their interdependence, is a system of forces in which laws derive from the configuration of the overall system, the energy that the field possesses, and the direction of the forces in play. A mutation in the direction of the force results in a mutation in behavior. To understand behavior ($B$), we must consider, for each type of psychological event (actions, emotions, expressions, needs, ideals, cognitive structure, etc.), the overall situation of the moment, that is, the structure and state of the person ($P$) and the psychological environment ($E$) at a given time: $B = f(PE)$.

From this, the concept of "living space" emerges, which is the relationship between the person ($P$) and the psychological environment ($E$). The environment is understood in psychobiological terms (quasi-physical, quasi-social, quasi-mental structure), and therefore, every fact that has a psychobiological existence must find a place in this field, and only facts that find such a place have dynamic effects (i.e., are causes of events). In this regard, Lewin considered the relationship between environment and needs and assumed the existence of direct relationships between the momentary state of the individual and the structure of the individual's psychological environment. The psychological environment, even when it remains the same, depends on individual characteristics and the degree of development of the individual but also on the individual's momentary condition (the actual state of individual's needs at a given time). Within the range of facts existing at a given time, we find the facts that are located in the border area (or frontier). According to Lewin (1935), the individual is, dynamically, a relatively closed system. Therefore, the intensity with which the environment affects the individual is determined by the structure and the forces that characterize a situation and also by the functional solidity of the borders between the living space and the outside world in a process of continuous interchange through perceptual processes. This area is important for understanding changes in the field and the direction in which they may occur. From here, it emerges how context is understood in terms of what is psychologically significant to the individual.

According to Lewin, when studying the fundamental dynamic relationships between the individual and the environment, it is necessary to constantly keep in mind the overall real situation in its concrete individuality. For this reason, methods of individual-environment analysis that rely exclusively on statistical methods (obtaining numerical values to, for example, characterize the position of an individual within a group) tend to return descriptive analyses with levels of abstraction that make it impossible to study the relationship or concrete position of the individual in a comprehensive and well-defined situation. Therefore, from a dynamic perspective, scientific research must be anchored in everyday life to improve and activate valid social interventions (action research).

Bronfenbrenner's (1979) ecological model has had important implications for understanding the relationship between developmental and environmental systems. Like Lewin, Bronfenbrenner argued for the importance of studying social behaviors as they occur in real-life contexts, thus orienting research in social and developmental psychology toward an ecological perspective of analyzing everyday life contexts. Bronfenbrenner's perspective considers the developing person, the person's environment, and particularly the evolving interaction between the developing person and the environment. Development is defined in terms of enduring change in the way a person perceives and treats the environment (Bronfenbrenner, 1979). The ecological environment is conceptualized as a set of structures, each within the other, like a series of Russian dolls (see Fig. 1):

Bronfenbrenner understood context in terms of the developmental environment by articulating it into levels, the innermost of which is the immediate environment that contains the developing person.

1. The microsystem or environment in which the individual lives, i.e., the family, the peer world, school, or work (or, as is often the case for research purposes, the laboratory or testing room).

The next level requires going beyond individual settings and looking at the relationships between levels. Such interconnections can be as crucial to development as the events that take place within a given setting:

2. The mesosystem encompasses the relationships between microsystems. A child's ability to learn to read in elementary school may depend on how the child is taught and on the nature of connections between school and family.

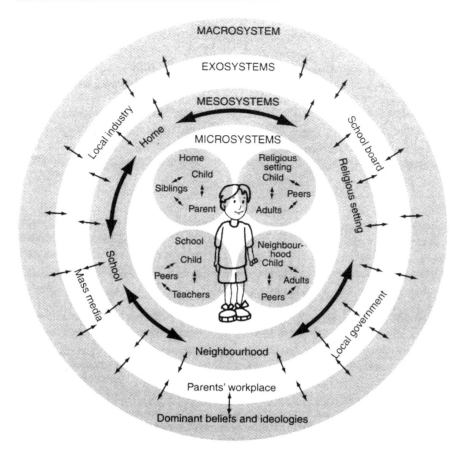

**Fig. 1** The ecological environment. (Figure scanned from Penn, 2005)

The third level evokes the hypothesis that a person's development is profoundly influenced by events that occur in environments in which the person is not present and does not directly experience:

3. The exosystem. Among the most powerful influences affecting child development are the working conditions of the parents.

The last level concerns all environments and consists of the superstructural pattern of all three levels: a given culture or subculture(s) with particular reference points from a developmental point of view to belief systems, lifestyles, opportunities, nationality, ethnic groups, etc. Within any culture or subculture, settings of a given type – such as houses, streets, or offices – tend to be similar, whereas across cultures they are markedly different. Within each society or subculture, there is a pattern in the organization of each type of setting. Furthermore, an alteration of the structure of settings in a society produces, in turn, corresponding changes in behavior and development (Bronfenbrenner, 1979):

4. The macrosystem or culture in which the individual lives. For example, according to Bronfenbrenner, a change in maternity ward practices that affects the relationship between the mother and infant may produce effects that are still detectable 5 years later. A severe economic crisis that occurs can have a positive or negative impact on the subsequent development of a child throughout life, depending on the age of the child at the time the family experienced financial constraints. An example of how a change at the macrosystem level results in a restructuring of different settings with effects on behavior and development is that of COVID-19. The arrival of the pandemic brought about a series of changes at the socio-ecological level (family, school, peer group), which resulted in a modification of the living environment and children's behavior, impacting the emotional level. Sprang and Silman (2013) found that levels of posttraumatic stress were four times higher in children who had experienced quarantine than in those who had not.

Finally, Bronfenbrenner considers time in the environmental changes caused by events or transitions across a person's lifespan. Time is present several times in the multidimensional structure of his model:

5. The macrochronological systems. For example, the increase in the number of working mothers, divorced parents, or extended families.

In analyzing various systems, it is necessary to consider the role of ecological transitions, understood as shifts in role or setting, that occur over a person's lifespan. The development of ecological transitions involves role shifts, particularly in the behavioral expectations associated with particular positions in society. This principle applies to the developing person and others in their world, as roles have the power to alter the way a person is treated and influence that person's actions, feelings, and thinking. According to Bronfenbrenner, a child is more likely to learn to talk in an environment that contains roles in which adults are required to talk to children (e.g., school) or that encourage or allow others to do so (such as when one parent does chores so that the other can read a story to the child).

Bronfenbrenner and Evans (2000) and Bronfenbrenner (2005) expanded his model to include biological influences. The bioecological model includes the role of the dimensions of continuity and change in the biopsychological characteristics of humans, both as individuals and as groups.

In analyzing the micro- and macro-dimensions of environmental systems, Bronfenbrenner is credited with emphasizing the role of the relationships between individual environments in development, since these environmental interconnections can be as decisive for development as the events that take place within a given context (again, see Fig. 1).

## Context in Cultural-Historical Perspective and the Theory of Activity

That context, understood in terms of the sociocultural environment, influences the development of higher psychic functions cannot be fully understood without reference to the theories of Lev Semënovič Vygotsky and the Russian cultural-historical school. Vygotsky (1934) theorized a social nature of the mind, stating that it represents a set of social relations that become functions of personality and forms of its structure. For Vygotsky, development can be understood in the historical-cultural context from which it originates. In this context, through communication and social interactions, the child evolves and appropriates cultural tools, including language. Development is a consequence of the external learning situations to which the child is subjected. In this sense, context represents the place capable of activating the potential of the individual. One of the principles at the basis of the cultural-historical approach concerns human activity which, according to Vygotsky, is socially mediated. An example is given by the relationship between thought and language, where the latter is characterized by being both a product of historical evolution (active in communication) and a system of cultural mediation of cognitive functions. The individual, through communication, appropriates the signs and meanings produced by a given society. This mediation between thought and language (which in this case is configured as a social device of thought itself) allows the individual to act in that society in a culturally appropriate and effective way. Returning to the previously described principle, it is clear that the tools provided by the social and cultural context are at the origin of the individual's mental functioning. The appropriation of these tools does not occur in isolation but through relationships with others, which is also mediated by these devices – it is in interaction that higher mental functions originate. The schemas that the individual uses to interpret the physical and social world are the result of the social and communicative interactions to which they are subjected. From this perspective, the set of such relationships (and communications) allows individuals to act in society, adapt to it, and modify their behavior accordingly. Mental processes and categories are mediated by pre-existing devices in specific cultural contexts and historical moments. For Vygotsky (1934), cognitive skills are deeply influenced by and originate from the social and cultural context; they depend on learning and knowledge that is built by interaction with others.

For this reason, Vygotsky emphasized the importance of studying psychological processes in the practical activities of everyday social life, mediated by culture, artifacts, and the contexts within which they occur. Aleksej Nicolaevič Leont'ev agreed with Vygotsky that psychological processes are grounded in activity and that attention should be centered on action as the primary unit of analysis. Leont'ev disseminated and expanded on Vygotsky's studies on human action through the elaboration of the psychological theory of activity (Leontiev, 1977) (This theory was deepened and developed by Engeström (1987, 1991)). According to Leontiev (1977, p. 62), "the object of an activity is its motive"; this object shapes the activity itself, which is articulated in actions that generate operations within a given social context

(Manzi et al., 2021). The concept underlying the theory is that all psychological processes develop through activity, with action representing the only possible unit of analysis. As described above, however, this is always mediated by cultural tools. The analysis does not aim so much to understand the meaning behind action but, rather, aims to study goal-oriented activities.

Activity on the psychological plane is understood as a unit of life, mediated by mental reflection, by an image whose true function is to orient the subject in the objective world (Leontiev, 1977). Therefore, activity cannot be considered separately from social relations and social life; rather, it is a system that obeys the system of relations of a given society. Outside of these relations, human activity does not exist. Activities are articulated by a series of actions that, according to this theory, are undertaken consciously to achieve a purpose, through a series of operations generated by the action itself. Such operations, which represent the ways through which action is realized, are automatic and independent of the characteristics of the activity itself. The operations are produced by the action in a determined context of socio-cultural activity. Taken in isolation, away from the context of activity that generated them, such actions lose their meaning (Engeström & Blackler, 2005; Leontiev, 1977; Ligorio & Pontecorvo, 2010; Nardi, 2005; Sannino, 2011; Zucchermaglio, 1996). Leontiev, in agreement with Vygotsky, showed how psychological processes can be adequately studied, on the condition that we understand their dimensions of meaning and activity.

## From Bruner to Music: The Mind as a Generator of Sense and Meaning Within a Cultural Dynamic

Jerome Bruner (1990) attached considerable importance to culture as it shapes the minds of individuals. From his perspective, individual expression of culture is about creating meanings and assigning meanings within different contexts and on particular occasions. Such meaning-making involves placing encounters with the world in their appropriate social and cultural contexts. Indeed, although meanings are "in the mind," they derive their definitions from the culture in which they are created. It is this cultural location of meanings that ensures their negotiability and, ultimately, their communicability. Individuals internalize the cultural system of which they are part, consisting of symbols, beliefs, concepts, and values. This language (handed down from generation to generation) is the tool that allows the individual to know, interpret, and negotiate the meanings of reality. The development of knowledge and skills takes the form of an interactive process in which people learn from each other. This is made possible through language and the use of intersubjectivity, the human ability to understand the minds of others through language, gesture, and/or other means. From here emerges the socio-constructivist view of development and knowledge, which is attributed to an essentially social nature; development is conditioned by culture and the use of artifacts within a given context.

Bruner (1990) focused on the processes of acquisition and interpretation of the world, as he sought to understand how individuals construct their knowledge of reality and the meanings attributed to it. The search for meaning is the way through which individuals appropriate and interpret the cultural systems to which they belong. During this continuous process of interpreting reality, the self, and others, individuals build and develop their knowledge of the world. From this process, culture emerges as an integral part of the individual. For this reason, it seems essential to understand individual psychological functioning within its social and cultural context: mind, context, and culture are difficult to distinguish (Bruner, 1986, 1990; Cole, 1996; D'Andrade, 1992; Shweder, 1990; Valsiner, 1989a; Valsiner, 1989b; Wertsch, 1991).

Bruner was not alone in moving in this direction. For example, in an attempt to integrate different psychoanalytic theories, Graham Music (2016) indicates how the mind works according to inter- and intra-subjective modalities identifiable from the beginning in the relationship between infant and caregiver. Music highlights how even before language develops, the embryo and then the newborn can communicate with the mother and/or caregiver through precise mental functions that allow decoding the meaning and significance of their interactions. These functions, called reflexive function and affective tuning, are not related to mere technical instrumentation but find their value and specificity in the cultural process in which they are activated. That is, it is the context of interaction between caregiver and infant that determines how the child develops, which determines the activation of some genes rather than others but also the very possibility of living an experience and defining it as traumatic. In this sense, Music speaks of cultural nature, highlighting how culture is a factor that marks the development of a child's mind and, in particular, the main developmental stages, from life in utero to adolescence. In doing so, he uses concepts such as genes and environment, trauma, neglect or resilience, the development of language, play and memory, and, finally, moral principles and prosocial skills. Moving in this direction highlights how developmental modes and different theories of growth and development (e.g., attachment theory) are affected by cultural variability and contexts. Through a series of longitudinal and cross-cultural studies, Music highlights how the mind is culturally/context dependent in its functioning both in purely biological aspects (genes) and cognitive processes (learning, attention, etc.) related to the mental systems of the construction of reality. Moreover, other psychoanalytic authors have highlighted empirically how context is nothing more than a shared affective symbolization made possible through collusion between minds – a system of sharing in the construction of reality based on systems of attributions of meaning (with affective codes such as friend/enemy, inside/outside, high/low) and significance (Andrisano Ruggieri, 2015; Andrisano Ruggieri et al., 2014; Andrisano Ruggieri & Pecoraro, 2014; Carli, 2008; Salvatore & Scotto di Carlo, 2005).

From this perspective, the context is never the physical environment but a psychic space that indicates the inter- and intra-subjective dimension of the mind's functioning, in which the active codes of meaning and significance determine the construction of a specific reality that can be seen, for example, in the mode of interaction between people as well as in the exercise of specific activities. Contexts are always variable because they are inscribed and defined by the dynamic between minds, which generates a specific cultural dimension.

## An Example of Using the Dependent Context of the Mind in Psychology Teacher Training

We hope that it will now be useful to provide the reader with an example of how we introduce theories of the dependent context of the mind in our psychology courses for future teachers. Specifically, we use the film *Dangerous Minds* to show students that "the individual does not exist" and that the mind is a relational matrix based on contextual dynamics. We hope that, either before or after reading about this example, the reader will watch the film because we think that doing so will enhance understanding of the content of this chapter.

The film is based on a true story and is set in the United States. The protagonist, Louanne Johnson (played by Michelle Pfeiffer), is a former Marine and divorcee with a Ph.D. degree, who hopes that teaching will help her to make sense of her life following the end of her relationship with her husband. With the help of her friend and colleague, Hal, she applies for a job teaching literature at a California high school, run by Principal Grandey. Her application is accepted immediately because few teachers were willing to teach the mostly Chicanos and African-American students of both sexes who were undisciplined, uninterested in education, and involved in gangs and drugs. The student leader of the literature class is Emilio Ramirez, the proudest and most unfriendly but also the most intelligent. Louanne finds herself in a whirlwind of hooligans. Mocked and humiliated, she finds it impossible to employ any standard teaching methods.

Being white, Louanne is immediately called "White Bread" by the students. It is evident in the dynamic that the teaching/learning setting does not follow the classic canons, as we normally know them. Louanne's systematic denigration highlights how teaching is organized through a systematic attribution of meaning based on the friend/enemy dichotomy. To the pupils in the class, the school and the teachers are enemies; for the school, these kids are an annoying problem. This leads to indifference: they are the black sheep who must adapt to the rules of the system. The result is a tug-of-war between the students and the school.

Louanne's class was designated as "special," which in the United States reflects a politically correct way of referring to students who are problematic in some way; in other countries, these students would more likely be referred to as "difficult." Both "special" and "difficult" refer to an idea of an individual mind in the system of attribution of meaning, disconnected from the context, in which the meaning of "difficult" and "special" does not imply a different action of the teacher in the modulation of the teaching and learning setting.

In other words, "special" and "difficult" do not immediately call into play the competence of the teacher and thus the teacher's ability to manage the teaching relationship in this situation. It recalls a dynamic between minds, a collusive system. On the contrary, in the film as in reality, the attribution of responsibility is entrusted to the individual student or to the class. Thus, the need to reshape action because of the context, and the culture active in that context, is denied.

This is how the school administration behaves toward the special class, treating it as something different, as a school within a school, ignoring the specificity of the demand for instruction, education, and training. The school and the various teachers, reasoning in terms of predefined teaching/learning settings, fail in their social mandate because they pursue goals established a priori, that is, without taking into account the contextual variability of the forces in the field (using Lewin's terminology) or the different ecological levels (using Bronfenbrenner's terminology).

Louanne also falls into this trap at the beginning, as she tries to research and deepen her use of different teaching techniques. However, it is now evident that such techniques are based on the assumption of environmental and contextual invariance. For example, if your washing machine breaks down, you can call a technician who can repair it because he or she can establish what is broken, what needs to be fixed, and then fix it. But in education, we are talking about a defined variability environment and context.

Therefore, Louanne quickly realizes that all those techniques are useless because they are inapplicable. All that remains is for her to consider the system of attribution of meaning and the significance of which the contextual variability appears dense. She therefore decides to take a different approach. She declares that she is a former Marine on leave and that she knows how to use karate. From that moment, the class is interested in Louanne, because being street kids, strongly accustomed to fighting with their peers, finds it useful to learn karate. Karate, therefore, appears to be the pretext to redefining the teaching action through the need to establish a negotiated teaching/learning setting, that is, capable of defining methodological objectives based on the construction of competence to learn rather than to state objectives. In this case, the technique is constructed because of the educational objectives that are modified by the systems of attribution of sense and meaning active in the context.

Louanne explains the key to the song "Mr. Tambourine Man" to the boys: In this song, Bob Dylan talks about a drug mule, a subject that teases the boys because it is as close to their reality as karate. At the same time, on the subject of poetry, Louanne considers it useful to talk about the "other" Dylan, the poet Dylan Thomas. The students thus begin to develop skills to understand poetry in its deeper meaning. At the same time, Louanne tries to build an alliance with "Don Emilio," the class leader, and with the students' families. As per the models of analysis of context described earlier, it is evident that the models of Lewin and Bronfenbrenner appear useful not only in understanding the forces operating in this educational field but also how the context defines itself based on cultural processes in the interactions between the school and the families and the families with the children. Each level determines a level of signification based on the same sense, a violent conflict between social classes, ethnic groups, and the school world.

## Some Concluding Remarks

People do not grow in a social vacuum. The learning objectives of this chapter were to provide conceptual and theoretical tools to analyze and understand the influence of social dimensions, socioeconomic status, and sociocultural context on people's lives, to activate appropriate social interventions from context analysis. The study of context follows theories that focus more on some elements of the mind-context relationship and show how individuals participate in systems of coordinated actions, attributing specific meanings to them, and are strongly conditioned by social and cultural contexts. What emerges is a reading of context that emphasizes the role of culture (Bruner, 1990) and how cultural contexts influence the structuring of cognitive activities. Particular reference was made to the ways in which individuals attribute meaning to the experiences in which they are involved. The ways in which individuals interpret and orient their cognitive activity are inextricably linked to these contexts.

Education and culture cannot be analyzed and understood in isolation and separated from each other but must be understood in terms of uniqueness. Therefore, it is necessary to ask ourselves the function that education has in culture and the role that culture has in people's lives. Bruner (1996) has repeatedly pointed out that the mind could not exist without culture, as the evolution of the mind is linked to the development of a way of life in which knowledge is represented by a symbolism shared by members of a given cultural community, upon which the social context is built and organized. Therefore, human activity can only be fully understood from the analysis of the social and cultural context and the framework of thought within which it takes place (Bruner, 1990; Mollo, 2021; Perret-Clermont, 2001).

## References

Andrisano Ruggieri, R. (2015). Theory of mind: Overcoming the dichotomy between culture and nature. *Europe's Journal of Psychology, 11*(4), 742–745. https://doi.org/10.5964/ejop.v11i4.1054

Andrisano Ruggieri, R., & Pecoraro, N. (2014). Family business dynamics: Generational change as identity transition. In S. Salvatore, A. Gennaro, & J. Valsinier (Eds.), *Mulitentric identitis in globalizing word* (pp. 133–160). IAP – Information Age Publishing.

Andrisano Ruggieri, R., Pozzi, M., & Ripamonti, S. (2014). Italian family business cultures involved in the generational change. *Europe's Journal of Psychology, 10*(1), 79–103. https://doi.org/10.5964/ejop.v10i1.625

Bronfenbrenner, U. (1979). *The ecology of human development*. Harvard University Press.

Bronfenbrenner, U. (2005). The bioecological theory of human development. In U. Bronfenbrenner (Ed.), *Making human beings human: Bioecological perspectives on human development* (pp. 3–15). Sage. (Original work published in 2001).

Bronfenbrenner, U., & Evans, G. W. (2000). Developmental science in the 21st century: Emerging questions, theoretical models, research designs and empirical findings. *Social Development, 9*(1), 115–125. https://doi.org/10.1111/1467-9507.00114

Bruner, J. (1996). *The culture of education*. Harvard University Press.

Bruner, J. S. (1986). *Actual minds, possible worlds*. Harvard University Press.

Bruner, J. S. (1990). *Acts of meaning*. Harvard University Press.

Carli, R. (2008). *Culture giovanili. Proposte per un intervento psicologico nella scuola*. Franco Angeli.

Carli R., Paniccia R. M. (2004). *L'Analisi della Domanda*. Il Mulino.

Cole, M. (1996). *Cultural psychology. A once and future discipline*. Harvard University Press.

D'Andrade, R. (1992). Schemas and motivation. In R. D'Andrade & C. Strauss (Eds.), *Human motives and cultural models* (pp. 23–44). Cambridge University Press.

Engeström, Y. (1987). *Learning by expanding: An activity-theoretical approach to developmental research*. Finland Orienta-Konsultit.
Engeström, Y. (1991). Activity theory and individual and social transformation. *Multidisciplinary newsletter for activity theory,* 1991a7/8617
Engeström, Y., & Blackler, F. (2005). On the life of the object. *Organization, 12*, 307–330.
Grossen, M. (1988). *L'intersubjectivité en situation de test*. Delval.
Grossen, M., & Perret-Clermont, A.-N. (1984). Some elements of social psychology of operational development of the child. *The Quarterly Newsletter of the Laboratory of Comparative Human Cognition, 6*, 51–57.
Iannaccone, A., & Zittoun, T. (2014). Overview: The activity of thinking in social spaces. In A. Iannaccone & T. Zittoun (Eds.), *Activities of thinking in social spaces*. Nova Publisher Inc.
Leontiev, A. N. (1977). *Activity, consciousness, personality*. Prentice-Hall.
Lewin, K. (1935). *A dynamic theory of personality*. McGraw-Hill.
Lewin, K., Baccianini, M., & Palmonari, A. (1972). *Teoria e sperimentazione in psicologia sociale*. Il mulino.
Ligorio, M. B., & Pontecorvo, C. (2010). *La scuola come contesto*. Carocci.
Manzi, F., Savarese, G., Mollo, M., & Iannaccone, A. (2021). Editorial: Sociomateriality in children with typical and/or atypical development. *Frontiers in Psychology, 11*.
Mead, G. H. (1934). *Mind, self and society*. University of Chicago Press.
Mollo, M. (2021). *Academic cultures: Psychology of education perspective*. Hu Arenas. https://doi.org/10.1007/s42087-021-00238
Music, G. (2016). *Nurturing natures. Attachment and Children's emotional, sociocultural and brain development*. Routledge.
Nardi, B. A. (2005). Objects of desire: Power and passion in collaborative. *Activity, Mind, Culture, and Activity, 12*(1), 37–51. https://doi.org/10.1207/s15327884mca1201_4
Penn, H. (2005). *Understanding early childhood development: Issues and controversies*. Bell & Bain Ltd..
Perret-Clermont, A.-N. (2001). Psychologie sociale de la construction de l'espace de pensée. In J.-J. Ducret (Ed.), *Actes du colloque Constructivismes: usages et perspectives en éducation, Genève, 4–8 Septembre 2000* (pp. 65–82). SRED.
Perret-Clermont, A.-N. (2004). The thinking spaces of the young. In A.-N. Perret-Clermont, C. Pontecorvo, L. Resnick, T. Zittoun, & B. Burge (Eds.), *Joining society: Social interactions and learning in adolescence and youth* (pp. 3–10). Cambridge University Press.
Renzo, C., & Paniccia, R. M. (2004). *Analisi della domanda. Teoria e tecnica dell'intervento in psicologia clinica*. Il Mulino.
Salvatore, S., & Scotto di Carlo, M. (2005). *L'intervento psicologico per la scuola. Modelli, metodi, strumenti*. Firera & Liuzzo Publishing.
Sannino, A. (2011). Activity theory as an activist and interventionist theory. *Theory & Psychology, 21*(5), 571–597.
Schubauer-Leoni, M. L., Bell, N., Grossen, M., & Perret-Clermont, A.-N. (1989). Problems in assessment of learning: The social construction of questions and answers in the scholastic context. *International Journal of Educational Research, 13*(6), 671–668.
Shweder, R. A. (1990). Cultural psychology- what is it? In J. W. Stigler, R. A. Shweder, & G. Herdt (Eds.), *Cultural psychology. Essays on comparative human development* (pp. 27-66). Cambridge University Press.
Sprang, G., & Silman, M. (2013). Posttraumatic stress disorder in parents and youth after health-related disasters. *Disaster Medicine and Public Health Preparedness, 7*(1), 105–110. https://doi.org/10.1017/dmp.2013.22
Valsiner, J. (1989a). *Human development and culture: The social nature of personality and its study*. Lexington Books.
Valsiner, J. (1989b). Collective coordination of progressive empowerment. In L. T. Winegar (Ed.), *Social interaction and the development of children's understanding* (pp. 7–20). Ablex.

Vygotsky, L. S. (1934). *Thought and language*. Moscow/Leningrad, Russia: Sozekgiz.
Wertsch, J. V. (1991). A socio-cultural approach to socially shared cognition. In L. Resnick, J. Levine, & S. Teasley (Eds.), *Perspectives on socially shared cognition* (pp. 85–100). Hyattsville, MD: American Psychological Association.
Wundt, W. (1900). *Compendio di psicologia*. C. Clausen.
Zucchermaglio, C. (1996). *Vygotskij in azienda: apprendimento e comunicazione nei contesti lavorativi*. Nuova Italia Scientifica.

# Psychology in Teacher Education

## Susanne Narciss and Joerg Zumbach

## Contents

| | |
|---|---|
| Introduction | 809 |
| Purposes and Rationale of Psychology in Teacher Education Curricula | 810 |
|     Frameworks for Professional Standards and Competences for Teacher Education Worldwide | 811 |
|     The Role of Psychology in Teacher Education: Core Teaching and Learning Objectives | 818 |
| Core Contents and Topics of Psychology Programs in Teacher Education | 820 |
|     Psychological Topics, Concepts, and Research Areas Relevant for Teacher Education | 822 |
|     Selecting and Organizing Topics, Content-Material, and Activities for a Psychology Course | 822 |
| Teaching, Learning, and Assessment of Psychology in Teacher Education: Approaches and Strategies | 828 |
|     Approaches for Promoting the Acquisition of Basic Psychological Knowledge | 831 |
|     Approaches for Promoting a Deeper Understanding of Applying Psychology into Teaching | 832 |
|     Approaches for Promoting an Epistemic Understanding of How Psychological Findings Are Generated | 834 |
|     Assessment Approaches | 835 |
| Challenges and Lessons Learned | 836 |

---

S. Narciss (✉)
School of Science - Faculty of Psychology, Psychology of Learning and Instruction, Technische Universitaet Dresden, Dresden, Sachsen, Germany
e-mail: susanne.narciss@tu-dresden.de

J. Zumbach
Department of Educational Research, University of Salzburg, Salzburg, Austria
e-mail: Joerg.Zumbach@sbg.ac.at

© Springer Nature Switzerland AG 2023
J. Zumbach et al. (eds.), *International Handbook of Psychology Learning and Teaching*,
Springer International Handbooks of Education,
https://doi.org/10.1007/978-3-030-28745-0_68

Teaching, Learning, and Assessment Resources ............................................. 839
  Tips for Teaching ................................................................. 839
  Recommended (Text)Books for Teaching Psychology in Teacher Education Programs ... 839
  Online Resources ................................................................. 839
Cross-References ................................................................... 842
References ......................................................................... 842

#### Abstract

Teachers should be empowered to act as deliberate professionals, i.e., guiding their actions in an adaptive way to the affordances of educational situations by carefully choosing purposes and goals, by ethical and cultural considerations, as well as by conceptual and technical knowledge. The core goal of teaching psychology in teacher education and vocational programs is to contribute to the education of such deliberate professionals. With theoretical and empirical insights in areas such as human learning, cognition, and motivation; personality and social development; testing and measurement; individual diversity, group differences, and special needs; research on social and cultural factors in instructional contexts; and classroom management, teachers' professional development, and school effectiveness, educational psychology provides an important basis for the initial education of teachers. Yet, given the restricted time and space for psychology courses in initial teacher education, the curriculum and syllabus design for these programs poses several challenging issues, in particular how to deal with the trade-off between breadth and depth in covering scientific psychological insights and their various potential applications in teaching contexts.

This chapter aims at providing international perspectives and insights into the core goals, as well as evidence-based practices and approaches of teaching psychology in teacher education programs. Starting with an introduction to the rationale for teaching psychology in teacher education programs, the chapter offers a summarizing overview of frameworks of professional teacher standards from all over the world, as well as recommendations for teaching psychology, and especially educational psychology, in teacher education programs. Next, core contents and topics of psychology for (pre-service) teachers are analyzed and presented based on a review of respective textbooks being used in countries around the world. Evidence-based instructional suggestions for implementing teaching, learning, and assessment are also provided. Finally, the relevance of psychology teaching in teacher education programs is emphasized, particularly with regard to transferring psychological knowledge and theories into educational practice and understanding psychological epistemology.

#### Keywords

Teacher education · Educational psychology · Teaching standards · Teacher competences · Educational practice · Transfer · Competence

## Introduction

Teaching psychology to prospective and in-service teachers is a highly relevant field of psychology learning and teaching in countries all around the world. The overarching goal in this field is to contribute to the development of (future) teachers' professional knowledge and competences in order to empower them as reflective practitioners, efficient problem-solvers, and lifelong learners in their future professional work and life as teachers.

The definition of teacher professionalism remains a much debated issue that is increasingly discussed not only locally or nationally but also globally (Menter & Flores, 2021). Teaching is a very complex and challenging professional field. According to Anderson et al. (1995), the multidimensionality, uncertainty, and social and ethical nature of teaching contribute to this complexity: Classroom situations are multidimensional because many events occur simultaneously and often require teachers to make trade-offs (e.g., balancing individual and class-wide needs or breadth vs. depth of content coverage). Furthermore, due to the diversity of students and teaching situations and to the dynamic changes taking place in global society, teachers must always deal with some degree of uncertainty about best tactics and strategies and thus have to constantly monitor and adjust their teaching acts. Finally, teachers' choices must also take into account societal and ethical values and goals, such as providing equal educational opportunities for all students. Accordingly, a core issue of teacher education programs is how they can address the complexities of teaching in order to help teachers to develop professional knowledge and competences for mastering these multifaceted and complex challenges.

Educational psychological knowledge can contribute in many ways to prepare teachers to master the challenges of this complex professional field in terms of evidence-based reflection and deliberate action (e.g., Anderson et al., 1995). For example, that knowledge can inform decisions regarding (a) the instructional design of learning environments, (b) the assessment and evaluation of learning and teaching, and (c) the selection and continuous adaptation of strategies for teaching heterogeneous groups of learners.

Thus, educational psychology courses are core components of teacher education programs and reviews. These courses have been included in teacher education for at least a century (e.g., Woolfolk Hoy, 2000), and psychological research and knowledge inspired several changes and reforms in teaching (e.g., by drawing attention to the conditions and effects of teaching for deep and generative understanding).

Over the last decades, the studies run within the Program for International Student Assessment (PISA) have attracted much attention to teachers' professional knowledge and competences and how their development can be improved. Furthermore, a meta-analysis of meta-analyses (Hattie, 2009) has attracted researchers' and education policy makers' attention to the role of teachers and to teacher factors that contribute to effective student learning. This has resulted in a remarkable accumulation of educational research on teacher education (see, e.g., recent special issues edited by Mayer & Oancea, 2021; Menter & Flores, 2021). Moreover, PISA as well as continent-wide major policy programs such as the European Bologna Process (Bologna Working Group, 2005) have called for a worldwide harmonization of conceptual developments and changes regarding the standards and competences in the field of teaching and learning (Menter & Flores, 2021). This has resulted, among other things, in the specification of international frameworks of core educational objectives referred to as twenty-first-century skills (e.g., the comparative analysis by Voogt & Roblin, 2012, or Partnership for twenty-first Century Skills [P21], 2015). Addressing the twenty-first-century skills in learning and instruction requires that teachers are not only able to teach content in the context of their local classroom, but do so in a way such that students acquire the essential skills for working and living in today's world. These include learning and innovations skills such as (a) critical thinking, complex problem-solving, communication, and collaboration in diverse (multicultural) groups; (b) information, media, and technology skills such as information literacy, media literacy, and ICT literacy; and (c) life and career skills such as self-regulation, leadership, and social and cross-cultural competency.

Most recently, global social challenges have raised important educational affordances and issues related to educational equality and social justice that will contribute to further changes in views of teacher professionalism (e.g., Flores & Swennen, 2020; Menter & Flores, 2021). For example, rising awareness of global migration streams as well as of racism, sexism, and other kinds of social discrimination has increased attention to the urgent need to address educational equality and social justice in teaching and learning. Furthermore, the global Covid-19 pandemic has revealed the vital importance of being able to implement strategies for online teaching and learning. Moreover, an increase in the frequency of disastrous weather extremes has highlighted the need to develop ways of ensuring a sustainable future. Addressing these social challenges in a rapidly changing world adds at least three competency fields to teacher education programs, namely, competences for implementing inclusive learning environments, for digitalization of teaching and learning, and for teaching and reflecting the values and issues of sustainability.

## Purposes and Rationale of Psychology in Teacher Education Curricula

As already mentioned, a major aim of educational psychology courses within teacher education programs is to help future teachers learn how they can use psychological knowledge and evidence to deal with the complexity of teaching. To identify and specify more concretely the core teaching and learning goals in this field, we will summarize and compare international frameworks of professional teaching standards and/or competences. Based on this review and comparison, core teaching and learning goals for the psychology curriculum targeting teacher students will be presented.

## Frameworks for Professional Standards and Competences for Teacher Education Worldwide

Ever since the World Education Forum in Dakar in 2000, the development of teaching standards has been an important topic on the global education agenda. The aim has been to improve the quality of education in order to equip learners with the competences for effective participation in today's societies and economies. Hence, professional standards of teaching as well as teaching competency frameworks have been developed worldwide in order to specify the necessary knowledge, skills and strategies, values and attitudes, as well as teaching activities that contribute to successful professional behaviors in the field of learning and instruction. These standards provide the basis for teacher education and for promoting teachers' continued professional development (Centre of Study for Policies and Practices [CEPPE], 2013). Furthermore, they provide a yardstick that enables teachers to track their professional conduct in relation to the various competency domains of teaching (e.g., instructional design, classroom organization and management, and learning assessment and feedback). This subsection reviews and compares selected teacher standards and competency frameworks from different regions of the world, including Australia, Europe, Southeast Asia, Africa, and the USA.

### Australian Standards

The Australian Education Standards Authority (NSW Education Standards Authority [NESA], 2014) identifies seven standards related to teacher competences and assigns them to the three professional sub-domains of knowledge, practice, and engagement (see Table 1). Work on the development of the Australian Professional Standards for Teachers started in 2009 and was finalized in July 2010. In December 2010 the standards were endorsed by the Ministerial Council for Education, Early Childhood Development and Youth Affairs.

### European Conceptions of Teacher Standards and Competences

The teacher competency framework of the European Commission (2013; see Table 2) distinguishes three professional facets that are further described by several competency aspects. Given the federal system in Europe, this framework is considered to serve as a basis for the national discussions and developments of teacher standards, while respecting national traditions and policies.

### Southeast Asia Standards

The Southeast Asia Teacher Competence Framework (SEA-TCF) consists of 4 essential, 12 general, and 31 enabling competences (see Table 3). The development of the SEA-TCF started in August 2007 and was iteratively further improved through 2017 and adopted in July 2018. It provides standards for teaching professionals of the 11 member countries of the Southeast Asian Ministers of Education Organization (SEAMEO) (Teachers' Council of Thailand, 2018).

**Table 1** Overview on Australian professional standards for teachers (NESA, 2014)

| Professional domain | *Standards* and focus areas |
|---|---|
| Knowledge | 1. *Know students and how they learn*<br>– Physical, social, and intellectual development and characteristics of students<br>– Understand how students learn<br>– Students' diverse linguistic, cultural, religious, and socioeconomic backgrounds<br>– Strategies for teaching Aboriginal and Torres Strait Islander students<br>– Differentiate teaching to meet the specific learning needs of students across the full range of abilities<br>– Strategies to support full participation of students with disability<br>2. *Know content and how to teach it*<br>– Content and teaching strategies of the teaching area<br>– Content selection and organization<br>– Curriculum, assessment, and reporting<br>– Understand and respect Aboriginal and Torres Strait Islander people to promote reconciliation between Indigenous and Non-Indigenous Australians |
| Practice | 3. *Plan for and implement effective teaching and learning*<br>– Establish challenging learning goals<br>– Plan, structure, and sequence learning programs<br>– Use teaching strategies<br>– Select and use resources<br>4. *Create and maintain supportive and safe learning environments*<br>– Support student participation<br>– Manage classroom activities<br>– Manage challenging behavior<br>– Maintain student safety<br>– Use ICT safely, responsibly, and ethically<br>5. *Assess, provide feedback, and report on student learning*<br>– Assess student learning<br>– Provide feedback to students on their learning<br>– Make consistent and comparable judgments<br>– Interpret student data<br>– Report on student achievement |
| Engagement | 6. *Engage in professional learning*<br>– Identify and plan professional learning needs<br>– Engage in professional learning and improve practice<br>– Engage with colleagues and improve practice<br>– Apply professional learning and prove student learning<br>7. *Engage professionally with colleagues, parents/carers, and community*<br>– Meet professional ethics and responsibilities<br>– Comply with legislative, administrative, and organizational requirements<br>– Engage with parents/carers<br>– Engage with professional teaching networks and broader communities |

## US Standards and Competences for Teachers

In the USA, the National Board for Professional Teaching Standards (NBPTS) was founded in 1987 with the objective to advance the quality of teaching and learning (NBPTS, 2016). Based on research and practitioner expertise, the NBPTS members

**Table 2** Teacher competences – perspectives from research and policy (European Commission, 2013)

| | Competence aspects |
|---|---|
| **Knowledge and understanding** | Subject matter knowledge |
| | Pedagogical content knowledge (PCK), implying deep knowledge about content and its structure:<br>- Knowledge of tasks, learning contexts, and objectives<br>- Knowledge of students' prior knowledge and recurrent subject-specific learning difficulties<br>- Strategic knowledge of instructional methods and curricular materials |
| | Pedagogical knowledge (knowledge of teaching and learning processes) |
| | Curricular knowledge (knowledge of subject curricula) |
| | Educational sciences foundations (intercultural, historical, philosophical, psychological, sociological knowledge) |
| | Contextual, institutional, organizational aspects of educational policies |
| | Issues of inclusion and diversity |
| | Effective use of technologies in learning |
| | Developmental psychology |
| | Group processes and dynamics, learning theories, motivational issues |
| | Evaluation and assessment processes and methods |
| **Skills** | Planning, managing, and coordinating teaching |
| | Using teaching materials and technologies |
| | Managing students and groups |
| | Monitoring, adapting, and assessing teaching/learning objectives and processes |
| | Collecting, analyzing, and interpreting evidence and data (school learning outcomes, external assessment results) for professional decisions and teaching/learning improvement |
| | Using, developing, and creating research knowledge to inform practices |
| | Collaborating with colleagues, parents, and social services |
| | Negotiation skills (social and political interactions with educational stakeholders, actors, and contexts) |
| | Reflective, metacognitive, interpersonal skills for learning individually and in professional communities |
| | Adapting to educational contexts characterized by multilevel dynamics with cross-influences (macro-level, government;, meso-level, school contexts; microlevel, classroom and student dynamics) |
| **Dispositions: beliefs, attitudes, values, commitment** | Epistemological awareness (issues concerning features and historical development of subject area and its status, as related to other subject areas) |
| | Teaching skills through content |
| | Transferable skills |

(continued)

**Table 2** (continued)

| | Competence aspects |
|---|---|
| | Dispositions to change, flexibility, ongoing learning, and professional improvement, including study and research |
| | Commitment to promoting the learning of all students |
| | Dispositions to promote students' democratic attitudes and practices, as European citizens (including appreciation of diversity and multiculturality) |
| | Critical attitudes to one's own teaching (examining, discussing, questioning practices) |
| | Dispositions to teamworking, collaboration, and networking |
| | Sense of self-efficacy |

developed and iteratively revised Five Core Propositions and Standards describing the knowledge, skills, and attitudes that enable proficient teachers to empower student learning (see also Thorpe, 2014). A first version of the Five Core Propositions and Standards was published in 1989 and an updated version appeared in 2016 (see Table 4 for a summary). The NBPTS emphasizes in the introduction to the description of the updated version that the five core propositions have proven their value and that the update of the explications of the propositions has mainly been of stylistic nature.

Driven by the affordances of twenty-first-century education needs and based on current research on teaching and learning, the Interstate Teacher Assessment and Support Consortium (InTASC) of the Council of Chief State School Officers (CCSSO) (2013) developed the *InTASC Model Core Teaching Standards*. These standards further specify the NBPTS's five core propositions and emphasize the key themes of "Personalized Learning for Diverse Learners," "A Stronger Focus on Application of Knowledge and Skills," "Improved Assessment Literacy," "A Collaborative Professional Culture," and "New Leadership Roles for Teachers and Administrators" (CCSSO, 2013; pp. 4–5; see Table 5). The *InTASC Model Core Teaching Standards* groups ten standards into four categories: learners and learning, content, instructional practice, and professional responsibility.

### African Framework of Standards and Competences for the Teaching Profession

The African Framework of Standards and Competences for the Teaching Profession provides a guiding baseline of common references for the teacher qualification frameworks of the 55 member states of the African Union. Its key purpose is to serve as a common reference point for teacher qualification in Africa. In order to promote the comparability with international teacher qualification frameworks, the teaching standards and qualities of the teaching profession have been developed in alignment with the relevant global qualification levels and competency frameworks (e.g., the International Classification of Education, ISCED 2011 developed by the UNESCO Institute for Statistics, 2012, or the European Qualifications Framework (EQF), European Commission, 2018). Accordingly, as summarized in Table 6, the

**Table 3** Overview on the Southeast Asia Teacher Competence Framework (SEA-TCF; SEAMEO)

| Essential competence | *General* and enabling competences |
|---|---|
| 1. **Know and understand what to teach** | 1.1 *Deepen and broaden the knowledge base on what is taught*<br>– Master subject content<br>– Use research-based knowledge<br>1.2 *Understanding educational trends, policies, and curricula*<br>– Update myself on new educational trends<br>– Study educational policies and how they affect my teaching<br>1.3 *Updating knowledge on local, national, regional, and global developments*<br>– Understand how to implement the curriculum<br>– Check new changes in education environment |
| 2. **Helping students learn** | 2.1 *Knowing students and how they learn*<br>– Identify my students' needs and strengths to help them learn better<br>– Understand how my students learn<br>– Value what makes students unique<br>2.2 *Using the most effective teaching and learning strategies*<br>– Select appropriate teaching and learning strategy<br>– Design clear and effective lessons my students can understand<br>– Create a positive and caring learning space<br>2.3 *Assessing and feedback on students' learning*<br>– Design assessment process and tools<br>– Monitor my students' progress and provide appropriate support<br>– Use results from assessment to improve instruction |
| 3. **Engaging the community** | 3.1 *Partner with parents and caregivers*<br>– Build a support network<br>– Create a welcoming space<br>– Sustain the partnership<br>3.2 *Involve the community to help students learn*<br>– Engage parents and caregivers to be partners in learning<br>– Design learning activities using community conditions, local wisdom, tradition, knowledge<br>3.3 *Encourage respect and diversity*<br>– Accept what makes people different<br>– Practice inclusion and respect in the classroom |
| 4. **Becoming a better teacher every day** | 4.1 *Knowing myself and others*<br>– Continue to grow by knowing myself more<br>– Become more aware and responsible for my emotions and health<br>– Nurture my relationships with care and respect<br>4.2 *Practicing human goodness in my work and my life*<br>– Be kind and compassionate<br>– Inspire my students and colleagues by setting my best example<br>– Nurture my students' confidence on what they can do and become<br>4.3 *Mastering my teaching practice*<br>– Keep alive my passion for teaching<br>– Take responsibility in my own personal and professional growth<br>– Inspire other teachers by setting an example |

**Table 4** Overview on the "Five Core Propositions" and their descriptors explicating the related teacher competences (NBPTS, 2016)

| Proposition | Descriptors |
| --- | --- |
| Commitment to students and their learning | • Recognize individual differences in their students and adjust their practice accordingly<br>• Understand how students develop and learn<br>• Treat students equitably<br>• Know that teacher's mission transcends the cognitive development of students |
| Knowledge of the subject area and how to teach it to students | • Appreciate how knowledge in subject area is created, organized, and linked to other disciplines<br>• Command specialized knowledge of how to convey a subject to students<br>• Generate multiple paths to knowledge |
| Responsibility for managing and monitoring student learning | • Call on multiple methods to meet instructional goals<br>• Support student learning in varied settings and groups<br>• Value student engagement<br>• Regularly assess student progress<br>• Engage students in learning |
| Systematic thinking about practice and learning from experience | • Make difficult choices that test their professional judgment<br>• Use feedback and research to improve their practice and positively impact student learning |
| Member of learning communities | • Collaborate with other professionals to improve school effectiveness<br>• Work collaboratively with families<br>• Work collaboratively with community |

framework distinguishes five professional domains, namely, knowledge and understanding, skills, values and attributions, partnerships, and leadership (African Union, 2019). These standards address traditional issues such as mastery of the teaching area, teaching design, and learner feedback as well as emerging issues such as inclusivity, climate change, and gender equity.

These standards for professional teacher/teaching from various regions around the world reveal that over the last decade, well-structured comprehensive frameworks for teacher qualification have been developed. Because one pillar inspiring their development and iterative improvement originated in the UNESCO framework *International Standard Classification of Education* (UNESCO Institute for Statistics, 2012), the standards are rather similar in their overall structure of superordinate domains. More specifically, all of them emphasize that teachers' major professional goal is to help all students learn. Accordingly, they consider teachers' knowledge and understanding of the learners, as well as their knowledge and understanding of the subject matter and how to teach it, as essential professional competences for the successful application of their further professional skills and practices. Furthermore, there is general agreement that teachers' professional values, attitudes, and beliefs as well as their continued professional growth constitute core competencies for successful teaching.

**Table 5** Summarizing overview on *InTASC Model Core Teaching Standards* (CCSSO, 2013; pp. 8–9)

| Category | *Standards* – descriptions |
|---|---|
| Learner and Learning | 1. *Learner development*<br>– Understanding of how learners grow and develop<br>– Recognizing that patterns of learning and development vary individually within and across the cognitive, linguistic, social, emotional, and physical areas<br>– Designing and implementing developmentally appropriate and challenging learning experiences<br>2. *Learning differences*<br>– Understanding of individual differences and diverse cultures and communities<br>– Ensuring inclusive learning environments that enable each learner to meet high standards<br>3. *Learning environments*<br>– Working with others to create environments that<br>  (a) Support individual and collaborative learning<br>  (b) Encourage positive social interaction, active engagement in learning, and self-motivation |
| Content | 4. *Content knowledge*<br>– Understanding the central concepts, tools of inquiry, and structures of the discipline(s) that are taught<br>– Creating learning experiences that make the discipline accessible and meaningful for learners to assure mastery of the content<br>5. *Application of content*<br>– Understanding of how to connect concepts and use differing perspectives to engage learners in critical thinking, creativity, and collaborative problem-solving related to authentic local and global issues |
| Instructional practice | 6. *Assessment*<br>– Understanding and using multiples methods of assessment to<br>  (a) Engage learners in their own growth, to monitor learner progress<br>  (b) Guide the teacher's and learner's decision-making<br>7. *Planning for instruction*<br>– Planning instruction that supports every student in meeting rigorous learning goals by drawing upon knowledge of content areas, curriculum, cross-disciplinary skills, and pedagogy, as well as knowledge of learners and the community context<br>8. *Instructional strategies*<br>– Understanding and using a variety of instructional strategies to<br>  (a) Encourage learners to develop deep understanding of content areas and their connections<br>  (b) Build skills to apply knowledge in meaningful ways |
| Professional responsibility | 9. *Professional learning and ethical practice*<br>– Engaging in ongoing professional learning<br>– Using evidence to continually evaluate practice<br>– Adapting practice to meet the needs of each learner<br>10. *Leadership and collaboration*<br>– Seeking appropriate leadership roles and opportunities to take responsibility for student learning<br>– Collaborating with learners, families, colleagues, other school professionals, and community members to ensure learner growth and to advance profession |

**Table 6** Overview of the domains and descriptors of expected competences of initial teacher education of the African Framework of Standards and Competences for the Teaching Profession (African Union, 2019)

| Domain | Descriptors of standards and competences |
|---|---|
| **Professional knowledge and understanding** | 1. Knowledge and understanding of human development and the learner<br>2. Knowledge and understanding of the curriculum<br>3. Knowledge and understanding of the subject matter<br>4. Knowledge and understanding of interdisciplinary learning<br>5. Knowledge and understanding of education theory, pedagogy, and teaching practice<br>6. Knowledge and understanding of learner assessment, feedback, monitoring, and evaluation of the learner<br>7. Knowledge and understanding of education-related policies and legislation<br>8. Knowledge and understanding of digital technologies for teaching and learning |
| **Professional skills and practices** | 9. Effective teaching and learning<br>10. Effective classroom organization and management<br>11. Effective learner assessment<br>12. Effective administration of learning<br>13. Effective use of technologies for teaching and learning<br>14. Guidance and counseling, support, school health, and safety |
| **Professional values, attributes, and commitment** | 15. Awareness and respect for learners' diversity<br>16. Respect for learners' rights and dignity<br>17. Respect for school systems and colleagues<br>18. Role model for learners<br>19. Commitment to continued professional development |
| **Professional partnerships** | 20. Partnerships with learners, parents, carers, guardians, communities, and stakeholders |
| **Professional leadership** | 21. Leadership and management through commitment to the school's vision, high-impact teaching and learning, transparency, accountability, and respect for colleagues and learners |

Despite similarities in their overall structure, the frameworks differ to some extent in how much detail and elaboration is devoted to the competences related to (a) diversity, cultural understanding, and inclusion, as well as (b) adoption of technology for learning and instruction. The Australian, African, European, and US frameworks include these competences, while they are not explicitly mentioned in the Southeast Asian framework.

## The Role of Psychology in Teacher Education: Core Teaching and Learning Objectives

The summarizing overview of the international frameworks of professional teacher standards reveals that prospective teachers must acquire a wide array of knowledge, understanding, and skills and, thus, competences related to issues of learning and teaching in diverse social and cultural contexts.

To further specify core goals for teaching and learning psychology in pre-service teacher education, we will use as starting points the European Qualification Framework for Higher Education (European Commission 2018; see Table 7) as well as the revised version of the *InTASC Model Core Teaching Standards* published by the US Council of Chief State School Officers (2013; see Table 5).

The EQF objectives reveal that knowledge and critical understanding provide the foundation of thinking and acting reflectively in complex professional fields that not only require the ability to apply routinely learned strategies but also competences to integrate information and knowledge to make decisions in highly complex situations, to communicate and collaborate, and to deal with changes in professional requirements.

As mentioned above, teaching is a complex field in which a routine application of practical strategies has limitations in many situations. There is empirical evidence that teachers' beliefs and their knowledge of psychological concepts and principles related to the understanding of students' learning and instructional practices are associated with their interpretations and judgments of classroom events (e.g., Fives & Buehl, 2012) as well as with students' perceptions of instructional quality (Koenig

**Table 7** Summarizing overview on EQF-objectives for Higher Education (first and second HE cycle)

| Cycle | Objective | Description |
|---|---|---|
| 1 | Knowledge and understanding | • Comprehensive, specialized, factual, and theoretical knowledge<br>• Awareness of the boundaries of that knowledge<br>• Critical understanding of theories and principles |
| 2 | Applying knowledge and understanding | • Application of knowledge and understanding in a manner that indicates a professional approach to work or vocation<br>• Competences for identifying, analyzing, and solving problems<br>• Ability to devise and sustain arguments within field of study |
| 3 | Making informed judgments | • Ability to gather and interpret relevant data<br>• Ability to evaluate and present information and concepts from relevant data<br>• Ability to arrive at informed judgments that include reflection on relevant social, scientific, or ethical issues<br>• Ability to integrate knowledge in order to handle complexity |
| 4 | Communication and collaboration | • Competences for communicating information, ideas, problems, and solutions to both specialist and nonspecialist audiences |
| 5 | Professional awareness and lifelong learning | • Identify and address learning needs for further knowledge<br>• Ability for lifelong self-regulated learning |

& Pflanzl, 2016). Psychological research provides concepts, findings, and principles that can challenge naïve beliefs and thinking about learning and instructional practices. Accordingly, researchers have repeatedly emphasized the importance of providing future teachers with a strong foundation of psychological knowledge to help them to understand the rationale and boundary conditions of instructional practices and current assumptions about complex learning (e.g., Anderson et al., 1995; Darling-Hammond, 2006; Good & Levin, 2001; Patrick, Anderman, Bruening, & Duffin, 2011; Willingham, 2017; Woolfolk Hoy, 2000).

Aligned with the Framework for Teacher Education Standards, the core purpose of psychology modules and courses within teacher education programs is to help future teachers learn how they can use psychological knowledge and evidence to promote all students' learning and to deal with the complexity of tailoring evidence-based instructional practices to their students' needs.

Inspired by the generic EQF-objectives for Higher Education and Frameworks for Teacher Education Standards, we identified the following overarching learning goals for psychology courses in initial teacher education programs (HE levels 1 and 2):

- Knowing and critically understanding psychological findings in the core areas that are necessary to understand students' learning, thinking, motivation, development, and social and emotional behavior, as well as their development, individual differences, and diverse backgrounds
- Knowing and critically understanding psychological concepts, approaches, findings, and principles undergirding instructional practices and strategies (e.g., assessment, instructional design, and classroom management)
- Applying basic knowledge and understanding to analyze and identify patterns of learners' conditions and contexts
- Applying basic knowledge and understanding to examine if and how instructional strategies or learning environments can be rooted in psychological principles and findings
- Making informed judgments by integrating the basic knowledge and understanding of psychological findings to select, gather, and interpret relevant learner attributes as well as instructional context data in order to draw implications for improving instructional practices
- Being able to communicate psychological findings related to factors influencing students' learning, as well as psychologically founded principles and implications for instructional practices and strategies

## Core Contents and Topics of Psychology Programs in Teacher Education

While there has long been general agreement on the important role of educational psychology for teachers (e.g., Anderson et al., 1995; Patrick et al., 2011; Woolfolk Hoy, 2000), teacher education programs vary considerably in how much time they devote to psychology courses. Consequently, the kinds of psychological knowledge and skills that can be included in these programs also vary considerably. It is challenging to design curricula for psychology programs with limited time frames that address in a meaningful way the core purposes and overarching objectives described above. To identify psychological contents and topics of high relevance for teacher education, researchers and policy makers have taken several approaches.

For example, Snowman (1997) reviewed 10 educational psychology textbooks published after 1990 in the USA and asked 20 expert educational psychology teachers to rank order the psychological topics of those textbooks in terms of their relevancy for teaching. His review revealed that the textbooks cover a wide variety of topics and provide numerous classroom applications to illustrate how the findings and principles related to these topics can be used to support students' learning. It also revealed that the educational psychology instructors rated most topics as relevant and gave the highest ratings to areas such as motivation, learning processes, cognitive and social-emotional development, the role of educational psychology in teaching, classroom measurement, affective and social processes, and cultural differences.

Another explored what educational psychology topics are considered highly relevant by 48 German experts from 3 fields of teacher education (e.g., Lohse-Bossenz, Kunina-Habenicht, & Kunter, 2013). To create a clustered list of topics for this study, the authors inspected official documents of educational foundation courses of the federal state of Hessen (Germany). This list included 17 topics for the content area of *learning*, 13 for the content area of *development*, and 13 for the content area of *assessment*. Results of this study confirmed that the three content areas are considered to be key areas that should be included in educational psychology programs for teacher education.

The Coalition for Psychology in Schools and Education of the American Psychological Association has synthesized psychological research to identify the top 20 psychological principles that enhance teaching and learning in school contexts. These principles are categorized into five areas of psychological functioning (see American Psychological Association, Coalition for Psychology in Schools and Education [APA-CPSE], 2015), namely:

1. Thinking and learning: How do students think and learn (principles 1–8)?
2. Motivation: What motivates students (principles 9–12)?
3. Social-emotional learning: Why are social context, interpersonal relations, and emotional well-being important for student learning (principles 13–15)?
4. Classroom management: How can classroom behavior be best managed (principles 16–17)?
5. Assessment: How can teachers effectively assess student progress (principles 18–20)?

Finally, national or international qualification frameworks or models of teaching as a profession have served as valuable sources for identifying core content areas (e.g., Anderson et al., 1995; Darling-Hammond & Bransford, 2005; Woolfolk Hoy, 2000).

## Psychological Topics, Concepts, and Research Areas Relevant for Teacher Education

Adopting an international perspective on the issue of how to identify highly relevant psychological topics for teacher education, we analyzed the tables of contents of comprehensive recent textbooks from the USA, Europe (Germany), Australia, China, and South Africa (see Table 8).

Our initial analysis of the tables of contents indicated that all the selected comprehensive textbooks cover a wide variety of psychological topics relevant for promoting teaching and learning but that they have organized the topics in different ways. In order to identify similarities and differences in the order and the depth of topic coverage, we assigned the chapters of the selected textbooks to ten major content areas, namely, *Introduction; Learning and Behavioral Management; Information Processing, Memory, and Cognition; Motivation and Emotion; Student Differences and Diversity; Developmental Theories and Differences; Social Factors, Interaction, and Communication; Creating Environments for Learning and Teaching; Assessment, Evaluation, and Feedback;* and *Teacher Characteristics, Beliefs, and Attitudes.*

Table 8 reveals that though there are variations in the order and the depth of coverage among the textbooks, mostly all textbooks addressed the ten major content areas at least to some extent. The variations in the order and depth of covering the different content areas can be partly explained by the differences in professional teacher standard and competency frameworks. For example, the Snowman and McCown textbook has been developed in line with the InTASC Standards (see Table 5), whereas the Chinese textbook reflects the Southeast Asian framework of teacher competences (see Table 3). Additionally, the variations in organizing the content might be due to the large number of relevant psychological topic areas and their interconnectedness when it comes to their application in instructional contexts.

## Selecting and Organizing Topics, Content-Material, and Activities for a Psychology Course

The issue of selecting and organizing relevant content areas and topics and material and activities that are aligned with the learning objectives of courses are of high relevance for developing well-organized courses on a specific topic or content area. Addressing this issue can be done in various ways. First, textbooks or textbook chapters that provide a meaningful structure of the content area together with resources for learning activities can serve as a starting point. Second, instructional design approaches or frameworks such as elaboration theory (Reigeluth, 2018), the 4C/ID model (Frerejean et al., 2019), and Merrill's First Principles of Instructions (Merrill, 2002; see also ▶ Chap. 49, "First Principles of Instruction Revisited," by Merrill, this volume) can provide a basis for developing meaningful course structures and organizing instructional content and material. Third, teacher competency frameworks such as the Technological, Pedagogical and Content Knowledge model

**Table 8** Summarizing overview on topics of selected comprehensive psychology textbooks for teacher education

| Psychological topics and findings | USA Snowman and McCown (2014) | Germany Urhahne, Dresel, and Fischer (2019) | Australia McInerney (2014) | China Qi and Rude (2019) | South Africa Irma and Ebersöhn (2004) |
|---|---|---|---|---|---|
| Introduction | Applying Psychology to Teaching (pp. 2–22) Educational psychology Potential and limits of research in educational psychology Teaching – art or/and science? | Preface | My education lab | Introduction (Part I) Educational psychology Research methods in educational psychology History of educational psychology | Relevance of the book Aims Assumptions Children |
| Learning and behavioral management | Operant conditioning (pp. 237–261) Basic concepts Educational applications Social cognitive theory (pp. 294–342) Model, basic concepts Self-regulated learning | Learning and behavior (pp. 3–16) Classical conditioning Operant conditioning Self-regulated learning (pp. 68–86) Brain and learning (pp. 87–107) Informal learning (pp. 126–144) | Stimulating effective learning (Part I; Chap. 6, pp. 170–207) Learning theory Social cognitive theory Self-regulation and learning Theory and research into practice | Theories of learning (Part III) Behavioral Cognitive Constructive Humanistic | The learner (pp. 13–145) Cognition and learning Health and well-being Behavior Learning styles |
| Social factors, interaction and communication | Role of social interaction on cognitive development (pp. | Social processes in school (pp. 421–465) Social interaction and communication | Addressed in subchapters of Part II, Chap. 6; Part III; Chap. 13 Teacher expectations | Classroom social factors (Part of Chap. 15: Classroom management) Behavioral management | Social context (pp. 167–289) Families Group work |

(continued)

Table 8 (continued)

| Psychological topics and findings | USA Snowman and McCown (2014) | Germany Urhahne, Dresel, and Fischer (2019) | Australia McInerney (2014) | China Qi and Rude (2019) | South Africa Irma and Ebersöhn (2004) |
|---|---|---|---|---|---|
|  | 45–46) Social approach to teaching (pp. 488–494) | Social structures and processes Social attitudes in school context | and student motivation (pp. 235–237) Social, emotional, and moral development | (Part of Chap. 15: Classroom management) | Community development Inclusive education Culture |
| Information processing, cognition, memory | Information processing theory (pp. 262–293) Information processing view Human memory models Why we forget Metacognition Technology – information processing tool | Memory and knowledge acquisition (pp. 23–52) Memory definition – models Recall, retrieval, and forgetting Knowledge acquisition Science learning (pp. 145–161) | Information processing (Part 1; Chap. 4, pp. 108–147) Information processing and constructivism Perception and effective learning Prior knowledge, epistemic beliefs Learning strategies Remembering | Information processing (Chaps. 9–12 included in Part IV – Psychology of learning) Knowledge acquisition Problem-solving – creativity Self-regulated learning Moral cognition | Information processing theories Cognition and learning (pp. 13–28) Memory (pp. 125) |
| Developmental theories and differences | Theories of development (pp. 25–74) Psychosocial development Cognitive development Moral development Age level differences (pp. 75–114) | Development in childhood and adolescence (pp. 231–258) Models and Conditions of Development Psychosexual and social development Cognitive and speech development | Developmental theories (Part I; Chap. 2, pp. 38–74) Piaget/Vygotsky Theories of mind Developmental needs of children (Part III; Chaps. 11, 12, 13) Learning and physical/motor development Personal development | Development of the learners (Chap. 2 included in Part II – Psychology of the learner) Cognitive development Development of personality Development of moral cognition (Chap. 12 included in Part IV – Psychology of learning) | Theory of human development (included in chapter "Culture"; pp. 258–271) |

| | Preschool – kindergarten Primary grades Elementary school Middle school High school | Motivational and emotional development | Social, emotional, and moral development | | |
|---|---|---|---|---|---|
| Motivation and emotion | Motivation and perceptions of self (pp. 383–420) Behavioral view Social cognitive view Other cognitive views Humanistic view Role of self-perceptions Motivating (….) with technology | Emotion (pp. 185–199) Definition – basic emotions Individual emotional experiences Emotions in schools Motivation (pp. 207–221) Basic concepts – frameworks Expectancies and values Course of action | Managing effective learning (Part II; Chap. 7, pp. 208–247) Motivation: cognitive perspectives Self-motivated learning Expectancy-value-approach Attribution theory Peer influence Teacher expectations and motivators | Learning motivation (Chap. 8 included in Part IV – Psychology of Learning) Motivation theories Individual factors Situational factors | Emotions and emotional intelligence for educators (pp. 31–43) |
| Student differences and diversity | Understanding student differences (pp. 115–149) Intelligence Learning styles Gender differences, bias Addressing cultural and socioeconomic diversity (pp. 150–190) Multiculturalism | Intercultural learning (pp. 107–114) Basic concepts Intercultural psychology Intercultural openness in schools: challenges and prospects Intelligence, creativity, and giftedness (pp. 166–184) Students with special | Cultural dimensions (Part II; Chap. 9, pp. 288–312) Social constructivism and multiculturalism School achievements of minority groups Multicultural education Indigenous minority education | Individual differences (Chap. 3 included in Part II – psychology of the learners) Intelligence Learning styles Children with special needs | Inclusive education (pp. 230–246) Culture (pp. 258–271) |

(continued)

Table 8 (continued)

| Psychological topics and findings | USA Snowman and McCown (2014) | Germany Urhahne, Dresel, and Fischer (2019) | Australia McInerney (2014) | China Qi and Rude (2019) | South Africa Irma and Ebersöhn (2004) |
|---|---|---|---|---|---|
| | Ethnicity and social class Accommodating student variability (pp. 191–236) Historical developments Ability grouping Inclusion – legislation (IDEA) Students with special needs | needs (pp. 565–617) Dyslexia, dyscalculia, ADHD Mental and social disorders Prevention and intervention | | | |
| Assessment, evaluation, and feedback | Assessing students' capabilities (pp. 503–593) Assessment of classroom learning Understanding standardized assessment Learning from teaching | Assessment, evaluation, and research in learning and instruction (pp. 471–506) Assessment and testing – basics Assessment of learning Evaluation and quality assurance Research methods Feedback techniques (p. 347) | Measurement and evaluation for effective learning (Part II; Chap. 10, pp. 314–350) Principles – validity, reliability Learning objectives – taxonomies Measurement strategies Educational outcome evaluations | Assessment in the classroom (Chap. 14 included in Part V - Psychology of Instruction) Classroom evaluation Traditional methods Non-traditional methods Use of classroom review | Assessment and intervention (pp. 317–331) Educational psychological assessment Educational psychological intervention and therapy |
| Creating environments for learning and teaching | Classroom management (pp. 421–457) Approaches to | Teaching and instruction (pp. 333–407) Learning and instruction – input- | Addressed in Parts I; III e. g., Effective teaching and learning (Part I; Chap. 1, | Effective instruction (Chap. 13 included in Part V – Psychology of Instruction) Effective instruction and | Adaptation of learning environments to meet |

|  | classroom management<br>Preventing problems<br>Dealing with problems<br>Violence, bullying<br>Approaches to instruction (pp. 458–502)<br>Behavioral – direct instruction<br>Cognitive and constructivist<br>Humanistic<br>Social approach to teaching | process-product-frameworks<br>Effective teaching and instruction<br>Teaching and learning with multimedia | pp. 2–37)<br>Instructional design and theories (Part I; Chap. 6, p. 197)<br>Classroom implications of humanistic perspectives (pp. 399–405)<br>Information and communication technologies (Part III; Chap. 14, pp. 1–20) | instructional design<br>Teaching aims and standards<br>Classroom management (Chap. 15 included in Part V)<br>Physical environment<br>Social environment<br>Approaches and methods | the needs of the learner |
| --- | --- | --- | --- | --- | --- |
| Teacher characteristics, beliefs, attitudes | Learning from teaching (pp. 578–647)<br>Skill improvement<br>Inquiry skills improvement<br>Technology for reflective inquiry | Teacher competences and professional development (pp. 395–407)<br>Teaching requirements<br>Competence models<br>Teacher professional development | Effective teaching and learning (Part I; Chap. 1, pp. 2–32)<br>Teaching requirements<br>Teacher professional standards<br>Teacher effectiveness and learning<br>Teaching skills/teacher motivation | Psychology of the teacher (Part VI – Chap. 16)<br>The ideal teacher<br>Professional qualities<br>Psychological health<br>Growth and development | Missing |

(TPACK; Koehler & Mishra, 2009) can ground decisions about how to select and organize topics, material, and activities. Finally, a combination of several of these approaches can inform course design.

Regardless of what approach is used for selecting and organizing topics and developing course structure, instructors have to align their course goals with specific learning objectives as well as with course outcomes and the content, material, and learning activities related to these outcomes. Table 9 illustrates how we used the core competences of the European Qualifications Framework to align the course goals and learning objectives to learning outcomes, content, and activities, for the topic area of formative assessment and feedback. Notice that, to help student teachers to build a contemporary psychological and pedagogical perspective on psychological concepts, the course includes both theories and empirical findings related to the topics of formative assessment and feedback, as well as opportunities for reflecting and discussing (individually and collaboratively) evidence-based formative assessment and feedback practices and strategies, as well as instruments and case vignettes.

## Teaching, Learning, and Assessment of Psychology in Teacher Education: Approaches and Strategies

Psychology instruction (in all fields and areas) requires a planning, implementation, and evaluation process that should follow professional guidelines and is based on scientific rules and theories of memory and learning (Sweller, Ayres, & Kalyuga, 2011; Zumbach, 2021). Following instructional design (ID; not to be confused with instructional design theories), this process includes needs assessment, analysis of learning, assessment of learner characteristics, choice of learning content, choice of didactical approach, design and use of instructional media, design of learning assessment procedures, etc. (Van Merriënboer & Kirschner, 2013). Another crucial aspect when planning and conducting teaching is a continuous evaluation (formative and summative) of the whole procedure and its individual components (Deibl, Zumbach, Geiger, & Neuner, 2018). Here, the concept of constructive alignment (CA) might be a helpful tool to synchronize different parts of the process of planning and implementing learning environments (Biggs, 2012). CA distinguishes between the learning outcomes that students are expected to achieve, teaching methods, and assessment methods. Teaching and assessment methods should be aligned according to the intended learning outcomes (Wang, Su, Cheung, Wong, & Kwong, 2013).

Consequently, the first step in designing a course based on the idea of CA is to define learning objectives. Decisions about teaching and evaluating assessment methods in an aligned system of instruction follow (Biggs, 2014). As described by Deibl et al. (2018, p. 296), "This should ideally be a fully criterion-referenced system where the objectives define what to teach, how to teach, and how to assess performance. Thus, there have to be precise learning objectives with the teaching methods supporting the students effectively in order to accomplish these objectives." In order to align these three basic and mutually dependent components, learning assessments have to represent the objectives (Biggs, 2014). Taken together, these considerations

**Table 9** Alignment of a course goal, content and activities, and learning objectives by the European Qualification Framework – Higher Education

**Major course goal**
Develop student knowledge, understanding, competences in the field of formative assessment and feedback

| Course outcomes – content – material | Learning objectives | European Qualification Framework – Higher Education | | | | |
|---|---|---|---|---|---|---|
| | | Knowledge and understanding | Application skills | Informed judgment | Communication | Learning skills |
| Explain key terms related to formative assessment and feedback | Define what formative assessment is in contrast to summative assessment | ☐ | | | | |
| | Define quality criteria for assessment (objectivity, reliability, and validity) | ☐ | | | | |
| | Define feedback – formative feedback | ☐ | | | | |
| | Define competence – competence-based assessment | ☐ | | | | |
| Describe key models related to formative assessment and feedback | Describe Reinhold's formative assessment cycle (Reinholz, 2016) | ☐ | | | | |
| | Describe interactive tutoring feedback model (Narciss, 2008, 2017) | ☐ | | | | |
| | Describe 3 core-questions feedback model (Hattie & Timperley, 2007) | ☐ | | | | |
| Summarize key research findings on formative assessment and feedback | Describe major findings from seminal meta-analyses and reviews on formative assessment and feedback (e.g., Bennett, 2011; Kluger & DeNisi, 1996; Shute, 2008; Black & Wiliam, 2009; Evans, 2013) | ☐ | | | | |
| Describe design principles for formative assessment and feedback strategies | Describe core steps of designing a formative assessment strategy | ☐ | ☐ | | | |
| | Describe core principles of designing a formative feedback strategy | ☐ | ☐ | | ☐ | ☐ |

(continued)

**Table 9** (continued)

| Major course goal: Develop student knowledge, understanding, competences in the field of formative assessment and feedback | | European Qualification Framework – Higher Education |||
|---|---|---|---|---|
| | Identify feedback components and sources that can be used to design a formative feedback strategy | ☐ | | |
| Analyze typical instruments for formative assessment and feedback | Analyze and discuss on quality features of formative assessment instruments | ☐ | ☐ | ☐ |
| | Analyze and discuss on quality features of formative feedback instruments | ☐ | ☐ | ☐ |
| | Analyze and discuss on quality features of competency evaluation forms | ☐ | ☐ | ☐ |
| Analyze feedback scenarios with a focus on feedback strategies using external feedback sources: teacher, peer | Analyze and discuss the structure of the scenario based on the findings from the formative assessment cycle | ☐ | ☐ | |
| | Analyze and discuss to what extent the scenario meets the principles derived from the interactive tutoring feedback model | ☐ | ☐ | |
| | Analyze and discuss the scenario based on Hattie's feedback model | ☐ | ☐ | |
| Analyze feedback scenarios with a focus on the feedback receiver (self-assessment – internal feedback; feedback perception) | Analyze, reflect, and discuss features of the scenario with regard to the issue of how to promote accurate self-assessment | ☐ | ☐ | ☐ |
| | Analyze, reflect, and discuss features of the scenario with regard to the issue of how different learners might differ in their perceptions of the feedback | ☐ | ☐ | ☐ |
| | Analyze, reflect, and discuss features of the scenario with regard to the issue of how to support learners in using feedback for their further learning | ☐ | ☐ | ☐ |

imply that different objectives, needs, methods, assessments, and the like have to be planned correspondingly and carefully.

Several instructional design (ID) approaches have been developed for effective teaching and learning. They range from transmission-focused to problem-based and to socio-constructive (for overviews see Reigeluth, 1999, 2018). Space limits do not allow us to summarize all of them here, but let us consider some examples of approaches that are most appropriate for particular teaching goals and for teaching situations that range from large classes to small-group learning and to supervised and reflective learning by doing.

## Approaches for Promoting the Acquisition of Basic Psychological Knowledge

Courses at an introductory level are frequently provided for the whole cohort of students. For such courses with sometimes up to 1000 students, teacher-centered approaches such as lectures might be applicable and appropriate. Modern information technologies allow to provide them to be taught online (e.g., using massive open online courses, MOOCs) or in a blended format. One prominent approach to designing courses for larger classes is direct instruction, which is commonly used worldwide and provides a rationale for systematically planning and implementing courses based on a sequence of activities that are both teacher- and student-centered (Stockard, Wood, Coughlin, & Rasplica Khoury, 2018). The core design of direct instruction consists of four elements. First comes a teacher-led introduction, where students' prior knowledge is activated through a summarizing repetition of the content from preceding lessons. In a second step, the teacher presents new learning objectives and then explains new content in a clear and detailed way. This step can include oral presentations, demonstrations, illustrations, and the like. The third stage includes practicing and applying the new knowledge in the classroom. In an introductory psychology lecture, guided practice with classroom cases, or working on application questions and discussing their answers individually (e.g., by using clickers), in pairs, in small groups, or class-wide can provide opportunities for practice with formative feedback. For very large groups of students, such practice activities can also be provided in accompanying tutorial groups. The fourth stage of direct instruction involves individual practice combined with (individualized) feedback. To this end students can, for example, be provided with practice tasks and worked-out solutions of these tasks.

Analyses such as that provided by Klahr and Nigam (2004) or the meta-analysis by Stockard et al. (2018) reveal that direct instruction is a highly effective approach to teaching and learning in schools and universities. Yet, there are further ways to design rather teacher-centered instruction, and direct instruction does not address how to organize or (re)arrange content (e.g., following elaboration theory; Reigeluth, 1999). It is rather a basic framework of how to design classroom instruction in an organized manner.

## Approaches for Promoting a Deeper Understanding of Applying Psychology into Teaching

In order to deepen students' understanding and transfer of psychological knowledge into teaching contexts, instructional approaches targeting the acquisition of complex skills are needed. One prominent example is the four-component instructional design model (4C/ID; see Van Merriënboer & Kester, 2014). The approach has been designed for the training and acquisition of complex skills. The four components compromise learning tasks, part-task practice, supportive information, and procedural information and are based on the four learning processes of induction, elaboration, knowledge compilation, and strengthening. In order to design and conduct instruction following the 4C/ID approach, teachers have to first decompose the skills and abilities that form the overall learning objectives into sub-skills. In a next step, the skills and knowledge required to apply these (part) skills must be analyzed. Subsequently, appropriate instructional strategies for task parts, as well as the whole task, must be selected. Finally, all these elements are combined in the design of the learning environment. For the design of learnings tasks, Van Merriënboer (2012) suggests providing learning experiences that are authentic and based on real-life tasks. These should be sequenced from easy to difficult with adaptive learner support (i.e., scaffolding) for each stage of the sequence. The part-task practice should contribute to the proceduralization of knowledge by means of additional practice. Part tasks should be embedded within the context of the whole task and, thus, provide meaningful learning environments. Learners are supported by additional information. A core rationale here is to support learning and performance in problem-solving and reasoning with regard to the given tasks. This supportive information should be specified and adapted to the learning tasks and should be continuously accessible to the learners. Finally, procedural information must be designed and provided as a basis for learning and to allow acquisition of routine. This procedural information must also be linked to each (part) learning task and presented just in time when needed by learners.

The 4C/ID is one example of a generic model that allows teachers to plan, implement, and evaluate learning environments for complex learning domains such as teacher education. It also gives instructional designers considerable freedom in their choice of instructional (or didactical) strategies that will support the accomplishment of learning objectives.

Problem-based learning and inquiry-based learning are instructional approaches useful for targeting deep understanding and transfer of psychological knowledge in teacher education. They are widespread and effectively implemented in many disciplines (including psychology) and universities worldwide. Both approaches use prepared cases or problems that require problem-solving as well as self-regulated learning (for further details see ▶ Chaps. 50, "Problem-Based Learning and Case-Based Learning," by Zumbach and Prescher and ▶ 51, "Inquiry-Based Learning in Psychology," by Lippmann in this volume).

Modern information technology also allows the use of digitally simulated learning environments, with different classroom scenarios for teacher training.

Bradley (2020) differentiates among virtual puppetry simulations, multiuser virtual environments, and single-user simulations. In virtual puppetry simulations, actors (e.g., other students) take the role of learners in virtual online classes and simulate the classroom for pre-service teachers to deal with. In multiuser virtual environments, multiple users can interact synchronously and, thus, train together. Finally, single-user simulations are closed system and system responses to learners' action are predetermined, but they also provide possibilities for interactions among pre-service teachers and the simulated students (Albright, 2020; Bradley, 2020). Such approaches are similar to what has been referred to as "microteaching." "Microteaching" is a collective term for approaches, techniques, and arrangements that include the real-time simulation or practice with real students and allows training teachers in specific situations in controlled settings with video recording and feedback based on these recordings (e.g., Ostrosky et al., 2013).

Further approaches to reflective, practice-based learning from experience include practica, internships (e.g., Hoveid & Hoveid, 2019; Janssen, Westbroek, & Doyle, 2014), and service learning (see ▶ Chap. 53, "Service Learning," by Bringle et al., this volume). The cognitive apprenticeship approach (Collins, Brown, & Newman, 1989) provides a solid instructional framework to support reflective practice-based learning. The basic idea behind this approach is that a learner is successively guided toward expertise by expert mentors. This is usually done by having the apprentice participate in the activities of the mentor. The instructional design is based on a repertoire of methods which can be applied in parallel or in sequence (cf. Collins et al., 1989):

- (Cognitive) Modeling: Here the experts show how they solve sample problems or perform sample tasks. It is important that the expert describes all relevant aspects and "thinks aloud" during the modeling process so that the learner can understand what is going on.
- Coaching: Learners take over some parts or tasks as experts provide (verbal) support and help.
- Scaffolding: Experts provide scaffolds for the learners, including, for example, hints about how to proceed or how to overcome difficulties.
- Fading: As the learner develops more expertise, the expert gradually provides less guidance.
- Articulation: Learners and teachers describe their thoughts. When teachers do so, students can better understand what might otherwise be hidden knowledge and can use that knowledge to build their own expertise. When learners articulate their thoughts, mentors are better able to detect gaps in students' knowledge, the presence of misunderstandings, or incorrect assumptions and then intervene accordingly.
- Reflection: Reflecting on one's behavior and thinking is a metacognitive strategy that helps learners to appreciate important aspects of their skill development, to evaluate their progress, and to take corrective action if necessary.
- Exploration: Learners are encouraged to engage in self-directed explorations, experiences, and problem-solving. This phase is crucial to promote knowledge transfer.

There are many studies that emphasize the effectiveness of the cognitive apprenticeship approach, especially the importance of scaffolding (Torp & Sage, 2002), and reflection (e.g., Barron et al., 1998).

## Approaches for Promoting an Epistemic Understanding of How Psychological Findings Are Generated

Cognitive apprenticeship also plays an important role in another aspect of psychology in teacher education: the role of epistemology of psychology itself. While most teacher training programs worldwide include the content domains that future teachers will teach, psychology and especially educational psychology is often considered only a supplementary discipline and is thus given very limited time and space in the curriculum. Thus, it is hard for pre-service teachers to understand the different methodologies within their subjects and also to understand how psychology works as an academic discipline and how psychological science knowledge is generated, validated, and revised or extended (Moser, Zumbach, Deibl, Geiger, & Martinek, 2021). However, it is crucial that future teachers understand how psychological research is conducted and what implications can and cannot be drawn from it. So it is important to introduce students to psychological research methods, for example, through research-based courses or inquiry-based learning. This does not mean that trainee teachers should be able to conduct their own psychological research, but they should at least understand how this field and its research works (i.e., to understand the epistemology of psychology). This understanding enables them, first, to identify, understand, and apply psychological research results to their field. At the same time, it can provide a valuable basis for reflecting on their teaching practices and conducting their own research on its effectiveness, e.g., in terms of action research and the scholarship of teaching and learning (SoTL).

The scholarship of teaching and learning is an approach of evidence-based self-driven research that aims at analyzing, understanding, reflecting on, and improving one's own teaching (e.g., Felten, 2013). To be more specific, Potter and Kustra (2011, p. 2) define SoTL as "the systematic study of teaching and learning, using established or validated criteria of scholarship, to understand how teaching (beliefs, behaviors, attitudes, and values) can maximize learning, and/or develop a more accurate understanding of learning, resulting in products that are publicly shared for critique and use by an appropriate community."

Action research is also dedicated to analyzing one's own teaching in order to gain insights and understanding about what happens in one's own classes and how to improve instruction. Clark, Porath, Thiele, and Jobe (2020, p. 8f.) describe action research as "a process for improving educational practice. Its methods involve action, evaluation, and reflection. It is a process to gather evidence to implement change in practices. (...) Action research develops reflection practices based on the interpretations made by participants. (...) Action research is iterative; plans are created, implemented, revised, then implemented, lending itself to an ongoing process of reflection and revision. (...) In action research, findings emerge as action develops and takes place; however, they are not conclusive or absolute, but ongoing."

A minor difference between SoTL and action research can be found in the implications of each strategy: While SoTL focuses mainly on analyzing what happens, action research is rather a formative evaluation approach that contributes to quality management and, thus, improvement of teaching and learning (see also Stringer, 2008). Nevertheless, the two approaches overlap and are important not only for educating pre-service teachers but also to for encouraging those teachers to implement them in their own teaching careers.

## Assessment Approaches

As is the case in any other field of psychology teaching and learning, the constructive alignment of learning objectives, instructional approach, and assessment is crucial to obtain reliable and valid information on teaching and learning processes and outcomes. In teacher education programs, this alignment is of even greater significance because the number of students is much bigger than in the psychology programs (at the first author's university, there are 1000 education students vs. 120 BA-psychology students each year). Further, education students' own assessment experiences during their studies help to shape the beliefs, standards, and strategies that will guide how they will later assess their teaching processes and outcomes. Providing high-quality assessment experiences should therefore be an important goal in teacher education programs. Ideally, teachers of psychology in those programs are aware that their teaching and assessment activities serve as models for their education students, and so they will want to offer a variety of examples of high-quality assessment strategies and procedures.

It is important to differentiate two target domains of assessment. The first is assessment of learners' products and process of knowledge, skill, and competence acquisition. The second is assessment of the quality or effectiveness of the learning environment or core factors of it.

Irrespective of the target of assessment, both formative and summative assessment must be considered. Summative assessment is mostly used at the end of a teaching or learning phase and aims at capturing the current state of learning or of teaching quality in terms of a score such as a grade. Formative assessment is used several times during the teaching or learning phase and serves to identify the strengths, but also the areas in need of improvement, and provides information on how to improve the quality of learning or teaching.

### Assessment of Students' Learning, Knowledge, and Competences

Many kinds of educational measurement and testing can be used to assess students' learning progress and success (for an overview see Brookhart & McMillan, 2019), and both formative and summative approaches can be used in combination.

Approaches to summative assessment can include, for example, tests consisting of multiple-choice items, constructed response items, (short) essays, oral examinations, case-based applied problem-solving assignments, adaptive testing, and others (see also Table 9 above or ▶ Chap. 54, "Assessment of Learning in Psychology," by Blalock, Rainey, and Halonen, this volume). In alignment with the core standards and competences summarized in section "Frameworks for Professional Standards and Competences for Teacher Education Worldwide," summative assessment should address at least student teachers' knowledge and understanding of psychological concepts, approaches, and findings as well as their competences in reflecting and evidence-based judgment and argumentation with this knowledge (see EQF framework, section "Frameworks for Professional Standards and Competences for Teacher Education Worldwide"). For big cohorts of students, these competences can be economically and reliably assessed using, for example, case vignettes that serve as the stem for several multiple-choice test questions. There is empirical evidence that such vignette assessment tasks can be as effectively implemented for training and assessing student teachers' competences as reflective essay writing in combination with classroom observations (e.g., Jeffries & Maeder, 2011).

Formative assessment strategies have been found to contribute significantly to students' learning at all levels of education (e.g., Hattie, 2009). Thus, student teachers should be provided with numerous opportunities to experience formative assessment strategies and practices. Approaches to formative assessment include (vignette-based) assignments with instructors' feedback, peer feedback, and/or self-generated feedback supported by feedback scripts and clear rubrics or competency evaluation sheets. Furthermore, if applied not only at the end of a teaching or learning phase, most summative assessment approaches can be implemented in a formative way as well, as long as they are complemented by formative feedback strategies (Bennett, 2011).

### Assessment of Courses

Summative and formative assessment approaches should also be applied for improving instructional design of psychology courses and curricula in teacher education. Such approaches are commonly used under the aegis of student evaluation of teaching (SET), but can also include feedback from peers and others. To offer reliable and valid assessment data, the previously mentioned principles of alignment of course goals, learning objectives, and assessment criteria are crucial as well. This requires developing and using different assessment instruments for different course formats. Results from summative or formative evaluations following the alignment principles can be used for course development and improvement, but also for action research and research within the context of SoTL (see above).

## Challenges and Lessons Learned

Curriculum design and implementation are challenging tasks that require addressing several alignment issues, including the alignment of the goals and affordances of (a) the academic discipline with those of the diverse professional fields in which the graduates of this discipline will work, (b) the curriculum with the goals and resources of the local settings, and (c) the curriculum with the goals and capabilities of the target students. Furthermore, the current state of the art in an academic domain is constantly progressing, professional domains are constantly changing in accordance with societal affordances and/or technical developments, and students' diverse goals and capabilities are always changing as well (cf. Narciss, 2019).

Recent research has contributed to major developments within the areas of teacher education and psychology. Especially relevant are the meta-meta-analysis by Hattie (2009) and several large-scale studies (e.g., PISA, PERLS, and others), and the implications of that research have contributed significantly to the field in the form of competence-based teaching and assessment, among other things. One core outcome of all of these studies has been to make more prominent the importance of psychology for teachers and teacher education. Nevertheless, as already mentioned, there are still some constraints that limit the teaching of psychology in teacher education. These include limits on the position and amount of psychology in teacher education curricula in many programs. When the number of courses designated for psychology in teacher education is too small, they will not meet the requirements for psychological knowledge that is required of today's teachers. The result can appear as problems such as failure to address the common and stable psychological misconceptions (cf. De Bruyckere, Kirschner, & Hulshof, 2019; Dekker, Lee, Howard-Jones, & Jolles, 2012; Rato, Abreu, & Castro-Caldas, 2013) that are not only prevalent among pre-service teachers but also among expert teachers.

Teachers should be empowered to act as deliberate professionals, i.e., guiding their actions in an adaptive way to the affordances of educational situations by carefully choosing purposes and goals, by ethical and cultural considerations, as well as by conceptual and technical knowledge. The core goal of teaching psychology in teacher education and vocational programs is to contribute to the education of expert teachers who will be able to retrieve psychological knowledge and apply it to the complex situational demands they are faced with in instructional contexts. In other words, we need to teach and train psychologically literate and competent teachers, in order to empower them as efficient problem-solvers and lifelong learners for their future professional work and life.

In order to accomplish this goal, student teachers should be provided with opportunities for learning, understanding, and applying a broad range of psychological concepts, methods, and empirical evidence and to link that knowledge and understanding to evidence-based professional applications in school contexts (see Table 8). Hence, educational psychologists teaching in teacher education programs are faced with the challenging question of how to offer teacher students access to scientific psychological concepts, methods, and empirical evidence that they can use to develop their professional knowledge and competences. This question is also relevant in other domains of psychology learning and teaching, but the previously mentioned limits on psychology content within teacher education programs create unique challenges. Moreover, psychology scholars do not always have practical experience in teaching at schools and therefore need to learn how teachers can use psychological knowledge. Thus, psychology teachers in teacher education programs are faced with several challenges when selecting curriculum content as well as when organizing and implementing the teaching and learning of this content. A first challenge relates to the trade-off between breadth and depth of covering the potential range of topics. Deciding for covering broadly the whole range of topics may lead to a superficial memorization of content as opposed to reaching a deep understanding of psychological insights and their applicability in school situations. When this happens, superficially memorized knowledge is unlikely to be transferred to professional practice. However, although covering psychological topics in greater depth will likely help students attain deeper knowledge and better understanding of its practical implications, doing so inevitably places limits on how many such topics can be addressed in a given amount of time. A mix of breadth and depth can be created by providing introductory lectures (accompanied by tutorials) and at least one or two in-depth courses, in which at least one topic can be worked on intensively.

A second challenge relates to the issue of how to identify and select those psychological topics and findings that are most reliable and of highest relevance for classroom teaching and learning. Some topics might seem relevant and prominent from a practical perspective (e.g., learning styles), yet there are no reliable empirical findings supporting them (e.g., De Bruyckere et al., 2019). Others are highly interesting from a psychological science perspective but either have little or no relevance for teaching or may not yet be extensive enough or stable enough to be of full value. Fortunately, over the last decade, several comprehensive textbooks and online resources have been developed that can scaffold dealing with this challenge (see 6.2).

A third challenge relates to the issue of how to provide students with opportunities to link foundational psychological knowledge to professional teacher tasks through evidence-based reflection and deliberate action within a one-semester time frame at a university (i.e., psychology teaching is rarely integrated in school contexts). The approaches presented in section "Approaches for Promoting a Deeper Understanding of Applying Psychology into Teaching" can serve as a basis for dealing with this challenge (see also Table 9; or Narciss, Hammer, Damnik, Kisielski, & Körndle, 2021).

Teacher education programs face at least three additional challenges (Patrick et al., 2011, p. 71) that have to be addressed more or less constantly: (a) communicating the relevance of educational psychology research to the wider education community, (b) developing collaborative relationships with colleagues in teacher education programs that support a common discourse and shared vision of effective teacher preparation, and (c) documenting the ways that educational psychology courses make a difference to the practice of graduating teachers and to the educational experiences of their K–12 students.

Finally, (future) teachers need to be made aware that educational psychology cannot provide recipes or prescriptions. They need to understand instead that psychology can provide concepts, models, and theoretical and empirical findings that teachers can use to better understand the rationale and boundary conditions of (their) teaching practices and behaviors, as well as to explore ways how to improve them. And because research in psychological science is constantly progressing, these teachers must be helped to understand that there will always be new psychological knowledge to learn and apply. This means that they should be encouraged to engage in the kind of lifelong learning that can keep them updated about the latest developments in psychological research that is relevant to educational practice.

## Teaching, Learning, and Assessment Resources

### Tips for Teaching

The issue of identifying core instructional principles for teaching psychology in higher education has been addressed by various groups of researchers (e.g., Elvira, Imants, Dankbaar, & Segers, 2017; Mohamed, Valcke, & De Wever, 2017). Elvira and colleagues used a literature review to extract ten instructional principles that we consider very thoughtful, and thus we offer it here in Table 10.

### Recommended (Text)Books for Teaching Psychology in Teacher Education Programs

The five comprehensive textbooks outlined in Table 8 are all valuable resources for teaching educational psychology to student teachers. We consider the two following textbooks as very inspiring because they provide both a research-based coverage of the subject and implications of research findings for educational practice in various school settings. The books offer also access to valuable online study and teaching resources:

- Snowman, J., & McCown, R. (2015). *Psychology applied to teaching*. Boston, MA: Cengage Learning.
- McInerney, D. M. (2013). *Educational psychology: Constructing learning*. New York, NY: Pearson.

The following three books can serve as resources for combatting misconceptions about learning and education:

- Holmes, J. D. (2016). *Great myths of education and learning.* New York: John Wiley & Sons.
- De Bruyckere, P., Kirschner, P. A., & Hulshof, C. D. (2015). *Urban myths about learning and education.* Amsterdam: Academic Press.
- De Bruyckere, P., Kirschner, P. A., & Hulshof, C. (2019). *More urban myths about learning and education: Challenging eduquacks, extraordinary claims, and alternative facts.* London: Routledge.

### Online Resources

https://www.battelleforkids.org/networks/p21/frameworks-resources

**Table 10** Instructional principles for psychology teaching (summarized from Elvira et al., 2017)

| Principle | Instructional activities |
|---|---|
| *Transforming theoretical/conceptual knowledge into experiential/practical knowledge* | |
| 1. Support epistemological understanding | – Introduce concepts early to prevent development of naïve theories and oversimplification<br>– Emphasize the complexity, uncertainty, and dynamic development of knowledge<br>– Engage students in critical thinking |
| 2. Provide opportunities to differentiate between and among concepts | – Provide repeated encounters with concepts in several different contexts<br>– Make students compare and contrast concepts in different contexts<br>– Expose the knowledge and reasoning embodied in professional context(s) |
| 3. Practice with a variety of problems to enable students to experience complexity and ambiguity | – Provide both typical and atypical problems<br>– Gradually increase complexity of problems until they resemble situations that arise in practice |
| 4. Enable students to understand how particular concepts are connected | – Make the connections explicit between concepts<br>– Focus on higher-order concepts to provide guidance for novices<br>– Provide opportunities to identify or isolate specific subcomponents of a concept |
| 5. Target for relevance | – Apply repeatedly knowledge to real cases<br>– Provide opportunities for exploring professional activities<br>– Provide tasks requiring similar cognitive activities as required in the workplace |
| *Explicating procedural/experiential knowledge into conceptual/theoretical knowledge* | |
| 6. Share inexpressible knowledge | – Initiate small-group discussions<br>– Use cognitive modeling by thinking aloud |
| 7. Pay explicit attention to prior knowledge | – Instruction should target (naïve) misconceptions<br>– Take into account prior knowledge from adjacent domains |
| *Reflecting on both practical and conceptual knowledge by using self-regulative knowledge* | |
| 8. Supporting students in strengthening their problem-solving strategies | – Communicate the great value of qualitative processes during problem-solving<br>– Guided practice or coaching |
| 9. Evoke reflection | – Encourage generation of solution processes, and make students compare their solutions to expert solutions<br>– Encourage the discussion of differences among solutions in comparison to expert solution<br>– Provide formative feedback |

(continued)

**Table 10** (continued)

| Principle | Instructional activities |
|---|---|
|  | – Encourage peer feedback<br>– Encourage self-feedback strategies |
| 10. Facilitating the development of metacognitive knowledge (learning strategies) and skills (self-monitoring, planning, and evaluation) | – Explicitly teach metacognitive strategies<br>– Witness the value of self-monitoring<br>– Provide possibilities to plan, monitor, and evaluate work<br>– Highlight similarities across domains to encourage students to use metacognitive skills across the curriculum |

The website of the Partnership for twenty-first Century Learning Group provides informative resources describing the framework of twenty-first-century skills and learning, as well as twenty-first-century support systems required for effective learning in the twenty-first century. These include twenty-first Century Standards, Assessments of twenty-first Century Skills, twenty-first Century Curriculum and Instruction, twenty-first Century Professional Development, and twenty-first Century Learning Environments. The P21 frameworks were compiled by teachers, education experts, and leaders in business and are in use both in the USA and abroad.

https://www.apa.org/ed/schools/teaching-learning

Accessible, easy-to-use, and evidence-based resources that are considered supportive to teachers and school professionals including counsellors and administrators. The Center for Psychology in Schools and Education creates these resources so as to enhance the application of psychological science in school programs and policies for schools and pre-K to 12 education.

https://www.apa.org/ed/schools/teaching-learning/top-twenty/principles

These top 20 principles have been derived from psychological research to support evidence-based teaching and learning in pre-K to 12. The principles are student-focused, learning-focused, and assessment- and feedback-focused.

https://www.esplat.org/

ESPLAT is the European Society for Psychology Learning and Teaching. It provides resources and information about different teaching topics, including psychology in teacher education.

https://journals.sagepub.com/home/plj

The *Psychology Learning and Teaching* (PLAT) journal is specifically dedicated to publishing research and practice in psychology learning and teaching, including research in the area of psychology in teacher education.

http://teachpsych.org/

The Society for the Teaching of Psychology offers a wide variety of resources for psychology teachers including resources for teacher education.

http://www.efpta.org/home/

The European Federation of Psychology Teachers' Associations provides many different resources for teaching psychology in secondary education.

## Cross-References

▶ Assessment of Learning in Psychology
▶ First Principles of Instruction Revisited
▶ Formative Assessment and Feedback Strategies
▶ Inquiry-Based Learning in Psychology
▶ Service Learning
▶ Problem-Based Learning and Case-Based Learning

## References

African Union. (2019). *African framework of standards and competences for the teaching profession*. Addis Ababa, Ethiopia: African Union Commission.

Albright, G. (2020). Introduction to PK12 professional development role-play simulation technology. In E. Bradley (Ed.), *Games and simulations in teacher education* (pp. 7–17). Cham, Switzerland: Springer.

American Psychological Association, Coalition for Psychology in Schools and Education. (2015). *Top 20 principles from psychology for preK–12 teaching and learning*. Retrieved from http://www.apa.org/ed/schools/cpse/top-twenty-principles.pdf

Anderson, L. M., Blumenfeld, P., Pintrich, P. R., Clark, C. M., Marx, R. W., & Peterson, P. (1995). Educational psychology for teachers: Reforming our courses, rethinking our roles. *Educational Psychologist, 30*(3), 143–157.

Barron, B. J., Schwartz, D. L., Vye, N. J., Moore, A., Petrosino, A., Zech, L., & Bransford, J. D. (1998). Doing with understanding: Lessons from research on problem- and project-based learning. *Journal of the Learning Sciences, 7*, 271–311.

Bennett, R. E. (2011). Formative assessment: A critical review. *Assessment in Education: Principles, Policy & Practice, 18*(1), 5–25.

Biggs, J. (2012). What the student does: Teaching for enhanced learning. *Higher Education Research & Development, 31*(1), 39–55.

Biggs, J. (2014). Constructive alignment in university teaching. *Review of Higher Education, 1*, 5–22.

Black, P., & Wiliam, D. (2009). Developing the theory of formative assessment. Educational Assessment, Evaluation and Accountability (formerly: Journal of Personnel Evaluation in Education), 21(1), 5–31.

Bologna Working Group. (2005). *A framework for qualifications of the European higher education area* (Bologna Working Group Report on Qualifications Frameworks). Copenhagen: Danish Ministry of Science, Technology and Innovation. Retrieved from http://ecahe.eu/w/index.php/Framework_for_Qualifications_of_the_European_Higher_Education_Area

Bradley, E. (2020). Introduction. In E. Bradley (Ed.), *Games and simulations in teacher education* (pp. 1–6). Cham, Switzerland: Springer.

Brookhart, S. M., & McMillan, J. H. (Eds.). (2019). *Classroom assessment and educational measurement*. London, UK: Routledge.

Centre of Study for Policies and Practices in Education. (2013). *Learning standards, teaching standards and standards for school principals: A comparative study*. Chile: Organisation for Economic Cooperation and Development. https://doi.org/10.1787/5k3tsjqtp90v-en

Clark, S., Porath, S., Thiele, J., & Jobe, M. (2020). *Action Research*. Manhattan, KS: New Prairie Press. https://newprairiepress.org/ebooks/34

Collins, A., Brown, J. S., & Newman, S. E. (1989). Cognitive apprenticeship: Teaching the crafts of reading, writing, and mathematics. In L. B. Resnick (Ed.), *Knowing, learning, and instruction* (pp. 453–494). Hillsdale, NJ: Erlbaum.

Council of Chief State School Officers. (2013, April). Interstate teacher assessment and support consortium. In *TASC model core teaching standards and learning progressions for teachers 1.0: A resource for ongoing teacher development*. Washington, DC: Author.

Darling-Hammond, L. (2006). Constructing 21st-century teacher education. *Journal of Teacher Education, 57*(3), 300–314.

Darling-Hammond, L., & Bransford, J. (2005). *Preparing teachers for a changing world: What teachers should learn and be able to do*. San Francisco, CA: Jossey-Bass.

De Bruyckere, P., Kirschner, P. A., & Hulshof, C. (2019). *More urban myths about learning and Education: Challenging eduquacks, extraordinary claims, and alternative facts*. London, UK: Routledge.

Deibl, I., Zumbach, J., Geiger, V., & Neuner, C. (2018). Constructive alignment in the field of educational psychology: Development and application of a questionnaire for assessing constructive alignment. *Psychology Learning and Teaching, 17*(3), 293–307. https://doi.org/10.1177/1475725718791050

Dekker, S., Lee, N. C., Howard-Jones, P., & Jolles, J. (2012). Neuromyths in education: Prevalence and predictors of misconceptions among teachers. *Frontiers in Psychology, 3*, 429. https://doi.org/10.3389/fpsyg.2012.00429

Elvira, Q., Imants, J., Dankbaar, B., & Segers, M. (2017). Designing education for professional expertise development. *Scandinavian Journal of Educational Research, 61*(2), 187–204. https://doi.org/10.1080/00313831.2015.1119729

European Commission. (2013). *Supporting teacher competence development for better learning outcomes*. Luxembourg, Luxembourg: European Commission.

European Commission. (2018). *European qualifications framework: Supporting learning, work and cross-border mobility*. Luxembourg, Luxembourg: European Commission.

Evans, C. (2013). Making sense of assessment feedback in higher education. *Review of Educational Research, 83*(1), 70–120.

Felten, P. (2013). Principles of good practice in SoTL. *Teaching and Learning Inquiry, 1*(1), 121–125.

Fives, H., & Buehl, M. M. (2012). Spring cleaning for the "messy" construct of teachers' beliefs: What are they? Which have been examined? What can they tell us? In K. R. Harris, S. Graham, T. Urdan, S. Graham, J. M. Royer, & M. Zeidner (Eds.), *APA educational psychology handbook (Individual differences and cultural and contextual factors)* (Vol. 2, pp. 471–499). Washington, D.C.: American Psychological Association. https://doi.org/10.1037/13274-019

Flores, M. A., & Swennen, A. (2020). The COVID-19 pandemic and its effects on teacher education. *European Journal of Teacher Education, 43*(4), 453–456. https://doi.org/10.1080/02619768.2020.1824253

Frerejean, J., Van Merriënboer, J. J., Kirschner, P. A., Roex, A., Aertgeerts, B., & Marcellis, M. (2019). Designing instruction for complex learning: 4C/ID in higher education. *European Journal of Education, 54*(4), 513–524.

Good, T. L., & Levin, J. R. (2001). Educational psychology yesterday, today, and tomorrow: Debate and direction in an evolving field. *Educational Psychologist, 36*(2), 69–72.

Hattie, J. (2009). *Visible learning: A synthesis of over 800 meta-analyses relating to achievement*. New York, NY: Routledge, Taylor & Francis.

Hattie, J., & Timperley, H. (2007). The power of feedback. *Review of Educational Research, 77*(1), 81–112.

Hoveid, H., & Hoveid, M. (2019). *Making education educational: A reflexive approach to teaching*. Cham, Switzerland: Springer.

Irma, E., & Ebersöhn, L. (2004). *Keys to educational psychology*. Capetown, South Africa: UCT Press.

Janssen, F., Westbroek, H. B., & Doyle, W. (2014). The practical turn in teacher education: Designing a preparation sequence for core practice frames. *Journal of Teacher Education, 65*(3), 195–206.

Jeffries, C., & Maeder, D. W. (2011). Comparing vignette instruction and assessment tasks to classroom observations and reflections. *The Teacher Educator, 46*(2), 161–175. https://doi.org/10.1080/08878730.2011.552667

Klahr, D., & Nigam, M. (2004). The equivalence of learning paths in early science instruction: Effects of direct instruction and discovery learning. *Psychological Science, 15*(10), 661–667. https://doi.org/10.1111/j.0956-7976.2004.00737.x

Kluger, A. N., & DeNisi, A. (1996). The effects of feedback interventions on performance: A historical review, a meta-analysis, and a preliminary feedback intervention theory. *Psychological Bulletin, 119*(2), 254–284.

Koehler, M., & Mishra, P. (2009). What is technological pedagogical content knowledge (TPACK)? *Contemporary Issues in Technology and Teacher Education, 9*(1), 60–70.

Koenig, J., & Pflanzl, B. (2016). Is teacher knowledge associated with performance? On the relationship between teachers' general pedagogical knowledge and instructional quality. *European Journal of Teacher Education, 39*(4), 419–436.

Lohse-Bossenz, H., Kunina-Habenicht, O., & Kunter, M. (2013). The role of educational psychology in teacher education: Expert opinions on what teachers should know about learning, development, and assessment. *European Journal of Psychology of Education, 28*(4), 1543–1565.

Mayer, D., & Oancea, A. (2021). Teacher education research, policy and practice: Finding future research directions. *Oxford Review of Education, 47*(1), 1–7.

McInerney, D. M. (2014). *Education psychology constructing learning* (6th ed.). Frenchs Forest, NSW, Australia: Pearson.

Menter, I., & Flores, M. A. (2021). Connecting research and professionalism in teacher education. *European Journal of Teacher Education, 44*(1), 115–127.

Merrill, M. D. (2002). First principles of instruction. *Educational Technology Research and Development, 50*(3), 43–59.

Mohamed, Z., Valcke, M., & De Wever, B. (2017). Are they ready to teach? Student teachers' readiness for the job with reference to teacher competence frameworks. *Journal of Education for Teaching, 43*(2), 151–170.

Moser, S., Zumbach, J., Deibl, I., Geiger, V., & Martinek, D. (2021). Development and application of a scale for assessing pre-service teachers' beliefs about the nature of educational psychology. *Psychology Learning & Teaching, 20*(2), 189–213. https://doi.org/10.1177/1475725720974575

Narciss, S. (2008). Feedback strategies for interactive learning tasks. In J. M. Spector, M. D. Merrill, J. J. G. Van Merrienboer, & M. P. Driscoll (Eds.), *Handbook of research on educational communications and technology* (3rd ed., pp. 125–144). Mahaw, NJ: Lawrence Erlbaum.

Narciss, S. (2017). Conditions and effects of feedback viewed through the lens of the interactive tutoring feedback model. In D. Carless, S. M. Bridges, C. K. Y. Chan, & R. Glofcheski (Eds.), *Scaling up assessment for learning in higher education* (pp. 173–189). Singapore, Singapore: Springer.

Narciss, S. (2019). Curriculum design for (non-) psychology programs–a reflection on general and specific issues, and approaches on how to address them: Comment on Dutke et al., 2019. *Psychology Learning & Teaching, 18*(2), 144–147.

Narciss, S., Hammer, E., Damnik, G., Kisielski, K., & Körndle, H. (2021). Promoting prospective teacher competences for designing, implementing, evaluating, and adapting interactive formative feedback strategies. *Psychology Learning & Teaching, 20*(2), 261–278.

National Board for Professional Teaching Standards. (2016). *What teachers should know and be able to do*. Retrieved March 08, 2020, from https://www.nbpts.org/standards-five-core-propositions/

NSW Education Standards Authority. (2014). *Australian professional standards for teachers*. Sydney, NSW, Australia: Author.

Ostrosky, M. M., Mouzourou, C., Danner, N., & Zaghlawan, H. Y. (2013). Improving teacher practices using microteaching: Planful video recording and constructive feedback. *Young Exceptional Children, 16*(1), 16–29.

Partnership for 21st Century Skills. (2015). *Framework for 21st century learning*. Washington, DC. Retrieved from http://www.p21.org/storage/documents/docs/P21_framework_0816.pdf.

Patrick, H., Anderman, L. H., Bruening, P. S., & Duffin, L. C. (2011). The role of educational psychology in teacher education: Three challenges for educational psychologists. *Educational Psychologist, 46*(2), 71–83. https://doi.org/10.1080/00461520.2011.538648

Potter, M. K., & Kustra, E. (2011). The relationship between scholarly teaching and SoTL: Models, distinctions, and clarifications. *International Journal for the Scholarship of Teaching and Learning, 5*(1). Online: http://www.georgiasouthern.edu/ijsotl.

Qi, C., & Rude, L. (2019). Educational Psychology (3rd. Edition). Beijing, China: Higher Education Press.

Rato, J. R., Abreu, A. M., & Castro-Caldas, A. (2013). Neuromyths in education: What is fact and what is fiction for Portuguese teachers? *Educational Research, 55*(4), 441–453.

Reigeluth, C. M. (1999). The elaboration theory: Guidance for scope and sequence decisions. In C. M. Reigeluth (Ed.), *Instructional-design theories and models* (pp. 425–453). Mahwah, NJ: Lawrence Erlbaum.

Reigeluth, C. M. (2018). Lesson blueprints based on the elaboration theory of instruction. In C. M. Reigeluth (Ed.), *Instructional theories in action* (pp. 245–288). New York, NY: Routledge.

Reinholz, D. (2016). The assessment cycle: A model for learning through peer assessment. *Assessment & Evaluation in Higher Education, 41*(2), 301–315.

Shute, V. J. (2008). Focus on formative feedback. *Review of Educational Research, 78*(1), 153–189.

Snowman, J. (1997). Educational psychology: What do we teach, what should we teach? *Educational Psychology Review, 9*, 151–170. https://doi.org/10.1023/A:1024740512959

Snowman, J., & McCown, R. (2014). *Psychology applied to teaching*. Stamford, CT: Cengage Learning.

Stockard, J., Wood, T. W., Coughlin, C., & Rasplica Khoury, C. (2018). The effectiveness of direct instruction curricula: A meta-analysis of a half century of research. *Review of Educational Research, 88*(4), 479–507.

Stringer, E. T. (2008). *Action research in education*. Upper Saddle River, NJ: Pearson Prentice Hall.

Sweller, J., Ayres, P., & Kalyuga, S. (2011). *Cognitive Load Theory*. Amsterdam, The Netherlands: Springer.

Teachers' Council of Thailand. (2018). *South East Asia Teachers Competence Framework (SEA-TCF)*. Bangkok, Thailand: Teachers' Council of Thailand.

Thorpe, R. (2014). Sustaining the teaching profession. *New England Journal of Public Policy, 26*(1), 1–16.

Torp, L., & Sage, S. (2002). *Problems as possibilities: Problem-based learning for K-16 education* (2nd ed.). Alexandria, Egypt: Association for Supervision and Curriculum Development.

UNESCO Institute for Statistics. (2012). *International standard classification of education: ISCED 2011* (Comparative Social Research, 30). https://hdl.voced.edu.au/10707/240136.

Urhahne, D., Dresel M., & Fischer, F. (2019). *Psychologie für den Lehrberuf* [Psychology for the teaching profession]. Berlin, Germany: Springer.

Van Merriënboer, J. J. G. (2012). Four-component instructional design. In N. M. Seel (Ed.), *Encyclopedia of the sciences of learning*. Boston, MA: Springer. https://doi.org/10.1007/978-1-4419-1428-6_414

Van Merriënboer, J. J. G., & Kester, L. (2014). The four-component instructional design model: Multimedia principles in environments for complex learning. In R. E. Mayer (Ed.), *The Cambridge handbook of multimedia learning* (pp. 104–148). Cambridge, UK: Cambridge University Press. https://doi.org/10.1017/CBO9781139547369.007

Van Merriënboer, J. J. G., & Kirschner, P. A. (2013). *Ten steps to complex learning: A systematic approach to four-component instructional design* (2nd ed.). New York, NY: Routledge.

Voogt, J., & Roblin, N. P. (2012). A comparative analysis of international frameworks for 21st century competences: Implications for national curriculum policies. *Journal of Curriculum Studies, 44*(3), 299–321. https://doi.org/10.1080/00220272.2012.668938

Wang, X., Su, Y., Cheung, S., Wong, E., & Kwong, T. (2013). An exploration of Biggs' constructive alignment in course design and its impact on students' learning approaches. *Assessment & Evaluation in Higher Education, 38*(4), 477–491.

Willingham, D. T. (2017). A mental model of the learner: Teaching the basic science of educational psychology to future teachers. *Mind, Brain, and Education, 11*(4), 166–175.

Woolfolk Hoy, A. (2000). Educational psychology in teacher education. *Educational Psychologist, 35*(4), 257–270.

Zumbach, J. (2021). *Digitales Lehren und Lernen* [Digital teaching and learning]. Stuttgart: Kohlhammer.

# Teaching Psychology in Secondary Education

## High School Psychology in the United States

Rob McEntarffer and Kristin Whitlock

## Contents

| | |
|---|---|
| Introduction | 848 |
| History: How Did We Get Here? | 849 |
| US High School Psychology Course Curriculum and Instruction | 851 |
| Challenges | 854 |
| Hope for the Future | 856 |
| Implications for Non-US Psychology Teachers | 858 |
| Conclusion | 860 |
| Cross-References | 861 |
| References | 861 |

### Abstract

This chapter focuses on the teaching of introductory psychology in secondary education (high schools) in the United States and recommendations that may be useful for university-level psychology teachers based on the US high school psychology experience. The chapter summarizes the historical origins of US high school psychology, discusses national organizations and curriculum guidance documents relevant to high school psychology curriculum/instruction, and describes what is typically taught in high school psychology courses. The end of the chapter focuses on potential implications for international college psychology teachers and hopes for the future of US high school psychology.

---

R. McEntarffer (✉)
Lincoln Public Schools, Lincoln, NE, USA
e-mail: rmcenta@lps.org

K. Whitlock
Davis High School, Kaysville, UT, USA

© Springer Nature Switzerland AG 2023
J. Zumbach et al. (eds.), *International Handbook of Psychology Learning and Teaching*,
Springer International Handbooks of Education,
https://doi.org/10.1007/978-3-030-28745-0_39

**Keywords**

High school psychology · Secondary school psychology · Introductory psychology · Teaching psychology · International psychology

## Introduction

In the United States, millions of secondary education (high school) students take an introductory psychology course every year. Psychology has been a part of the American high school experience for over a hundred years and is taught in all 50 US states (Keith, Hammer, Blair-Broeker, & Ernst, 2013). This widespread exposure to psychology in high school may be a uniquely American phenomenon: it is difficult to find reliable information about how prevalent psychology courses are in high schools worldwide, but statistics from the College Board may be an indication. The College Board Advanced Placement (AP) program is a series of course curricula and end-of-course tests that students can choose to participate in for the purpose of earning university credit during their high school career. In the United States, the College Board lists 9,692 high schools as offering an Advanced Placement psychology course (College Board, 2020). Across the 10 most populous non-US countries (see Fig. 1), only 191 high schools total are listed in the same College Board database. The International Baccalaureate (IB) program reports that there were 22,789 students who took an IB Psychology course in 2020 (International Baccalaureate Organization, 2020). About half of IB students attend school in the United States, so it is safe to assume that about 11,000 of these high school students who took the IB course are in the United States (the IB organization does not report this information specifically). If these dramatic differences between the numbers of AP and IB Psychology courses in the United States and other countries are an indication of the trend in the international prevalence of high school psychology courses, then the US high school psychology course experience may be at least somewhat unique. Examining the history, curriculum, and outcomes of this course may be useful for psychology instructors in order to add to the international perspective on psychology teaching.

In this chapter, we seek to "tell the story" of US high school psychology courses for international readers because parts of this story may be useful for teachers of psychology outside the United States. The authors of this chapter have been teaching high school psychology in the United States for 44 years combined, and we have been involved in efforts at the national level to help US psychology teachers improve curriculum and instruction. In many ways, our teaching careers are intertwined with the story of US high school psychology. We begin the chapter with a brief summary of the historical origins of US high school psychology and discuss US national organizations and position statements that currently influence US high school psychology curriculum and instruction. Then we describe the range of learning goals most common in high school psychology courses and identify potential implications for university psychology teachers. We end the chapter with discussions

| Rank | Country | Number of AP Psychology courses |
|---|---|---|
| 1 | China | 155 |
| 2 | India | 6 |
| 3 | United States | 9,692 |
| 4 | Indonesia | 6 |
| 5 | Pakistan | 3 |
| 6 | Nigeria | 4 |
| 7 | Brazil | 2 |
| 8 | Bangladesh | 1 |
| 9 | Russia | 1 |
| 10 | Mexico | 13 |

**Fig. 1** Advanced placement psychology courses in the top 10 most populous countries. (Source: https://apcourseaudit.inflexion.org/ledger)

of implications for non-US psychology teachers and hopes for the future of US high school psychology.

## History: How Did We Get Here?

Several histories of high school psychology courses document how this class began and evolved in the United States (Benjamin Jr., 2001; Coffield & Engle, 1960; Engle, 1967; Griggs, Jackson, & Meyer, 1989; Keith et al., 2013; Ragland, 1992; White, Marcuella, & Oresick, 1979). For the purposes of this chapter, it may be useful to focus on how the US high school psychology course evolved from its origins to a course based on the science of psychology.

Psychology may have been offered in some US high schools since at least 1895, and a nationwide survey in 1960 reported that the course was offered in 39 states

(Coffield & Engle, 1960). This same report indicated that the number of psychology courses was increasing nationwide. The authors explained that "the trend of today is toward a more intense development of science, psychology cannot be offered" and this trend may have been preventing the course from expanding further (Coffield & Engle, 1960, pg. 352). The "competition" between high school psychology courses and "real" or "hard" science courses has apparently existed for the entire history of the high school psychology course.

Engle (1967) noted that high school textbooks with the word "psychology" in the title first appeared in 1889 and noted that one of the factors limiting the number of high school psychology courses was the lack of trained teachers. It is likely that the training these teachers were missing was training in teaching a science course. The relative lack of previous instruction in science emerged in another survey (White et al., 1979), which indicated that high school psychology courses were more likely to include topics such as personal problems and family living rather than topics like biological bases of behavior and statistics. One decade later, a similar survey (Griggs et al., 1989) found that most high school psychology courses focused on developmental and personality concepts rather than addressing a full survey of typical university introductory psychology courses and that this specific focus for high school psychology courses likely was caused by "limited training of the instructors" (pg. 120). In this survey, teachers reported that their university courses and teaching methodology courses focused on history content and instruction with very few courses in social sciences.

Ragland (1992) found that the psychology course was still not the main focus for most teachers assigned to teach high school psychology. These teachers' "teaching identities" were not solely or mainly centered on psychology. Most teachers reported that the majority of their teaching day was devoted to a variety of courses other than psychology. By 2009, researchers documented an increase in the quality of US high school psychology courses as indicated by increasing numbers of high school teachers with a psychology background in their undergraduate careers and some evidence that experiences in high school psychology courses were associated with higher achievement in university psychology courses (Hedges & Thomas, 2009). A more recent summary describing the history and state of the US high school psychology course (Keith et al., 2013) acknowledged the historical lack of science preparation of high school psychology teachers, but documented a change due to the "golden era" of training for high school psychology teachers between 1992 and 1999. They referred to this period as a golden era because of the wealth of training opportunities available specifically for high school psychology teachers. These training opportunities and resources included a new AP Psychology course and curriculum, National Science Foundation (NSF)-supported training workshops for teachers, and support from the American Psychological Association (APA) for the development of national standards. The authors of this chapter enter the story during this "golden age." Both authors attended an NSF-funded workshop at Texas A&M University in the summer of 1994. This month-long training experience changed who we were as teachers and launched us toward lifelong careers dedicated to high school psychology.

This brief review of the history of the US high school psychology course highlights a theme that will recur several times during this chapter: in the past, high school psychology courses focused on a narrow band of what some psychologists might call "applied" topics rather than the breadth of topics included in an undergraduate psychology survey course. This specificity may have been due to a lack of science training for high school psychology teachers and few resources devoted specifically to high school psychology teachers. As training opportunities increased, so did the variety and scope of high school psychology courses. Current US high school psychology courses are more focused than they have been in the past on the science of psychology.

## US High School Psychology Course Curriculum and Instruction

The US high school psychology course emphasized different aspects of psychology throughout its history. The learning objectives and curriculum for the course have evolved toward a focus on the science of psychology and making sure students are exposed to a survey of the breadth of psychological research areas. In this section of the chapter, we will describe the most common goals of current US high school psychology courses and some of the continuing challenges relevant to the content of this course.

A well-taught introductory psychology course provides instructors, at all educational levels, an opportunity to introduce students to the concepts that explain our cognition and behaviors. In that journey, students learn the principles that guide scientific discovery and begin to discriminate between empirical findings and the psychological misconceptions prevalent in the media. students learn the vocabulary that helps them connect personal experience to the world around them. Students learn the difference between correlation and causation, the importance of sampling and random assignment to research, and how to analyze data using statistics and practice reading graphs. Students are consumers of psychological information, and this class, in high school or university, provides students with tools to think critically about these sources and discern fact from unsubstantiated claims.

In addition, students learn the vocabulary that helps them connect personal experience to the world around them. Students begin to realize how psychology can help solve many troubling problems facing the world. They may become increasingly sensitive to the influence of bias on their perceptions and recognize the cognitive fallacies that hinder good decision-making. Experiences in this course may transform a student's perception of themselves and their relationships with others. They learn effective ways of coping with stress and research-based ways of increasing their personal well-being. Students also learn the basic principles of learning and the fragile nature of memory. These concepts have the potential to transform their lives. For many high school students, this class may be their only formal exposure to these principles.

Other students may continue their education at the university level where they may major in psychology and possibly choose to pursue a graduate degree; thus, this class serves as an important starting point in the educational pipeline. A high-quality high school course may serve as the beginning of the pipeline for committed, excited undergraduate psychology majors. High school psychology courses can give students enough information and experiences with psychology to convince them that this is the area they want to focus on in university, and they may start their university experience committed to studying psychology because they already made an informed decision in high school. These students will be familiar with some of the vocabulary and skills they will need to be successful in university psychology classes. Research findings are mixed regarding whether high school students with psychology experience perform better in university-level psychology classes. Studies do not find strong relationships between past experience in high school psychology and success as measured by course grades, but high school psychology courses seem to be associated with increased familiarity with important terms that help undergraduates be more confident in their university-level courses (Carstens & Beck, 1986; Hedges & Thomas, 1980). College Board-sponsored research indicates that students who are successful on the AP Psychology test are more likely to succeed in psychology university courses (Wyatt, Jagesic, & Godfrey, 2018), but it is not clear that the specialized training students experience in AP Psychology courses is similar enough to non-AP courses to confer the same benefit in university courses.

Even though some research studies do not find clear evidence of increased academic success that can be attributed to high school psychology courses, one benefit is clear: all former high school psychology students who enter university already convinced that they are interested in psychology will inevitably increase the chances they will major in psychology and commit to courses in the department. These students may experience many of the same academic struggles all new university students experience, but they at least know they are interested in the science of psychology, and this increased interest may benefit those students and the university. These students may be more likely to seek out research and leadership opportunities in psychology departments and commit to psychology as their area during their undergraduate experience.

The benefits of taking a psychology course in high school may differ widely based on the students, their experiences, and future goals. Diversity is also reflected in the widely different contexts in which the course is taught. Some teachers are working in large urban or suburban high schools with thousands of adolescent students, while others may be working in small rural schools that serve students from kindergarten to high school. Some instructors teach in private religious schools, in public schools, or in publicly funded charter schools. Many teach this course in a semester, while others complete this course in a year. Some classes are taught primarily through lecture, while others use a more active learning approach. Many teachers incorporate class demonstrations of basic principles as a primary means to illustrate core concepts, where others incorporate lab experiences into the curriculum. In many schools, students can enroll in university-level psychology courses while still in high school, such as the AP or IB programs. Increasingly, students may enroll in Concurrent Enrollment (CE), also called Dual Enrollment, courses at their local high schools that allow them to earn university credit from participating schools of higher education.

In addition to the varied contexts in which this course is taught, the students themselves are incredibly diverse. Their different cultural, ethnic, and racial backgrounds shape their perception of concepts presented in class and how they apply these principles to their everyday lives. Students' academic interest and abilities differ widely. In one class, some students may be reading at a university level, while others struggle to read. Teachers provide academic accommodations for students with 504 or Individual Educational Plan (IEP) designations as required by law. These designations require an official diagnosis of a disability that may interfere with learning or a pattern of past academic challenges for specific students. Students with 504 or IEP designations have documentation for teachers regarding what accommodations or modifications should be available to them during instruction and for assessments.

Students also vary widely in their expectations of the course. Because many are exposed to media portrayals of psychologists as therapists, they assume that the course will focus primarily on mental health topics. Students' motivations for enrolling in the course vary widely. Some students, because of trauma in their own lives, seek out this class to help them understand their experiences. Some are curious based on psychological information they read online, fiction they have read, or media portrayals of psychological illness. Some students may know psychologists from their family or through other social contacts, and these relationships sparked their interest. Others have no interest in the course material at all, but are hoping for an "easy" class that will fill an elective credit toward graduation.

Amidst this diversity, teachers of psychology must decide what should be emphasized during the short period they have their students in their class. This is not an easy task as historically there has been little guidance in this area. In the United States, psychology is an elective course, meaning that students are not required to take this course to graduate from high school. Because of this, little attention has been given to setting standards to guide important curriculum decisions. Instructors are also divided in their beliefs of what the overall learning goals of the course should be. In other words, should the focus of the course be on teaching the specific content of psychology or should the emphasis be on helping students acquire scientific reasoning, critical thinking skills, and/or the skills that make them more marketable in the world of work?

For most of the history of the high school psychology course, curriculum standards for what should be taught were not sufficiently addressed by either social studies or science curriculum standards. In 1999, the APA formally addressed this omission with their approval of the *National Standards for High School Psychology Curricula* (hereafter referred as "the Standards"). This standards document provides needed guidance about the overall content and skills that should be included in the course. The Standards divide the content of psychology into seven broad domains with "scientific inquiry" emphasized because of its importance in conveying the scientific nature of the field.

While the Standards are revolutionary, useful, and easily available, APA still faces challenges in making teachers aware of their existence and in widespread adoption of these standards by individual states. To date, 34 states have no curriculum standards for this course. Three states (Alabama, Florida, and Tennessee) have standards based on APA's, one state (Utah) refers its teachers directly to the Standards, six states (Indiana, Kansas, Oklahoma, Texas, North Dakota, and Wisconsin) have standards that roughly align or overlap with APA's Standards, and North Dakota and Wisconsin reference APA's Standards in theirs. Georgia has psychology standards that may align to APA's but not as clear as the states above. Four states (Arkansas, Maryland, Vermont, and Illinois) have standards aligned in various ways to the College, Career, and Civic Life (C3) Framework for Social Studies State Standards from the National Council for the Social Studies (NCSS). Three states (Iowa, Mississippi, and North Carolina) have standards, but they are not aligned with APA. One state, New Hampshire, briefly mentions psychology in their "minimum standards for public school approval," but psychology doesn't seem to be in their curriculum standards (E. Leary, personal communication, November 10, 2020). Thus, even with the Standards, it is unclear what is actually being taught in high school psychology courses in the United States. It is unclear as to why it is so difficult to bring cohesiveness to the teaching of this course with this valuable resource in place. It may partly be due to the broad and sometimes overwhelming amount of content. It may be due to the lack of training or the turnover in those teaching the course. In addition, there is still confusion over where this course belongs; in other words, is this a science or a social studies class? Lingering misconceptions about the nature of psychology influence the treatment this course receives at the state and local levels where curricular decisions are often made.

## Challenges

Part of the challenge of teaching the science of psychology at the high school level is reflected in an inaccurate perception of the discipline as a whole. Many within the general public, as well as those in other scientific disciplines, do not view psychology as science. Psychology is often omitted, or inconsistently recognized, as a STEM (science, technology, engineering, and mathematics) discipline or viewed as a "soft science." This basic misunderstanding of the scientific nature of the field is recognized by the APA as one of its strategic goals: to "Elevate the public's understanding of, regard for, and use of psychology" (American Psychological Association, 2021).

While there are those who question psychology's place within science, others have recognized the vital interdisciplinary role that it plays. Psychology is a "hub" science (Cacioppo, 2007), along with physics, chemistry, earth sciences, mathematics, medicine, and the social sciences, as a discipline whose empirical research findings are often cited by researchers in other fields. Psychological science provides unique insights into a range of cognitive and behavioral phenomena that informs and leads to developments in other disciplines.

While it is difficult to judge just how widespread the misperception of psychology is in the context of kindergarten through 12th grade (K12) schools, it has shaped psychology's status as an elective course, its placement primarily within the Social Studies department, the relative lack of attention paid by state boards of education and national organizations regarding curriculum standards, and the insufficient training many teachers receive to teach a science course. While scholarship on the history of the high school psychology course does not often address which department high school psychology is assigned to, some teacher education programs direct teachers who want to teach psychology to obtain a "broad-field" social studies certification rather than a specific certification in teaching science (University of Nebraska, Lincoln, n.d.). This certification requirement means that high school psychology teachers are far more likely to have more undergraduate coursework in other "social studies" courses, like history, than they are to have extensive coursework in other sciences.

The American Psychological Association (2017) has found that credentialing (academic qualifications required to teach specific courses in US schools) of high school psychology teachers is highly variable. Twenty-four states do not require a psychology credential, meaning that any qualified teacher can teach this course. This may mean that the teacher has little or no academic preparation in psychology. Fourteen states do offer a psychology teaching credential; however, teachers do not have to have this credential in order to teach the course. Only 13 states currently require a credential in psychology (American Psychological Association, 2018). Without sufficient training in science, essential understandings of the nature of this discipline may be lost as teachers struggle with concepts they are not well trained to teach.

Also, placing psychology in high school social studies departments may lead to less obvious changes in the curriculum of the course. Some K12 schools and districts develop curricula within discipline areas. A social studies curriculum director is likely to include different content and skills in a high school psychology curriculum than is a science curriculum director. High school psychology teachers rarely only teach psychology as part of their teaching load, and content/skills from the other courses they teach during the day may influence the pedagogies and examples these teachers use in their psychology classrooms. It may be impossible to determine why the majority of high school psychology courses "live" in high school social studies departments rather than science departments, but this reality influences the nature of the high school psychology courses, who gets to teach these courses, and how the courses are perceived by others.

National K12 curriculum organizations also reflect conflicting visions of where the high school psychology course belongs. The National Council for the Social Studies (NCSS) is the largest social studies curriculum organization in the United States. NCSS mentions psychology in its definition of social studies (National Council for the Social Studies, n.d.-a), but psychology is NOT listed in the "disciplinary tools and concepts" along with Civics, Economics, Geography, and History (National Council for the Social Studies, n.d.-b). The College Board lists AP Psychology in the "History and Social Sciences" section rather than in the general

"Sciences" section of their curriculum page (CollegeBoard, n.d.). A search for the term "psychology" in the Next Generation Science Standards (National Science Teachers Association, n.d.) reveals no mention of psychology in the hundreds of pages of that curriculum. Documents from these major national teaching and curriculum organizations represent the underlying reality that in high school curriculum and practice, psychology "lives" in the world of social studies, not science, and this placement may influence the scope and potential of the high school psychology course.

## Hope for the Future

Even in the context of these challenges, there is hope for the future of this course. The APA and College Board continue to move forward with policies and curricula that advance the teaching of this discipline as science. The APA's National High School Psychology Standards (American Psychology Association, August, 2011), due to expire in December 2021, are currently under revision with a projected release date of February, 2022. These revised standards will continue to emphasize the central importance of scientific inquiry and will describe connections between psychological themes and content and the Next Generation Science Standards. As these connections are clarified, state departments of education may be more likely to formally adopt the APA's Standards and move toward approving psychology as a science course. This change would allow students to earn science credit toward graduation. In addition, the College Board is already taking steps to move the AP Psychology exam from its current designation as a "History and Social Science" Exam to a "Science" exam (A. Fineburg, personal communication, January 12, 2021). Such steps would ameliorate the "non-science" status of this high school psychology course and help it find its true home among the other sciences. As the number of students taking psychology continues to increase, this is a necessary step in changing entrenched misconceptions. It will take time for these practical and attitude shifts to occur. Even among psychology teachers, these changes may bring some potential discomfort. Psychology teachers primarily see themselves as social studies teachers. With a shift in course designation to a science class, many may be concerned about whether they have the appropriate credentials, knowledge, and skills to teach the course.

Realizing the transformative potential of high school psychology, the APA sponsored the first ever National Summit on High School Psychology Education in July 2017 at Weber State University in Ogden, Utah (American Psychological Association, 2017). The purpose of the summit was to examine the state of high school psychology and create initiatives, programs, and other resources to advance its teaching. Seventy instructors representing all educational levels from across the United States were involved. Participants were divided into eight working groups (Psychology as a Science, Skills that Promote Flourishing, National Standards for High School Psychology Curricula, Assessing Student Knowledge and Skills in Psychology, Credentialing and Identifying the High School Psychology Teacher,

Ongoing Professional Development, Diversity and Access, and Technology and Online Learning). Each group was tasked with identifying areas of need and developing necessary resources. As a result of the landmark event, over 40 products ("deliverables") were created. These ranged from Advocacy Toolkits to assist teachers in approaching policymakers about credentialing and course designation; Assessment Guides assisting teachers in developing appropriate and effective assessments; lesson plans focusing on metacognitive, transferable, and well-being skills; compilations of professional development opportunities; a video on the value of high school psychology for students of all backgrounds; and vetted technology tools to help teachers address the needs of their classrooms. At the conclusion of the Summit, the Teachers of Psychology in Secondary Schools (TOPSS), the voice of high school teachers within the APA, became responsible for making these resources widely available.

One of the deliverables is tied directly to the issue of addressing the misperception of the discipline of psychology. The first working group, Psychology as a Science, provided a report called *High School Psychology is Science* (American Psychological Association, 2017). This report first provides a general overview of the connection between psychology and the other sciences. It also provides a brief history of the high school psychology course along with a discussion of the challenges facing the course and the positive outcomes for teaching psychology as science. The document also tackles several common misperceptions that lead people to believe psychology is not a science. With the goal of increasing the recognition of psychology as science, the report ends with specific recommendations, including credentialing issues. For example, the report suggests that if an instructor is determined to be qualified to teach psychology, what academic department they are employed in is not a key issue. This assurance should allay the fears of many instructors that if the course moves to the science department, they will not be able to teach the course. Another suggestion included in the report is that TOPSS create effective laboratory exercises that parallel the Next Generation Science Standards to increase student's awareness of the scientific nature of the discipline. Psychology students, like students in other scientific disciplines, need to learn the techniques of hypothesis testing and analyzing data to draw valid conclusions. Another Summit deliverable was designed to help reach this goal: the Society for the Teaching of Psychology (Division Two of the APA) published *Promoting Psychological Science: A Compendium of Laboratory Exercises for Teachers of High School Psychology* (Miller, 2018). This set of lab exercises addresses most of the content domains in introductory psychology giving students the opportunity to plan and carry out psychological investigations.

Soon after the National Summit on High School Psychology, the APA's Board of Educational Affairs (BEA) formed the Introductory Psychology Initiative (IPI) (American Psychology Association, 2018). The purpose of this initiative is to make recommendations for all major aspects of introductory psychology across all instructional levels. Members were divided into four working groups: Student Learning Outcomes (SLOs) and Assessment, Course Models and Design, Teacher Training and Development, and Student Success and Transformation. The first phase of the project, beginning in 2018, was to review existing research, conduct a national survey of instructors, and gather data, including feedback from listening sessions conducted at regional conferences. Phase 2, beginning in 2019, included the recruitment of faculty across diverse educational settings, to pilot test the recommendations of the working groups and develop case studies that illustrate the influence the implementation of these recommendations had at the different institutions. Phase 3 included presentations of the research findings and recommendations at the APA Convention in August of 2020.

The SLOs developed by the IPI working group are available to preview online (American Psychological Association, 2020) and will be discussed in more detail in an upcoming APA publication (Halonen, Thompson, Whitlock, Landrum, & Frantz, in press). Rather than prescribe specific content that must be taught in this course, the SLOs focus on three broad skills that students should develop as a result of taking this class. These skills include being able to identify basic concepts and research findings (define and explain basic psychological concepts, interpret research findings, and apply psychological principles to personal growth and everyday life) and to solve problems using psychological methods (draw logical and objective conclusions; describe the advantages and limitations of various research strategies; design, conduct, or evaluate psychological research; and counter unsubstantiated statements, opinions, or beliefs using psychological science). The third skill involves the ability to provide examples of psychology's integrative themes. This thematic approach departs from more traditional methods, but allows instructors maximum flexibility in selecting content. Instead of asking students to memorize isolated concepts, the focus is on connecting specific content to broader ideas with the hope that these ideas will linger with students long after the course concludes.

The IPI project provides instructors with some preliminary resources (American Psychological Association, 2019) of how to design a course around themes. Instructors are encouraged to select specific content based on student interest or instructor expertise that connect to these broader ideas. For example, to illustrate the integrative theme "Psychology explains general principles that govern behavior while recognizing individual differences," instructors may wish to discuss the factors that influence intelligence, resilience, personality testing, supertasters, or synesthesia. The hope is that long after students forget most or all of the definitions, experiments, or theories they learned in the course, these themes will still resonate and help them successfully navigate the psychological information they are exposed to everyday.

## Implications for Non-US Psychology Teachers

The history and current status of high school psychology courses in the United States leads us to conclude that this course may be a valuable experience for secondary education students outside the United States, and psychology teachers in other countries can learn from challenges and successes in the United States to build or expand similar programs internationally. Specifically, evidence presented in this chapter indicates that the high school psychology course benefits from ongoing, strong central/national resources, teacher training programs, and continued involvement from high school psychology teachers.

The history of the high school psychology course demonstrates the need for high-quality, state, or national resources for high school teachers. For much of our history, high school psychology courses varied widely in scope and learning objectives. High school students were as likely to encounter a course based on personality or personal adjustment as they were to experience a survey of the science of psychology. The examples of national resources mentioned earlier in the chapter (from organizations such APA/TOPSS and the College Board) strengthen the high school psychology course. Since many high school psychology teachers do not have extensive course work in the science of psychology, these high-quality, research-based national documents give high school psychology teachers a solid ground to stand on. Teachers can count on these resources to be based on current research and reflect the consensus of the field. Many high school psychology teachers are the only staff member assigned to a psychology class in their school, so these national documents help communicate to these isolated teachers what the scope of an introductory psychology class should be, as well as provide references and other support as teachers plan their lessons. Specifically, the national standards from APA/TOPSS (American Psychology Association, August, 2011) and College Board AP Psychology course description (College Board, 2020) provide detailed curriculum information for high school psychology and Advanced Placement psychology teachers. Teachers from outside the United States who are interested in establishing or strengthening high school psychology programs could begin by finding or developing these "bedrock," central resources teachers can use as the bases of their high school courses.

In addition to resources, the US high school psychology course benefitted from continuing high-quality training opportunities. During the "golden age" of the development of the course (Keith et al., 2013), university psychology faculty were able to obtain grants from the National Science Foundation for summer workshops on university campuses. These multiple week-long experiences provided high school psychology teachers with an "immersion" experience. Teachers lived on campus and attended courses that represented the full range of the science of psychology. For many teachers, this workshop was their first opportunity to focus solely on university-level psychology content and instruction. These NSF-funded workshops trained a generation of high school psychology teachers who went on to seek out leadership and other service opportunities in national high school psychology organizations (this generation includes the co-authors of this chapter). The legacy of these training opportunities continues with week-long APA-funded experiences at other university campuses. Other training opportunities also exist for high school psychology teachers: APA/TOPSS sponsors shorter workshops and continually provides high-quality instructional materials (Clark University, n.d.; Oregon State University, 2019). The College Board continually updates the AP Psychology Course Exam Description (College Board, 2020) and organizes day- and week-long workshops for AP Psychology teachers. Less formal opportunities now exist for high school psychology teachers seeking support and information: the AP Psychology Teachers Facebook page (Facebook, 2020) includes more than 6,000 teachers and features multiple questions and answers hourly. Teachers from outside the United States who are interested in supporting high school psychology programs should consider establishing ongoing training opportunities grounded in university-level science-based psychology content so that high school teachers can compensate for a lack of background in psychology coursework and stay current in their field.

Another lesson to be learned from the story of the high school psychology course is that the strength of high school psychology depends on the continued involvement of high school psychology teachers. At every stage in the journey from the beginning of the high school psychology course until now, national organizations and resources emerged from the involvement and effort of high school psychology teachers, supported by university psychology researchers and teachers. The APA recognized the importance of involving high school psychology teachers in their efforts as long ago as the 1970s: the APA established the Clearinghouse for Precollege Psychology and began publishing a newsletter in order to share materials created by and for high school psychology teachers (Keith et al., 2013). The emergence and continued efforts of TOPSS depend on the involvement of high school psychology teachers: the TOPSS board is made up of high school psychology teachers and includes one university psychology instructor as an advisor. The College Board institutionalized high school teacher involvement in the structure of the scoring system for the AP Psychology exam: half the leadership and other roles for the scoring process for the written portion of the AP exam are reserved for high school psychology teachers. Teachers from outside the United States who are interested in supporting high school psychology programs should remember to enlist, empower, and enable high school psychology teachers to develop and lead efforts to strengthen high school psychology programs.

## Conclusion

High school students in the United States have been experiencing some version of a psychology course for over a hundred years. The prevalence and content of this course has changed over time. The current high school psychology teacher community is a strong group of teachers dedicated to helping young people understand the breadth of the science of psychology and how these ideas can help them understand human thinking and behavior. High school psychology teachers are committed to a philosophy of "giving psychology away" (Miller, 1969). Formal and informal teacher communities share materials nationwide through social networks and offer advice, guidance, and support daily. Some high school psychology teachers are beginning to work with university faculty to take a possible next step in our discipline: help non-psychology teachers understand how principles of cognitive psychology can help students learn and teachers teach (Chew, 2020).

It may be useful for psychology teachers outside the United States to investigate local high school psychology courses and seek out high school teachers. A strong high school psychology program can benefit higher education institutions by increasing student interest in the science of psychology and helping to better prepare undergraduate students who may take university psychology courses. In addition, forming relationships with high school psychology teachers can benefit university psychology faculty. We are a fun bunch of people, and we are always excited to establish professional relationships with university psychology teachers.

## Cross-References

▶ Basic Principles and Procedures for Effective Teaching in Psychology
▶ Educational Psychology: Learning and Instruction
▶ First Principles of Instruction Revisited
▶ Psychology in Social Science and Education
▶ Psychology in Teacher Education
▶ Teaching Introductory Psychology
▶ Teaching of General Psychology: Problem Solving
▶ Teaching Psychology in Secondary Education
▶ Teaching the Foundations of Psychological Science

## References

American Psychological Association. (2017, July). *APA summit on high school psychology education*. APA Summit on High School Psychology Education. Retrieved January 4, 2021, from https://www.apa.org/ed/precollege/topss/high-school-summit?tab=1

American Psychological Association. (2018, August). *Advocacy toolkit for the psychology teaching credential*. Advocacy Toolkit for the Psychology Teaching Credential. Retrieved January 4, 2021, from https://www.apa.org/advocacy/education/psychology-teaching-credential

American Psychological Association. (2019, July). *The APA introductory psychology initiative*. The APA Introductory Psychology Initiative. Retrieved January 5, 2021, from https://www.apa.org/ed/precollege/undergrad/introductory-psychology-initiative/pilot

American Psychological Association. (2020, July). *APA Introductory Psychology Initiative (IPI) student learning outcomes for introductory psychology (Draft, July 2020)*. APA Introductory Psychology Initiative (IPI). Retrieved January 5, 2021, from https://www.google.com/url?q=https://www.apa.org/ed/precollege/undergrad/introductory-psychology-initiative/student-learning-outcomes.pdf&sa=D&ust=1609795481504000&usg=AOvVaw1H0BtZr6_9_2SpZzYWRaz_

American Psychological Association. (2021). *IMPACT APA American Psychological Association strategic plan*. IMPACT APA American Psychological Association Strategic Plan. Retrieved January 4, 2021, from https://www.apa.org/about/apa/strategic-plan

American Psychology Association. (2011, August). *National standards for high school psychology curricula*. National Standards for High School Psychology Curricula. Retrieved November 10, 2020, from https://www.apa.org/education/k12/national-standards

American Psychology Association. (2018, January). *The APA introductory psychology initiative*. The APA Introductory Psychology Initiative. Retrieved January 4, 2021, from https://www.apa.org/ed/precollege/undergrad/introductory-psychology-initiative

Benjamin, L. T., Jr. (2001). A brief history of the psychology course in American high schools. *American Psychologist, 56*(11), 951–960. https://doi.org/10.1037/0003-066X.56.11.951.

Cacioppo, J. T. (2007) The Structure of Psychology, Association for Psychological Science Presidential Column, December 2007
Carstens, C. B., & Beck, H. P. (1986). The relationship of high school psychology and natural science courses to performance in a college introductory psychology class. *Teaching of Psychology, 13*(3), 116–118. https://doi.org/10.1207/s15328023top1303_3.
Chew, S. (2020, May 27). *Teaching study skills (not just study tips) in introductory psychology.* American Psychology Association. Retrieved November 17, 2020, from https://www.apa.org/ed/precollege/psychology-teacher-network/introductory-psychology/study-skills
Clark University. (n.d.). *American Psychological Association-Clark University workshop for high school teachers.* American Psychological Association-Clark University Workshop for High School Teachers. Retrieved January 15, 2021, from https://www.clarku.edu/departments/psychology/events/american-psychological-association-clark-university-workshop-for-high-school-teachers/
Coffield, K. E., & Engle, T. L. (1960). High school psychology: A history and some observations. *American Psychologist, 15*(6), 350–352. https://psycnet.apa.org/doi/10.1037/h0049317.
College Board. (2020). *AP psychology course and exam description.* AP Psychology The Course. Retrieved November 10, 2020, from https://apcentral.collegeboard.org/courses/ap-psychology/course
CollegeBoard. (n.d.). *AP course and exam pages.* AP Course and Exam Pages. Retrieved December 21, 2020, from https://apcentral.collegeboard.org/courses
Engle, T. L. (1967). Teaching psychology at the secondary school level: Past, present, possible future. *Journal of School Psychology, 5*(3), 168–176. https://doi.org/10.1016/0022-4405(67)90037-4.
Facebook. (2020). *AP psychology teachers.* AP Psychology Teachers Private Group. Retrieved November 17, 2020, from https://www.facebook.com/groups/556665311050841
Griggs, R. A., Jackson, S. L., & Meyer, M. E. (1989). High school and college psychology: Two different worlds. *Teaching of Psychology, 16*(3), 118–120. https://doi.org/10.1207/s15328023top1603_3.
Halonen, J. S., Thompson, J. L., Whitlock, K. H., Landrum, E. R., & Frantz, S. (in press). In R. R. Gurung & G. Neufeld (Eds.), *Measuring Meaningful learning in introductory psychology: The IPI student learning outcomes* (Transforming introductory psychology: Expert advice on teaching, training, and assessing the course). American Psychological Association.
Hedges, B. W., & Thomas, J. H. (1980). The effect of high school psychology on pre-course knowledge, midterm grades, and final grades in introductory psychology. *Teaching of Psychology, 7*(4), 221–223. https://doi.org/10.1207/s15328023top0704_6.
Hedges, W., & Thomas, J. H. (2009). The effect of high school psychology on pre-course knowledge, midterm grades, and final grades in introductory psychology. *Teaching of Psychology, 7*(4), 221–223. https://doi.org/10.1207/s15328023top0704_6.
International Baccalaureate Organization. (2020). *The IB diploma programme final statistical bulletin.* The IB Diploma Programme Final Statistical Bulletin. Retrieved January 4, 2021, from https://www.google.com/url?q=https://www.ibo.org/contentassets/bc850970f4e54b87828f83c7976a4db6/dp-statistical-bulletin-may-2020-final-en.pdf&sa=D&ust=1609795481477000&usg=AOvVaw13M9kvaDveJnEzvFgO9MXf
Keith, K. D., Hammer, E. Y., Blair-Broeker, C. T., & Ernst, R. M. (2013). High school psychology: A coming of age story. *Teaching of Psychology, 40*(4), 311–317. First Published October 7, 2013 Research Article. https://doi.org/10.1177/0098628313501044.
Miller, G. (1969). Psychology as a means of promoting human welfare. *American Psychologist, 24*, 1063–1075.
Miller, R. L. (2018). *Promoting psychological science: A compendium of laboratory exercises for teachers of high school psychology.* Promoting Psychological Science: A Compendium of Laboratory Exercises for Teachers of High School Psychology. Retrieved January 15, 2021, from https://teachpsych.org/ebooks/promotingpsychscience

National Council for the Social Studies. (n.d.-a). *College, Career, and Civic Life (C3) framework for social studies state standards.* About C3. Retrieved December 21, 2020, from https://www.socialstudies.org/standards/c3

National Council for the Social Studies. (n.d.-b). *National curriculum standards for social studies: Executive summary.* National Curriculum Standards for Social Studies: Executive Summary. Retrieved December 21, 2020, from National Curriculum Standards for Social Studies: Executive Summary

National Science Teachers Association. (n.d.). *Next generation science standards.* Next Generation Science Standards. Retrieved December 21, 2020, from https://www.nextgenscience.org/

Oregon State University. (2019, April 1). *SPS to host APA/APF/Oregon State university psychological science workshop for high school psychology teachers.* SPS to host APA/APF/Oregon State University Psychological Science Workshop for High School Psychology Teachers. Retrieved January 15, 2021, from https://liberalarts.oregonstate.edu/news/sps-host-apaapforegon-state-university-psychological-science-workshop-high-school-psychology-teachers

Ragland, R. G. (1992). Teachers and teacher education in high school psychology: A national survey. *Teaching of Psychology, 19*(2), 73–78. https://doi.org/10.1207/s15328023top1902_2.

University of Nebraska, Lincoln. (n.d.). *Secondary social sciences.* Secondary Social Sciences. Retrieved January 15, 2021, from https://cehs.unl.edu/tlte/secondary-social-sciences/

White, K. M., Marcuella, H., & Oresick, R. (1979). Psychology in the high schools. *Teaching of Psychology, 6*(1), 39–42. https://doi.org/10.1207/s15328023top0601_12.

Wyatt, J., Jagesic, S., & Godfrey, K. (2018). *Postsecondary Course Performance of AP® exam takers in subsequent coursework.* College Board – Current Research. Retrieved December 17, 2020, from https://aphighered.collegeboard.org/research-reports

# Psychology in Work and Organizational Education

## 35

Pedro F. Bendassolli, Sonia Gondim, and Fellipe Coelho-Lima

## Contents

| | |
|---|---|
| Introduction | 866 |
| A Cross-Sectional Definition of Work | 867 |
| Work in Context | 869 |
| A Portfolio of Topics for WOP Teaching | 870 |
| The Ethical Dimension of WOP Teaching | 872 |
| Decision-Making: Designing a Teaching Plan | 873 |
| Challenges and Perspectives | 878 |
| References | 879 |

### Abstract

The purpose of this chapter is to provide guidelines for the teaching practice of disciplines related to Work and Organizational Psychology (WOP), applied to different fields of knowledge other than psychology. We begin by sensitizing teachers to the permeability of human work as an object of study, and a field of problematization of the psychological phenomenon in any context where it occurs. Work is a phenomenon that crosses human life and is present in any professional practice. As such, the main mission of a professor in charge of teaching the contents of this area is to understand work as a central axis whose effects are noticeable in the diverse facets of human life's contextual expressions. Our starting point is work characterization: what is this phenomenon, and which elements allow us to handle it in a cross-sectional perspective of human life. In the proposed model, we conceptualize work as an intentional action, with several ramifications in key psychological dimensions, such as those involving performance, development, health, and affectivity. By theorizing the 'work'

P. F. Bendassolli (✉) · F. Coelho-Lima
Universidade Federal do Rio Grande do Norte, Natal, Brazil

S. Gondim
Universidade Federal da Bahia, Salvador, Brazil

© Springer Nature Switzerland AG 2023
J. Zumbach et al. (eds.), *International Handbook of Psychology Learning and Teaching*,
Springer International Handbooks of Education,
https://doi.org/10.1007/978-3-030-28745-0_41

phenomenon, instead of the concepts used by the WOP area, the chapter stimulates a debate on the very nature and dissemination of knowledge. This is because, in this psychology sub-area, what we usually find are theories of medium or low reach, unable to encompass the wider phenomenon of connection between work and other psychological phenomena. In addition, without a central driver, it is up to the teacher to navigate in the ocean of concepts and techniques so widespread in the field, which makes professional qualification unstable and floating. However, in order to allow the teacher to interact with WOP scientific narratives, we present some matches between concepts used by this area and the central dimensions of the work phenomenon. Next, we develop a guide to orient the teacher in making decisions on which strategies to use to stimulate teaching and debate around this proposal, which conceives work and its connection with key psychological phenomena.

**Keywords**

Work · Meaning of work · Organizational psychology · Competences

## Introduction

Human work represents a challenge for teaching and learning processes. Working is not just an isolated activity, but takes part in a set of actions that, coordinated, result in some reality transformation, either in the form of a new product, or changes in other people. The human being, although endowed with physical and cognitive resources that enable him/her to use complex procedures, is not born with the necessary skills to exercise them. Unlike other animals, many of whom are great "workers," the human being enjoys a wide plasticity, with reflections in complex learning systems, throughout life.

Therefore, when we consider teaching topics related to work and organizations, we are talking about a process that crosses the species itself, since the human agent, when becoming a qualified worker, participates in building his/her own humanity and our civilization's. The very concept of "organization," as an objectified form (a material instance and a set of institutionalized rules and procedures), brings the work implicitly. In fact, a brief historical dive can bring to light the different forms of work organization experienced by the human being. From slavery, with its radical dependence on manual labor, to the intensely intellectual work of scientists and writers, in autonomous and creative arrangements, going through industrial work (and its machine-dependence), we see a great diversity of ways to institutionalize work, that is, to materialize it, with remarkable implications for (formal) teaching and learning processes.

Our proposal, in this chapter, goes in a different direction from several manuals that address topics on Work and Organizational Psychology, from now on called WOP. In those manuals, what we find is a more or less institutionalized set of concepts for apprehending a wide range of phenomena, whose integration they rarely discuss or demonstrate. This is because they do not always take into account a substantive view of work. For example, we can discuss "motivation," or "leadership," but it is rare to show to what extent, on a more general level, both relate to the same phenomenon: the act of working. This chapter proposes an alternative path. First, it presents a cross-sectional definition of work, by describing it as a phenomenon that crosses the human experience itself, which has agents capable of building their own "environment," their own culture, their own tools, their own future. Second, starting from this transversal notion of work, it proposes a generic roadmap in order to think about a series of topics of interest for teaching and developing competencies related to the act of working.

Essentially, our proposal is to consider *human action* as intentional, a point of articulation between psychology, organizations, and work. The latter consists precisely of a type of activity oriented to generating results in reality. Around this type of action, a series of devices converge – personal, interpersonal, social, institutional –, which function as mediation points for the referred action. Then, their results are appropriated by the subject himself and by third parties. This action is permeated by affections, by cognitive constructions, and by facilitating or hindering contextual elements.

Therefore, from the idea of work as an intentional action, we can think of topics such as psychological development, understood as the increasing capacity of the agent to manage his/her context and organize regulatory mental schemes, both internal and external. We can think of performance, as the meeting between a planned action and an action executed in specific circumstances. The performance consists, at the same time, of the descriptive (what happened or did not happen) and evaluation elements of the action (we reached or not a target previously set as necessary/intended). We can think that health is also at the action's origin, here considered as the subject's ability to be active and exercise its agency. In addition, we can also think about the ethical and moral aspects involved in generating work results.

In the next section, the chapter strengthens this definition of work initially outlined. Then, it presents itself as a counterpoint to a concrete and specific context, calling attention to the importance of thinking of work in a universal (or cross-sectional) way, but also local. Next, it suggests topics or subjects articulated with the suggested work dimensions, including those related to the ethics of teaching, and progresses with more specific and practical considerations for the preparation of a WOP teaching plan, its challenges and perspectives.

## A Cross-Sectional Definition of Work

We find the definition of work – as an intentional action that requires mediation to promote personal, material, and social changes – in the writings of several intellectuals and thinkers (e.g., Friedman & Naville, 1962; Hesiod, 2018; Marx & Engels, 2012; Vygotsky, 1997). This definition is opposed to views aligned with the etymological origin of the word "work" and Greek mythology (Leal, 1997), which associate work with a form of divine punishment, emptying its character of central value in society, which would distance us qualitatively from other animals (Blanch, 2006). One reason for this devaluation has to do with the differences in social status of the types of work that prevail in our society, since there is a small number of jobs capable of promoting human development and social justice, in opposition to the vast majority of jobs without social value and personal meaning.

However, regardless of how work is done under objective conditions, many of which deprive it from intrinsic meaning, we can assume that working consists of engaging in a conscious and intentional activity, to achieve valuable personal and social goals. Work is at the base of the economy (production and consumption of goods and services), of the world materiality (use and reuse of resources, with effects on the ways of doing), of the legal order (rights and duties of work and at work), and of shared social norms (moral conduct in social relationships). In addition, it is essential for the development of human potentials (psychological needs), and a milestone in the insertion of the human being in a universe of symbols and meanings that characterizes culture (Bendassolli & Gondim, 2019).

Figure 1 is a graphical representation of what we consider a promising approach for disciplines oriented to WOP, with an expanded definition of work at the center. We start from the principle that the human being is an active agent in the process of changing the reality. He makes use of material, affective, cognitive, and volitional resources to make a mediation capable of generating a partial or total transformation (personal, interactional, material, or social). However, social and cultural variability can hinder, to some degree, the intentional action in its purpose of change. Moreover, macroeconomic, social, technological, political, legal, and moral conditions have favored or hampered the full achievement of work.

This expanded understanding of work, considering its function and economic, social, historical, political and, therefore, psychological repercussions, is what

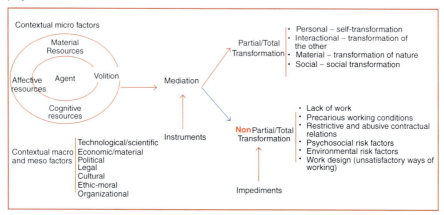

**Fig. 1** Work as a mediated transforming human action

generally supports the way by which the various subfields that make up WOP address this phenomenon. Hence, this is the main landmark for understanding the importance of WOP for training professionals from other areas, who work directly with the issue of Work and Organizations, as we next explore in more detail.

## Work in Context

In the previous section, we highlighted the definition of work as a cross-sectional category of human existence (Fig. 1). However, work is also a situated, contextual phenomenon. The way this main activity of human transformation is valued and socially organized varies greatly. Therefore, besides considering work transversality, which in itself is a form of idealization for organizing our reflection, there is another important element in a teaching-learning proposal in this field. It needs to take into account not only a unified definition of work, but also the local specificities of each country, which determine how work is institutionalized, thus creating demands for teaching and learning.

Therefore, in training courses where topics of WOP are relevant, we must acknowledge that work contexts vary a lot. On the other hand, this proposal, which conceives work as a cross-sectional activity (Fig. 1) shows that, despite the different contexts, the key dimensions of the phenomenon remain. For example, although countries differ in the way of structuring work, either due to different levels of technological maturity, or to different forms of social organization, the agent still has to engage in the actions needed for transformation, and his/her work is the means to enable it. If, in one context, mediation instruments use robots, and in others they still depend on "live" work (visible physical effort), the common factor is the need to use mediation instruments (natural or built), thus having to learn how to operate them efficiently.

Similarly, if we consider the way organizations are structured, we will find significant variations between different realities, internal to countries and, above all, when comparing them. For example, the organization may consist merely of a digital platform for work intermediation (crowdwork, people's mobile applications, and delivery). Back to Fig. 1, we can choose some possible impacts on teaching and learning processes. First, new skills are needed, and by skills, we understand the set of cognitive knowledge and the subjective mobilizations necessary to operate effectively in the material reality, like using new tools for virtual work mediation. Equally, as we observe in Latin American countries, such work organization through virtual networks may end up by penalizing workers' social organization, by interfering in their sociability processes, organization in union classes, and workers' rights and protection (Fig. 1, macro factors).

Finally, let us consider one more example. There was an increase in workers' mobility among countries, which increased the chances of working in a country other than the one where the basic vocational training took place. The recognition of this new reality raised efforts in an attempt to unify standards of scientific and practical qualification in some parts of the world. A more visible example is the

European Union's Erasmus Program (https://ec.europa.eu/programmes/erasmus-plus/about_en), which became effective in 1980. The training and education support program proposed a standardization for people qualification as a response to globalization, and facilitated their movement among European countries.

These examples make evident the challenge imposed on teaching topics related to the field of work, especially that of seeking greater balance between macro trends in phenomena related to work and organizations, and local specificities, combining the "ideal" transversality (intended abstract and comprehensive category) of work and its institutionalization in specific contexts.

## A Portfolio of Topics for WOP Teaching

As we suggest, the choice of which subjects to teach in higher education courses on WOP must take into account the cross-sectional definition of work provided previously. It also needs to consider the contextual influences for the materialization of such a work. In other words, our proposal is that the central teaching axis be work itself as a psychological and social *phenomenon*, carried out by agents and using mediation instruments, with the aim of transforming themselves and the social elements of which they are part. We show the synthesis of this proposal as questions (Fig. 2).

Our starting point (first question) regards why human beings work. A professional, regardless of his/her area of expertise, must know how to theorize and understand what leads the human agent to invest in an act of reality transformation by benefiting from self-transformation. Economic, material, motivational, social, political, religious, and psychological aspects unleash movements toward goals that we intend to achieve in social life. There is a set of motivational theories to include in the teaching program. The choice of theories to address is based on epistemological, theoretical, and methodological fundamentals of the discipline's professor and on the analysis of the local reality where she works.

There are two possible ways for choosing the phenomena to discuss, which should guide the development of competencies. The first concerns the cognitive, affective, motivational, and behavioral processes that lead the person to start and keep a transformational action. Concepts such as the meaning and sense of work, work engagement, and work value are some examples that seek to explain the quality

**Fig. 2** Key elements for decision-making on including WOP phenomena in a teaching program

of human action engagement. The second refers to the contextual meso and macro factors that favor or hinder this action (Fig. 1). This implies that the teacher must be able, at least, to move through different fields of knowledge. For example, wider economic systems, labor legislation, and social and cultural norms can help the student understand the influence of factors where human action takes place.

The second question brings to the discussion the different work contexts in global and local reality, as mentioned previously. The range of options here is even more challenging for choosing what to include in the program. Depending on the reality, the teacher needs to characterize the types of formal and prevailing work in his/her local reality, for instance, the higher or lower prevalence of informal work; or the different social pressures to favor certain categories or work arrangements, with their respective impacts on the type and quality of the necessary skills. The objective is not to provide an exhaustive analysis, but to make the student incorporate to his/his repertoire theoretical and empirical elements of work contexts, in his/her immediate reality, and assume a critical attitude, by being able to envision interconnections between the local context and global issues, since work is, in itself, a twofold local and global phenomenon.

Therefore, in this case, the choice of phenomena consists in the characterization of modalities, arrangements, and contexts where the work (potential human action for transformation) takes place in a given society. It requires the teacher to consider the global work scenario, assessing the relevance, adequacy, and applicability of some theoretical models for the context of his/her local reality. Theories that address the organization as phenomena and other organizational forms of work are available in the scientific literature of the area, but it is necessary to evaluate how well they serve as a lens to analyze the concrete reality.

The third question strongly relates to the second, since it asks about ways of doing or hindering work. There are multiple forms of work organization, work designs, methods, and resources that can contribute to the success or failure of its full execution. Work is a social act, but also reflective and productive. It is reflective to the extent that every human being thinks to some degree about his/her work, with more or less freedom to make changes to achieve his/her initially planned objectives. This is because some works withdraw from the individual his/her power to plan what and how to do, and the quality of what will be produced. Contextual variables at the macro level (labor legislation, economy, technology) and at the meso level (organizations and institutional forms of work organization) can become an impediment to performing the work as a transformation action.

The fourth and final question that supports the criteria for choosing phenomena to include in the discipline program regards the consequences and results of work for the person, for social interactions, and for society in general. What we want to highlight here is that the teacher needs to choose phenomena and topics that address the facet of work as a social action, and the consequences of such action. Task performance and the distinct behaviors that favor it must be addressed. Here, we emphasize work as a productive act that should have a social impact, in order to really achieve its purpose of transformation. We return to this topic in the next section.

Furthermore, among the results of the work on the agent, those on his/her health, both physical and mental, stand out. The act of working implies the possibility of transformation, of yourself and the other, and of the surrounding material and social reality; but there is also the possibility of failure, of error, permeated by different levels and types of impediment. A hampered work affects health directly. Such impediment may arise from the circumstances of work organization, and also from disease-causing social processes, when we prioritize results to the detriment of human well-being. The topic of stress at work, burnout, and several other ways of restricting the quality of life are essential aspects to discuss in a training activity in this field.

## The Ethical Dimension of WOP Teaching

In the previous section, we presented some guiding questions for choosing topics to develop with students, with a transversal definition of work as a central element. However, there is an additional dimension to place on the scene, and it refers to the ethical-moral aspects of the very act of teaching the topics previously mentioned. According to our definition (Fig. 1), the human agent is the central point, but not as a worker who simply generates profit, but as a major player of his/her own activity, being the first beneficiary of its results, if there were not processes of intense work exploitation and expropriation over time and still today, widely documented. Abstract work is not what sets the world in motion, but real (concrete) work, performed by natural persons.

Thus, the teacher must take into account that, when engaging in processes for competence development in this field, he/she deals at all times with important ethical-moral implications. Especially with the human radicality of live work, and not only with instrumental aspects, of performance, productivity, and process optimization, as if they were simply mechanical devices to adjust, seeing knowledge only through its practical, operational dimension. Thus, meeting management demands of any kind – from changes in the organization of work to modifications in its technical and technological basis – has effects on the people who carry out these activities. Hence, the debates listed by WOP contribute not only to recognizing the humanity of this work, in general, but of the people who work in their uniqueness.

In our view, teaching and developing competencies in WOP should rely on the unity between instrumental dimension, focused on results, and ethical-moral dimension, focused on the recognition of the agent's centrality and his/her intentional (implied) action in the world. For example, when an engineer proposes a new work organization, new technological arrangements, or when new managerial routines are developed, the motivation that seems to come to the forefront regards the direct effects of such changes on performance, on the result seen only in its economic dimension, as the gain for shareholders and controllers. Often, teaching focuses primarily on such aspects of work activity, without apparently involving the people directly affected by the changes – but only or mainly considering machines, equipment, instruments, standards, and systems. However, to achieve the expected effect, it is essential to take into account the persons who carry out the activity.

In other words, any change in the work process should assume the active involvement of workers in a given organization. Otherwise, as many studies on organizational change show (Beer & Walton, 1987; Burke, 2017; Stouten, Rousseau, & Cremer, 2018), the trend is a resistance to such changes, or even their failure. The teaching process should sensitize the students, future professionals/managers, for these aspects of the work experience. The teacher can, for example, address the classical separation between those who think about work and those who do it, an issue inherited from Taylor's scientific administration, in the distant nineteenth century, which created a gap between professionals (often those dedicated to intellectual work) and workers (a synonym for manual workers) (Bravermann, 1998). If, from the standpoint of working conditions, we observe differences between them, they disappear when we consider the position they assume within the production process – both are workers selling their workforce.

In short, the contents developed for WOP need to go beyond the optimization of work results (for the others, the owners of the means of production), and address the development of human agents, including their critical and reflective potential, with each student seeing himself/herself as a worker. Finally, to make them notice and question the effects of phenomena such as job precarization, moral harassment, conflicts at work, and exploitation.

## Decision-Making: Designing a Teaching Plan

In this final section, we focus on some more practical and instrumental considerations regarding the development of a teaching plan for WOP, aimed at professional qualification.

The starting point of a plan, whatever the topic, is the explanation of the instructional objectives that express competencies to achieve at the end of the learning process (Bloom, 1956; Krathwohl, 2002; Vaughan, 1980). Instructional objectives are formulations that clearly state the learning goal at the end of a planned educational process, which also serve as a basis for the evaluation processes. Competence can be defined as an articulated set of knowledge, skills, and attitudes (values) that favor a qualified performance, which reveals the effective capacity to deal with the diverse challenging and problematic situations of daily life (Fleury & Fleury, 2001). For instructional purposes, it is necessary to take into account that, in higher education, the focus is mainly on knowledge acquisition, particularly in the cognitive domain. This domain has four dimensions of knowledge and six levels of increasing complexity.

In its revised version (Krathwohl, 2002), the first dimension of knowledge is the factual, in which the learner gets familiarity with essential terms and concepts. The second dimension regards conceptual knowledge, which refers to the ability of using concepts in schemes, structures, and models. The third is procedural knowledge, which concerns the ability to use methods and techniques and apply them in practice.

The fourth and final dimension is metacognitive knowledge, which refers to the capacity for reflective, critical, and in-depth elaboration on the various levels of knowledge, by using previous repertoires to give opinions on the best models and methods, or to create new ones. There are six levels of increasing complexity that can be targets of the teaching-learning process: memorization (recognizing and remembering), understanding (interpreting, comparing, exemplifying), application (using concepts in different situations), analysis (differentiating, decomposing, organizing), evaluation (judging and assigning value), and creation (generalizing and producing new theoretical perspectives).

We already mentioned the key aspects that support knowledge on work as a cross-sectional phenomenon of human life – why; how; in what contexts the human being works; and what would be the consequences of this work for him, for human interactions, and for society. When considering these aspects, the teacher must define the knowledge dimensions that are relevant to his/her context (considering the course he/she teaches), and the levels of complexity that students should achieve.

In higher education, the student is expected to go far beyond the levels of complexity related to memorization and understanding. The expectation is that they will be able to analyze, apply, evaluate, and even try new theoretical elaborations on phenomena related to WOP, in their various manifestations. However, considering the complexity of the topics suggested in this chapter, especially in terms of integrating knowledge around a transversal view of work (Fig. 1), the teacher could focus on the first two dimensions of skill development: the factual and the conceptual. Thus, complexity can be attached to the first four levels: memorization, understanding, analysis, and application. Building a learning diagram can help the teacher choose the content to address in the discipline, and the educational strategies (Fig. 3).

Let us resume Fig. 2 to help the teacher in his/her process of building the teaching-learning plan. This figure contains four guiding questions and three sets of related phenomena. At the end, students should be able to answer, at least in part, the four questions in Fig. 2: why does the human being work? Where and in what contexts does this work take place in their immediate reality, and how does it differ from other countries' reality? Which are the main factors that hinder or facilitate human transforming action? What are the results and consequences of work for the person, for human interactions, and for society?

When considering that the intended levels of learning complexity would be the factual and the conceptual, the first step we suggest to the teacher, for each of the questions in Fig. 2, is to identify the relevant conceptual topics. For example, regarding the question "why does the human being work," he/she can discuss the "meaning of work" concept (Bendassolli & Tadeo, 2017), debating its historical aspects; he/she can also promote a conceptual discussion on work centrality, although it is relative, according to the culture and countries. Alternatively, he/she can promote a reflection on the material and social bases that explain each person's need for work (in the form of selling his/her workforce), or the philosophical bases of work, as an activity for transforming the reality based on culture (Bendassolli, 2016).

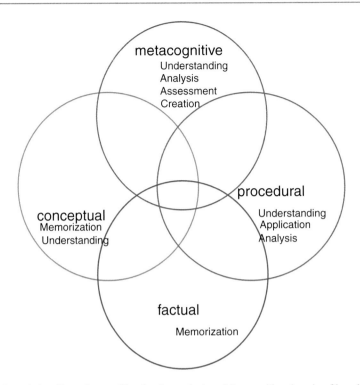

**Fig. 3** Knowledge dimensions and levels of complexity of the cognitive domain of learning in the revised Bloom's Taxonomy

The second step, after examining in detail the concept of the chosen topic, regarding the respective question in Fig. 2, is to move on to the corresponding factual aspects. Here it is important that the teacher help the student understand that the conceptual facets of the topic of discussion are rooted in objective aspects of his/her own life reality, regardless of the country and the conditions in which he/she lives. When discussing the meaning of work, the teacher can use resources extracted from daily newspapers, internet news, examples culturally shared between teacher and students, or present data and statistics, when available and relevant – for example, studies inspired by the Meaning of Work Research Team (MOW, 1987) bring data that compare different countries with respect to the meaning of work.

Furthermore, as shown in Fig. 3, the factual level of skills development takes place through memorization, understanding, analysis, and application. Therefore, still considering our example on the meaning of work as a conceptual topic for discussion, the teacher would debate data or facts related to the practical repercussions of the concept. Then, in his/her available time with the students, he/she could suggest a case analysis, and explore with them how problems or setbacks in the processes of attributing meaning could affect some key dimensions of the work management process. Some studies show that, by having difficulty to find meaning at work, a person can become discouraged, or do it in a purely instrumental, superficial way, with potential impacts on mental health and even on task performance

Therefore, a third step would be for the teacher to use some active teaching methodology, such as the case study, or to promote a panel with the students, dividing them in small groups, with the task of thinking on the implications for the worker for being prevented or removed from a meaningful work. Activities that invert the teacher's place, as the holder of knowledge, to the student, as a leading player in the creation of strategies for application and action, based on the conceptual inputs presented, also contribute to the processes of knowledge memorization and retaining.

The teacher should notice that the level of complexity of the themes associated with the questions in Fig. 2 is not homogeneous. Let us consider a second topic – factors that hinder work activity. First, there is the task of conceptualizing a hindering factor. As we suggested in the correspondent section, we will consider the issue of work design. This is an investigation path in the literature, and, essentially, its objective is to point out which organizational elements of the work can enhance the action and which prevent it. A line of reflection regards working conditions (EurWork, 2011). Working conditions refer to material elements (physical working environment, machinery, equipment, etc.), social (how management organizes the work, task division, etc.), psychological (level of work motivation, well-being, meaning of work, etc.), economic (wage compensation), among several others that affect work results. After defining working conditions and their content, the next step, following the previous example on work meaning, is to discuss with the students ways to apply this concept. Here it is possible to use some measurement instrument consistent with the model of working conditions (for example, EurWork, 2011).

However, there are ways of addressing the issue of impediments other than just using the concept of working conditions. The teacher can choose a more qualitative discussion, and share with the students reflections from authors linked to what in France is known as "work clinics" (Lhuilier, 2016). In some perspectives, as in "activity clinics" (Clot, 2009), impediment does not refer only to external aspects of work activity (such as stimuli from the physical or material environment), but also to its intrinsic aspects. For instance, an activity or work can be prevented when there are conflicts regarding what is understood as the most appropriate way to do the work, especially in the context of a collective activity, where the interdependence of different agents is essential.

The choice of which concept to discuss in a particular facet of the transversal work phenomenon (Fig. 2) thus depends on the teacher's analysis of the level of complexity he/she wants to adopt in his/her approach and teaching process. By "complexity," in this case, we refer to the fact that the teacher wishes, by his/her experience or even through his/her perception of the ability of a given group of students, regarding certain concepts, to choose approaches that are not "mainstream" within the field, as would be, for example, that of working conditions. By choosing perspectives that deviate from the typical manuals of the area, the teacher will have the challenge of "translating" these concepts, although they have a promising

| Questions | Concepts | Suggestions of books and organizations to consult |
|---|---|---|
| Why does the human being work? | Sense and meaning of work<br>Human motivation<br>Work centrality<br>Values<br>Social and professional identity | Latham, G. P. (2012). *Work Motivation: History, theory, research and practice* (2nd ed). Sage Publications: Thousand Oaks, CA.<br>Yeoman, R., Bailey, C., Madden, A., & Thompson, M. (2019). *The Oxford Handbook of Meaningful Work* |
| Where and in what contexts does the human being work? | Working conditions<br>Organizational behavior<br>Work organization<br>New ways of working | International Labor Organization<br>https://www.ilo.org/global/lang-en/index.htm<br>European Foundation for the Improvement of Living and working Conditions<br>https://www.eurofound.europa.eu/<br>European Statistical System<br>https://ec.europa.eu/eurostat<br>Scandhra, T.A. (2019) *Essentials of organizational behavior. An evidence-based approach* (2nd ed.). Sage Publications.<br>D' Cruz, P., Noronha, E., Caponecchia, C., Escartin, J., Salin, D., & Tuckey, M.R. (2021). *Dignity and inclusion at work*. Springer. |
| What are the ways to do the transforming or prevented action? | Work design<br>Work clinics | Ones, D. A., Anderson, N., Viswesvaran, V., & Sinangil, H.K. (2018) *The Sage Handbook of industrial, Work and Organizational Psychology* (2nd ed.). 3 v.<br>Dejours, C., Deranty, J-P., Renault, E., & Smith, N.H. (2018). *The return of work in critical theory: Self, society and politics*. New York: Columbia University Press. |
| What are the results or consequences of work for the person, for social interactions, and for society? | Well-being at work<br>Burnout | Schaufelli, W.B., Malasch, C., & Marek, T. (2018). *Professional burnout. Recent developments in theory and research*. Routledge. |

**Fig. 4** Suggestions of references for consultation to compose a teaching plan on WOP topics

application, allowing, in addition, an expansion of the student's focus of competence development.

Complexity also arises from the fact that, when choosing concepts that depend on a theoretical framework unfamiliar to the average student, the teacher will have to start by addressing the general bases of these concepts (for example, in the case mentioned above, he/she will have to define "work activity" first, and then "extrinsic" and "intrinsic" elements). As mentioned earlier, the institutionalization of work varies according to cultural contexts; likewise, concepts more or less familiar to the teacher also vary according to his/her country's context; after all, researchers who live there, and in theory are more likely to reflect the reality of that context, created such concepts. The teacher's choice for approaching the concepts, through which he/she will meet the aspects suggested in Fig. 2, depends on his/her own experience, beliefs, and on his/her assessment of the students' profile, to whose formation he/she is supposed to contribute.

For illustration purposes, we built Fig. 4, where the teacher can check some books to support his/her teaching plan, based on the questions in Fig. 2. We emphasize that the choice of texts for basic use in the disciplines should take into account the instructional goals, students' profile, the context of the course, and the teacher's level of mastery to deal with work-related themes, theories, methodologies, and phenomena.

## Challenges and Perspectives

Throughout this chapter, we defended what a teacher of a discipline on labor and organizations would achieve, in quality of teaching and contribution, if instead of merely adopting a set of topics and concepts more or less "consecrated" in the WOP manuals, he/she organized or situated them within a wider and fundamental "map": the very definition of work. By assuming this map as the organizational unit for curricula choice and design, the concepts are organically presented and, ideally, make more sense to students. Moreover, we share the definition of competencies, as composed of conceptual and factual elements, the latter represented by the possibility of connection between the theory and episodes of reality that it explains.

Our proposal also highlighted, as far as possible, the importance of the teacher being aware of the ethical and moral dimension of the contents taught, especially when considering that working is not merely reproducing techniques and procedures to achieve a result, but to immerse in a set of social and cultural norms and values. The student himself sometimes does not realize that he/she is a worker, or that he/she is driven to the labor market as such. Therefore, all suggestions are also valid for making students create metacognitions related to their own condition as a worker: why they work, what hinders their work, where their work takes place, and the consequences of their work on others, on themselves (health, well-being, meaning), and on society (quality of work, division of work results, etc.).

Teaching WOP subjects to students other than psychology students has the potential to provoke a reflection that, especially in more technical courses (engineering, medicine, technology etc.), may not have another space to occur. The student, due to social and cultural factors, often thinks of teaching only as the acquisition of conceptual, procedural, and practical knowledge. The teacher, on the other hand, must make a commitment to remind him/her of other important elements in skills development. These are the capacity for self-reflection, and the development of meta-skills that allow each student to critically assess the meaning of those concepts in his/her life, on one side, and their meaning on the phenomenon under discussion (work and organizations, in this case). In other words, it would be the ability to create from what you receive, which may be a great challenge of the education process, regardless of the subarea.

In addition, how to evaluate the education process? First, it is important to consider that the learning assessment process, based on the concept of competencies already suggested, can capture the level of mastery acquired by the students in order to answer satisfactorily to each of the questions in Fig. 2. We can proceed with an evaluation simply to assess the level or amount of information memorized by the student. Here, the focus would be on a type of summative assessment (Taras, 2005). If we consider the complexity of other levels of skills development, such as the ability to apply knowledge or to create new knowledge, the evaluation process should monitor transfer processes, that is, the autonomy and proficiency with which the student, faced with concrete problems of work contexts, is able to translate the acquired knowledge into creative and effective solutions. Evaluations based on case studies, as well as group evaluations, may be relevant strategies in this context.

Finally, it is important that the teacher, when addressing topics related to the world of labor from the perspective of psychology (in this case, WOP) always remembers that his/her preferences dictate the topics that he/she feels prepared or competent to teach. However, the WOP area (certainly, other areas of psychology have similar issues) is a multidisciplinary area, with influences from different fields, and, in general, has narrow concepts – in the sense given to this term by science sociologists, like concepts developed and oriented to deal only with certain aspects of the phenomenon. For example, the concept of "work commitment": it deals only with why and how people engage in the work, get involved or not, and what are the consequences of such engagement on their performance.

However, the phenomenon that this concept seeks to describe comprises only one facet of the reasons people work (Fig. 2). In other words, the choice of a facet of the phenomenon, reflected in its materialization in a concept ("commitment") is just *one* of a series of other possibilities. Although this may seem commonplace, ignoring this aspect is equivalent to presenting students with concepts, as if they could fully encompass the phenomena. This is a cognitive trick, since the student (or even the teacher) considers that the concept is the phenomenon, when, in fact, it is the reverse. In an area like WOP, the risk of falling for this trick cannot be ignored.

In conclusion, we sought to offer guidelines for the teaching practice of disciplines related to Work and Organizational Psychology (WOP), applied to different fields of knowledge other than psychology. Our intention was to sensitize teachers on the importance of human work as an object of study and a field of problematization of the psychological phenomenon, in any context where it takes place. We hope to have provided information of sufficient quality and quantity to enable the teacher to prepare his/her own teaching plan, taking into account the best balance between global and contextual aspects of work as a phenomenon, and the learning needs of the students under his/her responsibility.

It is relevant to warn that the choice of topics demands an ethical commitment from the teacher, and his/her ability to understand the relationship between concepts and phenomena. Failing to do this can, at best, lead to a partial development of skills by students; and, in the worst case, lead students to believe that there are "recipes" ready for each situation they experience at work and within organizations. It is a common anguish, in WOP teaching contexts: the belief in the existence of techniques and procedures capable of minimizing or simply erasing the complexity of the relationship between work, agent, and organizations. Starting from a cross-sectional definition of work can assist in this process, but it is also a construction, and it is up to the teacher to do the same as his/her students: innovate, creating his/her own resources for reflection and knowledge transmission.

## References

Bendassolli, P. F. (2016). Work and culture: Approaching cultural and work psychology. *Culture & Psychology, 23*(3), 372–390.

Bendassolli, P., & Gondim, S. (2019). Work as a cultural phenomenon. In P. Bendassolli (Ed.), *Culture, work and psychology: invitations to dialogue* (pp. 3–19). Charlote: IAP.

Bendassolli, P. F., & Tateo, L. (2017). The meaning of work and cultural psychology: Ideas for new directions. *Culture & Psychology, 24*(2), 135–159.
Blanch, J. M. (2006). El trabajo como valor en las sociedades humanas. In A. Garrido-Luque (Coord.), *Sociopsicología del trabajo* (pp. 57–97). Barcelona: Editorial UOC.
Bloom, B. (1956). *Taxonomy of educational objectives: The classification of educational goals – Handbook 1: Cognitive Domain.* New York: David McKay.
Braverman, H. (1998). *Labor and monopoly capital: The degradation of work in the twentieth century.* New York: Monthly Review Press.
Burke, W. W. (2017). *Organization change: Theory and practice.* California: Sage publications.
Clot, Y. (2009). *Travail et pouvoir d'agir.* Paris: PUF.
D'Cruz, P., Noronha, E., Caponecchia, C., Escartín, J., Salin, D., & Tuckey, M. R. (2021). *Dignity and inclusion at work.* Singapore: Springer.
Dejours, C., Deranty, J.-P., Renault, E., & Smith, N. H. (2018). *The return of work in critical theory: Self, society and politics.* New York: Columbia University Press.
European Observatory of Working Life – EurWork. (2011, 04 May). Solidarity principle. *European Foundation for The Improvement of Living and Working Conditions.* Retrieved from https://www.eurofound.europa.eu/observatories/eurwork/industrial-relations-dictionary/solidarity-principle
Fleury, M. T. L., & Fleury, A. (2001). Construindo o conceito de competência. *Revista de administração contemporânea, 5*(SPE), 183–196.
Friedmann, G., & Naville, P. (1962). *Traité de sociologie du travail.* Paris: Armand Colin.
Hesiod. (2018). *Works and days.* London: Penguin Books.
Krathwohl, D. R. (2002). A revision of bloom's taxonomy: An overview. *Theory Into Practice, 41*(4), 212–218.
Latham, G. P. (2012). *Work motivation: History, theory, research and practice* (2nd ed.). Thousand Oaks: Sage Publications.
Leal, J. C. (1997). *Os deuses eram assim.* Duque de Caxias: Mil Folhas.
Lhuilier, D. (2016). Psychopathologie du travail contemporain: nouveaux défis cliniques. *Trabalho (En) Cena, 1*(1), 84–97.
Marx, K., & Engels, F. (2012). *The communist manifesto.* Connecticut: Yale University Press.
Meaning of Work International Research Team – MOW. (1987). *The Meaning of working.* London: Academic Press.
Ones, D. A., Anderson, N., Viswesvaran, V., & Sinangil, H. K. (2018). *The sage handbook of industrial, work and organizational psychology.* Thousand Oaks: Sage Publications.
Scandhra, T. A. (2019). *Essentials of organizational behavior. An evidence-based approach.* Thousand Oaks: Sage Publications.
Schaufelli, W. B., Malasch, C., & Marek, T. (2018). *Professional burnout. Recent developments in theory and research.* London: Routledge.
Stouten, J., Rousseau, D. M., & Cremer, D. (2018). Successful organizational change: Integrating the management practice and scholarly literatures. *Academy of Management Annals, 12*(2), 752–788.
Taras, M. (2005). Assessment–summative and formative–some theoretical reflections. *British Journal of Educational Studies, 53*(4), 466–478.
Vaughan, C. A. (1980). Identifying course goals: domains and levels of learning. *Teaching Sociology, 7*(3), 265–279.
Vygotsky, L. S. (1997). *The collected works of LS Vygotsky: The history of the development of higher mental functions* (Vol. 4). New York/London: Plenum Press.
Yeoman, R., Bailey, C., Madden, A., & Thompson, M. (Eds.). (2019). *The Oxford handbook of meaningful work.* London: Oxford University Press.

# Psychological Literacy and Learning for Life    36

Julie A. Hulme and Jacquelyn Cranney

## Contents

| | |
|---|---|
| Introduction | 882 |
| Purposes and Rationale | 883 |
| Context | 883 |
| Employability as an Outcome of Psychology Education | 884 |
| Thinking Like a Psychologist | 885 |
| Psychological Literacy and Psychologically Literate Citizenship | 886 |
| Implications for Psychology Education | 888 |
| Approaches and Strategies | 889 |
| Psychologically Literate Educators | 889 |
| Thinking Like a Psychologist | 891 |
| Application of Psychological Principles to Personal Goals | 891 |
| Application of Psychological Principles to Professional Goals | 892 |
| Application of Psychological Principles to Community, Societal, and Global Goals | 895 |
| Curriculum Renewal | 897 |
| Challenges and Lessons Learned | 899 |
| Concluding Thoughts | 903 |
| Teaching, Learning and Assessment Resources | 903 |
| Tips | 903 |
| Further Readings | 904 |
| Cross-References | 905 |
| References | 906 |

J. A. Hulme (✉)
School of Psychology, Keele University, Keele, Staffordshire, UK
e-mail: j.a.hulme@keele.ac.uk

J. Cranney
Psychology, University of New South Wales, Sydney, NSW, Australia
e-mail: j.cranney@unsw.edu.au

© Springer Nature Switzerland AG 2023
J. Zumbach et al. (eds.), *International Handbook of Psychology Learning and Teaching*,
Springer International Handbooks of Education,
https://doi.org/10.1007/978-3-030-28745-0_42

**Abstract**

There is a growing motivation within the higher education sector to ensure that undergraduate programs produce graduates who are employable, and who contribute to society. Within psychology, the developing concept of psychological literacy has been utilized to meet this agenda, and psychology curricula are increasingly focused on teaching students to apply psychology to meet their personal, professional, and societal goals. In this chapter, we introduce the related concepts of psychological literacy and psychologically literate citizenship, and review some of the salient literature. We suggest that teaching for psychological literacy provides the opportunity to enhance students' scientific literacy, critical thinking, employability, and global citizenship, and we present some practical ways in which educators around the globe have taught their students to become psychologically literate, drawing on case studies as well as published literature. Finally, we explore the lessons we have learned from our review of the relevant literature and of these practices, and offer a critical perspective on the current state of the discipline, in terms of psychology education. In recognizing and valuing the opportunities presented by the framework of psychological literacy, we suggest that we need to reflect upon the nature of psychology and its position as a discipline, and to develop our own psychological literacy. In particular, we must grow our respect for diversity and inclusive practices, and be collegiate in further developing and disseminating our thinking and practices around psychological literacy. We hope that this chapter will provoke a continued discussion of the ways in which psychological literacy can promote students' "learning for life," and will serve as a call to action for the psychology education community to further develop our thinking and practices in this field.

**Keywords**

Psychological literacy · Personal development · Employability · Global citizenship · Curriculum

## Introduction

According to Horan (2018), higher education serves three fundamental purposes: to preserve eternal truths (i.e., to disseminate important subject knowledge); to create new knowledge (through research and development activities); and to perform a service to humanity (i.e., to facilitate the application of both new and old knowledge for the public good). Likewise, Boyer (1990, pp. 77–78) suggests that:

> The aim of education is not only to prepare students for productive careers, but also to enable them to live lives of dignity and purpose; not only to generate new knowledge, but to channel that knowledge to humane ends; not merely to study government, but to help shape a citizenry that can promote the public good. Thus, higher education's vision must be widened if the nation is to be rescued from problems that threaten to diminish permanently the quality of life.

In this chapter, we will explore the ways in which psychology education, through the related lenses of psychological literacy and psychologically literate citizenship, can be utilized to deliver these aims and purposes to psychology students, with a particular focus on undergraduate education. First, we will provide some historical context, exploring the evolving focus of psychology education in recent years, and briefly introducing the theoretical concepts of psychological literacy and psychologically literate citizenship. We will then focus in more depth on what psychological literacy brings to students in terms of the purposes of higher education, before considering some practical strategies, challenges, and opportunities in the delivery of psychological literacy within psychology education.

## Purposes and Rationale

### Context

Traditional undergraduate psychology education, in many countries, is the foundation level of study that prepares students for subsequent professional training as a psychologist at postgraduate level. As such, it has focused primarily upon the delivery of core content, such as social, cognitive, biological, and developmental psychology, and upon the ability to conduct research and analyze data. It could be argued that, historically, psychology fulfilled the first two of Horan's fundamental purposes, leaving the application of psychology for the public good to be studied in specific professional contexts (such as clinical and educational psychology). However, in countries that follow this model of psychological education and training (e.g., the UK, Australia, the USA), it is apparent that a majority of psychology graduates follow alternative career paths beyond psychological research and registered practice as a psychologist, with only around 20% entering psychology professions. Psychology graduates outside of professional psychology pursue diverse careers, including health and social care, education, local government, management, and commerce. As such, undergraduate psychology needs to be broad-based, preparing graduates for varied and unknown career pathways.

At the same time, the world is changing, with the rapid development of new knowledge, technology, job roles and career paths, and new societal problems to solve (Maree, 2017). In this context, psychology educators must equip students with the skills, knowledge, and attributes to be prepared for career changes and transitions. That is, students need to be able to apply their psychological education to the challenges and opportunities in these changing situations, including being able to learn new knowledge and skills. Increasingly, there are calls for higher education to deliver "value" to graduates, which is often translated into economic value in terms of graduate earnings. Psychology graduates frequently seek careers that "make a difference" to society, including helping others (Bromnick & Horowitz, 2013). As a result, these graduates may not accrue large salaries, but may make a significant contribution to the "public good." This tension was recognized recently in the UK-government commissioned Augar review of post-18 education, which called for government to:

consider the economic value for students and the economy of different higher educational routes, for different people. However, we are clear that successful outcomes for both students and society are about more than pay. Higher levels of education are associated with wider participation in politics and civic affairs, and better physical and mental health. We also understand the social value of some lower-earning professions such as nursing and social care, and the cultural value of studying the Arts and Humanities. (Augar, 2019, p. 87)

To some extent, this debate echoes long-standing arguments about the value of higher education and the nature of employability, which can be argued to be about much more than the ability of graduates to be employed. For example, Yorke (2006, p. 8) defined employability as: "... a set of achievements – skills, understandings and personal attributes – that make graduates more likely to gain employment and be successful in their chosen occupations, which benefits themselves, the workforce, the community and the economy." This widely used definition of employability recognizes the social value of graduate employability skills, alongside those directly associated with gaining employment.

Nevertheless, there is a need for psychology educators to consider ways of enhancing their students' employability, alongside their ability to contribute to the public good. Following a brief discussion of employability in psychology, we will turn our attention to the concepts of psychological literacy and psychologically literate citizenship as useful frameworks to facilitate the delivery of the knowledge, skills, and attributes associated with both economic and social value.

## Employability as an Outcome of Psychology Education

In light of the above-mentioned challenges, it is worth reflecting on the skills that employers desire in the graduates that they employ. Typically, these include self-management and emotional intelligence, business awareness, leadership, critical thinking, problem solving, communication, team work, literacy, numeracy, and technological competence (Oliver & de St Jorre, 2018).

Although psychology education, as described by the majority of international professional and subject-related bodies, should be well-placed to teach these skills (American Psychological Association [APA], 2013; Australian Psychology Accreditation Council [APAC], 2019; BPS, 2019; Quality Assurance Agency [QAA], 2016), we need to ensure that students learn them. Reddy, Lantz, and Hulme's (2013) guidelines for psychology educators cite Gaunt's (unpublished) framework for understanding graduate employability in terms of the "4 A's": that is, awareness (or acknowledgement), acquisition, application, and articulation. In this model, it is proposed that graduates need all "4 A's" in order to optimize their employability: to be *aware* of the existence of a skill, and to acknowledge its value; to *acquire* the skill, and to be able to put it into practice; to *apply* the skill in new contexts and to solve unfamiliar problems; and to be able to *articulate* their skills in a way that is relevant to an employer or other interested audience. Development of the "4 A's" is not proposed to be linear; students may acquire skills of which they are not fully aware, or they may be able to apply a skill but be unable to articulate it. Traditional, more didactic methods of higher education may facilitate the development of skills awareness and acquisition, but may be less effective in supporting students' ability to apply and articulate their skills. This is evident from research in Australia, suggesting that recent graduates may lack "business awareness" and struggle to solve complex problems (Sarkar, Overton, Thompson, & Rayner, 2016), and from the UK, where employers report that transferability of skills to the workplace and graduates' ability to articulate at interview what they can contribute to a role are problematic (Pollard et al., 2015).

We know that "transfer of learning" to new contexts (e.g., applying psychological theory and research findings to new situations) is a challenging task and requires practice (Worrell et al., 2010). Given the changing nature of our world, including employment contexts, this kind of skill practice would seem to be important for all graduates, and particularly for psychology graduates, given their diverse and changing career destinations. This perspective also aligns with Barnett's (2011) notion of lifelong and lifewide learning: that is, students need to be given opportunities to learn how to integrate their learning across multiple formal and informal contexts, as well as within their everyday lives, throughout the lifespan. From a practical perspective, psychology educators should focus on scaffolding students' capacity to apply their growing knowledge of psychological topics, as well as their skills in research, critical thinking, and interpersonal skills, to increasingly complex human problems. Students then need to articulate these capacities in a way that potential employers understand. This requires the metacognitive capacities of employability, that is, aspects of the "4 A's."

## Thinking Like a Psychologist

As noted above, psychology students are required to become scientifically literate and capable of evaluating information, taking an evidence-based approach to problem solving using psychology. However, based on research in the UK, Hulme and Kitching (2017) suggest that there are particular challenges around this for psychology students, who may study psychology to understand their personal life experiences, which may relate to mental ill health, addictions, previous psychological treatments, or relationship difficulties:

> Psychology is an unusual discipline, drawing on natural sciences, social sciences and philosophy (Quality Assurance Agency, 2016). It encompasses all aspects of what it is to be human, covering biology and neuropsychology, social interaction and cultural context, cognitive processing, development from pre-birth to death, all of the things that humans share in common, and all of the ways in which we are diverse. As such, it touches on the life experiences of each and every one of us, and at the same time requires us to study those experiences within an academic context. (Hulme & Kitching, 2017, p. 4)

Popular psychology and self-help techniques are easily accessible to students through social media and can encourage students to look for simple answers to complex questions. They may bring their "life to psychology"; to look for confirmation within their academic learning of the things that they believe to be true about themselves, based on their personal experiences. This can create a barrier to scientific and critical thinking. As psychology educators, we must encourage students to learn first about the evidence base provided by psychology, and then take that into their everyday lives, to apply psychology to the personal, professional, and societal issues that they face – or to "bring psychology to life." It is important to recognize the personal relevance of students' lives to psychology and to facilitate their self-awareness of the ways in which this personal meaning can impact on their ability to evaluate evidence, and make informed decisions.

Thus, while traditional undergraduate psychology education has emphasized the learning outcomes of knowledge comprehension and a moderate level of research skill (including research-associated critical thinking, statistical analysis, and ethics), there is a growing emphasis internationally on shifting psychology-naive students from a pop-psychology orientation to a psychological scientist orientation, which continues to be a major challenge for both traditional and modern approaches to psychology education. This shift can be captured in terms of "thinking like a psychologist": students must, initially, recognize that psychology requires a different way of thinking that is more than "common sense," and subsequently acquire the skills to apply psychological knowledge to evaluate information, make decisions, and solve problems. Note that in many countries, "psychologist" is a legally protected term, but within the context of this educationally oriented chapter, we are referring to the mindset that should be uniquely associated with the acquisition of psychological knowledge, skills, and attitudes; similarly, educators in other disciplines are encouraging students' professional identification with their discipline by using terms like "thinking like an astronomer" (Hulme & De Wilde, 2014).

Thus psychology education can be viewed as a process that confers key employability skills upon successful students, some of which are captured within the ability to "think like a psychologist": to draw upon psychological knowledge, to think critically, and to apply knowledge in new contexts, based upon the psychological evidence base. Collectively, the knowledge, skills, and attributes associated with psychology education have been extensively described through the concepts of psychological literacy and psychologically literate citizenship, upon which we will now focus.

## Psychological Literacy and Psychologically Literate Citizenship

The term psychological literacy was first coined by Boneau (1990), who collated the views of psychology text book authors to determine the most important concepts and terms within the discipline of psychology at that time. However, recognizing that subject content is fluid and constantly evolving, more recently, the concept has been redefined, in line with Cranney and Dunn's (2011) definition of literacy as "domain knowledge that is used adaptively" (p. 8); that is, people apply knowledge and skills from a discipline (e.g., psychology, information technology, health) to achieve desired goals in their everyday lives.

**Table 1** The components of psychological literacy (McGovern et al., 2010, p. 11)

|   | Psychological literacy |
|---|---|
| 1. | Having a well-defined vocabulary and basic knowledge of the critical subject matter of psychology |
| 2. | Valuing the intellectual challenges required to use scientific thinking and the disciplined analysis of information to evaluate alternative courses of action |
| 3. | Taking a creative and amiable skeptic approach to problem solving |
| 4. | Applying psychological principles to personal, social, and organizational issues in work, relationships, and the broader community |
| 5. | Acting ethically |
| 6. | Being competent in using and evaluating information and technology |
| 7. | Communicating effectively in different modes and with many different audiences |
| 8. | Recognizing, understanding, and fostering respect for diversity |
| 9. | Being insightful and reflective about one's own and others' behavior and mental processes |

McGovern et al. (2010) were the first to define psychological literacy in this way, which encompasses components beyond Boneau's (1990) knowledge-centric definition. They outlined nine attributes that might be acquired by undergraduate students of psychology (see Table 1).

The knowledge, skills, and attributes contained within McGovern et al.'s list have been differently interpreted by different professional bodies around the globe, but there is some consensus that psychological literacy encompasses psychological subject knowledge, scientific literacy, information literacy, critical thinking, ethics, reflective skills, and an ability to apply psychology to issues in everyday life. This list has much in common with our previous list of desirable employability skills.

A broader definition that neatly captures this was proposed by Cranney and colleagues (e.g., Cranney & Dunn, 2011; Cranney & Morris, in press), who suggested that psychological literacy is the capacity to intentionally and adaptively use psychology to achieve personal, professional, and societal goals. Similarly, Murdoch (2016) discusses psychological literacy in terms of the "ethical application of psychological skills and behaviour" (p. 189), which is comprised of: the psychology-specific aspects of a set of "generic literacies" (e.g., critical thinking, statistical literacy, multicultural literacy); psychology-specific skills and knowledge; and the ability to apply all of these skills and knowledge to personal, occupational, and societal issues.

The importance of the application of psychology to "personal, occupational and societal goals" is thus a recurring theme within the psychological literacy literature. McGovern et al. (2010) suggested that this common interest in taking a psychologically informed approach to solving global problems in a pro-social and ethical way could be described within a separate, but related concept, of psychologically literate citizenship. Effectively, psychologically literate citizenship combines the basic concept of psychological literacy, with the more expansive concept of global citizenship. According to Oxfam (1997), global citizens are people who:

- Are aware of the wider world and have a sense of their own role as world citizens
- Respect and value diversity

- Have an understanding of how the world works economically, politically, socially, culturally, technologically, and environmentally
- Are outraged by social injustice
- Participate in and contribute to the community at a range of levels from the local to the global
- Are willing to act to make the world a more equitable and sustainable place
- Take responsibility for their actions

The above definition is imbued with value statements, and it could be argued that every individual needs to periodically examine their value system so that they know its origins and how it relates to their sense of morality and related ethics (see Morris, Cranney, Baldwin, Mellish, & Krochmalik, 2018, Chaps. 3 and 9). McGovern et al.'s (2010) definition of psychologically literate citizens as "critical scientific thinkers and ethical and socially responsible participants in their communities" (p. 10) is less heavily value-laden, but as critical thinkers, we should interrogate and then come to an understanding of the place of words such as "ethical and socially responsible" (see Miller, 1969).

## Implications for Psychology Education

Our core argument here is that a moderate level of psychological literacy should be the general outcome of studying psychology. Such an achievement should meet all three of Horan's (2018) prescribed fundamental purposes of higher education: to preserve eternal truths; to create new knowledge; and to perform a service to humanity (through the application of psychological principles to achieving personal, professional, and societal goals, with an emphasis on solving societal problems). Most current societal problems, such as climate change, health inequalities, and global terrorism, can be argued to be caused by human behavior (Halpern, 2010; Miller, 1969), and so the more that community leaders – particularly our psychology graduates – know about ways to influence human behavior, the more capable they are of solving those problems (Banyard & Hulme, 2015). How well are we preparing our psychology graduates for this kind of role in our society?

In considering how we teach psychological literacy within a classroom, we must both (a) recognize the relevance of psychology to students' personal lives, and (b) facilitate their self-awareness of the ways in which this personal meaning can impact on their ability to evaluate evidence and to make informed decisions. In this regard, psychological literacy may be a threshold concept (Meyer, Land, & Baillie, 2010), transforming the ways in which students perceive psychology as a discipline and its applicability to everyday life, as well as offering a set of outcomes that can be attained through successful study of psychology (McGovern et al., 2010; see Table 1).

However, change at the level of the individual educator is unlikely to be sufficient in facilitating the development of psychologically literate students. As Halpern et al. (2010) argued, curriculum renewal is necessary to support psychology educators in creating a coherent curriculum with psychological literacy as the primary outcome. Otherwise, we risk minimal impact upon students. There has been some success in the UK because psychological literacy is explicitly required in undergraduate psychology programs (BPS, 2019; QAA, 2016). Teaching strategies being implemented to meet this requirement range from the minimal (e.g., "I'll mention at the end of my lecture on attention how this is relevant to mobile phone use while driving") to the substantial (e.g., problem-based learning approaches with relevant problems to be solved, such as reducing car accidents resulting from driver mobile phone use). Nevertheless, it is clear that curriculum renewal is under way as a result of this "stick" approach. The BPS is also rewarding good practice, by awarding a prestigious annual prize to departments with the "most innovative programme" (a "carrot" approach).

Next, we outline some practical strategies to facilitate the delivery of psychological literacy and psychologically literate citizenship, on the part of individual educators and small teaching teams, and then at the level of the whole curriculum.

## Approaches and Strategies

Thus far, we have discussed the importance of preparing students for learning, throughout life and across their different activities and interests (lifelong and lifewide learning; Barnett, 2011), through the delivery of psychological literacy, in the interests of developing their employability and their ability to contribute to societal good. Here, we consider effective ways to develop students' psychological literacy. We address this first by reflecting on the importance of becoming psychologically literate educators, and then by providing examples of teaching practices, and curriculum renewal.

### Psychologically Literate Educators

Hulme (2014) argued that there are three main principles that must be considered in order to successfully deliver psychological literacy. Firstly, we must recognize for ourselves the relevance of psychology to everyday life, and the ways in which we can apply it in different contexts. In other words, we must become psychologically literate. This is consistent with Dunn, Cautin, and Gurung's (2011, p. 15) claim that: "Promoting psychological literacy entails reorienting what and how we teach students in a way that emphasizes psychology's relevance." Given that many psychology academics themselves experienced as students a curriculum that focused entirely on theory and research, this requires a shift in thinking and pedagogy (Hulme & Winstone, 2017).

Secondly, Hulme (2014) suggested, we need to ensure that psychological literacy is embedded throughout the curriculum, through a process of constructive alignment (Biggs, 1996). Thus, program learning outcomes signal the importance of psychological literacy to students; program content and learning activities allow students to practice and develop their psychological literacy; and assessments effectively measure students' competence on the key aspects of psychological literacy that were signaled in the learning outcomes.

Finally, Hulme (2014) proposed that educators must also model psychological literacy to our students, to facilitate social learning. This requires reflection on applications of psychology within our own professional lives, such as providing an evidence base for our teaching practices, solving problems, informing our everyday interactions with students, and ensuring that inclusivity, respect for diversity, and ethics underpin our educational and research activities (Bernstein, 2011; Cranney & Dunn, 2011a; McGovern, 2011).

Let us briefly consider our own orientations as psychology educators, and the psychological evidence base from which we might draw, based on these suggestions. If we are psychologically literate educators, we are committed to being reflective practitioners, and to using evidence-based approaches in our practice (see Bernstein, 2011). We know that human behavior is determined by environment-person interactions, and as educators, we have significant influence on the curriculum environment. Thus, we could consider different evidence-based approaches to shaping the curriculum environment in a way that supports student learning. For example, we could implement learning, teaching, and assessment strategies consistent with the seven Higher Education Learning Framework evidence-based principles described by Carroll et al. (2018). One such principle is "Leverage the social dynamics of learning to enhance the learning experience" (p. 1); this could be implemented by incorporating peer-learning activities into tutorials. Alternatively, one could apply Self-Determination Theory (Ryan & Deci, 2000) to shape the curriculum environment in a way that supports students' needs for autonomy, competence, and relatedness, thus supporting student motivation and successful learning (e.g., see Enhancing Student Wellbeing, 2016). A slightly different approach is to focus on providing students with opportunities to develop their self-management skills. Self-management is the capacity to strive effectively toward meaningful goals, and to be flexible in the face of set-backs. For students, these skills include time-management, effective study strategies, and emotional regulation. These skills have relevance for students' personal and professional development, and can be delivered in ways that enable academic content and skills to be intertwined.

We will now explore some specific student-centered learning, teaching, and assessment strategies that facilitate the development of students' psychological literacy, which are informed by principles of psychological literacy. We suggest that a fundamental aspect of acquiring psychological literacy is developing and implementing a mindset that equips students to "think like a psychologist." Thus, we first describe a sample strategy for encouraging the development of this capacity. Then, we give examples of how to provide students with opportunities to practice application of psychological principles to personal, professional, and societal goals. Finally, we give examples of whole-program curriculum approaches.

## Thinking Like a Psychologist

For students to successfully navigate the modern world, both in their personal and professional lives, the skills of critical thinking, information literacy, and evaluation of evidence are essential. Beyond graduation, these skills incorporate scientific literacy, but also broader skills such as analyzing language and other types of qualitative evidence; thus, the skills provide a toolkit which facilitates future learning, employment, and problem solving.

### Example 1 An Introductory Exercise in Designing and Undertaking Psychological Research

This exercise has been run successfully within the tutorial program of a core first-term unit (Introduction to Psychological Applications) for Bachelor of Psychology students at the University of New South Wales (UNSW), Australia. The essential ingredients are well-designed support for team-work and research skill capability building, allowing for the satisfaction of the student needs for autonomy, competence, and relatedness (Ryan & Deci, 2000). Despite ethical constraints, teams of students can choose a research question within specified topics (= autonomy). There is a low-stakes assessment (e.g., teams undertake a deconstruction of a research article), as well as ample opportunities within tutorials (e.g., exercises in oral presentation) to practice their research-related skills and to check group dynamics prior to the final oral presentation of their completed research project (= competence). There are also many team-building exercises along the way (= relatedness), and we have found that these experiences promote peer friendships, which ease transition to university and support successful learning throughout students' entire program. Moreover, undertaking a research exercise, whereby students must distill a sensible hypothesis, operationalize variables, test human participants, and make sense of their data, is a fast and furious – but feasible – way for first-year students to successfully acquire a beginner's scientific mindset. This experience greatly advantages students as they progress through their degree, and could be delivered during the first year of any psychology program.

## Application of Psychological Principles to Personal Goals

As discussed above, psychologically literate individuals are able to intentionally apply psychological knowledge to achieve their personal, professional, and societal goals. Personal goals include performing well in their studies and at their workplaces, creating and maintaining positive relationships, and pursuing their interests (Morris et al., 2018).

### Example 2 Designing, Implementing and Evaluating a Self-Behavior-Change Program

This exercise is the major individual assignment for a flipped classroom unit on the Psychological Science of Resilience at UNSW. The unit covers the psychological science of topics such as stress and emotional regulation, general academic skills such as time management and study strategies, and communication skills such as active listening. Learning is supported by an accessible "textbook" specifically written for this course, *The Rubber Brain* (Morris et al., 2018). For this assignment, students choose a behavior that they wish to change (= autonomy, competence); in the past, these behaviors have ranged from skill building, such as learning how to horse-ride or study more effectively, to health behaviors such as exercising more, to esoteric personal goals such as learning more about one's ancestral culture. Students (a) initially undertake and report on a motivational strategy (GROW model; Morris et al., 2018) regarding why they want to pursue the goal; (b) measure, report, and reflect upon their wellbeing and self-efficacy before and after the assignment; (c) identify and attempt to implement evidence-based strategies for achieving their goal, including a consideration of potential barriers and solutions; (d) complete weekly progress reports and a final report, which includes a measure of the intended behavioral change and the intervention strategy; and (e) partner with another student to discuss their progress in class each week. The exercise allows students to gain a personal experience of a program of attempted behavior change (under supervision of the instructor), including methods of evaluation of that program. We are aware that similar exercises are delivered elsewhere (e.g., Psychology of Happiness and Wellbeing, Keele University), and they could be widely implemented. Students acquire an appreciation of how psychological principles can be applied to their everyday lives, alongside a taste of science in terms of evidence-based strategies and outcome evaluation.

## Application of Psychological Principles to Professional Goals

Cranney and Dunn (2011) also suggest that students will be able to apply psychology to help them to achieve their professional goals. Here, we explicitly consider the ways in which psychology is relevant to students' professional development, and how this can be delivered effectively through psychology education.

### Example 3 Exercise in Evidence-Based Study Skills

Given the lifelong and lifewide nature of learning (Barnett, 2011) and the rapidly changing career landscape that often involves extended training, we suggest that study skills are a professional skill that can and should be further developed during university study. In interactive group work during the UNSW unit mentioned above (Example 2), students share with their peers their usual approaches to study. They then consider the findings of Dunlosky, Rawson, Marsh, Nathan, and Willingham's (2013) review of the effectiveness of ten learning strategies, whereby only two have received an acceptable level of support from methodologically rigorous studies. In their groups, students then choose a learning strategy that has not yet received adequate support, and design an experimental study to test the effectiveness of that strategy, which they share with the class. This exercise encourages students to reflect on the effectiveness of the learning approaches they currently utilize and to recognize that quality, not quantity, of study is important for success.

## Example 4 Career Development Learning (CDL) in First and Final Years

Bachelor of Psychology students at UNSW are introduced to CDL, via the unit Introduction to Psychological Applications (see Example 1). A psychology careers expert lectures on pathways to professional psychology, as well as "career literacy" in terms of evidence-based systematic approaches to job search, constructing resumes and cover letters, and interviewing for positions (this knowledge is assessed in the final exam). Tutorials build on this material using engaging interactive activities. In addition, lectures are given by experts in forensic psychology, clinical psychology, and business psychology (examinable), and videos of professional psychologists in diverse fields are made available. In the final year, all psychology major students take a core capstone unit (Research and Psychological Applications) whereby a major focus is CDL, with three components: (1) advanced careers lectures and tutorials providing systematic approaches to constructing resumes and cover letters, informational interviews, and interviewing for positions; (2) lectures by experts in fields where psychology graduates could find a variety of careers positions; and (3) a CDL portfolio assignment whereby students first carry out an informational interview with a person in a role that they aspire to, and then undertake activities related to achieving that goal, such as recording their relevant knowledge, skills, and experience and identifying further relevant CDL activities. This personalized approach to CDL has been well received (Cranney & Morris, 2018).

A similar approach emphasizing personal development as an essential component of CDL was espoused by Lantz (2011), in her Psychology Student's Employability Guide. The guide draws upon the career psychology literature, scaffolding students' reflections about their own strengths and weaknesses, and matching their skills, attributes, and values to possible careers to which they aspire. Students are encouraged to formulate action plans throughout their undergraduate programs, to strengthen areas of weakness, check their understanding of particular career roles, and gain experience that is relevant to their preferred career route.

Overall, these activities fit with the "4 A's" framework by providing opportunities for students to: increase their awareness of and acquire further career-relevant knowledge, skills, and experience; apply that knowledge and skill in situations such as the informational interview; and acknowledge that knowledge and skill in the form of their CDL portfolio or their responses to the activities in Lantz's (2011) guide.

## Example 5 Work-Integrated Learning (WIL)

The capstone course in Example 4 provides students with a metacognitive and integrative conceptualization of their skill acquisition during their psychology education. Another strategy is WIL, which could involve a local research laboratory or partnership with potential employers, either (a) "in-house," where employers have a project that can be worked on without students leaving the classroom, or (b) within a workplace (Cranney & Morris, in press).

(a) WIL in the classroom – Making a Difference with Psychology

Making a Difference with Psychology is an elective module in the final year of the undergraduate psychology program at Keele University, UK. The module was designed to facilitate students' understandings of the application of psychology to professional goals, particularly for students who wish to pursue careers outside professional psychology. The learning outcomes, teaching activities, and assessment encourage students to apply psychology to employment-relevant contexts. Early sessions on leadership are delivered via interactive lectures, and teaching then moves to group work and active learning strategies, considering issues such as science communication, or raising aspirations in deprived youth. Towards the end of the module, students use problem-based learning to explore issues relating to education and professional training, taking the perspective of teachers and trainers. Throughout, external speakers who are also employers contribute to the teaching (for example, a British Army Major talks about leadership in the military, while the lecturer supports students to connect the talk to their psychological knowledge). In this way, students are scaffolded to move from being consumers of information to becoming independent learners who can think critically, evaluate, and apply knowledge. The final session is dedicated to the psychology of recruitment, and focuses on interview and selection procedures, to equip students for their postgraduation job searches.

The assessment includes a formative presentation, in which students work in groups, based on their problem-based learning activities, to present a solution to an education or training provider. The students provide peer feedback on the persuasiveness of their suggested approach and the likelihood that they might be employed by the target company as consultants to deliver their proposed project. The summative assessment is authentic; students are presented with an invitation to tender for business, requiring them to provide a detailed written plan that meets the needs of the employer, and to write a psychologically informed rationale explaining the evidence that underpins their chosen approach. Recent examples of assessment have included: (a) a project from Shaftesbury Young People, who support looked-after young people to apply to university; and (b) a marketing project for Keele's postgraduate programs (leading to a successful campaign that was used by the university the following year). In the first years of its delivery, the module recruited poorly, but we have worked with our students to ensure its relevance to their professional goals; it now recruits well. Student evaluations are positive; they find the content stimulating and inspiring, despite finding the problem-based aspects challenging at first.

(b) WIL in the workplace: UK Placements

Many universities recognize the benefits of offering work-based activities during a program of undergraduate study. Some examples of different models of doing this are provided as case studies within Reddy et al.'s (2013) employability guide. At Huddersfield University, in the UK (case study 12), students study a module in which they reflect on the relevance of psychology to a (loosely) work-relevant context of their choice: this might be a part-time job that they undertake during their studies, a voluntary placement, or even caring for relatives. Students are assessed via a reflective portfolio. This model ensures accessibility and inclusion, due to the broad definition of "work" that is adopted, which ensures that the majority of students are able to engage.

An increasing number of institutions, including Aston University in the UK (see case studies 17 and 18; Reddy & Moores, 2006; Reddy et al., 2013), offer full-year work placement opportunities. In this model, the usual 3-year English degree is increased to 4 years, with the year between second and third year being spent in a workplace. At Aston, the significance to students of adding an extra year to their degree program, in terms of extending their studies, delaying graduation, and increased expense, is recognized. Through a second-year module, students explore possible career choices, and ways of optimizing the benefits from their placement year, prior to deciding to go on placement. On return to university, students take a module in which they consolidate their learning from their placement, revising their career plans, and re-assessing their competencies relating to employability. Reddy and Moores (2006) report substantial benefits to students, including improved student grades, and students report improved confidence and preparedness for graduate-level employment as a result of the placement experience.

Both of these kinds of WIL experiences explicitly remind students of the need to intentionally apply – to a work context and their own professional goals – the psychological knowledge and skills that they have acquired throughout their degree program. However, there are resource issues for WIL, especially where students are required to gain experience in genuine workplaces, because the university must take responsibility for occupational health and safety. Close partnerships with employers are helpful in developing placements, and learning contracts and other procedures are usually necessary (e.g., in Example 5b); thus, dedicated staff are required to support delivery.

## Application of Psychological Principles to Community, Societal, and Global Goals

A number of institutions have devised ways of incorporating psychological literacy at the level of the community, society, or even globally, within their programs. Hulme and Kitching (2016) reported that UK university psychology educators were being increasingly pushed by students, institutions, their professional body, and government, to incorporate more of this type of learning within the curriculum. However, they also suggested that developing these types of learning could be resource intensive and difficult with large student numbers. As one participating educator said: "Engagement with communities, organisations and business has to be a way forward. How psychology does that is an interesting one...in mainstream psychology, how do we develop what we are terming civic engagement...?" (p. 16). In this section, we describe some examples of strategies that have been used to deliver this aim successfully.

**Example 6 Psychology in Education**
At Keele University, the elective module Psychology in Education is taken by between 50 and 100 third-year (final year) undergraduate students each year. The module covers a range of topics related to the application of psychology to different educational issues, from early years through to higher education. During the module, students have an opportunity to volunteer with local education providers. For example, in the nearby community of Stoke-on-Trent, there is a known challenge around raising literacy levels, and students can choose to participate in the *Stoke Reads* project, to raise literacy levels and enjoyment of reading among young children.

Other projects have included initiatives to reduce bullying in local schools, and to destigmatize mental health and encourage help-seeking behaviors among students at Keele (leading to a very successful "Look After Your Mate" campaign by the Keele Students' Union). Each project was associated with an assessment (students chose one from a selection) reviewing the psychological literature relating to the topic, and developing psychologically informed interventions to address these community issues. Students report finding the project-based approaches challenging at first, but they gradually gain confidence, and recognize that their ability to apply psychology to their local community, as well as to their possible subsequent training and employment, is enhanced by these activities. The projects benefit the local community, and strengthen links between the psychology department, the university, and the surrounding area, which is recognized as a region of social and economic deprivation.

**Example 7 International Community Psychology Projects**
Akhurst and Mitchell (2012; and Case Study 29 of Reddy et al., 2013) designed a community psychology project in partnership between York St John University, UK, and a number of international universities on three continents, to give students global perspectives and experiences which were also work-relevant. Students worked on overseas community-based projects, accompanied by a tutor, alongside local academics and community partners. Examples included working with children with communicative and developmental disorders in the USA, educational projects with children in South Africa, and developing community skills in India. Akhurst and Mitchell reported multiple benefits: students developed cross-cultural awareness, engaged deeply and emotionally with the psychological elements of the learning experience, and became more committed to future "helping" roles and activities relating to social justice.

**Example 8 Development of Cultural Responsivity**
Cultural responsivity is the capacity and motivation to learn about another culture, so that one can interact in a more respectful way with people of that culture. This capacity is foundational to working with/for diverse groups. The dispossession and oppression of First Nations peoples (e.g., in North America and Australia) and the migration of people away from war zones and genocide (e.g., Syrian people fleeing to Europe) have had disastrous consequences for those peoples, exacerbated by the prejudice displayed by the invading or "receiving" cultures (respectively). The application of evidence-based skills derived from psychological sciences could

help to negotiate more positive cultural contact. Indeed, "cultural competency" has been identified by employers and psychology educators as a desirable skill set (e.g., Reddy et al., 2013).

Dudgeon, Darlaston-Jones, and Clark (2011) describe a unit which meets these purposes. It includes a 4-week immersion in a remote Australian Aboriginal community as part of a respectful working partnership with the Gelganyem Youth and Community Wellbeing Programme. The students "travel with a staff member and are engaged in a range of activities from the delivery of out-of-school programs, helping with breakfast club, developing grant applications, and other community needs *identified by the community*" (p. 85, italics added). This immersion experience is bracketed by thorough preparation activities and debrief activities and assessments. As a result of these and other learning experiences, graduates attain a high level of cultural responsivity and are "in demand" for human services positions in the public service and not-for-profit sectors (L. Darlaston-Jones, 15 June 2016, personal communication).

## Curriculum Renewal

The example approaches and strategies discussed above illustrate good practices in delivering elements of psychological literacy within the psychology curriculum at module/unit level, or within the practice of individual educators. However, while such innovations support the delivery of psychological literacy, it is desirable to renew the entire curriculum, at program level, to ensure that students have optimal opportunities to develop their knowledge, skills, and attributes. According to Halpern et al. (2010), curricula designed for psychological literacy should:

- Reinforce the scientific underpinnings of psychology
- Include content for the core domains of psychology (we note that these are similar but differently named by professional bodies from different countries)
- Provide opportunities for applied learning, including WIL and problem-solving experiences
- Include assessments that promote critical thinking and different methods of communication
- Be structured so that students' development of higher-level thinking skills is progressive throughout the course
- Have clearly articulated program-level learning outcomes, that are aligned to teaching and assessment
- Be delivered by pedagogically trained teachers
- Include knowledge and skills delivery that are relevant to students' lives, to facilitate a contribution to public good

These principles are closely aligned to those we have already discussed. Broadly speaking, Halpern et al.'s (2010) proposals relate to our conceptualizations of:

thinking like a psychologist; applying psychology to personal, professional, and societal goals; and psychologically literate educators. Dunn et al. (2011) propose similar principles for curriculum design, but include an additional level of review, recommending that the departmental teaching team needs to refresh its understanding of their mission, and align the curriculum renewal to this. Operationalizing program-level, rather than module-/unit-level learning outcomes, requires a collegiate approach, with strong leadership that emphasizes the value of psychological literacy as a core principle at the heart of the curriculum.

The Psychology Department at Stirling University have provided a useful example of curriculum review with a view to developing psychologically-literate citizens (Hulme et al., 2015; Watt, 2013). Watt (2013), as program lead, reflects on this process in some detail, remarking on the importance of motivating both staff and students to engage with the renewal process, and of working collaboratively with students to ensure that the curriculum both meets their needs, and allows them to progressively develop as independent learners, with increasing skills to apply psychology to their goals. The program facilitates learning by trial and error; students are able to make mistakes, and are encouraged to work hard to play to their strengths and to develop their areas of weakness. By their final year, students are able to: take responsibility for their own learning, effectively supporting and being supported by their peers; lead their own research projects in teams; in some cases, deliver teaching to students in earlier years of the program; and even help to develop their own modules. Watt describes a need to build students' confidence through scaffolding, and also to build staff confidence in the ability of students to apply psychology competently and reliably. The project has been a resounding success: the program received the BPS Innovative Programmes Award in 2014, and students report that they develop leadership capabilities, employability, and psychologically literate citizenship, which facilitate their learning, development, and societal contribution well beyond graduation (Hulme et al., 2015).

A slightly different approach was taken when reviewing the psychology curriculum at Keele University (unpublished). The leadership team at Keele convened a curriculum review group to update the curriculum and ensure that it delivered the requirements for BPS accreditation, while also integrating psychological literacy and employability throughout. Curriculum "theme leads" for each of the core areas of psychology (QAA, 2016) reviewed coverage of each element that covered their topic, across all levels of the program. Curriculum structure was checked to ensure that students were able to demonstrate broad coverage of psychological knowledge in the first year, and then across the subsequent 2 years, display progressive development of knowledge and skills and the ability to apply psychology. A key feature of the revised curriculum focused on the final-year elective modules (including *Making a Difference in Psychology* and *Psychology in Education*, described previously). Single Honours and Major students could choose up to three electives, and other students (studying another subject alongside psychology) could choose one. Each elective focused on applications of different areas of psychological content knowledge. This allowed students to choose areas of psychology that interested them, thus increasing student engagement and relevance to future aspirations. However, all of these modules were designed in similar ways, so that each has learning outcomes, teaching activities, and assessments that facilitate students' abilities to apply psychological knowledge to problem solving. Thus, all students learn the same core knowledge early in the program and are scaffolded, through second year, to develop their skills in applying psychology. In final year, they can choose to specialize in particular areas, and to develop their psychological literacy more fully in those areas that are relevant to them. Single Honours students thus gain more practice in the skills of psychological literacy than those doing less psychology, but every student has the opportunity to develop psychological literacy to some extent. This is consistent with Halonen, Dunn, Baker, and McCarthy's (2011) suggestion that departments should plan for differential exposure to psychological literacy within the program, depending on whether students are studying psychology as their main specialism or alongside other subjects. The curriculum review was facilitated by teaching team discussions and "away" days, to ensure some consensus of opinion amongst teaching staff, and consistent with Dunn et al.'s (2011) recommendations discussed above.

Based on these experiences, we endorse the principles proposed by Halpern et al. (2010) and Dunn et al. (2011), and suggest that program leaders should adopt collegiate approaches to working with teaching teams and students to agree on important principles relating to the design of the curriculum. Scaffolding is required to move students towards independent learning approaches, gradually and progressively, throughout the program. Likewise, constructive alignment of learning outcomes, activities and assessments is essential. Program-level learning outcomes must align to unit/module learning outcomes, and all must refer explicitly to key aspects of psychological literacy. Teaching and learning activities must allow students to practice the relevant skills of psychological literacy, and to learn from mistakes. Finally, assessments must allow students to demonstrate their psychological literacy, by measuring their ability to apply psychological knowledge and skills to their personal, professional, and societal goals. As psychologically literate educators (Bernstein, 2011), we recognize that regular evaluations, analysis of student performance, and revisions of teaching help to ensure that the curriculum delivers the program learning outcomes and ensures that graduates are able to acquire attributes that are consistent with psychological literacy.

## Challenges and Lessons Learned

In delivering psychological literacy as "learning for life," we have learned much about what helps students (and educators) to learn effectively. In this section, we share some of those lessons, and consider some challenges that require further attention. In reflecting on these points, we hope to elucidate the ways in which psychology can help students to become graduates who can solve problems in everyday life, who will continue to develop through lifelong and lifewide learning, and thus can thrive in a changing world.

Firstly, in terms of lessons learned, we believe that teaching for psychological literacy provides considerable opportunities. Students who are facilitated to "think like a psychologist" are equipped with good skills in scientific literacy and critical thinking. In this regard, psychology prepares them well for further scientific training, as well as developing a broader skill base. Indeed, Trapp et al. (2011) describe psychology as a "STEM+" subject. Given the diversity of students who study psychology, and especially the high proportion of female students, psychological literacy may facilitate increased participation in science for otherwise under-represented groups, and as such impact greatly on the scientific literacy of the general population. Thus, psychology could be considered as a "gateway" science, creating opportunities for graduates to engage further with other aspects of science. Our experiences have demonstrated both the value of this for students, and the importance of making the scientific nature of psychology explicit within the curriculum. Likewise, we would suggest that "thinking like a psychologist" allows one to question not only published research reports and claims in the media but also one's own way of thinking, and the latter is the greatest cognitive, emotional, and motivational challenge (Halpern, 1998; Morris et al., 2018).

The diversity of psychology students also creates opportunities for learning about equality, diversity, and inclusion in wider society, and the application of psychological knowledge to the development of intercultural competency. Respect for and value of diversity is an important component of psychological literacy (McGovern et al., 2010) and is especially important at a time of global migration, international trade, and racial and religious tensions, and in light of gender inequality, mental health challenges, and inequities for those with disabilities. Education that develops psychological literacy taps into psychology students' desire to help others (Bromnick & Horowitz, 2013), and even increases this desire (Akhurst & Mitchell, 2012). We are increasingly aware of the benefits of educating for psychologically literate citizenship in terms of meeting the goal of higher education that serves the public good (Boyer, 1990; Horan, 2018).

However, psychology students do not always find learning to be psychologically literate easy. Learning in general, and acquiring a "psychologically literate mindset" in particular, is challenging, both for psychology students and for psychology educators. There are "desirable difficulties" (Worrell et al., 2010, p. 132) in effective and meaningful learning that frame learning as a joint responsibility (and at best, a partnership): students must expend quality effort to acquire new knowledge and skills, and educators must provide evidence-based teaching and assessment strategies to effectively support and provide opportunities for student learning (Halpern et al., 2010). These opportunities must encourage students to try, potentially fail, but then learn from those failures. The benefit of desirable difficulties is evident from our evaluations, such as those from *Making a Difference* and *Psychology in Education*, above, where students initially struggle with the applied nature of the learning, but subsequently report that these modules transform their thinking and develop their confidence. A key lesson here is the importance of scaffolding, and the need to reassure students that learning higher-level psychological literacy skills is difficult, but will be worthwhile, and is achievable with support.

We suggest that the challenges are related to the rewards, as epitomized in this quote from George Bernard Shaw: "Life is not meant to be easy, my child; but take courage: it can be delightful."

Within this chapter, we have explored a number of ways of ensuring that education for psychological literacy can be successful and create opportunities to develop students' ability to apply psychology to their personal, professional, and societal goals. This benefits not only the students themselves, but also wider society. However, a number of challenges are also apparent.

Firstly, much of the psychological literacy work, including our own position within this chapter, relates to a strong claim that psychology is a science. In particular, there is a sense that knowledge is derived from the scientific method, particularly an experimental approach which includes random assignment of participants to conditions, the control of potentially confounding variables, and some level of scientific objectivity. However, it is important to note that psychology as a discipline draws upon a wide range of research methods, including those that might be perceived to be "stereotypically" scientific, and those that are less positivistic, including qualitative methods. It is important that we must not undermine the value of the diverse methodologies that are recognized within psychology; different methodologies provide valuable insights and perspectives on the complexity of human experience. Psychologically literate students also need to recognize their own subjectivity, and the way that this can affect their interpretation and evaluation of information, even that which is traditionally scientific. For this reason, we have chosen to talk here about "thinking like a psychologist," rather than "thinking like a scientist"; we hope that this captures the richness of empirical evidence available within the discipline as a whole. However, challenges remain, in that the discourse of "psychology as science" permeates the discipline to a large extent, and this can create barriers to students' engagement with the wider range of psychological methods, as well as a perception that qualitative research is somehow less rigorous than experimental approaches (Povee & Roberts, 2014). The psychology education community must find ways to encourage students (and colleagues) to appreciate the heterogeneity of research in the discipline.

A further challenge relates to cultural responsivity and relativity. We acknowledge that the contents of this chapter are biased by our Western World views, and we welcome critiques and extensions of these discussions from colleagues in diverse cultures, particularly around the value-laden conceptualization of psychological literacy and psychologically literate citizenship. While encouraging our students to develop intercultural competence, we are aware that this is very much a "work in progress" for us too. In Australia and the USA, psychology educators are keen to better reflect the perspectives of First Nations people (e.g., Darlaston-Jones, 2015), while in the UK, South Africa, and Canada, for example, the international and ethnic diversity of the student body has motivated considerable work to "decolonise the curriculum." This increased attention to cultural diversity is welcome, and we would encourage our colleagues to continue the work, individually and across the global discipline community. The international sharing of insights and practices in this regard is essential in our attempts to become psychologically literate educators who ourselves respect and value diversity in our classrooms.

Relatedly, the development of psychologically literate educators more broadly presents a challenge. Psychological literacy is new to many psychology educators (Hulme & Winstone, 2017) and indeed, is a "threshold concept" (Meyer et al., 2010) for educators as well as for students. In order to deliver psychological literacy effectively, there is a need for psychology-specific academic development and learning on the part of psychology educators. Just as we must create and share strategies to help students acquire the concept, we must do the same for our colleagues. There is a challenge here for psychology professional and subject-related bodies to promote psychological literacy not only through accreditation processes but also through offering resources and accessible continuing professional development opportunities.

Throughout this chapter, we have argued that psychology undergraduate students will acquire (and be aware of, apply, and be able to articulate) a "moderate level of psychological literacy." This raises the question of what is really meant by "a moderate level of psychological literacy"? In his criticism of educational systems in the Western World, Nadal Ravakant (Ravakant & Navukant, 2017) argues that all students should "learn the basics" (including learning to think better, to achieve psychological health, and to have healthy relationships) really well. Subsequently, Ravakant suggests, students should be allowed to pursue only those topics that interest them. Similarly, we suggest (consistent with Halonen et al., 2011) that the psychology major should consist of: (a) a fundamental set of minimal attributes (knowledge, skills, attitudes), supported by at least one cornerstone course which includes an introduction to "thinking like a psychologist"; followed by (b) significant choice in topics that build upon those foundations; and then (c) a capstone experience whereby students have opportunities for integrative learning, with a high level of choice and autonomy to ensure engagement and deep learning. As such, psychology graduates will acquire a "spiky profile" of psychological attributes: they may excel in some components of psychological literacy, while exhibiting minimal knowledge and skills in other areas. The challenge here, then, is that our current perspectives on psychological literacy may imply: "a relatively well-integrated and functional set of schemas that across individuals may show some variability in expression, but in terms of central tendency, can be recognized and assessed as 'psychological literacy'" (Cranney & Dunn, 2011, p. 8). The reality, from a student and educator perspective, may be that some aspects of psychological literacy are aspirational (Murdoch, 2016), and some students may never acquire the full set of associated attributes. Indeed, perhaps the most important element of psychological literacy might be the development of reflective skills and self-awareness, enabling the student themselves to be aware of their own strengths and weaknesses. We would argue that all psychology students should be given opportunities to engage with all of the different components of psychological literacy, and to determine the relevance of each for themselves. Further work is required to establish whether a "threshold" level of achievement against the different skills can be, or should be, determined, and to determine how, or if, we can measure that achievement. Some researchers have attempted to measure psychological literacy (e.g., Heritage, Roberts, & Gasson, 2016), but this is still in its early stages, and debate around how psychological literacy can be operationalized is ongoing. Further work in this area presents an exciting challenge for the psychology education community.

Indeed, as psychology educators, we face a similar challenge in regard to our own personal and professional development. As Cranney and Morris (in press) suggest: "No one is ever 'fully' psychological literate—this is impossible. But we choose our own areas of our lives where we want to apply psychology to achieve our personal, professional, and societal goals. Of particular relevance to us as psychology educators is to apply the knowledge and skills of psychology to the educational context, and become 'scientist-educators'." Only in addressing this challenge, we suggest, will we fully capitalize on the lessons we are learning, and truly develop the principles of education for psychological literacy.

## Concluding Thoughts

In conclusion, then, psychological literacy is still a relatively new concept within psychology education, and as such, there are still lessons to learn and challenges to overcome. However, we have argued that the opportunities presented by delivering psychology education through the lens of psychological literacy are immense. For society, psychological literacy offers a means of ensuring that higher education is fit for its purposes of preserving knowledge, creating new knowledge, and serving the public good (Horan, 2018). For educators, it offers a means to teach psychology in a way that is rewarding, engaging, and enables us to continue to learn and develop our own psychological understanding and skills. Perhaps most importantly, for students, psychological literacy enables them to develop as lifelong and lifewide learners, and facilitates their engagement with science, critical thinking, and civic issues, albeit to varying extents. In this way, our psychology graduates are well prepared for the uncertain future of a changing world; they are able to "learn for life."

## Teaching, Learning and Assessment Resources

If you are now keen to increase the focus on psychological literacy within your teaching practice, we hope you will find these tips and additional resources useful.

## Tips

1. Start out by thinking about what you want students to know and do; try to ensure that you give them an opportunity to practice with support in class, and that your assessments measure the same knowledge and skills.
2. If engaging students in active and problem-based learning seems daunting at first, start by thinking of examples of the way that the psychology content you are teaching can be applied to everyday life – and encourage your colleagues to do the same. Don't try to change everything all at once – take steps, and learn as you go.
3. Try to involve students in the process of renewing your classes, assessments, and curricula. Students can be extremely creative, providing you with lots of ideas

– and working with them in partnership can give them a sense of ownership over their learning, which can facilitate their engagement.
4. Like students, educators' learning can be facilitated by working with other educators. Find like-minded colleagues at your university or elsewhere, and work in partnership to renew your curricula. Consider observing others' classes, or asking them to observe yours, and give you some ideas on what you can do to increase the focus on application and psychological literacy.
5. Reflect on your own position as a psychologically literate educator: to what extent are you applying psychology to your teaching and assessment practices, and how do you model psychological literacy to your students? If you think there is room for improvement in some areas, consider exploring some of the further reading suggestions below, to develop your thinking and practices in the areas you think need most work.

## Further Readings

1. Cranney, J., & Dunn, D. (2011a). *The psychologically literate citizen: Foundations and global perspectives*. New York, NY: Oxford University Press.
   - The definitive source to develop your thinking about education for psychological literacy, covering definitions, cultural perspectives, and suggestions for practice.
2. Morris, S., Cranney, J., Baldwin, P., Mellish, L., & Krochmalik, A. (2018). *The rubber brain: A toolkit for optimising your study, work, and life*. Bowen Hills, QLD: Australian Academic Press.
   - Provides useful content and techniques for helping students to apply psychology to their own personal and professional development, helping them to learn effectively. The practical exercises – relevant either to the subject matter or to general skills that facilitate successful completion of assessments – could be integrated into almost any psychology unit.
3. Cranney, J., Morris, S., & Baldwin, P. (n.d.). Psychological literacy. Retrieved from http://www.psychliteracy.com/
   - A useful website collating a plethora of resources, information and insights into psychological literacy from around the world.
4. Mair, C., Taylor, J., & Hulme, J. A. (2013). *An introductory guide to psychological literacy and psychologically literate citizenship*. York, UK: Higher Education Academy. Retrieved from https://www.heacademy.ac.uk/knowledge-hub/psychology-education-psychological-literacy
   - A practically-focused introduction to the concepts of psychological literacy and psychologically-literate citizenship, with ideas about ways in which different core topics in psychology can be applied to everyday life.
5. Taylor, J., & Hulme, J. A. (2015). Psychological literacy: A compendium of practice. Retrieved from http://eprints.bournemouth.ac.uk/22906/4/psychological_literacy_compendium_final2._amended.pdf
   - A set of case studies from the UK, illustrating the ways in which some educators have delivered psychological literacy to their students.

6. Taylor, J., & Hulme, J. A. (2018). International edition of the psychological literacy compendium. Retrieved from http://eprints.bournemouth.ac.uk/30425/1/International%20edition%20Psychological%20Literacy%20Compendium%20Final.pdf
   - Building upon Taylor and Hulme (2015), this international edition of the compendium includes additional case studies, from the UK and the rest of the world.
7. Halpern, D. (1998). Teaching critical thinking for transfer across domains: Dispositions, skills, structure training, and metacognitive monitoring. *American Psychologist, 53*, 449–455.
   - This article is ground-breaking in the sense that it points to the motivational aspect of critical thinking – that is, in order to engage in critical thinking – possibly the most commonly stated graduate outcome for Western universities – one must be motivated to do so, because it takes effort! The highlighting of the metacognitive aspects of critical thinking underline this point. Examination of one's own thinking, of course, is fundamental to progress in any domain of one's life.
8. Halpern, D. (2010). *Undergraduate education in psychology: A blueprint for the future of the discipline*. Washington, DC: APA.
   - This collection contains McGovern et al.'s (2010) ground-breaking chapter, as well as many other useful chapters specifically written to support psychology educators.
9. Dunlosky, J., Rawson, K., Marsh, E. J., Nathan, M. J., & Willingham, D. T. (2013). Improving students' learning with effective learning techniques: Promising directions from cognitive and educational psychology. *Psychological Science in the Public Interest, 14*(1), 4–58.
   - A review of the psychological literature to inform learning and teaching practices using evidence from psychological science.
10. Harré, N. (2018). *Psychology for a better world: Working with people to save the planet*. Auckland, New Zealand: Auckland University Press.
    - An intriguing exploration of the ways in which psychology can be applied to the global environmental crisis, illustrating one aspect of psychologically-literate citizenship.

## Cross-References

▶ Basic Principles and Procedures for Effective Teaching in Psychology
▶ Inquiry-Based Learning in Psychology
▶ Problem-Based Learning and Case-Based Learning
▶ Service Learning
▶ Teaching Introductory Psychology
▶ Teaching of General Psychology: Problem Solving
▶ Teaching the Foundations of Psychological Science

# References

Akhurst, J., & Mitchell, C. (2012). International community-based work placements for UK psychology undergraduates: An evaluation of three cohorts' experiences. *Psychology Learning and Teaching, 11*(3), 401–405. https://doi.org/10.2304/plat.2012.11.3.401.

American Psychological Association. (2013). APA Guidelines for the undergraduate psychology major: Version 2.0. Retrieved from http://www.apa.org/ed/precollege/about/undergraduate-major.aspx

Augar, P. (2019, May 30). Independent panel report to the review of post-18 education and funding. Retrieved from https://assets.publishing.service.gov.uk/government/uploads/system/uploads/attachment_data/file/805127/Review_of_post_18_education_and_funding.pdf

Australian Psychology Accreditation Council. (2019). Accreditation standards for psychology programs: Effective 1 January 2019, Version 1.2. Retrieved from https://www.psychologycouncil.org.au/sites/default/files/public/Standards_20180912_Published_Final_v1.2.pdf

Banyard, P., & Hulme, J. A. (2015). "Giving psychology away": How George Miller's vision is being realised by psychological literacy. *Psychology Teaching Review, 21*(2), 93–101.

Barnett, R. (2011). Lifewide education: A new and transformative concept for higher education. In N. J. Jackson (Ed.), *Learning for a complex world: A lifewide concept of learning, education and development*. Bloomington, IN: AuthorHouse.

Bernstein, D. (2011). A scientist-educator perspective on psychological literacy. In J. Cranney & D. S. Dunn (Eds.), *The psychologically literate citizen: Foundations and global perspectives* (pp. 281–295). New York, NY: Oxford University Press.

Biggs, J. (1996). Enhancing teaching through constructive alignment. *Higher Education, 32*, 347–364. https://doi.org/10.1007/bf00138871.

Boneau, C. A. (1990). Psychological literacy: A first approximation. *American Psychologist, 45*, 891–900. https://doi.org/10.1037//0003-066x.45.7.891.

Boyer, E. L. (1990). *Scholarship reconsidered: Priorities of the professoriate*. San Francisco, CA: Carnegie Foundation for the Advancement of Teaching.

BPS. (2019, January). Standards for the accreditation of undergraduate, conversion and integrated Masters programmes in psychology. Retrieved from https://www.bps.org.uk/sites/bps.org.uk/files/Accreditation/Undergraduate%20Accreditation%20Handbook%202019.pdf

Bromnick, R., & Horowitz, A. (2013). Reframing employability: Exploring career-related values in psychology undergraduates. Proceedings of the HEA STEM conference, Birmingham, UK. Retrieved from https://www.heacademy.ac.uk/system/files/resources/reframing_employability_exploring_career-related_values_in_psychology_undergraduates.pdf

Carroll, A., Lodge, J. M., Bagraith, R., Nugent, A., Matthews, K., & Sah, P. (2018). *Higher education learning framework matrix – An evidence-informed model for university learning*. Brisbane, QLD: The University of Queensland. Retrieved from https://www.slrc.org.au/wp-content/uploads/2018/05/HELF-isbn.pdf

Cranney, J., & Dunn, D. S. (2011). Psychological literacy and the psychologically literate citizen: New frontiers for a global discipline. In J. Cranney & D. S. Dunn (Eds.), *The psychologically literate citizen: Foundations and global perspectives* (pp. 3–12). New York, NY: Oxford University Press.

Cranney, J., & Morris, S. (2018). Undergraduate capstone experiences and psychological literacy. In G. J. Rich, A. Padilla-Lopez, L. K. de Souza, L. Zinkiewicz, J. Taylor, & J. L. S. B. Jaafar (Eds.), *Teaching psychology around the world: Volume 4* (pp. 306–327). Newcastle upon Tyne, UK: Cambridge Scholars Press.

Cranney, J., & Morris, S. (in press). Psychological literacy in undergraduate psychology education and beyond. In P. Graf & D. Dozois (Eds.), *Handbook on the state of the art in applied psychology*. Hoboken, NJ: Wiley.

Darlaston-Jones, D. (2015). (De)Constructing paradigms: Creating a psychology curriculum for conscientisation education. *The Australian Community Psychologist, 27*(1), 38–48.

Dudgeon, P., Darlaston-Jones, D., & Clark, Y. (2011). Changing the lens: Indigenous perspectives on psychological literacy. In J. Cranney & D. S. Dunn (Eds.), *The psychologically literate citizen: Foundations and global perspectives* (pp. 72–90). New York, NY: Oxford University Press.

Dunlosky, J., Rawson, K., Marsh, E. J., Nathan, M. J., & Willingham, D. T. (2013). Improving students' learning with effective learning techniques: Promising directions from cognitive and educational psychology. *Psychological Science in the Public Interest, 14*(1), 4–58. https://doi.org/10.1177/1529100612453266.

Dunn, D., Cautin, R. L., & Gurung, R. A. R. (2011). Curriculum matters: Structure, content, and psychological literacy. In J. Cranney & D. S. Dunn (Eds.), *The psychologically literate citizen: Foundations and global perspectives* (pp. 3–12). New York, NY: Oxford University Press.

Enhancing Student Wellbeing. (2016). Enhancing student wellbeing: Resources for educators. Retrieved from http://unistudentwellbeing.edu.au/

Halonen, J. S., Dunn, D. S., Baker, S., & McCarthy, M. A. (2011). Departmental program approaches for educating psychologically literate citizens. In J. Cranney & D. Dunn (Eds.), *The psychologically literate citizen: Foundations and global perspectives*. New York, NY: Oxford University Press.

Halpern, D. (1998). Teaching critical thinking for transfer across domains: Dispositions, skills, structure training, and metacognitive monitoring. *American Psychologist, 53*, 449–455. https://doi.org/10.1037/0003-066x.53.4.449.

Halpern, D. (2010). *Undergraduate education in psychology: A blueprint for the future of the discipline*. Washington, DC: American Psychological Association.

Halpern, D. F., Anton, B., Beins, B. C., Bernstein, D. J., Blair-Broeker, C. T., Brewer, C., et al. (2010). Principles for quality undergraduate education. In D. Halpern (Ed.), *Undergraduate education in psychology: A blueprint for the future of the discipline*. Washington, DC: American Psychological Association.

Heritage, B., Roberts, L., & Gasson, N. (2016). Psychological literacy weakly differentiates students by discipline and year of enrolment. *Frontiers in Psychology, 7*, 162. https://doi.org/10.3389/fpsyg.2016.00162.

Horan, S. (2018, March 14). What are universities for? Report for the Halpin Partnership. Retrieved from https://www.halpinpartnership.com/debate/what-are-universities

Hulme, J. A. (2014). Psychological literacy: From classroom to real world. *The Psychologist, 27*, 932–935.

Hulme, J. A., & De Wilde, J. (2014). *Tackling transition in STEM disciplines: Supporting the Science, Technology, Engineering and Mathematics (STEM) student journey into higher education in England and Wales*. York, UK: Higher Education Academy. Retrieved from https://www.heacademy.ac.uk/system/files/resources/hea_tackling_transitions_in_stem.pdf

Hulme, J. A., & Kitching, H. J. (2016). Teaching and learning issues in the disciplines: Psychology. Retrieved from https://www.bps.org.uk/sites/bps.org.uk/files/Member%20Networks/Divisions/DARTP/Teaching%20and%20Learning%20Issues%20in%20the%20Disciplines%20Psychology.pdf

Hulme, J. A., & Kitching, H. J. (2017). The nature of psychology: Reflections on university teachers' experiences of teaching sensitive topics. *Psychology Teaching Review, 23*(1), 4–14.

Hulme, J. A., Skinner, R., Worsnop, F., Collins, E., Banyard, P., Kitching, H. J., Watt, R., & Goodson, S. (2015). Psychological literacy: A multifaceted perspective. *Psychology Teaching Review, 21*(2), 13–24.

Hulme, J. A., & Winstone, N. E. (2017). Do no harm: Risk aversion versus risk management in the context of pedagogic frailty. *Knowledge Management & E-Learning: An International Journal, 9*(3), 261–274. https://doi.org/10.34105/j.kmel.2017.09.016.

Lantz, C. (2011). *The psychology student's guide to employability*. York, UK: Higher Education Academy. Retrieved from https://www.heacademy.ac.uk/system/files/employability_guide_0.pdf

Maree, K. (2017). The psychology of career adaptability, career resilience, and employability: A broad overview. In K. Maree (Ed.), *Psychology of career adaptability, employability and resilience*. Cham, Switzerland: Springer.

McGovern, T. V. (2011). Virtues and character strengths of psychologically literate faculty. In J. Cranney & D. Dunn (Eds.), *The psychologically literate citizen: Foundations and global perspectives* (pp. 296–305). New York, NY: Oxford University Press.

McGovern, T. V., Corey, L. A., Cranney, J., Dixon, W. E., Jr., Holmes, J. D., Kuebli, J. E., Ritchey, K., Smith, R. A., & Walker, S. (2010). Psychologically literate citizens. In D. Halpern (Ed.), *Undergraduate education in psychology: Blueprint for the discipline's future* (pp. 9–27). Washington, DC: American Psychological Association.

Meyer, J. H. F., Land, R., & Baillie, C. (2010). *Threshold concepts and transformational learning*. Rotterdam, The Netherlands: Sense Publishers.

Miller, G. (1969). Psychology as a means of promoting human welfare. *American Psychologist, 24*(12), 1063–1075. https://doi.org/10.1037/h0028988.

Morris, S., Cranney, J., Baldwin, P., Mellish, L., & Krochmalik, A. (2018). *The rubber brain: A toolkit for optimising your study, work, and life*. Bowen Hills, QLD: Australian Academic Press.

Murdoch, D. D. (2016). Psychological literacy: Proceed with caution, construction ahead. *Psychology Research and Behavior Management, 9*, 189–199. https://doi.org/10.2147/prbm.s88646.

Oliver, B., & de St Jorre, T. J. (2018). Graduate attributes for 2020 and beyond: Recommendations for Australian higher education providers. *Higher Education Research & Development, 37*(4), 821–836. https://doi.org/10.1080/07294360.2018.1446415.

Oxfam. (1997). *A curriculum for global citizenship*. Oxford, UK: Oxfam.

Pollard, E., Hirsh, W., Williams, M., Buzzeo, J., Marvell, R., Tassinari, A., … Ball, C. (2015). *Understanding employers' graduate recruitment and selection processes* (BIS research paper 231). Retrieved from https://core.ac.uk/download/pdf/74379837.pdf

Povee, K., & Roberts, L. (2014). Qualitative research in psychology: Attitudes of psychology students and academic staff. *Australian Journal of Psychology, 66*(1), 28–37. https://doi.org/10.1111/ajpy.12031.

QAA. (2016, October). Subject benchmark statement for psychology. Retrieved from https://www.qaa.ac.uk/docs/qaa/subject-benchmark-statements/sbs-psychology-16.pdf?sfvrsn=af95f781_8

Ravakant, N., & Navukant, N. (2017). Naval Ravakant: The knowledge project. Farnam Street Media Inc. Retrieved from https://www.farnamstreetblog.com/2017/02/naval-ravikant-reading-decision-making/

Reddy, P., Lantz, C., & Hulme, J. A. (2013). *Employability in psychology: A guide for departments*. York, UK: Higher Education Academy. Retrieved from https://www.heacademy.ac.uk/knowledge-hub/employability-psychology-guide-departments

Reddy, P. A., & Moores, E. (2006). Measuring the benefits of a psychology placement year. *Assessment and Evaluation in Higher Education, 31*(5), 551–567. https://doi.org/10.1080/02602930600679555.

Ryan, R. M., & Deci, E. L. (2000). Self-determination theory and the facilitation of intrinsic motivation, social development, and well-being. *American Psychologist, 55*, 68–78. https://doi.org/10.1.1.335.6945&rep=rep1&type=pdf.

Sarkar, M., Overton, T., Thompson, C., & Rayner, G. (2016). Graduate employability: Views of recent science graduates and employers. *International Journal of Innovation in Science and Mathematics Education, 24*(3), 31–48.

Trapp, A., Banister, P., Ellis, J., Latto, R., Miell, D., & Upton, D. (2011). *The future of undergraduate psychology in the United Kingdom*. York, UK: Higher Education Academy. Retrieved from https://www.heacademy.ac.uk/knowledge-hub/future-undergraduate-psychology-united-kingdom

Watt, R. (2013). Developing the psychologically-literate citizen at the University of Stirling. Retrieved from https://www.heacademy.ac.uk/sites/default/files/resources/Watt-developing-psyc-lit-Stirling-v2.pdf

Worrell, F. C., Casad, B. J., Daniel, D. B., McDaniel, M., Messer, W. S., Miller, H. L., Jr., Prohaska, V., & Zlokovich, M. S. (2010). Promising principles for translating psychological science into teaching and learning. In D. Halpern (Ed.), *Undergraduate education in psychology: A blueprint for the future of the discipline*. Washington, DC: American Psychological Association.

Yorke, M. (2006). *Employability in higher education: What it is – What it is not*. York, UK: Higher Education Academy. Retrieved from https://www.heacademy.ac.uk/knowledge-hub/employability-higher-education-what-it-what-it-not

# 37. Psychology in Professional Education and Training

Christoph Steinebach

## Contents

| | |
|---|---|
| Introduction | 912 |
| Purpose of the Curricula in Vocational Education and Further Education in a Changing World | 913 |
|     Social Change | 913 |
|     Change in the Professional World | 913 |
|     Change in the Comprehension of Learning | 914 |
|     Change in Learning Environments | 914 |
|     Requirements for Education | 915 |
| Rationale, Basic Concepts, and Objectives of Vocational Education and Further Education | 915 |
|     Theory-Based Versus Practice-Integrated | 915 |
|     Formal Versus Informal | 916 |
|     General Versus Vocationally Specific | 917 |
|     Efficiency Versus Personal Growth | 918 |
|     Literacy Versus Citizenship | 918 |
| Teaching, Learning, and Assessment in Vocational Education and Further Education | 919 |
|     Professional Socialization | 919 |
|     Personality Development | 920 |
|     Optimal Development | 921 |
|     Learning | 922 |
|     Competence Development | 923 |
| Challenges and Lesson Learned: Course Design and Didactics | 927 |
|     Experiential Learning and Inquiry-Based Learning | 928 |
|     Hybrid Forms of Teaching | 929 |
|     Vocational Guidance and Counseling | 930 |
|     Subjects and Contents | 931 |
|     Evaluation | 931 |
| Psychologists as of Teachers | 932 |
| Outlook: Innovation of Continuing Education and Psychology for Non-psychologists | 933 |

C. Steinebach (✉)
ZHAW Zurich University of Applied Sciences, School of Applied Psychology, Zürich, Switzerland
e-mail: Christoph.Steinebach@zhaw.ch

© Springer Nature Switzerland AG 2023
J. Zumbach et al. (eds.), *International Handbook of Psychology Learning and Teaching*, Springer International Handbooks of Education,
https://doi.org/10.1007/978-3-030-28745-0_43

| | |
|---|---|
| Teaching, Learning, and Assessment Resources | 934 |
| Tips and Questions | 934 |
| Further Readings | 935 |
| Cross-References | 936 |
| References | 937 |

### Abstract

Psychology plays a special role in vocational education in many respects. In the course of rapidly developing professional and educational worlds, its importance continues to grow. This change corresponds to a new understanding of psychological courses in vocational education and training. For individuals, as well as for institutions and organizations, the changes in the world of work can lead to orientation crises. Interest in psychological content is increasing.

Psychological reflection of the vocational biography, psychological training offers, as well as the psychological career-related counseling are of special importance here. From this, recommendations can be derived to offers, to their goals, and to their didactics. Psychological theories help to grasp the meaning of the offers. From a psychological point of view, vocational training is a learning, development, and socialization process. Learning opens up opportunities for personality formation and optimal development in a changing professional world.

The reflection of psychological competences offers the possibility for a competence-oriented description of programs. It also shows that the usual focus of psychological competences on social skills falls short. Psychology in academic studies and further education requires a didactic approach that enables self-determined learning in formats that are independent of time and place. This results in special tasks for didactics and the monitoring of learning processes. This is also associated with special challenges for teachers. The impact of psychological offerings in higher and further education can be seen, among other things, in the extent to which "psychological literacy" promotes personal development, innovation in the workplace, and social participation.

### Keywords

Vocational education · Continuing education · Social change · Competence models · Career resilience · Psychological literacy

## Introduction

With the interest to apply psychology to education, to the professional world or to health promotion, the question of its teaching for people in different professions also arose. Therefore, the roots of these offers go back to the foundation of the first psychotechnical institutes in Europe at the beginning of the last century (Carpintero & Herrero, 2002; Suter, 1935). Also, even today a multitude of changes in society as a whole and in the professional world make psychological training courses attractive and necessary.

For a long time now, a wide variety of offers in very different formats with different designs have enjoyed great popularity. Special interests, questions, and competences of the participants pose particular challenges to the didactics. After all, it is necessary to harmonize professional profiles, individual needs and interests, competence profiles, contents, and didactics. In this way, psychology makes an important contribution to training "non-psychologists" personally and professionally for the special challenges of work life during their studies and in further education.

## Purpose of the Curricula in Vocational Education and Further Education in a Changing World

### Social Change

In the course of their lives, people have to cope with a variety of challenges in different areas of life. Many of these challenges are to be expected as tasks in the course of life. Others are unexpected and can be associated with crises. Since the turn of the last millennium, at least four central "megatrends" have been mentioned: globalization, pluralization, acceleration, and knowledge orientation (Renn, Chabay, van der Leeuw, & Droy, 2020; on acceleration, Rosa, 2017). The concern to avoid or manage global risks (World Economic Forum, 2020), the focus on fundamental societal development goals (United Nations, 2020), and the quest to improve quality and efficiency bring new demands for individuals, teams, and institutions. Rapidly knowledge becomes obsolete and requires continuous updating and optimization.

It is important to keep in mind that teaching and learning in vocational education and training differ significantly in the various countries and cultures. These differences also represent different cultural norms, values, and beliefs that influence individual learning, individual development, and career biography. Conversely, it can also be assumed that such individual changes can lead to cultural change (Albert & Trommsdorff, 2014).

### Change in the Professional World

In the world of work, too, positive development, satisfaction and well-being are only conceivable if individuals face up to the given challenges. Resilience manifests itself in successful self-development and environmental empowerment (Steinebach, 2015). It is important not to lose sight of one's own path and goals while worrying about one's professional career. "Career adaptability" becomes a prerequisite for "career satisfaction and career success." As Maree (2017) suggests, referring to Hartung and Cadaret, "career adaptability is (the) key to developing career resilience and changing the self in fluctuating career contexts, leading to the successful accomplishment of career development tasks and career transitions as well as the resolution of career- and work-based traumas" (Maree, 2017, 6). In this context, the world of work has always been changing. However, terms like "Work 4.0" or

"Industry 4.0" stand for a change that is happening very fast and is very fundamental (cf. Ahrens & Gessler, 2018).

Continuing education is an adequate response to these challenges. From the company's perspective, continuing education then appears to be a sensible investment that secures competitive advantages and influence, supports strategic adaptation, strengthens resources, enables participation, and solves operational problems (on the theories of continuing education, see Käpplinger, 2018).

## Change in the Comprehension of Learning

At school, in university, and in continuing vocational training, learning and personal development today are in many respects a self-designed and self-responsible processes. Learning succeeds particularly well when learners have the impression that they are working on solving real problems. Existing knowledge should be awakened, and new insights should be secured and consolidated. In a strong practical reference, the benefit of theoretical knowledge for practical action should become clear. At the same time, the transfer of knowledge into practice should also ensure that the new knowledge is sustainably anchored in the learners' lifeworld (Jenkins & Healey, 2005). What "institutional strategies to link teaching and research" can succeed in this? (Jenkins & Healey, 2005, 1). Research-based learning is most likely to meet this understanding of learning (Zumbach & Astleitner, 2016). On the one hand, because the learning process can be understood as research, and on the other hand, because one needs to understand research in order to stay up to date with the latest knowledge. In professional education, we also view psychology as empirical science and evidence-based practice. Therefore, learning opportunities must teach how psychological expertise worthy of the label "evidence-based" is generated (Jenkins & Healey, 2005, 22).

## Change in Learning Environments

The understanding of teaching and learning described above suggests a special design of the learning environment in studies and further education. At the micro level, courses require special forms of didactics. The connection between the university as a place of learning and the other learning and living environments of the course participants is a particular challenge. More and more, the workplace is being understood as a place of learning. This means that cooperation between companies and external training providers, e.g., universities, is becoming increasingly important. At the meso level, it is a matter of designing the continuing education course in such a way that the competences acquired in the modules build on one another in a meaningful way. At the exo level, universities must present themselves as an institution for the acquisition and recognition of competences. In this context, it proves to be a challenge that not only the continuing education landscape but also universities are under strong pressure to change. Especially since they themselves are also involved in the local and regional context at the macro level (Braun, Weiß, & Seidel, 2014).

## Requirements for Education

Current discussions about higher education and continuing vocational training point to a variety of very fundamental societal changes. This makes it difficult to give recommendations on necessary competences and skills (Wilson, 2019). The relationship between "theory" and "practice" plays a special role in understanding societal change, individual development, needs, and the design of psychological offerings in vocational education. "Theory" is considered the link between research, teaching, and practice.

The reference to the learners' own development and personal responsibility makes it clear that education is more than knowledge. Education aims at basic skills of understanding the world and thus also at competences to decide on good actions as a basic question of ethics (Mittelstraß, 2002; Pfadenhauer, 2013).

Professional action always has an impact on others. Knowledge helps to be able to assess the consequences of one's own actions and to justify one's own actions. Thus, theoretical knowledge is essential for meeting ethical requirements in research and professional action (Doylea & Buckley, 2014). Students learn what ethical research guidelines must be considered. They learn that research in the applied sciences serves evidence-based practice and enables practice-based theory development. They learn that theory is always individual and intersubjective. They increasingly understand practice as experience in a concrete environment and learn to understand the interactions between theory and practice. All this is combined with the question of whether the chosen procedure is ethically justifiable. Against this background, research-based learning also imparts knowledge about the dangers of deliberate falsification and bona fide manipulation in research, about the rules of peer review and scientific self-control. This makes it clear that when we integrate research-based learning into vocational education and training, it is not only techniques and tools that become the topic. We also convey an attitude of scientific honesty and thus also promote a corresponding scientific culture of the university or institution.

## Rationale, Basic Concepts, and Objectives of Vocational Education and Further Education

### Theory-Based Versus Practice-Integrated

Professionals face a highly complex and rapidly changing world. In this situation, they expect psychology as a science to provide answers to their questions (Narciss, 2019). The close connection between research, theory, teaching, and practice is a wonderful ideal. However, the practical implementation is not easy (Zumbach & Astleitner, 2016). For each learning field with its own competence profiles, it will be necessary to clarify (a) the relationship between research and teaching, (b) which competences and metacompetences should be taught at which educational level, (c) which special challenges for professional ethics and research ethics exist in this subject in particular, and (d) with which subject-specific didactics psychological competences should be taught to students and participants in continuing education with their own individual or professional profiles. In all of this, the learning process with its specific phases must be taken into account (Zumbach & Astleitner, 2016).

The currently common biopsychosocial model of human development can help reduce complexity and order the relevant factors. From this systemic perspective, human development is understood as a process explained by changes at the biochemical, neurophysiological, emotional, and cognitive levels. These interconnected systemic processes, following the work of Uri Bronfenbrenner (1917–2005) are in turn embedded in different environmental systems, usually distinguished as micro-, meso-, exo-, and macrosystems. Levels and processes change over time. Not infrequently, complex adaptation processes become necessary here. This is especially true for ecological transitions (e.g., from school to work, from one employment to another), where the relationships between requirements, activities, and roles change (Schmidt-Lauff, 2018; Steinebach, 2013; Steinebach, Eberhardt, Kotrubczik, Majkovic, & Zinsli, 2014; Steinebach, Steinebach, & Brendtro, 2012).

The perfectly reasonable reference to the complexity of the problem and the relevant conditions often triggers skepticism and dissatisfaction (Steinebach, 2019). However, skepticism might be also seen as an expression of critical thinking. Associated with this approach is the insight that theories are at best maps that never represent reality one-to-one but can nevertheless provide orientation ("theories-are-maps," Erikson & Erlandson, 2015, p. 3). Thus, transfer to everyday life becomes a major challenge. In order to promote the transfer, the everyday life is didactically included. Practice becomes the place of learning to ensure the transfer of theory into everyday life (Eckert & Kadera, 2018). In this context, everyday life then stands for the physical and social aspects of the context, for the real occurrences and their social construction (Gerstenmaier & Mandl, 2018).

**Formal Versus Informal**

Meanwhile, when it comes to acquiring specific skills, vocational training often seems to be disconnected from formal offerings. With informal learning, occupational activities, social relationships in the workplace, in-company training, and human resource development become more important. It is emphasized that skills are not acquired only to the usual settings of instruction (Rintala et al., 2019). Learning often occurs independently of specific times (e.g., problem-based), places (e.g., job-dependent), and social situations (e.g., dialogue with competent co-workers). Especially in continuing education, learning is thus highly self-determined, individualized, and dependent on individual dispositions and resources, environmental offers and incentives, as well as social support in learning and living environments (Thalhammer & Schmidt-Hertha, 2018).

Flexibilization and individualization are also considered desirable in formal offerings. At the level of continuing education, for example, courses are now also offered as "open studies." For the most part, offerings at the university level do not require prior degrees. It may be, however, that professional prerequisites are required. To acquire these prerequisites, as well as for the "open studies" courses themselves, existing formal learning opportunities can be opened up to those interested.

Due to the concern to describe learning in all its facets and to finally be able to confirm the acquisition of competences, a distinction is made between formally, non-formally, and informally acquired competences. Competences are considered to be formally acquired if they have been imparted within the framework of regulated educational programs. This can be the case, for example, in the context of bachelor's and master's degree programs or in the context of curricular continuing education programs. Non-formally acquired competences are competences that were acquired apart from regular educational programs. This usually includes in-company training. Informally acquired competences are all those skills and abilities that have been acquired in everyday life, whether at work or in free time. The fact that informally acquired competences are also of particular importance for professional development is not new. What is new, however, is the concern to also document these competences and to credit them as equivalent to formally acquired competences (Council of the European Union, 2012; Harteis & Heid, 2018). This is not only intended to promote learning in the workplace. It is also intended to increase permeability between vocational education and tertiary education. However, this requires appropriate standards and recognition processes (Winterton, Delamare Le Deist, & Stringfellow, 2006; Schröder & Denbostel, 2019).

## General Versus Vocationally Specific

The scope and structure of psychological courses in higher and further education differ depending on which competences are to be imparted. The distinction between sub-competences and competences, key competences and meta-competences alone makes it clear that very different abilities and skills can be the subject of psychological offerings. Due to the variety of meanings and the many overlaps with everyday language, a pragmatic definition of "competence" is obvious. Competences are then understood as characteristics of individuals or groups, of institutions, or organizations. Competences are needed to achieve given goals. They are manifested in actions that are appropriate to the situation. From these actions are inferred (a) general cognitive competences, (b) specialized cognitive competences, (c) a competence-performance model, (d) a modified competence-performance model, (e) motivated action tendencies, (f) objective and subjective self-concepts, (g) action competence, (h) key competences, and (i) meta-competences (Weinert, 2001). Emphasized is that basic competences are important across different fields of action. They cannot be defined by a specific subject matter. Here Weinert speaks of domain-general competences, metacognitive competences, competence-relevant motivational attitudes, and competence-relevant volitional skills (Weinert, 2001).

Competence models are not static. They evolve with the concerns of people and the requirements of work. Currently, "entrepreneurship" is considered an important competence in which "innovation skills" are particularly relevant (Deitmer, 2019). In addition, "Work 4.0" places special demands on communication with customers ("connectivity and creativity" as competences, Kim, 2019, p. 191).

## Efficiency Versus Personal Growth

Continuing professional development is about learning measures that are more or less planned, more or less structured, more or less self-directed, self-responsible and self-financed, and more or less recognized. One can think of seminars, courses, trainings, guidance and supervision, coaching, job rotation, job shadowing, and much more (Käpplinger, 2018). In all of these, psychological skills can also be taught.

In many ways, psychological knowledge can be helpful in solving problems in very different professional situations and fields of work. Therefore, the decision to pursue psychological learning opportunities may be motivated by a desire to become more effective in one's profession. To be distinguished from this would be the desire to grow personally. It is about learning how to use one's potential for one's own development and for life as a whole. Personal fulfillment, well-being, and health are important goals. The concerns of professional effectiveness and personal growth are also the subject of self-determination theory (Deci & Ryan, 2015). In this theory, self-determination, autonomy, and experience of competence are understood as basic needs. People are particularly motivated to address goals and perform actions when they feel that these goals and actions serve to satisfy their basic needs. "Satisfaction of these basic needs promotes optimal motivational traits and states of autonomous motivation and intrinsic aspiration" (Deci & Ryan, 2015, 486). The basic assumptions of this theory can also be applied to career development. We then speak of "career self-determination," "career autonomy," and "career competence" (Chen, 2017, 330). Thus, the pursuit of autonomy reflects the self-concept and professional identity, one's own interests, as well as the meaning of the professional activity. With the experience of being able to act competently in one's career, self-efficacy and thus individual resilience also grow.

## Literacy Versus Citizenship

In today's world, what does a person need to achieve goals, acquire knowledge, realize his or her potential, and participate in society? The answer to this question is "literacy" (United Nations Educational, Scientific and Cultural Organization, 2019). Literacy encompasses many different skills in a wide range of areas that are not limited to cognitive skills alone. For a more precise clarification of what is meant by "psychological literacy," on the one hand, the definitions of "literacy" are used, and on the other hand, "citizenship" becomes an important determinant.

"Citizenship" refers to the ability to actively participate in the life of the community and society as a whole and to assume responsibility. This is also based on intercultural competence and a comprehensive understanding of the world.

Psychological literacy encompasses a wide range of specialist knowledge and thus also knowledge of the conceptual world of psychology. Human actions can be reflected, analyzed, and developed; problems are reflected upon openly, creatively, and from a professional distance. Psychological theories are applied in the analysis of information and the evaluation of techniques as well as in the development of solutions to problems. "Psychological Literacy" is also demonstrated in the ability to communicate appropriately in different situations, taking into account the diversity of people and their living conditions. It is manifested in a prudent and reflective attitude towards oneself and others and is also the basis for ethical action (Cranney & Dunn, 2011; ▶ Chap. 36, "Psychological Literacy and Learning for Life").

When it comes to designing programs (Dunn, Cautin, & Gurung, 2011), it is generally assumed that such competences can only be taught in a comprehensive study of psychology. "... psychological literacy is a core component of graduate literacy in general, and ... the psychologically literate citizen is a core component of the global citizen ..." (Cranney & Dunn, 2011, p. 10.). On the other hand, "literacy" is also talked about in other fields of practice and sciences. And we can assume that psychological competences certainly play a role in these fields. For example, someone who works as an engineer and has leadership responsibility for his or her team will be interested in developing his or her own leadership competences and will be happy to acquire psychological competences in the process. Therefore, we should not define "psychological literacy" too narrowly and create a general educational ideal in which psychological competences also have their place.

## Teaching, Learning, and Assessment in Vocational Education and Further Education

### Professional Socialization

Psychological theories of socialization try to shed light on the contribution of the environment to the development of the personality, of cognitions, emotions, and behavior. In this context, family, school, and professional institutions are considered important instances of socialization. With reference to Niklas Luhmann (1927–1998), we can assume that social processes without corresponding structures would appear disorderly and chaotic. Social processes appear chaotic to the observer, who lacks any category to judge them. Within the process of socialization, we learn to bring order into chaotic social processes, to read and understand them better. Socialization ensures the possibility of remaining capable of action over the course of one's life and of pursuing one's own goals in social responsibility. "The term *Socialization* is used to describe the very general, anthropologically based facts of the social shaping of reliable social relationships and the intergenerational transmission of social knowledge of action ..." (translated by the author, emphasis in original, Grundmann, 2017, 64).

Personality and identity thereby represent physical, emotional, and cognitive resources, as well as possibilities and limitations of environmental systems (Tomlinson & Jackson, 2019). In reflecting on one's competences, one learns more about one's personality. However, people also process their external reality largely through social interaction and communication with others. Transferred to executive education, this means that their current behavior can be understood as the result of a (self-)reflected socialization process. Knowledge, their personality profile, and social skills are expressed in their leadership style. The effects of leadership behavior are reflected in the commitment, willingness to learn, and, for example, the assumption of responsibility by those led. And this has consequences for general communication, for learning in the company, for the planning of processes up to the productivity and growth of the company (von Rosenstiel, 2018; articles in Lippmann, Pfister, & Jörg, 2019). Colleagues, one's team, supervisors, and professional development offerings assume the function of direct mediators of external reality in professional life. They provide patterns of appropriation and processing of external reality via conversation, instruction, guidance, and training.

## Personality Development

Vocational training follows formal and informal paths. Formal education tends to be determined by institutionalized rules and serves the systematic transmission of knowledge. Informal education is rooted in everyday situations and mostly uses implicit pedagogy. In different cultures, the effects of formal versus informal education vary. "These differences are presumably related to several factors, including differences in educational systems, teaching and learning styles, time use, cultural values, and relations between informal and formal education" (Trommsdorff & Dasen, 2001, p. 3006). This also applies to the development and socialization of emotionality and social behavior (Albert & Trommsdorff, 2014; Trommsdorff, 2012).

Professional socialization and education take place in an immediate social and cultural context, and yet socialization processes and their engagement are highly individual. In the ideal of self-determined learning, everyone can, based on their own personality and developmental history, actively engage with individual preferences, objectives, and assistance, and thus explore their own potential and use it for their own vocational education and development. New norms and trends or emerging risks give rise to individual reflection and reorientation. Personal experience offers little security. Problems of action and orientation are increasingly seen as problems of the individual. Those who fail are seen as having little resilience. "Burnout" becomes the recognized way out. Some experience developments in this field of tension as delightful "surfing"; for others, the "feeling of life on the slippery slope" (Rosa, 2017) triggers anxiety and depression. Concern for one's own well-being becomes a central challenge of individual developmental. According to Ryff and

Keyes (1995), self-acceptance, positive social relationships, autonomy, control over the environment, meaning in life, and personal growth are considered important needs or values. When we have a positive attitude toward ourselves, experience warm, satisfying, trusting relationships, are concerned about the well-being of others, lead a self-determined and independent life, can resist social pressures, experience ourselves as competent, have goals in life and can thus give direction to our lives, and are open to new experiences, we feel good.

Admittedly, it is not easy to achieve and maintain this well-being under the pressure of the rapidly changing world of work. In this time of change and contradictions, conflicts can hardly be avoided. The decoupling of thinking, feeling, and physical experience can become a problem. Workplace health promotion interventions, e.g., with a focus on mindfulness and mindful leadership, are designed to counteract this (Knafla & Schär, 2019). Learners can benefit from reflecting on their socialization and coming to terms with their own values. They use thinking about themselves to promote their own competences in dealing with the complexity and dynamics of social relations and to support the competence development of their peers.

## Optimal Development

Referring to relevant models of developmental psychology (Brandtstädter, 2015; Steinebach, 2006), we would assume that evaluations of one's own development take place in the life course, for example, in dealing with particular developmental tasks ("How can I advance my career?"). There is an initial attribution of events to the individual ("I put myself out there! I'm really good at that!"), or to external stable or variable factors ("I can rely on my family, they'll support me!" "I must be lucky!"). Values, developmental goals, and control beliefs ("I can do something about that!") also factor into the assessment. With the broader consideration of competences, this attribution of personal and situational factors expands to include the acquisition, consolidation, or diffusion of competences. Here, the conception of competence as a self-organizing disposition takes on a decisive significance. Especially in the reflection of one's own potential, it is important to be able to self-critically define special opportunities for professional development.

What competences do people possess that come fairly close to the goal of autonomous and at the same time socially responsible self-determination? Brandtstädter (1980) mentiones:

- An ongoing and differentiated review of one's own behavior
- An internal environmental model that reflects and explains aspects of the environment in a differentiated way
- An internal self-model that adequately reflects one's own feelings and behavioral potentials
- A self-critical and experience-open attitude as a prerequisite for flexible changes of the internal environmental and self-model

- A high degree of "exploratory variability and spontaneity" (translated by the author, Brandtstädter, 1980, p. 219)
- The capacity for self-reinforcement with regard to the environmental and self-ideal
- The extensive personal autonomy of one's own evaluative criteria and standards
- A reluctance to accept instructions or role expectations
- The willingness to change the self- and environmental ideal if necessary
- A positive self-assessment and evaluation
- A willingness to change perspectives, empathize, and consider the interests of others

From the point of view of developmental psychology, vocational training and counseling should make it possible to reevaluate one's own life story and thus also the issues, phases, and events that are difficult at present or in retrospect. One's own weaknesses and strengths, but also the obstacles and supportive potentials of the environment should be reflected upon. By processing past experiences and developmental crises, a personal and social reorientation becomes possible for the person. The reassessment is supported by information on general development and current development conditions, risks, and opportunities.

## Learning

"Acquiring competencies is hardly comparable with learning as knowledge acquisition. Competencies are described as learnable but not teachable. ... Methodical notes about competency acquisition or about didactic conceptions of imparting competency are usually of a rather general character, which is often not least due to a rather vague competency concept" (Barth, Godemann, Rieckmann, & Stoltenberg, 2007). In professional development, situations are conceivable in which behavioral-cognitive theories as well as theories of situated learning are helpful (Steinebach, Süss, Kienbaum, & Kiegelmann, 2016). Of particular importance then are cognitive and constructivist theories of learning in which construction, action, schema formation are reflected under personal, social, and societal conditions (Ludwig, 2018). Such reconsideration then certainly has implications for the design of learning opportunities. Madson, Zaikman, and Hughes (2020), for example, recommend making greater use of offerings in "team-based learning" for teaching psychological competences.

Learning – and thus education – happens earlier and naturally before, during, and after (and in) schooling, apprenticeships, or in the early years of employment. Especially the constructivist theories of self-directed learning are helpful to grasp educational processes in their complexity therein. Successful learning opportunities offer sufficient room for self-directed learning in authentic challenging situations and thus address motivation and emotion in a special way (Merrill, 2002). However, motivation and positive emotions alone are not sufficient, but they are also of great importance in the development of social competences – compared to planning or

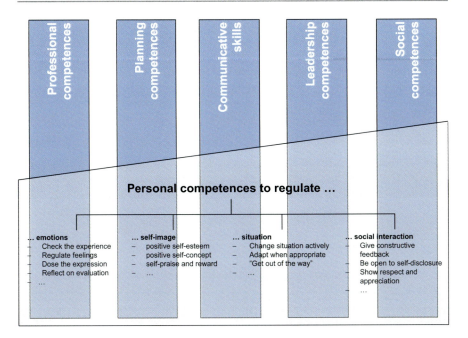

**Fig. 1** Psychosocial competences for the workplace (cf. Steinebach et al., 2016)

technical competences (Barth et al., 2007; Diener, Thapa, & Tay, 2020). Furthermore, it is important to be able to learn to understand a subject matter through exploration and observation, to be active in the learning process, and to be able to control this action oneself (Mayer, 2019; Steinebach, 2005). "Personal competence" here means appropriate forms of situation regulation, self-regulation, interaction regulation, and emotion regulation (Arnold, Pätzold, & Ganz, 2018, Diener et al., 2020; Heyse, Erpenbeck, Coester, Ortmann, & Sauter, 2019; Steinebach & Steinebach, 2013, see Fig. 1). Whereby all forms of self-regulation are to be understood as culture-based, i.e., they have to correspond to the cultural context with its views on appropriate self-regulation (Trommsdorff, 2009).

## Competence Development

"The trend towards competence-based ICVT (Initial and Continuing Vocational Training) development is not only observed at the national level within countries but also at an international level" (Mulder, Weigel, & Collins, 2006, p. 8). Even though concepts of competence-based education permeate the professional world and continuing vocational training after the "competency-based turn" of the 1990s (Ahrens & Gessler, 2018), competences are controversially discussed. "The term 'competency' echoes throughout the country. ... However, no agreement exists about what (key) competencies actually are, which are of importance and how the approach of competence acquisition finds its way into higher education." (Barth et al., 2007, 417; Zeuner, 2018). The use of the concept of competence also supports other developments, such as increasing self-responsibility in the learning process, the inclusion of practice as a place of learning, recourse to previously acquired knowledge, and the development of new learning theories that emphasize self-direction of learning as well as cognitive and social construction of knowledge (Mulder et al., 2006). Diversity in understanding concepts is matched by diversity in theories (Mulder, 2019). We usually assume that personal competence is partly related to professional competence, partly related to methodological competence, but certainly related to social competence. Just as there is an overarching personal competence, we could also assume an overarching research competence. This would then most likely still play a role for professional competence, or also for the evaluation and development of methods, i.e., for methodological competence (cf. Steinebach et al., 2014). Personal competences also require meta-competences, in which knowledge about one's own competences is reflected. Competences to act professionally in the narrower sense include professional competences and planning competences (cf. Tippelt, 2018; Winterton et al., 2006).

There is agreement in describing job-related competences as prerequisites that are necessary to cope with complex, mostly occupational tasks. According to Erpenbeck and von Rosenstiel (2017), competences do not represent arbitrary abilities to act in any number of domains, but rather abilities or dispositions "that allow for meaningful and fruitful action in open, complex, sometimes chaotic situations, that is, that enable self-organized action under mental and representational uncertainty" (p. 6). In this context, the ability to understand the consequences of one's own actions in terms of their impact on the environment and individual responsibility for sustainable use of resources is gaining importance ("higher education for sustainable development," Barth et al., 2007, p. 416). Competences thus include skills, knowledge, and qualifications, but cannot be reduced to these. Overarchingly, it can be stated that in the psychological tradition, competences are conceived as learnable context-specific performance dispositions "that functionally relate to situations and requirements in specific domains" (Klieme & Hartig, 2007, p. 17).

The examination of one's own learning, one's own values and experiences, as well as reflection on how to deal with and cope with complex demanding situations (e.g., through supervision or intervision) supports the development of one's own potential and the learning process in the acquisition and deepening of competences. This openness in the contribution of the individual as well as in the different places of learning is also reflected in the recognition of informally acquired competences in the European Qualifications Framework (EQF; critically Mulder & Winterton, 2017). In the EQF, personal competences and national qualifications become comparable across all educational sectors and qualification levels. Learning outcomes are described and systematized on the basis of knowledge, skills, and competences (see Table 1). Knowledge refers to the respective factual, experiential, and theoretical knowledge. Skills refer to all knowledge and experience necessary for the successful performance of a specific task or occupation. Competence means the ability to use knowledge, skills and personal, social and/or methodological abilities in work and

**Table 1** Selected psychological competences for other professions

| Competences: psychological competences[a] | Knowledge: subjects of psychology | Skills: topics and professional fields | Interface of psychological competences, knowledge, and skills to other professions |
|---|---|---|---|
| **Part I** | | | |
| • Has the necessary foundational knowledge of psychological concepts, constructs, theories, methods, practice, and research methodology to support competence.<br>• Has the necessary specialized knowledge of psychological concepts, constructs, theory, methods, practice, and research methodology relating to own areas to support competence.<br>• Adopts an evidence-based orientation to the provision of assessments, interventions, service delivery, and other psychological activities.<br>• Identifies assessment or evaluation needs in individuals, groups, communities, organizations, systems, or society.<br>• Consults psychological and other relevant research to inform practice.<br>• Selects, designs, or develops assessments or evaluations, using methods appropriate for the goals and purposes of the activity.<br>• Resolves ethical dilemmas in one's professional practice using an appropriate approach.<br>• Consults peers, supervisors, or other relevant sources when appropriate. | Learning and cognition | Design of learning processes based on theories of learning and thinking. | Economy and behavior economics |
| | Perception and motivation | Reflection on the influences of perception and motivation on thinking, feeling, and behavior. | Health promotion, security engineering |
| | Biological psychology | Evaluation of physiological processes associated with various aspects of experience and behavior. | Biology |
| | Psychophysiology | Evaluation of the influences of various pharmaceuticals on physiology, experience, and behavior. | Pharmacology |
| | Neuropsychology | Describe neurological processes and their psychological effects. | Neurology |
| | Social psychology | Understanding social processes in, e.g., dyads, groups, and organizations. | Social education, social work, cultural consultant |
| | Life span developmental psychology | Consideration of special needs in education and counseling across the life span. | Social work, gerontology |
| | Personality psychology | Selection, implementation, and evaluation of psychodiagnostic tools. | Psychiatry |

(continued)

**Table 1** (continued)

| Competences: psychological competences[a] | Knowledge: subjects of psychology | Skills: topics and professional fields | Interface of psychological competences, knowledge, and skills to other professions |
|---|---|---|---|
| **Part II** | | | |
| • Integrates assessment and other information with psychological knowledge to guide and develop psychological interventions.<br>• Has the necessary basic skills to support competence in psychological practice.<br>• Has the necessary specialized skills to operate in own areas of psychological practice to support competence.<br>• Works with knowledge and understanding of the historical, political, social, and cultural context of clients, colleagues, and relevant others.<br>• Resolves ethical dilemmas in one's professional practice using an appropriate approach.<br>• Works and communicates effectively with all forms of diversity in clients, colleagues, and relevant others.<br>• Establishes, maintains, and develops appropriate working relationships with clients and relevant others.<br>• Establishes, maintains, and develops appropriate working relationships with colleagues in psychology and other professions.<br>• Works with knowledge and understanding of the historical, political, social, and cultural context of clients, colleagues, and relevant others. | Statistics and research methods | Evaluating empirical data and critically assessing research methods | Statistics and computer science |
| | Biostatistics | Reflection on problems in considering high complexity of factors and interactions including neural bases | Cognitive and neuroscience |
| | Educational psychology | Design of teaching and learning across the life span | Education |
| | Organizational and media psychology | Optimizing conditions of behavior and experience in work environments and organizations | Management, marketing, business, human resource management |
| | Work, traffic, and engineering psychology | Design of conditions and processes of human–machine interaction | Safety professions |
| | Health psychology | Promotion of health and well-being in prevention and rehabilitation | Nursing, physiotherapy |
| | Sport psychology | Promotion of body perception, movement processes, motivation and training in amateur and professional sports | Sports teacher, trainer |
| | Clinical psychology | Diagnosis and therapy of mental disorders | Psychiatry |
| | Forensic psychology | Diagnosis and therapy of deviant behavior. | Law and criminology |
| | Counselling psychology | Counseling and communication of individuals and systems | Social education, theology |

(continued)

**Table 1** (continued)

| Competences: psychological competences[a] | Knowledge: subjects of psychology | Skills: topics and professional fields | Interface of psychological competences, knowledge, and skills to other professions |
|---|---|---|---|
|  | Social psychology, community psychology, environmental psychology | Promotion of togetherness in culture and community | Urban planning, architecture |

[a]International Association of Applied Psychology & International Union of Psychological Science, 2016

life situations for professional and personal development. Here, for example, independence and willingness to take responsibility, learning competence, communicative and social competences are taken into account. Table 1 provides an overview of competences, knowledge, and skills, and relates them to other professions. Even if, as is usually the case, various levels of proficiency remain unnoticed here, it is actually only a graduation from low to high proficiency that makes it possible to speak of excellence (e.g., to high performance Worrell, Olszewski-Kubilius, & Subotnik, 2019) and, for example, to offer continuing education courses at an "advanced level" (Barrick, 2019). It should be noted that a focus on one or another competence and the negative evaluation of low levels of competence can also lead to social exclusion of those who are considered "incompetent" (see on Ableism and Prejudice Nario-Redmond, 2019; Debray & Spencer-Oatey, 2019, Morgan, 2019).

## Challenges and Lesson Learned: Course Design and Didactics

Psychological competences for other professions complement the respective specific competence profile with further aspects. "Curricula for non-psychologists should be (a) specific to the profession of the target group, (b) specific to the needs and (c) work processes of the target group and (d) limited to the professional field of the target group. Although psychology curricula for non-psychology students need to be limited regarding their breadth, they should (e) maintain the depth and multi-perspectivity required for understanding psychological phenomena" (Dutke et al., 2019, S. 111–112). This also requires a basic knowledge of the nonpsychological discipline or at least the involvement of experts from the other profession in curriculum development.

Psychologists are asked to develop psychological competences, learning objectives, and teaching methods "from silos to bridges" (Linden, 2015). For example, if the goal is to build "shaping competence" in Higher Education for Sustainable Development (ESD), the "goal ..., is to promote personality development, enabling a person to be able to cope with complex situations, to be able to act upon reflection and to make decisions. It is also about being able to take on responsibility, to consider ethical standards when acting and to be able to judge consequences.

Learning processes which consider the requisites of such a new learning culture can be characterized on the basis of three consequences: (1) Competence-orientation. ... This requires a normative framework for the justified selection of such competences in the same way as an educational concept is necessary which offers contents for developing competences and helps to identify learning opportunities. (2) Societal orientation. ... Learning takes place in real-life situations which question and change societal living. (3) Individual centering. Learning by the individual is seen to be active in the societal context" (Barth et al., 2007, 419). In all of this, it is the case that the target groups in lifelong learning are very heterogeneous because educational biographies are very diverse. At the same time, however, a close interlocking of initial education and continuing education is required (Jütte & Bade-Becker, 2018). The different living and working environments lead to a high need for coordination, if necessary, also with employers. Which forms of learning opportunities are therefore particularly promising?

## Experiential Learning and Inquiry-Based Learning

"Experiential learning" builds on particular learning experiences. These address the whole person and require that prior learning and life experiences be utilized. The activation of prior knowledge and the reflection of lessons learned are of particular importance. In this context, "single loop learning" and "double loop learning," as "widely accepted cyclical models of learning illustrate the links between two types of learning: 'single-loop' learning about obtaining knowledge to solve specific problems based on existing premises; and 'double-loop' learning about establishing new premises such as mental models and perspectives" (Winterton et al., 2016, p. 6). It becomes possible to integrate learning experiences into existing knowledge and to further develop one's own knowledge in terms of a qualitatively better understanding (Barth et al., 2007). Here, the proximity to the concept of inquiry-based learning also becomes clear.

A variety of recommendations show how research can be integrated into teaching. For example, why is "inquiry-based learning" (Spinath, Seifried, & Eckert, 2014) a good way to teach knowledge and skills in higher education? Not only since the work of David Merrill (2002, 2008) we know that learning is sustainably supported when learners try to solve real problems, when existing knowledge is activated as a basis for new knowledge, when new knowledge is generated with the applications, when the new knowledge is applied by the learner, and when the new knowledge is integrated into the learner's life world. Those who integrate research into teaching ensure that learners engage with real problems, that theory-based knowledge is activated, that not only is more knowledge developed and consolidated in an evidence-based manner, but that practical skill is fostered. Now, various types and degrees of linking research and teaching are conceivable. The resulting forms of teaching are mostly located with reference to Jenkins and Healey (2005) in an axis cross of student self-activity on the one hand and content vs. process issues on the other (cf. Jenkins & Healey, 2005; Tremp & Hildbrand, 2012).

**Hybrid Forms of Teaching**

The term "hybrid" has different roots and thus different facets of meaning. It expresses that different elements are brought together or mixed. Or it emphasizes that something particularly powerful is created by the combination. Hybrid forms of teaching generally refer to the combination of analog and digital teaching. In the course of globalization and technological change, not least in "Work 4.0," special opportunities are seen in the combination of analog and digital. Blended learning generally refers to the supplementation of classroom events with online offerings. This includes internet forums, chats, podcasts, videos, and work with various communication and learning platforms. All of this can be used in the service of knowledge transfer and competence building. The "Cognitive Theory of Multimedia Learning" and the "Adaptive Control of Thought- (ACT-) and Script Theory" provide a good theoretical framework here (Kollar & Fischer, 2018). They are a foundation for innovative instructional approaches such as (1) the cognitive apprenticeship approach, (2) psychology of instructional design (ID) approach, (3) problem-based learning, and (4) knowledge building (Kollar & Fischer, 2018).

Particular opportunities are provided by learning opportunities in which learning is independent of location and time, in which social interaction can be designed flexibly, and in tools that enable virtual simulation of professional situations. For example, electronic learning diaries, virtually staged problem situations with clients and patients, digital settings for simulating practical professional tasks, and the use of information platforms are now being used in studies and further education.

From the point of view of educational psychology, various decisions have to be made when considering the appropriate design of hybrid forms of teaching: The question arises, for example, whether the chosen offerings follow a behaviorist, a cognitivist, or a constructivist perspective. Accordingly, the methods will be oriented towards questions and answer selection, tutorials and adaptive systems, or simulations and serious games (Zumbach, Rammerstorfer, & Deibl, 2020).

When choosing suitable media, it is important to decide whether the offerings should be online or offline. Here it is necessary to choose between CD-ROM and offers via websites on learning platforms. From a didactic point of view, the question of whether learning is synchronous or asynchronous is interesting. For example, face-to-face classes or group work require agreements on time and place, but independent, rather informal research and practice ("hands on") can certainly take place synchronously (Renner et al., 2020). In addition to didactic questions, there are also economic challenges. E-learning offerings have led to a very fundamental change in the continuing education landscape. Due to high costs, errors in management, and a lack of competences, even simple successes had to be hard fought for (Attwell, 2019).

## Vocational Guidance and Counseling

Psychological counseling in the field of vocational education follows different concerns: It serves the orientation in the choice of profession; it looks for solutions for occurring problems and helps to cope with difficulties; it helps in the choice of suitable offers; it is an offer for the reflection of goals in case of decreasing or missing motivation and much more; it is an offer for students before or during their career choice, for students and participants in further education, for instructors and trainers as well as for teachers at universities (Mendzheritskaya, Ulrich, Hansen, & Heckmann, 2018; Schreiber, 2020). In vocational education, psychological counseling promotes the ability for self-development and self-education, not only in studies and continuing education but also in everyday professional life, thus supporting success in the profession and satisfaction with one's own professional development (Grant, 2013).

"Psychological counseling is a non-patronizing process in which problems of those seeking advice in their behavior, actions, and experiences are clarified with reference to psychological theories in a setting designated as counseling through information and reflection and where attempts at solutions are accompanied" (translated by the author, Steinebach, 2006, p. 13). From this understanding, the person seeking advice is considered the expert for his or her life situation, and the counsellor is considered the expert for the process. He or she is responsible for (1) the relationship between the person seeking advice and the person giving advice. (2) Psychological counseling in education and training focuses on concrete questions and problems of the person seeking advice. Here it distinguishes itself from psychotherapy, which focuses on severe mental health problems. (3) Counseling is understood as a holistic offer, which deals with the behavior, actions, and experiences of those seeking advice. (4) The psychological perspective is shown by using psychological theories and current research results to explain problems and to work out solutions. (5) Under the maxim of informed consent, it is ensured that the person seeking advice is always oriented during the process about what is being done and why. (6) Different methods ensure that a new view of the existing problems succeeds, strengths become clear, and solutions are addressed (Kiel, 2020). Such methods accompany the process until solutions are stable and new competences have been consolidated.

In the field of vocational training, psychological counseling can be understood as complementary. It is then an offer that accompanies the vocational (further) training and helps to avoid or solve possible problems. In addition, psychological counseling can also be understood as a very individual learning offer. It teaches problem-solving skills that make it possible to master future solutions on one's own. From this point of view, in the field of vocational education counseling and coaching (Passmore & Sinclair, 2020) are understood very similarly (Möller, Beinicke, & Bipp, 2019). Regardless of different theoretical or methodological emphases, counseling and coaching promote self-determination and resilience in addressing difficult career challenges (Maree, 2017).

## Subjects and Contents

There are a variety of psychological subjects and contents that represent an important offer for personnel of other professions and fields of work. Some of the offerings are of interest regardless of the specific field of work. These include courses on stress management, conflict management, or mediation. They offer opportunities to reflect on and build on one's own resources and personal strengths. The corresponding modules sometimes also introduce students to techniques of meditation and mindfulness.

Competences in communication and mediation can also be part of offerings to promote competences in counseling. Modules here teach basics, but also specific knowledge and skills in the use of particular media (e.g., online counseling) or in the application of particular counseling strategies (e.g., systemic counseling).

However, the teaching of psychological content in the broad field of counseling also focuses on career-related counseling and on organizational processes. In these courses, competences in career counseling and the design of development and change processes in organizations are developed. Competences for reflection and reorientation of the professional biography with individuals or also the analysis, consultation, and accompaniment of special situations of a team or an organization are imparted.

Different offers are also aimed at people who have taken on a special role in their organization. In this field, we include human resource management trainings or further education for leaders. Here, self-management, but also health promotion at the workplace, personnel psychology, counseling and support of employees, interview techniques and new leadership models, leadership of individuals and teams, or diversity in leadership are topics.

Other offerings and content are aimed specifically at members of different professions, for example, police officers and security forces (e.g., trauma psychology), trainers in sports (e.g., on mental skills), engineers in particularly safety-relevant workplaces.

All of these and a variety of other offerings help participants take a new look at themselves and the "human factor" in their professional and work fields.

## Evaluation

Evaluation is a complex issue. It poses the question of the impact, effectiveness, and efficiency of training courses. It is about short- and long-term effects, about the design of the offers as well as the courses as a whole, and last but not least about the transfer. Psychological offers in continuing education also face the challenge of presenting psychology as an evidence-based science. The evaluation of one's own actions in continuing education thus becomes a question of one's own credibility. By asking about the fit of learning objectives, didactics, and resources, evaluation serves to assure quality (e.g., Ditton, 2018; Zumbach & Astleitner, 2016). The focus of evaluation can be narrow or broad. The biopsychosocial model helps identify important factors. At the same time, it calls for considering the learning culture and work environment as relevant environmental aspects. Analyzing and changing the learning environment as well as the workspace as a learning space becomes a topic (Fleige & Robak, 2018; Stang, Bernhard, Kraus, & Schreiber-Barsch, 2018).

With the goal of evaluating, one's own learning and the learning of the learning group, the evaluation of one's own learning process can itself become the subject of teaching. This is where teaching, learning, and research come together. If we understand research competence as an important professional competence, it is indispensable to teach students these competences. However, we must keep in mind that not everyone who graduates sees their future in psychological research. For them, it is about research skills that are useful in their everyday professional lives. Professional practitioners should be interested in research findings. They should also know that research is human-made, and mistakes are possible. With healthy skepticism, they should be able to reflect on current research findings in terms of their relevance to practice. Professional practitioners should know that cognitive processes in everyday life and in research are often similar, but in some respects research findings can also be superior to subjective assessments. Both are important: research criticism, but also self-criticism. By linking research and teaching, we should succeed in making learners curious about current research. We can assume that this will succeed especially if lecturers are seen as models, as experts who exemplify the transfer of evaluation results into practice and for practice with enthusiasm and thoughtfulness. In this sense, the goal is to foster an evaluative competence in which reflection is informed by curiosity and expertise. Which didactics are most likely to ensure this is certainly an empirical question.

## Psychologists as of Teachers

What makes psychologists good teachers in continuing education? What competences are needed? Connected to these questions is a universe of other questions. Many also serve the effort to better grasp psychological and educational competences, competence profiles, and competence promotion (see, for example, Ludwig, 2018). In addition, there seems to be a need to call for expertise in counselling as well as teaching (Mendzheritskaya et al., 2018; Schiersmann, 2018). Expertise is also expected in those professional fields for which psychological competences are to be taught in a complementary manner (Loo, 2019). Knowledge and skills related to the professional field, didactic skills, own continuing education, and a network appropriate to the teaching field are considered important (Broad, 2019). Finally, all social changes read not only for learners but also for teachers. And they have intensified in the time of the COVID-19 pandemic (Boeren, Roumell, & Roessger, 2020).

All of this suggests a very challenging competence profile for psychologists in continuing education. The challenge is all the greater when learning psychology takes place in informal settings. Especially in informal settings, the roles are often not clear. Nevertheless, the goal must be to strive for evidence-based behavior change even in "recovery-oriented systems" and to positively change the social, societal, and political frameworks (▶ Chap. 36, "Psychological Literacy and Learning for Life"; Ponce, Carr, Miller, Olezeski, & Silva, 2019). In all of this, continuing education, as well as psychology in continuing education, is also under public scrutiny. It is necessary from there that psychologists can prove their competences, also over appropriate standards in the own further training (Taylor & Neimeyer, 2015).

It is also important for psychologists working as continuing educators to engage in their own continuing education and to take advantage of appropriate formal offerings. In addition, it seems important to reflect on one's own informal learning, one's own experiences. Reflection supports the acquisition of competences, especially outside the professional field, and learning processes take place. Thus, the organizational conditions that provide the framework for all teaching programs also become an important topic. Structures and processes, strategy and finances must be aligned in such a way that they support the competence development of teachers.

## Outlook: Innovation of Continuing Education and Psychology for Non-psychologists

The preceding considerations make it clear: Continuing education in psychology for non-psychologists is an exciting, but also very demanding professional and research field. Continuing education is oriented toward current conditions and the changes in which the world of work stands. In addition, there are individual challenges and needs that make psychological learning content and competences interesting for participants. This also gives rise to requests for psychology. Often there is a lack of standards for courses and continuing professional development (CPD), not only for non-psychologists but also for psychologists and probably also for psychologists in continuing education. Therefore, it is necessary to develop the needs and the cut, the offers, and the didactics with the participants and their employers.

In further education as a psychological offer, the professional and specialist associations are of particular importance. It is necessary to design competence profiles, to formulate standards, and to secure these nationally and internationally. This requires not only political commitment but also research. After a phase of discussing different theories, models, and concepts, it seems necessary to bring together the available knowledge on continuing education and lifelong learning (Käpplinger, 2018). This concerns "competence" as a concept as well as theories on learning and instruction, on the interconnectedness of learning and guidance, and on diversity in learning and professional biographies (Migliore, 2019 on diversity). The focus should be on strengthening learner and instructor self-reflection (Pachner, 2018). The call for "frameworks," "taxonomies," "recognition," "acquisition," "assessment," and "new concepts" on the "to-do-list" (Mulder, 2019) makes connecting teaching and research a strategic concern in continuing education in psychology. Research questions can arise in teaching and solutions can be developed in the classroom. However, this requires that we secure such teaching strategically and structurally, but also financially. Thus, the connection between teaching and research must be anchored in the vision, mission, and strategy of the university or the institution. The pedagogical foundations and curricula are to be further developed in the sense of linking research and teaching. Structural measures are to facilitate collaboration between researchers and teachers (Braun et al., 2014). Where particular didactic challenges arise, staff should be further developed (cf. Jenkins & Healey, 2005). Before that, however, a major challenge remains we need to know more about promoting specific psychological competences in nonpsychological professions. The call from the 1960s "Give Psychology away!" (Banyard & Hulme, 2015) is not enough. After all, today we are talking about specific psychological content in highly specialized nonpsychological professional fields. This brings benefits to the practice of very different professions. But it should not stop at this occupation-specific use of psychology. The general promotion of psychological competences and "psychological literacy" will also have an impact on companies, communities, and society. And this will open up new perspectives on what is humanly possible (Banyard & Hulme, 2015) in order to be able to lead a life of dignity, self-determination, and social responsibility, also at work.

## Teaching, Learning, and Assessment Resources

### Tips and Questions

(1) How do you think continuing education programs that promote psychological competences have changed in the wake of the COVID-19 pandemic? Think about changes in goals, didactics, and methods.
(2) Psychology for non-psychologists: What learning content absolutely must be taught in face-to-face situations in the field and definitely cannot be taught virtually?
(3) Take a look at the ESPLAT European Society for Psychology Learning and Teaching website (https://www.esplat.org). How do you think the professional identity of a school psychologist differs from that of a psychology teacher?
(4) Educational policy (e.g., https://europa.eu/europass/en/validation-non-formal-and-informal-learning) demands the recognition of informally and non-formally acquired competences for formal education. When you think of psychological competences, what informally acquired psychological competence would you possibly recognize? How would you validate that someone actually has this competence?
(5) Which psychological offerings in job-related continuing education particularly support the SDGs of the United Nations (https://sdgs.un.org/goals)?

## Further Readings

1. Broad, J. H. (2019). Pedagogical issues in vocational teachers' learning: The importance of teacher development. In: McGrath, S., Mulder, M., Papier, J. & Suart, R. (Eds.): *Handbook of vocational education and training. Developments in the changing world of work* (Vol. 2, pp. 1769–1786). Springer Nature Switzerland.
    - Psychologists are not necessarily good teachers by themselves. What is important in order to be able to teach psychology and convey psychological content?
2. Chen, C. P. (2017). Career Self-Determination Theory. In: Maree, K. (Ed.): *Psychology of career adaptability, employability and resilience* (pp. 329–347). Springer International Publishing.
    - Self-determination theory is a good aid to understanding why people make decisions and then implement the decisions they make. Here, this theory is applied to career-related decisions.
3. Dutke, S. Bakker, H., Sokolova, L., Stuchlikova, I., Salvatore, S. & Papageorgi, I. (2019). Psychology curricula for non-psychologists? A framework recommended by the European Federation of Psychologists' Associations' Board of Educational Affairs. *Psychology Learning & Teaching*, 18(2), 111–120.
    - Psychology for non-psychologists is rarely critically reflected upon. In this paper, an analysis of the development and current situation of corresponding offerings is provided. In addition, recommendations are given on how the field should develop in the future.
4. Erikson, M. G., & Erlandson, P. (2015). *Theories as maps: Teaching psychology. Beyond mind and behavior.* Scholarship of Teaching and Learning in Psychology. Advance online publication. 1–8.
    - Psychology is often considered to be very "theory-heavy." What is the significance of theories in psychology and how can the metaphor of theories as "maps" help to create a better understanding?
5. Kim, S. Y. (2019). The fourth industrial revolution: Trends and impacts on the world of work. In: McGrath, S., Mulder, M., Papier, J. & Suart, R. (Eds.): *Handbook of vocational education and training. Developments in the changing world of work.* (Vol. 1, pp. 177–194). Springer Nature Switzerland.
    - The change in the course of „Work 4.0" reaches into all areas of society. In this paper, lines of development and influences are highlighted.
6. Maree, K. (2017). The Psychology of career adaptability, career resilience, and employability: A Broad Overview. In: Maree, K. (Ed.): *Psychology of career adaptability, employability and resilience* (pp. 3–11). Springer International Publishing.
    - Organizational and societal changes pose a variety of challenges to the individual. This article shows how career development, resilience, and professional success interact.

7. Migliore, M. C. (2019). Older workers' vocational learning: Taking activities and personal senses into account. In: McGrath, S., Mulder, M., Papier, J. & Suart, R. (Eds.): *Handbook of vocational education and training. Developments in the changing world of work* (Vol. 2., pp. 1001–1018). Springer Nature Switzerland.
   - Offers of career-related continuing education, also in psychology, must be geared to the respective target groups. In doing so, the diversity of people must be taken into account. This article shows how this can be done for continuing education of older employees.
8. Mulder, M. (2019). Foundations of competence-based vocational education and training. In: McGrath, S., Mulder, M., Papier, J. & Suart, R. (Eds.): *Handbook of vocational education and training. Developments in the changing world of work*. (Vol. 2., pp. 1167–1192). Springer Nature Switzerland.
   - From a technical and educational policy point of view, competence orientation is an important feature of vocational training. Basics for education and training are shown here.
9. Wilson, R. (2019). Skills forecasts in a rapidly changing world: Through a glass darkly. In: McGrath, S., Mulder, M., Papier, J. & Suart, R. (Eds.): *Handbook of vocational education and training. Developments in the changing world of work*. (Vol. 1, pp. 3-21). Springer Nature Switzerland .
   - Often enough it is the demand to orientate offers towards future developments. In this way, employees as well as organizations are well prepared for upcoming changes. Whether and how this can succeed, however, must be critically questioned.
10. Worrell, F. C., Olszewski-Kubilius, P., & Subotnik, R. F. (2019). The psychology of high performance: Overarching themes. In: Subotnik, R.F., Olszewski-Kubilius, P. & Worrell, F. C. (Eds.): *The psychology of high performance: Developing human potential into domain-specific talent* (pp. 369–385). American Psychological Association.
    - In the discussion about competences, little attention has been paid to the question of whether a competence is only weakly or even very strongly developed. This question is explored in the article on high performance.

## Cross-References

▶ First Principles of Instruction Revisited
▶ Inquiry-Based Learning in Psychology
▶ Problem-Based Learning and Case-Based Learning
▶ Psychological Literacy and Learning for Life
▶ Teaching Engineering Psychology
▶ Teaching of Work and Organizational Psychology in Higher Education

## References

Ahrens, D., & Gessler, M. (2018). Von der Humanisierung zur Digitalisierung: Entwicklungsetappen betrieblicher Kompetenzentwicklung. In D. Ahrens & G. Molzberger (Eds.), *Kompetenzentwicklung in analogen und digitalisierten Arbeitswelten, Kompetenzmanagement in Organisationen* (pp. 157–172). Springer.

Albert, I., & Trommsdorff, G. (2014). The role of culture in social development over the lifespan: An interpersonal relations approach. *Online Readings in Psychology and Culture, 6*(2), 1–30.

Arnold, R., Pätzold, H., & Ganz, M. (2018). Weiterbildung und Beruf. In R. Tippelt & A. von Hippel (Eds.), *Handbuch Erwachsenenbildung/Weiterbildung* (6th ed., pp. 931–945). Springer VS.

Attwell, G. (2019). E-learning at the workplace. In S. McGrath, M. Mulder, J. Papier, & R. Suart (Eds.), *Handbook of vocational education and training. Developments in the changing world of work* (Vol. Vol. 1, pp. 923–947). Springer Nature Switzerland.

Banyard, P., & Hulme, J. A. (2015). Giving Psychology away: How George Miller's vision is being realised by psychological literacy. *Psychology Teaching Review, 21*(2), 93–101.

Barrick, R. K. (2019). Competence and excellence in vocational education and training. In S. McGrath, M. Mulder, J. Papier, & R. Suart (Eds.), *Handbook of vocational education and training. Developments in the changing world of work* (Vol. 2, pp. 1155–1166). Springer Nature Switzerland.

Barth, M., Godemann, J., Rieckmann, M., & Stoltenberg, U. (2007). Developing key competencies for sustainable development in higher education. *International Journal of Sustainability in Higher Education, 8*(4), 416–430.

Boeren, E., Roumell, E. A., & Roessger, K. M. (2020). COVID-19 and the future of adult education: An editorial. *Adult Education Quarterly, 70*(3), 201–204.

Brandtstädter, J. (1980). Gedanken zu einem psychologischen Modell optimaler Entwicklung. *Zeitschrift für Klinische Psychologie und Psychotherapie, 28*(3), 209–222.

Brandtstädter, J. (2015). *Positive Entwicklung. Zur Psychologie gelingender Lebensführung*. Springer Spektrum.

Braun, E., Weiß, T., & Seidel, T. (2014). Lernumwelten in der Hochschule. In T. Seidel & A. Krapp (Eds.), *Pädagogische Psychologie* (pp. 433–453). Beltz.

Broad, J. H. (2019). Pedagogical issues in vocational teachers' learning: The importance of teacher development. In S. McGrath, M. Mulder, J. Papier, & R. Suart (Eds.), *Handbook of vocational education and training. Developments in the changing world of work* (Vol. 2, pp. 1769–1786). Springer Nature Switzerland.

Carpintero, H., & Herrero, F. (2002). Early applied psychology: The early days of the IAAP. *European Psychologist, 7*(1), 39–52.

Chen, C. P. (2017). Career self-determination theory. In K. Maree (Ed.), *Psychology of career adaptability, employability and resilience* (pp. 329–347). Springer International Publishing.

Council of the European Union. (2012). *Council Recommendation of 20 December 2012 on the validation of non-formal and informal learning (2012/C 398/01)*. (https://www.cedefop.europa.eu/files/Council_Recommendation_on_the_validation_20_December_2012.pdf).

Cranney, J., & Dunn, D. S. (2011). Psychological Literacy and the psychological literate citizen. New frontiers for a global discipline. In J. Cranney & D. S. Dunn (Eds.), *The psychologically literate citizen. Foundations to global perspectives* (pp. 3–12). Oxford University Press.

Debray, C., & Spencer-Oatey, H. (2019). 'On the same page? Marginalisation and positioning practices in intercultural teams. *Journal of Pragmatics, 144*, 15–28.

Deci, E., & Ryan, R. (2015). Self-determination theory. In J. Wright (Ed.), *International encyclopedia of the social & behavioral sciences* (Vol. 21, 2nd ed., pp. 486–491). Elsevier.

Deitmer, L. (2019). Innovation skills in apprentice training. In S. McGrath, M. Mulder, J. Papier, & R. Suart (Eds.), *Handbook of vocational education and training. Developments in the changing world of work* (Vol. 1, pp. 121–137). Springer Nature Switzerland.

Diener, E., Thapa, S., & Tay, L. (2020). Positive emotions at work. *Annual Review of Organizational Psychology and Organizational Behavior, 7*(1), 451–477.

Ditton, H. (2018). Evaluation und Qualitätssicherung im Bildungsbereich. In R. Tippelt & B. Schmidt-Hertha (Eds.), *Handbuch Bildungsforschung* (4th ed., pp. 757–777). Springer VS.

Doylea, E., & Buckley, P. (2014). Research ethics in teaching and learning. *Innovations in Education and Teaching International, 51*(2), 153–163.

Dunn, D. S., Cautin, R. L., & Gurung, R. A. (2011). Curriculum matters: Structure, content, and psychological literacy. In J. Cranney & D. S. Dunn (Eds.), *The psychologically literate citizen. Foundations to global perspectives* (pp. 15–26). Oxford University Press.

Dutke, S., Bakker, H., Sokolova, L., Stuchlikova, I., Salvatore, S., & Papageorgi, I. (2019). Psychology curricula for non-psychologists? A framework recommended by the European Federation of Psychologists Associations Board of Educational Affairs. *Psychology Learning and Teaching, 18*(2), 111–120.

Eckert, T., & Kadera, S. (2018). Der sozialökologische Ansatz in der Erwachsenenbildung. In R. Tippelt & A. von Hippel (Eds.), *Handbuch Erwachsenenbildung/Weiterbildung* (6th ed., pp. 185–203) Springer VS.

Erikson, M. G., & Erlandson, P. (2015). Theories as maps: Teaching psychology. Beyond mind and behavior. Scholarship of Teaching and Learning in Psychology. Advance online publication. 1–8.

Erpenbeck, J., & von Rosenstiel, L. (2017). *Handbuch Kompetenzmessung* (3rd ed.) Schäffer-Poeschel Verlag.

Fleige, M., & Robak, S. (2018). Lehr-Lernkultur in der Erwachsenenbildung. In R. Tippelt & A. von Hippel (Eds.), *Handbuch Erwachsenenbildung/Weiterbildung* (6th ed., pp. 623–641) Springer VS.

Gerstenmaier, J., & Mandl, H. (2018). Konstruktivistische Ansätze in der Erwachsenenbildung und Weiterbildung. In R. Tippelt & A. von Hippel (Eds.), *Handbuch Erwachsenenbildung/Weiterbildung* (6th ed., pp. 221–233) Springer VS.

Grant, A. M. (2013). The efficacy of coaching. In J. Passmore, D. B. Peterson, & T. Freire (Eds.), *The Wiley- Blackwell handbook of coaching & mentoring psychology* (pp. 15–39). New York: Wiley Blackwell.

Grundmann, M. (2017). Sozialisation – Erziehung – Bildung: Eine kritische Begriffsbestimmung. In R. Becker (Ed.), *Lehrbuch Bildungssoziaiologie* (pp. 63–88). Springer.

Harteis, C., & Heid, H. (2018). Bildungsarbeit in Wirtschaft und Betrieb. In R. Tippelt & B. Schmidt-Hertha (Eds.), *Handbuch Bildungsforschung* (4th ed., pp. 565–585). Springer VS.

Heyse, V., Erpenbeck, J., Coester, S., Ortmann, S., & Sauter, W. (2019). *Kompetenzmanagement mit System*. Waxmann.

International Association of Applied Psychology & International Union of Psychological Science (2016). *International declaration on core competences in professional Psychology*. https://iaapsy.org/site/assets/files/1476/ref_competences_iaap_2016.pdf., 11–14.

Jenkins, A., & Healey, M. (2005). *Insitutional strategies to link teaching and research*. The Higher Education Academy.

Jütte, W., & Bade-Becker, U. (2018). Weiterbildung an Hochschulen. In R. Tippelt & A. von Hippel (Eds.), *Handbuch Erwachsenenbildung/Weiterbildung* (6th ed., pp. 821–836) Springer VS.

Käpplinger, B. (2018). Theorien und Theoreme der betrieblichen Weiterbildung. In R. Tippelt & A. von Hippel (Eds.), *Handbuch Erwachsenenbildung/Weiterbildung* (6th ed., pp. 679–695). Springer VS.

Kiel, V. (2020). *Analoge Verfahren in der systemischen Beratung. Ein integrativer Ansatz für Coaching, Team- und Organisationsentwicklung*. Vandenhoeck & Ruprecht.

Kim, S. Y. (2019). The fourth industrial revolution: Trends and impacts on the World of work. In S. McGrath, M. Mulder, J. Papier, & R. Suart (Eds.), *Handbook of vocational education and training. Developments in the changing world of work* (Vol. Vol. 1, pp. 177–194). Springer Nature Switzerland.

Klieme, E., & Hartig, J. (2007). Kompetenzkonzepte in den Sozialwissenschaften und im erziehungswissenschaftlichen Diskurs. *Zeitschrift für Erziehungswissenschaft, 8*, 11–29.

Kollar, I., & Fischer, F. (2018). Digitale Medien für die Unterstützung von Lehr-/Lernprozessen in der Weiterbildung. In R. Tippelt & A. von Hippel (Eds.), *Handbuch Erwachsenenbildung/ Weiterbildung* (6th ed., pp. 1553–1568). Springer VS.

Knafla, I., & Schär, M. (2019). Verhaltensauffälligkeit, psychische Störungen und Führung. In E. Lippmann, A. Pfister, & U. Jörg (Eds.), *Handbuch Angewandte Psychologie für Führungskräfte: Führungskompetenz und Führungswissen* (pp. 911–935). Springer.

Linden, W. (2015). *From silos to bridges: Psychology on the move. Canadian Psychology/ Psychologie Canadienne, 56*(1), 1–5.

Lippmann, E., Pfister, A., & Jörg, U. (Eds.). (2019). *Handbuch Angewandte Psychologie für Führungskräfte* (5th ed.). Springer.

Loo, S. (2019). Vocational teachers knowledge, experiences, and pedagogy. In S. McGrath, M. Mulder, J. Papier, & R. Suart (Eds.), *Handbook of vocational education and training. Developments in the changing world of work* (Vol. 2, pp. 1611–1625). Springer Nature Switzerland.

Ludwig, J. (2018). Lehr-Lerntheoretische Ansätze in der Erwachsenenbildung. In R. Tippelt & A. von Hippel (Eds.), *Handbuch Erwachsenenbildung/Weiterbildung* (6th ed., pp. 257–274) Springer VS.

Madson, L., Zaikman, Y., & Hughes, J. S. (2020). Psychology teachers should try team-based learning: Evidence, concerns, and recommendations. *Scholarship of Teaching and Learning in Psychology, 61*(1), 53–68.

Maree, K. (2017). The Psychology of career adaptability, career resilience, and employability: A Broad Overview. In K. Maree (Ed.), *Psychology of career adaptability, employability and resilience* (pp. 3–11). Springer International Publishing..

Mayer, R. E. (2019). How multimedia can improve learning and instruction. In J. Dunlosky & K. A. Rawson (Eds.), *The Cambridge handbook of cognition and education* (pp. 460–479). Cambridge University Press.

Mendzheritskaya, J., Ulrich, I., Hansen, M., & Heckmann, C. (2018). *Gut beraten an der Hochschule: Wege zum besseren Lehren und Lernen*. Kohlhammer Verlag.

Merrill, M. D. (2008). Reflections on a four-decade search for effective, efficient and engaging instruction. In M. W. Allen (Ed.), *Michael Allens 2008 e-Learning Annual* (Vol. 1, pp. 141–167). Wiley Pfeiffer.

Merrill, M. D. (2002). First principles of instruction. *Educational Technology Research and Development, 50*(3), 43–59.

Migliore, M. C. (2019). Older workers vocational learning: Taking activities and personal senses into account. In S. McGrath, M. Mulder, J. Papier, & R. Suart (Eds.), *Handbook of vocational education and training. Developments in the changing world of work* (Vol. 2, pp. 1001–1018). Springer Nature Switzerland.

Mittelstraß, J. (2002). Bildung und ethische Maße. In N. Killius, J. Kluge, & L. Reisch (Eds.), *Die Zukunft der Bildung* (pp. 151–170). Suhrkamp.

Möller, H., Beinicke, A., & Bipp, T. (2019). Wie wirksam ist Coaching? In A. Beinicke & T. Bipp (Eds.), *Strategische Personalentwicklung. Meet the Expert: Wissen aus erster Hand* (pp. 165–188). Springer.

Morgan, H. M. (2019). *Underdog entrepreneurs: A framework of success for marginalized and minority innovators*. Springer Nature.

Mulder, M. (2019). Foundations of competence-based vocational education and training. In S. McGrath, M. Mulder, J. Papier, & R. Suart (Eds.), *Handbook of vocational education and training. Developments in the changing world of work* (Vol. 2, pp. 1167–1192). Springer Nature Switzerland.

Mulder, M., Weigel, T., & Collins, K. (2006). The concept of competence in the development of vocational education and training in selected EU member states. A critical analysis. *Journal of Vocational Education and Training, 59*(1), 65–85.

Mulder, M., & Winterton, J. (2017). Introduction. In M. Mulder (Ed.), *Competence-based vocational and professional education. Bridging the worlds of work and education* (pp. 1–43). Springer Nature.

Narciss, S. (2019). *Curriculum design for (non-) psychology programs–a reflection on general and specific issues, and approaches on how to address them: Comment on Dutke et al., 2019. Psychology Learning and Teaching, 18*(2), 144–147.

Nario-Redmond, M. R. (2019). *Ableism: The causes and consequences of disability prejudice.* John Wiley & Sons.

Pachner, A. (2018). Lehren in der Erwachsenen- und Weiterbildung. In R. Tippelt & A. von Hippel (Eds.), *Handbuch Erwachsenenbildung/Weiterbildung* (6th ed., pp. 1439–1456). Springer VS.

Passmore, J., & Sinclair, T. (2020). What is coaching? In J. Passmore & T. Sinclair (Eds.), *Becoming a coach* (pp. 7–13). Springer.

Pfadenhauer, M. (2013). Competence – more than just a buzzword and a provocative term? Towards an internal perspective on situative problem-solving capacity. In S. Blömeke, O. Zlatkin-Troitschanskaia, C. Kuhn, & J. Fege (Eds.), *Modeling and measuring of competencies in higher education: Tasks and challenges* (pp. 81–90). Sense Publishers.

Ponce, A. N., Carr, E. R., Miller, R., Olezeski, C. L., & Silva, M. A. (2019). *Psychologists as educators: Creating change in community mental health. Professional Psychology: Research and Practice, 50*(6), 427–433.

Renn, O., Chabay, I., van der Leeuw, S., & Droy, S. (2020). Beyond the indicators: Improving science, scholarship, policy and practice to meet the complex challenges of sustainability. *Sustainability, 12*(2), 578.

Renner, B., Wesiak, G., Pammer-Schindler, V., Prilla, M., Müller, L., Morosini, D., Mora, S., Faltin, N., & Cress, U. (2020). Computer-supported reflective learning: how apps can foster reflection at work. *Behaviour & Information Technology, 39*(2), 167–187.

Rintala, H., Nokelainen, P., & Pylväs, L. (2019). Informal workplace learning. In S. McGrath, M. Mulder, J. Papier, & R. Suart (Eds.), *Handbook of vocational education and training. Developments in the changing world of work* (Vol. 1, pp. 729–742). Springer Nature Switzerland.

Rosa, H. (2017). *Beschleunigung: die Veränderung der Zeitstrukturen in der Moderne.* Suhrkamp Verlag.

Ryff, C. D., & Keyes, C. L. M. (1995). The structure of psychological well-being revisited. *Journal of Personality and Social Psychology, 69*(4), 719–727.

Schiersmann, C. (2018). Beratung im Kontext von Weiterbildung. In R. Tippelt & A. von Hippel (Eds.), *Handbuch Erwachsenenbildung/Weiterbildung* (6th ed., pp. 1495–1512). Springer VS.

Schmidt-Lauff, S. (2018). Zeittheoretische Implikationen in der Erwachsenenbildung. In R. Tippelt & A. von Hippel (Eds.), *Handbuch Erwachsenenbildung/Weiterbildung* (6th ed., pp. 319–338). Springer VS.

Schreiber, M. (2020). *Wegweiser Im Lebenslauf. Berufs-, Studien- und Laufbahnberatung in der Praxis.* Kohlhammer.

Schröder, T., & Dehnbostel, P. (2019). Enhancing permeability between vocational and tertiary education through corporate learning. In S. McGrath, M. Mulder, J. Papier, & R. Suart (Eds.), *Handbook of vocational education and training. Developments in the changing world of work* (Vol. 1, pp. 603–625). Springer Nature Switzerland.

Spinath, B., Seifried, E., & Eckert, C. (2014). Forschendes Lehren: Ein Ansatz zur kontinuierlichen Verbesserung von Hochschullehre. *Journal Hochschuldidaktik, 25*(1–2), 14–16.

Stang, R., Bernhard, C., Kraus, K. & Schreiber-Barsch, S. (2018). Lernräume in der Erwachsenenbildung. In: Tippelt, R. & von Hippel, A. (Eds.): \ (6 643–658). Springer VS.

Steinebach, C. (2005). Neue Theorie – neue Praxis? Perspektiven der Hochschuldidaktik aus psychologischer Sicht. In C. Steinebach (Ed.), *Psychologie Lehren und Lernen. Beiträge zur Hochschuldidaktik* (pp. 13–22). Universitätsverlag Winter.

Steinebach, C. (2006). Beratung und Entwicklung. In C. Steinebach (Ed.), *Handbuch Psychologische Beratung* (pp. 37–56). Klett-Cotta.

Steinebach, C. (2013). Beratung. Stärkenorientierte Gespräche. In C. Steinebach & K. Gharabahi (Eds.), *Resilienzförderung im Jugendalter. Praxis und Perspektiven* (pp. 51–68). Springer.

Steinebach, C. (2015). Resilience. In J. D. Wright (Ed.), *International Encyclopedia of the Social & Behavioral Sciences* (Vol. 20, 2nd ed., pp. 555–560). Elsevier.

Steinebach, C. (2019). Teaching non-psychologists: The third step. Comment on Dutke et al., 2019. *Psychology Learning and Teaching, 18*(2), 131–133.

Steinebach, C., Eberhardt, D., Kotrubczik, H., Majkovic, A., & Zinsli, M. (2014). Reflexion persönlicher Kompetenzentwicklung. Die Auseinandersetzung mit dem eigenen Potenzial als Sozialisationsprozess und Grundlage für Gesundheit und Wohlbefinden. In B. Sieber-Suter (Ed.), *Kompetenzmanagement. Erfahrungen und Perspektiven zur beruflichen Entwicklung von Lehrenden in Schule und Weiterbildung* (pp. 20–31). hep-Verlag.

Steinebach, C., & Steinebach, U. (2013). Gleichaltrige: Peers als Ressource. In C. Steinebach & K. Gharabaghi (Eds.), *Resilienzförderung im Jugendalter. Praxis und Perspektiven* (pp. 93–109). Springer.

Steinebach, C., Steinebach, U., & Brendtro, L. K. (2012). Peerbeziehungen und Gesundheit im Jugendalter. In C. Steinebach, D. Jungo, & R. Zihlmann (Eds.), *Positive Psychologie in der Praxis* (pp. 153–161). Beltz.

Steinebach, C., Süss, D., Kienbaum, J., & Kiegelmann, M. (2016). *Basiswissen Pädagogische Psychologie*. Weinheim: Beltz.

Suter, J. (1935). Rück- und Ausblick. In H. Spreng (Ed.), *Psychotechnik. Angewandte Psychologie* (pp. 201–214). Max Niehans Verlag.

Taylor, J. M., & Neimeyer, G. J. (2015). *Public perceptions of Psychologists professional development activities: The good, the bad, and the ugly. Professional Psychology: Research and Practice, 46*(2), 140–146.

Thalhammer, V., & Schmidt-Hertha, B. (2018). Bildungsforschung zum informellen Lernen. In R. Tippelt & B. Schmidt-Hertha (Eds.), *Handbuch Bildungsforschung* (4th ed., pp. 947–966). Springer VS.

Tippelt, R. (2018). Professionsforschung und Bildung. In R. Tippelt & B. Schmidt-Hertha (Eds.), *Handbuch Bildungsforschung. Springer Reference Sozialwissenschaften* (pp. 649–666). Springer VS.

Tomlinson, M., & Jackson, D. (2019). Professional identity formation in contemporary higher education students. *Studies in Higher Education, 46*(4), 1–16.

Tremp, P., & Hildbrand, T. (2012). Forschungsorientiertes Studium – universitäre Lehre: Das «Zürcher Framework» zur Verknüpfung von Lehre und Forschung. In T. Brinker & P. Tremp (Eds.), *Einführung in die Studiengangentwicklung* (pp. 101–116). Bertelsmann.

Trommsdorff, G. (2009). Culture and development of self-regulation. *Social and Personality Psychology Compass, 3*(5), 687–701.

Trommsdorff, G. (2012). Development of "agentic" regulation in cultural context: The role of self and world views. *Child Development Perspectives, 6*(1), 19–26.

Trommsdorff, G., & Dasen, P. (2001). Cross-cultural study of education. In N. J. Smelser & P. B. Baltes (Eds.), *International encyclopedia of the social and behavioral sciences* (pp. 3003–3007). Elsevier.

United Nations (2020). *SDGs Learning, Training & Practice. 2020 Edition Report*. UNITAR. https://sdgs.un.org/sites/default/files/2020-09/26938SDG_Learning_HLPF_Publication.pdf.

United Nations Educational, Scientific and Cultural Organization (2019). *UNESCO Strategy for Youth and Adult Literacy (2020-2025)*. https://unesdoc.unesco.org/ark:/48223/pf0000371411?posInSet=2&queryId=fab6406f-989c-4049-b36b-a2fb1c00bda3.

von Rosenstiel, L. (2018). Weiterbildung von Führungskräften. In R. Tippelt & A. von Hippel (Eds.), *Handbuch Erwachsenenbildung/Weiterbildung* (6th ed., pp. 1345–1361). Springer VS.

Weinert, F. E. (2001). Concept of competence: A conceptual clarification. In D. S. Rychen & L. H. Salganik (Eds.), *Defining and selecting key competencies* (pp. 45–65). Hogrefe & Huber Publishers.

Wilson, R. (2019). Skills forecasts in a rapidly changing world: Through a glass darkly. In S. McGrath, M. Mulder, J. Papier, & R. Suart (Eds.), *Handbook of vocational education and training. Developments in the changing world of work* (Vol. 1, pp. 3–21). Springer Nature Switzerland.

Winterton, J., Delamare Le Deist, F., & Stringfellow, E. (2006). *Typology of knowledge, skills and competences: Clarification of the concept and prototype. Cedefop Reference series; 64*. Luxembourg: Office for Official Publications of the European Communities.

World Economic Forum. (2020). *The global risks report 2020*. World Economic Forum.

Worrell, F. C., Olszewski-Kubilius, P., & Subotnik, R. F. (2019). The psychology of high performance: Overarching themes. In R. F. Subotnik, P. Olszewski-Kubilius, & F. C. Worrell (Eds.), *The psychology of high performance: Developing human potential into domain-specific talent* (pp. 369–385). American Psychological Assoziation.

Zeuner, C. (2018). Internationale Perspektiven der Erwachsenenbildung. In R. Tippelt & A. von Hippel (Eds.), *Handbuch Erwachsenenbildung/Weiterbildung* (6th ed., pp. 659–678). Springer VS.

Zumbach, J., Rammerstorfer, L., & Deibl, I. (2020). Cognitive and metacognitive support in learning with a serious game about demographic change. *Computers in Human Behavior, 103*, 120–129.

# Teaching Sport and Exercise Psychology

## 38

### Robert Weinberg and Joanne Butt

## Contents

| | |
|---|---|
| Introduction | 945 |
|    Definition and Brief History of Sport and Exercise Psychology | 945 |
|    Current Issues and Future Directions | 945 |
| Purposes and Rationale of the Curriculum | 946 |
| Core Contents and Topics of Sport and Exercise Psychology | 949 |
|    Historical Perspectives | 949 |
|    Knowledge Development | 950 |
|    Individual Differences | 950 |
|    Group Dynamics | 952 |
|    Leadership | 952 |
|    Psychological Skills | 953 |
|    Exercise Motivation and Well-Being | 953 |
|    Psychology of Injury | 954 |
|    Character/Moral Development and Aggression | 954 |
| Teaching, Learning, and Assessment in Sport Psychology: Approaches and Strategies | 955 |
|    Flipping the Classroom | 955 |
|    Turning a Class Into a Team | 956 |
|    UNIFORM Program | 956 |
|    Assessment Considerations in Sport Psychology | 957 |

---

R. Weinberg (✉)
Department of Sport Leadership and Management, Miami University, Oxford, OH, USA
e-mail: weinber@miamioh.edu

J. Butt
School of Sport & Exercise Sciences, Liverpool John Moores University, Liverpool, UK
e-mail: j.butt@LJMU.ac.uk

© Springer Nature Switzerland AG 2023
J. Zumbach et al. (eds.), *International Handbook of Psychology Learning and Teaching*,
Springer International Handbooks of Education,
https://doi.org/10.1007/978-3-030-28745-0_44

Challenges and Lessons Learned .............................................................. 958
Teaching, Learning, and Assessment Resources ............................................. 959
References .................................................................................... 960

### Abstract

The purpose of this chapter is to highlight how the field of sport and exercise psychology has evolved, especially from a curriculum point of view, and how this has influenced the teaching of sport and exercise psychology, including innovative strategies for assessment and approaches to teaching. After providing a brief history and current and future issues within the field, the purposes and rationales for curriculum development are discussed. The influences of the Association for Applied Sport Psychology (AASP) in the United States and the British Psychological Association and the Health and Care Professions Council in the United Kingdom on curriculum development and accreditation of programs helped determine the focus of curriculum development. Specifically, if individuals wanted to be certified in applied sport psychology, they had to complete certain courses and had a certain amount of supervised experiences. Next the core content areas that make up the field of sport and exercise psychology are discussed. These include many topic areas including individual differences (e.g., anxiety, personality, motivation), group dynamics (group cohesion, social loafing, group roles and norms), exercise related to well-being, adherence, and addictive behaviors, burnout, moral development, psychological skills, and psychology of injury. Strategies to enhance assessment and teaching/learning are offered including flipping the classroom, breaking classes into teams, teaching psychological skills through the use of Transtheoretical Model principles, as well as innovative ways to perform formative and summative assessments. These teaching strategies are followed by a discussion of some of the major challenges and lessons learned regarding the teaching of sport and exercise psychology. These challenges include determining the necessary requirements of becoming an accredited sport psychology graduate program as curriculum development will likely accreditation requirements for those universities wanting graduate-level accreditation as well as providing both more applied and theoretically oriented curriculum for those individuals wanting careers in applied sport psychology as well as those wanting to focus on becoming a university faculty member. Furthermore, future curriculums will need to include information geared toward professionals wanting to focus more on counseling or clinical interventions vs. those interested in sport performance.

### Keywords

Sport psychology · Certification · Psychological skills · Research · Exercise behavior change

# Introduction

## Definition and Brief History of Sport and Exercise Psychology

Sport and exercise psychology is the scientific study of people and behaviors in sport and exercise contexts and the practical application of that knowledge (Gill, Williams, & Reifsteck, 2017). More recently, there has been interest in specifically defining applied sport psychology as a subfield of performance psychology which puts the focus on the practice and profession of sport psychology (cf. Portenga, Aoyagi, & Cohen, 2017). Typically, the field can be also defined by two overarching objectives: (a) to understand how psychological factors affect an individual's (or team's) physical performance and (b) to understand how participation in sport and exercise affects a person's psychological development, health, and well-being. Modern sport psychology dates back to the 1890s (Kornspan, 2012) with some of the early work on social facilitation and cyclists (Triplett, 1898). Colman Griffith, with his extensive research and application with athletes at the University of Illinois, is known as the father of American sport psychology (Kroll & Lewis, 1970). Many scholars (e.g., Kornspan, 2015) point to the first World Congress in Sport Psychology held in in Rome in 1965 as the formal beginnings of sport psychology as it was the first time athletes, coaches, researchers, and others formally got together to discuss the psychological aspects of sport.

## Current Issues and Future Directions

Over the years, the growth of sport psychology has now included exercise psychology. Specifically, instead of only studying psychological factors in sport and competitive settings, the field now incorporates psychological factors related to exercise (specific content will be discussed later in the chapter). Because it is a growing field, there have been a number of issues or trends that are shaping the field currently and will probably continue to provide direction in the future.

- Tension between academic (research) and applied sport psychology still exists. Although improving, there needs to be more interaction between researchers and practitioners, focusing on the science-practitioner model.
- Tension between psychology-trained (and licensed) psychologists and kinesiology-trained (specializing in sport psychology but not licensed) psychologists in administering psychologically based interventions with athletes and other performers (e.g., first responders, business people, artists, doctors, police, etc.).
- There are opportunities for advanced training in psychology departments, counseling/clinical psychology, versus through kinesiology departments, sport/exercise psychology (Peterson, Brown, McCann, & Murphy, 2012). This divide leads to issues in what to call a person working with athletes on mental skills/

issues as well as competency issues (what minimum training and knowledge is required to work with an athlete population).
- Competency issues being addressed through a revised certification program including coursework, practical mentored experiences, and an exam administered by the Association for Applied Sport Psychology so one can call themselves a Certified Mental Performance Consultant (Watson & Portenga, 2014).
- Multidisciplinary research with experts in other kinesiology subdisciplines (e.g., exercise physiology, biomechanics, motor learning) as well as other disciplines (e.g., nursing, engineering, social work) to study big issues facing society such as the obesity epidemic or enhancing positive youth development (Weinberg & Gould, 2019).
- Increases in globalization and cultural diversity. New knowledge and best practices are rapidly being developed in a host of Asian, European, and South American countries. Understanding the differences and diversity among cultures is becoming more and more essential for successful sport psychology practitioners.
- The positive psychology movement which focuses on the development of positive attributes such as happiness, optimism, and hope (Seligman & Csikszentmihalyi, 2002) has really always been part of the field of sport psychology, but it has been enhanced in the past several years.

## Purposes and Rationale of the Curriculum

Sport psychology classes at the university level started to develop in earnest in the late 1960s into the 1970s. This growth was accelerated in the 1980s and 1990s and continues today at both undergraduate and graduate levels. At undergraduate level, sport psychology and psychology of coaching classes are usually a requirement or an elective class within a kinesiology/sport science department for students majoring in some sport science curriculum (e.g., sports medicine, exercise science, sport management, coaching). There are only a few schools nationwide where students can actually major in sport psychology at the undergraduate level (e.g., West Virginia University). At graduate level, there are a number of universities that offer either master's or doctoral degrees specializing in sport psychology, and these are highlighted in a publication from the Association for Applied Sport Psychology titled Directory of Graduate Programs in Applied Sport Psychology (Burke, Sachs,, & Tomlinson, 2018).

Sport and exercise psychology curriculums in the United States have generally not been aligned with, or constrained by, any competency models, accreditation bodies, or professional standards. However, in many countries, there has been a movement toward establishing a competency-based qualification for the training and development of applied sport psychologists (cf. Fletcher & Maher, 2013), which often includes a specified taught curriculum offered by institutions. As one example of this process, the two-stage qualification to become a registered sport and exercise psychologist in the United Kingdom is described later in this chapter. As far back as

2003, in a position statement on behalf of the International Society of Sport Psychology (ISSP), the increase in sport psychology practitioners across the globe was noted, in addition to the influx of academic programs available (Tenenbaum, Lidor, Papaianou, & Samulski, 2003). Thus, developments in competencies focusing on occupational standards, knowledge, and specific skills continue to be at the forefront of professional practice issues in sport and exercise psychology, especially in Europe (e.g., Hutter, Van der Zande, Rosier, & Wylleman, 2018). Specific to the United States, based on both the American Psychological Association (APA) (2002), and Association for Applied Sport Psychology (AASP) (2010) codes of ethics regarding issues of competence, there are expectations for individuals teaching sport and exercise psychology. For example, the APA states in Sect. 2.01 of the ethics code that (a) "Psychologists provide service, teach and conduct research with populations and in areas only within the boundaries of their competence, based on their education, training supervised experience, consultation, study, or professional experience" (2002, p. 5). This standard regarding competence in teaching echoed in the AASP code of ethics Principle A (2010). The standard of being up to date is the essence of competence in knowing one's subject matter. This could be achieved via coursework, reading the literature, attending conferences, participating in continuing education workshops, webinars, etc. However, competence could also be demonstrated in the use of technology and in actual teaching methods. Thus, although the teaching of sport and exercise psychology is not constrained by accreditation standards, teachers do need to maintain competence in the field as demonstrated by the above examples.

However, it would be remiss if there was no discussion in this chapter about certification of sport psychologists and accreditation of sport psychology graduate programs as they relate to the teaching of sport psychology. First, certification of sport psychologists has been administered by AASP since 1989. The certification process (which has been updated and now includes an exam) includes a variety of coursework (i.e., sport psychology, research methods, professional ethics, psychopathology, counseling, sport science, diversity and culture, psychological foundations of behavior) as well as 400 hours of mentored practical experience in applied sport psychology. Many schools, which have a graduate specialization in sport psychology, try to offer most (if not all) of the classes that students need to be certified in applied sport psychology. However, there are no specific requirements about the specific content of these courses. For example, besides having a sport psychology course in the curriculum (focusing on some aspects of sport psychology content), there is no specification as to exactly the content of the course, who teaches the course (do they need to be AASP certified), or the methods employed to teach the class. Therefore, the certification process has had little influence on the teaching of sport psychology (just as long as it is a required part of the graduate curriculum). Nonetheless, the debate on developing "Accredited graduate programs" in the United States has been ongoing over many years (cf. Quartiroli, 2014).

However, recently, AASP has added an exam component to becoming certified in applied sport psychology. In essence, starting in 2018, besides requiring specific coursework, a person who wants to be certified by AASP (now called a Certified

Mental Performance Consultant CMPC) needs to pass an exam in applied sport psychology. The exam will target many of the areas noted above but also focus on the research and practice related to becoming a competent CMPC. Therefore, specific areas of competency will be required, and it is likely that courses in sport and exercise psychology will need to incorporate these knowledge areas into their curriculum so that individuals will be properly prepared to take and pass the exam to become a CMPC. In addition, for many years, there has been discussion of accreditation of sport psychology graduate programs. This is an ongoing discussion and will probably have some standards attached to the courses in the programs, but at this time this is still in the discussion stage.

While it is not the purpose of this chapter to compare sport and exercise psychology teaching and learning from other countries, it is interesting to briefly mention the training pathway that has been developed in the United Kingdom, as sport and exercise psychology amalgamated into the British Psychology Society (BPS) along with other divisions of psychology such as health, clinical, social, and forensic. Prior to this movement occurring in approximately 2007, a training pathway for certification similar to the United States existed with the British Association for Sport and Exercise Science (BASES). However, when the BPS adopted the Division of Sport and Exercise Psychology, a specific training pathway to qualification (becoming a registered sport and exercise psychologist legislated by the Health and Care Professions Council) was developed. The foundation psychology requirement (Graduate Basis for Chartered status; GBC) is initially obtained from studying an undergraduate degree in psychology, which covers a range of core topics (e.g., individual differences, developmental psychology, biological psychology, research methods). Undergraduate students studying outside of psychology (e.g., sport science degrees) must obtain these key areas of knowledge via alternative options (such as short courses, conversion diplomas, top-up psychology in developmental and bio-psychology) if they want to pursue the full practitioner qualification. Obtaining an accredited master's degree with the BPS (which emphasizes theoretical knowledge rather than applied practice) is the first stage toward qualification. The Training and Standards Partnership Committee (BPS Division of sport and exercise psychology) ensures that universities offering accredited master's programs are adhering to the specified curriculum and that teaching staff are appropriately qualified. Re-accreditation visits take place every 5 years. Stage 2 part of the qualification requires supervised experience (normally 2–3 years) with a registered supervisor as trainees work toward achieving competency across four key roles (ethics, applied practice, research project and skills, dissemination of work). Following the submissions of training logs, practice hours, reflective practice, case studies, and supervisor interactions, candidates attend a viva with two independent assessors who have been periodically assessing submitted work during the 2–3-year period. The latest development in the training pathway has occurred within BASES where students can now opt to take their supervised practical experience through SEPAR (Sport and Exercise Psychology Accreditation Route). The end product of taking the training pathway with either the BPS or BASES leads to registration as a sport and exercise psychologist legislated by the Health and Care Professions Council (HCPC).

As noted earlier, within the United States, since there are no specific competencies thrust upon the teaching of sport psychology by outside agencies, what might be some core teaching and learning objectives and competencies to be included in sport psychology classes? Although some textbooks in sport psychology focus more on research (e.g., Horn & Smith, 2019) and some more on application (e.g., Orlick, 2008), most textbooks take a scientific-practitioner perspective (e.g., Weinberg & Gould, 2019). The superordinate learning objectives of the scientist-practitioner model involve taking a research-to-practice approach. Specifically, the objective is to understand sport psychology research and theory and then be able to apply this knowledge to practical sport settings. In essence, research should inform practice although at times practice could lead to specific sport psychology research endeavors.

The other superordinate goals focus more on specific sport psychology content put in the form of two questions. These include (a) to understand how psychological factors affect an individual's physical performance (performance enhancement focus) and (b) to understand how participation in sport and exercise settings affect an individual's psychological development, health and well-being (mental health focus). An example of a question regarding performance enhancement would be "what is the effect of anxiety on penalty kicks in soccer?" For the mental health perspective, a question would be "what is the relationship of regular exercise to reductions in depression and anxiety?" Although coaches and athletes are generally more interested in the performance enhancement aspect of sport psychology, probably in the long run, the effect of one's participation on their psychological development and mental health is most likely the more important aspect.

## Core Contents and Topics of Sport and Exercise Psychology

To determine core content and topics in sport and exercise psychology, it is again instructive to take a close look at the current popular textbooks in the field focusing on content that appears to cut across both more applied-oriented and more research-oriented as well as research-to-practice texts. In addition to core content and topics, we will briefly discuss the major theories, themes, models, and research paradigms that build the core of what students need to learn.

## Historical Perspectives

An understanding of the history of sport psychology along with current issues and future directions is typically the first chapter in many texts (e.g., Gill et al., 2017; Weinberg & Gould, 2019; Williams, 2014). Some critical aspects of history that are usually covered include Norman Triplett's research on social facilitation and cycling in the 1890s, Coleman Griffith's extensive research and practice in the 1920s and 1930s giving him the title of father of American sport psychology, Franklin Henry providing a scientific approach to the study of sport psychology, the formal beginning of sport psychology in 1965 with the first International Congress in Sport Psychology in Rome, the establishment of professional applied and scholarly organizations in the 1970s and 1980s, and the multidimensional and global nature of sport psychology in the 2000s. Present and future issues and trends in sport psychology (some noted earlier) include such things as cultural diversity, ethics and competency, limited full-time positions for applied sport psychologists, importance of counseling and clinical training to help enhance the mental health of athletes, focus on positive psychology, and focus on specific specializations (e.g., exercise psychology, positive youth development, performance excellence outside of sport – business, music, military).

## Knowledge Development

In most sport psychology texts, there is a chapter that focuses on how knowledge is derived. There are scientifically derived knowledge and professional practice knowledge. Both of these are important. Students learn the difference between professional practice knowledge which is usually guided by trial-and-error learning and scientific knowledge which is derived by experiments and studies using the scientific method. Throughout the years, there has been a gap between scientific and professional practice knowledge. However, more recently, there has been an attempt to integrate professional practice and scientific knowledge. For example, the RE-AIM model (Glasgow, Vogt, & Boles, 1999) outlines five factors that interact to affect knowledge transfer. These include (a) reach (who the program affects), (b) efficacy (program outcomes), (c) adoption (who uses the program), (d) implementation (is the program delivered as specified), and (e) maintenance (sustaining the program over time).

In terms of paradigms, most knowledge in sport psychology in the 1960s and 1970s was quantitative with the focus on laboratory research. However, in a seminal article (Martens, 1979) entitled "Smocks to Jocks," the importance of gathering data in field (realistic) settings was championed in addition to the already laboratory research. This led to many studies being conducted in the field as well as a start to more qualitative research, which started appearing in the literature in the late 1980s and has now a strong foothold into the development of sport psychology knowledge. Qualitative research along with emergence of case studies has provided sport psychology with more depth and richness of data that was missing with purely quantitative studies.

## Individual Differences

How people are different is one of the central themes throughout all of psychology and thus is one of the themes in most sport psychology courses. Although the specific individual differences somewhat vary among different textbooks and courses, some of the mainstay topics include personality, motivation, confidence, and anxiety.

**Personality** Literally hundreds of articles on sport personality have been published although most as the field started to gain prominence in the 1960s and 1970s (Vealey, 2002). Although the trait approach dominated the early research on personality (as it did in mainstream psychology), currently the interactional perspective, which takes a person-by-situation approach, is the dominant paradigm as it accounts for the most variance in behavior. Along with the interactional approach, the other contemporary approach to personality gaining the most support is the phenomenological approach. This is similar to the interactional approach. However, the interactional approach focuses on fixed traits or dispositions as the primary determinants of behavior, whereas the phenomenological approach focuses on individuals' understanding and interpretation of themselves and their environment. In essence, individuals' subjective experience and personal views of the world and of themselves are seen as critical. Many of the most prominent theories in sport psychology such as self-determination, achievement goal, cognitive evaluation, and social cognitive fall within the phenomenological framework (these theories will be discussed further in relation to their place within the themes of sport psychology).

**Motivation** A very popular individual difference variable is motivation for both researchers and practitioners. There are a number of influential theories that attempt to understand how motivation affects performance as well as other important variables such as persistence, choice of activities, and affective and cognitive responses. These include such theories as achievement motivation (Atkinson, 1974), achievement goal (Dweck, 1986; Nicholls, 1984), attribution (Weiner, 1985), self-determination (Deci & Ryan, 1985), and competence motivation (Weiss & Amorose, 2008). These encompass many individual differences such as intrinsic vs. extrinsic motivation, task vs. ego orientation, high vs. low achievers, and high vs. low self-esteem. In accordance with the scientist-practitioner model, these theories provide practical information for motivating different types of performers based on their unique personalities and individual differences.

**Anxiety/Arousal** Anxiety is a critical component if an athlete wants to perform at high levels. Many studies have been conducted investigating high- vs. low-anxiety individuals in their performance of a variety of strength, endurance, fine motor, coordination, speed, and balance tasks (Mellalieu, Hanton, & Fletcher, 2006). There are many theories which attempt to explain the arousal-performance relationship including drive theory, the inverted-U hypothesis, multidimensional anxiety theory, catastrophe theory, individualized zones of optimal functioning, and reversal theory. Although they provide different predictions, as a group, there are some consistencies which help practitioners/coaches help their performers to play up to their potentials. One point in relation to individual differences is the notion (especially highlighted by the zones of optimal functioning) that different individuals have different optimal levels of anxiety. For example, some perform their best at high levels, whereas others perform their best at low levels. In addition, research has revealed that the way an athlete interprets his anxiety is probably more important than their amount of anxiety (Jones, 1995).

**Confidence** Of all the individual difference variables, confidence is probably the one that most consistently is related to increased performance. For example, the individual attribute that comes up most consistently when studying mental toughness is confidence (Gucciardi, Hanton, & Fleming, 2017). A construct highlighted by the research and theorizing of Bandura (1977), self-efficacy, is seen as similar to confidence (although some differences) and have helped in the development of sport confidence (Vealey, 2001). Individuals high vs. low on sport confidence have demonstrated differences in performance, affect, cognitions, and behavior. Although self-efficacy and sport confidence were originated as individual difference variables, group/team concepts have been developed (i.e., team efficacy) as well as efficacy attached to a certain individual (i.e., coaching efficacy).

## Group Dynamics

Besides individual differences, a major thrust within sport psychology is the focus on groups and group/team dynamics. Many different topics are included in this area such as the differences between groups and teams, theories regarding how groups are formed, group structure, group roles, role clarity, role acceptance, and role conflict, as well as group norms and norms for productivity. The relationship of individual to team performance is critical in sport, and Steiner's model of actual and potential productivity (Steiner, 1972), the Ringelmann effect (Ingham, Levinger, Graves, & Peckham, 1974), and social loafing (Heuze & Brunel, 2003) all address this critical issue in sport.

However, the topic of group/team cohesion is the one group area that most coaches are interested in developing. Defining task vs. social cohesion comes first and then a conceptual model for the personal, environmental, leadership, and team factors that influence cohesion (Carron, 1982). Measurement of task and social cohesion via sociograms and the Group Environment Questionnaire (Widmeyer, Brawley, & Carron, 1985) is critical to test the effectiveness of team building programs. The cohesion-performance relationship has received the most attention, and it is moderated by the type of measurement (task vs. social cohesion) and task demands (individual vs. team) (Carron, Coleman, Wheller, & Stevens, 2002). From an applied perspective, strategies for enhancing team cohesion by coaches and athletes as well as team building programs have been emphasized.

## Leadership

Different approaches to leadership are emphasized from those emanating outside of sport including the trait, situational, behavioral, and interactional approaches. Models of leadership specific to sport include the cognitive-mediational model of leadership (Smoll & Smith, 1989), the multidimensional model of sport leadership (Chelladurai, 2007), and most recently the transformational model of leadership in sport (Turnnidge & Cote, 2016). Effective leadership is seen as having four components including leader qualities, leadership styles, follower qualities, and situational factors.

## Psychological Skills

A core aspect of most sport and exercise psychology texts is the focus on mental skills. Mental skills for performance enhancement have been one of the key aspects of applied sport psychology. This usually takes the form of chapters on goal setting, imagery, arousal regulation, and attentional focus. For arousal regulation, different somatic, cognitive, and multimodal techniques such as progressive relaxation, the relaxation response, and cognitive-affective stress management are typically discussed. Different imagery theories are highlighted such as psychoneuromuscular, bioinformational, and symbolic learning (see Weinberg, 2008, for a review) as well as developing an imagery training program such as PETTLEP (Physical, Environment, Task Type, Timing, Learning, Emotion, Perspective) (Holmes & Collins, 2001). Goal setting uses Locke's (1968) original theory and over 500 studies to develop goal setting principles and effective goal setting programs in sport and exercise settings. The psychological skill of focused concentration includes performers understanding concepts such as situation awareness, attentional selectivity, attentional capacity, attentional alertness, and shifting attentional focus (Weinberg & Gould, 2019). Changing self-talk and one's focus of attention through techniques such as mindfulness (Kabat-Zinn, 2003) and rational emotive behavior therapy (Ellis, 1994) are critical for maintaining appropriate attentional focus.

## Exercise Motivation and Well-Being

As noted earlier, sport psychology has grown and incorporated exercise as part of its title and focus. Although some texts focus only on sport psychology, while other focus exclusively on exercise psychology, most combine both sport and exercise psychology. Two of the areas within exercise psychology that receive the most attention are typically exercise motivation and exercise and psychological well-being. Exercise motivation typically focuses on the concept of exercise adherence since approximately 50% of people starting an exercise program drop out within 6 months. In addition, large percentages of adults around the world are either overweight or obese (Afshin et al., 2017). Because of the serious health effects of being overweight and obese, many theories and models have been developed or applied to try and predict adoption and adherence to exercise. These include the Health Belief Model, Theory of Planned Behavior, Social Cognitive Theory, Self-Determination Theory, Ecological Model, and Transtheoretical Model (see Weinberg, 2018, for a review). In addition to the models and theories, much research has focused on the determinants of exercise adherence including personal factors, demographic variables, environmental factors, cognitive and personality variables, social environment physical environment, physical activity characteristics, and leader qualities. Finally, different strategies and approaches highlighting this area include behavior modification approaches, reinforcement approaches, decision-making approaches, cognitive-behavioral approaches, social support approaches, and intrinsic approaches.

There is an abundant literature attesting to the physiological benefits of exercise. However, research within exercise psychology has demonstrated the positive influence of exercise on psychological well-being. The two mental health variables that have received the most attention are anxiety and depression, and research has consistently revealed exercise to reduce both of these negative mental states (see reviews by Mutrie, 2001; Landers & Arent, 2001). Exercise has also been shown to enhance mood, improve cognitive functioning, improve well-being in many different chronic diseases, and generally enhance quality of life (Weinberg & Gould, 2019).

## Psychology of Injury

Part of exercise psychology typically in sport and exercise psychology textbooks is the psychology of injury. Early research focused on predicting, from a psychological perspective, who would be more likely to be injured with models focusing on antecedent variables, perceived stress, and coping skills (Andersen & Williams, 1986). In recent years, the focus has changed to using psychological skills such as relaxation, goal setting, and imagery to help performers during the rehabilitation process.

## Character/Moral Development and Aggression

The related topics of moral development and aggression seem particularly important today with off-the-field issues that many athletes appear to be having with violence, sexual assaults, and other illegal behavior. Then there are the sport-related issues of bullying and hazing. So, the issue of "does sport build character or characters" has been a focus of much research investigating the relationship between sport participation and delinquency as well as gang behavior (Spruit, van der Put, van Vugt, & Stams, 2017; Spruit, van der Put, van Vugt, van der Stouwe, & Stams, 2016). Since a lot of the amoral behavior in sport has a physical component, as well as the need to be positively aggressive within sports, aggression theories appear relevant. Instinct theory, the frustration-aggression theory, and social learning theory have been used to help explain why, how, and under what conditions aggrieve behavior is probable. Applying research to enhance moral behavior in sport and decrease negative aggression is typically highlighted in sport and exercise psychology texts.

## Teaching, Learning, and Assessment in Sport Psychology: Approaches and Strategies

Thus far, the focus of this chapter has been on the core content areas to be included within sport psychology courses as well as some historical background, purposes, and rationale for the curriculum. But how will this information be taught and conveyed to students to optimize their learning? First, it should be noted that there is really a dearth of written information (e.g., journal articles, books, book chapters) on the teaching of sport psychology. There have been some sessions dedicated to teaching strategies at the annual AASP Conference, as well as an interest group within AASP but not much written content specific to the teaching of sport psychology. Therefore, the approaches, strategies, and assessments for teaching sport psychology will primarily come from the above: AASP sources, generally known effective teaching practices, as well as in-depth discussions with colleagues about their teaching practices of sport psychology.

### Flipping the Classroom

A technique that has gained some traction in terms of teaching is the "flipped classroom." This strategy basically means that events that normally take place inside the classroom now take place outside the classroom and vice versa (Bergmann & Sams, 2012). If students learn basic content outside the classroom, then time inside the classroom can be used for active learning strategies such as case studies, role-playing, and team projects. For example, outside of class, students might be asked to read a chapter in their textbook, take an online quiz, and participate in an electronic discussion board where students react to a couple of thought-provoking questions (e.g., should a coach have his/her athletes set individual goals in a team sport?) and interact with each other responding to different posts. In this way, they would be prepared to come to class with some knowledge learned outside the classroom. In class, for example, if the outside homework focused on effective goal setting in sport, students could be divided into teams/groups and each given a different question related to goal setting. After meeting for, say, 10–15 min, each group reports to the class on how they responded to their goal setting question. Some of these questions might include (a) discuss the differences between outcome, process, and performance goals and apply the use of these to different types of teams (younger vs. older, skilled vs. unskilled, competitive vs. non-competitive); (b) discuss the process of setting goals on a team sport including how goals are set, the role of the coach, and individual vs. team sports; and (c) discuss the principles of effective goal setting and provide examples of how they would be implemented. Of course, an instructor could employ a classroom that was totally flipped, as noted above, as well a partially flipped classroom where, for example, the instructor might selectively and intentionally lecture on difficult and complex material or use some sessions for keynote lectures but other sessions for active learning strategies.

## Turning a Class Into a Team

A teaching strategy that is taken from the practice of sport psychology and social psychological research (Tuckman, 1965) is the making of a team or taking a group and making it into a team. Eggleston (2009) provides some suggestions for using and applying Tuckman's research to the classroom. The basic premise of Tuckman's research is that groups go through four different stages to become a team. The stages are forming, storming, norming, and performing. Teams are first formed so that hopefully they are heterogeneous and relatively equal and they create a team name, team colors, and maybe a team saying. In the storming phase, teams are given different assignments to be discussed in class, with competitions between teams highlighted as well as choice of captains within teams which usually creates some conflict. In the norming stage, the instructor gives each team some rules and strategies for the completion of successful team projects. Communication among teammates can be enhanced outside of class through a course management system (e.g., blackboard, canvas), e-mails, and other technology. In the performing stage, teams will present their projects (usually 2–3) to the rest of the class throughout the semester. Projects that are presented might use PowerPoint or YouTube videos, create brochures, conduct coaching clinics in sport psychology, role-play interactions between coaches and athletes, etc. The concept of working in teams can also be applied when helping sport psychology students learn to work from a multidisciplinary sport science perspective. From an applied perspective, preparing students for working with athletes and teams is important as they might be required to work as part of a multidisciplinary sport science support team or when engaging in case formulation. In this instance, team case study work can be used, and sport psychology students can work in teams with students majoring in physiology, strength and conditioning, and nutrition to identify an athlete's key strengths and areas for improvement. This also an effective way of students learning the process of goal setting as this can become an extension of moving beyond identifying areas to work on and how to form a training plan.

## UNIFORM Program

One of the main thrusts of applied sport psychology is to teach psychological skills such as anxiety management, goal setting, self-talk, and imagery. A 12-week curriculum called UNIFORM has been shown to be effective in teaching these mental skills (cf. Gilbert, Moore-Reed, & Clifton, 2017). The program uses a unique teaching approach called the Game Plan Format, which is based in the Transtheoretical Model of behavior change. More specifically, facilitators use a multi-method approach (i.e., interactive education sessions, in-class assignments, films/video footage, take-home adherence strategy tasks, physical activities, and journaling) to help the participants learn the skills and apply them to their sport and daily lives. Research has shown that varsity student-athletes undergoing a psychological skills intervention increased their use of these psychological skills when compared to a control group.

## Assessment Considerations in Sport Psychology

Assessment and feedback for learning rather than just assessing for progress have become increasing popular topics when discussing the important aspect of the student learning experience (cf. Brown & Knight, 1994). Formative assessments are designed to help students meet the learning outcomes of the class/module and considered a strategy to engaging learners. It is a method that is also known to enhance self-evaluation and self-reflection on learning which are important skills for sport psychology students to develop if they are to pursue careers in teaching, in applied sport psychology consultancy, or in research. The strategy of peer feedback (cf. Nicol, Thomson, & Bresline, 2014) can easily be embedded into formative assessment strategies and further provide opportunities for students to learn through a reflective process about their own work and their peers. In sport psychology, one example for formative assessments might include keeping a reflective practice diary while taking internship credit. In this example, students would receive periodic feedback on their use of literature and evidenced-based research and how their knowledge can inform the next phase of their internship work. A second example might be centered on the research side of sport psychology where the final summative assessment is to submit a lab report or research report. Students can undertake three or four formative assessments in this process and receive feedback on literature searching, using literature to develop a rationale for the research, data collection, and analysis. Summative assessments can still be used to evaluate the knowledge, and a grade can be produced commensurate with students' standard of achievement. In sport psychology, more traditional-based assessments (e.g., tests, essays, oral presentations) can be effective for summative assessments especially as understanding theoretical knowledge of sport psychology and the science underpinning intervention is crucial before students are able to learn how to start to apply that knowledge as a practitioner.

When considering the broad spectrum of career options for students who have studied sport psychology (e.g., research/further qualifications, applied consultancy, coaching, lecturing), it is important to consider "blended learning" options, not just for engagement and learning but as a way for students to become more familiar with using technology. Using technology has become part of sport psychology work, especially when working as a practitioner/consultant where searching for innovative ways to engage athletes and coaches in education is becoming a key skill. Blended learning (cf. Ward & LaBranche, 2003) typically involves a mixture of traditional face-to-face classroom strategies and the use of different technologies, such as video/audio streaming, and learning platforms, such as a Padlet, or electronic discussion boards. The use of Socrative has become popular in recent years where students can engage in the classroom through responding to a live quiz using their mobile phones and results can be shown immediately. For sport psychology students, the use of technology (beyond traditional blended learning activities) could involve creating a research-to-practice blog, developing a webpage, or even creating a professional development profile (e.g., LinkedIn profile).

## Challenges and Lessons Learned

Since sport and exercise psychology is a relatively new field (compared to other areas of psychology), there are several challenges that we currently face as well as those in the future in terms of curriculum development and teaching. Despite the challenges, we have learned a great deal as curriculum has been developing at a rapid pace to stay abreast of the rapid research and applied changes and advances in the field. As noted earlier, a main focus in the field (spearheaded by the Association for Applied Sport Psychology) was to develop a certification program which would recognize sport psychology professionals in terms of their experiences and expertise. The requirements of certification have changed (e.g., an exam has been added to course work and applied practicum experience), and one of the challenges is to continue to develop curriculum especially at the graduate level. Besides trying to provide some "teeth" (standards) into becoming certified in applied sport psychology, there is also a move to provide accreditation to graduate programs in sport psychology. Thus, a challenge for the future is to determine the necessary requirements of becoming an accredited sport psychology graduate program as curriculum development will likely follow accreditation requirements for those universities wanting graduate-level accreditation.

Because the majority of new graduate students are interested in consulting with athletes (or other performers), it will be incumbent upon many graduate programs to develop curriculum that will be aligned with not only becoming certified in sport psychology but also becoming an accredited graduate program. However, graduate work in sport psychology is based on a scientist-practitioner model. Therefore, as curriculum develops, it needs to both meet the needs of those graduate students wanting more of an applied focus as well as providing a theoretical and empirical underpinning of theories and research that informs the practice of applied sport psychology and provides future researchers and teachers the knowledge to be not only cutting-edge in research but also cutting-edge in teaching.

Along these lines, in terms of practitioners of sport psychology, one of the key challenges is to provide clear career paths (via curriculum development) for those individuals wanting to be able to work on mental health issues of athletes (focus on clinical or counseling psychology typically through a psychology department) versus those who want to focus on performance enhancement (focus on studying sport psychology through a kinesiology department). In recent years, there has been increased interest in the mental health of athletes especially at the college level, and these athletes have pressure to perform well both in the classroom and on the athletic field and thus are often stressed not having enough time and energy to spend on each endeavor. There are only a very few universities that have a graduate sport psychology specialization/practicum while studying counseling psychology through a psychology department or where a graduate counseling degree can be obtained alongside a kinesiology (sport psychology) PhD degree. It seems logical that curriculum needs to be developed and enhanced so that more of these combined psychology and kinesiology programs can meet the needs of our current and future students. After providing empirical research and theory, teachers could then utilize a number of hands-on teaching techniques to give students experience using the research/theory to inform practice such as role-playing, mock interviews, simulations, group/team competitions, and the inverted (flipped) classroom.

## Teaching, Learning, and Assessment Resources

This Special Interest Group from the Association of Applied Sport Psychology is committed to the improvement of the teaching and learning process in sport and exercise psychology. Topics of interest include (a) the tools and strategies employed by instructors (e.g., curriculum design, innovative activities), (b) empirical research on the teaching and learning of sport and exercise psychology, and (c) professional and ethical issues related to the assessment and evaluation of sport exercise psychology students, courses, and instructors.

http://tamieggleston.com/uploads/3/6/1/9/3619199/aaspnews23-1(2).pdf

This article uses social psychology research on the stages of group formation applied to sport psychology classes. The author discusses breaking up her sport psychology classes into teams with 5–7 students per team. Activities and assignments are provided which use the different stages of group/team formation.

**Eggelston, T. (2015). Adventures with flipping: Students will flip over a sport psychology class that incorporates flipped classroom strategies. Association for Applied Sport Psychology Newsletter, 30 (1) 10–12.**

This article discusses the strategy of flipping the classroom where events that normally take place inside the classroom now take place outside the classroom. Students learn basic content outside the classroom so they are prepared to lead the class and/or partake in active learning classroom activities.

**Smith, G. (2007, March). Going for the Gold: Using Sports Psychology to Improve Teaching and Learning. Association for Psychological Science. Observer.**

This article focuses on using active learning through sport psychology principles. Specifically using Olympic designations of bronze, silver, and gold, different learning activities are developed with increasing levels of difficulty and risk with degree of difficulty and risk increasing from bronze to gold.

**Cruickshank, A., Martindale, A., & Collins, D. (2018). Raising our game. The necessity and progression of expertise-based training in sport psychology. Journal of Applied Sport Psychology, 30, 1–19.**

This article focuses on the training in applied sport psychology. Presently, our training focuses on enhancing competence. However, the authors argue that our training should focus on professional expertise rather than simply competence. Ways in which expertise-based training can be implemented are also discussed.

**Gilbert, J., Moore-Reed, S., & Clifton, A. (2017). Teaching sport psychology for now and the future? The psychological UNIFORM with high school varsity athletes.**

This article focuses on the delivery of a 12-week curriculum (called UNIFORM) taught to high school athletes. This curriculum focused on teaching psychological skills (e.g., relaxation, imagery, goal setting, self-talk). Results revealed that athletes were able to learn these skills and then employ them in actual competition. Athletes still used the skills 4 months after the intervention was completed.

**Forneris, T., Conley, K., Danish, S., & Stoller, L. (2014). Teaching life skills through sport: Community-based programs to enhance adolescent development. In J. Van Raalte & B. Brewer (eds.) Exploring sport and exercise psychology (third ed.) pp. 261–276.**

This chapter focused on teaching life skills to adolescents through sport in community-based settings. A unique part of this program is that peer leaders (usually high school students) are taught how to integrate life skills into the teaching of sport skills. Because life skills are being taught, the more similar the teachers to the students in their life experiences and skill level, the more the students will learn. In essence, a coping model is preferred over a mastery model.

## References

Afshin, A., Forouzanfar, M., Retisma, M., Sur, P., Estep, K., Lee, A., et al. (2017). Health effects of overweight and obesity in 195 countries over 25 years. *New England Journal of Medicine, 377*, 213–227.

American Psychological Association. (2002). *Ethical principles of psychologists and codes of conduct*. Washington, DC: American Psychological Association.

Andersen, M., & Williams, J. (1986). A model of stress and athletic injury: Prediction and prevention. *Journal of Sport and Exercise Psychology, 10*, 294–306.

Association for Applied Sport Psychology. (2010). *AASP code of principles and standards*. Retrieved from http://www.appliedsportpsych.org/about/ethics.

Atkinson, J. (1974). The mainstream of achievement-oriented activity. In J. Atkinson & J. Raynor (Eds.), *Motivation and achievement* (pp. 13–42). New York: Halstead.

Bandura, A. (1977). Self-efficacy: Toward a unifying theory of behavioral change. *Psychological Review, 84*, 191–215.

Bergmann, J., & Sams, A. (2012). *Flip your classroom: Reach every student in every class every day*. Washington D.C: International Society for Technology in Education.

Brown, S., & Knight, P. (1994). *Assessing learners in higher education*. London: Kogan Page.

Burke, K., Sachs, M., & Tomlinson. (2018). *Directory of graduate programs in applied sport psychology* (12th ed.). Indianapolis, IN: Association for Applied Sport Psychology.

Carron, A. (1982). Cohesiveness in sport groups: Interpretations and considerations. *Journal of Sport Psychology, 4*, 123–138.

Carron, A., Coleman, M., Wheller, J., & Stevens, D. (2002). Cohesion and performance in sport: A meta-analysis. *Journal of Spot and Exercise Psychology, 23*, 168–188.

Chelladurai, P. (2007). Leadership in sports. In G. Tennenbaum & R. Eklund (Eds.), *Handbook of sport psychology* (3rd ed., pp. 113–135). Hoboken, NJ: Wiley.

Deci, E., & Ryan, R. (1985). *Intrinsic motivation and self-determination in human behavior.* New York: Plenum Press.

Dweck, C. (1986). Motivational processes affecting learning. *American Psychologist, 41*, 1040–1048.

Eggleston, T. (2009). Making a class a team. *Association for Applied Sport Psychology Newsletter, 23*, 26–28.

Ellis, A. (1994). The sport of avoiding sports and exercise: A rational emotive behavior therapy perspective. *The Sport Psychologist, 8*, 248–261.

Fletcher, D., & Maher, J. (2013). Toward a competency-based understanding of the training and development of applied sport psychologists. *Sport, Exercise, and Performance Psychology, 2*(4), 265–280.

Gilbert, J. N., Moore-Reed, S. D., & Clifton, A. M. (2017). Teaching sport psychology for now and the future? The psychological UNIFORM with high school varsity athletes. *The Sport Psychologist, 31*(1), 88–100.

Gill, D., Williams, L., & Reifsteck, E. (2017). *Psychological dynamics of sport and exercise* (3rd ed.). Champaign, IL: Human Kinetics.

Glasgow, R., Vogt, T., & Boles, S. (1999). Evaluating the public health impact of health promotion interventions: The RE-AIM framework. *American Journal of Public Health, 8*, 1322–1327.

Gucciardi, D., Hanton, S., & Fleming, S. (2017). Are mental toughness and mental health contradictory concepts in elite sport? A narrative review of theory and evidence Journal of Science and Medicine in Sport. Doi.org/https://doi.org/10.1016/j.jams.2016.08.006.

Heuze, J., & Brunel, P. (2003). Social loafing in a competitive contest. *International Journal of Sport and Exercise Psychology, 1*, 246–263.

Holmes, P., & Collins, D. (2001). The PETTLEP approach to motor imagery: A functional equivalence model for sport psychology. *Journal of Applied Sport Psychology, 13*, 60–83.

Horn, T., & Smith, A. (2019). *Advances in sport and exercise psychology* (3rd ed.). Champaign, IL: Human Kinetics.

Hutter, R. V., van der Zande, J. J., Rosier, N., & Wylleman, P. (2018). Education and training in the field of applied sport psychology in Europe. *International Journal of Sport and Exercise Psychology, 16*(2), 133–149.

Ingham, A., Levinger, G., Graves, J., & Peckham, V. (1974). The Ringelmann effect: Studies of group size and group performance. *Journal of Experimental Social Psychology, 10*, 371–384.

Jones, G. (1995). More than just a game: Recent development and issues in competitive anxiety and sport. *British Journal of Psychology, 86*, 449–478.

Kabat-Zinn, J. (2003). Mindfulness-based interventions in context: Past, present and future. *Clinical Psychology: Science and Practice, 10*, 144–156.

Kornspan, A. (2012). History of sport and performance psychology. In S. Murphy (Ed.), *The Oxford handbook of sport and exercise psychology* (pp. 3–23). Oxford, UK: Oxford University Press.

Kornspan, A. (2015). John D. Lawther: Contributions in the psychology of sport. *The Sport Psychologist, 29*, 346–357.

Kroll, W., & Lewis. (1970). America's first sport psychologist. *Quest, 1S*(3), 1–4.

Landers, D., & Arent, S. (2001). Physical activity and mental health. In R. Singer, H. Hausenblas, & C. Janelle (Eds.), *Handbook of sport psychology* (2nd ed.). New York: Wiley.

Locke, E. (1968). Toward a theory of task motivation incentives. *Organizational Behavior and Human Performance, 3*, 157–189.

Martens, R. (1979). About smocks to jocks. *Journal of Sport Psychology*, 94–99.

Mellalieu, S., Hanton, S., & Fletcher, D. (2006). A competitive anxiety review: Recent directions in sport psychology research. In S. Hanton & S. Mellalieu (Eds.), *Literature reviews in sport psychology* (pp. 1–45). New York: Nova.

Mutrie, N. (2001). The relationship between physical activity and clinically-defined depression. In S. Biddle, K. Fox, & S. Boucher (Eds.), *Physical activity, mental health and psychological Wellbeing* (pp. 46–62). London, UK: Routledge & Kegan Paul.

Nicholls, J. (1984). Concepts of ability and achievement motivation. In C. Ames & R. Ames (Eds.), *Research on motivation in education: Student motivation* (pp. 39–73). New York: Academic Press.

Nicol, D., Thomson, A., & Bresline, C. (2014). Rethinking feedback practices in higher education: A peer review perspective. *Assessment & Evaluation in Higher Education, 39*(1), 102–122.

Orlick, T. (2008). *In pursuit of excellence* (4th ed.). Champaign, IL: Human Kinetics.

Peterson, C., Brown, C., McCann, S., & Murphy, S. (2012). Sport and performance psychology: A look ahead. In S. Murphy (Ed.), *The Oxford handbook of sport and performance psychology* (pp. 741–753). Oxford, UK: Oxford University Press.

Portenga, S. T., Aoyagi, M. W., & Cohen, A. B. (2017). Helping to build a profession: A working definition of sport and performance psychology. *Journal of Sport Psychology in Action, 8*(1), 47–59.

Quartiroli, A. (2014). The perceived value of the association for applied sport psychology certification and certification exam: A survey of sport and exercise psychology professionals. *Athletic Insight, 6*(3), 245.

Seligman, M., & Csikszentmihalyi, M. (2002). Positive psychology: An introduction. *American Psychologist, 55*, 5–14.

Smoll, F., & Smith, R. (1989). Leadership behavior in sport: A theoretical model and research paradigm. *Journal of Applied Sport Psychology, 19*, 1522–1551.

Spruit, A., van der Put, C., van Vugt, E., & Stams, G. (2017). Predictors of intervention success in a sports-based program for adolescents at-risk of juvenile delinquency. *International Journal of Offender Therapy and Cognitive Criminology, 122*. https://doi.org/10.1177/0306624X17698055.

Spruit, A., van der Put, C., van Vugt, E., van der Stouwe, G., & Stams, G. (2016). Sport participation and juvenile delinquency: A meta-analytic review. *Journal of Youth and Adolescence, 4*, 655–671.

Steiner, I. (1972). *Group process and productivity.* New York: Academic Press.

Tenenbaum, G., Lidor, R., Papaianou, A., & Samulski, D. (2003). ISSP position stand: Competencies (occupational standards, knowledge, and practice) and their accomplishment (learning specification, essential knowledge, and skills) in sport and exercise psychology. *International Journal of Sport and Exercise Psychology, 1*, 155–166.

Triplett, N. (1898). The dynamogenic factors in pacemaking and competition. *American Journal of Psychology, 9*, 507–553.

Tuckman, B. (1965). Developmental sequence in small groups. *Psychological Bulletin, 63*, 384–399.

Turnnidge, J., & Cote, J. (2016). Applying transformational leadership theory to coaching research in youth sports. A systematic literature review. *International Journal of Sport and Exercise Psychology.* https://doi.org/10.1080/1612197X2016.1189948.

Vealey, R. (2001). Understanding and enhancing self-confidence in athletes. In R. Singer, H. Hausenblas, & C. Janelle (Eds.), *Handbook of sport psychology* (2nd ed., pp. 550–565). New York: Wiley.

Vealey, R. (2002). Personality and sport behavior. In T. Horn (Ed.), *Advances in sport psychology* (pp. 43–82). Champaign, IL: Human Kinetics.

Ward, J., & LaBranche, G. A. (2003). Blended learning: The convergence of e-learning and meetings. *Franchising World, 35*, 22–23.

Watson, J., & Portenga, S. (2014). An overview of the issues affecting the future of certification in sport psychology. *Athletic Insight, 6*, 261–276.

Weinberg, R. (2008). Does imagery work? Effects on performance and mental skills. *Journal of Imagery Research in Sport and Exercise, 3*, 1–20.

Weinberg, R. (2018). Theories and models of behavior change applied to exercise: Research and practice. In S. Razon & M. Sachs (Eds.), *Applied sport psychology: The challenging journey from motivation to adherence* (pp. 37–48). New York: Routledge.

Weinberg, R., & Gould, D. (2019). *Foundations of sport and exercise psychology*. Champaign, IL: Human Kinetics.

Weiner, B. (1985). *An attribution theory of achievement and emotion (Psychological review)*. New York: Springer Verlag.

Weiss, M., & Amorose, A. (2008). Motivational orientations and sport behavior. In T. Horn (Ed.), *Advances in sport psychology* (3rd ed., pp. 115–154). Champaign, IL: Human Kinetics.

Widmeyer, N., Brawley, L., & Carron, A. (1985). *The measurement of cohesion in sport teams: The group environment questionnaire*. London, ON: Sports Dynamics.

Williams, J. (2014). *Sport psychology: Personal growth to peak performance*. New York: McGraw Hill.

# Family Therapy 39

## Clinical Supervision as a Sociocultural Generative Practice

Maria Elisa Molina, Pablo Fossa, and Viviana Hojman

## Contents

| | |
|---|---|
| Triadic Perspective | 966 |
| Triadic Perspective of Semiotic Mediation | 967 |
| Clinical Supervision Modalities | 968 |
| Generalization and Contextualization | 969 |
| Levels of Semiotic Construction | 970 |
| Guidance Process in a Temporality Frame | 971 |
| Dialogicity | 972 |
| Diversity of Dialogues and Aims | 973 |
| The Person of the Therapist: From An Individual and Structural to a Dialogical and Temporal Understanding | 974 |
| The Clinical Supervision as Collaborative Learning | 975 |
| Conclusion | 976 |
| Cross-References | 977 |
| References | 977 |

### Abstract

The present chapter understands *clinical supervision* as a sociocultural practice that concerns the construction of meanings and relationships in the field of family therapy, by means of which learning and transformation emerge. This process takes three modalities: the narrative, the live supervision, and the scene supervision, with different aims. The process entails a significant personal relationship together with knowledge and skill learning. It is developed in motion at a multilevel and reciprocal dialogue from individual to culture spheres. The chapter elaborates on the dynamics of the supervision activity from the theoretical frame of Cultural and Semiotic Mediation Psychology. It makes a revision of different

M. E. Molina (✉) · P. Fossa · V. Hojman
Universidad del Desarrollo de Chile, Santiago, Chile
e-mail: memolina@udd.cl

© Springer Nature Switzerland AG 2023
J. Zumbach et al. (eds.), *International Handbook of Psychology Learning and Teaching*,
Springer International Handbooks of Education,
https://doi.org/10.1007/978-3-030-28745-0_46

concepts proposing the process of the therapist's training as triadic, dialogical, and generative of signs and meanings.

**Keywords**

Clinical supervision · Triadic model · Dialogical model · Semiotic mediation

The present article understands *clinical supervision* as a sociocultural practice that concerns the construction of meanings and relationships, in the field of family therapy, by means of which learning and transformation emerge. This practice comprises pedagogic strategies carried out for the effective functioning of educational programs. As a teaching action, clinical supervision aims at the development of knowledge, skills, and abilities. However, it differs from teaching being the personal relationship more significant than the aim of enhancing knowledge and skills in clinical practice. On the other hand, it is also a *process in motion*. As a human interaction, it creates new practices and leads to new ideas, knowledge, or theories that enable the dialogue among the professional, disciplinary, local, and historical context of contemporary human life.

The chapter aims theoretically analyzing this practice in order to enable understanding from a systemic and semiotic perspective. This approach will focus on some concepts such as triadic process, semiotic mediation, generalization-contextualization, temporality frame, and dialogicity.

## Triadic Perspective

The clinical supervision process considers dynamically at least three actors: agent, (*the agent* (or team), who is the trainer), addressee (the apprentice who is the *addressee*), object (different focal points, that third party which is in turn the *object* of construction) (Fig. 1).

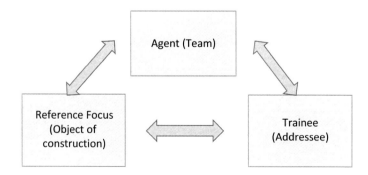

**Fig. 1** The triadic model of clinical supervision

These *construction objects* include the consultant system, the training path of the practitioner, the therapeutic relationship, the supervisory relationship, and the discipline and interdiscipline – psychological, anthropological, sociological, and ethical. The consultant system means the individual and the relational system, particularly the family system, that seeks psychological help. The *training path of the practitioner* entails the trajectory of actions, duties, and behaviors displayed in the course of the formation. The therapeutic relationship is the aspects related with the quality of the bond between therapist and clients at therapy. The supervisory relationship refers to the interpersonal and affective aspects that enable as well as affect the learning process. The discipline and the interdiscipline address the field of knowledge comprised in the process of clinical supervision.

The training path of the supervised is the main construction object, which needs focusing on aspects of effectiveness, on the skills to carry out a helping relationship, on the process of reflection, and on flexibility to adapt to the situations that occur at the consultation of individuals and groups that are in trouble (Gilbert & Evans, 2000). This learning occurs from the beginning of the therapist training as a development of personal aspects of the therapist in a relational context, which includes permanent feedback of individual and intersubjective aspects.

The supervised-supervisor is a holistic relationship in which the *object* is included (the problem of the consultants, the technique, the theory, the understanding of the relationship, and so on), composing the triadic structure that co-evolves where each part is definable in terms of the two others (Simao, 2012; Zittoun, Gillespie, Cornish, & Psaltis, 2007). Then, agent (subject), addressee (other), and object conform a whole unit in a co-genetic dynamic. This understanding is isomorphic with the triadic metaphor proposed by Pierce, on which the generative process of unlimited semiosis is based (Rosa, 2007).

At a higher level, the triadic structure constitutes a unit in the experience of learning, training, and guidance, displaying generative actions and meaning construction. The dynamic consists of a dyad, basically a dialogical relationship of part and counterpart – an Ego and an Alter (Marková, 2003) – that displays movements towards an immediate future, which are directed to the object of construction. The third of the relationship is emergence, a created and renewed object that along with it modifies the relationship with and between the dyad, projecting the dialogue forward.

## Triadic Perspective of Semiotic Mediation

This triadic model is inherent to the training process in its emphasis on psychological development seen as mutual interdependence between positions, not like static and individual structures that undergo events of change, but ongoing process of continuous transformation (Valsiner, 2014; Zittoun et al., 2007). Taking Vygotsky's proposal, a useful reference is the mediation model through the *subject-other-object* triangle. Considering this theoretical assumption, the dynamics of the triangle lead to the process of semiotic mediation, that is, the creation of the sign (Vygotsky, 1978). In order to adapt, human beings construct signs, so the possibility of accessing the world is from a sign-dependent mind (Innis, 2012). This proposal entails the psychological foundation of the semiotic process by way of which the self exists and is built in semiosphere (Valsiner, 2014). Accordingly, the process of the therapist's training is triadic, dialogical, and generative of signs and meanings.

## Clinical Supervision Modalities

The clinical supervision can take three modalities based on the object of analysis: (1) the narrative, (2) the live supervision, and (3) the therapeutic scene. The supervision of the narrative carries out a clinical discussion after the therapeutic meeting. This practice conducts joint discussions and reflections between the supervisor and the supervised, which may include a team of colleagues, around the descriptions, perceptions, ideas, and feelings of the supervised. This process aims to facilitate the visualization of therapeutic skills in the professional in training as well as resources and potential in the consulting system through continuous decision-making. The supervision of the therapeutic session is a second modality referred to as *live supervision*. This activity takes place since the origins of the systemic model of family therapy, where the teamwork of therapists, co-therapists, supervisors, and peers constructed the theoretical approach, using a one-way vision mirror (we will refer to this kind of supervision further on this chapter). The *scene supervision*, third modality, considers the observation and review of brief videotaped excerpts from the session and allows focusing on reflection and analysis of therapeutic interventions. The reflection at this context allows elaborating distinctions regarding psychotherapeutic techniques and interactions from the relational systemic model, referring to the organization of the relationship, the quality of reciprocal exchange, and the positions that the therapist takes respect to each interlocutor. In the *scene supervision*, the therapist chooses a relevant moment of the session – previously video recorded – and observes it together with the supervisor and the team. The supervisor positions himself with the peers as observers of the interaction, with the purpose of analyzing the wide variety of the interaction including details, nonverbal aspects, or subtleties that bring new perspectives of that encounter. The supervised has an equivalent perspective when observing the video-recorded interaction in which he was an active participant, now from a meta-position. It entails a psychological distancing as the interaction is observed that enables reflection, while on the other hand, as he/she loses distance, he/she manages the feelings of being evaluated or criticized in his/her skills. The discussion and analysis of chosen moments of the session promotes to monitoring of microprocess at the therapeutic encounter, distinguishing actions, interactions, gestures, and words, arranged in sequences of dialogical construction.

## Generalization and Contextualization

The process of clinical supervision develops a semiotic process of meaning construction. It is developed around the therapist's narratives with the aim of searching new understandings around the problem and the possibilities of overcoming it. The new meanings include values – such as health/non-health, responsibility, intention, care, risk, resources, and other concepts. The process follows a trajectory motivated by value adding and decision-making (Lehmann, Murakami, & Klempe, 2019). The specific therapeutic situation and problems of the consultants become the objects of elaboration and co-construction in supervision as the therapist in training edits the narrative. This kind of work elaborates on the life meanings of the consultants from their discourses, which the therapist categorizes and contextualizes. At the team meeting, these elaborations have a conversation with other possibilities, understandings, approximations, and definitions, in the search for clarity around the role of the therapist as to the decisions to make in therapy. Those possibilities come from the personal and professional experiences of each of the team members, the theoretical background of the discipline, as well as the local and global social context. It entails a semiotic process of meaning making such as proposed by Valsiner (2006, 2014) that carries out mutual feed-forward loops between contextualization and generalization/abstraction as well as between pleromatization and schematization.

> The increasing richness of experience leads to the formation of over-abundant pleromatic signs – with the need to cope with the richness through schematization. The generalizing abstraction of the schematized kind leads to emergence of new richness of experiential side – leading further to new pleromatic signs, which feed into further abstraction from that semiotic richness through schematization (Valsiner, 2006, p. 14).

Pleromatization refers to the undifferentiated, ambiguous, holistic, and abundant experience, which addresses both to the experiences of the professional in training and to the uncertainties of the consultants. The supervision process would carry out a sequence of transition between an experience as a whole and its categorization that at the same time constrains it, loose aspects of the experience, but leads to decision-making for the immediate future and solving the feeling of uncertainty.

The exercise of visualizing possibilities and formulating new meanings and actions is the stimulus to the continuing work that the therapist will do with the consultants. These understandings and generalized categories will act as starting points for new dialogues, to enable the pleromatic semiosis – the experience in its wholeness – and push for the meaning construction at the therapeutic context. This approach does not see the motive of consultation as fixed or static but in transformation and movement and the therapeutic process as generative. Additionally, the therapeutic dialogue interprets what the consultants live and the holistic field of meaningful actions (ibid., P.10) by signs and categories like metaphor or hypothesis. This process allows psychological understanding, which could be analogous to diagnosis.

Training includes developing skills related to the semiotic process. The semiotic model offers a theoretical and methodological framework for the clinical supervision process. The micro-process describes trajectories of meaning construction that unfold as chains where each new constructed sign establishes a dialogic relationship with another immediately previous one (Josephs, Valsiner, & Surgan, 1999). The relationships between the meanings constructed are of similarity, opposition, and ambivalence, which stimulate the progress of the process and the decisions that are made in the therapeutic conversation to regulate tension and uncertainty. This analysis allows to appreciate how the therapeutic relationship is being carried out, where the foci are placed, is the therapist focused on the contributions of the consultants and their affections, or is he/she diverting the relevant foci according to the way in which the tension is regulated. A central aspect for the maintenance of dialogue and the generation of meanings is that the semiotic tension fluctuates between intermediate levels, in such a way as to favor the creative impulse. An excessively stressed semiotic tension raises an emotional tension with it that can lead to a decrease in the generation of alternatives, to deviate attention or leave the field of meanings under construction and get relief. The micro-process analysis of the therapy allows reviewing the construction describing how the therapist tunes in with the levels of elaboration of the consultants and delivering conceptual tools for the exploration of the moments of difficulty and change in therapy.

## Levels of Semiotic Construction

The emotional climate or atmosphere that develops in the therapeutic scenario is an important aspect of the formation of systemic therapists, since beyond the individual emotions of consultants and therapists, they reflect a perception of feelings, affections, or shared experiences, as preverbal, ambiguous, and diffuse states. It is the pleromatization of the therapeutic system. That includes even aspects of great intensity at key moments of the therapeutic encounter. Constructing meanings and bringing generalization contribute to the development of a perception of congruency to the consultants and the therapist.

One aspect to develop in the trainee is learning to recognize different signs, such as the use the consultants made of the physical environment (space), their gestures, body movements and dispositions, and then the verbal contents. That implies to learn the ability to respond to the experience of pleromatization paying attention to some part of the hyper-richness totally of experience – the climate – and selecting some details to elaborate it through abstraction and categorization. A first experience with the other could emerge from a pleromatic sign based on intuition, from more undifferentiated levels of experience, to take the construction towards planes of explicitness, definition, contextualization, and then generalization. This process takes different types of sign and levels of affective semiosis from a primary level of physiological activation to the categorical designation of feelings or emotions, followed by generalization, and then hypergeneralization (Valsiner, 2006, 2014, 2017). The pleromatic sign could emerge at the physiological or at the hyper-generalized layer.

For example, intuition emerges at the physiological level, while the notions of freedom, love, or loyalty are constructed at a hypergeneralized level. The affective experience on a first preverbal level is holistic and ideosyncratic. As it is processed and categorized, it advances at the level of generalization and loses its unique and ideosyncratic character. As the construction advances at a hypergeneralized level, it get to a new form of holistic experience at the macrogenesis process of culture. Distinguishing the different levels of hierarchy and abstraction of the sign allows orienting the reflection around the therapeutic dialogue by offering semiotic tools for mobilizing the emergence of possibilities. Participants in a dialogue can lead it by increasing or decreasing generalization, around particular, unique, ordinary, or shared aspects.

## Guidance Process in a Temporality Frame

In the clinical supervision, different thinking heads analyze the possibilities for the therapeutic scenario. The therapist in training participates at the discussion and experiences (in the first person), the learning activity, and the relational process of co-construction. It is the pattern of supervision, a useful tool for the therapeutic reflection. Supervision is a process of guidance that is developed in a temporality frame through a regulated, organized trajectory that implies more than instances of reflection. It also involves accompanying a pilgrimage that describes sequences of transient stabilities, transitions, and passages (border crossings) towards objectives that mean new self-positions for those who participate (Marsico, 2016). In that accompany and be accompanied, the supervisor applies a cultural function, through mutual interdependence with the supervised and the object of the training. The effects of this function regulate the construction of images and concepts around himself as a professional, therapeutic skills, and social role. This function also involves the object of construction, the problem of the consultants, the therapeutic and supervisory relationship, and the discipline. The actions appealed by social purposes include dispositions and intentions of the actors towards constructing the professional discipline and knowledge, but also around the construction of adult role in society, or the practice of guiding and leadership roles. The process of clinical supervision as well as that of therapy is a process of thinking on the edge (Aristegui, 2015; Marsico, 2016). One objective is to develop in the supervised the ability to be in the process, attentive to the here-and-now, when flowing on the meeting at the continuous taking decisions – self-positioning – based on the relationship with recent, or more remote past, to enhance future possibilities. This is relevant, insofar as only the supervised person is in the emerging consultant-therapist relationship. The supervisor's action is catalyzer for this construction process. As catalyzer, it establishes limits and regulations for external suggestions – contributions from the therapist in training, team members, and members of the consulting system – to be compatible with their elaborations concerning the needs of the process, facilitating the connection between previously disconnected notions, and enabling the transition of meanings among intersubjective spheres. The abductive reasoning favors the meaning emergence. It differs from deductive or inductive thinking, as the ability to construct hypotheses, offering them as possibilities in dialogue (Rosa, 2007).

## Dialogicity

Different visions converge in the work at the clinical supervision. For instance, at the live supervision, the supervisor together with some peers observe the interaction between the therapist and the family, while another team observes the interaction between supervisor and supervised therapeutic system. The Milan group was the pioneer of this modality, demonstrating at the team meeting after the session that different observers, from their different positions, provide very different visions and descriptions of what they observe (Elkaim, 1985). The supervisor, as observer of the therapeutic session, must face the immediacy of the activity that leads him to focus more on the effect of the interventions and on the trajectory of the therapeutic interaction, orienting (through his interventions by a cytophone) towards certain directions and not others, depending on the objectives to achieve for that particular meeting. From his/her role, he/she "dialogues" with two interlocutors or recipients, on the one hand with the therapeutic system as a relational organization, and on the other with the therapist in training, from his/her intentions and behavioral, emotional, and cognitive dispositions. On the other hand, the team that observes the supervision system will focus more on the constructions, distinctions, the interaction between the different actors, supervisor-therapist-members of the consulting system, and the ways in which they are organized. The richness of this process is the inclusion of wide possibilities of variability in the analysis perspectives. The actors share the object of co-construction of the clinical supervision and the display of the therapeutic session. Different dialogues approach this object: the therapist with the consulting system, the therapist with his supervisor, the supervisor with the therapeutic system, and the team with the supervision system – supervisor-supervised (see scheme). Every dialogue entails internal and external exchanges. For example, the therapist maintains an external exchange with his consultants and the supervisor, while internalizing voices and evoking other previously internalized towards the generation of ideas and meanings that contribute to the construction of the ongoing therapeutic process (Fig. 2).

This dialogical model allows expanding the range of possibilities for the life of the consultants and offering dialogical chains of explicit and implicit levels for developing understandings and conceptualizations. Those understandings go beyond what the team and each participant manage to categorize, enunciate, and explain in common. The therapeutic and supervision scene displays a pleromatic construction. Dialogue implies openness toward different positions where each participant enters into a relation of co-determination, in the transience of experience and uncertainty of the future. In this dialogical space, permanence and movement are shaped in a mutual relationship. From this perspective, learning experience implies a process of internalization of alter positions or positions referred to the other. The supervisor provides a position, a sign, that brings new resources to the self-image

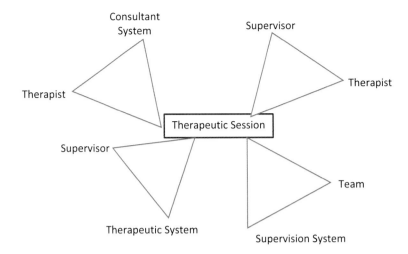

**Fig. 2** Relational pattern of the live supervision based of the organization of multiple voices in dialogical tryad around the therapeutic session

and ideas of the trainee (built on imaginations and signs) to perceive himself as an agent with skills, knowledge, and autonomy in his role as a therapist.

The supervisor is not a specialist who manages predetermined information, as he/she does not guide a pre-established itinerary. He/she is an actor that subjectively adopts positions and provides meanings for the process of transformation. The dialogicity at the here and now disposes the relationship between diversity of meanings to produce semiotic tension with asymmetry. That asymmetry pushes the actors to take positions in the dialogue in the search for a novelty that results in overcoming that tension.

Part of teamwork involves an exchange of different or opposite positions. For example, in the case of a particular case, a student can focus on how to favor the change expected by the index patient; another may be focused on the meanings and emotions of the family that hinder change, while another can elaborate on the meanings and function of the symptom in the organization and family history. Looking from different perspectives allows connecting partial and individual visions of different problems and leads to systemic and complex thinking.

## Diversity of Dialogues and Aims

The supervisee copes with different objectives that he or she needs to balance with the mediation of the supervisor. On one hand, there are emotional needs such as the feeling of being capable, approved, confirmed, validated, and supported by the supervisor. It is an objective to the supervisor as well to help to construct self-trust and confidence in the trainee that will allow him/her to be calm and take advantage of his resources to prioritize and be attentive to the needs of the consultants. In order to enhance these feelings, he or she will construct the confidence in his/her ability to think and decide on what to do in the therapeutic context.

On the other hand, the specialized discipline knowledge is the content the trainee needs to assimilate. The knowledge comprehends *the signs* that the therapist needs to focus in order to have significant information about the consultants and their problems, *the techniques* that help to address the signs, and *the thoughts* that come from the theoretical perspective used for constructing meanings and understanding about selves, others, and relationships and difficulties, pain, and relief. Usually, the supervision open conversation focuses on knowledge. On the other hand, the not said – the subtext – is expressed probably through gestures, postures, accent, and tone of voice and is concerned with affects, emotions, values, and particularly opposition and diversity. The supervisor is challenged to address the not said and the opposition, not referring directly but circumventing it with meanings and topics slightly related to the problems the consultants have. The supervisor needs to manage the emotional tension and at the same time allow the construction of new knowledge related to the discipline. His/her function is to regulate these explicit and implicit dialogues that make arise emotional tension as well as semiotic tension of the conceptual construction. The emotional climate of the discussion will manifest the congruency of this regulation –mediation – and how the focus related with emotional needs and knowledge assimilation is kept in the meaning construction.

In addition, and on the other side, the supervisor manages two agendas in his mind: A personal agenda of own professional development and the aims of helping the trainee to develop psychotherapeutic competences. So, the professional in training in his/her turn acts as a mediator of the inner dialogues of the supervisor, between his personal needs and his role.

Every interaction entails at least two objects of meaning construction: the explicit content of the elaboration, in this case the concepts concerning psychotherapy, and the emotional definition of the relationship (Watzlawick, Beavin, & Jackson, 2002). The last issue entails fuzzy feelings about acceptance, validation, or sympathy that lead to define the relationship as collaborative, friendly, authoritarian, conflictive, or hostile.

## The Person of the Therapist: From An Individual and Structural to a Dialogical and Temporal Understanding

An aspect of clinical supervision is the attention to the therapist, as the subjective experiences affect the quality of the resulting professional action. The intergenerational model proposed by the psychiatrist Murray Bowen (Kerr, 1984) has been considered useful for that purpose. It postulates the learning of patterns of interpersonal behavior within the family of origin, which would be brought by the therapist to interactions with patients, supervisors, and peers. From this conceptualization, clinical psychological formation would be aimed at making the supervisor aware of these patterns and developing strategies that allow him to interrupt the models that govern them (Harber & Hawley, 2004). Considering the concept of intergenerational transmission and differentiation, this model raises a debate between repetition/transformation dynamics, differentiation/undifferentiation, and evolution/stagnation and stresses notions of functionality or dysfunctionality of behaviors and relationships. The assumption of patterns and repetition does not seem to agree with the concept of open systems. The concept of pattern repetition comprises an ontological notion of static entity in the absence of transformation or development. The theoretical proposals of these models are based on a broad clinical trajectory and psychotherapeutic experience. Using their contributions can be useful reconceptualizing them in a relationship of inclusive opposites (Valsiner, 2014) of structure/process, stability/transformation where dialogue, change and temporality are integrated. From there, we can explain that transgenerational processes display recursive relationships between systems and self-positions in time living, that is in the local and temporal context. On the other hand, the proposal of invisible loyalties (Boszormenyi-Nagy, 1997) and resistance to the differentiation of the family of origin does not seem consistent with the conceptualization of development defined by differentiation. Differentiation implies building identity and creating personal postures and refers to the construction of the self. The dialogical model (Ribeiro & Gonçalves, 2011) regards the self as a multivoiced space that is built through the internalization of the "others." The self-construction addresses two complementary and included processes of belonging and differentiation. It is an open and dynamic process, which goes on with temporality as it revises lived experiences with the family of origin editing them by means of a reconstructive memory. The process transforms each evocation in the very action of remembering. The cultural, semiotic, and dialogical perspective contributes to overcome the view of dysfunction and transgenerational transmission as obstacles for transformation and fixed entities as it points at new horizons of novelty and diversity.

On the other hand, relational practices associated with significant moments in personal histories reveal complex processes of cultural regulation that seek to ensure the inclusion of members to its institution, such as the family. But still, there are other institutions related with the local contexts and its values that regulate ways of living, relationships, coexistence, religious beliefs, and so on. The notion of cultural regulation becomes part of the analysis of self-construction in which relational phenomena are transforming processes between personal, local, and more global contexts.

## The Clinical Supervision as Collaborative Learning

The dialogical conceptualization also finds a basis in the development of conversational and language-based models (Gergen, 2006). These, known as constructionist models, define supervision not by an expert role of the trainer. It incorporates the observer as part of the system, visualizing the supervisor as part of the therapeutic one. The supervision intends to the therapist to develop curiosity and collaboration. These ideas are also consistent with humanistic models of psychotherapy. The humanist models point to the development of a reflexive process, highlighting the action of sense construction which is not instrumental (Aristegui, 2015). This view of psychotherapy takes the perspectives of reflexivity and flexibility, in relation to meaning construction and sense of one's life, the self, and its environment, opened to possibilities, and generating novelty. The dynamics of semiotic process that enable that flexibility are tension, ambivalence, and psychological distancing. They operate in this process facilitating the collaboration and elaboration of the senses of self and life (Molina & Del Río, 2009). The focus is no longer on a reality that needs to be discovered and known – because it is preexisting – but rather a reality that is built with others, is co-constructed, and is part of what does not yet exist, which belongs to the possibilities of the near future, *what should be* (Valsiner, 2014). A formation that is theoretically based on a circular thought, recognizing that there are no certainties but hypotheses, enables collaboration in practice and prevents dynamics of rivalry among the participants of that process.

The not-knowing position questions the idea of *generality* as an ontological value and emphasizes *particularity*. The non-expert position of the supervisor implies a respect towards a person and his experience as "other" who responds, demands, and brings possibilities to the expansion of horizons (Tateo, 2016). This co-construction, consequently, manifests itself in an idiosyncratic way, space-temporarily located, that is, contextualized and unique (De Luca Picione & Valsiner, 2017). Therefore, from this perspective, the supervisor is a collaborator in a mutual search for ideas generation and knowledge development, in the course of an interaction between supervised and the rest of the team in a peer relationship. Therapy and clinical supervision are similar processes of dialogue and co-construction, but not isomorphic: Clinical supervision is not therapy. The above implies that the training process is more focused on the meanings of therapy and supervision and less on intimate personal aspects of the supervised. Focusing on the individual sphere of the therapist could lead to restricting the possibilities for new conversations and introducing new limits in a scenario of greater intimacy, where the person of the therapist receives attention in a relational organization that ceases to be symmetric. The focus, in such a case, would be on his/her privacy but not towards the intimacies of the team members, who remain as external distanced observers of the process, with less active participation.

## Conclusion

We have referred to the process of clinical supervision and training of systemic therapists as a continuum of experience and knowledge generation. The result of this moving process makes the disciples become diffusers and developers of the therapeutic thinking and knowledge.

The training process integrates diverse goals, such as training in skills, internalizing rules of the therapeutic process, as well as exercising creativity and self-confidence to be in the here-and-now of the exchange and construction. It is at the same time following and disobeying the supervisor guidance in order to cross borders to enhance knowledge and experience. From this perspective, change is not a goal, but to generate possibilities of meanings, asymmetries, and tensions, seeking the trainee develops confidence in them and becomes their own agent. Agent, in a broad sense of the term, is a subject that positions him/herself from its intentions and subjectivities and relates to another, allowing the other to question and provoke him/her in order to receive answers.

The main activity is creation, where expectations need to be regulated and assumptions questioned, so difference becomes the purpose. Like every constructive process, many times we think of what we intend to build as something to discover, as if it were already somehow, somewhere. To develop ideas and imagining, the future entails the cognitive processes needed to enter that creation, but not for those goals to be achieved but to experience that the new experiences exceed the anticipated.

## Cross-References

▶ Cultural Psychology
▶ Community Psychology and Psychological Distress
▶ Developmental Psychology: Moving Beyond the East–West Divide
▶ Epistemology of Psychology
▶ Qualitative Methodology
▶ The Methodology Cycle as the Basis for Knowledge

## References

Aristegui, R. (2015). Social constructionism and discussion of paradigms in psychology: Indeterminacy, holism and language games vs. In *Theory pictorial language*. Ohio, Taos: Institute Publications/WorldShare Books.
Boszormenyi-Nagy, I. (1997). Response to "are trustworthiness and fairness enough? Contextual family therapy and the good family". *Journal of Marital and Family Therapy, 23*(2), 171–173.
De Luca Picione, R., & Valsiner, J. (2017). Psychological functions of semiotic borders in sense-making: Liminality of narrative processes. *Europe's Journal of Psychology, 13*(3), 532–547.
Elkaim, M. (1985). *Formaciones y prácticas en terapia familiar*. Buenos Aires: Ediciones Nueva Visión.
Gergen, K. (2006). *Therapeutic realities: Collaboration, oppression, and relational flow*. Chagrin Falls, Ohio: The Taos Institute Publications.
Gilbert, M. C., & Evans, K. (2000). *Supervision in context. Psychotherapy supervision: An integrative relational approach to psychotherapy supervision*. Maidenhead, BRK, England: Open University Press.
Harber, R., & Hawley, L. (2004). Family of origin as a supervisory consultative resource. *Family Process, 43*(3), 373–390.
Innis, R. (2012). Meaningful connections: Semiotics, cultural psychology, and the forms of sense. In J. Valsiner (Ed.), *The oxford handbook of culture and psychology*. London; Oxford University Press.
Josephs, I. E., Valsiner, J., & Surgan, S. E. (1999). The process of meaning construction. In J. Branstställter & R. M. Lerner (Eds.), *Action & self-development* (pp. 257–282). Thousand Oaks, Ca: Sage.
Kerr, M. (1984). Theoretical base for differentiation of self in one's family of origin. *The Clinical Supervisor, 2*(2), 3–36.

Lehmann, O., Murakami, K., & Klempe, S. (2019). A qualitative research method to explore meaning-making processes in cultural psychology. *Sozialforschung/Forum: Qualitative, Social Research, 20*(2). https://doi.org/10.17169/fqs-20.2.3190

Marková, I. (2003). *Dialogicality and social representations*. Cambridge: Cambridge University Press.

Marsico, G. (2016). The borderland. *Culture & Psychology, 22*(2), 206–215. https://doi.org/10.1177/1354067X15601199

Molina, M. E. & Del Río, M. T. (2009). Dynamics of psychotherapy processes. J. Valsiner, P. Molenaar, M. Lyra N. Chaudhary. Handbook dynamic process methodology in the social and developmental science, New York: Springer-Verlag.

Ribeiro, A. P., & Gonçalves, M. M. (2011). Maintenance and transformation of problematic self-narratives: A semiotic-dialogical approach. *Integrative Psychological and Behavioral Science, 45*, 281–303.

Rosa, A. (2007). Acts of psyche: Actuations as synthesis of semiosis and action. In J. Valsiner & A. Rosa (Eds.), *The Cambridge handbook of sociocultural psychology* (pp. 205–237). New York, NY, US: Cambridge University Press. https://doi.org/10.1017/CBO9780511611162.013

Simao, L. (2012). The other in the self: A triadic unit. In J. Valsiner (Ed.), *The oxford handbook of culture and psychology*. London: Oxford University Press.

Tateo, L. (2016). Toward a cogenetic cultural psychology. *Culture & Psychology, 22*(3), 414–423.

Valsiner, J. (2006, June). The overwhelming world: Functions of pleromatization in creating diversity in cultural and natural constructions. International summer school of semiotic and structural studies, Imatra.

Valsiner, J. (2014). *An invitation to cultural psychology*. London, New Delhi: Sage.

Valsiner, J. (2017). *Between self and society: Creating psychology in a new key*. Tallinn: ACTA Universitatis Tallinnensis.

Vygotsky, L. S. (1978). *Mind in society: The development of higher psychological processes*. London: Harvard University Press.

Watzlawick, P., Beavin, J., & Jackson, D. (2002). *Teoría de la comunicación humana: Interacciones, patologías y paradojas*. Herder: Barcelona.

Zittoun, T., Gillespie, A., Cornish, F., & Psaltis, C. (2007). The metaphor of the triangle in theories of human development. *Human Development, 50*, 208–229.

# Medical Education

**40**

Ricardo Gorayeb and M. Cristina Miyazaki

## Contents

| | |
|---|---|
| History of Psychology in Medical Schools | 981 |
| Barriers to Integrating Psychology in Medical Schools | 982 |
| Overcoming Barriers to Teaching Psychology in Medical Schools | 982 |
| Teaching Psychology in Medical Schools | 984 |
| Conclusions | 988 |
| References | 989 |

### Abstract

Behavioral and social variables play an important role on health and illness. If future physicians are to care effectively for their patients using the biopsychosocial model of healthcare and can identify and deal adequately with the stress associated with medical school and the practice of medicine, then psychology has much to contribute to the medical school curriculum. However, there are several barriers to integrating psychology in medical schools, such as irrelevant course objectives to medical practice and the predominance of the biomedical model. Overcoming these barriers requires integrating psychology in healthcare to improve outcomes, such as increasing patients' healthy behaviors and treatment adherence. This chapter presents a brief history of psychology in medical schools, barriers to integrate psychology into medical education, and recommendations to overcome these barriers and integrate psychology into the medical curriculum. It proposes contributions from psychology to medical education based on the different roles played by physicians.

---

R. Gorayeb (✉)
School of Medicine, São Paulo University, Ribeirão Preto, Brazil

M. C. Miyazaki
School of Medicine, FAMERP, São José do Rio Preto, Brazil
e-mail: cmiyazaki@famerp.br

**Keywords**

Psychology in medical education · Barriers to teaching psychology in medical schools · Overcoming barriers to teaching psychology in medical schools · Physicians' roles and psychology's contribution to medical education

The role of behavioral and social variables in the etiology, prevention, evolution, treatment, and rehabilitation of diseases with high prevalence rates is now well established in the literature (Braveman & Gottlieb, 2014; U.S. Department of Health and Human Services, 2020; Saunders, Barr, McHale, & Hamelmann, 2017). Behavioral and social variables also have an important role on other problems present in healthcare systems, such as healthcare disparities, errors, patient safety, and health professionals' mental health (Association of American Medical Colleges, 2011).

Medical students, therefore, must be prepared to deal with important challenges related to social and behavioral issues, including taking care of their own health, during and after training (Puthran, Zhang, Tam, & Ho, 2016). This concern is present in the Global Standards for Quality Improvement for Medical Education (World Federation for Medical Education, 2020), a guide to the development and evaluation of medical education that can be applied and modified to different settings. Some of the key questions regarding curriculum content, according to the Global Standards for Quality Improvement for Medical Education, are which components of behavioral and social sciences (BSS) should be included in the medical curriculum, why they should be included, and how much time is allocated for each component.

According to Harden and Carr (2017), BSS must be integrated into the medical school curriculum if future medical doctors are to provide integrated biopsychosocial care. The use of the biopsychosocial model, proposed in the late 1970s (Engel, 1977), remains a challenge for the expansion of the biomedical model, still widely used in health. Despite criticisms, the biopsychosocial model has significantly influenced teaching, practice, research, and public policies in health in different countries (Farre & Rapley, 2014; Wade & Halligan, 2017). Thus, it is important to understand how social and behavioral components have been included in medical education.

An adapted definition of Behavioral and Social Sciences, based on the National Institutes of Health Office of Behavioral and Social Sciences Research (OBSSR), is provided by the Association of American Medical Colleges (2011):

> The Behavioral and Social Sciences are defined as the sciences of behavior, including individual psychological processes and behavioral interactions, and the sciences of social interaction, including familial, cultural, economic, and demographic. The core areas focus on the understanding of behavioral or social processes and on the use of these processes to predict or influence health outcomes or risk factors (p. 6).

Psychology, therefore, is one of the subjects often included in medical school curricula. A brief history of the teaching of psychology in medical schools is given below.

## History of Psychology in Medical Schools

Reports on the relevance of psychology in medical education date from the end of the nineteenth century and beginning of the twentieth century. According to Dearborn (1901), from the Tufts Medical School, physicians need to take psychology during medical school since medical practice is concerned with individuals having body and mind. The first departments of medical psychology in medical schools around the world date from the early 1950s (Cripa, 2019; Matarazzo, 1994; Robiner, Hong, & Ward, 2020).

The Flexner Report published in 1910 – with a critique of medical education in America and taking the German model as an example – greatly improved medical schools in America and placed scientific knowledge at the center of medical education. However, despite its benefits, excellence in science was not balanced with excellence in clinical care. Quoting Edmund Pellegrino, Duffy (2011) points out that "doctors had become neutered technicians with patients in the service of science rather than science in the service of patients" (p. 275).

The publication of the Flexner Report was followed by intense debate over the medical curriculum. Despite psychologists' efforts, psychology was not included as a basic course in the medical curriculum at the time (Pickren, 2007). According to psychologist Fred Wells (1913, p. 177) "... if psychology is to be successfully taught to medical students, it must afford them something they can use." Moreover, psychologists' partners at the time – psychiatrists and neurologists – were not included among the leaders of medical education (Pickren, 2007).

In the second half of the twentieth century, psychology was increasingly included in medical education in the United States (Matarazzo, Carmody, & Gentry, 1981). The development of solid clinical skills in the field, research data showing the contribution of psychology in the prevention, treatment, and rehabilitation of health problems, as well as the development of health psychology, strongly contributed in showing the important role of psychology and psychologists in healthcare (Pickren, 2007).

In Europe, higher education reform, through the Bologna Declaration, 1999, aimed to achieve greater compatibility and comparability among higher education systems, eliminating obstacles to the free mobility of students, teachers, and scientists. An analysis of 32 European medical schools from 18 countries, during the reform implemented after the Bologna Declaration, concluded that "about two-thirds of the curriculum included Psychology as a separate course, although this was recommended by the Advisory Committee on Medical Training of the European Union" (Dušek & Bates, 2003, p. 28).

According to Visser (2009) "to practice evidence-based medicine, doctors must know how psychological and behavioral factors influence health and illness: medicine should be taught from a biopsychosocial perspective. However, this does not appear to be the case. The hidden curriculum makes a separation between the 'need to know' biomedical sciences, and the 'nice to know' behavioural and social sciences" (p. 20).

Although teaching psychology has advanced since its insertion in medical schools, many obstacles are still present.

## Barriers to Integrating Psychology in Medical Schools

Despite evidence about the relevance of behavioral or psychological factors to health and illness, psychology is not yet a fundamental component of the medical curriculum. Different schools still choose which aspects of psychology to include in their curriculum and how. In addition, the acceptance and appreciation of psychology by medical students is still low, and the discipline is seen as "soft and fluffy" (Galagher, Wallace, Nathan, & McGrath, 2015, p. 91).

Identifying the barriers to integrating psychology in medical schools is relevant, since this identification enables outlining strategies to overcome them. Table 1 shows some of these barriers.

## Overcoming Barriers to Teaching Psychology in Medical Schools

If psychology is to be properly integrated into the medical curriculum, its relevance for the practice of medicine must be acknowledged by managers and educational policy makers – those responsible for allocating time for psychology into the curriculum. To achieve this goal, psychology must be integrated into medical practice, and clinicians and psychology faculty members must learn to cooperate (Tabatabaei et al., 2016).

**Table 1** Barriers to integrating psychology into the medical curriculum

1. Little knowledge about the role of psychology in the medical curriculum
2. Discipline objectives are not relevant to medical practice
3. Inefficient leadership
4. Resistance to change and to curriculum change
5. Lack of:
    Qualified teachers
    Adequate financial resources
    Consensus between medical and psychology professors
    Power by psychology professors
    Space assigned to the discipline
    Well-defined objectives
    A systematic integration of psychology in all stages of medical education (vertical integration)
6. Predominance of the biomedical model in medical education and practice
7. Existence of a hidden curriculum with inadequate role models during clinical courses
8. Students' negative attitude towards the discipline (e.g., unhelpful, subjective, "soft and fluffy," "nice to know" but not "need to know," not agreeable to medicine, does not have a big role like other disciplines)

*Note*: Data are from Daltro, Jesus, Bôas, & Castelar, 2018; Galagher et al., 2015; Institute of Medicine, 2004; Litva & Peters, 2008; Ouakinin, 2016; Russell, Teijlingen, Lambert, & Stacy, 2004; and Tabatabaei, Yazdani, & Sadeghi, 2016.

Professionals from several areas are part of healthcare teams and able to show how different professions – including psychology – can contribute to better patient care. The growth of health psychology, as a field of practice and research, has provided an excellent opportunity for psychologists to work with other healthcare professionals, including physicians from different areas (Duarte, Miyazaki, Blay, & Sesso, 2009; Gorayeb, Borsari, Rosa-e-Silva, & Ferriani, 2012; Lutfiyya, Chang, McGrath, Dana, & Lipsky, 2019; Ward, Shaffer, & Testa, 2018).

Interprofessional work can show the relevance and contribution of different professions to improved care, effective treatment, and cost reduction in healthcare systems. Although research about benefits of team-based work in the area is still needed, healthcare systems in several countries advocate for it (Lutfiyya et al., 2019; Nguyen et al., 2020; Robiner et al., 2020). A medical professor who sees the benefits of interprofessional work in their practice will advocate for this kind of collaboration and is an adequate (and good) role model for medical students.

The term "hidden curriculum," also known as "informal curriculum," "medical culture and enculturation," and "institutional values," is frequently highlighted as one possible cause why "psychology as a discipline continues to struggle for space and acceptance against the biomedical sciences in the medical curriculum," regardless of when it is taught during the course (Galagher et al., 2015, p. 98). Psychology must show its relevance to the practice of medicine to change from a low status subject and become accepted and valued in medical education. Thus, some important questions must be answered: What psychology should medical students learn? How should it be taught? And when?

Helping medical students integrate psychology content to their medical practice is central since there is growing evidence that psychological and social factors are relevant for health and disease. However, a more practical approach has been recommended in place of teaching psychological theories, which often make little sense to students (BeSST, 2010; Galagher et al., 2015).

Clinical teaching scenarios may help medical students understand how several disciplines can significantly contribute to patient care.

- Example: A woman with recently diagnosed breast cancer seeks a physician to help her deal with the situation and develop a "health strategy." She complains to a medical student that she is receiving treatment options instead of health strategies.
- How can psychology contribute with the case?
  - Identifying the emotional, cognitive, and social consequences of the diagnosis
  - Recognizing the influence of those consequences on clinical outcomes
  - Determining which important decisions concerning treatment the patient must make and how these decisions will impact the patient's coping style (AAMC, 2011)

Besides knowledge on behavioral sciences, faculty must adopt new teaching methodologies, like moving from lectures to small group problem-based learning. Career development programs must be established to promote strong leadership and competent faculty, necessary for the advancement of behavioral sciences in medical education (e.g., time away from other commitments to focus on improving skills) (Institute of Medicine, 2004).

Several reports (e.g., AAMC, 2011; BeSST, 2010; Institute of Medicine, 2004) and scientific literature from around the world (Benbassat, Baumal, Borkan, & Ber, 2003; Cordingley et al., 2013; Harden & Carr, 2017; McKinley & Ghaffarifar, 2021; Robiner et al., 2020) have advocated for the relevance of social and behavioral sciences on medical education. According to Daltro et al. (2018), psychology should promote competence for a reflexive, ethical, and humanistic practice, especially in patient-physician interactions.

The Behavioral and Social Science Matrix (AAMC, 2011) – based on the Canadian Medical Education Directions for Specialists or CanMEDS (Frank, 2005; Frank, Snell, & Sherbino, 2015) and the Institute of Medicine's (IOM), 2004 document for behavioral and social sciences knowledge and skills – helps assess medical students and physicians on their clinical approach of patients (Table 2). Thus, it follows that psychology faculty in medical schools should be familiar with the matrix.

Physicians' roles and behavioral and social knowledge shown on Table 2 (AAMC, 2011; Frank, 2005; Frank et al., 2015) indicate several necessary skills and competences to practice medicine that may be developed during medical school. Medical education accreditation requires similar skills and competences approved by WHO member states. Several organizations have endorsed the relevance of behavioral and social knowledge among physicians (WHO, 2016; World Federation for Medical Education, 2020).

One of the objectives of the WHO (2016) Global Strategy on Human Resources for Health: Workforce 2030 is that "by 2020, all countries will have established accreditation mechanisms for health training institutions" (p. 17). This will facilitate "global labour mobility and the international recruitment of health workers from low-resource settings" (p. 12).

## Teaching Psychology in Medical Schools

According to the American Association of Medical Colleges (AAMC, 2011), "A complete medical education must include, alongside physical and biological science, the perspectives and findings that flow from the behavioral and social sciences" (p. 4). Several organizations in different countries have recommended the inclusion of behavioral and social sciences in the medical curriculum to improve patient care and public health (e.g., AAMC, 2011; General Medical Council – GMC, 2015). Psychology contributions to medical education can be grouped in several categories, as presented in Table 3. Indications of material regarding each topic will be briefly presented to complement Table 3.

An evidence-based consensus behavioral sciences curriculum was developed by Cordingley et al. (2013) with the participation of medical practitioners, psychologists, and medical educators. It is important to note that those experts agreed that medical

**Table 2** Physicians' competency according to CanMEDS and IOM

**Physician roles according to CanMEDS**
**Medical expert:** Integrates "all of the CanMEDS roles, applying medical knowledge, clinical skills, and professional values in their provision of high-quality and safe patient-centered care" (p. 14)
For example, clinical reasoning, compassion, medical expertise, patient safety
**Communicator:** Establishes "relationships with patients and their families that facilitate gathering and sharing information for effective healthcare" (p. 16)
For example, active listening, attention to psychosocial aspects of illness, empathy
**Collaborator:** Conducts effective work "with other healthcare professionals to provide safe, high quality, patient-centered care" (p. 18)
For example, constructive negotiation; respect for other physicians and members of the healthcare team
**Leader:** Contributes with others "to a vision of a high-quality health care system and takes responsibility for the delivery of excellent patient care" (as clinician, administrator, scholar, teacher) (p. 20)
For example, effective committee participation; negotiation; personal leadership skills
**Health advocate:** Commits to improve health
For example, "work with patients and their families to increase opportunity to adopt health behaviors"; "work with a community or population to identify the determinants of health that affects them" (p. 23)
**Scholar:** Commits to excellence in practice through lifelong "learning, teaching others, evaluating evidence, and contributing to scholarship" (p. 24)
**Professional:** Commits "to the health and well-being of individual patients and society ethical practice, high personal standards of behaviour, accountability to the profession and society, physician-led regulation, and maintenance of health" (p. 26)
**IOM behavioral and social sciences knowledge domains with examples**
**Patient behavior:** Patients' verbal and nonverbal clues about feelings
**Mind-body interactions:** Psychosocial aspects of pain
**Physician role and behavior:** Convey HIV results without assumptions that could endanger the therapeutic relationship
**Physician-patient interaction:** Establish rapport to build a partnership
**Health policy, economics, and systems (including population health):** Address issues of patients' access to care
**Social and cultural context:** Identify community resources useful to patients

*Note*: Data are from AAMC, 2011; Frank, 2005; Frank et al., 2015; Harden & Carr, 2017

students needed only "to achieve sufficient understanding of a topic to inform their practice and decision making," and not to become psychology specialists.

- **Core Knowledge**
  - *Biopsychosocial approach*: The biopsychosocial approach clarifies the link between psychological and social factors on health and illness, which are determined by multiple factors at different levels. Using the biopsychosocial model requires the inclusion of psychological and social factors on medical education and should lead to better healthcare training. Ayers and de Visser (2021) discuss how to teach and use the biopsychosocial model on medical and healthcare education, using clinical cases as examples.
  - *Concepts of health, illness, and disease*: By discussing several definitions of health, its implication for treatment, and different clinical cases, Ayers and de

**Table 3** Psychology contributions to medical education

**Core knowledge**
- Biopsychosocial approach
- Concepts of health, illness, and disease
- Psychological or behavioral factors that contribute to health and illness
- Psychological responses to illness
- Psychosocial development across the lifespan
- Stress and coping
- Cognitive functions in health and illness
- Behavioral change and treatment adherence
- Management of patients with dependence issues
- Psychosocial aspects of pain

**Professional practice**
- Effective communication skills
- Self-care (e.g., stress management)
- Personal values and attitudes
- Teamwork skills

*Note:* Data from AAMC, 2011; Ayers & de Visser, 2021; Cordingley et al., 2013; General Medical Council, 2015; Ouaquinin, 2016

Visser (2021) show the importance of psychology for treating the person, not just the disease.

- ***Psychological or behavioral factors that contribute to health and illness***: These factors are discussed by Taylor (2017), who also presents an overview of health promotion, changing health habits, and several approaches to health behavior change (cognitive-behavioral approach to health behavior change; the transtheoretical model, changing health behaviors through social engineering, and venues for health habit modification).
- ***Psychological responses to illness***: People hold individual beliefs (which may or may not be accurate) about Illness that will shape the way they respond to it (e.g., information they give to health professionals, choice of treatment, treatment adherence). Known as the self-regulation model of illness behavior, the five dimensions of illness representation include identity (symptoms, label), timeline (time to develop and duration), consequences, causes, and controllability (Petrie & Weinman, 1997). Ayers and de Visser (2021) present all five dimensions of illness representation and present cases to illustrate their influence on how people manage their illness according to their beliefs (see also Martin, Haskard-Zolnierek, & DiMatteo, 2010).
- ***Psychosocial development across the lifespan***: Cognitive and social development from conception to death and its influence on health and illness (e.g., Center on the Developing Child at Harvard University, 2016)
- ***Stress and coping***: Definition and physiology of stress, chronic stress, coping, social support, resilience, and coping strategies. This is an important topic to medical students (medical education and practice are related to high levels of stress) and may be also used to teach them to identify their own stress and to use coping strategies to manage it in a positive way (Taylor, 2017).

- *Cognitive functions in health and illness*: Memory, learning, sleep and consciousness, attention, perception, and language (e.g., cognitive aspects of aging, effects of sleep deprivation). Sleep deprivation is also an important topic for medical students who have a high prevalence of sleep problems (Azad et al., 2015). The discussion about sleep is also an opportunity to identify students at risk for sleep disorders and refer them to professionals.
- *Behavioral change and treatment adherence*: These are important aspects of healthcare. Helping patients to change behaviors that compromise health and promoting treatment adherence are important parts of a physicians' work. Ayers and de Visser (2021) and Taylor (2017) comprehensively present the behavioral and social factors associated with the main causes of morbidity and mortality (WHO, 2020). These authors also discuss strategies to understand and improve patient adherence. Martin et al. (2010), especially Chaps. 6 (Relationships and communication between caregivers and patients) and 7 (Effective collaboration with patients – on a tight schedule), are of particular interest for future physicians.
- *Managing dependent patients*: Substance use is an important and prevalent health issue. Substance users seek healthcare services for several problems, and physicians can identify and refer those patients for adequate care. The "Mental health professionals' guide to understanding harmful substance use," in Schumacher and Williams (2020), written for mental health professionals working in medical settings, is useful to understand the distinction between "substance use and harmful substance use as well as the signs and symptoms of substance use disorders" (p. 11).
- *Psychosocial aspects of pain*: Although pain is one of the most common reasons to see a physician, it remains undertreated. Rosenberg (2012) provides a comprehensive paper on the subject, which may help medical students understand the complexity of the problem, the strategies used to assess pain, and the need to refer many patients to pain specialists.

– **Professional Practice**
- *Effective communication skills*: Healthcare practice occurs through social interaction, so effective communication is essential for all healthcare professionals. In most medical schools, teaching communication skills is centered on the doctor-patient relationship and uses roleplaying (Skelton, 2017). Several good books have been published on this subject (e.g., Silverman, Kurts, & Draper, 2013). Skelton (2017) offers many suggestions of readings, relevant websites, and online teaching resources. When psychologists teach communication skills, it would be useful to partner-up with physicians who can be role models for students. Other issues like family interviewing, interviews with patients on different stages of development (e.g., children, adolescents), angry patients, breaking bad news, talking with grieving families, and discussing advanced directives should also be included in communication skills training. When teaching communication skills, one must also include (when not already included on other sections of the curriculum) other types of communication, such as relationship with colleagues, other healthcare professionals, community, critical reading, writing (e.g., reports), and self-presentation (e.g., clothes).

- **Self-care**: Stress, anxiety, and depression among medical students and physicians are well documented (Institute of Medicine, 2004). In medical school, students should learn stress management strategies to reduce psychological distress and anxiety; to recognize risk factors and signs of depression, anxiety, burnout, and substance abuse; and to know when to seek professional help. Medical students should also learn "to adopt wellness strategies that promote … wellbeing, … to create healthy, intimate relationships, to clarify personal values, and to openly discuss realistic strategies for creating balance in their lives" and include this in their professional lives (Institute of Medicine, 2004, p.71). Psychologists, because of their training, are in a good position to promote, as part of the medical school curriculum or as extra-curriculum activities, the well-being and emotional health of students.
- **Personal values and attitudes**: The personal values of medical students and physicians play an important role in their attitudes towards and interactions with others and influence their clinical decisions (Moyo, Goodyear-Smith, Weller, Robb, & Shulruf, 2016). Students should have opportunities to reflect and discuss (e.g., support groups) their difficult experiences during training and express their feelings, as well as learning from the experience of other students.
- **Teamwork skills**: Effective teamwork and interpersonal communication skills are essential for patient safety. Characteristics of effective teams include common purpose, measurable goals, effective leadership, effective communication, good cohesion, and mutual respect (WHO, 2012). Some of the necessary skills to be an effective team member (e.g., effective communication skills) may be taught by psychologists during medical school. However, teamwork skills training is often learned in multidisciplinary learning environments that include other healthcare students and/or professionals (e.g., nurses, social workers), active learning strategies, and feedback (Chakraborti, Boonyasai, Wright, & Kern, 2008). Interprofessional education is advocated by the World Health Organization (2010) as a key step to improve healthcare services. If health professionals learn to work collaboratively while they are still students, they will "enter the workplace as a member of the collaborative practice team" (WHO, 2010, p. 10). Psychologists in medical schools can help other faculty members train future generations of healthcare professionals in a collaborative and interprofessional way (Miyazaki, Gorayeb, Santos Junior, & Nakao, 2017).

## Conclusions

Behavioral sciences are an important component of medical education, and psychology can contribute to ensure that medical students develop relevant skills to become effective practitioners. However, psychologists teaching in medical schools must ensure they include contents that will be useful to medical practice. Health psychology contributes greatly to medical practice by helping future physicians develop skills that benefit patients, for example, how to improve adherence to medical regimens, and themselves, for instance, how to effectively manage the stress associated to the practice of medicine. This will lead to more efficient professionals and improve patients' quality of life.

## References

Association of American Medical Colleges. (2011). *Behavioral and social science foundations for future physicians. Report of the Behavioral and Social Science Expert Panel.* Retrieved form: https://www.aamc.org/system/files/d/1/271020-behavioralandsocialsciencefoundationsforfuturephysicians.pdf

Ayers, S., & de Visser, R. (2021). *Psychology for medicine and healthcare* (3rd ed.). London: Sage.

Azad, M. C., Fraser, K., Rumana, N., Abdullah, A. F., Shahana, N., Hanly, P. J., & Turin, T. C. (2015). Sleep disturbances among medical students: A global perspective. *Journal of Clinical Sleep Medicine, 11*(1), 69–74. https://doi.org/10.5664/jcsm.4370

Behavioural & Social Sciences Teaching in Medicine (BeSST) Psychology Steering Group. (2010). *A core curriculum for psychology in undergraduate medical education.* Available at: https://s3.eu-west-2.amazonaws.com/assets.creode.advancehe-document-manager/documents/hea/private/core-curriculum-for-psychology-undergrad-medical-education_1568036673.pdf

Benbassat, J., Baumal, R., Borkan, J. M., & Ber, R. (2003). Overcoming barriers to teaching the behavioral and social sciences to medical students. *Academic Medicine: Journal of the Association of American Medical Colleges, 78*(4), 372–380. https://doi.org/10.1097/00001888-200304000-00009

Braveman, P., & Gottlieb, L. (2014). The social determinants of health: It's time to consider the causes of the causes. *Public Health Reports, 129*(Suppl 2), 19–31. https://doi.org/10.1177/00333549141291S206

Center on the Developing Child at Harvard University. (2016). *From best practices to breakthrough impacts: A science-based approach to building a more promising future for young children and families.* Retrieved from https://developingchild.harvard.edu/resources/from-best-practices-to-breakthrough-impacts/

Chakraborti, C., Boonyasai, R. T., Wright, S. M., & Kern, D. E. (2008). A systematic review of teamwork training interventions in medical student and resident education. *Journal of General Internal Medicine, 23*(6), 846–853. https://doi.org/10.1007/s11606-008-0600-6

Cordingley, L., Peters, S., Hart, J., Rock, J., Hodges, L., McKendree, J., & Bundy, C. (2013). What psychology do medical students need to know? An evidence based approach to curriculum development. *Health and Social Care Education, 2*(2), 38–47. https://doi.org/10.11120/hsce.2013.00029

Cripa, J. A. (2019, February 6). USP é pioneira na criação do Departamento de Psicologia Médica [University of São Paulo in Ribeirao Preto is a pioneer in the creation of the Department of Medical Psychology]. *Jornal da USP.* Retrieved from: https://jornal.usp.br/artigos/usp-e-pioneira-na-criacao-do-departamento-de-psicologia-medica/#:~:text=O%20Departamento%20de%20Psicologia%20M%C3%A9dica,do%20ensino%20m%C3%A9dico%20no%20Brasil

Daltro, M. R., Jesus, M. L. S., Bôas, L. M., & Castelar, M. (2018). Ensino da psicologia em cursos de medicina no Brasil [Teaching psychology in medical schools in Brazil]. *Arquivos Brasileiros de Psicologia, 70*(2), 38–48. http://pepsic.bvsalud.org/pdf/arbp/v70n2/04.pdf

Dearborn, G. V. N. (1901). Psychology and the medical school. *Science, 14*(343), 129–136. https://doi.org/10.1126/science.14.343.129

Duarte, P. S., Miyazaki, M. C., Blay, S. L., & Sesso, R. (2009). Cognitive behavioral group therapy is an effective treatment for major depression in hemodialysis patients. *Kidney International, 76*, 414–421. https://pubmed.ncbi.nlm.nih.gov/19455196/

Duffy, T. P. (2011). The flexner report – 100 years later. *Yale Journal of Biology and Medicine, 84*, 269–276. https://pubmed.ncbi.nlm.nih.gov/21966046/

Dušek, T., & Bates, T. (2003). Analysis of European medical schools' teaching programs. *Croatian Medical Journal, 44*(1), 26–31. https://pubmed.ncbi.nlm.nih.gov/12590425/

Engel, G. L. (1977). The need for a new medical model: A challenge for biomedicine. *Science, 196*(4286), 129–136. https://pubmed.ncbi.nlm.nih.gov/847460/

Farre, A., & Rapley, T. (2014). The new old (and old new) medical model: Four decades navigating the biomedical and psychosocial understanding of health and illness. *Healthcare, 5*(4). https://doi.org/10.3390/healthcare5040088

Frank, J. R. (Ed.). (2005). *The CanMEDS 2005 physician competency framework. Better standards. Better physicians. Better care.* Ottawa: The Royal College of Physicians and Surgeons of Canada. Retrieved from: http://www.ub.edu/medicina_unitateducaciomedica/documentos/CanMeds.pdf

Frank, J. R., Snell, L., Sherbino, J, (Eds). (2015). *CanMEDS 2015 physician competency framework.* Ottawa: Royal College of Physicians and Surgeons of Canada. Retrieved from: http://www.ub.edu/medicina_unitateducaciomedica/documentos/CanMeds.pdf

Galagher, S., Wallace, S., Nathan, Y., & McGrath, D. (2015). 'Soft and fluffy': Medical students' attitudes towards psychology in medical education. *Journal of Health Psychology, 20*(1), 91–101. https://pubmed.ncbi.nlm.nih.gov/23988684/

General Medical Council. (2015). *Outcomes for graduates (Tomorrow's Doctors).* Retrieved from: https://www.gmc-uk.org/-/media/documents/outcomes-for-graduates-jul-15-1216_pdf-61408029.pdf

Gorayeb, R., Borsari, A. C. T., Rosa-e-Silva, A. C. J. S., & Ferriani, R. A. (2012). Brief cognitive behavioral intervention in groups in a Brazilian assisted reproduction program. *Behavioral Medicine, 38*, 29–35. https://pubmed.ncbi.nlm.nih.gov/22676628/

Harden, J., & Carr, J. E. (2017). Social and behavioural sciences in the medical school curriculum. In J. A. Dent, R. M. Harden, & D. Hunt (Eds.), *A practical guide to medical teachers* (pp. 180–187). Edinburgh: Elsevier. https://core.ac.uk/download/pdf/35276612.pdf

Institute of Medicine. (2004). *Improving medical education: Enhancing the behavioral and social science content of medical school curriculum.* Washington, DC: The National Academies Press. https://doi.org/10.17226/10956

Litva, A., & Peters, S. (2008). Exploring barriers to teaching behavioral and social sciences in medical education. *Medical Education, 42*, 309–314. https://onlinelibrary.wiley.com/doi/10.1111/j.1365-2923.2007.02951.x

Lutfiyya, M. N., Chang, L. F., McGrath, C., Dana, C., & Lipsky, M. S. (2019). The state of the science of interprofessional collaborative practice: a scoping review of the patient health-related outcomes based on literature published between 2010 and 2018. *Plos One, 14*(6), e0218578. https://doi.org/10.1371/journal.pone.0218578

Martin, L. R., Haskard-Zolnierek, K. B., & DiMatteo, M. R. (2010). *Health behavior change and treatment adherence. Evidence-based guidelines for improving healthcare.* Oxford: OUP. https://psycnet.apa.org/record/2010-03911-000

Matarazzo, J. D. (1994). Psychology in a medical school: A personal account of a department´s 35-year history. *Journal of Clinical Psychology, 50*(1), 7–36. https://www.ohsu.edu/sites/default/files/2019-06/Matarazzo-1994-PDF.pdf

Matarazzo, J. D., Carmody, T. P., & Gentry, W. D. (1981). Psychologists on the faculties of United States schools of medicine: Past, present and possible future. *Clinical Psychology Review, 1*, 293–317. https://www.sciencedirect.com/science/article/pii/0272735881900088?via%3Dihub

McKinley, D. W., & Ghaffarifar, S. (2021). The necessity of examining patients' social behavior and teaching behavior change theories: Curriculum innovations induced by the COVID-19 pandemic. *BMC Medical Education, 21*(1), 150. https://doi.org/10.1186/s12909-021-02582-2

Miyazaki, M. C., Gorayeb, R., Santos Junior, R., & Nakao, R. (2017). O trabalho do psicólogo em equipes de saúde [Psychologists' working in healthcare teams]. In: Sociedade Brasileira de Psicologia, R. Gorayeb, M. C. Miyazaki, & M. Teodoro (Orgs.). *PROPSICO Programa de*

*Atualização em Psicologia Clínica e da Saúde*: Ciclo 1 (pp.43-76). Porto Alegre: Artmed Panamericana.

Moyo, M., Goodyear-Smith, F. A., Weller, J., Robb, G., & Shulruf, B. (2016). Healthcare practitioners' personal and professional values. *Advances in Health Sciences Education, 21*, 257–286. https://link.springer.com/article/10.1007/s10459-015-9626-9

Nguyen, K. H., Chien, A. T., Meyers, D. J., Li, Z., Singer, S. J., & Rosenthal, M. B. (2020). Team-based primary care practice transformation initiative and changes in patient experience and recommended cancer screening rates. *INQUIRY: The Journal of Health Care Organization, Provision, and Financing, 57*, 1–8. https://www.ncbi.nlm.nih.gov/pmc/articles/PMC7453437/

Ouakinin, S. (2016). Teaching psychology in medicine: The context, methodologies, and doctor's professional identity. *Acta Médica Portuguesa, 29*(12), 869–874. https://doi.org/10.20344/amp.8384

Petrie, K. J., & Weinman, J. A. (1997). *Perceptions of health & illness*. Amsterdan: Harwood Academic Publishers.

Pickren, W. (2007). Psychology and medical education: A historical perspective from the United States. *Indian Journal of Psychiatry, 49*, 179–181. https://doi.org/10.4103/0019-5545.37318

Puthran, R., Zhang, M. W. B., Tam, W. W., & Ho, R. C. (2016). Prevalence of depression amongst medical students: A meta-analysis. *Medical Education, 50*(4), 456–468. https://doi.org/10.1111/medu.12962

Robiner, W. N., Hong, B. A., & Ward, W. (2020). Psychologists' contributions to medical education and interprofessional education in medical schools. *Journal of Clinical Psychology in Medical Settings.* https://doi.org/10.1007/s10880-020-09730-8

Rosenberg, M. (2012). Undertreated pain epidemic: Multi-modality approach to pain management. *Journal of Managed Care Medicine, 15*(1), 30–37. https://www.namcp.org/journals/jmcm/articles/15-1/Undertreated%20Pain.pdf

Russell, A., Teijlingen, E., Lambert, H., & Stacy, R. (2004). Social and behavioural science education in UK medical schools: Current practice and future directions. *Medical Education, 38*, 409–417. https://pubmed.ncbi.nlm.nih.gov/15025642/

Saunders, M., Barr, B., McHale, P., & Hamelmann, C. (2017). *Key policies for addressing the social determinants of health and health inequities.* Copenhagen. WHO Regional Office for Europe (Health Evidence Network (HEN) Synthesis report 52). Retrieved from: https://www.who.int/publications/i/item/9789289052658

Schumacher, J. A., & Williams, D. C. (2020). *Psychological treatment of medical patients struggling with harmful substance use.* Washington, DC: American Psychological Association. https://doi.org/10.1037/0000160-002

Silverman, J., Kurts, S., & Draper, J. (2013). *Skills for communicating with patients* (3rd ed.). London: Radcliffe.

Skelton, J. R. (2017). Clinical communication. In J. A. Dent, R. M. Harden, & D. Hunt (Eds.), *A practical guide to medical teachers* (5th ed., pp. 188–194). London: Elsevier.

Tabatabaei, Z., Yazdani, S., & Sadeghi, R. (2016). Barriers to integration of behavioral and social sciences in the general medicine curriculum and recommended strategies to overcome them: A systematic review. *Journal of Advances in Medical Education and Professionalism, 4*(3), 111–121. https://pubmed.ncbi.nlm.nih.gov/27382578/

Taylor, S. E. (2017). *Health Psychology* (10th ed.). New York: McGraw-Hill.

*The Bologna Declaration of 19 June 1999: Joint declaration of the European Ministers of Education.* Retrieved from: https://www.eurashe.eu/library/bologna_1999_bologna-declaration-pdf/

U.S. Department of Health and Human Services (2020). *Healthy people 2030.* Retrieved from https://health.gov/healthypeople

Visser, R. (2009). Psychology in the medical curriculum: "need to know" or "nice to know". *The European Health Psychologist, 11*, 20–23. https://www.ehps.net/ehp/index.php/contents/article/view/ehp.v11.i2.p20/942

Wade, D. T., & Halligan, P. W. (2017). The biopsychosocial model of illness: a model whose time has come. *Clinical Rehabilitation, 31*(8), 995–1004. https://doi.org/10.1177/0269215517709890

Ward, W., Shaffer, L. A., & Testa, E. G. (2018). Pediatric psychologists' collaboration in a National Pediatric Obesity Initiative: A case study in interprofessional collaboration. *Journal of Clinical Psychology in Medical Settings, 25*(4), 367–389. https://doi.org/10.1007/s10880-018-9540-4

Wells, F. L. (1913). The advancement of psychological medicine. *Popular Science Monthly, 82*, 177–186.

World Federation for Medical Education. (2020). *Basic medical education WFME global standards for quality improvement. The 2020 Revision.* Retrieved from: https://wfme.org/standards/bme/

World Health Organization – WHO. (2010). *Framework for action on interprofessional education & collaborative practice.* Retrieved from: http://apps.who.int/iris/bitstream/handle/10665/70185/WHO_HRH_HPN_10.3_eng.pdf;jsessionid=5D00FD42D9C26B3B3154CCE77009253E?sequence=1

World Health Organization – WHO. (2012). *Being an effective team player.* Retrieved from:https://www.who.int/patientsafety/education/curriculum/course4_handout.pdf

World Health Organization – WHO. (2016). *Global strategy on human resources for health: Workforce 2030.* Retrieved from: https://www.who.int/hrh/resources/global_strategy_workforce2030_14_print.pdf?ua=1

World Health Organization – WHO. (2020). *World health statistics 2020: Monitoring health for the SDGs, Sustainable Development Goals.* Geneva: WHO. Retrieved from: https://apps.who.int/iris/bitstream/handle/10665/332070/9789240005105-eng.pdf?sequence=1&isAllowed=y

# Psychology of Art

## 41

Lia da Rocha Lordelo

## Contents

| | |
|---|---|
| Introduction | 994 |
| Purposes and Rationale of the Curriculum in Psychology of Art | 994 |
| Classic Approaches to the Intersection "Art" and "Psychology" | 995 |
| Psychoanalysis and Its Outspreads | 995 |
| The Contribution of Carl Gustav Jung | 997 |
| Lev. S. Vygotsky and His Legacy on Psychology of Art | 998 |
| Gestalt Psychology: Art and Perception | 999 |
| Beyond the Classics: Recent Approaches Interfacing Psychology and Art | 1000 |
| A Shift in Focus: From Objects to People | 1001 |
| Psychology of Art's Focus on People: A Performative Turn | 1002 |
| Some Teaching, Learning, and Assessment Resources | 1004 |
| Articulate Theoretical Interests Within Psychology to Contents in Classroom | 1004 |
| Consider the Profile of the Classroom | 1004 |
| Work with Seminal Texts Using Visual/Audio/Literary "Resources" | 1004 |
| Stimulate Fruition | 1005 |
| Reading References | 1005 |
| From within | 1005 |
| From Outside Psychology | 1006 |
| Cross-References | 1007 |
| References | 1007 |

### Abstract

This chapter presents an introductory overview on the psychology of art, a field of expertise almost as old as Psychology itself. The first theoretical section outlines classic contributions for the area, like psychoanalysis, analytical psychology, Gestalt theory, and the contribution of the soviet cultural-historical school of psychology, represented by Lev S. Vygotsky. The second part briefly highlights more recent

L. da Rocha Lordelo (✉)
Federal University of Recôncavo of Bahia, Santo Amaro da Purificação, Brazil
e-mail: lialordelo@ufrb.edu.br

© Springer Nature Switzerland AG 2023
J. Zumbach et al. (eds.), *International Handbook of Psychology Learning and Teaching*,
Springer International Handbooks of Education,
https://doi.org/10.1007/978-3-030-28745-0_48

contributions widely disseminated in several theoretical approaches within current Psychology; these last contributions appear closely connected to historic transformations in the art world as from the end of the nineteenth century. It is our goal, with this chapter, to provide psychology teachers with a more sophisticated understanding of artistic human experience – however broad that phenomenon might seem.

**Keywords**

Art · Psychology · Artists · Aesthetic experience · Art appreciation · Aesthetics

## Introduction

Psychology of art is a field of expertise almost as old as Psychology itself, as it can be seen through one of its pioneers´ contribution on the subject. In 1876, Gustav Fechner published on Aesthetics (Fechner, 1876), and this is one of his early works in Psychology. Another classic contribution comes from Sigmund Freud's *Delusion and Dream in Jensen's Gradiva* (1907), one of his most important analyses of literary works. However old – in relation to scientific psychology – psychology of art might be, its relevance is still up for discussion, as scholars argue (Dickie, 1962; Reber, 2008; Lindel & Mueller, 2011). Recent research in the field has attempted, mainly from different theoretical perspectives, such as cognitive, cultural, neuropsychological, phenomenological, and evolutionary ones, to integrate art theory/aesthetics and psychological findings in order to have a more sophisticated understanding of artistic human experience – however broad that phenomenon might seem. The scope of that definition – artistic experience – will be defined according to each specific theoretical and methodological perspective – which is a common procedure in many branches of psychology itself.

However unique all these approaches in psychology of art are, in terms of definition of their main object, their most usual methods of research and practical application, they seem to be united by a few common points: first, that art is a controversial, but unique and crucial feature of human experience (Leder, Gerger, Dressler, Schabman, 2012), dating back from human species´ first traces on the planet. Second, is that, as much as artists, also philosophers, economists, and anthropologists, psychologists can and must appreciate, study, and try to understand art from their own point of view. Third, neither psychologists nor any of these scholars will be ever able to give full, definite explanations on what art is, under the risk of deflating or simply wearing out its value and meaning.

## Purposes and Rationale of the Curriculum in Psychology of Art

Considering that psychology of art is not a mandatory course in Psychology undergraduate curriculums in general,[1] learning about it must go beyond the acknowledgment of different psychological theories. There are naturally a great number of

---

[1] That is the reality in most Psychology undergraduate, graduate, and postgraduate courses in my country of origin, Brazil.

questions formulated by these branches: how does art give meaning to our lives? More specifically, how does being an artist interfere in people's attitudes and their coping with professional or health issues? And yet, which psychological processes are involved in the appreciation of a work or art (be it a song, a poem, or a painting)? How do factors such as artistic experience or expertise, economic status or cultural background influence that appreciation process? Which specific parts of the brain are responsible for that? Are there significant differences in the process of appreciation of art pieces as distinct from each other as, let's say, a Renaissance painting by Italian artist Michelangelo and a large-scale light installation by Danish artist Olafur Eliasson? Are famous, genial artists simply born with their talents?

The list of questions is endless. Psychology students interested in psychology of art will be able to formulate adequate (although partial) answers to these questions in light of the specific theories that address these issues. But perhaps more importantly, they should also be able to appreciate art works in a less naive, more careful way, precisely because they are able to think of the questions described above. In the end, all these questions come down to a simple statement: relating to a work of art (watching, listening to it, making it with one's own hands) is mainly an act of interest (Coli, 2011), and psychologists can help this uniquely human act to be cultivated, cherished, and enriched. Psychology of art can and must be extremely useful in the art education field, reminded that artists are being formed in independent art academies and institutes, as well as in undergraduate courses at universities,[2] since the middle of the last century. Besides contributing to developing artists, psychology of art is decisive in artistic mediation processes in general, which includes art teaching for children and teenagers in elementary and high school educational levels, and above all aesthetic and educational programs in art museums and institutions, as well as less formal contexts of art appreciation.

## Classic Approaches to the Intersection "Art" and "Psychology"

### Psychoanalysis and Its Outspreads

Psychoanalysis, although remaining a somewhat controversial approach in scientific psychology, particularly in some countries, constitutes one of the first and most significant contributions to the psychology of art. It is actually sintomatic that, on the verge of the twentieth century in central Europe, one could trace connections between psychoanalysts and artists from several expressions. The admiration was mutual. Sigmund Freud would write to famous Austrian writer Arthur Schnitzler, who he greatly admired: "I have gained the impression that you have learned through intuition – though actually as a result of sensitive introspection – everything that I have had to unearth by laborious work on other persons"

---

[2] The "institutionally accredited artist" (Firunts, 2016) first appeared on the scene, in the USA, in the 1960s. This is an important landmark for the professionalization in the arts field: artists starting to be formed, trained, and doing research in formal, academic settings.

(Kupper & Rollman-Branch, 1959). French author Anaïs Nin, another great admirer of psychoanalysis, wrote a preface to Otto Rank's Art and Artist (Nin, 1968). Although Freud had initially analyzed psychopathic personality types on a theatrical stage a year before,[3] he definitely devoted more efforts torward the analyses of literary and visual works (Freud, 1970, 2012). Apart from his historical analysis of Jensen's Gradiva (Freud, 1907), one of his most important works is about the day-dreaming of creative writers (1908). In that analysis, Freud shows himself intrigued by the fact that writers usually can't explain to themselves or the audience how they come up with the material with which they work, or which are their sources. He then parallels the creative writer with the child at play; probably because the imaginary processes at stake in doing literature are initially present in childhood. "The creative writer does the same as the child at play. He creates a world of phantasy which he takes very seriously – that is, which he invests with large amounts of emotion – while separating it sharply from reality" (Freud, 1908, p. 421). In the next excerpt, one can see the principles of psychoanalysis more clearly expressed in the mechanism of day-dreaming, which would explain artistic creation:

> As people grow up, then, they cease to play, and they seem to give up the yield of pleasure which they gained from playing. But whoever understands the human mind knows that hardly anything is harder for a man than to give up a pleasure which he has once experienced. ***Actually, we can never give anything up; we only exchange one thing for another. What appears to be a renunciation is really the formation of a substitute or surrogate.*** [emphasis added] In the same way, the growing child, when he stops playing, gives up nothing but the link with real objects; instead of playing, he now phantasies. He builds castles in the air and creates what are called day-dreams. (Freud, 1908, p. 423)

The basic difference between the child's play and the adult's phantasy, which are determined by desires, is that the child wishes he or she were a grownup; and the adults fantasize for unfulfilled desires, of which they are usually ashamed.

There is one last exciting comment in Freud's work. He claims that these products of imagination are changing throughout a person's life. These phantasies and day-dreams must fit reality, which means there is a strong connection between phantasy and time – the individual in the course of his or her development.

Otto Rank, a psychoanalyst colleague who eventually distanced himself intellectually (and personally, later on) from Freud's emphases on the Oedipal complex, is also known for contributions to the psychology of the artist. He claimed that scientific psychology had failed to explain artistic creativity and that would have led us to dismiss psychological contributions to the study of art. In opposition, he was deeply interested in art, but strictly related to the problem of personality development, and believed that the urge to create did not find expressions only in works of art, but also in mythology and religion (an idea that would be also explored by Jung) (Nin, 1968): "In any case we can say of all artistic creation that the artist not

---

[3] This work remains unpublished to the present day.

only creates his art, but also uses art in order to create" (Rank, 1989, p. 7). In his most important book on the subject, *Art and the Artist* (Rank, 1989), he especially dedicated himself to changes on the meaning of art forms, analyzing primitive art collections as much as abstract modern art.

Ernst Kris, a trained psychoanalyst but historically connected to the ego psychology school, along with names such as Anna Freud, Erik Erikson, and Carl G. Jung, was also an art historian who became renowned by his book *Psychoanalytic explorations in art* (Kris, 1968). His analysis of German sculptor Franz Messerschmidt remains famous to present days, as he links aspects of the artist's schizofrenic personality to features of his natural-sized busts, with strong facial expressions inspired by his own.

Psychoanalysis is probably the first important and popular theoretical contribution, within Psychology, to art theory. However, that theoretical force was heavily supported by clinical, psychopathological studies – as is the case of sculptor Messerschmidt. In his case, for instance, Kris would say that that childhood experiences influenced all the artist's thoughts, dreams, and artistic creations. For Brazilian art theorist Ostrower, traumas and past experiences can, of course, influence, but not determine overall a creative situation (Ostrower, 1999). In her opinion, to believe in that assertion is to ignore art's own language and standards; to use or apply psychoanalytic concepts and methods to the art world is to reduce that world. That constitutes a relevant issue in the psychology of art, for, we mentioned earlier, it is not reasonable for Psychology to give full, definite explanations on what art is. Nonetheless, psychoanalysis' insights into the minds of creative artists and how these people constitute their motivations for creation still stand as exciting contributions to the field of artistic creation.

## The Contribution of Carl Gustav Jung

The cooperation and mutual admiration between Freud and Jung has been widely documented – particular through their personal correspondence (Freud & Jung, 1976), as have been their disagreement and estrangement. Jung would object to the necessary sexual nature of traumas advocated by Freud, and would, within time, develop his own psychological concepts, such as collective uncounscious, archetypes, which are central for when analytical pscyhology studies art.

One of Jung's major disagreements in relation to Freud's approach to the analysis or works of art, according to Quiroga Mendez (2010), was his reductionist view on that analysis.

> Neuroses and psychoses are likewise reducible to infantile relations with the parents, and so are a man's good and bad habits, his beliefs, peculiarities, passions, interests, and so forth. It can hardly be supposed that all these very different things must have exactly the same explanation, for otherwise we would be driven to the conclusion that they actually are the same thing. *If a work of art is explained in the same way as a neurosis, then either the work of art is a neurosis or a neurosis is a work of art.* [emphasis added] (Jung, 1978a, p. 67)

The collective unconscious, manifested through archetypes, would be a source from which all artistic experience would be generated, but it is important to pay attention to art's symbolic nature. Art is symbolic because, like other phenomena such as myths and spiritual beliefs, it is a human experience capable of putting someone in contact with his or her collective unconscious, which generates between conscious and unconscious dimensions a process of connection or communication that engenders a third, necessary and common element for both (Mendez, 2010, p. 57). It is also important to stress that Jung believed that a pathological condition could not explain the quality or success of a work of art. His analytical approach to art, although centered on psychological processes of integration of unconscious and conscious experiences, did not try to lay down the artist on the psychoanalytic couch, but was rather interested on art in a transpersonal, transgenerational scale (Gaillard, 2010): art is mainly linked to the progressive transformations of a culture within time, through successful generations:

> The normal man can follow the general trend without injury to himself; but the man who takes to the back streets and alleys because he cannot endure the broad highway will be the first to discover the psychic elements that are waiting to play their part in the life of the collective. Here the artist's relative lack of adaptation turns out to his advantage; it enables him to follow his own yearnings far from the beaten path, and to discover what it is that would meet the unconscious needs of his age. (Jung, 1978a, p. 83)

## Lev. S. Vygotsky and His Legacy on Psychology of Art

If Vygotsky's approach to art is not his most important legacy to psychological studies, it is certainly crucial to his own entrance in Psychology (Van der Veer & Valsiner, 1996). His academic training was in Law and History, but the years working as teacher in his hometown made him interested in psychological and pedagogical issues that led to building a research program that later became known as the Cultural-Historical Psychology school, along with other fundamental Soviet scholars, such as Alexis Leontiev and Alexander Luria. Vygotsky received his doctoral degree with a dissertation on the psychology of art (Vigotski, 2001), which was based on a previous essay on William Shakespeare's Hamlet, written when he has 19 years old (Vigotski, 1999). And while it is true that his approach, as Freud's (Ostrower, 1999) can be considered quite logocentric (Smagorinsky, 2011), focusing for the most part on literature, Vygotsky's attention to theater – which is a practice also traditionally focused on language – is uncommon among psychologists interested in art. This is understandable in part because visual arts and literature are more popular artistic languages in general; but that also points to some of Vygotsky's very original contributions: he showed interested in the psychology of the actor, that is, the process of constructing a theatrical character and how to express these emotions on stage. These concerns are strictly linked to Konstantin Stanislavski's (2013a, b) system of interpretation; specifically, Vygotsky referred to *perezhivanie*, a concept roughly translated as "emotional experience," in several of his writings (1994, 1999,

2001). If on a certain level *perezhivanie* was described as an emotional state of the creating artist, explaining the intrinsic emotional character of a work of art, on a deeper level Vygotsky's notion intended to define a set of emotions inherent to human performance, highlighting the understated role of emotions in human development and building a connection between emotion and imagination (Smagorinsky, 2011; Gonzalez Rey, 2018). "This means that, in essence, all our fantastic experiences take place on a completely real emotional basis. We see, therefore, that emotion and imagination are not two separate processes; on the contrary, they are the same process" (Vygotsky, 1971, p. 210).

It is also important to notice one significant feature of Vygotsky´ contribution to art that distinguishes it particularly from the psychoanalytic approach. In what can be considered a highly developmental approach, he envisioned art as a method for building life, claiming that "(a)rt is the organization of our future behavior. It is a requirement that may never be fulfilled but that forces us to strive beyond our life toward all that lies beyond it" (Vygotsky, 1971, p. 253). That orientation toward the future was very different from classic psychoanalytic views, which attempted to understand connections between artistic practices of artists and their personalities, linking the formation of those to experiences that had happened in their past.

This developmental view we are referring to will grow into psychological approaches to art, imagination, and creative processes within contemporary cultural psychology, as we will see in the reading references.

## Gestalt Psychology: Art and Perception

As the history of Psychology teaches us, Gestalt theory came along as a kind of third force in a context where the first behavioral psychologists were confronting idealistic approaches in the field, in the very beginning of the twentieth century. The very basic notion of Gestalt theory – that the whole is different from the sum of its parts – turned out to be, from the very beginning, extremely appealing for those willing to understand how we appreciate art. The theoretical system developed by German/Austrian[4] psychologists Wolfgang Köhler, Max Wertheimer, and Kurt Koffka understood perception in a holistic, integrated manner that would not, for that matter, completely decompose a painting in order to analyze it. Instead, according to its most basic tenet, the whole picture would be more important than its elements – texture, color, spatial composition, and so on. The laws of perception, initially proposed by Wertheimer (1923), but further developed by the others, such as proximity, continuity, similarity, etc., could be found very clearly especially in the case of visual works; and also in music, which was the object of investigation of one other seminal

---

[4]Although the three scholars were trained in universities in Germany and Austria, Köhler was originally born in Estonia; and Wertheimer was born in Prague, in Austro-Hungary at the time. And eventually, with after the First World War, all of them went to the United States and constituted their lives there.

research paper by von Ehrenfels (1890) for constituting Gestalt psychology. Interestingly, by stating that "(t)he Gestalt-Theorie is more than a theory of perception; it is even more than a mere psychological theory" (Koffka, 1922), gestaltists believed there was more to Gestalt than to only identify and describe basic psychological processes. Rudolf Arnheim (1986), who became a central figure in Gestalt psychology applied to the study of art, made reference to that singular theoretical undertaking within Psychology, which at the same time, tried to make sense of phenomena outside the realms of traditional psychological science:

> Finally, although gestalt psychologists in what may be called their polemical period had to concentrate many of their demonstrations and discussions on the organizational and self-regulatory aspects of gestalt structure, they were very much concerned from the beginning with the biological, cognitive, and aesthetic reward of gestalt processes, namely the creation of well-functioning, stable, and clarifying patterns in nature, science, and art--a perfection difficult or impossible to obtain otherwise. (Arnheim, 1986, p. 823)

It is from Arnheim, one of the most influential books on art and visual perception (Arnheim, 2005), widely used in university courses, especially in visual arts. As an art theorist, in his studies, he was concerned with showing that Gestalt was not only a theory of perception of form, but that the qualitative aspect of what was being perceived was extremely linked to the degree of internal articulation of stimuli patterns and conditions of actualization of the perceptive field (Ferraz & Kastrup, 2010). "Rather than limiting itself to offering a method of combining and segregating perceptual shapes, gestalt theory is concerned primarily with the complex dynamics of organization in field situations, be they physical or psychological" (Arnheim, 1986, p. 823). This is probably the reason why Gestalt became so central for analyzing visual works of art.

## Beyond the Classics: Recent Approaches Interfacing Psychology and Art

The theoretical contributions listed above are not, of course, the only ones existing in Psychology's first 70 years of existence – that is, mainly from its origin in 1870s until the 1950s. But they certainly stand out as the ones that became most popular within Psychology – and especially in the case of Psychoanalysis, outside it, to a wider audience constituted by artists, art critics, and art enthusiasts. These contributions are enrooted in specific epistemological and methodological orientations that refer to the very constitution of Psychology – the first schools of thought that appeared in European countries in the end of the nineteenth century. But since these first efforts, other ways to explore the psychology of art have emerged from distinct theoretical points of view, from predominantly philosophical psychological approaches to approaches that integrate scientific fields such as neurology and theory of evolution, viewing human artistic experiences as an interdisciplinary object of investigation.

One important thing that needs to be addressed is that what we call "psychology of art" is actually a field as diverse as is the field we have learned to call "psychology." Aesthetic appreciation; artistic experience; artistic behavior; aesthetic orientation torward artifacts; passive and active exposure to artworks; creative processes are some of the terms or phenomena addressed to within this field, and we can say that they can all be, for different reasons, included as possible topics when studying psychology of art.

## A Shift in Focus: From Objects to People

Art as an autonomous field was well established until the nineteenth century, as an object *par excellence* studied by Art History or Aesthetics – a branch of Philosophy. Nonetheless, the creation of psychology of art as a field might have been a consequence of the insertion of the person in that equation, whether as a passive audience or a creative artist. This means there was a shift in focus: while art historians and philosophers would focus on the work or art and built frameworks and criteria of analysis based on it – constituting and identifying art schools, periods, recurring motives and styles; psychologists began to try to understand how people related to these motives and styles, how they experienced them and how or if these impacted in their lives.

This is how, for instance, psychologists connected to phenomenology have attempted to provide with a psychological perspective such a philosophical tradition as art appreciation with contributions from Martin Heidegger (2007) and Maurice Merleau-Ponty (1962; 2013). For authors interested in this approach (Roald, 2008), the emphasis on phenomenological psychology is on actual, lived human experience; they also stress that "(t)he questions of the nature of art and of its appreciation cannot, however, exist independently" (Roald, 2008, p. 190). So, experience is crucial. Live, dynamic, concrete experiences in the life-world. Other experiential accounts evoke contributions of John Dewey (1934), Mikhail Bakhtin (1984, 1990), and Vygotsky, already mentioned here, to focus on "embodied, felt, emotional, intellectual, and intersubjective" sense-making processes (Sullivan & McCarthy, 2009). Another distinctive feature of these experiential approaches to appreciation of art is their preference for qualitative methodologies and their sensitivity to single variations of human experience, instead of looking at patterns of appreciation that constitute generalizable, abstract scientific principles on the subject.

That methodological feature contrasts immensely with other contemporary approaches in the field, namely, evolutionary and cognitive neuroaesthetic ones. Nadal and Skov (2013) claim that it might be hasty to talk about art from the beginning of the history of humanity; but we might refer to neurobiological substrates of aesthetic experience as a field of inquiry existing for a couple of centuries now. They define neuroaesthetics as "experimental studies of brain mechanisms involved in the appreciation of art and aesthetics" (Nadal & Skov, 2013, p. 2). Moreover, it can be defined as

> the study of the neural processes [underlying] the psychological processes that are evoked in the creator or the viewer of the object in the course of interacting with it. These psychological processes may involve perceptual, sensory, cognitive, emotional, evaluative, and social

aspects among others, all of which are presumed to have a biological—neural— basis. (Skov & Vartanian, 2009, p. 3)

Researchers in the field of neuroaesthetics believe that the boundaries between art and not art, as well as focusing on art objects specifically, go against the proper understanding of aesthetic experience, for, as they say, "notions of art, artist, and artwork are culturally and historically contingent, as are the criteria used to distinguish what is an artwork from what is not, or what is an art form from what is not" (Nadal & Skov, 2013, p. 5). Evolutionary approaches contribute to that discussion reminding us that art in non-Western societies, or what we call art, are not exclusively (sometimes, not at all) centered on objects and permeate a much broader range of activities – celebrations, rituals, and other events (Zaidel, Nadal, Flexas, and Munar, 2013). That distinction and other significant archaeological evidence suggest a biological ancestral origin for these reactions we call aesthetic appreciation. According to De Smedt and Cruz (2010, p. 697), these current scientific investigations on art reflect recent theoretical and conceptual developments in psychology, in particular the decline of behaviorism and the growing influence of evolutionary theory. Another example of recent theoretical contribution within that tendency is the cognitive models of art appreciation developed by Leder, Belke, Oeberst, and Augustin (2004), in which authors propose an influential framework of aesthetic experiences and aesthetic judgments, through a cognitive model of information-processing stages; there are, of course, other contributions within that theoretical orientation, especially dedicated to connecting artistic creation and reception (Tinio, 2013).

That change in the object of inquiry and also in theoretical frameworks might situate another subtle change when it comes to the majority of investigations in the psychology of art: if, in the first classic theoretical endeavors, psychologists tended to focus almost exclusively in world famous works and artists – from Freud's analysis of Michelangelo's Moses (Freud, 1955), for instance, but also in several other analyses which explore the works of artists like Pablo Picasso and James Joyce (Jung, 1978b) or Paul Cezanne (Arnheim, 2005); the most recent theoretical efforts have replaced that interest in artists and works that constitute landmarks in the history of Western art for an interest in more anonymous creators. In a sense, to be interested in anonymous – that is, not recognized by wide audiences and prestigious critics – artists is a consequence of that already mentioned shift in focus (from objects to people) as well as a clear recognition that the standards for defining what is (good, worthy of analysis) art and what is not are culturally, economically, and historically defined.

## Psychology of Art's Focus on People: A Performative Turn

Focusing on how people are and act in the world using an aesthetic perspective is a recent, exciting development in the psychology of art. That change has probably also been guided by what we must ackowledge as a performative turn in the arts in general, according to Fischer-Lichte (2008). Throughout the twentieth century,

(...) the dissolution of boundaries in the arts, repeatedly proclaimed and observed by artists, art critics, scholars of art, and philosophers, can be defined as a performative turn. Be it art, music, literature, or theatre, the creative process tends to be realized in and as performance (Fischer-Lichte, 2008, p. 22)

That performative turn, as I stated before (Lordelo, 2018), is conceptually linked to the linguistic turn that took place in Philosophy as well as in Linguistics in the beginning of the twentieth century. Scholars working under that framework would start to claim there could be no radical distinction between language and the world, for it is the words and symbols we use that establish the reality as we live it. One of the most relevant contributions in that field comes from John Austin (1962) and his speech acts theory. To sum up, the theory set the grounds to understanding that speaking always involves acting; the performative, as theorized by Austin and other seminal authors such as Judith Butler (1988), also has the ability to destabilize and even collapse binary oppositions – speaking X acting, world X language, etc. Fighting against these dichotomies has substantial implications for a new understanding not only in the arts in general, but especially in the way we, psychologists, might view human aesthetic experience – but not only. Scholars in this field such as Schechner (2006) explain that we can find performances in many situations (seen separately or intertwined): in daily life, sports, sex, in rituals, business situations, etc., and also in art itself. From this claim, it is possible to conclude that performance is a broad concept that includes art, but does not limit itself to it. In a way, for Schechner, not everything is meant to be performance, but virtually everything can be seen as performance.

These contributions from Philosophy and Performance Studies are crucial for new, integrated ways of approaching psychology of art, mainly because it becomes virtually impossible for psychologists to ignore the changes through which artistic languages have gone. Artists like Allen Kaprow (1993), part of the influential Fluxus Group,[5] have written on the subject, saying that art cannot be seen as something people do – separately from their lives and how they understand themselves. Within that logic, art becomes a diffuse activity, completely linked to life. In one of his essays, he defends the idea of a lifelike art, as opposed to artlike art. Art ceases to be seen as something we do, for it constitutes who we are. In a very broad sense, performance can exist only as actions, interactions, and relationships, continuously marking and changing our identities (Goffman, 1959; Schechner, 2006). For instance, the notion of performativity, which became so seminal for Gender Studies, refers, somehow, to that: these scholars state that gender is not a fact, but a construction, and the "body becomes its gender through a series of acts which are renewed, revised, and consolidated through time" (Butler, 1988, p. 523).

---

[5] Fluxus was a group founded in New York City in the 1960s, by influential artists such as Allen Kaprow, Nam Jum Paik, John Cage, Joseph Beuys, Yoko Ono, and others who were interested in experimental, interdisciplinary art projects.

It is an exciting but challenging turn for the psychology of art to deal with such vibrant theoretical contributions, which come directly from transformations in our understandings of artistic works and processes.

## Some Teaching, Learning, and Assessment Resources

As we have seen throughout this chapter, psychology of art is a wide, heterogeneous field filled with classic psychological references. Nonetheless, it has recently not only been injected with theoretical approaches that call for an interdisciplinary attitude within the area, but also been challenged with contributions from outside of Psychology that are connected to paradigmatic changes in the understandings of artistic practices that took place in the twentieth century. Considering that overview, we present some recommendations for psychology of art teachers in their daily study and practice:

### Articulate Theoretical Interests Within Psychology to Contents in Classroom

We have mentioned before that theoretical diversity in the psychology art refers to a great extent to the diversity in Psychology itself. It is also worth reminding that this is not a mandatory set of theories of course for a Psychology degree. That means that each course in psychology of art might reflect the theoretical inclinations and, most of all, interests and curiosities among the students taking that class.

### Consider the Profile of the Classroom

Contents and discussions in the psychology of art can be of interest not only for psychology students, but also for artists or art students – in literature, music, performing arts, etc. It is important, then, to adjust contents of the course. We know there is a great contribution for visual arts within Gestalt Psychology, as there are important psychoanalytical, junguian concepts that raise important issues concerning creative processes for literary artists, for example. These choices are worth making, for the benefit of the course.

### Work with Seminal Texts Using Visual/Audio/Literary "Resources"

We have become acquainted, throughout this chapter, with several classic texts within psychology of art. These should be definitely present in a psychology of art course. In addition, paintings, installations, plays, and songs are more than aid resources; they are integral part of the theoretical content of the class, mainly because they constitute one of the objects of interest in the field. So it is highly important that art works and artists, their profiles or biographies, permeate the classes; not only those who are quoted in the texts that are read and discussed, but also some that look similar – and sometimes, for an analytical contrast – and radically different.

## Stimulate Fruition

There is hardly any point in teaching about the psychology of art if one does not show any interest in an art piece, whichever it is. Therefore, as teachers, it is part of our task to estimulate that interest – whether through showing art works in the classroom, or drawing attention to specific artists that relate to the contents in the course, or maybe even drawing attention to an exhibition or dance piece that is being shown in town. That act of interest and engagement is crucial for any good learning in the psychology of art.

## Reading References

These texts and books are other references that might be interesting to get to know, for they are not mentioned in this introductory chapter; the references within Psychology represent new, exciting ways to articulate psychological issued with artistic ones; and the ones outside it help us comprehend more clearly transformations in the arts, especially since the last century, as well as contemporary debates they generate:

## From within

1. May, R. (1980). The courage to create. New York: Bantam Book.

Humanist psychologist, artist, and theologist Rollo May is the author of this small gem in which he gives a sensitive account of how human courage and creation are interconnected throughout the course of our existence, beginning with some core definitions of these concepts and, in a second moment, using his experience with clinical cases.

2. Abbey, E. (2007). Perceptual uncertainty of cultural life: becoming reality. In: J. Valsiner & A. Rosa (Eds.) The Cambridge Handbook of Sociocultural Psychology. Cambridge: Cambridge University Press.
3. Abbey, E. (2012). Ambivalence and its transformations. J. Valsiner (ed.) Oxford Handbook of Culture and Psychology. Oxford: Oxford University Press.

Emily Abbey's theory of poetic motion derives from cultural psychological new theoretical contributions on human development, which is here described as a movement of constant overcoming of uncertainties not only between the past and the present, but also between the present and the future, through a continuous process of meaning construction. Poetic motion is the movement to make sense of this dynamic tension between literal and imagined domains.

4. Freeman, M. (1993). Finding the muse: a sociopsychological inquiry into the conditions of artistic creativity. New York: Cambridge University Press.
5. Freeman, M. (1999). Culture, narrative and the poetic construction of selfhood. Journal of Constructive Psychology, 12, 99–116.

After writing a book in which he explores conditions under which artists create, Mark Freeman went on other topics such as the poetic construction of selfhood. Through defining poiesis as the process of recreation via imagination (Freeman, 1999, p. 15), the author proposes a concept that serves art as well as psychology.

## From Outside Psychology

6. Gombrich, E. (2006). The story of art. London: Phaidon Press.

First published in 1950, this book is a comprehensive treatise by one of the most influential art critics of the twentieth century. Although mainly centered in visual works, Gombrich's book covers thousands of years of works of art in Western societies and it still is an unavoidable introductory reference on art appreciation.

7. Benjamin, W. (2010). *The Work of Art in the Age of Mechanical Reproduction.* North Charleston: Createspace Independent Publishing Platform.

This seminal text by philosopher and critical theorist Walter Benjamin, written in the 1930s, is crucial for understanding the transformations in the arts that began to take place in the end of the nineteenth century, starting with the invention of photography.

8. Bourdieu, P.; Darbel, A.; Schnapper, D. (1997). *The Love of Art: European Art Museums and Their Public.* Cambridge: Polity Press.

French sociologist Pierre Bourdieu, besides having written on other important subjects, developed highly relevant analyses of how people learn, for instance, to attend museums, and then to appreciate art. His sociological lessons also teach us that social and economic backgrounds are strictly related to people's artistic tastes and judgments.

9. Schechner, R. (2006). *Performance studies: an introduction.* New York & London: Routledge.

This introductory book by performance director and theorist Richard Schechner, already quoted in the chapter, is a great initial presentation on what performance is. This helps us understand why such a concept and practice became such a major artistic paradigm in dance, visual arts, poetry, and virtually any other arts.

10. Bourriaud, N. (2002). *Relational aesthetics*. Paris: Les Presses du réel.

Bourriaud's book presents a highly original contribution to the once traditional field of aesthetics. Relational aesthetics takes into account people's – artists and audience – personal, affective relation to works of art; and once we understand that, it becomes easier for us not only to see how contemporary artists create their works, and to realize we are part of these works somehow.

## Cross-References

▶ Community Psychology and Psychological Distress
▶ Cultural Psychology
▶ Developmental Psychology: Moving Beyond the East–West Divide
▶ Epistemology of Psychology
▶ Qualitative Methodology
▶ The Methodology Cycle as the Basis for Knowledge

## References

Abbey, E. (2007). Perceptual uncertainty of cultural life: Becoming reality. In J. Valsiner & A. Rosa (Eds.), *The Cambridge handbook of sociocultural psychology*. Cambridge: Cambridge University Press.
Abbey, E. (2012). Ambivalence and its transformations. In J. Valsiner (Ed.), *Oxford handbook of culture and psychology*. Oxford: Oxford University Press.
Arnheim, R. (1986). The two faces of gestalt psychology. *American Psychologist, 41*(7), 820–824.
Arnheim, R. (2005). *Arte e percepção visual: uma psicologia da visão criadora. Nova versão*. São Paulo: Pioneira Thomson Learning.
Austin, J. (1962). *How to do things with words*. Oxford: Oxford University Press.
Bakhtin, M. M. (1984). *Problems of Dostoevsky's poetics*. (C. Emerson, Ed. and Trans.). Minneapolis: University of Minnesota Press. (Original work published 1929).
Bakhtin, M. M. (1990). *Art and answerability: Early philosophical essas by M. M. Bakhtin*. (M. Holquist, Ed., V. Liapunov, Trans). Austin, TX: University of Texas Press.
Benjamin, W. (2010). *The work of art in the age of mechanical reproduction*. North Charleston: Createspace Independent Publishing Platform.
Bourdieu, P., Darbel, A., & Schnapper, D. (1997). *The love of art: European art museums and their public*. Cambridge: Polity Press.
Bourriaud, N. (2002). *Relational aesthetics*. Paris: Les Presses du réel.
Butler, J. (1988). Performative acts and gender constitution: An essay in phenomenology and feminist theory. *Theatre Journal, 40*(4), 519–531. (Dec., 1988).
Coli, J. (2011). *O que é arte*. São Paulo: Editora brasiliense.

De Smedt, J., & Cruz, H. D. (2010). Toward an integrative approach of cognitive neuroscientific and evolutionary psychological studies of art. *Evolutionary Psychology, 8*(4), 695–719.

Dewey, J. (1934). *Art as experience*. New York: Perigree Books.

Dickie, G. (1962). Is psychology relevant to aesthetics? *Philosophical Review, 71*(3), 285–302.

Fechner, G. T. (1876). *Vorschule der Ästhetik [Primary school of aesthetics]*. Leipzig: Breitkopf & Härtel.

Ferraz, G., & Kastrup, V. (2010). Coexistência de formas e forças: a atualidade das contribuições Gestaltistas ao campo da arte. *Psico, Porto Alegre, PUCRS, 41*(4), 423–431.

Ficher-Lichte, E. (2008). *The transformative power of performance: A new aesthetics*. Abingdon: Routgledge.

Firunts, M. (2016). Staging professionalization lecture-performances and para-institutional pedagogies, from the postwar to the present. *Performance Research, 21*(6), 19–25. https://doi.org/10.1080/13528165.2016.1240924

Freeman, M. (1993). *Finding the muse: A sociopsychological inquiry into the conditions of artistic creativity*. New York: Cambridge University Press.

Freeman, M. (1999). Culture, narrative and the poetic construction of selfhood. *Journal of Constructive Psychology, 12*, 99–116.

Freud, S. (1907). Delusions and dreams in Jensen's 'Gradiva'. Standard edition 9:7–95. *Gesammelte Werke, 7*, 31–125.

Freud, S. (1908). Creative writers and day-dreaming. *Standard Edition, 9*, 143–153.

Freud, S. (1955). The Moses of Michelangelo. (1914). In *The standard edition of the complete psychological works of Sigmund Freud* (Vol. XIII). London: The Hogarth Press and the Institute of Psychoanalysis.

Freud, S. (1970). *Leonardo Da Vinci e uma lembrança de sua infância (1910)*. Obras Completas (Vol. XI, pp. 55–124). Rio de Janeiro: Imago.

Freud, S. (2012). O Moisés de Michelangelo (1914). In *Totem e tabu, contribuição à história do movimento psicanalítico e outros textos (1912–1914)*. São Paulo: Companhia das Letras. Tradução de Paulo César de Souza. (Sigmund Freud, Obras Completas, v. 11).

Freud, S, & Jung, C. G. (1976). *Correspondência completa*. McGuirre, W. (Org.). Trad. Leonardo Fróes e Eudoro Augusto Maciera de Souza. Rio de Janeiro, Brazil: Imago.

Gaillard, C. (2010). Jung e a arte. *Pro-Posições, Campinas, 21*(2), 121–148. maio/ago. 2010.

Goffman, E. (1959). *The presentation of self in everyday life*. New York: Anchor Books.

Gombrich, E. (2006). *The story of art*. London: Phaidon Press.

González Rey, F. L. (2018). Vygotsky's "the psychology of art": A foundational and still unexplored text. *Estudos de Psicologia (Campinas), 35*(4), 339–350. https://doi.org/10.1590/1982-02752018000400002

Heidegger, M. (2007). *A origem da obra de arte* (p. 70). São Paulo: Edições.

Jung, C. G. (1978a). On the relation of analytical psychology to poetry. In C. G. Jung (Ed.), *The spirit in man, art and literature* (4th ed.). Princeton: Princeton University Press.

Jung, C. G. (1978b). *The spirit in man, art and literature* (4th ed.). Princeton: Princeton University Press.

Kaprow, A. (1993). *Essays on blurring art and life*. Berkeley/Los Angeles: University of California Press.

Koffka, K. (1922). Perception: An introduction to the Gestalt-theorie. *Psychological Bulletin, 19*, 531–585.

Kris, E. (1968). *Psicanálise da arte*. São Paulo: Editora Brasiliense.

Kupper, H. I., & Rollman-Branch, H. S. (1959). Freud and Schintzler – (Doppelgänger). *Journal fo the American Psychoanalytic Association, 7*(1), 109–126.

Leder, H., Belke, B., Oeberst, A., & Augustin, D. (2004). A model of aesthetic appreciation and aesthetic judgments. *British Journal of Psychology, 95*, 489–508.

Leder, H., Gerger, G., Dressler, S. G., & Schabmann, A. (2012). How art is appreciated. *Psychology of Aesthetics, Creativity, and the Arts, 6*(1), 2–10.

Lindell, A. K., & Mueller, J. (2011). Can science account for taste? Psychological insights into art appreciation. *Journal of Cognitive Psychology, 23*(4), 453–475. https://doi.org/10.1080/20445911.2011.539556

Lordelo, L. d. R. (2018). Poetics within performance art: The developmental nature of artistic creative processes. In O. Lehman, N. Chaudhary, A. C. Bastos, & E. Abbey (Eds.), *Poetry and imagined worlds: Creativity and everyday experience*. Palgrave MacMillan.

May, R. (1980). *The courage to create*. New York: Bantam Book.

Merleau-Ponty, M. (1962). *Phenomenology of perception*. London: Routledge & Keagan Paul. (Original work published 1945).

Merleau-Ponty, M. (2013). *O olho e o espírito*. São Paulo: Cosac Naify Portátil.

Nadal, M., & Skov, M. (2013). Introduction to the special issue: Toward an interdisciplinary neuroaesthetics. *Psychology of Aesthetics, Creativity, and the Arts, 7*(1), 1–12.

Nin, A. (1968). Foreword. In O. Rank (Ed.), *Art and artist: Creative urge and personality development*. New York: Norton Paperback.

Ostrower, F. (1999). *Acasos e criação artística*. Rio de Janeiro: Editora Campus.

Quiroga Mendez, P. (2010). Arte y psicología analítica, una interpretación arquetipal del arte. *Arte, Individuo y Sociedad, 22*(2), 49–62.

Rank, O. (1989). *Art and artist: Creative urge and personality development*. New York: Norton Paperback.

Reber, R. (2008). Art in its experience: Can empirical psychology help assess artistic value? *Leonardo, 41*(4), 367–372.

Roald, T. (2008). Toward a phenomenological psychology of art appreciation. *Journal of Phenomenological Psychology, 39*, 189–212.

Schechner, R. (2006). *Performance studies: An introduction* (2nd ed.). New York/London: Routledge.

Skov, M., & Vartanian, O. (2009). Introduction: What is neuroaesthetics. In M. Skov & O. Vartanian (Eds.), *Neuroaesthetics* (pp. 1–7). Amityville: Baywood.

Smagorinsky, P. (2011). Vygotsky's stage theory: The psychology of art and the actor under the direction of Perezhivanie. *Mind, Culture, and Activity, 18*(4), 319–341. https://doi.org/10.1080/10749039.2010.518300

Stanislavsky, K. (2013a). *An actor prepares*. London: Bloomsbury.

Stanislavsky, K. (2013b). *Building a character*. London: Bloomsbury.

Sullivan, P., & McCarthy, J. (2009). An experiential account of the psychology of art. *Psychology of Aesthetics, Creativity, and the Arts, 3*(3), 181–187.

Tinio, P. P. L. (2013). From Artistic Creation to Aesthetic Reception: The Mirror Model of Art. *Journal for Aesthetic, Creativity, and the Arts, 7*(3), 265–275.

Van der Veer, R., & Valsiner, J. (1996). *Vygotsky: uma síntese*. São Paulo: Edições Loyola.

Vigotski, L. S. (1999). *A tragédia de Hamlet: o príncipe da Dinamarca*. São Paulo: Martins Fontes.

Vigotski, L. S. (2001). *Psicologia da Arte*. São Paulo: Martins Fontes.

von Ehrenfels, C. (1890). Uber 'Gestaltqualitäten'. *Vierteljahrsschrift für wissenschaftliche Philosophie, 14*, 249–292.

Vygotsky, L. S. (1971). *Psychology of art*. New York: MIT Press.

Vygotsky, L. S. (1994). The problem of the environment. In R. V. Veer & J. Valsiner (Eds.), *The Vygotsky reader* (pp. 338–354). Cambridge, MA: Blackwell.

Vygotsky, L. S. (1999). On the problem of the psychology of the actor's creative work. In *The collected works of L. S. Vygotsky* (Vol. 6: Scientific legacy) (R. Rieber, Ed.; M. J. Hall, Trans.; pp. 237–244). New York: Plenum.

Wertheimer, M. (1923). Untersuchungen zur Lehre von der Gestalt, II [Investigations on the gestalt theory]. *Psychologische Forschung, 4*, 301–350.

Zaidel, D. H., Nadal, M., Flexas, A., & Munar, E. (2013). An evolutionary approach to art and aesthetic experience. *Psychology of Aesthetics, Creativity, and the Arts, 7*(1), 100–109.

# Psychology and Social Work Through Critical Lens

## 42

Maria Cláudia Santos Lopes de Oliveira and Tatiana Yokoy

## Contents

| | |
|---|---|
| Introduction | 1012 |
| Teaching and Learning Objectives of the Chapter | 1013 |
| Social Work in a Liquid Era | 1013 |
| Social Work: A Kaleidoscopic Concept | 1015 |
| Psychology and Social Work in Contemporary Societies: Overcoming a Traditional Stance | 1017 |
| Toward a Critical Stance on Social Sciences and Social Work: The Importance of the Sociocultural Turn | 1020 |
| Applied Psychology and Contexts of Practice in Social Work | 1023 |
| Healthcare and Social Work | 1024 |
| Family-Centered Social Care and the Active Participating Beneficiaries | 1027 |
| Social Work in Educational Settings | 1030 |
| Concluding Remarks | 1035 |
| References | 1036 |

### Abstract

Psychology around the world has undergone important changes along last decades. One of the most salient transformations has impacted both the science and psychologists' self-images as practitioners and researchers and provoked the slow displacement of the discipline's focus, from isolated individuals to individuals within groups and communities. Psychology today left the closed rooms of offices and clinics, and has gone outdoors, to work with community members and through the participation in communities' daily life. As a consequence of this empirical shift, theoretical novelties were required. Psychologists represent now

M. C. S. L. de Oliveira (✉)
Institute of Psychology, University of Brasília, Brasília, Brazil

T. Yokoy
School of Education, University of Brasília, Brasília, Brazil
e-mail: yokoy@unb.br

even more active agents within health, educational, social care system, and governmental and non-governmental programs. In this chapter we present and discuss the historical process of this sociocultural and epistemological rupture in Psychology and consider its impacts over applied social sciences today. We elaborate on contemporary challenges concerning social work and discuss the contribution critical psychological approaches can provide to enhance its impacts and outcomes in face of the very complex issues dealt by social policies in a globalized world.

**Keywords**

Sociocultural turn in psychology · Social work · Psychological care · Institutional psychology

## Introduction

Psychology around the world, as an applied and as a theoretical field, has undergone important changes along the two or three last decades, mainly. One of the most salient transformations has impacted both the social representations of this science and the self-images of psychologists as practitioners and researchers, and it refers to the slow displacement of the discipline's major focus, from isolated individuals to individuals within groups and communities.

While general psychology's main professional setting formerly used to be, and to a certain extent still is, the private locus of psychological therapy rooms, and psychologists' main subjects were psychiatric patients and individuals with mental illness or disorders, an important part of psychology today left the closed rooms of offices and clinics, and the cognitivist and behaviorist straight jacket has gone outdoors, to work with community members and participate in the community daily life. As a consequence, instead of the former solitude of an isolated practice, psychologists have now acquired a growing importance as social care professionals, members of multi/interdisciplinary teams engaged in a practice that aims at empowering people and changing their living conditions.

In its move to the side out of the most traditional settings, applied psychology seems to have expanded its influence and penetration as well. In these diverse settings psychologists now work together with different groups in both urban and rural contexts, and in multiple, innovative institutional settings and collective arrangements, such as community centers, after-school projects, workers unions, political movements, sports leagues, among other human collectives. As a consequence of this empirical shift, theoretical novelties were needed as well.

While psychologists represent now even more active agents within health, educational, social care system, within governmental and non-governmental programs, their insertion in public policies and community activism demanded a more interdisciplinary stance. The borders between psychology and other professions engaged in social care seem to have blurred, and psychological knowledge has now proved to play an important role not only within its own professional practice but also as part of the general theoretical and practical framework of other applied sciences and social care practitioners' education, especially as a source of important subsidy for their critical and ethical daily practice. Taking this dual aspect into consideration, we elaborate on contemporary challenges concerning social work and discuss the contribution critical psychological approaches can provide to enhance its impacts and outcomes in face of the very complex issues dealt by social policies in a globalized world. We also elaborate on what is (or should be) specific to psychologists participation in social work practices in collective settings, and the general contribution psychology as a science can provide to social care as a whole.

We present and discuss the roots of this historical, sociocultural, and epistemological rupture in Psychology and consider their impacts over applied social sciences today. We draw an overview of the relationships between psychology and social work in a more traditional view, considering their implicit values, theoretical basis, and practical implications. Then we focus on critical approaches in Psychology, analyzing their contribution to enhance social work current trends and practice. The last part of the chapter is dedicated to elaborate on some pedagogic implications of contemporary psychological trends in social work to teaching and learning psychology. We provide some illustrations based on cases and examples of good practices in social work, in order to illustrate its potential to induce development, personal and social transformations in contexts of health care; family-centered social assistance, and educational settings, in which creative ways of dealing with everyday challenges are analyzed in order to inspire practitioners who already work in this field and those who intend to develop a career in it.

## Teaching and Learning Objectives of the Chapter

In this chapter students are expected to:

- Understand the contribution of applied psychology to social work practice
- Identify similarities and differences between Psychology and Social Work, concerning their historic, philosophical and epistemological hallmarks
- Distinguish between traditional and critical psychological frameworks in social work

## Social Work in a Liquid Era

We should understand that the role played by social sciences and social care professions have significantly changed around the world in recent times. In fact, the world as a whole goes through important changes in terms of cultural, political, and economic distribution of resources, and understanding these changes is essential in terms of correctly interpreting their effects upon subjectivities. Nations that led important democratic achievements in the past are now dominated by conservative, populist, and moralist political trends. Few hands detain the major parcel of the wealth of the world and a vast parcel of the values-system nurtured by modern era – instrumental rationality, progress, rule-following, social order, etc. – have proved unsustainable, giving space for a new social era in which following Marx, together with Bauman, "all that is solid melts into air" (Bauman, 2000). The liquid modernity describes the condition of constant mobility and change imposed to identities, relationships, and economics in contemporary societies.

Social sciences are deeply affected by complex realities that have increased in the liquid modernity and are interconnected in a globalized world. Critical issues as international migration, interreligious conflicts, political conservatism, deeper socioeconomic inequalities, lack of access to healthcare and educational deficits are worldwide problems, and they demand of social scientists a critical stance before they intervene upon vulnerable social groups and individuals based on scientific goals, as well as on ethics and responsibility. Therefore, because capitalism is more wicked than ever and social inequalities are higher and higher around the world (Bauman, 2011), there is a growing interdependence between socioeconomic and political issues, for one side, and psychological suffering in its diverse facets, for the other side. It is recognized today that sociocultural and economic factors can affect individuals, families, and groups so profoundly that they should be necessarily included in the interpretive framework that will guide our practice as psychologists in social work teams. In this context, the various psychiatric disorders, the licit and illicit drugs abuse, the burnout syndrome, suicidal ideation, etc., cannot be interpreted just as effects of individual difficulties or solely related to intraindividual causes. Such problems are currently considered as symptoms of an intricate network of sociopolitical, cultural, economic, and personal factors deeply ingrained in the history of modern societies and aggravated in face of the paradoxical contemporary times. World Health Organization [WHO] (2018) recognizes that good mental health today as a basic human right (Puras & Gooding, 2019) and the access to mental health policies, which included psychological care, should be universally accessible. In line with international health policies, Psychology is currently recognized as a social resource people can use toward liberation (Sloan, 2002), which means that psychological knowledge and practice is expected to overcome the status of a "neutral" corpus of scientific knowledge and to perform a core role in societal development, promoting, together with other social care professions, vulnerable peoples' development, low income groups' empowerment, religious minorities' inclusion, the cultural development of communities and nations, and other relevant social outcomes, coherent with the objective of enhancing ethic, justice, and democracy in all societies.

We begin by briefly considering the history of social assistance in the Western world. Concerning this topic, an important epistemological turn occurred in social assistance, both as a profession and as a theoretical corpus, and this shift took place in Europe and the USA at some moment along the second half of the twentieth century, after worldwide wars.

Social assistance origin is located in Europe, marked by a very conservative stance, due to the weird fusion of scientific aspirations and Christian philanthropy. In search of a scientific and a moral basis, social assistance is influenced by the functional positivism, the primacy of professional neutrality, and the verticalism, objectivism, and the a-politicism of social actions, together with the impact of the religious moral order and confessionalism, related to Christian assistentialism. After the worldwide counter-hegemonic social movements in the sixties, a process during which social assistants' self-images suffered a deep conceptual reconfiguration, the original epistemological hallmarks of the discipline were rejected, giving birth to new perspectives in the field. As the main effect of this historical process, a more critical reflexive stance is assumed by scholars and professionals in the field, especially concerning its own ontological foundations and the recognition of its non-neutral role as part of the construction of a contradictory society, in which social assistants are, at the same time, social policing agents that intervene upon social relations and part of the society in which they intervene (Martins, 2016).

As for Psychology, we notice a very similar self-reflexive process of criticism taking place, especially by the mediation of emergent critical trends. Thanks to the dialogue of social psychology with feminism, post-structuralism, and decolonial studies coming from philosophy and other social sciences, it is now fully recognized the historical role played by mainstream psychological knowledge in the normalization, hierarchization, and moral regulation of individuals, by following the modern science trends of categorization, classification, and ordering, the most important side effect of which was the exclusion of individuals and groups and the expansion of social inequalities throughout the world.

In Brazil, for instance, since the colonial period (1500–1808), many groups (ex: native indigenous and African populations) were subjected to enslavement, disciplined and exploited by means of Christian evangelization, and other acculturation strategies (Lopes de Oliveira, 2019). This colonialist rationale is still present as part of the reality faced by social workers in our country (Alberto et al. 2014). Those who work in the social care facilities, for instance, deal with huge tensions between, on one side, the social protection constitutional principles, whose main focus is ensuring rights, fighting social inequalities and, on the other side, the charitable, clientelist and philanthropic institutional inheritances still operating within these facilities, together with the demands of a neoliberal zeitgeist, in which unfair and unhealthy work conditions, although illegal and unacceptable, are often found.

Although affected by critical ideas as it is, differently from other social and applied disciplines, in contemporary Psychology such ideas have not acquired a dominant status in the epistemological arena nor had a definitive role in transforming mainstream theoretical approaches. Indeed, critical epistemologies in Psychology today share with traditional epistemologies the landscape of psychological theory and practice and oddly occupy a disadvantageous position in it. Despite this, we understand that as our goal is to enhance a reflexive stance on social work, in which individuals and groups in contemporary societies are approached through ethical, responsible, and technical means at a time, a critical psychological standpoint is essential.

## Social Work: A Kaleidoscopic Concept

Social work is a wide sphere of human activity but there is not yet one well-accepted meaning concerning its scope, importance, and goals throughout the world. A brief analysis of the available literature coming from different countries shows that the concept "social work" is linked to, at least, three semantic fields. They are:

1. In the more general sense, *social work* refers to a broad set of actions and interventions different professionals perform together with individuals, groups, peoples, and communities, which intends to minimize social risks and vulnerability, and promote social change and/or the improvement of their living conditions and future achievements. These professionals are either representatives of the Government or non-governmental organization stakeholders. In this sense, social work is *a particular sphere of human activity* that is part of public social policies, implemented either by government or nongovernment programs.
2. The second perspective follows a French tradition inaugurated by authors as M. Foucault, F. Guatarri, P. Bourdieu, among others (cf. Donzelot, 1997; Jeaninne Verdès-Leroux, 1986). In this sense, *social work* is described as a by-product of Modern Age, which is intimately related to the birth of European Nation States and the consolidation of capitalism as a global mode of production. According to this perspective, the changes in the dynamics of economic production and the functioning of societies during the eighteenth century represented an important shift that impacted social life. Industrialism was an expensive social experiment that demanded efficiency and outcomes, based on the continuous supervision, control, and regulation of social activities and individuals, mainly upon scientific bases. Social sciences and social care practices emerged at that time in order to *prevent and control idleness and procrastination, social maladjustment, and rebellions, ensuring the full use of each individual's vital energy in service of keeping social order,* and promoting economic reproduction, at a time.
3. Finally, the third context of use of the term *social work*, the more specific one, refers to *a particular actor, the social worker* or "social assistant," a registered professional whose practice is regulated by the state. In this perspective, the scientific debate around social work is usually presented together with topics concerning their professional education, daily practices, challenges and social outcomes. Illustrative of this perspective, Ingleby (2010) refers to six roles attributed to social workers:
   - Preparing for and working with individuals, families, carers, groups, and communities.
   - Planning, carrying out, reviewing and evaluating social work practices.
   - Supporting individuals to represent their needs, views and circumstances.
   - Managing risks to individuals, families, carers, groups, community, self and colleagues.
   - Managing and being accountable, with supervision and support for social work practice within individual organizations.
   - Demonstrating professional competence in social work practice.

The three views referred above can dominate the different national contexts, depending on historical, epistemological, legal, and institutional aspects that guide social work everyday practice. In the sections of this chapter, considering contextual differences, we move between the three aforementioned perspectives. At times, we will set the focus on the changes applied Psychology has undergone after its emergence in the late years of the nineteenth century and will highlight its slow transition from an exclusive individualistic stance to a collective-oriented set of epistemologies, theories, and practices. At other times, we will emphasize the importance of Psychology scientific architecture, in special some branches of critical psychological approaches, and its role in feeding the development of professional competences of social workers and enhancing an ethical and emphatic stance on cared individuals and groups by social care agents (social assistants[1], pedagogues, psychologists, healthcare professionals, law agents, and others) (Conselho Federal de Serviço Social/Conselho Federal de Psicologia, 2007).

## Psychology and Social Work in Contemporary Societies: Overcoming a Traditional Stance

Social work attends different functions in contemporary societies, and social workers themselves share polysemic or even contradictory understandings of their role as social agents, not all of them committed to social empowerment and human development. For instance, Curado and Menegon (2009) interviewed social workers regarding their professional role. The results they achieved in the study were organized into four categories concerning social workers' practice: (a) offer an occasional aid to people whose incomes are below the federal poverty threshold (APA's 2021) and those in need of any social support at critical moments; (b) promote human rights and foster societal changes targeting at achieving social equality; (c) improve the strategies for social management; and (d) use care as an instrumental resource for seeking vote and reproducing patronage, the dependence of disadvantaged groups on charity and aid.

In professionals' conceptions, as we can see above, authors found out critical conceptions together with conservative, old-fashioned positions, as in categories (a) and (d). Furthermore, these more conservative categories do not meet the guidelines of the International Federation of Social Workers (2014, online), in which the important role of social work in promoting social justice and empowerment, is highlighted

> Social work is a practice-based profession and an academic discipline that promotes social change and development, social cohesion, and the empowerment and liberation of people. Principles of social justice, human rights, collective responsibility and respect for diversities are central to social work. Underpinned by theories of social work, social sciences, humanities and indigenous knowledge, social work engages people and structures to address life challenges and enhance well being. The above definition may be amplified at national and/or regional levels.

---

[1] In this chapter, we use the term "social worker" in reference to the set of social care professionals, while "social assistant" is exclusively adopted to refer to those graduated in this career and registered as professionals, even though this differentiation is not universally adopted in different national contexts.

One of the core features of social work is that its goals rarely would be translated into material acquaintances, mostly because the State, through social policies, is incapable of providing all the needs, which are demanded by vulnerable groups. Instead, its aimed effect involves intangible outcomes such as cared groups' improved autonomy, better strategies to cope with their own challenges, and the ability to find creative solutions to their daily problems and precariousness of material resources (Brazil, 2018). Accordingly, McLaughlin (2014, p. 1811) sums up social work as an endeavor

> to help people to live more successfully within their local communities by helping them find solutions to their problems. In doing so, social workers deal not only with individuals but with their families, neighbors, and friends, as well as with other organizations such as the police, medical professions, and schools. While predominantly concerned with the care and protection of those in need or at risk, it often involves the use of statutory powers over individuals, for example, in the removal of a child from its parents due to it being considered to be at risk of significant harm or the detention of someone against his or her will under mental health legislation.
> 
> The exact forms such interventions take, and the values that underpin them, will vary both historically and from country to country as sociopolitical and other cultural factors influence attitudes to, and provision for, the distressed and disadvantaged within a given society.

The historic development of social work as a practice points to the emergence of an interdisciplinary field whose scientific and practical fundamentals have been the object of intense political and epistemological dispute. Such disputes have opposed not only social scientists, but policy-makers, stakeholders, entrepreneurs, employers, and social care professionals, along the time. The first disputed topic concerns the very definition of social work, in face of the absence of a consensual definition of the scope of the social work agreed upon by different nations. In France, for instance, Rulac (2014) refers to the existence of an intense tension between social assistants and social scientists. The French practitioners are resistant to recognize the scientific basis of their practice and they prioritize the situated professional knowledge as the basis of a good intervention. Social sciences are perceived by them as excessively theoretical, and they would bring the marks of the divorce between theory and situated practice. One of the consequences of this skepticism regards science was the absence of a university degree in Social Work in that country until the year 2013.

In fact, France is not alone in this position. In different countries beyond in Europe (cf. Olivares, 2012, analyzing Chile) this specific profession has been lately institutionalized, or keep a blurred border with social sciences, even though these countries had social policing going on for long. They counted on specific agents in charge of the policies that targeted the social regulation and protection of vulnerable groups, families, and communities and one of the social care professions that will be required to perform this function is Psychology itself.

While social sciences are blamed for their scarce amount of empirical knowledge produced, concerning traditional Psychology the major problem is not the volume of empirical knowledge, but the excessive focus on individuals and on experiments conducted within artificial settings. Aspects associated with the occurrence of the two world wars, along the twentieth century, caused the transference of an important parcel of Psychology research groups from Europe to USA. For the one side, the scientific enterprise yielded in US laboratories had a superlative importance in the development and visibility of this science as a whole. For the other side, the seclusion of psychological knowledge within laboratories has pushed Psychology away from social reality and, particularly concerning this field's contribution to social work; at least US psychological major paradigms based on experimental behaviorism and cognitivism are definitely limited.

According to the traditional social division of sciences, Psychology was considered as the science of the psychological realm, no matter how many different and contrasting definitions of psychological realm we will find out within it. That is why for long time psychologists were kept apart from social work teams, even though these professionals continuously applied psychological concepts and instruments as resources, even though in a fragmented and superficial way. Psychological concepts (personality, attitudes, beliefs, motivation, etc.) and instruments (psychological tests, for instance) would help them to deal with supposedly subjective, intra-psychological dimensions of the conduct that interfered in one's social life. In other words, traditional Psychology helped social workers to deal with supposedly individual issues by using loose psychological categories, split notions of human development, and empirical instruments detached from theories (cf. Ingleby, 2010). We now recognize that the consumption of Psychological knowledge by traditional social assistants corroborated their own beliefs and prejudice, in special the idea that social problems were mostly associated with individual traumas, mental illnesses, deficits, etc. (Jensen, 2015) and/or moral dysfunctions, such as procrastination, laziness, and lack of goal-orientation.

Prado (2014) follows this path. The scholar argues that the main feature of the contribution historically provided by Psychology to social work was reductionism. The political basis of social phenomena was oversimplified by mainstream Psychology, interpreted as if caused by individual psychopathological traits, accordingly to classificatory and discriminatory agendas. Just recently, by the end of the twentieth century, Psychology really engaged in the debate and practice of social work in a more dialogical, interdisciplinary, and relevant manner. This novel stance brought fresh air to psychological practice within facilities such as prisons, asylums, hospitals, and schools.

As a consequence of this long-lasting reductionism, Afonso et al. (2012) highlights that social work still lacks a robust theoretical-methodological framework that go beyond both the psychologization of social problems and the objectivist views that usually offer weak practical solutions to everyday problems. Ahead of the complex social problems we deal with nowadays, the mere incorporation of psychology into social work without a deeper self-reflexive stance fuels in social workers these days the fear of a return to the "psychologization of the social question" (Afonso et al., 2012, p. 190). Taking the opposite way to this feared scenario, contemporary approaches in Psychology put under suspicious its own traditional individualistic and moralist vein, and search for new epistemologies that qualify services and support an empowering and inclusive perspective on social work.

## Toward a Critical Stance on Social Sciences and Social Work: The Importance of the Sociocultural Turn

The construction of a critical psychology requires clarification concerning the philosophical and epistemological standpoints of critical thinking. In a broad sense, critical humanities and social sciences imply the commitment with alternatives to traditional scientific perspectives in the interpretation of human beings and social problems. This means the de-naturalization of social issues and the adoption of an inquisitive stance toward conventional explanatory schemes that guided psychological interventions in the social world. Nissen (2012, p. 12) explains the three core aspects usually shared by critical psychological approaches:

(a) The "progressivist" use of psychology in social critique
(b) The "reflexivist" critique of psychology itself
(c) The "reconstructionist" building of alternatives to traditional psychology

According to Teo (2018)

> the term *critical* [original author's emphasis] itself has different meanings. For natural-scientific psychologists, the idea of critical thinking refers to the application of scientific process and practices to the world. Critical psychologists who understand themselves as following a political-economic analysis challenge psychology on the background of power, politics, and society (pp. vi-vii).

Critical scientists share a focus on social sustainability, foreseeing a society that rejects the hegemony of the Western neoliberal and capitalist market models. They search for the collective well-being and for a meaningful life for all, mediated by distributed economy, democracy, and justice (Natale et al. 2016). According to these authors, in order to be considered as a critical approach, an epistemology should include some core features, such as:

- The primacy on ecology
- The rejection of economic utilitarianism and developmentalism per se
- The commitment with human rights
- Listening the voices of minority groups
- The suspension of well-established truths and beliefs

Finally, critical scientific approaches lead an active effort to overcome exclusive Euro-American mainstream epistemologies and insert universal theoretical and empirical assumptions into brackets. By this attitude, they leave room for questions and interrogations; their attention is directed to those formerly unknown, or disregarded, "epistemologies of the South" (Santos, 2016, p. x), and to the knowledge produced in Africa and Latin America. Within a critical epistemology, these sites are increasingly recognized as producing interesting theoretical models, considered as valid not only to nourish the interpretation of their intricate local problems, but to guide innovative ways of analyzing other contexts' social phenomena as well, in a globalized world (Nwoye, 2014).

As a consequence, psychological critical perspectives impose a shift in the way we interpret and intervene upon human beings. Mental life is now conceived not as a universal, objective, steady state phenomenon (Valsiner, 2017). Instead, as far as human subjectivity is socially, historically, and culturally embedded, the psyche emerges in relation with humans unique experiences guided by, and oriented to, the complex network of semiotic relations, in the irreversible flux of time of a given society.

Critical psychology is based on questioning, "asking questions about psychology and raising questions about the questions that are asked has been identified as a process of reflexivity and interference" (Teo, 2018, p. 2). Inquiring, raising questions for which one has no simple answer is a trend that has been totally abandoned by traditional psychology. Nevertheless, according to a critical psychology, questioning the basis of a given scientific field is part of recognizing its sociocultural and historical basis *instead of* assuming it as a definitive corpus of true statements.

The sociocultural shift in Psychology articulated a set of theoretical, philosophical, and epistemological perspectives coming from humanities and social sciences. Such a shift did not give rise to a single or hegemonic theoretical model, but instead it generated a kaleidoscope of more or less articulated complementary perspectives, which have in common ideas concerning the inseparability of mind and culture; and the core role performed by sociocultural contexts in the production of subjectivity (Kirshner & Martin, 2010).

Together with classic thinkers, as the Italian philosopher Gianbattista Vico, who rejected this passive and responsive view of human beings and argued that humans' main hallmark is the *ingegno*, that is, their ability to be intentional and creative, imaginatively introducing new elements in pre-established relationships with others and with reality (Tateo, 2015), an important epistemological trend supporting sociocultural turn comes from constructionist approaches. Constructionism is a broad and diverse umbrella indeed, which common ground is the assumption that human knowledge and development are a shared experience, co-constructed upon social interaction. This umbrella covers, among other epistemological perspectives, the social constructionism, post-structuralism, discursive psychology, and feminist psychology (Harré, 2010).

Constructionist ideas have had an important impact on scientific thinking in psychology by radically problematizing the biological determinism of mental functioning and offering elements to defend the sociocultural and collective origin of the emotions, values, beliefs, and meanings that populate the human mind and give rise to psychological functions. These functions develop as part of social interaction patterns and are progressively incorporated and internalized, giving birth to the sense of personal identity.

Therefore, socioculture – in the form of historically constituted and socially assumed founding schemes, conventions, rules, myths, and narratives – is responsible for the form, the mode of organization (Shotter, 2010), as well as the hierarchical content of mental life. Constructionism avoids every possible use of internal categories to investigate the psychological world and embraces the idea that human conduct is organized in the form of stories or narratives, texts through which each subject constitutes a sense of continuity of the self in the timeline (Sarbin, 1986). Here, the sociocultural turn in psychology offers an important clue to social work: the storied nature of human conduct and the healing potential of dialogical settings in which intentional beings will construct a sense of selfhood, belonging, and historicity.

As we have already emphasized earlier in this chapter, for political reasons, the formation of the human and social sciences was characterized by the divorce of culture and subjectivity, turning the two into parts of distinct scientific fields (Sato & Valsiner, 2010). Cultural psychology makes an effort to reinsert subjectivity within culture. By bringing the concept of culture into the current debate on psychological processes, Cultural Semiotic psychology highlights the importance of meaning processes as guiding the co-construction of subjects and the social world.

In epistemological terms, the adherence to a cultural semiotic perspective suggests the union of approaches from the general psychology of dynamic phenomena with semiotics in order to understand how human systems (including the individual system, as well as groups, communities, nations, etc.) can position themselves proactively (and not just reactively, as some psychological approaches considers) in face of objects that become worthy of attention and semiotic elaboration, based on specific meanings previously created by communities and actively recreated by the subjects in their concrete interactions.

Cultural Semiotic psychology is considered as a branch of general psychology, and it provides analytical and empirical insightful ideas that favor a broad understanding of how human beings develop upon activity and semiotic movements within and between different layers of the sociocultural world. Cultural psychology suggests that the study of the psyche should adopt a idiographic perspective and highlight the (trans)formation of the person along unique developmental trajectories.

The historic role played by mainstream Psychology in its eagerness to desubjectify the subject, reducing it to static categories – focused on "being" rather than "becoming" and depriving it of its gestalt properties-, is problematized in Valsiner et al. (2016). According to authors, the main challenge general Psychology needs to face in order to improve its relevance as a critical science for social praxis are:

- Need for *a generic unit of analysis in psychology, which is a synthesis of the mutual oppositions* in a system
- Escape from harmony, repetition, and equilibrium and accept crisis, novelty, and tension as inherent moments of living systems
- The constant (re)generation of the psyche in the processes of acting, counteracting, and constructing a self-reflexive structure, mediated by signs that constantly produce new phenomena

In other words, both scientific and applied Psychology are being increasingly pushed to give up the bourgeois normative features that used to define its core principles as a liberal science. Psychology is currently demanded to assume a new frame based on situated knowledge, on practice-based competences developed within concrete spheres of living experience. A critical corpus of knowledge emerges that allows for Psychology's active participation in the construction of collective projects committed with the transformation and emancipation of groups and communities.

We understand that the ethos of critical psychology approaches offers important clues that should be considered by those implied in a contextualized, situated, practice in social work. In this new scenario, we must ask ourselves: which contribution critical psychology offers to social work?

## Applied Psychology and Contexts of Practice in Social Work

For a long time, the debate concerning social work and its distinct contexts of practice was led by social assistants, whose professional identity is related to their participation in the construction of social policies and their growing commitment with an ethical and empathic anchoring of daily practice. Later on, other applied social disciplines, including Psychology, pedagogy, laws, etc., were included in this debate and they participated in the organization of a new field of empirical and situated knowledge constructed around community-based interventions. However, this emergent field has never been a calm sea. Instead, social work is an arena of deep tensions derived from theoretical and methodological issues emerging in the intersection of its multiple founding and adjacent disciplines, as well as related to the intricate network of social problems that affects human beings in a globalized world (Brazil, 2015).

In democratic societies, social work plays a strategic role as a bridge between the state and citizens, by expanding the reach and impact of social policies while inducing social protagonism and citizenship. Considering the features of this complex panorama of social demands within the contemporary world, no solution is enough in itself. Instead, diverse integrated actions are necessary and their common ground is to connect the goods and services offered by public policies and their beneficiaries. Thus, the core function of social work is to trigger developmental processes that, starting from a diagnosis of local problems, needs, and contexts, enhance their living conditions and increase locals' social participation, authorship, and networks, by means of multiple, intersectoral actions, and different forms of intervention in the public's own territory.

These processes will certainly vary according to the context, the targeted public, and the issues participants understand as relevant at a given moment. Projects aiming at intervening on community relations, for instance, will focus on collective goals, such as preventing prejudice and power unbalance while strengthening co-authorship, community autonomy, political engagement, and socio-relational links within groups and individuals.

Psychologists in social work can follow many different epistemological and methodological orientations in face of the challenges related to service user's demands as well as those associated with the multidisciplinary and multi-professional character of the work, in which psychologists, social assistants, pedagogues, health professionals, lawyers, and others are engaged (Yokoy, 2021). Concerning just psychology, theoretical and practical knowledge comes from different sources as well, such as social psychology, community psychology, developmental psychology, institutional psychology, clinical psychology, organizational psychology, psychoanalysis, systemic theories, psychodrama, etc. Still, Yokoy (2021) presents some principles for social policies and indicates the emergence of new psychological practices that are convergent with the collective catalization of novel subjective, family, and community developmental trajectories. In this sense, Psychology today moves from individualism toward a culturally contextualized praxis that transforms and promotes people's concrete living conditions and the quality of social, ethnic-racial, gender, religious, and/or age relations. Institutional-based interventions by contemporary psychologists focus on diverse relevant topics and specific features of the territories.

Projects developed by multi-professional teams within educational, socio-educational, security, or healthcare facilities will share some goals and differ with regard to others. In a way or another, different strategies will be needed to achieve desired outcomes. Thus, methodologies in social work should be developed in terms of co-created projects that consider the history of that given territory, aiming at empowering people to face daily life issues and more and more complex future individuals and collective existential challenges (Brazil, 2015). This means a continuous construction in which both workers and the subjects attended by the work creatively participate and are collaboratively benefited by the outcomes they reach.

In the next section, we present the three main areas in which Psychologists have contributed to the achievement of social policies' aims and goals, especially those related to social inclusion, citizenship, and protection of human rights. They are: healthcare; family-centered social assistance; and educational settings.

## Healthcare and Social Work

Healthcare is a broad system of integrated activities related to the organization, financing, and delivery of health services at the primary, secondary, and tertiary levels (WHO, 2018). Promoting a healthy society is an increasingly expensive and complex undertaking. Sociopolitical factors – such as the increase in the world population, the greater longevity of people, and the new technological stuff necessary to support the Medical practice – together with behavioral factors – world population physical inactivity, incorrect eating habits, daily stress, etc. – turn healthcare into something necessary, but unattainable sometimes.

Countries in the world follow different trends concerning health system financing. The first category includes countries in which health assistance is universally government-funded, which means that healthcare is available to all citizens regardless of their income or employment status. In the second group are included those countries in which some people receive healthcare via primary private insurance, while people who are ineligible for it, from the government. In the third model, the universal public insurance system, health costs are usually divided among the government, employees, and employers. This means that people who don't have a legal contract of employment and/or can't register as unemployed may be ineligible for free healthcare. Finally, in a small albeit growing scope of nations, health is an exclusive private enterprise, converted into a very profitable business, of which most people are excluded, what risks not only their own lives but the community as a whole. Moreover, some countries included in the three other categories by WHO currently undergo political reforms that will soon result in a transition to models in which the government will have smaller participation in healthcare costs.

In this very contrasting scenario, the citizens' right to access healthcare policies in its different levels of action is under threat, which is a major issue for social work attention and psychologists. From the consequences of one's total exclusion of healthcare assistance to the support needed to deal with chronicle diseases and permanent impairments, for instance, the importance of inclusive social policies is undeniable, by means of ethical policies and engaged social workers. Furthermore, social workers are needed not only in the direct care of people, they should be integrated within different points of the health system, including the participation into health councils; in the elaboration, management, and evaluation of health policies; in the development of research projects that assess innovative care practices held within healthcare facilities, and others. As for psychologists in social work, they are expected to go far beyond an individualistic outpatient care limited to psychodiagnosis and individual/group psychotherapy. Although individual approaches are necessary in specific circumstances, psychologists are encouraged to have a growing participation in the solution of broader problems that impede the healthcare systems to being efficient and inclusive (Dimenstein, 2014; Spink et al. 2014), what involves getting out of the box, adopting different, creative context-sensitive, culturally inclusive strategies.

Principles as community participation, comprehensiveness, humanization, complexity, and interdisciplinarity are core aspects of the activities carried out by multi-professional teams, psychologists included, which work within healthcare systems (WHO, 2018). While social assistants pre-grad education is clearly attuned with these principles, psychology students' professional training is impacted by the challenge of surpassing historically rooted individualism in this field and having the opportunity to participate in and collaborate with multi-professional teams and community leaders in situated contexts of practice. Health promotion and healing practices deal with a diverse scope of situated knowledge, both scientific and non-scientific ones. The co-construction of collaborative interventions that lead to positive outcomes, from the standpoint of the users themselves, need considering the multiple, divergent realities in which health services operate. Culture-sensitive psychological techniques will add an important contribution to social work in healthcare contexts.

The National Health System in the authors' home country (Unified Health System-SUS, Brazil) is universally government-funded, what is considered as a great social achievement, considering our enormous territory, and the tremendous sociocultural and economic divergences within the cared population. Following WHO, the SUS is guided by principles as universality, integrality, and equity; therefore the same principles guide the social work of psychologists in healthcare. While universality refers to ensuring to all citizens the right of access to public health services, integrality speaks of the coordination of the diverse dimensions of health-disease process, including health promotion and protection, cure and rehabilitation, in equal conditions to different persons, regions, or communities, so that differences are not transformed into inequalities (Spink et al. 2014).

In search of good practices 1:

**Applying Integral Health Principles in Improving a Child's Adherence to Treatment**

A psychologist who works in a given health care service is requested to develop – together with nurses and the doctor – specific actions to improve a diabetic child's adherence to treatment. Considering the principle of integrality, it is essential to comprehend that infant diabetes is much more than an organic condition; diabetes implies in a set of life-long commitments, affecting the child's whole life trajectory and future horizons. Dealing with diabetes in childhood and adhering to treatment will probably involve difficulties as possible side effects of medication or parents' guilt in social settings such as birthday parties, for instance. Above all, team intervention will certainly interfere in family history, dynamics, affects and values, and in its participation in the sociocultural context, as a source of community support that can make lighter the load of the disease.

Hence, even if the initial focus of the team is this specific demand around the child's difficulties with adherence to treatment, social workers are expected to open their lens in order to include the whole family in their strategies, considering its integrality and in a contextualized way. Appropriately planning healthcare actions in this direction will certainly reduce psychosocial impacts of chronic illness; improve the child's quality of life; minimize undesirable effects of the health condition upon schooling; and help the family to strengthen its own coping strategies against the stressors associated with the illness *per se*. In sum, social workers should not ignore protocols, but they should also be aware of the impacts of human beings' uniqueness on social work and, as a consequence, that each case will probably require of the team specific solutions.

## Family-Centered Social Care and the Active Participating Beneficiaries

Psychologists in social assistance services are supposed to participate in interdisciplinary teams, the main goal of which is promoting subjective and collective changes, helping beneficiaries in overcoming social risks, as well as strengthening community bonds and families´ potentialities. In sum, enhancing individuals, families, groups, and communities' autonomy and protagonism (Conselho Federal de Serviço Social/ Conselho Federal de Psicologia, 2007).

A family-centered social care, as most of the social work practice based on a critical approach is not usually performed by an isolated professional and the client – this was the main feature of a clientelistic approach, indifferent to users autonomy and the community development. In critical social care, discussed earlier in this chapter, individuals, families, and communities are considered as social-historical agents that find in sociocultural concrete settings semiotic resources to develop in a bidirectional manner, by participating in social practices. So, to be effective, social work must articulate this network of intersectoral services in order to approach families in its integrality and complexity, and strengthen both its inner bonds and its sense of belonging in the community.

In contemporary times, we share a plural panorama of family arrangements, quite distinct from the bourgeois nuclear family structure typical of the Modern Age: extended families; couples with adopted kids; second partners with their own kids living together; intercultural religious families; families headed by grandparents, by single parents, by Same-assigned sex couples (APA's 2021), for instance. Following institutional reports (Brazil, 2012a), and academic works (Soares, 2012), all groups of people that recognize in each other's ties of blood, affection, and solidarity are considered as a family. Hence, a protective family dynamics can exist regardless of the specific features of its inner arrangements, and even independent of its socioeconomic features. Even so, social policies should intervene in order to prevent, to approach, and help to find an adequate solution whenever families face some crisis, mostly if this problem represents a possibility for victimization of women, children, and the Older population (APA's 2021).

These three groups are considered as prioritized groups by social policies due to the fact that they have specific material, legal, and emotional demands concerning social support. As for children and older people, their peculiar developmental conditions, and as for women, their struggles facing gender inequalities and violence. For these reasons, in most democratic countries, children are totally sheltered by the law, and their rights regarding public health, education, and social assistance are considered as the most relevant ones. In capitalist societies, for instance, children and adolescents suffer in a sharper way than adults the effects of the culture of consumption and also the impacts of the mechanisms of social exclusion that affect those families deprived of means for consumption. In fact, the earlier in life a person is exposed to deteriorated socioeconomic conditions, the longer she/he will remain affected by the perverse effects of poverty and its consequences on his/her development trajectories and that of the following generations, unless she/he is reached by the arms of protecting public social policies.

Children and adolescents can be condemned to social exclusion by many factors, other than the ones rooted in family's and community's scarcity of material resources.

Cultural features such as the prevalence of conservative values and beliefs that support parents' unquestionable authority upon their kids can also deprive children and adolescents of the chance to participate in the decisions that concern their lives and disturb their physical, cognitive, moral, or emotional developmental outcomes. Some examples are early school dropouts due to early adolescence marriage or child labor.

Taking these factors into account, families are one of the most important contexts of social work that, according to Brazil (2012b), involves the following principles:

(a) Critical awareness and research spirit on the part of professionals dealing with families.
(b) Knowledge of the territory, its potentials, resources, and vulnerabilities, in order to carry out preventive and proactive action.
(c) Knowledge about life cycles; ethnic, racial, and sexual orientation issues, as well as other specific topics that may define relations in the territory.
(d) Interdisciplinary and interprofessional approach, which makes it possible to understand families and territories according to sociological, anthropological, economic, psychological approaches, among others.
(e) Participation of service beneficiaries in the planning and evaluation of actions implemented with families.

It is important to highlight that everyone assisted by social work has their own rights: the right to learn how public policies services work; to express his/her interests and expectations; to participate in decision-making processes concerning the solution of their own problems; and – exception made to specific conditions determined by law – to decide about their own lives, including the alternative of not taking part in a given intervention or activity proposed by social workers, if she/he understands that the proposal violates or ignores his/her interests.

Social workers and psychologists should create together with service-users opportunities to democratic and protecting relations – within the family and with the staff – and prevent the proliferation of problems as segregation, subordination, and undervaluation. Below, we illustrate the importance of family-centered social work by means of two initiatives that focused upon the family system. They accomplished encouraging the collaborative participation of both direct beneficiaries (older people, people without housing (APA's 2021)) and their families.

In search of good practices 2:

**Reducing Violence Against older people in the Territory: A Family-Based Intervention**

The first case refers to an initiative held in a special social protection service for older people and their families in the south region of Brazil aiming at reducing statistics of victimization of older population in the territory (Appio & Tramontin,

(continued)

2012). One hundred and twenty-four older adults and 332 family members were accompanied in this social care facility and the multi-professional team had noticed in the months before an expressive increase in the number of reported episodes of violence against older people (mainly neglect, abuse, and abandonment by family members), followed by legal measures to ensure the victims' rights what, in most cases, meant their transference to nursing homes.

The team started by doing home visits and inviting family members to talking-meetings in the social care facility. They constructed together with each family group an "Individual Plan" that settled the main points to be approached and the main goals to be collaboratively achieved. Along the meetings with the families the staff could figure out that not only older adults but also the family members were exposed to harsh vulnerable conditions as well and endured concrete difficulties to cope with taking care of the older people, for example, when they retained the bank card what had a negative impact upon the whole family who would not count on his/her contribution to household expenses. According to the team, their option to dealing with issues of intra-familiar violence through approaches that engaged the whole family, instead of individual-oriented techniques, led to positive outcomes, especially because the strategy favored a sensitive look both to the victim and to the other family members' perspectives. This way the older adults' rights were protected and relations of care within the family context were favored, turning older people less vulnerable and preventing the aggravation of the episodes, which would probably lead to the future transference of the victimized member to nursing homes, on the expense of the government.

In search of good practices 3:

**Culture and the Inclusion of People Without Housing: An Aesthetic Approach of Reality**

This example portrays an innovative social project that combines information, local culture, and the purpose of socially including people living in the streets or under extreme social vulnerability. This project resulted in a serial magazine named "Traços Magazine," initiated in 2015 in Brasília, Brazil. Since then the magazine has won many awards and is part of the International Network of Street Papers (Street Publications). The idea was to unite local artists – poets, writers, musicians, designers, actors, directors, and photographers – invited to collaborate in the production of the reports, and the so-called "culture spokesperson," people without housing, whose function is to, after proper training, publicize and sell the magazine in places such as restaurants, bars, cinemas, and theaters. Together with this professional activity, spokesmen are offered personal care related to health issues (dental care, testing for sexually transmitted infections), mental health care (mostly related to alcohol

(continued)

and illicit drugs abuse, anxiety, depression, etc.), educational mentoring, and have the opportunity to participate in distinct cultural activities. This aspect favors the development of an aesthetic approach to reality, besides turning them more accurate in the paper of culture spokesperson. All these initiatives demand a huge intersectoral articulation of public and private efforts that engage social assistance, health care, education, and cultural profitable organizations: 100% of the magazine sales revenue is destined to beneficiaries. The agreement followed by partners is that at least 30% of the profits will mandatorily be used by spokesmen to acquire new magazines, so that she/he can start a new cycle of income generation, to finance future life plans and to support self-care and self-esteem individual projects.

After living in the streets for sometime, human beings experience negative social stigma and develop weak self-images and low self-esteem. Being ignored by other people or even being targeted by unpleasant, offensive attitudes will cause self-defensive and hostile conducts. Participants in the project showed a tendency to self-isolate and avoid social contact. The fact that each volume of the magazine dedicates few pages to portray the life history of one of them help spokesperson to voice their life and to position themselves as protagonists of the life and culture of the city, thus providing them visibility and social recognition. Lopes (2019) argues that the discursive line of the magazine functions as a counter-discourse that questions participants' marginalization processes, their social exclusion, and the social stigmas they are exposed to, expanding personal and professional perspectives, promoting social visibility, and community bonds. After participating in the Traços Magazine project for sometime, most participants not only experienced changes in their appearance and attitudes, many managed to get fixed housing, jobs, would pay for their own food, and maintain self-care initiatives. In some cases, family bonds were restored and they went back to the family home. Mental health treatment helped many of them to overcome substance use disorders (APA's 2021). Those who needed legal assistance obtained it with the project help as well.

## Social Work in Educational Settings

Psychology has constructed a long-lasting relationship with the educational environment. The demands posed by schools and the wide scope of problems related to teaching and learning have contributed to the development of psychological instruments – like intelligence and personality tests – and to the psychological science as a whole. However, especially at first, this relationship was characterized by an individualized, remedial and curative emphasis (Guzzo et al. 2014). School difficulties lived by children were approached by mainstream Psychology in terms of cognitive, mental problems, and the solutions for these problems were searched inside their mind. We now understand that all human beings are equipped with a natural ability to learn, no exception made. Learning is a complex mental function and it is so essential for the survival and development of human beings, so necessary to cope with the threats and challenges faced along one's life course, that in the absence of a hard brain injury or a severe intellectual disability, the fact that some children just do not succeed in school tasks should be necessarily put under suspicion. Hence, learning problems at school should be necessarily interpreted together with other factors, such as family issues, social vulnerabilities, economic hierarchies, and other concrete difficulties lived by young apprentices in daily life. And this is where school social workers come in. For instance, in regions with lower Human Development Indexes (HDI), school dropouts are a bigger problem than it is in higher HDI, in an intimate relation with problems such as child labor, domestic and community violence, drug trafficking, etc. These professionals have important roles within schools, supporting teachers and pupils, as policy-makers, and in the administration of educational policies.

In democratic societies, at least, schooling is a universal opportunity, a basic experience shared by most of the population at a certain interval of the life course. Considering this aspect, each school represents in itself a knot in the educational policies system and, at the same time, a context in which children, adolescents, and their families can be accessed by other social policies. Thus, the longer the school career and the more qualified the educational experiences children and young people are exposed to in schools, the less they will depend on other social policies and the government, in the future. Hence, social workers are demanded to intervene both within schools and in permanent dialogue with schools, especially when these professionals take part in intersectoral policies, which are by their nature related to education, health, social assistance, justice, etc., at once.

Considering the vast literature existing on educational psychology focusing on regular schools and the role of school social workers (Dupper, 2008; Openshaw, 2008), in the remaining of this section we will focus on a particular educational context in which social workers, psychologists included, perform a core role in achieving desired goals: juvenile justice. Juvenile justice in the international context is an intersectoral policy, intrinsically related to many other social policies, as education, healthcare, social assistance, public security, and justice (Watts & Hodgson, 2019).

The core aspects and principles guiding juvenile justice in the world nowadays mentions humanitarian treatment to young people who violated the law, emphasizing the importance of school opportunities and professional training, together with the efforts to strengthen family and community bonds and their growing commitment with the problems of their immediate sociocultural context, in a participatory, emancipatory perspective (Decker & Marteache, 2017).

Thus, to cohere with these principles, local policies should guarantee that school opportunities have a central importance within juvenile justice, if they expect young people to reach innovative developmental trajectories as a consequence of the legal sanction, uniting the physical, mental, moral, spiritual, and social dimensions of subjectivity (Lopes de Oliveira, 2003, 2014, 2016; Paiva and Cruz, 2014).

One of the greatest challenges countries face regarding juvenile justice today involves a creative solution for reaching the best equilibrium between the effectiveness of the legal measures imposed to young offenders as a consequence of their criminal act, for a side, and the high costs and the many undesired psychosocial side effects of custodial legal measures, for the other. The imbalance between the two plates of the scale pushes young people in the opposite direction of the humanitarian principles enumerated before. Whenever legal measures fail, young people not only practice novel offenses, but these offenses tend to be more serious and involve even more violence, demanding even more severe penalties as a consequence (Lopes de Oliveira & Yokoy, 2012).

A second big issue endured by social workers in juvenile justice refers to the racial and socioeconomic selectivity within the socio-educational system, a visible effect of the deep tension installed in it between promoting human rights and reproducing criminalization, poverty, and stigmatization of minority groups. For instance, in most Western developed and developing countries, the number of black people in jail is higher than in Caucasian ones. Social workers deal with negative social representations about young people and should work to overcome this condition, preventing the effects of these negative representations on the social evaluation of young people's behaviors and attitudes. Thanks to a racial selectivity, more often than whites, black young people are usually interpreted in association with criminality, even when they are just expressing joviality and joy (Paiva & Cruz, 2014).

Social work multi-professional teams, psychologists included, have as their main role to construct together with their peers and the adolescents they attend, novel developmental trajectories that exclude adolescents' dependence on criminal activities and promote their living in healthy and secure conditions. Social workers accomplish different functions in juvenile justice, some of which will target the adolescents themselves; others will engage different actors within the system, such as security agents and management personal. Concerning the adolescents, there are custodial and noncustodial legal measures, and professionals are responsible for supervising and going along with them during the time they comply with the legal measure, and define – together with adolescents and their parents – a set of goals for an individualized socio-educational plan, based on the elements previously investigated and the character of the offense itself. This includes the following steps:

(a) Learn about his/her legal process, and stay up to date with any novelties or required reports concerning the measure itself and the protection of the adolescents' rights.
(b) Gather information about the adolescent and his/her family system, their intergeneration history, inner structure, and emotional links.
(c) Check if the adolescent is already assisted by the healthcare and educational system and, if necessary, refer them and their families to the proper social policies.
(d) Supervise adolescents along with planned educational, cultural, sports, and professional training activities, and evaluate in collaboration with them the reached and not yet reached outcomes.

(e) Observe school frequency and academic performance, in dialogue with teachers and school counselors.
(f) Make it clear what are the adolescents' rights and duties and construct with them a commitment with following rules. Inform him/her about the consequences of rule-breaking.
(g) Evaluate, together with security agents, issues of misbehavior, indiscipline, and other occurrences along custody, based on general rules and sensitive to each unique case, choosing the most effective attitude to take in each case.
(h) Monitor peer relations within the institution, to prevent rebellions and other circumstances that may risk adolescents' safety and life.
(i) Highlight the adolescents' main achievements, and whenever legally allowed, indicate his/her release, or the transference to a less severe penalty, in order to favor better results with less harm on their subjectivity.
(j) Collaborate with the institutional effort to follow the adolescents after release until they are fully inserted in a context of minimum social protection, preventing thus the occurrence of new episodes that may lead them back to custody.

As for other actors in the juvenile justice system, social workers intervene in issues of organizational climate, promoting mutual collaboration within the teams and preventing/intervening in issues of competition, individualism, or lack of empathy; they can lead permanent education workshops to construct with the staff symbolic resources and competences necessary to work and discuss other issues that may compromise the quality of service and the effectiveness of collaboration between professionals working in different points of socio-educational care, or the attachment with the adolescents.

In the authors' home country, research projects conducted by Yokoy and Rengifo-Herrera (2020), Andrade (2017), and Cunha (2019) show that, after a long history of oppression and discrimination regarding juvenile offenders within local juvenile justice, some meaningful changes are taking place within it, and this transformation is feeding better expectations regarding the future outcomes of socio-educational system.

First of all, they noticed a slow renewal of the staff after the retirement or the dropout of tougher educators, whose self-images were more aligned with that of security agents. The profile followed by the recently recruited educators, which coexists with the more traditional ones, is attuned with human rights principles so that they aim not only to blame and punish offenders, but they are sensitive to the adolescents' social needs and educational and professional expectations. Moreover, they seem motivated to engage in initiatives aiming at their professional development, which is essential in order to improve socio-educational achievements.

Secondly, they found that social workers within juvenile justice are unsatisfied with more traditional approaches and they are more and more in search of alternative practices in justice that help them intervene in a more effective way. Techniques related to Restorative justice (Aertsen & Pali, 2017; Marshal, 2018), nonviolent communication (Rosenberg, 2005), and peace culture (Branco & Lopes de Oliveira, 2018) are among the new tendencies adopted. Although far from generalized throughout the system, the successful results obtained through pilot-experiences based on such alternative practices, are encouraging a growing number of social workers to follow the direction of this innovative field of practice.

Finally, we notice a slow but significant cultural transition within the socio-educational system concerning the preference for noncustodial, instead of custodial sanctions. For a long time, depriving freedom was considered as the best alternative in cases of a juvenile offense. Around 20 years ago, fortunately, the many undesired consequences of long-term imprisonment (cf. Goffman, 2009), such as stigma, social isolation, emotional disorders, and the worsening of violent behavior, were finally considered, and the sentencing of noncustodial sanctions grew and overcame the custodial ones.

Social workers, psychologists included, together with recognizing adolescents agency and autonomy, are expected to adopt cultural-inclusive practices that take into account the severe sociocultural constraints endured by juvenile offenders and the impact of these constraints over their own developmental trajectories, as well as their families and peers. Cultural sensitivity is necessarily co-constructed in the context of collaborative activities and projects that engage not only the adolescents but their families and meaningful community members as well, besides schools, health services, and other equipment within the territory.

According to Paiva and Cruz (2014), cultural sensitivity and inclusiveness are the most important parts of a radical shift in juvenile justice, which means overcoming traditional socio-educational perspectives, based on controlling or punishing the body in order to change the mind of the offenders, and meet a novel perspective based on coexistence, empathy, collaboration, and mutual recognition. This perspective coheres with the idea that adolescents have the right to access socialization settings that contribute to improve reflexivity, autonomy, citizenship, and prepare them to transform their living conditions.

We are not arguing that provoking such a shift in the way juvenile offenders position themselves and are positioned by society and the justice system is an easy task. It is hard to genuinely touch their heart; difficult to develop discursive forms that not only grasp their minds but stir up their motivational system and engage them in a vivid dialogue with social workers as well. It is almost impossible to make them focus on their future, mainly if the horizon is beyond a few months. Most have negative self-representations and denote a great difficulty to imagine and project alternative futures to the "thug life." For most, violence has turned into their main source of identity and social acknowledgment. Thus, social workers who intend to be helpful to adolescents in the construction of new existential possibilities need to be able to find out in the adolescents the potentialities they are unable to see in themselves, a possible first step in the way along which they will reinterpret their role in the family, proximal community, and in society.

The example below illustrates the effort made by a group of social workers to co-construct with offenders and community members a community-based project to improve adolescents' participation and citizenship. The social workers work in a noncustodial sanctions (community services and supervised probation) facility, part of the juvenile justice system of the Federal District, Brazil.

In search of good practices 4: **"Soccer of the Hood"**[2]

The social workers dealt with a huge difficulty to construct, together with the adolescents they attended, a genuine engagement and responsibility regarding the fulfillment of the legal sentence, after their have committed a light infraction. How to overcome families' concrete difficulties (ex: unemployment, school dropout, discrimination) and community precariousness while taking into account adolescents' desires, dreams, and affections, transforming all of this into a meaningful project, from the standpoint of the cared adolescents? Since long adolescents complained of the scarcity of sportive, cultural, and leisure activities in the community. The team decided to innovate supervised probation in that facility, uniting soccer practice and social protagonism with the main goals of socioeducation.

The "soccer of the hood" project includes a set of activities around soccer playing (training, practicing, organizing, and participating in community championships). Adolescents under probation participate in all the project's activities, which involve the steps of planning, executing, evaluating, sharing decisions, and searching for means to improve the project itself. The project engages them in democratic and collective experiences, together with the other adolescents of the community, social workers, and other community leaders, in a respectful and responsible way.

The fact that they are recognized as trustworthy subjects, full of potentialities to be explored instead of useless, unrecoverable offenders gets to slowly change their self-images. Participants offer each other mutual support, exchange other personal experiences than criminal ones, and discuss about their idols and models with which they identify (for instance, Brazilian national team soccer players *versus* well-known drug dealers of the neighborhood). As a consequence they get to foresee social alternatives to gather social acknowledgment if not by the ostentation of guns, or expensive tennis shoes.

## Concluding Remarks

In this chapter we explored the historical, conceptual, and theoretical challenges posed to the interaction of psychology and social work, when they are part of institutional-based, or community-based programs. We argued that in a globalized, interconnected world, social work should be informed by critical approaches in social sciences and humanities, meaning the endless effort to use psychological

---

[2] To other informations about the "Soccer of the Hood" project, please access: https://www.instagram.com/uamaparanoa (Instagram); https://www.facebook.com/uamaparanoaitapoa/ (Facebook); or, search in Youtube "Soccer of the Hood: a project that makes a difference" (Futebol da Quebrada: um projeto que faz a diferença), a video produced by adolescents and social workers (https://www.youtube.com/watch?v=BmxI9SA2cW4)

knowledge as a tool for the social critique, for the critique of psychology itself, and the critique as the main pillar in the construction of a different building to psychological science.

Having these three points in mind, we presented a general overview of the branch of the critical thinking that guides our epistemological framework, which follows the track of the sociocultural turn and, more specifically, is based on the cultural-semiotic psychology. In a few words, this approach offers a broad understanding of how human beings develop upon activity and semiotic movements within and between different layers of the sociocultural world. Individuals are considered as social-historical agents that find in cultural settings the semiotic resources to their own development and the cultural recreation, by their active co-participation in social practices in which meanings can be negotiated.

The three contexts of practice herein described are illustrative of the different possibilities for social workers, psychologists included, insertion in institutions, groups, and collective settings. Beyond their specific features, the three spheres of activity pose common challenges to multi-professional teams in social work, such as: to face the complexities of social work as a collective, multi-professional enterprise; to construct democratic and creative work processes and sensibilities; and recognizing diversity of individual, family, and community cultures. Besides, it is important to collaborate in a network of services that promotes social protection, significant experiences to enhancing the exercise of citizenship, assuring human rights and favoring psychosocial changes in individuals, families, and communities.

In order to deal with the challenges inherent to social work, a critical, ethical, and political formation for psychologist is demanded, as well as an ethical-political analysis of contemporary societies. We hope this chapter has contributed to provide literature for the formation in Psychology, departing from sociocultural and critical perspectives, and articulated to the empirical contexts in which the social work develops.

## References

Aertsen, I., & Pali, B. (2017). *Critical restorative justice*. Bloomsbury.
Afonso, M. L. M., Vieira-Silva, M., Abade, F. L., Abrantes, T. M., & Fadul, F. M. (2012). Psychology in the unified system of social welfare. *Pesquisas e Práticas Psicossociais, 7*(2), 189–199.
Alberto, M. de F. P., Freire, M. L., Leite, F. M., & Gouveia, C. N. N. A. (2014). As políticas públicas de assistência social e a atuação profissional dos(as) psicólogos(as) [Public social assistance policies and the professional performance of psychologists]. In I. F. de Oliveira, & O. H. Yamamoto (Eds.), *Psicologia e políticas sociais: Temas em debate* (pp. 127–174.). Editora da Universidade Federal do Pará.
American Psychological Association. (2021). Inclusive language guidelines. https://www.apa.org/about/apa/equity-diversity-inclusion/language-guidelines.pdf
Appio, M., & Tramontin, V. G. (2012). Serviço de proteção social especial para pessoas idosas e suas famílias [Special Social Protection Service for elderly people and their families]. *EntreLinhas- Conselho Regional de Psicologia do Rio Grande do Sul, 57*, 10–10.
Bauman, Z. (2000). *The liquid modernity*. Polity Press.

Bauman, Z. (2011). *Collateral damage: Social inequalities in a global age*. Polity Press.
Branco, A. U., & Lopes de Oliveira, M. C. S. (2018). *Alterity, values and socialization: Human development within educational contexts*. Springer.
Brazil. (2012a). *Norma Operacional Básica do Sistema Único de Assistência Social- NOB/SUAS* [Basic Operating Standard of the Unified Social Assistance System- NOB/SUAS]. Ministério do Desenvolvimento Social e Combate à Fome. https://www.mds.gov.br/webarquivos/public/NOBSUAS_2012.pdf
Brazil. (2012b). *Trabalho social com famílias do Serviço de Proteção e Atendimento Integral à Família– PAIF* [Social work with families of the Service of Protection and Integral Assistance to the Family– PAIF]. Ministério do Desenvolvimento Social e Combate à Fome. http://www.mds.gov.br/webarquivos/publicacao/assistencia_social/Cadernos/Orientacoes_PAIF_2.pdf
Brazil. (2015). *Documento técnico orientador para subsidiar o seminário nacional sobre trabalho social com famílias na Política Nacional de Assistência Social* [Guiding technical document to support the national seminar on social work with families in the National Social Assistance Policy]. Ministério do Desenvolvimento Social e Combate à Fome. https://aplicacoes.mds.gov.br/sagirmps/ferramentas/docs/Produto%203%20-%20TSF_MIOTO.pdf
Brazil. (2018). *Contribuições para o Aprimoramento do PAIF- Gestão, família e território em evidência* [Contributions to the Improvement of PAIF- Management, family and territory in evidence]. Ministério do Desenvolvimento Social. http://www.mds.gov.br/webarquivos/arquivo/assistencia_social/consulta_publica/Contribuicao%20para%20o%20Aprimoramento%20do%20PAIF%20final.pdf
Conselho Federal de Serviço Social, & Conselho Federal de Psicologia (2007). *Parâmetros para atuação de assistentes sociais e psicólogos(as) na Política de Assistência Social* [Parameters for the performance of social workers and psychologists in the Brazilian Social Assistance Policy]. Conselho Federal de Serviço Social, & Conselho Federal de Psicologia.
Curado, J. C., & Menegon, V. S. M. (2009). Gênero e os sentidos do trabalho social [Gender and the meanings of social work]. *Psicologia & Sociedade, 21*(3), 431–441.
Decker, S. H., & Marteache, N. (2017). *International handbook of juvenile justice*. Springer.
Dimenstein, M. (2014). A Psicologia no campo da saúde mental [Psychology in the field of mental health]. In I. F. de Oliveira, & O. H. Yamamoto (Eds.), *Psicologia e políticas sociais: Temas em debate* (pp. 75–125). Editora da Universidade Federal do Pará.
Donzelot, J. (1997). *The policing of families*. John Hopkins.
Dupper, D. (2008). *School Social Work: Skills and interventions for effective practice*. Wiley.
Goffman, E. (2009). *Asylums: Essays on the social situation of mental patients and other inmates*. Aldine Transaction. (Original work published 1961)
Guzzo, R. S. L., Mezzalira, A. S. da C., & Moreira, A. P. G. (2014). Desafios, ameaças e compromissos para os psicólogos: As políticas públicas no campo educativo [Challenges, threats and commitments for psychologists: public policies in the educational field.]. In I. F. de Oliveira, & O. H. Yamamoto (Eds.), Psicologia e políticas sociais: Temas em debate (pp. 215–238). Editora da Universidade Federal do Pará.
Harré, R. (2010). Public sources of the personal mind: Constructionism in context. In S. R. Kirschner, & J. Martin (Eds.), *The sociocultural turn in Psychology: The contextual emergence of mind and self* (pp. 31–45). Columbia University Press.
Ingleby, E. (2010). *Applied Psychology for Social Work*. Learning Matters.
International Federation of Social Workers. (2014). *Global definition of Social Work*. https://www.ifsw.org/what-is-social-work/global-definition-of-social-work/
Jensen, M. (2015). Catalytic models developed through social work. Integrative *Psychological and Behavioral Science, 49*(1), 56–72.
Kirshner, S., & Martin, J. (2010). The sociocultural turn in Psychology: An introduction and an invitation In S. R. Kirschner, & J. Martin (Eds.), *The sociocultural turn in Psychology: The contextual emergence of mind and self* (pp.01–28). Columbia University Press.
Lima, A. C. (2019). *Futebol das quebradas: A promoção do desenvolvimento e a construção de práticas inovadoras de atendimento socioeducativo* [Soccer of the Hood: Promoting

development and the construction of innovative socioeducational care practices] [Trabalho de Conclusão de Curso, Universidade de Brasília]. Biblioteca Digital da Produção Intelectual Discente. https://bdm.unb.br/handle/10483/22662

Lopes de Oliveira, M. C. S. (2003). Inserção escolar no contexto das medidas socioeducativas: "Sem a escola, a gente não é nada" [School insertion in the context of socioeducational sanctions: "Without school, we are nothing"]. In M. F. O. Sudbrack, M. I. G. Conceição, & M. T. da Silva (Orgs.), *Adolescentes e drogas no contexto da justiça* (pp. 293–307). Plano.

Lopes de Oliveira, M. C. S. (2014). Da medida ao atendimento socioeducativo: Implicações conceituais e éticas [From socioeducational sanction to socioeducational care: Conceptual and ethical implications]. In I. L. Paiva, C. Souza, & D. B. Rodrigues (Orgs.), *Justiça juvenil: Teoria e prática no sistema socioeducativo* (pp. 79–100). Editora da Universidade Federal do Rio Grande do Norte.

Lopes de Oliveira, M. C. S. (2016). A ação socioeducativa no contexto da justiça juvenil: Interlocuções com a psicologia escolar [Socioeducational action in the context of juvenile justice: Interlocutions with school psychology]. In M. N. Viana, & R. Francischini (Eds.), *Psicologia Escolar: Que fazer é esse?* (pp. 124–136). Conselho Federal de Psicologia.

Lopes de Oliveira, M. C. S. (2019, August 19-23). *Living by and despite violence and vulnerability: Contributions of semiotic cultural psychology to communities and subjectivities* [Panel oral presentation]. The International Conference in Theoretical Psychology, Copenhagen, DN. https://conferences.au.dk/istp2019

Lopes de Oliveira, M. C. S., & Yokoy, T. (2012). Education, peace or jail culture? What is promoted by institutions in charge of adolescents involved with criminal activities. In A. U. Branco, & J. Valsiner (Eds.), *Cultural psychology of human values* (pp. 239–264). Information Age.

Lopes, L. P. S. (2019). Análise discursiva da Revista Traços: Revista cultural e projeto social [Discursive analysis of Traços Magazine: Cultural magazine and social Project]. *VERBUM-Cadernos de Pós Graduação, 8*(2), 181–201.

Marshal, T. F. (2018). *Restorative justice: An overview.* Conventry Lord Mayor Committee for Peace and Reconciliation.

Martins, L. R. (2016). The thinking of Jeannine Verdès-Leroux and the social work: A critique rescue. *Serviço Social & Sociedade, 127*, 514–532.

McLaughlin, K. (2014). Social work. In T. Teo (Ed.), *Encliclopaedia of Critical Psychology* (pp. 1812–1815). Springer.

Natale, A., Matino, S., Procentese, F., & Arcidiacono, C. (2016). De-growth and critical community psychology: Contributions towards individual and social well being. *Futures, 78–79*, 47–56.

Nissen, M. (2012). *The subjectivity of participation: Articulating social work practice with Youth in Copenhagen.* McMillan.

Nwoye, A. (2014). African psychology, critical trends. In T. Teo (Ed.), *Encliclopaedia of Critical Psychology* (pp. 57–68). Springer.

Olivares, S. I. (2012). Challenges to social work in a field of labor with difuse professional limits. *Barbarói, 15*(2), 163–172.

Openshaw, L. (2008). *Social work in schools: Principles and practice.* Guilford Press.

Paiva, I. L. de, & Cruz, A. V. H. (2014). A Psicologia e o acompanhamento de adolescentes em conflito com a lei [Psychology and monitoring of adolescents in conflict with the law]. In I. F. de Oliveira, & O. H. Yamamoto (Eds.), *Psicologia e políticas sociais: Temas em debate* (pp. 175–214.). Editora da Universidade Federal do Pará.

Prado, M. A. M. (2014). Psicologia e Política: Entre preterições, críticas e resistências [Psychology and Politics: Between deprecations, criticisms and resistances]. In I. F. de Oliveira, & O. H. Yamamoto (Eds.), *Psicologia e políticas sociais: Temas em debate* (pp. 09–15). Editora da Universidade Federal do Pará.

Puras, D., & Gooding, P. (2019). Mental health and human rights in 21st century. *World Psychiatry, 18*(1), 42–43.

Rodrigues, C. D., Oliveira, V. C. de, & Rocha, R. L. S. (2017). Brazil. In S. H. Decker, & N. Marteache (Eds.), *International Handbook of Juvenile Justice* (pp. 71–89). Springer.

Rosenberg, M. (2005). *The Heart of Social Change: How You Can Make a Difference in Your World*. Puddle Dancer Press.

Rulac, S. (2014). Social work and social intervention in France: The state of the knowledge. *Cadernos de Pesquisa, 44*(154), 876–890.

Santos, B. de S. (2016). *Epistemologies of the South: Justice against epistemicide*. Routledge.

Sarbin, T. R. (1986). The narrative as a root metaphor for Psychology. In T. R. Sarbin (Ed.), *Narrative psychology: The storied nature of human conduct* (pp. 3–21). Praeger Publishers/Greenwood Publishing Group.

Sato, T., & Valsiner, J. (2010). Time in life and life in time: Between experiencing and accounting. *Ritsumeikan Journal of Human Sciences, 20*(1), 79–92.

Shotter, J. (2010). Inside our lives together: A neo-Wittgensteinian Constructionism. In S. R. Kirschner, & J. Martin (Eds.), *The sociocultural turn in Psychology: The contextual emergence of mind and self* (pp. 45–67). Columbia University Press.

Sloan, T. (2002). Psicologia de la liberacion: Ignacio Martín-Baró. *Interamerican Journal of Psychology, 36*, 353–357.

Soares, R. P. (2012). *A concepção de família da política de assistência social: Desafios à atenção a famílias homoparentais* [The concept of family in social assistance policy: Challenges for the attention to homoparental families]. [Master's Dissertation, Universidade de Brasília]. Repositório Institucional da Universidade de Brasília. https://repositorio.unb.br/handle/10482/11113

Spink, M. J., Brigagão, J. I. M., & Nascimento, V. L. V. do. (2014). Psicólogos(as) no SUS: A convivências necessárias com as políticas de saúde [Psychologists in the SUS: The necessary coexistence with health policies]. In I. F. de Oliveira, & O. H. Yamamoto (Eds.), *Psicologia e políticas sociais: Temas em debate* (pp. 47–73). Editora da Universidade Federal do Pará.

Tateo, L. (2015). Gianbattista Vico and the psychological imagination. *Culture & Psychology, 21*(20), 145–161.

Teo, T. (2018). *Outlines of theoretical psychology: Critical investigations*. Palgrave Macmillan.

Valsiner, J. (2017). *From methodologies to methods in human psychology*. Springer.

Valsiner, J., Marsico, G., Chaudhary, N., Sato, T., & Dazzani, V. (2016). *Psychology as a science of human being: The Yokohama manifesto*. Springer.

Verdès-Leroux, J. (1986). *Trabalhador social: Prática, habitus, ethos, formas de intervenção* [Social worker: Practice, habitus, ethos, forms of intervention]. Cortez.

Watts, L., & Hodgson, D. (2019). *Social justice theory and practice for social work: Critical and philosophical perspectives*. Springer Nature.

World Health Organization (2018). *Mental health, human rights and standards of care. Assessment of the quality of institutional care for adults with psychosocial and intellectual disabilities in the WHO European Region*. https://www.who.int/europe/publications/i/item/9789289053204

Yokoy, T. (2021). Atuação do(a) psicólogo(a) na política de assistência social: Desafios enfrentados e práticas emergentes [Psychologist's role in social assistance policy: Reflections on the challenges faced and indicators for the construction of emerging practices]. In A. F. do A. Madureira, & J. Bizerril (Orgs.), *Psicologia & Cultura: Teoria, pesquisa e prática profissional* (pp. 271–304). Cortez.

Yokoy, T., & Rengifo-Herrera, F. J. (2020). Affective-Semiotic Fields and the Dialogical Analysis of Values and Interpersonal Relations in Socio-educational Contexts. In M. C. S. Lopes-de-Oliveira, A. U. Branco, & S. F. D. C. Freire (Eds.), *Psychology as a Dialogical Science: Self and Culture Mutual Development* (pp. 95–114). Springer Nature Switzerland.

# Learning and Teaching Geropsychology

43

Thomas Boll

## Contents

| | |
|---|---|
| Introduction | 1042 |
|     Geropsychology Research | 1043 |
|     Professional Geropsychology and Geropsychology Teaching | 1043 |
| Purposes and Rationale of the Curriculum in Geropsychology | 1045 |
|     Qualification for Understanding and Solving Age-Related Problems | 1045 |
|     Diversity of Study Programs: Challenge for Curriculum Development in Geropsychology | 1046 |
|     Core Learning and Teaching Objectives in Geropsychology: Content Dimensions | 1047 |
| Core Contents and Topics of Geropsychology | 1052 |
|     Theoretical Foundations | 1052 |
|     Normative Foundations | 1057 |
|     Methodical Foundations | 1058 |
|     Settings of Geropsychological Work | 1060 |
| Linking of Courses to Modules Within Study Programs | 1061 |
|     Modules of Geropsychological Study Programs | 1061 |
|     Arranging Course Sequences over Several Semesters | 1062 |
| Teaching, Learning, and Assessment in Geropsychology: Approaches and Strategies | 1062 |
|     Learning Outcomes, Teaching, and Assessment: Issues of Alignment | 1062 |
|     Different Target Students: Geropsychology in Non-psychological Study Programs | 1065 |
| Challenges and Lessons Learned | 1066 |
|     Research and Practical Application | 1066 |
|     Teaching and Practical Application | 1067 |
|     Research and Teaching | 1067 |
| Teaching, Learning, and Assessment Resources | 1067 |
|     Tips for Geropsychology Teaching | 1067 |

T. Boll (✉)
Department of Cognitive, and Behavioural Sciences, Institute for Lifespan Development, Family, and Culture, University of Luxembourg, Esch-sur-Alzette, Luxembourg
e-mail: thomas.boll@uni.lu

© Springer Nature Switzerland AG 2023
J. Zumbach et al. (eds.), *International Handbook of Psychology Learning and Teaching*, Springer International Handbooks of Education,
https://doi.org/10.1007/978-3-030-28745-0_50

Annotated References for Further Reading .............................................. 1068
URL-links to Teaching, Learning, and Assessment Resources .......................... 1072
Cross-References ................................................................... 1072
References ......................................................................... 1073

### Abstract

This chapter presents a broad overview about the essential aspects of learning and teaching geropsychology in tertiary education. After an introduction to the scope of geropsychology and the need for geropsychology education, the objectives and basic principles of geropsychology curricula are discussed. Their overall goal is to qualify students and/or professionals to understand and solve psychological aspects of problems of older people in the contexts of practical application, research, and teaching. Specific teaching and learning objectives in geropsychology are described in terms of underlying content dimensions (e.g., areas of acting, functioning, and development of older people; basic components of practical geropsychological acting; target groups and settings) and levels of competency to be acquired (e.g., uni-, multi-structural, relational, and extended abstract level). This is followed by an overview of the core topics of geropsychology. These refer to theoretical (e.g., basic concepts of age, aging, and older population; action competence of older people; challenges in later life; resources for adaptation; problems of people providing services to older adults), normative (ethical and legal), and methodical foundations (research, assessment, evaluation, and intervention methods). This is followed by sections on linking main learning objectives and core topics of geropsychology to courses within study programs (psychological or non-psychological) and about the relations between teaching, learning, and assessment in geropsychology. This chapter concludes with information about resources for these issues including relevant URL links, tips for teaching, and annotated references to further reading.

### Keywords

Aging · Older adulthood · Clinical practice · Geropsychology · Geropsychology training · Mental health services · Professional competence · Professional standards

## Introduction

Geropsychology (also known as gerontopsychology, psychology of aging, or psychological gerontology) is still rather young compared to other subfields such as differential, social, organizational, and clinical psychology. Yet, it is already so well developed, distinct, and relevant that it deserves a chapter of its own in this International Handbook on Psychology Learning and Teaching. Its subject area is large enough and well definable. So, there is a consensus between both Anglo-American (*Society in Clinical Geropsychology*) as well as European geropsychological organizations (*Standing Committee on GeroPsychology* by the *European Federation of Psychologists' Associations (EFPA)* that geropsychology addresses mental and behavioral phenomena of aging (as a change process), of older people (as a certain age group), and of old age (as a late stage of life) in research, applied fields, and teaching (https://geropsychology.org; http://geropsychology.efpa.eu/introduction/). The section on core contents of geropsychology later in this chapter will mention concrete topics more in detail. The tasks of the discipline are clear. As a subfield of psychology, geropsychology, like its parent discipline, aims at describing, explaining, and optimizing the phenomena that fall within its purview. Today, geropsychology has a strong research and a strong practice branch as indicated by several criteria.

## Geropsychology Research

Numerous psychological university departments in the USA, Europe, Australia, and other parts of the world host specialized institutes or professorships for geropsychology often associated with or part of the institutes for lifespan developmental psychology which have provided and further provide important contributions to geropsychological research. In addition, there are geropsychology research groups at non-university research institutes (e.g., Max Planck Institute for Human Development in Berlin/Germany). Moreover, there are several specialized peer-reviewed journals of geropsychology (e.g., *GeroPsych – The Journal of Gerontopsychology and Geriatric Psychiatry*; *Psychology & Ageing*; *The Journals of Gerontology, Series B: Psychological Sciences*) and further gerontological journals that regularly publish articles with geropsychological research results. Multi-volume encyclopedias and handbooks further document the breadth and depth of the geropsychological knowledge that has been accumulated so far (e.g., *Encyclopedia of Geropsychology* edited by Pachana, 2017; *Oxford Encyclopedia of Psychology and Aging* edited by Knight, 2019). Additional relevant sources are mentioned in the annotated references to further reading near the end of this chapter. Finally, the existence of specific scientific and/or professional organizations in various parts of the world makes a strong case for geropsychology as a developed discipline. For instance, in the USA, this is the *Society in Clinical Geropsychology*, which is housed under the APA Division 12, Section 2 (https://geropsychology.org), in Europe the *Standing Committee on GeroPsychology* by the *European Federation of Psychologists' Associations (EFPA)* (http://geropsychology.efpa.eu/standing-committee-/), and in Australia the *Psychology and Ageing Interest Group (PAIG)* of the *Australian Psychological Society (APS)* (https://groups.psychology.org.au/paig/).

## Professional Geropsychology and Geropsychology Teaching

Geropsychology has also been increasingly established as a field of professional psychology and teaching especially in the USA as indicated by the following developments or publications: (1) Recognition of the *American Board of*

*Geropsychology (ABGERO)* (https://abgero.org/) as a specialty within the *American Board of Professional Psychology (ABPP)*, which is the decisive committee for professional certifications within America; psychologists certified in geropsychology are called "specialist geropsychologist" *or* "ABGERO specialist" (55 people listed on the website in December 2021); (2) publication of *Pikes Peak Model for training in Professional Geropsychology* (Knight, Karel, Hinrichsen, Qualls, & Duffy, 2009); (3) development of a geropsychology training organization called *Council of Professional Geropsychology Training Programs (CoPGTP;* Hinrichsen, Emery-Tiburcio, Gooblar, & Molinari, 2018) (http://copgtp.org) with 71 member programs listed on the website in December 2021, many of which are in line with the *Pikes Peak Model for Training in Professional Geropsychology*; (4) publication of *Guidelines for Psychological Practice with Older Adults* (American Psychological Association, 2014); and (5) publication of *Psychologists in Long-Term Care (PLTC) Guidelines for Psychological and Behavioral Health Services in Long-Term Care Settings* (Molinari et al., 2021).

There is no comparable European-wide documentation of professionalization and teaching activities available yet. However, the programmatic position of the EFPA Standing Committee is already strikingly comprehensive: "Expertise and knowledge of geropsychology will be necessary for all fields of applied psychology since ageing represents a transversal dimension that is important for many if not all domains of individual functioning. Geropsychology should thus be an integral part of all psychological training throughout Europe. Knowledge in GeroPsychology should be provided for different target groups" (Standing Committee on GeroPsychology by the European Federation of Psychologists' Associations, 2021). In relation to teaching, however, a German survey with psychological and psychotherapeutic institutes (Kessler, Agines, Schmidt, & Mühlig, 2014) indicates that several bachelor programs of psychology offer a very low and master programs of psychology a moderate amount of geropsychological teaching content mostly as part of modules on life-span developmental psychology. In contrast, according to the same study and a study by Becker et al. (2020), psychotherapy training institutes offer a higher proportion of geropsychology courses or course content.

However, it is very likely that this situation will change soon, given the radical move in psychotherapy education in Germany in 2020 from a postgraduate format (which required a previous diploma or master's degree) to a *consecutive bachelor's* and *master's* format. This new mode will give geropsychological training much a higher weight than it had in the previous psychotherapy education and in previous bachelor and master programs in psychology. The new licensing and the associated bachelor's and master's regulations for psychotherapists state very clearly that they must acquire knowledge about mental disorders and the practice of psychotherapy (including preventive and rehabilitative measures) also *with older people*; the wording of the new regulation explicitly singles out this subgroup from the general group of adults (Approbationsordnung für Psychotherapeutinnen und Psychotherapeuten (PsychThApproO), 2020). This should increase the demand for geropsychology teaching in these highly attractive study programs. In view of the increasing discrepancy between the demand for geropsychologically well-trained professionals and the supply, which is already too low now, more geropsychology teaching and learning is urgently needed (Moye et al., 2019).

Geropsychology is also taught in *non-psychological* bachelor and master programs. This is especially true for the study of gerontology, in which geropsychology is one of the central pillars along with geriatric medicine, sociology of aging, and nursing science (Kessler et al., 2014). There is also a need and a place for teaching geropsychology in social work and nursing science programs. Indeed, their graduates also provide services to older adults. Providers and recipients would both benefit from improved geropsychological training for this staff.

## Purposes and Rationale of the Curriculum in Geropsychology

### Qualification for Understanding and Solving Age-Related Problems

The core mission of geropsychology teaching in the tertiary sector is to qualify students to handle the challenging tasks in their future work with, for, or about seniors. These may be in the area of research, applied practice, teaching, or all three. The tasks usually arise in the context of professional work, sometimes also in a voluntary activity or purely on private initiative.

Geropsychological research, teaching, and application are interrelated in the following ways: Research provides the conceptual, methodical, and normative tools for solving (or preventing) problems in the experience and behavior of older people or of other persons providing services to older people (e.g., family members, professional caregivers). In general, the better the existing tools from previous geropsychological research (and practice), and the better these tools are conveyed to those who are or will be involved in senior-related work, the more effectively the problems of the older people and others affected can be solved or prevented. Standards and guidelines exist for both research and application practice in relation to older adults to assure quality work (American Psychological Association, 2014; Molinari et al., 2021). A guideline for teaching and learning geropsychology does not yet exist, but may emerge from this chapter.

Because geropsychology has a strong application focus, it is advisable to base proposals for teaching and learning geropsychology on a closer look at the structure of acting in geropsychological research and practical casework. Drawing on a praxeological model of applied developmental psychology (Montada, 1984), geropsychological acting can be described as including six basic questions and steps: What is the problem to be addressed (problem description)? How did the problem come about (analysis of problem conditions)? What will be the further development of the problem (prognosis of the problem course)? What is the desired outcome (goal setting and its justification)? How can the objectives be achieved (intervention)? Were the goals achieved (evaluation of intervention outcome)? These steps build on each other. For example, to analyze the conditions of a problem, the problem must first be identified. The prognosis of the problem course and the goals set may vary depending on the identified conditions of the problem. Interventions often aim at modifying the previously identified problem conditions. Evaluation of interventions involves checking the extent to which the goals set in a previous step have been achieved.

The above structure of geropsychological action is amazingly simple and informative at the same time. If one fills its abstract elements with concrete content, it becomes clear that age-related problems are very diverse with regard to the target persons concerned and their areas of life, experiences, actions, functions and their development. The same is true for the conditions of these problems as well as the available and still to be developed possibilities of intervention. The settings of applied geropsychological work are also heterogeneous (e.g., private households, locations for paid work of older employees, care institutions, policy-making, and public administration). This complexity makes tertiary education in geropsychology a challenging task. It requires the teaching and learning of knowledge and skills for the appropriate, competent, and successful implementation of all six steps in relation to the various problems faced by the aforementioned people in different settings. With this in mind, the relevant geropsychological contents and competencies to be taught and learned will be outlined (see sections "Core Learning and Teaching Objectives in Geropsychology: Content Dimensions" and "Core Contents and Topics of Geropsychology").

## Diversity of Study Programs: Challenge for Curriculum Development in Geropsychology

The organization of learning objectives must take into account the heterogeneity of the demands of the study programs in terms of amount and content of geropsychology learning and teaching. Some programs aim at training their students primarily to be *researchers* and others more to be *practitioners* who provide services to older people. Further, study programs differ in the *levels of qualification* (e.g., Bachelor, Master, PhD). Then, some study programs offer *initial training* in geropsychology or provide *additional training* for graduate psychologists (clinical or otherwise) who want to be better equipped to work with older people. Finally, some programs offer *major training* in geropsychology, whereas others offer *minor training* for students from other disciplines (e.g., gerontologists, social workers, nursing scientists). Rather than formulating a single list of learning objectives for all programs, an approach is used that allows for the flexible generation of different sets of learning objectives, depending on the purposes of the programs and the needs of the students.

To this end, a heuristic approach and mode of presentation are adapted here that have been used successfully in the development and presentation of a curriculum on educational psychology (Brandtstädter et al., 1974). This involves decomposing learning goals into underlying conceptual dimensions: Six basic *content* dimensions (Dimension A to F) and a 7th dimension (Dimension G) of *types and levels of competencies* to be acquired. Each dimension can take on several qualitative values. In a later step, the sets of learning objectives of specific geropsychological study

# 43 Learning and Teaching Geropsychology

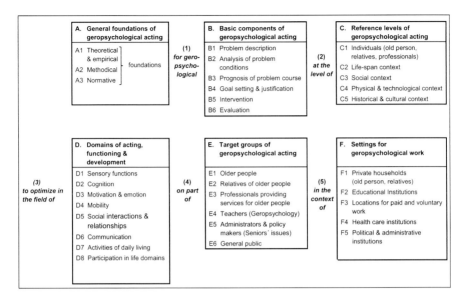

**Fig. 1** Six dimensions and their links to organize the content areas of geropsychology learning and teaching objectives

programs can be generated by combining selected values on some or all of these seven dimensions, as will become clearer more below (see Fig. 1).

## Core Learning and Teaching Objectives in Geropsychology: Content Dimensions

To specify the content of goals of geropsychology learning and teaching, (A) "General foundations of geropsychological acting" is used as initial dimension. These foundations are then further specified in the subsequent dimensions in relation to (B) "Basic components of geropsychological acting," (C) "Reference levels of geropsychological acting," (D) "Domains of acting, functioning, and development," (E) "Target groups of geropsychological acting," and (F) "Settings of geropsychological work."

### Dimension A: General Foundations of Geropsychological Acting

This dimension results from the previously mentioned fact that geropsychological acting requires theoretical, methodical, and normative knowledge.

A1 Theoretical foundations: General theories of aging, theories and empirical findings on functioning, and development in various domains from sensory and cognitive functioning to activities of daily living and participation

A2 Methodical foundations: Major *research* methods (e.g., from hypothesis formulation, data collection, and analysis to interpretation and publication), strategies for developing and using such methods, and methods of *applied* geropsychological acting (e.g., from problem description to ... to intervention and outcomes evaluation)

A3 Normative foundations: Ethic, legal, academic, and professional standards for geropsychological acting in research and practice; norms of bodily and mental functioning and development of older adults, their relatives, and the professionals dealing with them

Theoretical, methodical, and normative knowledge, as just described, form the scientific basis for the various steps of geropsychological acting to be explained in the next section.

## Dimension B: Basic Components of Geropsychological Acting

As indicated above, the general structure of geropsychological acting involves six interrelated steps, which build on each other:

B1 Problem description: Identification of is-ought-discrepancies in the acting, functioning, and development of the geropsychologically relevant target groups. This may refer to existing problems to be corrected or impending ones to be prevented. It can also refer to the optimal use or design of remaining potentials or newly emerged opportunities.

B2 Analysis of problem conditions: Construction of causal models of major kinds of age-related problems of acting, functioning, and development; case-specific analysis of the conditions of practical problems

B3 Prognosis of problem course: A prognosis is required to determine whether a given problem tends to endure or may even worsen (versus will diminish spontaneously) without intervention; a prognosis is also required as an estimation of risks for the future occurrence of certain problems and for considering the demand for preventive interventions of risk reduction.

B4 Goal setting and justification: Critical analysis of norms for functioning and development in old age in general (e.g., "positive aging"); case-specific goal setting and justification for dealing with problems of the relevant target groups in terms of attainability, desirability, and compatibility with other goals of the target persons and their relationship partners and possible negative side effects of pursuing envisioned goals

B5 Intervention: Development and evaluation of corrective and preventive interventions for major problems of the relevant target persons; case-specific application, adaptation, or new development of interventions for given practical problems

B6 Evaluation: Development of general evaluation criteria and strategies; case-specific evaluation of interventions in relation to previously set goals; negative results as a reason to return to previous steps of the geropsychological workflow (e.g., analysis of problem conditions, goal setting, intervention)

## Dimension C: Reference Levels of Geropsychological Acting

The aforementioned steps of problem description, analysis of problem conditions, prognosis, goal setting, intervention, and evaluation can refer to five levels of the professional action space. These include three major kinds of individuals and four kinds of context (cf. Diehl & Wahl, 2020):

C1 Individuals (Older adults, relatives, professionals): Geropsychological actions do not only refer to the older adults. In addition, they may also refer to their relatives and to professionals as relationship partners and/or support providers.

C2 Life-span developmental context: An individual's current functioning and development is linked to his/her past and (anticipated) future functioning and development.

C3 Social context: This includes different social environments such as family, work, civic organizations, communities, and social relationships with its relevant actors (e.g., family members, coworkers, friends, neighbors, co-residents in nursing homes).

C4 Physical and technological context: Various living and dwelling options as barriers or opportunities for functioning and development (that might provide different access to public services); access to communications media and to assistive devices compensating older people' declines and supporting other target persons work

C5 Historical and cultural context: Major historical events (e.g., wars, economic crises, epidemics); economic, legal, and administrative conditions (e.g., pension, health and long-term care systems); and "sociocultural trends" (e.g., changing values)

## Dimension D: Domains of Acting, Functioning, and Development

Geropsychological acting is ultimately in the service of optimizing the acting, functioning, and development of the major target persons (e.g., older people, relatives, professionals) in several domains, as applicable. Eight ones are suggested here which are commonly considered in geropsychology and are much in line with the domains of functioning, activities of daily living, and participation included in the International Classification of Functioning, Disability, and Health (ICF) by the WHO (2001).

D1 Sensory functions: Basic seeing and hearing functions, pain, and conceptually guided perceptual functions (e.g., basic recognizing and interpreting)

D2 Cognition: Knowledge, memory and intelligence functions, problem-solving strategies, and orientation. These dimensions include both cognitive *content* (e.g., what is believed, desired, or intended) and underlying cognitive processes (e.g., storing and retrieving information).

D3 Motivation and emotion: Needs, desires, and goals (fulfilled and frustrated) as driving forces for acting, positive and negative emotions, and subjective well-being

D4 Mobility: Fine hand use; changing and maintaining body position; carrying, moving, and handling objects; walking and moving; and moving around using transportation and driving oneself

D5 Social interactions and relationships: Older adults' social interactions with people in general and particular social relations with "relatives" and with professionals working for older people

D6 Communication: Comprehending and producing verbal and nonverbal messages and use of communication devices

D7 Activities of daily living: Self-care and domestic life activities and activities of recreation and leisure

D8 Participation in major life domains: Education, work, economic, social, and civic life

**Dimension E: Target Groups of Geropsychological Acting**

Geropsychological actions may be directed at the following kinds of persons:

E1 Older people: This is the target group to whom attempts to optimize functioning and development primarily refers.

E2 Relatives of older people: The term "Relatives" is understood in a broad sense that includes family members as well as other close persons (e.g., neighbors, friends, colleagues) as relationship partners and/or support providers.

E3 Professionals providing services to older people: Geriatricians, geriatric nurses, speech therapists, occupational therapists, physiotherapists, social workers, geropsychologists, and geragogues/trainers for older people

E4 Teachers: Geropychology teachers for students of different qualification levels

E5 Administrators and policy makers (dealing with seniors' issues): People working at local, regional, or national levels who analyze the situation of older people, prepare reports, develop plans for seniors, and implement appropriate measures to improve their situation

E6 General population: Geropsychologists could research relevant phenomena (e.g., views about aging) and initiate campaigns to change problematic variants (e.g., age stereotypes).

**Dimension F: Settings for Geropsychological Work**

The contexts in which geropsychologists work towards optimizing the functioning, acting, and development of target persons are rather diverse. The starting points, requirements, and boundary conditions for geropsychological acting differ significantly depending on the respective setting.

F1 Private households (of older persons and of their relatives)

F2 Educational institutions: These may provide education for older people or for people living or working with older people

F3 Locations for paid and voluntary work of older persons: Industry, service companies, and public institutions

F4 Healthcare institutions: These institutions are diverse, too, and include general and geriatric hospitals, rehabilitation clinics and centers, day care facilities, retirement, and nursing homes

F5 Political and administrative institutions: Geropsychologists may contribute to the analysis of the situation of older people, their relatives, and relevant professionals (e.g., senior reports) at local, regional, or national levels and may be involved in deriving measures for improvement (e.g., senior plans for various societal levels).

## Dimension G: Level of Competencies

Describing learning objectives only in terms of content areas such as "Methodological foundations of geropsychological assessment of older persons' cognitive performance" (e.g., A2/B2/C1/D2) is incomplete. This leaves open what a student should be "able to do" in relation to a given content (e.g., to list, to classify, to apply to a problem, to improve). Thus, an appropriate description of learning objectives must combine a *content area* with one or more types/levels of *competences* to be acquired.

Dimension G considers four levels of competence based on the well-known "Structure of Observed Learning Outcomes (SOLO)" by Biggs and colleagues (e.g., Biggs & Tang, 2011). Each level is characterized by a certain kind of understanding and performance.

G1 Unistructural level: One or a few aspects of the task are taken up and used (understanding as nominal). Student can identify, name, define, and list elements of a content domain and perform simple procedures.

G2 Multistructural level: Several aspects of the task are recognized but dealt with independently (understanding as knowing about). Student can classify; describe; talk about a reasonable amount of content, and perform more complex procedures. But they can not apply or transfer easily.

G3 Relational level: The components of a content domain are integrated into a whole, with each part contributing to the overall meaning (understanding as appreciating relationships). Student can explain causes, predict, apply a theory, etc. to a familiar problem or domain.

G4 Extended abstract level: The integrated whole at the relational level is re-conceptualized at a higher level of abstraction, which enables generalization to a new area, or is reflexively applied to oneself (understanding as far transfer, and as involving metacognition). Student can generalize, hypothesize, evaluate decisions, improve a practice, apply a theory to a new problem or domain, generate new approaches to . . ., and formulate a new theory.

In most cases, teachers in tertiary education want their students to finally reach the higher levels of this competence hierarchy (e.g., relational; extended abstract). A progression in the passage of a study program can be described as a progression in the levels of competencies, and this also applies to the gain of a master's over a bachelor's qualification (cf., Brabrand & Dahl, 2009).

# Core Contents and Topics of Geropsychology

## Theoretical Foundations

The following remarks on the theoretical foundations of geropsychological acting focus on older people as the most important target group. These are supplemented in subsection "Problems of Other Target Groups: Relatives of Older People and Professionals" with some comments on the basics of acting in relation to the other target groups (e.g., relatives of older people, professionals providing services for older people).

## Basic Concepts of Age, Aging, and the Aged
- "Old age" as a phase in the life course: Major subcategories of old age: third, fourth, and fifth age (Diehl & Wahl, 2020)
- Descriptive concepts of age: Chronological age, biological age, functional age, psychological/subjective age
- Different age metrics: Distance from birth, distance from death (Schilling, 2017)
- Normative concepts of aging: Pathological, normal, and optimal aging (Gerok & Brandtstädter, 1992), positive (successful, productive, etc.) aging (e.g., Wahl, 2020), and cultural norms of positive aging (Kitayama, Berg, & Chopik, 2020)
- Aging as individual life-span developmental process (Baltes, 1987)
- Views on aging, aging stereotypes, and ageism (e.g., Kornadt & Rothermund, 2015; Pinquart & Wahl, 2021)

## Action Competence of Older People

### Acting in Everyday Life
- Narrow view: Confined to basic (BADL; self-care) and instrumental (IADL; household management) activities of daily living (e.g., Lawton & Brody, 1969); critique of this limited scope (Verbrugge, 2016)
- Broader view: Comprehensive scheme of activities in daily living and participation of the "International Classification of Functioning, Disability and Health (ICF)" by WHO (2001)
- From biomedical model of ICD to biopsychosocial model of ICF: Role of personal and environmental factors for effect of diseases on activities of daily living and participation in life domains
- Applications of the ICF (e.g., geriatric assessment; rehabilitation; transdisciplinary communication, cooperation, and documentation; development of assistive technologies (ATs); analysis of use of ATs and their effectiveness

## Personal self-Regulation of Development
- Basic action-theoretical concepts: desires, beliefs about means, actions (Brandtstädter, 2006)
- Major desires and goals of older people; major domains of older people's acting
- Experience and actions of older people in relation to major events and transitions in their life course such as retirement, illness, and death of close caregivers, as well as their own aging, becoming ill, functionally impaired, activity limited, participation restricted, disabled, and dependent on others, moving into a nursing home and facing their own finitude
- Models of intentional self-development and developmental regulation
  - Two process model of assimilation (tenacious goal pursuit) and accommodation (flexible goal adjustment) (e.g., Brandtstädter, 2009; Rothermund & Brandtstädter, 2019); basic assumptions and further extensions (e.g., explanation of depression and well-being paradoxes)
- Other models of developmental regulation:
  - Model of selection, optimization, and compensation (e.g., Freund & Baltes, 2000)
  - Motivational theory of life-span development (Heckhausen, Wrosch, & Schulz, 2010)
- Limits of intentional acting in old age (e.g., dementia) and its consequences: joint acting, supported acting, acting on behalf of old person (legal representative).

## Challenges in Later Life: Demands for Adaptation

### Age-related Diseases and Geriatric Syndromes (Including Causes and Risk Factors)
- Major bodily illnesses (e.g., diabetes, hypertension, heart insufficiency, stroke, arthrosis, cataract, macular degeneration, osteoporosis, Morbus Parkinson) and mental disorders (e.g., dementia, anxiety, depression)
- Chronicity and progression of diseases; multimorbidity
- Polypharmacy; physical, mental, and behavioral side effects of medication
- Impact of the aforementioned disorders on bodily and mental functioning, activities of daily living, and participation in important life domains (see ICF by WHO, 2001)
- Major "geriatric syndromes": immobility, instability, incontinence, cognitive problems, malnutrition, frailty, pressure ulcers, sleep disorders, depression and suicidality, isolation (Inouye, Studenski, Tinetti, & Kuchel, 2007)
- Psychological significance of geriatric disorders and syndromes:
  - Objects of evaluation, emotional responding and acting of patients and their relatives
  - Limitation of resources of older people

- Influencing factor on geropsychological assessments
  - Influencing factor on goal setting and interventions: In addition to curing diseases (if possible), the main focus is on maintaining and restoring functional capacity, independence, and quality of life.
- Challenging behavior (e.g., aggressive, agitated behavior; resistance to nursing interventions)

### Normative Life Transitions
(Lichtenberg & Mast, 2015, Vol. 2, Sect. II)

- Life domains with age-graded development
  - Work: (mandatory) retirement, post-retirement "work" (paid and unpaid); transition out of post-retirement work period
  - Family: empty nest, grandparent roles, death of relatives (e.g., parents, older siblings, spouse)
  - Community: Voluntary engagement and its motivation (e.g., altruism, generativity)
  - Self: One's leisure time, cultural activities, travelling, education; healthy lifestyle, preparation for illness and death (health and care proxy, advance directive, testament)

### Historical Events and Changes
(Diehl & Wahl, 2020; Gerstorf et al., 2020)

- Definition and dimensions; role of birth cohorts for understanding life-span development and aging
- Major kinds of historical factors and changes
  (a) Extended access to resources (e.g., education, professional career, health care)
  (b) Changes in social and family life (e.g., larger and diversified social networks)
  (c) Proliferation of knowledge and technology (e.g., digitalization)
  (d) Changing Zeitgeist regarding societal definitions of social roles, attitudes, and age norms (e.g., age norms, views on aging)
  (e) Economic crisis
  (f) Wars, collapse, and reshaping of political systems, epidemias and pandemias
- Mode of operation of historical influences
  - Provide development opportunities and constraints
- Developmental outcomes of historical changes
  - Increase of life expectancy over last decades
  - Increased cognitive test performance
  - Subjective well-being and control beliefs
  - Change of dynamic personality constructs (e.g., life goals, concern for others, civic orientation)
  - Changing views on aging

### Non-normative Life Transitions
(Cohen, Murphey, & Prather, 2019)

- General definition of critical life events and dimensions for describing them
- Examples of not necessarily age-related critical life events in the domains of social relationships (e.g., loss of family members and friends; late life divorce; accidents), work (e.g., loss of employment despite desire to continue), and health
- Demands resulting from confrontation with critical life events:
  - Adaptation to the event, its implications and consequences

## Resources for Adaptation of Older People

### Personal Resources
(Diehl & Wahl, 2020, Chap. 2)

Normal cognitive development in old age and its relation to competencies of everyday life

- Major theoretical perspectives:
    Age-related slowing, deficit in inhibition of irrelevant information, deterioration of working memory, reduction of attentional resources
- Conceptual distinctions among intelligence and memory constructs
  - Mechanics (fluid) versus pragmatic (crystalized) intelligence
  - Working memory, episodic vs. semantic memory, declarative vs. procedural memory; executive functioning;
  - Wisdom
- Empirical findings on age-related cognitive development:
  - Mechanic versus pragmatic cognitive performance
  - Episodic versus semantic memory
  - Wisdom
- Interindividual differences regarding cognitive aging and plasticity
- Relation between age-related cognitive decline and autonomous living
- Predictors of cognitive aging
- Effectiveness of cognitive trainings across age

### Social Resources
(Sharifian, Sol, Zahodne, & Antonucci, 2022)

- Social relations theories:
  - Convoy model
  - Socioemotional selectivity theory
  - Strength and vulnerability integration model
- Differentiation of structural, functional, and evaluative dimensions of social relationships

- Differentiation based on relationship type
  - Family versus friendships in later life
  - "Weak" ties (church-related ties, neighbors)
- Means of communication
  - Benefits and costs of social technology use in older adults
- Clinical applications and recommendations

## Physical and Technological Resources

(Diehl & Wahl, 2020, Chap. 1 and selected parts of subsequent chapters)

- Physical/living environments:
  - Goal of "aging in place" (aging in familiar private home environment and neighborhood)
  - Various new housing arrangements as new options (e.g., assisted housing, multigenerational housing, different long-term care solutions)
- Technological environments and tools of older people ("Gero-technology"): new assistive technologies (ATs) and new media
  - Definition of ATs, major variants, and examples
  - Use of ATs: promoting and inhibiting internal and external factors
- Effects of living environments and of (the use of) technology on maintaining health, physical and cognitive functioning, subjective well-being, safety, autonomous living, and social connectedness

## Problems of Other Target Groups: Relatives of Older People and Professionals

Subsections "Basic Concepts of Age, Aging, and the Aged" to "Resources for Adaptation of Older People" referred to the theoretical foundations for geropsychological action towards the most important target group, i.e., older persons. In this subchapter, a few remarks follow on selected topics relevant to the other two important target groups.

## Family Caregivers of Older People: For Example, Caregiver Burden and Gain

(Schulz, Beach, Czaja, Martire, & Monin, 2020)

- Stages from initial taking over of caregiver role to death of care recipient
- Caregiver burden and caregiver gain
- Impact of caregiving on health, work, private life, financial security, social relations of caregivers
- Risk factors for adverse outcomes
- Support structures for family caregivers
- Interventions for family caregivers

## Professional Caregivers of Older People: For Example, Concerns of Long-Term Care (LTC) Staff

(Chenoweth & Lapkin, 2018)

- Job stress, burnout, and job turnover
- Lack of professional and societal recognition
- Threats to nursing leadership and disempowerment of nurses
- Factors associated with LTC staff satisfaction and retention
- Strategies for improving the supply and retention of LTC staff

## Normative Foundations

### Ethical Foundations

(Bush, Allen, & Molinari, 2017)

- Major ethical issues and challenges (e.g., respecting dignity, autonomy vs. beneficence; sharing confidential information with other family members and in interdisciplinary teams; conflict of interest between old person and other family members; consent in the context of assessment, goal setting, intervention, research; maintenance of one's professional competence)
- Resources for ethical decision-making (e.g., professional ethics codes, professional guidelines, position papers of professional organizations, ethics committees)
- Ethical decision-making model in geropsychology
- Application examples for ethical decision-making

### Legal Foundations

(Klie, 2017, 2021; Pachana, 2017: selected articles)

The legal regulations relevant for geropsychological work may differ from country to country and change across time. Therefore, only those kinds of issues that present legal challenges and are often legally regulated are mentioned. Readers (teachers) can flesh this out, taking into account the specific regulations that apply in their country.

- Older persons as legal subjects (capacity to manage legal affairs, informed consent to assessment and treatment, advanced directives, legal guardianship, liberty rights, rights to privacy and confidentiality, legal entitlements to geropsychological and related services, and its reimbursement)
- Offenses against older people: Neglect, abuse, and exploitation (Pillemer, Burnes, Riffin, & Lachs, 2016)
- Legislation governing the major institutions and services for older people (e.g., hospitals, rehabilitation centers, long-term care institutions, mobile care services) and private care services to protect vulnerable older persons

- Regulations against age discrimination
- Legal obligations of geropsychologists (e.g., professional secrecy, documentation of professional work)
- Liability issues (e.g., malpractice and delegation errors by geropsychologists)

## Methodical Foundations

### Research Methods and Resources
(Knight, 2019, Section 2: Lifespan developmental methodology and analyses; Weil, 2017)

### Overview of Research Process Related to Ageing and Older People
- Development of research question, theoretical conceptualization, method and design selection, data collection, data analysis, interpretation of results, reporting findings
- Specifics of research with older adults

### Choosing a Research Method and a Design
- Qualitative, quantitative, and mixed methods
- Cross-sectional, longitudinal, and combined designs

### Analyzing Data and Reporting Findings
- Traditional qualitative and quantitative data analysis and corresponding software
- Emerging new methods and designs
- Interpreting and reporting findings in articles, presentations, and grant proposals

### Applied Geropsychological Assessment and Evaluation Methods
(Hinrichsen, 2019; Knight & Pachana, 2015; Lichtenberg & Mast, 2015, volume 2)

### General Issues
- Relating assessment and evaluation to the major steps of geropsychological acting (e.g., assessment methods used for problem description and analysis of problem conditions, basis for goal setting, prognosis and intervention)
- Problems in applying assessment methods developed for younger populations, reflection on risks and need to apply, and adaptation of the methods to older people

### Data Sources and Access Options
- Clinical interviewing of older adults and informants
- Self-report and other report questionnaires
- Cognitive performance testing
- Behavioral observation
- Psychophysiological measuring
- Functional behavior analysis

## Selected Problem Areas
- Mental disorders
- Major transitions in later life

## Intervention Methods
(Diehl & Wahl, 2020, Chap. 7; Hinrichsen, 2019; Knight & Pachana, 2015)

### General Issues
- Basing interventions on problem description, analysis of problem conditions, goal getting
- Major distinctions and decisions:
  - Purposes: Preventive vs. corrective interventions
  - Target points for interventions: Older persons and their context
  - Intervention agents: Geropsychologists and others of multi-professional geriatric teams (e.g., geriatricians, physiotherapists, occupational therapists, speech therapists, educators)
- Specific considerations when implementing interventions with older adults (e.g., sensory, cognitive, and motivational requirements of interventions); adaptation of key interventions to the situation of older people

### Preventive interventions
- Interventions goals: Long life in best possible health, independent living, high a level of well-being
- Stages: Primary, secondary, and tertiary prevention
- Strategies: Reduction of risk factors, increase of protective factors/resilience
- Target persons: Older people, family carers, professional care providers
- Examples of interventions: Preparation for retirement, active aging programs, cognitive and physical training and developmental counseling, and interventions in relation to nursing home, private home modifications, and improvement of community infrastructure

### Corrective interventions
- Interventions goals: Reduction of mental disorders, restoring bodily and mental functioning, maintaining independence and well-being despite multi-morbidity, and adaptation to critical life events
- Strategies: Modification of problem conditions, strengthening of ressources
- Primary targets: Older people. Additional targets: Family carers and professional care providers
- Examples of interventions:
  - For older people: Psychotherapy, cognitive and physical training, reality orientation programs, home modifications, and improvement of community infrastructure
  - For family caregivers: Increasing their knowledge about older people's problems and stress reduction

- For professional caregivers: Increasing knowledge about work-related conditions, increasing job satisfaction, stress reduction, and job enrichment

## Settings of Geropsychological Work

(O'Shea Carney, Gum, and Zeiss (2015); Pachana, 2017, selected articles: e.g., on Home-Based Care and Primary Care Settings for Delivery of Geropsychology Services to Older Persons; respite care, age-friendly communities, housing solutions for older adults, ergonomics and demographics, learning in older adults, social politics for aging societies, long-term care, assisted living).

### Private Households (old person, relatives)
- Relevance: Most important setting for older people with and without care needs
- Forms and structures of professional work:
  - Domestic care services
  - Home visits to prevent institutionalization

### Educational Institutions
- For older people and their relatives: institutions of adult or health education
- For professionals currently or in future working for older people

### Work Locations for Older People
- For paid work
- For voluntary work

### Healthcare Institutions
These facilities are the most important settings for geropsychological services for older adults with various types of support needs depending on diseases, functional impairments, and activity limitations of older people.

- Major kinds of institutions:
  - General, geriatric, and psychiatric hospitals
  - Rehabilitation centers/clinics
  - Day care centers, nursing homes
  - Hospices
- Attributes of the aforementioned institutions:
  - Attributes of specific target groups of older people admitted to and living in the respective institutions
  - Target groups beyond older adults: relatives of older people, professional staff
  - Kinds of geropsychological and other services offered
  - Goals and competence profiles of the major groups of professional staff providing them (e.g., physicians, certified nurses, social workers, geropsychologists, occupational therapists, speech therapists, physiotherapists, educators)

- Structures and modes of cooperation in multiprofessional teams (e.g., responsibilities and leadership, joint geriatric assessment, goal setting, interventions, and evaluation; referrals, case/team meetings)
- Legal and administrative regulations (incl. reimbursement) for institutions

## Linking of Courses to Modules Within Study Programs

## Modules of Geropsychological Study Programs

The following modules bundle the thematically related courses into building blocks for geropsychology study programs. Of course, the full range of core topics from the section on "Core Contents and Topics of Geropsychology" cannot be included into the limited space of a single program. Larger portions can, of course, be accommodated in consecutive programs leading to bachelor's, master's, and doctoral degrees. Even then, some selection of topics for courses is still inevitable.

- Module 1 *(Basic concepts of age, aging, and older people)*: Includes a course on these concepts and courses on intentional self-development in adulthood, on geropsychology as a discipline, and on the structure of the given study program.
- Module 2 *(Research methods)*: Designed to build up competencies in *research methods*. The courses provide an overview of basic methods of scientific working and the research process as well as courses on methods of qualitative and quantitative data collection and analysis and the presentation of research results. The implementation of a concrete research project (bachelor's/master's/PhD thesis) completes the module.
- Module 3 *(Assessment and intervention methods)*: Refers to the major *components of geropsychological acting*, in particular, geropsychological assessment (problem description, analyses of problem causes, prognosis of problem course) and intervention (goal setting, intervention, evaluation). Some courses may focus on single components and their variants (e.g., overview of assessment methods, overview of intervention methods); other courses may combine multiple components in relation to major age-related problems (e.g., theory, assessment, and intervention related to cognitive problems of older people).
- Module 4 *(Domains of acting, functioning, and development in age)*: Courses deal with the different domains of acting, functioning, and development of older people (e.g., cognitive functioning and declines; motivation and emotion; social relationships, isolation and loneliness; activities of daily living and related declines).
- Module 5 *(Problems of aging in different target groups)*: Courses that cover analysis and intervention of age-related problems in different target groups (e.g., health risks and prevention in older people; care giver burden and gain of family members; job stress and job turnover among professional staff; adaptation of the home environments and technology use in response to age-related decline)

- Module 6 (*Settings of geropsychological work*): Analysis and solution of concrete practical problems in different settings of geropsychological work. Courses on gerontological practice at the community level, in acute elder care and rehabilitation, in long-term care facilities, as well as in in administrative and political organizations

## Arranging Course Sequences over Several Semesters

In each semester, it is advisable to combine courses from several of the six modules listed in section "Modules of Geropsychological Study Programs," e.g., courses on (1) specific areas of acting, functioning, and development, (2) specific components of geropsychological acting (e.g., assessment, intervention), (3) specific target groups, or (4) specific settings of geropsychological work. Combinations of courses that impart theoretical knowledge with those that teach methodical or practical skills create variety and allow cross-references. They also show that the program provides knowledge and skills that are relevant to practice, which enhances motivation to study.

Courses offered in successive semesters should build on each other. Those that provide an overview (e.g., on age-related problems) should precede those that provide more detailed and in-depth training (e.g., on specific geropsychiatric disorders). Courses that provide basic geropsychology action skills (e.g., to conduct assessments or interventions) should precede those that address their integration into complex geropsychological workflows (e.g., case seminars with specific clients in specific settings).

## Teaching, Learning, and Assessment in Geropsychology: Approaches and Strategies

### Learning Outcomes, Teaching, and Assessment: Issues of Alignment

Having covered the learning themes and content of geropsychology in detail, the question arises as to what goals should guide teaching activities, what teaching activities should be used, and how the achievement of learning goals should be assessed. The concept of "constructive alignment" (e.g., Biggs, 2014; Biggs & Tang, 2011) establishes a systematic link between the three entities (see Fig. 2).

### Intended Learning Outcomes

If the teacher applies the concept of constructive alignment to geropsychology learning, teaching, and assessment, then the first step is to define what students should learn in a given unit (e.g., a course). Such "intended learning outcomes" include (1) what students should be able to do, (2) at what level of understanding and performance, (3) with the given content, and (4) in what context. The teacher characterizes the intended level of a certain learning outcome with reference to

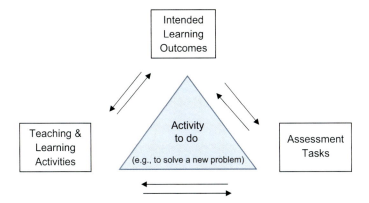

**Fig. 2** Alignment between intended learning outcomes, teaching and learning activities, and assessment tasks

one of four qualitative labels of the Structure of Observed Learning Outcomes (SOLO) taxonomy, to which four sets of activities of increasing complexity correspond (activity verbs in brackets): *unistructural* (e.g., to identify, name, define, list; perform simple procedure), *multistructural* (e.g., to classify; to describe; perform more complex procedure), *relational* (e.g., to explain causes, predict, apply a theory to a familiar domain or problem), and e*xtended abstract level* (e.g., to hypothesize, evaluate decisions, improve a practice, apply a theory to a new domain or problem, formulate a new theory). For example, for a course on "ethical issues in aging," the learning outcomes might be that upon completion students will be able to do the following:

- *Recite* existing ethical principles and frameworks relevant for geropsychological work with older people in institutional settings.
- *Describe and classify* ethically appropriate versus ethically questionable acting in nursing homes.
- *Explain causes* of ethically questionable acting in own institution.
- *Evaluate* whether and why a concrete care decision is problematic from an ethical point of view, and if so, *design an appropriate solution*.

To formulate the intended learning outcomes of one's courses, teachers will find valuable methodical help in Chap. 7 of Biggs and Tang (2011).

## Teaching and Learning Activities

The word "constructive" in "constructive alignment" reflects the theoretical view that knowledge is constructed through the activities of the learner and that the key to good teaching is to get the learner to engage in activities most suited for reaching the intended learning outcomes in question. The intended learning outcomes should therefore guide the choice of such instructional activities appropriate to engage students in activities that correspond the intended learning outcomes (in terms of type, content, and level of understanding and achievement). Thus, with reference to the above example, instructors should create teaching situations in which students can *recite, describe and classify, explain causes of, evaluate a problem, and design a solution of* the ethical or unethical issues identified in the learning objectives.

For a wide range of students, the traditional lecture and tutorial have only very limited stimulation potential for raising levels of understanding and performance. Fortunately, there are better alternatives for reaching these outcomes (see Biggs & Tang, 2011, Chaps. 8 and 9 for general considerations and further concrete suggestions). A first one for teaching declarative knowledge (in large classes) are interactive forms of lecturing that include working with concept maps, forming learning partnerships with other students, writing minute papers, thinking aloud modeling, and the deliberate use of changing activities within lectures. A second group of teaching/learning activities is particularly relevant for conveying *functioning knowledge*, which is knowledge that informs the learner what to do and how to act better in concrete situations especially in professional contexts (e.g., how to provide better services to older people). Here, relevant teaching and learning activities require learners to *apply* knowledge to given domains and to solve problems in *case-based* and *problem-based* as well as *workplace teaching/learning* which all are particularly relevant for geropsychology teaching and learning.

Teaching/learning in the workplace plays a major role, e.g., in internships, which are part of many study programs. This form of teaching/learning is even more important for students in part-time study programs, who work in the respective professional fields alongside their studies and have particularly good opportunities to regularly apply their newly acquired knowledge to real professional practice. Instead of simply letting these forms of learning run alongside teaching and learning at the university, it would be better to link them systematically to the respective courses in the form of reflexive, case- and problem-based teaching, and learning.

## Assessment Tasks

Intended learning outcomes should be further aligned with the adequate kind of *assessment* tasks, which should determine whether these learning outcomes have in fact been reached as is done in criterion-referenced testing. The most important issue is that the assessment tasks should focus on the extent to which students can perform those activities in relation to the content and context that co-define the intended learning outcomes. That means with respect to the example above, assessment tasks should assess the extent to which students can *recite, describe and classify, explain causes of, evaluate a problem, and design a solution of* the ethical or unethical issues stated in the above learning objectives. This has some implications on how to design the respective tasks. In any case, clear assessment criteria have to be established for each task and learning outcome. Assessment formats will differ depending on whether declarative or functioning knowledge is assessed and which levels of understanding and performance should be covered. Whereas written formats (of which there are several) are well-suited to assess both low and high levels of learning outcomes, multiple choice formats usually assess only low level learning outcomes. Teachers who want to design and use their own assessments for declarative knowledge and functioning knowledge in the context of constructive alignment will find valuable methodical help in Chaps. 11 and 12 of Biggs and Tang (2011).

## Different Target Students: Geropsychology in Non-psychological Study Programs

The core task of geropsychological learning and teaching in the tertiary sector, namely, to qualify students to better cope with the demanding tasks in their respective professional fields, also applies to geropsychology education in non-psychological study programs. A transfer of considerations by Dutke et al. (2019a, 2019b) and Narciss (2019) for designing psychology curricula for non-psychology students leads to the following guidelines here. Geropsychological curricula should, first, be specific to the *professional needs* and *work processes* of the non-psychological target groups dealing with issues related to older people (e.g., gerontologists, social workers, nursing scientists). This requires sufficient information on these topics from the best available sources. These can be provided by relevant documents (e.g., descriptions of study programs and professional tasks) or – even better – by experts from the relevant academic and professional fields, with whom close cooperation is therefore recommended. In addition to people with many years of experience in senior specialist or management functions, it is also advisable to explicitly consult part-time students here as further experts on the needs, tasks, and work processes of their practical field.

Curricula for non-psychological programs require a very careful selection and adaptation of geropsychological content and competencies to be taught and learned, to actually increase the qualification of non-psychological target groups for completing *their* specific professional tasks which by and large are not identical with those of full-fledged geropsychologists. On the other hand, geropsychological curricula for non-psychologists should not be so limited that they severely impair a deeper understanding of geropsychological phenomena and related research results. Therefore, a basic knowledge of geropsychological research methods should still be taught so that students from a non-psychology study program can understand and evaluate the results of relevant research in this field, without becoming necessarily enabled to conduct high-level studies of this kind themselves.

Admittedly, non-psychologists should also learn something *about* geropsychologists' core competencies. This knowledge is important, for example, so that a non-psychologist can better advise or decide whether an older person should be referred to a geropsychologist for further assessment and intervention. However, it is not readily appropriate, given existing professional roles and rules, to teach non-psychology students or professionals the key geropsychological competencies to autonomously assess older adults or to provide psychotherapeutic treatment to them. Here it becomes apparent that the issue of geropsychology learning and teaching in non-psychology programs can quickly touch on issues of professional self-concepts, powers, and responsibilities vis-à-vis other professions providing services to older people and related persons. These general procedural guidelines should suffice here, and no concrete geropsychology curricula for non-psychology courses are proposed. In addition to the fundamental issues just touched upon, the development of these curricula would also have to take into account the often very specific local conditions of the fields of practice as well as the educational institutions. This can be better handled by the respective locally formed cooperation teams.

## Challenges and Lessons Learned

The initial view of this chapter on the relationship between geropsychological research, teaching, and application was simply linear: Research provides the conceptual, methodical, and normative tools, which are transmitted by teaching to students/practitioners, who then apply them to solve the practical psychological problems of the relevant target groups. It now turns out that it is more fruitful to regard the relationship between the three entities as multidirectional (Fig. 3).

## Research and Practical Application

Researchers can strive to gain practically useful knowledge from the outset. For example, they can follow principles for constructing practically useful theories by (1) *identifying practically relevant problems* to be solved; (2) building theories with causal factors, mediators, moderators, and outcomes as essential components; and (3) including *modifiable key variables* as suitable targets for interventions (Berkman & Wilson, 2021). In this process, practitioners can provide researchers with pertinent information about relevant practical problems and – later – the applicability of findings in practice settings. Researchers can also serve practitioners by making the implications of their findings for application highly visible in their publications and

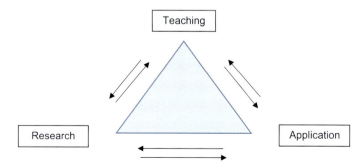

**Fig. 3** Multidirectional relationships between geropsychological research, teaching, and application

conference presentations. Relevant journals can catalyze these processes by encouraging consideration of application issues in the scope statement of their journals (e.g., formulating better policies, developing better practices to serve older adults), by including relevance to practice in their publication criteria, or by requiring "Implications for practical applications" parts in the discussion sections of their articles.

## Teaching and Practical Application

Teachers should also try to identify the problems in various practical application areas and define the knowledge and competencies needed to solve these problems in order to make carefully targeted choices for teaching content and learning assessments. Teachers should consult practitioners about this. Conversely, practitioners should not hesitate to ask teachers to convey such knowledge and skills that are needed to solve problems in professional practice. Which research findings are most relevant to practical application is probably clearest to those teachers who are researchers and practitioners in one person. Teachers who are not should use other sources to obtain the corresponding information. Study program directors are well advised to do likewise and, in addition, to include practitioners/persons from key application areas on the teaching staff and steering committees of their programs.

## Research and Teaching

Researchers should already consider the relevance of their results as possible content for teaching in their research-oriented publications. They could point this out by including instructive figures or tables that summarize the main research findings in an instructive way that can be easily picked up for teaching purposes. Further options are parts in the discussion sections of research papers ("Implications for Teaching") and the writing of textbooks for teachers and students of geropsychology. Each chapter covering a major content area should include a final subsection with considerations for teaching. Active collaboration between researchers as authors of textbooks and students as well as teachers as users of these works should help to achieve these goals. Editors and publishers may catalyze this process in their respective policies.

## Teaching, Learning, and Assessment Resources

## Tips for Geropsychology Teaching

### Organizing and Updating Curricula
- Observe continuously changing demands of practical fields to update curricula if necessary
- Observe continuously new developments in research and update curricula if relevant

- Use feedback from involved groups to improve curricula (e.g., workshop with students, teachers, stakeholders in the field; survey with students and alumni)
- Admission of students in application oriented study programs: Strive for composition of students representing a broad range of occupational settings (e.g., geriatric hospitals /wards, rehabilitation centers, domestic care services, nursing homes, administrations).

### Organization of the Semester-by-Semester Schedule of Classes
- Encourage both teachers and students to bring current topics from their professional fields into courses (to improve ability for applying new knowledge to solve practical problems)
- Supplement thematically fixed courses by ones that allow flexible adaptation to upcoming relevant topics (e.g., "New developments in geropsychological research and practice")
- Composition of teaching staff in application-oriented programs: some of them should be both researchers and practical appliers of knowledge.

### Kinds of Teaching and Learning Activities
- Learning and teaching activities: Use a variety of formats and allow students to work both individually and in groups to achieve their credits depending on the course content and learning objectives
- Internships: Encourage / require your part-time students to complete internships in areas that are markedly different from their current field of work
- Bachelor's and master's theses: Encouraging students to choose as topics practical problems that they have already encountered in their workplace or will encounter in the future and that may be a suitable target for innovation.

## Annotated References for Further Reading

### Handbooks/Encyclopedias
- Lichtenberg, P. A. & Mast, B. T. (Eds.) (2015). *APA handbook of clinical geropsychology*. Washington, DC: American Psychological Association.

This research and practice oriented manual includes two volumes (1343 pages in total). Volume 1 covers the history and current status of the field, various aspects of normal aging and diversity in aging.

Volume 2 covers the assessment and treatment in relation to a broad range of mental disorders in ageing as well as to the major transitions in later life.

- Knight, B. G. (Ed.) (2019). *The Oxford Encyclopedia of Psychology and Aging*. Oxford: Oxford University Press.

This mainly research oriented work – available digitally and in print (3 volumes: 1864 pages in total) – provides a broad overview of psychology and aging in

5 sections. (1) Theories and Conceptual Models including perspectives from neighboring disciplines like biology and sociology of aging, (2) Lifespan Developmental Methodology and Analyses including designs, biological and behavioral data collection, basic and advanced methods of data analyses. (3) Cognitive Aging and Neuroscience covering research on brain organization, cognitive performance and interventions, (4) Aging in a wide range of Social-Physical-Technical-Cultural Environments. (5) Clinical Geropsychology of assessment and therapy of major behavioral and mental disorders.

- Pachana, N. (Ed.) (2017). *Encyclopedia of Geropsychology.* Singapore: Springer. This encyclopedia – available digitally and in print (3 volumes, 2250 pages in total) – is addressed to researchers, practitioners and students. It provides a comprehensive coverage of the entire breadth of the field of geropsychology and its major subareas of normal and pathological functioning and development in ageing, their diversity and context, global and specific theories of aging, various methods of geropsychological research, assessment and intervention, ethical and legal issues as well as settings of applied geropsychological work. These issues are covered in relatively brief individual articles by international and multidisciplinary authors. Contributions from (gero)psychology are supplemented by those from neuroscience, social science, population health, public policy, epidemiology and demography and medicine.
- Pantel, J., Bollheimer, C., Kruse A., Schröder, J., Sieber, C. & Tesky, V.A. (Eds.) (2021). *Praxishandbuch Altersmedizin: Geriatrie – Gerontopsychiatrie – Gerontologie [Practical Handbook of Geriatric Medicine: Geriatrics – Gerontopsychiatry – Gerontology].* Stuttgart: Kohlhammer.

Even though this interdisciplinary and application-oriented handbook contains the word „geropsychology" neither in its title nor subtitle, its covers a lot of topics that are geropsychological in nature or otherwise relevant for geropsychological practice in 4 sections (1004 pages). (I) Basics (e.g. demographic change, concepts of healthy and pathological aging, plasticity and cognitive reserve), (II) Diagnosis and treatment of geriatric syndromes (e.g. immobility, instability, incontinence, malnutrition, delirium, dementia and minor cognitive impairment, sleep disorders, depression and suicidality), (III) Geriatric aspects of selected medical disciplines (e.g., cardiology, neurology, ophthalmology), (IV) Cross-cutting topics (e.g., geriatric assessment, psychotherapy, psychosocial and non-pharmacological interventions, geriatric teams and support structures, palliative and spiritual care, prevention, rehabilitation, ethical and legal aspects, transcultural aspects).

**Textbooks**
- Diehl, M. & Wahl, H.-W. (2020). *The psychology of later life: A contextual perspective.* Washington, DC: American Psychological Association.

This book (284 pages) combines an up-to-date overview of development in old age in 5 domains with an introduction and application of a theoretical perspective that strongly focuses on the role of 3 major developmental contexts (life-span, social-physical-technological, historical-cultural). After the introduction of this perspective 5 separate chapters then present the development in old age in 5 domains (cognition and every day competencies; personality; motivation, emotion and well-being; self-perception of aging; successful ageing). An additional chapter is devoted to behavioral interventions in adult development and ageing. Each chapter includes a section that describes the importance of the 3 contexts explained above for the development in the 5 domains considered followed by dialogue with another expert in the given field.

- Boll, T., Ferring, D. & Valsiner, J. (Eds.) (2018). *Cultures of care in aging.* Charlotte, NC: Information Age Publishing.

This book deals with elder care as influenced by many factors of the person in need of care, the care giver(s), and the micro-, and macro-social as well as the cultural context. It includes contributions from authors in geropsychology, other gerosciences and cultural psychologies in 4 sections (442 pages): (A) Contexts (e.g., demographic trends, history of professional care, home care policies, concepts of positive aging,) (B) Individuals' stance toward care (e.g., Effects of caring on families, cultural influences on older persons' care-related preferences), (C) Between informal and formal care (e.g., scientific and legal concepts of care dependency, informal caregivers in long-term care, suffering and compassion in caregiving relationships), and (D) Future issues (e.g., self-care assistive technologies, personnel recruitment and retention; quality assurance; culturally competent care). In each section, the set of contributions by geropsychologists and other geroscientists is followed by a commentary from cultural psychologists.

- Hinrichsen, G. A. (2019). *Assessment and Treatment of Older Adults: A Guide for Mental Health Professionals.* Washington, DC: American Psychological Association. This practice-oriented, handy book (233 pages) addresses mental health professionals either new or experienced in working with older adults. The author has comprehensive experience in geropsychological research, teaching, practice and professional organizations. Basic explanations about working with older adults as well as facts about aging and the lifespan developmental perspective are followed by two overviews of assessment and treatment of older adults. This is further exemplified regarding late life depression and anxiety as well as cognitive impairment and drug abuse. Two appendices about useful resources and relevant assessment screening instruments complete the book.

## Journal Articles
- American Psychological Association. (2014). Guidelines for psychological practice with older adults. *American Psychologist, 69*(1), 34-65. doi:10.1037/a0035063

These guidelines are designed to assist psychologists in assessing their own readiness to work with older adults and to enhance their knowledge, skills, and experience in this field through continuing education. The guidelines aim at providing practitioners with (a) a frame of reference for *clinical work* with older adults and (b) basic information and further guidance in the areas of attitudes, general aspects of aging, clinical issues, assessment, intervention, consultation, professional issues, and continuing education and training relevant to working with this group. This paper provides recommendations in the areas of awareness, knowledge, and clinical skills seen as applicable to this work, rather than prescribing specific training methods to be followed.

- Molinari, V., Edelstein, B., Gibson, R., Lind, L., Norris, M., O'Shea Carney, K., Bush, S. S., Heck, A. L., Moye, J., Gordon, B. H., & Hiroto, K. (2021). Psychologists in Long-Term Care (PLTC) Guidelines for Psychological and Behavioral Health Services in Long-Term Care Settings. *Professional Psychology: Research and Practice, 52*(1), 34–45. https://doi.org/10.1037/pro0000298

Psychologists in Long-Term Care (PLTC) Guidelines Revision Task Force present PLTC guidelines based on the original prescriptive Standards for Psychologists in Long-Term Care Facilities organization. The content of the PLTC Standards was updated and the format changed from prescriptive standards to aspirational guidelines. First, general guidelines regarding knowledge and skills in LTC (e.g., education and training, understanding of LTC systems, end-of-life care) are presented, followed by specific guidelines covering the basic psychological service activities in LTC (e.g., referral, assessment, treatment, ethical issues, and advocacy). The PLTC guidelines are aimed at providing guidance to psychologists who work or plan to work in long-term care and to assist them in their continuing education efforts.

**Journals with Regular Contributions on Geropsychological Topics**
- American Psychologist
- European Journal of Ageing
- European Psychologist
- GeroPsych – The Journal of Gerontopsychology and Geriatric Psychiatry
- Innovation in Aging
- Journal of Aging Studies
- Journal of Applied Gerontology
- Journal of Cross-Cultural Gerontology
- Journal of Gerontological Nursing
- Journal of Nutrition, Health and Aging
- Journal of Mental Health and Aging
- Psychology and Aging
- Research on Aging
- The Journals of Gerontology, Series B: Psychological Sciences
- Zeitschrift für Gerontologie und Geriatrie

## Journals with Contributions Relevant for Teaching Geropsychology

- Educational Gerontology
- Gerontology and Geriatrics Education
- Psychology Learning and Teaching
- Training and Education in Professional Psychology

## URL-links to Teaching, Learning, and Assessment Resources

- American Board of Professional Psychology – Speciality Board Geropsychology (https://www.abpp.org/Applicant-Information/Specialty-Boards/Geropsychology.aspx)
- APA Divison 20 (Adult development and teaching) – Graduate studies directory (https://www.apadivisions.org/division-20/publications/graduate-studies)
- APA office on aging, the focal point for APA activities pertaining to aging: https://www.apa.org/pi/aging
- Council of Professional Geropsychology Training Programs (CoPGTP; http://copgtp.org): lists 14 doctoral & practicum programs, 24 predoctoral internship programs, 3 postlicensure programs, 17 postdoctoral training programs in geropsychology, 1 associate member, 2 international members (https://copgtp.org/members/member-list/)
- GeroCentral: collaborative effort between the APA Division 12, Section II: Society of Clinical Geropsychology and Division 20: Adult Development & Aging, along with the Council of Professional Geropsychology Training Programs (CoPGTP), Psychologists in Long Term Care (PLTC), and the APA Committee ON Aging (CONA) to bring together available resources for geropsychology training, service provision, policy, and research, including online assessment of geropsychology competencies, in a central internet location (https://gerocentral.org/)
- Psychologists in Long-Term Care (http://www.pltcweb.org/index.php)
- Society of Clinical Geropsychology (https://geropsychology.org/).

## Cross-References

▶ Community Psychology and Psychological Distress
▶ Cultural Psychology
▶ Developmental Psychology
▶ Formative Assessment and Feedback Strategies
▶ Problem-Based Learning and Case-Based Learning
▶ Psychological Assessment and Testing
▶ Psychology and Social Work Through Critical Lens
▶ Psychology in Health Science
▶ Psychology in Professional Education and Training
▶ Psychology in Work and Organizational Education

▶ Psychology of Special Needs and Inclusion
▶ Qualitative Methodology
▶ Small Group Learning
▶ Teaching the Foundations of Psychological Science
▶ The Methodology Cycle as the Basis for Knowledge

**Acknowledgments** I dedicate this chapter to Prof. Dr. Dieter Ferring (1958–2017), who founded the Master's program in Gerontology at the University of Luxembourg.

## References

American Psychological Association. (2014). Guidelines for psychological practice with older adults. *American Psychologist, 69*(1), 34–65. https://doi.org/10.1037/a0035063

Approbationsordnung für Psychotherapeutinnen und Psychotherapeuten (PsychThApproO) in der Fassung vom 4. März. (2020). [Licensing regulations for psychotherapists (PsychThApproO) version of 4th March, 2020]. *Bundesgesetzblatt (BGBL), I,* 11, 448-483.

Baltes, P. B. (1987). Theoretical propositions of life-span developmental psychology: On the dynamics between growth and decline. *Developmental Psychology, 23*(5), 611–626. https://doi.org/10.1037/0012-1649.23.5.611

Becker, T., Martin, F., Wilz, G., Risch, A. K., Kessler, E.-M., & Forstmeier, S. (2020). Psychotherapie im höheren Lebensalter in der Psychotherapieausbildung. Eine Bestandsaufnahme [Psychotherapy with Older Adults in Psychotherapy Training. A Survey]. *Zeitschrift für Klinische Psychologie und Psychotherapie, 49*(3), 172–181. https://doi.org/10.1026/1616-3443/a000593

Berkman, E. T., & Wilson, S. M. (2021). So useful as a good theory? The practicality crisis in (social) psychological theory. *Perspectives on Psychological Science, 16*(4), 864–874. https://doi.org/10.1177/1745691620969650

Biggs, J. (2014). Constructive alignment in university teaching. *HERDSA Review of Higher Education, 1*, 5–22.

Biggs, J. B., & Tang, C. (2011). *Teaching for Quality Learning at University* (4th ed.). Maidenhead: McGraw Hill Society for Research into Higher Education & Open University Press.

Boll, T., Ferring, D., & Valsiner, J. (Eds.). (2018). *Cultures of care in aging*. Charlotte, NC: Information Age Publishing.

Brabrand, C., & Dahl, B. (2009). Using the SOLO taxonomy to analyze competence progression of university science curricula. *Higher Education, 58*, 531–549. https://doi.org/10.1007/s10734-009-9210-4

Brandtstädter, J. (2006). Action perspectives on human development. In R. M. Lerner (Ed.), *Handbook of Child Psychology: Theoretical models of human development* (Vol. 1, 6th ed., pp. 516–568). New York, NY: Wiley.

Brandtstädter, J. (2009). Goal pursuit and goal adjustment: Self-regulation and intentional self-development in changing developmental contexts. *Advances in Life Course Research, 14*, 52–62. https://doi.org/10.1016/j.alcr.2009.03.002

Brandtstädter, J., Fischer, M., Kluwe, R., Lohmann, J., Schneewind, K. A., & Wiedl, K. H. (1974). Entwurf eines heuristisch-taxonomischen Schemas zur Strukturierung von Zielbereichen pädagogisch-psychologischer Forschung und Lehre [Design of a heuristic-taxonomic scheme for structuring goal areas of educational-psychological research and teaching]. *Zeitschrift für Entwicklungspsychologie und Pädagogische Psychologie, 6*, 1–18.

Bush, S. S., Allen, R. S., & Molinari, V. A. (2017). *Ethical practice in geropsychology*. Washington, DC: American Psychological Association.

Chenoweth, L., & Lapkin, S. (2018). Personnel recruitment and retention in long-term eldercare. In T. Boll, D. Ferring, & J. Valsiner (Eds.), *Cultures of care in aging* (pp. 315–346). Charlotte, NC: Information Age Publishing.

Cohen, S., Murphey, M. L. M., & Prather, A. A. (2019). Ten surprising facts about stressful life events. *Annual Review of Psychology, 70*, 577–597. https://doi.org/10.1146/annurev-psych-010418-102857

Diehl, M., & Wahl, H.-W. (2020). *The psychology of later life. A contextual perspective.* Washington, DC: American Psychological Association.

Dutke, S., Bakker, H., Sokolova, L., Stuchlikova, I., Salvatore, S., & Papageorgi, I. (2019a). Psychology curricula for non-psychologists? A framework recommended by the European Federation of Psychologists' Associations' Board of Educational Affairs. *Psychology Learning and Teaching, 18*(2), 111–120. https://doi.org/10.1177/1475725718810929

Dutke, S., Bakker, H., Sokolova, L., Stuchlikova, I., Salvatore, S., & Papageorgi, I. (2019b). Going too Far or Not Far Enough? The Framework for Psychology Curricula for Non-psychologists revisited – Reply to Comments. *Psychology Learning and Teaching, 18*(2), 148–153. https://doi.org/10.1177/1475725719838889

Freund, A. M., & Baltes, P. B. (2000). The orchestration of selection, optimization, and compensation: An action-theoretical conceptualization of a theory of developmental regulation. In W. J. Perrig & A. Grob (Eds.), *Control of human behaviour, mental processes and consciousness* (pp. 35–58). Mahwah/NJ: Erlbaum.

Gerok, W., & Brandtstädter, J. (1992). Normales, krankhaftes und optimales Altern: Variations- und Modifikationsspielräume [Normal, pathological, and optimal aging: Margins of variation and modification]. In P. B. Baltes & J. Mittelstraß (Eds.), *Zukunft des Alterns und gesellschaftliche Entwicklung. Akademie der Wissenschaften zu Berlin. Forschungsbericht 5 [The future of aging and societal development. Academy of Sciences Berlin, Research Report 5]* (pp. 356–385). Berlin: de Gruyter.

Gerstorf, D., Hülür, G., Drewelies, J., Willis, S. L., Schaie, K. W., & Ram, N. (2020). Adult development and aging in historical context. *American Psychologist, 75*, 525–539. https://doi.org/10.1037/amp0000596

Heckhausen, J., Wrosch, C., & Schulz, R. (2010). A motivational theory of life-span development. *Psychological Review, 117*, 32–60. https://doi.org/10.1037/a0017668

Hinrichsen, G. A. (2019). *Assessment and Treatment of Older Adults: A Guide for Mental Health Professionals.* Washington, DC: American Psychological Association.

Hinrichsen, G. A., Emery-Tiburcio, E. E., Gooblar, J., & Molinari, V. A. (2018). Building foundational knowledge competencies in professional geropsychology: Council of Professional Geropsychology Training Programs (CoPGTP) recommendations. *Clinical Psychology: Science and Practice, e12236.* https://doi.org/10.1111/cpsp.12236

Inouye, S. K., Studenski, S., Tinetti, M. E., & Kuchel, G. A. (2007). Geriatric syndromes: clinical, research, and policy implications of a core geriatric concept. *Journal of the American Geriatric Society, 55*(5), 780–791. https://doi.org/10.1111/j.1532-5415.2007.01156.x

Kessler, D. E.-M., Agines, S., Schmidt, C., & Mühlig, S. (2014). Qualifikationsmöglichkeiten im Fachgebiet Gerontopsychologie. [Qualification offers in geropsychology. A baseline study]. *Zeitschrift für Gerontologie und Geriatrie, 47*(4), 337–344. https://doi.org/10.1007/s00391-013-0553-1

Kitayama, S., Berg, M. K., & Chopik, W. J. (2020). Culture and well-being in late adulthood: Theory and evidence. *American Psychologist, 75*(4), 567–576. https://doi.org/10.1037/amp0000614

Klie, T. (2017). Das Recht und die Lebensphase Alter [The law and the life phase of old age]. *Zeitschrift für Gerontologie und Geriatrie, 50*, 275–280. https://doi.org/10.1007/s00391-017-1254-y

Klie, T. (2021). Rechtliche Aspekte [Legal aspects]. In J. Pantel, C. Bollheimer, A. Kruse, J. Schröder, C. Sieber, & V.A. Tesky (Hrsg.), *Praxishandbuch Altersmedizin: Geriatrie –*

*Gerontopsychiatrie – Gerontologie* [Practical Handbook of Geriatric Medicine: Geriatrics – Gerontopsychiatry – Gerontology] (pp. 955-976). Stuttgart: Kohlhammer.

Knight, B. G. (Ed.). (2019). *The Oxford Encyclopedia of Psychology and Aging*. Oxford: Oxford University Press.

Knight, B. G., & Pachana, N. A. (2015). *Psychological assessment and therapy with older adults*. Oxford, England: Oxford University Press.

Knight, B. G., Karel, M. J., Hinrichsen, G. A., Qualls, S. H., & Duffy, M. (2009). Pikes Peak model for training in professional geropsychology. *American Psychologist, 64*, 205–214. https://doi.org/10.1037/a0015059

Kornadt, A. E., & Rothermund, K. (2015). Views on aging: domain-specific approaches and implications for developmental regulation. *Annual Review of Gerontology and Geriatrics, 35*, 121–144. https://doi-org.proxy.bnl.lu/10.1891/0198-8794.35.121

Lawton, M. P., & Brody, E. M. (1969). Assessment of older people: selfmaintaining and instrumental activities of daily living. *Gerontologist, 9*, 179–186. https://doi.org/10.1093/geront/9.3_part_1.179

Lichtenberg, P. A., & Mast, B. T. (Eds.). (2015). *APA handbook of clinical geropsychology* (Vol. 2 volumes). Washington, DC: American Psychological Association.

Molinari, V., Edelstein, B., Gibson, R., Lind, L., Norris, M., O'Shea Carney, K., ... Hiroto, K. (2021). Psychologists in Long-Term Care (PLTC) Guidelines for Psychological and Behavioral Health Services in Long-Term Care Settings. *Professional Psychology: Research and Practice, 52*(1), 34–45. https://doi.org/10.1037/pro0000298

Montada, L. (1984). Applied developmental psychology: Tasks, problems, perspectives. *International Journal of Behavioral Development, 7*, 267–286. https://doi.org/10.1177/016502548400700302

Moye, J., Karel, M. J., Stamm, K. E., Qualls, S. H., Segal, D. L., Tazeau, Y. N., & DiGilio, D. A. (2019). Workforce analysis of psychological practice with older adults: Growing crisis requires urgent action. *Training and Education in Professional Psychology, 13*(1), 46–55. https://doi.org/10.1037/tep0000206

Narciss, S. (2019). Curriculum design for (non-)psychology programs – a reflection on general and specific issues, and approaches on how to address them: Comment on Dutke et al., 2019. *Psychology Learning and Teaching, 18*(2), 144–147. https://doi.org/10.1177/1475725719831498

O'Shea Carney, K., Gum, A. M., & Zeiss, A. M. (2015). Geropsychology in interprofessional teams across different practice settings. In P. A. Lichtenberg, B. T. Mast, B. D. Carpenter, & J. Loebach Wetherell (Eds.), *APA handbook of clinical geropsychology, Vol. 1. History and status of the field and perspectives on aging* (pp. 73–99). Washington, DC: American Psychological Association. https://doi.org/10.1037/14458-005

Pachana, N. (Ed.). (2017). *Encyclopedia of Geropsychology*. Singapore: Springer.

Pachana, N. A., & Yeo, G. (2019). Interprofessional training and practice: The Need for More Engagement, Training, and Research in Geropsychology. In O. Braddick (Ed.), *Oxford Research Encyclopedia of Psychology*. https://doi.org/10.1093/acrefore/9780190236557.013.426

Pantel, J., Bollheimer, C., Kruse, A., Schröder, J., Sieber, C., & Tesky, V. A. (Eds.). (2021). *Praxishandbuch Altersmedizin: Geriatrie – Gerontopsychiatrie – Gerontologie [Practical Handbook of Geriatric Medicine: Geriatrics – Gerontopsychiatry – Gerontology]*. Stuttgart: Kohlhammer.

Pillemer, K., Burnes, D., Riffin, C., & Lachs, M. S. (2016). Elder abuse: global situation, risk factors, and prevention strategies. *Gerontologist, 56*, S194–S205. https://doi.org/10.1093/geront/gnw004

Pinquart, M., & Wahl, H. W. (2021). Subjective Age From Childhood to Advanced Old Age: A Meta-Analysis. *Psychology & Aging, 36*(3), 394–406. https://doi.org/10.1037/pag0000600

Rothermund, K., & Brandtstädter, J. (2019). Dual process theory of assimilation and accomodation. In D. Gu & M. E. Dupre (Eds.), *Encycloepedia of Gerontology and Population Aging*. Basel: Springer Nature. https://doi.org/10.1007/978-3-319-69892-2_96-1

Schilling, O. K. (2017). Distance-to-death research in Geropsychology. In N. A. Pachana (Ed.), *Encyclopedia of Geropsychology*. Singapore: Springer. https://doi.org/10.1007/978-981-287-080-3_125-1

Schulz, R., Beach, S. R., Czaja, S. J., Martire, L. M., & Monin, J. K. (2020). Family caregiving for older adults. *Annual Review of Psychology, 71*, 635–659.

Sharifian, N., Sol, K., Zahodne, L. B., & Antonucci, T. C. (2022). Social relationships and adaptation in later life. *Reference Module in Neuroscience and Biobehavioral Psychology*, B978-0-12-818697-8.00016-9. https://doi.org/10.1016/B978-0-12-818697-8.00016-9

Standing Committee on GeroPsychology by the European Federation of Psychologists' Associations. (2021, December 22). *Introduction geropsychology*. Retrieved from http://geropsychology.efpa.eu/introduction/

Verbrugge, L. M. (2016). Disability experience and measurement. *Journal of Aging and Health, 28*(7), 1124–1158. https://doi.org/10.1177/0898264316656513

Wahl, H.-W. (2020). Aging successfully: Possible in principle? Possible for all? Desirable for all? *Integrative Psychological & Behavioral Sciences, 54*(2), 251–268. https://doi.org/10.1007/s12124-020-09513-8

Weil, J. (2017). *Research design in aging and social gerontology: Quantitative, qualitative, and mixed methods*. New York: Routledge.

World Health Organization. (2001). *International classification of functioning, disability, and health: ICF*. Geneva, Switzerland: World Health Organization.

# Psychology of Special Needs and Inclusion

## 44

Mirella Zanobini, Paola Viterbori, and Maria Carmen Usai

## Contents

| | |
|---|---|
| Introduction | 1078 |
|    Special Needs and Disability from a Cultural Perspective | 1078 |
|    Inclusion and Inclusive Education Around the World | 1079 |
| The Psychological Issues Connected to Inclusion | 1081 |
|    Attitudes Toward Inclusion in Peers and Adults | 1082 |
|    Inclusion and Participation | 1085 |
|    Inclusion and Well-Being | 1086 |
|    The Satisfaction of Families Toward School Inclusion | 1087 |
| Implications for Learning and Teaching | 1088 |
|    How to Promote Inclusive Attitudes | 1088 |
|    How to Build an Inclusive Environment | 1090 |
|    Inclusive Teaching Practices | 1092 |
| References | 1093 |

### Abstract

Special educational needs refer to the conditions in which a student has to be provided with the necessary measures to overcome any learning obstacle. In this chapter, special educational needs are explored in different sections that share the same idea on the extreme relevance of cultural aspects in influencing inclusion. After introducing the regulatory framework, a review of inclusion measures and advancement in different countries is presented. The second part of this chapter addresses the psychological aspects related to the inclusion of students with special educational needs. Key factors for positive outcomes in inclusive education include peer and adult attitudes toward individuals with special educational needs, as well as participation in in-class activities, school well-being, and family satisfaction toward school inclusion. The third part is aimed at describing

M. Zanobini (✉) · P. Viterbori · M. C. Usai
Department of Educational Sciences, University of Genova, Genova, Italy
e-mail: mirella.zanobini@unige.it; paola.viterbori@unige.it; maria.carmen.usai@unige.it

© Springer Nature Switzerland AG 2023
J. Zumbach et al. (eds.), *International Handbook of Psychology Learning and Teaching*,
Springer International Handbooks of Education,
https://doi.org/10.1007/978-3-030-28745-0_52

methods and strategies that have proven to be effective in promoting inclusion. In particular, measures to foster inclusive attitudes and create an inclusive environment are illustrated. In conclusion, inclusive teaching strategies are reviewed.

**Keywords**

School inclusion · Inclusive attitudes · Inclusive practices · Participation · Well-being

## Introduction

The present chapter addresses the concept of inclusion as it has been covered by psychological literature focused on students with special needs. The main focus will be on the school and psychological issues connected to students with special educational needs and their inclusion in school. Given the many facets of the terms special needs and inclusion and their underlying concepts, the first part of the chapter will attempt to delineate the principal meanings of the terms, in relation to cultural and theoretical differences.

## Special Needs and Disability from a Cultural Perspective

It is not always simple to understand each other when speaking about special educational needs (SENs). In a very broad sense, everyone is unique, and consequently, everyone could be a carrier of special needs. Especially in educational contexts, it is widely accepted that a "good teacher" should adapt their teaching methods to each student's individual needs. However, when are a student's needs considered special? In addition, how do SENs and disabilities differ?

As you can imagine, there is no single answer to these questions. In an article published in 2012, Giangreco, Doyle, and Suter (2012) proposed a comparison between the American and Italian special education systems, highlighting the proportion of students considered with disabilities and with SENs in the two countries, among other differences. US inclusion-oriented schools at that time identified approximately 14% of their students as having disabilities and another 16% as having some other kind of SENs, while the investigation of 16 Italian schools found an average of 3.8% students with certified disabilities and 5.5% with other SENs (with a wide range from 1% to 15%). The reason for these wide differences has to be rooted in the different inclusion criteria. Students enrolled in inclusive settings in the American context tended to have, in most cases, learning or language disorders and mild disabilities. Simultaneously, significant delays in literacy or math were considered SENs. In contrast, Italian legislative provisions follow relatively stringent criteria in certifying a disability, and students with severe intellectual, physical, or multiple disabilities attend regular schools. The concept of SENs is generally less well defined and can be interpreted in different ways. Nepi et al.

(2013), referring to UNESCO's classification system, defined SENs as "any situation in which extra resources become necessary in order to provide a student with the tools needed to overcome a barrier to learning." In this direction, different kinds of SENs can be identified: physical or mental disabilities, learning or behavioral problems, and difficulties related to poor social, cultural, or economic contexts. The Organization for Economic Cooperation and Development (OECD, 2003) presented three cross-national categories derived from educational statistics: disabilities, learning, and behavioral difficulties, and social disadvantages. The intention was to create a common data set among participating countries that share a common goal, namely, to create an education system suitable for including all students and achieving equitable outcomes while maintaining cultural diversity and improving quality instruction.

In conclusion, both when consulting the scientific literature and when it comes to educational approaches favoring disabilities, developmental disorders, and SENs, it is therefore important to fully understand which population is being referred to. We can state that SENs possibly derive from different conditions, and attitudes toward considering individual needs as "special" or "normal" can also vary concerning cultural factors. For example, although a medical certification is required in the presence of a mental, physical, sensory disability, or neurodevelopmental disorder in Italy, personalized school planning is also provided for disadvantaged situations associated with sociocultural factors or conditions of temporary disability without the requirement of diagnostic labeling.

## Inclusion and Inclusive Education Around the World

Before attempting to exemplify how inclusive education works in different countries, it is important to examine different meanings of the term. Historically, the term integration preceded the actual widespread acceptance of the term "inclusion." In the 1970s, at the beginning of cultural and political movements aimed at guaranteeing access to mainstream schools for children with disabilities, the main objective was to "insert" or "integrate" children attending separate school structures into less restrictive environments. For example, in the UK in 1978, the Warnock Report on SENs recommended, "The principle of educating handicapped and non-handicapped children together, which is described as 'integration' in this country and 'mainstreaming' in the United States of America, and is recognised as part of a much wider movement of 'normalisation' in Scandinavia and Canada, is the particular expression of a widely held and still growing conviction that, so far as is humanly possible, handicapped people should share the opportunities for self-fulfilment enjoyed by other people" (p. 99). The authors of the report distinguished three types of integration: *physical location*, which is when special units or classes are set up in ordinary schools; *social integration*, which is when children attend a special class or unit and share activities with peers; and *functional integration*, which is intended as joint participation in educational programs with fellow students. Even in Italy, the beginning of integration largely was initiated by families who wished to avoid the marginalization of their children (Barzaghi, 2019) and was a part of a broader democratization movement in the country, realized through the abolition of psychiatric institutes (Basaglia law, 180/1978) and special classes (law 517/1977).

Avramidis and Norwich (2002) stated that when the term integration is used, the emphasis is on the individual child's ability to adapt to an unchanged school environment. Inclusion goes beyond the idea of assimilating children with disabilities into the existing traditional school system and emphasizes the need for a change in the school context to accommodate all types of students.

Many authors agree that the Salamanca Declaration (UNESCO 1994) was the turning point toward an international commitment to avoid segregated educational solutions and promote inclusive school environments for every child, regardless of the severity of the condition. Moreover, starting from this event, the term inclusion began to take the place of "integration." Another crucial event in this process was the publication of the International Classification of Functioning, Disability and Health (ICF: WHO, 2001), which radically changed the concept of disability, thereby emphasizing the role of contextual variables in influencing human functioning beyond the type and levels of impairment. This transformation also brought about a dramatic change in the use of words; the term "handicap" disappeared, and an emphasis was instead placed on participation and the relative limits due to personal or environmental barriers (see paragraph 2.2). However, it was not until 2006 that the right of persons with disabilities to full and unquestioned participation in the life of their communities was internationally sanctioned. Article 24 of the United Nation Convention on the Rights of Persons with Disabilities (UNCRPD) affirms that "States Parties recognise the right of persons with disabilities to education. With a view to realizing this right without discrimination and on the basis of equal opportunity, States Parties shall ensure an inclusive education system at all levels and lifelong learning." It additionally states that States Parties shall ensure "Persons with disabilities are not excluded from the general education system on the basis of disability, and that children with disabilities are not excluded from free and compulsory primary education, or from secondary education, on the basis of disability." In 2010, the European Union ratified the convention, and currently, the ratification of the Convention by 175 states around the world makes it a law in those countries.

Despite the progress, the application of these principles as concrete implementations of school inclusion in different countries and different local realities is still uneven and sometimes far from actual realization. Kiel et al. (2020) highlighted that it is possible to distinguish different inclusion concepts from a narrow definition, where inclusion refers only to students with disabilities, to a broad definition focused on all students' diversity. In the latter case, teaching is tailored to students' individual needs both through different learning objectives and with differentiated tasks that are tuned to students' needs, learning strategies, and achievement levels. In the same vein, Nilholm (2020) identified four uses of the term inclusion in the research on this topic: inclusion can denote the place of education; in addition, it can require that the social and academic needs of pupils with disabilities are met; the third definition applies to all students, with or without SENSs; lastly, inclusion involves the creation of communities in school.

Even considering only the meaning relating to all children's attendance in the common school, there are still considerable differences today. The European Agency for Development in Special Needs Education has classified European countries into three categories according to their policies and practices for the schooling of children with disabilities and the extent of exceptions to the mainstreaming principle. Some countries, such as Italy and Sweden, apply a full-inclusion model, where almost all pupils and students with SENs attend ordinary schools. In other countries, such as Austria, two distinct systems are maintained. Learners there who are officially labeled as having SENs attend either special schools or inclusive settings, with their parents maintaining the right to choose the kind of schooling they prefer for their child. Most countries (such as Denmark, France, Ireland, and England) currently have a multitrack system with various inclusion approaches, including specialized structures, specialized classrooms, and mainstream classrooms. Despite these differences, in most European countries and around the world, the attendance of disabled students in normal classes has increased, while the percentage in separate school settings has decreased (Schwab, 2017).

Given the achievement of this important goal, some questions remain unanswered, such as how can we fully apply the principles of equity, dignity, well-being, and full participation in school life derived from the application of the UN convention and how can we build truly inclusive environments that involve all pupils and create communities in schools? We will try to address these issues in the third section.

## The Psychological Issues Connected to Inclusion

As highlighted in the previous chapter, inclusive education currently constitutes a challenge for many countries. In many European countries, the inclusive education trend started with agreements such as the Salamanca Statement (UNESCO 1994) and the UNCRPD (2006). School inclusion is currently a reality in many of these countries and all over the world.

Many studies have shown the positive outcomes of inclusive education, especially for children with intellectual disabilities. Inclusive placements (compared to segregated placements) generally reduce problematic behaviors, produce more positive academic outcomes, increase social interactions with peers, and promote better self-concepts (Vianello & Lanfranchi, 2011). Moreover, an advantage was also found for students without disabilities in terms of social and academic skills.

Nevertheless, some authors claim that the student's presence in regular classes per se cannot guarantee access to a shared curriculum (Obiakor et al. 2012) and that is important to distinguish between physical inclusion and social inclusion. D'Alessio (2011) and Zanobini (2013) suggested micro exclusions can also be found in the so-called fully inclusive settings.

The aims of the subsequent paragraphs are, on the one hand, to highlight how personal and environmental variables relate to the attitudes of peers and adults and, on the other hand, to describe the possible pragmatic and psychological outcomes – in terms of children's participation and well-being and parental satisfaction – regarding different levels of inclusiveness.

## Attitudes Toward Inclusion in Peers and Adults

This section considers the perceptions of peers and adults in different roles (teachers, parents of classmates, and other members of the school and community) toward children with various kinds of SENs. We will try to understand which factors contribute to building these attitudes.

The literature concerning attitudes generally considers a multidimensional, three-component model with behavioral, affective, and cognitive attitude components (Vignes et al., 2008). However, not all the authors agree on the possibility of measuring the three dimensions separately (Armstrong et al., 2017). Regarding the focus of this chapter, children's attitudes toward peers with disabilities can be explored, for example, by presenting children with different vignettes describing a hypothetical classmate who has physical, cognitive, sensory, or behavioral problems and submitting the related assertions to be evaluated. The behavioral component concerns behavior intentions toward peers with a disability (i.e., "I would invite John to a sleep over at my house). The affective component reflects personal feelings such as fear, shame, and joy (i.e., "I would be happy to have Mark as my friend"), and the cognitive aspect relates to knowledge and beliefs toward individuals with various kinds of disabilities or SENs (i.e., "I think Jenny likes many things").

Research exploring the inclusive attitudes of peers has produced mixed results. For example, Nepi et al. (2013) found that in Italy, despite the full inclusion model adopted in this country, students with SENs attending both primary and secondary schools experienced less acceptance from peers, especially in challenging conditions. A questionnaire completed by classmates indicated a greater percentage of rejection toward students with a disability or other SENs in the "study condition," where students were asked to express how much they liked to do school work with each classmate, compared to the "play condition." In a review of studies aimed at analyzing students' attitudes toward peers with developmental disabilities, the variables underlying these attitudes, and the outcome in terms of social participation, De Boer et al. (2010) found an average tendency toward neutral attitudes. Nevertheless, whereas some students showed very positive attitudes, a group of children embraced negative attitudes that could make life at school very difficult for a peer with a disability.

Students who undergo less peer acceptance are at risk of experiencing feelings of loneliness and a lesser sense of belonging to the school community. Many studies have focused on the variables relating to students' inclusive attitudes to analyze which personal and environmental factors can influence their inclusiveness levels to prevent these consequences. In this vein, we can consider three types of factors: personal variables related to children with typical development (gender, age, knowledge and understanding of disabilities, acquaintances and friendships with a peer with SENs), personal variables related to children with SENs (the type of SENs, the presence of behavioral problems), and environmental variables (the attitudes of teachers or parents, school characteristics).

Regarding gender, an advantage is usually found for girls (de Boer et al., 2010), with females expressing more positive attitudes than males but not in every condition (Laws & Kelly, 2005). In the few studies considering the effect of age, older peers hold more positive attitudes when a significant difference is found (De Boer et al., 2010). No correlation with age has been found in other studies (Laws & Kelly, 2005).

In summary, the results concerning the role of age and gender are inconsistent. It is important to remember that a positive attitude does not always translate into positive behaviors. Cultural reasons may drive girls to manifest greater acceptance when requested. Similarly, as children grow older, they become more aware of the social desirability of an inclusive attitude. Acquiring additional concrete knowledge and experience in the field of disabilities could better help explain interindividual differences. Indeed, most of the literature indicates that direct contact and interaction with people with disabilities are associated with more positive attitudes, possibly because contact reduces anxiety and enhances empathy toward individuals with disabilities (Armstrong et al., 2017). Nevertheless, some studies have found that simple experience with a classmate with a disability does not influence peer attitudes, while friendliness with a peer with SENs is correlated with more positive attitudes (de Boer et al., 2010). Although most research has found that children with SENs generally have fewer friends than their typically developing peers, research on friendship quality shows mixed results. At least in some cases, students with SENs may not have many friends but do have one or two high-quality friends in terms of companionship (spending free time together), intimacy (sharing private thoughts and feelings), and support (helping each other).

Most research concerning attitudes, peer acceptance and friendship has investigated possible differences based on the type of disability or SENs. Overall, the results show that behavioral difficulties are associated with worse attitudes (see, for example, the review of Woodgate et al., 2019). In the same vein, more positive peer attitudes were found toward children with physical or intellectual disabilities than children with behavioral problems (Laws & Kelly, 2005) and children with cognitive difficulties rather than children with ADHD.

Behavioral problems seem to influence the overall quality of inclusion more than cognitive difficulties, academic skills, or physical problems (de Boer et al. 2013). The disruptive characteristics of children with inappropriate behaviors have a strong impact on class life and can be perceived as voluntary rather than the result of SENs (Litvack et al., 2011). This can then trigger a lower level of acceptance not only by peers but also by teachers. In general, severe conditions in terms of the cognitive, emotional, or behavioral characteristics of students with SENs confront teachers with difficult tasks and can adversely affect their perceptions and attitudes. In turn, a teacher's ability to create an inclusive climate at school could influence children's attitudes and perceptions toward peers with disabilities or other kinds of SENs.

It is well known that teachers' attitudes can be strongly relevant to success in implementing inclusive education. However, research analyzing this topic does not always agree on this variable's actual weight and the key factors influencing the attitudes themselves. Among the aspects considered potentially involved are the teachers' years of active experience in inclusive educational contexts and their knowledge in the field of disability.

Moreover, teachers' professional self-efficacy is considered a crucial factor in implementing inclusive attitudes. It largely depends on teachers' perceptions of whether they possess adequate skills to successfully include different kinds of students. Especially when teachers must cope with severe cognitive disabilities and with problematic behaviors, the sense of being efficacious in their own profession is strictly linked to the possession of training in the field of developmental disorders. Other variables, such as age or previous teaching experience, appear to be less important in contributing to teachers' attitudes.

We can conclude that teachers' attitudes toward disabled children and their full inclusion in mainstream education are necessary for building an inclusive educational community, but it is not enough. Without adequate knowledge and teaching skills, teachers with positive attitudes may have limited possibilities to promote the process of inclusion in their own classes. Moreover, the ability to foster successful peer relationships is critical to ensure all children's successful inclusion and support their social and emotional development (Laws & Kelly, 2005).

From these premises, we can conclude that many variables concerning students and teachers, who are key actors in the school inclusion process, can influence the process itself. Nevertheless, these protagonists do not act in a closed system. Thus it is important to highlight which aspects of the external community and school organization can contribute to constructing an inclusive class climate.

In this vein, parents are a fundamental part of the inclusion process. The literature on parents' perceptions has primarily considered the parents of children with disabilities by analyzing their satisfaction with school inclusion; we will consider this topic in-depth in Sect. 2.4. However, research about other parents is scarce. A study by de Boer and Munde (2015) highlighted that parents generally declare positive attitudes toward children with disabilities, but the findings showed some important differences as well. Attitudes were less positive toward children with profound intellectual and multiple disabilities compared to children with sensory, physical, or mild disabilities. Moreover, greater acceptance characterized mothers rather than fathers and younger parents compared to older ones. Another study aimed to compare the inclusiveness profiles of parents of children with and without SENs attending kindergarten (Schmidt et al., 2020) and found a generally positive attitude. However, parents of children with SENs showed higher openness to the inclusion of children with different SENs types than the other parents. The former tends to emphasize the benefits and positive social effects of inclusion in regular classrooms rather than negative effects on children with and without SENs. Nevertheless, the disability severity in this case also influenced parental attitudes, with more negative evaluations toward the inclusion of students with intellectual disabilities. The authors suggest that preschool services, in particular, can play an important role in increasing parental awareness and knowledge of various kinds of disabilities as well as in decreasing misconceptions concerning inclusive education.

What seems particularly frightening to parents, similar to what happens for teachers, is the fear that teachers do not have sufficient skills to deal with the most challenging situations. Especially when children with behavioral or severe intellectual disorders are enrolled, parents may worry that their children will receive less attention from teachers and that classmates with a disability hold back their children's learning.

Of course, teachers' competence is not the only ingredient for successful inclusion. Teachers' ability to put their skills to good use correlates with the tendency of schools to make the necessary changes for accommodating all types of students. First, cooperation between teachers with different roles appears to be a crucial factor. In an inclusive school, specialized teachers and curricular teachers work together toward a common goal, namely, to put every child in the best conditions to achieve learning goals and gain full participation in classroom activities. Both personalized educational plans and changes in the environment, schedules, and timing are required to achieve this.

Soukakou (2012), who described the factors involved in an inclusive class profile at the preschool level, highlighted the extent to which adults adapt spaces, furniture, and materials to promote children's learning and social experiences in class as an indicator of environmental adaptation. Furthermore, the author considered the importance of other factors: planning and monitoring the achievement of individual goals; the adaptation of group activities to promote individual involvement; the guiding and scaffolding of adults in play activities; adults' support for social communication; and the extent to which the transitions between the times of the school day are organized and adapted to prepare children for scheduled activities. In sum, "inclusive education is not only about teaching students with and without SENs in one classroom, it is about striving for inclusive communities that foster the social integration and school well-being of all students" (Heyder et al., 2020, p. 7).

## Inclusion and Participation

When thinking about school inclusion, the focus is not only on the placement in the classroom in the sense of spatial location, but also on the best conditions for social involvement and learning at school. In this sense, social participation or "involvement in life situations," as defined in the ICF, is considered the gold standard indicator of a successful implementation of inclusion in a school context.

In a recent literature review, Maciver et al. (2019) defined the multidimensional nature of the participation construct in terms of involvement in structured (e.g., sport) and unstructured (e.g., play) activities and engagement not only in classroom activities but also in the wider school community. "Participation includes school events, trips, teams, clubs, relationships with adults and friendships with peers." Furthermore, the effectiveness of participation cannot be assessed only in terms of physical presence and activities performed but also in terms of the involvement, motivation, and fulfilment of all participants. The key question is as follows: which factors favor each student's participation in school life in this broad sense?

To answer this question, Maciver and colleagues considered both personal and environmental variables. The first set of variables is grouped into identity (described as self-perception, preferences, internalization of roles, habits, and routines), experiences of body and mind (pain, fatigue, anxiety, and mood), and competence (expressed by making choices, persistence, and skills in various domains).

The second set concerns the quality of the contexts in terms of opportunities and constraints.

First, adults' quality is analyzed in terms of knowledge, skills, and attitudes and the ability to provide participation opportunities and model positive roles for students. Furthermore, the collaboration between staff is seen as an opportunity (instead of poor communication between adults, which is an obstacle to participation). As shown above, the quality of peers, which takes shape as positive attitudes, friendship, and support, can also promote the participation of children with SENs. The quality of the structures and organization, responding to all students' needs and characterized by flexibility and the presence of coherent and predictable routines, constitutes another element in favor of participation. Additionally, the quality of spaces and objects, available, accessible, and suitable, is considered another ingredient necessary for all students' full participation.

In light of the multidimensional nature of participation, it is appropriate to add the community's quality, thereby allowing for wider participation, both inside and outside the school. In this direction, we have already mentioned the role of the families of classmates. To feel part of the class, it is important to attend birthday parties or other occasions to visit peers' homes and share in sports or other recreational activities with peers after school hours. To achieve this goal, people, associations, and organizations of various kinds must be considered open and accessible to all.

In conclusion, participation in this broad sense allows the child to experience a sense of belonging to the school and out-of-school community. Furthermore, participation in a wide range of activities promotes children's self-determination and learning new skills. It is also associated with positive health and developmental outcomes, including a better sense of well-being and greater life satisfaction.

## Inclusion and Well-Being

It has been stressed that school inclusion cannot be conceived as a simple physical location in regular classes. Therefore, it is very important to analyze how the inclusion and participation of students with disabilities are related to every student's well-being. Students' well-being is currently considered a priority objective and an indicator of the quality of the teaching process.

Research that investigates well-being usually highlights the multidimensional nature of the construct. Govorova et al. (2020) reported that in the context of the PISA (Programme for International Student Assessment), well-being is described according to five domains: cognitive (achievement of knowledge and skills by students), psychological (commitment, a sense of belonging, and the realization of one's aspirations), physical (good health and participation in sports activities), social (experiencing meaningful relationships inside and outside of school), and material (availability of the necessary resources). In the research by Simmons et al. (2015), which involved 606 students aged 6–17, participants answered the question: "What constitutes an ideal school for well-being?" Respondents cited different characteristics of the organization and climate at school: good communication and relationships, feelings of safety and security, and opportunities for students to play active roles in their education.

How can a school achieve these goals? The possible strategies that the school can implement at various levels will be examined in more detail in the third section.

Here, we try to clarify the possible relationship between well-being and inclusion. As we have seen, most research shows that peer and adult attitudes and involvement in life situations are crucial for students with SENs to achieve a sense of belonging related strictly to their psychological well-being. Nevertheless, there is a lack of research aiming to understand the possible correlations between the school well-being of typically developing children and their attitudes toward inclusion. It is plausible to believe that students who are satisfied with their academic achievements, and perceive themselves as autonomous and accepted by classmates, teachers, and parents, may in turn have a favorable and inclusive attitude toward the most fragile children (Zanobini and Viterbori, 2021). Therefore, the strong relationship between inclusive attitudes of peers and students' well-being with learning difficulties (Tobia & Marzocchi, 2011) can also characterize students with typical development.

Although it is difficult to determine the direction of the influence between school well-being and different aspects of inclusion, the research findings tell us that well-being in school is significantly correlated with, or even predicts, a sense of belonging at school, active involvement in school activities, and student satisfaction level (Yang et al., 2019).

## The Satisfaction of Families Toward School Inclusion

Traditionally, family studies have highlighted the increased demands of rearing a child with a disability and the resulting distress. Nevertheless, the cognitive appraisal of the situation is crucial for family adjustment. Many studies have shown that positive and negative appraisals co-occur and that the proportions of each appraisal can predict parental well-being (Trute & Hiebert-Murphy, 2002). Family adjustment and well-being are affected not only by the child's specific condition but also by the environmental characteristics.

A study aimed at exploring parental perceptions of services for children with autism (Al Jabery et al., 2014) showed an average satisfaction level. In particular, the items that presented a lower level of satisfaction concerned the cost of services, professional-parent collaboration (in terms of adequacy and frequency of collaboration), and the adequacy of parental involvement in the child's education.

When a child with a disability enters school, parents have to cope with new challenges. Marginalization constitutes a risk for their children with disabilities and their families due to such issues as less availability of time, poor sharing of interests, problems and activities with other families, and fear of rejection and external judgment. Despite these difficulties, parents of children with disabilities usually demonstrate a positive disposition toward inclusion. They generally believe that inclusive education may enhance their children's self-concept, ameliorate their learning skills, and better prepare their children for the real world. A study focusing on factors affecting parental perspectives (Leyser & Kirk, 2011) showed that parents recognize the positive effects of inclusion on classmates and are likely to accept individual differences more when attending an inclusive setting. The concerns of parents of children with and without SENs are generally related to the availability of specialized services and qualified personnel.

Research on the levels of parent satisfaction regarding the inclusive education of their children with disabilities (Zanobini et al., 2017) has showed that these parents generally hold positive perceptions about inclusive educational placement. However, there are some interesting differences. First, emotional regulation evaluated by teachers was significantly associated with all measures of parental satisfaction. As mentioned previously, difficulties in self-regulatory behaviors and emotional responses can be negatively correlated with peer and adult attitudes and consequently undermine parental satisfaction. Moreover, parents with lower educational levels tend to be more satisfied than parents with higher education concerning school services, particularly in the degree of cooperation between the adults involved in the educational and rehabilitation process. It also seems particularly important to underline how some parents identify an element of criticality in relationships with classmates and their families in the face of otherwise high levels of satisfaction in many areas of school inclusion.

These results show the importance of paying attention to multiple factors in the design of inclusive school environments. These include knowledge and familiarity with various types of disorders for all individuals directly or indirectly involved in the educational process, and solid training for all teachers, enabling them not to be overwhelmed in the most complex situations. Additionally, the active involvement of all children and their families, taking into account individual and sociocultural differences, is an important factor, as is the ability to draw on the school's resources and that of the entire community.

## Implications for Learning and Teaching

### How to Promote Inclusive Attitudes

As previously indicated, the successful implementation of inclusion is largely dependent on teachers who need to have both appropriate skills and knowledge and certain values and attitudes to work effectively in inclusive settings. Empirical research has suggested that training can positively affect teachers' skills, knowledge, and attitudes toward children with SENs. For example, Tristani and Basset-Gunter's (2020) systematic review showed that a positive attitudinal response is promoted by diverse intervention strategies that included course-based, workshop, practicum, and blended approaches. A change in inclusive attitudes may derive from a better knowledge and understanding of the disability and from the acquisition of specific teaching skills and strategies, such as how to adjust the physical environment, make curriculum adaptations, and handle various types of difficult behaviors (off-task, noncompliant, and isolating, among others).

In sum, training programs can positively impact teachers' attitudes toward the inclusion of children with SENs, particularly when these programs a) include fieldwork and classroom-based observation and direct contact with children with SENs; b) provide the acquisition of knowledge, strategies, and skills, which in turn increase teachers' perceived competence and reduce anxiety and stress; and c) promote reflection about how stereotypes, perceptions, attitudes, and beliefs may negatively affect teaching behavior and teacher–student interactions.

Finally, teachers' attitudes toward the inclusion of children with SENs depend on the availability of effective equipment, teaching materials, and advice and help from other teachers or specialists. This means that attitudes may also be influenced by educational environment-related variables, suggesting that teachers' attitudes may become more positive with the provision of adequate resources and support (Avramidis & Norwich, 2002).

In addition to teachers, classmates also play an important role in promoting inclusion. In particular, children's positive attitudes toward peers with SENs are significant prerequisites for fostering social participation in schools and the success of inclusive learning environments. Empirical research has suggested that interventions aimed at increasing children's disability awareness can improve the knowledge, attitudes, and acceptance of people with disabilities (Lindsay & Edwards, 2013). These interventions include different approaches, such as social contact and simulation.

Social contact interventions derive from Allport's theory (1954), which suggests that negative attitudes may be reduced by creating positive interactions between members of different social groups. Under specific circumstances, positive contact can reduce anxiety about intergroup contact and elicit emotions such as empathy toward outgroup members. The mere presence of students with disabilities in classrooms or schools may not be sufficient to develop positive attitudes; it is the intensity and quality of contacts that better explain attitudes than the type of classroom (e.g., Schwab, 2017). For example, contact has to be frequent, interactive, focused on common goals, meaningful, and pleasant.

A systematic review of 35 studies found a positive association between children's direct interactions with people with disabilities and their attitudes toward disability (MacMillan et al., 2014). Similarly, Armstrong et al. (2017), in their meta-analysis, showed that both direct and indirect (for example, reading storybooks) contact experiences improved children's attitudes toward peers with SENs.

Simulation is another approach used to enhance children's understanding of the difficulties peers with disabilities may encounter. Simulation-based interventions allow children without a disability to experience situations, perceptions, and interactions from the perspective of a child with a disability. For example, Pivik et al.

(2002) used virtual reality to provide children with a better understanding of what it is like to move around in a wheelchair and experience concrete obstacles such as stairs or objects too high to reach and attitudinal barriers such as inappropriate comments.

Other interventions used multiple components, such as multimedia activities (presentations, movies, and class activities) combined with social contact. Lindsay and Edwards (2013) suggested that common elements of successful interventions include disrupting stereotypes and creating awareness of the barriers people with disabilities encounter. In addition, interventions that included multiple and interactive activities, social contact with an individual with a disability, and several sessions over a longer period, rather than short duration approaches, appear to be more effective.

Finally, positive parental attitudes toward inclusion can also facilitate the implementation of inclusive policies (De Boer et al., 2010) since schools find it difficult to promote inclusion without the support of parents of both typical children and children with SENs. In addition, parents shape children's attitudes and orientations toward peers with SENs so that children whose parents show positive attitudes might be more likely to accept peers with SENs in inclusive classrooms. Although it is recognized that parents play an important role in the implementation and success of inclusive policies and practice, research focusing on interventions that may promote positive attitudes toward inclusion in parents is lacking. Nevertheless, it has been suggested that parents could be involved in disability awareness interventions with their children or become more involved in inclusive school activities so that they can become aware of the chances of inclusive practice for all children (Paseka & Schwab, 2020).

## How to Build an Inclusive Environment

Inclusive learning environments allow children, independent of their condition and characteristics, to feel in control and comfortable at school, to participate and make friendships and to learn and achieve. This entails that different inclusion components should be considered to create an inclusive environment, such as physical, social, and academic aspects of inclusion (Obiakor et al., 2012). These components allow the creation of environments that promote a sense of belonging and well-being at school, as well as high levels of student engagement and achievement.

Physical inclusion refers to the possibility for all students to have equitable access to services and activities. For example, students with motor disabilities or sensory impairments have specific needs regarding mobility, sense of direction, and safety when moving around, and children with autism often experience difficulties in sensory processing, such as hypersensitivity to noise, smells, or lighting that makes them feel uncomfortable. Therefore, physical inclusion involves those changes and arrangements that allow children with SENs to feel safe and promote learning, participation, and autonomy. Methods for adapting the classroom environment may include offering alternative seating options, changing classroom arrangements to help children better concentrate on school activities, reducing the noise level, or adjusting the lighting.

Social and emotional inclusion refers to the opportunity to make friends with peers, participate in community activities, and engage in leisure and play. Children with disabilities are often marginalized and are at increased risk of being isolated or bullied, and their opportunities for social participation are reduced compared to typical children. To reach social inclusion, it is not sufficient to allow children with SENs to attend regular classes. Schools need to address the culture of negative attitudes toward disability that lead to prejudice and discrimination and to develop strategies that help children know each other and experience positive interactions and relationships. Specific interventions have been developed to enhance social inclusion, such as the Circle of Friends approach (Frederickson & Turner, 2003) and various peer support interventions (Carter et al., 2015). These approaches contribute to higher levels of active engagement for students with and without disabilities, increase social interactions, decrease problem behaviors for students with disabilities, and promote the acquisition of functional skills.

Academic inclusion refers to all the actions that promote the participation of students with SENs in the teaching–learning process of their classroom. Several approaches have been developed to promote academic inclusion, such as Universal Design for Learning (Rose & Meyer, 2002). These approaches are based on the idea that all students respond better to responsive teaching that acknowledges variabilities in students' abilities, interests, and needs; provides multiple ways of representing content; promotes students' expression; and engages students' motivation. In addition, specific materials, assistive technology, small-group instruction, visual support, and different accommodations can be provided to make learning accessible and allow the students to demonstrate what they know.

Implementing learning environments that embed these inclusive characteristics depends on educational policies and schools' ability to effectively implement these policies in their specific context. The UNESCO Guide for Ensuring Inclusion and Equity in Education (2017) has provided a policy framework for establishing inclusive education systems. The guide was intended to help countries embed inclusion and equity in educational policy and put into practice the principle that "every learner matters and matters equally." Developing policies that embrace an inclusive approach involves recognizing that students' difficulties may arise from aspects of the education system itself, such as the specific characteristics of education systems, the forms of teaching provided, the learning environment, and how students' achievement is supported and evaluated.

Once policies are established, the implementation of inclusive education occurs at the school and classroom levels. First, schools need to analyze their own characteristics, values, and practices; identify the weaknesses that may occur; and set priorities for change. Different kinds of assessment tools that can assist schools in the evaluation process are now available. For example, the Index for Inclusion (Booth & Ainscow, 2011) provides a planning framework to facilitate school evaluation for inclusion in three dimensions: creating inclusive cultures, producing inclusive policies, and evolving inclusive practices. For each dimension, a series of indicators are provided to help schools identify their own strengths and weaknesses and develop a plan reflecting inclusive aims and the priorities identified. This process needs the school leader's support, who should demonstrate inclusive values, motivation, autonomy, and trust in school staff.

Finally, a relevant aspect of the implementation of inclusive education is teacher training. A lack of training is identified as a key barrier to inclusion by teachers (Glazzard, 2011) who often perceive inclusive education as a top-down recommendation rather than a participatory process. Teacher training on SENs must be organized to prepare regular teachers to work with all kinds of students so that they do not feel overwhelmed when meeting children with SENs. Providing training to all teachers, including pre-service teachers, enhances the awareness that it is within each teachers' professional role to include all children in their classroom, including those with SENs and that inclusion is not just the domain of support teachers.

## Inclusive Teaching Practices

Inclusive teaching strategies refer to teaching approaches intended to address the needs of students with different backgrounds, learning styles, and abilities. These strategies promote inclusive learning environments in which all students feel equally valued and embrace a student-centered approach and a view of the teacher as a facilitator to learning rather than an information provider. Generally, teachers who can use a wide range of teaching strategies and are flexible in their teaching approach are more likely to succeed in inclusive classrooms. Characteristics such as attention to planning, good communication skills, high expectations toward students, and demonstrating respect for all learners are common to effective teachers.

Jordan and McGhie-Richmond (2014) identified several general dimensions in the practice of effective teachers:

1. Classroom management: Effective teachers establish rules for routines, such as starting and completing activities, and rules for behavior, make sure that all the students understand the rules, and are committed to fostering student independence. They require self-regulation and responsibility, and as a result, they are not the center of the classroom's control because students are expected to know who is to do what, when, and how.
2. Time management: Effective teachers use time effectively. Having established rules and routines, minimal time is spent directing students. In addition, they protect themselves and students from distractions and communicate clear expectations for lessons and transitions.
3. Lesson presentation: Effective teachers use flexible teaching strategies, materials, and tools, including technology. They make sure that students are aware of the lesson's objectives, make connections with past learning, are clear about expectations, frequently check for understanding, and promote students' participation.

4. Large group and whole-class instruction, small group, and individual instruction: Effective teachers can manage teaching and interactions at the class and individual level.
5. Prevalent teaching style: Effective teachers promote students' engagement and interact positively with all students by engaging students in dialogue that extends students' thinking at high cognitive engagement levels.
6. Classroom tone: Effective teachers promote respect, mutual support, collaboration, and encourage taking responsibility for learning.

It should also be noted that teachers' implementation of inclusive teaching practices is affected by the school's culture and the teachers' beliefs, such as their personal views about ability and disability. Teachers with "entity" beliefs hold that ability is rather fixed and poorly responsive to learning. In contrast, teachers with "incremental" beliefs hold that ability can develop and increase over time under the right learning conditions. Similar beliefs have been found in regard to explaining students' disability (Jordan et al., 2010). Some teachers think that a disability is a fixed condition that is intrinsic to the child and scarcely influenced by instruction; conversely, others recognize that a disability is partly created by society and thus feel responsible for reducing barriers and increasing access to learning. These differences in teacher beliefs are related to differences in instructional practices and different propensity to inclusion. For example, teachers who hold a malleable view of disability are more likely to use student-centered instruction and less likely to motivate their students through extrinsic sources such as grades.

## References

Al Jabery, M. A., Arabiat, D. H., Al Khamra, H. A., Betawi, I. A., & Jabbar, S. K. A. (2014). Parental perceptions of services provided for children with autism in Jordan. *Journal of Child and Family Studies, 23*(3), 475–486. https://doi.org/10.1007/s10826-012-9703-0

Allport, G. (1954). *The nature of prejudice*. Cambridge, MA: Addison-Wesley Publishing.

Armstrong, M., Morris, C., Abraham, C., & Tarrant, M. (2017). Interventions utilising contact with people with disabilities to improve children's attitudes towards disability: A systematic review and meta-analysis. *Disability and Health Journal, 10*(1), 11–22. https://doi.org/10.1016/j.dhjo.2016.10.003

Avramidis, E., & Norwich, B. (2002). Teachers' attitudes towards integration/inclusion: a review of the literature. *European Journal of Special Needs Education, 17*(2), 129–147. https://doi.org/10.1080/08856250210129056

Barzaghi, C. M. (2019). Gli alunni con disabilità nella scuola di tutti. Il tortuoso percorso dall'integrazione all'inclusione. In M. Zanobini & M. C. Usai (Eds.), *Psicologia della disabilità e dei disturbi dello sviluppo: elementi di riabilitazione e d'intervento*. Milano, Italy: Franco Angeli.

Booth, T., & Ainscow, M. (2011). *The index for inclusion* (3rd ed.). Bristol, UK: Centre for Studies on Inclusive Education.

Carter, E. W., Moss, C. K., Asmus, J., Fesperman, E., Cooney, M., Brock, M. E., . . . Vincent, L. B. (2015). Promoting inclusion, social connections, and learning through peer support arrangements. *Teaching Exceptional Children, 48*(1), 9–18. https://doi.org/10.1177/0040059915594784

D'Alessio, S. (2011). *Inclusive education in Italy. A criticalaAnalysis of the policy of Integrazione Scolastica*. Rotterdam, The Netherlands: Sense Publishers.

de Boer, A., & Munde, V. S. (2015). Parental attitudes toward the inclusion of children with profound intellectual and multiple disabilities in general primary education in the Netherlands. *The Journal of Special Education, 49*(3), 179–187. https://doi.org/10.1177/0022466914554297

De Boer, A., Pijl, S. J., & Minnaert, A. (2010). Attitudes of parents towards inclusive education: A review of the literature. *European Journal of Special Needs Education, 25*(2), 165–181. https://doi.org/10.1080/08856251003658694

de Boer, A., Pijl, S. J., Post, W., & Minnaert, A. (2013). Peer acceptance and friendships of students with disabilities in general education: The role of child, peer, and classroom variables. *Social Development, 22*(4), 831–844. https://doi.org/10.1111/j.1467-9507.2012.00670.x

Frederickson, N., & Turner, J. (2003). Utilizing the classroom peer group to address children's social needs: An evaluation of the Circle of Friends intervention approach. *The Journal of Special Education, 36*(4), 234–245. https://doi.org/10.1177/002246690303600404

Giangreco, M. F., Doyle, M. B., & Suter, J. C. (2012). Demographic and personnel service delivery data: Implications for including students with disabilities in Italian schools. *Life Span and Disability, 15*(1), 93–123.

Glazzard, J. (2011). Perceptions of the barriers to effective inclusion in one primary school: Voices of teachers and teaching assistants. *Support for Learning, 26*(2), 56–63. https://doi.org/10.1111/j.1467-9604.2011.01478.x

Govorova, E., Benítez, I., & Muñiz, J. (2020). Predicting student well-being: Network analysis based on PISA 2018. *International Journal of Environmental Research and Public Health, 17*(11), 4014. https://doi.org/10.3390/ijerph17114014

Heyder, A., Südkamp, A., & Steinmayr, R. (2020). How are teachers' attitudes toward inclusion related to the social-emotional school experiences of students with and without special educational needs? *Learning and Individual Differences, 77*, 1–11. https://doi.org/10.1016/j.lindif.2019.101776

Jordan, A., & McGhie-Richmond, D. (2014). Identifying effective teaching practices in inclusive classrooms. In C. Forlin & T. Loreman (Eds.), *International Perspectives on Inclusive Education: Vol. 3. Measuring inclusive education* (pp. 133–162). Bingley, UK: Emerald Group Publishing. https://doi.org/10.1108/S1479-363620140000003023

Jordan, A., Glenn, C., & McGhie-Richmond, D. (2010). The Supporting Effective Teaching (SET) project: The relationship of inclusive teaching practices to teachers' beliefs about disability and ability, and about their roles as teachers. *Teaching and Teacher Education, 26*(2), 259–266. https://doi.org/10.1016/j.tate.2009.03.005

Kiel, E., Braun, A., Muckenthaler, M., Heimlich, U., & Weiss, S. (2020). Self-efficacy of teachers in inclusive classes. How do teachers with different self-efficacy beliefs differ in implementing inclusion? *European Journal of Special Needs Education, 35*(3), 333–349. https://doi.org/10.1080/08856257.2019.1683685

Laws, G., & Kelly, E. (2005). The attitudes and friendship intentions of children in United Kingdom mainstream schools towards peers with physical or intellectual disabilities. *International Journal of Disability, Development and Education, 52*(2), 79–99. https://doi.org/10.1080/10349120500086298

Leyser, I., & Kirk, R. (2011). Parents' perspectives on inclusion and schooling of students with Angelman Syndrome: Suggestions for educators. *International Journal of Special Education, 26*(2), 79–91.

Lindsay, S., & Edwards, A. (2013). A systematic review of disability awareness interventions for children and youth. *Disability and Rehabilitation, 35*(8), 623–646. https://doi.org/10.3109/09638288.2012.702850

Litvack, M. S., Ritchie, K. C., & Shore, B. M. (2011). High-and average-achieving students' perceptions of disabilities and of students with disabilities in inclusive classrooms. *Exceptional children, 77*(4), 474–487. https://doi.org/10.1177/001440291107700406

Maciver, D., Rutherford, M., Arakelyan, S., Kramer, J. M., Richmond, J., Todorova, L., ... Forsyth, K. (2019). Participation of children with disabilities in school: A realist systematic review of psychosocial and environmental factors. *PloS one, 14*(1), e0210511. https://doi.org/10.1371/journal.pone.0210511

MacMillan, M., Tarrant, M., Abraham, C., & Morris, C. (2014). The association between children's contact with people with disabilities and their attitudes towards disability: a systematic review. *Developmental Medicine & Child Neurology, 56*(6), 529–546. https://doi.org/10.1111/dmcn.12326

Nepi, L. D., Facondini, R., Nucci, F., & Peru, A. (2013). Evidence from full-inclusion model: The social position and sense of belonging of students with special educational needs and their peers in Italian primary school. *European Journal of Special Needs Education, 2*(3), 319–332. https://doi.org/10.1080/08856257.2013.777530

Nilholm, C. (2020). Research about inclusive education in 2020 – How can we improve our theories in order to change practice? *European Journal of Special Needs Education, 1-13*. https://doi.org/10.1080/08856257.2020.1754547

Obiakor, F. E., Harris, M., Mutua, K., Rotatori, A., & Algozzine, B. (2012). Making inclusion work in general education classrooms. *Education and Treatment of Children, 35*(3), 477–490. https://doi.org/10.1353/etc.2012.0020

Organization for Economic Cooperation and Development (OECD). (2003). *Students with Disabilities, Difficulties and Disadvantages: Statistics and Indicators for Curriculum Access and Equity*. Paris, France: OECD.

Paseka, A., & Schwab, S. (2020). Parents' attitudes towards inclusive education and their perceptions of inclusive teaching practices and resources. *European Journal of Special Needs Education, 35*(2), 254–272. https://doi.org/10.1080/08856257.2019.1665232

Pivik, J., McComas, J., MaCfarlane, I., & Laflamme, M. (2002). Using virtual reality to teach disability awareness. *Journal of Educational Computing Research, 26*(2), 203–218. https://doi.org/10.2190/WACX-1VR9-HCMJ-RTKB

Rose, D., & Meyer, A. (2002). *Teaching every student in the digital age*. Alexandria, VA: ASCD.

Schmidt, M., Krivec, K., & Bastič, M. (2020). Attitudes of Slovenian parents towards pre-school inclusion. *European Journal of Special Needs Education, 35*(5), 696–710. https://doi.org/10.1080/08856257.2020.1748430

Schwab, S. (2017). The impact of contact on students' attitudes towards peers with disabilities. *Research in Developmental Disabilities, 62*, 160–165. https://doi.org/10.1016/j.ridd.2017.01.015

Simmons, C., Graham, A., & Thomas, N. (2015). Imagining an ideal school for wellbeing: Locating student voice. *Journal of Educational Change, 16*(2), 129–144. https://doi.org/10.1007/s10833-014-9239-8

Soukakou, E. P. (2012). Measuring quality in inclusive preschool classrooms: Development and validation of the Inclusive Classroom Profile (ICP). *Early Childhood Research Quarterly, 27*(3), 478–488. https://doi.org/10.1016/j.ecresq.2011.12.003

Tobia, V., & Marzocchi, G. M. (2011). Il benessere nei bambini con disturbi specifici dell'apprendimento e nei loro genitori: uno studio pilota con il questionario sul benessere scolastico-versione per genitori [The wellbeing of children with specific learning disabilities and their parents: a pilot study with the Questionnaire on the School Wellness-parents' version]. *Ricerche di psicologia, 4*, 499–517. https://doi.org/10.3280/RIP2011-00400

Tristani, L., & Bassett-Gunter, R. (2020). Making the grade: Teacher training for inclusive education: A systematic review. *Journal of Research in Special Educational Needs, 20*(3), 246–264. https://doi.org/10.1111/1471-3802.12483

Trute, B., & Hiebert-Murphy, D. (2002). Family adjustment to childhood developmental disability: A measure of parent appraisal of family impacts. *Journal of Pediatric Psychology, 27*(3), 271–280. https://doi.org/10.1093/jpepsy/27.3.271

UNESCO (1994). The Salamanca Statement and Framework for Action on Special Needs Education. *World Conference on Special Needs Education: Access and quality*. Salamanca, Spain, 7-10 June 1994.

UNESCO. (2017). *A guide for ensuring inclusion and equity in education*. Paris, France: United Nations Educational, Scientific and Cultural Organization. Retrieved at https://unesdoc.unesco.org/ark:/48223/pf0000248254

United Nations General Assembly Session 61 Resolution 106. *Convention on the Rights of Persons with Disabilities* A/RES/61/106 13 December 2006

Vianello, R., & Lanfranchi, S. (2011). Positive effects of the placements of students with intellectual developmental disabilities in typical class. *Life Span and Disability, 14*(1), 75–84.

Vignes, C., Coley, N., Grandjean, H., Godeau, E., & Arnaud, C. (2008). Measuring children's attitudes towards peers with disabilities: A review of instruments. *Developmental Medicine & Child Neurology, 50*(3), 182–189. https://doi.org/10.1111/j.1469-8749.2008.02032.x

Warnock, H. M. (1978). *Special Educational Needs: Report of the Committee of Enquiry into the Education of Handicapped Children and Young People*. London, UK: Her Majesty's Stationery Office.

Woodgate, R., Gonzalez, M., Demczuk, L., Snow, W., Barriage, S., & Kirk, S. (2019). How do peers promote social inclusion of children with disabilities? A mixed-methods systematic review. *Disability and Rehabilitation, 42*(18), 2553–2579. https://doi.org/10.1080/09638288.2018.1561955

World Health Organization. (2001). *The International Classification of Functioning, Disability and Health (ICF)*. Geneva: WHO, Switzerland. http://www.who.int/classifications/icf/en/

Yang, Q., Tian, L., Huebner, E. S., & Zhu, X. (2019). Relations among academic achievement, self-esteem, and subjective well-being in school among elementary school students: A longitudinal mediation model. *School Psychology, 34*(3), 328-340. https://doi.org/10.1037/spq0000292

Zanobini, M. (2013). Some considerations about inclusion, disability, and special educational needs: A reply to Giangreco, Doyle and Suter (2012). *Life Span and Disability, 16*(1), 83–94.

Zanobini, M., Viterbori, P., Garello, V., & Camba, R. (2017). Parental satisfaction with disabled children's school inclusion in Italy. *European Journal of Special Needs Education*. https://doi.org/10.1080/08856257.2017.1386318

Zanobini, M. & Viterbori, P. (2021). Students' well-being and attitudes towards inclusion. *European Journal of Special Needs Education*. https://doi.org/10.1080/08856257.2021.1920213

# Teaching the Psychology of Religion and Spirituality

**45**

Timothy A. Sisemore

## Contents

| | |
|---|---|
| Introduction | 1098 |
| What Is the Psychology of Religion and Spirituality? | 1098 |
|    Defining the Psychology of Religion and Spirituality | 1098 |
|    A Brief History of the Psychology of Religion and Spirituality | 1099 |
|    Major Content Areas of the Psychology of Religion and Spirituality | 1101 |
| Teaching the Psychology of Religion and Spirituality as an Undergraduate Course | 1105 |
|    Contexts for the Course | 1105 |
|    Possible Course Texts | 1106 |
|    Suggested Attitudes for Teaching PRS | 1107 |
|    Instructional Strategies | 1108 |
|    Introducing PRS in the General Psychology and Related Undergraduate Curriculum | 1108 |
|    PRS in the Graduate Curriculum | 1112 |
| Summary | 1112 |
| References | 1113 |

### Abstract

This chapter introduces the field of the psychology of religion and spirituality, defining its domain and presenting some of the key areas of research it offers. It discusses how these can be shaped into an undergraduate class on the topic and provides basic suggestions on how the literature of the psychology of religion and spirituality can be integrated into other undergraduate courses. Finally, suggestions are offered for teaching psychology of religion at the graduate level.

### Keywords

Psychology · Religion · Spirituality · Undergraduate courses · Graduate courses

T. A. Sisemore (✉)
St. Louis Behavioral Medicine Institute, St. Louis, MO, USA
e-mail: timothy.sisemore@uhsinc.com

© Springer Nature Switzerland AG 2023
J. Zumbach et al. (eds.), *International Handbook of Psychology Learning and Teaching*,
Springer International Handbooks of Education,
https://doi.org/10.1007/978-3-030-28745-0_53

## Introduction

As you perused the Table of Contents of this Handbook, you might have been surprised to see that there is a chapter on the psychology of religion and spirituality. Indeed, the editors are commended for their thoughtfulness in including this chapter. Many, particularly Western, colleges and universities are so afraid of appearing to promote religion that they neglect the major role it plays in the lives of most people. Most psychology departments do not offer a course in the area, despite a long and rich history of scientific study in the area.

Another reason for this may be the notable disparity between psychologists and the general public on religious belief. For example, Delaney, Miller, and Bisonó (2013) found that clinical psychologists continued to be considerably less religious than the general population in America, while religion is largely considered to be beneficial. Their survey found psychologists as less likely to see their religion as very important (21% vs 55% in the public) and only half as likely to believe in God at all (32% vs 64%). While this only reflects on clinical psychologists, the trend seems evident across the spectrum of the field of psychology.

Religion and spirituality remain vital aspects of the lives of most persons around the world. It is hard to say we understand humans if we do not have some understanding of the nature of religion in their lives – how this affects their goals, relationships, values, coping, and self-images. Yet, not only are there few courses in the psychology of religion, but most psychology textbooks severely undervalue the role of faith in the lives of most people, giving only brief mention to faith despite the formative role it plays for so many. The field of the psychology of religion has produced many valuable findings yet often they languish in the psychology of religion journals, their value ignored by (or at least hidden from) the broader field of psychology.

This chapter will introduce the field of the psychology of religion, defining its domain and presenting some of the key areas of research it offers. It will discuss how these can be shaped into an undergraduate class on the topic. Space will only permit some basic suggestions on how the literature of the psychology of religion can be integrated into other undergraduate courses. Finally, suggestions are offered for teaching psychology of religion at the graduate level.

## What Is the Psychology of Religion and Spirituality?

We begin our discussion by looking at the field itself: defining it, briefly charting its history, and surveying some of the major content areas in it.

### Defining the Psychology of Religion and Spirituality

Looking back into history, the topics of psychology as we know it were often seen as a subset of religion, with ancient texts covering themes of what goes on in the mind and emotions, and which behaviors are to be encouraged and which to be discouraged. It spoke of meaning and purpose and of relationships (see Hill et al., 2000). Wisdom for life is offered in all of the great religious traditions, so psychology – as technically the "word on the soul" by its etymology – originated in religion. Philosophers weighed in, of course, Plato and Aristotle, among others, musing on human nature and behavior. The Enlightenment turned this around as science became the primary lens through which humans gained knowledge. It was inevitable that they would turn the lens on themselves and their practices, and so was born the modern discipline of psychology.

We will shortly turn to our brief history of the psychology of religion, but first a word on terminology. Religion is the traditional term used for the area we are discussing, coming from the Latin root *religio* that carried the notion of a bond, typically between an individual and a higher power (Hill et al., 2000). The precise meaning has been debated, but overall has included both an individual and institutional level (Pargament, Mahoney, Exline, Jones, & Shafranske, 2013). Given the anti-institutional sentiment in the West in particular, the term "spirituality" (rooted in *spiritus*, breath of life) gained ground as an alternative to religion. Sisemore (2016) summarized the contrasting connotations of the two terms by describing religion as related to ideas of being institutional, external, objective, old, fixed, and frozen, requiring a deity, and including a moral code. Much of this no longer aligned with the highly individualistic Western culture. In contrast, spirituality connotes individual, internal, subjective, newness, flexibility, and dynamism, does not require a deity, and does not entail a moral code. Spirituality has also been an Eastern phenomenon, too, with many forms of faith excluding a deity as such.

The rise of the term "spirituality" led to considerable debate in the field, though most people describe themselves as religious and spiritual (Marler & Hadaway, 2002). But the focus has been on the "spiritual but not religious" category, with 18% of Americans claiming this option (Pew Forum on Religious and Public Life, 2012). Hood (2003) argued that a subset of this group might better be termed "spiritual *against* religion" where spirituality frees from the bondage of religion. All of these groups fall within the purview of the psychology of religion.

We will follow the lead of Pargament et al. (2013) who define spirituality as simply "the search for the sacred" (p.14), with "sacred" being more than a higher power but including any aspect of life that might manifest the divine. They define religion as "the search for significance that occurs within the context of established institutions that are designed to facilitate spirituality" (p. 15). As such, then, spirituality is the broader term with religion being a subset of it, though one might argue there could be religion without spirituality.

## A Brief History of the Psychology of Religion and Spirituality

The relationship between science and faith has long been conflictual – the tragedy of Galileo being a prime example. However, the tension only mounts when science moves toward religion itself as occurs when secular psychology turns to try to explain religion and religious behavior. We will note some of the pivotal points in this story, admittedly neglecting many important events and authors in the service of brevity.

**William James** The connection between the young scientific discipline of psychology and an interest in people's religious behavior could not have been more intimate than it being the focus on a set of lectures by the founding president of the American Psychological Association, William James (Nelson, 2009). The lectures occurred in Edinburgh from 1899 to 1902 and were published as *The Varieties of Religious Experience* (James 1902/1961). Consistent with his (and psychology's) individualistic tendencies, *Varieties* examined the religious experience of particular persons – primarily exceptional experiences – from a psychological viewpoint. The work has been immensely influential, praised for its giving credibility to the psychological study of religion, its being supportive of faith, and looking at experience from outside the norm foreshadowed the recent turn to spirituality. Negatively, James avoided more normative experiences such as prayer and the influence of the religious community and may have overemphasized the role of emotion (Sisemore, 2016).

**Sigmund Freud** One of the most significant figures in Western history, Freud stepped boldly into the psychology of religion, largely using his theoretical systems to psychologize and explain away religion and religious experience. Three of his works were strongly focused on religion: *Totem and Taboo* (1913/1950), *Moses and Monotheism* (1939/1955), and *The Future of an Illusion* (1923/1961), this likely being his most influential work on religion as he blatantly labeled religious faith as an "illusion" and replaced it with scientific human reasoning. While James had been detached and rather neutral in his view of religious experience, Freud now used science not only to explain but to debunk religious faith, drawing battle lines in this debate that continue to this day.

**Freud's Successors** Several of Freud's disciples strayed from his pure atheistic position and looked more favorably on the spiritual and religious. Carl Jung rejected his father's Christian faith (Nelson, 2009) but it was influential, and Jung studied other religions and argued that religion was largely valuable. His theories might best be described as a form of Gnosticism as God is relegated to an archetype in Jung's theory of personality. Erik Erikson developed a methodology called psychohistory, using psychoanalytic theory to explain significant figures from the past. In *Young Man Luther* (1962), Erikson examines a major religious figure and notes not only the influence of his early childhood but his ongoing development in adulthood. (And did the same with spiritual icon Mahatma Gandhi [Erikson, 1969].) Object relations theory, too, gives space for a God image that acts as a transitional object from parents to broader life (Winnicott, 1990).

**Psychology of Religion in Other Models of Psychology and Today** The phenomenological/humanistic approach to psychology emerged in the mid- twentieth century and included several figures who considered religion. Gordon Allport came from a Protestant family and became a significant scholar at Harvard (Wulff, 1997). He introduced important categories of intrinsic and extrinsic faith (in *The Individual and His Religion*, 1950) and wrote a seminal book on racial prejudice (*The Nature of Prejudice*, 1954/1958) that included theory on why some religious persons are prejudiced and why some are not. Another humanist, Erich Fromm (1950/1967), stressed the need to move from authoritarian religion to humanistic religion, a faith that focuses on human strength and so moves away from traditional forms of religion.

The coming of behaviorism had little impact on the study of religion other than to essentially discard it from attention. When cognitive psychology came to the fore, again the focus was more on persons and thoughts than just behavior, though now potentially the impact of religious thoughts might be considered.

All the while, however, the psychology of religion was becoming its own field with scholars devoting their careers to studying the role of religion (and subsequently spirituality) in the lives of individuals. Social psychology joined the pursuit and much literature has emerged on how religious community interacts with individuals (Sisemore, 2016, Chapter 12) and even broader culture (Sisemore, 2016, Chapter 13).

Most of the work being done flows from an empirical model based on Western scientific psychology, yet in recent years there is movement toward a more emic perspective on the field, working from indigenous perspectives and broadening the focus to include more from other religions (Sisemore & Knabb, 2020a) and even to examine the psychology of being secular (e.g., Streib & Klein, 2013). Finally, there has been a strong movement to consider the clinical implications of the psychology of religion, as exemplified by the inauguration of the journal *Spirituality in Clinical Practice*. Numerous journals publish articles on the psychology of religion and spirituality, and many psychological organizations have a division to focus on this. For example, the American Psychological Association hosts Division 36, The Society for the Psychology of Religion and Spirituality. There is also the Society for the Scientific Study of Religion composed largely of social psychologists and publishing one of the most prestigious journals in the field.

## Major Content Areas of the Psychology of Religion and Spirituality

The domain of PRS is quite broad as religion and spirituality impact many areas of the lives of those who hold to them. My goal in the paragraphs that follow is simply to summarize the areas and cite a sample finding so that I can communicate a "taste" of the field. This list is by no means exhaustive but hopefully is representative of the work done in PRS.

**Development and Religion and Spirituality** Religious faith and spirituality play a significant role in development for many individuals and families, if not for most. Some (e.g., Barrett, 2012) argue there is scientific evidence that seeking something "bigger" than ourselves is possibly even built in at birth. Many families raise children into a faith and place them in communities that support and encourage them in that belief. Marriage is often seen as a religious act, and religion and spirituality impact adults in their family and work lives. Though this may be a generational effect, for now religion may be more salient in the lives of old adults than any other group.

One sample area of research in this area is the way that attachment theory, rooted in the work of John Bowlby (1969), has been applied to religious relationships. This work might have been started by Kirkpatrick and Shaver (1990) but it has grown considerably and is summarized in the recent landmark work of Granqvist (2020). Granqvist and Dickie (2006) track how attachment to parents translates to attachment to God and changes through development, moving from more parent-focus to God-focus as God becomes a secure object (in the optimal version) and safe haven.

**Conversion and Deconversion** One of the fascinating things in religion is the sometimes-dramatic conversion of a person from non-faith to religious faith, or a change from one faith to another, or even from a posture of faith to non-faith. The first two of these are generally called conversions while the latter is referred to as deconversion. These are sometimes quite remarkable and sudden while at other times gradual and subtle. Arguably the leading theorist of conversion is Rambo (Rambo & Bauman, 2012) who sees conversion beginning in the broad context of the individual and running through a crisis, quest, and encounter with the religious group, interaction with them, and then a commitment to the group leading to the ensuing consequences. Studies are also ongoing about the reverse process of leaving a faith, exemplified by Streib's Deconversion Project (Streib, Hood Jr., Keller, Csöff, & Silver, 2009) which looks at narratives of those who deconvert and found themes such as the pursuit of autonomy, feeling debarred from paradise (disappointed with the faith), finding a new frame of reference, and some who live lifelong quests, trying various religions.

**The Psychology of Religious Experience** As noted earlier, this is in a sense where the psychology of religion began as James (1902/1961) lectured on psychological explanations of religious experience. Since then, the field has broadened to look at things ranging from the more typical experience of prayer, meditation (including mindfulness), and rituals, to more unusual things such as serpent handling and mystical experience. Hood and his colleagues (e.g., Hood & Williamson, 2008) have offered fascinating insight into how some Christian believers take literally a disputed text of the Bible and in faith handle serpents to express it. Hood is sympathetic in general, seeing this as a strong demonstration of faith – even when these worshippers are occasionally bitten and even die.

**Religion and Mental/Physical Health** Another large body of research in PRS examines how religious faith and spirituality impact health – often for the better but sometimes for the worse. The Society for the Psychology of Religion and Spirituality (APA Division 36) recently focused their annual conference on the topic (2020). The hope, community, and good habits espoused by religious often play positive roles in promoting good health, though spiritual crisis during illness can have the opposite effect (e.g., Exline & Rose, 2013). Meditation and mindfulness are also garnering considerable attention for their health benefits. Let us focus on prayer. It has benefits to physical health by helping cope with stress, giving a sense of control and promoting relaxation, and thereby reduces cardiovascular issues, though the literature is less conclusive regarding cancer and HIV/AIDS (summarized by Sisemore, 2016, p. 198). The benefits to a sense of well-being are also strong, with 60% of studies summarized by Kimball (2013) showing positive effects. For some, though, prayer can increase anxiety depending on one's view of God (Spilka & Ladd, 2013).

**Cognitive Science of Religion** This is a broad area that looks to see how religion appears in the brain and cognitive processing. It fits with a literature that has examined how religious acts and experience show in the brain and how cognitive processes inform and react to religious and spiritual activity and ritual. It is a very cross-disciplinary area of PRS as it intersects with neuroscience, development, cognition, chemistry, and even evolutionary psychology. An example is Barrett's (2012) work mentioned earlier that suggests children to be naturally predisposed to see agency in the world. For instance, they more readily see something like the Grand Canyon as made by God than by the forces of nature. Based on this, Barrett says, it is almost as if parents raising children not to believe in a God who has agency must undo this tendency. An older illustration of this is the infamous Good Friday Experiment (Pahnke, 1966) conducted by Timothy Leary where seminary students were randomly given a placebo or psilocybin prior to going to worship. Needless to say, those receiving the hallucinogen had more remarkable experiences that day – except for one in particular who had a very upsetting experience. The goal was to explore how physiological states impact spiritual experience.

**Religious Practices** We looked at some unusual experiences, but psychologists of religion also examine more routine religious and spiritual practices for what they are: regular parts of life and spiritual maintenance and growth. We noted earlier how prayer can help with health issues, but activities such as prayer have a deeper meaning than simply physical benefits. Religious practices, often referred to as rituals, can occur individually or in community. Rituals can also range to such things as bar and bat mitzvahs for Jews, the Hajj for Muslims, and Easter for Christians, to give some basic illustrations. Other rituals might include fasting or feasting, times of celebration, or mourning. Research shows that these have impacts ranging from creating a synchrony among participants, to a channeling of sexuality, to delaying death, being a means of contacting the supernatural, focusing attention, creating a sense of vulnerability yet support, and promoting the community (these are summarized in Sisemore, 2016, p. 283–4).

**Religion and Coping and Meaning** Two key functions of religion and spirituality are to provide a sense of meaning to life in general and events in particular and to provide a way to cope with the challenges of life. PRS has looked at these extensively and found that religion generally promotes coping but can lead to spiritual crisis when events challenge it. Kenneth Pargament has arguably been the leader in research in this area, defining religious coping as "a search for significance in times of stress" (Pargament, 1997, p. 90). This leads to efforts to conserve the significance of the sacred or to transform the significance of the sacred, with such positive coping leading to some of the health benefits mentioned earlier. Should these strategies fail, there is a spiritual crisis that can be devastating to the individual.

Crystal Park (e.g., Park, Edmondson, & Hale-Smith, 2013) has pioneered research on meaning and its relationship to religion, finding that religion fits well as a meaning system as it integrates well with peoples' self-definition, daily living, and life goals. Challenges to this push the person to integrate them into meanings or to adapt meanings (Park, 2013). Between these approaches, we can learn how religion gives life meaning and enables people of faith to cope with life's challenges, though admittedly sometimes this leads to spiritual struggle.

**Religion in Communities** Historically faith communities have been vital to many cultures and shape the individuals within them, partly through rituals as we noted before. This is less clear in the West given how it is shaped by individualism but clearly holds true for many religions – including Christianity in many cases. I previously explained (Sisemore, 2016, p. 276–278) how religious communities provide moral cohesion, a sense of belonging and a sense of transcendence. Religious community can be controversial as seen with what the field calls new religious movements, often popularly called "cults." Other controversial issues current in this field are the role of non-heterosexuals in many religious communities given many sacred texts speak against sexuality outside of marriage between a male and female, conflicting with current views of sexual and gender diversity.

**Religion and Spirituality in Clinical Practice** There is a growing emphasis on taking the findings in PRS and applying them to clinical work by psychologists and other mental health professionals. When people of faith face mental health challenges, they generally desire to include their faith in psychotherapy. This can be a challenge as mental health professionals are generally less religious than the general public (developed in Shafranske, 1996). Models have been developed from specifically religious perspectives, such as Knabb et al. (2019) from a Christian worldview and al-Karam (2018) from a Muslim one, though other religions are rapidly developing models of therapy built on their worldviews while (in many cases) incorporating evidence-based treatments.

Pargament (2007) has developed a broad model of psychotherapy named "spiritually oriented psychotherapy" built around the notion of seeing problems through a spiritual lens, useful for all forms of religion and spirituality. There are several religious and spiritual interventions that have empirical support (Plante, 2009) including prayer, meditation, clarifying meaning, bibliotherapy, participating in rituals, and acting in accordance with religious ethics and promoting forgiveness, gratitude, and kindness – including acts of sympathy and charity. Others include accepting self and others and appreciating the sacredness of life. Applications of PRS to psychotherapy are being actively researched and form a vital part of the field today.

This cursory review of some of the areas of work underway in the psychology of religion and spirituality is intended simply to give the reader a flavor of the dimensions of the area and the fascinating findings emerging – findings that are immensely practical and particularly impacting clinical work with persons of faith.

## Teaching the Psychology of Religion and Spirituality as an Undergraduate Course

We turn now to consider the actual teaching of PRS in postsecondary education. We will consider the primary approach of teaching it as a freestanding course of its own, then turn to how important elements of PRS can be incorporated into other courses, and then conclude with some thoughts on teaching PRS at the graduate level.

### Contexts for the Course

There are, of course, quite a variety of educational institutions, but when it comes to religion there is somewhat of a bifurcation into religious institutions and state or other secular schools. Nielsen and Silver (2015) address the significance of this issue, with the former sometimes promoting a specific religion (or even a specific version of a religion – such as a Baptist university promoting the Baptist version of the Christian faith), while sectarian schools may be commissioned carefully to avoid any semblance of endorsing a specific religion. Indeed, this may lead at times to a hesitance to even offer a course in PRS. Yet to avoid doing so can leave a significant deficit in a college's curriculum given the significant and vital role religion plays in the life of many (if not most) people and thus to neglect it is to fail to fully understand persons and some communities.

One of the problems that Nielsen and Silver (2015) point out, however, is that the preponderance of research in PRS is from Christian populations given most has been conducted in the West where Christianity is the most common religion. Yet, much of this research is done with deference to other faiths and the trends are changing (see, e.g., Sisemore & Knabb, 2020a). Nielsen and Silver (2015) suggest that professors consider the accreditation standards of the school and requirements for being able to teach a course given there may be a need to show some background in PRS in order to teach the course. Even at that, instructors will need to be self-aware of their own faith (or secularity) and its impact on the course and be prepared for the potential reactions of students from varying backgrounds with regard to faith, particularly as this is often a troubling topic and may bring up unpleasant memories for some who have had negative experiences with religion and religious groups. Conversely, Nielsen (2012) notes that many believing student may enroll for such a course in an effort to affirm their own beliefs.

The context of a faith-based institution may alter the approach to the course and its content. Religiously based schools vary widely on how open they are to presentation of contrasting views of faith and to letting their own views be examined by scientific psychology. Addressing these issues in advance with school administration will be important. Clarifying with students how the course fits into the school's philosophy will also be essential to the success of the course. A PRS class may challenge students' beliefs but also may lead to a deeper appreciation of faith through closer examination of how it functions in life and serves psychological as well as spiritual functions.

Another contextual issue is in what department to teach PRS. Obviously, a psychology department is most common and natural. But religion has many sociological dimensions and much of the research is done by sociologists and social psychologists. It could also, then, be offered in a sociology department. A PRS course might also be housed in an anthropology department as through it we learn of different cultures and people groups. PRS can also be located as a course in a religious studies or theology department and could be adapted to different approaches to the material depending on how the department frames the course and its role in the curriculum.

## Possible Course Texts

While some instructors will prefer to assemble a set of articles or media for their courses, there is a solid set of options for textbooks that can organize material and make supplements of articles and media less central. We will briefly note a few.

Paloutzian (2016) is a traditional text focused on undergraduates that has recently been updated and is a manageable resource for undergraduates. Written by a leader in the field, it challenges students to see how religion can shape meaning through the changes of life. Paloutzian fulfills the book's title well as a warm welcome to the field, though some may see it as less positive toward faith than other texts.

Sisemore (2016) is written explicitly with the goal of being an undergraduate text and is organized to support that. It is intentionally two-pronged, presenting the empirical research but also having a more qualitative aspect in giving voice to people of differing faiths (and atheism) to illustrate key points.

Nelson (2009) may be stronger on theory and explanation and thus less clearly focused on the empirical literature, though he gives this adequate coverage. Its strength is giving detail to ideas and has made some effort to be more intentional in discussing Eastern religions than the others. It is becoming a little dated, however.

Hood, Hill, and Spilka (2018) are clearly the dominant text in the field as evident in its being in its fifth edition. I mention it last only because it is more of a graduate text and may be a challenge to most undergraduate students. It is, nonetheless, the

# 45 Teaching the Psychology of Religion and Spirituality

standard for the most information, and its empirical approach keeps it extremely focused on the scientific literature which it thoroughly and fairly covers.

Also notable are two handbooks that offer excellent summaries of topics in the area, though these may be best suited as sources for supplemental readings than as textbooks. Pargament (2013) is the editor-in-chief of the American Psychological Association's massive two-volume *Handbook of Psychology, Religion, and Spirituality*. Other than its sheer comprehensiveness, Pargament's work is noteworthy in that the entire second volume is dedicated to applied areas of PRS and thus of utility for those with more clinical interests.

Paloutzian and Park (2013) have also published an outstanding source for summaries of many of the vital areas of PRS. While not as thorough as Pargament (2013), this book is manageable enough to consider as a text if an instructor wants focused summaries of topics and to connect them through customized lecture. This could be a flexible approach is the instructor know the field well enough.

Beyond these, there are numerous books on topics in PRS in addition to the growing body of journal literature. Many professors will want to direct their students to the primary literature at some point for the sake of making them familiar with original sources and how the data is developed in research.

## Suggested Attitudes for Teaching PRS

We mentioned above how the philosophy of a course in PRS will vary depending on the type of institution it is offered in. So will the stance of the instructor. I venture to suggest a few attitudes that may enhance the experience across a range of settings.

First, there will need to be some openness. For people of faith, there is often anxiety in having science examine this treasured part of their lives. Others will seek to use science to discount the faith of others. Instructors in the class will want to create a space for students to speak freely with a sense that the divergent perspectives will be respected. An atmosphere of curiosity and understanding is to be preferred.

Second, for this to occur, the instructor does well to model humility in approaching the discipline of PRS. A humble approach acknowledges the problems of epistemology in the area, and that science, committed as it is to the observable and measurable, is not equipped to answer ultimate religious questions (Sisemore & Knabb, 2020b). While PRS can describe religious/spiritual behavior, emotions, and attitudes, it is not equipped to decide basic questions such as whether there is a God, etc. The instructor may wish to model a humble approach to facilitate the openness just described.

Finally, the instructor will want to be particularly respectful – especially to students who do not share the instructor's position regarding faith. There are such things as religious micro-aggressions where one person subtly insults or dismisses the faith of others. In a day when we are increasingly working to respect cultural differences, religion and spirituality should not be omitted as worthy of cultural respect.

From this, the atmosphere of the class should be one of understanding and engaging, not of judging. Students, too, can bring biases and, as we all know, feelings run strong around the issue of religion. PRS is a form of scholarship and as such should keep a posture of detachment and eagerness to understand.

## Instructional Strategies

As with any course, the instructor must engage students and utilize effective pedagogy. While the standard methods of lecture, exam, papers, etc. play a role, I offer a few other suggestions for structuring the class. A wonderful resource was created by Kevin Ladd (https://osf.io/vsua9/) which lists a variety of syllabi in the area of PRS, and I encourage you to consult this for ideas on overall structure of your course.

Nielsen (2012) surveyed a number of psychology of religion courses and found some of the major assignments used. We will omit more typical ones (such as a research paper, though it was the most commonly used). Personal reflection assignments were also common. Here one could be asked to reflect on course content in light of a personal experience or reflect more generally on their (non)spiritual journey in some way. Similarly, one could assign students to write a spiritual autobiography. Experiential activities are commonly used, and these may range from trying a meditative technique to attending a worship service of a group different from one's own background to interviewing a practitioner of a different faith. Another interesting task is to have students watch films and consider them from the perspective of PRS. For example, in the past I have had students watch the Academy Award winning *Chariots of Fire* and compare how the two lead characters used faith in differing ways in their pursuit of Olympic gold. One could also stage a debate between differing points of views on certain topics or have students design an empirical study of a topic covered in class.

To Neilsen's list, I would add students could be asked to complete a project in the community where they attend a meet with a spiritual leader or assist with a community project of a religious/spiritual group. One might also hold class symposia (also preparing them for this common format of presenting research) by assigning small groups a topic and having them break it down for several presentations around the theme. Finally, instructors might invite guest speakers who have either done research in an area of PRS or who could describe their spirituality or spiritual experience. Similarly, numerous clips are available on YouTube and other Internet sources to show religious practices and spiritual experiences.

You, of course, may have other, better ideas and creativity is encouraged. Hopefully, some of these suggestions may inspire your ingenuity.

## Introducing PRS in the General Psychology and Related Undergraduate Curriculum

PRS is an orphan in psychology in some ways. There is not a doctorate in the field, though there are some related programs. For instance, the University of Denver and

Iliff School of Theology offer a joint Ph.D. program in the study of religion, and Religion and Psychological Studies is one of its concentrations (https://www.du.edu/duiliffjoint/current-students/concentrations/religion-psychological-studies). Several clinical psychology programs offer doctoral degrees in clinical psychology from a specific religious perspective, though this is not really the same as the psychology of religion. This lack of a formal route to becoming a psychologist of religion mean scholars in the field may be social psychologists, personality psychologists, developmental psychologists, philosophers of psychology, or clinical psychologists by training. This implies that PRS connects to various areas in the broader realm of psychology, despite not having a direct route to becoming an expert in the field.

Despite this, textbooks in other major areas of psychology overlook the PRS literature and the importance of religion in general and in so doing offer incomplete views of their topics. A rare exception is Krull's (2019) introductory psychology text that includes an entire chapter on the psychology of religion. Conscientious professors of a variety of classes may wish to include a section on how PRS overlaps with their classes at points. As already observed, PRS can be relevant to sociology, religion, anthropology, and also ethics, social work, counseling, philosophy, world religions, and diversity studies. These instructors merely need to ask themselves, "How do religion and spirituality intersect with the content area of the course?" A brief reflection will likely yield some important ways PRS is germane to the course – even though the standard texts may overlook it.

Space will not permit a review of all possible courses in all disciplines where the literature of PRS is relevant, but I offer a brief list of typical courses in an undergraduate psychology curriculum and a point of connection with the PRS literature.

**Abnormal Psychology** There is a fascinating history of research on distinguishing religious experience and belief from psychopathology, particularly psychosis. PRS has also produced a solid body of research on the positive and negative impacts of religion and spirituality on mental health.

**Personality Psychology** The differences between intrinsic (faith valued for itself) and extrinsic (faith as pragmatic, serving external purposes) religiosity are important in understanding how faith is incorporated into personality more than just being some behaviors. For many people, religion and spirituality are core components of a sense of self, making it challenging to understand who they are without considering the role of their faith.

**Community Psychology** Historically faith occurred predominantly in community, only recently, and in the West primarily, has it been more of an individualistic phenomenon. In the United States, for example, the church is a core source of community for many black Americans. Often such faith shapes the larger community and so is vital to understanding its functioning.

**Statistics and Research Methods** Understanding what psychologists of religion have done to explore something as "invisible" as faith demonstrates the flexibility of research methods. Religion is a ripe field for utilizing qualitative methods to build theory about religious behavior, and mixed methods approaches are giving insight into the complexities of those without faith who have often been assumed to be homogeneous in their atheism (see Sisemore, 2016, p. 137–142 for a summary).

**Tests and Measures** For instance, my colleagues and I took an explicitly theological concept, grace, and developed a measure for it and then demonstrated its utility in understanding individual functioning and its role in coping with mental illness (Bufford, Sisemore, & Blackburn, 2017). There are numerous other examples of creatively operationalizing religious variables to make them researchable.

**Social Psychology** We have already noted that many researchers in PRS are social psychologists. Earlier we noted the work of Hood and colleagues (e.g., Hood & Williamson, 2008) in studying serpent handling groups. Much work has also been done on the role of fundamentalism as a form of religion and the magnetism of new religious movements. Ritual is also a key feature of social life – often for the non-religious as well!

**Industrial/Organizational Psychology** People do not check their faith at the door of their places of business. Muslim businesses may pause operations at times of prayer; conflict can ensue if a hajib or yarmulke is worn into a place of business, or if an employee wants to place a crucifix by their office door. Does faith impact life in the workplace? Is it possibly a resource businesses might incorporate more effectively? These are only a few of the areas where PRS impacts industrial/organizational psychology.

**Positive Psychology** This is a natural area of overlap with PRS given the long history of religion promoting virtues. Positive psychologists can hardly study core areas like forgivingness, gratitude, and happiness without considering the roles faith and spirituality play, whether for better or worse.

**Biological or Physiological Psychology** PRS has long examined the activity of the brain during spiritual experience, noting the areas which are active during prayer, meditation, and other aspects of faith expression. We noted earlier the Good Friday experiment (Pahnke, 1966) and this opens the door to other interconnections of worship and physiology such as the use of peyote in indigenous American spirituality. Mystical experiences are also intriguing in their impact on physiology – or vice versa.

**Cognitive Psychology** In addition to Barrett's (2012) argument for children as intuitively seeking causation beyond the physical, other areas here are the study of body and spirit and why so many see humans as including a spiritual element. Cognitive scientists of religion have also looked at ritual and particularly the role of linguistics in rituals and at how persons of faith attribute life events to the divine that others attribute to more material causes.

**Human Development** Already one of the more cross-disciplinary domains of psychology, the role of religion and spirituality in changes throughout the lifespan are not to be overlooked. There are myriad areas to consider here, from cognitive development and faith and morality, to the role of parents in transmitting faith traditions, to the challenges as children often leave or change faiths as they move into adulthood.

**History of Psychology** We skimmed the surface of the history of PRS earlier but given the fact that vital players in history like James, Freud, and Jung have spoken to the psychology of religion, a thorough history of psychology course could not overlook examining these areas and how psychology and religion in general have had a tumultuous relationship.

**Ethics of Psychology** Though more likely to be in a graduate course, psychology has an impact on ethics, particularly in tracing the move from a religious ethic to one based on consensus such as in the American Psychological Association. How are religious issues to be treated in psychotherapy? What are we to do with the conflicts between some forms of religion and the broad range of gender and sexuality diversities? How are conflicts between religious belief and ethical standards to be handled?

**Philosophical Psychology** The problem of ethics has largely been seen as a philosophical one, and the psychology of religion and spirituality can offer insight into the impact of diverging epistemologies in science and religion (as attempted in Sisemore & Knabb, 2020a). How do views about faith inform the development of ethics?

**Learning and Memory** This may be one of the more thinly related areas to PRS, but one must learn one's religion and hold memories of religious experience. Here religion might learn from psychology how to make sermons more memorable or how to teach the faith to people in religious communities.

**Sensation and Perception** Good work has been done in PRS on the intersection of sense and the spiritual, examining what exactly goes on during mystical experiences or other strange phenomena such as near death experiences. When a person claims "God spoke to me" or the like, what does that actually mean in terms of what is sensed and perceived?

**Clinical** We need only to point to the large second volume of Pargament (2013) that is devoted to clinical application of PRS. Should therapy be more spiritually oriented for people of faith? How should faith be incorporated in understanding and treating mental health concerns? How is psychology to be integrated with specific faiths? It is hard to imagine a comprehensive course on clinical psychology that ignores faith as a part of the problem and/or solution for many clients.

This quick survey is illustrative of the many ways that the PRS literature can be tapped to enhance education across the spectrum of psychology given that faith is such a vital and central part of the lives of so many people.

## PRS in the Graduate Curriculum

One may occasionally find a PRS course in a graduate curriculum, and as noted above, on occasion it is an area of focus in a graduate program, albeit more often in religion schools than psychology schools. It is included in some psychology doctoral programs in clinical psychology, particularly as associated with Christian-focused programs (e.g., it is offered currently at Regent University in Virginia (https://www.regent.edu/school-of-psychology-and-counseling/program/psyd-in-clinical-psychology/#programs-program_courses)).

Given the recent surge in research in applied psychology of religion, it is quite apropos to doctoral programs in clinical psychology (and related non-psychology clinical and counseling programs). Given that the American Psychological Association (2003) has encouraged the use of culturally appropriate interventions in therapy, and religion and spirituality are seen as cultural dimensions. It would seem incumbent on doctoral psychology programs to directly address working with religion persons, but there is relatively little emphasis on this – even though psychologists have developed a set of empirically derived competencies for working with religious and spiritual clients (Vieten et al., 2016) and the Society for the Psychology of Religion and Spirituality has an active task force working toward adapting these as guidelines for all applied psychologists. These flow from PRS and so this content will need to be covered somewhere in graduate programs if psychologists are to be trained to use culturally appropriate interventions with people of faith. This also entails an awareness of working with persons from a variety of faith backgrounds (Sisemore & Knabb, 2020a) and knowing more emic approaches to understanding faith. Much the same can be said for students in social work, counseling, and marriage and family therapy.

In non-clinical psychology programs, PRS can broaden the understanding of the content area along the lines noted in the list of courses above, though in more detail. It also can fill out the background of students in religious studies programs and even those who are pursuing pastoral degrees and clinical pastoral education.

## Summary

The psychology of religion and spirituality has struggled to find a home in the broader field of psychology, yet offers extremely important insights into human behavior, but as individuals and as groups. If we are to understand humans in their fullness – as psychology purports to do – then we must study and understand the role of religion and spirituality in humans and our cultures. Colleges and universities are encouraged to consider adding a course in PRS to their curricula, and professors in other areas of psychology are urged to incorporate relevant findings from PRS in their courses in psychology. Maybe even some schools will pioneer the field and develop doctoral programs in PRS. Clinically oriented graduate programs might consider how to equip their graduates to serve people of faith as a form of diversity. Finally, I hope this chapter has given enough of a taste of the field to pique an interest in further study in PRS by the reader.

## References

Allport, G. W. (1950). *The individual and his religion*. New York: Macmillan.
Allport, G. W. (1958; original, 1954). *The nature of prejudice*. New York: Doubleday.
American Psychological Association. (2003). Guidelines for multicultural education, training, research, practice, and organizational change for psychologists. *American Psychologist, 58*, 377–402.
al-Karam, C.Y. (Ed.). (2018). Islamically integrated psychotherapy: Uniting faith and professional practice. West Conshohoken, PA: Templeton Press.
Barrett, J. L. (2012). *Born believers: The science of children's religious belief*. New York: Free Press.
Bowlby, J. (1969). *Attachment and loss: Vol. 1. Attachment*. New York: Basic Books.
Bufford, R. K., Sisemore, T. A., & Blackburn, A. M. (2017). Dimensions of grace: Factor analysis of three grace scales. *Psychology of Religion and Spirituality, 9*, 56–69. Supplemental materials at https://doi.org/10.1037/rel0000064.supp
Delaney, H. D., Miller, W. R., & Bisonó, A. M. (2013). Religiosity and spirituality among psychologists: A survey of clinician members of the American Psychological Association. *Spirituality in Clinical Practice, 1*(S), 95–106. https://doi.org/10.1037/2326.4500.1.S.95
Erikson, E. H. (1962). *Young man Luther: A study in psychoanalysis and history*. New York: W. W. Norton.
Erikson, E. H. (1969). *Gandhi's truth: On the origins of militant nonviolence*. New York: W. W. Norton.
Exline, J. J., & Rose, E. D. (2013). Religious and spiritual struggles. In R. F. Paloutzian & C. L. Park (Eds.), *Handbook of the psychology of religion and spirituality* (2nd ed., pp. 380–398). New York: Guilford.
Freud, S. (1950). *Totem and taboo: Some points of agreement between the mental lives of savages and neurotics*. London: Routledge and Paul. (Original work published 1913.).
Freud, S. (1955). *Moses and monotheism*. New York: Vintage Books. (Original work published 1939.).
Freud, S. (1961). *The future of an illusion*. New York: W.W. Norton. (Original work published 1923.)
Fromm, E. (1967). *Psychoanalysis and religion*. New York: Bantam Books. (Original work published 1950).
Granqvist, P., & Dickie, J. R. (2006). Attachment and spiritual development in childhood and adolescence. In E. C. Roehlkepartain, P. E. King, L. Wagener, & P. L. Benson (Eds.), *The handbook of spiritual development in childhood and adolescence* (pp. 197–210). Thousand Oaks, CA: Sage.
Granqvist, P. E. (2020). *Attachment in religion and spirituality: A wider view*. New York: Guilford.
Hill, P. C., Pargament, K. I., Hood, R. W., Jr., McCullough, M. E., Swyers, J. P., Larson, D. B., & Zinnbauer, B. J. (2000). Conceptualizing religion and spirituality: Points of commonality, points of departure. *Journal for the Theory of Social Behavior, 30*, 52–77.
Hood, R. W., Jr., Hill, P. C., & Spilka, B. (2018). *The psychology of religion: An empirical approach* (5th ed.). New York: Guilford.

Hood, R. W., Jr., & Williamson, W. P. (2008). *Them that believe: The power and meaning of the Christian serpent-handling tradition*. Berkeley, CA: University of California Press.

Hood, R. W. (2003). The relationship between religion and spirituality. In A. L. Griel & D. G. Bromiley (Eds.), *Defining religion: Investigating the boundaries between the sacred and the secular* (pp. 241–264). Oxford, UK: Elsevier Science.

James, W. (1961). *The varieties of religious experience*. New York: Macmillan. (Original work published 1902).

Kimball, B. M. (2013). A practical meta-analysis of prayer efficacy in coping with mental health. *Master of Social Work Clinical Research Papers*. Paper 208. Retrieved from http://sophia.stkate.edu/msw_papers/208

Kirkpatrick, L. A., & Shaver, P. R. (1990). Attachment theory and religion: Childhood attachments, religious beliefs, and conversion. *Journal for the Scientific Study of Religion, 29*, 315–334. In R. F. Paloutzian & C. L. Park (Eds.), *Handbook of the psychology of religion and spirituality* (2nd ed., pp. 118–137). New York: Guilford.

Knabb, J. J., Johnson, E. L., Bates, M. T., & Sisemore, T. A. (2019). *Christian psychotherapy in context: Theoretical and empirical explorations in faith-based mental health*. New York: Routledge.

Krull, D. S. (2019). *Psychological science: A conversational approach* (2nd ed.). Matthews, NC: Kona Publishing.

Marler, P. L., & Hadaway, C. K. (2002). "Being religious" or "being spiritual" in America: A zero-sum proposition? *Journal for the Scientific Study of Religion, 41*, 289–300.

Nelson, J. M. (2009). *Psychology, religion, and spirituality*. New York: Springer.

Nielsen, M. E. (2012, Summer). Teaching psychology of religion at a state university. *Society for the Psychology of Religion and Spirituality Newsletter: American Psychological Association Division, 36*(2), 2–5.

Nielsen, M. E., & Silver, C. F. (2015). Strategies and resources for teaching psychology of religion. In D. Dunn (Ed.), *The Oxford handbook of undergraduate psychology education* (pp. 577–587). New York: Oxford.

Pahnke, W. (1966). Drugs and mysticism. *International Journal of Parapsychology, 8*, 295–314.

Paloutzian, R. F. (2016). *Invitation to the psychology of religion* (3rd ed.). New York: Guilford.

Paloutzian, R. F., & Park, C. L. (Eds.). (2013). *Handbook of the psychology of religion and spirituality* (2nd ed.). New York: Guilford.

Pargament, K. I. (1997). *The psychology of religion and coping: Theory, research, and practice*. New York: Guilford.

Pargament, K. I. (2007). *Spiritually integrated psychotherapy: Understanding and addressing the sacred*. New York: Guilford.

Pargament, K. I. (Ed. in Chief, 2013). *APA handbook of psychology, religion, and spirituality (2 Vols.)*. Washington, D.C.: American Psychological Association.

Pargament, K.I., Mahoney, A., Exline, J.J., Jones, J.W., & Shafranske, E.P. (2013). Envisioning an integrative paradigm for the psychology of religion and spirituality. In K.I. Pargament (Ed.-in-Chief), *APA handbook of psychology, religion, and spirituality: Vol. 1: Context, theory, and research* (pp. 3–19). Washington, D.C.: American Psychological Association.

Park, C. L. (2013). Trauma and meaning making: Converging conceptualizations and emerging evidence. In J. A. Hicks & C. Routledge (Eds.), *The experience of meaning in life: Classic perspectives, emerging themes, and controversies* (pp. 61–76). New York: Springer.

Park, C. L., Edmondson, E., & Hale-Smith, A. (2013). Why religion? Meaning as motivation. In K. I. Pargament (Ed.-in-Chief), *APA handbook of psychology, religion, and spirituality: Vol. 1: Context, theory, and research* (pp. 157–171). Washington, D.C.: American Psychological Association.

Pew Forum on Religion and Public Life. (2012, October 9). Religion and the unaffiliated. Retrieved from www.pewforum.org/2012/10/09/nones-on-the-rise-religion/

Plante, T. G. (2009). *Spiritual practices in psychotherapy: Thirteen tools for enhancing psychological health*. Washington, DC: American Psychological Association.

Rambo, L. R., & Bauman, S. C. (2012). Psychology of conversion and spiritual transformation. *Pastoral Psychology, 61*, 879–894.

Sisemore, T. A. (2016). *The psychology of religion: From the inside out.* Hoboken, NJ: John Wiley & Sons.

Sisemore, T. A., & Knabb, J. J. (Eds.). (2020a). *The psychology of world religions and spiritualities: An indigenous perspective.* West Conshohocken, PA: Templeton Press.

Sisemore, T. A., & Knabb, J. J. (2020b). Seeing religions and spiritualities from the inside: Problems for Western psychology that can be addressed with an indigenous psychological perspective. In T. A. Sisemore & J. J. Knabb (Eds.), *The psychology of world religions and spiritualities: An indigenous perspective* (pp. 3–28). West Conshohocken, PA: Templeton Press.

Spilka, B., & Ladd, K. L. (2013). *The psychology of prayer: A scientific approach.* New York: Guilford.

Streib, H., Hood, R. W., Jr., Keller, B., Csöff, R.-M., & Silver, C. (2009). *Deconversion: Qualitative and quantitative results from cross-cultural research in Germany and the United States (research in contemporary religion, Vol. 4).* Göttingen, Germany: Vandenhoeck & Ruprecht.

Streib, H., & Klein, C. (2013). Atheists, agnostics, and apostates. In K.I. Pargament (Ed.-in-Chief), *APA handbook of psychology, religion, and spirituality: Vol. 1: Context, theory, and research* (pp. 713–728). Washington, D.C.: American Psychological Association.

Vieten, C., Scammell, S., Pierce, A., Pilato, R., Ammondson, I., Pargament, K. I., & Lukoff, D. (2016). Competencies for psychologists in the domains of religion and spirituality. *Spirituality in Clinical Practice, 3*, 92–114. https://doi.org/10.1037/scp0000078

Winnicott, D. W. (1990). *The maturational process and the facilitating environment.* London: Karnac Books.

Wulff, D. M. (1997). *Psychology of religion: Classic and contemporary* (2nd ed.). New York: John Wiley & Sons.

# Epistemology of Psychology

**46**

Gordana Jovanović

## Contents

Introduction .................................................................. 1118
Positivist Epistemology ........................................................ 1120
Critiques of Positivism ........................................................ 1122
Another History of Knowing Subject and Known Objects ............................ 1128
Epistemic Situation in Psychology .............................................. 1132
A Lesson to Be Learnt ......................................................... 1138
References .................................................................... 1139

### Abstract

After a brief introduction of the term epistemology, the chapter presents an historical overview of most influential epistemological positions, pointing out especially those aspects that have proved to be relevant to psychology or which could be relevant to its future development. Positivism seems to be an indispensable starting point given its dominance in the first half of the twentieth century, even though it first appeared as a scientific program in the mid nineteenth century, in philosophy of Comte. As a new version of positivism named logical positivism or logical empiricism (Vienna Circle) provoked quite different critiques over decades (Popper, Quine, Husserl, Critical Theory, hermeneutics, feminist theories, communitarian epistemology), it follows a section dealing with critiques of positivist claims of certainty, of induction as a preferred mode of generating knowledge, of the unity of sciences, of atomistic representational model of knowledge, and of individualistic subject of knowing. Additionally it is referred

---

Gordana Jovanović is independent academic

G. Jovanović (✉)
Belgrade, Serbia
e-mail: gorda.jovanovic@gmail.com

© Springer Nature Switzerland AG 2023
J. Zumbach et al. (eds.), *International Handbook of Psychology Learning and Teaching*,
Springer International Handbooks of Education,
https://doi.org/10.1007/978-3-030-28745-0_54

to another, humanistic epistemic culture shaped in Renaissance under the influence of revival of the ancient Greek and Latin cultural legacy, which however remained less influential in shaping further developments. In spite of that, at the turn of the twentieth century, there were philosophers and psychologists (Dilthey, Wundt) who argued for a necessity to distinguish natural and human sciences and, correspondingly, to acknowledge that social and human sciences require specific modes of knowing (understanding) oriented toward grasping meaning of human experience and symbolic products objectified in human historical and sociocultural worlds. Summarizing implications of different epistemological positions for psychology, it is stated that epistemology of psychology is characterized, on the one hand, by a substantial influence of positivism and its natural-science model of knowledge, and on the other hand, by challenges posed by psychology's subject matter to positivism. In conclusion, it is argued for a holistic, historically based and culturally shaped relational model of knowledge capable to integrate value dimension as an indispensable feature of human experience and human activity. In this way psychology and consequently teaching psychology can do justice to their subject matter – experience and activity of human beings as historical, social, and cultural beings living in a man-made world.

**Keywords**

Epistemology · Positivism · Hermeneutics · Signification · Popper · Dilthey · Wundt · Habermas

## Introduction

The term "epistemology," derived from two Greek roots – "ἐπιστήμη, *epistēmē*" (meaning – knowledge, understanding) and "λόγος, logos" (meaning – account, thought, reason) – is usually translated as theory of knowledge. The first appearance of the English term in the 1840s was a translation of the German term "Wissenschaftslehre" (literally – theory of science) introduced by German philosopher Johann Gottlieb Fichte (1762–1814), and elaborated in his main work under the title *Wissenschaftslehre* (1804).

From the very beginning the term epistemology has been associated with both a broader and a narrower meaning, referring either to knowledge in general or to scientific knowledge only. Either way, it was probably not an exaggeration when Karl Popper a half of century ago stated: "The phenomenon of human knowledge is no doubt the greatest miracle in our universe" (Popper, 1972, p. vii). But if a miracle, human knowledge has shared the destiny with other miracles in human world – never being completely deciphered.

Generally, to know means to have a kind of mental state. Mental states that underlay knowing belong to a category of states named beliefs. Clearly, not any belief counts as a knowledge. A belief needs an association with truth in order to qualify to be considered knowledge. However, even not just a true belief is knowledge. To know requires from the subject who claims to know to provide a valid justification for the truth claim. "For true beliefs to count as knowledge, it is necessary that they originate in sources we have good reason to consider reliable. These are perception, introspection, memory, reason, and testimony" (Steup & Neta, 2020, no pagination). Even though to this basic definition of knowledge as a justified true belief some additional condition could be added (as it is possible to imagine situations where a subject can have a justified true belief and in spite of that not knowing), a process of acquiring knowledge certainly presupposes a subject involved in that process (knowing subject, knower) and object(s) at which subject's knowing activity is directed (known objects could be of different kinds – to know that, to know how, or to know facts or individuals) (Baergen, 2006).

However, this simple structure of epistemic situation consisting of subject and object of knowing is just an abstraction from broader contexts of both the subject and object of knowing. There are different levels of mediation operating at the locus of subject of knowing – structure and functioning of its sense organs, cognitive schemes, its motivation, expectations, social position, psychological and other beliefs, symbolic capital available to it, and a general world view of its culture or epoch. The object of knowing is also part of a physical or sociocultural environment, it can be visible or hidden, or even repressed, it can be saturated with positive, desirable, or negative, adverse connotations, and with cultural, historical meanings in general. Both the process of knowing and its results, namely, knowledge, are shaped by plurality of contexts, including those a knower might not be aware of. It is the task of epistemological studies to take into account all these complexities, even though this is quite a challenging task, even at a descriptive level, not to speak of tasks to justify truth claims made under such conditions.

If epistemology is understood as a theory of scientific knowledge, i.e., where the object of knowing is a particular form of knowledge itself, the epistemic situation becomes even more complex. Scientific knowledge presupposes use of specific methods in the process of acquiring and verifying knowledge; the process itself is highly standardized and most importantly includes community of scientists as an indispensable reference agency. Even though scientific procedures are designed to reduce the influence of subjective factors of the scientists in order to achieve a supposedly objective account, it is clear that no scientist can assume God's view perspective, but is embedded into their culture, including scientific culture and their epochal agendas. At a quite basic level no science can escape language and its formative role in shaping even the basic processes of acquiring and transmitting knowledge, starting with the very naming of the observed phenomena (see, for example, Cassirer, 1923/1975).

From the history of epistemological conceptions, very different even opposed ones, it is possible to learn that a seemingly simple epistemic situation in which a knowing subject tries to know an object, is a microcosmos of a much broader world. When it comes to scientific knowledge, the position of psychology as science becomes additionally complicated as knowing subject belongs to its subject matter as well, and its object of knowing is also of a specific nature – the object is actually a subject, a conscious and self-conscious subject capable of using language and interpreting signs in the world (Piaget, 1972b).

This chapter presents an overview of most influential epistemological positions from a historical perspective, pointing out especially those aspects which have proved to be relevant to psychology or which could be relevant to its future development. Positivism is an indispensable starting point first given its dominance in the first half of the twentieth century and second, in view of quite different critiques it provoked over decades. However, it is referred also to another, humanistic epistemic culture shaped in Renaissance under the revival of ancient Greek and Latin cultural legacy, but this humanist epistemic culture remained less influential in shaping further developments. Summarizing implications of those epistemological positions to psychology, it could be stated that epistemology of psychology is characterized, on the one hand, by a substantial influence of positivism and its natural-science model of knowledge, and on the other hand, by challenges psychology's subject matter poses to positivism. The structure of this chapter is shaped according to these lines in order to demonstrate the importance of historical context for understanding scientific theories and formative role of critical accounts in development of science. Both historical consciousness and critical attitude are teaching goals whose relevance transcends any particular scientific field or topic.

## Positivist Epistemology

As the knowledge acquisition is a process taking place between epistemic subject and object to be known, it is clear that it depends on both sides, with their narrower or broader contexts and on all the methods, i.e., tools used by the knower in the process of knowing. Therefore at the very beginning some pressing questions appear: are all objects (i.e., natural, mental, social phenomena) the same in their epistemic position, are all methods and validity criteria suitable for all objects to be known. Answers to these questions define different epistemological positions.

Positive answers characterize positions, which argue that there are no substantial differences among phenomena in the world when they are the objects of knowledge. Consequently positive answers support the model of unity of science regardless of the objects they study, which means that there are no differences between natural and social or human sciences. The most influential position of this kind is logical positivism, which dominated philosophies, theories of science, and sciences themselves in the first half of the twentieth century, even though its roots are older. An immediate ancestor of the name root stems from French positivism of the mid-nineteenth century (positivisme, from positif – in philosophical meaning "imposed by experience," something that is posited). However, positivism remained committed to historically even older epistemological position of empiricism. Logical positivism is used as a description of the epistemological position formulated in the first decades of the twentieth century within the so-called Vienna Circle. Another description – logical empiricism – includes Vienna Circle but also Berlin school and some other philosophical centers in other parts of the world. Logical positivism and logical empiricism claim that genuine knowledge is based on sensory experience of objects that are part of an independently existing reality. If knowledge is not immediately based on sensory experience, it should be possible to reduce it to sensory experience. Thus, positivism is interested in positive facts only for which empirical evidence can be provided by sensory experience. Only propositions describing positive facts can be considered meaningful propositions, claims logical positivism.

Both historically and in its revived version, which was flourishing in the Vienna Circle – with the main representatives Moritz Schlick (1882–1936) and Rudolf Carnap (1891–1970) – positivism argues that the only valid knowledge is scientific knowledge, which has to replace metaphysical knowledge. Historically, this was the idea of French philosopher and sociologist Auguste Comte (1798–1857) who first in modern times formulated a program of "positive philosophy," as he called it in a series of texts published between 1830 and 1852 under the title *Cours de philosophie positive*.

While arguing for empirically founded scientific knowledge, which would expel theological or metaphysical assumptions of knowledge, Comte at the same time claimed that the purpose of knowledge is improvement of human life and society. Comte was committed to the Enlightenment idea of progress of knowledge and humankind. In his *Discours sur l'Esprit positif* (1844/1865) Comte described intellectual features of positivism, as he understood it, which showed explicit educational and social purpose of positive philosophy: "the proper function of intellect is the service of the social sympathies; the word positive connotes all the highest intellectual attributes and will finally have moral significance" (Comte, 1865, p. vii). After that Comte discussed social aspects of positivism defining in that chapter "the political motto of positivism as order and progress," and progress as "the development of order" (ibid. p.viii). In the further chapters Comte examined "the action of positivism upon the working classes," then "the influence of positivism upon women," "the relation of positivism to art" (ibid, pp. ix-xi). These features qualify Comte's positivism as an expansive social positivism.

The scope of positivism in its twentieth century version was much narrower, as the name logical positivism suggests. Similarly to Comte, Vienna Circle, a group of philosophers and scientists nominally led by Moritz Schlick, relied on model of natural sciences, but contrary to Comte, members of the Vienna Circle referred strongly to mathematics as well in order to achieve objectivity and accuracy of knowledge, i.e., statements expressing knowledge. They argued that only statements that can be verified are proper, meaningful statements. Verification can occur empirically through reference to sensory experience. This is the way how facts are generated. Only two kinds of meaningful statements are possible: analytic and synthetic. While in analytic statements meaning is completely contained in the subject of the statement, synthetic statements have a content, which requires an external verification – by reference to sensory experience. The program they pursued normatively expelled all a priori assumptions.

In spite of striking differences in the scope, both versions of positivism, Comte's positivism and Vienna Circle positivism, share empiricism and scientism – a view that only scientific knowledge is a valid knowledge and that valid knowledge needs empirical verification. It should be noted however that the very fact that Comte's positivism and Vienna Circle positivism are in many important aspects very different theories, could be understood as an early announcement that positivism is not a position that can stand up to absolutist certainty claims it has advanced.

## Critiques of Positivism

Even though arguments against positivism were raised already in the 1930s (for example, in Critical Theory of society or early Frankfurt School (Horkheimer, 1937), then in Husserl's (1859–1938) *Die Krisis der europäischen Wissenschaften und die transzendentale Phänomenologie (Crisis of European Sciences and Transcendental Phenomenology)*, by the mid-twentieth century several new critiques appeared, which contributed to the demise of positivism from its previous dominant position. In addition to critical theorists who continued the critique of positivism even after its demise – Theodor Adorno (1903–1969), Habermas (born 1929) – there were serious objections provided by Karl Popper (1902–1994), Willard van Orman Quine (1908–2000), and from a different perspective by Ludwig Wittgenstein (1889–1951) (1953) and Thomas Kuhn (1922–1996) (1962).

The first doubts on the very possibility of certainty and objectivity claims positivism has advanced as the validity criteria of knowledge came from the field that was considered to exemplify the certainty and objectivity of knowledge – natural sciences. Physicists working on subatomic particles (Werner Heisenberg, Niels Bohr) realized that it is not possible to accurately describe subatomic processes and moreover that it is not possible to determine them independently from the observation as observation changes them.

Further questionings of positivist claims were articulated by philosophers. Karl Popper criticized the logic of scientific research adopted by positivism, then the method of verification and the role ascribed to induction in generating inferences, which then became parts of scientific laws. He was especially concerned about "a major philosophical problem: the problem of induction" (Popper, 1972, p. 1) and he thought he had solved it, and that already in 1930s, which means at the best times of Vienna Circle. However, the problem of induction is much older than Vienna Circle. As a matter of fact, inductive inferences have a strong common sense background in beliefs in regularities on the grounds of the past repeated observations. The problem of induction entered philosophy very early – already in Aristotle and Cicero. In modern times David Hume (1711–1776) addressed human understanding (*An Enquiry Concerning Human Understanding*, 1748/1998), as a problem of justified beliefs. From that standpoint Hume identified two problems related to induction: a logical and a psychological problem. From a logical point of view it is not justified to make any expectations and consequently conclusions about the future events on the grounds of experiences of the past repeated events. To Hume, even the inclusion of degrees of probability into expectation cannot solve the logical problem of induction. As humans in spite of that believe that the events of which they have no experience will repeat in the future as they were repeatedly experienced in the past,

Hume concluded that human understanding is based on an irrational faith. Thus, implications of induction are epistemological skepticism and irrationalism.

Poppers solution to the problem of induction – and induction is certainly not just a major philosophical problem, it is no less a major problem in all sciences, even though it is, surprisingly enough, hardly addressed by them – should avoid these difficulties. Instead of the positivist verifiability principle of meaningfulness and truthfulness of statements, which is necessarily entangled with the inherent problems of induction and therefore "all theories remain guesses, conjectures, hypotheses" (Popper, 1972, p. 13), Popper introduced what he called a "negative approach" – instead of verification, what is needed is falsification, i.e., the very possibility of falsification.

Before that move, Popper translated "all the subjective or psychological terms, especially 'belief' etc. into *objective* terms. Thus, instead of speaking of a 'belief', I speak, say, of a 'statement' or of an explanatory theory...and instead of an 'impression', I speak of an observation statement' or of a 'test statement'; and instead of the 'justification of a belief, I speak of 'justification of the claim that a theory is true', etc.," (Popper, 1972, p. 6; italics in original). It is striking that some steps in Popper's questioning of positivist epistemological claims, i.e., his translation work, led him very close to the behaviorist psychology whose manifesto was published by John Watson in 1913 – "Psychology as the Behaviorist Views It." Behaviorist psychology expelled from psychology any terms referring to subjective states. But behaviorism went even further translating speech into a verbal response, as it operates with stimulus and response only because they are accessible to external observation. As mental states are not available to external observation, terms referring to them were not allowed into the program of a psychology "as behaviorist views it." Popper does not refer to Watson even in his later or latest works. Instead he translated Hume's logical problem of induction into objective, formal terms, but then following the principle of transference applied his solution to Hume's psychological problem of induction. Popper believes that his solution to the problem of induction eliminates irrationalism, which is a necessary consequence of Hume's approach to induction. Popper describes his approach stressing the difference:

> The fundamental difference between my approach and the approach for which I long ago introduced the label 'inductivist' is that I lay stress on *negative arguments,* such as negative instances or counter examples, refutations, and attempted refutations - in short criticism – while the inductivist lay stress on *'positive instances'*, from which he draws 'non-demonstrative *inferences*' and which he hopes will guarantee the 'reliability' of the conclusion s of these inferences. (Popper, 1972, p. 20)

Popper's critique of some of the core claims of the Vienna Circle positivism was nevertheless advanced from the common standpoint of scientism that insists on a sharp demarcation between scientific and nonscientific statements and acknowledges validity to scientific knowledge only. Vienna Circle used verifiability as a criterion of demarcation, while Popper criticized that criterion and argued for falsifiability instead, but both criteria served the same goal – determination of scientific statements and their demarcation from other types of statements. Scientism is a position that claims that nonscientific statements (Popper's examples: metaphysical, psychoanalytic, Marxist theory) are not meaningful statements. Thus, not just knowledge but the meaning itself is reduced to scientific statements only.

The second very important critique of logical positivism was formulated by analytic philosopher Willard Van Orman Quine (1908–2000). In *Two dogmas of empiricism* (1951), considered by some philosophers the most important paper in the twentieth century philosophy, Quine attacked two core theses of logical positivism – he called them dogmas as suggested by the very title of his paper. The first is the belief that there is a sharp distinction between analytic and synthetic truth statements (meaning of analytic statements is contained in the very subject of the statement independently of the facts, while meaning of synthetic statements depends on facts that have to be established). Historically, the distinction goes back to Leibniz (1646–1716), Hume (1711–1776), and Kant (1724–1804), but was reappropriated by modern logical positivism. The second target of Quine's critique is positivist reductionism as a standpoint claiming that "each meaningful statement is equivalent to some logical construct upon terms which refer to immediate experience" (Quine, 1951, p. 20). As in both theses or dogmas of logical positivism meaning is the core issue, Quine had to offer a different theory of meaning – instead of a reductionist theory he argued for a holistic theory. It holds that a reference to a whole theory is needed instead of focus on singular statements. This means that it is not possible to decompose a theory into singular statements subjected to empirical verification by immediate sensory experience. The holistic claim of system-dependence of statements has consequences for the status of analytic and synthetic distinction making it untenable. A simple example: a definition of a concept appearing in an analytic statement depends on language use outside of the statement and precedes it.

Quine also argued against contrasting common sense and scientific knowledge, pointing out that "Science is not a substitute for common sense but an extension of it" (1957, p. 229). This claim is especially important to social and human sciences. Quine included them into his broader concept of science, which is not restricted to natural sciences only, even though natural sciences are understood by Quine as well as paradigmatic sciences. His position is described as naturalism, which expresses his view that sciences provide account of reality, not an a priori philosophy. The same applies to epistemology, which is founded on science.

What are the implications of those critiques of logical positivism for sciences? They converge in insights that epistemological quests for certainty followed by reductionism and elementarism are not tenable on both logical and empirical grounds. These critical insights are even more important as they were formulated from the standpoint of scientism. However, scientism itself is also subjected to critique – in phenomenology (Husserl), in hermeneutics (Gadamer), in Critical Theory from its first generation (Adorno, Horkheimer, Marcuse) to contemporary representatives (Habermas), in contemporary socio-constructionist, qualitative approaches, in feminism.

His seminal study *The Crisis of European Sciences and Transcendental Phenomenology* (whose first part was published in 1936 in Belgrade because Husserl was prevented from publishing in Nazi Germany) Edmund Husserl started by a diagnosis of his time: "The positivistic reduction of the idea of science to mere factual science. The 'crisis' of science as the loss of its meaning for life" (Husserl, 1936/1970, p. 5).

> The exclusiveness with which the total world-view of modern man, in the second half of the nineteenth century, let itself be determined by the positive sciences and be blinded by the "prosperity" they produced, meant an indifferent turning-away from the questions which are decisive for a genuine humanity. Merely fact-minded sciences make merely fact-minded people. (Husserl, 1936/1970, pp. 5–6)

While the original positivism considered itself as a step forward in development of humanity, as a vehicle of progress, Husserl saw that development as a fatal loss, i.e., as a regression. While positivism praised the strength and purity of facts, Husserl warned of "fact-minded sciences" and "fact-minded people" alike. While Husserl's contemporary logical positivism was eager to establish rules for meaningful statements, Husserl was concerned with meaning for life, or rather with "struggle for the meaning of man" (ibid, p. 14).

But Husserl claimed that even for the sake of objectivity a radical turn to subjectivity is needed:

> Only a radical inquiry back into subjectivity – and specifically the subjectivity which *ultimately* brings about all world-validity…can make objective truth comprehensible and arrive at the ultimate ontic meaning of the world… Thus it is not the being of the world as unquestioned, taken for granted, which is primary in itself… rather, what is primary in itself is subjectivity, understood as that which naively pregives the being of the world and then rationalizes or (what is the same thing) objectifies it. (ibid, p. 69)

However, to Hans-Georg Gadamer (1900–2002), it is not subjectivity in itself, which would provide insights into meaning of man as any understanding necessarily presupposes as its very condition of the possibility some pre-understanding, or prejudice (Vorurteil) as inherited and given in tradition, history. Even though history is a human achievement, as Gadamer stated it:

> In fact history does not belong to us; we belong to it… Long before we understand ourselves through the process of self-examination, we understand ourselves in a self-evident way in the family, society and state in which we live. The focus of subjectivity is a distorting mirror. The self-awareness of the individual is only flickering in the closed circuit of historical life. (2006, p. 278)

Historicity of man has implications for sciences dealing with historicity, which means for human sciences. To Gadamer, there is no doubt that human sciences are substantially different from natural sciences. To know historical world and to know individual in the historical world requires different conception of knowledge itself: "Understanding is to be thought of less as a subjective act than as participating in an event of tradition" ( ibid. p. 291). In other words, both subject and object in epistemic situation of human sciences have different status comparing to natural sciences.

In the last decades the turn away from individual knowing subject and individualistic epistemology led to a conceptualization of a new epistemological program. Martin Kusch (2002) argues for a new position in epistemology, which he calls communitarian epistemology. It is strongly socially oriented, but in some important aspects it is different from the existing social epistemology, which is very much interested in science policy and in programs that should complement the dominant individualistic epistemology. However, according to Kusch's communitarian epistemology, there is no isolated individual knower. Knowledge is fundamentally social – it depends on epistemic communities as it "marks a social status... Social statuses exist only in so far as there are communities that constitute, impose or grant these statuses...." (p. 1).

It is not so difficult to recognize here Thomas Kuhn's (1962) account of scientific knowledge as constituted by scientific community, i.e., his concept of paradigm as a set of beliefs, assumptions, rules defining the subject matter of study, methods of research, and interpretation of results accepted by a relevant scientific community. As Kusch himself admitted he has generalized Kuhn's account from scientific knowledge to knowledge in general. The other admitted intellectual debts of Kusch's communitarian epistemology go to important figures of the program of sociology of scientific knowledge (Barry Barnes, David Bloor, Harry Collins, and Steven Shapin) and their philosophical interlocutors (Mary Hesse, David Hume, Peter Winch, and Ludwig Wittgenstein). Interestingly, the founding figure of sociology of knowledge Karl Mannheim is not mentioned.

Along the lines of arguing for social foundations of knowledge and relying on feminist scholarships feminist epistemology was formulated, questioning many assumptions of traditional epistemology, including its supposed value-neutrality. Instead, feminists claim that "science is politics by other means (Harding, 1991, p. 308) and therefore raise the questions "whose science, whose knowledge." It is for the sake of knowledge and science that feminist epistemology argues for necessity to include reflection on the standpoint of knowing subject as a condition of possibility of objectivity (Haraway, 1988). In view of Sandra Harding, one of the leading feminist scholars, this has consequences for natural sciences as well:

> The same social forces that shape nature-as-an-object-of-knowledge and other parts of culture also shape us and our scientific accounts...
> The natural sciences must incorporate the critical, self-reflexive methods beginning to emerge in the social sciences in order to block the intuitive, spontaneous consciousness of nature and inquiry to which all of us, but especially scientists, are susceptible. The natural sciences, I have argued, are a particular kind of social science and should be so conceptualized. Only in this way can a strong objectivity be activated, one that insists on socially situated science and on scientific rather than "folk" accounts of those social situations. (1991, pp. 308–309)

Feminist epistemologies transcend the realm of knowledge in two directions – on the one hand, when arguing that science and knowledge in general are socially situated (in choice of subject matter, of knowing agent, methods, criteria of evaluation and interpretation) and on the other hand, when requiring a transformative, emancipatory role for science, which itself should be transformed, including the transformed logic of research, with a different position of both the subject and object of knowledge. Therefore, "the subject/agent of feminist knowledge is also the subject/agent of every other liberatory knowledge project...Thinking from women's lives provides crucial resources for the reinvention of sciences for the many to replace sciences that are often only for the elite few" (Harding, 1991, p. 310–312).

However, before the feminist epistemological program was articulated, the transcendence of realm of knowledge was accomplished philosophically at the very core of knowledge, i.e., as far as conditions of the possibility of knowledge are concerned. Instead of Kantian a priori transcendental conditions of the possibility of experience (for example, forms of space and time), Habermas argued for a reinterpretation of Kant's philosophy in terms of linguistic and pragmatic turn in order to overcome methodological individualism of the previous foundational project. The new a priori conditions include intersubjectivity of language and communication, which are historically created but fulfill the transcendental role of constituting the very possibility of knowledge. Habermas distinguishes three types of knowledge interests, which express a general relation of humans to their natural and social world in the process of self-formation of humankind. It is within that context shaped by interest in controlling nature (instrumental interest) or in establishing and preserving communication and joint activities among members of a community (practical interest) that knowledge of respective domains is constituted. Critical theory is led by emancipatory interests in overcoming existing limits and distorting processes at both individual and societal level. Therefore to Habermas "a radical critique of theory of knowledge is possible only as social theory" (1972, p.vii).

However, in his book *Erkenntnis und Interesse, (Knowledge and Human Interest),* which he described as a study on the prehistory of positivism, Habermas reconstructs historical transformations of theory of knowledge from its previous privileged position within modern philosophy: "the philosophy of science that has emerged since the mid nineteenth century as the heir of the theory of knowledge is methodology pursued with a scientistic self-understanding of the sciences. 'Scientism' means science's belief in itself: that is, the conviction that we can no longer understand science as one form of possible knowledge, but rather must identify knowledge with science" (1972, p. 4).

Consequences of the disappearance of the classical theory of knowledge with its core question of "how is knowledge possible" and its replacement by methodology "which restricts itself to the pseudo-normative regulation of established research" (ibid. p. 4) affect both philosophy and sciences, contributing to the strengthening of positivist attitude to knowledge and science. As defined by Habermas, positivism means "that we disavow reflection" (p. vii). In that way a possible source of change is removed, which explains a relative longevity of positivism, especially in the form of scientific or rather scientistic methodology. Indeed, as noted by Steinmetz (2005) there is "positivism's uncanny persistence in the human sciences up to the present moment" (p. 2).

Psychology is a good example of such tendencies as it is keeping on positivist assumptions even after they were abandoned in the natural sciences, for example, in post-Newtonian physics. Even though by mid-twentieth century psychology abandoned behaviorism as the main home of positivism in psychology, psychology's dominant epistemology remained reduced to methodology, which continued to operate with its stimulus-response research model.

It is true, since 1970s a shift in psychological methodology could be identified. Sometimes it is called "a quiet methodological revolution" brought about by qualitative approaches, which oppose positivist assumptions (Denzin & Lincoln, 2018, p. vii, Flick, 2014). Nevertheless, it remains the critical diagnosis advanced by Habermas that methodology has replaced epistemology. Even though qualitative approaches insist on reflexivity as a necessary procedure in acquiring scientific knowledge, requests for reflexivity are not sufficient to reclaim epistemology, in the sense of critical inquiry into conditions of possibility of valid knowledge.

As a consequence of all those developments, accounts of knowledge have gradually become more complex, dynamic, holistic, pluralistic, and relativistic. At the same time reductionism and elementarism are still defended as effective scientific strategies in acquiring knowledge, including psychological knowledge.

## Another History of Knowing Subject and Known Objects

Plato strictly separated the world of ideas and material, sensory world. Sensory organs can observe contingent things, but they cannot realize a necessary truth. It is only an immaterial and immortal soul that can acquire a true knowledge, claimed Plato in *Phedo* (387–367B.C./1955, 95e ff). Therefore, in Plato's view, soul is the only valid epistemic agency. In this way Plato formulated an important epistemic principle, the principle of similarity – it is possible to know only through similarity of subject and object of knowledge.

In spite of quite substantial differences between Aristotle's philosophy and philosophy of his teacher Plato, Aristotle (350BC/2006) also endorsed a kind of epistemological principle of similarity. In his treatise *On the Soul* he stated: "in the case of objects which involve no matter, what thinks and what is thought are identical; for speculative knowledge and its object are identical" (429b 16). A contemporary philosopher Charles Taylor interprets these statements as representing a different model of knowledge compared to epistemology of modern times, which he described as a representational model:

> The most important traditional view was Aristotle's, according to which when we come to know something, the mind (*nous*) becomes one with the object of thought. Of course this is not to say that they become materially the same thing, rather mind and object are informed by the same *eidos*. Here was conception quite different from the representational model…The basic bent of Aristotle's model could much better be described as participational: being informed by the same *eidos*, the mind participates in the being of the known object, rather than simply depicting it. (1995, p. 3)

While Plato and Aristotle formulated it in terms of soul and the idea of truth, eidos, this epistemic principle has been reiterated through the history in different terms, but nevertheless it was keeping on important hermeneutic insight that at least some shared base is needed as a condition of the possibility of knowledge and understanding. This principle defines both possibilities and limits of knowledge, or rather dialectics of possibilities and limits of knowledge. The results of the process of knowing are not just a known object but also a changed subject of knowing. When applied to any future hermeneutic endeavor, to new interpretations of previously already interpreted texts, this provides the conditions of possibility and meaningfulness of such endeavors even before they start. No understanding or knowing could be considered closed, final. Thus, any temporary limit of knowing is at the same time a possibility for a new knowing. Temporary limits can be overcome by different means. Institutionalized knowledge acquisition, i.e., education plays a crucial role in that regard.

The legacy of ancient Greek thoughts on knowledge includes a whole range of epistemological positions – from agnosticism and skepticism to empiricism and rationalism. All of them have had successors – up to our times. Indeed, questions on knowledge and a quite prominent place given to them have shaped a quite influential tradition – from ancient to modern times. The rise of natural sciences in the seventeenth century influenced greatly the development of empiricist strand of epistemology, although not under the name of epistemology, which was introduced, as already mentioned, only in the nineteenth century.

Before the rise of modern sciences of nature and new models of knowledge and new values inscribed in them, there was a very special historical epoch that announced a radical shift in understanding the world and position of humans in it when compared to the previous medieval feudal world. Clearly, understanding of knowledge was also affected. "Educational ideals and practice were transformed" (Hankins, 2007, p. 338).

This epoch was characterized by its strong appeal to revive ancient Greco-Roman cultural legacy. Even though the new attitude and new mood started already in the fourteenth century, in Italian cities, the very name of that epoch, namely, Renaissance took a longer way before it became firmly adopted in the nineteenth century.

Renaissance is closely associated with humanism thanks to its shift to humans as central figures in building a new world and a new world view. Humans became also central figures of intellectual and artistic interests and subject matters of studies called *studia humaniora, or studia humanitatis*, which focused on literature, languages, art, and history. The concept of humanitas itself was taken from Cicero. Renaissance humanists believed that studying poetry and art can be formative in moral education of individuals and in cultivating communal life: "The humanist movement first gained moral authority when Petrarch gave it the purpose of inculcating virtue and eloquence. Humanists were in principle committed to nurturing the patriotism, prudence, and civic virtue of social elites..." (Hankins, 2007, p. 342).

New discoveries – of the New World – and technical innovations – printing – changed conditions of acquiring and transmitting knowledge which, liberated from the absolutism of Church authority, became a concern of more and more people when pursuing their mundane interests. The plurality of new ideas and revived old ideas instigate a spirit of criticism to which everything could and was subjected. In result every certainty was undermined. Alexandre Koyré (1892–1964) describes the consequences of the new situation: "Deprived of its traditional patterns and rules of judgment and of choice, man finally feels himself lost in an alien and uncertain world, a world in which nothing is certain and everything is possible" (Koyré, 1971, p, ix). The sixteenth century had its thinkers who were able and courageous enough to think their time.

Michel Montaigne (1533–1592) agreed with the skeptical epochal diagnosis about a lack of any certainty. He decided to turn away from the external world for about a decade and to try to find certainty in himself. Thanks to inherited wealth he could afford this turn, but after a thorough examination he had to admit that he could not find any certainty in himself either. His *Essays* (1580–1588/1923), a new literary genre he introduced, documented his thought journeys. But he was able to accept such an uncertain state of affairs, moreover from his skeptical position he argued for reconciliation of conflicting parties, including Catholic and Reformist confessions.

There is a historically important lesson – skepticism as an epistemological position, which questions any possibility of certain true knowledge does not have necessarily destructive consequences. Quite the contrary, it can foster humility and tolerance in both epistemological and sociopolitical issues. However, it should be noted that these are just potentials of skepticism. In the further historical development skepticism was abandoned for the sake of finding certain foundations of knowledge and strict rules for true judgments.

Thus, in the seventeenth century, which is considered by some authors as the second phase of modernity, the first being Renaissance humanism, instead of skepticism a strong quest for certainty started shaping approaches to knowledge. That quest was motivated also by devastating consequences of religious wars in Europe. Instead of competing perspectives, it was argued for a universal certain foundation of knowledge. Both philosophy and emerging sciences of nature were committed to such an attitude. Under such conditions humanist legacy of tolerance to variety of perspectives and skepticism to any imposition of unquestionable authority was easily forgotten or even repressed as a potential threat to the new epistemological and a general epochal agenda.

In modernity, as a project of laying down foundations for a new world, epistemological questions were considered very important. Clearly, knowledge is indispensable in any human activity. Moreover, knowledge is constitutive to it. In philosophy René Descartes (1596–1650) started building new foundations with a self-imposed radical doubt in all previous knowledge he acquired in the best schools of his time. Instead Descartes was looking for a new "method of rightly directing one's Reason and of seeking truth in the Sciences" (Descartes 1637/1971a, b, p. 5):

> The first was never to accept anything as true if I had not evident knowledge of its being so; that is, carefully to avoid precipitancy and prejudice, and to embrace in my judgment only what presented itself to my mind so clearly and distinctly that I had no occasion to doubt it. (p. 20)

Descartes (1637/1971) confessed: "My first task must be to establish such certainty" (p. 23). He found that certainty in his mind, in his thinking I, as formulated in his famous *cogito ergo sum* (I am thinking, therefore I exist). But he advanced that to "a general rule that whatever we conceive very clearly and very distinctly is true" (p. 32). Descartes explicates what that general rule meant to him: "and since my method was not bound up with any special subject matter, I hoped to apply it to the problems of other sciences as usefully as I had in algebra" (p. 23).

Descartes self-confident program of laying down rules for acquiring true knowledge, based on clear and distinct ideas of a thinking mind, has brought about certainty. But at the same time that program excluded from the domain of knowledge everything that cannot be subjected to fixed general rational rules. As rightly pointed out by Stephen Toulmin (1992):

> The ideals of reason and rationality typical of the second phase of Modernity were, thus, intellectually perfectionist, morally rigorous, and humanly unrelenting. Whatever sorts of problem one faced, there was a supposedly unique procedure for arriving at the correct solution. That procedure could be recognized only by cutting away the inessentials, and identifying the abstract core of 'clear and distinct' concepts needed for its solution. Unfortunately, little in human life lend itself fully to the lucid, tidy analysis of Euclid's geometry or Descartes' physics. (p. 200)

Such a program provoked critique though. For example, Giambattista Vico (1668–1744) questioned superiority of knowledge of nature and values associated with it as demonstrated by developments of modern natural science since the seventeenth century. Instead Vico (1725/1984) claimed that humans know better what they have created: "the universal principle of his theory of knowledge, that the condition under which a thing can be known is that the knower should have made it, that the true is identical with the created: *verum ipsum factum*" (Croce, 1913, p. 5). History is what humans create. Therefore Vico has been praised as one of the founders of philosophy of history. To Habermas, "In a certain way, the philosophy of history begins early in the eighteen century with Vico's famous explication of the *topos verum et factum convertuntur*" (1973, p. 242).

By formulating a new epistemic principle – *verum est factum* Vico opposed Cartesianism, its rationalist epistemology, which based truth on clear and distinct ideas of thinking subject (Descartes 1637). He also opposed Cartesian focus on individual thinking subject, pointing instead to the world, and especially languages humans created as a precious source of knowledge. This is missing in Descartes' philosophy, even though Descartes could provide proofs for the existence of material things while starting from thinking subject, i.e., res cogitans. In the sixth meditation of his *Meditations on First Philosophy* Descartes undertakes a complex process of reasoning referring also to God, who "is not deceitful" and concludes finally "corporeal things must exist" (Descartes, 1642/1971, p. 116). It should be noted in this context that in the second meditation Descartes, after examining "the nature of human mind," concluded that "it is better known than the Body" (Descartes, 1642/1971, p. 66). Vico went further or rather out into the human historical world, which in his view can be better known to humans as it is created by humans themselves.

Vico (1709/1990) was also concerned with pedagogical implications of Cartesianism. Instead of striving for certainty and excluding all uncertain aspects of human experience from the scope of true knowledge, Vico argues for necessity to return to old wisdom. "He appeals to the sensus communis, common sense, and the humanistic ideal of eloquentia.... But the most important thing in education is still something else – the training in the sensus communis, which is not nourished on the true but on the probable, the verisimilar" (Gadamer 1960/2006, pp. 17–19).

In the late nineteenth and at the beginning of the twentieth century several German philosophers and psychologists – Wilhelm Dilthey (1833–1911), Heinrich Rickert (1863–1936), Wilhelm Wundt (1832–1920), Wilhelm Windelband (1848–1915) – were engaged in arguing that human sciences (Geisteswissenschaften) are different from natural sciences, but not inferior compared to them. They insisted on a distinction between natural and human sciences justifying that claim by pointing out that phenomena studied by natural, on the one side, and social and human sciences, on the other side, are fundamentally different. Consequently, the epistemic situation, i.e., relation between the subject and object of knowledge is different as well as the methods used in the process of acquiring knowledge (Jovanović, 2010). The famous debate Erklären vs Verstehen (explanation – understanding debate) started its long journey. The distinction was programmatically formulated by Wilhelm Dilthey: "We explain nature, but we understand the soul" (1894/1974, p. 144). However, psychology in its main stream remained close to natural science epistemology, imposing it on phenomena belonging to human kinds, not natural kinds (Danziger, 1999; Hacking, 1994).

## Epistemic Situation in Psychology

Phenomena studied by psychology belong to a domain of phenomena to which – or more precisely to most of them – humans in their ordinary lives have or can have access. This general or widespread accessibility of objects of psychology – one could metaphorically call it a kind of their democratic distribution – has necessarily consequences for psychology as a science, which constructs its subject matter out of such phenomena. Among those phenomena there is a particular class of phenomena – experiences – to which only subjects of such experiences have access. The epistemologically privileged access to mental states available to subjects, bearers of those states, poses a challenge to psychology as a scientific endeavor. The history of psychology witnesses quite different, even opposed answers to such a challenge, including the exclusion of subjective experiences from psychology's subject matter (Jovanović, 2010).

Further features of phenomena out of which psychology constructs its subject matter are derived from the fact that subjects of mental states live in communities together with other members. Moreover, communities provide the very conditions of possibility of being human (Wundt, 1900–1920). Communities are not just an external physical environment from which stimuli evoke reactions in organisms. It is rather a human-made world, consisting also of material objects, but more importantly it is constituted through different kinds of activities of its members who produce specific facts, social facts on which social ontology is based whose main feature is its dependence on human activities (Searle, 1995). These activities include quite important signification acts, speech acts being their basic form. Thus humans develop activities and produce outcomes that cannot be described in terms of physical processes. Therefore natural science model cannot be appropriate to describe phenomena of psychic and social life. They transcend themselves as they refer to extra physical domains, to realms of signification and meaning as their defining features, while physical dimensions have just an auxiliary function, they are means in processes of signification, in meaning-making processes. Thus, the definition of humans as animal symbolicum should be extended to include symbolic world as well (Cassirer, 1923/1975); Jovanović, 2019a, b; Valsiner, 2014b).

There is also a temporal extension of humans as they transcend not just their physical space, but also physical time. In the same way as signification allows to transcend the physical space, it allows to transcend the present time and include symbolic representations of the past and the future. It is cultural inheritance based on objectified meaning-making processes that substantially shapes humans.

Living in historical, social, and cultural worlds humans use tools provided by those worlds in order to develop to historical, social, and cultural beings, i. e, to think, feel, and act in accordance with logical, social, or cultural norms and values. As life in a community requires exchange and coordination among its members, it is clear that the immediate epistemologically privileged access to mental states available to subjects of those states only needs to be complemented by other mediated modes and means of knowing mental states of other subjects (Dilthey, 1894/1974; 1883/1988).

Thus, additionally to the general democratic distribution of phenomena out of which psychology constructs its subject matter – these are mental states and their expressions in conduct and in objectified material as well as symbolic forms – there is a distribution of processes of knowing those phenomena between, on the one side, the subjects of experience who can know some of those phenomena as they have an immediate access to their own mental states and, on the other side, other subjects who can have only a mediate access to the mental states of other subjects and that thanks to the fact that those mental states are expressed in forms which are available to others – as bodily expressions, as language, as cultural forms (art, religion, system of philosophical, and scientific ideas, including psychological ones, i.e., psychology as a set of scientific discourses).

These features characterize quite specific and indeed very complex ontological and, related to that, epistemological landscape that psychology has to deal with. Clearly, ontological and epistemological questions are basic questions that have consequences for psychology as a science. In other words, the ways in which psychology addresses psycho-ontological and epistemological questions shape psychology. Different ways of addressing those questions constitute different psychologies.

History of psychology is a history of different psychologies as they were developed over time under different historical and sociohistorical conditions. However, history of psychology is not a neutral record of psychologies as they existed in their times. Quite the contrary, history of psychology is also a record of misrepresentation, misrecognition, or even repression of psychological ideas (Jovanović, 2021). Therefore it is not enough to study just an original version of a theory. Sometimes, it is reception of the ideas and theories, regardless how partial or one-sided or even biased they might be, which proved to be more powerful in shaping the further developments than a theory in its author's version. Thus, the relevance of history of psychology transcends just a historiographic interest. It is highly relevant to shed more light on basic processes of acquiring knowledge and acknowledging scientific knowledge. Even though at the core these are basic hermeneutic processes, they are mediated and entangled with the whole life worlds of authors and interpreters.

Therefore, to discuss teaching and learning psychology – which is the subject matter of this book – necessarily requires reflection on explicit but also latent ontological and epistemological assumptions adopted by psychological theories. The starting question is – What kind of psychology is taught and consequently learnt. In the educational context with its inherent normative dimension normative dimensions of psychology's knowledge and interpretations become more visible and therefore urge to be reflected upon. Understandably, normative dimensions of psychology are expressions of more general evaluative features of human psychic functioning and of human world in general (Wundt, 1921). Those ontological features of human world pose quite a challenge to a traditional self-understanding of science as based on a dichotomy of facts and values and declared a value-free endeavor (Putnam, 2002). However, the intentional exclusion of evaluative dimensions from human psychic and other forms of activity does not mean that such a discursive gesture indeed expels values from human psyche and human world. If they are excluded from scientific inquiry they will remain in spheres of life and world, which are less accessible to public deliberation and therefore stronger resistant to a possible change.

It is evident from these briefly described ontological and epistemological peculiarities of the phenomena out of which psychology constructs its subject matter that psychology must face quite challenging tasks if it wants to do justice to all the complexities of the phenomena it is expected to study. Therefore different strategies of reducing complexities have been applied in the history of psychology – exclusion of some phenomena, selection of a just few features of the phenomena, translation of holistic patterns into a sum of a few elements, exclusion of developmental time dimension, decontextualization, assuming an allegedly objective standpoint.

These epistemological strategies have their particular outcomes and more general implications for psychology as a science and its role in shaping self-understanding of humans in modern world.

From the quite broad repertoire of epistemological positions formulated over a long period of history, psychology has adopted only some of them, and only rarely it has explicated the adopted position. Psychology shared a general turn toward experience and away from traditional metaphysical categories, like soul. Thus, empiricism would be somehow a natural choice.

However, experience as a starting point or subject matter of psychology does not necessarily implicate adoption of positivist empiricism, as usually assumed. The case of the founding father of psychology Wilhelm Wundt is telling in that regard.

He argued that experience is a common subject matter of all sciences, including both natural sciences and "mental sciences," psychology being one of them. Empirical psychology arose after attempts at metaphysical explanations of psyche and it turned to experience instead:

> every concrete experience immediately divides into *two factors*: into a *content* presented to us, *and our apprehension of this content*. We call the first of these factors *objects of experience*, the second *experiencing subject*. This division points out two directions for the treatment of experience. One is that of the *natural sciences*, which concern themselves with the objects of experience, thought of as independent of the subject. The other is that of *psychology*, which investigates the whole content of experience in its relations to the subject and in its attributes derived directly from the subject. (Wundt, 1897, pp. 2–3; italics in original)

However, Wundt argued that in spite of its turn to experience, psychology should not be separated from philosophy. As a matter of fact, its links to philosophy are neither just temporary nor just historical. In his inaugural lecture *Über den Einfluss der Philosophie auf die Erfahrungswissenschaften (On the influence of philosophy on the empirical sciences)* Wundt stated that "psychology stands close to philosophy through its history, and through the nature of its problems" (Wundt, 1876, p.4). In his engaged writing *Psychology's Struggle for Existence* (1913) Wundt argued that a separation from philosophy would threaten psychology. "Discussion of theory of knowledge makes the beginning of any scientific psychology if it does not want to stay on the surface of randomly listed observations" (Wundt, 1913, p. 31).

Unfortunately, Wundt's conceptualization of psychology, including its relation to philosophy has been to a great extent repressed or misunderstood (Jovanović, 2021). One of the consequences of such a reception of the founding father of psychology is also the status of epistemological issues in psychology.

There is, however, a noteworthy exception to the status of epistemology in psychology. Following the scientific ethos Jean Piaget (1896–1980) argued for necessity to replace epistemology as a philosophical, (and this meant for him speculative) endeavor by a scientifically founded theory of knowledge. He called it genetic epistemology: "Genetic epistemology attempts to explain knowledge, and in particular scientific knowledge, on the basis of its history, its sociogenesis, and especially the psychological origins of the notions and operations upon which it is based" (Piaget, 1970, p. 1). However, sociogenesis of scientific knowledge remained just mentioned, and Piaget's genetic epistemology has become developmental psychology, i.e., psychology of ontogenetic development transferred to a theory of scientific knowledge. Even though Piaget's critique of "the myth of the sensory origin of scientific knowledge" (Piaget, 1972a, p. 45) and his constructivist account of knowledge – knowledge is a process of construction taking place between a subject and object to be known – undermine positivist epistemology, his genetic epistemology can hardly grasp the specificity of historical and cultural objects.

In spite of the specificity of its subject matter, psychology for most parts of its history joined other sciences in adopting positivism, scientism, and methodolatry. Psychology was not alone in such choices, but it seems that it remained longer faithful to such commitments while other sciences started questioning positivism much earlier. Behaviorism was certainly an important bearer of positivism in psychology in the first half of the twentieth century. With its radical program of psychology as a natural science of behavior behaviorism – from its manifesto formulated by John Watson (1913) through its neo versions, which allowed, additionally to stimulus and response as the main elements of explanatory accounts, to introduce variables mediating between stimulus and response – remained faithful to the main commitments of positivism – model of natural science as the only scientific model of knowledge and requests to found knowledge on observable facts only.

Even after the demise of behaviorism as a psychological school based on positivism, i.e. after 1960s, psychological methodology remained mostly positivist in its foundations – following the idea of a unity of science, operating basically with the stimulus-response model, even when dealing with symbolic, verbal material, which by definition cannot be described in physical terms referring to observable fact. Meaning is not an observable fact but a referential process taking place between a sign producer, the sign it uses, and the object signified by a sign. Understanding a sign presupposes processes of interpretation. As stated by Charles Sanders Peirce: "Nothing is a sign unless it is interpreted as a sign" (Peirce, 1931–1958, 2.308).

Acknowledging an interpretive status to knowing subject, known object, and the world humans live in is a defining standpoint of the alternative methodology that emerged as a consequence of critiques of positivism and insights into limits of quantitative methodology. Again, compared to other social sciences, psychology was relatively late in adopting qualitative methodology (Flick, 2014; Jovanović, 2011). This is even more surprising as psychology's subject matter is knowing subject, which is necessarily an interpreting subject. By adopting natural science model, which means by treating human kinds as natural kinds, psychology has distorted its subject matter or even forgotten it. This was the consequence of the methodolatric belief that methods have priority over subject matter.

With such an attitude psychology takes share in modern agenda, which prioritized methods of acquiring knowledge in order to distinguish science from religious or speculative knowledge. However, while abandoning medieval theologically founded worldview and generally prioritizing methods – just to remind that Descartes's writing marking the beginning of modern philosophy was devoted to method (*Discourse on the Method*) – modernity expelled purposes not just from understanding nature as it was conceived in medieval theology based on Aristotelian physics, but surprisingly enough started transferring a purposeless view or at the best marginalization of purposes to the study of humans as well. A search for causes of events became a universal research agenda. But causes are not enough to explain human affairs as humans have intentions, they set goals which determine their actions. Thus, different explanatory models are needed in order to explain humans.

Even within the classical theory of science there were authors arguing for necessity to include teleological explanation into scientific repertoire. A further shift occurred with distinction between explanation and understanding, in its origin country Germany known as Erklären-Verstehen debate. Understanding refers to objects of knowledge, which are defined not by their physical feature but by the meaning they express. To understand a meaning of a simple sign means that the sign is interpreted in relation to what it signifies. The relation between a sign and signified is not a causal relation, but a hermeneutic, interpretive one:

> A sign, or *representamen*, is something which stands to somebody for something in some respect or capacity. It addresses somebody, that is, creates in the mind of that person an equivalent sign, or perhaps a more developed sign. That sign which it creates I call the *interpretant* of the first sign. (Peirce, 1932, §2.228; italics in original)

The plurality of interpretants created by signs in minds of humans shapes the subjective world of humans interacting with physical and symbolic worlds in which they live. This is the subject matter of psychology as a science of humans, of their subjective world and their activity objectified in historical, social and cultural worlds. It is to such a subject matter that psychology needs to adopt and develop epistemology which would do justice to its subject matter. If the adopted methodology fails to generate knowledge on its subject matter, it loses its purpose.

Indeed, adopted epistemology and methodology have both enabling and constraining roles in all sciences.

However, even after the demise of behaviorism as a dominant psychological school and even in spite of some turns having been invested with high expectations (for example, qualitative turn), it seems that the main stream of psychology is continuing its scientific journey – away from the phenomena of human experience and activity that it is supposed to study and closer toward neurons, as demonstrated by the rise of neuropsychology. A lack of reflection or even a strong disdain for reflection of assumptions adopted by psychology in its program of separation from philosophy has been complemented with strong epistemological, methodological, and theoretical individualisms which isolate both psychological object to be known and psychology itself from historical, social, and cultural contexts, which are not just external contexts but provide the very conditions of possibility of both its object and psychology as science itself. With an attitude of scientific solipsism it is not so easy to psychology to recognize that its scientism is serving more other than proper scientific purposes:

> Psychology has become an arena for a complex social game of a fashion of appearing "scientific" at the expense of alienation of the data from the phenomena and the data makers from the theoretical and philosophical issues that were fundamental concerns for their predecessors at Baldwin's time. (Valsiner, 2014a, p. 4)

The basic and unique structure of human experience is its intentionality, its directedness toward objects – this is the crucial insight introduced into psychology by Franz Brentano (even though first formulated already by medieval stoics, for example Acquinas) and explored further by Edmund Husserl in his phenomenological philosophy. The immediate experience as given to the experiencing subject is the only proper source of knowledge of consciousness, claimed phenomenology.

However, conditions of possibility of human consciousness are not in individual consciousness. As stated by Jerome Bruner (1915–2016):

it is culture and the search for meaning that is the shaping hand ...the central concept of a human psychology is meaning and the processes and transactions involved in the construction of meanings...to understand man you must understand how his experiences and his acts are shaped by his intentional states...the form of these intentional states is realized only through participation in the symbolic systems of culture. Indeed the very shape of our lives – the rough and perpetually changing draft of our autobiography that we carry in our minds – is understandable to ourselves and to others only by virtue of those cultural systems of interpretation. But culture is also constitutive of mind. By wirtue of this actualization in culture, meaning achieves a form that is public and communal rather than private and autistic. (Bruner, 1990, p. 23; 33)

As much as humans are intentional beings living in a symbolic universe of signifying signs, it is clear that epistemology of psychology must include teleological explanations and interpretations as its indispensable epistemological tools. Moreover, in order to reach and grasp unconscious psychic functions which are involved in construction of meanings, psychology needs not just hermeneutics, but a depth hermeneutics, able to understand the meaning of states and activities of which their subjects are not aware. For that reason, Habermas (1972) greatly appreciated psychoanalysis as a unique epistemological (and therapeutic) endeavor, which requires self-reflection.

A comprehensive epistemology of psychology is probably the most demanding epistemological project. Consequently, it is a challenge to teaching and learning psychology as it has to deal not just with the actual but also with a not-yet existent, but mostly needed –also as a gesture of epistemic justice to humans as knowing subjects and known objects of psychological knowledge and as creators of unique universe of meanings objectified in cultural worlds.

## A Lesson to Be Learnt

The history of epistemological conceptions shows features that resemble history of other forms of human engagement with the world, natural, social, and subjective alike. It has shown that epistemological self-confidence, i.e., trust in human capability to know the world – nature, other human fellows, and their communities and cultures – easily becomes transformed into power to impose, command, exploit, appropriate, or possess, or even destroy. In his "ecology of mind" Gregory Bateson (1904–1980) warned of the catastrophic consequences of epistemic – and related to that moral – arrogance of humans in their relationship to nature and their human fellows, in families, cities, societies, or on the earth (1972). Epistemic justice – acknowledgment of existence of certain phenomena, acknowledgment of their specific ways of being, acknowledgment of rights and capabilities of epistemic objects that happen to be human subjects (Habermas, 1972; Jovanović, 2019c; Piaget, 1972b) – is a presupposition for social justice. At the same time, only a just society can provide an equal access to education as a privileged place of acquiring knowledge as a relational not dualistic experience in a never ending striving to understand the meaning of human existence in plurality of its activities and changing forms and imagined possible worlds.

## References

Aristotle (2006). *On the soul*. (J. A. Smith, Trans.). Digireads.com. https://ia802609.us.archive.org/17/items/aristotledeanima005947mbp/aristotledeanima005947mbp.pdf. (Original work written 350B.C).
Baergen, R. (2006). *Historical dictionary of epistemology*. Lanham, MD: The Scarecrow Press.
Bateson, G. (1972). *Steps to an ecology of mind*. San Franciso, CA: Chandler Publishing Company.
Bruner, J. (1990). *Acts of meaning*. Harvard University Press.
Cassirer, E. (1975). *The philosophy of symbolic forms. Language*. (R. Mannheim, Trans.).Yale University Press. (Original work appeared 1923).
Comte, A. (1865). *A general view of positivism*. (J. H. Bridges, Trans.). Trübner and Co. https://ia800908.us.archive.org/20/items/ageneralviewpos00comtgoog/ageneralviewpos00comtgoog.pdf
Croce, B. (1913). *The philosophy of Giambattista Vico*. (R. Collingwood, Trans.). The Macmilla Company. (Original work published 1911).
Danziger, K. (1999). Natural kinds, human kinds and historicity. In W. Maiers et al. (Eds.), *Challenges to theoretical psychology* (pp. 24–32). Captus Press.
Denzin, N. & Lincoln, I. (Eds.) (2018). *The SAGE handbook of qualitative research* (5) SAGE. Los Angeles, CA
Descartes, R. (1971a). Discourse on the method. In *Descartes philosophical writings* (E. Anscombe & P. T. Geach, Eds. and Trans). (pp. 5–58). Bobb-Merrill Educational Publishing. (Original work published 1637).
Descartes, R. (1971b). Meditations on first philosophy. In *Descartes philosophical writings* (E. Anscombe & P. T. Geach, Eds. and Trans). (pp 59–124). Bobb-Merrill Educational Publishing. (Original work published 1641).
Dilthey, W. (1974). Ideen über eine beschreibende und zergliedernde Psychologie. In: W. Dilthey: *Die gestige Welt: Einleitung in die Philosophie des Lebens* (*Gesammelte Schriften, B. 5*) (pp. 139–240). Teubner. (First edition published 1894).
Dilthey, W. (1988). *Introduction to the human sciences: An attempt to lay a foundation for the study of society and history*. (R. Betanzos, Trans.). Harvester Wheatsheaf. (Original work published 1883).
Flick, U. (2014). *An introduction to qualitative research* (5th ed.). Los Angeles, CA: SAGE.
Gadamer, H.-G. (2006). *Truth and method*. (J. Weinsheimer & D. Marshall, Trans.). Continuum. (Original work published 1960).
Habermas, J. (1972). *Knowledge and human interest* (J. Shapiro, Trans.). Beacon Press. (Original work published 1968).
Habermas, J. (1973). *Theory and praxis*. (J. Viertel, Trans.). Beacon Press.
Hacking, I. (1994). The looping effects of human kinds. In D. Sperber, D. Premack, & A. J. Premack (Eds.), *Causal cognition: A multi-disciplinary approach* (pp. 351–383). Clarendon Press.
Hankins, J. (Ed.). (2007). *The Cambridge companion to Renaissance philosophy*. Cambridge, UK: Cambridge University Press.
Haraway, D. (1988, Autumn). Situated knowledges: The science question in feminism and the privilege of partial perspective. *Feminist Studies, 14*(3), 575–599.
Harding, S. (1991). *Whose science? Whose knowledge? Thinking from woman's lives*. Cornel University Press.
Horkheimer, M. (1937/2002). Traditional and critical theory. In *Critical theory. Selected essays* (pp. 188–244). (M. O'Connell et al., Trans.). Continuum.

Hume, D. (1998). In T. L. Beauchamp (Ed.), *An enquiry concerning human understanding*. Oxford University Press. (Original work published 1748).
Husserl, E. (1970). *The crisis of European sciences and transcendental phenomenology. An introduction to phenomenological philosophy*. (D. Carr, Trans.). Northwestern University Press. (Original work published 1936).
Jovanović, G. (2010). Historizing epistemology in psychology. *Integrative Psychological & Behavioral, 44*, 310–328. https://doi.org/10.1007/s12124-010-9132-9
Jovanović, G. (2011). Toward a social history of qualitative research. *History of the Human Sciences, 24*(2), 1–27. https://doi.org/10.1177/0952695111399334
Jovanović, G. (2019a). Cultural psychology as a human science. In G. Jovanović, L. Allolio-Näcke, & C. Ratner (Eds.), *The challenges of cultural psychology. Historical legacies and future responsibilities* (pp. 15–36). Routledge.
Jovanović, G. (2019b). The repression of cultural psychology in the history of psychology. In G. Jovanović, L. Allolio-Näcke, & C. Ratner (Eds.), *The challenges of cultural psychology. Historical legacies and future responsibilities* (pp. 169–185). Routledge.
Jovanović, G. (2019c). Wundt's forgotten legacy and epistemological foundations of critical psychology. In K. Murakami, J. Cresswell, T. Kono, & T. Zitoun (Eds.), *The ethos of theorizing* (pp. 96–105). Captus University Press.
Jovanović, G. (2021). How psychology repressed its founding father Wilhelm Wundt. *Human Arenas, 4*, 32–47. https://doi.org/10.1007/s42087-021-00186-2
Koyre, A. (1971). Introduction. In *Descartes philosophical writings* (E. Anscombe & P. T. Geach, Eds. and Trans). (pp. vii–xliv). Bobb-Merrill Educational Publishing.
Kuhn, T. (1962). *The structure of scientific revolutions*. University of Chicago Press.
Kusch, M. (2002). *Knowledge by agreement: The program of communitarian epistemology*. Oxford, UK: Oxford University Press.
Montaigne, M. (1923). *Essays* (C. Cotton, Trans.; W.R. Hazlitt, Ed.) Navarre Society. (Original work published 1580-1588). https://ia802902.us.archive.org/3/items/essaysofmontaign0001unse_p9k9/essaysofmontaign0001unse_p9k9.pdf
Peirce, C. S. (1931–1958). In C. Harshorn & P. Weiss (Eds.), *Collected papers*. Cambridge, MA: Harvard University Press.
Piaget, J. (1970). *Genetic epistemology*. (E. Cuckworth, Trans.). Columbia University Press.
Piaget, J. (1972a). *Psychology and epistemology. Towards a theory of knowledge*. Penguin.
Piaget, J. (1972b). *Epistémologie des sciences de l'homme*. Gallimard.
Plato. (1955). *Phaedo*. (R. S. Bluck, Trans.). Routledge & Kegan Paul. (Original work written between 387 and 376 B.C.)
Popper, K. (1972). *Objective knowledge. An evolutionary approach*. Oxford University Press.
Putnam, H. (2002). *The collapse of the fact/value dichotomy and other essays*. Cambridge, MA: Harvard University Press.
Quine, W. V. (1951). Two dogmas of empiricism. *Philosophical Review, 60*, 20–43. https://doi.org/10.2307/2181906
Quine, W. V. (1957). The scope and language of science. *British Journal for the Philosophy of Science, 8*, 1–17. Northwestern University Press.
Searle, J. (1995). *The construction of social reality*. Penguin.
Steinmetz, G. (Ed.) (2005). *The politics of method in the human sciences. Positivism and its epistemological others*. Durham, NC: Duke University Press.
Steup, M., & Neta, R. (2020). Epistemology. In Zalta, E (Ed.), *The Stanford encyclopedia of philosophy*. https://plato.stanford.edu/archives/fall2020/entries/epistemology/
Toulmin, S. (1992). *Kosmopolis*. Chicago, IL: The University of Chicago Press.
Valsiner, J. (2014a). Needed for cultural psychology: Methodology in a new key. *Culture & Psychology, 20*(1), 3–30. https://doi.org/10.1177/1354067X13515941
Valsiner, J. (2014b). *An invitation to cultural psychology*. Sage.
Vico, G. (1990). *On the study of methods of our time* (E. Gianturco, Trans.). Cornel University Press. (Original work published 1709).

Vico, G. (1984). *The new science* (T. Bergin & M. Fisch, Trans). Cornel University Press. (Original work published 1725, third edition. 1744).
Watson, J. (1913). Psychology as the behaviorist views it. *Psychological Review, 20*, 158–177. https://psychclassics.yorku.ca/Watson/views.htm
Wittgenstein, L. (1953). *Philosophical investigations* (G. E. M. Anscombe, Trans.). Oxford: Basil Blackwell.
Wundt, W. (1876). *Über den Einfluß der Philosophie auf die Erfahrungswissenschaften. Akademische Antrittsrede*. W. Engelmann.
Wundt, W. (1897). *Outlines of psychology*. (C. H. Judd, Trans.). Williams & Norgate, Stechert.
Wundt, W. (1900–1920). *Völkerpsychologie*. Eine Untersuchung der Entwicklungsgesetze von Sprache, Mythus und Sitte. (10 Vol.). Enke.
Wundt, W. (1913). *Die Psychologie im Kampf ums Dasein*. Kröner.
Wundt, W. (1921). *Logik der Geisteswissenschaften. Vierte umgearbeitete Auflage*. Enke.

## Further reading

Adriana Kaulino, Teresa Matus (2021) Theoretical proposal for the relationship between epistemology and ethics in psychology. *T&P, 31*(2), 237–253. https://doi.org/10.1177/09593543211002267
David Borges Florsheim, Lívia Mathias Simão (2021) Towards rethinking the primacy of foundationalism: Epistemology, dialogue, and ethics in psychopathology. *T&P, 31*(2), 161–178. https://doi.org/10.1177/0959354320976918
Fairweather, A., & Zagzebski, L. (2001). *Virtue epistemology. Essays on epistemic virtue and responsibility*. Toronto, ON: Oxford University Press.
Goldman, A. (1985). The relation between epistemology and psychology. *Synthese, 64*(1), 29–68.
Grimm, S. (2016). How understanding people differs from understanding the natural world. *Philosophical Issues. A Supplement to Nous*, 209–225. https://doi.org/10.1111/phis.12068
Grimm, S., Baumberger, C., & Ammon, S. (Eds.) (2017). *Explaining understanding*. New York, NY: Routledge.
Medina, J. (2013). *The epistemology of resistance. Gender and racial oppression, epistemic injustice, and resuistant imaginations*. New York, NY: Oxford University Press.
Neisser, U. (1976). *Cognition and Reality: Principles and Implications of Cognitive Psychology*. San Francisco, CA: W. H. Freeman and Company.
Peiwei Li (2021) Knowing as being: Psychology, limits to knowledge, and an ethics of solidarity. *T&P, 31*(2), 199–219. https://doi.org/10.1177/0959354320978703
Pita King, Darrin Hodgetts, Danilo Silva Guimarães (2021) Towards rethinking the primacy of epistemology in psychology: Introduction to the special section. *Theory and Psychology, 31*(2), 153–160. https://doi.org/10.1177/09593543211003161
*Theory and Psychology* (2021, Vol 31 (2). Special section towards rethinking the primacy of epistemology in psychology.
Tore Dag Bøe (2021) Ethical realism before social constructionism. *T&P, 31*(2), 220–236. https://doi.org/10.1177/09593543211004756
Veronica Hopner, James H. Liu (2021) Relational ethics and epistemology: The case for complementary first principles in psychology. *T&P, 31*(2), 179–198. https://doi.org/10.1177/0959354320974103

# Psychology in Health Science

**47**

Giulia Savarese, Luna Carpinelli, and Tiziana Marinaci

## Contents

| | |
|---|---|
| Introduction | 1144 |
| Purposes and Rationale of the Curriculum in Health Psychology | 1146 |
| From the Clinical Model to "Functional" Well-Being | 1150 |
| Core Contents and Topics of Psychology in Health Science | 1152 |
| Functional Competency | 1153 |
| Foundational Competency | 1153 |
| Teaching, Learning, and Assessment in Health Psychology | 1155 |
| Challenges and Lessons Learned | 1161 |
| Teaching, Learning, and Assessment Resources | 1162 |
| Cross-References | 1165 |
| References | 1165 |

### Abstract

This chapter discusses the characteristics, training programs, strengths, and critical aspects of health psychology, as it is taught in educational courses that concern health sciences. This document overviews the central theme of the issue: the adaptation of psychology to academic medical doctors. The first section addresses the history, fundamental objectives, and models of teaching and learning in health psychology. Then, we describe standards for professional sectors for university education, predominantly in a psychology degree, and graduate and postgraduate courses. We also describe theoretical approaches and strategies; survey the evidence for teaching, learning, and assessing fundamental skills; and lay out the best solutions for teaching and learning in psychology. Finally, we describe curriculum design and implementation, and recommendations for both psychology teachers and students.

G. Savarese (✉) · L. Carpinelli · T. Marinaci
Department of Medicine, Surgery, and Dentistry 'Scuola Medica Salernitana', University of Salerno (Italy), Fisciano/Baronissi, Italy
e-mail: gsavarese@unisa.it; lcarpinelli@unisa.it; tizianamarinaci@gmail.com

**Keywords**

Health science · Teaching · Learning · Assessment resources

## Introduction

Health psychology is a relatively recent and rapidly expanding discipline that explores the psychological and behavioral aspects associated with changes in health and disease in humans. The thematic horizon of this discipline is the study of psychological factors that are related to how people stay healthy, why they become ill, and how they respond to becoming ill (Tran, 2013).

This is a relatively new subfield of psychology that initially grow within important historical, social, and cultural changes: the discarding of a strictly biomedical conception of health – typically thought of as the mere absence of disease – in conjunction with a growing awareness of the role that psychological and social factors play in the treatment and maintenance of many diseases.

The possibility of realizing the ideal of "health for all" (Mahler, 1981), proposed by the World Health Organization, moved early health psychologists towards a more holistic view of the concepts of health and disease, and informed Engel's (1977) biopsychosocial model, which remains an important lens into traditional health psychology.

Health psychology was formally established as a discipline in the late 1970s, when section 38 – labeled Health Psychology (1979) – was created within the American Psychological Association (APA). This formal recognition was followed in 1980 by the definition of the field of studies and research, as formulated by Matarazzo, the first president of the American Health Psychology section:

> Health psychology is the aggregate of the specific educational, scientific, and professional contributions of the discipline of psychology to the promotion and maintenance of health, the prevention and treatment of illness, and the identification of etiologic and diagnostic correlates of health, illness and related dysfunction and to the analysis and improvement of the health care system and health policy formation. (Matarazzo, 1980, p. 815)

To date, the psychology of health, as a discipline, encompasses research on medical, nursing, social work, community care and health, patients' perspectives throughout the life cycle (combined with the perspectives of health workers and patients' families), the "culture" of health, social determinants of psychophysical well-being, and disparities in health based on demographic characteristics, such as social class and gender. The health psychology division of the APA is dedicated to the promotion and maintenance of good health, and the prevention and treatment of illness. Health psychologists study issues that prevent people from practicing healthy behaviors and designs programs to assist individuals. These programs may be designed to help people stop smoking, lose weight, manage stress, prevent cavities, or stay physically fit. Medical centers, hospitals, health maintenance organizations, rehabilitation centers, public health agencies, and private practices are possible employment settings for health psychologists (the APA Guidelines for Graduate and Postgraduate Psychology, 2020). Health psychology studies numerous psychological and social factors that are important for health-care systems to understand, such as the reasons that many patients do not fully cooperate with medical advice, errors in medical decision-making, or challenges in interpersonal relationships. Furthermore, it studies the effects of emotions, personality, and motivation on healing.

Health psychology teaching occurs at both the undergraduate and postgraduate levels and is experienced by both mainstream psychology students and those studying other health-related subjects (Ogden, 2012).

The education and training guidelines in professional psychology health service specialties were endorsed as a policy of the American Psychological Association in 2012. These guidelines have the potential for broad impact on the field by providing both a structure and recommendations for the consistent usage of language – definitions and terminology – to reduce current descriptive inconsistencies across education and training programs in professional psychology. The guidelines were not designed to define the specifics of the training or practice of individual psychologists; they are to be used only to describe programmatic structure in a consistent manner (Rozensky et al. 2015).

In Europe, generally, professional training in health psychology consists of a master's or advanced degree in health/medical psychology.

In America, the "National Institutes of Health" (2020) reported that most states require psychologists to hold a doctorate in psychology, have completed an extensive internship, and have accrued at least 2 years of professional experience in the field as part of a postdoctoral program. In addition to holding a mandatory state license, health psychologists can also obtain voluntary certification from the American Board of Professional Psychology.

In Asia, there is a degree in health psychology awarded by universities and colleges that lasts 3–7 years (website: https://www.bachelorstudies.com/Bachelor/Health-Care/Asia/).

The "South African College of Applied Psychology" (SACAP) (2020) reported that the health psychology bachelor's degree is a specialty within the discipline of psychology that is concerned with individual behaviors and lifestyles affecting physical health.

In Australia, the graduate certificate in health psychology explores health behaviors and connections with quality of life (website: https://www.open.edu.au/degrees/graduate-certificate-in-health-psychology-curtin-university-cur-hpy-gce).

A health psychology course is present in a lot of training curricula, for example, in medicine, nursing, motor, and physical disciplines. The broad focus is on the relationships between biopsychosocial processes (such as cognitions, emotions, and behavior, psychophysiological stress systems, and brain functioning) and health outcomes. More specifically, topics of interest are the prevention of disease and promotion of health and the diagnosis and treatment of psychological aspects of chronic somatic diseases.

Rarely, there are school training courses in health/medical psychology (website: https://www.psychologydegree411.com/degrees/health-psychology/). In the "Society for Health Psychology" (2020), it is possible to take public health and nursing classes (e.g., epidemiology and health policy), go to conferences (and watch health psychology pre-conferences at larger, more general conferences), and also seek out summer courses that are offered from time to time on related topics by national organizations.

Therefore, above all, health psychology has a clinical purpose and training is mainly associated with psychologists. For this reason, this chapter was centered on training in psychology.

## Purposes and Rationale of the Curriculum in Health Psychology

In the report "EuroPsy: A Framework for Education and Training of Psychologists in Europe" (2011), which was approved by the *European Federation of Psychologists' Associations* (EFPA) General Assembly in 2011, the first education phase is typically devoted to orienting students in the various subspecialties of psychology. This may also include related disciplines. The second phase prepares students for independent professional practice as a psychologist. This portion of the curriculum may be undifferentiated and prepare students for further PhD training or for employment as a "general practitioner" in psychology. Alternatively, it may be differentiated and prepare students for practice within a particular professional area of psychology, such as clinical or health psychology, educational or academic psychology, or work and organizational psychology.

The aim of the internship (referred to as the "stage" in some European countries) is to provide introductory professional field training that enables students to integrate theoretical and practical knowledge, to learn procedures related to psychological knowledge, to begin practicing under supervision, and to be able to reflect upon and discuss their own and other people's activities and begin working in a setting with professional colleagues.

The third phase in the professional education of psychologists consists of supervised practice within a particular area of professional psychology. This professional field training seeks to prepare for independent practice as a licensed (or equivalent) psychologist, to develop working roles as a professional psychologist based on one's unique training and personality, and to consolidate the integration of theoretical and practical knowledge.

The curriculum must have a duration of at least 5 years (300 ECTS – university credits); this may be divided among 180 units for the first phase and 120 units for the second phase (which matches the Bologna "3 + 2" structure of Bachelor's + Master's). However, universities and countries differ in the structure of their education systems. The duration of the third phase (supervised practice) must be at least 1 year (60 ECTS) or its equivalent. This amounts to a total length of 6 years or 360 ECTS.

A distinction is made between four broad professional contexts: "clinical and health," "education," "work and organizations," and "other." The first three categories encompass a wide range of activities, whereas the "other" category refers to all other contexts.

There are numerous primary competences that any psychologist should be able to demonstrate. These can be grouped into seven functional categories that relate to professional activities: goal specification, assessment, development, intervention, evaluation, communication, and enabling. There are nine additional enabling competences related to professional activity in general (professional strategy, continuing professional development, professional relations, research and development, marketing and sales, account management, practice management, quality assurance, and self-reflection); a practicing psychologist should demonstrate these in addition to the primary competences (EuroPsy: A Framework for Education and Training of Psychologists in Europe, 2011).

In the report "Mutual Evaluation of Regulated Professions: Overview of the *Regulatory Framework in the Health Services Sector* – Psychologists and Related Professions" (2015), the training requirements in most cases include completion of 5 years of a postsecondary training program. Often, a master's degree in psychology is required, which is then followed by a mandatory traineeship or professional experience. Mandatory traineeship is required in 8 of 17 countries (Belgium, France, Finland, Iceland, Italy, Liechtenstein, Portugal, and Sweden); whereas state-level examination was reported for only 3 of 17 countries (Denmark, Italy, and Sweden). No information is available for Croatia, Norway, and Greece.

In the area of psychology in health care, three member states report regulation using reserved activities – namely Finland, Slovakia, and Iceland. Two other countries (the Netherlands and the UK) reported the use of title protection without any reserved activities. Five member states (Austria, the Czech Republic, Malta, Slovenia, and Spain) protect both the use of the title and have reserved activities in this profession. Reserved activities reported by the member states are mostly generic, but in some instances they are specific (for example, see Slovakia concerning family and marital counseling, and Spain concerning issuance of various licenses and permits). In Lithuania, reserved activities relate to the provision of publicly funded health-care services. In the Czech Republic, activities are those in clinical psychology, but under the supervision of clinical psychologists. The training requirements in most cases include completion of 4–7 years of a postsecondary training program; often a master's degree in psychology or health psychology is required, sometimes followed by a mandatory traineeship, professional experience, or additional qualification course. Mandatory traineeship is required in 4 of 9 countries (Czech Republic, Malta, Slovenia, and Spain), whereas state-level examination was reported for only 2 of 9 countries (Austria and Slovenia).

The American Psychological Association, in the "National Standards for High School Psychology Curricula," proposes guidelines for the organization of the curriculum. The released document delineates the contents and performance standards that guide teachers in designing instruction. The standards are hierarchically organized to respond to increasing levels of specificity, such as domain standards, content standards, and performance standards. The domains represent overarching thematic areas that encompass broad areas of psychological knowledge and study;

the standard areas are unit topics that represent closely related theories and findings regarding more specific areas of knowledge and study; finally, the content standards are specific topics that teachers can use as starting points to build lessons (American Psychological Association (APA), 2011). As the same document suggests, the various domains are not envisioned within a rigid organization of the curricula – on the contrary, the general purpose of the project is to support teachers in a multiple-level conceptual organization, thus allowing teachers themselves "to keep the overarching themes in mind while they teach more specific content each day" (ibid. p. 2).

Each of these areas refers to a primary topic or unit in psychology. The respective standard areas within each general domain are listed in Fig. 1 and these are: scientific inquiry; biopsychology; development and learning; sociocultural context; cognition; individual variations; and applications of psychological science.

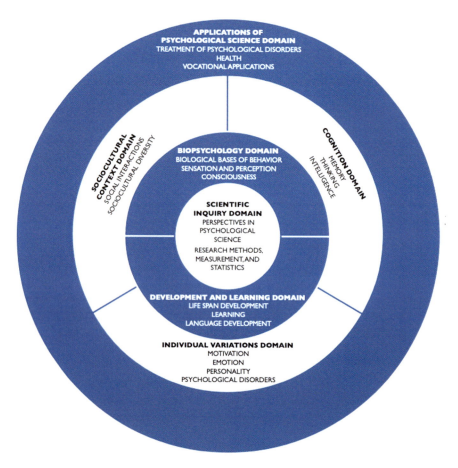

**Fig. 1** Graphical illustration of the national standards for high school psychology curricula (APA, 2011)

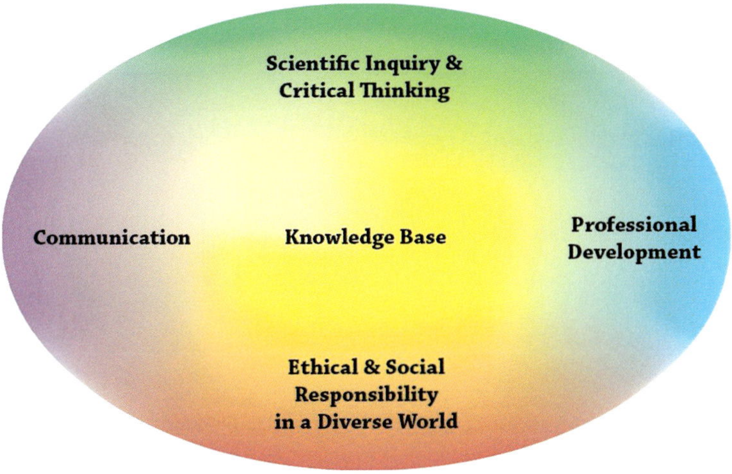

**Fig. 2** Graphical Illustration of the "Psychology: Major Competencies," the APA Board of Educational Affairs Task Force (APA, 2011 – revised 2013)

Content standards and performance standards represent more specific sublevels that refer to each domain and are grouped within each standard area.

Regarding "Psychology: Major Competencies," the APA Board of Educational Affairs Task Force also indicated five inclusive goals (see Fig. 2) for the undergraduate major.

Each goal contains an appropriate range of explicit student learning outcomes that incorporate action verbs and measurement potential:

GOAL 1: KNOWLEDGE BASE
    1.1 Describe key concepts, principles, and overarching themes in psychology
    1.2 Develop a working knowledge of psychology's content domains
    1.3 Describe applications of psychology
GOAL 2: SCIENTIFIC INQUIRY AND CRITICAL THINKING LEARNING GOALS AND OUTCOMES
    2.1 Use scientific reasoning to interpret psychological phenomena
    2.2 Demonstrate psychology information literacy
    2.3 Engage in innovative and integrative thinking and problem-solving
    2.4 Interpret, design, and conduct basic psychological research
    2.5 Incorporate sociocultural factors into scientific inquiry
GOAL 3: ETHICAL AND SOCIAL RESPONSIBILITY IN A DIVERSE WORLD
    3.1 Apply ethical standards to evaluate psychological science and practice
    3.2 Build and enhance interpersonal relationships
    3.3 Adopt values that build community at local, national, and global levels

GOAL 4: COMMUNICATION
  4.1 Demonstrate effective writing for various purposes
  4.2 Exhibit effective presentation skills for various purposes
  4.3 Interact effectively with others
GOAL 5: PROFESSIONAL DEVELOPMENT
  5.1 Apply psychological content and skills to career goals
  5.2 Exhibit self-efficacy and self-regulation
  5.3 Refine project management skills
  5.4 Enhance teamwork capacity
  5.5 Develop a meaningful professional direction for life after graduation (The APA Guidelines for the Undergraduate Psychology Major, 2011)

The APA "Guidelines for the Graduate and Postgraduate Psychology Major" (2011) encompasses master's and doctoral psychology programs (The APA Guidelines for Graduate and Postgraduate Psychology, 2020). The APA "Graduate and Postgraduate Education and Training" (2011) states that for psychologists to competently serve all members of the public now and in the future, professional psychology training programs must strive to ensure that psychology trainees demonstrate acceptable levels of knowledge, skills, and awareness to work effectively with diverse individuals. To prepare professional psychologists to serve a diverse public, the requirements must be commitment to a supportive training environment; transparency in educational expectations, policies, and procedures; establishing and maintaining standards for professional competence to protect the public; the professional standards to protect the public; and competent ethical practice and referral.

## From the Clinical Model to "Functional" Well-Being

The first orientation can essentially be traced back to a real clinical model in which health is negatively understood as the absence of disease; disease is then defined by the conspicuous presence of pathological signs and symptoms. The model focuses on the dimension of treatment in relation to the conditions of overt pathology or a concrete threat of disease, minimizing prevention and the patient's role in treatment. Consistent with the clinical model is that of the well-being–malaise continuum. In this conception, well-being is a positive state that can be pursued by moving beyond a central, neutral point to the positive end of the continuum, where it is possible to improve the levels of physical and mental health and well-being. On the contrary, passing the central point in the opposite direction (towards the negative end of the continuum) one encounters disability and illness, crossing different decremental levels of abilities and functional conditions. However, this is a dichotomous model, in which health and disease are clearly differentiated and are substantially opposite and mutually exclusive.

A defining characteristic of life is the ability to function. Functionality – at physical, mental, and social levels – is an integral part of health. In turn, this has internal manifestations for performance and social expectations. Loss of function can be a sign or symptom of a disease, and a good indicator that people require health intervention. It is easy to think that health and well-being consist of a lack of disease, and to consider malaise and disease to be interchangeable terms. "Dis-ease" literally means "without ease." It can be defined as the failure of a person's active mechanism to adequately counteract stimuli and stress, resulting in functional or structural disorders. This definition constitutes an ecological concept of disease that uses multiple factors to determine the cause of a disease rather than describing a single cause. This multifactorial approach increases the likelihood of addressing multiple intervention points to improve health.

It is precisely this broadening of perspective, therefore, that challenges the dichotomous conception of health/illness or well-being/sickness and requires a decisive orientation towards complexity. It is no longer realistic to restrict attention exclusively to clinical levels or individual factors; it is necessary to establish the concept of health with models based on social and environmental parameters.

The best-articulated evolutionary approach is probably represented by the ecological model of health, which is oriented primarily to supporting interventions and processes of health promotion at the individual family level within a community, and eventually at a societal level; this model devotes particular attention to quality of life and the social determinants of health. However, this approach is also approached through multiple concepts and lines of conceptual development, which can be categorized as having three prevailing directions: (a) from the model of role performance to capabilities; (b) from the adaptive model to overcoming the "normal pathological" dichotomy; and (c) from the eudaimonic model to the perspective of psychological well-being.

In detail, these can be described as follows:

*From the model of role performance to capabilities:* The role performance model defines health in terms of an individual's ability to play a role in family and work (or school) contexts, or in social and community life. This capacity is measured by performance according to expectations and social norms. In this view, "disease" is the failure to fulfill one's role at the level expected by society. This model is the basis for occupational health or occupational health assessment, certifications for physical activities at school, or for sick leave from work. The idea of a "patient role" is a vital component of the model. The role of the patient is indeed relevant in current systems of care (devis Italy, 2011; Shillling, 2002). This model is best expressed in the need to place health within the framework of functionalist dimensions linked to modern social and economic organization, with social models of functioning linked precisely to the role performance perspective as a fundamental variable for productivity in and of economic and social systems. In many ways, this position can be redefined in a contemporary context by focusing on the relationship between the social positions and resources that characterize the system of relations in the contemporary world. From this perspective, health refers to Amartya Sen's perspective of "capabilities": "different people have different needs and different abilities or possibilities to transform resources into" functioning, "that is, into real achievements in improving their health and own perspectives in the life project" (Shillling, 2002).

*From the adaptive model to overcoming the "normal pathological" dichotomy*: The adaptive model proposes that health is essentially measured by a person's ability to adapt positively to social changes and to the cultural models with which a person comes into contact. Illness occurs when a person fails to adapt to changes that challenge their physical, psychological, and social functioning. However, this reading seems to propose a distinction between health as adaptation and disease as a lack of adaptation; that is, it re-proposes a dichotomy between "normal" adaptation processes and "pathological" conditions characterized by an inability to adapt.

*From the eudaimonic model to the perspective of psychological well-being*: A eudaimonic approach considers a high level of well-being to be the equivalent of optimal health and strongly emphasizes interaction between the psychological, social, physical, and spiritual aspects of life and the environment, which help a person achieve goals and create meaning. The disease is regarded as denervation or wasting – a lack of involvement in life. This conception also refers to the question of the definition of well-being; the ambiguity contained in the expression "subjective well-being" also refers to the need to specify the relationship between resources and personal and social well-being. The broadening of the perspectives that intervene in these representations remains insufficiently comprehensive to overcome a certain one-sidedness; however, the perspectives pose the need for an ecological model of health that recognizes the interconnection between people and their physical and social environments.

From an ecological perspective, health is multidimensional, extending from the individual to the surrounding community, and encompassing the context within which a person functions. It incorporates a systemic approach in which the actions of part of the system influence the functioning of the whole. This view of health expands the concept of well-being, recognizing that social and environmental factors can promote health and healthy behavior.

## Core Contents and Topics of Psychology in Health Science

Rodolfa et al. (2005) describe competency development in professional psychology by providing two *domains of professional competency*: foundational and functional competency. The foundational competency domain embodies what professional psychologists do, including reflective practice (self-assessment), scientific knowledge, methods, relationships, ethical and legal standards and policy, individual and cultural diversity, and interdisciplinary systems. This domain of competency prepares professionals for acquiring functional competency. Functional competency focusses on skills and knowledge that are vital for performing the psychologist role. This includes assessment and diagnosis of cases, intervention, consultation, research and evaluation, supervision and teaching, and management and administration. These characterize the everyday function of professional psychologists. This model is useful across the stages of professional development, including doctoral education, postdoctoral training, and continuing competency (de-Graft Aikins et al., 2019). Further details on the two competency domains are given below:

## Functional Competency

Functional competency focusses on adequate training in diagnosis, assessment, clinical decision-making, case management, research, and teaching.

## Foundational Competency

Four areas of foundational competency are explored: intellectual, emotional, cultural, and professional. We also explore challenges faced by practitioners (de-Graft Aikins et al., 2019).

We have identified four foundational competency areas that are unique to the practice of clinical health psychology and represent competency areas that clinical health psychologists acquire above and beyond those enumerated in the benchmarks document. The first is engagement in reflective self-assessment regarding one's degree of competency for working in health systems. The second involves basing practice on the biopsychosocial model, using the best available evidence and considering patients' individual differences, values, and preferences. The third foundational competency area (identified by Tempe Summit participants as being distinctive to clinical health psychology) is reliance on interdisciplinary collaboration in caring for patients and implementing practice-based research. The final foundational area of competence uniquely associated with practicing clinical health psychology is comprehension of the ethical and legal standards specifically associated with the health-care system (Larkin & Klonoff, 2014).

Generally, the primary recommendations are "to reduce the factual content of programmes, contextualise the learning and make better use of modern teaching and learning methods" (Cordingley et al., 2013).

## Health Psychologist Job Requirements

To practice as an independent psychologist in the USA, a five-year doctoral degree in clinical or counseling psychology is necessary. During the training period, a standard one-year internship or residency specializing in health psychology must be completed. Doctoral and internship coursework must be completed from an APA-accredited program. Postdoctoral work may also be required and is available through medical centers, health programs, and universities.

In addition to a graduate degree, health psychologists must meet licensure or certification requirements within their state. Licensing requirements vary by state but typically include a graduate degree and passing an exam. Health psychologists must complete continuing education units, in state-specific durations, to renew or maintain their licenses.

Health psychology constitutes a disciplinary field of training, research, and professional applications concerning cognitive, affective/emotional, psychosocial, behavioral, social, and cultural factors that are at the origin of people's health (salutogenesis). These factors concern the promotion and maintenance of health from a biopsychosocial perspective, the prevention and treatment of diseases and their psychological correlates, the analysis and improvement of health protection systems, and the development of health policies in favor of communities. In particular, some of the primary lines of investigation concern the identification of relevant behaviors for health (for example, risky and self-protective behaviors); risk perception and its effects on behavior throughout human development; beliefs, attitudes, intentions, and reactions to health and disease conditions; social representations of health and disease; emotions and their regulation in relation to health and disease, with specific regard to affective dysregulations; the relationships between stress, health, and disease; psychosocial coping strategies and resources; psychological and social well-being and quality of life in various social classes; the promotion of healthy lifestyles, disease prevention, and the most effective techniques to accomplish these purposes; compliance with therapeutic prescriptions; factors that facilitate or hinder treatments; interpersonal relationships in health practice, specifically the patient–therapist relationship; communicative competence in health practice (for example, communication with the patient and the family unit); proper functioning of the interprofessional health team; the health of the social health operator and family caregivers; the organization of health-care services and interventions; the evaluation of prevention programs and health promotion in various social contexts (school, work, and community); and the interaction of health psychology with other adjacent professional fields (e.g., medical psychology, psychosomatic medicine, and behavioral medicine).

At the operational level, health psychologists plan, implement, and evaluate the programs, interventions, and treatments.

The classic interventions aim at developing healthy lifestyles and skills for coping with stressful conditions; the psychoeducational interventions regard health and disease (carried out both individually and in institutional settings such as schools or working contexts); the other interventions promote individual development and psychophysical well-being throughout the entire lifespan, and community empowerment programs give individuals and social groups greater control over their health and enhance their quality of life.

The individual and group treatments correct unhealthy behavior (for example, persistence in smoking, consumption of drugs and alcohol, improper eating habits, and lack of physical exercise); the individual and group treatments are used for the best management of disease conditions, particularly chronic diseases such as diabetes or hypertension.

Although relatively common theoretical and practical frameworks exist, health psychology differs from clinical psychology in that it is more directly focused – on personal and social resources that can help people build and control their health by adopting healthy lifestyles; on the causes of and prevention methods for disorders; and on the processes of changing people's attitudes and conduct with respect to risks, disease management, reaction to stress, and pursuit of a state of well-being.

The international literature categorizes health psychology into *five major cognitive and practical subspecialties*. Clinical health psychology is linked to behavioral medicine; its clinical practice is oriented towards behavioral change through psychotherapeutic or psychoeducational treatment for individuals or small groups.

Community health psychology develops interventions and programs to promote physical and mental health at the community level. Public health psychology interacts with other health sciences, such as medicine and epidemiology, to promote health at the population level, with a specific interest in vulnerable and at-risk social groups. Critical health psychology focusses on social, cultural, gender, and socioeconomic inequalities in health systems, access to services, and health policies; this subspecialty seeks initiatives and programs to promote social change and improvements in equity and social justice. Occupational health psychology integrates with the psychology of work and organizations to change work factors that affect workers' physical and mental health. Adopting an interdisciplinary perspective, health psychologists collaborate with numerous professionals: doctors, epidemiologists, health sociologists, nurses, dieticians, rehabilitation therapists, other psychological health workers, educators, and social communication specialists.

## Teaching, Learning, and Assessment in Health Psychology

### Approaches and Strategies
*Evidence-based practice* (EBP) requires educators to inject significant new content into research, design, and methodology courses, and to further integrate research and practicum training (Bauer, 2007). The knowledge base is usually generated by applying particular inclusion criteria (for example, regarding the design type or type of outcome assessment); these criteria generally describe the impact of particular service practices on child, adolescent, or family outcomes. A scientist/practitioner training model is crucial, with a focus on teaching the basic principles of careful EBP selection. Selecting an appropriate EBP requires an understanding of the core psychological processes involved in various problems and disorders (in addition to the pertinent risk and protective factors) and the theoretical framework guiding the intervention. The procedures for evaluating an intervention should also match the problem features that are likely to change as a function of the intervention (Kratochwill & Shernoff, 2004).

Evidence-based practice in psychology merely requires process learning, with a focus on "just-in-time" knowledge. Despite a focus on the critical appraisal process in training, and the realization that just-in-time knowledge is important in many clinical situations, EBP also demands mastery of a core knowledge base. Clinicians must have broad knowledge of the science of behavior, the relationships between behavior and health, and the mechanisms of behavior change. Education and training must include a special focus on biological, cognitive, affective, and cultural factors that affect health and health-care delivery, in addition to issues surrounding diversity. This knowledge, which is foundational for all APA-accredited professional psychology programs, is essential for interpreting clinical observations, evaluating whether research results are appropriate to the current clinical situation, and integrating research findings with clinical expertise and patient values (Collins Jr, Leffingwell, & Belar, 2007).

Learning strategies can facilitate the design and implementation of intervention programs and procedures. An effective learning strategy is any cognitive, affective, or behavioral activity that facilitates encoding, storing, retrieving, or using knowledge. There are four important *categories of learning strategies*: knowledge acquisition, comprehension monitoring, active study strategies, and support strategies (Weinstein & Macdonald, 1986).

Good practices for effective teaching and learning are as follows (Nilson, 2016):

Lecture: The instructor presents material and answers questions that arise.

Interactive lecture: Lectures are presented with breaks of 2–15 min for student activities (such as answering a multiple-choice objective item, solving a problem, comparing and filling in lecture notes, debriefing a minicase, completing a pair-share exercise, or conducting a small-group discussion) every 12–20 min.

Recitation: Students answer knowledge and comprehension questions.

Directed discussion: A class discussion follows a generally orderly question set that the instructor has crafted to lead students to certain realizations or conclusions, or to help them meet a specific learning outcome.

Writing and speaking exercises: These informal assignments and activities, usually in class and ungraded, help students learn material, clarify their thinking, or make progress on a formal assignment.

Classroom assessment techniques: These informal assignments and activities, usually in class and ungraded, show the instructor how well students are mastering new material; these often overlap with writing and speaking exercises.

Group work/learning: Students complete a learning activity or create a product in small groups of 2–6 in or out of class; the instructor must carefully manage these activities.

Student-peer feedback: Students give mutual feedback on a written or orally presented product, usually a written draft or practice speech.

Cookbook science labs: Pairs or triads of students conduct a traditional, often predictable experiment following prescribed, cookbook-like procedures.

Just-in-time teaching: The instructor adjusts class activities and lectures to respond to misconceptions, as revealed by students' electronic responses to conceptual questions; this is an extension of electronic daily quizzes to motivate students to complete class readings.

Case method: Students apply course knowledge to devise one or more solutions to problems presented in a realistic story or situation; this is an individual, small-group, or class activity.

Inquiry-based or inquiry-guided learning: Students learn or apply material to meet a challenge, answer a question, conduct an experiment, or interpret data.

Problem-based learning: Student groups conduct outside research on student-identified learning issues (unknowns) to devise one or more solutions to difficult problems presented in a realistic story or situation.

Project-based learning: Students (as individuals or in groups) apply course knowledge to produce a report (written or oral), process or product design, research or program proposal, or computer code; this is often paired with cooperative learning.

Role plays: Students act out instructor-assigned roles, improvising the script in a realistic and problematic social or interpersonal situation.

Simulations: Students play out, either face to face or on a computer, a hypothetical social situation that abstracts key elements from reality.

Service learning with reflection: Students learn from performing community service and systematically reflecting on it.

Fieldwork and clinicals: Students learn how to conduct research and make sound professional judgments in real-world situations (Nilson, 2016).

Fieldwork may involve any of the following:

(a) Assessment of health promotion needs and priorities in the context of population subgroups, such as children, young people, or the elderly, within communities and organizations.
(b) Consultancy for analyzing psychological and behavioral risk factors and protection for biopsychosocial health in various social contexts of reference.
(c) Diagnosis of personality characteristics and assessment of personal characteristics, psychosocial resources, needs, and expectations at various age stages, using quantitative (inventories and tests) and qualitative (direct situation observation, clinical interviews, narrative interviews, and focus groups) techniques.
(d) Selection, construction, adaptation, standardization, administration, and interpretation of psychological investigation tools for psychodiagnostic synthesis (tests, inventories, and questionnaires on cognitive skills, interests, motivations, personalities, attitudes, group and social interactions, pathological syndromes, and psychological fitness for specific tasks and conditions).
(e) Psychoeducational interventions and social skills training for health promotion, health management, and healthy behavior among individuals, groups, and organizations.
(f) Psychotherapy and behavioral rehabilitation interventions for restoring biopsychosocial well-being among individuals, families, and social groups within a community context.
(g) Individual and group counseling to facilitate effective management of stressful situations to prevent long-term adverse health effects and promote better adaptation and quality of life.
(h) Individual and group counseling to correct unhealthy behaviors and increase compliance with therapeutic treatments, especially in the presence of chronic diseases.
(i) Counseling and psychological support for hospitalized patients, their families, and staff.
(j) Design, implementation, and evaluation of tools, interventions, and programs for community health promotion and the prevention of diseases and discomfort, with specific regard to educational, associative, and work contexts.
(k) Implementation of research/action programs within the community to involve citizens in developing health policies and formulating improvement objectives for prevention and treatment.

(l) Individual and group supervision interventions for various health operators to enhance communication skills and team functioning, and prevent burnout (Medichini et al., 2016).

**Online Teaching and Learning**

Online teaching and learning methods for health psychology necessitate several considerations. Upton and Cooper (2006) have described their experiences, saying that it is possible to ensure that students can access appropriate material for their course and level of study. "This material is developed around the concept of smaller *content chunks*, which can be combined into whole units of learning (topics), and ultimately, a module. Consequently, the key aim of this development is to stimulate and engage students, promoting better involvement with the academic material, and hence better learning. It is hoped that this was achieved through the development of material including linked programs and supporting material, small Java Scripts and basic email, forms, and HTML additions" (Upton & Cooper, 2006).

In the specific case of online health psychology, many authors have suggested designing the learning and teaching environment to promote greater student participation and engagement, thereby increasing deep learning among students. Some have suggested that web-based learning appeals to students both on and off campus. Online health psychology teaching material includes a range of health psychology resources coordinated through the *Blackboard Virtual Learning Environment (VLE)* (Upton & Cooper, 2004).

Blackboard is an online learning system that provides the functionality required to successfully manage distance, web-enhanced, or hybrid education programs. In essence, it provides a ready-made online shell for tutors to populate with content, together with a set of commonly used online tools. The range of facilities available in Blackboard are organized under the following headings:

- Announcements – to provide students with details of new online content, timetable changes, course reminders, etc.
- Course information – details on the syllabus, timetable, assessment procedures, and other course administration information
- Staff information – including photos and contact information for tutors
- Course material – flexible management of content such as lectures notes, handouts, presentations, and (as in this case) web pages
- Assignments – online summary and formative computer-marked assessments and tutor-marked essay assignment titles
- Communication tools – email, asynchronous discussion board, and synchronous chat (Upton & Cooper, 2004)

Upton and Cooper (2006) have reported an example of implementing online teaching:

*Interactivity*: A range of activities directed via web-based instructions with instantaneous feedback, provided with tutor–learner interaction.

*Individualization for students and cohorts*: A series of "gates" introduced to monitor and direct progression based on the cohort and skill/knowledge level of an individual student. Small chunks of information heighten student interest and lead them to more information.

*Relevance of material*: Differing pages and topics developed based on a student's professional course.

*Student expectancy*: Refers to the learners' perception of success and how much they consider it to be under their control; consists of several short quizzes based on the presented material prior to the final assessment.

*Satisfaction*: Intrinsic motivations enhanced via the interactive and light-hearted nature of the material, with external rewards developed.

*Responses to stress*: A small JavaScript program (a programming language for use in web pages to enable the use of dynamic content) in which students press a button and highlight an increasingly stressed response. There is thus an interaction between the computer and the learner; consequently, this small program increases the learner's stress response and provides relevant learning experience.

*Email exercises*: Small-scale exercises are presented throughout the web pages, which encourages students to assimilate their learning. These are completed on forms and emailed to the tutor. An instant response is provided, along with a more considered response within five working days. This is also a learner–tutor interaction that enables asynchronous discussion.

*Games*: A range of games are presented that have been developed to engage students, enhance learning, and allow for some light-hearted relief. For example, there are crosswords, hangman games, word searches, and jigsaw scramblers for pictorial health psychology models. In addition, the development of popular games such as "Who wants to be a health psychologist millionaire?" is under development.

*All pages*: All units begin with aims, essential materials, and access to further information on how to use pages. Links to a reference list and glossary are presented throughout.

*Links to external sources*: The full power and extent of the Internet is used. Students are directed to readings from an external source, which they must read, analyze, and respond to.

*Questionnaires*: A series of questionnaires (e.g., examining stressful life events or gender) are presented, marked, and given appropriate comments through a JavaScript programming language. This is another computer–learner interaction that presents learners with information in an informative and engaging manner and facilitates learning development rather than simply teaching.

*Exercises*: Each topic chunk ends with a short (four- or five-item) multiple-choice test that allows students to assess their learning. Feedback and directions are provided.

*Graphs*: Several graphs illustrating key points are presented throughout the pages. Each of these asks the student to interpret and respond (e.g., by clicking on the graph to indicate when an event occurred). Instant feedback is provided.

Thus, several key elements must be tackled to develop new material. Despite the numerous benefits of online learning, there are also potential drawbacks, notably including a reliance on student initiative and motivation, a need for a greater examination of the material, and an evaluation of how to present material to best engage the learner (Upton & Cooper, 2006). Disadvantages must also be considered and lecturers must be cautious in their enthusiasm for the subject to avoid overloading students with too much information.

In the same way that a traditional course is constrained by the number of contact hours, online courses are limited by the number of learning hours (Upton & Cooper, 2004).

## Assessment

The guiding principles for assessing competence have been developed by members of the Task Force on the Assessment of Competence in Professional Psychology, sponsored by the American Psychological Association (APA). *The Board of Educational affairs* (BEA) has also established a Task Force on the Assessment of Competencies in Professional Education, Training, and Credentialing.

This movement has actually led to a major shift in the way the tasks, methods, and expected outcomes of vocational training are viewed today (McCutcheon, 2009). As Miller (1990) has pointed out, the assessment of competence in the training and career period of a professional psychologist facilitates the determination of what one knows, if one knows how, if one shows how, and how one does.

In summary, the guiding principles and recommendations for the assessment of competence promoted by the BEA try to overcome a simply summative approach of competence, to leave space for a more holistic approach, which is able to take into account the complexity and the dynamism of professional training in psychology.

The focus is on the acquisition of skills that go through all stages of the professional life span and which, more generally, are able to build a "culture of the competence of assessment," including the knowledge bases, practices, and ethics of the profession, through a continuous process of integration and revaluation. Simultaneously, this comprehensive approach is capable of enhancing the self-reflection and self-assessment process, and taking into account interpersonal functioning and professional development, in addition to individual and cultural diversity.

Overall, therefore, this represents a base of principles that, taken together, provide a valuable guide to understand and measure the development of students in terms of their actual performance.

## Best Solutions for Teaching and Learning in the Psychology Area

In 1999, in Bologna (Italy) the Ministers of Education from 29 European countries agreed and committed to a vision of a *European Higher Education Area* (EHEA) where university-level education would follow shared principles to ensure high quality and comparability.

At present, the EHEA is made up of a group of 48 countries following the so-called Bologna Process directives to achieve these goals, implementing systems with three cycles of higher education qualifications (Bachelor's, Master's, and

Doctoral degrees), in addition to the introduction of the European Credit Transfer and Accumulation System (ECTS), facilitating student mobility between EHEA countries. The introduction of the EHEA has implied changes in higher education at all levels. It is therefore necessary to learn about the experience of teachers, who are one of the main players in this process (Ariza, Quevedo-Blasco, Ramiro, & Bermúdez, 2013).

It is clear that the EHEA has brought about important changes at all levels of higher education.

In this regard, Ariza et al. (2013) focused on teachers' experience, investigating their level of satisfaction with various aspects of the EHEA (for example, their views and attitudes about the process, and how the change affected their method of teaching) and identify possible needs that prevent them from performing their tasks well.

Among the respondents, 48.64% wanted to express their personal opinion in more detail and make suggestions for improvement (for further information, see the contents of Table 4 in Ariza et al., 2013, p. 203).

There are many key points to be strengthened, including establishing a curriculum common to all European universities; improving teacher training on new teaching techniques; and increasing financial funding for scholarships and research.

## Challenges and Lessons Learned

We believe that the teaching of undergraduate health psychology should be evidence based, teaching theories with both empirical support and community and policy applications. Understanding methods such as randomized control trials is critical to appreciating how behavioral medicine interventions work. Similarly, a working knowledge of how stress affects multiple organ systems, culminating in allostatic load (McEwen, 2004), is essential for understanding the biopsychosocial model, which has been the guiding paradigm of the field since its inception. Although each professor has the freedom to design a customized syllabus, our data suggest that cornerstone topics must be covered for students to have a basic knowledge of the field – for example, models and strategies for health behavior change, stress and coping processes, and chronic illness and adjustment. Students would also benefit from being well versed in biobehavioral relationships linking cognition, behavior, and affect with disease. Whether incorporating key topics or a specific topic sequence will lead to better learning outcomes for students remains an empirical question.

Conveying these strengths, in addition to the central topics within health psychology, should be a priority for instructors; introductory topical psychology courses that create awareness of the field should also be considered (Panjwani, Gurung, & Revenson, 2017).

Designing curricula for psychology nonmajor programs requires tackling alignment issues for a program that is smaller and more poorly resourced than a major program. Thus, challenges related to the selection of curriculum content, and the organization and implementation of curriculum delivery, are far more pronounced. This holds true, in particular, for the trade-off between breadth versus depth and multi-perspectivity. Moreover, psychology scholars mostly have limited expertise in professional fields outside the core psychology fields. Therefore, the challenge of aligning a psychology curriculum with the requirements of external professional fields is significant. Collaborating with nonpsychology experts to tackle this challenge is one possible approach to address this issue. Another approach would be using existent general and specific resources for curriculum design. For example, the *European Qualifications Framework for Higher Education (EQF;* for a comprehensive description see Hernández-Encuentra and Sánchez-Carbonell, 2005) provides general guidance regarding the overarching question mentioned above by distinguishing five core qualification goals for higher education.

Furthermore, (inter)national standards and competency frameworks, in addition to handbooks on teaching in the respective domain, may serve as valuable resources for analyzing the epistemic and practical needs of a professional domain. Finally, existent curricula may serve as a starting point. Thus, we briefly outline how the trade-off between breadth and depth has been addressed in the psychology curriculum of the teacher education program at TU Dresden. The curriculum consists of two mandatory modules that can be complemented by optional courses and a scientific thesis (Staatsexamensarbeit) under the guidance of a psychology scholar teaching in the teacher education program. The first mandatory module overviews the core scientific concepts, methods, and empirical evidence considered highly relevant in the professional field through three main lectures. The second provides a set of problem-oriented seminars covering school-relevant psychology topics, from which students select two courses to deepen their psychological knowledge and competences in at least two psychology fields (Narciss, 2019).

## Teaching, Learning, and Assessment Resources

### Advice for Supporting Teaching

Ware et al. (1993) provided a comprehensive review of advising in psychology and suggested that there are five key components: advising relationships, content areas, resources and training, student diversity, and evaluation. Johnson and Morgan outlined several goals that we considered when designing a plan. They wanted to (a) increase the effectiveness of face-to-face advising by reducing time spent on basic information; (b) increase the depth of advising interaction between faculty and students; (c) provide consistent and correct information in a timely manner; (d) increase and vary the types of information delivery systems; (e) focus on program requirements, career information, and planning as the most important content provision; (f) make advising resources more visible; and (g) evaluate our progress.

Johnson and Morgan (2005) described the components of an *advising coordinator.* Their department endorsed the position as a permanent part of staffing. The faculty member in this position advises all new majors, conducts outreach to students in the residence halls, supervises peer advisors, coordinates a mass-advising day each semester, and organizes a graduate school information session in the fall and a career night in the spring. They also conduct in-service training on advising for faculty. Finally, the coordinator teaches a one-credit orientation to the major course (Johnson & Morgan, 2005).

For the *advising plan*, the strategy was to hold advising sessions for freshmen in the residence halls. In addition, freshmen are electronically blocked from registering until they have met with an advisor. Finally, a letter is mailed to all incoming freshmen containing advice on navigating the major and directing them to our website tutorials and information (Johnson & Morgan, 2005).

For the *administrative changes*, a policy was instituted whereby students must meet with an advisor before declaring the major. Before meeting with an advisor, new majors must also complete a web-based tutorial. As a second administrative change, a prerequisite of "declared major" was created for our fundamental sophomore/junior-level experimental psychology course. The department chair sends emails to all declared majors regarding staffing changes, advising and curricular information, and course sequencing advice (e.g., a change in the semester of a once-per-year course offering). The chair also sends a letter to all students who have just declared, indicating their assigned advisor and detailing the advising-related events offered every year. Prominent whiteboards installed in the main classroom area give psychology majors updated information (e.g., club meetings, course changes, and guest speakers). Administrators mail postcard reminders about major events such as mass advising. Finally, an extensive website links students to other useful psychology-related sites (Johnson & Morgan, 2005).

For *mass advising*, the university sends computerized progress reports, updated each semester, to students through their advisors. However, students are not required to meet with their assigned advisors. In response to students' complaints about locating their advisors, a 3-h mass advising session was initiated. This session is offered each semester and guarantees students that they will receive their report and be able to meet with an advisor, even if not their assigned advisor (Johnson & Morgan, 2005).

For the *interactive web advising tutorial*, a mandatory interactive web advising tutorial was launched. This includes three components: general advising, program advising, and career advising. The three interactive components require approximately 45 min to complete. Students complete forms (e.g., their educational goals) and quizzes (e.g., True or False: A course in statistics is required for a psychology degree) that promote interaction with the material (Johnson & Morgan, 2005).

**Recommendations for Psychology Teachers**

A course is intended to meet the following learning outcomes in the psychology major:

1. Describe, compare, and contrast major theoretical perspectives in psychology.
2. Distinguish observations from conclusions, and distinguish theories and findings based on evidence from those without support.
3. Give an oral presentation in front of a class or conference audience.

4. Explain how research helps develop the knowledge base within psychology.
5. Examine major ethical issues and standards for psychological research and practice, and determine the circumstances in which specific behaviors would or would not be ethical (Anderson, 2006).

## Recommendations for Students

1. Read the syllabus and abide by the requirements.
2. Organize, summarize, and rewrite lecture notes in a way that makes sense and clarifies ideas.
3. Because students recall handwritten information better than typed information, students should handwrite their class notes.
4. Review lecture notes regularly and apply the various concepts learned to situations/examples in real life.
5. Read assigned chapters, take notes, and self-quiz with each section to reinforce and verbalize the main ideas; form a study group to explain material to each other, quiz each other, and practice.
6. Apply concepts and ask questions about anything you do not understand.
7. Come to class regularly and engage with the materials and assignments; do not miss lectures and exercises.
8. Submit a hard copy of assignments/papers during class on the due date.
9. Ask questions when in doubt about anything (Wachholtz, 2017).

## Assessment Resources for Supporting Psychology Teachers and Constructing a Learning Environment

In 1996, under the leadership of high school psychology teacher Laura Maitland, a group from *Teachers of Psychology in Secondary Schools (TOPSS)* and several college advisors described a science-centered model for high school courses that would provide rigor and flexibility. Consistent with the original plan to create a living document that would undergo systematic revision, a second task force revised the model in 2005. They articulated outcomes consistent with five domains in psychology (methods, biopsychological, developmental, cognitive, and variations in individual and group behavior) (Dunn, McCarthy, Baker, Halonen, & Hill IV, 2007).

It is crucial to construct a learning environment that supports reflection and cooperation between group members. Here, the need is for formative rather than summative assessment, particularly in the initial stages of a problem-based learning curriculum. Helping students concentrate on assessment criteria paradoxically may encourage them to adopt a strategic approach and focus on the superficial aspects of their assessment tasks, rather than engaging in meaningful learning activity. One solution might be to reconceptualize assessment criteria as "learning criteria," using Biggs' principle of constructive alignment in curriculum development and delivery (Norton, 2004). Biggs (1987) proposed the *3P model*, with three fundamental learning stages: presage, process, and product. Presage factors are those prior to learning; process factors relate to the learning process; and product or performance factors refer to the learning outcome gained. Based on these three stages, Biggs

(1987) proposed a tool for measuring students' learning approach in tertiary levels, called the *Study Process Questionnaire (SPQ)*. The questionnaire operationalizes these approaches through their constituent motives and strategies. There are 42 items; each item represents either a surface motive, surface strategy, deep motive, deep strategy, achieving motive, or achieving strategy. The items in the SPQ have been revised and validated, producing 20 items. The surface approach is generally associated with memorizing facts and reproducing information; the deep approach often involves understanding meanings and utilizing information; and the achieving approach is merely the pursuance of good grades. Biggs, Kember, and Leung (2001) revised the SPQ into the R-SPQ-2F (with 20 items) by examining only two factors: surface and deep. This new model is claimed to have good psychometric qualities of internal reliability, consistency, and validity (Astika & Sumakul, 2020).

## Cross-References

▶ Medical Education
▶ Psychology in Social Science and Education
▶ Psychology of Special Needs and Inclusion

## References

African College of Applied Psychology (SACAP). (2020). Website: https://www.sacap.edu.za/blog/applied-psychology/applied-psychology/

American Psychological Association. (2011). *National standards for high school psychology curricula*. Washington, DC: Author. Website: https://www.apa.org/education/k12/psychology-curricula.pdf

American Psychological Association. (2013). National standards for high school psychology curricula. *The American Psychologist, 68*(1), 32.

American Psychological Association. (2016). Guidelines for the undergraduate psychology major: Version 2.0. *The American Psychologist, 71*(2), 102.

Anderson R. A. (2006). Website: https://teachpsych.org/resources/Documents/otrp/syllabi/ra06healthf.pdf

Ariza, T., Quevedo-Blasco, R., Ramiro, M. T., & Bermúdez, M. P. (2013). Satisfaction of health science teachers with the convergence process of the European higher education area. *International Journal of Clinical and Health Psychology, 13*(3), 197–206.

Astika, G., & Sumakul, T. Y. (2020). Students'profiles through learning approaches using Biggs'study process questionnaire. *ELTR Journal, 3*(1), 46–54.

Bauer, R. M. (2007). Evidence-based practice in psychology: Implications for research and research training. *Journal of Clinical Psychology, 63*(7), 685–694.

Biggs, J. B. (1987). Study process questionnaire manual. Melbourne: Australian Council for Educational Research. *ELTR Journal, 4*(1), 36–42.

Biggs, J. B., Kember, D., & Leung, D. Y. (2001). The revised two-factor Study Process Questionnaire: R-SPQ-2F. *British Journal of Educational Psychology, 71*, 133–149.

Collins, F. L., Jr., Leffingwell, T. R., & Belar, C. D. (2007). Teaching evidence-based practice: Implications for psychology. *Journal of Clinical Psychology, 63*(7), 657–670.

Consiglio ordine psicologi (CNOPP) – Italy. *Report: Lo Psicologo della salute Classificazione EUROPSY Clinical and Health Psychology – (Clinica, Salute e Benessere).* Website: https://www.psy.it/allegati/aree-pratica-professionale/psicologo_della_salute.pdf

Cordingley, A. (Ed.). (2013). *Self-translation: Brokering originality in hybrid culture.* A&C Black: London.

de-Graft Aikins, A., Osei-Tutu, A., Agyei, F., Asante, P. Y., Aboyinga, H., Adjei, A., ... & Edu-Ansah, K. (2019). Competence in professional psychology practice in Ghana: Qualitative insights from practicing clinical health psychologists. *Journal of Health Psychology.* Website: https://journals.sagepub.com/doi/pdf/10.1177/1359105319859060?casa_token=JmpdLp2cFjcAAAAA:jTmfCH5YHbTnSAUgXAevVUg9NfrjPn8VY2q7en88gzZz54mlUhiaCy3LOOpgxJarwiwUw7ekv2E9A

Dunn, D. S., McCarthy, M. A., Baker, S., Halonen, J. S., & Hill, G. W., IV. (2007). Quality benchmarks in undergraduate psychology programs. *American Psychologist, 62*(7), 650.

Engel, G. L. (1977). The need for a new medical model: A challenge for biomedicine. *Science, 196*, 129–136.

EuroPsy: A framework for education and training of psychologists in Europe. (2011). Report. Website: http://www.inpa-europsy.it/

Hernández-Encuentra, E., & Sánchez-Carbonell, J. (2005). The Bologna process and lifelong education: Problem-based learning. *Higher Education in Europe, 30*(1), 81–88.

Johnson, E. J., & Morgan, B. L. (2005). Advice on advising: Improving a comprehensive university's program. *Teaching of Psychology, 32*(1), 15–18.

Kratochwill, T. R., & Shernoff, E. S. (2004). Evidence-based practice: Promoting evidence-based interventions in school psychology. *School Psychology Review, 33*(1), 34–48.

Larkin, K. T., & Klonoff, E. A. (2014). *Specialty competencies in clinical health psychology.* OUP Us: Oxford.

Mahler, H. (1981). The meaning of health for all by the year 2000. *World Health Forum, 2*(1), 2–21.

Matarazzo, J. D. (1980). Behavioral health and behavioral medicine: Frontiers for a new health psychology. *American Psychologist, 35*(9), 807.

McCutcheon, S. R. (2009). Competency benchmarks: Implications for internship training. *Training and Education in Professional Psychology, 3*(4S), S50.

McEwen, B. S. (2004). Protection and damage from acute and chronic stress: allostasis and allostatic overload and relevance to the pathophysiology of psychiatric disorders. *Annals of the New York Academy of Sciences, 1032*(1), 1–7.

Miller, G. E. (1990). Assessment of clinical skills/competence/performance. *Academic Medicine, 65*(Suppl), S63–S67.

Narciss, S. (2019). Curriculum design for (non-) psychology programs–a reflection on general and specific issues, and approaches on how to address them: Comment on Dutke et al., 2019. *Psychology Learning & Teaching, 18*(2), 144–147.

National Institutes of Health. (2020). Website: researchtraining.nih.go

Nilson, L. B. (2016). *Teaching at its best: A research-based resource for college instructors.* Wiley. Website: https://www.spu.ac.th/tlc/files/2016/02/Teaching-at-its-best.pdf

Norton, L. (2004). Using assessment criteria as learning criteria: A case study in psychology. *Assessment & Evaluation in Higher Education, 29*(6), 687–702.

Ogden, J. (2012). *Health psychology: A textbook.* Maidenhead, UK: McGraw-Hill Education.

Panjwani, A. A., Gurung, R. A., & Revenson, T. A. (2017). The teaching of undergraduate health psychology: A national survey. *Teaching of Psychology, 44*(3), 268–273.

Report: Mutual evaluation of regulated professions: Overview of the regulatory framework in the health services sector – psychologists and related professions. Report based on information transmitted by Member States discussion in the meeting of 6 March 2015 file:///C:/Users/Savarese%20Giulia/Downloads/ME_-_update_-_FINAL_report_psychologists_-_to_be_published.pdf

Rodolfa, E., Bent, R., Eisman, E., Nelson, P., Rehm, L., & Ritchie, P. (2005). A cube model for competency development: Implications for psychology educators and regulators. *Professional Psychology: Research and Practice, 36*(4), 347.

Rozensky, R. H., Grus, C. L., Nutt, R. L., Carlson, C. I., Eisman, E. J., & Nelson, P. D. (2015). A taxonomy for education and training in professional psychology health service specialties: Evolution and implementation of new guidelines for a common language. *American Psychologist, 70*(1), 21.
Shilling, C. (2002). Culture, the 'sick role' and the consumption of health. *British Journal of Sociology, 53*(4), 621–638.
Society for health psychology. (2020). Website: https://societyforhealthpsychology.org/councils-committees/education-training-council/
The APA Graduate and Postgraduate Education and Training. (2020). Website: https://www.apa.org/ed/graduate/
The APA Guidelines for the graduate and post-graduate Psychology. (2020). Website: https://www.apa.org/careers/resources/guides/college-students
The APA Guidelines for the Undergraduate Psychology Major. (2011). Website: https://www.apa.org/ed/precollege/about/learning-goals.pdf
Tran, V. (2013). Health psychology. In M. D. Gellman & J. R. Turner (Eds.), *Encyclopedia of behavioral medicine*. New York, NY: Springer.
Upton, D., & Cooper, C. D. (2004). Online health psychology: Do students need it, use it, like it and want it? *Psychology Learning & Teaching, 3*(1), 27–35.
Upton, D., & Cooper, C. (2006). Developing an on-line interactive health psychology module. *Innovations in Education and Teaching International, 43*(3), 223–231.
Ware, J. E., Snow, K. K., Kosinski, M., & Gandek, B. (1993). SF-36 health survey. Manual and interpretation guide. Boston: The Health Institute, New England Medical Center, 10–6.
Wachholtz, A. (2017). *Programme of course of health psychology*. University of Colorado Denver. Denver (USA).
Website: https://www.bachelorstudies.com/Bachelor/Health-Care/Asia/
Website: https://www.psychologydegree411.com/degrees/health-psychology/
Website: https://www.open.edu.au/degrees/graduate-certificate-in-health-psychology-curtin-university-cur-hpy-gce
Weinstein, C. E., & Macdonald, J. D. (1986). Why does a school psychologist need to know about learning strategies? *Journal of School Psychology, 24*(3), 257–265.

## URLS References

http://citeseerx.ist.psu.edu/viewdoc/download?doi=10.1.1.473.8449&rep=rep1&type=pdf
http://www.inpa-europsy.it/moduli/EuroPsy%20Regulations%20July%202011.pdf
https://onlinelibrary.wiley.com/doi/pdf/10.1348/000709901158433?casa_token=CDIq8o_AeZoAAAAA:SPhh-poQCQdX_2zHaL2FVVeNebBazAL6cQt1u-Kl9XGDmr874qnGbTDlxKoCkMF796Hbm36IxpkeOg
https://societyforhealthpsychology.org/training/training-resources/teaching-resources-for-health-psychology/
https://teachpsych.org/page-1603066
https://teachpsych.org/resources/Documents/otrp/syllabi/aw17health.pdf
https://teachpsych.org/resources/Documents/otrp/syllabi/rubric%20revision%20FINAL%20with%20header.pdf
https://www.apa.org/education/k12/national-standards
https://www.psychologicalscience.org/members/teaching
https://www.redalyc.org/pdf/337/33727852004.pdf
https://www.tandfonline.com/doi/abs/10.1080/02796015.2004.12086229

# Part III

# General Educational and Instructional Approaches to Psychology Learning and Teaching

# Basic Principles and Procedures for Effective Teaching in Psychology

# 48

Douglas A. Bernstein

## Contents

| | |
|---|---|
| Characteristics of Effective Teachers | 1173 |
| Preparing Your Courses | 1173 |
|    Setting Goals | 1173 |
|    Choosing Course Materials | 1175 |
|    Creating a Syllabus | 1176 |
|    Setting Up Your Grading System | 1178 |
| Evaluating Student Learning | 1179 |
|    Tests and Quizzes | 1180 |
|    Writing Assignments | 1182 |
|    Applying the Psychology of Learning to Student Evaluation | 1182 |
| The First Day of Class | 1183 |
|    Exploring Your Classroom | 1183 |
|    Establishing Yourself as a Teacher | 1184 |
| Developing Your Teaching Style | 1185 |
|    Effective Lecturing | 1186 |
|    Answering and Asking Questions | 1187 |
|    Promoting Class Discussion | 1188 |
|    Conducting Classroom Demonstrations | 1189 |
| Faculty-Student Relationships | 1189 |
|    The Ethical Use of Teacher Power | 1189 |
|    Dealing with Student Requests, Complaints, and Problems | 1190 |
|    Dealing with Student Behavior Problems | 1192 |
| Assessing and Improving Your Teaching | 1193 |
|    Evaluations by Students | 1193 |
|    Evaluations by Colleagues | 1194 |

---

D. A. Bernstein (✉)
Department of Psychology, University of South Florida, Tampa, FL, USA
e-mail: douglas.bernstein@comcast.net

© Springer Nature Switzerland AG 2023
J. Zumbach et al. (eds.), *International Handbook of Psychology Learning and Teaching*, Springer International Handbooks of Education,
https://doi.org/10.1007/978-3-030-28745-0_55

Self-Evaluation ............................................................................. 1194
Integrating Teaching into Your Academic Life .............................................. 1194
References ................................................................................. 1196

**Abstract**

This chapter is designed for the many new, or relatively inexperienced, psychology teachers who find themselves underprepared to assume their role in the classroom. It begins with an overview of the general principles underlying effective teaching in higher education and goes on to offer specific suggestions that are particularly relevant in teaching psychology. Topics include setting course goals, choosing reading assignments, writing a course outline, setting up a grading system, evaluating student learning, developing a teaching style, establishing and maintaining rapport with students, evaluating one's teaching skills, and integrating teaching in one's academic life.

**Keywords**

Teaching · Effective teaching · Course planning · Course evaluation · Student-teacher relationship

Many new psychology teachers in the United States enter their first classrooms with extensive content knowledge learned in graduate school, but with little or no formal preparation for their teaching role (Boice, 1996; Boysen, 2011; Buskist, 2013; Buskist, Tears, Davis, & Rodrigue, 2002; Chew et al., 2018; Mervis, 2001). This situation is at least as common in other countries (e.g., Padilla-Lopez et al., 2018). These first-time teachers may be asked to offer courses (that may or may not be within their primary area of expertise) without being told what topics to cover or how to create a syllabus (course outline), choose readings, prepare and conduct lectures and class activities, evaluate students' performance, or handle grading complaints. They may know nothing about what to do in the face of classroom disruptiveness, requests for special consideration, and students' needs for mental health services. They have to learn these and many other teaching skills by applying their wits and guts through trial and error, informed perhaps by the examples set by their own teachers, and whatever informal advice and readings they might find. No wonder so many graduate students and first-year teachers feel anxious, unprepared, or underprepared for their teaching responsibilities (Buskist, 2013; Davis & Huss, 2002; Meyers & Prieto, 2000; Wimer, Prieto, & Meyers, 2004).

This chapter is designed to help if you are one of those people. It presents some basic principles for effectively teaching psychology offers suggestions for applying those principles in as you plan, conduct, and evaluate your courses. The relevance of some of the advice contained here may vary depending on international differences in teaching cultures and traditions, psychology curricula, student characteristics, institutional policies, and other factors, but most of the material has universal applicability.

## Characteristics of Effective Teachers

In the 1990s, a great deal of research in the United States found that the teacher behaviors most strongly associated with student learning are *enthusiasm*, *clarity*, and *good rapport* with students (e.g., Feldman, 1998; Junn, 1994; Lowman, 1998; McKeachie, 2001; Murray, 1997; Teven & McCroskey, 1996). More recent research has confirmed the importance of these behaviors and identified many others that are related to them (e.g., Beers, Hill, Thompson, & Tran, 2014; Hativa, 2013; Keeley, Ismail, & Buskist, 2016; Weimer, 2013a).

The 28 behaviors that are most consistently seen in excellent teachers formed the basis for an observation instrument called the Teacher Behaviors Checklist (TBC; Buskist et al., 2002; Keeley, Smith, & Buskist, 2006; see Table 1).

Factor analysis of the TBC revealed two main dimensions: (1) being caring and supportive and (2) having professional competency and communication skills (Keeley et al., 2006). In other words, whatever else you do, your chances of becoming an effective teacher are better if you care about your teaching and about your students, if you know your subject matter, and if you can clearly express what you know.

You can see video clips illustrating several categories of desirable teacher behavior at https://bit.ly/2VIOivF (Landrum & Stowell, 2013). If you watch some of these clips or observe other effective teachers in action, you will surely notice that they don't all follow the same script. Each has found a pathway to effective teaching that fits within the framework of their own personalities. Keep this in mind. You do not have to conform to someone else's ideal of a "good teacher" in order to be one. Students tend to like and respect teachers who display almost any interpersonal style as long as that style is authentic and as long as it is clear that the teacher is knowledgeable and cares about them and about teaching. The key to effective teaching, then, is to find your own way to communicate to students your caring, your content knowledge, your motivation, and your good intentions. The following sections suggest specific ways to do this.

## Preparing Your Courses

Careful planning and preparation are vital if you are to minimize your teaching anxiety and maximize your teaching effectiveness.

## Setting Goals

Your course goals should reflect both what you want your students to learn in the course and the purpose the course is designed to serve in your departmental and institutional curriculum.

You might begin thinking about your goals by taking the Teaching Goals Inventory (TGI; https://tgi.its.uiowa.edu/; Angelo & Cross, 1993). It lists 53 student

**Table 1** The Teacher Behaviors Checklist

| |
|---|
| 1. Accessible (posts office hours, gives out phone number and email information) |
| 2. Approachable/personable (smiles, greets students, initiates conversations, invites questions, responds respectfully to student comments) |
| 3. Authoritative (establishes clear course rules; maintains classroom order; speaks in a loud, strong voice) |
| 4. Confident (speaks clearly, makes eye contact, and answers questions correctly) |
| 5. Creative and interesting (experiments with teaching methods; uses technological devices to support and enhance lectures; uses interesting, relevant, and personal examples; not monotone) |
| 6. Effective communicator (speaks clearly/loudly; uses precise English; gives clear, compelling examples) |
| 7. Encourages and cares for students (provides praise for good student work, helps students who need it, offers bonus points and extra credit, and knows student names) |
| 8. Enthusiastic about teaching and about topic (smiles during class, prepares interesting class activities, uses gestures and expressions of emotion to emphasize important points, and arrives on time for class) |
| 9. Establishes daily and academic term goals (prepares/follows the syllabus and has goals for each class) |
| 10. Flexible/open-minded (changes calendar of course events when necessary, will meet at hours outside of office hours, pays attention to students when they state their opinions, accepts criticism from others, and allows students to do make-up work when appropriate) |
| 11. Good listener (doesn't interrupt students while they are talking, maintains eye contact, and asks questions about points that students are making) |
| 12. Happy/positive attitude/humorous (tells jokes and funny stories, laughs with students) |
| 13. Humble (admits mistakes, never brags, and doesn't take credit for others' successes) |
| 14. Knowledgeable about subject matter (easily answers students' questions, does not read straight from the book or notes, and uses clear and understandable examples) |
| 15. Prepared (brings necessary materials to class, is never late for class, and provides outlines of class discussion) |
| 16. Presents current information (relates topic to current, real-life situations; uses recent videos, magazines, and newspapers to demonstrate points; talks about current topics; and uses new or recent texts) |
| 17. Professional (dresses nicely [neat and clean shoes, slacks, blouses, dresses, shirts, ties] and no profanity) |
| 18. Promotes class discussion (asks controversial or challenging questions during class, gives points for class participation, and involves students in group activities during class) |
| 19. Promotes critical thinking/intellectually stimulating (asks thoughtful questions during class, uses essay questions on tests and quizzes, assigns homework, and holds group discussions/activities) |
| 20. Provides constructive feedback (writes comments on returned work, answers students' questions, and gives advice on test-taking) |
| 21. Punctuality/manages class time (arrives to class on time/early, dismisses class on time, presents relevant materials in class, leaves time for questions, keeps appointments, and returns work in a timely way) |
| 22. Rapport (makes class laugh through jokes and funny stories, initiates and maintains class discussions, knows student names, and interacts with students before and after class) |

(continued)

**Table 1** (continued)

| |
|---|
| 23. Realistic expectations of students/fair testing and grading (covers material to be tested during class, writes relevant test questions, does not overload students with reading, teaches at an appropriate level for the majority of students in the course, and curves grades when appropriate) |
| 24. Respectful (does not humiliate or embarrass students in class, is polite to students [says thank you and please, etc.], does not interrupt students while they are talking, and does not talk down to students) |
| 25. Sensitive and persistent (makes sure students understand material before moving to new material, holds extra study sessions, repeats information when necessary, and asks questions to check student understanding) |
| 26. Strives to be a better teacher (requests feedback on his/her teaching ability from students, continues learning [attends workshops, etc. on teaching], and uses new teaching methods) |
| 27. Technologically competent (knows how to use a computer, knows how to use email with students, knows how to use overheads during class, and has a Web page for classes) |
| 28. Understanding (accepts legitimate excuses for missing class or coursework, is available before/after class to answer questions, doesn't lose temper at students, and takes extra time to discuss difficult concepts) |

competencies and gives you the opportunity to rate the importance of each of them in your course. The TGI generates an instant report that summarizes the goals that you rated as "essential," "very important," "important," or "unimportant" and allows you to compare your responses with those of thousands of other teachers.

The results of the TGI – and your reflections on it – should clarify what you want your students to learn and thus help you to plan your courses accordingly. For example, if you think it is important for your students to develop critical thinking skills, you will probably plan a course that allows them to critique and debate the validity of research results. If you want to give students collaborative learning experiences, you might plan to have them work in teams to summarize research articles or solve course-related problems. If you simply want to assure that students understand the terms and concepts you present in the course, you will probably create exams and class activities that test those skills.

The goals for your course will also be influenced by the role it plays in your department and on your campus. Is it a prerequisite for other courses and, if so, what are they? What courses, if any, are prerequisites for yours? Is your course part of a specialized sequence? Awareness of what your students should already know will help you establish a starting point and determine the appropriate level for your class presentations, activities, and reading assignments. Knowing what your department or institution expects students to learn in your course will also help you decide what to cover (and what to skip) and what level of detail is appropriate.

## Choosing Course Materials

Once you have established the goals for your course, the next task is to decide which learning materials you want your students to use. In the United States, Canada, and some countries in Europe and elsewhere, this involves choosing a textbook; in other countries, it involves creating a list of readings. Whatever the case, if you have not taught the course before, begin the selection process by reexamining the materials you learned from when you took the course yourself, and then review the materials previously assigned by your local colleagues. You can also explore the readings chosen by teachers at institutions similar to yours by visiting their departments' home pages and then following links to the relevant online syllabi. At the website of the Society for the Teaching of Psychology (STP), you will find additional reading lists on the Project Syllabus page at the Office of Teaching Resources in Psychology (OTRP) (https://bit.ly/2CYYsBd). Rating forms and other sources of advice about choosing textbooks are also available (e.g., Bernstein, Frantz, & Chew, 2020; Weimer, 2013b).

There are plenty of options if you want to use reading materials other than, or in addition to, a textbook, including sets of readings that can be assembled in custom-designed course packets from companies such as CoursePackets.com, Cognella, and XanEdu. You can create books of reading through sources such as the American Psychological Association's Custom Course Books (https://bit.ly/2QB46gf), and you may also be able to find additional resources through the websites of the European Federation of Psychology Teachers' Associations. If you wish to assign downloadable material, be sure that you understand relevant national and international copyright laws and restrictions that may apply (Davis, 2009; Hilton, 2003).

As you select your course materials, keep track of the total number of pages you plan to assign. Don't underestimate your students' abilities, but be reasonable. A comprehensive reading list might seem ideal at the beginning of the term, but it may not serve your goals if, in the context of all their other courses, students will not have time to read everything you assign, let alone think deeply about it (Davis, 2009).

## Creating a Syllabus

Psychology teachers in some countries do not provide students with a syllabus, or course outline, but this is standard practice in North America and elsewhere. Consider doing so even if it is not traditional where you teach, because a syllabus has considerable value in promoting communication with your students. Distributing a syllabus on the first day of class (or on a course website beforehand) shows that you are organized and have other attributes seen in effective teachers, including being prepared and enthusiastic. A well-constructed syllabus serves as a preview and road map of the course and tells students what they can expect from you and what you will be expecting of them. Creating a syllabus can help you, too, because it forces you to think carefully about many details – including class projects, guest speakers, quiz, exam, and term paper assignments and deadlines, missed-deadline and make-up exam policies, and the like – that might otherwise slip through the cracks until students ask about them.

When deciding what to include on your syllabus, err on the side of completeness. The more information about the course you provide, the fewer questions you will have to answer in class and the easier it will be to refer students to the syllabus. The Project Syllabus website mentioned earlier contains numerous sample syllabi and a link to "Pointers for Preparing Exemplary Syllabi." As you will see there, your syllabus should include at least the following information:

1. The name, number, and title of your course (e.g., Psychology XXX, Cognitive Psychology)
2. The days, time, and location of class meetings (e.g., MWF, 10 a.m., room XX, Psychology Building)
3. Your name, office address, and how to contact you (if you include your personal phone number, indicate the hours during which calls are welcome)
4. Your scheduled office hours (these may not be traditional in your country, but they provide yet another way to communicate caring about your students)
5. The name(s), office location(s), phone number(s) or email addresses, and office hour(s) of anyone who will be helping you teach the course
6. A brief summary of the course and your goals in teaching it. For example:

*This course offers an introduction to the more applied areas of psychology, including research methods, developmental psychology, learning and memory, thinking and intelligence testing, health psychology, personality, psychological disorders and their treatment, and social psychology. Throughout the course, you will be encouraged to develop your ability to think critically about psychology and about topics outside of psychology. You will get much more out of the lectures and discussions if you complete the assigned readings before each class.*

7. A list of all required and recommended readings and other materials, along with information about whether, and where, any of these materials can be found on reserve in the library or elsewhere.
8. A list of what will occur at each class meeting, along with the readings or other assignments to be completed before each meeting.
9. A description of *exactly* how student performance will be evaluated and how final grades will be determined. List the number of exams and quizzes, whether they will be essay, multiple- choice, short-answer, or whatever, the number of items on each, how much each will contribute to the final grade, and whether grades will be affected by class attendance and participation.
10. A list of your course policies and rules of etiquette. These can include things such as "Please enter quietly if you come to class late," "No eating or drinking in class, please," "Late assignments will incur a 50 percent penalty," "Silence all mobile phones," and the like. In short, spell out everything you do and do not want to happen in class, and the consequences of rule violations. Some of these policies will be unfamiliar to your students, so don't leave them guessing, or discovering them the hard way.

## Setting Up Your Grading System

Systems for evaluating student performance on course assignments and for arriving at final grades vary widely across the world, but there is one universal truth: most students care at least as much about how they will be graded as about what they are learning. There is no single best grading system, but there are some "golden rules" of grading that effective teachers everywhere tend to follow.

First, grading systems should be *accurate*, meaning that course grades reflect each student's level of performance as measured by clear criteria. Second, grading systems should be *fair*, and just as important, they should be *perceived* as fair. Your students should be confident that all those whose total scores, or percentage of available points, fall within certain ranges will receive certain grades. Third, grading systems should be *stable*, meaning that the system described at the beginning of the course is not subject to unannounced, unpredictable, or repeated changes.

Following these "golden rules" will make it easier to follow a final one, namely, that grades should be *defensible*. Your grading system should allow you to explain and justify – to students or anyone else who has a right to ask – how and why each student's grade was determined. If you heed these basic rules, you will find teaching less stressful, not only because your students will know what to expect, and thus be less likely to argue about grades, but also because you will be far less vulnerable to charges of capricious grading.

**Types of Grading Systems.** Assuming that – as is true in some places – you are not required to have a fixed distribution of grades in your course, the first step in setting up your grading system is to decide whether to use a norm-referenced system (also referred to as "grading on a curve"), a criterion-referenced system (also called "absolute" or "standards of excellence" grading), or some combination of the two.

*Norm-referenced* grades can be assigned using a planned distribution in which students who are, say, in the top 10 percent of the distribution of points earned get As; the next 20 percent get Bs, the next 40 percent get Cs, the next 20 percent get Ds, and the bottom 10 percent get Fs. Notice that, in this system, all possible grades will be assigned, but the actual number of points associated with each grade will vary from class to class, depending on how well the best students do. *Criterion-referenced* grades are assigned individually, regardless of the performance of any other student, or the class as a whole. The simplest form of criterion-referenced grading gives an A to anyone who earns, say, 90 percent of the points available in the course, or on a particular assignment; a B to those earning, say, 80–89 percent; and so on.

The advantages of criterion-referenced grading are that (1) students are evaluated on an absolute scale determined by the instructor's definition of what constitutes mastery of course material, (2) final grades indicate the degree to which students achieved that mastery, and (3) because students are not competing against each other, they tend to be more cooperative (Ory & Ryan, 1993). Potential disadvantages of criterion-referenced grading include the fact that it can be difficult to determine what criteria are valid in a given course, especially when you are teaching it for the first time. For example, is it reasonable to expect students to achieve at the 90 percent level, given the difficulty of the material? If no one reaches that level, will you be comfortable assigning no As?

Norm-referenced grading has the advantage of rewarding students whose academic performance is outstanding relative to the class. It can also prevent grade distortions when, for example, even the best students perform poorly because a test or other assignment was flawed in some way. In such cases, the best of the poor performances would still earn As, whereas under a criterion-based system, everyone might receive an F. Norm-referenced grading can, however, lead to some unfortunate consequences, especially when there is little variability in the performance of a given class. Under such a system, even if all your students earned at least, say, 80 percent of the points available, some of them would still receive Cs, Ds, and Fs. And even if none of your students scored above 50 percent on any graded assignment, some of them would still get As, Bs, and Cs. In these (thankfully rare) cases, anyone unfamiliar with the characteristics of the class in question could easily be misled about the meaning of norm-referenced grades (Ory & Ryan, 1993).

*Hybrid* grading approaches are designed to exploit the strengths of both norm-referenced and criterion-referenced systems. In a modified norm-referenced system, for example, the benchmark for assigning grades is not based strictly on the overall point distribution (e.g., wherein the top 10 percent get A grades) but on the *average score* of the best students in the class. To establish this benchmark, the teacher calculates the mean of the scores earned by the top 10 percent of all students. If there are 50 students in the class, for example, the benchmark would be the mean score earned by the top five students. To earn an A, students would have to earn at least 95 percent of the benchmark, earning a B would require 85 percent of the benchmark, a C would require 75 percent of the benchmark, and so on. This hybrid system (a) allows all students to earn an A if they do well enough, (b) does not penalize students for poorly designed evaluation instruments, and (c) requires a high absolute level of achievement, not just a high relative standing within the class, to earn a high grade, and (d) can be used for any graded assignment, whether it be a quiz, an exam, or total points at the end of the term.

## Evaluating Student Learning

Effective teachers link their grading systems to their course objectives and goals for student learning (Astin & Antonio, 2012; Suskie, 2018), a link that has been described as "teaching what you are grading and grading what you are teaching" (Walvoord & Anderson, 2010). This does not mean that you should teach only what will be on your exams but that you should evaluate students on the most important content in your courses. Further, your evaluations should ideally contribute to the learning process, helping students to discover what they do and do not yet know and what skills they have and have not yet developed (Brookfield, 2006).

Evaluation can be done in many ways and at various points in time. Graded or ungraded quiz and exam scores, comments on draft versions of term papers or research plans, and other kinds of evaluations that take place during a course provide *formative feedback* that comes in time for students to use it to improve their performance. End-of-course evaluations such as scores on final exams, term papers, and research reports provide *summative feedback* that tells the story of what a student learned – as measured by those evaluative instruments. Overall, the greater the number of evaluative components that go into determining a final grade, and the more varied those components are, the more valid the final grade is likely to be (e.g., Davis, 2009; Suskie, 2018; Svinicki & McKeachie, 2014; Walvoord & Anderson, 2010).

## Tests and Quizzes

The most commonly employed option for evaluating student performance is the written test and, its briefer cousin, the written quiz. These can be constructed in essay, short-answer, or multiple-choice formats.

Essay and short-answer tests can be constructed relatively quickly, they provide an assessment of students' writing ability, and they can present tasks that require high level analysis of course material, including problem-solving skills and complex thinking (Erickson, Peters, & Strommer, 2006). Essay tests can be scored using analytical or global quality methods (Ory & Ryan, 1993). The *analytical scoring method* is usually easier to defend when students raise challenges. It requires that you to write an "ideal answer," also known as a *grading rubric*, that contains specified elements with predetermined point values. You then compare each student's essay to the ideal answer and award points according to which, and how many, specified elements are present (Ory & Ryan, 1993). In the *global quality* scoring scheme, you assign a score to each student based on either the total quality of the response relative to other student responses or in relation to your own criteria (Ory & Ryan, 1993).

The main disadvantage of essay and short-answer tests is that they take an enormous amount of time to evaluate systematically. Before deciding on the essay or short-answer format, therefore, estimate how much time it will take to grade each question, increase that estimate to be on the safe side, and multiply the result by the number of students in your class. Then multiply that figure by the number of tests to be given in the course, and decide whether the resulting time commitment is realistic in light of your other academic responsibilities.

If the time required for grading essay or short-answer tests is likely to be unmanageable, consider using a multiple-choice format for some or all student performance evaluations. Multiple-choice tests completed on paper forms can be quickly scored by optical scanners, and those completed on a computer can be scored electronically and then downloaded into a computer-based gradebook. In addition, the difficulty level and other information about each multiple-choice item's performance can be assessed by item analysis programs available through most exam scoring software.

Among the disadvantages of multiple-choice tests are that they take a long time to write and an even longer time to write well (Jacobs & Chase, 1992; Ory & Ryan,

1993). Further, no matter how careful you are, some items may be misunderstood, interpreted in unexpected ways, or vulnerable to double meanings, all of which can confuse students and lead them to make inquiries during the test and raise challenges afterward. One way to minimize these problems, and also to spread out the item-writing workload, is to write two or three multiple-choice items immediately after each class period, when the material and students' reactions to it are fresh in your mind (e.g., Erickson & Strommer, 1991). This strategy helps ensure that all important material covered in class is also covered on the exam. It might also result in higher quality items that are more closely linked to your learning goals, because you will be concentrating more intensely on each item's wording, clarity, accuracy, and difficulty level than might be the case during a last-minute item-writing marathon.

Regardless of the format you choose, analyze your tests and quizzes using a *table of specifications* (Jacobs & Chase, 1992; Ory & Ryan, 1993; see Table 2). Each row of this table should represent one concept, phenomenon, principle, theory, or other content elements to be tested. Each column should represent a cognitive skill to be demonstrated, such as defining terms, comparing concepts, applying principles, analyzing information, and the like. Each of the table's cells thus represents the intersection of a particular bit of course content and the level of skill being tested. You can use this table to plan the content and level of the items you are about to write (or choose from a test-item bank). If you have already written or chosen a set of items, enter a digit representing each item into the cell that best represents its content and level. Tests and quizzes need not assess every possible concept at every possible cognitive level, but the resulting pattern of entries will tell you how well the test or quiz covers the lectures and assigned readings and at what level.

You may want to consult references on item-writing (e.g., Bernstein, Frantz & Chew, 2020; Jacobs & Chase, 1992; Ory & Ryan, 1993) before drafting your items. Also, before duplicating or posting any test or quiz for distribution, have it reviewed for typographical errors, double meanings, and other problems by an experienced colleague and also by someone who can read it from the perspective of a student.

**Table 2  A sample table of specifications.** This small table of specifications was created to plan a ten-item quiz on the principles of learning. Notice that, here, three items test basic knowledge (definitions), three more test deeper understanding, and four test students' ability to apply what they know about the concepts tested. Many teachers create tables like this one using Bloom's revised taxonomy of cognitive skills (Anderson & Krathwohl, 2001; Bloom, Englehart, Furst, Hill, & Krathwohl, 1956; Jacobs & Chase, 1992)

| Content | Knowledge | Cognitive skills Comprehension | Application |
|---|---|---|---|
| Classical conditioning | 1 | 1 | 2 |
| Shaping | | | 1 |
| Reinforcement | 1 | 1 | |
| Observational Learning | | 1 | |
| Latent learning | | | 1 |
| Cognitive processes | 1 | | |

## Writing Assignments

Making writing assignments will help your students to improve their writing and will help you to better evaluate their knowledge of course material. In small classes, these might include a ten-page term paper, whereas larger enrollments might only permit one-page assignments that can be graded relatively quickly using the analytical approach mentioned earlier. You might assign several of these "mini-papers" to cover a broad spectrum of course material.

As with exams and quizzes, your writing assignments should be tied to your learning objectives, and as already noted, it is essential that you develop grading rubrics for each of them. Discussions of rubrics, and templates for constructing them, are available elsewhere (e.g., Reddy & Andrade, 2010; Stevens & Levi, 2012).

## Applying the Psychology of Learning to Student Evaluation

The fact that most students forget most of what they hear or read in a course within a few weeks or months (e.g., Landrum & Gurung, 2013; Rickard, Rogers, Ellis, & Beidleman, 1988) is consistent with the results of laboratory research on human learning and memory. While there is no way to ensure that students will forever remember everything you teach in your courses, research in cognitive psychology suggests that certain evaluation procedures might help students to retain course information longer and in a more useable format (Ambrose, Bridges, DiPietro, Lovett, & Norman, 2010; Bjork, 1979, 1999).

**Massed versus Distributed Practice.** Long-term retention is improved when students engage in numerous study sessions (*distributed practice*) rather than when they "cram" during a single session on the night before a quiz or exam (*massed practice*) (e.g., Bjork, 1979; Cepeda et al., 2006; Dunlosky, Rawson, Marsh, Nathan, & Willingham, 2013). With this in mind, consider giving enough exams and quizzes that students will be reading and studying more or less continuously. You can also promote distributed practice by including a few unannounced quizzes. If you are concerned that such quizzes will create a stressful classroom atmosphere, consider instead sprinkling your lectures with quick questions about both current content and content from earlier in the course.

**Retrieval Practice: The Testing Effect.** There is overwhelming evidence that the more students practice retrieving information, especially in different settings, the more they will learn and the longer they will retain it (Dunlosky et al., 2013; Karpicke & Blunt, 2011; Roediger & Karpicke, 2006a, 2006b; Rohrer & Pashler, 2010). This *testing effect* occurs even when students receive no feedback on the results of the test (Roediger & Karpicke, 2006a). In other words, frequent testing can promote learning as well as assess it.

**Desirable Difficulties.** Robert Bjork (2013) coined the term *desirable difficulties* to describe training conditions that are difficult for the student, appear to impede performance during training, but result in long-term retention. He argues that to be most effective in the long run, we should intertwine the concepts to be learned rather than teaching them in separate blocks. If material is important, says Bjork, it should not just be "covered" and then dropped; it should be presented throughout the course and interwoven with other concepts.

You can take advantage of desirable difficulties by giving cumulative exams and quizzes that require students to retrieve information about past as well as current course material. Similarly, you can teach your content as an integrated whole, rather than in separate units. So, in a course on biological psychology, you could present neurotransmission as it relates not only to neural communication, but also to learning, drug effects, stress and coping, and mental disorders. Creating desirable difficulties requires doing things (like cumulative testing and shuffled reading assignments) that students may not like at first, but as in the case of frequent testing, they will accept and even appreciate your research-based methods if you describe them as pathways to long-term retention of information.

**Prompt Feedback.** Learning is enhanced when students receive prompt and constructive feedback that helps them to identify and correct their mistakes (e.g., Chickering & Gamson, 1987, 1991; Dinham, 1996). If many days, or even weeks, pass between taking a test and receiving feedback on it, an important learning opportunity will have been missed. At the very least, you should describe and discuss in class the most frequently missed items (on multiple-choice and short-answer tests) and the most misunderstood concepts on essay tests. You should also offer to have individual discussions with students about their exam results and/or provide an opportunity for students to work individually or in groups, in class or outside of class, to find the correct answers and correct their mistakes. This process can help them learn more from the exam they just took and may improve their scores if they are tested on the same material later.

## The First Day of Class

Once you have established your goals for teaching your course, selected your teaching materials, set up your grading system, and created your syllabus, it is time to prepare for the first day of class. The anxiety that you might feel on that day can stem partly from the fact that you are going to be meeting a group of strangers. Once you and your students get to know one another and begin to form a working relationship, class sessions typically become much less stressful, and a lot more enjoyable and productive. Luckily, there are some things you can do both before and during the first class meeting to hasten this process.

### Exploring Your Classroom

Visit each of your classrooms at least a week before the new term begins to familiarize yourself with their layouts and systems. If a room is normally locked, be sure you have the key. Locate the switches for lighting, projection screens, temperature, and anything else that you will need to control during class. Does everything work properly? Is there a podium or table for your notes and other teaching materials and equipment? If you will want to darken the room during audiovisual presentations, be sure that window shades work properly. If you plan to use a chalkboard, dry-erase board, or flip chart, confirm that there is chalk or felt-tipped pens, and just in case, plan to bring your own supply. Finally, be sure that there is enough seating in the room to accommodate all the students enrolled in your class. Contact the appropriate campus office to report any malfunctions or request any items you will need.

If a room is equipped with audiovisual devices, be sure you know how they operate and where spare parts such as projection bulbs are located. If you are not sure about any of these things, contact the campus office that services instructional equipment, and while you are at it, ask for information about Internet passwords, any lock codes needed to access stored equipment, and the like. If you will be using your own projector, laptop computer, or other equipment, check the location of electrical outlets, and decide if you will need an extension cord, perhaps with multiple receptacles. If you plan to stream videos from the Internet, make sure the campus network is fast enough to do so. If it isn't, put the videos on your computer's hard drive. If possible, try out all your presentation slides, videos, and audios to be sure that no hidden problems will interfere with your presentation.

## Establishing Yourself as a Teacher

The first day of class will be your first opportunity to shape your students' perceptions of you, to establish your rules for the course, and to illustrate the kind of classroom environment you want to create. Some teachers assume that students will like them better if, on the first day of class, they merely distribute a syllabus, describe the course's grading system, make a reading assignment, and dismiss the students early. However, this strategy can give the impression that you don't see class time as particularly valuable, that you may not care much about teaching (or them), and that they can expect you to do most of the talking while they sit passively and listen. Like other kinds of first impressions, once formed, these perceptions and expectations are difficult to change (Kassin, Fein, & Markus, 2017). Here are some tips for establishing a more desirable impression.

First, arrive early, with everything you will need for the entire class period, including sample copies of the reading materials you will be assigning. Put your name, and the name and number of your course, on the chalkboard, overhead projector, or computer screen. While waiting for class to begin, greet and chat with students as they enter. These simple things suggest that you care enough about your teaching to show up on time, fully prepared.

Second, once class begins, introduce yourself, and perhaps say a few words about your background, your academic and scholarly activities, maybe even your hobbies and other outside interests. This information helps to establish you as a person as well as a teacher. You might also let your students know how to address you, as Dr., Mr., Miss, Mrs., Ms., Professor, or perhaps by your first name.

Third, distribute your syllabus and go over its most important elements. Once you have covered the course basics, ask for questions by saying something like "OK, what questions do you have for me?" This way of asking conveys your expectations that there will be questions and your interest in answering them. Simply saying "Any questions?" suggests that you hope there are not any. After you invite questions, scan the classroom so as to further demonstrate that you want students to respond. Be sure to wait long enough for students to work up the nerve to raise their hands (believe it or not, some students will be as nervous in addressing you as you are in addressing them!). If no one asks a question, have a few in mind to get the ball rolling, for example, "You might be wondering if the exams are cumulative (or whether attendance is mandatory, or what to do if you have to leave class early, or how to choose a paper topic, or where the lab is)." Then give the answers in a friendly way. In short, if you want your students to feel free to ask questions throughout the course, offer them genuine opportunities to do so on the first day, and then reward them when they respond.

Finally, you can encourage your students to participate actively in your course by planning something for the first day that requires them to do so. For example, if your class is small, ask the students to say a few words about themselves and their interests, perhaps including something about themselves that is unique, or about why chose to take your class. In larger classes, you can ask students to form small groups in which they introduce themselves and their interests, and possibly exchange contact information that could help establish study groups. You can also simply ask students to call out the topics they are most interested in learning about, and then write each one on the classroom display and say a few words about whether, and when, those topics will be covered in the course (McKeachie, 1986).

Another good first-day option is to present some course content. There may not be much time left to do this, but a short preview of particularly interesting material can whet the students' appetite for what you will be covering later. For example, you can present a case study, problem, or controversy and ask the students to form small groups to analyze, solve, or discuss it (Erickson & Strommer, 1991). You might even administer a short quiz designed to test students' knowledge of – or misconceptions about – the content of your course. If you have two minutes left at the end of the first class, ask your students to jot down and turn in their reactions. This little exercise not only shows that you care what your students think, it also provides you with immediate feedback on how the first day went (McKeachie, 1986).

Whatever else you do in that first class, be sure to bring it to an organized conclusion by assuring the students that you will never keep them past the end of the time period, and reminding them of the topic of the next class and the assignment(s) they are to complete for it.

## Developing Your Teaching Style

Just as no two personalities are exactly alike, no two teachers have exactly the same teaching style. In developing yours, you might at first find yourself imitating some of your favorite teachers. That strategy might help to some extent, but in the long run it is best to simply be yourself. Being genuine is a good first step in developing your teaching style, but you will also need to have skill at presenting lectures, asking and answering questions, generating class discussion, and conducting classroom demonstrations and activities.

## Effective Lecturing

Becoming a good lecturer takes some effort, and though there is no guaranteed prescription for achieving this goal, there are some guidelines (e.g., Smith & Valentine, 2012).

First, decide what content you want to cover in each lecture, and then prepare more material than you will need. Overpreparation will assure that you have plenty to talk about if nervousness causes you to speak too quickly, or if some part of the lecture is not working and you decide to skip ahead. Although you should *prepare* a lot of material, don't try to *cover* too much of it in any single class (Zakrajsek, 1998). Remember that students don't learn through lectures alone. They also learn through reading, talking to teachers and fellow students, and doing lab work, class projects, papers, and other activities. So don't feel obligated to rush your lectures in order to cover everything in detail. If you try to do so, you will be exhausted, and your students will be overwhelmed. There is evidence that most students can only comprehend three to five major points in a 1-hour lecture, and four to five major points in a 90-minute lecture (Lowman, 1995). The best lecturers tend to concentrate on those few important points and to present them in several ways to assure that everyone understands.

Second, as you prepare your notes, keep in mind that students' attentiveness is usually high at first but fluctuates over time (Bunce, Flens, & Neiles, 2010; Davis, 2009; Johnstone & Percival, 1976; McKeachie, 1999; Risko et al., 2012; Wilson & Korn, 2007). With this in mind, consider organizing each class period in four to five segments of ten to fifteen minutes each, and plan something near the end of each segment that is likely to recapture attention. For example, pose a problem, a dilemma, a mystery, or a question or assign a class activity. Audiovisual stimuli help hold attention, too, so don't depend on your words alone to hold students' attention. A compelling photo or a dramatic video can bring even day-dreaming students back to class. Remember, also, that you can lose students' interest if you use unfamiliar terms without defining them and showing how they are spelled. To help hold your students' attention as you lecture, scan the room and make eye contact with everyone from time to time. Sprinkle your lectures with vivid, offbeat, or funny examples of, or analogies to, the concept or phenomenon or principle that you are describing. Despite your best efforts, though, you will have a few students who appear bored, fall asleep, or leave class early. This happens to even the best teachers, so don't be too hard on yourself when it happens to you.

Third, as you lecture, be sure that all your students can see and hear you. In larger classes, or if you have a soft voice, you may need a microphone. Don't sit or stand where you can't be seen from certain seats. Moving around the room a bit as you lecture can help you to hold attention, but be aware that rapid or repetitive pacing can be distracting.

It is ideal to present each lecture as a fascinating, spontaneous story, without depending heavily on notes or appearing to give a canned speech. Reaching this level of comfort and smoothness takes time and practice, however, and some people are better at it than others. To help reach your own full potential, present some or all of your lectures to an audio or video recording device, and then review the recordings to identify any mannerisms, vocal patterns, disfluencies, or repetitious words or phrases that might be distracting or annoying. Then repeat all or part of each lecture to see if you can improve it. You will be amazed at how much easier it is to give a lecture in class when it is not the first time you tried it.

As you lecture, keep checking on your students' reactions. Do they appear to understand you or are they confused? Are they "with you" or are they thinking of other things? Students' facial expressions and posture will tell you a lot about their level of interest and involvement, but show your students you care how the lecture is going by stopping now and then to ask something like "OK, what terms have I used that you don't understand?" or "What questions do you have at this point?" or "Am I going too fast? Too slow?" You might also ask a question about something you just talked about; the quality of the students' responses will help you to assess how clearly you presented that content.

Finally, bring each lecture to an organized close by summarizing its key points or asking the students to do so. And don't hesitate to generate some curiosity about your next lecture by offering a "tease" about something it will contain. "Next time, we'll find out how many of you are colorblind."

## Answering and Asking Questions

If your lecturing style lets students know that you truly want them to understand the course material, they will inevitably ask questions. The way you handle those questions can solidify or undermine your relationship with the class. First, listen carefully to each question – without interrupting – to be sure you understand it. Second, reward students for asking questions by looking at them in a friendly way as they speak and perhaps telling them that they have asked a good question. Third, if you can answer the question, do so. If not, don't be afraid to say that you are not sure of the answer. Above all, don't demean the questioner or make up an answer. Instead, promise to provide an answer at the next class or via email to the group. Then keep your promise! Students don't expect you to know everything there is to know about psychology, and they will appreciate your openness and willingness to find answers for them. (You can also encourage the class to do their own research on particularly interesting questions, but don't make it mandatory; otherwise students will perceive the assignment as punishment for asking questions.)

Some new teachers hesitate to ask questions of their students in class for fear that no one will respond. You can minimize this problem by (a) asking questions that students will need some time to think about and (b) as mentioned earlier, giving them enough time (at least five seconds) to think of a response. If your "wait time" is too short, the students will not only find it hard to answer your question but may get the message that you don't really want them to try. It is ideal if all students generate a response, even if they don't verbalize it (Abel & Roediger III, 2018). You can promote this level of engagement by asking everyone to jot down an answer and perhaps giving them a minute or so to share their answer with a classmate before you ask a volunteer to respond. Comparing answers with another student first may make it easier for even relatively shy students to speak up.

## Promoting Class Discussion

Like other classroom skills, learning how to generate discussion of course material takes some practice. Here are just a few guidelines (for more details, see Bernstein, Frantz, & Chew, 2020, and Forsyth, 2003).

First, if discussions of particular topics are planned for certain class sessions, tell your students what reading or other preparation is required. You might also want to hand out a list of questions on which discussion will focus or assign students to write a "one-minute paper" about the discussion topic immediately beforehand to ensure that they have given it at least a minimal amount of thought.

Second, let your students know if there are to be discussion rules – such as about raising hands before speaking. If highly charged topics are to be discussed, you will also want to explain that there is no place in class for racist, sexist, homophobic, or other ad hominem remarks.

Third, begin each discussion with a clear focus. For example, you might start by asking students to comment on or analyze a reading assignment, a newspaper story, a controversial idea, a case study, or a clinical interview. You can pose a specific question about this material, or just ask students to react to it. As the students begin to speak, encourage their participation by nodding your head, making eye contact with the speakers, and, especially in large classes, rephrase what they have said to be sure everyone heard it. If others do not join in, ask the class to react to what has been said. Keep track of key points by silently writing them where everyone can see them, but once the discussion develops, don't feel obligated to respond to every comment – or at least leave plenty of "wait time" before doing so. If you don't dominate the situation, your students will eventually begin to respond to each other. If you fill brief silences with a mini-lecture, discussion will probably dry up (Brookfield & Preskill, 1999).

Fourth, remember that some discussions start more easily in small groups (Erickson & Strommer, 1991). Thus, you might want to divide larger classes into groups of three to six, have them discuss a topic for a while, and then ask a representative from each group to report on the results and invite reactions from other groups.

Finally, end the discussion a few minutes before the end of class period so that you will have time to clear up any misconceptions or misinformation that might have been created, to summarize the most important points raised, and to suggest additional reading or Internet research that will help students follow up on what they have learned.

## Conducting Classroom Demonstrations

Telling students about the course material is important, but the material can be made more memorable if you conduct demonstrations that allow students to experience a concept or phenomenon for themselves. To take just one example, after lecturing about the "blind spot" at the point where the optic nerve exits the human eye, you can take a minute to allow each student to find his or her own blind spot. There are more opportunities than you might think to use demonstrations. Websites associated with many psychology textbooks are filled with ideas and detailed instructions for conducting demonstrations. General tips for using demonstrations can be found in journals such as the Society for the Teaching of Psychology's *Teaching of Psychology,* through its Facebook group, through the PsychTeacher listserv, and by asking colleagues in your department and elsewhere to tell you about demonstrations that they have found useful. Having a large set of demonstrations available can help to maintain student engagement by spicing up and reinforcing the content of virtually every lecture. Just remember to rehearse every new demonstration before trying to use it in class. Procedures that seem simple on paper can be complex and tricky in practice.

## Faculty-Student Relationships

Most students will enter your courses with positive expectations about you and with high hopes of enjoying themselves and doing well. These expectations provide the foundation for a good learning experience and a good teaching experience. The suggestions presented so far should help you build on that foundation by offering a well-organized course in a consistent, planful, and caring manner. But as described earlier, your success as a teacher also depends on creating positive, constructive relationships with your students. Let's now consider some suggestions for doing so, and for preventing and dealing with the relationship problems that can arise.

## The Ethical Use of Teacher Power

Even if you have never taught before, your students will (correctly) perceive you as having power and authority, if for no other reason than that you will be assigning grades. The power differential that pervades all aspects of your relationship with students is valuable because, for one thing, it allows you to conduct your class according to your plan. Students do not want you to abdicate your authority, but it is important that you do not abuse your power (Keith-Spiegel, et al., 1993; Wilson, Smalley, & Yancey, 2012).

For example, it goes without saying that you should not have romantic relationships with your students. Even when initiated with the best of intentions on both sides, such relationships contain inherently coercive elements that can be harmful to students. Further, once the relationship becomes public (as it eventually will), it will undermine your relationship with the rest of the class by raising doubts about your character and the fairness of your grading system.

You should also be careful not to inadvertently impose your political, moral, or religious beliefs upon students. It is all too easy to err in this regard, because the views you express in a lecture or discussion will carry the weight of authority, and students may feel coerced to accept them – or even adopt them – on papers and exams, at least.

You should also try to create a classroom atmosphere in which all your students feel accepted and included. For example, use classroom examples that are diverse enough to let your students know that you don't presume they are all born in your country, heterosexuals, members of your dominant ethnic, racial, and religious groups, or of one particular gender. Avoid even well-intentioned remarks or jokes that are likely to be offensive to any subgroup of students. If you plan small group discussions in class, *assign* students to those groups rather than letting them self-select in a way that might be too homogeneous or that excludes certain individuals based on gender, ethnicity, disability, or whatever. On quiz and exam questions, use ethnically diverse names for hypothetical people and make sure that the examples and terms used are gender balanced and familiar to everyone. For example, students who are not Jewish might be clueless about a test item that refers to a Seder.

## Dealing with Student Requests, Complaints, and Problems

Inevitably, some of your students will come to you with requests, excuses, and problems. How well you are prepared for these encounters and how you handle them is another aspect of your teaching style. Remember, first, that you do not have to accommodate every request or accept every excuse in order to preserve good relationships with your students. If students perceive that you make your decisions carefully, fairly, and reasonably, even an unwelcome outcome need not harm faculty-student rapport. In fact, dealing with students in a firm but fair fashion can go a long way toward reinforcing students' perceptions of you as a caring teacher.

**Student Disabilities.** In the United States, at least, more students than ever are reporting special needs related to learning disabilities, attention deficit hyperactivity disorder, and the like (Vickers, 2010). Accommodating these students typically involves allowing them extra time or providing a distraction-free location in which to take quizzes or exams. Your department administrators and the campus rehabilitation center (if you have one) can provide advice and guidelines about how best to respond to requests from these students.

**Excuses.** When students offer excuses for failing to show up for a class, a quiz, or an exam, or missing the deadline for a term paper or other assignment, take a firm, rational, but caring approach. Accept the excuse, but before offering a make-up exam or other accommodation, ask for verification using a form like the one shown in Table 3. This authoritative solution tends to reduce the number of students who offer phony excuses (Bernstein, 1993).

**Table 3** **Excuse documentation form.** You can use a form like this to help students establish the legitimacy of their excuse for missing an exam. You can create versions of this form for dealing with excuses relating to any academic situation

**Application for a Psychology [course number] Make-Up Examination**
**Fall/Spring/Summer Semester, 20xx**
**[Your Name Here]**

After completing the information requested below and obtaining the necessary signature(s), please return this form to me. Once I have verified the accuracy of the information you have provided, and confirmed that your reason for requesting a make-up exam is acceptable in accordance with the policies of my course, the department, and the university, an alternate exam date, time, and place will be arranged. All make-up exams will take place after the regular exam.

Important note: Unless you are requesting a make-up exam because of a last-minute illness or emergency, this form must be turned in at least 5 days before the date of the regularly scheduled exam. If you miss this deadline you will not be eligible for a make-up exam.

Please provide the following information:
I, _____certify that I am unable to take the Psychology xxx exam scheduled for_____ , 20xx because (please be clear and specific when describing your reason and be sure to obtain a confirming signature):

[Leave about half a page blank here]

Your name:_____       Your signature: _____
Your ID# _____        Your phone number: _____
Your e-mail address:_____
Confirmed by (please print name):_____
Signature: _____
Position or relationship to student:_____
Telephone number:_____
E-mail address:_____

**Complaints About Test Items**. When you return multiple-choice tests or quizzes in class, some students who are unhappy with their scores may shout out questions about items they missed and argue with you about correct answers. This process can create chaos in the classroom and tension in the teacher. To prevent such conflict and maximize student learning, rank the test's items from most-missed to least-missed. Then, after returning the results, tell the class that you will now review the items, beginning with the most-missed. Present the items in large font on your computer display or transparencies, one at a time, and explain why each correct answer is correct. For short quizzes, review all the items. For longer exams, review the 10 to 20 most difficult items – or whatever number you have time to cover; this will address the vast majority of questions; you can invite students to discuss other items during your office hours or by appointment.

**Table 4** A test item review form. Allowing students to submit forms like this one not only eases tension and emotional distress during in-class test reviews, but it lets students know that you will seriously consider their questions, comments, and alternative interpretations about item grading

Request to Review Grading of An Exam Item

Name_____     Student ID #_____
Instructor's Name_____     Section_____
Item #_____     Test Form_____

I believe that response option ____ should also be considered correct because:

[Leave page blank here]


I found supporting evidence on page(s) _____ in the textbook or in the following source below.

If students have questions that are easily answered, answer them. If they raise more involved objections, ask them to fill out and return a test item review form such as the one shown in Table 4. Tell them that you will read all submitted forms and announce your final decisions in class. Typically, only students with well thought-out complaints will take the time to complete these forms. If you decide that a complaint is valid, announce that you will give credit to everyone whose response deserves it. If you reject an appeal, announce that, too, and if you have time, jot a brief response on all review request forms before returning them to the students.

A different version of the same system can be used to handle complaints about grades on essay exams or other written assignments. Here, too, it is important to give your students time to reflect on their grade and your reasons for assigning it before they raise objections (Svinicki, 1998). So ask students to carefully re-read their written work and your comments about it and then – if they still feel you have been unfair or misguided – to resubmit the work along with a detailed statement indicating why you should reconsider your grading decision. Requiring students to carefully evaluate both their writing and your response to it tends to prevent complaints by students who become aware of the mistakes or misstatements that led to the grade they received. At the same time, reading the reasons that students offer when requesting an improved grade gives you the opportunity to thoughtfully reconsider your earlier judgment and to correct any mistakes you might have made.

## Dealing with Student Behavior Problems

Some students occasionally display annoying, disruptive, irresponsible, or otherwise inappropriate behavior. The most common of these "classroom incivilities" involve talking during lectures, making disparaging remarks, failing to silence cell phones, using phones to talk or text, and the like (Bjorklund & Rehling, 2010). It is important to deal with inappropriate behaviors as soon as you detect them and to make your first steps firm, but not extreme (Knepp, 2012). For example, in the case of inappropriate talking, you can ask the offending student if something you said was unclear, you can stroll over near the offender while lecturing, and you can ask individual offenders to discuss the situation with you after class (see Bernstein, Frantz, & Chew, 2020, Goss, 1995, and Mann et al., 1970 for a more detailed list of potential classroom problems and how to deal with them).

Whatever tactics you choose, remember that the way you deal with one student's problematic behavior can have a ripple effect on other students' perceptions of you (Kounin, 1977; Silvestri & Buskist, 2012). If your methods are reasonable and measured, they will solidify your standing as an authoritative, but fair, teacher. If they are excessive, capricious, or abusive, you run the risk of alienating the entire class. If you are in doubt about how to handle particular classroom behavior problems, underreact the first time, and then seek advice from more experienced colleagues about what to do next. If you encounter students whose behavior suggests a mental disorder or other serious problem, seek advice from your campus student counseling center or a local mental health facility.

## Assessing and Improving Your Teaching

Your teaching skills will improve with practice, especially if you collect and pay attention to evaluative feedback on how you are doing. Like the evaluations you give your students, evaluations of your teaching can be *summative* (e.g., end-of-term evaluations designed to "grade" your teaching) or *formative* (e.g., comments from students or others designed to guide your teaching during the term).

## Evaluations by Students

The third or fourth week of classes is an ideal time to ask your students to evaluate your course and your teaching because you will probably have given and returned a quiz or some other graded assignment. Their evaluations need not be elaborate or time-consuming. You can simply ask students to list three things they like about the class so far, three things they don't like, and three things they would like to see changed.

To promote honest and thoughtful responses, be sure to explain that the evaluations are anonymous and that you will use the feedback to improve *this* course as well as your teaching skills in general. You won't want to, or be able to, follow every student recommendation and correct every perceived fault, but after you have read and considered these formative evaluations, take a few minutes in class to thank your students for their comments, discuss their feedback, and explain any changes you will (or won't) be making.

Even the best teachers leave some students dissatisfied, and because new teachers, especially, tend to agonize over negative comments, it is a good idea to review formative comments systematically. Categorize them as Positive Comments, Negative Comments, Suggestions for Improvement, and Factors Beyond My Control. A comment that "lectures are interesting" would go in the Positive Comments category, while "quizzes are difficult" could go in either the Negative Comments or Positive Comments category, depending on how much you want to challenge your students. "I hate having class at 8:00 a.m." would go into the Factors Beyond My Control category. "I wish you would keep a lecture outline on the screen" would go in the Suggestions for Improvement category. Now count the number of students making each kind of statement. If only one person claims the pace of class is too slow, the problem probably lies with that student, so during your class discussion of student feedback, ask whoever made that comment to visit you. If *all* but one student finds the class boring, you will want to consider ways to address the problem. When in doubt about how to respond to student feedback, discuss it with an experienced colleague or someone at your campus instructional development office, if you have one.

## Evaluations by Colleagues

Constructive feedback from more experienced teachers can be of enormous benefit in improving your teaching, so consider asking a colleague to visit one or two of your classes. Meet with the visitor beforehand to describe your goals for the class to be observed, outline and explain the methods you will be using, and identify the aspects of your teaching that you are most interested in improving. After the visit, arrange another meeting to discuss the visitor's observations.

## Self-Evaluation

Watching yourself teach is another valuable way to evaluate your teaching (Centra, 1993), so you might want to arrange to make periodic videos in your classes. Watch these videos in private first, then in the company of a colleague or teaching expert in order to identify your teaching strengths and weaknesses and discuss ideas for improvement.

## Integrating Teaching into Your Academic Life

If this chapter has left you wondering how you will find the time to deal with everything that it takes to be an effective teacher while still meeting all the other academic and nonacademic obligations you face, you are not alone. No matter how much time you plan to devote to teaching responsibilities, it will be less than you need. New teachers, especially, will find that it always takes longer than they think it will to plan class sessions, meet with students (or answer their email), grade exams or papers, set up and administer record-keeping systems, accommodate students with special needs, and the like. As you gain experience and build your arsenal of teaching materials, methods, and systems, teaching will become progressively easier and less time-consuming, though it will never be effortless or without occasional problems.

Teaching can best be integrated into your academic life by following a few basic rules. First, save everything. Don't delete or discard grade rosters, exams, quizzes, papers, student correspondence, the results of student evaluations, or anything else related to a course for at least 2 years and perhaps longer. Having these materials handy may save a lot of time and trouble when a student asks to see a hand-scored paper from the last term or claims that there was an arithmetical error on a final grade.

Second, keep good records about how each class went, not only in terms of what worked and what didn't, but also whether you were ahead or behind the schedule listed in the syllabus. Spend a few minutes after each class marking your class notes to remind yourself what to do, and what not to do, the next time you teach that material or conduct that demonstration. Also note how much material you actually covered during each class, so you can compare it to what you had planned to cover. These few minutes of *post-mortem* reflection can help you to avoid mistakes and fix problems, thus saving time when you start planning the next version of the course. In addition, create a physical or electronic folder for each class session and use it to store the notes, presentation slides, and other materials that you used, or plan to use, for that session. These folders can also be used to file newspaper articles, notes on good examples or interesting applications of concepts, and any other information that will help you to update and freshen each class session the next time it comes around.

Third, create your own versions of the forms presented above for dealing with student excuses and complaints about test items. Developing form-driven routines for handling these matters will not only save you time but also reduce the number of ad hoc decisions that you have to make each time you teach.

Fourth, build a directory of useful phone numbers, email addresses, and websites that will help you to refer students to various kinds of help, to campus services and facilities, and to sources of additional course-related information. Having these handy – and keeping copies on your smartphone as well as at the office – can make discussions and email exchanges with students more efficient and more valuable.

Finally, don't try to re-invent the wheel. Whatever you encounter in your courses – whether it is students calling you at midnight or dogs mating in your classroom – has probably already happened to other teachers. So find a senior mentor in your department, and take advantage of that person's knowledge and expertise. By doing so, and by taking to heart the other advice offered in this chapter, your teaching experience can be one of the most rewarding aspects of your academic life. And if it is, remember to do what you can to pass on what you have learned to those new teachers who, with sweaty palms and hopeful hearts, will follow in your footsteps.

# References

Abel, M., & Roediger, H. L., III. (2018). The testing effect in a social setting: Does retrieval practice benefit a listener? *Journal of Experimental Psychology: Applied, 24*(3), 347–359.

Ambrose, S., Bridges, M., DiPietro, M., Lovett, M., & Norman, M. (2010). *How learning works: Seven research-based principles for smart teaching.* San Francisco, CA: Jossey-Bass.

Anderson, L. W., & Krathwohl, D. R. (2001). *A taxonomy for learning, teaching and assessing: A revision of Bloom's taxonomy.* New York, NY: Longman Publishing.

Angelo, T., & Cross, K. P. (1993). *Classroom Assessment techniques: A handbook for college teachers* (2nd ed.). San Francisco, CA: Jossey-Bass.

Astin, A., & Antonio, A. (2012). *Assessment for excellence: The philosophy and practice of assessment and evaluation in higher education* (2nd ed.). Lanham, MD: Rowman & Littlefield with American Council on Education.

Beers, M., Hill, J., Thompson, C. A., & Tran, P. (2014). La formation dans l'enseignement de la psychologie pour les étudiants de cycle supérieur: les compétences essentielles pour les nouveaux enseignants (Graduate training in the teaching of psychology: Essential skills for new instructors). *Pratiques Psychologiques, 20*(3), 181–196.

Bernstein, D. A. (1993). Excuses, excuses. *APS Observer, 6*, 4.

Bernstein, D. A., Frantz, S., & Chew, S. L. (2020). *Teaching psychology: A step by step guide* (3rd ed.). New York, NY: Routledge.

Bjork, R. A. (1979). An information-processing analysis of college teaching. *Educational Psychologist, 14*, 15–23.

Bjork, R. A. (1999). Assessing our own competence: Heuristics and illusions. In D. Gopher & A. Koriat (Eds.), *Attention and performance XVII. Cognitive regulation of performance: Interaction of theory and application* (pp. 435–459). Cambridge, MA: MIT Press.

Bjork, R. A. (2013). Desirable difficulties perspective on learning. In H. Pashler (Ed.), *Encyclopedia of the mind.* Thousand Oaks, CA: Sage Reference.

Bjorklund, W., & Rehling, D. (2010). Student perceptions of classroom incivility. *College Teaching, 58*(1), 15–18.

Bloom, B. S., Englehart, M. D., Furst, E. J., Hill, W. H., & Krathwohl, D. R. (1956). *Taxonomy of educational objectives: The classification of educational goals.* New York, NY: David Mckay.

Boice, R. (1996). *First-order principles for college teachers: Ten basic ways to improve the teaching process.* Boston, MA: Anker.

Boysen, G. A. (2011). The prevalence and predictors of teaching courses in doctoral psychology programs. *Teaching of Psychology, 38*, 49–52.

Brookfield, S. (2006). *The skillful teacher: On technique, trust, and responsiveness in the classroom* (2nd ed.). San Francisco, CA: Jossey-Bass.

Brookfield, S., & Preskill, S. (1999). *Discussion as a way of teaching: Tools and techniques for democratic classrooms.* San Francisco, CA: Jossey-Bass.

Bunce, D., Flens, E., & Neiles, K. (2010). How long can students pay attention in class? A study of student attention decline using clickers. *Journal of Chemical Education, 87*, 1438–1443.

Buskist, W., Tears, R., Davis, S. F., & Rodrigue, K. M. (2002). The teaching of psychology course: Prevalence and content. *Teaching of Psychology, 29*, 140–142.

Buskist, W. (2013). Preparing the new psychology professoriate to teach: Past, present, and future. *Teaching of Psychology, 40*(4), 333–339.

Centra, J. (1993). *Reflective faculty evaluation: Enhancing teaching and determining faculty effectiveness.* San Francisco, CA: Jossey-Bass.

Cepeda, N., Pashler, H., Vul, E., & Wixted, J. (2006). Distributed practice in verbal recall tasks: A review and quantitative synthesis. *Psychological Bulletin, 132*(3), 354–380.

Chew, S. L., Halonen, J. S., McCarthy, M. A., Gurung, R. A. R., Beers, M. J., McEntarffer, R., & Landrum, R. E. (2018). Practice what we teach: Improving teaching and learning in psychology. *Teaching of Psychology, 45*, 239–245.

Chickering, A., & Gamson, Z. (1987). Seven principles for good practice in undergraduate education. *AAHE Bulletin, 39*(7), 3–7.
Chickering, A., & Gamson, Z. (1991). Applying the seven principles for good practice in undergraduate education. *New Directions for Teaching and Learning, 47*, 1–69.
Davis, S., & Huss, M. (2002). Training graduate teaching assistants. In S. F. Davis & W. Buskist (Eds.), *The teaching of psychology: Essays in honor of Wilbert J. McKeachie and Charles L. Brewer*. Mahwah, NJ: Erlbaum.
Dinham, S. (1996). What college teachers need to know. In R. Menges & M. Weimer (Eds.), *Teaching on solid ground* (pp. 297–313). San Francisco, CA: Jossey-Bass.
Dunlosky, J., Rawson, K., Marsh, E., Nathan, M., & Willingham, D. (2013). Improving students' learning with effective learning techniques: Promising directions from cognitive and educational psychology. *Psychological Science in the Public Interest, 14*(1), 4–58.
Erickson, B., & Strommer, D. (1991). *Teaching college freshmen*. San Francisco, CA: Jossey-Bass.
Erickson, B., Peters, C., & Strommer, D. (2006). *Teaching first-year college students*. San Francisco, CA: Jossey Bass.
Feldman, K. (1998). Identifying exemplary teachers and teaching: Evidence from student ratings. In K. Feldman & M. Paulsen (Eds.), *Teaching and learning in the college classroom* (2nd ed., pp. 391–414). Boston, MA: Pearson Custom Publishing.
Forsyth, D. (2003). *The professor's guide to teaching: Psychological principles and practices*. Washington, DC: American Psychological Association.
Goss, S. (1995). Dealing with problem students in the classroom. *APS Observer, 8*(26-27), 29.
Hativa, N. (2013). *Student ratings of instruction: Recognizing effective teaching*. Charleston, SC: Oron Publications.
Hilton, J. (2003). *You can run but you cannot hide: What every teacher needs to know about copyright*. Presented at the National Institute on the Teaching of Psychology, St. Petersburg Beach, FL.
Jacobs, L., & Chase, C. (1992). *Developing and using tests effectively*. San Francisco, CA: Jossey-Bass.
Johnstone, A., & Percival, F. (1976). Attention breaks in lecture. *Education in Chemistry, 13*, 49–50.
Junn, E. (1994). Experiential approaches to enhancing cultural awareness. In D. Halpern (Ed.), *Changing college classrooms* (pp. 128–164). San Francisco, CA: Jossey-Bass.
Karpicke, J., & Blunt, J. (2011). Retrieval practice produces more learning than elaborative studying with concept mapping. *Science, 333*, 772–775.
Kassin, S., Fein, S., & Markus, H. R. (2017). *Social psychology* (10th ed.). Boston, MA: Cengage Learning.
Keeley, J. W., Ismail, E., & Buskist, W. (2016). Excellent teachers' perspectives on excellent teaching. *Teaching of Psychology, 43*(3), 175–179.
Keeley, J., Smith, D., & Buskist, W. (2006). The teacher behaviors checklist: Factor analysis of its utility for evaluating teaching. *Teaching of Psychology, 33*, 84–91.
Keith-Spiegel, P., Wittig, A., Perkins, D., Balogh, D., & Whitley, B. (1993). *The ethics of teaching: A casebook*. Muncie, IN: Ball State University.
Knepp, K. (2012). Understanding student and faculty incivility in higher education. *The Journal of Effective Teaching, 12*(1), 32–45.
Kounin, J. (1977). *Discipline and group management in classrooms*. Huntington, OH/New York, NY: Robert E. Krieger Publishing Company.
Landrum, R. E., & Gurung, R. A. R. (2013). The memorability of introductory psychology revisited. *Teaching of Psychology, 40*(3), 222–227.
Landrum, R. E., & Stowell, J. R. (2013). The reliability of student ratings of master teacher behaviors. *Teaching of Psychology, 40*, 300–303.
Lowman, J. (1995). *Mastering the techniques of teaching* (2nd ed.). San Francisco, CA: Jossey-Bass.

Lowman, J. (1998). What constitutes masterful teaching. In K. Feldman & M. Paulsen (Eds.), *Teaching and learning in the college classroom* (2nd ed., pp. 503–513). Boston, MA: Pearson Custom Publishing.

Mann, R. D., Arnold, S., Binder, J., Cytrynbaum, S., Newman, B., Ringwald, B., & Rosenwein, R. (1970). *The college classroom: Conflict, change, and learning*. New York, NY: Wiley.

McKeachie, W. J. (1986). *Teaching tips: Strategies, research, and theory for college and university teachers* (8th ed.). Boston, MA: Houghton Mifflin.

McKeachie, W. J. (1999). *Teaching tips: Strategies, research, and theory for college and university teachers* (10th ed.). Boston, MA: Houghton Mifflin.

McKeachie, W. J. (2001). *McKeachie's teaching tips: Strategies, research, and theory for college and university teachers* (11th ed.). Boston, MA: Houghton Mifflin.

Mervis, J. (2001). Student survey highlights mismatch of training, goals. *Science, 291*, 408–409.

Meyers, S. A., & Prieto, L. R. (2000). Training in the teaching of psychology: What is done and examining the differences. *Teaching of Psychology, 27*, 258–261.

Murray, H. (1997). Effective teaching behaviors in the college classroom. In R. Perry & J. Smart (Eds.), *Effective teaching in higher education: Research and practice* (pp. 171–204). New York, NY: Agathon.

Ory, J., & Ryan, K. (1993). *Tips for improving testing and grading*. Newbury Park, CA: SAGE Publications.

Padilla-López, A., de Souza, L. K., Zinkiewicz, L., Taylor, J., Binti Jaafar, J. L. S., & Rich, G. (2018). *Teaching psychology around the world* (Vol. 4). Newcastle Upon Tyne, UK: Cambridge Scholars Publishing.

Reddy, Y., & Andrade, H. (2010). A review of rubric use in higher education. *Assessment & Evaluation in Higher Education, 35*(4), 435–448.

Rickard, H. C., Rogers, R., Ellis, N. R., & Beidleman, W. B. (1988). Some retention, but not enough. *Teaching of Psychology, 15*, 151–152.

Risko, E. F., Anderson, N., Sarwal, A., Engelhardt, M., & Kingstone, A. (2012). Everyday attention: Variation in mind wandering and memory in a lecture. *Applied Cognitive Psychology, 26*(2), 234–242. https://doi.org/10.1002/acp.1814

Roediger, H., & Karpicke, J. (2006a). Test-enhanced learning: Taking memory tests improves long-term retention. *Psychological Science, 17*, 249–255.

Roediger, H., & Karpicke, J. (2006b). The power of testing memory: Basic research and implications for educational practice. *Perspectives on Psychological Science, 1*, 181–210.

Rohrer, D., & Pashler, H. (2010). Recent research on human learning challenges conventional instructional strategies. *Educational Researcher, 39*, 406–412.

Silvestri, M., & Buskist, W. (2012). Conflict in the college classroom: Understanding, preventing, and dealing with classroom incivilities. In W. Buskist & V. Benassi (Eds.), *Effective college and university teaching: Strategies and tactics for the new professoriate* (pp. 135–143). Los Angeles, CA: SAGE.

Smith, D., & Valentine, T. (2012). The use and perceived effectiveness of instructional practices in two-year technical colleges. *Journal on Excellence in College Teaching, 23*(1), 133–161.

Stevens, D., & Levi, A. J. (2012). *Introduction to rubrics: An assessment tool to save grading time, convey effective feedback, and promote student learning* (2nd ed.). Sterling, VA: Stylus Publishing.

Suskie, L. (2018). *Assessing Student Learning: A Common Sense Guide* (3rd ed.). San Francisco, CA: Jossey-Bass.

Svinicki, M. (1998). Helping students understand grades. *College Teaching, 46*, 101–105.

Svinicki, M., & McKeachie, W. (2014). *McKeachie's teaching tips: Strategies, research & theory for college and university teachers* (14th ed.). Belmont, CA: Wadsworth, Cengage Learning.

Teven, J., & McCroskey, J. (1996). The relationship of perceived teacher caring with student learning and teacher evaluation. *Communication Education, 46*, 1–9.

Vickers, M. (2010). Accommodating college students with learning disabilities: ADD, ADHD, and dyslexia. Pope Center on Higher Education. Retrieved from www.popecenter.org/acrobat/vickers-mar2010.pdf.

Walvoord, B., & Anderson, V. J. (2010). *Effective grading: A tool for learning and assessment in college* (2nd ed.). San Francisco, CA: Jossey-Bass.

Weimer, M. (2013a, February 6). Defining teaching effectiveness. *Faculty Focus*. Retrieved from www.facultyfocus.com/articles/teaching-professor-blog/defining-teaching-effectiveness/.

Weimer, M. (2013b). Choosing and using textbooks. *The teaching professor blog*. Retrieved at https://www.facultyfocus.com/articles/teaching-professor-blog/choosing-and-using-textbooks/

Wilson, J. H., Smalley, K. B., & Yancey, C. T. (2012). Building relationships with students and maintaining ethical boundaries. In R. E. Landrum & M. A. McCarthy (Eds.), *Teaching ethically: Challenges and opportunities* (pp. 139–150). Washington, DC: American Psychological Association.

Wilson, K., & Korn, J. (2007). Attention during lectures: Beyond ten minutes. *Teaching of Psychology, 34*, 85–89.

Wimer, D. J., Prieto, L. R., & Meyers, S. A. (2004). To train or not to train; that is the question. In W. Buskist, B. C. Beins, & V. W. Hevern (Eds.), *Preparing the new psychology professoriate: Helping graduate students become competent teachers* (pp. 2–9). Retrieved from: http://teachpsych.org/resources/e-books/pnpp/html/pnpp01.html

Zakrajsek, T. (1998). Developing effective lectures. *APS Observer, 11*, 24–26.

## Recommended Readings

Bernstein, D. A., Frantz, S., & Chew, S. L. (2020). *Teaching psychology: A step by step guide* (3rd ed.). New York, NY: Routledge.

Curzan, A., & Damour, L. (2000). *First day to final grade: A graduate student's guide to teaching*. Ann Arbor, MI: University of Michigan Press.

Davis, B. (2009). *Tools for teaching* (2nd ed.). San Francisco, CA: Jossey-Bass.

Forsyth, D. (2003). *The professor's guide to teaching: Psychological principles and practices*. Washington, DC: American Psychological Association.

Royce, D. D. (2000). *Teaching tips for college and university instructors: A practical guide*. Saddle River, NJ: Prentice Hall.

# First Principles of Instruction Revisited

## 49

M. David Merrill

## Contents

| | |
|---|---|
| Introduction | 1202 |
| Historical Context and Rationale | 1203 |
| Design Issues and Approaches | 1204 |
|     Instructional Design Theory | 1204 |
|     Instructional Goals | 1204 |
|     Elements of Content | 1205 |
|     Instructional Interaction | 1205 |
|     Instructional Strategies | 1206 |
|     Problem-Solving Model | 1206 |
|     Problem-Progression Model | 1210 |
|     First Principles of Instruction | 1211 |
| Evaluation Issues and Approaches | 1214 |
|     Levels of Instructional Strategy | 1214 |
|     Measurement of Complex Task or Problem-Solving Performance | 1216 |
|     Pebble-in-the-Pond Model for Instructional Design | 1217 |
| Core Findings and Current Trends | 1219 |
|     Are First Principles of Instruction Widely Implemented? | 1220 |
|     Do First Principles of Instruction Promote More $e^3$ Instruction? | 1220 |
|     Are First Principles of Instruction Useful to Evaluate Existing Instruction? | 1222 |
| Challenges, Lessons Learned, and Implications | 1223 |
|     Challenges and Lessons Learned in Developing a Prescriptive Instructional Design Theory | 1223 |
|     Implications for Learning and Teaching Psychology | 1224 |
| Teaching, Learning, and Assessment Resources | 1225 |
|     Learning Events Review Rubric | 1225 |
|     Syllabus Review Checklist | 1225 |
| Bibliography | 1225 |
|     Complete Description of First Principles of Instruction | 1225 |
|     Pebble-in-the-Pond Model of Instructional Design | 1228 |
|     Research Support for First Principles of Instruction | 1229 |

M. D. Merrill (✉)
Utah State University, St. George, UT, USA

| | |
|---|---|
| Demo Courses That Were Specifically Developed by Applying First Principles of Instruction | 1230 |
| Cross-References | 1230 |
| References | 1231 |

### Abstract

First Principles of Instruction were introduced by the author in 2002. He asserted that implementation of these principles promotes effective, efficient, and engaging ($e^3$) instruction and that failure to implement these principles results in less effective, less efficient, and less engaging instruction. These principles and their corollaries are Merrill's attempt to develop a prescriptive theory of instructional design. He subsequently elaborated these principles and their implementation in several articles since the initial paper. This chapter brings together some of the more important elaborations of this theory including its historical background and rationale, a summary of the *First Principles of Instruction*, levels of instructional strategy, the challenge of measurement for complex problem-solving performance, the *Pebble-in-the-Pond* model for instructional design based on First Principles of Instruction, assessing the quality of existing instruction, and a summary of some of the research exploring the benefits and constraints of applying the *First Principles of Instruction*.

### Keywords

Instructional design · Instructional design theory · Instructional content · Instructional interaction · Instructional strategies · Problem-solving · Problem-centered · Tell-show-ask-do · DOidentify · DOexecute

## Introduction

As a child, the author's father demonstrated that a beautiful painting could be created using only three colors: red, yellow, and blue. He learned that only a few elements could be combined into complex outcomes. At the end of his undergraduate studies, a class on number theory helped him realize there are many different types of number systems beyond base 10 and that number systems are merely logical systems to help up explain the world around us. In graduate school, a comment by B.F. Skinner provided a guide for the author's professional life. "What I've tried to do," explained Skinner, "is make only a few assumptions and then see how much of human learning we can explain with only these assumptions." The author realized that all the different theories about learning didn't have to agree; that, just like there were many different number systems, there were many different theories of learning; and that, like number systems, these were inventions to help us explain the world. He also realized that just like a painting could be created with only three crayons, effective learning could be explained by combining only a few fundamental elements. Early in his career, it occurred to him that one could build a logical system, a theory, about instruction. This chapter presents his attempt to build such a theory for instructional design (Merrill, 1994, 2017a, b).

## Historical Context and Rationale

In 1972, the invitation to contribute a chapter to Volume 1 of the American Educational Research Association *Annual Review of Research in Education* provided the author with an opportunity to attempt developing a logical system, a theory, about instruction. With one of his first graduate students, Richard C. Boutwell, they proposed a two-dimensional, behavior by content, task classification system. They also proposed a classification of instructional variables for promoting higher cognitive instructional outcomes such as acquiring real-world concepts, e.g., the psychology concepts of positive and negative reinforcement, or executing complex procedures, e.g., putting a dog into a harness for conducting a classical conditioning experiment, or solving a real-world problem, e.g., diagnosing a mentally disturbed client. These constituted their attempt "to make only a few assumptions and then see how [they might be able to unambiguously describe instructional strategies using these classifications]." The remainder of this chapter reviewed instructional research studies using these classifications and instructional variables to describe the instructional strategies involved (Merrill & Boutwell, 1973).

Brigham Young University established an Instructional Psychology PhD program in collaboration with the Instructional Research and Development Laboratory. During the 1970s, many research studies conducted within this PhD program tested hypotheses related to the instructional variables and task classification system identified in Merrill and Boutwell (1973). During this period, BYU was awarded a major research contract from the National Science Foundation to develop a computer-based instruction system called TICCIT, Two-way Interactive Computer-Controlled Instructional Television (Merrill, Schneider, & Fletcher, 1980). The research team agreed to build a system with built-in instructional design based on the instructional variables previously identified. This system was unique in that it implemented learner control not just of content but also of the instructional strategies involved. During this project in consultation with his colleagues, the author attempted to formalize an instructional design theory which was called *Component Display Theory* (Merrill, 1983, 1987a, b, 1994).

Charles Reigeluth published a collection of papers on instructional design theories and models (Reigeluth, 1999), in order to provide an overview on the many kinds of instructional theories that instructional designers need to be familiar with to select the best approach or combination of approaches that they felt were appropriate for their particular instructional situation. The author challenged Dr. Reigeluth suggesting that while these different theories stressed different aspects of instruction and used different vocabulary to describe their model and methods, fundamentally, at a deep level, they were all based on a common set of principles. Dr. Reigeluth kindly suggested that he didn't think that the assumption was correct, but he challenged the author, "if you feel strongly about it that perhaps you should try to find evidence for that assumption."

The author took the challenge and reviewed these instructional design theories to identify prescriptive principles that are common to the various theories. A second purpose for this review was to determine the extent to which *Component Display Theory* principles were consistent with these prescriptive principles. The result was the publication of the often-referenced paper on First Principles of Instruction (Merrill, 2002a). The author has spent the time since in refining his proposition in a series of papers and chapters on First Principles of Instruction (Merrill, 2006a, b, 2007a, b, 2009a, b, 2013, 2020; Francom, Bybee, Wolfersberger, Mendenhall, & Merrill, 2009; Francom, Wolfsberger, & Merrill, 2009; Mendenhall et al., 2006; Merrill & Gilbert, 2008). In 2013, he published his book, *First Principles of Instruction*, that elaborated these principles, provided a set of suggestions for how these principles might be implemented in various models of instruction, and provided a wide variety of instructional samples that illustrate the implementation of First Principles in a wide range of content areas and at different levels of education including training, public schools, and higher education (Merrill, 2013). In 2020, he wrote a revised edition of this book that simplified the presentation to make it more accessible to interested educators (Merrill, 2020).

## Design Issues and Approaches

### Instructional Design Theory

Early in his career, the author determined that there is a difference between learning theory and instructional theory. Learning theory is about what the learner does to acquire some knowledge or skill; instructional theory is about what the instructor does to promote acquisition of some knowledge or skill. Learning theory is descriptive in that it explains how learning occurs. Instructional theory is prescriptive in that it prescribes what the instructor does to promote effective, efficient, and engaging ($e^3$) learning. Instruction is effective to the degree that the learning goals are accomplished by the learner, it is efficient when effective learning occurs in the shortest time possible, and it is engaging when learners demonstrate a desire to learn more. This chapter focuses on instructional design theory and does not attempt to interrelate these two types of theory.

### Instructional Goals

There have been many attempts to identify categories of content or knowledge that can be learned from instruction. Bloom (1956) represented one of the earliest attempts to define a taxonomy of cognitive knowledge to be learned: knowledge, understanding, applying, analyzing, evaluating, and creating. Gagne (1965, 1970, 1977, 1985) identified categories of learning outcomes including verbal association, multiple discrimination, concept learning, principle learning, and problem-solving.

# 49 First Principles of Instruction Revisited

Anderson and Krathwohl (2001) identified four kinds of content or knowledge to be taught: factual knowledge, conceptual knowledge, procedural knowledge, and conditional knowledge. The audience for *First Principles* is instructional designers. The author and his colleagues found that these designers, many of whom are not trained in psychology, often found terms like *concept* or *procedure* difficult to understand. After careful consideration, the author and his colleagues decided to use everyday terms that were easier for these practitioners to grasp. Therefore, *First Principles* identified five kinds of content to be taught: *information-about* (factual knowledge), *part-of* (factual knowledge), *kind-of* (conceptual knowledge), *how-to* (procedural knowledge), and *what-happens* (conditional knowledge) (see Table 1 column 1). These categories of knowledge are appropriate for most subject matter areas and are independent of the specific content of the different areas. Most of the cognitive skills in almost all subject matter areas can be described using these five categories of content or knowledge to be learned.

## Elements of Content

Content can be represented at two levels: a general *information* level and a specific *portrayal* level (see Table 1 row 1). Information applies to many different situations. Portrayals or examples apply to a specific object or situation. Both levels of representation are necessary for $e^3$ learning to occur. Too much instruction is information rich but example poor; that is, we provide lots of information that applies to a wide range of situations, but we fail to provide sufficient specific illustrations of the ideas presented by the information. The cells in Table 1 are the specific content elements representing information and portrayals appropriate for each type of content (see Merrill, 2013, Chapter 3).

## Instructional Interaction

Instructors can provide opportunities for interacting with the content in four different instructional interaction modes: *Tell*, *Show*, *Ask*, and *DO* (Table 2). The interaction

**Table 1** Instructional content

| Knowledge outcome | General information | Specific portrayal |
|---|---|---|
| Information-about | Facts, associations | NA |
| Part-of | Name, description | Location of parts with regard to a specific whole |
| Kind-of | Definition – list of defining property values | Instances – specific examples and non-examples that illustrate property values |
| How-to | Steps and sequence | Illustrate a specific example of the procedure |
| What-happens if | Conditions and consequences | Illustrate a specific example of the process |

**Table 2** Instructional interaction modes

| Demonstration | Tell | Show |
|---|---|---|
| | Provides information | Provides portrayal |
| Application | Ask | DO |
| | Requires recall or recognition of information | Requires using information with a specific portrayal |

mode *Tell* presents information to the student. Information can be presented in many ways: speech, text, graphics, animation, and video. The interaction mode *Show* demonstrates portrayals or specific examples of the information. Portrayals can also be demonstrated in many ways: auditory, text, graphics, animation, and video.

The interaction mode *Ask* requires the learner to remember general information. You are familiar with tests that require learners to remember information. Such remember-tests are a primary way to assess student learning. However, *Ask* fails to assess a learner's ability to recognize a new portrayal, perform a new task, or solve a new problem. The interaction mode *DO* requires the learner to apply the general information to a specific object or situation. The interaction mode *DO* enables the instructor to assess a learner's ability to recognize a new portrayal ($DO_{identify}$), perform a new task ($DO_{execute}$), or solve a new problem (see Merrill, 2013, Chapter 4).

## Instructional Strategies

When instructional interactions are combined with elements of instructional content, they form *instructional events* (see the cells in Table 3). A set of instructional events for a given type of content comprise an *instructional strategy* for teaching a particular kind of knowledge. Thus, each row in Table 3 identifies an instructional strategy for each type of knowledge outcome (see Merrill, 2013, Chapter 5).

## Problem-Solving Model

The study of problem-solving is an important area of psychology, and there had been significant research to investigate how both novices and experts solve problems. This research also investigated how to promote general problem-solving skills in both novices and experts. The model of problem-solving presented here is not an attempt to promote general problem-solving skill but rather an attempt to provide tutorial guidance to help students acquire the skills necessary to solve a specific class of problems important to a given subject matter domain. Relating the learning theory on problem-solving and the instructional prescription for tutoring students in solving a particular class of problems is beyond the scope of this chapter.

A problem-centered approach differs from problem-based learning or case-based learning as they are typically described in the instructional literature (e.g., Savery,

# 49 First Principles of Instruction Revisited

**Table 3** Instructional strategies

|  | Information |  | Portrayal |  |
|---|---|---|---|---|
|  | Tell | Ask | Show | DO |
| Information-about | Tell associations | Ask associations |  |  |
| Part-of | Tell name + description | Ask name + description | *Show* location | DO identify location |
| Kind-of | Tell definition | Ask definition | *Show* examples | DOid identify examples |
| How-to | Tell steps and sequence | Ask steps and sequence | *Show* specific steps in sequence | DOex execute steps in sequence |
| What-happens | Tell conditions + consequence | Ask conditions + consequence | *Show* conditions + consequence | Do predict consequence or Do find missing or faulted conditions |

2006; Tawfik & Kolodner, 2016). A problem-centered approach is much more structured. It involves presenting a specific whole complex problem to the learners, demonstrating successful completion of the problem, providing information plus demonstration plus application for each of the component skills required by the problem, and then showing learners how these component skills apply to the problem. This is a guided approach to problem-solving as recommended by Kirschner, Sweller, and Clark (2006).

Instructional strategies for the different kinds of knowledge outcomes can be combined to form a model for teaching a specific problem-solving skill (Fig. 1). This problem-solving instructional model was constructed by combining the instructional events previously identified and described into a coherent whole that leads to the ability to solve a given class of problem within a specific subject matter domain. A primary component of problem-solving is a set of *conditions* that when true lead to the desired *consequence* or problem solution. We identified this particular type of problem-solving skill as *what-happens*. This *what-happens* component skill requires learners to predict the consequence from a set of conditions or to find faulted or missing conditions when there is an unanticipated consequence.

In order to identify conditions that lead to a problem solution, learners must be able to determine if the condition shares all the necessary *properties* required to lead to the consequence. This *kind-of* component skill is prerequisite to being able to identify the conditions in a problem-solving situation. When conditions are not adequate or missing, then it is necessary for learners to execute *steps* that modify inadequate conditions or supply the missing conditions required for the consequence or problem solution. This how-to component skill is the third component of a problem-solving strategy. However, learners cannot execute appropriate steps until they are able to recognize those properties that characterize an adequate execution of the step such that it produces the desired condition. This is another *kind-of* prerequisite for a model of problem-solving (see Merrill, 2013, Chapter 6).

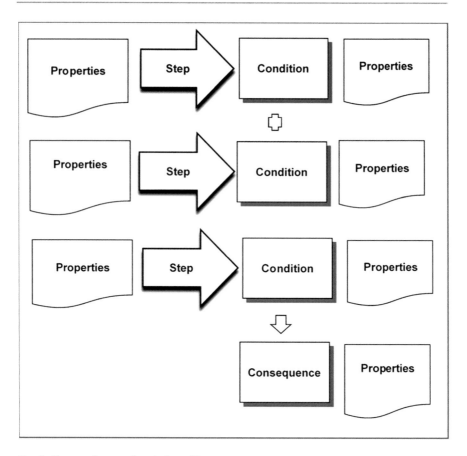

**Fig. 1** Content elements for whole problem

A model of problem-solving requires an integrated combination of at least three different component skills: what-happens, how-to, and kind-of. Some conditions may also require prerequisite information-about or part-of component skills. The demonstration and application required to acquire a problem-solving skill therefore involve the prescriptive strategies for each of the component skills involved in the problem-solving task (see Merrill, 2013, Chapter 6).

Helping a daughter with an eating disorder is an example of a problem-solving task. There are certain conditions, when accomplished, that increase the probability that the daughter can overcome her eating disorder. Figure 2 summarizes the elements of this task. K. Melvin, a nurse who works with eating disorders, suggested the conditions that can lead to overcoming the eating problem: the young woman demonstrates the symptoms of an eating disorder, she recognizes the problem, she accepts treatment, and she undergoes a period of recovery. Teaching this complex problem-solving skill requires several different instructional strategies. The instruction focuses on the steps (how-to) that parents should take that lead to each of the

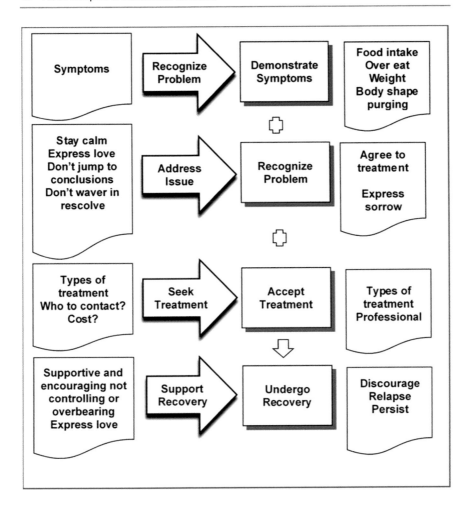

**Fig. 2** Content elements for eating disorder treatment

conditions. The step for the first condition is to recognize the symptoms that indicate that there is a problem. But before the parent can acquire this step, they must first learn to recognize the symptoms when they observe them (kind-of). The properties they need to learn to recognize include dramatic reduction of food intake or excessive overeating, preoccupation with weight or body shape, dramatic weight loss or gain, and evidence of purging behaviors (vomiting, fasting, laxative or diuretic use, over-exercising). Once they recognize that there is a problem, the next step is to address the issue with their daughter to help her acknowledge that she has a problem. The properties for this step are challenging to execute and are oversimplified here for brevity but include express love, stay calm, listen, don't jump to conclusions, and more. When the daughter acknowledges that she has a problem, then the next step is to seek professional treatment. The properties for this step include knowing what types of treatment are available, knowing who to contact, and knowing how to pay for the treatment. When the treatment has concluded, the daughter will be in a period of recovery. The important step for a parent during this recovery period is to provide support. The properties of this support include being supportive and encouraging rather than controlling or overbearing, expressing love, and more.

Helping a daughter overcome an eating disorder is a complex problem-solving task. The presentation here is extremely abbreviated and simplified for our purposes. Hopefully it is sufficient to demonstrate the problem-solving strategy advocated by First Principles of Instruction.

## Problem-Progression Model

Finally, problem-solving models for a progression of increasingly complex problem portrayals can be combined into a model for a problem-centered module or course (see Fig. 3; see Merrill, 2013, Chapter 7).

*First Principle of Instruction* deliberately chose the term problem-centered rather than problem-based. There is a large literature on problem-based learning, but the instructional model from that literature differs with the instructional model illustrated in Fig. 3. (1) In problem-based learning (PBL), learners set their own goals or outcomes; in problem-centered learning (PCL), the instructional outcome is set by the instructional system. For First Principles of Instruction, one of the defining

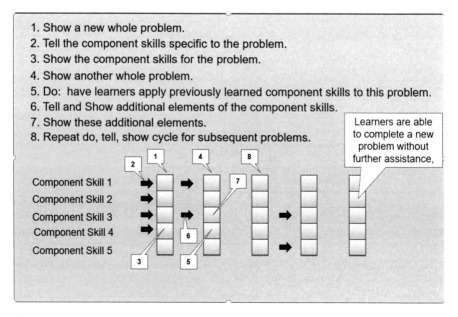

**Fig. 3** Model for problem-centered module or course

characteristics of instruction is that it is goal-oriented. (2) In PBL, students seek for information; in PCL, the information required is provided by the instruction. (3) In PBL, problems must be ill-structured; in PCL, problems can be either ill-structured or well-structured. (4) In PBL, collaboration among student is required; in PCL, collaboration is encouraged but not essential. (5) In PBL, student self-assessment and peer assessment are required; in PCL, student or peer assessment is encouraged but not required. (6) Both stress the need for real-world problems. (For a description of problem-based learning, see Savery, 2006.) Problem-based learning too often provides minimal guidance to students, and research has shown that problem-based learning often fails to accomplish its goals because of this lack of guidance. First Principles of Instruction combines a tutorial guided approach to the teaching of problem-solving in specific knowledge domains (see Kirschner et al., 2006).

## First Principles of Instruction

As a result of his review of instructional design theories (Merrill, 2002a), he identified five general principles of instruction: the activation principle, the demonstration principle, the application principle, the integration principle, and the problem-centered principle (see Fig. 4). Merrill (2007a) analyzed additional research and instructional design theories that provide more conceptual and empirical support for these principles.

Figure 4 arranges these principles to show a cycle of instruction, to indicate that when activation, demonstration, application, and integration are implemented in that order in the context of solving one or more real-world problems, the instruction is more effective, efficient, and engaging in promoting the acquisition of the ability to solve complex problems or complete complex tasks.

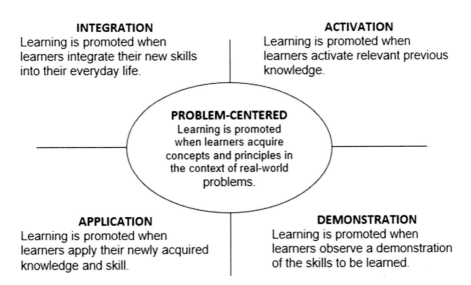

**Fig. 4** First Principles of Instruction

These principles are very general and can be applied in many ways in a variety of instructional situations. Merrill (2002a) identified corollaries for each principle that elaborate additional concepts that need to be considered that restrict the implementation of these principles. Merrill (2007a) identified empirical research that supported and elaborated each of these corollaries and some additional considerations. The following paragraphs, quoted from Merrill (2007a, pp. 65–69), present these corollaries as a series of questions. The following paragraphs also cross-reference the First Principles of Instruction corollaries with the instructional design theory described previously. The reader is encouraged to consult Merrill (2002a, 2007a) for details of the supporting instructional design theories and related empirical research that support these principles and their corollaries.

**Problem-Centered (Let Me Do the Whole Task!)**
- Does the instruction involve authentic real-world problems or tasks?
- In place of a formal objective, does the instruction show the learners the whole task they will be able to do or the whole problem they will be able to solve as a result of completing the instruction?
- Does the instruction teach the components of the problem or task and then help the learner use these components in solving the whole problem or doing the whole task?
- Does the instruction involve a progression of problems not just a single application?

**Activation<!–ITerm100--?> (Where Do I Start?)**
- Does the instruction direct learners to recall, relate, describe, or apply prior knowledge from relevant past experience that can be used as foundation for the new knowledge? If learners have limited prior experience, does the instruction provide relevant experience that can be used as a foundation for the new knowledge?
- Does the instruction help learners see its relevance and to have confidence in their ability to acquire the knowledge and skill to be taught?
- Does the instruction provide or encourage the recall of a structure that can be used to organize the new knowledge?

**Demonstration (Don't Just Tell Me; Show Me!)**
- Does the instruction demonstrate (show examples of) what is to be learned rather than merely telling information about what is to be learned?
- Are the demonstrations (examples) consistent with the content being taught? (see Table 3)
  - Are there examples and non-examples for kinds-of (concepts)?
  - Are there demonstrations for how-to (procedures)?
  - Are there visualizations for what-happens (processes)?
- Are some of the following learner guidance techniques employed?
  - Is learner's attention directed to relevant information?
  - Are multiple representations included and explicitly compared?

- Are learners assisted to relate the new information to the structure that was recalled or provided?
• Are the media relevant to the content and used to enhance learning?

**Application (Let Me Do It!)**
• Do learners have an opportunity to practice and apply their newly acquired knowledge or skill?
• Are the application (practice) and assessment (tests) consistent with the stated or implied objectives? (see Table 3)
  - Does information-about (factual knowledge) practice require learners to recall or recognize information?
  - Does parts-of (factual knowledge) practice require learners to locate, name, and/or describe each part?
  - Does kinds-of (conceptual knowledge) practice require learners to identify new examples of each kind?
  - Does how-to (procedural knowledge) practice require learners to do the procedure?
  - Does what-happens (conditional knowledge) practice require learners to predict a consequence of a process given condition or to find faulted conditions given an unexpected consequence?
• Is the practice followed by corrective feedback and an indication of progress not just right-wrong feedback?
• Does the application or practice enable learners to access context-sensitive help or provide coaching when they are having difficulty in solving the problem or doing the task? Is coaching gradually diminished with each subsequent task until learners are performing on their own?

**Integration (Watch Me!)**
• Does the instruction provide techniques that encourage learners to integrate (transfer) the new knowledge or skill into their everyday life?
• Does the instruction provide an opportunity for the learner to publicly demonstrate their new knowledge or skill?
• Does the instruction provide an opportunity for learners to reflect on, discuss, and defend their new knowledge or skill?
• Does the instruction provide an opportunity for learners to create, invent, or explore new and personal ways to use their new knowledge or skill?

**Implementation**
[Considerations for implementing the instruction, not a First Principle]

• Does the instruction facilitate learner navigation through the learning task?
• Is the degree of learner control appropriate for the learning goals and your learners?
• Is collaboration used effectively?
• Is the instruction personalized?

## Evaluation Issues and Approaches

### Levels of Instructional Strategy

First Principles of Instruction provide a guidance for designing $e^3$ instruction. However, these principles can also be used to assess the $e^3$ potential of existing instruction. The author has had the opportunity to review many courses. Figure 5 illustrates a common instructional sequence that he has observed. You may have also observed this common instructional sequence and may have used a variation of this sequence in your own courses. The course or module consists of a list of topics representing the content of the course. Information about the topic is presented, represented by the arrows. Occasionally a quiz or exercise is inserted to help illustrate the topic, represented by the boxes. The sequence is to teach one topic at a time. At the end of the course or module, there is a culminating final test or in some cases a final project that asks the students to apply the topic to complete some task or solve some problem.

Sometimes this sequence is very effective in enabling students to gain skills or to learn to solve problems. Too often, however, this sequence is ineffective and not engaging for students. The effectiveness of this sequence and the degree of engagement it promotes for learners depend on the type of learning events that are represented by the arrows and the boxes in this diagram.

There are many different types of instructional events (see Table 3). Perhaps the most frequently used instructional event is to present information or *Tell*. This *Tell* can take many forms including lectures, videos, textbooks, PowerPoint presentations, etc. The next most frequent instructional event is to have learners remember what they were told, what they read, or what they saw. This remember instructional event is labeled *Ask*.

If in Fig. 5 the presentation instructional events (arrows) are labeled with *Tell* and the practice or test instructional events (boxes) are labeled with *Ask*, then this module is not going to be very effective and most likely will not prepare learners to

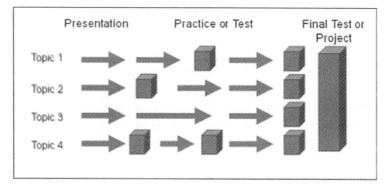

**Fig. 5** Common instructional sequence

adequately complete a project using the content taught. If the last event is an *Ask* final exam rather than a final project, then students may be able to score well on the final exam, but this does little to prepare them to apply the ideas taught to the solution of a complex problem or completion of a complex task.

Merrill (2006a) suggested that applying First Principles one by one provides a scaled set of instructional strategies each one more effective than its predecessor. Bernstein (2018) advocates active learning as contrasted with passive learning but indicates that the question is not just "Does active learning work?" but that a more nuanced comparison is required to indicate the relative contribution of active learning. The following scaled set of instructional strategies represents hypotheses that might help provide insight into active learning. Merrill (2006a) presents these scaled strategies as a series of hypotheses. Following are the scaled hypotheses quoted from Merrill (2006a; pp. 272–279).

Figure 5 representing a *Tell-Ask* instructional strategy is considered an information-only level 0 strategy. Even though it is the least effective and engaging instructional strategy, it is the most commonly used (see Barclay, Gur, & Wu, 2004; Margaryan, Bianco, & Littlejohn, 2015; Merrill, 2020).

Hypothesis 1: A level 1 instructional strategy that adds consistent demonstration to a level 0 information-only strategy promotes a higher performance level on complex tasks [Demonstration Principle].
- Hypothesis 1.1: Adding learner guidance to demonstration promotes an additional increment in the level of efficient and effective performance on complex tasks.
- Hypothesis 1.2: Relevant media included in a demonstration promotes learning efficiency, effectiveness, and engagement. Irrelevant media included in a demonstration results in a decrement in learning efficiency, effectiveness, or engagement.

Hypothesis 2: A level 2 instructional strategy that adds consistent application with corrective feedback to a level 1 instructional strategy consisting of information plus demonstration promotes an additional level of performance on complex real-world tasks [Application Principle].
- Hypothesis 2.1: Adding gradually diminishing coaching to application promotes an additional increment in learning efficiency, effectiveness, and engagement.

Hypothesis 3: A level 3 instructional strategy that consists of a problem-centered instructional strategy that includes consistent demonstration and consistent application with corrective feedback promotes an additional increment in the level of performance on problem-solving and complex tasks [Problem-Centered Principle].
- Hypothesis 3.1: Adding task progression to a task-centered instructional strategy promotes an additional increment in learning efficiency, effectiveness, and engagement.

Hypothesis 4: Providing or recalling relevant experience promotes an additional increment in learning efficiency, effectiveness, and engagement when added to a level 1, level 2, or level 3 instructional strategy [Activation Principle].

Hypothesis 5: Providing activation-structure promotes an additional increment in learning efficiency, effectiveness, and engagement when added to level 1, level 2, or level 3 instructional strategies [Activation Principle].

Hypothesis 6: Adding reflection-integration to any of the above instructional strategies promotes an additional increment in learning efficiency, effectiveness, and engagement [Integration Principle].

Hypothesis 7: Adding create-integration to any of the above instructional strategies promotes transfer of the newly acquired knowledge and skill to performance on similar tasks in the real world beyond the instructional situation [Integration Principle].

Hypothesis 8: Adding go-public-integration to any of the above instructional strategies promotes engagement that in turn promotes an additional increment in learning efficiency, effectiveness, and engagement [Integration Principle].

## Measurement of Complex Task or Problem-Solving Performance

First Principles of Instruction form an integrated set of prescriptions, which are designed to promote the acquisition of all the knowledge and skill necessary for the learner to complete whole, integrated, complex tasks. The common types of measurement that require learners to remember-what-I-told-you, or to perform individual steps in isolation from the whole procedure, or to make isolated predictions from a limited set of circumstances are not sufficient forms of measurement to get at the complexity of real-world tasks or to assess the contributions of instructional strategies based on these First Principles of Instruction. Adequate measurement of performance in complex real-world tasks requires that we can detect increments in performance demonstrating gradually increased skill in completing a whole complex task or solving a whole complex problem (Merrill, 2006a, p. 269). The literature refers to this form of assessment as competency-based assessment, measuring how the learner can perform real-world tasks and solve real-world problems that they will encounter long after the instruction has ended (Hager, Gonczi, & Athanasou 1994).

Three possible approaches for designing scaled measurement of performance in a complex task are briefly described in Merrill (2006a, p 270).

1. Identify a progression of tasks, arranged so that the number or complexity of operations required for completion increases incrementally. The learner then completes the tasks in succession until [he/she] is unable to complete a task. Appropriate scoring measures the highest level in the progression of tasks at which the student completes the whole task in an acceptable manner.
2. For complex tasks that don't lend themselves to a progression, the learners are given a task with various levels of coaching available. When the learner is unable to proceed, the first level of coaching is provided. If the learner has difficulty, the second level of coaching is provided and so forth until the learner is able to complete the task. The score is an inverse of the amount of successively more

elaborate coaching required for the student to solve the problem or complete the task.
3. [A single staged complex task is involved.] "Each stage toward the complete solution requires an incremental increase in expertise . . . . The student is scored on the number of stages completed toward the problem solution."

## Pebble-in-the-Pond Model for Instructional Design

The Pebble-in-the-Pond model of instructional design (Merrill, 2002b, 2007b) was developed to provide a more appropriate approach for designing problem-centered instruction than the more typical ISD model (Dick, Carey, & Carey, 2009). The Pebble-in-the-Pond model of instructional design attempts to overcome of the limitations of the more traditional Instructional Systems Development (ISD) model of instruction design

**Principle-Oriented.** The steps emphasized in the Instructional Systems Development (ISD) procedure are not what lead to an $e^3$ learning consequence; rather, it is the products that these steps produce that are the conditions for the desired learning outcomes. The Pebble-in-the-Pond model prescribes the instructional products that are the conditions that result in an $e^3$ learning consequence.

**Content-First.** A content-first approach designs with the *portrayals of the content* rather than with *information about the content*. The Pebble-in-the-Pond approach begins the design process with a portrayal of an instance of the problem learners will learn to solve. This problem is a portrayal of the goal to be accomplished, rather than an abstract description of the problem and its solution.

**Problem-Centered.** The Pebble-in-the-Pond approach provides a portrayal of an actual problem and a demonstration of its solution that is more easily understood by learners than an abstract statement describing the problem.

**Prototyping.** The Pebble-in-the-Pond model produces a prototype mock-up that includes actual content material and that allows learner interaction with the instructional strategies, rather than an abstract design document.

In the Pebble-in-the-Pond model (Fig. 6), the pebble is an instance of a real-world problem. The resulting ripples are the elements of instructional design. Ripple 1 is a demonstration and application of one instance of the problem. Ripple 2 is a demonstration or application for each instance in a progression of problems. Ripple 3 is a demonstration and application for each of the component skills required to solve the problems. Ripple 4 is strategy enhancement – a structural framework and/or peer interaction. Ripple 5 is design finalization including interface, navigation, and supplemental materials. Ripple 6 is formative evaluation and revision (see Merrill, 2013, Chapter 11, p. 271).

**Designing a problem prototype** includes the following activities:

- Identify the content area, primary goal, and learner population for the instruction.
- Identify a class of problems that, when solved, accomplish the learning goal.

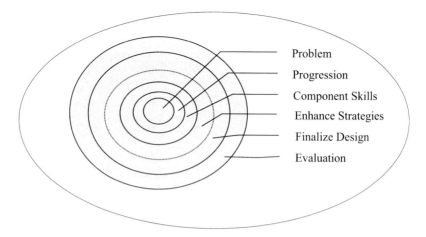

**Fig. 6** Pebble-in-the-Pond instructional design

- Collect a sample of problem portrayals.
- Identify the content elements – consequence, conditions, steps, and properties – of your problems.
- Design a prototype demonstration for a portrayal of the problem.
- Design a prototype application for a portrayal of the problem.

**Designing a problem progression** includes the following activities:

- Design a progression of divergent problem portrayals from simple to complex.
- Identify the component skills required to solve each problem portrayal in the sequence.
- Adjust the progression to include sufficient opportunity for learners to acquire all of the desired component skills.

**Designing component skills** includes the following activities:

- Determine the distribution of demonstration and application for each condition and step required for the portrayals in the progression.
- Based on this strategy distribution, design demonstration and application instructional events for each condition and step of the portrayals in the problem progression.
- Use the Course Critique Checklist to check the adequacy of the instructional strategies you have designed.

**Designing structural framework** enhancement includes the following activities:

- Design a structural framework.
- Design guidance based on this structural framework.

- Design coaching based on this structural framework.
- Design reflection based on this structural framework.

**Designing peer interaction** enhancement includes the following activities:

- Assign peer interaction groups.
- Design peer sharing for activation.
- Design peer discussion for demonstration.
- Design peer collaboration for application.
- Design peer critique for integration.

**Finalize your functional prototype** by completing the following steps:

- Review your course using the Course Critique Checklist.
- Design missing course components.
- Design a title page and introductory learning events.
- Design a structural framework for guidance and coaching.
- Design peer interaction for use with groups of learners.
- Design overall course structure.
- Design an appealing appearance.
- Design unambiguous navigation and directions.
- Design links or supplemental representations for extensive portrayals.
- Design take-away materials for future learner review.

Take the following steps to **implement adequate assessment**:

- Identify assessment opportunities and design response events for gathering learner performance data.
- Design or revise response events to identify specific data that will be collected.
- Design or modify your functional prototype so that it will collect and save learner performance data.
- Conduct ongoing evaluation to acquire learner interaction and performance data including professional review, one-on-one trials, and small group trials.
- Use your evaluation data to engage in ongoing revision of your functional prototype.

## Core Findings and Current Trends

The following papers review the instructional design theories that were reviewed and from which First Principles of Instruction were derived and summarize research support for many of the propositions of First Principles of Instruction: Merrill, 2002a, 2007a; and Merrill, 2013, Chapter 21. Some studies that directly tested First Principles of Instruction are reviewed below (see also

Merrill, 2013, Chap. 22). More recent studies from around the world are referenced at the end of this section.

## Are First Principles of Instruction Widely Implemented?

A study by Barclay et al. (2004) analyzed over 1400 web sites in 5 countries that claimed to provide instruction on marriage relationships. A few of these sites implemented the application principle or the demonstration principle, but most of these sites do not implement any of these principles.

MOOCs are a recent very popular way to deliver instruction. How well do these *massive open online courses* implement First Principles of Instruction? Margaryan and her colleagues (Margaryan et al., 2015) carefully analyzed 76 MOOCs representing a wide variety of content sponsored by several different institutions to determine the extent that these courses implemented First Principles of Instruction. There overall conclusion was that most of these courses failed to implement these principles.

The author reviewed 129 syllabi representing courses taught by 52 faculty members at an International American University (Merrill, 2020). The syllabi were divided into four types: inadequate, typical, instructional, and problem-centered. A typical syllabus often includes remember or ambiguous objectives, a topic-centered schedule, *tell-ask* learning assignments, and a final experience or test. An instructional syllabus includes *DO-identify* or *DO-execute* objectives, a task-centered schedule, *DOid* or *DOex* assignments, and a final activity that required completing *DOid* or *DOex* tasks. A problem-centered syllabus includes problem-centered objectives, a problem-progression schedule, assignments involving solving whole problems or doing whole tasks, and a final activity requiring a doing new whole task or solving a new whole problem. A typical syllabus fails to implement First Principles of Instruction; an instructional syllabus implements levels 1 and 2 from First Principles of Instruction; a problem-centered syllabus implements level 3 from First Principles of Instruction. The findings showed that there were 7 inadequate syllabi, 82 traditional syllabi, 27 instructional syllabi, and 13 problem-centered syllabi. The faculty that submitted instructional and problem-centered syllabi had all participated in workshops provided by the author on First Principles of Instruction.

## Do First Principles of Instruction Promote More e³ Instruction?

A study conducted by NETg, a company that sells instruction to teach computer applications, compared their off-the-shelf version of their Excel instruction, which is topic-centered, with a problem-centered version of this course, which was developed based on First Principles of Instruction. Participants in the experiment came from several different companies that were clients of NETg. The assessment for both groups consisted of developing a spreadsheet for three real-world Excel problems.

The problem-centered group scored significantly higher (89% vs 69%), required significantly less time to complete the problems (29 min vs 49 min), and expressed a higher level of satisfaction than the topic-centered group. All differences are statistically significant beyond the .001 level (Thompson Inc., 2002).

A doctoral student at Florida State University completed a dissertation study comparing a topic-centered course teaching Flash programing with a problem-centered course. This study was carefully controlled so that the variable was merely the arrangement of the skill instruction in the context of problems or taught skill-by-skill. The learning events for both groups were identical except for the order and context in which they were taught. On a transfer Flash problem that required students to apply their Flash programing skills to a new problem, the problem-centered group scored significantly higher than the topic-centered group and felt the instruction was more relevant and resulted in more confidence in their performance. The problem-centered group also reported reduced cognitive load for the transfer task. There was no time difference between the two groups for completing the final project (Rosenberg-Kima, 2012).

Frick and his associates developed an online MOOC (massive open online course) on plagiarism based on First Principles of Instruction (see https://plagiarism.iu.edu). Frick and Dagli (2016) assessed the performance of 2016 students in this course to determine the effect of First Principles of Instruction. Students could study all of part of the tutorials in preparation for the test. An assessment instrument enabled students to indicate which First Principles they experienced during their study of the tutorials. The authors provide the following results:

In the graduate student (GR) group, participants who agreed that they experienced First Principles of Instruction and ALT were about five times more likely to be high masters, when compared to those who did not agree that they experienced First Principles and ALT. Similarly, participants in the high school and undergraduate (H&UG) student group who agreed that they experienced First Principles of Instruction and ALT were about three times more likely to achieve high mastery than did those who did not agree. Moreover, based on the relative contribution of each principle, the H&UG test takers relied more on the demonstration and application principles to achieve mastery, while the GR students tended to experience all First Principles of Instruction; in addition, GR students rated their experience of the authentic problems principle and the integration principle more highly than other First Principles for achieving mastery (Ibid p.271).

The authors conclude that:

> These findings are consistent with Merrill's claims and his prediction that First Principles of Instruction promote learning. Results from Study 1 indicate that employing First Principles of Instruction in the design of MOOCs is likely to yield high-quality instruction and satisfaction with MOOCs, as well as to promote what students learn within MOOCs.

The conclusion that can be drawn from these studies of First Principles of Instruction is that courses based on First Principles do facilitate learning effectiveness, efficiency, and learner satisfaction.

Following is a sample of research studies that implemented First Principles of Instruction in a wide variety of subject matter content and in a number of different countries.

Emamiyan et al. (2016). Ardebil Medical University, Tehran, nursing students divided into experimental and control groups. The experimental group that received instruction that implemented First Principles of Instruction performed better than the control group in both recall and application.

Jalilehvand (2016). Tehran Iran – high school boys. A biology class that implemented First Principles of instruction was compared to a "conventional method" group. Findings indicated that students of the experimental group were better than the control group students in terms of four components of creativity.

Jghamou et al. (2019). University Hassan II de Casablanca. ELECTRE 1 is a method for selecting among various training alternatives. In this approach, the corollaries of First Principles of Instruction are the criteria applied to each pair of training alternatives to determine if they are equivalent or if one is better than the other. This decision tool is then used to select the best training alternatives for two large companies.

Lo and Hew (2017). University of Hong Kong. First Principles of Instruction was used to design two flipped classrooms in mathematics. Significant learning gains are reported for both groups.

Lo, Lie, and Hew (2018). University of Hong Kong. First Principles of Instruction were used to design flipped classrooms. The levels of student achievement were improved in Chinese language, mathematics, and physics.

Nelson (2015). Brigham Young University. Three essential reading texts for museum educators were reviewed to the extent that they included First Principles of Instruction.

Truong, Elen, and Clarebout (2019). Hanoi University, Vietnam. Developed a coding scheme to use to review the extent to which courses implement First Principles of Instruction. They applied this instrument to the analysis of an intensive English language course.

Tu and Snyder (2017). Santa Monica College and Nova Southeastern University. A blended college-level statistic course was designed guided by First Principles of Instruction. The course promoted conceptual understanding in terms of literacy, reasoning, and thinking statistically.

Yorganci (2020). Ataturk University, Turkey. Three courses, e-learning, blended learning, and flipped learning, versions of a mathematics course were designed using First Principles of Instruction. The flipped learning group's achievement scores were higher than the other groups.

## Are First Principles of Instruction Useful to Evaluate Existing Instruction?

Collis and Margaryan (2005a, b) used First Principles of Instruction as a foundation to develop assessment criteria to measure the quality of 60 corporate training courses for a multinational company. They used their First Principles instrument for formative evaluation when courses were being developed and for post-course evaluation for those already developed. They concluded First Principles could "serve as an evaluation framework for quality improvement of training oriented towards business needs and workplace tasks" (p. 734).

Frick and his associates (Frick, Chadha, Watson, Wang, & Green, 2008; Frick, Chadha, Watson, Wang, & Green, 2009; Frick, Chadha, Watson, & Zlatkovska, 2010a, b; Frick & Dagli, 2016; Frick, Watson, Cullen, & Han, 2002) designed a student evaluation questionnaire that had student indicate whether the course being evaluated included First Principles of Instruction. The correlations all show that the extent to which First Principles are included in a course correlates with student rating of instructor quality and their rating of satisfaction with the course. Students also spent more time on task and were judged by their instructors to have made more learning progress when the courses involved First Principles of Instruction.

Tanner (2015) explored "a validation of a First Principles-based rubric as a quality standard, which can be used to measure inherent course quality based on its pedagogical design. This study answers Merrill's (2009a) stated need to verify these principles in a wide variety of settings, audiences, and subject matter domains. This study also sought to examine relationships among accepted measures of expertise and course developers' application of Merrill's (2002a, b, 2009a, 2013) *First Principles of Instruction* to provide further insight into instructional designer expertise, and the possibility of validating existing measures of that expertise" (Tanner, 2015, p. 3).

Tanner found significant correlations between application of First Principles of instruction and self-assessed knowledge of instructional design concepts which included adult learning, multimedia theory, instructional design theory, and level of instructional design knowledge. He found that First Principles of Instruction could be used in instructor-led classrooms, online, and blended (combined lecture and online). He also found that First Principles were more easily applied in some disciplines than others. He concluded that this research validated the use of a First Principles of Instruction rubric (see Merrill, 2009b) as a quality standard for measuring inherent pedagogical quality based solely on the course's design.

## Challenges, Lessons Learned, and Implications

### Challenges and Lessons Learned in Developing a Prescriptive Instructional Design Theory

There are some areas of human expertise that are so pervasive that everyone feels that they can already perform the tasks; all it requires is common sense. After Merrill (2002a, b) was published, it was not uncommon to be told, "I agree with First Principles, I'm already using these principles in my instruction." On some occasions, the speaker would offer the opportunity to review or critique their instruction. In almost every case, my review revealed that what the instructional designer thought was *demonstration* fell far short of what I thought I had described as demonstration and that what the instructional designer thought was "application" failed to meet my criteria for $e^3$ application. Demonstration and application are common words, and many people upon reading these words assume that they know what they mean and thus equate their design activities with these principles. These instructional designers seemed to have skipped or forgotten the corollaries that accompanied these principles. This observation of instruction that was thought to implement First Principles, but failed to do so, was verified by carefully conducted survey studies. These studies attempted to determine the extent to which existing instruction implemented First Principles of Instruction. Each of these survey studies found that most of the courses surveyed did not implement these principles (Barclay et al., 2004; Margaryan et al., 2015; Merrill, 2020).

First Principles is an attempt to present a prescriptive instructional design theory that can be used as a guide for designing or evaluating instruction. To be as precise as possible, a theory must carefully define the concepts and propositions involved. This requires concise and consistent terms referring to these concepts and propositions. In formulating my *Component Display Theory*, I used concise but esoteric terms (*expository generality, inquisitory generality, expository instance, inquisitory instance*) with the hope that these unusual terms would require readers to attend to the referents for these terms without confusing them with more common vocabulary (Merrill, 1983). Readers often complained that there was too much jargon that was difficult to understand or remember. Therefore, in the later versions of this theory, I used everyday terms (*Tell information, Ask information, Show example, Do example*). Because these terms are so common, readers often assume they know what they mean and fail to restrict their meaning to the precise concepts of the theory.

## Implications for Learning and Teaching Psychology

I have not had the opportunity to review the psychology classes in several universities or even all the psychology classes in a single university. However, the reviews of courses to determine the use of First Principles of Instruction cited in this chapter have shown that most of these courses implement only a level 0 instructional strategy. Therefore, I'm confident that a review of psychology courses, except at the highest graduate level, is also most likely to implement primarily a level 0 instructional strategy, that is, they likely do not implement *First Principles of Instruction*. If this is the case, then I'm also confident that adding appropriate demonstration (*show*) and appropriate application (*DO*) would significantly increase the $e^3$ learning outcome of these courses. A recent article in *Psychology Learning & Teaching* (Stark, 2018) described an attempt to introduce more effective *demonstration* via worked examples into a course. This indicates that there is some effort to implement First Principles in the teaching of psychology.

While many of the courses reviewed gave lip service to involve problem-solving, most did not implement a level 3 problem-centered instructional strategy. While problem-based learning is often described in the professional literature (Savery, 2006), the reviews reported in this chapter found that most of the courses reviewed

# 49 First Principles of Instruction Revisited

did not involve problem-solving or when they did it was very inadequately implemented. I'm confident that this may also be true of psychology courses. Implementing a guided problem-centered strategy, especially in introductory classes, will likely increase the $e^3$ learning in these courses. Rumain and Geliebter (2020) describe a "process-oriented guided-inquiry learning-based curriculum for experimental psychology laboratory" which is a good example of implementing a level 3 problem-centered instructional strategy.

## Teaching, Learning, and Assessment Resources

To facilitate the use of First Principles of Instruction, the author provided a set of rubrics for reviewing the adequacy of the instructional events in an existing course or in a course that is under development (Merrill, 2009b). Table 4 is the rubric for demonstration instructional events, and Table 5 is the rubric for application instructional events.

## Learning Events Review Rubric

## Syllabus Review Checklist

Merrill (2020) developed a Syllabus Review Checklist to determine the extent to which the syllabus of a university course reflected the use of First Principles of Instruction. The checklist was accompanied by a documentation which explained and elaborated the items on the checklist. Table 6 is an abbreviated syllabus for a course in Descriptive and Illustrative Drawing. Table 7 is the checklist that was used to review this syllabus.

## Bibliography

The following sources will provide more detailed description, examples, and research supporting First Principles of Instruction.

## Complete Description of First Principles of Instruction

Merrill (2002a, b) The initial paper introducing First Principles of Instruction and citing the instructional design theories on which these principles were based.

    Merrill (2009a) A second look at First Principles of Instruction that tried to present a more complete description of the theory.

    Merrill (2013) My attempt to present a complete description of First Principles of Instruction directed at those who evaluate existing instruction or develop new instruction. One important feature of this book is the many examples illustrating

**Table 4** Demonstration e³ quality rubric

| | Tell | Show | Multimedia | Guide | >3 | Structure |
|---|---|---|---|---|---|---|
| Kinds | Does the demonstration tell learners the name and **definition** of each category? | Does the demonstration show learners **examples** of each category? | Does the demonstration use effective multimedia principles? | Does the demonstration provide guidance by highlighting **discriminating properties** or by showing **matched examples** among categories? | Does the demonstration include at least **three examples** from each category? | Does **guidance** during demonstrations show learners how the defining properties and portrayals relate to an organizing structure? |
| How to | Does the demonstration tell learners the **steps and sequence** in the procedure? | Does the demonstration show a specific instance of the task and **demonstrate each of the steps** required to complete the task? | Does the demonstration use effective multimedia principles? | Does the demonstration provide **guidance** by calling attention to the execution of each step? | Is the procedure demonstrated in a **progression** of at least three increasingly difficult situations? | Does **guidance** during demonstrations show learners how the steps in the procedure relate to an organizing structure? |
| What happens | Does the demonstration tell learners the **conditions and consequence** of the process? | Does the demonstration show the **process** in a specific real or simulated situation? | Does the demonstration use effective multimedia principles? | Does the demonstration provide **guidance** by helping learners relate the events in the process to the conditions and consequence? | Is the demonstration of the process repeated for a **progression** of at least three increasingly complex scenarios? | Does **guidance** during demonstrations show learners how the conditions and consequence relate to an organizing structure? |
| Whole task | Does the demonstration describe a **whole problem** or task indicating some of the major steps involved? | Is the **whole task** or problem demonstrated to the learners? | Does the demonstration use effective multimedia principles? | Are the **component skills** of the whole task demonstrated to learners in the context of the whole task using a problem- or task-centered instructional strategy? | Is there a **progression** of at least three increasingly difficult whole tasks or problems demonstrated to the learners? | Does **guidance** during demonstrations show learners how the steps in the whole task relate to an organizing structure? |

© M. David Merrill

## 49 First Principles of Instruction Revisited

**Table 5** Application e³ quality rubric

| | Ask | Do | Feedback | Coach | >3 | Peer interaction |
|---|---|---|---|---|---|---|
| Kinds | Are learners asked to remember the definition? | Does the application require learners to classify new examples? | Does the application provide corrective feedback that focuses learners' attention on discriminating properties? | Does the application provide coaching early in the sequence and gradually withdraw this coaching as the application continues? | Does the application require learners to classify a series of three or more divergent examples? | Does the application allow for peer collaboration and peer critique? |
| How to | Are learners required to remember the steps in the sequence? | Does the application require learners to do the task by executing each step in a real or simulated situation? | Does the application provide intrinsic feedback and extrinsic feedback? | Are tasks early in the progression coached and is this coaching gradually withdrawn as for successive tasks in the progression? | Does the application require learners to do a simple to complex progression of at least three tasks? | Does the application allow for peer collaboration and peer critique? |
| What happens | Are learners required to remember the conditions and consequence of the process? | Are learners required to predict the consequence? OR are learners required to troubleshoot an unexpected consequence in a specific situation? | Are learners able to receive intrinsic feedback by being able to test their predictions or test their troubleshooting? | Is coaching provided for problems early in the progression and gradually withdrawn as the progression continues? | Are learners required to make predictions or troubleshoot a series of at least three increasingly complex problems? | Does the application allow for peer collaboration and peer critique? |
| Whole task | Are learners asked to remember information about the whole problem or task? | Do learners have to apply the component skills to the completion of a new whole task or problem? | Are learners able to receive intrinsic feedback on their performance by seeing the consequences of their activities? | Is coaching provided for problems early in the progression and gradually withdrawn as the progression continues? | Are learners required to solve a progression of at least three increasingly complex whole problems or tasks? | Does the application allow for peer collaboration and peer critique? |

© M. David Merrill

**Table 6** Syllabus for Descriptive and Illustrative Drawing

**Course Description:** This course introduces students to the fundamental principles of observational and analytical drawing. Various representational and analytical approaches are explored through assignments that encourage the development of skills needed to effectively represent and communicate visual information.

**Learning Outcomes:**
- Comprehend the significance of line as the fundamental element in multimedia and communication.
- Visualize and technically illustrate the characteristics and attributes of lines.
- Display more proficiency in free hand drawing.
- Approach and apply drawing as a universal visual language.
- Demonstrate an increased sense of art appreciation.

**Course Schedule/Topics:**

| Week | Activities | Course materials/tools | |
|---|---|---|---|
| 1 – 2 | Drawing as a fundamental skill in multimedia and communication<br>Unit 1: Basic reasons for drawing and the abilities developed from it<br>Unit 2: Defining the line and analyzing its anatomy<br>Unit 3: Visual rhetoric in line drawing | Derwent tinted charcoal pencil (white) | 2 |
| | | Lily drawing pencil 101 (3B), (4B), (5B), (6B) | 2 each |
| | | Charcoal pencil: Camlin neutral | 2 |
| 3 – 4 | The effects of line<br>Unit 1: The emotional and structural attributes of line, texture, and shape<br>Unit 2: The uses of Lines to express a variety of phenomena<br>Unit 3: Line connotations<br>Unit 4: The study of Facial expressions with lines | White charcoal | 2 |
| | | Gioconda charcoal pencil | 2 |
| | | Surwin 6151 pencil (2B) | 2 |
| | | Staedtler Noris Club pencils (144) assorted color | 1 pk |
| | | Graphite pencils | 2 |
| 5 – 6 | Ways of seeing<br>Unit 1: Laws of composition<br>Unit 2: Mark making with pencil | White drawing cardboards | 10 pc |
| | | Black drawing cardboards | 10 pc |
| 7 – 8 | Understanding perspective<br>Unit 1: The fundamental law of perspective<br>Unit 2: The study of perspective as visual illusion<br>Unit 3: The technique of perspective drawing | Black glossy cardboards | 10 pc |
| | | Drawing pads | 10 |
| | | Erasers | 10 |
| 9 | The characteristics of drawing materials and tools | | |
| 10 | Tonality and the illusion of 3D<br>Unit 1: Common variations in the tonal scale<br>Unit 2: The techniques of tonking and pointillism | **Assessment Criteria:**<br>All drawings and illustrations will be evaluated on the following criteria:<br>• Technical skill and creativity<br>• Originality in approach of visual representation<br>• Clear visual and aesthetic expression<br>• Strong portfolio of exhibition quality. | |
| 11 | Composition in drawing | | |
| 12 | The technique of still life drawing | | |
| 13 | Studies in plant life | | |
| 14 | Studies in figure drawing | | |
| 15 | The study of broad structures | | |

**Required Reading:** Ruskin J. (2001). *The Elements of Drawing*. New York: Dovers Publishers
**Recommended Reading:** . . .

the technical terms, the propositions, and the models of First Principles of Instruction.

Merrill (2020) A revised edition of the 2013 book that attempts to provide a more readable and concise presentation of First Principles of Instruction for Instructional Developers.

## Pebble-in-the-Pond Model of Instructional Design

Merrill (2002b) The initial paper introducing the Pebble-in-the-Pond Model of Instructional Design.

Merrill (2007b) A more complete presentation of the Pebble-in-the-Pond model for instructional design with an example illustrating this development procedure.

Levels of Instructional Strategy

**Table 7** Syllabus Review Checklist for Descriptive and Illustrative Drawing

| Inadequate | Typical | Instructional | Problem centered | | Comments |
|---|---|---|---|---|---|
| | | | | Reviewer Dave Merrill | |
| | | | | Date | |
| | | | | Faculty | |
| | | | | Course  Descriptive and Illustrative Drawing | |
| | | | | **Objectives** | "Comprehend the significance of" is ambiguous; "Visualize and technically illustrate" is DOex; "Display proficiency" is DOex; "Approach and Apply" is ambiguous but might mean DOex in apply. Why are these DOex objectives? Why are they more effective? |
| ☐ | | | | None | |
| | ☒ | | | Remember or ambiguous | |
| | | ☒ | | DOid or DOex | |
| | | | ☐ | Problem-centered | |
| | | | | **Schedule** | Appears to be organized around tasks to accomplish but because only topics are listed rather than assignments we don't know. But the fact that drawing materials are required and that a rubric for evaluating drawings is given leads one to suspect that each of these topic areas involved one or more drawing tasks. What would be a better schedule? |
| ☐ | | | | None | |
| | ☐ | | | Topic-centered | |
| | | ☒ | | Task-centered | |
| | | | ☐ | Problem progression | |
| | | | | **Assignments** | No assignments are listed; this would be a great addition to the schedule. But the fact that materials are required and a rubric for evaluating drawings is given suggests that there are a number of specific tasks required for each of these topic areas. Why would the syllabus significantly improve if these assignments were specified and described? |
| ☐ | | | | None | |
| | ☐ | | | Tell/Ask activities | |
| | | ☒ | | DOid or DOex tasks | |
| | | | ☐ | Whole problem task | |
| | | | | **Final activity** | No indication is given about how grades will be determined, but the rubric suggests that drawings will be evaluated and that they provide the basis for evaluation. Why? How could this syllabus be modified to provide very powerful instructional syllabus? Ans: If the specific drawing assignments were identified and described |
| ☐ | | | | None | |
| | ☐ | | | Final paper and/or test | |
| | | ☒ | | DOid or DOex tasks | |
| | | | ☐ | New problem-solving task | |

**Comments**: Note that this is not problem-centered because it appears that the course consists of a set of individual drawing assignments that may or may not be related to a greater whole. I suspect not.

Merrill (2006a, b) suggests that the application of First Principles is cumulative; as each principle is implemented in succession, the quality of the resulting instruction improves.

## Research Support for First Principles of Instruction

Merrill (2002a) This initial paper that cites the theories and research from which First Principles of Instruction were derived.

Merrill (2007a) This paper takes each of the propositions of First Principles of Instruction and cites research findings supporting each principle.

Merrill (2013) Chapters 21 and 22. These chapters summarize indirect and direct support for First Principles of Instruction.

Checklists for using First Principles of Instruction to evaluate existing instruction or guide development of new instruction.

Merrill (2009b) This paper presented a checklist for using First Principles of Instruction to evaluate the quality of instructional products. The evaluation of Collis and Margaryan (2005a, b) was an expansion and modification of this checklist. The work of Tanner (2015) also concluded that this checklist was a valid tool for assessing the quality of instruction based on IT design.

## Demo Courses That Were Specifically Developed by Applying First Principles of Instruction

- (Francom, Bybee, et al., 2009) Biology 100 course redesigned based on First Principles of Instruction for a general education course in an international university.
- (Mendenhall et al., 2006) Entrepreneur Course based on First Principles of Instruction for college students in developing countries.
- The most successful course designed using First Principles of Instruction is "How to Recognize Plagiarism: Tutorials and Tests" designed and administered by Ted Frick and his associates at Indiana University. In 2016, the original course developed in 2002 was completely revised based on First Principles of Instruction (see https://plagiarism.iu.edu). In September 2019, Dr. Frick provided the following information to me about this course: "FYI, the numbers of students using our plagiarism tutorials and tests (IPTAT) is astonishing—since 2016 we've had over 60 million page views, over 3 million register from over 200 countries, and approaching 600,000 who have passed a Certification Test." In the frequently asked questions associated with this course, they cite the following information: "Undergraduate and advanced high school students are 3 times more likely to pass a Certification Test, if first they successfully do *most or all* of the tutorials. Master's and doctoral students are 5 times more likely to pass, if they complete the tutorials first. Students who do not complete the tutorials and practice tests are between 90 and 95 percent likely to *fail* their first Certification Test."

## Cross-References

▶ Basic Principles and Procedures for Effective Teaching in Psychology
▶ Educational Psychology: Learning and Instruction
▶ Problem-Based Learning and Case-Based Learning

## References

Anderson, L. W., & Krathwohl, D. R. (2001). *A taxonomy for learning, teaching and assessing: A revision of Bloom's Taxonomy of educational objectives*. New York, NY: Longman.

Barclay, M. W., Gur, B., & Wu, C. (2004). The impact of media on the family: Assessing the availability and Quality of instruction on the World Wide Web for enhancing marriage relationshjips. In *Paper presented at the World Congress of the Family: Asia Pacific Dialogue, Kuala, Malaysia*.

Bernstein, D. A. (2018). Does active learning work? A good question, but not the right one. *Scholarship of Teaching and Learning in Psychology, 4*(4), 290307.

Bloom, B. S. (1956). *Taxonomy of educational objectives, handbook: The cognitive diomain*. New York, NY: Dvid McKay.

Collis, B. M., & Margaryan, A. (2005a). Design criteria for work-based learning: Merrill's first principles of instruction expanded. *British Journal of Educational Technology, 36*(5), 725–738.

Collis, B. M., & Margaryan, A. (2005b). Merrill plus: Blending corporate strategy and instructional design. *Educational Technology, 45*(3), 54–58.

Dick, W., Carey, L., & Carey, J. O. (2009). *The systematic design of instruction* (7th ed.). Hoboken, NJ: Pearson.

Francom, G., Bybee, D., Wolfersberger, M., Mendenhall, A., & Merrill, M. D. (2009). A task-centered approach to Freshman-level general biology. *Bioscene, Journal of College Biology Teaching, 35*(1), 66–73.

Francom, G., Wolfsberger, M., & Merrill, M. D. (2009). Task-Centered peer-interactive redesign. *TechTrends, 533*, 35–100.

Frick, T., Chadha, R., Watson, C., Wang, Y., & Green, P. (2009). College student perceptions of teaching and learning quality. *Educational Technology, Research and Development, 57*(5), 705–720.

Frick, T., Chadha, R., Watson, C., & Zlatkovska, E. (2010a). Improving course evaluations to improve instruction and complex learning in higher education. *Educational Technology Research and Development, 58*(2), 115–136.

Frick, T., Chadha, R., Watson, C., & Zlatkovska, E. (2010b). *New measures for course evaluation in higher education and their relationships with student learning*. Denver, CO: Paper presented at the annual meeting of the American Educational Research Association. Retrieved from https://www.indiana.edu/~tedfrick/TALQ.pdf.

Frick, T., & Dagli, C. (2016). MOOCs for research: The case of the Indiana University plagiarism tutorials and tests. *Technology, Knowledge and Learning, 21*(2), 255–276. https://doi.org/10.1007/s10758-016-9288-6.

Frick, T., Watson, C., Cullen, T., & Han, S. (2002). 5-Star instructional design evaluation of web-based instruction in medical science. In M. Simonson & M. Crawford (Eds.), *Annual proceedings of selected research and development papers presented at the national convention of the association for educational communications and technology* (Vol. 1, pp. 167–172). Dallas, TX.

Gagne, R. M. (1965, 1970, 1977, 1985). *The conditions of learning and theory of instruction*. New York, NY: Holt, Rinehart & Winston.

Hager, P., Gonczi, A. and Athanasou, J. (1994). General issues about the assessment of competence. Assessment and Evaluation in Higher Education, 19, 1, 3-16.

Merrill, M. D. & Gilbert, C. G.(2008). Effective peer interaction in a problem-centered instructional strategy. *Distance Education, 29*(2), 199–207.

Kirschner, P. A., Sweller, J., & Clark, R. E. (2006). Why minimal guidance during instruction does not work: An analysis of the failure of constructivist discoverym, problem-based, experiential, and inquiry-based teachihng. *Educational Psychologist, 41*(2), 75–86.

Margaryan, A., Bianco, M., & Littlejohn, A. (2015). Instructional quality of massive open online courses (MOOCs). *Computers and Education, 80*, 77–83.

Mendenhall, A., Buhannan, C. W., Suhaka, M., Mills, G., Gibson, G. V., & Merrill, M. D. (2006). A task-centered approach to entrepreneurship. *TechTrends, 53*(3), 84–89.

Merrill, M. D. (1983). Component Display Theory. In C. M. Reigeluth (Ed.), *Instructional design theories and models; An overview of their current status* (pp. 279–333). Hillsdale, NJ: Lawrence Erlbaum Associates.

Merrill, M. D. (1987a). A lesson basded on Component Display Theory. In C. M. Reigeluth (Ed.), *Instructional design theories in action* (pp. 201–244). HIllsdale, NJ: Lawrence Erlbaum Associates.

Merrill, M. D. (1987b). The new Component Display Theory; instructional design for courseware authoring. *Instructional Science, 16*, 19–34.

Merrill, M. D. (1994). *Instructional design theory*. Engle Wood Cliffs, NJ: Educational Technology Publicatiions.

Merrill, M. D. (2002a). First principles of instruction. *Educational Technology Research and Development, 50*(3), 43–59.

Merrill, M. D. (2002b). A pebble-in-the-pond model for instructional design. *Performance Improvement, 41*(7), 39–44.

Merrill, M. D. (2006a). Hypothesized performance on complex tasks as a function of scaled instructional strategies. In J. Elen & R. E. Clark (Eds.), *Handlking complexity in learning environments: Theory and research* (pp. 265–281). Amsterdam, The Netherlands: Elsevier.

Merrill, M. D. (2006b). Levels of instructional strategy. *Educational Technology, 40*(4), 5–10.

Merrill, M. D. (2007a). First principles of instruction: A synthesis. In R. A. Reiser, J. V. Dempsey, R. A. Reiser, & J. V. Dempsey (Eds.), *Trends and issues in instructional design and technology* (Vol. 2, 2nd ed., pp. 62–71). Upper Saddle River, NJ: Merrill/Prentice Hall.

Merrill, M. D. (2007b). A task-centered instructional strategy. *Journal of Research on Technology in Education, 40*(1), 33–50.

Merrill, M. D. (2009a). First principles of instruction. In C. M. Reigeluth & A. Carr (Eds.), *Instructional design theories and models: Building a common knowledge base* (Vol. III, pp. 41–56). New York, NY: Routledge Publishers.

Merrill, M. D. (2009b). Finding e3 (effective, efficient, and engaging) instruction. *Educational Technology, 49*(3), 15–26.

Merrill, M. D. (2013). *First principles of instruction: Identifying and designing effective, efficient, and engaging instruction*. San Francisco, CA: Pfeiffer.

Merrill, M. D. (2017a). A 50+ year search for effective, efficient and engaging instruction. Acquired Wisdom Series (S. Tobis, J. D. Fletcher, & D. Beliner, Eds.). *Educationa Review, 24*. Retrieved from https://doi.org/10.14507/er.v24.2220.

Merrill, M. D. (2017b). A 50+ year search for effective, efficient and engaging instruction. In S. Tobias, J. D. Fletcher, & D. C. Berliner (Eds.), *Educational review: Acquired wisdom: A publication series to preserve and transmit the knowledge and skills of distinguished educational researchers* (Vol. 24, pp. 1–31) Retrieved from edrev.asu.edu.

Merrill, M. D. (2020). A syllabus review check-list to promote problem-centered instruction. *TechTrends, 64*, 105–123.

Merrill, M. D. (2020). First Principles of Instruction: Revised Edition. Association for Educational Communications and Technology.

Merrill, M. D. (2020) First Principles of Instruction, Revised Edition. Association for Educational Communications and Technology

Merrill, M. D., & Boutwell, R. C. (1973). Instructional development: Methodology and research. In F. N. Kerlinger (Ed.), *Review of research in education* (Vol. 1, pp. 95–131). Itasca, IL: F. E. Peacock Publishers.

Merrill, M. D., & Gilbert, C. G. (2008). Effective peer interaction in a pforlbm-centered instructional strategy. *Distance Education, 29*(2), 199–207.

Merrill, M. D., Schneider, E. W., & Fletcher, K. A. (1980). *TICCIT*. Englewood Cliffs, NJ: Educational Technology Publications.

Reigeluth, C. M. (1999). *Instructional design theories and models: A new paradigm of instructional theory* (Vol. II). Mahwah, NJ: Lawrence Erlbaum Associates, Publichers.

Rosenberg-Kima, R. (2012). *Effects of task-centered vs. topic-centered instructional strateghy approaches on problem-solving – Learning to program flash.* Tallahassee, FL: Florida State University. Retrieved from mdavidmerrill.com/.

Rumain, B. & Geliebter, A. (2020) A process-oriented guided-inquiry learning-based curriculum for the experimental psychology laboratory. Psychology Learning & Teaching. online publication ttps://doi.org/10.1177/1475725720905973.

Savery, J. R. (2006). Overview of problem-based learning: Definitions and distinctions. *Interdisciplinary Journal of Problem-Based Learning, 1*, 9–20.

Stark, E. K. R. (2018). Learning scientific explanations by means of worked examples -- promoting psychology students' explanation competence. Psychology Learning & Teaching, 17(2) pp 144-165.

Tanner, R. S. (2015). *Application of first principles of insruction: A correlational study of design expertise and implied course quality.* Capella University. Ann Arbor Michigan: ProQuest LLC.

Tawfik, A. A. , & Kolodner, J. L. (2016). Systematizing Scaffolding for Problem-Based Learning: A View from Case-Based Reasoning. Interdisciplinary Journal of Problem-Based Learning, 10(1). Available at: https://doi.org/10.7771/1541-5015.1608

Thompson Inc. (2002). *Thompson job impact study: The next generation of learning.* Napperville, IL: NETG.

# Problem-Based Learning and Case-Based Learning

## 50

Joerg Zumbach and Claudia Prescher

## Contents

| | |
|---|---|
| Introduction | 1236 |
| Purposes and Rationale | 1238 |
| Design Issues and Approaches | 1240 |
|     Problems and Cases in PBL | 1240 |
|     Structure of the PBL Process | 1241 |
|     Tutoring PBL | 1242 |
|     Small-Group and Self-Directed Learning | 1243 |
|     Scheduling PBL and Other Organizational Issues | 1244 |
|     Grading in PBL | 1245 |
| Evaluation/Research Issues and Approaches in PBL and Their Results | 1246 |
|     Comparison of Efficiency and Effectiveness Between PBL and Traditional Curricula | 1246 |
|     Moderators in PBL Evaluation | 1247 |
|     Comparison Between Different Settings of PBL | 1248 |
|     Meta-review on PBL | 1248 |
| Current Trends | 1248 |
| Challenges, Lessons Learned, and Implications for Learning and Teaching Psychology | 1249 |
| Teaching, Learning, and Assessment Resources Associated with PBL | 1250 |
| Cross-References | 1250 |
| References | 1250 |

### Abstract

Problem-based learning (PBL) is a learner-centered small-group learning approach that supports active learning. This chapter provides core definitions of PBL and other forms of case-based learning. To be precise, several aspects of

---

J. Zumbach (✉)
Department of Educational Research, University of Salzburg, Salzburg, Austria
e-mail: joerg.zumbach@plus.ac.at

C. Prescher
Technische Universität Dresden, Dresden, Germany
e-mail: claudia.prescher@tu-dresden.de

© Springer Nature Switzerland AG 2023
J. Zumbach et al. (eds.), *International Handbook of Psychology Learning and Teaching*, Springer International Handbooks of Education,
https://doi.org/10.1007/978-3-030-28745-0_58

designing PBL are described, such as problem design, process structure, small-group learning, tutoring, and others. Research and evaluation of PBL compared to traditional approaches are summarized mostly based on meta-analyses.

### Keywords

Problem-based learning; Case-based learning; Tutoring; Small-group learning; Active learning

## Introduction

Learning with cases and problem-based learning have a long tradition in teaching psychology, especially concerning clinical and abnormal psychology, but also educational psychology. Case-based learning refers to using cases in teaching and learning. It integrates several instructional approaches such as problem-based learning (PBL) or the case method.

Learning with cases is a stimulating approach that fosters active learning, applied problem-solving, and knowledge transfer. Problem-based learning as a kind of case-based teaching and learning originated in North-American medical schools (Servant & Schmidt, 2016; Wood, 2003). It is a curricular and an instructional format. The introduction of PBL was based on considerations of how to change instructor-led higher education into student-centered higher education. The major rationale for these considerations was based upon observations that instructor-led higher education does not enable active learning and, thus, does not contribute to students' abilities and competences in areas of problem-solving or transfer. Consequently, the Canadian McMaster University decided to change their medical education program by moving away from the lecture-based teaching approach toward PBL (Hillen, Scherpbier, & Wijnen, 2010). At first, approaches of introducing PBL were mostly limited to medical education programs in northern America. In the course of time, it has spread worldwide as an instructional and a curricular approach throughout different disciplines and programs (Koh, 2016).

The basic idea of PBL as an instructional approach is to have small tutor-guided groups solve a problem. This guided process can be described as follows (see also Dolmans & Schmidt, 2010): Students in a small group receive a description of a problem or are presented with a case that they have to solve. First, the group starts analyzing the case/problem including aspects or subproblems that are involved; they are supported by a tutor (Moust, 2010). Then, students contribute to these aspects with their prior knowledge and formulate hypotheses about the problem and possible solutions. Next, these hypotheses and ideas are structured, and students identify open issues they need to work on in order to solve the problem. This process ends with formulating learning objectives. After this small-group session, students work self-directed in order to accomplish these learning objectives by using secondary sources such as literature (e.g., textbooks, Internet resources, etc.), accompanying courses and lectures, and contact with experts. At the beginning of the next tutor-guided small-group meeting, students present their newly acquired knowledge and discuss these contributions in order to solve the case or problem. Finally, the whole process starts all over again by discussing the next problem (Hung & Amida, 2020).

PBL serves as an instructional, small-group learning approach that can be used as a single episode within a larger course or curriculum. However, PBL can also be used on a more general level, such as encompassing a whole curriculum (e.g., Verheggen & Snellen-Balendong, 2010). In this case, desired competences and learning objectives from courses are covered by a sequence of problems allowing students to accomplish these objectives by solving the problems they are presented with. This requires some basic decisions that are crucial to implementing PBL on this level (for an overview see van Berkel, Scherpbier, Hillen, & van der Vleuten, 2010):

- Carefully designing ill-structured problems that contribute to accomplishing the learning objectives. This requires that objectives are merged in a problem or case description.
- Developing a staff or tutor handbook providing background knowledge about the problems, their nature, and underlying learning objectives. This should help tutors to ensure that the core phenomena of problems are correctly addressed.
- Providing required resources for small-group learning by training tutors to guide students rather than to teach them and providing adequate numbers of classrooms.
- Developing class schedules that differ from traditional schedules: As different courses are merged together and self-directed small-group learning is essential, the most important elements of the class schedule are small-group meetings. As these group sessions end up in self-generated learning objectives, enough time for self-directed learning is necessary between these sessions. Accompanying courses (e.g., introductory lectures and courses, skills labs, etc.) have to be arranged around the small-group meeting hours.
- Providing students with resources for self-regulated learning, such as having access to (online) libraries, experts, etc. and eventually trainings in how to apply effective self-directed learning and corresponding cognitive and meta-cognitive learning strategies.
- Adapting assessment strategies and approaches, following the principles of constructive alignment. Therefore, a close coordination of learning objectives, learning activities, and assessment is essential.

However, there are also other types of instructional case-based approaches. They differ in the degree to which they are teacher-led or student-centered. Figure 1 depicts the continuum between teacher-centered and student-centered case-based learning approaches.

Following Barrows (1986), one of these forms is known as lecture-based cases, where students do not actively work on cases or problems. Instead, examples or applications of the instructional material are shown. However, case-based lectures place cases or problems at the beginning of lectures or units within lectures, thereby forming the basis for the respective lecture. During the lecture, theoretical and

**Fig. 1** Teacher-centered and student-centered case-based learning approaches

practical background that helps solve the problem is provided by the instructor. Usually, the lecturer provides the solution to the problem at the end of the lesson. Consequently, student participation increases when using the case method (also known as the Harvard method; see also Henry & Foss, 2015), because students have to prepare for lectures in advance using recommended literature. During the lectures, teachers present cases/problems and actively involve students in solving these cases/problems via direct requests. This approach is similar to flipped classroom approaches. That is, students have to prepare lessons at home using instructor-provided material (e.g., instructional video clips or reading tasks; e.g., Abeysekera & Dawson, 2015). Then, exercises and application of content are done face to face in class. Hence, the modified case method is an approach where multiple case/problem solutions are presented and discussed. However, problem-based learning is more student-centered and two different approaches can be distinguished. On the one hand, basic problem-based learning refers to single or small-group learning where the case/problem initiates the problem-solving process without necessarily discussing the case/problem again after an individual learning phase. On the other hand, this chapter refers to closed-loop reiterative PBL where the full cycle, as described above, is applied. This also involves tutor-guided small-group problem-solving and small-group problem-solving discussions after individual learning phases.

We have to note here that all these approaches are prototypic descriptions of or recommendations on how to design instruction. There are also other instructional approaches that are similar and can be combined with the methods mentioned above, including service learning (that could be also conducted as a PBL format), challenge-based learning, learning by design, and others.

## Purposes and Rationale

Problem-based learning has originally been introduced in order to promote active learning and transfer of learning (see also ▶ Chap. 49, "First Principles of Instruction Revisited," by Merrill, this volume). Some of the design elements making PBL such as active learning approach (e.g., Silverthorn, 2020) are (1) active and applied problem-solving, (2) small-group learning, and (3) instructional guidance.

First, PBL means active problem-solving including knowledge acquisition in applied and meaningful contexts. This means that knowledge acquisition is necessary in order to explain cases or solve problems. Thus, PBL provides situated learning environments that are more likely to promote transfer than learning environments that do not promote active learning.

Second, if conducted properly PBL fosters cognitive, motivational, and affective processes during learning (Gillies, 2007). Concerning these aspects, small groups are stable across time, because small-group composition usually does not change during a term. Within the group, cognitive benefits derive from different aspects (e.g., Mende, Proske, & Narciss, 2021) including learning from other learners who provide information and/or explain things, providing one's own perspectives, activating pre-knowledge, and elaborating on one's own knowledge. These processes of explanation and elaboration are also beneficial from a metacognitive perspective, because reflection on one's knowledge also helps detect need for further elaboration or knowledge acquisition strategies. In addition, communication and argumentation skills are fostered here. From a socio-emotional perspective, stable groups also provide member support and group well-being; hence, they establish a positive-affective learning environment that is also determined by positive interdependency. Finally, the gap between education and professional life is becoming smaller: whereas in professional contexts, working in teams is the standard practice, in educational programs learners are usually working alone. Therefore, PBL also prepares students for careers after educational programs by training and practicing teamwork.

Third, if necessary, instructional guidance is provided by tutors supervising the PBL process. Kirschner, Sweller, and Clark (2006) argue that PBL as self-directed learning environment is not effective due to its explorative character that is not compatible with human cognitive structures. On the other hand, Hmelo-Silver, Duncan, and Chinn (2007) claim that PBL is compatible with humans' cognitive architecture due to its implicit and explicit levels of guidance. In closed-loop reiterative PBL approaches, the process of collaborative problem-solving is highly structured and divides the process up into several stages. In addition, tutors make sure that core learning objectives specified in the curriculum or the syllabus will be identified and accomplished.

From a cognitive perspective, learning with cases and/or problem-solving contributes to learners' development from novices to experts. A basic paradigm that helps explain this transition is the case-based reasoning (CBR) paradigm (Kolodner, 1993, 1997). Concerning expertise research, findings reveal that experts (i.e., people that are regarded as "experts" within their field and have practiced in their area of expertise for about 10 years or more) show different strategies and characteristics than naive or novice persons (Hambrick, 2019). Following CBR, experts possess a huge amount of knowledge within their area of expertise. This knowledge is domain-related, well organized, and characterized by huge mental libraries. During problem-solving, experts retrieve problem-relevant information from these libraries and develop and apply plans in order to solve the problem. New knowledge that is relevant here is indexed and integrated in mental libraries. These indexes also store information about the problem's/case's target and context. When faced with a similar problem, the solution-related case can be found and activated via these cues. Hence, experts are excellent problem-solvers within their domain, enabling them to focus on important aspects of a problem, to use their working memory more efficiently (by means of chunking, based on their prior knowledge), and to activate problem-solving strategies they already have from prior problem-solving (when compared to novices). In sum, PBL supports this process of acquiring case-related knowledge, thereby supporting novice learners on their way to become experts (ten Cate & Durning, 2018).

## Design Issues and Approaches

Case-based learning in psychology classrooms can be fostered in different ways. For instance, closed-loop reiterative PBL can be implemented as a form of case-based instruction. However, there are several aspects related to the design of problems and cases, as well as to structuring, and tutoring PBL processes that need to be considered.

## Problems and Cases in PBL

First, the design of the problem itself is an important factor. Here, the term "problem" is used in a broader sense, because the trigger for problem-solving might not necessarily be perceived as a genuine "problem" by learners. For instance, if a case from clinical or abnormal psychology is presented, students might not really experience the case as a problem but rather as a description (which it actually is). Consequently, the problem as such arises during small-group discourses. Regardless of whether a problem is immediately recognized or not, it forms the core of PBL consequently triggering all subsequent processes of group discussion, work, and self-regulated learning. According to Schmid and Moust (2010), there are four categories of knowledge resulting in four kinds of problem categories:

- Explanatory knowledge (theories) that corresponds with explanation problems
- Descriptive knowledge (facts) and fact-finding problems
- Procedural knowledge (knowledge of how to do things) and strategy problems
- Subjective knowledge (personal convictions or attitudes of the learner that are covered by moral dilemma resolution problems)

Schmidt and Bouhuijs (1980) provide another typology of problems. They distinguish types of action necessary to solve a problem. Thus, they suggest (patient) problems, strategy tasks, action tasks, discussion tasks, and study tasks. According to Schmid and Moust, a problem task requires an explanation that explores and describes the phenomena represented by the problem. A strategy task is defined as an explanation type of assignment, i.e., students are supposed to find explanations for the phenomena described in the story. Learners are expected to take a certain perspective following a "what if" task (e.g., "What would you do if you were in the position of, e.g., the physician, the lawyer, the engineer?"; Schmid & Moust,

2010, p. 4). In contrast, an action task requires an active approach or an activity that involves the students. Discussion tasks focus on students' subjective opinions and the exchange of (different) opinions. Last, study tasks require individual study with textbooks or other resources (Schmidt & Bouhuijs, 1980).

Schmid and Moust (2010) also suggest central design issues for problems, leading to the following core design aspects in Table 1.

Table 1 shows that there are two kinds of aspects: formal and instructional aspects. Formal aspects make it easier for students to get an overview of the problem; however, instructional aspects focus on how to work with the problem. This includes cognitive (e.g., activation of prior knowledge) as well as motivational and scaffolding approaches (e.g., limitation of learning objectives and/or domain).

Problems are "fuzzy" representations of learning objectives and competences students are supposed to accomplish and acquire via successful problem-solving (e.g., Sockalingam, Rotgans, & Schmidt, 2011). Here, the term "fuzzy" means that they do not directly reflect the core objectives but aim at them leaving room for students' self-generated learning goals. Thus, it is crucial that problems are carefully designed in order to match course objectives or curricula so that learners can identify core objectives and work toward reaching them (Hung, 2016; Mpofu, Das, Murdoch, & Lanphear, 1997). This process needs to be supported by tutors, if students are missing core learning objectives.

The presentation format of problems can vary broadly. It ranges from so-called "standardized patients" (i.e., real people introduced or trained to behave following a pre-given script), video cases, text-based cases or problems, simulations, and others (e.g., Yoon et al., 2016).

## Structure of the PBL Process

Closed-loop reiterative PBL is an instructional approach where learners are supported by flexible adaptation of guidance (Schmidt, Loyens, Van Gog, & Paas, 2007). This guidance is warranted by several design issues like the design of problems and cases (see above), by tutors, by other (traditional) courses

**Table 1** Design aspects of problems

| | |
|---|---|
| Formal aspects | A clear title of the problem |
| | A clear body text of the problem |
| | A clear body of providing the instructions and tasks |
| | A clear indication of how to provide the outcome(s) of the problem-solving process |
| Instructional aspects | A clear instruction about what to do with the problem |
| | Activation of and connection to students' pre-knowledge |
| | Activation of curiosity and motivation |
| | Limitation to a small number of learning issues/objectives that are clearly communicated to students |
| | Limitation to certain learning domains that are not too complex in order to understand/learn them within a given time |

accompanying PBL courses, and by structures guiding the PBL process. There are several approaches to structure small-group meetings during small-group learning. One of the most prominent was provided by Schmidt (1983), known as the seven-step method (see also Camp, van het Kaar, van der Molen, & Schmidt, 2014; Van Til & van der Heijden, 2009; there are also other approaches like the five-step approach; e.g., Shyu, 2001). These seven steps are as follows:

Step 1: Clarifying concepts: Facilitating understanding of the problem/case (e.g., if terms are unfamiliar or the text is unclear)
Step 2: Defining the problem: Identifying the main theme; analyzing the problem and recognizing the most important (sub)problems, topics, or phenomena in order to support formulation of subsequent hypotheses
Step 3: Analyzing the problem/brainstorming: Collecting ideas; providing individual answers or explanations and hypotheses to the topics identified and arguments for these answers; activating pre-knowledge; stimulating associative thinking
Step 4: Problem analysis/systematic classification: Discussing thoughts and contributions from the first stages, prioritizing topics and explanations, and agreeing upon the most important hypotheses and preliminary answers/solutions to the problem; organizing and structuring explanations, answers, and ideas, summarizing them under superordinate categories, adding or deleting ideas
Step 5: Formulating learning objectives: Defining the most important open issues and formulating learning objectives; reflecting on the problem and the progress in solving it
Step 6: Individual and self-directed learning: Selecting information resources based on the learning objectives formulated in Step 5; planning the procedure and providing a report
Step 7: Discussing solutions: Providing their insights, correcting each other (if necessary), explaining their thoughts; collaboratively finding problem solutions/explanations; documenting this process and reflecting on it; starting a new cycle with a new problem

This process can be (re)iterative via presenting a sequence of several problems that are based on the prior ones during a course or a curriculum. In addition, these steps are a rough guide, offering possibilities for modified implementation.

**Tutoring PBL**

The PBL process is a structured process for collaborative problem-solving, as described above. In order to maintain the structure of the process and to guide students through it, groups are usually supported by tutors; hence, tutors are facilitators. That is, tutors do not teach; instead, they scaffold and guide students throughout the problem-solving process. Consequently, tutors need a complex set of competences in order to support students in reaching multiple goals at more or less the same time. Though there is a debate on whether tutors should be knowledgeable in the domain(s) of the course or the curriculum (e.g., Zumbach & Spraul, 2007), moderation skills are out of question. Barrows explains (1988, p. 44): "There is no question that the ideal situation is for the tutor to be an expert both as tutor and in the discipline being studied by the students . . . if this is not possible, the next best tutor is the teacher who is good at being a tutor, as described here, though not an expert in the discipline being studied." The combination of both competence in guiding and moderating learner expertise and competence or expert knowledge in the field that is studied seems to be promising. Barrows (1988) also suggests that if it is necessary to choose between a moderator and an expert (without moderation skills), moderation skills should be preferred over content expertise. The worst combination is a tutor "who is an expert in the area of study, but a weak tutor" (p. 44). Further research shows that a combination of domain expertise and tutoring skills is beneficial for student learning and group cooperation (Groves, Régo, & O'Rourke, 2005; Zumbach & Spraul, 2007).

McCaughan (2013) defines a set of skills and activities that a tutor has to accomplish during tutoring, including supporting learners throughout all stages of the learning process. This is done via activities such as scaffolding, pushing students to deeper levels of understanding, not interfering in learners' statements (even if they might not be entirely correct), not acting as an expert or information source, encouraging and stimulating discussions, being responsible for learning with students, encouraging students' progress, supporting metacognitive actions and strategies, supporting reflection, providing feedback, etc. Tutors also ensure that students continue working on the problems' central phenomena or learning objectives. Especially tutors without domain knowledge need support in this field. Therefore, handbooks serve to support these tutors as well as expert tutors. They address the most important issues concerning the respective problem or case.

Another core function of tutors is grading. Besides other approaches of educational measurement, like testing and applied problem-solving, in many PBL programs, tutors also evaluate small-group members. These evaluations are part of leaners' grades (Dodds, Orsmond, & Elliott, 2001; Sa, Ezenwaka, Singh, Vuma, & Majumder, 2019).

## Small-Group and Self-Directed Learning

Problem-based learning is a steady change between collaborative small-group learning and self-directed individual learning. Though there is no consensus on how small or large a small group should be, the group sizes should allow each member of the group to participate and to contribute to the group's progress. There are many advantages and disadvantages to small-group learning. On the one hand, successful group learning leads to positive interdependency of group members (Johnson & Johnson, 2004; Teng & Luo, 2015). On the other hand, social loafing, ganging-up, and other well-known negative types of behavior hinder effective group work (see Johnson & Johnson, 2004 for an overview). Dolmans and Schmidt (2006) summarize different positive aspects of small-group learning during PBL, thereby differentiating cognitive and affective effects. Cognitive effects include activation of prior knowledge, information recall, collaborative knowledge building, causal reasoning or theory building, and conceptual change initiated by cognitive conflict leading to collaborative learning construction. In contrast, positive influence of group discussions on students' interest in the subject matter is an affective effect. Nevertheless, authors also describe negative effects like superficial group discussions caused by lack of motivation. In this case, effective tutoring, providing positive interdependency (e.g., by means of grading – see below – but also by providing appropriate problems/tasks), and a positive affective tone in small-group discussions can contribute to reducing social loafing and enhancing group productivity (Teng & Luo, 2015).

## Scheduling PBL and Other Organizational Issues

When leaving "traditional" formats and medium-size or large classes and switching to PBL, there are not only obstacles from an instructional point of view but also on the organizational level. First, small groups need more space than large groups such as closed rooms or spaces where groups can work without being interrupted. Thus, the infrastructure regarding meeting rooms must be appropriate. Second, small groups need more tutors than one large group with one lecturer. Hence, when introducing PBL, more tutors are needed. Besides faculty-led tutorial groups, there is also research and practice in using students as tutors in groups. Most of these students are from higher classes that are financially rewarded or academically credited for their work. A study by Kassab, Abu-Hijleh, Al-Shboul, and Hamdy (2005) compared student-led versus faculty-led tutorial groups. The study revealed comparable academic outcomes of student- and faculty-tutored groups. Student tutors were rated higher in providing feedback and in understanding students' difficulties in tutorials. Additionally, atmosphere, decision-making processes, and support for the group leader were rated higher in these groups. Johansen, Martenson, and Bircher (1992) report that student teachers act more like colleagues than like superiors. Also, more advanced student tutors are better at enhancing group productivity than less experienced student tutors. Concerning faculty members, student teachers need training for their role as group facilitators (Johansen et al., 1992; Kassab et al., 2005).

Problem- and case-based learning can be integrated into higher education in different ways (see above), including "single-shot" episodes within classes (e.g., PBL as one instructional approach among others in the same class), PBL throughout a whole class/course, or as a curriculum approach. PBL as a curriculum approach includes disintegrating borders between domains and classes in favor of cross-disciplinary PBL. This can be realized via accompanying classes, labs, and other course formats. Hence, moving away from "traditional" class scheduling is necessary. Wong (2003) describes the difference between lecture-based learning and problem-based learning in teaching law as follows: among others, the number of lecture hours was reduced from 28 to 4 h per semester in one field. The University of

York (n.d.) describes their weekly schedule, starting on Thursday with two problems in two tutorial groups, the third problem starting on Friday. Over the weekend and on Monday, there is time for self-directed study. On Tuesday, there is a recap session. Wednesday is again dedicated to self-directed study. On Thursday, there is the last round of tutorial groups with final discussions. Afterward, new problems are introduced and the cycle starts all over again. This example shows how different the schedule of PBL curricula is compared to traditional lecture-based curricula.

## Grading in PBL

Grading is a crucial function in education throughout different stages and forms of formalized education (for an overview see Kubiszyn & Borich, 2007). With regard to PBL as a different instructional format compared to "traditional" classes and curricula, grading and assessment needs to be carefully designed. Here, "constructive alignment" supports planning adequate forms of educational assessment (Biggs, 1996; Deibl, Zumbach, Geiger, & Neuner, 2018). Constructive alignment refers to three basic dimensions in teaching and learning and their interrelationships: learning objectives, instructional approaches, and grading. Aligning these three constructs means that the learning content and its underlying objectives need to be reflected in the didactical/instructional method used and in the way assessment of leaners' performance is designed. That is, these three dimensions of teaching and learning have to match. Having students solve problems from week to week and finally using a multiple-choice exam in order to generate their grades is pointless. Instead, alternative forms of educational assessment need to be applied and combined (Nendaz & Tekian, 1999). For instance, continuous assessment of students during tutorial groups, applied problem-solving exams, and appropriate standardized exams that include measurement of understanding, problem-solving, and transfer are alternative types of assessment that can be used in PBL. Gijbels, Dochy, Van den Bossche, and Segers (2005; see also Nendaz & Tekian, 2009) list a set of assessment methods that are used in different PBL programs: modified essay questions, progress tests, free recall, standardized patient simulations, essay questions, short-answer questions, multiple-choice questions, oral examinations, rating of performance-based testing, and case-based examinations. Modified essay questions refer to standardized questions about problems that are sequentially ordered. That is, after answering a question, students receive new information; then, the next question is asked; and so forth. In progress tests, a large set of standardized questions are developed, addressing course or curriculum objectives. Students can access these questions at several stages of their progress in order to get feedback or to assess their current knowledge on the respective topic. Concerning students' retrieval strategies and knowledge structures, free recall is a possible assessment strategy. Standardized patient simulations serve to assess students' knowledge and clinical skills. Usually, these are judged on the basis of essay, open questions, multiple-choice questions, oral exams, performance ratings, and/or case-based examinations. Case-based examinations are conducted by presenting cases/problems to students and assessment of their declarative as well as procedural knowledge (also by possible combinations of open questions, essays, oral exams, multiple-choice questions, and others; Gijbels et al., 2005).

As these examples reveal, there is a broad range of possibilities, alternatives, and combinations of educational assessment and grading. Nevertheless, despite the lack of general practical recommendations on assessment in PBL settings (Nendaz & Tekian, 1999), from an instructional design perspective, many possibilities open a broad range of methods that support constructive alignment.

## Evaluation/Research Issues and Approaches in PBL and Their Results

Since the introduction of PBL in the 1960s, a huge body of research on this instructional format has evolved. Especially in medical education, many studies have analyzed the difference between "traditional" curricula and PBL programs on student outcomes. Thus, also some meta-analyses (and also a meta-meta-analysis) were published over the years. Almost all these meta-analyses compare effects of PBL with traditional teaching (e.g., lecture-based learning). Within these meta-analyses, four central research areas can be identified:

1. Comparison of efficiency and effectiveness between PBL and traditional learning (teacher-centered, lecture-based) for different disciplines:
   - Mathematics, science, technology, geography, physics, chemistry, English, and life sciences for school level (Batdı, 2014a, b)
   - Medicine (incl. dental medicine and pharmacy) and health sciences in higher education (Colliver, 2000; Galvao, Silva, Neiva, Ribeiro, & Pereira, 2014; Gao et al., 2016; Huang, Zheng, Li, Li, & Yu, 2013; Sayyah, Shirbandi, Saki-Malehi, & Rahim, 2017; Zhang et al., 2018)
   - Medicine and related disciplines in higher education (Dochy, Segers, van den Bossche, & Gijbels, 2003)
2. Moderators that have effects on learning outcomes within PBL like disciplines, PBL methods, types of problems (Dochy et al., 2003; Walker & Leary, 2009)
3. Comparison between different settings of PBL (e.g., digital case scenarios vs. paper case scenarios; Gavgani, Hazrati, & Ghojazadeh, 2015)
4. A meta-review (Strobel & van Barneveld, 2009) addressing basic concepts of learning and their measurement in meta-analyses regarding learning outcomes in PBL

## Comparison of Efficiency and Effectiveness Between PBL and Traditional Curricula

Most meta-analyses in this field are located within higher education addressing medical education. Only the meta-analyses provided by Batdı (2014a, b) address secondary education. Almost all of the reported meta-analyses refer to indicators for performance, such as academic achievement scores (Batdı, 2014a), theoretical and practical knowledge/skills (Huang et al., 2013; Colliver (2000); Dochy et al., 2003; Zhang et al., 2018, Gao et al., 2016), and students grades or examination outcomes (Galvao et al., 2014; Sayyah et al., 2017). Batdı (2014b) reports additional outcomes, like students' attitudes toward PBL. The meta-analyses by Batdı (2014a), Huang et al. (2013), Galvao et al. (2014), Sayyah et al. (2017), Gao et al. (2016), and Zhang et al. (2018) show positive effects of PBL on achievement. Colliver (2000) reports only small effects and only for theoretical knowledge. Dochy et al. (2003) find positive effects on skill acquisition, but slightly negative effects on acquisition of declarative knowledge. Moderate (Batdı, 2014b) or no effects (Galvao et al., 2014) are reported for self-report data (attitudes and subjective evaluation). Despite the fact that single studies as well as the meta-analysis by Dochy et al. (2003) reveal partly negative or no effects of PBL on performance, other meta-analyses show an overall positive effect of PBL compared to traditional curricula (e.g., Galvao et al., 2014; Sayyah et al., 2017).

## Moderators in PBL Evaluation

Two of these meta-analyses tried to identify moderators of effect of PBL. Dochy et al. (2003) as well as Walker and Leary (2009) included studies predominantly in the medical field but also from teacher education, social sciences, allied health, business, engineering, and science. Dochy et al. (2003) examined – among other variables – expertise of students, retention period, and type of assessment in PBL. Students' expertise in the sense of prior knowledge seems to have a limited impact on learning outcomes. Moreover, significant benefits of PBL were only found in the second year of PBL programs. In all other years, from first to fifth, no differences or worse academic performances were identified. Regarding measurement of success, academic performance of PBL compared to traditional programs was worse when assessed immediately after the courses. However, these differences are counterbalanced after a longer period of time concerning declarative knowledge. Further examination of procedural knowledge shows significantly better learning outcomes in PBL programs assessed right after courses and in delayed testing.

Walker and Leary's (2009) meta-analysis included 82 single studies (concentrating on medical education) focusing on moderator analyses in PBL, different problem types, and kinds of assessment. In medical education effect sizes were comparably low ($d = 0.085$). Stronger effects were found in teacher education, social sciences, healthcare, and business studies. Studies in science and engineering revealed small effect sizes or no significant effects. Inconsistencies were found concerning academic performance of PBL programs compared to traditional programs. These inconsistencies regard declarative knowledge and procedural knowledge (principles and application ($d$ from 0.2 to 0.33). Analysis also shows that mainly diagnostic types of problems were used, especially in medical fields. Other types of problems were rarely used, such as design problems, dilemmas, or troubleshooting problems.

Design problems had the strongest effects on learning outcomes, whereas other problem types had small effects, e.g., troubleshooting, diagnosis problems, and dilemmas. Descriptive analysis revealed that closed-loop PBL leads to better academic performance than other PBL methods; however, there are only a limited number of studies mentioning the PBL method used in their examinations.

## Comparison Between Different Settings of PBL

A meta-analysis by Gavgani et al. (2015) compares effects of different PBL settings. They included five studies from the field of medical education comparing paper-based case scenarios with digitally provided scenarios and their impact on clinical reasoning and satisfaction. No differences were found between paper-based cases and digitally provided scenarios on clinical reasoning, but they discovered that satisfaction of students in digital-based learning environments is higher.

## Meta-review on PBL

In their synthesis of meta-analyses on the effects of PBL, Strobel and van Barneveld (2009) examined effects on different levels of educational assessment. They included eight meta-analyses and reviews that were qualitatively analyzed. Strobel and van Barneveld (2009) discovered that the temporal perspective is essential: while traditional teaching approaches focus on immediate effects, PBL focuses on the acquisition of competences from a sustainable perspective. They concluded that PBL supports long-term retention in terms of skill development and satisfaction of students and teachers, whereas traditional approaches contribute to better test performance immediately after courses. Thus, PBL is significantly more effective than traditional instruction in training competent and skilled practitioners and promoting long-term retention of knowledge and skills.

## Current Trends

How will PBL change in the future? Two areas of development regarding PBL are further development of the PBL approach itself and classification and embedding of PBL within larger learning environments.

**Trends Within the PBL Approach** In the original PBL approach, each small learning group is supposed to have a tutor. To make PBL attractive for larger learning groups, the concept of floating tutors has emerged (i.e., one tutor tutoring more than one group at the same time; Salari, Roozbehi, Zarafi, & Tarmazi, 2018). Another trend is to use digital learning environments (cf. Gavgani et al., 2015). This refers to distributed PBL using computer-mediated communication such as videoconferencing and other digital learning scenarios (e.g., simulations). For instance, presenting cases as interactive learning material forms a well-established digital learning environment, especially in the field of medical education. Also, in psychology education cases can be presented using (interactive) video material or simulations.

**Trends Regarding the Framing and Contextualization of PBL** As described above, problem-based learning can be used and designed as learning environment in different ways. There are two major approaches that can be distinguished:
1. PBL as a didactic method that is (partly) used in teaching
2. PBL as a curricular approach

Nevertheless, PBL can also be varied by combining it with other curricular approaches and teaching methods on a group level as well as an individual level (e.g., service learning, project-based learning, challenge-based learning, and others). What these approaches have in common is that PBL requires and stimulates active learning. For example, PBL can be used to stimulate learning processes (e.g., in the sense of challenge-based learning). Embedding learning objectives in applied and relevant contexts leads to sustainable learning processes (and, following Carl E. Wiemann – Nobel Laureate in Physics in 2001 – learning is not a passive process; learning must be active).

## Challenges, Lessons Learned, and Implications for Learning and Teaching Psychology

In conclusion, PBL is an active learning approach that overcomes known problems from traditional teaching (such as inert knowledge) that stimulates active and self-regulated learning. All of these are important prerequisites for the development of professional competence. Therefore, we tested and piloted PBL scenarios in each of our teaching areas (psychology courses for students of psychology and for students in the teacher training program, respectively; e.g., Zumbach, 2003; Hemker, Prescher, & Narciss, 2017). Our experiences show that:

- PBL works well in both analog and digital spaces, as long as adequate support and feedback is provided. This includes support for knowledge communication.
- If people with little prior knowledge take PBL courses, tutors should have expertise in the domain along with moderating skills. If the learners already have a certain amount of prior knowledge, tutors only need to have skills in facilitating small-group learning and in supporting problem-solving.
- Students who have no prior PBL experience should be introduced to the PBL method.
- PBL seminars in the teacher training program for psychology were highly welcomed by students. The exposure to realistic practical problems from the school context was experienced positively. However, one of the challenges of using PBL in teacher education is heterogeneous target groups (e.g., elementary schools, high schools, grammar schools, and vocational schools, each specializing in different school subjects). For these heterogeneous groups of students,

differentiation, e.g., via individualized supporting information and feedback, is absolutely needed.

Our experiences are consistent with the findings of the meta-analyses mentioned above, and they provide encouragement for the use of PBL in psychology education for all audiences.

## Teaching, Learning, and Assessment Resources Associated with PBL

- The interdisciplinary journal of PBL: This journal publishes articles dealing with the study, analysis, or application of PBL. The journal is published twice a year. It is available online for free: https://docs.lib.purdue.edu/ijpbl/
- Challenge-based learning: Provides a framework to work on real-world problems collaboratively and to develop solutions together. The focus is on acquiring and linking knowledge: www.challengebasedlearning.org
- van Berkel, H., Scherpbier, A., Hillen, H., & van der Vleuten, C. (Eds.) (2010). *Lessons from Problem-based Learning*. Oxford: Oxford University Press. Open Access: https://oxford.universitypressscholarship.com/view/10.1093/acprof:oso/9780199583447.001.0001/acprof-9780199583447
- Victorian Curriculum and Assessment Authority (Australia): This side provides suggestions for teaching psychology, e.g., using PBL: https://www.vcaa.vic.edu.au/curriculum/vce/vce-study-designs/Psychology/advice-for-teachers/Pages/Index.aspx
- Yale University: At Yale University's website, PBL is described, and links are provided to examples of problems and cases for various fields: https://poorvucenter.yale.edu/strategic-resources-digital-publications/strategies-teaching/case-based-learning

## Cross-References

▶ First Principles of Instruction Revisited
▶ Service Learning
▶ Small Group Learning

## References

Abeysekera, L., & Dawson, P. (2015). Motivation and cognitive load in the flipped classroom: Definition, rationale and a call for research. *Higher Education Research & Development, 34*(1), 1–14. https://doi.org/10.1080/07294360.2014.934336

Barrows, H. S. (1986). A taxonomy of problem-based learning methods. *Medical Education, 20*, 481–486.

Barrows, H. S. (1988). *The tutorial process*. Southern Illinois University School of Medicine.

Batdı, V. (2014a). A meta-analysis study comparing problem based learning with traditional instruction. *Elektronik Sosyal Bilimler Dergisi, 13*(51), 346–364. https://doi.org/10.17755/esosder.12812

Batdı, V. (2014b). The effects of a problem based learning approach on students' attitude levels: A meta-analysis. *Educational Research and Reviews, 9*(9), 272–276. https://doi.org/10.5897/ERR2014.1771

Biggs, J. (1996). Enhancing teaching through constructive alignment. *Higher Education, 32*, 347–364.

Camp, G., van het Kaar, A., van der Molen, H., & Schmidt, H. (2014). *PBL: Step by step*. Department of Educational Development and Research, Maastricht University.

Colliver, J. A. (2000). Effectiveness of problem-based learning curricula: Research and theory. *Academic Medicine, 75*(3), 259–266.

Deibl, I., Zumbach, J., Geiger, V., & Neuner, C. (2018). Constructive alignment in the field of educational psychology: Development and application of a questionnaire for assessing constructive alignment. *Psychology Learning and Teaching, 17*(3), 293–307. https://doi.org/10.1177/1475725718791050

Dochy, F., Segers, M., Van den Bossche, P., & Gijbels, D. (2003). Effects of problem-based learning: A meta-analysis. *Learning and Instruction, 13*, 533–568.

Dodds, A. E., Orsmond, R. H., & Elliott, S. L. (2001). Assessment in problem-based learning: The role of the tutor. *Annals of the Academy of Medicine Singapore, 30*, 66–70.

Dolmans, D. H. J. M., & Schmidt, H. G. (2006). What do we know about cognitive and motivational effects of small group tutorials in problem-based learning? *Advances in health sciences education, 11*(4), 321–336.

Dolmans, D. H. J. M., & Schmidt, H. G. (2010). The problem-based learning process. In H. van Berkel, A. Scherpbier, H. Hillen & C. van der Vleuten (Eds.), *Lessons from problem-based Learning.* : Oxford University Press. Retrieved 9 Dec. 2020, from https://oxford.universitypressscholarship.com/view/10.1093/acprof:oso/9780199583447.001.0001/acprof-9780199583447-chapter-003.

Galvao, T. F., Silva, M. T., Neiva, C. S., Ribeiro, L. M., & Pereira, M. G. (2014). Problem-based learning in pharmaceutical education: A systematic review and meta-analysis. *The scientific World Journal*. https://doi.org/10.1155/2014/578382

Gao, X., Luo, S., Mu, D., Xiong, Y., Guanjian, L., & Wan, C. (2016). Effects of problem-based learning in paediatric education in China: A meta-analysis. *Journal of Evidence Based Medicine, 9*(3), 136–143. https://doi.org/10.1111/jebm.12190

Gavgani, V. Z., Hazrati, H., & Ghojazadeh, M. (2015). The efficacy of digital case scenario versus paper case scenario on clinical reasoning in problem based learning: A systematic review and meta-analysis. *Research and Development in Medical Education, 4*(1), 17–22. https://doi.org/10.15171/rdme.2015.003

Gijbels, D., Dochy, F., Van den Bossche, P., & Segers, M. (2005). Effects of problem-based learning: A meta-analysis from the angle of assessment. *Review of educational research, 75*(1), 27–61.

Gillies, R. M. (2007). *Cooperative learning: Integrating theory and practice*. Sage.

Groves, M., Régo, P., & O'Rourke, P. (2005). Tutoring in problem-based learning medical curricula: The influence of tutor background and style on effectiveness. *BMC Medical Education, 5*(1), 1–7.

Hambrick, D. Z. (2019). Expertise. In R. Sternberg & J. Funke (Eds.), *The psychology of human thought: An introduction* (pp. 235–254). Heidelberg University Press.

Hemker, L., Prescher, C., & Narciss, S. (2017). Design and evaluation of a problem-based learning environment for teacher training. *Interdisciplinary Journal of Problem-Based Learning, 11*(2), 10. https://docs.lib.purdue.edu/ijpbl/vol11/iss2/10/

Henry, C., & Foss, L. (2015). Case sensitive? A review of the literature on the use of case method in entrepreneurship research. *International Journal of Entrepreneurial Behaviour & Research, 21*(3), 389–409.

Hillen, H., Scherpbier, A., & Wijnen, W. (2010). *History of problem-based learning in medical education.* Retrieved 9 Dec. 2020, from https://oxford.universitypressscholarship.com/view/10.1093/acprof:oso/9780199583447.001.0001/acprof-9780199583447-chapter-002.

Hmelo-Silver, C. E., Duncan, R. G., & Chinn, C. A. (2007). Scaffolding and achievement in problem-based and inquiry learning: A response to Kirschner, Sweller, and Clark. *Educational Psychologist, 42*(2), 99–107.

Huang, B., Zheng, L., Li, C., Li, L., & Yu, H. (2013). Effectiveness of problem-based learning in Chinese Dental Education: A meta-analysis. *Journal of Dental Education, 77*(3), 377–383. https://doi.org/10.1002/j.0022-0337.2013.77.3.tb05482.x

Hung, W. (2016). All PBL starts here: The problem. *Interdisciplinary Journal of Problem-Based Learning, 10*(2). https://doi.org/10.7771/1541-5015.1604

Hung, W., & Amida, A. (2020). Problem-based learning in college science. In J. Mintzes & E. Walter (Eds.), *Active learning in college science* (pp. 325–340). Springer.

Johansen, M. L., Martenson, D. F., & Bircher, J. (1992). Students as tutors in problem-based learning: Does it. *Medical Education, 26*, 163–165.

Johnson, D. W., & Johnson, R. T. (2004). Cooperation and the use of technology. In D. H. Jonassen (Ed.), *Handbook of research on educational communications and technology* (pp. 785–812). Lawrence Erlbaum Associates.

Kassab, S., Abu-Hijleh, M. F., Al-Shboul, Q., & Hamdy, H. (2005). Student-led tutorials in problem-based learning: Educational outcomes and students' perceptions. *Medical Teacher, 27*(6), 521–526.

Kirschner, P. A., Sweller, J., & Clark, R. E. (2006). Why minimal guidance during instruction does not work: An analysis of the failure of constructivist, discovery, problem-based, experiential, and inquiry-based teaching. *Educational Psychologist, 41*, 75–86.

Koh, G. C. (2016). Revisiting the 'Essentials of problem-based learning'. *Medical Education, 50*(6), 596–599.

Kolodner, J. L. (1993). *Case-based reasoning.* Morgan Kaufman.

Kolodner, J. L. (1997). Educational implications of analogy. *American Psychologist, 52*(1), 57–66.

Kubiszyn, T., & Borich, G. (2007). *Educational testing and measurement* (8th ed.). Wiley.

McCaughan, K. (2013). Barrows' integration of cognitive and clinical psychology in PBL tutor guidelines. *Interdisciplinary Journal of Problem-Based Learning, 7*(1). https://doi.org/10.7771/1541-5015.1318

Mende, S., Proske, A., & Narciss, S. (2021). Individual preparation for collaborative learning: Systematic review and synthesis. *Educational Psychologist, 56*(1), 29–53. https://doi.org/10.1080/00461520.2020.1828086

Moust, J. (2010). The role of the tutor. In H. van Berkel, A. Scherpbier, H. Hillen & C. van der Vleuten (Eds.), *Lessons from problem-based learning.* : Oxford University Press. Retrieved 9 Dec. 2020, from https://oxford.universitypressscholarship.com/view/10.1093/acprof:oso/9780199583447.001.0001/acprof-9780199583447-chapter-006

Mpofu, D. J. S., Das, M., Murdoch, J. C., & Lanphear, J. H. (1997). Effectiveness of problems used in problem-based learning. *Medical education, 31*(5), 330–334.

Nendaz, M. R., & Tekian, A. (1999). Assessment in problem-based learning medical schools: A literature review. *Teaching and learning in medicine, 11*(4), 232–243.

Sa, B., Ezenwaka, C., Singh, K., Vuma, S., & Majumder, A. (2019). Tutor assessment of PBL process: Does tutor variability affect objectivity and reliability? *BMC Medical Education, 19*(1), 76.

Salari, M., Roozbehi, A., Zarafi, A., & Tarmazi, A. R. (2018). Pure PBL, Hybrid PBL and Lecturing: Which one is more effective in developing cognitive skills of undergraduate students in pediatric nursing course? *BMC Medical Education, 18*(195). https://doi.org/10.1186/s12909-018-1305-0

Sayyah, M., Shirbandi, K., Saki-Malehi, A., & Rahim, F. (2017). Use of a problem-based learning teaching model for undergraduate medical and nursing education: A systematic review and meta-analysis. *Advances in Medical Education and Practice*, 691–700. https://doi.org/10.2147/AMEP.S143694

Schmidt, H. G. (1983). Problem-based learning: Rationale and description. *Medical Education, 17*, 11–16.

Schmidt, H. G., & Bouhuijs, P. A. (1980). *Onderwijs in taakgerichte groepen*. Spectrum.
Schmidt, H. G., Loyens, S. M., Van Gog, T., & Paas, F. (2007). Problem-based learning is compatible with human cognitive architecture: Commentary on Kirschner, Sweller, and Clark. *Educational Psychologist, 42*(2), 91–97.
Schmidt, H., & Moust, J. (2010). Designing problems. In H. van Berkel, A. Scherpbier, H. Hillen & C. van der Vleuten (Eds.), *Lessons from problem-based learning*. : Oxford University Press. Retrieved 11 Jan. 2021, from https://oxford.universitypressscholarship.com/view/10.1093/acprof:oso/9780199583447.001.0001/acprof-9780199583447-chapter-005
Servant, V., & Schmidt, H. G. (2016). Revisiting 'Foundations of problem-based learning: Some explanatory notes'. *Medical Education, 50*(7), 698–701.
Shyu, S. Y. (2001). How to turn the students into research masters by internet-online project learning and instructional innovation. *Taiwan Education, 607*, 25–34.
Silverthorn, D. U. (2020). When active learning fails… and what to do about it. In J. Mintzes & E. Walter (Eds.), *Active learning in college science* (pp. 985–1001). Springer.
Sockalingam, N., Rotgans, J., & Schmidt, H. G. (2011). Student and tutor perceptions on attributes of effective problems in problem-based learning. *Higher Education, 62*(1), 1–16.
Strobel, J., & van Barneveld, A. (2009). When is PBL more effective? A Meta-synthesis of Meta-analyses comparing PBL to conventional classrooms. *Interdisciplinary Journal of Problem-based Learning, 3*(1), 44–58. https://doi.org/10.7771/1541-5015.1676
ten Cate, O., & Durning, S. J. (2018). Understanding clinical reasoning from multiple perspectives: A conceptual and theoretical overview. In O. ten Cate, E. Custers, & S. Durning (Eds.), *Principles and practice of case-based clinical reasoning education. Innovation and change in professional education* (pp. 35–46). Springer.
Teng, C. C., & Luo, Y. P. (2015). Effects of perceived social loafing, social interdependence, and group affective tone on students' group learning performance. *The Asia-pacific education researcher, 24*(1), 259–269.
University of York (n.d.). York Law School. Guide to Problem-Based Learning. Retrieved 24 Feb. 2021 from https://www.york.ac.uk/media/law/documents/pbl_guide.pdf
van Berkel, H., Scherpbier, A., Hillen, H., & van der Vleuten, C. (Eds.). (2010). *Lessons from problem-based learning*. Oxford University Press.
Van Til, C., & van der Heijden, F. (2009). *PBL study skills. An overview*. Department of Educational Development and Research, Maastricht University.
Verheggen, M., & Snellen-Balendong, H. (2010). Designing a problem-based learning medical curriculum. In H. van Berkel, A. Scherpbier, H. Hillen & C. van der Vleuten (Eds*.), Lessons from problem-based learning*. : Oxford University Press. Retrieved 9 Dec. 2020, from https://oxford.universitypressscholarship.com/view/10.1093/acprof:oso/9780199583447.001.0001/acprof-9780199583447-chapter-004.
Walker, A., & Leary, H. (2009). A problem based learning meta analysis: Differences across problem types, implementation types, disciplines, and assessment levels. *Interdisciplinary Journal of Problem-Based Learning, 3*(1). https://doi.org/10.7771/1541-5015.1061
Wong, Y. J. (2003). Harnessing the potential of problem-based learning in legal education. *The Law Teacher, 37*(2), 157–173.
Wood, D. F. (2003). Problem based learning. *BMJ, 326*(7384), 328–330.
Yoon, B. Y., Choi, I., Choi, S., Kim, T.-H., Roh, H., Rhee, B. D., & Lee, J. T. (2016). Using standardized patients versus video cases for representing clinical problems in problem-based learning. *Korean Journal of Medical Education, 28*(2), 169–178.
Zhang, S., Xu, J., Wang, H., Zhang, D., Zhang, Q., & Zou, L. (2018). Effects of problem-based learning in Chinese radiology education: A systematic review and meta-analysis. *Medicine., 97*(9). https://doi.org/10.1097/MD.0000000000010069
Zumbach, J. (2003). *Problembasiertes Lernen*. Waxmann.
Zumbach, J., & Spraul, P. (2007). The role of expert and novice tutors in computer mediated and face-to-face problem-based learning. *Research and Practice in Technology Enhanced Learning, 2*(2), 161–187.

# Inquiry-Based Learning in Psychology

## 51

Marie Lippmann

## Contents

| | |
|---|---|
| Introduction | 1256 |
|     Professional and Scientific Issues and Objectives | 1257 |
|     Historical Context | 1257 |
| Purposes and Rationale | 1258 |
| Design Issues and Approaches | 1259 |
|     Phases of Inquiry-Based Learning: The Inquiry Cycle | 1259 |
|     A Synthesis of Existing Inquiry Phases and Cycles | 1260 |
| Evaluation/Research Issues and Approaches Associated with the Topic | 1262 |
| Core Findings and Future Trends | 1264 |
|     The Cognitive Dimension of Inquiry | 1264 |
|     The Guidance Dimension of Inquiry | 1265 |
|     Effects of Cognitive Demands and Guidance Within IBL | 1265 |
|     Implications for Learning and Teaching | 1266 |
|     Two Questions Remain: What Type of Guidance Is Adequate, and for Whom? | 1267 |
|     Further Implications for Learning and Teaching | 1270 |
|     IBL in Higher Education: Facilitating Factors and Constraints | 1271 |
| IBL and Computers: Tools for Successful Inquiry and Learner Collaboration | 1273 |
|     Tools Supporting the Orientation Phase | 1274 |
|     Tools Supporting Questioning in the Conceptualization Phase | 1274 |
|     Tools Supporting Hypotheses Building in the Conceptualization Phase | 1274 |
|     Tools Supporting Exploration in the Investigation Phase | 1274 |
|     Tools Supporting Data Interpretation | 1275 |
|     Tools Supporting the Conclusion Phase | 1275 |
| Challenges, Lessons Learned, and Implications | 1276 |

M. Lippmann (✉)
California State University, Chico, CA, USA
e-mail: mlippmann@csuchico.edu

© Springer Nature Switzerland AG 2023
J. Zumbach et al. (eds.), *International Handbook of Psychology Learning and Teaching*,
Springer International Handbooks of Education,
https://doi.org/10.1007/978-3-030-28745-0_59

Teaching, Learning, and Assessment Resources Associated with the Topic .................. 1277
  Reading Resources ................................................................... 1277
  Web Resources: Tools Supporting IBL Processes ........................................ 1278
Cross-References ....................................................................... 1279
References ............................................................................. 1279

**Abstract**

Inquiry-based learning (IBL) is an educational approach in which learning is facilitated by engaging students in complex, authentic questions, or problems. In IBL, students typically apply methods and practices comparable to those of professional scientists. These methods and practices include the formulation of research questions and hypotheses and the testing of said hypotheses by means of observation or empirical tests and experimenting. This process guides learners toward discovering new causal relations. Learning in IBL is based on an active construction of knowledge, and the learner's own responsibility for discovering new information is emphasized. The role of the professor or teacher is usually that of a facilitator. The effectiveness and efficacy of IBL have been continuously challenged over the past decades. Critics have proposed that IBL does not provide sufficient structure to help learners understand and apply important concepts and procedures of science. This chapter comes to the conclusion that it is essential to employ some level of guidance within IBL settings to help learners accomplish subtasks and overarching goals, and to effectively learn from the IBL activities. For IBL in Higher Education, the conclusions of this chapter highlight the importance of departmental and institutional support for transiting from teacher-led, traditional instructional approaches to IBL, with a focus on fostering dialogue about IBL principles and IBL effectiveness.

**Keywords**

Inquiry-based learning (IBL) · IBL design · IBL in higher education · IBL in psychology education · IBL and technology · IBL tools

## Introduction

Inquiry-based learning (IBL) is an educational approach in which learning is facilitated by engaging students in complex, authentic questions or problems (Lee, Greene, Odom, Schechter, & Slatta, 2004; Spronken-Smith, Walker, Batchelor, O'Steen, & Angelo, 2011). In IBL, students typically apply methods and practices comparable to those of professional scientists (Keselman, 2003; Pedaste et al., 2015). These methods and practices include the formulation of research questions and hypotheses and the testing of said hypotheses by means of observation or empirical testing and experimenting. This process guides learners toward discovering new causal relations (Pedaste et al., 2015; Pedaste, Mäeots, Leijen, & Sarapuu, 2012). Learning in IBL is based on an active construction of knowledge (Lee et al.,

2004; Spronken-Smith et al., 2011), and the learner's own responsibility for discovering new information is emphasized (de Jong & van Joolingen, 1998; Pedaste et al., 2015). The role of the professor or teacher is usually that of a facilitator (Lee et al., 2004; Spronken-Smith et al., 2011).

## Professional and Scientific Issues and Objectives

As educator and researcher, Joerg Zumbach (2003) states, based on a proverb of unknown origin: "Tell me, and I will listen; show me, and I will understand; involve me, and I will learn." This notion has echoed through the field of instructional psychology for the last five decades, and psychologists and educational scientists agree that learner involvement is key to successful learning (Freeman et al., 2014; Lazonder & Harmsen, 2016). Consequently, there has been increasing interest in, and demand for, teaching approaches, which connect knowledge to its applications (Barron & Darling-Hammond, 2010). The primary goal is to equip learners with the skills required to master the demands of the rapidly changing work environments of the twenty-first century. Teachers, researchers, and policy-makers have thus been calling for learner-centered educational approaches, anchored in authentic application-based contexts (European Commission, 2007; National Research Council, 2000; NCREL, 2003; American Association for the Advancement of Science, 1993; Organization for Economic Co-Operation and Development, 2009; Barron & Darling-Hammond, 2010; Mullis, Martin, Ruddock, O'Sullivan, & Preuschoff, 2009; Levy & Murnane, 2004). Inquiry-based learning (IBL), as an educational approach, satisfies these interests and demands because it features authentic inquiry processes and focuses on building a scientifically literate community (Pedaste et al., 2015).

## Historical Context

Inquiry-based learning (IBL) originated from the work of educational philosopher John Dewey (1859–1952), who played a key role in the educational reform in the first half of the twentieth century (Lazonder & Harmsen, 2016). Dewey proposed that instead of focusing on rote memorization of facts, education should equip learners with the skills to think and act scientifically (Lazonder & Harmsen, 2016; National Research Council, 2000). After the discovery learning movement in the 1960s and based on the notion that learning is best facilitated when a "whole heartedness of purpose was present" (Kilpatrick, 1918; Barron & Darling-Hammond, 2010), IBL was implemented on a large scale in educational practice (Lazonder & Harmsen, 2016).

Inquiry-based methods were originally adopted as an engaging way to learn science content (Bruner, 1961; Bruner, Goodnow, & Austin, 1956), but the focus gradually shifted toward an emphasis of cultivating science process skills (Kuhn, 2005; Klahr, 2000; Lazonder & Harmsen, 2016). Earlier and more recent reviews on IBL reflect those shifts in focus. Bittinger (1968) and Hermann (1969), for example, found IBL to be more effective when compared with expository forms of instruction, particularly with regard to the transfer of the learned material to novel contexts and situations. Mere retention of learned facts was sometimes superior in expository methods (Lazonder & Harmsen, 2016). Bittinger (1968) found the transfer advantage of IBL in both laboratory and regular classroom settings, albeit effects were less pronounced in the classroom. Hermann (1969) first raised the issue of the role of guidance for successful IBL, a notion that has since received much attention in both research and practice (Hmelo-Silver, Duncan, & Chinn, 2007; Lazonder & Harmsen, 2016). More recent reviews focus more on the actions learners perform during an inquiry, thereby reflecting learner activities, and the quality of the products that the learners generate during that inquiry, thereby reflecting performance success (D'Angelo et al., 2014; Lazonder & Harmsen, 2016). It is important to note that there seems to be a lack of consensus on the kind of instructional strategies encompassed in the definition of IBL (Alfieri, Brooks, Aldrich, & Tenenbaum, 2011). Some researchers propose that IBL is an umbrella term for various educational strategies, including project-based learning, problem-based learning, and design-based learning (Barron & Darling-Hammond, 2010). From this perspective, the common denominator of these strategies is that they provide learners with opportunities to develop new knowledge and skills in the context of complex (mainly project-oriented) tasks, which require sustained engagement, research, collaboration, the activation of resources, and the development of an ambitions product (Barron & Darling-Hammond, 2010). The instructional incentive of said strategies is to facilitate learners' ability to analyze, think critically, solve complex problems, and communicate their insights effectively in the context of authentic and contextualized problems (Barron & Darling-Hammond, 2010).

Other researchers propose a more narrow definition of IBL, differentiating IBL from project-based, problem-based, and design-based Learning. Lazonder and Harmsen (2016), for example, define IBL as a method in which learners conduct experiments, observe phenomena, or collect data to infer the principles, which are underlying a particular topic or domain. In this conceptualization of IBL, learners' investigations are typically guided by one or more research questions (determined by the learners themselves or provided by the teacher), and the investigations are carried out in alignment with the scientific method and can be performed with tangible materials, existing databases, virtual labs, or computer simulations (Lazonder & Harmsen, 2016). To differentiate IBL from project-based, problem-based, and design-based learning, the latter, narrower definition of IBL will be used for the purposes of this chapter.

## Purposes and Rationale

This chapter aims to provide insights from instructional psychology on the topic of IBL research and practice, to provide a basis for an application of IBL to psychology learning and teaching. IBL will be examined in terms of existing design issues and approaches, research issues and approaches associated with the topic of IBL, and core findings and future trends. Conclusions are drawn with regard to challenges and lessons learned, and implications are discussed. Finally, teaching, learning, and assessment resources associated with IBL are provided. The overarching goal of this chapter is to guide readers through the history and development of IBL as a concept and a practice, and to provide frameworks for addressing current IBL topics, relative to considerations for future directions.

## Design Issues and Approaches

Inquiry-based learning (IBL) aims to engage learners in a process of authentic scientific discovery (Pedaste et al., 2015). From an educational viewpoint, this complex scientific process is comprised of smaller units, which are logically connected and draw the learners' attention to important aspects of their scientific inquiry (Pedaste et al., 2015). These individual interconnected units are defined as inquiry phases, and their connections form inquiry cycles (Pedaste et al., 2015).

## Phases of Inquiry-Based Learning: The Inquiry Cycle

Research in learning and teaching has proposed a number of inquiry phases and cycles (Pedaste et al., 2015). Table 1 presents examples of inquiry phases, as suggested by researchers over the past nine decades.

An apparent distinction between the examples pertains to whether an inquiry cycle starts with an inductive empirical or data-informed approach (e.g., Bybee et al., 2006) or a deductive theory-guided approach (e.g., White & Frederiksen, 1998, as cited in Pedaste et al., 2015). In some cases, inductive and deductive approaches are combined

**Table 1** Examples of inquiry phases

| Year | Authors | Inquiry phases |
|---|---|---|
| 1933 | Dewey, J. | Defining a problem; formulating a hypothesis; conducting tests |
| 1969 | De Groot, A. | Observation; induction; deduction; testing; evaluation |
| 1988 | Klahr, D. and Dunbar, K. | Search hypothesis: generate and induce frames; test hypothesis: formulate experiment, make prediction, run experiment |
| 1992 | de Jong, T. and Njoo, M. | Analysis; hypothesis generation; testing; evaluation |
| 1998 | White, B.Y. and Frederiksen, J.R. | Question; predict; experiment; model; apply |
| 2002 | Justice, C., et al. | Knowledge building; formulating research question; formulating hypotheses, resource allocation; information assessment; synthesis; communication; evaluation; self-reflection |
| 2006 | Bybee, R. et al. | Engagement; exploration; explanation; elaboration; evaluation |

within an inquiry cycle (e.g., Klahr & Dunbar, 1988). Klahr and Dunbar (1988) even propose that the scientific reasoning process is generally comprised of a dual search in two spaces, hypothesis space (deductive) and experiment space (inductive).

The way inquiry cycles are set up typically implies an ordered sequence of phases (Pedaste et al., 2015). In spite of this sequencing of phases, IBL should not be considered a uniform, linear, prescribed process, because the way the phases connect to one another is context-dependent (Pedaste et al., 2015). In the inquiry cycle introduced by Justice et al. (2002), for example, one single inquiry phase (self-reflection) is connected directly to all other phases because self-reflection is presumed to be equally important in each phase. In addition, the arrangement of phases within an inquiry cycle may vary, depending on the nature of the phases (Pedaste et al., 2015). As de Jong and Njoo (1992) outline, some phases can be considered transformative (i.e., when an inquiry process directly generates or changes information) or regulative (i.e., when an inquiry process manages the learning process).

## A Synthesis of Existing Inquiry Phases and Cycles

In a recent systematic literature review, which took into account 32 articles published in academic journals in the time from 1972 until 2012, Pedaste et al. (2015) set out to answer the questions:

(1) Which inquiry phases are necessary for IBL?
(2) How should these phases be arranged within an inquiry cycle?

In a first step, the authors assessed the variety of inquiry phases, which resulted in a list of 109 terms for inquiry phases (Pedaste et al., 2015). Because these 109 terms overlapped to a considerable extent, the authors then grouped the terms according to similar criteria by comparing definitions and eliminating redundancies, thereby reducing the initial list of 109 terms to 34 terms (Pedaste et al., 2015). The remaining 34 terms were sequenced and reorganized into 11 distinct inquiry phases, which were then merged into 5 general inquiry phases and a set of sub-phases (Pedaste et al., 2015). The resulting phases are illustrated in Fig. 1.

Pedaste et al. (2015) define the *orientation* phase as the process of instantiating curiosity for a topic and posing a learning challenge with a problem statement. The *conceptualization* phase is defined as the process of generating theory-informed research questions and/or hypotheses, with the sub-phases of *questioning* (i.e., the process of deriving research questions relative to the stated problem) and *hypotheses generation* (i.e., the process of deriving hypotheses relative to the stated problem; Pedaste et al., 2015). The authors operationalize the *investigation* phase as the process of planning and implementing the data collection and analyzing the data (Pedaste et al., 2015). The investigation phase is comprised of the sub-phases of *exploration* (i.e., the process of systematic data collection based on the research questions), *experimentation* (i.e., the process of

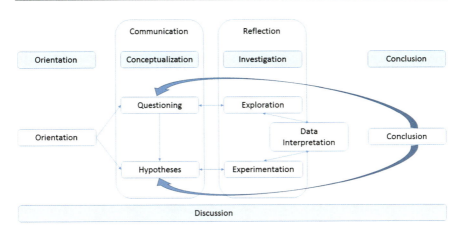

**Fig. 1** Inquiry phases and cycle, framework adapted from Pedaste et al. (2015)

planning and implementing an experiment with the goal of testing hypotheses), and *data interpretation* (i.e., the process of deriving new insights from the data collection; Pedaste et al., 2015). The conclusion phase pertains to the process of arriving at conclusions based on the data, relative to hypotheses and research questions (Pedaste et al., 2015). Finally, the *discussion* phase is defined as the process of communicating these data-informed conclusions to others and/or regulating the inquiry process by means of reflection. The sub-phases of the discussion phase are comprised of *communication* (i.e., the process of presenting outcomes of an inquiry phase or the entire inquiry cycle to others, with the aim of gathering feedback) and *reflection* (i.e., the process of evaluating and describing specific inquiry phases or the entire inquiry cycle; Pedaste et al., 2015). Overall, this inquiry cycle is similar to others, but is different in that it is based on terms which have been derived as core terms from previous works (e.g., Bell, Urhahne, Schanze, & Ploetzner, 2010; Bruce & Casey, 2012; Corlu & Corlu, 2012; Kuhn & Dean, 2008; Steinke & Fitch, 2011; Wecker, Kohnle, & Fischer, 2007). Pedaste et al. (2015) further elaborate their inquiry cycle by instantiating it as an inquiry-based learning framework, which proposes that learning within the inquiry cycle occurs along three possible pathways (Table 2).

In conclusion, this inquiry-based learning framework introduced by Pedaste et al. (2015) presents a contemporary, synthesized view on IBL. It is based on a systematic literature review of existing IBL inquiry phases and cycles and can be utilized to facilitate an effective and efficient IBL process (Pedaste et al., 2015). The proposed framework takes into account the strengths of the reviewed IBL approaches while minimizing the influence of rare variations of inquiry cycles (Pedaste et al., 2015). With the help of this framework, educators are able to structure and organize complex IBL processes, with the added benefit of being able to implement this framework across a variety of educational contexts, including virtual and real-world learning environments (Pedaste et al., 2015).

**Table 2** Pathways in the inquiry cycle, as suggested by Pedaste et al. (2015)

| | Pathway | Special characteristics |
|---|---|---|
| | \multicolumn{2}{l}{A discussion phase can overlap with – and influence – any of the phases described below at any given time within the inquiry cycle} |
| (a) | Orientation – questioning – exploration – questioning – exploration – data interpretation | The loop between questioning and exploration can be repeated more than once. Alternatively, it is possible to move directly from the initial exploration to data interpretation. Communication and reflection can occur additionally in each phase |
| (b) | Orientation – hypotheses – experimentation – data interpretation – hypotheses – experimentation – data interpretation – conclusion | The loop between hypotheses, experimentation, and data interpretation can be repeated more than once. Alternatively, it is possible to move directly from the initial data interpretation to conclusion. Communication and reflection can occur additionally in each phase |
| (c) | Orientation – questioning – hypotheses – experimentation – data interpretation – hypotheses – experimentation – data interpretation – conclusion | The loop between hypotheses, experimentation, and data interpretation can be repeated more than once. Alternatively, it is possible to move directly from the initial data interpretation to conclusion. A revision of the questioning phase might be necessary, but it is more likely that hypotheses are revised. Communication and reflection can occur additionally in each phase |

## Evaluation/Research Issues and Approaches Associated with the Topic

The effectiveness and efficacy of IBL have been continuously challenged over the past decades (Furtak, Seidel, Iverson, & Briggs, 2012; Kirschner, Sweller, & Clark, 2006; Mayer, 2004). Critics have proposed that IBL does not provide sufficient structure to help learners understand and apply important concepts and procedures of science (e.g., Kirschner et al., 2006; Mayer, 2004). The critics of IBL typically advocate for expository, direct forms of instruction, in which teachers present knowledge in the form of carefully designed lectures and verification-oriented laboratory exercises (Kirschner et al., 2006). The rationale for the critics' recommendations is based on their understanding of IBL as an educational strategy in which teachers are taking a hands-off approach to the learning process of their students, while said students are engaging in almost entirely self-directed of dubious value (Kirschner et al., 2006). In their argumentation, they often categorize IBL along with other educational approaches, such as problem-based learning and discovery learning, under umbrella terms such as "minimally guided instruction," describing settings in which leaners discover and explore scientific phenomena without instructor guidance (Kirschner et al., 2006). However, not all researchers agree with this "hands-off" definition of IBL, but argue that IBL must be differentiated from unguided discovery learning because IBL approaches are typically thoroughly scaffolded (Hmelo-Silver, Duncan, & Chinn, 2007). Advocates of IBL agree with opponents of minimally guided instruction approaches in that there is relatively little evidence suggesting that minimally guided instruction approaches foster learning to a considerable degree (Hmelo-Silver et al., 2007). However, the advocates of IBL do not agree that IBL does in fact classify as a minimally guided instruction approach (Hmelo-Silver et al., 2007) because IBL approaches provide scaffolding by means of instructor guidance. In IBL, learners construct knowledge and acquire domain-specific reasoning skills and practices by collaboration and engagement in investigations (Hmelo-Silver et al., 2007). Those investigations typically revolve around authentic scientific questions, and emphasis is placed on active engagement in the learning process and collaborative learning in the sense that students develop evidence-based explanations and communicate their insights (Hmelo-Silver et al., 2007). However, the instructor plays a key role in facilitating that learning process and often provides important content knowledge whenever it is required (Hmelo-Silver et al., 2007). This content knowledge may even be provided by the instructor strategically via direct instruction (Krajcik, Czerniak, & Berger, 1999; Schmidt, 1983; Schwartz & Bransford, 1998), but it is provided on a just-in-time basis and only when it becomes necessary in order for the students to be able to proceed (Edelson, 2001; Hmelo-Silver et al., 2007).

While the debate between advocates of IBL and direct forms of instruction continues, researchers have turned to investigate the effectiveness of IBL with regard to the specific conditions that affect learning processes and outcomes (Furtak et al., 2012). Such studies often follow an experimental or quasi-experimental design in which a control group receives instruction via lecture and an experimental group engages in IBL, with varying levels of guidance and scaffolding (Furtak et al., 2012). The learning outcomes between control and experimental group are typically compared with regard to conceptual understanding, and a number of meta-analyses of reforms in science education found IBL to be relatively more effective than lecture-based direct instruction (Bredderman, 1983; Schroeder, Scott, Tolson, Huang, & Lee, 2007; Shymansky, Hedges, & Woodworth, 1990; Weinstein, Boulanger, & Walberg, 1982). However, even in those meta-analyses, IBL was not defined in a consistent manner and varied greatly in the amount and types of support provided by the instructors (NRC, 1996; 2001). The variability in the way IBL has been operationalized is detrimental to the construct validity of IBL in meta-analyses. That is the case because the generalizability of the inferences that can be made after combining effect sizes is sensitive to (a) the selected sample, (b) the operationalization of the outcome measures, and (c) the way that IBL was defined (Furtak et al., 2012; Shadish, Cook, & Campbell, 2002). Coding IBL as either present or absent does not take into account the range of activities and cognitive processes learners engage in and ignores the different levels of scaffolding and guidance provided by instructors (Hmelo-Silver et al., 2007).

## Core Findings and Future Trends

To determine whether the cognitive demands placed upon learners within IBL settings, and the level of guidance provided by instructors, affect learning processes and learning outcomes, Furtak et al. (2012) introduce a framework that takes into account the cognitive features of IBL activities and the degree of guidance provided to the students who engage in the IBL activities. Both aspects, the cognitive dimension of inquiry and the guidance dimension of inquiry, are introduced and discussed in the following, based upon the framework proposed by Furtak et al. (2012).

## The Cognitive Dimension of Inquiry

Based on Duschl's (2003, 2008) operationalization of IBL, Furtak et al. (2012) propose the following cognitive dimensions of inquiry: (a) conceptual structures/cognitive processes learners employ during scientific reasoning, (b) epistemic frameworks which are utilized whenever scientific knowledge is constructed and evaluated, and (c) social interactions which affect how knowledge is represented, shared, and discussed. Furtak et al. (2012) then add a fourth category, which the authors view as a subdivision of Duschl's (2003, 2008) epistemic domain and which they refer to as the procedural domain. The four domains that comprise the cognitive dimensions of inquiry are further explained in Table 3.

**Table 3** Domains within the cognitive dimension of inquiry according to Furtak et al. (2012)

| | Domain | Definition | Cognitive IBL features within domain |
|---|---|---|---|
| 1 | Conceptual domain | Scientific theories, facts, principles, i.e., the body of knowledge regarding science | Relate to prior knowledge, tap into students' mental models, provide conceptual informative tutorial feedback |
| 2 | Epistemic domain | Knowledge on how to generate scientific theories, facts, and principles by means of collecting evidence | Refer to the nature of science, draw evidence-based conclusions, generate and adapt theories |
| 3 | Social domain | Communicative and collaborative processes by which knowledge on scientific theories, facts, and principles is constructed | Take part in class discussions, debate scientific ideas, present knowledge, work collaboratively |
| 4 | Procedural domain | Methods of discovering scientific theories, facts, and principles, i.e., asking questions, designing experiments, collecting and interpreting data | Generate scientific questions, design experiments, apply scientific procedures, record data, represent data, take a hands-on approach |

**Fig. 2** The guidance dimension of inquiry, relative to student involvement in the guidance process. (Adapted from Furtak et al., 2012)

## The Guidance Dimension of Inquiry

In addition to the cognitive dimension of inquiry, Furtak et al. (2012) propose that IBL settings vary depending on the level of guidance that is provided to the student. They conceptualize the guidance dimension as a continuum, varying from teacher-led traditional instruction, via teacher-guided inquiry, to student-led inquiry/discovery (Fig. 2).

Based on this continuum, Furtak et al. (2012) identified three distinct types of guidance contrasts to make this continuum available for comparisons:

(a) Teacher-led traditional instruction versus student-led inquiry
(b) Teacher-led traditional instruction versus teacher-guided inquiry
(c) Teacher-guided inquiry versus student-led inquiry

## Effects of Cognitive Demands and Guidance Within IBL

Grounded in this framework distinguishing between cognitive and guidance dimensions of inquiry, Furtak et al. (2012) conducted a meta-analysis in which they coded 37 experimental and quasi-experimental studies published in the period of 1996–2006. A main goal of their meta-analysis was to determine which cognitive and guidance dimensions were compared and contrasted in the studies, in order to arrive at more nuanced interpretations of results, and to derive implications for teaching practice and future research. For each of the 37 studies, the authors assessed which cognitive feature(s), and which guidance features, were present in experimental and control groups. They found that the 37 studies included in their review had an average effect size of .50 (SD = 0.56). With regard to the cognitive dimensions, the authors found that 10 out of the 37 studies employed all 4 of the cognitive domains in their experimental IBL groups. In other words, the participants in the experimental groups in those ten studies were required to generate knowledge on scientific theories, facts, and principles; they needed to develop an understanding of how those theories, facts, and principles are generated and communicated, and they were required to apply scientific methods in a hands-on approach. Seven out of the 37 studies required students to generate knowledge and communicate it. Six studies only required students to generate knowledge. Five studies required students to generate scientific knowledge, come to an understanding how to generate it, and apply scientific methods. Ten different combinations of cognitive domains were found in the experimental groups in total. For the control groups, the researchers found that 21 studies included conceptual scientific knowledge and 8 different combinations of cognitive features (Furtak et al., 2012).

In many studies, the cognitive domains were intertwined within the IBL procedure and applied to varying degrees to both experimental and control groups. For example, in a study conducted by Chang and Mao (1999), students in the experimental group collaborated in teams to collect data (procedural domain), discussed and presented that data (social domain), and generated explanations based on the data (epistemic domain), in the context of the topic of the sun-moon-earth system (conceptual domain). Students in the control group, in contrast, experienced a combination of lectures and demonstrations on the same topic (conceptual domain). As demonstrated in this example, the control groups often employed at least one of the cognitive features that were also present in the experimental groups. Furtak et al. (2012) therefore refrained from interpreting the effect sizes of those studies solely based on the cognitive inquiry domains present in the experimental groups, but instead determined the difference between the cognitive domains in experimental and control groups via contrasts, relative to each other. In the example from the study of Chang and Mao (1999), the conditions contrasted in were coded as conceptual, epistemic, social, and procedural (experimental group) versus conceptual (control group). The researchers found that the three studies that explicitly contrasted the cognitive epistemic domain of inquiry produced the largest mean effect on student learning (.75). The second largest effect size (.72) was found for studies contrasting a combination of epistemic, social, and procedural domains. The most commonly contrasted domain was the social domain, which produced the lowest effect size (.11), as compared to the other contrasts (Furtak et al., 2012).

For the guidance dimension of inquiry, the researchers found that the ten studies explicitly contrasting teacher-led traditional instruction with teacher-guided inquiry produced a higher mean effect size (.65) than the five studies contrasting teacher-led traditional instruction with student-led inquiry/discovery (.25). The six studies contrasting teacher-guided inquiry with student-led inquiry/discovery produced the smallest mean effect size (.01). When combining the cognitive and guidance dimensions in one analysis, the researchers found the largest effect sizes (.80) for studies contrasting teacher-led traditional instruction versus teacher-guided inquiry when those studies varied a combination of epistemic domain, social domain, and procedural domain (Furtak et al., 2012).

## Implications for Learning and Teaching

The results of this meta-analysis (Furtak et al., 2012) demonstrate an overall positive effect of IBL on student learning. By taking into account the cognitive demands of different IBL approaches, as well as varying levels of instructor support, the researchers were able to show that it is important to specify features of IBL settings, rather than attempting to market IBL as a "one size fits all" type of paradigm. This notion is supported by the considerable variability in effect sizes that different combinations of cognitive demands and instructor support produced.

With regard to the cognitive dimension of IBL, it was found that studies contrasting the epistemic domain and studies contrasting a combination of epistemic, social, and procedural domains produced the largest effect sizes. This means that it is particularly important to involve learners in constructing, developing, and explaining scientific rationales and procedures, to help learners understand, and engage in, science (Furtak et al., 2012).

With regard to the guidance dimension of IBL, the researchers found that the subset of ten studies contrasting teacher-guided inquiry with teacher-led traditional instruction produced effect sizes that were twice as large as the five studies that contrasted student-led inquiry (discovery) with teacher-led traditional instruction (Furtak et al., 2012). This evidence suggests that teacher-guided inquiry IBL settings have a more positive effect on student learning than student-led IBL settings that are more discovery oriented. With regard to the ongoing debate about the general effectiveness of IBL (Kirschner et al., 2006; Mayer, 2004; Klahr & Nigam, 2004; Hmelo-Silver et al., 2007), this finding highlights an important aspect.

It is inappropriate to group teacher-guided IBL settings with unguided student-led discovery approaches, because teacher-guided IBL approaches are twice as effective as student-led discovery approaches (Furtak et al., 2012). It is noteworthy, however, that this meta-analysis still revealed that even if teacher-guided and student-led IBL approaches are grouped together, these approaches still benefit student learning more than teacher-led traditional instruction (Furtak et al., 2012), thus highlighting the importance of furthering IBL settings as a viable means of constructing knowledge inside and outside the classroom.

## Two Questions Remain: What Type of Guidance Is Adequate, and for Whom?

Having established the cognitive demands and some general notions on guidance within IBL approaches, a glaring question remains: What type of guidance is adequate, and for whom? As Lazonder and Harmsen (2016) point out in their recent meta-analysis, this question can only be answered when taking into account developmental differences in scientific reasoning, as well as a more nuanced typology of guidance. Scientific reasoning is a core cognitive demand in IBL settings and encompasses the four cognitive dimensions of inquiry comprised of the conceptual domain, the epistemic domain, the social domain, and the procedural domain (Furtak et al., 2012). Overall, scientific reasoning can be summarized as the application of scientific methods of inquiry to reasoning situations (Kuhn, & Franklin, 2006). Scientific reasoning is not a skill which we are born with, but rather a skill set which develops over time. Table 4 is adapted from the meta-analyses by Lazonder and Harmsen (2016) and provides an overview of a number of skills involved in scientific reasoning, relative to their development from childhood into adulthood.

**Table 4** Scientific reasoning skills and developmental milestones according to Lazonder and Harmsen (2016)

| Reasoning skill | Developmental milestones |
| --- | --- |
| Formulating hypotheses | Skill to develop hypothesis develops during elementary school age (Piekny & Maehler, 2013) |
| | Children prior to adolescence often formulate only one plausible hypothesis based on their prior beliefs (Klahr, Fay, & Dunbar, 1993) |
| | Adolescents are more likely to consider multiple hypotheses and are able to generate implausible hypotheses along with plausible ones (Klahr et al., 1993) |
| | The ability to formulate hypotheses matures around the age of 12, but inducing alternative or novel hypotheses from data remains a challenge across age groups (Klahr et al., 1993) |
| Design experiments | Five years are not yet capable of distinguishing between probing a hypothesis and generating an effect, but this skill increases around the age of 6 (Piekny, Gruber, & Maehler, 2014; Sodian, Zaitchik, & Carey, 1991) |
| | With support, 6- to 7-year-olds are able to test relationships between variables (Chen & Klahr, 1999; Varma, 2014) |
| | Most learners only acquire this skill around the age of 10 (Kanari & Millar, 2004; Schauble, Glaser, Duschl, Schulze, & John, 1995) |
| | Through middle childhood and adolescence, children continuously improve their ability to develop experimental comparisons and become increasingly able to transfer this skill to a variety of domains (Chen & Klahr, 1999; Koerber, Sodian, Kropf, Mayer, & Schwippert, 2011; Veenman, Wilhelm, & Beishuizen, 2004) |
| Evidence evaluation | The ability to differentiate between perfect covariation and non-covariation evidence emerges during preschool and early elementary school years (Koerber et al., 2011; Piekny & Maehler, 2013) |
| | Preschool children of 4 to 5 years of age are already capable of understanding perfect covariation as causation (Koerber, Sodian, Thoermer, & Nett, 2005; Piekny et al., 2014) |
| | The more demanding ability to interpret imperfect covariation starts developing in early childhood, develops slowly, and is hardly ever fully understood by individuals, even in adulthood (Kuhn, Amsel, & O' Loughlin, 1988) |

In summary, Lazonder and Harmsen (2016) suggest that children around the age of 5 start being able to generate hypotheses, conduct simple experiments, and evaluate evidence. These skills constitute some basic cognitive requirements for engaging in IBL processes, thereby rendering children around the age of 5 ready to participate in simplified IBL settings. Young learners who operate at very basic cognitive levels of inquiry are likely to need different levels of guidance than older learners in order to be successful, which highlights the importance of further specifying and elaborating on the guidance dimension of inquiry (Lazonder & Harmsen, 2016).

Lazonder and Harmsen (2016) define guidance as any type of assistance offered before or during IBL activities, aiming to simplify, support, or elicit certain scientific reasoning skills. Because younger (or generally less experienced) learners typically require more explicit guidance than older (or more experienced) learners, it is important to provide a framework which classifies guidance features based on their explicitness or extensiveness, rather than focusing solely on the cognitive skills or demands that are necessary to succeed within a particular IBL environment (Lazonder & Harmsen, 2016). With this notion in mind, Lazonder and Harmsen (2016) propose the following typology of guidance within IBL settings, which they adapted from previous works of De Jong and Lazonder (2014):

- *Process constraints* are restrictions to the comprehensiveness of a learning task and are directed at learners who are capable of performing and regulating basic IBL processes but who lack the experience to perform under more demanding circumstances.
- *Status overviews* highlight task progress and are directed at learners who are able to engage in basic IBL processes, but lack the ability to plan, and are unable to monitor their learning progress, relative to their learning goals.
- *Prompts* are reminders to perform a certain action and are aimed at learners who are capable of performing that action but unable to do so at their own initiative.
- *Heuristics* are reminders to perform an action and provide information on how to perform that action and are directed at learners who are unsure about how and when a certain action should be performed.
- *Scaffolds* are explanations or directions on how to tackle particularly demanding parts of an action and are directed at learners who do not yet have the ability to perform the entire action on their own or who do not remember how to perform that action.
- *Explanations* specify how to perform an action and are directed at learners who do not yet know just how to perform that action.

Based on this framework, Lazonder and Harmsen (2016) determined 72 studies to include in their meta-analysis, which aimed at determining the effectiveness of the different types of guidance on learning activities, performance success, and learning outcomes, relative to learners' ages.

They identified 72 studies to be included in their analyses. Measures of learning activities (i.e., the utilization of inquiry skills within the IBL process) were reported in 20 out of the 72 studies. The overall effect size of guidance on learning activities ranged between 0.44 and 0.88, thus indicating a medium to large effect. The overall effect of guidance on learning activities did not depend on the specificity or type of guidance, but the results revealed an interaction between type of guidance and learner age. Process constraints, which are the least directive type of guidance, were more beneficial for adolescents (d = 0.94) than for children (d = 0.78). Scaffolds, which provide more specific guidance, were more effective for teenagers (d = 3.62) than for adolescents (d = 0.70). However, none of these descriptive differences reached statistical significance.

Performance success was operationalized via the products, which learners generated during their IBL process, and was reported in 17 out of the 72 studies (Lazonder & Harmsen, 2016). The results again revealed an overall positive effect of guidance (d = 0.71). Learners who received guidance outperformed unguided learners by more than half a standard deviation, which produced a significant difference between those two groups (p < .001). Larger effect sizes were associated with more specific guidance (p = .030), and explanations were more effective than all the other less specific types of guidance combined (p = .033). No effect was found for scaffolds, but heuristics were more effective than their less specific alternatives (p = .043). Prompts were as effective as status overviews and process constraints combined (p = .401), and status overviews were less effective than process constraints (p = .023). However, the results also revealed that no type of guidance was particularly effective relative to the age of learners, thereby indicating that the different types of guidance have similar positive effects on performance success in children, teenagers, and adolescents (Lazonder & Harmsen, 2016).

Learning outcomes were reported in 60 out of the 72 studies included in the meta-analysis (Lazonder & Harmsen, 2016). The overall effect size of guidance on learning outcomes (d = 0.50) indicated a moderate effect. The type of guidance had no significant effect. That is, all six types of guidance were equally effective in facilitating learning outcomes. The effectiveness of the different types of guidance was unrelated to age groups, indicating that children, teenagers, and adolescents benefited from the different types of guidance to comparable extents (Lazonder & Harmsen, 2016).

In summary, the meta-analysis by Lazonder and Harmsen (2016) emphasized the overall effectiveness of guidance in IBL settings, thereby supporting the previous findings of Furtak et al. (2012). However, their analyses did not result in a clear conclusion as to whether specific types of guidance yield more promising effects for some learners over others. In spite of a moderating effect in performance success, different types of guidance did not lead to differences in learning activities and learning outcomes. Both, learning activities and learning outcomes, were enhanced by each type of guidance to similar extents. For all practical purposes, this means that less specific types of guidance, such as process constraints or status overviews, are already helpful to young learners with low inquiry skills. Reversely, older, more experienced learners are able to benefit from specific types of guidance, such as scaffolds and explanations (Lazonder & Harmsen, 2016).

## Further Implications for Learning and Teaching

Critics of IBL have argued that guidance that is more specific will result in higher learning outcomes and have thus argued for high levels of instructional guidance in general (Kirschner et al., 2006). Typical examples for high levels of instructional guidance, which have been successfully incorporated into IBL settings and which have been advocated for by IBL critics (Kirschner et al., 2006), include worked examples and process worksheets (De Vries, Van der Meij, & Lazonder, 2008; Mulder, Lazonder, & De Jong, 2014). Using the framework introduced by Lazonder and Harmsen (2016), worked examples would classify as explanations, and process worksheets would classify as heuristics and would thus categorize as different types of guidance. However, based on their meta-analysis, Lazonder and Harmsen (2016) argue that both types of guidance, in spite of differing in terms of specificity, would yield comparable positive effects on IBL processes and learning outcomes.

In essence, this finding means that "strong guidance" does not equal "specific" guidance. Other aspects, such as duration and frequency of guidance, might be more important to optimize the IBL process and related learning outcomes.

Based on the meta-analyses by Furtak et al. (2012) and Lazonder and Harmsen (2016), it is recommended to employ some level of guidance within IBL settings to help learners accomplish subtasks and overarching goals and to effectively learn from the IBL activities. This means that whenever learners engage in scientific inquiry processes, instructors should take care to provide the learners with adequate guidance. However, it is important to note that adequate guidance does not equal highly specific guidance, as often suggested by IBL critics. In addition, instructors are not required to select a particular type of guidance based on assumptions related to the age of their students or the student's prior expertise within IBL settings (Lazonder & Harmsen, 2016). Instead, instructors are able to base their guidance choices on factors such as the learners' prior topic knowledge, familiarity with certain inquiry skills, or the student-instructor ratio (Lazonder & Harmsen, 2016).

## IBL in Higher Education: Facilitating Factors and Constraints

IBL has been increasingly applied to university settings, with the goal to move toward more student-centered learning (Biggs, 1999; Ramsden, 2003) and to bridge the gap between teaching and research (Boyer Commission, 1999; Brew, 2006; Healey & Jenkins, 2009). In 2011, a meta-analysis examined ten studies, which had been conducted within a multi-institutional research project examining IBL settings within undergraduate university education in New Zealand (Spronken-Smith et al., 2011). The specific aim was to determine facilitating factors and constraints of IBL within undergraduate education and to draw conclusions that would be helpful to educators across the world. The ten studies included in the meta-analysis followed a mixed-methods approach. The studies included case study data, instructor and student interviews, classroom observations, focus groups, in-class feedback sessions, and quantitative survey data (Spronken-Smith et al., 2011).

Based on a triangulation of evidence across data sources, Spronken-Smith et al. (2011) identified three factors, which facilitated the effectiveness of IBL in undergraduate education, pertaining to instructor attributes, course design attributes, and institutional/departmental attributes. The authors further identified five barriers constraining the effectiveness of IBL in undergraduate education, pertaining to institutional buy-in, support in the transition toward IBL, coping with different assessment products, challenges in self-reflection skills, and institutional/departmental barriers. Table 5 provides an overview of those facilitating factors and constraints and their components.

**Table 5** Facilitating factors and constraints for IBL in undergraduate education, adapted from Spronken-Smith et al. (2011)

| Facilitating factors for IBL in undergraduate education | |
|---|---|
| Factor | Specific aspects |
| Instructors | Instructor supports student-centered teaching philosophy |
| | Instructor skilled in self-reflection |
| | Instructor has personal interest in the scientific method |
| | Instructor is ready to challenge departmental norms |
| | Instructor is trained in IBL or seeks support from experienced faculty |
| Course design | Courses allow for open-ended questions |
| | Courses focus on collaborative learning |
| | Courses focus on active student engagement |
| | Courses focus on student-centered learning, with instructor guidance |
| | Courses provide scaffolds for inquiry skills |
| Institutional/departmental facilitating factors | IBL course implementation is easier if the whole program is student-centered |
| | Support of IBL by administration |
| | Sufficient resources (faculty, staff, and learning spaces) |
| | Development opportunities for faculty and staff |
| Constraints for IBL in undergraduate education | |
| Departmental and institutional buy-in | Lack of access and funds for faculty/staff development programs |
| | Lack of mentoring opportunities provided by IBL experienced faculty |
| | Lack of peer mentoring approaches |
| Transition support | Lack of appropriate induction for faculty, staff, and students |
| | Lack of departmental/institutional consensus on how to transition from teacher-led, traditional instructional approaches toward IBL |
| Coping with different assessment products | Lack of flexibility in how to assess learning progress and learning outcomes |
| | Lack of clear assessment criteria |
| Self-reflection challenges | Lack of reflection exercises built into course structures |
| | Lack of examples for effective self-reflection to model appropriate strategies |
| Institutional/departmental constraints and barriers | Lack of showcasing good practice examples |
| | Lack of emphasis on positive IBL outcomes |
| | Lack of dialogue about IBL and its underlying principles |
| | Lack of instructor education on the potential and working mechanisms of successful IBL in undergraduate education |

In summary, this meta-analysis highlights the importance of departmental and institutional support for transiting from teacher-led, traditional instructional approaches to IBL (Spronken-Smith et al., 2011), with a focus on fostering dialogue about IBL principles and IBL effectiveness. Associated with this institutional and departmental support are resources necessary for facilitating the successful implementation of IBL, such as access to faculty and staff development programs, and appropriate learning spaces, to establish what could be paraphrased as an IBL corporate culture with universities. On the course level, it is important that collaborative learning and inquiry with instructor guidance are structurally possible and supported by the individual instructors by focusing on student-centered learning and showing authentic and genuine understanding of, and enthusiasm for, scientific inquiry processes (Spronken-Smith et al., 2011).

## IBL and Computers: Tools for Successful Inquiry and Learner Collaboration

Computer tools can support learners in successfully completing inquiry cycles (Bell et al., 2010). One reason is that computers assist in the performance of routine processes, such as calculating, sorting, and visualizing data, thereby freeing cognitive resources for higher-order thinking processes necessary for successful IBL (Bell et al., 2010; Lehtinen, 2003; van Joolingen, de Jong, Lazonder, Savelsbergh, & Manlove, 2005). A second reason is that computers can be controlled by learners and utilized to research and access information independently and without relying on the instructor (Bell et al., 2010; Lehtinen, 2003; van Joolingen et al., 2005). Different computer tools are optimized to support different phases within inquiry cycles. The following section introduces and discusses exemplar computer tools, relative to the phase of the inquiry cycle they support. Fig. 3 provides an overview of those tools, relative to the inquiry phase they support.

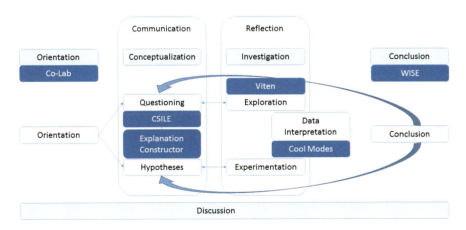

**Fig. 3** Examples of computer tools supporting different inquiry phases

## Tools Supporting the Orientation Phase

Computer tools are able to aid cognitive processes in the orientation phase by eliciting learner interest, stimulating interest, and focusing attention on relevant information (Bell et al., 2010; Hmelo & Day, 1999). An example is the Co-Lab project (van Joolingen et al., 2005; www.co-lab.nl), which assists learners in developing a first impression of what an inquiry-based investigation could look like. In the Co-Lab project "Greenhouse effect," learners first encounter an assignment, which encourages them to explore their environment, experiment with a simple simulation of sun-earth configurations, and build a basic model of greenhouse processes (Bell et al., 2010; van Joolingen et al., 2005). This helps learners to orient within this topic domain but leaves plenty of freedom to explore and develop their own research questions (Bell et al., 2010).

## Tools Supporting Questioning in the Conceptualization Phase

Because complex scientific topics can typically not be investigated in just one attempt, computer tools can be helpful in prompting continued questioning (Bell et al., 2010). An example for such a tool is the Computer-Supported Intentional Learning Environment (CSILE, Scardamelia & Bereiter, 1994). This learning environment offers a knowledge-building tool, which allows learners to add notes to a community database. The learning environment prompts learners to label their notes, based on the "thinking type" the notes relate to, which can be "question," "my theory," or "plan." The learning environment provides definitions of each thinking type and supports learners in collaborative learning efforts and facilitates continuous, iterative questioning throughout the inquiry process (Scardamelia, Scardamalia, 2002).

## Tools Supporting Hypotheses Building in the Conceptualization Phase

An example for a computer tool, which supports the formation and generation of hypotheses, is the ExplanationConstructor (Sandoval, 2003; Sandoval & Reiser, 2004). This tool offers multiple features. One feature is "The Organizer," which learners can use to develop questions and link their questions to potential explanations. Using another feature, learners can then elaborate on their questions and explanations by linking the explanations to evidence, such as data diagrams. Another feature, the "Explanation Guide," explicitly highlights the most important components of a scientific explanation (Sandoval & Reiser, 2004).

## Tools Supporting Exploration in the Investigation Phase

Learners often have difficulties conducting investigations because they do not know which variables to attend to and how to conduct efficient and conclusive experiments and seek out to confirm their original hypotheses, rather than testing it (Bell et al., 2010; de Jong & van Joolingen, 1998). Computer tools can aid the investigation process by reducing the complexity of scientific phenomena and drawing attention to the relevant variables (Bell et al., 2010; van Joolingen et al., 2005). In the Viten project (www.viten.no), for example, different representations of information can be accessed. The project "On Thin Ice" incudes an animation demonstrating the fundamental structure of the earth's radiation balance and how this radiation balance is impacted by fossil fuel combustion, deforestation, volcanic eruptions, and traffic (Bell et al., 2010). Learners are also able to access time series data from expert projections and links to web resources with further information. The Viten project thus encourages learners to explore various types of information by employing rich multimedia functionality (Bell et al., 2010).

## Tools Supporting Data Interpretation

Data analyses and interpretation are important to test one's hypotheses against gathered information and evidence (Bell et al., 2010). To accomplish that, data needs to be represented in an appropriate format suitable to the planned analysis. Cool Mode (Pinkwart, 2003; 2005) is a computer tool, which allows for dynamic representations of data and supports data interpretation with diagrams and tables. Learners have the additional option to add notes to data windows (Lingnau et al., 2003). By utilizing multiple layers and windows flexibly, Cool Mode is able to display different features simultaneously, such as graph windows and note windows, thereby facilitating data interpretation (Bell et al., 2010; Manlove, Lazonder, & de Jong, 2007).

## Tools Supporting the Conclusion Phase

Computer support in the conclusion phase takes place on different levels. On a basic level, features like electronic notebooks, as provided by the WISE (Web-based Inquiry Science Environment, Slotta, 2004), are equipped with prompts challenging learners to reflect on their conclusions more deeply, to view their findings from different perspectives, or to apply their results to a transfer problem. For a more in-depth reflection on their own conclusions, the WISE engages learners in complex, transfer-oriented modeling tasks (Bell et al., 2010). An example is derived from the "Too fast, too furious" module within WISE. First, learners simulate the motions of both driver and airbag in a crash scenario to learn about the risks of using airbags and the underlying physical principles. Learners are prompted to capture their learning in an electronic notebook and then asked to reflect on what they have learned. In a next step, learners are required to generate conclusions on the role of collision speed, driver's body height, and a car's crash zone. The next assignment is to write a report to the fictitious "Insurance Institute for Highway Safety" and to include recommendation for the design of cars and airbags (Bell et al., 2010). In a final step, learners are prompted to consider multiple simulations of car crashes, relative to comparable physical models from other scientific domains, and to derive conclusions related to general issues of modeling (Bell et al., 2010; Slotta, 2004).

There are many more tools available for each of the inquiry phases. In summary, it is worthy to note that the main advantage of computerized IBL support is based on an optimization of IBL processes, perhaps comparable to that of instructor guidance. That is not to say that computer support is equivalent to instructor guidance. Rather, computer support and instructor guidance share a number of helpful features, such as focusing learners' attention on relevant information, scaffolding IBL processes, and encouraging continuous inquiry.

## Challenges, Lessons Learned, and Implications

Psychologists and educational scientists agree that learner involvement is key to successful learning (Freeman et al., 2014; Lazonder & Harmsen, 2016). In the rapidly changing work environments of the twenty-first century, educational approaches must equip learners with skills necessary to engage in lifelong learning under ever-changing conditions. Teachers, researchers, and policy-makers have thus been advocating for learner-centered educational approaches, embedded in authentic application-based contexts (European Commission, 2007; NCREL, 2003; OECD, 2009; Barron & Darling-Hammond, 2010; Mullis et al., 2009). Inquiry-based learning (IBL), as an educational approach, satisfies these interests and demands because it features authentic inquiry processes and focuses on building a scientifically literate community (Pedaste et al., 2015), which makes IBL an ideal candidate for the teaching of psychology in the context of higher education.

The effectiveness and efficacy of IBL have been continuously challenged over the past decades (Kirschner et al., 2006; Mayer, 2004). Critics have proposed that IBL does not provide sufficient structure to help learners understand and apply important concepts and procedures of science (e.g., Kirschner et al., 2006; Mayer, 2004). The critics of IBL typically advocate for expository, direct forms of instruction, in which teachers present knowledge in the form of carefully designed lectures and verification-oriented laboratory exercises (Kirschner et al., 2006). Based on the meta-analyses by Furtak et al. (2012) and Lazonder and Harmsen (2016), this chapter comes to the conclusion that it is essential to employ some level of guidance within IBL settings to help learners accomplish subtasks and overarching goals and to effectively learn from the IBL activities. This means that whenever learners engage in scientific inquiry processes, instructors should take care to provide the learners with adequate guidance. However, it is important to note that adequate guidance does not equal highly specific guidance, as often suggested by IBL critics (Kirschner et al., 2006). In essence, the work of Lazonder and Harmsen (2016) showed that "strong guidance" does not equal "specific" guidance. Other aspects, such as duration and frequency of guidance, might be more important to optimize the IBL process and related learning outcomes.

For IBL in higher education, the conclusions of this chapter highlight the importance of departmental and institutional support for transiting from teacher-led, traditional instructional approaches to IBL (Spronken-Smith et al., 2011), with a focus on fostering dialogue about IBL principles and IBL effectiveness. Associated with this institutional and departmental support are resources necessary for facilitating the successful implementation of IBL, such as access to faculty and staff development programs, and appropriate learning spaces, to establish what could be paraphrased as an IBL corporate culture with universities. On the course level, it is important that collaborative learning and inquiry with instructor guidance are structurally possible and supported by the individual instructors by focusing on student-centered learning and showing authentic and genuine understanding of, and enthusiasm for, scientific inquiry processes (Spronken-Smith et al., 2011).

There are many computer tools available to support learners throughout each of the inquiry phases (Bell et al., 2010). With regard to those tools, it is worthy to note that the main advantage of computerized IBL support is based on an optimization of IBL processes, perhaps comparable to that of instructor guidance. That is not to say that computer support is equivalent to instructor guidance. Rather, computer support and instructor guidance share a number of helpful features, such as focusing learners' attention on relevant information, scaffolding IBL processes, and encouraging continuous inquiry.

In conclusion, IBL is an effective approach to meet the demands of teaching in higher education in the twenty-first century and, thus, the teaching of psychology at universities. Learners benefit from guidance within the IBL process. It is up to instructors to determine the level of specificity and the type of guidance they choose to implement, relative to the learners' prior knowledge. Institutions and departments are powerful allies in the implementation of IBL at the course and university level and the facilitation of positive IBL outcomes.

## Teaching, Learning, and Assessment Resources Associated with the Topic

Below you will find a list of ten recommended further reading references and URLs about relevant teaching, learning, and assessment resources that you may find inspiring for teaching and learning.

## Reading Resources

Bell, T., Urhahne, D., Schanze, S., & Ploetzner, R. (2010). Collaborative inquire learning: models, tools, and challenges. *International Journal of Science Education, 32*(3), 349 – 377. https://doi.org/10.1080/09500690802582241.
  In this article, the authors introduce a number of computer tools to assist learners in the successful completion of different phases within the inquiry process. A particular benefit of this work is that it highlights not the tool itself, but its functions, relative to the inquiry cycle.

Furtak, E.M., Seidel, T., Iverson, H., & Briggs, D. (2012). Experimental and quasi-experimental studies of inquiry-based science teaching: A meta-analysis. Review of Educational Research, 82(3), 300 – 329. https://doi.org/10.3102/0034654312457206.

In this meta-analysis, the authors introduce a framework for the evaluation of IBL settings, relative to their cognitive demands and their degree of guidance, thus contributing to more nuanced explanations relative to the ongoing debate on the overall effectiveness of IBL.

Lazonder, A.W. & Harmsen, R. (2016). Meta-analysis of inquiry-based learning: Effects of guidance. *Review of Educational Research, 86*(3), 681 – 718. https://doi.org/10.3102/0034654315627366.

In this meta-analysis, the authors revisit the historic debate about the importance of guidance within IBL settings, and elaborate on previous research by investigating effects of different types of guidance, relative to learner age and IBL experience.

Pedaste, M., Mäeots, M., Siiman, L.A., de Jong, T., van Riesen, S.A.N., Kamp, E.T., Manoli, C.C., Zacharia, Z.C., & Tsourlidaki, E. (2015). Phases of inquiry-based learning: Definitions and the inquiry cycle. *Educational Research Review, 14,* 47 – 61. https://doi.org/10.1016/j.edurev.2015.02.003.

In this overview article, the authors discuss different approaches to defining inquiry phases and inquiry cycles based on previous research and current directions.

## Web Resources: Tools Supporting IBL Processes

www.viten.no
   The Viten project offers web-based learning resources K 8–12. Various tools can be utilized to support specific phases within the IBL process.

www.co-lab.nl
   Co-Lab offers a large platform for complex learning environments supporting IBL processes, targeting various phases of IBL cycles.

https://www.mindmeister.com/
   MindMeister is a popular web tool learners can use to create mind maps and brainstorm complex topics. Mind maps can include a wide variety of multi-media including text, images, icons, links, and attachments. MindMeister also supports offline editing and syncing. Mind maps can be exported to Word, PowerPoint, and PDF and in the form of an image.

http://edu.glogster.com/?ref=com
   Glogster is a web tool and mobile app allowing learners to create free interactive posters, or Glogs. A "Glog" (graphics blog) is an interactive multimedia image. Glogster provides educators and learners with the technology to create online multimedia posters – with text, graphics, photos, videos, sounds, drawings, and data attachments.

http://www.videonot.es/
   VideoNotes is a free web tool that allows learners to take notes on a video they are watching. The notes are synchronized with the video that is being watched. VideoNotes is integrated into Google Drive, which means that students are able to save their notes directly to their Drive account and access, edit, and work on their notes anytime they want. All the notes are time-stamped.
http://edpuzzle.com/
   Edpuzzle enables learners to utilize specific information from videos, insert audio notes, or record over a video with one's own voice. Learners can also add questions and notes to their multimedia collages.

## Cross-References

▶ Basic Principles and Procedures for Effective Teaching in Psychology
▶ First Principles of Instruction Revisited
▶ Problem-Based Learning and Case-Based Learning
▶ Technology-Enhanced Psychology Learning and Teaching

## References

Alfieri, L., Brooks, P. J., Aldrich, N. J., & Tenenbaum, H. R. (2011). Does discovery-based instruction enhance learning? *Journal of Educational Psychology, 103*(1), 1–18. https://psycnet.apa.org/doi/10.1037/a0021017.

American Association for the Advancement of Science. (AAAS). (1993). *Benchmarks for science literacy.* New York, NY: Oxford University Press.

Barron, B., & Darling-Hammond, L. (2010). Prospects and challenges for inquiry-based approaches to learning. In H. Dumont, D. Istance, & F. Benavides (Eds.), *The nature of learning: Using research to inspire practice* (pp. 199–225). Paris, France: Centre for Educational Research and Innovation (OECD).

Bell, T., Urhahne, D., Schanze, S., & Ploetzner, R. (2010). Collaborative inquiry learning: Models, tools, and challenges. *International Journal of Science Education, 32*(3), 349–377. https://doi.org/10.1080/09500690802582241.

Biggs, J. (1999). *Teaching for quality learning at university.* Maidenhead, UK: The Society for Research into Higher Education & Open University Press.

Bittinger, M. L. (1968). A review of discovery. *The Mathematics Teacher, 61*(2), 140–146. Reston, VA: National Council of Teachers of Mathematics.

Boyer Commission. (1999). *Reinventing undergraduate education: A blueprint for America's research universities.* Stony Brook, NY: Carnegie Foundation for the Advancement of Teaching.

Bredderman, T. (1983). Effects of activity-based elementary science on student outcomes: A quantitative synthesis. *Review of Educational Research, 53*(4), 499–518. https://doi.org/10.3102/00346543053004499.

Brew, A. (2006). *Research and teaching: Beyond the divide.* London, UK: Palgrave Macmillan.

Bruce, B. C., & Casey, L. (2012). The practice of inquiry: A pedagogical 'sweet spot' for digital literacy? *Computers in the Schools, 29*(1–2), 191–206. https://doi.org/10.1080/07380569.2012.657994.

Bruner, J. S. (1961). The act of discovery. *Harvard Educational Review, 31*(2), 21–32.

Bruner, J. S., Goodnow, J. J., & Austin, G. A. (1956). *A study of thinking*. New York, NY: Wiley.
Bybee, R. W., Taylor, J. A., Gardner, A., Van Scotter, P., Powell, J. C., Westbrook, A., & Landes, N. (2006). *The BSCS 5E instructional model: Origins and effectiveness* (pp. 88–89). Colorado Springs, CO: BSCS.
Chang, C.-Y., & Mao, S.-L. (1999). Comparison of Taiwan science students' outcomes with inquiry-group versus traditional instruction. *Journal of Educational Research, 92*(6), 340–346. https://doi.org/10.1080/00220679909597617.
Chen, Z., & Klahr, D. (1999). All other things being equal: Acquisition and transfer of the control of variables strategy. *Child Development, 70*(5), 1098–1120. https://doi.org/10.1111/1467-8624.00081.
Corlu, M. A., & Corlu, M. S. (2012). Scientific inquiry based professional development models in teacher education. *Educational Sciences: Theory and Practice, 12*(1), 514–521.
D'Angelo, C., Rutstein, D., Harris, C., Bernard, R., Borokhovski, E., & Haertel, G. (2014). *Simulations for STEM learning: Systematic review and meta-analysis*. Menlo Park: SRI International.
De Jong, T., & Lazonder, A. W. (2014). The guided discovery learning principle in multimedia learning. In R. E. Mayer (Ed.), *The Cambridge handbook of multimedia learning* (2nd ed., pp. 371–390). New York, NY: Cambridge University Press.
de Jong, T., & Njoo, M. (1992). Learning and instruction with computer simulations: Learning processes involved. In E. De Corte, M. C. Linn, H. Mandl, & L. Verschaffel (Eds.), *Computer-based learning environments and problem solving* (pp. 411–427). Berlin/Heidelberg, Germany: Springer.
De Jong, T., & Van Joolingen, W. R. (1998). Scientific discovery learning with computer simulations of conceptual domains. *Review of Educational Research, 68*(2), 179–201. https://doi.org/10.3102/00346543068002179.
De Vries, B., Van der Meij, H., & Lazonder, A. W. (2008). Supporting reflective web searching in elementary schools. *Computers in Human Behavior, 24*(3), 649–665. https://doi.org/10.1016/j.chb.2007.01.021.
Duschl, R. A. (2003). Assessment of inquiry. In J. M. Atkin & J. Coffey (Eds.), *Everyday assessment in the science classroom* (pp. 41–59). Arlington, VA: NSTA Press.
Duschl, R. A. (2008). Science education in three-part harmony: Balancing conceptual, epistemic, and social learning goals. *Review of Research in Education, 32*(1), 268–291. https://doi.org/10.3102/0091732X07309371.
Edelson, D. C. (2001). Learning-for-use: A framework for the design of technology-supported inquiry activities. *Journal of Research in Science Teaching, 38*(3), 355–385. https://doi.org/10.1002/1098-2736(200103)38:3%3C355::AID-TEA1010%3E3.0.CO;2-M.
European Commission: Science, Economy, and Society. (2007). *Science education now: A renewed pedagogy for the future of Europe*. Office for Official Publications of the European Communities.
Freeman, S., Eddy, S. L., McDonough, M., Smith, M. K., Okoroafor, N., Jordt, H., & Wenderoth, M. P. (2014). Active learning increases student performance in science, engineering, and mathematics. *Proceedings of the National Academy of Sciences, 111*(23), 8410–8415. https://doi.org/10.1073/pnas.1319030111.
Furtak, E. M., Seidel, T., Iverson, H., & Briggs, D. C. (2012). Experimental and quasi-experimental studies of inquiry-based science teaching: A meta-analysis. *Review of Educational Research, 82*(3), 300–329. https://doi.org/10.3102/0034654312457206.
Healey, M., & Jenkins, A. (2009). Developing undergraduate research and inquiry. In *Research report to the higher education academy*. York, UK: Higher Education Academy.
Hermann, G. (1969). Learning by discovery: A critical review of studies. *Journal of Experimental Education, 38*(1), 58–72. https://doi.org/10.1080/00220973.1969.11011167.
Hmelo, C., & Day, R. (1999). Contextualized questioning to scaffold learning from simulations. *Computers & Education, 32*(2), 151–164.
Hmelo-Silver, C. E., Duncan, R. G., & Chinn, C. A. (2007). Scaffolding and achievement in problem-based and inquiry learning: A response to Kirschner, Sweller, and Clark (2006). *Educational Psychologist, 42*(2), 99–107. https://doi.org/10.1080/00461520701263368.

Justice, C., Warry, W., Cuneo, C., Inglis, S., Miller, S., Rice, J., & Sammon, S. (2002). *A grammar for* inquiry: Linking goals and methods in a collaboratively taught social sciences inquiry course. The Alan Blizzard Award Paper: The Award Winning Papers. Canada: MrGraw-Hill Ryerson.

Kanari, Z., & Millar, R. (2004). Reasoning from data: How students collect and interpret data in science investigations. *Journal of Research in Science Teaching, 41*(7), 748–769. https://doi.org/10.1002/tea.20020.

Keselman, A. (2003). Supporting inquiry learning by promoting normative understanding of multivariable causality. *Journal of Research in Science Teaching, 40*(9), 898–921. https://doi.org/10.1002/tea.10115.

Kilpatrick, W. H. (1918). The project method. *Teachers College Record, 19*(4), 319–335.

Kirschner, P. A., Sweller, J., & Clark, R. E. (2006). Why minimal guidance during instruction does not work: An analysis of the failure of constructivist, discovery, problem-based, experiential, and inquiry-based teaching. *Educational Psychologist, 41*(2), 75–86. https://doi.org/10.1207/s15326985ep4102_1.

Klahr, D. (2000). *Exploring science: The cognition and development of discovery processes*. Cambridge, UK: The MIT Press.

Klahr, D., & Dunbar, K. (1988). Dual space search during scientific reasoning. *Cognitive Science, 12*(1), 1–48. https://doi.org/10.1207/s15516709cog1201_1.

Klahr, D., Fay, A. L., & Dunbar, K. (1993). Heuristics for scientific experimentation: A developmental study. *Cognitive Psychology, 25*(1), 111–146. https://doi.org/10.1006/cogp.1993.1003.

Klahr, D., & Nigam, M. (2004). The equivalence of learning paths in early science instruction: Effects of direct instruction and discovery learning. *Psychological Science, 15*(10), 661–667. https://doi.org/10.1111/j.0956-7976.2004.00737.x.

Koerber, S., Sodian, B., Kropf, N., Mayer, D., & Schwippert, K. (2011). The development of scientific reasoning in elementary school age: Understanding theories, designing experiments, interpreting data. *Zeitschrift für Entwicklungspsychologie und Pädagogische Psychologie, 43*, 16–21. https://doi.org/10.1026/0049-8637/A000027.

Koerber, S., Sodian, B., Thoermer, C., & Nett, U. (2005). Scientific reasoning in young children: Preschoolers' ability to evaluate covariation evidence. *Swiss Journal of Psychology, 64*(3), 141–152. https://doi.org/10.1024/1421-0185.64.3.141.

Krajcik, J. S., Czerniak, C., & Berger, C. (1999). *Teaching children science: A project-based approach*. Boston, MA: McGraw-Hill College.

Kuhn, D. (2005). *Education for thinking*. Cambridge, UK: Harvard University Press.

Kuhn, D., Amsel, E., & O'Loughlin, M. (1988). *The development of scientific thinking skills*. Orlando, FL: Academic Press.

Kuhn, D., & Franklin, S. (2006). The second decade: What develops (and how). In W. Damon, R. M. Lerner, D. Kuhn, & R. Siegler (Eds.), *Handbook of Child Psychology: Vol. 2. Cognition, Perception, and Language* (6th ed., pp. 953–994). Hoboken, NJ: Wiley.

Kuhn, D., & Dean, J. (2008). Scaffolded development of inquiry skills in academically disadvantaged middle-school students. *Journal of Psychology of Science and Technology, 1*(2), 36–50.

Lazonder, A. W., & Harmsen, R. (2016). Meta-analysis of inquiry-based learning: Effects of guidance. *Review of Educational Research, 86*(3), 681–718. https://doi.org/10.3102/0034654315627366.

Lee, V., Greene, D., Odom, J., Schechter, E., & Slatta, R. W. (2004). What is inquiry guided learning? In V. S. Lee (Ed.), *Teaching and learning through inquiry: A guidebook for institutions and instructors* (pp. 3–16). Sterling, VA: Stylus.

Lehtinen, E. (2003). Computer-supported collaborative learning: An approach to powerful learning environments. In E. De Corte, L. Verschaffel, N. Entwisthle, & J. Van Merrienboer (Eds.), *Powerful learning environments: Unravelling basic components and dimensions* (pp. 35–54). Oxford, UK: Elsevier.

Levy, F., & Murnane, R. J. (2004). Education and the changing job market. *Educational Leadership, 62*(2), 80–84.

Lingnau, A., Kuhn, M., Harrer, A., Hofmann, D., Fendrich, M., & Hoppe, H. U. (2003). Enriching traditional classroom scenarios by seamless integration of interactive media. In V. Devedzic, J. Spector, D. Sampson, & D. Kinshuk (Eds.), *Advanced learning technologies: Technology enhanced learning* (pp. 135–139). Los Alamitos, CA: IEEE Computer Society.

Manlove, S., Lazonder, A. W., & de Jong, T. (2007). Software scaffolds to promote regulation during scientific inquiry learning. *Metacognition and Learning, 2*(2–3), 141–155.

Mayer, R. E. (2004). Should there be a three-strikes rule against pure discovery learning? *American Psychologist, 59*(1), 14–19.

Mulder, Y. G., Lazonder, A. W., De Jong, T., Anjewierden, A., & Bollen, L. (2012). Validating and optimizing the effects of model progression in simulation-based inquiry learning. *Journal of Science Education and Technology, 21*, 722–729. https://doi.org/10.1016/j.learninstruc.2013.08.001.

Mulder, Y. G., Lazonder, A. W., & De Jong, T. (2014). Using heuristic worked examples to promote inquiry-based learning. *Learning and Instruction, 29*, 56–64. https://doi.org/10.1016/j.learninstruc.2013.08.001.

Mullis, I. V. S., Martin, M. O., Ruddock, G. J., O'Sullivan, C. Y., & Preuschoff, C. (2009). *TIMSS 2011 assessment frameworks*. Amsterdam, NL: International Association for the Evaluation of Educational Achievement.

National Research Council. (1996). *National science education standards*. Washington, DC: National Academies Press.

National Research Council. (2000). *Inquiry and the national science standards*. Washington, DC: National Academy Press.

National Research Council. (2001). *Inquiry and the national science education standards*. Washington, DC: National Academy Press.

NCREL. (2003). *21st century skills: Literacy in the digital age*. North Central Regional Educational Laboratory (NCREL). Retrieved December 19, 2019, from https://pict.sdsu.edu/engauge21st.pdf

Organization for Economic Co-Operation and Development (OECD). (2009). *Annual report.* Published under responsibility of the Secretary-General of the OECD. Retrieved December 19, 2019, from https://www.oecd.org/newsroom/43125523.pdf

Pedaste, M., Mäeots, M., Leijen, Ä., & Sarapuu, T. (2012). Improving students' inquiry skills through reflection and self-regulation scaffolds. *Technology, Instruction, Cognition and Learning, 9*(1–2), 81–95.

Pedaste, M., Mäeots, M., Siiman, L. A., De Jong, T., Van Riesen, S. A., Kamp, E. T., et al. (2015). Phases of inquiry-based learning: Definitions and the inquiry cycle. *Educational Research Review, 14*, 47–61. https://doi.org/10.1016/j.edurev.2015.02.003.

Piekny, J., Gruber, D., & Maehler, C. (2014). The development of experimentation and evidence evaluation skills at preschool age. *International Journal of Science Education, 36*(2), 334–354. https://doi.org/10.1080/09500693.2013.776192.

Piekny, J., & Maehler, C. (2013). Scientific reasoning in early and middle childhood: The development of domain-general evidence evaluation, experimentation, and hypothesis generation skills. *British Journal of Developmental Psychology, 31*(2), 153–179. https://doi.org/10.1111/j.2044-835X.2012.02082.x.

Pinkwart, N. (2003). A plug-in architecture for graph based collaborative modeling systems. In U. Hoppe, F. Verdejo, & J. Kay (Eds.), *Shaping the future of learning through intelligent technologies. Proceedings of the 11th conference on artificial intelligence in education* (pp. 535–536). Amsterdam, The Netherlands: IOS Press.

Pinkwart, N. (2005). *Collaborative modeling in graph based environments*. Berlin, Germany: dissertation.de.

Ramsden, P. (2003). *Learning to teach in higher education*. London, UK: Routledge/Falmer.

Sandoval, W. A. (2003). Conceptual and epistemic aspects of students' scientific explanations. *Journal of the Learning Sciences, 12*(1), 5–51. https://doi.org/10.1207/S15327809JLS1201_2.

Sandoval, W. A., & Reiser, B. J. (2004). Explanation-driven inquiry: Integrating conceptual and epistemic support for scientific inquiry. *Science Education, 88*(3), 345–372. https://doi.org/10.1002/sce.10130.

Scardamalia, M. (2002). Collective responsibility for the advancement of knowledge. In B. Smith (Ed.), *Liberal education in a knowledge society* (pp. 67–98). Chicago, IL: Open Court.

Scardamalia, M., & Bereiter, C. (1994). Computer support for knowledge-building communities. *The Journal of the Learning Sciences, 3*(3), 265–283. https://doi.org/10.1207/s15327809jls0303_3.

Schauble, L., Glaser, R., Duschl, R. A., Schulze, S., & John, J. (1995). Students' understanding of the objectives and procedures of experimentation in the science classroom. *Journal of the Learning Sciences, 4*(2), 131–166. https://doi.org/10.1207/s15327809jls0402_1.

Schmidt, H. G. (1983). Problem-based learning: Rationale and description. *Medical Education, 17*(1), 11–16. https://doi.org/10.1111/j.1365-2923.1983.tb01086.x.

Schroeder, C. M., Scott, T. P., Tolson, H., Huang, T. Y., & Lee, Y. H. (2007). A meta-analysis of national research: Effects of teaching strategies on student achievement in science in the United States. *Journal of Research in Science Teaching: The Official Journal of the National Association for Research in Science Teaching, 44*(10), 1436–1460. https://doi.org/10.1002/tea.20212.

Schwartz, D. L., & Bransford, J. D. (1998). A time for telling. *Cognition and Instruction, 16*(4), 475–522. https://doi.org/10.1207/s1532690xci1604_4.

Shadish, W., Cook, T., & Campbell, D. (2002). *Experimental and quasi-experimental designs for generalized causal inference*. Boston, MA: Houghton Mifflin.

Shymansky, J. A., Hedges, L. V., & Woodworth, G. (1990). A reassessment of the effects of inquiry-based science curricula of the 60's on student performance. *Journal of Research in Science Teaching, 27*(2), 127–144. https://doi.org/10.1002/tea.3660270205.

Slotta, J. D. (2004). The web-based inquiry science environment (WISE): Scaffolding knowledge integration in the science classroom. In M. C. Linn, E. A. Davis, & P. Bell (Eds.), *Internet environments for science education* (pp. 203–231). Mahwah, NJ: Lawrence Erlbaum.

Slotta, J. D., Jorde, D., & Holmes, J. (2007). *Learning from our peers in international exchanges: When is worth doing, and how can we help it succeed?* Unpublished Manuscript.

Sodian, B., Zaitchik, D., & Carey, S. (1991). Young children's differentiation of hypothetical beliefs from evidence. *Child Development, 62*(4), 753–766. https://doi.org/10.1111/j.1467-8624.1991.tb01567.x/.

Spronken-Smith, R., Walker, R., Batchelor, J., O'Steen, B., & Angelo, T. (2011). Enablers and constraints to the use of inquiry-based learning in undergraduate education. *Teaching in Higher Education, 16*(1), 15–28. https://doi.org/10.1080/13562517.2010.507300.

Steinke, P., & Fitch, P. (2011). Outcome assessment from the perspective of psychological science: The TAIM approach. *New Directions for Institutional Research, 2011*(149), 15–26. https://doi.org/10.1002/ir.377.

van Joolingen, W. R., de Jong, T., Lazonder, A. W., Savelsbergh, E. R., & Manlove, S. (2005). Co-Lab: Research and development of an online learning environment for collaborative scientific discovery learning. *Computers in Human Behavior, 21*(4), 671–688. https://doi.org/10.1016/j.chb.2004.10.039.

Varma, K. (2014). Supporting scientific experimentation and reasoning in young elementary school students. *Journal of Science Education and Technology, 23*(3), 381–397. https://doi.org/10.1007/s10956-013-9470-8.

Veenman, M. V. J., Wilhelm, P., & Beishuizen, J. J. (2004). The relation between intellectual and metacognitive skills from a developmental perspective. *Learning and Instruction, 14*(1), 89–109. https://doi.org/10.1016/j.learninstruc.2003.10.004.

Wecker, C., Kohnle, C., & Fischer, F. (2007). Computer literacy and inquiry learning: When geeks learn less. *Journal of Computer Assisted Learning, 23*(2), 133–144. https://doi.org/10.1111/j.1365-2729.2006.00218.x.

Weinstein, T., Boulanger, F. D., & Walberg, H. J. (1982). Science curriculum effects in high school: A quantitative synthesis. *Journal of Research in Science Teaching, 19*(6), 511–522. https://doi.org/10.1002/tea.3660190610.

White, B. Y., & Frederiksen, J. R. (1998). Inquiry, modeling, and metacognition: Making science accessible to all students. *Cognition and Instruction, 16*(1), 3–118. https://doi.org/10.1207/s1532690xci1601_2.

Zumbach, J. (2003). *Problembasiertes Lernen (problem-based learning)*. Münster, Germany: Waxmann Verlag.

# Small Group Learning 52

Ingo Kollar and Martin Greisel

## Contents

| | |
|---|---|
| Introduction | 1286 |
| Purposes and Rationale | 1287 |
| Design Issues and Approaches | 1290 |
| (The Combination of) Individual Learning Prerequisites for Successful Group Learning | 1290 |
| Group Processes for Successful Small Group Learning | 1291 |
| Instructional Conditions for Successful Small Group Learning | 1292 |
| Research Issues and Related Approaches | 1294 |
| Core Findings and Current Trends | 1295 |
| Challenges, Lessons Learned, and Implications for Learning and Teaching Psychology | 1296 |
| Teaching, Learning, and Assessment Resources Associated with Research on Small Group Learning | 1297 |
| Cross-References | 1299 |
| References | 1299 |

### Abstract

Small group learning has been shown to be an effective study method across a variety of disciplines, including psychology. The goal of this chapter is to provide an overview over research on small group learning to explain its potential with respect to teaching and learning psychology. The chapter starts with a description of motivational, neo-Piagetian, neo-Vygotskian, and cognitive theoretical approaches that explain why small group learning can be an effective learning

---

Chapter to be published in Zumbach, J., Bernstein, D. A., Narciss, S., & Marsico, G. (in prep.). *International Handbook of Psychology Learning and Teaching*. New York: Springer.

---

I. Kollar (✉) · M. Greisel
Lehrstuhl für Psychologie m.b.B.d. Pädagogischen Psychologie, University of Augsburg, Augsburg, Germany
e-mail: ingo.kollar@uni-a.de; martin.greisel@uni-a.de

method. Based on evidence that indicates that learners do not always benefit from small group learning, the following section introduces four kinds of scaffolding approaches that have been shown to be powerful means of improving learning processes and outcomes of small group learning. These are (a) the jigsaw method, (b) the peer feedback approach, (c) collaboration scripts, and (d) group awareness tools. Next, the chapter gives an overview over important research issues and related approaches. After that, core findings and current trends in research on small group learning are reported. The chapter ends with a description of the consequences that can be drawn for the teaching and learning of psychology.

**Keywords**

Collaborative learning · Knowledge acquisition · Skill acquisition · Interactive activities · Jigsaw method · Peer feedback · Collaboration scripts · Group awareness tools

## Introduction

As an instructional approach, small group learning has been around both in research and in practice for a very long time. In a way, already Socrates' dialogue method can be regarded as an instance of small group learning: By asking thought-provoking questions, one interaction partner stimulates the reasoning of the other partner, which hopefully leads to "insight" or, more profanely, to knowledge acquisition. More typical, though, are groups that are less hierarchical, so that the single group members engage in collaboration in a more equal way and at a more similar level. This becomes, for example, apparent in Dillenbourg's (1999) definition, according to which small group learning "is a situation in which two or more people learn or attempt to learn something together" (p. 1).

Even though sometimes under different labels (such as collaborative learning, cooperative learning, or team learning), the approach is widely used across different age groups from pre-school children (see Barclay & Breheny, 1994) to adults (de Hei, Tabacaru, Sjoer, Rippe, & Walenkamp, 2020); in different educational institutions such as primary schools (McNaughton, Crick, Joyce-Gibbons, Beauchamp, Young, & Tan, 2017) and universities (De Wever, van Keer, Schellens, & Valcke, 2011); in different learning settings including informal (Zheng, Zhang, & Gyasi, 2019), formal (e.g., Weinberger, Stegmann, & Fischer, 2010), and work-place settings (e.g., Selleck, Fifolt, Burkart, Frank, Curry, & Hites, 2017); and in both face-to-face (e.g., De Backer, Van Keer, & Valcke, 2020) and digital learning contexts (e.g., Yoon, Anderson, Park, Elinich, & Lin, 2018). Also, having students learn subject matter information in small groups is used across a wide range of disciplines, in the sciences (e.g., Sobocinski, Järvelä, Malmberg, Dindar, Isosalo, & Noponen, 2020), as well as in the humanities (e.g., Wang, Kollar, & Stegmann, 2017) and even in interdisciplinary teams (Rummel & Spada, 2005).

The goal of this chapter is to provide an overview over key theoretical assumptions, design issues, research issues, and empirical findings from instructional research on small group learning.

## Purposes and Rationale

The key assumption of proponents of researchers in the field is that learning in small groups may support individual learners in the acquisition of (a) subject matter knowledge (i.e., the content information that is to be learned and discussed within the group) and of (b) socio-communicative skills (e.g., argumentation; see Andriessen, Baker, & Suthers, 2003), at least when certain conditions are met. This assumption has been advocated from a range of different theoretical perspectives. From a motivational perspective, small group learning can be effective with respect to individual knowledge and skill acquisition when it is clear that (a) the group can reach a desired external reward for which (b) the contributions of each single group member are relevant (e.g., when the reward is only given when all single group members have reached a certain individual learning gain from prior to after collaboration; see Slavin & Tanner, 1979). That way, an interdependence between group members is created that will make it likely that the single learners support each other in their learning processes, because attaining the reward is attractive to every single group member (see also Johnson & Johnson, 2018).

From a neo-Vygotskian perspective, small group learning has a strong potential to support individual knowledge and skill acquisition because it may trigger so-called socio-cognitive conflicts: The idea is that through learning with one or more peers, different viewpoints on a topic will become visible. In case that some learning partners hold different views, socio-cognitive conflicts emerge. In Piagetian terms, such socio-cognitive conflicts cause a disequilibrium in the peers' cognitive systems, and they will strive to get back to a status of equilibrium. If they do so through accommodation, resolving the socio-cognitive conflict leads to significant restructuring processes in the learners' cognitive systems (see de Lisi & Golbeck, 1999).

From a neo-Vygotskian perspective, peer learners may provide each other a so-called zone of proximal development (ZPD) during collaboration. This will happen when the learning partners assist each other in an engagement in learning activities that are just a little above their actual competence level, by externalizing (e.g., through dialogue) their thought processes. Through this externalization by one learner, their peers will internalize these new practices, which is in itself a learning process that would not happen if they would study in isolation (see Hogan & Tudge, 1999).

Over the past two decades, the rather coarse-grained assumptions derived from Piagetian and Vygotskian theory have been complemented by research that takes a closer look at the kinds of processes and activities learners engage in during collaboration and investigates what kinds of activities are in particular related to cognitive change. An exemplary theoretical framework that argues for a very high potential of collaborative learning for knowledge acquisition is the ICAP framework proposed by Chi and Wylie (2014). This framework differentiates four kinds of visible learning activities that individuals may engage in during learning. In a passive mode of engagement, learners only receive information. An example would be to listen to a lecture. In an active mode of engagement, learners are physically active. An example would be to take verbatim notes during a lecture. In a constructive mode of engagement, students are also physically active, but create learning products that go beyond just a reproduction of the information they were presented. In the lecture context, this would, for example, be the case when a student creates a concept map of the main concepts that were presented in the lecture. Finally, in an interactive mode of engagement, students exchange viewpoints, questions, arguments, or comments and that way build on each other's reasoning. The basic assumption of the ICAP framework is that an engagement in these four different kinds of visible activities goes along with different levels of (invisible) cognitive processing. When students are passive, the most likely cognitive processes are processes of isolated storing of the perceived learning material. While being active, learners will typically engage in integrative processes by which new information is assimilated in existing schemata. When students are constructive, they typically engage in the creation of knowledge. And when they are interactive, they ideally jointly co-construct knowledge. That way, the cognitive processes that are typical for an engagement in each activity type become increasingly elaborated from passive to interactive.

Even though the ICAP model is not without criticism (see Renkl, 2011), there is empirical evidence that seems to support its assumptions. For example, Wekerle et al. (2022) asked $N = 381$ students who took part in a broad range of different university courses to indicate to what extent their teachers prompted an engagement in passive, active, constructive, and interactive learning activities. Also, they asked for students' subjective learning gains in each of their courses. Results showed that a higher engagement in interactive activities was more strongly related to learning outcomes than a higher engagement in the subordinate activities. In an experimental study that used objective knowledge tests, Menekse, Stump, Krause, and Chi (2013) found further support for the ICAP hypothesis. In this study, $N = 120$ engineering students received a text that explained a set of engineering concepts and included several graphs and figures to help student understand the content better. Participants were randomly distributed across four conditions: In the passive condition, students were instructed to read the text aloud. They were not allowed to highlight text content or to take notes. In the active condition, participants received highlighters and were instructed to highlight the most important text passages. In the constructive condition, students did not receive the complete text but instead only the graphs and figures and were instructed to produce written explanations of them. Finally, in the interactive condition, the same task as in the constructive condition was presented, but was to be solved by student dyads (instead of individuals as in the constructive condition). Before and after the respective tasks, students received a pre-test and a post-test they were asked to solve individually. Results were completely in line with the ICAP hypothesis: Students from the interactive condition reached the highest pre-post gains, followed by participants from the constructive condition, who were followed by students from the active condition. Participants from the passive conditions reached significantly lower scores than students from all other conditions.

One question that follows from research on the ICAP model is: Are all activities that learners engage in during small group learning per se "interactive" or is there a specific feature of interactive activities that sets them apart from passive, active, and constructive activities? Regarding the first part of this question, the answer clearly is "no": Of course, when collaborating with others, learners will often also engage in activities other than interactive ones. For example, a common phenomenon is that learners split the task in parallel sub-tasks and distribute them equally within the group, resulting in each group member working on their own without much interaction.

With respect to the second part of the question above, the answer is "yes": There is one main feature of interactive activities that sets them apart from the other kinds of activities that are differentiated in the ICAP model. An activity is only then interactive, if the peer engaging in that activity builds on contributions from her learning partners (see also Teasley, 1995). Thus, during an argumentative dialogue between two learners, for example, developing a counterargument on a peer's previously uttered argument would be regarded as an interactive activity, while a completely new argument that is introduced to the discourse would "only" count as a constructive activity, because it does not build on a contribution of a learning partner. Empirical evidence showing that this differentiation really matters for learning comes from a study by Vogel, Kollar, Ufer, Reichersdorfer, Reiss, and Fischer (2016): In their study, $N = 101$ mathematics freshmen were asked to work in dyads on a set of mathematical proof problems. Their collaborative discourse was recorded and analyzed on the basis of the ICAP model, with a focus on an engagement in constructive and interactive activities. After collaboration, students individually took a post-test to measure their argumentation skills. Regression analyses showed that students' engagement in interactive activities predicted their post-test performance, whereas an engagement in constructive activities did not. Furthermore, the study showed that an engagement in interactive activities was only beneficial for the learning partner who actually produced such interactive activities. Being exposed to a learning partner who shows an interactive engagement without showing interactive activities oneself however did not seem to be significantly related to one's own learning.

Taking the definition of interactive activities into account according to which interactive activities are activities by which students build on the contributions of their learning partner(s), generating counterarguments however is only one example for an interactive activity. Other interactive activities that have been described as being conducive for learning are, for example, student-generated explanations (King, 2007) and cognitive modelling (Palincsar & Brown, 1984), especially when following respective questions or requests from the learning partner(s).

Taken together, there are good theoretical and empirical reasons to assume that small group learning has a high potential to foster student learning. While, from a neo-Piagetian perspective, the elicitation and solution of socio-cognitive conflicts (typically through discourse) is regarded as the main motor for learning, neo-Vygotskians regard the mutual provision of a zone of proximal development between the learners as the main driving force. The cognitive perspective further provides more specific assumptions concerning what learning activities go along with high-level cognitive processes that play a significant role for individual knowledge and skill acquisition.

## Design Issues and Approaches

Despite the described theoretical and empirical reasons that make small group learning appear as an effective learning method, some studies also found negative effects of small group learning on knowledge acquisition, compared to individual learning. In a study by Weinberger et al. (2010), for example, triads vs. individual educational science students were asked to analyze three authentic educational problem cases by aid of a psychological theory within a computer-based learning environment. In the triadic condition, group members had the opportunity to view each other's case analyses and to provide each other with feedback. However, this interactive process was not further scaffolded. In the individual condition, students analyzed these cases individually, i.e., without receiving feedback or questions from peers. In a subsequent knowledge test that asked participants to analyze another case individually, students who had learned in groups received significantly lower scores than students who had solved the previous three cases individually.

These and other findings (e.g., Barron, 2003) indicate that small group learning is not an effective learning method per se. Instead, it appears that certain conditions must be met in order to make it successful. First, individual learning prerequisites and their combination within the group have an influence on the successfulness of small group learning. Second, groups need to engage in certain processes to reach high-level outcomes. And third, there are instructional conditions that may support groups to attain such outcomes. In the following, we elaborate on these conditions more deeply.

## (The Combination of) Individual Learning Prerequisites for Successful Group Learning

First, there are person- and group-related preconditions for successful small group learning. For example, Jurkowski and Hänze (2012) showed that students with more developed social competences benefitted more from collaborative learning than students with less developed social competences. Also, students who were only mildly assertive performed better after collaboration than students low or high in assertiveness. In a more recent study, Kelsen and Liang (2019) found evidence for extraversion and partially also conscientiousness to be positive prerequisites for successful collaborative learning. In a study with psychology students, Cummings and Sheeran (2019) found that students low in neuroticism and with high prior academic achievement benefit the most from peer-assisted study sessions. In a study that investigated how to best combine students with different personality traits, Bellhäuser, Konert, Müller, and Röpke (2018) further found that groups that were heterogeneous with respect to both conscientiousness and extraversion rated their productivity higher and invested more time than groups that were homogeneous with respect to one or both of these personality traits. With respect to the successful completion of group assignments, it was best when groups were heterogeneous with respect to either conscientiousness or extraversion; groups that were heterogeneous with respect to both, however, did not do better than groups who were only heterogeneous with respect to one of the two. Thus, several individual learner characteristics seem to have an influence on the successfulness of small group learning in terms of learning gains.

## Group Processes for Successful Small Group Learning

At the group level, especially self-organized study groups have been argued to be more satisfied with their collaboration when they manage to (a) arrive at shared representations of what their actual regulation problems are, (b) select regulation strategies that have the potential to immediately (rather than indirectly) tackle these problems, and (c) apply regulation strategies with a high intensity (see Melzner, Greisel, Dresel, & Kollar, 2020). Whether such groups are also more successful with respect to knowledge acquisition, however, is still subject to further research.

In a comprehensive research program, the group around Järvelä further showed that successful groups are more effective than less successful groups in coordinating their regulation efforts across three different social levels: First, even though collaborating with others, each individual group member needs to regulate her own learning during collaboration. For example, when she notices a lack of understanding of an important concept on her side, she may decide to look this concept up by aid of an online search engine. According to Järvelä and Hadwin (2013), regulative processes such as this are located at the "self"-level. Second, within groups, a single group member may regulate another group member's learning process. For example, when one group member does not notice her own lack of understanding, another group member might do so and thus point her peer to this lack of understanding and explain the concept in question to her. In Järvelä and Hadwin's (2013) terms, this would be an instance of regulation at the "co"-level. Third, the whole group may attempt to jointly regulate its collective learning process. For example, at the beginning of their collaboration, the group members may negotiate how to approach the task and jointly develop a plan for their collaboration. According to Järvelä and Hadwin (2013), this would be an instance of regulation at the "shared" level.

As mentioned, there is ample research on how groups regulate their learning at the different social levels, with the strongest emphasis of research on the "shared" level. For example, using a qualitative case study approach, Malmberg, Järvelä, Järvenoja, and Panadero (2015) describe a group of four educational science students who are supposed to analyze a case that describes a student with motivational problems. One student begins by sharing her own experiences as a pupil which to her seem to be similar to the problems of the student in the case description. Her fellow students ridicule her, which creates a socio-emotional problem. The group then proceeds to solve this socio-emotional problem at the shared level through joint discussion, which finally happens. In another study, De Backer et al. (2020) further showed that not all types of regulation at the shared level are conducive for knowledge acquisition. Using latent class analyses on coded video data from 64 Educational Sciences students who worked in a peer tutoring learning scenario, they found that socially shared regulation was especially effective when it followed an "interrogative" discourse type in which one student would elicit a thought-provoking trigger on which peers reacted with elaborative contributions. In contrast, engaging in an "interfering" type of socially shared regulation in which single students strongly and mostly negatively influence collaboration by interrupting the course of actions turned out to undermine post-test performance. Overall, thus, both individual- and group-level prerequisites and processes seem to have an influence on the successfulness of small group learning.

## Instructional Conditions for Successful Small Group Learning

Unfortunately, by far not all learners have the described individual preconditions that are conducive for successful small group learning at their disposal (e.g., Bellhäuser et al., 2018). Likewise, it has been shown numerous times that groups' spontaneous (i.e., un-guided) way of collaborating very often is suboptimal (see Weinberger et al., 2010). It therefore is not surprising that one of the most well-researched topics on small group learning focuses on how to scaffold collaborative learning (see Kollar, Wecker, & Fischer, 2018). For the purpose of this chapter, four prominent approaches are described in more detail: (a) the jigsaw approach, (b) the peer feedback approach, (c) the collaboration script approach, and (d) the group awareness approach.

### The Jigsaw Approach

The basic idea of the jigsaw approach as developed by Aronson, Blaney, Stephan, Sikes, and Snapp (1978) is to stimulate elaborated discussion within small groups by (a) creating knowledge differences between learners and (b) arranging and rearranging groups by composing them in ways that stimulate in-depth discussion within these groups almost naturally. For that sake, the whole group of learners (e.g., a psychology seminar) is first split up into groups of five to six students each. Then, every member of each group receives a segment of the material that is the topic of the lesson to study individually. That way, knowledge differences between single group members are created. Next, all students that read the same segment come together in so-called "expert" groups. In these groups, students discuss their segment with each other in-depth, in order to arrive at the deepest possible understanding. After that, the students return to their original groups, which now consist of experts regarding each and every segment. Now, the task is to mutually help each other to get a clear understanding of all the segments that the individual students have become experts on during the expert group stage. By re-arranging the groups like this, an engagement in interactive activities such as questioning, explaining, reacting to counterarguments, etc. becomes almost inevitable, which – as predicted in the ICAP model (Chi & Wylie, 2014) – is likely to result in a deep understanding of the topic.

Even though it was originally developed for high school classrooms, the jigsaw approach has also been used in university education. For example, Baken, Adams, and Rentz (2020) found the jigsaw approach to foster biology undergraduate students' knowledge acquisition in comparison to an unstructured small group learning condition which were both implemented in a laboratory course. Similar results have been found for further higher education contexts and disciplines as well (e.g., Alrassi & Mortensen, 2020).

**The Peer Feedback Approach**
Receiving elaborated feedback on one's own performance is a very powerful way to promote learning (see Hattie, 2009). Research on peer feedback investigates to what extent such feedback can also be provided by peers (as compared to teachers) and how such peer feedback can be improved by adding further guidance during the process of peer feedback (e.g., Gielen, Tops, Dochy, Onghena, & Smeets, 2010).

Deiglmayr (2018) differentiates between three phases of the peer feedback process. First, students perform a task for which they are going to receive peer feedback. Already during this phase, peer feedback can have a positive effect: As research indicates, already the expectation that one's performance will be assessed by a peer afterward may lead to better task performance than when no such expectation exists (Topping, 1998). Second, one or several peers formulate feedback on their peer's task performance. Here, research has shown that learners may also benefit from providing (and not only from receiving) peer feedback, especially when they are supported on how to give high-quality feedback (e.g., by following certain feedback criteria; see Alqassab, Strijbos, & Ufer, 2018). And third, students receive peer feedback and (ideally) incorporate it in their revision of the task. Empirical studies showed that the reception of high-quality peer feedback alone is not sufficient for the receiver to benefit from it. Rather, learning effects are especially likely when the feedback receiver engages in deep processing of that feedback (Wichmann, Funk, & Rummel, 2018).

**The Collaboration Script Approach**
Collaboration scripts are scaffolds that provide learners in small groups with detailed instruction on the kinds and sequence of activities and roles they are supposed to engage in during small group learning (Fischer, Kollar, Stegmann, & Wecker, 2013). Optimally, the activities and roles that are distributed are complementary to each other, so that an engagement in truly interactive activities in the sense of the ICAP model is prompted. For example, when arguing about a scientific topic, a collaboration script may prompt one learner of a dyad to produce an argument, while the other learning partner is supposed to carefully listen to that argument and to critically evaluate its validity. Afterwards, that learner is prompted to provide a counterargument, which is now to be critically evaluated by the first speaker. At the end, the script may prompt both learners to find an argument that would combine their perspectives.

Collaboration scripts such as this have been studied extensively in the past, especially in research on computer-supported collaborative learning (e.g., Näykki, Isohätälä, Järvelä, Poysa-Tarhonen, & Häkkinen, 2017). A meta-analysis by Vogel et al. (2016) showed that when compared to unstructured collaboration, computer-supported collaboration scripts have positive effects both on learners' acquisition of domain-specific knowledge and even more on the acquisition of cross-domain skills.

**The Group Awareness Approach**

Just as collaboration scripts, also group awareness tools have extensively been studied in research on computer-supported collaborative learning (e.g., Janssen & Bodemer, 2013). The idea of this approach is to (a) measure certain individual learning prerequisites (e.g., prior knowledge) or group processes (e.g., the homo-/heterogeneity of the single group members' contributions) and to (b) mirror this information back to the group, hoping that the group resp. its members will adapt its/their learning to this information. In one study, Schnaubert and Bodemer (2019) created dyads of students who first individually read a text that was assigned to them (one for each student). Then, students individually answered a knowledge test that included binary true-false questions that referred to the two texts and were asked to indicate whether they were confident that their answer was correct (again using a binary true-false format). During their subsequent collaboration, the two learning partners worked on a multi-touch table on which the information about each other's knowledge ratings (cognitive group awareness tool) and confidence ratings (metacognitive group awareness tool) were displayed. Results showed that both kinds of information had a strong influence on collaboration processes. When students had disagreed on a knowledge test question, the presentation of this conflict via the cognitive group awareness tool led the group to more extensively discuss this item than when no such information was presented. When the metacognitive group awareness tool displayed the information that group members were unsure of their answers, this information led groups to discuss topics associated with these knowledge test items more intensively. Yet, none of the two group awareness tools had an effect on a subsequent knowledge post-test.

The main message from all this is that to be an effective method for knowledge and skill acquisition, small group learning needs to be appropriately scaffolded. The four approaches just described all have been shown to be powerful in this regard and should especially be applied when learners or groups do not exhibit learning prerequisites or processes that have been shown to be important for the successfulness of small group learning.

# Research Issues and Related Approaches

It probably has become obvious from the previous section that one main issue in research on small group learning refers to how to scaffold collaborative learning in a way that students are supported with regard both to the quality of collaboration and to individual knowledge and skill acquisition. Thereby, especially computer-supported scaffolds and tools seem to be of interest these days (Chen, Wang, Kirschner, & Tsai, 2018; see following section).

Another important strand of research refers to the question what actually constitutes high-quality collaboration and how it relates to individual knowledge and skill acquisition as well as to different parameters of the quality of group products. It thus is not surprising that a lot of research on small group learning intensively looks at collaboration processes that unfold within small groups, typically using established or newly developed coding schemes (e.g., Weinberger & Fischer, 2006) or applying inductive analytical techniques such as content analysis (Mayring, 2014).

The strong interest in analyzing collaborative learning processes has also inspired the development of new analytical techniques, especially ones that take the temporal nature of such data into account. For example, Epistemic Network Analysis (Shaffer, Collier, & Ruis, 2016) allows to analyze coded collaborative learning activities with different grain sizes that makes it possible to detect relations between different activities which may only be fruitful (or harmful) for learning when shown in timely relation to each other.

In general, thus, research on small group learning can be characterized as a very active, dynamic, and multi-faceted field that brings together researchers from different disciplines with different methodological backgrounds.

## Core Findings and Current Trends

The dynamic and multidisciplinary nature of small group research makes it challenging to identify its core findings and current trends. When it comes to core findings, results from meta-analyses that synthesized the effects of collaborative vs. individual or whole-class learning seem to be of specific importance. For example, based on the results of 37 studies conducted in undergraduate STEM classes, Springer, Stanne, and Donovan (1999) found a mean effect size of $d = 0.51$ of small group learning on achievement and a mean effect size of $d = 0.55$ on attitudes (toward learning STEM material), when compared to non-collaborative forms of classroom instruction. In another meta-analysis, Kyndt et al. (2013) found similar results. Yet, they found larger effects of small group learning compared to regular classroom instruction in STEM classes compared to social sciences and language education. Also, they found larger effects for university students than for high school students.

A trend that has already started about 20 years ago but that still sparks a lot research interest refers to the question how digital technologies can be used to realize and scaffold small group learning. In fact, there is a whole research community with its own conference and its own journal that revolves around this question (see Cress, Rosé, Wise, & Oshima, 2021). In a meta-analysis that synthesized key findings from this research, Chen et al., (2018) found computer-supported collaborative learning to have a medium effect size of $d = 0.42$ on knowledge gain, of $d = 0.64$ on skill acquisition, and of $d = 0.38$ on student perceptions, when compared to computer-supported individual learning. Furthermore, when looking at the effects of computer use vs. no computer use in collaborative learning settings, they consistently reported positive effects of computer use on a broad range of dependent variables such as knowledge gain ($d = 0.45$), skill acquisition ($d = 0.53$), student perceptions ($d = 0.51$), group task performance ($d = 0.89$), and social interaction ($d = 0.57$). Finally, they found positive effects of extra technology-mediated learning environments or tools (such as computer-supported collaboration scripts or group awareness tools) compared to CSCL without such tools for knowledge gain ($d = 0.55$). Thus, it appears that digital technologies bear quite some potential when it comes to foster learning among students (see also ▶ Chap. 56, "Technology-Enhanced Psychology Learning and Teaching").

One particular trend in this context lies in current attempts to make machine learning algorithms and text mining methods usable for the assessment and scaffolding of (computer-supported) small group learning (see Rosé & Ferschke, 2016). The basic idea of related efforts is to use human-coded discourse data to train computer algorithms in reliably coding further discourse material from collaborating groups and to feed this information back into the computer-supported learning environment in a way that the group receives adaptive collaboration support. First results in this direction seem to be promising (see, e.g., Daxenberger, Csanadi, Ghanem, Kollar, & Gurevych, 2018).

## Challenges, Lessons Learned, and Implications for Learning and Teaching Psychology

This chapter has shown that small group learning has considerable potential as a method to be used in psychology learning and teaching. In fact, as current research indicates, small group learning seems to be an interesting method for the learning and teaching of psychological concepts and theories (e.g., Rumain & Geliebter, 2020; Yalch, Vitale, & Ford, 2019).

Even though it may be expected that many psychology students have rather positive learning prerequisites in terms of general cognitive ability, prior achievement, or personality traits such as conscientiousness, empirical research that has been conducted in this as well as in other academic fields at the undergraduate and graduate level demands psychology teachers not to be overly optimistic that small group learning will automatically go well in this population. In fact, also among university students (and even among those studying psychology), positive effects of scaffolding collaboration during small group learning have frequently been reported (e.g., Chen et al., 2018). Thus, psychology teachers should be well-prepared to employ appropriate scaffolding techniques when they intend to use small group learning in their classes, and these scaffolds should in particular be aimed at triggering student engagement in interactive activities (see Chi & Wylie, 2014).

A particular challenge in this respect though is how to assess what and how much scaffolding students need and – even more importantly – to provide adaptive support, that is, to fade support out and in as the group needs it. While Wang et al. (2017) have shown that groups of university students might actually be not too bad in deciding what kinds of support they need at what time and in adapting that support to their own needs, high expectations are placed in the possibilities of machine learning and text mining algorithms to provide automated and adaptive support. It will be interesting to see whether and when such developments become affordable and applicable in practice of teaching and learning.

Further, small group learning cannot only be realized within the limits of the classroom. Also, especially when it comes to preparing for exams, students often deliberately form study groups. For such groups to be successful, it seems to be important that the group has a high awareness and develops shared perceptions of different problems that may occur during collaboration and to apply regulation strategies that have the potential to immediately resolve these problems (see Melzner et al., 2020).

To sum up, if small group learning involves student engagement in interactive activities – be it externally scaffolded or spontaneously shown by the students – it is an effective method to be employed in psychology curricula to help students acquire key content from the discipline.

## Teaching, Learning, and Assessment Resources Associated with Research on Small Group Learning

Chen, J., Wang, M., Kirschner, P. A., Tsai, C.-C. (2018). The role of collaboration, computer use, learning environments, and supporting strategies in CSCL: a meta-analysis. *Review of Educational Research, 88*(6), 799–843. ▶ https://doi.org/10.3102/0034654318791584

This article presents a meta-analysis on the basis of 425 empirical studies published between 2000 and 2016 in the field of CSCL. Results demonstrate that in computer-supported settings, collaborative learning has positive effects on various learning outcomes when compared to individual learning. Also, when collaborative learning is realized, higher effects are reached when students use computers during collaboration as compared to when they do not. And finally, the study provides evidence for the effectiveness of tools and scaffolds that are specifically designed to support collaboration.

Chi, M. T. H., & Wylie, R. (2014). The ICAP framework: Linking cognitive engagement to active learning outcomes. *Educational Psychologist, 49*(4), 219–243. ▶ https://doi.org/10.1080/00461520.2014.965823

This article introduces the ICAP framework, which offers a cognitive explanation for the high potential that small group learning has for knowledge acquisition. According to the ICAP hypothesis, the likelihood that learners will engage in high-level cognitive processes increases the more they engage in interactive activities such as reacting to counterarguments, answering questions, or giving peer feedback. An important implication is that student engagement in such activities should be prompted if groups do not show them spontaneously.

De Wever, B., van Keer, H., Schellens, T., & Valcke, M. (2011). Assessing collaboration in a wiki: The reliability of university students' peer assessment. *The Internet and Higher Education, 14*(4), 201–206. ▶ https://doi.org/10.1016/j.iheduc.2011.07.003

This article provides an excellent example on how to implement small group learning in large lectures. The authors split $N = 659$ first-year students into groups of about eight students each and had them create wikis on the learning content. Each learner was then asked to assess the writing of their group mates. ICCs showed that these intra-group ratings showed a high consistency, indicating that peer assessment can reliably be used in wiki-based learning environments, even in large lectures.

Dillenbourg, P. (1999). What do you mean by collaborative learning? In P. Dillenbourg (Ed.), *Collaborative learning: Cognitive and computational approaches* (pp. 1–19). Amsterdam: Elsevier.

This book chapter provides an in-depth discussion of key concepts of research on small group learning. It also shows how diverse different implementations of small group learning can be. Further, the chapter provides an overview over different theoretical perspectives on collaborative learning, as well as on its effects on learning processes and outcomes. It is one of the most heavily cited contributions in research on collaborative learning.

Janssen, J., & Bodemer, D. (2013). Coordinated computer-supported collaborative learning: Awareness and awareness tools. *Educational Psychologist, 48*(1), 40–55. ▸ https://doi.org/10.1080/00461520.2012.749153

This article provides an overview over a specific kind of scaffold for small group learning, namely, group awareness tools. Group awareness tools mirror information on individual learning-relevant prerequisites or collaborative processes back to the group. As the article shows, even though effects on knowledge acquisition are rather rare, group awareness tools may have strong effects on how the group members act with each other. Therefore, group awareness tools can be considered as a rather implicit way of scaffolding small group learning.

Järvelä, S., & Hadwin, A. F. (2013). New frontiers: Regulating learning in CSCL. *Educational Psychologist, 48*(1), 25–39. ▸ https://doi.org/10.1080/00461520.2012.748006

This is a seminal article that provided a new theoretical perspective on the question how small groups regulate their learning. It differentiates three levels at which regulation processes may take place within groups: At the self-level, individual students regulate their own learning. At the co-level, single group members regulate other group members' learning. And at the shared-level, the group members jointly negotiate their learning process. This differentiation has been taken up by a large number of studies, which have shown that successful small groups are more effective in regulating their learning across these three levels.

Rummel, N. & Spada, H. (2005). Learning to collaborate: an instructional approach to promoting collaborative problem-solving in computer-mediated settings. *The Journal of the Learning Sciences, 14*(2), 201–241. ▸ https://doi.org/10.1207/s15327809jls1402_2

This article presents an empirical study that compares the effects of worked examples and of collaboration scripts to structure small group learning in dyadic interdisciplinary teams, each consisting of a medical student and a psychology student each. While the two scaffolds had differential effects on various process measures, both were comparable in their (positive) effects on knowledge acquisition. This study also provides an exemplary account for the richness of process data that can be used when studying small group learning.

Vogel, F., Wecker, C., Kollar, I., & Fischer, F. (2017). Socio-cognitive scaffolding with collaboration scripts: a meta-analysis. *Educational Psychology Review, 29*(3), 477–511. ▶ https://doi.org/10.1007/s10648-016-9361-7

This article presents a meta-analysis on the effects of computer-supported collaboration scripts (as compared to unstructured computer-supported collaboration) on the acquisition of domain-specific knowledge and cross-domain skills. Results show positive effect sizes for both outcome variables, but particularly larger effects on cross-domain skills. Further, the article reports findings that show that computer-supported collaboration scripts tend to be more effective the more they target student engagement in interactive activities and when they are combined with domain-specific support. Also, it provides preliminary evidence that shows that to be effective, computer-supported collaboration scripts need to be adjusted to learners' internal collaboration scripts.

Yalch, M. M., Vitale, E. M., & Ford, J. K. (2019). Benefits of peer review on students' writing. *Psychology Learning and Teaching, 18*(3), 317–325. ▶ https://doi.org/10.1177/1475725719835070

This study provides an excellent example on how small group learning may be implemented in psychology courses. $N = 59$ students had the task to write two scientific papers in the domain of child psychopathology. After attending a peer review workshop, each student was asked to provide feedback to two to three peers, using a scoring rubric that was provided by the course instructor. Results showed that the more critical students were of their peers' writing, the better their own grades were on their own writing.

## Cross-References

▶ Basic Principles and Procedures for Effective Teaching in Psychology
▶ Formative Assessment and Feedback Strategies
▶ Learning and Instruction in Higher Education Classrooms
▶ Technology-Enhanced Psychology Learning and Teaching

## References

Alqassab, M., Strijbos, J.-W., & Ufer, S. (2018). Training peer-feedback skills on geometric construction tasks: Role of domain knowledge and peer-feedback levels. *European Journal of Psychology of Education, 33*, 11–30. https://doi.org/10.1007/s10212-017-0342-0.

Alrassi, J., & Mortensen, M. (2020). Jigsaw group-based learning in difficult airway management: An alternative way to teach surgical didactics. *Journal of Surgical Education, 77*(4), 723–725. https://doi.org/10.1016/j.jsurg.2020.02.003.

Andriessen, J., Baker, M. J., & Suthers, D. D. (2003). Argumentation, computer support, and the educational context of confronting cognitions. In J. Andriessen, M. J. Baker, & D. Suthers (Eds.), *Arguing to learn: Confronting cognitions in computer-supported collaborative learning environments* (pp. 1–25). Dordrecht, Netherlands: Kluwer.

Aronson, E., Blaney, N., Stephan, C., Sikes, J., & Snapp, M. (1978). *The jigsaw classroom.* Beverly Hills, CA: Sage.

Baken, E. K., Adams, D. C., & Rentz, M. S. (2020). Jigsaw method improves learning and retention for observation-based undergraduate biology laboratory activities. *Journal of Biological Education*. https://doi.org/10.1080/00219266.2020.1796757.

Barclay, K. H., & Breheny, C. (1994). Letting the children take over more of their own learning: Collaborative research in the Kindergarten classroom. *Young Children, 49*(6), 33–39.

Barron, B. (2003). When smart groups fail. *Journal of the Learning Sciences, 12*(3), 307–359. https://doi.org/10.1207/S15327809JLS1203_1.

Bellhäuser, H., Konert, J., Müller, A., & Röpke, R. (2018). Who is the perfect match? Effects of algorithmic learning group formation using personality traits. *i-com, 17*(1), 65–77. https://doi.org/10.1515/icom-2018-0004.

Chen, J., Wang, M., Kirschner, P. A., & Tsai, C.-C. (2018). The role of collaboration, computer use, learning environments, and supporting strategies in CSCL: A meta-analysis. *Review of Educational Research, 88*(6), 799–843. https://doi.org/10.3102/0034654318791584.

Chi, M. T. H., & Wylie, R. (2014). The ICAP framework: Linking cognitive engagement to active learning outcomes. *Educational Psychologist, 49*(4), 219–243. https://doi.org/10.1080/00461520.2014.965823.

Cress, U., Rosé, C., Wise, A., & Oshima, J. (Eds.). (2021). *International handbook of computer-supported collaborative learning*. New York, NY: Springer.

Cummings, D. J., & Sheeran, N. (2019). Do academic motivation and personality influence which students benefit the most from peer-assisted study sessions? *Psychology Learning and Teaching, 18*(3), 244–258. https://doi.org/10.1177/1475725719840502.

Daxenberger, J., Csanadi, A., Ghanem, C., Kollar, I., & Gurevych, I. (2018). Domain-specific aspects of scientific reasoning and argumentation. In F. Fischer, C. Chinn, K. Engelmann, & J. Osborne (Eds.), *Scientific reasoning and argumentation: The roles of domain-specific and domain-general knowledge* (pp. 34–55). New York, NY: Routledge.

De Backer, L., Van Keer, H., & Valcke, M. (2020). Variations in socially shared metacognitive regulation and their relation with university students' performance. *Metacognition and Learning, 15*(2), 233–259. https://doi.org/10.1007/s11409-020-09229-5.

de Hei, M., Tabacaru, C., Sjoer, E., Rippe, R., & Walenkamp, J. (2020). Developing intercultural competence through collaborative learning in international higher education. *Journal of Studies in International Education, 24*(2), 190–211. https://doi.org/10.1177/1028315319826226.

De Lisi, R., & Golbeck, S. L. (1999). Implications of piagetian theory for peer learning. In A. M. O'Donnell & A. King (Eds.), *Cognitive perspectives on peer learning* (pp. 3–37). Mahwah, NJ: Erlbaum.

De Wever, B., van Keer, H., Schellens, T., & Valcke, M. (2011). Assessing collaboration in a wiki: The reliability of university students' peer assessment. *The Internet and Higher Education, 14*(4), 201–206. https://doi.org/10.1016/j.iheduc.2011.07.003.

Deiglmayr, A. (2018). Instructional scaffolds for learning from formative peer assessment: Effects of core task, peer feedback, and dialogue. *European Journal of Psychology of Education, 33*, 185–198. https://doi.org/10.1007/s10212-017-0355-8.

Dillenbourg, P. (1999). What do you mean by collaborative learning? In P. Dillenbourg (Ed.), *Collaborative learning: Cognitive and computational approaches* (pp. 1–19). Amsterdam, Netherlands: Elsevier.

Fischer, F., Kollar, I., Stegmann, K., & Wecker, C. (2013). Towards a script theory of guidance in computer-supported collaborative learning. *Educational Psychologist, 48*(1), 56–66. https://doi.org/10.1080/00461520.2012.748005.

Gielen, M., Tops, L., Dochy, F., Onghena, P., & Smeets, S. (2010). A comparative study of peer and teacher feedback and of various feedback forms in a secondary school writing curriculum. *British Educational Research Journal, 36*(1), 143–162.

Hattie, J. A. C. (2009). *Visible learning: A synthesis of over 800 meta-analyses related to achievement*. London: Routledge.

Hogan, D. M., & Tudge, J. R. H. (1999). Implications of Vygotsky's theory for peer learning. In A. M. O'Donnell & A. King (Eds.), *Cognitive perspectives on peer learning* (pp. 39–65). Mahwah, NJ: Erlbaum.

Janssen, J., & Bodemer, D. (2013). Coordinated computer-supported collaborative learning: Awareness and awareness tools. *Educational Psychologist, 48*(1), 40–55. https://doi.org/10.1080/00461520.2012.749153.

Järvelä, S., & Hadwin, A. F. (2013). New frontiers: Regulating learning in CSCL. *Educational Psychologist, 48*(1), 25–39. https://doi.org/10.1080/00461520.2012.748006.

Johnson, D. W., & Johnson, R. T. (2018). *Cooperative learning: The foundation for active learning.* Available on https://www.intechopen.com/books/active-learning-beyond-the-future/cooperative-learning-the-foundation-for-active-learning. Last accessed 02 Feb 2021.

Jurkowski, S., & Hänze, M. (2012). Kooperatives Lernen aus dem Blickwinkel sozialer Kompetenzen. Eine Untersuchung des Zusammenhangs sozialer Kompetenzen mit dem Lernerfolg, dem Unterrichtserleben und dem Gruppenarbeitsergebnis in verschiedenen kooperativen Lernumgebungen [Collaborative learning viewed from the perspective of social competences. An investigation of the relation of social competences with learning outcomes, perception of instruction, and products of collaborative learning in different learning environments]. *Unterrichtswissenschaft, 40*(3), 259–276.

Kelsen, B. A., & Liang, H.-Y. (2019). Role of the big 5 personality traits and motivation in predicting performance in collaborative presentations. *Psychological Reports, 122*(5), 1907–1924. https://doi.org/10.1177/0033294118795139.

King, A. (2007). Scripting collaborative learning processes: A cognitive perspective. In F. Fischer, I. Kollar, H. Mandl, & J. M. Haake (Eds.), *Scripting computer-supported collaborative learning: Cognitive, computational and educational perspectives* (pp. 14–37). New York, NY: Springer.

Kollar, I., Wecker, C., & Fischer, F. (2018). Scaffolding and scripting (computer-supported) collaborative learning. In F. Fischer, C. E. Hmelo-Silver, S. R. Goldman, & P. Reimann (Eds.), *International handbook of the learning sciences* (pp. 340–350). New York, NY: Routledge/Taylor & Francis.

Kyndt, E., Raes, E., Lismont, B., Timmers, F., Cascallar, E., & Dochy, F. (2013). A meta-analysis of the effects of face-to-face cooperative learning. Do recent studies falsify or verify earlier findings? *Educational Research Review, 10*, 133–149. https://doi.org/10.1016/j.edurev.2013.02.002.

Malmberg, J., Järvelä, S., Järvenoja, H., & Panadero, E. (2015). Promoting socially shared regulation of learning in CSCL: Progress of socially shared regulation among high- and low-performing groups. *Computers in Human Behavior, 52*, 562–572. https://doi.org/10.1016/j.chb.2015.03.082.

Mayring, P. (2014). *Qualitative content analysis: Theoretical foundation, basic procedures and software solution.* Klagenfurt, Austria: Beltz.

McNaughton, J., Crick, T., Joyce-Gibbons, A., Beauchamp, G., Young, N., & Tan, E. (2017). Facilitating collaborative learning between two primary schools using large multi-touch devices. *Journal of Computers in Education, 4*, 307–320. https://doi.org/10.1007/s40692-017-0081-x.

Melzner, N., Greisel, M., Dresel, M., & Kollar, I. (2020). Regulating self-organized collaborative learning: The importance of homogeneous problem perception, immediacy, and intensity of strategy use. *International Journal of Computer-Supported Collaborative Learning, 15*(2), 149–177. https://doi.org/10.1007/s11412-020-09323-5.

Menekse, M., Stump, G. S., Krause, S., & Chi, M. T. H. (2013). Differentiated overt learning activities for effective instruction in engineering classrooms. *Journal of Engineering Education, 102*(3), 346–274. https://doi.org/10.1002/jee.20021.

Näykki, P., Isohätälä, J., Järvelä, S., Poysa-Tarhonen, J., & Häkkinen, P. (2017). Facilitating sociocognitive and socio-emotional monitoring in collaborative learning with a regulation macro script – An exploratory study. *International Journal of Computer-Supported Collaborative Learning, 12*(3), 251–279. https://doi.org/10.1007/s11412-017-9259-5.

Palincsar, A. S., & Brown, A. L. (1984). Reciprocal teaching of comprehension-fostering and comprehension-monitoring activities. *Cognition and Instruction, 1*(2), 117–175. https://doi.org/10.1207/s1532690xci0102_1.

Renkl, A. (2011). Aktives Lernen: Von sinnvollen und weniger sinnvollen theoretischen Perspektiven zu einem schillernden Konstrukt [Active learning: About sensible and less sensible theoretical perspectives on a multifaceted construct]. *Unterrichtswissenschaft, 39*(3), 197–212.

Rosé, C., & Ferschke, O. (2016). Technology support for discussion based learning: From computer supported collaborative learning to the future or massive open online courses. *International Journal of Artificial Intelligence in Education, 26*, 660–678. https://doi.org/10.1007/s40593-016-0107-y.

Rumain, B., & Geliebter, A. (2020). A process-oriented guided-inquiry learning (POGIL)-based curriculum for the experimental psychology laboratory. *Psychology Learning and Teaching, 19*(2), 194–206. https://doi.org/10.1177/1475725720905973.

Rummel, N., & Spada, H. (2005). Learning to collaborate: An instructional approach to promoting collaborative problem-solving in computer-mediated settings. *The Journal of the Learning Sciences, 14*(2), 201–241. https://doi.org/10.1207/s15327809jls1402_2.

Schnaubert, L., & Bodemer, D. (2019). Providing different types of group awareness information to guide collaborative learning. *International Journal of Computer-Supported Collaborative Learning, 14*, 7–51. https://doi.org/10.1007/s11412-018-9293-y.

Selleck, C. S., Fifolt, M., Burkart, H., Frank, J. S., Curry, W. A., & Hites, L. S. (2017). Providing primary care using an interprofessional collaborative practice model: What clinicians have learned. *Journal of Professional Nursing, 33*(6), 410–416. https://doi.org/10.1016/j.profnurs.2016.11.004.

Shaffer, D. W., Collier, W., & Ruis, A. R. (2016). A tutorial on epistemic network analysis: Analyzing the structure of connections in cognitive, social, and interaction data. *Journal of Learning Analytics, 3*(3), 9–45. https://doi.org/10.18608/jla.2016.33.3.

Slavin, R. E., & Tanner, A. M. (1979). Effects of cooperative reward structures and individual accountability on productivity and learning. *The Journal of Educational Research, 72*(5), 294–298. https://doi.org/10.1080/00220671.1979.10885175.

Sobocinski, M., Järvelä, S., Malmberg, J., Dindar, M., Isosalo, A., & Noponen, K. (2020). How does monitoring set the stage for adaptive regulation or maladaptive behavior in collaborative learning? A multimodal analysis. *Metacognition and Learning, 15*(2), 99–127. https://doi.org/10.1007/s11409-020-09224-w.

Springer, L., Stanne, M. E., & Donovan, S. S. (1999). Effects of small group learning on undergraduates in science, mathematics, engineering, and technology: A meta-analysis. *Review of Educational Research, 69*(1), 21–51. https://doi.org/10.3102/00346543069001021.

Teasley, S. D. (1995). Talking about reasoning: How important is the peer in peer collaboration? In L. B. Resnick, R. Säljö, C. Pontecorvo, & B. Burge (Eds.), *Discourse, tools, and reasoning: Essays on situated cognition* (pp. 361–384). Berlin, Germany: Springer. https://doi.org/10.1007/978-3-662-03362-3_16.

Topping, K. (1998). Peer assessment between students in college and universities. *Review of Educational Research, 68*(3), 249–267. https://doi.org/10.3102/00346543068003249.

Vogel, F., Kollar, I., Ufer, S., Reichersdorfer, E., Reiss, K., & Fischer, F. (2016). Developing argumentation skills in mathematics through computer-supported collaborative learning: The role of transactivity. *Instructional Science, 44*(5), 477–500. https://doi.org/10.1007/s11251-016-9380-2.

Vogel, F., Wecker, C., Kollar, I., & Fischer, F. (2017). Socio-cognitive scaffolding with collaboration scripts: A meta-analysis. *Educational Psychology Review, 29*(3), 477–511. https://doi.org/10.1007/s10648-016-9361-7.

Wang, X., Kollar, I., & Stegmann, K. (2017). Adaptable scripting to foster regulation processes and skills in computer-supported collaborative learning. *International Journal for Computer-Supported Collaborative Learning, 12*(2), 153–172. https://doi.org/10.1007/s11412-017-9254-x.

Weinberger, A., & Fischer, F. (2006). A framework to analyze argumentative knowledge construction in computer-supported collaborative learning. *Computers & Education, 46*(1), 71–95. https://doi.org/10.1016/j.compedu.2005.04.003.

Weinberger, A., Stegmann, K., & Fischer, F. (2010). Learning to argue online: Scripted groups surpass individuals (unscripted groups do not). *Computers in Human Behavior, 26*(4), 506–515. https://doi.org/10.1016/j.chb.2009.08.007.

Wekerle, C., Daumiller, M., & Kollar, I. (2022). Using digital technology to promote higher education learning: The importance of different learning activities and their relations to learning outcomes. *Journal of Research on Technology in Education, 54*(1), 1–17. https://doi.org/10.1080/15391523.2020.1799455.

Wichmann, A., Funk, A., & Rummel, N. (2018). Leveraging the potential of peer feedback in an academic writing activity through sense-making support. *European Journal of Psychology of Education, 33*, 165–184. https://doi.org/10.1007/s10212-017-0348-7.

Yalch, M. M., Vitale, E. M., & Ford, J. K. (2019). Benefits of peer review on students' writing. *Psychology Learning and Teaching, 18*(3), 317–325. https://doi.org/10.1177/1475725719835070.

Yoon, S., Anderson, E., Park, M., Elinich, K., & Lin, J. (2018). How augmented reality, textual, and collaborative scaffolds work synergistically to improve learning in a science museum. *Research in Science and Technological Education, 36*(1), 1–21. https://doi.org/10.1080/02635143.2017.1386645.

Zheng, L., Zhang, X., & Gyasi, J. F. (2019). A literature review of features and trends of technology-supported collaborative learning in informal settings from 2007 to 2018. *Journal of Computers in Education, 6*, 529–561. https://doi.org/10.1007/s40692-019-00148-2.

# Service Learning

## An Innovative Pedagogy for the Psychology Curriculum

Robert G. Bringle, Roger N. Reeb, Luzelle Naudé, Ana I. Ruiz, and Faith Ong

## Contents

| | |
|---|---|
| Introduction | 1306 |
| Purposes and Rationale | 1308 |
|     Philosophical and Pedagogical Roots of Service Learning | 1308 |
|     Service Learning as Pedagogy in the Psychology Curriculum | 1309 |
| Design Issues and Approaches | 1310 |
|     Effective Service Learning Establishes Clear Educational Goals | 1311 |
|     Students Are Engaged In Tasks that Challenge Them | 1311 |
|     Service Tasks Have Clear and Significant Goals | 1312 |
|     Students Are Well Prepared for Their Service Activities | 1312 |
|     Student Reflection Before, During, and After Service | 1313 |
|     Maximize Student Voice in the Service Project | 1313 |
|     Valuing Diversity | 1314 |
|     Promote Collaboration with the Community | 1314 |

R. G. Bringle (✉)
Indiana University Purdue University Indianapolis, Indianapolis, IN, USA
e-mail: rbringle@iupui.edu

R. N. Reeb
University of Dayton, Dayton, OH, USA
e-mail: rreeb1@dayton.edu

L. Naudé
University of the Free State, Bloemfontein, South Africa
e-mail: naudel@ufs.ac.za

A. I. Ruiz
Alvernia University, Reading, PA, USA
e-mail: Ana.Ruiz@alvernia.edu

F. Ong
Ngee Ann Polytechnic, Singapore, Singapore
e-mail: Faith_ONG@np.edu.sg

© Springer Nature Switzerland AG 2023
J. Zumbach et al. (eds.), *International Handbook of Psychology Learning and Teaching*,
Springer International Handbooks of Education,
https://doi.org/10.1007/978-3-030-28745-0_61

Systematic Formative and Summative Evaluation .......................................... 1314
Assessment Enhances Student Learning ................................................... 1315
Acknowledge and Celebrate Students' Service Work .................................... 1315
Assessment and Research Issues ............................................................... 1315
Assessment and Research on Student Outcomes of SL ................................. 1315
Assessment and Research on Community Outcomes ..................................... 1316
Participatory Community Action Research as SL ........................................ 1317
Core Findings and Current Trends ............................................................ 1318
Core Findings ................................................................................. 1318
Trends ........................................................................................... 1319
Challenges, Lessons Learned, and Implications for Learning and Teaching Psychology .... 1321
Conclusion ......................................................................................... 1323
Cross-References ................................................................................. 1323
Teaching, Learning, and Assessment Resources ............................................ 1324
References .......................................................................................... 1325

### Abstract

Service learning (SL) is a high-impact pedagogy that integrates academic material, relevant community-based service activities, and critical reflection to achieve academic, social responsibility, and personal learning objectives in order to develop psychologically literate citizens. SL enhances knowledge and fosters social responsibility in students to democratically address challenges in diverse societies. SL rests on the sound pedagogical principles of active and experiential learning. This chapter focuses on the undergraduate psychology major; however, similar principles can be applied to other educational levels. Reaching educational goals is contingent on applying 11 essential elements to SL course design, implementation, and assessment, from establishing partnerships with the community to designing student reflection activities and celebrating their learning. This chapter highlights themes and issues in research, core findings, and trends, as well as challenges, lessons learned, and implications for learning, teaching, and community engagement. Finally, key resources are identified for SL.

### Keywords

Civic learning · Socially responsive knowledge · Reflection · Community partnerships · Ethics · Participatory community action research

## Introduction

Teaching psychology has a long history of learning by doing (e.g., laboratories, internships) but also an overreliance on lecturing as a dominant pedagogy. This pattern varies across levels of the curriculum (e.g., pre-college, undergraduate, graduate, continuing professional education), but the challenge remains for instructors to improve learning based on research. The best pedagogy will depend on the learning objectives and the context for learning. Altman (1996) proposed that the undergraduate psychology curriculum, which will be our primary focus, should support three learning domains: foundational knowledge (i.e., the core content and methods of psychology), professional knowledge (i.e., knowledge of the practice of psychology), and socially responsive knowledge (i.e., knowledge about society's issues and skills to address the problems). The latter domain is aligned with commentary among psychologists for the importance of producing "psychologically literate citizens" (Cranney & Dunn, 2011) or "citizen psychologists" (American Psychological Association, APA, 2018) who can connect their psychology education to being engaged in social and community issues. However, Reich and Nelson (2010) concluded:

> the goal of civic engagement among psychology faculty was certainly not widespread. More recent curriculum guidelines for undergraduate majors in psychology (APA, 2007) still place most emphasis on what Altman described as foundational knowledge. (p. 138)

This chapter focuses on service learning (SL), an underrepresented pedagogy within the psychology curriculum that has been largely ignored in discussions of improving teaching psychology (Cranney & Dunn, 2011; Halpern, 2010; Rich et al., 2018). SL is well-suited for not only enhancing socially responsive knowledge, civic learning, and social responsibility of psychology students but also enriching and improving all of their learning across the entire psychology curriculum, including foundational and professional knowledge. We define SL as:

> course-based, credit-bearing educational experience in which students (a) participate in mutually identified and organized service activities that benefit the community, and (b) reflect on the service activity in such a way as to gain further understanding of course content, a broader appreciation of the discipline, and an enhanced sense of personal values and civic responsibility. (Bringle & Clayton, 2012, p. 105; adapted from Bringle & Hatcher, 1996, p. 222)

This definition illustrates two key attributes of SL as a pedagogy: (a) being academic, it is distinct from volunteering and episodic co-curricular service; and (b) community partners collaborate with instructors to design, implement, and evaluate benefits. In our experience, "service learning" is inappropriately applied to some co-curricular programs, whereas we are limiting our focus to curricular integration of community-based activities into the psychology curriculum. This definition aligns well with definitions in other parts of the world, including Europe (e.g., Aramburuzabala, McIlrath, & Opazo, 2019; Europe Engage, n.d.), Asia (e.g., Xing & Ma, 2010), South America (e.g., CLAYSS, n.d.; Tapia, 2012), and Africa (e.g., Pacho, 2019). We understand that context matters and that educators around the world may use different frameworks and terminology (e.g., for "civic," "service," "service learning") (Aramburuzabala et al., 2019; Thomson, Smith-Tolken, Naidoo, & Bringle, 2011). Regardless of word choice, we agree with Furco and Norvell (2019), who reviewed various lists of essential elements of SL and stated "while there are fundamental definitions, elements, and principles of SL that apply no matter what the situation or context, the cultural fibre of the societies in which SL is practised will ultimately shape the overall character of the SL experience" (p. 32).

## Purposes and Rationale

SL is a pedagogical tool to enhance knowledge and foster a sense of social responsibility and competence in students so that, as global citizens, they can address the challenges of diverse and continuously evolving societies. The importance of social responsibility in higher education is reiterated in the United Nations Special Rapporteur Singh (2016):

> The 1998 World Declaration on Higher Education for the Twenty-First Century: Vision and Action ... called upon higher education institutions to give the opportunity to students to fully develop their own abilities with a sense of social responsibility, educating them to become full participants in democratic society and promoters of changes that will foster equity and justice. (para 109)

SL is rooted in American higher education's historical commitment to prepare local and national leaders (Harkavy & Hartley, 2010). With a growing emphasis on fostering what Altman (1996) called socially responsive knowledge in education, SL can empower universities to be a transformative force for cultural, economic, and social change across the globe (e.g., Cayuela, Alonso, Ballesteros, & Aramburuzabala, 2020). With SL's dual purpose of enhancing student development (learning, social responsibility, personal growth) and community benefits, it can (a) expand intellectual, social, and global horizons, (b) foster personal and professional growth, and (c) educate and prepare an informed and active socially responsible global citizenry.

## Philosophical and Pedagogical Roots of Service Learning

SL rests on the sound pedagogical principles of active and experiential learning of which Dewey, Lewin, and Piaget stand as the foremost "intellectual ancestors" (Kolb, 2015, p. 15). Kolb (2015) integrated these intellectual roots into a conceptual model to serve as a foundation for diverse forms of experiential learning, including SL (Bringle, Reeb, Brown, & Ruiz, 2016). SL connects students to life in communities and connects scholarly learning with experiences through reflection and social action in authentic community settings. SL is grounded in Dewey's progressive approach to experiential education, the social-constructivist perspectives of Piaget and Vygotsky, and the participatory and democratic approach of Lewin (e.g., action research) (Kolb, 2015). Another notable contribution to SL pedagogy is feminist epistemologies that emphasize connected knowing (Belenky, Clinchy, Goldberger, & Tarule, 1997), i.e., learning is a social-cultural process based on an ethic of care. SL creates democratic communities, and tensions between the self and others are bridged. SL links education to democratic citizenship, social action, and active engagement aimed at the public good, as echoed in Freire's emphasis on the development of critical awareness (Freire, 1968). For instance, in critical SL (Mitchell, 2008) and transformative learning theory (Mezirow, 2009), students are challenged to consider worldviews beyond their own, to reach a broadened sense of self with a deeper understanding of the notions of justice (as opposed to notions of charity), and to serve as social agents. SL is also regarded as a high-impact pedagogical practice (Kuh, 2008) that prioritizes student engagement in educationally purposeful activities, filled with rich academic challenges, supportive learning environments, and learning in diverse real-world settings (Bringle et al., 2016).

Notions of citizenship, democracy, and service are informed by political history, socioeconomic context, and power dynamics, implying variations in how SL is practiced. In the post-apartheid context of South Africa, for example, SL initiatives are situated in restorative practices, redress, and transformation (Thomson et al., 2011). In countries with colonial oppression and racialized histories, the term service might be associated with unequal, paternalistic, and charitable practices. More neutral terms (e.g., community interaction, community-based learning, and community engagement) are favored. In contrast to more individualistic philanthropic traditions, the Latin American context embeds SL in collaborative and collective action with the term "solidarity" (Regina & Ferrara, 2017). Also, the collectivist tradition and social ethic of *Ubuntu*, which is seen as an underlying principle in many African (Pacho, 2019) and South African (Bobo & Akhurst, 2019) SL initiatives, promotes society's common good in an interconnected manner.

## Service Learning as Pedagogy in the Psychology Curriculum

Across the globe, there are various guidelines for the design and delivery of psychology programs (e.g., Australian Psychological Society, 2015; EuroPsy, 2014; International Association of Applied Psychology, 2016); however, we will refer to the *APA Guidelines for the Undergraduate Psychology Major (Guidelines 2.0)* (APA, 2013) because they are aligned with other sets of guidelines. It is instructive to consider APA Learning Goals within the context of the three domains of knowledge (foundational, professional, socially responsive) identified by Altman (1996). Foundational knowledge refers to "the content concepts, theories, history, and methodology of a discipline" as well as "liberal education or cross-disciplinary knowledge intended to broadly educate students" (p. 374). APA Learning Goals 1 (Knowledge Base in Psychology) and 2 (Scientific Inquiry and Critical Thinking) coincide with what Altman called foundational knowledge. Professional knowledge, which coincides with APA Learning Goals 4 (Communication) and 5 (Professional Development), involves "practitioner skills and content in a field" including "vocationally oriented information and techniques" (p. 374). Socially responsive knowledge, which corresponds with APA Learning Goal 3 (Ethical and Social Responsibility in a Diverse World), involves the following emphases: (a) "educate students in the problems of society," (b) provide students with opportunities to "experience and understand first-hand social issues in their community," and (c) foster in students the "skills to act on social problems" (pp. 374–375). As Altman (1996) emphasized, "socially responsive knowledge leans heavily on both foundation knowledge and professional knowledge," with "the three types of knowledge intertwined and interdependent" (p. 375). Thus, educating psychologically literate citizens encompasses all three of Altman's knowledge domains.

SL is a powerful pedagogy for fostering psychologically literate citizens by pursuing all five of the APA Learning Goals and thereby also enhancing Altman's three knowledge domains (Bringle et al., 2016; Clayton, Bringle, & Hatcher, 2013a). Furthermore, relative to other pedagogical approaches, SL places a special emphasis on socially responsive knowledge, which can be enhanced in most psychology curricula. The United Nations (2020) propose 17 interconnected Sustainable Development Goals (SDGs) as "a call for action by all countries – poor, rich and middle-income – to promote prosperity while protecting the planet." The SDGs represent a "universal call to action to end poverty, protect the planet and improve the lives and prospects of everyone, everywhere." Based on available research, we contend that SL is the best pedagogical technique for educating psychology students to answer this call to action.

## Design Issues and Approaches

SL is an effective pedagogy to develop psychologically literate citizens. Reaching educational goals is contingent upon designing, implementing, and assessing high-quality SL courses. Typically, an existing psychology course is modified by integrating community-based activities into it. Bringle et al. (2016) provided examples for SL in introductory psychology, abnormal psychology, health psychology, social/personality psychology, developmental psychology, cognitive psychology, community psychology, research methods, interdisciplinary, and study abroad courses. Other examples for integrating SL into existing psychology courses are in the literature. Sometimes, all students engage in the community-based activities because the activities are viewed as integral to the course's learning objectives. Alternatively, students may be given a choice between a SL option and an alternative assignment (e.g., a research paper focused on a community issue). In all cases, the community-based activities are not simply an added requirement, but they have an educational rationale that is supported by their intentional integration into and coordination with other aspects of the course.

There are four types of potential community activities in SL courses: (a) direct service, (b) indirect service, (c) research, and (d) advocacy (Bringle et al., 2016). Direct service engages students face-to-face with residents or clients of a community organization. Examples include teaching at-risk children positive behaviors, participating in programs at a center for elderly persons experiencing dementia, or assisting community members who are experiencing mental illness or homelessness.

Indirect service involves students working behind the scenes to increase, enhance, or direct resources to support an organization, neighborhood, or government office to address a community issue. Examples include fundraising and/or crowdfunding, developing resource materials (e.g., brochures, instructional aids, web pages, social media platforms), or facilitating access to services (e.g., augmenting the collaboration between a homeless shelter and a health clinic).

In research, students use psychological methods (e.g., design, measurement, data analysis) in community-based research activities. Examples include collaborating with community partners to develop an assessment instrument and/or conduct a program evaluation. Alternatively, the research could be participatory community action research, wherein a team of individuals (faculty, students, and community partners) collaborate to conduct research that contributes to understanding social issues and social transformation.

Students doing advocacy apply psychological content to examine root causes of social issues and encourage transformative change in communities (e.g., increasing public awareness concerning an issue, changing policy, advocating for client rights, changing infrastructure to improve access to services). Activities could include conducting presentations in the community to increase awareness of a policy issue, obtaining support for a social change initiative, or assisting community members who are working for a cause (e.g., social media platforms, letters, e-mails, telephone calls, meetings with government officials or legislators).

Toole and Toole (1998) identified 11 essential elements for a SL course, and we will use them as a basis for discussing course design. High-quality SL courses that attend to each of these elements are an effective way of engaging both majors and nonmajors in their psychological courses and developing students' social awareness, knowledge, skills, and attitudes that are tied to the psychological curriculum.

## Effective Service Learning Establishes Clear Educational Goals

Designing a SL psychology course starts with the learning objectives from three domains: academic learning, socially responsive knowledge, and personal growth (Stokamer & Clayton, 2017). Figure 1 illustrates how these three domains can be independent or related learning objectives (e.g., leadership could be an academic topic, an area for studying leadership in community NGOs, or an area for personal growth). Linking students' service activities to the course's learning outcomes is what differentiates SL from volunteering. SL fully integrates academic content, course activities, reflection, and assessment with the community activities. Bringle et al. (2016) illustrated how SL courses from the undergraduate curriculum can be developed to contribute to all of the educational objectives in the five broad learning domains of the *APA Guidelines 2.0* (APA, 2013) in ways that promote socially responsive knowledge and personal growth in addition to foundational, academic competencies.

## Students Are Engaged In Tasks that Challenge Them

Not just any community-based activity is appropriate. Instructors and students must work with community partners to identify activities that are aligned with the course's

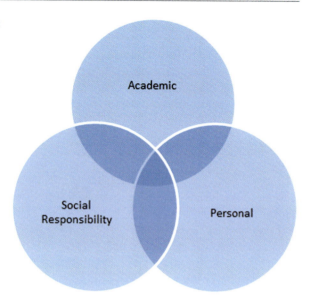

**Fig. 1** Learning domains that community service can enhance. (Adapted from Bringle et al. (2016, p. 71))

learning objectives and that benefit the community. One of the educational advantages of SL activities is challenging students to consider additional perspectives on the course content (i.e., academic learning), their communities (i.e., socially responsive knowledge), and themselves (i.e., personal learning). This works best when activities fit the students' skills and interests as well as the community's priorities.

## Service Tasks Have Clear and Significant Goals

Service activities should acknowledge an issue identified by the community, and the service objectives are then developed based on the context of the issue and the course's learning objectives. Furthermore, community-based activities should be designed and selected to be consistent with learning objectives. For example, as Boyle-Baise (2002) points out, "A charitable task probably will not generate insights for social change" (p. 33). Research finds that when service activities have clear goals, make significant contributions, and have an impact on oneself and others, students then gained greater social knowledge, civic dispositions, and skills (e.g., Billig, Root, & Jesse, 2005; Choo et al., 2019).

## Students Are Well Prepared for Their Service Activities

Student preparation for community-based activities was positively related to academic engagement, appreciation of academic content, civic engagement, and stronger civic disposition (Billig et al., 2005; Choo et al., 2019). Students also learn, often from a community representative, about where they will be serving – including strengths, assets, challenges, and social justice issues faced by community members.

The students' preparation consists of understanding the project and expectations and their roles and limitations (Chapdelaine, Ruiz, Warchal, & Wells, 2005). Some other substantial issues to consider may be transportation, safety, resources, and technology use (Jacoby, 2015). The practicalities of transportation and technology use and the dynamics of risk management and safety might vary vastly. For example, in countries with less economic, political, and social stability and more pronounced developmental challenges, the unequal distribution of wealth and resources (between students and community members but also within the student population) might pose challenges (Akhurst, 2017) that need to be addressed during the design of the SL course. More importantly, students need to be aware of the potential for personal changes that may result from the experiences. SL students should be supported as they reflect on their awareness of the world and the impact of the service on their understanding of themselves and others and as they navigate what may be uncomfortable personal and interpersonal experiences.

## Student Reflection Before, During, and After Service

A well-designed SL course requires students to reflect on and evaluate different perspectives and circumstances, which enhances their ability to think critically about social issues (Ash & Clayton, 2009). Higher-quality SL occurred when reflections were structured and regular; when the content of the reflection activities was aligned with the identified academic, civic, and personal outcomes (Astin et al., 2006; Dahan, 2016; Hatcher, Bringle, & Muthiah, 2004; Moely & Ilustre, 2014); and when reflections take various forms (e.g., written journals, in-class discussion, projects) (Astin et al., 2006; Dahan, 2016).

The DEAL Model for Critical Reflection (Ash & Clayton, 2009) comprises the following steps: (a) **d**escribe the experiences in detail; (b) **e**xamine the experiences from personal, civic, and/or academic perspectives; and (c) **a**rticulate **l**earning that has resulted. In the examine stage of DEAL, the prompts (e.g., for written reflection, in-class discussion) can be specific learning objectives derived from the *APA Guidelines 2.0* and aligned with academic learning, socially responsive knowledge, and/or personal growth. This approach to reflection provides authentic evidence of learning outcomes, and their products can be evaluated using Bloom's (1956) taxonomy. Bringle et al. (2016) provided many examples of DEAL reflection assignments for connecting community-based activities to facilitate academic learning, socially responsive knowledge, and personal growth.

## Maximize Student Voice in the Service Project

When students in a SL course are given more voice and ownership of the activities, they have improved self-concepts, are more politically engaged, and are more tolerant and appreciative of diversity (Morgan & Streb, 2001). Student voice can manifest itself when students elect to do SL when it is an option in a course, when they choose from a short list of service activities or sites, or when they work with the community organization to tailor activities to their interests. Students may also choose among ways to reflect on their service activities and demonstrate their learning (e.g., reflection essay, digital story, artistic expression).

## Valuing Diversity

SL engages students with individuals who are in some ways different from themselves. Bowman (2011) found in a meta-analysis that face-to-face diversity experiences (vs. didactic educational experiences) were related to enhanced civic attitudes. Pascarella et al.'s (2014) research found that exposure to diversity experiences fostered the development of cognitive growth and more complex modes of thought. Intentionally designed diversity experiences in SL courses, supported by appropriate reflection activities, provide powerful ways to enhance the education of students in ways that are not possible when learning is limited to books and the classroom.

## Promote Collaboration with the Community

Good SL does not have students learning *about* the community, doing activities *in* the community, nor doing activities *for* the community. Good SL has students doing activities *with* community partners in ways that develop respect for what they can learn from their community partners. This represents a tension that is embedded in discussions about SL that contrast charity orientations to community service with activities that are focused on social change, advocacy, and social justice. Indeed, the word "service" runs the risk of implying "haves" giving to "have nots" that undermines the aspiration that students and community partners are collaborating around a common interest and purpose. This also reflects a pattern that SL in the Northern Hemisphere is too often focused on student outcomes and charity orientations to community-based activities whereas SL in the Southern Hemisphere emphasizes action toward systemic community change and awareness of issues associated with power, oppression, and privilege (Tapia, 2012). Hamner, Wilder, and Byrd (2007) found that collaboration with clients in health promotion resulted in students' greater understanding of the community and appreciation for diversity and that clients were empowered with improved health habits and greater medical knowledge.

## Systematic Formative and Summative Evaluation

All good teaching has feedback systems designed to monitor how effectively the course has been implemented and to manage unexpected developments. These should solicit information from all relevant constituencies (e.g., students, community partners, residents/clients) to improve the course. Formative (i.e., questions asked in class and reflection) and summative evaluation (i.e., grading) should be developed to provide a basis to determine if intended objectives were met (Bringle et al., 2016).

## Assessment Enhances Student Learning

Assessment in SL should be purposeful and have clear standards. Walvoord and Anderson (1998) highlight four roles of assessment: evaluation, communication, motivation, and organization. In the context of SL, assessment serves these four roles: (a) evaluation provides information on student's learning and community activities; (b) communication conveys information to the students as well as instructors on the students' activities and learning and how they correspond to design; (c) motivation not only motivates the students but also shapes how they learn; and (d) organization denotes what is important and creates feedback opportunities during the learning experience. Most importantly, assessing learning establishes that the community-based activities are being engaged in for the sake of learning and acknowledges that the students can fulfill a role in their own learning.

## Acknowledge and Celebrate Students' Service Work

Because the nature of SL is often challenging and involves in-depth collaborative work with different individuals, instructors should identify multiple ways to recognize and celebrate the activities and outcomes that result from the course. These might occur within the course, through campus centers for SL, at the campus level, and in the community with community partners.

## Assessment and Research Issues

To maximize the likelihood that SL research will contribute to theory and practice, researchers must strive for the highest standards of evidence-based research on teaching and learning. To pursue the highest standards, chapters in Clayton et al. (2013a) and Clayton, Bringle, and Hatcher (2013b) discussed assessment methods and instruments for SL research, research approaches, and theory-based research for enhanced understanding of SL for students, faculty, institutions, communities, and partnerships. This section highlights major themes and issues in conducting research on SL. Most SL research has evaluated student outcomes. Nevertheless, research on community outcomes that provides guidance and recommendations for practice is important.

## Assessment and Research on Student Outcomes of SL

### Theory
Unfortunately, much of the research on SL has been atheoretical. Chapters in Clayton et al. (2013a, 2013b) consider the ways in which cognate theories can

inform and guide research on SL. Bringle (2003, 2017b) and Wilkenfeld, Lauckhardt, and Torney-Purta (2010) highlight examples of psychological theories that can inform SL research and practice (e.g., self-determination theory, intergroup contact theory, attribution theory, equity theory, social-cognitive theory, self-efficacy theory, and transtheoretical models of behavior change).

### Assessment

In assessing SL courses, traditional methods (e.g., multiple-choice exams) can have significant utility, as exemplified in a study by Reeb, Sammon, and Isackson (1999), but they may not tap higher-order thinking nor do they measure socially responsive knowledge or personal growth. Bringle, Phillips, and Hudson (2004), Peterson and Seligman (2004), and Robinson, Shaver, and Wrightsman (1991) compiled psychometric instruments that can be used in research on student outcomes of SL, including moderator and mediating variables. However, there is overreliance on self-report measures, and more research with authentic assessment and independent evaluation of outcomes is needed. For example, the DEAL Model (Ash & Clayton, 2009), reviewed earlier, can allow independent assessment of reflection products for improvements in academic learning, socially responsive knowledge, or personal growth (Ash & Clayton, 2009).

### Research Design

Experimental studies with random assignment that examine student outcomes in SL are rare, but some have been conducted (e.g., Brown, 2011a, b; Brown, Wymer, & Cooper, 2016). In experiments, strategies from psychotherapy outcome research (Kazdin, 1998) can identify active ingredients of SL courses. For example, in the package strategy, outcomes for students in a SL course with multiple components (e.g., different types of service, reflection, readings) are compared to outcomes of students in a section that lacks one component. Although pursuing experimental research will be an important contribution to research on SL, high-quality correlational research, quasi-experimental designs, and qualitative research will continue to contribute to understanding SL processes and outcomes. More attention also needs to be given to prospective longitudinal research designs that examine SL effects over time, larger sample sizes, and appropriate control or comparison groups.

## Assessment and Research on Community Outcomes

Although definitions of SL emphasize "benefit the community" (Bringle et al., 2016, p. 8), "There is a significant lack of research exploring community outcomes of service-learning, representing a surprising void in the literature" (Reeb & Folger, 2013, p. 389). Due to the complexity of community issues, research is best guided by a systems (ecological) framework (e.g., Christens & Perkins, 2008; Reeb et al., 2017) that delineates multiple levels, coordinates transdisciplinary collaboration, and guides projects to meet criteria of psychopolitical validity.

Psychopolitical validity incorporates two criteria in evaluating community projects: (a) "that psychological and political power be incorporated into community interventions" and (b) "that interventions move beyond ameliorative efforts and towards structural change" (Prilleltensky, 2008, p. 116). Because an ecological approach (a) assures assessment at multiple levels, (b) identifies connections among levels, and (c) recognizes that positive changes in one level may be deleterious at another, it is "a necessary concomitant to psychopolitical validity" (Christens & Perkins, 2008, p. 215). Future SL research needs to differentiate (a) outputs (e.g., number of people served), (b) outcome variables (e.g., alleviative/ameliorative, empowerment, transformative), and (c) process variables (e.g., mediators, moderators) (Reeb et al., 2017).

## Participatory Community Action Research as SL

Benefits of using participatory community action research (PCAR) in SL are noteworthy (Bringle et al., 2016; Reeb et al., 2017). PCAR is (Minkler & Wallerstein, 2003):

> A collaborative approach to research that equitably involves all partners in the research process and recognizes the unique strengths that each brings...[PCAR] begins with a research topic of importance to the community with the aim of combining knowledge and action for social change to improve community. (p. 6)

Strand, Cutforth, Stoecker, Marullo, and Donohue (2003) contend that "[PCAR], when used as a teaching strategy, is an exceptionally effective form of service learning ... appropriate for a variety of ... curricular levels" (p. 137). Principles for campus-community reciprocity, as detailed by Strand et al. (2003) and summarized by Bringle et al. (2016), are at the heart of PCAR:

(1) *Initiating partnerships*: (a) sharing an overall view, (b) developing mutual goals and strategies, and (c) increasing trust and respect
(2) *Guiding the development of partnerships*: (a) sharing power, (b) communicating clearly, (c) understanding and empathizing with one another, and (d) maintaining flexibility
(3) *Guiding outcomes of partnerships*: (a) addressing mutual needs and interests, (b) enhancing organizational capacity, and (c) developing long-term social change view and plans

Principles of reciprocity have pragmatic benefits (Reeb et al., 2017), such as tailoring a project to a particular community and incorporating multiple perspectives. PCAR SL promotes democratic participation, advocacy (referred to critical SL by Mitchell, 2008), and public policy. Minkler and Freudenberg (2010) reviewed (a) concepts and models for understanding policy making, (b) phases in utilizing PCAR in policy-making plans, (c) strategies and resources to strengthen policy initiatives, and (d) ways to identify allies and opponents in policy campaigns.

## Core Findings and Current Trends

Most research on SL has focused on student outcomes, with less attention on community benefits, community-campus partnerships, changes in instructors, and changes in departments and institutions of higher education (e.g., advancement criteria, infrastructure support, assessing learning across courses). This section summarizes research on student outcomes and delineates trends in SL pedagogy. Chapters in Clayton et al. (2013a, b) reviewed past research on SL for faculty, institutions, community, and partnerships.

## Core Findings

### Meta-Analyses

Celio, Durlak, and Dymnicki (2011) conducted a meta-analysis of pre-collegiate and collegiate students and found improvements associated with SL for attitudes toward self, school and learning, civic engagement, social skills, and academic performance. Yorio and Ye (2012) found similar results for understanding of social issues, personal insight, and cognitive development. Conway, Amel, and Gerwien (2009) conducted a meta-analysis of pre-collegiate, collegiate, and adult students and found SL was associated with positive outcomes in academic, personal, social, and citizenship domains. Focusing on changes in attitudes toward persons with disabilities, Case, Schram, Jung, Leung, and Yun (2020) found in a meta-analysis that SL with an adapted physical activity had a positive effect on changing attitudes toward persons with disabilities. Novak, Markey, and Allen (2007) compared courses with and without a SL component that included a quantitative measure of cognitive learning. The effect size attributable to SL indicated a 53% improvement in learning. Warren (2012) found a similar effect size. A review by Holsapple (2012) found that SL promoted a variety of diversity outcomes.

### Longitudinal Studies

Astin and Sax (1998), in a sample of 3,450 students attending 42 American institutions, found that SL had a strong impact on reported academic learning, life skill development, and civic responsibility upon graduation, after controlling for student characteristics. Ten years after entering the university, Astin et al. (2006) found SL was associated with students' post-graduation civic leadership, charitable giving, and political engagement. Kerrigan (2005) found that a senior-year SL course was associated with enhanced communication abilities, leadership skills, community involvement, understanding of diversity, and career development 3 years after graduation. Ruiz and Warchal (2013) found higher levels of community involvement after graduation for students who had engaged in SL and other service-oriented experiential activities during college.

### Authentic Evidence

Most research on student outcomes has relied on self-report measures, with fewer studies employing authentic evidence of learning that is independently evaluated.

Markus, Howard, and King (1993) compared students in SL and non-SL sections of a large political science course and found that learning and course grades were higher for SL students. Reeb et al. (1999) found that SL and non-SL students in abnormal psychology had similar levels of academic performance early in the semester, but SL students showed increasingly superior performance subsequently. Eyler and Giles (1999) conducted interviews focused on analyzing social problems, with interview transcripts rated by blind reviewers. Relative to students in non-SL courses and poorly implemented SL courses, students in well-implemented SL courses exhibited improvements in causal complexity, solution complexity, knowledge application, and personal political strategy. These results were replicated by Guo, Yao, Wang, Yan, and Zong (2016) in a psychology of learning course. Ash, Clayton, and Atkinson (2005) had raters evaluate written products from a SL course and found improvements across the semester on higher-order reasoning abilities and critical thinking. In a child psychology course, Miller and Yen (2005) found higher project grades and final examination scores for SL (vs. non-SL). Fleck, Hussey, and Rutledge-Ellison (2017) found similar knowledge gains due to SL (vs. non-SL) in a developmental research methods course.

## Course Characteristics

### Reflection
Research demonstrates that reflection plays a key role in student outcomes (Astin et al., 2006). Hatcher et al. (2004) found that regular reflection, structured reflection, and reflection focused on personal values were independently related to the quality of SL courses. Conway et al. (2009) found in a meta-analysis that structured reflection (vs. unstructured reflection) yielded larger effects.

### Types of Service
Brown et al. (2016) found in a social psychology course that direct service that facilitated autonomy-oriented helping (vs. indirect service and dependency-oriented helping) resulted in more positive views of social equality. Miller and Yen (2005) found higher final exam scores in a child psychology course for SL activities involving direct (vs. indirect) SL activities. Dahan (2016) found that reflection, direct service, and service duration (>30 hours of service) were related to positive change on civic attitudes.

## Trends

### Scaffolding Service Learning
Ti, Tang, and Bringle (2021) envisioned scaffolding SL courses across semesters so that subsequent courses can build upon earlier SL experiences. SL courses can also be scaffolded across disciplines (students from different disciplines collaborate on a community project), longitudinally over time (community projects are sustained by cohorts of students), across borders (complementary domestic SL and international

SL courses), and after graduation (SL is embedded in continuing education and for alumni).

### Assessing the Quality and Attributes of SL Course

Past research has too often treated SL as a monolithic, uniform, and standardized pedagogy when implemented and studied. This is illustrated in research in which SL courses are compared to non-SL courses. This approach fails to consider the variability that may exist in the quality and nature of SL courses (e.g., types of service activities, nature of reflection, learning objectives, discipline). Bringle, Hatcher, and Hahn (2019) and Furco and Matthews (2018) have both developed criteria for evaluating the quality of a SL course. These can be used in research to better understand which course attributes contribute to various outcomes (e.g., student learning, partnerships, community outcomes). In addition, research is beginning to examine moderator variables (e.g., what experiences and attributes students bring to a SL course) and mediating variables (e.g., changes in intervening variables associated with change in outcomes) that can extend research findings and the understanding for why outcomes are attained and for whom (Steinberg, Bringle, & McGuire, 2013).

### Internationalizing the Psychology Curriculum

A powerful hybrid pedagogy integrates study abroad with SL, which can enhance cross-cultural understanding, personal growth, and global civic learning (Bringle, Hatcher, & Jones, 2011). Through service activities that immerse students in a local culture, international SL emphasizes working with community partners to their benefit, learning about and from local cultures, regular and structured reflection, and consideration of power and privilege (Bringle et al., 2011). Niehaus and Crain (2013) documented superior outcomes for international SL relative to domestic SL.

### Other Hybrid Pedagogies

International SL is a hybrid pedagogy that intentionally integrates SL with study abroad. Other hybrid pedagogies integrate SL with practica and internships to produce civic internships and integrate SL with research courses to produce PCAR courses (Bringle, 2017a). SL contributes socially responsive knowledge, regular and structured reflection, reciprocal partnerships, diversity, and democratic values to hybrid courses.

### Enhancing Democratic Engagement in Service Learning

Inculcating democratic values into SL needs to have the following attributes: inclusive, participatory, collaborative with the participation of multiple constituencies, focus on public issues, contribute to progress on community issues, and embrace respect for different ways of knowing and different types of knowledge (Saltmarsh, Hartley, & Clayton, 2009). Democratic civic engagement, including SL, encompasses democratic processes and democratic purposes. The Council of Europe's (2016) *Competences for Democratic Culture* provided a conceptual model of civic competencies for learners if they are to participate effectively in a culture of democracy and live in culturally diverse democratic societies. A second monograph on pedagogy identified SL as one of the pedagogies that can develop these competencies (Council of Europe, 2017).

**eService Learning (eSL)**
Waldner, McGorry, and Widener (2012) identified four approaches to technologically supported distance SL education (i.e., eSL), each with its unique combination of activities, products, partnerships, strengths, and limitations:

> Hybrid Type I (service fully on site with teaching fully online), Hybrid Type II (service fully online with teaching fully on site), Hybrid Type III (a blended format with instruction and service partially online and partially on site), and extreme e-service-learning (100% of the instruction and service online). (p. 133)

Implementing eSL presents interesting possibilities for greater participation in SL, reconceptualizing partnerships, redefining collaboration, and redesigning critical reflection (Bringle & Clayton, 2020).

**Utility of SL in Preparing Students for the Existential Crisis of Climate Change**
Intergovernmental Panel on Climate Change (2019) documents evidence of climate change as an existential crisis. Research suggests that SL has utility in preparing students for the call for action (Schneller, 2008, p. 294): "service learning courses can increase awareness of environmental issues and community awareness; locus of control; environmental consciousness; conservation knowledge, . . . personal environmental actions; and enjoyment of nature."

## Challenges, Lessons Learned, and Implications for Learning and Teaching Psychology

There are several pathways that instructors follow and several factors that motivate them (political, moral, pedagogical, spiritual, and personal factors) to integrate SL into psychology courses (Bringle et al., 2016). The experiential, constructivist, and transformational approaches embedded in SL move learning outside of the classroom, decenter the teacher, and challenge the notion of absolute truths. These processes might be unfamiliar to some psychology instructors and may be regarded as counternormative (Clayton & Ash, 2004). Furthermore, working in partnership with community members and dealing with authentic real-world dilemmas that are often ill-structured and contradictory increases the quality of curricular design. It takes time and commitment to design a SL course and offer it. Instructors can benefit from assistance with course development from experienced SL instructors, particularly psychologists, and campus staff with SL expertise. Institutions may have manuals for instructors, and some organizations provide guidelines for good practice in SL (e.g., Europe Engage, Campus Compact, CLAYSS, The Forum on Education

Abroad, Council for the Advancement of Standards in Higher Education, National Youth Leadership Council).

Support for faculty development should start at the graduate level by preparing future instructors for work on civically engaged teaching, research, and professional service (Bringle et al., 2016). Furthermore, faculty development programs should focus on the characteristics of the instructors they support. For instance, although novice faculty may be more focused on the expectations of their departments, more advanced faculty may concentrate on scholarship or even mentoring. Some faculty members may also feel more comfortable and competent than others to design a SL course (e.g., adaptive leadership; building sustainable and mutually beneficial relationships) as well as communicating and negotiating power relationships and sharing decision-making (Preece, 2016). Faculty development programs may emphasize learning theories, funding, support to build communities of scholars, and preparation of promotion dossiers (Bringle et al., 2016). Support for faculty development is also available from regional associations listed in the GUNI book (see Resource section) as well as at conferences.

SL requires attention and responsibility to multiple constituencies, including students, instructors, administrators in the academic institution, and the community. The context (historical, political, economic, social, institutional, disciplinary) in which SL is practiced should be considered (Thomson et al., 2011). Sensitive race relations, differences in worldview, values, culture, and language should be respected. A guide, such as a code of ethics, provides a framework to determine the benefits to all the parties involved as well as potential risks. That is, to what extent will the SL activities benefit the community, the students, and other partners? Are there potential negative, unintended, and unexpected consequences of a well-intentioned service learning project? Chapdelaine et al. (2005) and Ruiz, Warchal, Chapdelaine, and Wells (2011) suggested that guiding principles should be based on codes of ethics that may be available from regional or national professional organizations. When a professional code of ethics is not available, the *Universal Declaration of Ethics Principles for Psychologists* (2008) may be consulted. This declaration includes four principles: (a) respect for the dignity of persons and peoples, (b) competent caring for the well-being of persons and peoples, (c) integrity, and (d) professional and scientific responsibilities to society. These principles align well with the feminist epistemology (Belenky et al., 1997) in which SL is embedded and the ethic of care promoted through SL.

These ethical principles are applicable to administrators, instructors, students, and community partners (Chapdelaine et al., 2005; Ruiz et al., 2011). Together the partners determine the roles and responsibilities of all parties involved; prepare a cost/benefit evaluation of the project; prepare students by clearly communicating learning outcomes, course requirements, and expectations; and model ethical behavior. Administrators focus on how SL aligns with the institutional mission and provide support for all involved. The instructors make sure that the community interests and course objectives are aligned, that there is a clear plan that is developed and shared with all parties, and that the students are prepared for the projects.

Partnerships with community organizations are essential to good SL course design. They need to be established prior to and during course design to ensure that the students' service activities are aligned not only with the course's learning objectives but also with community goals. The community partners, whether organizations or individuals, are influential in determining the nature of the community-based activities and the roles each partner plays. Particular attention needs to be focused on issues related to inclusive participation, diversity, and power imbalance. For example, promoting a social justice agenda in psychologists' training might have intricate implications in countries such as South Africa where inequality, social injustices, and structural constraints are severe and widespread. In these circumstances, power relations should be carefully managed, and care should be taken to not perpetuate inequity (Akhurst, 2017). Time and resources need to be allocated to negotiate partnerships in fluid circumstances and less-structured communities and for planning, preparation, and reflection before, during, and after the implementation of the SL course. After the scope and nature of the project are established by all the parties involved, each member takes on their roles and responsibilities. Then a plan is created with activities, goals, potential deadlines, and contingency plans, including how to provide formative and summative assessment. Although this may require a time commitment, dedication, and ethical inclination from faculty, it also challenges students to develop the ethical responsibility they need to function as psychologically literate and socially responsive global citizens (APA, 2013; Bringle et al., 2016).

## Conclusion

SL is an empirically established high-impact pedagogy that enhances foundational, professional, and socially responsive knowledge in students so that, as psychologically literate citizens, they are prepared to be engaged in the world. As an underdeveloped pedagogy for teaching psychology at all levels, it has the potential to enrich the curriculum, broaden learning objectives, enhance student motivation, prepare students for social issues in a diverse society, and contribute to the United Nations SDGs. Psychologists are well-positioned to contribute to the literature on SL through theory-based research that utilizes rigorous research methodology and assessment, including longitudinal research and research on community outcomes guided by a systems (ecological) perspective.

## Cross-References

- ▶ Assessment of Learning in Psychology
- ▶ Basic Principles and Procedures for Effective Teaching in Psychology
- ▶ First Principles of Instruction Revisited
- ▶ Formative Assessment and Feedback Strategies
- ▶ Inquiry-Based Learning in Psychology

## Teaching, Learning, and Assessment Resources

Bringle, R. G., Reeb, R., Brown, M. A., & Ruiz, A. (2016). *Service learning in psychology: Enhancing undergraduate education for the public good*. **American Psychological Association.**

> This book reviews the theory, research, and practice for SL, establishing it as an effective pedagogy that can help psychology departments meet the five key learning goals outlined in the *APA Guidelines 2.0*. Chapters provide specific implementation strategies in introductory, major, and capstone courses. They also examined faculty development, assessment, and scholarship and provide blueprints for department-wide civic engagement.

Bringle, R. G., Ruiz, A., Brown, M. A., & Reeb, R. (2016). **Enhancing the psychology curriculum through service learning.** *Psychology Learning and Teaching, 15*(3), 1–16.

> This article proposes that SL is the most potent pedagogy for developing well-rounded, psychologically literate citizens capable of meeting the learning goals for the undergraduate psychology major. SL is defined, rationales for SL are delineated, research demonstrating its efficacy is summarized, and ways in which SL contributes to academic learning, civic learning, and personal growth are described.

Chapdelaine, A., Ruiz, A., Warchal, J., & Wells, C. (2005). *Service-Learning Code of Ethics.* **Anker.**

> Envisioning an educational system that meets community concerns by cultivating in students a commitment to civic engagement, this book provides insights and tools for navigating the ethical dilemmas that arise during SL. Designed for administrators, instructors, and students, it contributes to meaningful reflection, class discussion, and values exploration by promoting SL as benefiting society and student development.

Cranney, J., & Dunn, D. (Eds) (2011). *The psychologically literate citizen: Foundations and global perspectives.* **Oxford University Press.**

> This edited book provides international responses that link traditional approaches in psychology to psychological literacy and psychologically literate citizens and offers practical suggestions for everyday teaching practice.

Global University Network for Innovation. (2014). *Higher education in the world 5: Knowledge, engagement and higher education: Contributing to social change.* **Palgrave MacMillan.**

> This volume contains an examination of community engagement in higher education, including SL, and regional developments from around the world.

Jacoby, B. (2015). *Service-learning essentials: Questions, answers, and lessons learned.* **Jossey-Bass.**

> This volume provides advice on basic and advanced issues related to the design, implementation, and assessment of service learning in higher education.

## References

Akhurst, J. (2017). Student experiences of community-based service learning during masters' level training, as related to critical community psychology practice. *Journal for New Generation Sciences, 15*, 1–20.

Altman, I. (1996). Higher education and psychology in the millennium. *American Psychologist, 51*, 371–378. https://doi.org/10.1037/0003-066X.51.4.371.

American Psychological Association. (2007). *APA Guidelines for the undergraduate psychology major*. Author.

American Psychological Association. (2013). *APA guidelines for the undergraduate psychology major: Version 2.0*. https://www.apa.org/ed/precollege/undergrad/index.aspx

American Psychological Association. (2018). *APA citizen psychologist*. https://www.apa.org/about/governance/citizen-psychologist

Aramburuzabala, P., McIlrath, L., & Opazo, H. (2019). *Embedding service learning in European higher education*. London, UK: Routledge.

Ash, S. L., & Clayton, P. H. (2009). Generating, deepening, and documenting learning: The power of critical reflection for applied learning. *Journal of Applied Learning in Higher Education, 1*, 25–48.

Ash, S. L., Clayton, P. H., & Atkinson, M. P. (2005). Integrating reflection and assessment to improve and capture student learning. *Michigan Journal of Community Service Learning, 11*(2), 49–60.

Astin, A. W., & Sax, L. J. (1998). How undergraduates are affected by service participation. *Journal of College Student Development, 39*, 251–263.

Astin, A. W., Vogelgesang, L. J., Misa, K., Anderson, J., Denson, N., Jayakumar, J., Saenz, V., & Yamamura, E. (2006). *Understanding the effects of service-learning: A study of students and faculty*. Report to the Atlantic Philanthropies.

Australian Psychological Society. (2015). *Australian curriculum: Psychological science*. https://www.psychology.org.au/Training-and-careers/psychological-science/

Belenky, M. F., Clinchy, B. M., Goldberger, N. R., & Tarule, J. M. (1997). *Women's ways of knowing: The development of self, voice, and mind*. New York, NY: Basic Books.

Billig, S., Root, S., & Jesse, D. (2005). *The impact of participation in service learning on high school students' civic engagement*. Center for Information & Research on Civic Learning and Engagement, Working Paper No. 33.

Bloom, B. S. (Ed.). (1956). *Taxonomy of educational objectives, handbook I: Cognitive domain*. New York, NY: David McCay.

Bobo, B., & Akhurst, J. (2019). 'Most importantly, it's like the partner takes more interest in us': Using Ubuntu as a fundamental ethic of community engagement partnerships at Rhodes University. *Alternation, 27*, 88–110. https://doi.org/10.29086/2519-5476/2019/sp27a4.

Bowman, N. A. (2011). Promoting participation in a diverse democracy: A meta-analysis of college diversity experiences and civic engagement. *Review of Educational Research, 81*(1), 29–68.

Boyle-Baise, M. (2002). *Multicultural service learning: Educating teachers in diverse communities*. New York, NY: Teachers College Press.

Bringle, R. G. (2003). Enhancing theory-based research on service-learning. In S. H. Billig & J. S. Eyler (Eds.), *Deconstructing service-learning: Research exploring context, participation, and impacts* (pp. 3–21). Greenwich, CT: Information Age Publishing.

Bringle, R. G. (2017a). Hybrid high-impact pedagogies: Integrating service-learning with three other high-impact pedagogies. *Michigan Journal of Community Service Learning, 24*(1), 49–63.

Bringle, R. G. (2017b). Social psychology and civic outcomes. In J. A. Hatcher, R. G. Bringle, & T. W. Hahn (Eds.), *Research on student civic outcomes in service learning: Conceptual frameworks and methods* (pp. 69–89). Sterling, VA: Stylus.

Bringle, R. G., & Clayton, P. H. (2012). Civic education through service-learning: What, how, and why? In L. McIlrath, A. Lyons, & R. Munck (Eds.), *Higher education and civic engagement: Comparative perspectives* (pp. 101–124). New York, NY: Palgrave.

Bringle, R. G., & Clayton, P. H. (2020). Integrating service learning and digital technologies: Examining the challenge and the promise. *Revista Iberoamerican de Education a Distancia, 23*(1), 43–65.

Bringle, R. G., & Hatcher, J. A. (1996). Implementing service learning in higher education. *Journal of Higher Education, 67*, 221–239.

Bringle, R. G., Hatcher, J. A., & Hahn, T. W. (2019). Practical wisdom for conducting research: An introduction. In J. A. Hatcher, R. G. Bringle, & T. W. Hahn (Eds.), *Practical wisdom for conducting research on service learning: Quality and purpose* (pp. 3–24). Sterling, VA: Stylus.

Bringle, R. G., Hatcher, J. A., & Jones, S. G. (Eds.). (2011). *International service learning: Conceptual frameworks and research*. Sterling, VA: Stylus.

Bringle, R. G., Phillips, M. A., & Hudson, M. (2004). *The measure of service learning: Research scales to assess student experiences*. Washington, DC: American Psychological Association.

Bringle, R. G., Reeb, R. N., Brown, M. A., & Ruiz, A. I. (2016). *Service learning and psychology: Enhancing undergraduate education for the public good*. Washington, DC: American Psychological Association.

Brown, M. A. (2011a). The power of generosity to change views on social power. *Journal of Experimental Social Psychology, 47*, 1285–1290.

Brown, M. A. (2011b). Learning from service: The effect of helping on helpers' social dominance orientation. *Journal of Applied Social Psychology, 41*, 850–871.

Brown, M. A., Wymer, J. D., & Cooper, C. S. (2016). The counter-normative effects of service-learning: Fostering attitudes toward social equality through contact and autonomy. *Michigan Journal of Community Service Learning, 23*(1), 37–44.

Case, L., Schram, B., Jung, J., Leung, W., & Yun, J. (2020). A meta-analysis of the effect of adapted physical activity service-learning programs on college student attitudes toward people with disabilities. *Disability and Rehabilitation*, 1–13.

Cayuela, A., Alonso, M., Ballesteros, C., & Aramburuzabala, P. (2020). *2019 Annual report of the European Observatory of Service-Learning in Higher Education*. https://www.eoslhe.eu/

Celio, C. I., Durlak, J., & Dymnicki, A. (2011). A meta-analysis of the impact of service-learning on students. *Journal of Experiential Education, 34*, 164–181.

Centro Latinoamericano de Aprendizaje y Servicio Solidario (CLAYSS). (n.d.). *What is "service learning"?* https://clayss.org/en/what-service-learning

Chapdelaine, A., Ruiz, A., Warchal, J., & Wells, C. (2005). *Service-learning code of ethics*. Bolton, MA: Anker.

Choo, J., Kong, T. Y., Ong, F., Shiuan, T. S., Nair, S., Ong, J., & Chan, A. (2019). What works in service-learning? Achieving civic outcomes, academic connection, career preparation, and personal growth in students at Ngee Ann Polytechnic. *Michigan Journal of Community Service Learning, 25*(2), 95–132.

Christens, B., & Perkins, D. D. (2008). Transdisciplinary, multilevel action research to enhance ecological and psychopolitical validity. *Journal of Community Psychology, 36*(2), 214–231.

Clayton, P. H., & Ash, S. L. (2004). Shifts in perspective: Capitalizing on the counter-normative nature of service-learning. *Michigan Journal of Community Service Learning, 11*, 59–70.

Clayton, P. H., Bringle, R. G., & Hatcher, J. A. (Eds.). (2013a). *Research on service learning: Conceptual frameworks and assessment* (Students and faculty) (Vol. 2A). Sterling, VA: Stylus.

Clayton, P. H., Bringle, R. G., & Hatcher, J. A. (Eds.). (2013b). *Research on service learning: Conceptual frameworks and assessment* (Communities, institutions, and partnerships) (Vol. 2B). Sterling, VA: Stylus.

Conway, J. M., Amel, E. L., & Gerwien, D. P. (2009). Teaching and learning in the social context: A meta-analysis of service learning's effects on academic, personal, social, and citizenship outcomes. *Teaching of Psychology, 36*, 233–245. https://doi.org/10.1080/00986280903172969.

Council of Europe. (2016). *Competences for democratic culture: Living together as equals in culturally diverse democratic societies*. Strasbourg, France: Council of Europe.

Council of Europe. (2017). *Council of Europe reference framework of competences for democratic culture (CDC)* (Guidance for implementation. 2. CDC and pedagogy) (Vol. *3*). Sttrasbourg, France: Council of Europe.

Cranney, J., & Dunn, D. (Eds.). (2011). *The psychologically literate citizen: Foundations and global perspectives*. New York, NY: Oxford University Press.

Dahan, T. A. (2016). Revisiting pedagogical variations in service-learning and student outcomes. *International Journal of Research on Service-Learning and Community Engagement, 4*(1).

Europe Engage. (n.d.). *Our definition of service-learning*. https://www.eoslhe.eu/europe-engage/

EuroPsy. (2014). *Tuning-EuroPsy: Reference points for the design and delivery of degree programmes in psychology*. https://www.efpa.eu/professional-development/tuning-europsy-_-tuning-educational-structures-in-europe

Eyler, J. S., & Giles, D. E., Jr. (1999). *Where's the learning in service-learning?* San Francisco, CA: Jossey-Bass.

Fleck, B., Hussey, H. D., & Rutledge-Ellison, L. (2017). Linking class and community: An investigation of service learning. *Teaching of Psychology, 44*, 232–239.

Freire, P. (1968). *Pedagogy of the oppressed*. New York, NY: The Seabury Press.

Furco, A., & Matthews, P. H. (2018, July). *Using a new, research-based tool to assess the quality of planning and implementation of service-learning courses*. Paper presented at the conference of the International Association for Research on Service Learning and Community Engagement, New Orleans, LA.

Furco, A., & Norvell, K. (2019). What is service learning? Making sense of the pedagogy and practice. In P. Aramburuzabala, L. McIlrath, & H. Opazo (Eds.), *Embedding service learning in European higher education: Developing a culture of civic engagement* (pp. 13–35). London, UK: Routledge.

Guo, F., Yao, M., Wang, C., Yan, W., & Zong, Z. (2016). The effects of service learning on student problem solving: The mediating role of classroom engagement. *Teaching of Psychology, 43*, 16–21.

Halpern, D. F. (Ed.). (2010). *Undergraduate education in psychology: A blueprint for the future of the discipline*. Washington, DC: American Psychological Association.

Hamner, J. B., Wilder, B., & Byrd, L. (2007). Lessons learned: Integrating a service learning community-based partnership into the curriculum. *Nursing Outlook, 55*(2), 106–110.

Harkavy, I., & Hartley, M. (2010). Pursuing Franklin's dream: Philosophical and historical roots of service-learning. *American Journal of Community Psychology, 46*, 418–427. https://doi.org/10.1007/s10464-010-9341-x.

Hatcher, J. A., Bringle, R. G., & Muthiah, R. (2004). Designing effective reflection: What matters to service learning? *Michigan Journal of Community Service Learning, 11*(1), 38–46.

Holsapple, M. A. (2012). Service-learning and student diversity outcomes: Existing evidence and directions for future research. *Michigan Journal of Community Service Learning, 18*(2), 5–18.

Intergovernmental Panel on Climate Change. (2019). *Summary for policy makers of IPCC Special Report on Global Warming*. https://www.ipcc.ch/2018/10/08/summary-for-policymakers-of-ipcc-special-report-on-global-warming-of-1-5c-approved-by-governments/

International Association of Applied Psychology. (2016). *International declaration on core competences in professional psychology*. https://iaapsy.org/policies-initiatives/ipcp-documents/

Jacoby, B. (2015). *Service-learning essentials: Questions, answers, and lessons learned*. San Francisco, CA: Jossey-Bass.

Kazdin, A. E. (1998). *Research design in clinical psychology* (3rd ed.). Boston, MA: Allyn & Bacon.

Kerrigan, S. (2005). College graduates' perspectives on the effect of capstone service-learning courses. In M. Martinez, P. A. Pasque, & N. Bowman (Eds.), *Multidisciplinary perspectives on higher education for the public good* (pp. 49–65). National Forum on Higher Education for the Public Good. Ann Arbor, MI.

Kolb, D. A. (2015). *Experiential learning: Experience as the source of learning and development.* Upper Saddle River, NJ: Pearson.

Kuh, G. D. (2008). *High-impact educational practices: What they are, who has access to them, and why they matter.* Washington, DC: Association of American Colleges and Universities.

Markus, G. B., Howard, J. P. F., & King, D. C. (1993). Integrating community service and classroom instruction enhances learning: Results from an experiment. *Educational Evaluation and Policy Analysis, 15*, 410–419.

Mezirow, J. (2009). Transformative learning theory. In J. Mezirow & E. W. Taylor (Eds.), *Transformative learning in practice: Insights from community* (pp. 18–31). Hoboken, NJ: Wiley.

Miller, K. K., & Yen, S. (2005). Group differences in academic achievement: Service learning in a child psychology course. *Psychology of Teaching, 32*, 56–58.

Minkler, M., & Wallerstein, N. (2003). *Community-based participatory research for health.* San Francisco, CA: Jossey-Bass.

Minkler, M., & Freudenberg, N. (2010). From community-based participatory research to policy changes. In H. Fitzgerald, K. Burack, & S. Seifer (Eds.), *Handbook of engaged scholarship: Contemporary landscapes, future directions: Volume 2: Community-campus partnerships* (pp. 275–294). Lansing MI: Michigan State University Press.

Mitchell, T. D. (2008). Traditional vs. critical service-learning: Engaging the literature to differentiate two models. *Michigan Journal of Community Service Learning, 14*(1), 50–65.

Moely, B. E., & Ilustre, V. (2014). The impact of service-learning course characteristics on university students' learning outcomes. *Michigan Journal of Community Service Learning, 21*(1), 5–16.

Morgan, W., & Streb, M. (2001). Building citizenship: How student voice in service-learning develops civic values. *Social Science Quarterly, 82*(1), 154–169.

Niehaus, E., & Crain, L. K. (2013). Act local or global?: Comparing student experiences in domestic and international service-learning programs. *Michigan Journal of Community Service Learning, 20*, 31–40.

Novak, J. M., Markey, V., & Allen, M. (2007). Evaluating cognitive outcomes of service learning in higher education: A meta-analysis. *Communication Research Reports, 24*(2), 149–157.

Pacho, T. (2019). Service-learning: An innovative approach to education in Africa. In J. K. Mugo, P. Namubiru-Ssentamu, & M. Njihia (Eds.), *The good education and Africa's future: Concepts, issues and options* (pp. 232–259). Nairobi, Kenya: Pauline's Publications Africa.

Pascarella, E. T., Martin, G. L., Hanson, J. M., Trolian, T. L., Gillig, B., & Blaich, C. (2014). Effects of diversity experiences on critical thinking skills over 4 years of college. *Journal of College Student Development, 95*(1), 86–92.

Peterson, C., & Seligman, M. E. P. (2004). *Character strengths and virtues: A handbook and classification.* Washington, DC: American Psychology Association.

Preece, J. (2016). Negotiating service learning through community engagement: Adaptive leadership, knowledge, dialogue and power. *Education as Change, 20*, 104–125. https://doi.org/10.17159/1947-9417/2016/562.

Prilleltensky, I. (2008). The role of power in wellness, oppression, and liberation: The promise of psychopolitical validity. *Journal of Community Psychology, 36*, 116–136.

Reeb, R. N., & Folger, S. F. (2013). Community outcomes in service learning: Research and practice from a systems perspective. In P. H. Clayton, R. G. Bringle, & J. A. Hatcher (Eds.), *Research on service-learning: Conceptual models and assessment* (Vol. 2B, pp. 389–418). Sterling, VA: Stylus.

Reeb, R. N., Sammon, J. A., & Isackson, N. L. (1999). Clinical application of the service-learning model in psychology: Evidence of educational and clinical benefits. *Prevention and Intervention in the Community, 18*, 65–82.

Reeb, R. N., Snow-Hill, N., Folger, S. F., Steel, A. L., Stayton, L., Hunt, C., O'Koon, B., & Glendening, Z. (2017). Psycho-ecological systems model: A systems approach to planning and gauging the community impact of engaged scholarship and service-learning. *Michigan Journal of Community Service Learning, 24*, 6–22.

Regina, C., & Ferrara, C. (2017). *Service-learning in Central and Eastern Europe: Handbook for engaged teachers and students.* CLAYSS. Centro Latinoamericano de Aprendizaje y Servicio Solidario.

Reich, J. N., & Nelson, P. D. (2010). Engaged scholarship: Perspectives from psychology. In H. E. Fitzgerald, C. Burack, & S. D. Seifer (Eds.), *Handbook of engaged scholarship: Contemporary landscapes, future directions. Volume 2: Community-campus partnerships* (pp. 131–147). East Lansing, MI: Michigan State University Press.

Rich, G., Padilla-López, A., Souza, L., Zinkiewicz, L., Taylor, J., & Jaafar, J. (2018). *Teaching psychology around the world* (Vol. 4). Newcastle upon Tyne, UK: Cambridge Scholars.

Robinson, J. P., Shaver, P. R., & Wrightsman, L. S. (Eds.). (1991). *Measures of personality and social psychological attitudes* (Vol. 1). London, UK: Academic.

Ruiz, A., & Warchal, J. (2013). Long-term impact of service-learning on alumni volunteer service activities. In P. Lin & M. Wiegand (Eds.), *Service-learning in higher education: Connecting the global to the local* (pp. 255–264). Indianapolis, IN: University of Indianapolis Press.

Ruiz, A., Warchal, J., Chapdelaine, A., & Wells, C. (2011). International service-learning: Who benefits? In P. Lin (Ed.), *Service-learning in higher education: National and international connections* (pp. 13–25). Indianapolis, IN: University of Indianapolis Press.

Saltmarsh, J., Hartley, M., & Clayton, P. H. (2009). *Democratic engagement white paper.* Boston, MA: New England Resource Center for Higher Education.

Schneller, A. J. (2008). Environmental service learning: Outcomes of innovative pedagogy in Baja California Sur, Mexico. *Environmental Education Research, 14*(3), 291–307. https://doi.org/10.1080/13504620802192418.

Singh, K. (2016). *Report of the Special Rapporteur on the right to education.* Geneva, Switzerland: United Nations Human Rights Council.

Steinberg, K., Bringle, R. G., & McGuire, L. E. (2013). Attributes of quality research in service learning. In P. H. Clayton, R. G. Bringle, & J. A. Hatcher (Eds.), *Research on service learning: Conceptual frameworks and assessment. Vol. 2A: Students and faculty* (pp. 27–53). Sterling, VA: Stylus.

Stokamer, S. T., & Clayton, P. H. (2017). Student civic learning through service learning. In J. A. Hatcher, R. G. Bringle, & T. W. Hahn (Eds.), *Research on student civic outcomes in service learning: Conceptual frameworks and methods* (pp. 45–65). Sterling, VA: Stylus.

Strand, K. J., Cutforth, N., Stoecker, R., Marullo, S., & Donohue, P. (2003). *Community-based research and higher education: Principles and practices.* San Francisco, CA: Jossey-Bass.

Tapia, M. N. (2012). Academic excellence and community engagement: Reflections on the Latin American experience. In L. McIlrath, A. Lyons, & R. Munck (Eds.), *Higher education and civic engagement: Comparative perspectives* (pp. 187–203). New York, NY: Palgrave.

Thomson, A. M., Smith-Tolken, A. R., Naidoo, A. V., & Bringle, R. G. (2011). Service learning and community engagement: A comparison of three national contexts. *Voluntas, 22*, 214–237. https://doi.org/10.1007/s11266-010-9133-9.

Ti, C., Tang, J., & Bringle, R. G. (2021). Initiating and extending institutionalization of service learning. *Journal of Higher Education Outreach and Engagement, 25*(2), 5–22.

Toole, J., & Toole, P. (1998). *The essential elements of service-learning practice.* St. Paul, MN: National Youth Leadership Council.

United Nations. (2020). *Sustainable development goals.* https://www.un.org/sustainabledevelopment/

*Universal Declaration of Ethical Principles for Psychologists* (3rd ed.). (2008). https://www.iupsys.net/about/declarations/universal-declaration-of-ethical-principles-for-psychologists/

Waldner, L. S., McGorry, S. Y., & Widener, M. C. (2012). E-service-learning: The evolution of service-learning to engage a growing online student population. *Journal of Higher Education Outreach and Engagement, 16*(2), 123–150.

Walvoord, B. E., & Anderson, V. J. (1998). *Effective grading: A tool for learning and assessment in college.* San Francisco, CA: Jossey-Bass.

Warren, J. L. (2012). Does service-learning increase student learning?: A meta-analysis. *Michigan Journal of Community Service Learning, Spring*, 56–61.

Wilkenfeld, B., Lauckhardt, J., & Torney-Purta, J. (2010). The relation between developmental theory and measures of civic engagement in research on adolescents. In L. R. Sherrod, J. Torney-Purta, & C. A. Flanagan (Eds.), *Handbook of research on civic engagement in youth* (pp. 193–219). Hoboken, NJ: Wiley.

Xing, J., & Ma, C. (Eds.). (2010). *Service-learning in Asia: Curricular models and practices*. Hong Kong: Hong Kong University Press.

Yorio, P. L., & Ye, F. (2012). A meta-analysis on the effects of service-learning on the social, personal, and cognitive outcomes of learning. *Academy of Management Learning & Education, 11*(1), 9–27.

# Assessment of Learning in Psychology

## Summative Strategies in Courses and Programs

Lisa Durrance Blalock, Vanessa R. Rainey, and Jane S. Halonen

## Contents

| | |
|---|---|
| Introduction | 1332 |
| Design Issues and Approaches of Summative Assessment | 1336 |
| Traditional Exams | 1336 |
| Integrative Papers | 1337 |
| Authentic Assessments | 1338 |
| Facilitating Successful Student Performance | 1340 |
| Evaluation/Research Issues Associated with Summative Assessment | 1341 |
| Establishing Validity of Summative Assessments | 1341 |
| Establishing Reliability of Summative Assessments | 1344 |
| Findings and Current Trends | 1346 |
| Challenges, Lessons Learned, and Implications for Learning and Teaching Psychology | 1348 |
| Conclusions | 1348 |
| Teaching, Learning, and Assessment Resources Associated with Summative Assessment | 1349 |
| Appendices | 1351 |
| Appendix A: A Summative Protocol for Introductory Psychology | 1351 |
| Appendix B: Example of a Speaking Rubric for Summative Assessment | 1353 |
| References | 1355 |

### Abstract

Summative assessment practices reveal whether students ultimately are successful in learning what we teach. In this chapter, we explore current insights about what summative practices reveal about effective teaching and learning in psychology's international contexts. We define summative practices and distinguish summative strategies from formative approaches, followed by discussing administrative concerns that help determine summative design choices. We offer exemplars at both the course and program levels to optimize gains from

L. D. Blalock (✉) · V. R. Rainey · J. S. Halonen
Department of Psychology, University of West Florida, Pensacola, FL, USA
e-mail: lblalock@uwf.edu

© Springer Nature Switzerland AG 2023
J. Zumbach et al. (eds.), *International Handbook of Psychology Learning and Teaching*,
Springer International Handbooks of Education,
https://doi.org/10.1007/978-3-030-28745-0_62

assessment for students and teachers alike. We identify the psychometric factors that influence the quality and success of summative designs. We close with an exploration of emerging contemporary issues and some "lessons learned" to optimize gains using summative assessment in psychology contexts.

**Keywords**

Assessment · Formative assessment · Summative assessment · Psychology capstone · Program evaluation

## Introduction

"How will I know if my students got it?" All serious educators entertain this fundamental question in the design and success of their courses. It is uncertain when the practice of incorporating examinations to measure learning began, but it is very clear that professors now almost automatically assume that assessment must be a prominent feature of their professional responsibilities. Assessing is simply part of our academic DNA. Because of their inherent interests in measuring behavior, psychologist-educators may envision greater opportunities associated with measuring the impact of a course on student learning. This chapter addresses the strategies psychologists use to measure whether their students "got it" and the purposes such measurement serves. Although the chapter derived from a collaboration by North American psychology colleagues in a regional comprehensive university, we trust that the content will be valuable across geographic and cultural boundaries.

Assessment practices have been flourishing in the past few years, in part as a response to complaints about the quality of what higher education has accomplished. Educators in North America have mandates to orchestrate their courses around student learning outcomes and to reflect a spirit of continuous improvement in the design and execution of the courses (Halonen, Beers, & Brown, In press). However, those pressures extend across the globe. For example, Boahin (2018) indicated that employers in Africa advocated that universities focus on developing competence in critical thinking and entrepreneurism among other outcomes in their programs to contribute to building a sturdier economy. Identifying evidence about whether students meet specified educational objectives in their programs or courses is the goal of summative assessment.

Part of the challenge of making sense of summative assessment practices across the globe is variable terminology used across contexts. In fact, from the vantage point of China, Cookson (2018, p. 930) characterized the field as suffering from "definitional anarchy." Although researchers have used various terms, such as practical assessment, authentic assessment, or high-impact assessment, *summative* assessment appears to be emerging as the most popular term to address whether or not student performance meets the expectations of the course instructor or department at some meaningful endpoint. That endpoint can conclude a learning experience, success in a course, or success in a program (Scriven, 1967).

Summative assessment involves various modalities. Some formats require students to render performance in a free-standing assessment experience before graduation, such as an exit or "leaving" examination or a performance review by an external monitor or assessor. Summative strategies can also be embedded in a course. As an example, many North American programs incorporate a final integrating experience in the curriculum, such as a senior seminar (a course that often involves independent and original research, including a thesis), a themed capstone (a course that intentionally focuses on helping students integrate their experiences across the curriculum in the context of studying a specific psychology topic in depth), or a practicum (an experiential course that allows students to try out specific psychology-related workforce skills). Regardless of the context, the results of a summative program assessment reflect the fitness of a curricular experience as a whole.

Contemporary practice in assessment makes a distinction between *formative* and *summative* assessment. In the case of formative assessment, instructors conduct performance measurement primarily to foster the growth of students' skills and knowledge or to make some kind of judgment about a student's learning capability. The primary benefit of assessment is directly to students, sizing up what students have achieved, pointing out where more development could occur, or determining optimal future educational pathways. Typically fairly informal, formative assessments tend to be low stakes in relation to what grade students will achieve. Formative assessment has been characterized as assessment *for* learning (McCarthy, 2015). However, Dirkson (2011) advocated faculty benefits since student performance implies where teaching might have fallen short. Formative assessment examples include making observations, homework, reflections, and self-evaluations.

In contrast, summative assessment provides an ultimate judgment on the quality of learning, resulting in high-stakes decisions. In the case of a course assessment, summative performance may determine student grades in the course. However, the results from a summative strategy could also be used to evaluate teacher effectiveness. If a summative assessment transpires at the program level, the primary purpose of the summative assessment facilitates external conclusions about the caliber of teaching and learning that has transpired in the program.

Summative assessments tend to be more formal and rigorous; they can be designed by the course instructor or imported into a course by the department. When the measurement target is program quality, students may participate in the assessment, but may not necessarily receive performance feedback or have it influence their grades. In contrast to formative assessment goals of measurement *for* learning, summative strategies have been characterized as assessment *of* learning (McCarthy, 2015). Examples of summative assessment include projects, portfolios, papers, exams, and state/national tests.

Scholars have debated the relative value of formative and summative assessments. For example, Wiggins (1993) emphasized that formative assessment focuses on improvement, whereas summative assessment is primarily an audit and suggested the evaluative emphasis may taint faculty enthusiasm for summative procedures. Taras (2005, p. 469) observed that formative assessment has been rendered an "antiseptic version" of summative assessment, which has become synonymous with judgments that may threaten self-efficacy and self-esteem for both students and teachers alike. Lau (2016) even suggested that a dichotomy has evolved that casts formative practices as "good" and summative practices as "bad." Consequently, the value of summative assessment viewed in such pejorative terms makes it easy to see why the summative vs. formative controversy has become so divisive and why summative strategies may have lost their central importance in favor of formative practices (Harlen, 2005). Dixson and Worrell (2016) observed that higher-stakes decisions require more robust psychometrics to ensure that conclusions drawn from the measurement are objective and justifiable.

Many instructors align with formative assessment strategies as the most effective learning technique due to its potential to encourage a growth mindset in students (Dweck, 2016; Taras, 2005). A comparison of international assessment practice (Berenbaum et al., 2015) identified that most countries represented in their review (including the UK, Australia, New Zealand, North America, and Norway) reported a much stronger commitment to the use of formative practices than summative approaches. The authors concluded that overreliance on summative practices reduces teacher autonomy and questioned the validity of drawing conclusions about program quality from the performance metrics that result from summative evaluations.

However, even within countries the educational context itself may demonstrate greater reliance on one form over the other (Tomas & Jessy, 2019). For example, in the UK, research-intensive settings tend to endorse summative practices, whereas other teaching-intensive contexts are more inclined to use a mix of assessment strategies. That pattern is also apparent in North American universities.

Hendrickson (2012), a North American scholar, provided a compelling argument about the relative value of formative over summative assessment. She argued that student placements in international academic rankings could be used as a form of external validation to measure summative assessment value. For example, Finland, which emphasizes the use of formative assessment, tends to head the list for academic achievement among countries of the world. In contrast, in the USA, which may be regarded as more summative-centric, has recently performed at mediocre levels in these comparisons. Hendrickson suggested that outcome is not accidental, but serves as an indictment of overreliance on summative practices.

Although many scholars suggest that an assessment process ideally should be able to serve both purposes, Knight (2010) argued the opposite. He distinguished formative strategies as "feedback" and summative strategies as "feed-out," so those purposes may not be compatible in a single measurement strategy. However, in our view, when a summative measurement takes place, there is no reason why this exercise cannot provide feedback to learners on how well they individually performed so that all stakeholders benefit; who receives the results is just one of many administrative variables that influence summative design and execution.

When achievement in a course is the primary motivation for testing, the instructor designs the best strategy for establishing what students have learned or learned to do in the course. Instructors must plan the mode, possibly the timing, and any potential weighting of a summative assessment. They may also determine whether a cumulative strategy would be preferable to assessing and combining smaller performances along the way (Lawrence, 2013). Psychology professors are much more likely to be intrinsically interested in the psychometrics that will be available if they are implementing quantitative measures.

Obviously, what summative strategy an instructor chooses will also be influenced by predictable constraints. For example, although an essay tapping higher-order thinking skills might be more effective in distinguishing deep cognitive gains from the course, instructors who have large class sizes typically opt for objective measures that are more easily graded. Program administrators tend to prefer easy assessment techniques to gather feedback on program quality. However, depending on its design, a summative measurement may not allow for targeted feedback for the program as a whole. In addition, the purpose of these assessments can often be misconstrued by faculty as a punishment for poor student performance, justifying why faculty may not be enthusiastic about engaging in summative practices for program evaluation.

Recently, psychology faculty in North America have experienced some institutional pressures to pursue "high-impact practices" (see Kuh et al., 2015); those experiences are likely to reflect corresponding high-impact assessment designs. Similarly, the instructor's personal preferences for assessment will surface and influence design choices. For example, faculty who find personal reflections or student journals too invasive will be disinclined to use personal reflection as a summative strategy, but they may seek other strategies to render fair grades and also get some direction on teaching improvements.

In contrast to course-level assessment, when summative measures address the curriculum quality hosted by a psychology program, design decisions become more complicated. Rather than exercising autonomous choice, an instructor may be obligated to impose assessments designed by other professors or publishers. Consequently, the success of summative options may be limited by the level of cooperation or collaboration that exists across department members. In North America, departments with available financial resources may import publisher-designed, nationally normed tests to gather the information the program needs and make comparisons in performance to other departments in the country to respond to accountability demands. Departments without resources may have to resort to building their own designs.

The purpose of this chapter is to explore the current state of summative assessment practices in psychology classrooms that reflect on both course and program achievement. Our experience as North American educators will be reflected in our perspective; however, we strive to reflect summative practices in other contexts as well. We begin with a brief discussion of traditional summative practices but move to describing more innovative, high-impact designs in both classroom and program contexts, highlighting the unique challenges associated with those efforts. We discuss the psychometric challenges involved in designing and delivering high-quality summative assessment, along with current trends in the literature. We offer tips for optimizing valid and reliable outcomes from summative assessment practices. Finally, we conclude with an annotated roster of references to support further investigation.

## Design Issues and Approaches of Summative Assessment

We cannot deny the utility of formative feedback in the college classroom. However, we also recognize that summative assessment is inherently a part of North American higher education practices, from the dreaded final exam week to the push being experienced in some specific contexts for more data to inform accountability initiatives. In this section, we will present summative assessment techniques as practiced at the college or tertiary level and the design issues that may come with these techniques. We will also discuss exemplary summative assessment techniques, at both the course level and the program level; in some cases, we propose how to infuse formative techniques naturally into these assessments.

Many educators promote backward design (see Fink, 2013) to develop sound assessment strategies. The first step in creating a summative assessment is to create or review course student learning outcomes (see Stanny, 2016 for tips on creating high-quality outcomes). Next, determine what kind of assessment is appropriate for each objective/goal. Focusing on the purpose of the assessment initially will align the assessment with course outcomes. Instructors can map out their outcomes and assessments to ensure they both cover all the necessary material and also promote evaluating many levels of knowledge across assessments (National Research Council, 2001; Svinicki & McKeachie, 2014). Finally, instructors should specify the purpose of the assessment to create clear expectations for students.

### Traditional Exams

Popular in North America, objective testing is traditional, although arguably the least creative way to assess students' knowledge. Ostensibly, the purpose of these assessments is to push students to learn the material and to hold them accountable for their learning. The prevailing belief among many academics is that without this kind of ultimate measurement, students would not be motivated to learn vital classroom information.

In many higher education classrooms, traditional exams dominate summative assessment. Although instructors can easily grade objective measures, these strategies entail an assortment of challenges. In some classrooms, summative exams may be the only assessments given throughout the academic term, which tends to involve some risk about the accuracy of conclusions drawn regarding what students actually learn. Some questions used in traditional exams may not clearly align with the course student learning outcomes. Most of the time, students are simply repeating memorized facts and relying on rote memorization (McTighe & Ferrara, 1998). Students may engage in a short, intensive review, but their emphasis is usually on capturing as many points as possible, rather than on learning. Upon completing the exam, students rarely review exam performance or course information (Wininger, 2005). Students may learn but quickly forget course content after the exam.

Timed exams create additional pressures because they suppress original insights (Elton & Johnston, 2002), which may prevent some students from demonstrating the depth of their learning. For students who fail summative assessments, the consequences may be more severe than just a poor course grade (Kitchen et al., 2006). In the wake of poor summative performance, students may simply repeat unsuccessful strategies in future contexts, blame the incompetence of the teacher or the test, or withdraw from the academic enterprise altogether.

Despite the fact that the more traditional summative techniques do not tend to foster a growth mindset, they can be useful when implemented in more innovative ways that capitalize on critical thinking and reflection techniques (Houston & Thompson, 2017). An exam could incorporate application questions, in which students must apply the information they learned to a case study. For example, a course in abnormal psychology could feature a final exam in which students must make a provisional diagnosis and treatment plan after getting some clinical information on a simulated client (Halonen, 2017).

Another traditional testing strategy involves posing questions that bring together different areas of information, forcing students to go beyond rote memorization. For instance, in a brain and behavior course, after learning about the process of how a brain "builds" a memory, students could be challenged with questions about what variables influence forgetting, encouraging them to think deeply about the process of memory formation.

One innovative variation on traditional testing strategies is to ask students to design their own exam questions (Berrett, 2019). Offering a brief instruction in Bloom's taxonomy (see Anderson & Krathwohl's, 2001 updated version) encourages scaffolding in learning and can help students develop greater savviness about test-taking skills. Collaborating on the development of test questions produces other benefits for students through gaining experience in teamwork skills. According to Berrett, this approach also is especially useful in developing a sense of community in online classes. Finally, metacognitive techniques can be applied to these exams to help students relearn missed information. For example, students can have the opportunity to review the exam questions for credit, explaining why they missed questions, and describing potential improvement strategies for the next exam.

## Integrative Papers

In North America, as well as many other countries, instructors may incorporate another traditional summative technique, the final paper, that requires more creativity and less time pressure. Final papers may also have formative checkpoints along the way with feedback from the instructor. However, a summative assignment may leave students in the dark about how exactly the instructor intends to grade the paper. Additionally, students frequently do not examine instructor feedback (Jollands,

McCallum, & Bondy, 2009), since instructors tend to return feedback during the last weeks of class when student motivation may be flagging.

Final papers may facilitate deeper student learning with some simple modifications. For example, a practice that emerged in many countries is the use of a grading "rubric," which provides students with detailed instructions about what will constitute success in their efforts. For example, a writing rubric for an experimental lab report might articulate the important areas of achievement that the student should develop in the lab report (e.g., clear statement of a hypothesis, accurate reporting of statistical findings, proper use of writing conventions, etc.) along with some means of distinguishing performances (does work in each area exceed, meet, or fail to meet the standard). In essence, the rubric answers the question of what instructors want out of student performance in a manner that should help students to understand how they will be graded (McCarthy, 2015).

Students can collaborate on the development of the rubric to enhance their understanding of what is expected. This rubric can then be used as a framework for self- and/or peer assessments, which also facilitates ownership in addition to higher-level reflection on their learning (APA, 2018). However, students benefit from explicit instruction on using the evaluation criteria and rendering constructive feedback. Building these self-assessment skills can lead to better outcomes after students graduate; they are better able to evaluate their work critically and develop self-directed learning skills (National Research Council, 2001).

Integrating summative papers with other assessments throughout the semester can help students improve these papers through feedback. For instance, creating a public speaking assignment in which students must present the main ideas in their papers will force students to process the feedback. The rubric for this presentation can include a criterion that says, "Improved the paper based on feedback from instructor." Or a low-stakes presentation due before the paper deadline and worth a minimal number of points can generate feedback to improve their papers. These strategies reinforce that formative assessments can facilitate even better performance during summative challenges.

## Authentic Assessments

Many (but not all) North American educators have recently embraced the value of designing learning experiences that are "high-impact," i.e., strategies that push students out of passive engagement with lectures into active learning strategies (Kuh, 2008). The value of moving into more active engagement has been demonstrated not just in improved retention of the content and skills associated with the course design (see Brown, Roediger, & McDaniel, 2014), but students who report learning from high-impact practices are more likely to persist in their studies to graduate. The ultimate purpose of a high-impact technique is to inspire passion in students and connect them to future career pathways (Houston & Thompson, 2017). With the movement toward more high-impact techniques in the classroom, the appeal of performance-based, authentic assessment techniques is also growing. We offer three examples that illustrate authentic assessment that can be used for summative purposes, sometimes at the course level and sometimes at both course and program levels.

An authentic assessment in introductory psychology demonstrates how both purposes can be achieved in an easily administered, objective strategy (see Appendix A). In North America, the introductory psychology course serves two purposes. Students who plan to major in psychology will enroll in the course to launch their studies, but nonmajors will also take the course to broaden their knowledge base. In our own undergraduate program, teachers of introductory psychology collaborated on a summative assessment using a flawed research design scenario and agreed to implement the design across sections, either embedded in a final exam or conducted as a freestanding test, mediated digitally.

Using fictional data, we provide a scatter diagram that pairs two sets of college student data: number of absences in college courses and reported stress levels. The protocol describes a process by which multiple researchers haphazardly gather data that produces a strong positive correlation. The researcher concludes that "stress causes higher rates of absence in college courses." A series of multiple-choice questions reveals whether students can *apply basic research methods in solving problems* (the course outcome) and provides specific information on their grasp of correlation, cause-and-effect claims, operational definitions, sample size, and control procedures, among other concepts. This exam also acquaints students with North American protocols for seeking approval of research, which transpires through a process managed by an institutional review board (IRB) and oversight. Performance results contribute both to student grades and judgments about teaching and learning quality across introductory sections.

Another example of authentic assessment requires the production of a portfolio that encompasses students' career development materials created across their university career. A career portfolio, consisting of a curriculum vitae or resume, cover letter, and career plan/backup plan, should generate significant motivation since, for most students, a job search will be looming after graduation. Using rubrics to evaluate each element represents a best practice approach. Another innovative way to assess and provide feedback is to have students present this portfolio to external assessors or monitors who are community professionals in their career areas of interest. The external assessor receives brief training about departmental standards, along with a rubric based on performance standards expected of undergraduate psychology majors (APA, 2013). Through this high-stakes technique, students can get to know professionals, ask questions, and receive high-value feedback from someone besides the instructor (Christopher, Baker, & Beins, in press). Other online platforms can use ePortfolios, where important past course work can be saved and showcased to future employers, along with the main career materials. Assessments can be done through the evaluation of the main materials or through a recorded student presentation of the ePortfolio.

Finally, students can engage in an integrative capstone project that incorporates the knowledge and skills gained in the academic major. For example, in a thematic capstone course focusing on psychology of the preschooler, students pair up to conceptualize an early childhood intervention that capitalizes on their shared interests (e.g., art, music, autism spectrum disorder). This project allows for creativity, the exploration of passions, and assessment of vital skills learned throughout their tenure in the psychology program. The major summative assessment pieces include a presentation of the intervention to the class and to a panel of community members involved in child development (e.g., Early Learning Coalition director, Department of Health member, pediatric nurse) and a paper outlining the theoretical basis and research that supports the intervention. In the presentations, students receive feedback from the instructor, students, and the community members. Peers use the presentation rubric to rate the presenters and provide feedback. All students must also self-assess their own performances using the rubric. These practices make all students aware of the rubric and requirements.

Additionally, low-stakes formative checkpoints provide useful feedback to the students. For instance, they must create catchy titles for their projects and develop introduction paragraphs and press releases, each worth a small number of points that contribute to their final grade. These checkpoints keep them on track and give them feedback on the vital components of their intervention, as well as their writing style. This combination of assignments optimizes the blend of formative and summative approaches.

## Facilitating Successful Student Performance

Rubrics created for capstone presentations and papers can easily be adopted across sections with different organizing themes if they are written generically to capture important components for program-level assessment purposes (see Appendix B for an example of a capstone writing rubric that provides both developmental feedback to students and input for program assessment needs). If faculty can collaborate on the design and implementation of performance criteria, the results contribute to program-level assessment techniques, determining how well students can write using proper conventions, think critically in evaluating psychological evidence, and present in a professional manner. The results of assessing these macro-level skills promote continuous improvement by supporting reforms in courses and experiences earlier in the curriculum (e.g., strengthening research methods, incorporating more instruction about writing standards in earlier classes, requiring more presenting in earlier classes).

Overall, summative assessment techniques can go beyond the traditional midterm/final exams featuring multiple-choice and essay questions. As pressures for high-impact practices proliferate in the postsecondary or tertiary environment, techniques for more innovative assessment protocols have also emerged. In particular, creating well-designed rubrics that students receive at the beginning helps in setting the precedent for the assessment (McCarthy, 2015), and instilling creativity in the classroom context fosters passion and connection to careers.

## Evaluation/Research Issues Associated with Summative Assessment

Given that the outcome of summative assessment can have a major impact on a student's progress or placement, faculty strive to implement assessments that are both valid (true representations) and reliable (consistent). In the context of a classroom, primary concerns regarding validity involve *content validity* (does the measure include the appropriate content?), *construct validity* (does the measure accurately represent the appropriate psychological concepts?), and *criterion validity* (does the test effectively correspond to some meaningful external measure?). Determining whether performance is consistent may involve repeated testing *(test-retest reliability)* or comparing one assessor's judgment against another *(interrater reliability),* among other types of reliability. Consistency in evaluating performance reliability can also relate to generalizability of an assessment across learning environments, settings, or students (National Research Council, 2001).

Table 1 provides a brief summary of the key questions that instructors should ask when developing a valid and reliable assessment. In the next section, we will discuss the kinds of reliability and validity for both objective and high-impact summative strategies, as well as the questions and strategies listed to provide guidance for how to create valid and reliable summative assessments. We will conclude with some strategies to enhance reliability and validity in summative strategies.

## Establishing Validity of Summative Assessments

Knight (2002, p. 278) notes that summative assessment is a "vexed business" because the lofty goals of higher education are not easily documented through assessment. To satisfy the demands of external stakeholders (e.g., taxpayers, governing bodies, accreditation organizations), adding high-stakes assessments can lead to conflict when results fall short of meeting those demands. Objective assessments distill broad educational experiences into a quantitative representation that may reduce claims of valid measurement. This emphasis can motivate instructors to "teach to the test," which may, ironically, produce higher quantitative scores but erode the overall quality of learning.

Summative performance may directly influence grades, but according to Kohn (1999), grading practices themselves, although widespread, are problematic since they can undermine motivation to learn. For example, letter grades, the most common expression of summative assessment in a North American course, can symbolize achievement, but many other factors can impact letter grades, such as work ethic. If students receive a C in a class or on an assessment, what does it really tell us about their performances? Certainly, their work was passable but not excellent, but in what areas were they most lacking? Did they struggle on multiple-choice questions but do well on written assessments? Is the grade a reflection of poor attendance? Or perhaps lack of access to resources? Distilling performance down to

**Table 1** Organizing questions to address summative psychometrics*

| Organizing questions to address summative psychometrics[a] |
| --- |
| What are my goals for the assessment? Does the assessment meet those goals? |
| Have I graded consistently? |
| Is there preexisting psychometric evidence of reliability and validity of this strategy? |
| Have I adequately covered this material in class or in readings? |
| How are internal factors impacting student performance (e.g., test anxiety, stress changes over the course of a term)? |
| What are the consequences of the assessment? Is the outcome justified based on the assessment outcome? |
| Can I make legitimate estimates about student knowledge based on the content of the assessment? |
| Do all students have a fair and equitable opportunity to demonstrate their learning, regardless of their heritage, educational background, or socioeconomic status? |
| Have students received adequate feedback on performance prior to a high-stakes assessment? |

[a]*Some of these questions are adapted from the* National Research Council *(2001)*

a single letter simply does not provide a full picture of that student's knowledge and skills (National Research Council, 2001).

What differentiates an A student from a C student? Maybe the A student showed better time management or teamwork skills. What about differentiating a B+ from a B? In this instance, not only is it harder to articulate a meaningful difference, but the importance of validity in assessment is even greater. All grade-rendering faculty know the angst involved in having hardworking students miss a grade cutoff by a point that might have a serious negative impact on the measures of overall performance. For example, in North America, students build a grade point average (GPA) in which grades translate to a number (A=4, B=3, and so forth). The strength of the GPA can sometimes be used to make important decisions about students, such as entrance into honor societies or admission into graduate programs. We provide these examples not to suggest doing away with letter grades, but rather to highlight the shortcomings of grades in capturing what learning has actually transpired in the course and to emphasize the importance of basing letter grades on valid and reliable assessments.

Although there are many kinds of validity, we argue that two kinds should take priority over others in course-level assessments: content validity and construct validity. Content validity evaluates whether or not the assessment includes the appropriate material. For example, your exam questions derive from assigned readings that are covered during the period represented in the exam and not from later reading assignments (APA, 2018). Construct validity evaluates whether or not the assessment measures the relevant constructs or skills you intended. If your questions use a vocabulary level that far exceeds the knowledge base of the students, you will not be able to assess student knowledge. If either of these validities are not met, the assessment will be fundamentally flawed.

In contrast, criterion validity becomes relevant when summative assessments represent program-level assessment. For example, the results from department-derived exit examinations could be correlated with success in graduate school. However, external correlations do not tend to be much of a concern for faculty managing student achievement in courses.

Approaches in establishing content and construct validity of summative assessments vary in effort and complexity. On the low-effort end of the spectrum, sometimes poor validity of a measure can be inferred based on student feedback and performance. Substantial email complaints or frequent questions asking for clarification regarding test items indicate a question or assessment may not have clarity, accuracy, or coherence sufficient to feel confident about the overall validity of the assessment instrument.

A higher-tech but still relatively low-effort way to evaluate validity is the use of item analysis features in automated grading systems (e.g., online learning management systems or Scantron machines). This practice evaluates distractors in multiple-choice tests to ensure those choices sufficiently distract. The discrimination index identifies questions that discriminate between high- and low-performing students. Similarly, if all students miss an individual item, the question likely did not ask content covered in instruction (content validity) or was not worded clearly (construct validity). Overall performance revealed in the class grade distribution can establish if the results distribute properly, indicating whether the assessment was too easy or hard and suggesting that a more comprehensive overall may be needed.

Instructors can solicit external review of their assessments to increase their efforts in establishing adequate psychometrics. For example, they can simply ask a student to read an assignment for clarity or a colleague to evaluate the appropriateness of the assessment. In core courses with multiple sections taught by more than one instructor (e.g., introduction to psychology, research methods), collaboratively creating common assessments has the potential for better quality summative assessments and improved reliability across sections.

Authentic assessment strategies and program-level evaluations call for criterion-related validity. In this validation strategy, results are compared to some external set of standards, a practice that is sometimes referred to as benchmarking. Comparing to standards established by an external entity ensures that the program is in step with the discipline. External evaluations can also come in more formal formats and procedures, such as the Quality Matters evaluations of online courses (Crews & Wilkinson, 2015) or the external marking model in the UK (British Psychological Society, 2019), though research does suggest consistency between external evaluators is an issue (Bloxham, den-Outer, Hudson, & Price, 2016). The use of criterion-driven strategies provides much richer evidence about the nature of the learning that has transpired, as well as where teaching might need to be improved. Enhancing criterion-related validity can be achieved through collaboration. Conferring with peers regarding the design of the assessment instrument, including the quality of the rubric that specifies performance expectations, can improve the legitimacy of conclusions drawn.

## Establishing Reliability of Summative Assessments

Although more straightforward conceptually, reliability may be harder to achieve than validity. The pressure to produce reliable results can drive assessments to be simple, rather than complex, which may make high-stakes assessments incompatible with education (Boud, 1995; Wiliam, 2020). Variations in evaluator experience and student internal states can influence whether consistency can be achieved (National Research Council, 2001; Wiliam, 2020). In addition, unexpected external forces (e.g., weather emergencies, pandemics) can disrupt assessments. Nonetheless, several approaches establish reliability in summative assessments.

Objective assessment strategies lend themselves to the clearest examples of reliability. The most common kind of reliability in a classroom setting is likely test-retest reliability, in which students produce similar results on multiple uses of the same test and/or questions. Establishing test-retest reliability may make more sense for a program-wide assessment that will serve many students and where assessment reporting will be required. However, repeated questions on course-level exams have the added benefit of promoting better long-term learning (Cepeda, Pashler, Vul, Wixted, & Rohrer, 2006). Split-half reliability could be used in a similar manner, though in this case the questions come from the same test and are split evenly between two halves. In larger classes where the instructor is using collections of test questions provided by textbook publishers to create multiple test versions, parallel forms reliability can be used to evaluate the similarity between the test versions. However, objective assessments that establish strong reliability often have lower construct and criterion validity, as they are unable to evaluate all aspects of student achievement. Thus, the higher reliability may lead to overconfidence in the quality of the assessment and its use.

In contrast, reliability for essay-based exam questions and authentic assessments should be more focused on establishing interrater reliability. That is, the instructor should take measures to ensure all graders, or raters, are grading consistently across students and across the semester. However, even in cases where the instructor is the sole grader, variations in internal states or external factors can lead to different grade outcomes, threatening the reliability of the assessment.

A key solution to establishing reliability for authentic assessments is using a rubric with well-defined criteria anchors that illustrate what performance looks like at each level. Rubrics can be holistic (e.g., students "exceed, meet, or fail to meet" established criteria) or analytic (e.g., points awarded for specific dimensions of performance). Analytic rubrics generally have better reliability than holistic rating scales. To improve validity, rubrics should be provided to students before they start working so they are aware of the expectations. Instructors can then use rubrics to grade assessments so that all students are evaluated on the same criteria. This practice can be powerful when using the same rubric across multiple sections of a course (see Appendix B for an example), improving both the reliability and validity of program-wide assessments.

Whereas rubrics provide better reliability, they can only do so when applied correctly. In cases where there are multiple graders within or across courses where interrater reliability is necessary, a calibration exercise is an effective tool in finding consensus. Here, instructors (or an instructor and a teaching assistant) all grade the same handful of papers (ideally that span the full range of performance) using the rubric and then compare their grades. They can work through discrepancies to reach agreement and attain interrater reliability. Although this approach cannot guarantee adequate reliability across or within graders, it greatly improves the odds that assessment will be more consistent across students and over time.

Providing feedback is a key part of effective rubric use as well, helping students see where they have room to improve. This approach is especially beneficial when students have the opportunity to revise the assignment. However, students often struggle to interpret feedback. For example, Duncan (2007) showed students found many comments on their work to be vague with a heavy emphasis on grammatical errors that failed to address larger areas for improvement. Grading features of learning-mediated systems that are popular in North America may provide some other options for effective feedback (McCarthy, 2015), but they can also be more burdensome on instructors. Regardless of the format of feedback, instructors should work to emphasize broad areas for improvement and avoid a heavy emphasis on grammar correction (unless grammar is the goal of the assessment). They should also work to better articulate feedback to avoid vague phrases (e.g., the ironically vague "improve clarity"; Duncan, 2007; McCarthy, 2015).

Although reliability is often discussed in terms of the consistency of the measure, it can also refer to the generalizability of an assessment or program to other contexts (National Research Council, 2001). Will the skills and knowledge assessed transfer outside of the classroom? This question is becoming more important for higher education as external stakeholders question the value of higher education. This challenge has been particularly pointed in North America since some of our politicians have questioned whether the psychology degree confers any real value to society at large (Halonen, 2011). On this front, it is important that instructors explicitly link classroom assessments to transferrable skills (Landrum & McCarthy, 2018) and that assessments are sufficiently varied so that students are given practice in a wide range of skills across the curriculum (National Research Council, 2001). Authentic assessments, such as portfolios, generally have better generalizability beyond the classroom as well.

Ultimately, experienced scholars who engage in summative assessment in the classroom may find they need to temper their expectations for reliability in summative assessments. Given the balance between validity and reliability (i.e., more objective measures providing better reliability but worse validity), a better approach is to accept lower reliability than we may expect in a research context and be aware of the limitations of our assessment. There are limits to what we can understand about student achievement in any one assessment, so instructors should take care to not place more value on a single assessment than is warranted (Wiliam, 2020). Instructors need to consider their constraints, assessment goals/outcomes, and purpose of the assessment to determine the correct balance of validity and reliability. These variables are almost guaranteed to vary across semesters, making summative assessment a highly dynamic process.

## Findings and Current Trends

Although we have attempted to make the case for effective summative assessment strategies, it would be misleading to see this argument as favoring summative over formative approaches. The best, but potentially most effortful, way to establish valid assessments is to rely on a variety of assessments that capture the range of student achievement (National Research Council, 2001).

Adopting a strategy with combined formative and summative assessment has several benefits. First, using several lower-stakes assessments to create an overall assessment will reduce student pressure and anxiety about performance on one large high-stakes assessment (Harlen, 2005). This approach has an overall benefit on accuracy and reliability as student performance is more reflective of their knowledge and skills. Second, using a variety of assessments allows instructors to evaluate different levels of knowledge (e.g., Anderson & Krathwohl, 2001) and ensures students are adequately meeting basic- and high-level knowledge standards. This outcome is especially important in scientific disciplines, such as psychology, because the nature of scientific inquiry requires a wide range of knowledge and skills (National Research Council, 2001). To determine if students are able to engage in scientific inquiry and problem-solving skills, they must first understand basic concepts, how to use those concepts in an appropriate context, and how to apply them in the planning, design, execution, analysis, and interpretation of an experiment. To evaluate all of these skills adequately, multiple assessments will provide the best, most valid, picture of student achievement.

Svinicki and McKeachie (2014) note that, just as in research, we should look for converging evidence of student achievement by providing multiple types of assessment. More varied and frequent assessments can also improve learning, particularly if the assessments are spaced out and emphasize understanding or application. Distributing assessments encourages students to space out their learning, which is beneficial for long-term retention (Cepeda et al., 2006). Additionally, Svinicki and McKeachie predicted that students will change their approach to learning based on how they will be assessed. Assessments focused on understanding and application will promote those skills outside of the assessment itself. Both spacing and promoting higher-level thinking allow for better retention and transfer of knowledge from one class or semester to the next, providing better program outcomes.

Another contemporary concern regarding summative assessment adequacy is linked to equity practices in the classroom (e.g., Hanafin, Shevlin, Kenny, & McNeela, 2007; Maringe & Sing, 2014; Volante, Schnepf, Jerrim, & Klinger, 2019), which is a growing concern in North American classrooms. Higher education is an expensive proposition, made even more challenging by the use of high-cost textbooks and computers to support course learning. As a consequence, North American students graduate with a substantial debt load, a fact that magnifies the importance of ensuring that students are being treated in an even-handed fashion. Establishing equitable conditions may be a concern, even in the absence of economic consequences. This problem is more difficult for an individual instructor to tackle solo; nonetheless, many North American faculty are vigilant in pursuing lower-cost or no-cost resources to promote equitable access. At our institution, the library works to secure a course reserve copy of every textbook in all undergraduate courses every term. This accommodation allows students who face financial hardship to get full access to texts.

Student facility in the language of instruction should also be considered when adopting an assessment strategy. Exams and assessments should be screened for any cultural references or idiomatic phrases that may not be shared by all students and thus limit understanding of the question (construct validity). This problem can include knowledge that does not span the generational divide. For example, in one question asking about the homunculus of the motor system, the first author (LDB) asked which famous person the somatosensory cortical homunculus most resembled (the correct answer being a famous classic rock icon). Although she thought this was a straightforward question (with a humorous answer), it turns out most contemporary students did not know who the icon was and got the question wrong!

A trend in North American education that grows out of concern for equity is the use of course materials and assessments that are accessible to all students (Steinfeld & Maisel, 2012). If students are not all able to access course materials, especially if that challenge arises from some physical limitations on the part of the student, it poses a major problem in establishing the validity of conclusions drawn from assessments based on those materials. In response to federal legislation, most North American universities have established roles for administrators to oversee "accommodations," strategies that level the playing field, such as allowing students with learning disabilities to have extended completion windows for exams. Other simple solutions include the following: providing class resources in cross-platform and screen reader-friendly formats (e.g., PDF), captioning any video resources (including any narrated lecture slides), using high-contrast instructional materials, avoiding problematic color combinations (e.g., using red and green to denote changes will be imperceptible to those with color deficiencies), and using good design principles (e.g., avoiding complicated layouts/graphics, using simple and clear language, using large, readable fonts). For more examples, posters developed by the UK Home Office offer universal design suggestions and come in a variety of different languages: https://accessibility.blog.gov.uk/2016/09/02/dos-and-donts-on-designing-for-accessibility/ (Pun, 2016). These simple steps allow for equal access to course materials and assessment and improve overall course design for all students.

Finally, we need to address affective factors that can influence summative student performance. Hirsch (2020) listed several adverse emotional effects of summative practice in a study of Swedish students, including undue pressures from demands for continuous improvement, navigating the aftermath of adverse results and saving face, managing optimal performance in time-pressured situations, and coping with the tension that results from feeling like their future hinges on a single performance. Hirsch indicated the pervasiveness of being measured discourages students from performing well and being motivated to learn and alienates teachers from enthusiastic participation in assessment.

## Challenges, Lessons Learned, and Implications for Learning and Teaching Psychology

We offer the following summary of recommendations that address challenges in developing and implementing sound summative assessments:

- *Engage in backward design strategies to ensure coherence between assessment and student learning outcomes or program goals.* Clarify your objectives to determine what evidence will satisfy that students have achieved your goals.
- *Where possible, adopt authentic assessment strategies over objective ones.* Students tend to invest more and generate more valid assessment results when meaningfully engaged in how we measure learning.
- *Incorporate technological strategies for summative practices to reduce faculty workloads.* Wherever possible, automating procedures can make assessment demands feel less overwhelming.
- *Actively evaluate psychometrics to improve future uses of the instrument.* Psychometrics provide feedback that lead to more defensible inferences from measurement when the instrument is deployed again.
- *Avoid drawing conclusions based on one performance.* It is simply bad practice to draw high-stakes conclusions on the basis of one data point.
- *Monitor your constructions for social equity concerns.* Strive to reduce obstacles that interfere with students' learning to enhance confidence in making valid interpretations of assessment results.
- *Clarify pathways for high-stakes decisions.* Provide meaningful context for letter grades to anchor student expectations to motivate students' best work.
- *Collaborate on common instruments used for program evaluation.* Sharing design and assessment responsibilities tends to sharpen summative practices and facilitate coherent curriculum delivery.
- *Expect rubrics to be refined potentially with each use.* No rubric will ever be perfect. Each administration should prompt some tweaking to improve its use.
- *Seek external validation/review to ensure clarity and accuracy.* Consider gathering assessment partners to improve external validation.
- *Anticipate potential legal entanglements from negative aftermath from high-stakes decisions.* Be clear about opportunities students can exercise to retest and possibly reclaim a pathway denied from the results of poor performance.

## Conclusions

In sum, we discussed summative techniques in this chapter, with an emphasis on moving toward high-impact assessments. We discussed the importance of developing instruments that produce performances with strong psychometric properties of validity and reliability. We also argued that innovative approaches benefit from a fusion of summative and formative techniques. Our recommendations for improving summative assessment include clarifying student learning outcomes and aligning them with assessment strategies. We also advocated infusing creativity in authentic assessment strategies to promote more enduring gains in learning. We pointed out the value of collaborating with others to monitor and improve evaluation strategies each term. Finally, we reinforced the importance of attending to social equity concerns as a way to make valid and reliable inferences about gains in student learning.

## Teaching, Learning, and Assessment Resources Associated with Summative Assessment

American Psychological Association (n.d.) *Teaching, Learning, and Assessment Resources associated with Summative Assessment. Teacher Assessment Guide.* https://www.apa.org/ed/precollege/topss/assessment-guide.pdf

This comprehensive introduction to assessment strategies provides a great resource for individuals who need a review of basic background about assessment practices. The work details contrasts between formative and summative assessment but also provides background information on test question design and psychometric interpretations. The American Psychological Association funded the guide, which is useful for both secondary and tertiary teachers.

Broadbent, J., Panadero, E., & Boud, D. (2018). Implementing summative assessment with a formative flavor: A case study in a large class. *Assessment and Evaluation in Higher Education,* 43(2), 307–322. https://doi:10.1080/02602938.2017.1343455

This paper discusses how summative assessment should have formative elements and how it can be transferred to a large class context without significantly adding to teacher workload. Providing exemplars and an annotated rubric with an explanation of how it is implemented (e.g., video explanation) helps students receive consistent information. The use of multiple, small, low-stakes, iterative assessments facilitates practice and builds skills over time. The balance between formative and summative assessment is important in promoting a learning environment, rather than a performance-based environment.

Harrison, C. J., Könings, K. D., Molyneux, A., Schuwirth, L. W. T., Wass, V., & van der Vleuten, C. P. M. (2013). Web-based feedback after summative assessment: How do students engage? *Medical Education, 47,* 734–744. https://doi:10.1111/medu.12209

Drawing from medical schools, this article discusses how to encourage optimal student performance, rather than mere minimal competence needed to pass an exam. This study examined how motivational variables affected how students processed feedback in a virtual learning environment. Overall, most students visited the website, but the most comprehensive users were those that scored highly on valuing feedback. Minimal users were those who just barely passed the exams.

Harlen, W. (2005). Teachers' summative practices and assessment for learning-Tensions and synergies. *The Curriculum Journal,* 16(2), 207–223. https://doi.org/10.1080/09585170500136093

Harlen discussed how assessments can be used for both summative and formative purposes. For instance, past summative assessments can be used to help students prepare for tests by reviewing their work and screening for weaknesses, helping in forming questions/rubrics, and student-to-student involvement in marking tests (i.e., test analysis; Carter, 1997). Overall, it is important to maintain distinct assessment types but also to create a type of synergy between the two.

Houston, D., & Thompson, J. N. (2017). Blending formative and summative assessment in a Capstone subject: 'It's not your tools, it's how you use them.' *Journal of University Teaching and Learning Practice,* 14(3).

This paper combined formative and summative assessment experiences in a paramedic capstone course, arguing for their interdependence. Connected activities included a topic pretest, problem-based learning, diagnostic exams with student contributions, and final oral exams with self-assessment components. Overall, students described positive impacts, including reviewing existing knowledge, improving critical thinking skills, and preparing for employment.

Knight, P. (August 25, 2010). Summative assessment in higher education: Practices in disarray. *Studies in Higher Education,* 27(3), 275–286. https://doi.org/10.1080/03075070220000662

Knight proposes that summative assessment practices are questionable on two grounds.

He charges that the technique overpromises results since design challenges could weaken confidence in conclusions drawn about performance. He also argues that the value of assessment practices on the whole has become suspect and advocates an overhaul of curricula. Knight discusses the differences between formative (feedback) and summative (feed-out) strategies.

Landrum, R. E., & McCarthy, M. A. (2018). Measuring the benefits of a bachelor's degree in psychology: Promises, challenges, and next steps. *Scholarship of Teaching and Learning in Psychology,* 4(1), 55–63. http://dx.doi.org/10.1037/stl0000101

This theoretical review paper takes a program-level look at how we should assess skills of psychology majors at graduation. They argue that the degree provides a strong preparation for a variety of workforce-ready skills, which are not often well-articulated. The authors propose a more centralized approach to assessment that tracks student progress via observable skills. This strategy would provide a well-rounded evaluation of each student's skills, knowledge, and abilities that the discipline could use for improving the public image of the major.

McCarthy, J. (2015). Evaluating written, audio and video feedback in higher education summative assessment tasks. *Issues in Educational Research,* 25(2), 153–169.

This study examines three different feedback formats for summative assessments in a college course: written, audio, and video. Students overwhelmingly preferred video feedback over written or audio feedback for its clarity and engaging quality. This finding was true across intersectional variables, including gender, nationality, and age. Audio feedback was the least preferred format.

Trotter, E. (2006). Student perceptions of continuous summative assessment. *Assessment and Evaluation in Higher Education,* 31(5), 505–521. https://doi:10.1080/02602930600679506

This study examined students' perceptions of a particular continuous summative assessment procedure (i.e., completing tutorial files). The majority of students found that this procedure motivated them throughout the semester in a continuous manner and felt that it helped to improve their learning. However, students receiving lower marks expressed less motivation to complete more of the tutorial assignments.

Wiliam, D. (2020). How to think about assessment. In S. Donarsky & T. Bennett (Eds.), *The researchED Guide to Assessment: An Evidence-informed Guide for Teachers* (pp. 21–36). John Catt Publishing.

This chapter provides a detailed look at reliability and validity in assessment. Wiliam emphasizes that trade-offs are necessary in any assessment as the goals of reliability and validity are often at odds with one another. He argues there is no perfect assessment and that the trade-offs must be balanced on a case-by-case basis in order to both support learning and assess it.

## Appendices

### Appendix A: A Summative Protocol for Introductory Psychology

**Proposal for Problem-Solving Measure for Introductory Psychology**
Outcome: Uses social science methods to solve problems based on 2018 Free-Response Question in Advanced Placement

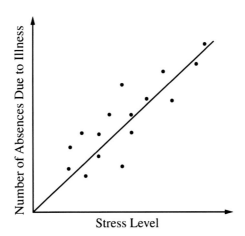

A team of researchers generated the data above by gathering information from college students at the end of the first semester on the relationship between class absence and perceived stress level. The research assistants were instructed to go into the commons and find first semester students to interview sometime during finals week. Stress was estimated on a 10-point scale with 10 representing the "most stress you could imagine." The researcher concluded that stress causes illness.

1. What is the name of the graphic used to illustrate the relationship between illness-related absences and stress levels?
   a. Histogram
   b. Frequency distribution
   c. Scatter diagram*
2. What was the sample size represented in the data?
   a. 15*.
   b. 30.
   c. Information supplied is insufficient to determine sample size.
3. What is the most plausible correlation coefficient that would correspond to the data presented in the graphic?
   a. -.92
   b. .00
   c. +.83*
4. What is the most likely threat to the quality of the data collected?
   a. Conducting the research at the end of the semester.
   b. Using a team of data collectors who may have differing styles.*
   c. The team of data collectors should have been one gender.
5. Is the operational definition of stress problematic?
   a. Yes. Imaginations are variable so it is not clear that participants are using the same scale in judging their stress.*
   b. No. If the scale is uniformly presented to the participants, it should produce legitimate data.
   c. Maybe. The operational definition will work fine for some participants but probably not as well for others.
6. What is the main reason we will have difficulty justifying that the findings of the sample study could be generalized to the population of first year college students at the university?
   a. The researchers didn't randomly select participants from the population.*
   b. The researchers didn't randomly assign participants from the population.
   c. The researchers didn't employ informed consent when they collected their data.
7. Is the researcher's claim that stress causes illness justified by this research?
   a. Yes. The relationship between stress and illness is strongly identified by the data.
   b. No. The sample size is too small to make this a legitimate claim.
   c. No. Correlation research doesn't produce evidence for causal claims.*
8. If a researcher wanted to convert this design into an experiment, why would an institutional review board likely have difficulty approving the proposal?
   a. Because college students need to have parental approval to participate in experimentation of any kind.
   b. Because researchers are violating ethical rules to do no harm since they would be manipulating stress levels.*
   c. Because IRB officials know this relationship is already firmly established in the psychology literature and they typically don't support replication studies.

9. Martin is introverted and unassertive. When he is approached by an aggressive research assistant, Martin figured out that the researcher was expecting him to report high levels of stress and absence. Although he had a stressful first semester, he didn't miss any classes but told the researcher that he missed a high number. This outcome is explained by which of the following concepts?
    a. Halo effect
    b. Demand characteristics*
    c. Placebo effects
10. The researcher suspects that these data may be problematic and repeats the strategy the next semester. This time the data demonstrate weaker connections between stress and illness-related absence. The difference in the results in the two data collections demonstrates which problem in good research design?
    a. Validity
    b. Parsimony
    c. Reliability*

## Appendix B: Example of a Speaking Rubric for Summative Assessment

**Capstone Speaking Rubric** Final score: _____ out of 100 points. *Score each category with a maximum of 10 points for grading purposes. Designate holistic score for department report.* **Presenter:**
Topic:
Review team:

### Holistic Performance Distinctions

| 3 Exemplary | Exceeds professional standards | 90–100% ( rating 9–10) |
|---|---|---|
| 2 Proficient | Achieves professional standards | 70–80% (rating 7–8) |
| 1 Developing | Fails to meet professional standards | <70 % (rating <7) |
| 0 Missing | Did not address | 0 |

| Area | Criteria | Grading: Score out of 10. Check off met criteria | Holistic score |
|---|---|---|---|
| Context | **Follows general project directions** | | |
| | _Chooses topic that fits assignment parameters | | |
| | _Adheres to recommended time constraints | | |
| | _Synthesizes empirical literature to create argument | | |

(continued)

| Area | Criteria | Grading: Score out of 10. Check off met criteria | Holistic score |
|---|---|---|---|
| **Introduction quality** | **Launches presentation effectively** | | |
| | _Introduces self to audience | | |
| | _Crafts compelling title | | |
| | _Clearly communicates thesis | | |
| | _Provides overview of intentions | | |
| **Thesis development** | **Effectively develops central idea** | | |
| | _Achieves appropriate breadth and depth | | |
| | _Develops coherence in argument (avoids introducing ideas) | | |
| **Organization** | **Produces effective flow in argument** | | |
| | _Sequences ideas to best advantage | | |
| | _Provides purposeful transitions | | |
| | _Acknowledges contradictory evidence, if needed | | |
| | _Completes appropriate multiple-choice question | | |
| **Conclusion** | **Ends presentation effectively** | | |
| | _Summarizes key ideas or themes | | |
| | _Avoids abrupt ending | | |
| | _Speculates about implications for the future | | |
| | _Manages Q&A with confidence | | |
| **Clarity and engagement** | **Establishes common ground with audience** | | |
| | *Tailors language to promote understanding* | | |
| | _Uses engaging, compelling word choice | | |
| | _Avoids jargon, vagueness | | |
| | _Avoids using deadening phrases, archaic forms (e.g., while, oftentimes) | | |
| **Quality of evidence/sources** | **Uses appropriate and relevant sources** | | |
| | _Chooses resources that fit purpose | | |
| | _Cites appropriate number, types of sources (e.g., scholarly sources) | | |
| | _Attributes ideas explicitly in presentation | | |

(continued)

| Area | Criteria | Grading: *Score out of 10. Check off met criteria* | Holistic score |
|---|---|---|---|
| **Disciplinary style** | **Adheres to APA presentation style** | | |
| | _Clearly represents scientific viewpoint | | |
| | _Emphasizes objectivity, precision, skepticism | | |
| | _Avoids personal testimony/ editorializing | | |
| | _Accurately conveys psychology content | | |
| **Delivery/format** | **Delivers articulate, polished message** | | |
| | _Demonstrates effects of rehearsal | | |
| | _Presents, rather than reads, presentation | | |
| | _Minimizes placeholders (um, like, you know) | | |
| | _Avoids distracting mannerisms | | |
| | _Uses technology smoothly | | |
| **Professionalism** | **Achieves professional presentation standards** | | |
| | _Meets specified project deadlines | | |
| | _Adopts professional appearance | | |
| | _Exhibits standard grammar and punctuation | | |
| | _Shares burden if presenting as group | | |

Please write in a narrative paragraph the strengths that you observed in the presentation
Please write in a narrative paragraph the areas that could have been better developed

# References

American Psychological Association. (2013). *APA guidelines for the undergraduate psychology major*. Version 2.0. https://www.apa.org/ed/precollege/about/psymajor-guidelines.pdf

American Psychological Association. (2018). *Teacher assessment guide*. http://pass.apa.org/assessment-resources/

Anderson, L. W., & Krathwohl, D. R. (2001). *A taxonomy for learning, teaching, and assessing: A revision of Bloom's taxonomy of educational objectives*. New York, NY/San Fransico, CA/London, UK: Longman.

Berenbaum, M., DeLuca, C., Earl, L., Heritage, M., Klenowski, V., Looney, A., Smith, K., Timperly, H., Volante, L., & Wyatt-Smith, C. (2015). International trends in the implementation of assessment for learning: Implications for policy and practice. *Policy Futures in Education, 13* (1), 117–140. https://doi.org/10.1177/1478210314566733.

Berrett, D. (2019, March 28). *Teaching*. Chronicle of Higher Education. https://www.chronicle.com/newsletter/teaching/2019-03-28

Bloxham, S., den-Outer, B., Hudson, J., & Price, M. (2016). Let's stop the pretense of consistent marking: Exploring the multiple limitations of assessment criteria. *Assessment & Evaluation in Higher Education, 41*(3), 466–481. https://doi.org/10.1080/02602938.2015.1024607.

Boahin, P. (2018). Competency-based curriculum: A framework for bridging the gap in teaching, assessment and the world of work. *Journal of Educational Assessment, 13*, 80–92.

Boud, D. (1995) Assessment and learning: Contradictory or complementary? In P.T. Knight (Ed.), *Assessment for learning in higher education*. Kogan page.

British Psychological Society. (2019). *Standards for the accreditation of undergraduate, conversion and integrated masters programmes in psychology*. British Psychological Society.

Brown, P. C., Roediger, H. P., III, & McDaniel, M. A. (2014). *Make it stick: The science of successful learning*. Dreamscape.

Carter, C. R. (1997). Assessment: Shifting the responsibility. *Journal of Secondary Gifted Education, 9*(2), Winter 1997/8, 68–75.

Cepeda, N. J., Pashler, H., Vul, E., Wixted, J. T., & Rohrer, D. (2006). Distributed practice in verbal recall tasks: A review and quantitative synthesis. *Psychological Bulletin, 132*(3), 354–380. https://doi.org/10.1037/0033-2909.132.3.354.

Christopher, A. N., Baker, S. C., & Beins, B. C. (in press). The role of assessment in capstone experiences. *Scholarship of Teaching and Learning*.

Cookson, C. J. (2018). Assessment terms half a century in the making and unmaking: From conceptual ingenuity to definitional anarchy. *Assessment and Evaluation in Higher Education, 43*(6), 930–942.

Crews, T. B., & Wilkinson, K. (2015). Online quality course design vs. quality teaching: Aligning quality matters standards to principles for good teaching. *Journal of Research in Business Education, 57*(1), 47–63.

Dirkson, D. J. (2011). Hitting the reset button: Using formative assessment to guide instruction. *Phi Delta Kappan, 92*(7), 26–31. https://doi.org/10.1177/003172171109200706.

Dixson, D. D., & Worrell, F. C. (2016). Formative and summative assessment in the classroom. *Theory into Practice, 55*, 153–159.

Duncan, N. (2007). 'Feed-forward': Improving students' use of tutors' comments. *Assessment & Evaluation in Higher Education, 32*(3), 271–283. https://doi.org/10.1080/02602930600896498.

Dweck, C. S. (2016). *Mindset: The new psychology of success*. Ballantine Books.

Elton, L., & Johnston, B. (2002). *Assessment in universities: A critical review of research*. Learning and Teaching Support Network Generic Centre. https://eprints.soton.ac.uk/59244/1/59244.pdf

Fink, D. (2013). *Creating significant learning experiences: An integrated approach to designing college courses (revised)*. Jossey-Bass.

Halonen, J. S. (2011). *Are there too many psychology majors?* White paper prepared for the staff of the state university system of Florida Board of Governors. Retrieved from http://www.cogdop.org/page_attachments/0000/0200/FLA_White_Paper_for_cogop_posting.Pdf

Halonen, J. S. (2017). Introductory psychology: A postmodern love story. In Dunn, D. S., & Hhand, B. M. (Eds.), *Thematic approaches for teaching introductory psychology*. San Francisco, CA: Cengage, publishers.

Halonen, J. S., Beers, M. J., & Brown, A. O. (In press). Assessment at the crossroads: How did we get here and what do we do now? *Scholarship of Teaching and Learning in Psychology*.

Hanafin, J., Shevlin, M., Kenny, M., & McNeela, E. (2007). Including young people with disabilities: Assessment challenges in higher education. *Higher Education, 54*, 435–448. https://doi.org/10.1007/s10734-006-9005-9.

Harlen. (2005). Teachers' summative practices and assessment for learning – Tensions and synergies. *The Curriculum Journal, 16*(2), 207–223. https://doi.org/10.1080/09585170500136093.

Hendrickson, K. A. (2012). Assessment in Finland: A scholarly reflection on one country's use of formative, summative, and evaluation practices. *Mid-Western Educational Researcher, 25*(1/2),

33–43. https://www.mwera.org/MWER/volumes/v25/issue1-2/v25n1-2-Hendrickson-GRADUATE-STUDENT-SECTION.pdf

Hirsch, A. (2020). When assessment is a constant companion: Students' experiences of instruction in an era of intensified assessment focus. *Nordic Journal of Studies in Educational Policy, 6*(2), 89–102. https://doi.org/10.1080/2002317.2020.1756192.

Houston, D., & Thompson, J. N. (2017). Blending formative and summative assessment in a capstone subject: 'It's not your tools, it's how you use them.'. *Journal of University Teaching and Learning Practice, 14*(3).

Jollands, M., McCallum, N., & Bondy, J. (2009, December). *If students want feedback, why don't they collect their assignments? 20th Annual Conference for the Australasian Association for Engineering Education.* https://search.informit.com.au/documentSummary;dn=919023650136289;res=IELENG

Kitchen, E., King, S. H., Robison, D. F., Sudweeks, R. R., Bradshaw, W. S., & Bell, J. D. (2006). Rethinking exams and letter grades: How much can teachers delegate to students? *Life Science Education, 5*(3), 270–280.

Knight, P. (2002). Summative assessment in higher education: Practices in disarray. *Studies in Higher Education, 27*(3), 275–286.

Knight, P. (2010). Summative assessment in higher education: Practices in disarray. *Studies in Higher Education, 27*(3), 275–286. https://doi.org/10.1080/03075070220000662

Kohn, A. (1999). *Punished by rewards: The trouble with gold stars, incentive plans, A's, praise, and other bribes.* Houghton-Mifflin.

Kuh, G. D. (2008). *High-impact educational practices: What they are, who has access to them, and why they matter.* Association of American Colleges and Universities.

Kuh, G. D., Ikenberry, S. O., Jankowski, N. A., Cain, T. R., Ewell, P. T., Hutchings, P., & Kinzie, J. (2015) *Using evidence of student learning to improve higher education.* National Institute for Learning Outcomes Assessment. Jossey-Bass.

Landrum, R. E., & McCarthy, M. A. (2018). Measuring the benefits of a bachelor's degree in psychology: Promises, challenges, and next steps. *Scholarship of Teaching and Learning in Psychology, 4*(1), 55–63. https://doi.org/10.1037/stl0000101.

Lau, A. M. S. (2016). 'Formative, good/summative, bad?': A review of the dichotomy in assessment literature. *Journal of Further & Higher Education, 40*(4), 509–525. https://doi.org/10.1080/0309877X.2014.984600.

Lawrence, N. (2013). Cumulative exams in the introductory psychology course. *Teaching of Psychology, 40*(2), 15–19. https://doi.org/10.1177/0098628312465858.

Maringe, F., & Sing, N. (2014). Teaching large classes in an increasingly internationalizing higher education environment: Pedagogical, quality, and equity issues. *Higher Education, 67*, 761–782. https://doi.org/10.1007/s10734-013-9710-0.

McCarthy, J. (2015). Evaluating written, audio and video feedback in higher education summative assessment. *Issues in Educational Research, 25*(2), 153–169.

McTighe, J., & Ferrara, S. (1998). *Assessing learning in the classroom.* National Education Association.

National Research Council. (2001). *Classroom assessment and the National Science Education Standards.* The National Academies Press. https://doi.org/10.17226/9847.

Pun, K. (2016, September 2). *Do's and dont's on designing for accessibility.* Accessibility in Government. https://accessibility.blog.gov.uk/2016/09/02/dos-and-donts-on-designing-for-accessibility/

Scriven, M. (1967). The methodology of evaluation. In R. W. Tyler, R. M. Gagne, & M. Scriven (Eds.), *Perspectives of curriculum evaluation* (pp. 39–83). Rand McNally.

Stanny, C. J. (2016). Revaluating Bloom's taxonomy: What measurable verbs can and cannot say about student learning. *Education Sciences, 6*(4), 37. https://doi.org/10.3390/educsci6040037.

Steinfeld, E., & Maisel, J. (2012). *Universal design: Creating inclusive environments.* Wiley.

Svinicki, M. D., & McKeachie, W. J. (2014). *In McKeachie's teaching tips: Strategies research, and theory for college and university teachers* (14th ed.). Cengage.

Taras, M. (2005). Assessment—Summative and formative—Some theoretical reflections. *British Journal of Educational Studies, 53*(4), 466–478.

Tomas, C., & Jessy, T. (2019). Struggling and juggling: A comparison of student assessment loads across research and teach-intensive universities. *Assessment & Evaluation in Higher Education, 44*(1), 1–10.

Trotter, E. (2006). Student perceptions of continuous summative assessment. *Assessment and Evaluation in Higher Education, 31*(5), 505–521. https://doi.org/10.1080/02602930600679506.

Volante, L., Schnepf, S. V., Jerrim, J., & Klinger, D. A. (2019). *Education policy & social inequality* (Vol. 4). Socioeconomic inequality and student outcomes. Springer.

Wiggins, G. P. (1993). *The Jossey-Bass education series. Assessing student performance: Exploring the purpose and limits of testing*. Jossey-Bass.

Wiliam, D. (2020). How to think about assessment. In S. Donarsky & T. Bennett (Eds.), *The researchED guide to assessment: An evidence-informed guide for teachers* (pp. 21–36). John Catt Publishing.

Wininger, S. R. (2005). Using your tests to teach: Formative summative assessment. *Teaching of Psychology, 32*(3), 164–166. https://doi.org/10.1207/s15328023top3203_7.

# Formative Assessment and Feedback Strategies

## 55

Susanne Narciss and Joerg Zumbach

## Contents

| | |
|---|---|
| Introduction | 1360 |
| Purposes and Rationale | 1360 |
|     Formative Assessment | 1361 |
|     Formative Feedback | 1363 |
| Design Issues and Approaches | 1365 |
|     Core Design Issues | 1366 |
|     Approaches Informing the Design of Formative Assessment and Feedback Strategies | 1366 |
| Research Issues, Core Findings, and Current Trends | 1370 |
|     Overview on Research Issues | 1373 |
|     Core Findings | 1375 |
|     Current Trends | 1376 |
| Challenges and Implications for Learning and Teaching Psychology | 1378 |
| Teaching, Learning, and Assessment Resources | 1379 |
|     Tips for Teaching and Learning | 1379 |
|     Recommended Readings | 1380 |
|     Online-Resources and Tools | 1381 |
| Cross-References | 1382 |
| References | 1382 |

### Abstract

Formative assessment and formative feedback strategies are very powerful factors for promoting effective learning and instruction in all educational contexts.

---

S. Narciss (✉)
School of Science - Faculty of Psychology, Psychology of Learning and Instruction, Technische Universitaet Dresden, Dresden, Sachsen, Germany
e-mail: susanne.narciss@tu-dresden.de

J. Zumbach
Department of Educational Research, University of Salzburg, Salzburg, Austria
e-mail: joerg.zumbach@plus.ac.at

© Springer Nature Switzerland AG 2023
J. Zumbach et al. (eds.), *International Handbook of Psychology Learning and Teaching*, Springer International Handbooks of Education,
https://doi.org/10.1007/978-3-030-28745-0_63

Formative assessment, as a superordinate term, refers to all activities that instructors and/or learners undertake to get information about teaching and learning that are used in a diagnostic manner. Formative feedback is a core component of formative assessment. If well designed and implemented in terms of a formative feedback strategy, it provides students and teachers with information on the current state of learning in order to help the further regulation of learning and instruction in the direction of the learning standards strived for. This chapter presents the issues in, as well as selected approaches for, designing formative assessment and feedback strategies. Based on recent meta-analyses and literature reviews, it summarizes core theoretical and empirical findings on the conditions and effects of formative assessment and feedback in (higher) education. Furthermore, it discusses challenges and implications for applying the current insights and strategies for effective formative assessment and feedback in higher education. Finally, suggestions on helpful resources are provided.

**Keywords**

Formative assessment · Assessment for learning · Formative feedback strategies

## Introduction

Formative assessment and formative feedback strategies are considered core components for promoting effective learning and instruction in all educational contexts (cf. Hattie, 2009). Within frameworks of formative assessment and feedback strategies, the learner is considered to be an active constructor of knowledge, and thus the formative function of feedback is emphasized. Formative assessment is an essential part of higher education. Formative assessment is an umbrella term for different approaches and strategies to monitor and improve students' self-regulated learning as well as the quality of instruction. As such, formative assessment can also be regarded as a set of cognitive and especially metacognitive strategies that contribute to meaningful learning (e.g., Hattie, 2009). From an evidence-based perspective, the extensive literature review provided by Black and Wiliam (1998) shows that well-designed formative assessment improves students' academic performance in school and in higher education across various fields (see also Black & McCormick, 2010).

## Purposes and Rationale

Assessment and feedback strategies can be implemented in a *summative* or *formative* way. If implemented in a summative way, they occur at end or after learners have been provided with an instructional unit. The main purpose of summative assessment is to capture the outcomes of this instructional unit via some kind of final exam. Mostly, the exam score is provided as feedback (▶ Chap. 54, "Assessment of Learning in Psychology," by Blalock, Rainey, and Halonen, this volume). If implemented in a *formative* way, assessment strategies provide students with opportunities for testing not only at the end but also during or even before learning in order to support their further learning progress by communicating valuable information about their current state of knowledge or learning. It is worth emphasizing that it is not the assessment items or tasks per se that are formative or summative, but *how* they are implemented and used (cf. Wiliam, 2006). Hence, one may well use multiple-choice exam items for formative purposes, if these items are provided before or during an instructional unit with the purpose of gathering information on how well students have understood the material, in order to guide the process of learning and instruction.

The main purpose of implementing assessment and feedback strategies in a formative way is to provide learners as well as teachers with information that can serve as an important basis for guiding and improving (*i.e., forming*) the process of learning and instruction. More specifically, formative assessment and feedback strategies can serve many purposes for both teachers and students, including the following ones:

– Elicit information about learning goals, intentions, and criteria for success.
– Elicit information about students' understanding, state of learning, state of knowledge, etc.
– Elicit information about the benefits and constraints of learning tactics and/or strategies.
– Elicit information about the benefits and constraints of instructional material and strategies.
– Provide information on the kinds of information and/or strategies that would be useful for moving forward in the learning process.
– Provide the basis for adapting instructional material and strategies to students' levels of knowledge and understanding.

Black and Wiliam's theory of formative assessment (Black & Wiliam, 2009) take up Sadler's (1989) key point that eliciting and using information about learning goals and student understandings are not only an instructor's task; peer and self-assessment are also important components of formative assessment (Black & Wiliam, 2009).

## Formative Assessment

Formative assessment includes all activities that instructors and/or learners undertake to get information about teaching and learning that are used in a diagnostic manner (Black & Wiliam, 1998; Boston, 2002). This diagnostic information can be used to improve teaching as well as learning and affects the planning, the process, and the outcomes of instructional situations. It includes a variety of methods, such as classroom observation, classroom discussions, students' work, and the like. As the term "formative" suggests, this kind of assessment is used to (re-)"form" the instructional and/or learning process, while "summative" assessments "sum" up outcomes. As already emphasized, summative assessment instruments (e.g., tests) and outcomes can also be used as information for formative assessment processes. Information retrieved from formative assessment provides the basis for feedback to everyone involved in the learning process (teachers, students, parents, etc.), which in turn should be used to improve the learning environment and its underlying processes and, thus, outcomes.

Several authors have conceptualized the formative assessment process as a cyclical process. For example, Natriello's (1987; see Fig. 1) model describes the evaluation process from a teacher's perspective in eight phases including (1) establishing the purpose of the evaluation, (2) assigning tasks to students, (3) setting criteria for student performance, (4) setting standards on student performance, (5) sampling information on student performance, (6) appraising student performance, (7) providing feedback on student performance, and (8) monitoring outcomes of the evaluation of students.

In their synthesis of feedback research in view of self-regulated learning, Butler and Winne (1995) adopted a cyclical conceptualization of formative assessment and feedback from a learner's perspective. In the context of peer assessment and peer feedback, this cyclical conceptualization of the formative assessment process has been, for example, picked up by Reinholz (2016). While these approaches mainly refer to assessment and feedback of learners, formative assessment can also refer to the design of learning environments itself. As a part of the instructional design process (see also ▶ Chap. 49, "First Principles of Instruction Revisited," by Merrill, this volume), formative assessment can also be applied to all stages of planning, conducting, and evaluating instruction (e.g., by means of peer feedback, student feedback, etc.) in order to improve instruction. This is closely related to action research which is defined by Clark et al. (2020, p. 8) as follows: "Action research is an approach to educational research that is commonly used by educational practitioners and professionals to examine, and ultimately improve, their pedagogy and practice. In this way, action research represents an extension of the reflection and critical self-reflection that an educator employs on a daily basis in their classroom." While action research is commonly described as a tool for improving teaching and learning in primary and secondary education, it can also be applied to higher education. In that sense, formative assessment also includes action research as an instrument for improving teaching and learning in psychology.

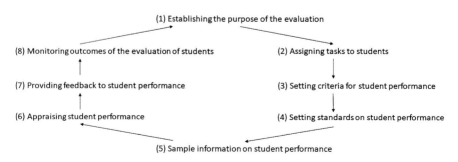

**Fig. 1** Formative assessment cycle according to Natriello (1987)

Nevertheless, the primary focus of this chapter is formative assessment for improving student learning. Here, information retrieved within the assessment cycle provides the basis for feedback to students and instructors. Following the model suggested by Natriello (1987; see Fig. 1), feedback is a core element for (future) learning and a student's progress.

## Formative Feedback

Feedback is a core component of formative assessment processes and has been identified as a powerful factor influencing learning in various instructional contexts, including higher education (e.g., Evans, 2013; Hattie & Gan, 2011; Hattie & Timperley, 2007; Morris, Perry, & Wardle, 2021; Shute, 2008). In instructional contexts, the term *feedback* refers to information which informs the learner about his/her actual state of learning or performance in order to support the regulation of the further process of learning in the direction of the standards being strived for (e.g., Narciss, 2008; Shute, 2008). This notion of feedback is inspired by cybernetic views of feedback (e.g., Wiener, 1954) and emphasizes that a core aim of feedback in instructional contexts is to reduce gaps between current and desired states of learning (Hattie, 2009; Ramaprasad, 1983; Sadler, 1989).

Within an instructional context, feedback can be provided by various external sources of information (e.g., teachers, peers, parents, computer-based systems) and/or by internal sources of information (i.e., information perceivable by the learner while task processing). External feedback strategies can be designed and implemented in many ways. In order to be effective, feedback content has to be processed and taken up meaningfully by the student. Accordingly, there is a complex interplay of internal and external factors that has to be taken into account when designing and investigating the effects of formative feedback strategies. To capture this interplay, Narciss (2008) has developed the interactive two-feedback loops model (ITFL model, also referred to as the interactive tutoring feedback model; Narciss, 2017).

The ITFL model suggests that feedback is considered as a multidimensional instructional activity that aims at contributing to the regulation of a learning process in such a way that learners acquire the knowledge and competencies needed to master learning tasks as well as the regulation of their learning (Narciss, 2013). The ITFL model considers external and internal feedback as core components of two intertwined feedback loops (see Fig. 2). By doing so, it draws attention to issues of how to design and implement *interactive* assessment and feedback strategies in such a way that the external feedback serves to empower students as self-regulated learners.

The ITFL model suggests that for efficient functioning of the intertwined feedback loops, the following components are crucial:

Internal and external feedback can only serve to close a gap between the standards strived for and a current state of learning if instructional goals, as well as the criteria indicating how well task requirements have been met (i.e., *control variables*), have

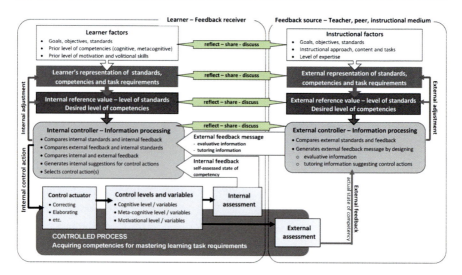

**Fig. 2** Interactive two-feedback loops model. (Narciss, 2017; reprinted with permission from Springer Nature)

been identified, and *standards* for these control variables have been specified as clearly as possible. This is relatively easy in domains with well-defined tasks but can be challenging in domains with ill-defined or complex tasks.

Students' and teachers' representations of instructional goals and criteria of successful task completion serve as a basis for determining the *reference values* in the respective loops. Discrepancies between these representations can occur depending on *learner and or instructional factors*. If there are such discrepancies, they will negatively influence the functioning of both feedback loops. Thus, it is worth providing opportunities for reflecting, sharing, and discussing the criteria and standards of high-quality task processing and completion within the given instructional context (e.g., teacher-to-student, peer-to-peer; student-to-teacher).

The accurate (i.e., reliable and valid) *assessment* of the current state of the control variable is a core prerequisite for generating competency-oriented, concrete, and actionable feedback in both feedback loops. With regard to the external loop, the quality of assessment instruments and strategies are crucial. Regarding the internal loop, students' skills in assessing their own learning and performance (i.e., in generating adequate *internal feedback*) need to be trained. This can be done by providing students with opportunities for self-assessment or also peer assessment. Hence, offering immediate external feedback might be criticized, because it may hinder students in self-assessing their task processing and in actively developing a grasp of criteria/standards.

The *external feedback message* is an important source of (a) calibrating the internal feedback and of (b) deriving control actions. Generating a formative external feedback message involves (a) comparing the external standards with the assessed state of competency and (b) using the result of this comparison to design evaluative information, as well as tutoring information pointing to the control action(s) necessary to achieve a higher level of competency.

The *internal processing* of the external feedback and the *generation of an internal control action* is a complex process. Students need to compare the external feedback, as well as their internal feedback with the standards being sought. Furthermore, they need to compare the external feedback with their internal feedback. Based on these comparisons, they have to figure out which control action(s) would contribute to close the gap and select the most adequate one.

In a formative assessment and feedback cycle, opportunities for applying the control action(s) in a further attempt with the task are generally offered in order to contribute to close the detected gap.

The ITFL model was originally developed for the design and investigation of *interactive tutoring feedback strategies* in (intelligent) computer-based tutoring systems (Narciss, 2008, 2013; Narciss et al., 2014). Here Narciss (2017, p. 174) states:

> Tutoring feedback strategies combine formative elaborated feedback with tutoring and mastery learning strategies. They provide formative evaluative feedback components that help the learners to become aware of any discrepancies that exist between their desired and their current state of competencies. Additionally, they provide (access to) elaborated feedback components (e.g., hints, explanations) that are aimed at supporting learners in acquiring the competencies necessary for mastering the learning tasks. In doing so *tutorial feedback strategies* offer (the access to) strategically useful information for task completion, without providing immediately the correct solution, and prompt the learner to apply this information to a next attempt in accomplishing the learning task and, thus, provide an individualized zone of proximal development. Furthermore, after successful task completion, they provide confirmatory positive feedback components. (a detailed description of such a tutorial feedback strategy is provided by Narciss & Huth, 2006)

However, the conceptual and empirical work on the ITFL model has also provided a basis for developing a competency framework for teacher education courses and higher education on formative feedback (Narciss, Hammer, Damnik, Kisielski, & Körndle, 2021) and for deriving prescriptive principles for designing formative feedback strategies (e.g., Narciss, 2006, 2012; Narciss, 2013).

## Design Issues and Approaches

The cyclical feedback frameworks summarized so far reveal that designing and implementing formative assessment and feedback strategies is a challenging task because of the complex interplay of external and internal loop factors in relation to the targeted instructional goals and tasks. Design issues relate to the quality of both the external and internal feedback loops. In the following sections, we will first provide an overview on the design issues and then outline selected approaches that provide suggestions on how to address these issues.

## Core Design Issues

In order to implement formative assessment and feedback strategies, teachers and learners need to develop an adequate understanding and representation of the relevant domain knowledge as well as competencies and specify the desired standards for these competencies. Thus, teachers have to analyze the conditions of the instructional context by consulting existing competency frameworks for the relevant domain and/or conducting, for example, cognitive task analyses. Second, they have to analyze the conditions and characteristics of the learner or, as more generally described, the feedback receiver, as well as the available feedback source(s) and measurement instruments. There are multiple sources and instruments that can provide information for feedback: interviews, tests, questionnaires, log-files, etc. Using the available information sources to provide formative feedback, instructors and learners have to be aware of the aim of the feedback. Based on these analyses, teachers may develop a formative assessment and feedback strategy, that is, a coordinated plan which integrates clear and decisive statements regarding the following issues (Narciss, 2012):

(a) What are the scope and functions of the assessment and feedback?
(b) When and how to reflect, share, and discuss the feedback scope and functions with the learners?
(c) When and how to reflect, share, and discuss success criteria and standards with the learners?
(d) When and how often should external assessment take place?
(e) What kind of external feedback sources are available?
(f) When and how often should internal assessment (i.e., students' self-assessment) be prompted?
(g) What kind of instruments or tasks can be used for the external and/or internal assessment?
(h) How can students be supported in using these instruments adequately?
(i) Given the selected functions and standards, what kind of elaborated information should the external feedback provide (*external feedback content*)?
(j) When and how should the selected feedback content be conveyed to the learner (*feedback timing and presentation*)?
(k) When and how to reflect, share, and discuss similarities and differences among the internal and external feedback?
(l) What kind of scaffolds can be provided to learners to support their processing of the external feedback and uptake of the external feedback?
(m) How can students be supported in generating and/or selecting adequate control actions?

## Approaches Informing the Design of Formative Assessment and Feedback Strategies

In the last decades, formative assessment and feedback has attracted growing interest in instructional contexts. Accordingly, a number of conceptual approaches have been developed that aim at informing the practice of formative assessment and feedback in (higher) education.

Wiliam and Thompson (2007), Wiliam (2010, p. 31) suggest five key strategies for designing formative assessment that address in a general way most of the issues raised above: "(1) clarifying, sharing, and understanding learning intentions and criteria for success (issues a, b, c); (2) engineering effective classroom discussion, questions, and tasks that elicit evidence of learning (issues d, e, f, g); (3) providing feedback that moves learners forward (issues i, j); (4) activating students as instructional resources for one another (issues k, l); and (5) activating students as the owners of their own learning (issues h, k, l, m)."

Clarifying the scope and functions of assessment and feedback, as well as sharing and understanding learning intentions, are crucial, because feedback is multifunctional, i.e., it can affect the learning process at various levels, and can therefore have numerous different functions (Narciss, 2008, 2013). It can, for example, acknowledge or confirm correct responses or high-quality learning outcomes and promote the acquisition of the knowledge and cognitive operations necessary for accomplishing learning tasks. Feedback can also contribute to correcting errors, misconceptions, or inadequate task processing strategies, prompt the application of metacognitive strategies (e.g., Butler & Winne, 1995; Mathan & Koedinger, 2005), or encourage students in maintaining their motivation (e.g., Narciss, 2004, 2008). In their feedback intervention theory, Kluger and DeNisi (1996) distinguish three regulation levels, a learning task level related to the processing of task details, a motivational task level, and a self-related meta-task level. Hattie and Timperley (2007) suggest that feedback works at four levels: (1) the task level, (2) the process level, (3) the self-regulation level, and (4) the self-level. Inspired by insights on self-regulated learning, Narciss (2008) suggests classifying the widely varying feedback functions as cognitive, meta-cognitive, and motivational. Several meta-analyses reveal that feedback effects can be detrimental if feedback messages are not task-related but provide person-related information, because the latter attract attention to the self-level (e.g., Hattie & Timperley, 2007; Kluger & DeNisi, 1996).

Regarding issues related to the design of the feedback content, a huge body of feedback research reveals that the abovementioned feedback functions have been addressed by a large variety of feedback types and strategies, which also vary widely regarding their content (for reviews see Hattie & Timperley, 2007; Mory, 2004; Narciss, 2008; Shute, 2008). External feedback content can consist of many different kinds of informative components, including the following:

- Knowledge of performance, providing learners with a summative feedback after they have responded to a set of tasks or accomplished a complex assignment (e.g., percentage of correctly solved tasks; number of errors; grade).
- Knowledge of result, providing learners with information on the correctness or quality of their actual response or outcome (e.g., correct/incorrect; flagging errors; good job).
- Knowledge of the correct response, providing the correct response or a sample solution to a given task.
- Elaborated feedback, providing additional information besides knowledge of results or knowledge of the correct response (e.g., hints, guiding questions,

explanations, worked examples). Since there is a variety of elaborated information that might be added to knowledge of results, Narciss (2008) suggests using at least five different categories in order to make a more subtle distinction regarding feedback types with elaborated feedback content:
- Knowledge about task constraints, offering information on task rules, task constraints, and/or task requirements.
- Knowledge about concepts, addressing conceptual knowledge by providing, for example, response-contingent hints on concept attributes, or attribute-isolation examples.
- Knowledge about mistakes, offering information on errors or mistakes (e.g., flagging location of errors; or providing hints on error type or error sources).
- Knowledge about how to process the task, addressing procedural knowledge (e.g., task-contingent hints about procedural skills or problem-solving strategies).
- Knowledge about meta-cognition, eliciting meta-cognitive knowledge and strategies necessary for self-regulating the learning process (e.g., topic-contingent hints about useful sources of information).

To design formative feedback strategies, several of these content types can be combined depending on the task, learner, and instructional conditions.

Feedback types also vary widely in the way they convey the feedback content to the learner. Addressing formal and technical issues related to the presentation of the feedback content requires decisions about the (a) feedback timing (e.g., immediate, delayed), (b) feedback scheduling (e.g., single try, multiple try, answer until correct), (c) codes and modes of feedback representation and delivery, and (d) adaptation strategy (e.g., non-adaptive, adaptive, adaptable, mixed-initiative, or shared-control adaptation).

Beaumont, O'Doherty, and Shannon (2011) developed a dialogic feedback framework that conceptualizes formative feedback also as part of a feedback cycle. It can inform addressing the engineering issues as well as the issues related to activating the learner as a participant in the assessment and feedback process. Beaumont and colleagues distinguish three phases of a dialogic feedback cycle (see Fig. 3).

1. A guided preparation phase in which students are provided with explanations, discussions, and exemplars in order to clarify task requirements, success criteria, and standards. The results from this phase can serve as feedforward for the task completion phase.
2. A guided in-task phase in which they are offered practice opportunities that should be scaffolded by generic feedback, pre-assessment tips, and/or peer assessment support.
3. The final feedback phase in which students should be provided with formative written feedback that refers clearly to the criteria and standards and are prompted to reflect and discuss it.

In each of these phases, dialogues among teachers and students should be included in order to iteratively develop a common ground concerning task requirements, as well as criteria and standards of assessment.

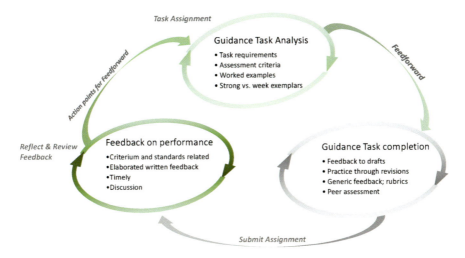

**Fig. 3** Dialogic feedback cycle. (Adopted from Beaumont et al., 2011)

Implementing a dialogic feedback cycle requires a kind of "feedback culture" that involves both instructors and learners, and by doing so continuously provides information that may serve to fine-tune the understanding of task requirements, possible shortfalls, and how to overcome them. Robinson, Pope, and Holyoak (2013) show that students have to become used to such feedback approaches, but the process can be supported by scaffolds that show students where and how to engage with the formative feedback (Price, Handley, & Millar, 2011).

Based on a thematic analysis of the research evidence on assessment feedback in higher education from 2000 to 2012, Evans (2013, pp. 80–83) derived the following principles of how to address effectively the feedback design issues:

1. *Feedback is a central, integral, and continuous process of student assessment.* This, in turn, is fostered by ensuring that relevant feedback is provided, that it is aligned with the task, and that it supports students in their productivity. In this context, performance assessment and the associated feedback should be constructively linked to learning objectives or aligned with them (in the sense of constructive alignment; Biggs & Tang, 2007). Feedback should not be isolated, but rather continuous and an integral part of the daily study routine, supporting students in an active working manner. In doing so, feedback should inform them about the learning process, encourage reflection, and promote self-directed learning.
2. *Assessment feedback guidance is explicit.* Feedback should inform students about principles of good (scientific) practice using examples and clear (evaluation) criteria.
3. *Greater emphasis is placed on feedforward compared to feedback activities.* Feedback is formative and not summative. Feedback should support and promote the learning process and be oriented toward the needs of learners.

4. *Students are engaged in and with the process.* Students should be able to comprehend the criteria and feedback practices and thereby develop their own skills regarding understanding and giving feedback.
5. *The technicalities of feedback are attended to in order to support learning.* Feedback must be appropriate to the method of performance review and adapted by students according to their level of performance. Accordingly, feedback should reflect what was done right, what was done wrong and why, and what can be done better and how. Feedback should also provide the opportunity for dialogue between students and lecturers.
6. *Training in assessment feedback/forward is an integral part of assessment design.* The higher education landscape is characterized by feedback of all kinds. As with review processes in everyday academic life, feedback on student performance must and can be practiced and, if necessary, should also be discussed and further developed collegially.

As detailed in Narciss (2017), the ITFL model also provides a rationale for the feedback principles suggested by authors who consider the learners' active participation and agency as central for effective assessment and feedback processes (e.g., Boud & Molloy, 2013; Carless, 2020; Carless, Salter, Yang, & Lam, 2011; Evans, 2013; Nicol, 2021; Nicol & Macfarlane-Dick, 2006; Wiliam, 2010). Table 1 provides a summarizing overview on those prescriptive principles for designing feedback strategies that can be explicitly linked to the components and assumptions of the ITFL model (for more details see Narciss, 2017).

To conclude, there are a number of conceptual frameworks and pedagogical approaches that served as a basis for deriving principles of good formative assessment and feedback practices. They all emphasize that learners have to be actively engaged in the assessment and feedback processes and that these processes should be viewed as cyclically linked. The principles are generically applicable to any performance in everyday university life, be it oral performance, for example, in the context of papers, written homework, laboratory assignments, or theses. Performance feedback, provided it is appropriate, informative, and meaningful, is thus one of the main proven effective factors in learning. However, in order for feedback to meet these criteria, continuous support from lecturers is important.

## Research Issues, Core Findings, and Current Trends

Assessment and feedback strategies have been the important topics in educational (psychology) research for more than a century. Accordingly, the body of theoretical as well as empirical papers is huge. Over the last decades, issues in formative assessment and feedback have received much attention, particularly in the field of higher education. This is reflected in a growing body of reviews and meta-analyses (e.g., Ajjawi et al., 2021; Evans, 2013; Morris et al., 2021; Van der Kleij & Lipnevich, 2021) as well as handbooks on formative assessment and feedback (e.g., Andrade & Cizek, 2010; Carless, Bridges, Chan, & Glofcheski, 2017;

**Table 1** Feedback design principles and exemplary approaches (adopted from Narciss, 2017)

| Feedback design principle | Approaches and examples of good practice |
| --- | --- |
| Distinction of an internal and external feedback loop | |
| Feedback strategies should be interactive rather than just focusing on transmitting external feedback | Ask-tell-ask-act strategy (e.g., French, Colbert, Pien, Dannefer, & Taylor, 2015) GROW strategy (e.g., Whitmore, 2010) Interactive tutoring feedback strategy (Narciss, 2008, 2013) |
| Controlled process – control levels and variables – standards and reference values for control variables | |
| Identify malleable and measurable variables that may serve as indicators of how well the process of task completion is currently running | Competence modeling (e.g., Fouad et al., 2009, 2022) Common core standards Assessment rubrics for written assignments Competency scales (e.g., counseling scale Lambie, Mullen, Swank, & Blount, 2018) |
| Select or specify the criteria and standards of high-quality task processing and completion | |
| Reflect, share, and discuss the criteria and standards of high-quality task processing and completion within instructional context (e.g., teacher-to-student, peer-to-peer; student-to-teacher) | Provide exemplars of diverse quality to make students actively engage in reflecting, sharing and discussing high vs. low levels of quality criteria Provide competency matrices with criteria for various levels, and make students reflect and discuss them |
| Assessment instruments and processes – internal an external | |
| Select or develop means/devices (e.g., assessment rubrics for written assignments) for assessing the current state of competency | Tabular presentation of assessment rubrics with Likert-like response options Competency matrices eliciting behavioral descriptors for various competence levels |
| Reflect, share, and discuss the assessment instruments | Provide worked examples of diverse quality to clarify if and how the assessment instrument can be applied to measure various levels of competency Provide occasions for peer assessment and/or peer feedback |
| Provide occasions for generating internal feedback before offering external feedback. | Prompt self-assessment with regard to the relevant assessment standards and make self-assessment overt Provide self-assessment work sheets (e.g., competency matrices, rubric tables) to help students to identify which of the criteria they have met as well as those they have not (yet) met |
| External assessment | Use assessment work sheets (e.g., competency matrices, rubric tables) to identify the current level of competency |
| Generate and provide external feedback | |
| Generate competency-oriented, concrete, and actionable external feedback message(s) | Apply W3-strategy to identify gaps and select or specify control actions that may contribute to close the gaps • What worked well? • What did not work well? • What can be done to …? |

(continued)

**Table 1** (continued)

| Feedback design principle | Approaches and examples of good practice |
|---|---|
| Provide information on the externally assessed level of performance in relation to the standards | Provide a tabular work sheet detailing standards/criteria, as well as external feedback with regard to the criteria (same structure as the internal feedback work sheet) |
| Internal processing of feedback and generating of control action ||
| Scaffold students in using the external feedback mindfully for (a) detecting gaps that have to be filled in order to meet the required standards and (b) deriving control actions to close these gaps | Provide a tabular work sheet detailing standards/criteria, internal as well as external feedback with regard to the criteria<br>Provide guiding questions for comparing standards with external and internal feedback<br>Prompt students to make a feedback action plan<br>Provide access to tutoring information (e.g., hints; guiding questions, worked examples) that may be used to identify control actions |
| Reflect, share, and discuss potential control actions for closing gaps between the current level of performance and the standards | Ask students to share and discuss their feedback action plan<br>Ask for a revision letter detailing what corrective actions to take in order to close the gaps<br>Collaborative revision of writing assignments based on feedback<br>Collaborative formulation of concrete suggestions for corrective action |
| Control action – cyclical processes of acting – assessing – feedback – information processing – controlling ||
| Offer the occasion for applying the selected corrective actions | Provide occasions for revision, another attempt of task completion, etc. |
| Prompt students to self-assess and generate internal feedback | Provide self-assessment work sheets (e.g., competency matrices, rubric tables) to help students to identify which of the criteria they have met, what has been improved, and what might still need improvement |
| Provide external feedback together with tutoring information (i.e., hints, guiding questions, explanations, analogies) to help students select and apply adequate corrective actions if they failed to do so without assistance | Elicit progress and emphasize successful attainments of high-quality standards<br>Emphasize<br>• What worked well<br>• What has been improved<br>• What can be done to further improve … |
| As in the first cycle, offer occasions for engaging in corrective actions which apply the tutoring feedback information | Provide occasions for revision, another attempt at task completion, etc. |

Henderson, Ajjawi, Boud, & Molloy, 2019; Nolan, Hakala, & Landrum, 2021; Winstone & Carless, 2019). Nevertheless, gaining an overview on the current state of the art on formative and assessment research is a challenging endeavor, because the issues have been addressed in several lines of research, including research on formative assessment, on formative feedback, on self-assessment, on peer assessment and peer feedback, as well as on technology-enhanced assessment and feedback strategies (see Lipnevich and Panadero (2021) and Panadero and Lipnevich (2021) for two recent attempts of integrating existing theoretical models and approaches on formative feedback).

## Overview on Research Issues

Figure 4 provides a heuristic overview of the numerous issues that can be addressed within the field of research on formative assessment and feedback (see also Narciss, 2013). It reveals that research on formative assessment and feedback is a complex endeavor and can address issues related to, for example:

(a) The (moderating) roles of three core sets of conditions that have to be considered when designing and evaluating formative assessment and feedback strategies, namely, the conditions of the feedback receiver, the feedback source, and the instructional feedback context.
(b) The role of factors influencing the quality of the internal and external assessment.
(c) The role of the three interrelated facets of an external feedback strategy that have to considered when designing a feedback strategy that is tailored to conditions and takes into account the external and, if possible, internal assessment factors.
(d) The (mediating) roles played by the perception, processing, and impact of feedback on levels of task performance, self-regulation, as well as self-concept.
(e) The potential effects that can be investigated on several levels (e.g., cognitive, meta-cognitive, motivational, affective) and with regard to performance or learning outcomes.

As shown in Fig. 4, research on formative assessment and feedback can focus on many aspects and (interacting) variables within a concrete (psychology) course or a specific instructional context. The concrete research issues as well as approaches depend on the research focus. For example, experimental studies focusing on the effects of various kinds of external feedback strategies or types have investigated if and how feedback design factors (e.g., content, timing, scheduling, and presentation modes) affect feedback efficiency in terms of improving students' performance and/or learning). Studies focusing on feedback perception and processing have investigated issues such as if and how students perceive and take-up feedback depending on features of (a) the feedback design (e.g., content or timing) and (b) the feedback source (e.g., peer vs. teacher).

Besides the issues that can be addressed in a specific instructional context, there are also many issues that may arise from superordinate levels that influence formative assessment and feedback. Such issues relate, for example, to the role of establishing a culture of assessment and feedback within and across classes, institutions, and what can be learned from international practice (e.g., Cranney, Hulme, Suleeman, Job, & Dunn, 2021). Research and design issues here can address how, for example, a culture of failure and/or a culture of feedback is possible and can

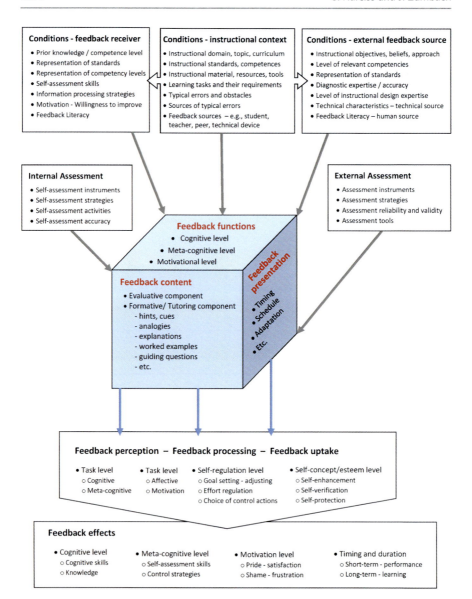

**Fig. 4** Heuristic research model eliciting design and research issues on formative feedback for an instructional context

contribute to effective formative assessment (e.g., Todd & Hammer, 2021). According to Bailey and Garner (2010), it seems that a feedback culture as an enacted top-down process does not lead to the desired effects. They conclude from their study (p. 196) that: "Teachers, like students, may experience a sense of disengagement with higher education practices ostensibly designed to support pedagogical and communicative interactions. Both parties may wonder if feedback is worth the paper it is written on."

## Core Findings

While there is a growing body of qualitative research on formative assessment and feedback in higher education, experimental studies in higher education contexts are rare (Evans, 2013; Morris et al., 2021). Thus, to date there is little experimental evidence on the conditions and effects of formative assessment and feedback strategies in these contexts (Morris et al., 2021). In their narrative synthesis of 28 studies (selected from 188 according to quality criteria), Morris and colleagues provide an overview on the empirical evidence regarding the main topics that have been addressed within these studies, including (1) content and delivery of formative assessment and feedback; (2) feedback timing and scheduling; (3) quizzing and testing; (4) peer assessment or peer feedback strategies; and (5) role of technology for providing feedback. In summary, their narrative synthesis reveals the following findings: Studies addressing issues within topic (1) vary in the types of feedback content they compare, their contexts are diverse, and they reveal that providing at least simple feedback is more effective than providing no feedback but that the effects of elaborated feedback vary depending on the characteristics of students and tasks. Studies addressing issues related to feedback timing provided rather mixed results. Studies on the assessment strategy of low stakes-quizzing and testing suggest that these strategies are promising. Studies on issues related to peer assessment and feedback suggest that their benefits depend on implementation factors. Studies investigating how technology-enhanced implementations of formative assessment and feedback strategies influence students' learning are of uneven quality and also provide a mixed picture. Thus, it is difficult to derive clear implications of their benefits and constraints; the authors emphasize that further high-quality studies on the causal link between technology-enhanced assessment and feedback are needed.

Interestingly, the synthesis provided by Morris et al. (2021) about research evidence on formative assessment and feedback effects in higher education overlaps considerably with the synthesis of findings from feedback research across all educational domains provided by Narciss (2008). Accordingly, the following conclusions are worth emphasizing:

Formative assessment and feedback strategies have be viewed as multi-dimensional instructional approaches. As depicted in Figs. 2 and 4, their effects occur through an interaction with the learner. This in turn means that the effects of various types of external feedback are not general, but only emerge depending on individual and context-related factors. For example, the amount of time it takes for errors to be eliminated with the help of external feedback depends on (a) the characteristics of the learner; (b) the quality of the external feedback design; (c) the type, complexity, and difficulty of the tasks; and (d) the type of error. In highly skilled learners, or with easy tasks or simple slips, simple outcome feedback might be sufficient to yield a correct response the next time or to improve learning. In learners with a low level of skill working on very complex and difficult tasks, or when errors are serious, it is possible that even elaborated formative feedback may not be sufficient for promoting mastery of the high demands.

How and on what levels of regulation learners perceive, process, and take up the information provided by the external feedback also significantly influences whether and how the effects of this information can unfold. The feedback processing should be mindful and requires that one have the competence to exploit feedback information in the service of one's own learning despite the potentially negative affective reactions that aspects of critical feedback might create. This competence has been referred to as feedback literacy (Carless & Boud, 2018). In addition to the cognitive dispositions of the learner (e.g., prior knowledge, strategic knowledge), individual motivational factors such as self-efficacy and perceived task values and individual meta-cognitive factors such as monitoring competencies and strategies play a role. Hence, in order to draw differentiated conclusions about the effects of various types of external feedback, not only cognitive but also individual motivational and meta-cognitive factors and the nature of individual feedback processing should be investigated.

Effects of feedback can occur on various levels (task, self-regulation, self-esteem) and can be more or less sustainable, i.e., range from short-term performance effects to long-lasting learning effects. Thus, to gain a differentiated picture of the benefits and constraints of various feedback strategies, evaluating their effects requires collecting data both during and after the treatment (Narciss, 2008).

## Current Trends

As summarized so far, a wide range of research on formative assessment and feedback strategies has been carried out in all instructional contexts, including higher education, and these research activities continue. After reviewing the core of recent research findings, we identified five trends we consider to be of particular interest for establishing effective formative assessment and feedback practices in psychology teaching and learning:

1. Empowering Students to Self-Assess and Generate Internal Feedback

Students in higher education have to self-regulate their learning. Since Butler and Winne's (1995) seminal synthesis of feedback and self-regulated learning, self-assessment and the ability to generate adequate internal feedback is considered a crucial factor for promoting self-regulated learning. Investigating the conditions and effects of self-assessment and internal feedback is still the focus of current research (e.g., Nicol, 2019; Nicol, 2021; Panadero, Lipnevich, & Broadbent, 2019).

2. Empowering Students to Peer-Assess and Generate Peer Feedback

Peer assessment and feedback strategies have been found to promote students' learning and performance if they are implemented adequately (e.g., Double,

McGrane, & Hopfenbeck, 2020; Li, Xiong, Hunter, Guo, & Tywoniw, 2020; Morris et al., 2021). However, many factors have to be taken into account, and thus, issues of how to promote peer assessment and feedback are still being addressed by current research. How peer assessment influences self-assessment is an important issue addressed by several research groups (e.g., Iglesias Pérez, Vidal-Puga, & Pino Juste, 2020; To & Panadero, 2019; Wanner & Palmer, 2018).

3. Empowering Students to Be Feedback Literate

As mentioned above, the mindful processing and taking up of the information provided by external feedback is crucial for the effectiveness of formative assessment and feedback. Carless and colleagues have developed the concept of *feedback literacy*, to refer to the competence of exploiting the feedback information in service of one's own learning despite the potentially negative affective reactions critical feedback aspects might prompt (e.g., Carless & Boud, 2018). Research on students' feedback literacy is still in its infancy but is receiving increasing attention in current research (e.g., Chong, 2021; de Kleijn, 2021; Winstone, Balloo, & Carless, 2022).

4. Empowering Teachers to Be Feedback Literate

Teachers' competences in designing and implementing effective formative assessment and feedback strategies (also referred to as teacher feedback literacy) have received increasing attention in research in recent years (e.g., Boud & Dawson, 2021). Some of the research in this field is linked to students' feedback literacy (e.g., Carless & Winstone, 2020; de Kleijn, 2021). Other research activities relate to issues of how to promote and support teachers in developing and applying the core competences in mastering the complex practice of formative assessment and feedback (e.g., Narciss et al., 2021; Wylie & Lyon, 2020).

5. Exploiting and Investigating the Potential of Modern Information Technologies

Modern information technologies increase the range of feedback strategies that can be implemented in instructional contexts. Technologies can, for example, support in various ways the phases of the assessment cycle. New, innovative interactive test-items using multimedia technology can be developed. Assessment instruments can be electronically implemented and delivered, for example, via learning platforms or in all kinds of online learning environments. Learner activities within online learning environments can be traced in logfiles, and learning analytics can be used to use these logfiles for assessment purposes. Results of data analyses can be visualized, and these visualizations can be used as components of interactive feedback strategies. Yet, as revealed by the experiences of the online shift due to the COVID-19 pandemic, as well as by recent research (e.g., Goldin, Narciss, Foltz, & Bauer, 2017; Spector et al., 2016; Wang & Han, 2021; Xiong & Suen, 2018), many issues related to formative e-assessment and feedback remain unanswered, and thus, this field of research needs, and will undoubtedly receive, intensive attention in future research.

## Challenges and Implications for Learning and Teaching Psychology

Implementing formative assessment and feedback strategies is a complex endeavor in which teachers and learners have to tackle a number of challenges, particularly in courses with an extremely unbalanced instructor-student ratio. In such courses, there are many practical difficulties that need to be taken care of, and solving these difficulties is very time-consuming, especially where there is a lack of sophisticated technologies. Thus, formative assessment has not yet received enough attention in such courses – and this holds true even for technology-enhanced environments such as massive open online courses (MOOCs; Xiong & Suen, 2018).

One suggested solution for tackling these challenges is using formative self- as well as peer assessment and feedback strategies. However, according to Wanner and Palmer (2018), successful self and peer assessment requires the development of students' capacities for using assessment criteria and giving feedback, as well as the continuous and timely involvement of the teacher. Thus, implementing self- and peer assessment is not simple for teachers or students. Accordingly, it is valuable to have many kinds of (collaborative) activities for developing and sharing strategies, tools, instruments, etc. that support the implementation of formative assessment and feedback strategies, especially in large courses (for a recent collection of such activities see Nolan et al., 2021).

The knowledge domains in all fields of psychology teaching and learning are very complex and thus more or less ill-structured. Developing and implementing formative assessment and feedback strategies for ill-structured knowledge domains is far more difficult than for well-structured domains, because it is challenging to identify and specify clear success criteria and their standards and develop a common ground regarding those criteria and standards. The shift to competency-oriented professional frameworks has added further challenges (e.g., Gonsalvez, Shafranske, McLeod, & Falender, 2021; Rodolfa & Schaffer, 2019). For example, designing reliable and valid assessment tasks and tools for professional competences is very demanding. A promising approach in the field of clinical psychology has been recently published by Gonsalvez and colleagues (Gonsalvez, Deane, Terry, Nasstasia, & Shires, 2021).

As mentioned in section "Current Trends," exploiting and investigating the potential of modern information and communication technologies (ICT) for formative assessment and feedback seems at first glance to be very promising. However, since so many technical as well as practical issues are still open, there is a lack of sophisticated tools. Moreover, technologies are mostly used to substitute traditional assessment practices by digital versions of them (e.g., Gikandi, Morrow, & Davis, 2011), and in many cases – rather than providing support – this creates an additional load on both teachers and learners. However, according to Puentedura's Substitution, Augmentation, Modification, and Redefinition (SAMR) model, the full exploitation of the potential of ICT would require that it is used to modify and redefine formative assessment and feedback by, for example, creating new assessment tasks and feedback strategies that would not be possible without these technologies (Puentedura, 2012; see also Redecker & Johannessen, 2013). Core issues and approaches in this direction have been published in the book *Re-imagining University Assessment in a Digital World* (Bearman, Dawson, Ajjawi, Tai, & Boud, 2020).

## Teaching, Learning, and Assessment Resources

## Tips for Teaching and Learning

Prescriptive principles for designing formative assessment and feedback strategies have been suggested by several authors. We have described some of them in section "Approaches informing the design of formative assessment and feedback strategies" and will not repeat them here. However, we want to share here the following ten tips extracted from *Common Formative Assessment: A Toolkit for PLCs at Work* by Kim Bailey and Chris Jakicic (2011) and published by Bill Ferriter in his Teaching Quality Blog (http://bit.ly/10Tips4FormAss).

1. ***Remember That Getting Information Quickly and Easily Is Essential***

    Assessment information is only valuable if you are actually willing and able to collect it and you can act on it in a timely manner. That simple truth should fundamentally change the way that you think about assessments.

2. ***Write Your Assessments and Scoring Rubrics Together Even If That Means You Initially Deliver Fewer Common Assessments***

    Collaborative conversations about what to assess, how to assess, and what mastery looks like in action are just as valuable as student data sets.

3. ***Assess ONLY the Learning Outcomes That You Identified as Essential***

    Assessing nonessential standards just makes it more difficult to quickly and easily get – and to take action on – information.

4. ***Ask at Least Three Questions for Each Learning Outcome That You Are Trying to Test***

    That allows students to fail a question and still demonstrate mastery. Just as importantly, that means a poorly written question won't ruin your data set.

5. ***Test Mastery of No More Than Three or Four Learning Targets per Assessment***

Doing so makes remediation after an assessment doable. Can you imagine trying to intervene when an assessment shows students who have struggled to master more than four learning outcomes?

6. ***Clearly Tie Every Single Question to an Essential Learning Outcome***

Doing so makes it possible to track mastery by student and standard. Your data sets have more meaning when you can spot patterns in mastery of the outcome – not the question.

7. ***Choose Assessment Types That Are Appropriate for the Content or Skills That You Are Trying to Measure***

Using performance assessments to measure the mastery of basic facts is overkill. Similarly, using a slew of multiple-choice questions to measure the mastery of complex thinking skills is probably going to come up short.

8. ***When Writing Multiple-Choice Questions, Use Wrong Answer Choices to Highlight Common Misconceptions***

The patterns found in the WRONG answers of well-written tests can tell you just as much as the patterns found in the RIGHT answers. If you fill your test with careless or comical distractors, you will miss out on an opportunity to learn more about your students.

9. ***When Writing Constructed Response Questions, Provide Students with Enough Context to Allow Them to Answer the Question***

Context plays a vital role in constructing a meaningful response to any question. Need proof? Suppose that a teenage daughter asks her parent, "Can I go to the mall with some friends tonight?" Will the parent ask a few questions before saying yes?

10. ***Make Sure That Higher Level Questions Ask Students to Apply Knowledge and/or Skills in New Situations***

A higher level question that asks students to apply knowledge in the same way as they have previously practiced becomes a lower level question.

## Recommended Readings

The following books view formative assessment and feedback as a shared enterprise offering teachers and students opportunities for developing their knowledge, competencies, and identities.

Bearman, M., Dawson, P., Ajjawi, R., Tai, J., & Boud, D. (Eds.). (2020). *Re-imagining university assessment in a digital world*. Singapore: Springer Nature

Carless, D., Bridges, S.M.; Chan, C.K.Y., & Glofcheski, R. (Eds.). (2017). *Scaling up assessment for learning in higher education*. Singapore: Springer Nature.

Nolan, S. A., Hakala, C. M., & Landrum, R. E. (Eds.). (2021). *Assessing undergraduate learning in psychology: Strategies for measuring and improving student performance*. Washington D.C.: American Psychological Association.

Winstone, N., & Carless, D. (2019). *Designing effective feedback processes in higher education: A learning-focused approach*. New York: Routledge.

## Online-Resources and Tools

The quickly growing field of formative assessment and feedback in higher education has inspired the development of numerous online resources and tools. The following URLs provide access to valuable resources and tools:

1. APA online resources: https://www.apa.org/ed/graduate/competency.html https://www.apa.org/ed/governance/bea/assess

    The APA Board of Educational Affairs has a rich section on issues of professional competencies and their assessment including "*The Assessment CyberGuide for Learning Goals and Outcomes*" compiled 2009 by Thomas Pusateri with assistance from Jane Halonen, Bill Hill & Maureen McCarthy.

2. https://stll.au.dk/en/resources/assessment-methods/innovative-assessment/

    This URL link is taken from the website of Aarhus University (Denmark), which describes innovative assessment methods as "hardly used methods of assessment at the Natural Sciences and Technical Sciences faculties." The website lists five innovative methods. These include portfolio, case study, innovative computer-based assessment, and objective structured practical/clinical exam.

3. https://www.open.edu/openlearn/ocw/mod/oucontent/view.php?id=106399&section=_unit1.2.2

    *Innovative Assessment Methods* is a free module offered by Open University (UK). The module equips learners with the skills that enable them to identify and create innovative assessment methods as well as identify enablers and hindrances to innovative assessment. Additionally, learners learn how to make use of assessment tools, as well as analyze the effectiveness of such tools. The module is to be completed in 4 weeks. Key topics that have been covered include competence-based curriculum, formative and summative assessment, and principles of pedagogical techniques.

4. https://www.queensu.ca/teachingandlearning/modules/assessments/31_s4_01_intro_section.html

Queen's University Canada offers a module called assessment strategies. The module comprises 11 sections and covers topics such as concept maps, concept tests, E-portfolios, and podcasts and vlogs as examples of innovative assessments. Diagnostic, formative, and summative are considered as assessment types. Other topics that have been included are assessment methods and assessment tools. The module helps learners to develop skills that enable them to design formative assessment techniques and criticize assessment methods.

5. Peerwise - https://peerwise.cs.auckland.ac.nz/

Peerwise is a free online tool in which students learn through teaching. Students create multiple-choice questions along with answers and explanations. Peers attempt to answer these questions and compare their answers against those of the authors. Peers can also leave a comment or agree/disagree with a previous comment. The platform has competitive features that allow participants to earn scores and badges based on their contribution.

## Cross-References

▶ Assessment of Learning in Psychology
▶ First Principles of Instruction Revisited
▶ Psychological Assessment and Testing
▶ Psychology in Professional Education and Training

## References

Ajjawi, R., Kent, F., Broadbent, J., Hong-Meng Tai, J., Bearman, M., & Boud, D. (2021). Feedback that works: A realist review of feedback interventions for written tasks. *Studies in Higher Education*. https://doi.org/10.1080/03075079.2021.1894115

Andrade, H., & Cizek, G. (Eds.). (2010). *Handbook of formative assessment*. New York: Routledge.

Bailey, R., & Garner, M. (2010). Is the feedback in higher education assessment worth the paper it is written on? Teachers' reflections on their practices. *Teaching in Higher Education, 15*(2), 187–198. https://doi.org/10.1080/13562511003620019

Bearman, M., Dawson, P., Ajjawi, R., Tai, J., & Boud, D. (Eds.). (2020). *Re-imagining university assessment in a digital world*. Springer.

Beaumont, C., O'Doherty, M., & Shannon, L. (2011). Reconceptualising assessment feedback: A key to improving student learning? *Studies in Higher Education, 36*, 671–687.

Biggs, J., & Tang, C. (2007). *Teaching for quality learning at university. What the student does* (3rd ed.). Maidenhead: McGraw-Hill.

Black, P., & McCormick, R. (2010). Reflections and new directions. *Assessment & Evaluation in Higher Education, 35*(5), 493–499.

Black, P., & Wiliam, D. (1998). Assessment and classroom learning. *Assessment in Education: Principles, Policy & Practice, 5*(1), 7–74.

Black, P., & Wiliam, D. (2009). Developing the theory of formative assessment. *Educational Assessment, Evaluation and Accountability, 21*(1), 5–31.

Boston, C. (2002). The concept of formative assessment. *Practical Assessment, Research, and Evaluation, 8*. https://doi.org/10.7275/kmcq-dj31. https://scholarworks.umass.edu/pare/vol8/iss1/9

Boud, D., & Dawson, P. (2021). What feedback literate teachers do: An empirically-derived competency framework. *Assessment & Evaluation in Higher Education*. https://doi.org/10.1080/02602938.2021.1910928

Boud, D., & Molloy, E. (Eds.). (2013). *Feedback in higher and professional education: Understanding it and doing it well*. London: Routledge.

Butler, D. L., & Winne, P. H. (1995). Feedback and self-regulated learning: A theoretical synthesis. *Review of Educational Research, 65*, 245–281.

Carless, D. (2020). From teacher transmission of information to student feedback literacy: Activating the learner role in feedback processes. *Active Learning in Higher Education*. https://doi.org/10.1177/1469787420945845

Carless, D., & Boud, D. (2018). The development of student feedback literacy: Enabling uptake of feedback. *Assessment & Evaluation in Higher Education, 43*(8), 1315–1325. https://doi.org/10.1080/02602938.2018.1463354

Carless, D., & Winstone, N. (2020). Teacher feedback literacy and its interplay with student feedback literacy. *Teaching in Higher Education*, 1–14. https://doi.org/10.1080/13562517.2020.1782372

Carless, D., Salter, D., Yang, M., & Lam, J. (2011). Developing sustainable feedback practices. *Studies in Higher Education, 36*(4), 395–407.

Carless, D., Bridges, S. M., Chan, C. K. Y., & Glofcheski, R. (Eds.). (2017). *Scaling up assessment for learning in higher education*. Singapore: Springer.

Chong, S. W. (2021). Reconsidering student feedback literacy from an ecological perspective. *Assessment & Evaluation in Higher Education, 46*(1), 92–104.

Clark, J., Porath, S., Thiele, J., & Jobe, M. (2020). *Action research*. NPP eBooks. 34. Online: https://newprairiepress.org/ebooks/34

Cranney, J., Hulme, J. A., Suleeman, J., Job, R., & Dunn, D. S. (2021). Assessing learning outcomes in undergraduate psychology education: Lessons learned from five countries. In S. A. Nolan, C. M. Hakala, & R. E. Landrum (Eds.), *Assessing undergraduate learning in psychology: Strategies for measuring and improving student performance* (pp. 179–201). Washington, D.C.: American Psychological Association. https://doi.org/10.1037/0000183-013

de Kleijn, R. A. (2021). Supporting student and teacher feedback literacy: An instructional model for student feedback processes. *Assessment & Evaluation in Higher Education*. https://doi.org/10.1080/02602938.2021.1967283

Double, K. S., McGrane, J. A., & Hopfenbeck, T. N. (2020). The impact of peer assessment on academic performance: A meta-analysis of control group studies. *Educational Psychology Review, 32*(2), 481–509.

Evans, C. (2013). Making sense of assessment feedback in higher education. *Review of Educational Research, 83*(1), 70–120.

Fouad, N. A., Grus, C. L., Hatcher, R. L., Kaslow, N. J., Hutchings, P. S., Madson, M. B., Collins, F. L., & Crossman, R. E. (2009). Competency benchmarks: A model for understanding and measuring competence in professional psychology across training levels. *Training and Education in Professional Psychology, 3*(4), 5–26. https://doi.org/10.1037/a0015832

Fouad, N. A., Hatcher, R. L., & McCutcheon, S. (2022). Introduction to the special issue on competency in training and education. *Training and Education in Professional Psychology, 16*(2), 109–111. https://doi.org/10.1037/tep0000408

Gikandi, J. W., Morrow, D., & Davis, N. E. (2011). Online formative assessment in higher education: A review of the literature. *Computers & education, 57*(4), 2333–2351.

Goldin, I., Narciss, S., Foltz, P., & Bauer, M. (2017). New directions in formative feedback in interactive learning environments. *International Journal of Artificial Intelligence in Education, 27*(3), 385–392. https://doi.org/10.1007/s40593-016-0135-7

Gonsalvez, C. J., Deane, F. P., Terry, J., Nasstasia, Y., & Shires, A. (2021). Innovations in competence assessment: Design and initial validation of the Vignette Matching Assessment Tool (VMAT). *Training and Education in Professional Psychology, 15*(2), 106–116. https://doi.org/10.1037/tep0000302

Gonsalvez, C. J., Shafranske, E. P., McLeod, H. J., & Falender, C. A. (2021). Competency-based standards and guidelines for psychology practice in Australia: opportunities and risks. *Clinical Psychologist, 25*(3), 244–259. https://doi.org/10.1080/13284207.2020.1829943

Hattie, J. A. (2009). *Visible learning. A synthesis of over 800 meta-analyses relating to achievement*. New York: Routledge.

Hattie, J. A., & Gan, M. (2011). Instruction based on feedback. In R. Mayer & P. Alexander (Eds.), *Handbook of research on learning and instruction* (pp. 249–271). New York: Routledge.

Hattie, J., & Timperley, H. (2007). The power of feedback. *Review of Educational Research, 77*, 81–112.

Henderson, M., Ajjawi, R., Boud, D., & Molloy, E. (Eds.). (2019). *The impact of feedback in higher education: Improving assessment outcomes for learners*. Singapore: Springer.

Iglesias Pérez, M. C., Vidal-Puga, J., & Pino Juste, M. R. (2020). The role of self and peer assessment in Higher Education. *Studies in Higher Education*, 1–10. https://doi.org/10.1080/03075079.2020.1783526

Kluger, A. N., & DeNisi, A. (1996). The effects of feedback interventions on performance: A historical review, a meta-analysis, and a preliminary feedback intervention theory. *Psychological Bulletin, 119*(2), 254.

Li, H., Xiong, X., Hunter, C. V., Guo, X., & Tywoniw, R. (2020). Does peer assessment promote student learning? A meta-analysis. *Assessment & Evaluation in Higher Education, 45*(2), 193–211. https://doi.org/10.1080/02602938.2019.1620679

Lipnevich, A., & Panadero, E. (2021). A review of feedback models and theories: Descriptions, definitions, and conclusions. *Frontiers in Education*. https://doi.org/10.3389/feduc.2021.720195

Mathan, S. A., & Koedinger, K. R. (2005). Fostering the intelligent novice: Learning from errors with metacognitive tutoring. *Educational Psychologist, 40*(4), 257–265.

Morris, R., Perry, T., & Wardle, L. (2021). Formative assessment and feedback for learning in higher education: A systematic review. *Review of Education, 9*(3). https://doi.org/10.1002/rev3.3292

Mory, E. H. (2004). Feedback research revisited. In D. H. Jonassen (Ed.), *Handbook of research on educational communications and technology* (2nd ed., pp. 745–783). Mahwah, NJ: Lawrence Erlbaum Associates.

Narciss, S. (2004). The impact of informative tutoring feedback and self-efficacy on motivation and achievement in concept learning. *Experimental Psychology, 51*(3), 214–228.

Narciss, S. (2006). *Informatives tutorielles feedback* [Informative tutorial feedback]. *Entwicklungs- und Evaluationsprinzipien auf der Basis instruktionspsychologischer Erkenntnisse*. Münster: Waxmann.

Narciss, S. (2008). Feedback strategies for interactive learning tasks. In J. M. Spector, M. D. Merrill, J. J. G. van Merrienboer, & M. P. Driscoll (Eds.), *Handbook of research on educational communications and technology* (3rd ed., pp. 125–144). Mahwah, NJ: Lawrence Erlbaum Associates.

Narciss, S. (2012). Feedback strategies. In N. Seel (Ed.), *Encyclopedia of the learning sciences* (Vol. F(6), pp. 1289–1293). New York: Springer.

Narciss, S. (2013). Designing and evaluating tutoring feedback strategies for digital learning environments on the basis of the interactive tutoring feedback model. *Digital Education Review, 23*, 7–26. Retrieved from http://greav.ub.edu/der

Narciss, S. (2017). Conditions and effects of feedback viewed through the lens of the Interactive Tutoring Feedback Model. In D. Carless, S. M. Bridges, C. K. Y. Chan, & R. Glofcheski (Eds.), *Scaling up assessment for learning in higher education* (pp. 173–189). Singapore: Springer.

Narciss, S., Hammer, E., Damnik, G., Kisielski, K., & Körndle, H. (2021). Promoting prospective teacher competencies for designing, implementing, evaluating, and adapting interactive formative feedback strategies. *Psychology Learning & Teaching, 20*(2), 261–278.

Narciss, S., & Huth, K. (2006). Fostering achievement and motivation with bug-related tutoring feedback in a computer-based training on written subtraction. *Learning and Instruction, 16*, 310–322.

Narciss, S., Schnaubert, L., Andres, E., Eichelmann, A., Goguadze, G., & Sosnovsky, S. (2014). Exploring feedback and student characteristics relevant for personalizing feedback strategies. *Computers & Education, 71*, 56–76.

Natriello, G. (1987). The impact of evaluation processes on students. *Educational Psychologist, 22*(2), 155–175.

Nicol, D. (2019). Reconceptualising feedback as an internal not an external process. *Italian Journal of Educational Research*, 71–84.

Nicol, D. (2021). The power of internal feedback: Exploiting natural comparison processes. *Assessment & Evaluation in Higher Education, 46*(5), 756–778.

Nicol, D. J., & Macfarlane-Dick, D. (2006). Formative assessment and self-regulated learning: A model and seven principles of good feedback practice. *Studies in Higher Education, 31*, 199–218.

Nolan, S. A., Hakala, C. M., & Landrum, R. E. (Eds.). (2021). *Assessing undergraduate learning in psychology: Strategies for measuring and improving student performance*. Washington, D.C.: American Psychological Association.

Panadero, E., & Lipnevich, A. (2021). A review of feedback typologies and models: Towards an integrative model of feedback elements. *Educational Research Review, 100416*. https://doi.org/10.1016/j.edurev.2021.100416

Panadero, E., Lipnevich, A., & Broadbent, J. (2019). Turning self-assessment into self-feedback. In M. Henderson, R. Ajjawi, D. Boud, & E. Molloy (Eds.), *The impact of feedback in higher education* (pp. 147–163). Cham: Palgrave Macmillan.

Price, M., Handley, K., & Millar, J. (2011). Feedback: Focusing attention on engagement. *Studies in Higher Education, 36*, 879–896.

Puentedura, R. (2012). *Building Upon SAMR*. www.hippasus.com/rrpweblog/archives/2012/09/03/BuildingUponSAMR.pdf

Ramaprasad, A. (1983). On the definition of feedback. *Behavioral Science, 28*, 4–13.

Redecker, C., & Johannessen, Ø. (2013). Changing assessment – Towards a new assessment paradigm using ICT. *European Journal of Education, 48*(1), 79–96.

Reinholz, D. (2016). The assessment cycle: A model for learning through peer assessment. *Assessment & Evaluation in Higher Education, 41*(2), 301–315.

Robinson, S., Pope, D., & Holyoak, L. (2013). Can we meet their expectations? Experiences and perceptions of feedback in first year undergraduate students. *Assessment & Evaluation in Higher Education, 38*, 260–272.

Rodolfa, E., & Schaffer, J. (2019). Challenges to psychology education and training in the culture of competence. *American Psychologist, 74*(9), 1118–1128. https://doi.org/10.1037/amp0000513

Sadler, D. R. (1989). Formative assessment and the design of instructional system. *Instructional Science, 18*, 119–144.

Shute, V. J. (2008). Focus on formative feedback. *Review of Educational Research, 78*, 153–189.

Spector, J. M., Ifenthaler, D., Sampson, D., Yang, L., Mukama, E., Warusavitarana, A., . . . Gibson, D. C. (2016). Technology enhanced formative assessment for 21st century learning. *Educational Technology & Society, 19*(3), 58–71.

To, J., & Panadero, E. (2019). Peer assessment effects on the self-assessment process of first-year undergraduates. *Assessment & Evaluation in Higher Education, 44*(6), 920–932.

Todd, J. S., & Hammer, E. Y. (2021). How to create a culture of assessment. In S. A. Nolan, C. M. Hakala, & R. E. Landrum (Eds.), *Assessing undergraduate learning in psychology: Strategies for measuring and improving student performance* (pp. 67–76). Washington, D.C.: American Psychological Association. https://doi.org/10.1037/0000183-006

Van der Kleij, F. M., & Lipnevich, A. A. (2021). Student perceptions of assessment feedback: A critical scoping review and call for research. *Educational Assessment, Evaluation and Accountability, 33*(2), 345–373.

Wang, D., & Han, H. (2021). Applying learning analytics dashboards based on process-oriented feedback to improve students' learning effectiveness. *Journal of Computer Assisted Learning, 37*(2), 487–499.

Wanner, T., & Palmer, E. (2018). Formative self-and peer assessment for improved student learning: the crucial factors of design, teacher participation and feedback. *Assessment & Evaluation in Higher Education, 43*(7), 1032–1047. https://doi.org/10.1080/02602938.2018.1427698

Whitmore, J. (2010). Coaching for Performance: *The principles and practice of coaching and leadership fully revised 25th anniversary edition*. Hachette UK.

Wiener, N. (1954). *The human use of human beings: Cybernetics and society.* Oxford: Houghton Mifflin.

Wiliam, D. (2006). Formative assessment: Getting the focus right. *Educational Assessment, 11*(3-4), 283–289.

Wiliam, D. (2010). An integrative summary of the research literature and implications for a theory of formative assessment. In H. Andrade & G. Cizek (Eds.), *Handbook of formative assessment* (pp. 18–40). New York: Routledge.

Wiliam, D., & Thompson, M. (2007). Integrating assessment with instruction: What will it take to make it work? In C. A. Dwyer (Ed.), *The future of assessment: Shaping teaching and learning* (pp. 53–82). Lawrence Erlbaum Associates.

Winstone, N. E., Balloo, K., & Carless, D. (2022). Discipline-specific feedback literacies: A framework for curriculum design. *Higher Education, 83*, 57–77. https://doi.org/10.1007/s10734-020-00632-0

Winstone, N., & Carless, D. (2019). *Designing effective feedback processes in higher education: A learning-focused approach*. London: Routledge.

Wylie, E. C., & Lyon, C. J. (2020). Developing a formative assessment protocol to support professional growth. *Educational Assessment, 25*(4), 314–330.

Xiong, Y., & Suen, H. K. (2018). Assessment approaches in massive open online courses: Possibilities, challenges and future directions. *International Review of Education, 64*, 241–263. https://doi.org/10.1007/s11159-018-9710-5

# Technology-Enhanced Psychology Learning and Teaching 56

Helmut Niegemann

## Contents

| | |
|---|---|
| Introduction | 1388 |
| Purposes and Rationale | 1388 |
| Design Issues and Approaches | 1389 |
|     Decision-Oriented Instructional Design (DO ID) Model | 1389 |
| Analyses | 1391 |
|     Analysis of the Addressees: Needs | 1391 |
|     Analysis of the Subject Matter | 1391 |
|     Analysis of the Resources | 1391 |
|     Formats | 1391 |
|     Content Structuring | 1394 |
|     Learning Tasks and Narration | 1394 |
|     Technical Aspects | 1394 |
|     Multimedia Design | 1396 |
|     Motivational and Emotional Design | 1396 |
|     Interaction Design | 1396 |
|     Time: Time Allocation | 1397 |
|     Graphics Design: Layout | 1398 |
|     Implementation | 1398 |
| Suitable E-Learning Formats for Psychological Contents | 1399 |
|     Online-Lectures: Mini-lectures | 1399 |
|     E-seminars (Webinars) | 1399 |
|     Simulations | 1399 |
|     Videos: Interactive Videos | 1400 |
|     Augmented Reality (AR)/Virtual Reality (VR)/Mixed Reality (MR) | 1400 |
|     MASL Multimedia-Assisted Self-Regulated Learning | 1400 |
| Conclusion, Challenges, and Current Trends | 1400 |
| Recommended Further Readings | 1401 |
| References | 1403 |

H. Niegemann (✉)
Saarland University, Educational Technology, Saarbrücken, Germany
e-mail: helmut.niegemann@uni-saarland.de

© Springer Nature Switzerland AG 2023
J. Zumbach et al. (eds.), *International Handbook of Psychology Learning and Teaching*, Springer International Handbooks of Education,
https://doi.org/10.1007/978-3-030-28745-0_64

## Abstract

The design and development of technology-enhanced psychology learning units underly the same principles as any other content. The specificity results from variables concerning the structure of the respective subject matter and variables of the learners. The chapter shows main aspects of the instructional design (ID) of multimedia-supported psychology teaching units to be considered in ID decisions. These aspects are bundled in the DO ID framework model; the focus here is on suitable formats of instruction and technical topics.

## Keywords

Instructional design · Formats · Simulation · Interactive videos

## Introduction

In 2020, due to the Corona pandemic, technology-enhanced learning and teaching changed from an optional, often occasional, or experimental format of teaching to the standard format. Many lecturers and professors had to flip their complete teaching habits and behavior in a short time. On the other hand, the use of multimedia-based teaching started in many domains of university teaching, including psychology, at least in Germany 20 years ago, when governmental programs fostered the use of computers and the Internet in universities. The favorite method of digital teaching has been recording normal lectures, more or less post-processed and made available on specific streaming servers in addition to or as a substitution for face-to-face lectures. Besides storage of learning material on learning platforms, other methods of technology-based teaching were quite seldom. There are several reasons (before the pandemic) for the slow adoption of the use of digital systems for teaching by professors and lecturers (not only) in psychology. One reason could be the lack of systematic knowledge and skills to use digital media efficiently in university teaching. The academic disciplines, which deal with the technological application of multimedia learning research, are educational technology (ET) and its sub-discipline instructional design (ID). Both are informed by instructional psychology and partly by computer science but being technological disciplines ET and ID normally do not just immediately apply results of psychological basic research. Technological statements need always to be specifically tested concerning side effects and the influence of moderating variables sometimes not taken into account by basic research. Criteria for the value of technological statements are not truth and reliability but the efficiency of problem-solving (Herrmann, 1979a, b; Bunge, 1998).

## Purposes and Rationale

This chapter tries to point out and to discuss efficient possibilities of technology-enhanced psychology teaching and learning structured by an ID framework model (DO ID model). After a short glance backward on ID as a discipline, a framework ID model is introduced which structures the presentation and discussion of the different facets of instructional design for technology-enhanced psychology teaching and learning. It should be made clear that instructional design is always a process of a series of interdependent *design decisions*, preferably based in general on theoretically based empirical findings and on the findings of thorough analyses concerning the specific conditions of the special case of conveying specific content to a specific group of people in a specific context. Being a framework model, the ID model focuses on aspects to be considered in the design; recommendations for specific design strategies can be found in specific ID models.

## Design Issues and Approaches

Although educational psychologists did research on teaching and learning since the beginning of the discipline more than 100 years ago, the development of educational or instructional technology was not part of the research programs for a long time. Educational (instructional) technology in its infancy was mostly technology, i.e., the focus has been on the use of audiovisual technical devices (Saettler, 1990) in education. This lasted in general the image of educational (instructional) technology for the public, but it does not correspond to the self-image of the discipline whose most important part is instructional design (ID). When ID started to get a technological academic discipline in the 1960s, theories and models were not at all concerned with the teaching and learning with computers or other media.

The AECT defined the discipline as "[...] the theory and practice of design, development, utilization, management, and evaluation of processes and resources for learning" (Seels & Richey, 1994).

One reason ID became more and more associated with the use of computer technology could be the permanent need to meticulously design computer-supported formats of teaching, while classroom teaching allows improvisation and many (experienced) teachers do not seem to like precise planning of their lessons.

Based on and inspired by theoretical approaches and models of Gagné and Briggs (1979); Morrison, Ross, and Kemp (2004); Smith and Ragan (2005); Klauer (1985); and Oser and Baeriswyl (2001), the author and his co-operates developed a framework ID model aimed to provide an orientation especially for practitioners designing multimedia-based learning environments. The model does not prescribe or proposes fixed paths to build technology-enhanced teaching units but emphasizes facets to be considered in making design decisions allowing large spaces for instructional creativity. We called it decision-oriented ID model (DO ID model).

## Decision-Oriented Instructional Design (DO ID) Model

The DO ID model (Fig. 1) is a framework model developed over the last 14 years (Niegemann, et al., 2008) to support instructional design by providing sound scientific information to make efficient ID decisions.

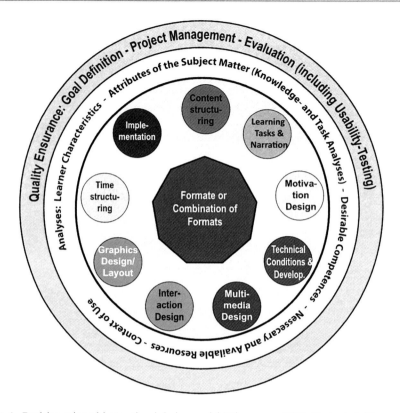

**Fig. 1** Decision-oriented instructional design model (Niegemann, 2020; Korbach & Niegemann, 2020)

The model represents three areas of instructional design: (1) A goal perspective and measures to ensure an appropriate standard of quality (external shell); (2) suitable procedures to analyze the needs, the relevant conditions, and the context of the planned instructional programs (second shell); and (3) the fields of concrete decisions to be made by instructional designers. As a framework model, DO ID could not be seen as concurrent to specific ID models (e.g., 4C/ID model, van Merriënboer, & Kirschner, 2018), instead it shows what aspects of design decisions should be considered and refers to relevant research findings.

Inside the two shells of the model, there are ten fields representing categories of decisions to be made in any instructional design process. The field in the very middle of the model represents the decision for a format, sub-formats, or a combination of formats. Formats are more or less schematic ways to convey the subject matter, e.g., e-lectures, webinars, computer-supported collaborative learning, serious games, explain videos, simulations, etc. The decision for a specific format, or a combination of formats, is the first decision, and many other decisions are swayed by it. The course of the further decisions is mostly not linear, many decisions and their respective consequences interact.

## Analyses

### Analysis of the Addressees: Needs

Generally, essential features of the addressees should be assessed. In case of psychology students at universities, there is a relative homogeneous group concerning prior knowledge, cognitive abilities, and motivation. In cases of psychology courses in further education prior knowledge, the motivation to enroll in the course and attitudes toward the subject matter and the teaching method should be assessed.

### Analysis of the Subject Matter

Teaching psychology as an academic domain comprehends theoretical knowledge but also procedural knowledge and strategic knowledge. Theoretical knowledge comprehends knowledge on relationships between concepts, including factual knowledge and conceptual knowledge.

Procedural knowledge is more differentiated concerning the structure of the abilities and skills, and it seems often not clearly separable from theoretical knowledge. Necessary competencies comprise developing hypotheses for research or diagnosing, designing empirical studies, developing and selecting tools and instruments for empirical studies (questionnaires, tests) or clinical use, application of tools and instruments, conducting statistical analyses, requiring statistical background knowledge, as well as the practical use of statistics software or even basic abilities in programming (e.g., R). The instructional challenges result not from the structure of the subject matter but from the pedagogical and instruction-specific relationships between the elements of the content.

Apart from the academic instruction, teaching clinical or counseling issues implies conveying behavioral skills ("soft skills") concerning the complete interaction with patients or clients.

### Analysis of the Resources

This step requires an alignment of the required and the available resources. Resources comprehend money, space, hard- and software tools, time, and competencies of colleagues or co-operates. Except for the payment of the staff involved, money is also needed to pay missing material, travelling, etc. Any ID project has to compare the available resources and the ones required. Shortage concerning resources constraints decision options.

## Formats

If there are no a priori decisions by principals, almost any instructional design process starts with a decision concerning the format of the instruction. Traditional theoretical content, especially overviews or introductions, are often conveyed via lectures. Deepening or consolidation of the subject matter could be possible by practicing self-regulated learning via reading texts and writing essays. There are also practical exercises concerning skills and the linking of theory and practice by working on more or less authentic tasks. Technology-based instruction contains a series of formats which partly are trials to fulfill the instructional functions of traditional formats, partly they are designed to optimize or enhance classical formats. To classify formats (originally named "models") systematically from an instructional psychology point of view, W. Schnotz and a group of colleagues and co-operates proposed a de- and re-construction of formats describing and analyzing them by typical facets (dimensions) Schnotz et al. (2004, 76 f.):

Facets (dimensions) relevant for learning as construction of representatives

- Organization of information (canonical – problem-based structure)
- Level of abstraction (decontextualization – contextualization)
- Use of knowledge (explication – application)

Facets (dimensions) relevant for learning as increasing participants and control of the learning process

- Locus of control (external regulation – self-regulation)
- Direction of channel (one-way – two-way communication)
- Mode of activity (receptive – productive)

Four more facets seem relevant to analyze and differentiate formats 15 years later:

- Social organization (individual learning – collaborative learning)
- Time structuring (singular units – sequence of connected units)
- Relation to real life (fictional – near to real)
- Kind and size of the device respective the display

The defining features of the different formats provide indications which format could be preferred depending on the learning objectives. Easy to grasp basic knowledge may be conveyed by video-lectures (with a possibility to ask questions via a forum), whereas complex topics which can be discussed under different views would need a format with bi-directional communication

A list of common formats in university and company education comprehends

- *Web-lectures, E-lectures:* records of normal lectures in classrooms or lecture rooms presented after the application of post-production techniques via streaming servers.
- *Mini-lectures:* E-lectures recorded by the trainer or professor at the desktop at home or in a studio, mostly much shorter than the conventional 45/60 or even 80/90 min; education companies offer the format in the context of MOOCs (massive open online courses) in many teaching subjects, including psychology.

- *Tutorial programs:* classical computer-based trainings, comprehending written and/or spoken texts, pictures, short videos or animations, and quizzes or other kinds of assessment.
- *Online-seminars, webinars:* Synchronous or asynchronous seminars; groups of learners present and discuss knowledge together.
- *Simulations:* Use of models of a section of reality to learn by doing and/or problem-solving and exercising complex skills riskless, sometimes supervised by a trainer.
- *Serious games:* Kinds of simulations containing features of games but designed to foster learning. Learning tasks in serious games are often wrapped into more or less fictitious stories.
- *Goal-based scenarios:* Kind of game-like simulation of a complex task; conveying information and requiring decisions by the learners, followed by feedback as natural consequences. Different from serious games, there should be no elements which are not closely related to the subject matter;
- *Computer-based collaborative learning (CSCL):* Collaborative learning with learners connected via a computer network instead of sitting in the same room. Often the collaboration is "scripted," i.e. there is some guidance for the learners concerning their tasks.
- *Problem-based learning; case-based learning*: Learners solve problems or work on realistic cases in virtual situations; e.g., in clinical training a virtual patient is presented and the learners have to make a diagnosis or to decide for therapeutically measures
- *Explaining videos*: Short videos explaining clearly a fact or a situation, often using cartoon-like drawings.

Hybrid formats are

- *Flipped classroom/inverted classroom:* Information is provided via video-lectures to follow at home, but come together physically to discuss or to work practically hand-in-hand
- *Performance support systems:* Combination of short instructions (different formats), help system, and supporting tools (e.g., prepared Excel sheets, templates, questionnaire items) (Rosenberg, 2018)
- *Multimedia-assisted self-learning (MASL):* Self-regulated learning with texts or other sources, guided by an application program with hints, guidelines, self-assessment tasks, and feedback

The list is not complete and there are some overlapping and fluent transitions. Serious games and goal-based scenarios will probably even in near future play no role in psychology teaching practice due to high costs of development.

Criteria for the selection of a suitable format could be (a) the matches of the above described facets, (b) characteristics of the respective content, and (c) the desired learner activities in the context of different learning tasks. This will be discussed later.

## Content Structuring

The structuring of the content follows often common textbooks. A major decision concerns always the *general instructional strategy*, i.e., the choice between an inductive (from the specific to the general) or deductive strategy (from the general to the specific). For *sequencing* decisions, the work of Reigeluth (1999) may be a fruitful guide. Considerations concerning *segmentation* are especially necessary if the format decision is for mini-lectures or micro-learning: How much information should be packed in one mini-lecture of, e.g., 15 min and how much on one page? How much in a micro-learning unit of 5 min? If learners use small displays and the displayed information can be controlled in advance by using an authoring system supporting features like fluent transition, the displayed portions of content should not be left to chance.

## Learning Tasks and Narration

Understanding theories and methodological relationships are common learning tasks in most psychology courses. The more application oriented the subject matter is, the more practical (procedural) are the learning tasks and require interactive design.

Psychologists know of the important role of stories (Schank, 1990) for recall; technology-based instruction allows support by pictures, animations, and short videos. Even very short stories can be supportive if they are suited to get the attention of the learners and have them actively deal with the topic. Explaining videos including simple stories have been shown to be successful in company learning and could be generated quite easily even without excellent drawing skills (Zander, Behrens, & Mehlhorn, 2020).

## Technical Aspects

For many professors and lecturers (not only) in psychology, a first question willing or forced to change the format of their teaching from the familiar face-to-face lectures, exercises, and seminars to online formats due to the pandemic regulations referred to the technical possibilities and resources. The origin of question mostly is "how can I use (which) technology to do my teaching as usual," i.e., the focus is understandably on the conservation of the familiar teaching methods, just by using technology.

The basic technical equipment consists of a desktop computer, at least a laptop. Most current computers have a built-in webcam and a microphone. While built-in webcams are often good enough to provide the image of the lecturer, the built-in microphones are mostly not sufficient for teaching tasks. Even rather cheap external microphones or headsets make a much better job. If pictures from printed material or physical material should be demonstrated a document camera could be useful investment. Separate loudspeakers could also be advantageous, although the light should not be neglected. Additional LED lights could avoid backlight or hard shadow effects in the face of the instructor. If the normal background of the workplace should not be seen by the learners, a blue (or green) screen could be used to show an individually selected or corporate identity compliant background picture. Some software products produce the same effect by AI technic.

The required software equipment depends partly on the format decision: In case of home or desktop made (mini-)lectures for asynchronous presentation, a recording software is required. Cost-free products are available (e.g., OBS) as well as commercial recording and production software (e.g., Camtasia, Capture). These software products allow records of the computer display (or a defined part of it) along with a picture of the speaker and the tone. The records offer possibilities of post-production (cutting, inserting assets like intros or outros, videos, etc.) and the record can be rendered into different formats (e.g., avi., .wmv, .mov, .mp4). Recording a sequence of slides with the spoken explanations of the instructor is also possible with common presentation software (e.g., Microsoft PowerPoint, Apple Keynote), including the production of a video, but without the speaker's picture.

To organize synchronous online-lectures, a video conferencing system is necessary. Probably all universities and most schools and education companies today have one or more conference systems licensed, e.g., Zoom, Teams, Webex, Adobe Connect, GoToMeeting, and Vitaro.

There rather small differences in the functionalities of these software. Helpful are

- Opportunities for participants to (virtually) put ones hand up
- The possibility to assign small groups of learners into different breakrooms to collaborate on a task
- Different opportunities for feedback during or after the end of a presentation
- The visibility of all participants during a session
- Chat functions

In case of the decision for the production of classical e-learning units (sequences of text, speech, pictures, animations, quizzes, and interactive work on tasks and problems with more or less rich feedback), an authoring system is necessary (e.g., Adobe Captivate, Articulate, Lectorate, iSpring). Authoring software allows to put all the categories of information presentation as well as some interactivity on the screen, and the pace of learning is mostly self-regulated by learners.

To offer all kinds of instructional presentations, a learning platform (learning management system, LMS) is essential. Widespread systems (e.g., Moodle, Canvas, Adobe Captivate Prime, easyLMS, NeoLMS; in Germany Ilias, OLAT) are quite similar concerning most functions. The LMS offer functionalities to present information in different formats:

- Discussing subject matter or other topics in forums
- To upload and download instructional materials
- To upload assignments
- To structure the evaluation and the grading of assignments

- To insert links to libraries
- To send e-mails or messages to all or a part of the participants
- To administrate the roles and rights of teachers, tutors, learners, etc.

Most LMS are compatible with worldwide accepted norms like SCORM (sharable content object reference model), LOM (learning objects metadata), or xAPI, and compliant learning programs are therefore interchangeable.

If images or photos should be digitally processed, changed, adapted, or optimized before included in an instructional unit, some kind of image processing software is required, e.g., GIMP (free), Photoshop, or Affinity.

Virtual reality (VR), augmented reality (AR), or mixed reality (MR) is already used for psychological research (Foreman, 2009); applications to use the technology are proposed in the same paper. Meaningful uses could be in clinical trainings or in observation trainings (e.g., in educational psychology, psychology of sports, organizational psychology).

## Multimedia Design

Designing e-learning raises questions on efficient ways to combine different codes. As research on these questions is well known in (educational) psychology since about 30 years and easily to get accessible, the practical recommendations derived from this research must not be outlined here (see Plass, Moreno, & Brünken, 2010; Mayer, 2021).

## Motivational and Emotional Design

Similar to multimedia design research, the foundations of motivational and emotional psychology could be assumed to be known to psychologists. Technological-oriented instructional theories and models concerning concrete ways to design motivating learning units or to optimize affects and mood of learners may be a domain rather familiar to instructional psychologists. Surveys of instructional design research in this area are provided by Keller and Deimann (2018) and Um et al. (2012).

## Interaction Design

Interaction design refers to design decisions concerning learner actions or activities on the one hand and the actions or activities of the technical system on the other hand. In many e-learning products, interactivity is actually quite poorly shaped. Learners are allowed to jump around between parts of a course, take quizzes or solve other tasks with drag and drop or filling in texts, and get rather simple feedback. There are many more learners' actions and much more specific and adaptive reactions by the system possible: Information-rich feedback (Narciss, 2008, 2020) includes feedback based on an analysis or diagnoses of the causes of failures, providing information and explaining why an answer is not correct. Learner's question asking is scarcely offered. There are several possibilities to realize question asking (Graesser et al., 1993): selecting from frequently asked questions or filling in domain specific "question stems" by drag and drop. Examples of question stems are "What is the cause of X?", "What is the result of the combination of X and Y?", "How do X and Y depend?". X and Y are gaps to be filled in by meaningful concepts from the relevant domain. Even asking (simple) questions in natural language could be offered without using AI technology. For many cases, the analysis of relevant key words by simple snippets of programming could be sufficient.

Theoretical models of interaction design have been proposed by Domagk, Schwartz, and Plass (2010) and Niegemann and Heidig (2020).

The analysis of learner input or tracking learner behavior could also be used as the basis for adaptive instruction. Depending on learners' behavior (navigation, clicking, keyboard input), additional or alternative information could be offered, or a different learning path could be generated (Ifenthaler & Drachsler, 2020; Kögler, Rausch, & Niegemann, 2020).

A rather seldom used interactive format are interactive videos: The learners' task is to detect features, moves, and patterns in a video. If a learner detected something, he or she clicks on the screen (if relevant on the location of the specified thing or person), the video stops, and a window opens requesting a description or explanation referring to the observation task. There are several examples in teaching psychology such an interactive video could fit. Another version of interactive videos shows an episode and requires the learner to make a decision deputizing for a character in the video. Depending on the decision (multiple choice), the video shows immediately or later the consequences of the decision as feedback.

Realization of more complex interaction requires more demanding authoring software or programing. Unfortunately, most current authoring systems refrain from the use of variables and capabilities to even simple programming. With such a system, it is no longer possible to address learners by their names, to compute numbers, to diagnose failures, etc.

## Time: Time Allocation

Carroll's model of teaching (1963; 1989) focuses on time as an important predicting variable in learning and instruction. Despite empirical evidence for successful technological application in the context of Bloom's mastery learning (Slavin, 1990), the control of time seems to play a rather minor role in instructional practice (schools, universities) and research today. Learning with digital technologies raises the question, how long information can be received without break until depletion respective a markable decrease in attention arises. This question is also relevant for usual teaching, but there are normally fixed organizational conditions (45, 60, 90 min for one unit) which have not to be observed if lectures are held online and offered asynchronously.

The question what length off a video lesson is optimal seems not easy to be answered. Obviously, there is a bunch of variables influencing the endurance of attention and information processing (Bradbury, 2016; Wilson & Korn, 2007).

Learning motivation, interest, physical resp. physiological state (tiredness, depletion), and features of the presentation (comprehensibility, enrichment, size, and contrast of the display) could have an impact.

Rather short lectures (mini-lectures: 10–20 min) could be a solution but raise further questions: what is the optimal length of pauses between the online lectures? Will longer time-distance and/or the kind of activities during breaks between the mini-lectures have an impact on the learning efficiency?

## Graphics Design: Layout

The most used presentation software for the academic teaching of psychology or other social sciences is PowerPoint or similar products. Multimedia presentations accompanying lectures, exercises, and seminars contain mostly written text and pictures. To be effective, common principles and criteria of graphics design and layout should be considered, even if divergent results from multimedia learning research sometimes still inhibit to express clear recommendations. Besides the huge corpus of multimedia learning research, there are traditional principles applied daily by graphics designers producing newspapers, commercial ads, and other written material (for an overview: Seidl 2020). The same criteria are applicable for e-learning presentations produced with authoring systems at least as long as we miss empirically based guidelines.

Even the use of technology in traditional university teaching (e.g., PowerPoint, electronic blackboards) requires some basic knowledge and skills to select appropriate sizes and styles of fonts as well as combinations of colors, etc.

## Implementation

Different from situations in the past when the implementation of digital instruction and learning in organizations and companies often required a lot of time and negotiations (Fishman & Penual, 2018), the digital learning innovations forced by the pandemic made e-learning and the use of instructional technology known in almost all areas. So, the problems to introduce new technologies can be expected to decrease considerably. Nevertheless, all stakeholders should be involved into the implementation strategy, and the information policy should be adapted to the specific needs and interests of the target group.

## Suitable E-Learning Formats for Psychological Contents

Due to the fact that many teachers acquired skills and abilities to design and develop e-learning sessions technically, there will probably be more online-teaching in psychology courses in the future then before the pandemic, but offline teaching formats will again dominate the teaching.

### Online-Lectures: Mini-lectures

Online or hybrid formats are especially suitable for content which changes only slowly, e.g., statistics and other methodological subject matter. The availability of mini-lectures in methodology courses could be advantageous in combination with exercises and formats of instruction and learning: Lectures could often not be synchronized with the progress in study projects of students, e.g., the computation of sample sizes is needed rather early in a term or study year, when students plan their projects, but it is taught systematically some weeks later. If all mini-lectures of a course are available from the beginning, and any time students can learn some content just in time they need it.

### E-seminars (Webinars)

A variation of the "flipped classroom" format could require students to produce their presentations as videos which are uploaded to the learning management systems a couple of days in advance of the final discussion. Experiences of the author during pandemic times especially in case of block seminars at two universities showed the students appreciated this format and agreed to use it further in normal times.

### Simulations

For more than 20 years, the use of simulation (e.g., case-based learning) has proven its worth in teaching different domains of medicine. Similar simulation environments are possible and, in some cases, already realized for psychology teaching (McMinn, 2009; Cleland, 2017; Chen, Kong, & Wei, 2020). For example, avatars representing patients or clients could be interviewed, and in combination with virtual results of tests, observations, or neuropsychological data (e.g., fMRT), students can learn diagnostics (psychotherapy/clinical psychology). Other applications are possible in social psychology (e.g., decision theory experiments) or organizational psychology. Serious games (games for learning) are technically a kind of simulation. In some psychology domains, simulation games concerning decision-making in complex situations had been used even 40 years ago (Dörner et al., 1983) for research and later for diagnostics (as part of assessment centers). A special kind of game for learning represents the format "goal-based scenarios" (Schank et al., 1999; Zumbach

2002). Actually, the use of simulations and games in everyday university teaching today is rather seldom; the development of appropriate games, simulations, or goal-based scenarios for learning is quite expensive.

## Videos: Interactive Videos

In teaching developmental psychology, the use of videos is usual, and a lot of material is easily available. This material is mostly used to demonstrate child behavior. Advanced technology has been developed for the systematic analysis of individual and group behavior in sports (Wilson 2008) (partly including the possibility of annotations into videos) and can be used in all domains where observation is part of the educational program (e.g., http://www.dartfish.com).

## Augmented Reality (AR)/Virtual Reality (VR)/Mixed Reality (MR)

Virtual reality generates 3D graphic environments which create in users impressions of being physically present in a virtual world and allows them to interact there with objects, characters, or persons in real time. Even if there are proposals to use VR in psychology (Foreman, 2009), the use of this technology in teaching is not (yet) usual.

Augmented reality allows to superimpose the natural visual perception by virtual images or texts to show hidden features or processes or to enrich the perceived environment by explanations or guidelines. Mixed reality combines the possibilities of VR and AR (Winn and Jackson 1999).

## MASL Multimedia-Assisted Self-Regulated Learning

A practicable way to combine self-regulated learning from texts and necessary guidance can be realized by a format invented first by the German expert of physics pedagogy Klaus Weltner in the 1970s, called "integrating guidance programme" (Weltner & Wiesner, 1973; Weltner, 1975). The idea is to guide learners in working with textbooks by proposing selected paragraphs to read, followed by quizzes or self-tests with feedback commentaries recommending or assigning re-reading or alternative presentations. While the method could be shown successful in university physics education, it was purely text based at that time, and getting feedback was somewhat uncomfortable and less adaptive. Multimedia guidance programs, available on tablets or smartphones, containing adaptive testing and rich feedback, could revitalize this format.

## Conclusion, Challenges, and Current Trends

There are many ways to foster and enhance teaching and learning psychology by (digital) technology. Most forms of application of digital technology is not specific to psychology, but as in other domains the efficiency of the use depends on the matching of the learning prerequisites of the learners and the features of the subject matter as well as the quality of the presentation. Educational technology can support the presentation of subject matter by making features or processes more salient or visible, allowing riskless learners' actions and experiences and allows flexibility of the instructional process in time and location. Collecting individual experiences with teaching psychology using digital technology could lead to new hypotheses concerning instructional technology not only in the domain of psychology. Technological research may differ in several aspects from mainstream nomological psychological research. External validity and criteria of efficiency play a greater role, and quasi-experimental methodology cannot longer be viewed as the stepchild of empirical research; new approaches (Reichardt, 2019) may provide the means for appropriate research design. After about 30 years of investigating mainly cognitive variables in multimedia learning, questions concerning the role and the impact of affective responses to information learners perceive in multimedia learning environments. Another challenge in technology-enhanced psychology teaching and learning will probably be the use of artificial intelligence-supported learning environments. Especially digitally conveyed subjects like statistics, diagnostics, etc. which change rather slowly learning analytics (Ifenthaler & Drachsler, 2020) could support adaptive learning. Other possible AI applications in psychology learning comprehend the simulation of patients in clinical situations and simulations of students in classrooms. Last but not least a renaissance of the use of simulation models (not only in cognition) for research and instruction (Dörner et al., 1983; Anderson, 1983, 1990) could change psychology learning in higher education.

## Recommended Further Readings

- Reiser, R. A. (2018). What field did you say you were in? Defining and naming our field. In R. A. Reiser & J. V. Dempsey (Eds.), *Trends and Issues in Instructional Design and Technology* (4th ed., pp. 1–7). New York: Pearson.
  *This contribution shows and discusses definitions of educational technology and instructional design as well as their change over time.*
- Merrill, M. D. (2002). *First principles of instruction.* Educational Technology Research and Development, 50(3), 43–59.
  *Probably one of the most cited articles in instructional design by one of the "founding fathers" of the discipline. A trial to summarize basic results of empirical research in instructional research for practise.*
- Reigeluth, C. M., Beatty, B. J., & Myers, R. D. (Eds.). (2017). *Instructional-Design Theories and Models* Volume IV. New York, London: Routledge/Taylor & Francis.
  *This is the 4th (and up to now the last) volume of a series of fundamental papers on instructional design. While the first volume about 40 years ago provided an overview over the most relevant theories and models of that time, volume 2 (1999) shows the progress in ID research and the development in the late 1990s, claiming a new paradigm of ID theories in the Information age. The purpose of the 3rd volume (2009) is a proposal to unify the different approaches*

in ID by building a common knowledge base and a common use of terms. The 4th volume takes a broader perspective and discusses what the authors call a "learner centered paradigm of education".
- Spector, J. M. (2016). *Foundations of educational technology: integrative approaches and interdisciplinary perspectives* (2nd ed.). New York: Routledge.

  *One of the best textbooks to get a comprehensive introduction into the field of learning and teaching from an application (i.e. technology) point of view. The book shows different approaches of the sciences of learning and theoretical as well as practical perspectives, both with example applications.*
- Domagk, S., Schwartz, R., & Plass, J. (2010). Interactivity in multimedia learning: An integrated model. Computers in Human Behavior, 26, 1024–1033.

  *Interactivity is a basic feature of technology-based learning environments. The authors deliver an integrated model to clarify the concept of interactivity including the user, the learning environment, and a system of connections and concepts that together make up interactivity. The model can help inform research, discussion, and design decisions on interactive multimedia instruction.*
- Keller, J. M., & Deimann, M. (2018). Motivation, volition, and performance. In R. A. Reiser & J. V. Dempsey (Eds.), *Trends and Issues in Instructional Design and Technology* (4th ed., pp. 78–86). New York: Pearson.

  *Keller's ARCS-model is one of the most successful dedicated ID models: It focuses on possibilities to initiate, to foster and to maintain the motivation of learners. Developed and evaluated since more than 50 years it has been shown helping instructional designers to find appropriate means to create motivating learning environments.*
- Plass, J. L., & Kaplan, U. (2016). Emotional Design in Digital Media for Learning. In S. Y. Tettegah & M. Gartmeier (Eds.), *Emotions, Technology, Design, and Learning* (pp. 131–161). Amsterdam/Boston: Elsevier/Academic Press.

  *Emotional design is an emergent aspect of ID research and development. Much earlier research focused on cognitive processes and outcomes and neglected affective responses to the information learners perceive. This chapter presents basics of learning and emotions and develops an integrated cognitive affective model of learning with multimedia (ICALM).*
- van Merriënboer, J. J. G., & Kirschner, P. A. (2018). Ten steps to complex learning. A systematic approach to four-component instructional design (3th ed.). New York: Routledge Taylor & Francis.

  *At least one of the most successfully applied specific instructional design models world-wide: an ID model dedicated to the design of cognitive complex learning tasks. Theoretically based on cognitive science theories and findings it meets the criteria of instructional psychology as well as the affordances of practitioners.*
- Graesser, A. C., Hu, X., & Sottilare, R. (2018). Intelligent Tutoring Systems. In F. Fischer, C. E. Hmelo-Silver, S. R. Goldman, & P. Reimann (Eds.), International Handbook of the Learning Sciences (pp. 246–255). New York: Routledge.

> From a computer science point of view, Intelligent Tutoring Systems (ITS) represent a gold standard in educational technology. They integrate different uses of Artificial Intelligent in education. This contribution describes the structure and the functions of Intelligent Tutoring Systems and discusses the challenges and limitations.

- McKenney, S., & Reeves, T. C. (2018). Conducting Educational Design Research (2nd ed.). New York: Routledge.

  > Research on instructional design and educational technology is different from research investigating basic relationships between variables. The authors present an approach which intertwines empirical investigation with systematic intervention development in the field and differentiate from older "action research" with rather weak methods.

## References

Anderson, J. R. (1983). *The architecture of cognition*. Cambridge, MA: Harvard University Press.

Anderson, J. R. (1990). *The adaptive character of thought (studies in cognition)*. New York: Taylor & Francis.

Bradbury, N. A. (2016). Attention span during lectures: 8 seconds, 10 minutes, or more? *Advantages in Physiology Education, 40*, 509–513.

Bunge, M. (1998). *Philosophy of science: From explanation to justification* (vol. 2). Boston, MA: Transaction Publishers: (1967, Springer)

Carroll, J. B. (1963). A model of school learning. *Teachers College Record, 64*, 723–733.

Carroll, J. B. (1989). The Carroll model. A 25-year retrospective and prospective view. *Educational Researcher, 18*(1), 26–31.

Chen, D., Kong, X., & Wei, Q. (2020). Design and development of psychological virtual simulation experiment teaching system. *Computer Applications in Engineering Education*. https://doi.org/10.1002/cae.22293

Cleland, J. (2017). Simulation-based education. The Psychologist (30, October). https://thepsychologist.bps.org.uk/volume-30/october/simulation-based-education (access february 2021)

Domagk, S., Schwartz, R., & Plass, J. (2010). Interactivity in multimedia learning: An integrated model. *Computers in Human Behavior, 26*, 1024–1033.

Dörner, D., Kreuzig, H. W., Reither, F., & Stäudel, T. (1983). *Lohhausen*. Huber, Bern/Stuttgart/Wien: Vom Umgang mit Unbestimmtheit und Komplexität.

Fishman, B., & Penuel, W. (2018). Design-based implementation research. In F. Fischer, C. E. Hmelo-Silver, S. R. Goldman, & P. Reimann (Eds.), *International handbook of the learning sciences* (pp. 393–400). New York: Routledge.

Foreman, N. (2009). Virtual reality in psychology. *Themes in Science and Technology Education, 2*(1–2). https://files.eric.ed.gov/fulltext/EJ1131318.pdf

Gagné, R. M., & Briggs, L. J. (1979). *Principles of instructional design*. New York: Holt, Rinehart & Winston.

Graesser, A. C., Person, N. K., & Huber, J. (1993). Question asking during tutoring and in the design of educational software. In M. Rabinowitz (Ed.), *Cognitive science foundations of instruction* (pp. 149–172). New York: Routledge. (eBook edition: 2020). https://doi.org/10.4324/9781315044712

Herrmann, T. (1979a). *Psychologie als problem. Herausforderungen der psychologischen Wissenschaft*. Stuttgart: Klett-Cotta.

Herrmann, T. (1979b). Pädagogische Pychologie als psychologische Technologie. In J. Brandtstädter, G. Reinert, & K. A. Schneewind (Eds.), *Pädagogische Psychologie: Probleme und Perspektiven* (pp. 209–236). Stuttgart: Klett-Cotta.

Ifenthaler, D., & Drachsler, H. (2020). Learning analytics. In H. Niegemann & A. Weinberger (Eds.), *Handbuch Bildungstechnologie* (pp. 515–534). Berlin, Germany: Springer.

Keller, J. M., & Deimann, M. (2018). Motivation, volition, and performance. In R. A. Reiser & J. V. Dempsey (Eds.), *Trends and issues in instructional design and technology* (pp. 78–86). New York: Pearson.

Klauer, K. J. (1985). Framework for a theory of teaching. *Teaching and Teacher Education, 1*(1), 5–17.

Kögler, K., Rausch, A., & Niegemann, H. (2020). Interpretierbarkeit von Logdaten in computerbasierten Kompetenztests mit großen Handlungsräumen. bwp@ Profil6. Berufliches Lehren und Lernen: Grundlagen, Schwerpunkte und Impulse wirtschaftspädagogischer Forschung. Hrsg. v. Karin Heinrichs, Kristina Kögler & Christin Siegfried, September 2020. https://www.researchgate.net/deref/https%3A%2F%2Fwww.bwpat.de%2Fprofil6_wuttke%2Fkoegler_etal_profil6.pdf

Korbach, A., & Niegemann, H. (2020). Microlearning via smartphones in VET for professional drivers: The case of securing cargo for international transport. In E. Wuttke, J. Seyfried, & H. Niegemann (Eds.), *Vocational education and training in the age of digitization. Challenges and opportunities* (pp. 183–201). Leverkusen: Barbara Budrich.

Mayer, R. E. (2021). *Multimedia learning* (3rd ed.). Cambridge/New York: Cambridge University Press.

McMinn, M. R. (2009). Ethics case-study simulation: A generic tool for psychology teachers. *Teaching of Psychology, 15*(2), 100–101. https://doi.org/10.1207/s15328023top1502_9

Morrison, G. R., Ross, S. M., & Kemp, J. E. (2004). *Designing effective instruction* (4th ed.). New York: Wiley.

Narciss, S. (2008). Feedback strategies for interactive learning tasks. In J. M. Spector, M. D. Merrill, J. van Merriënboer, & M. P. Driscoll (Eds.), *Handbook of research on educational communications and technology* (3rd ed., pp. 125–143). New York: L. Erlbaum Associates.

Narciss, S. (2020). Feedbackstrategien für interaktive Lernaufgaben. In H. Niegemann & A. Weinberger (Eds.), *Handbuch Bildungstechnologie* (pp. 369–392). Springer. https://doi.org/10.1007/978-3-662-54373-3_8-1

Niegemann, H. (2020). Instructional design. In H. Niegemann & A. Weinberger (Eds.), *Handbuch Bildungstechnologie* (pp. 95–152). Berlin: Springer.

Niegemann, H. M., & Heidig, S. (2020). Interaktivität und Adaptivität in multimedialen Lernumgebungen. In H. Niegemann & A. Weinberger (Eds.), *Handbuch Bildungstechnologie*. Berlin, Germany: Springer.

Niegemann, H. M., et al. (2008). *Kompendium multimediales Lernen*. Heidelberg, Germany: Springer.

Oser, F., & Baeriswyl, F. J. (2001). Choreographies of teaching: Bridging instruction to learning. In V. Richardson (Ed.), *Handbook of research on teaching* (4th ed., pp. 1031–1065). Washington, DC: American Educational Research Association.

Plass, J., Moreno, R., & Brünken, R. (Eds.). (2010). *Cognitive load theory*. Cambridge: Cambridge University Press.

Reichardt, C. S. (2019). *Quasi-experimentation: A guide to design and analysis*. New York: Guilford Press.

Reigeluth, C. M. (1999). The elaboration theory: Guidance for scope and sequence decisions. In C. M. Reigeluth (Ed.), *Instructional-design theories and models. A new paradigm of instructional theory* (pp. 425–453). Hoboken, NJ: L. Erlbaum Associates.

Rosenberg, M. J. (2018). Performance support. In R. A. Reiser & J. V. Dempsey (Eds.), *Trends and issues in instructional design and technology* (4th ed., pp. 132–141). New York: Pearson.

Saettler, P. (1990). *The evolution of American educational technology*. Englewood, Colorado: Libraries Unlimited, Inc.

Schank, R. C. (1990). *Tell me a story : A new look at real and artificial memory*. New York: Scribner.

Schank, R. C., Berman, T. R., & Macpherson, K. A. (1999). Learning by doing. In C. M. Reigeluth (Ed.), *Instructional-design – Theories and models. A new paradigm of instructional theory* (pp. 161–182). Mahwah, NJ: Erlbaum.

Schnotz, W., Eckhardt, A., Molz, M., Niegemann, H. M., & Hochscheid-Mauel, D. (2004). Deconstructing instructional design models: Toward an integrative conceptual framework for instructional design research. In H. Niegemann, D. Leutner, & R. Brünken (Eds.), *Instructional design for multimedia learning* (pp. 71–90). Münster, Germany: Waxmann.

Seels, B. B., & Richey, R. (1994). *Instructional technology: The definition and domains of the field*. Washington, D.C.: Association for Educational Communications and Technology.

Seidl, R. (2020). Grafikdesign: eine Einführung im Kontext multimedialer Lernumgebungen. In H. Niegemann & A. Weinberger (Eds.), *Handbuch Bildungstechnologie* (pp. 439–478). Berlin, Germany: Springer. https://doi.org/10.1007/978-3-662-54373-3_8-1

Slavin, R. E. (1990). Mastery learning re-reconsidered. *Review of Educational Research, 60*(2), 300–302.

Smith, P. L., & Ragan, T. J. (2005). *Instructional design* (3rd ed.). Hoboken, NJ: Wiley/Jossey-Bass.

Um, E. R., Plass, J. L., Hayward, E. O., & Homer, B. D. (2012). Emotional design in multimedia learning. *Journal of Educational Psychology, 104*(2), 485–498. https://doi.org/10.1037/a0026609

van Merriënboer, J. J. G., & Kirschner, P. A. (2018). *Ten steps to complex learning. A systematic approach to four-component instructional design* (3rd ed.). New York: Routledge Taylor & Francis.

Weltner, K. (1975). Das Konzept des integrierenden Leitprogramms - ein Instrument zur Förderung der Studienfähigkeit. *Informationen zur Hochschuldidaktik, H., 12,* 292–305.

Weltner, K., & Wiesner, H. (1973). Förderung von Selbstinstruktionstechniken im Hochschulunterricht durch integrierende Leitprogramme. Unterrichtswissenschaft(2/3), 111–120.

Wilson, B. D. (2008). Development in video technology for coaching. *Sports Technology, 1*(1), 34–40. https://doi.org/10.1080/19346182.2008.9648449

Wilson, K., & Korn, J. H. (2007). Attention during lectures: Beyond ten minutes. *Teaching of Psychology*, 85–89.

Winn, W., & Jackson, R. (1999). Fourteen propositions about educational uses of virtual reality. *Educational Technology* (July-August), 5–14.

Zander, S., Behrens, A., & Mehlhorn, S. (2020). Erklärvideos als format des E-learning. In H. M. Niegemann & A. Weinberger (Eds.), *Handbuch Bildungstechnologie* (pp. 247–258). Berlin, Germany: Springer. https://doi.org/10.1007/978-3-662-54373-3_8-1

Zumbach, J. (2002). Goal-Based Scenarios. Realitätsnahe Vorgaben sichern den Lernerfolg. In U. Scheffer & F. W. Hesse (Eds.), *E-Learning. Die Revolution des Lernens gewinnbringend einsetzen* (pp. 67–82). Stuttgart: Klett-Cotta.

# A Blended Model for Higher Education

## 57

M. Beatrice Ligorio, Francesca Amenduni, and Katherine McLay

## Contents

| | |
|---|---|
| Introduction | 1408 |
| Purposes and Rationale | 1409 |
| Design Issues and Approaches: The Blended Collaborative and Constructive Participation (BCCP) Model | 1410 |
| The Trialogical Learning Approach (TLA) | 1410 |
| Role-Taking (RT) | 1413 |
| The Jigsaw Method | 1415 |
| Evaluation: E-Portfolio and "Friend of Zone of Proximal Development" (ZPD) | 1418 |
| Core Findings and Current Trends | 1420 |
| Teaching and Learning Resources | 1422 |
| Challenges and Lessons Learned | 1423 |
| Cross-References | 1427 |
| References | 1427 |

### Abstract

The revised capability benchmark in professional psychology (APA, 2012) identified a set of core competencies for professional psychologists to develop during training. These competencies include professional identity, reflective practice, self-assessment, interpersonal relationship skills, and affective skills. In addition, psychologists' daily practice is increasingly shaped by the affordances of digital technologies. The global health emergency highlights the urgent need to advance professional psychologists' digital skills in different fields, from online

M. B. Ligorio (✉)
University of Bari, Bari, Italy
e-mail: mariabeatrice.ligorio@uniba.it

F. Amenduni
University of Rome 3, Rome, Italy

K. McLay
University of Queensland (AU), Brisbane, Australia

© Springer Nature Switzerland AG 2023
J. Zumbach et al. (eds.), *International Handbook of Psychology Learning and Teaching*,
Springer International Handbooks of Education,
https://doi.org/10.1007/978-3-030-28745-0_65

psychotherapy to school psychologists. The case study in this chapter explores the professional development of future human resources psychologists where a blended method – called Blended Collaborative and Constructive Participation (BCCP) – has been tested and developed.

This model allows students to directly experience several evidence-based methods for enhancing learning through digital technologies. The Trialogical Learning Approach improved the BCCP model by enriching evidenced-based techniques, such as Role-Taking and Jigsaw. The course is divided into two modules: Module 1 covers the course content, while Module 2 focuses on activities designed and performed in concert with agencies beyond the classroom.

Different methods are combined to assess students' learning outcomes and course effectiveness. In this chapter, we will describe how the e-portfolio is used and how introducing a specific role, called the friend of zone of proximal development, can support dyadic interaction that promotes self-direction toward new learning and professionalization.

While the impression may be that the course architecture is complex, the model we developed can be unpacked and recombined, depending on the specific contextual needs and affordances. We seek to make it clear that, to ensure the quality of a blended course, it is important to adhere to psycho-pedagogical bases. To do this, we provide several recommendations, including the importance of specific teacher training.

**Keywords**

Blended learning · Trialogical learning approach · Jigsaw · Role-Taking · Online collaboration · E-portfolio

## Introduction

The revised capability benchmark in professional psychology developed by the American Psychological Association (APA)[1] identified a set of core competencies for professional psychology that students should develop during their training. These competences include a focus on professional identity (Amenduni & Ligorio, 2017; Avedon & Grabow, 2010), reflective practice and self-assessment (Bruno & Dell'Aversana, 2017), interpersonal relationship skills (Pan, Zhong, Zhang, & Chang, 2020), and affective skills (Arifin & Ikhfan, 2018). Further to these competencies, the daily practice of psychologists is increasingly shaped by the affordances of digital technologies. Nothing illustrates this better than the global health emergency caused by COVID-19. From online psychotherapy (Erbe, Eichert, Riper, & Ebert, 2017) to school psychologists (Pham, 2014), the pandemic

---

[1] https://www.apa.org/ed/graduate/benchmarks-evaluation-system

has highlighted the critical need for professional psychologists in all fields to develop digital skills.

Technology is affecting content creation, social interaction, information acquisition, collaboration, and communication (Lenhart, Purcell, Smith, & Zickuhr, 2010; Thibaut, Curwood, Carvalho, & Simpson, 2015). Under this enormous pressure to innovate based on rapid technological diffusion, education is increasingly adopting digital tools to promote online spaces for learning. But this has not been a smooth or uniform process. Rather, online learning tools and approaches have been deployed in relation to variables such as socioeconomic context, teacher training, student attitudes and culture, organizational support, and many others. Therefore, educational research is constantly seeking to understand how to design effective educational tasks and how to use blended spaces productively. Indeed, blended learning has been a growing topic of research in higher education over the last decade (Bliuc, Ellis, Goodyear, & Piggott, 2011; Means, Murphy, & Baki, 2013; Sharpe, Benfield, & Roberts, 2006).

In a report published on the APA website (Naufel et al., 2018), five basic skill domains and 17 individual skills were identified as key to successful workforce preparation. These skills were identified through an analysis of online employment advertisements for psychologist positions. The so-called technological skills were included as one of the five basic skills, which were further operationalized as follows:

- *Flexibility/adaptability to new systems*: Be willing and able to learn and/or adapt to new computer platforms, operating systems, and software programs.
- *Familiarity with hardware and software*: Demonstrate competency in using various operating systems, programs, and/or coding protocols; troubleshoot technical errors; and use software applications to build and maintain websites, create web-based applications, and perform statistical analyses.

## Purposes and Rationale

One of the psychological professions shaped by the so-called digital transformation is *Work and Organizational Psychologists*. Recruitment, training, and development of human resources are among the traditional psychologist-based tasks which have been enhanced and transformed by digital technologies in the last 20 years (Egloffstein & Ifenthaler, 2017; Melanthiou, Pavlou, & Constantinou, 2015). Given this context, higher education (HE) programs aimed at the professional development of future human resources (HR) psychologists should include educational opportunities that enhance students' digital skills and literacy. We suggest that the case study presented in this chapter offers one way of achieving this goal, that is, a course in which technology is simultaneously the content and the method for teaching at a HE level. To demonstrate the value of this approach, we describe the course design and then provide an overview of the assessment tools, which not only evaluate the learning outcomes but also promote the digital skills that are arguably so critical in the contemporary context.

## Design Issues and Approaches: The Blended Collaborative and Constructive Participation (BCCP) Model

In this chapter, we propose the Blended Collaborative and Constructive Participation (BCCP) model we developed over more than 10 years of experimentation (Ligorio & Annese, 2010; Ligorio, Loperfido, Sansone, & Spadaro, 2011; Ligorio & Sansone, 2009; Sansone, Cesareni, Ligorio, Bortolotti, & Buglass, 2020). This model does not merely alternate between online and offline learning. Rather, there is cross-fertilization between online and face-to-face interactions. The first iteration of this model was introduced in 2005, and since then, several challenges have been considered in re-designing subsequent versions. Currently, the model divides the course into two modules, Module 1 (M1) covering the curricular content and Module 2 (M2) focusing on activities designed and performed in concert with companies operating in a field relevant for the course, for instance, e-learning companies or – for psychologists aiming to work in these fields – companies with human resources departments. Some psycho-educational techniques are included in this model, in particular, those that can be enhanced by the support of technology, such as Role-Taking (Cesareni, Cacciamani, & Fujita, 2016) and the Jigsaw method (Aronson & Patnoe, 2010). These techniques inspired the design of learning activities in the course.

In designing the BCCP method, several psycho-educational approaches were used as inspiration. Among those, the Trialogical Learning Approach (TLA) was particularly valuable. This approach worked as a practical and theoretical frame that enabled us to renew and adapt the psycho-pedagogical methods, such as Role-Taking (RT) and Jigsaw, to enrich the blended dimension of the model. In the following section, we describe the TLA in more detail and then explore how RT and Jigsaw were implemented by taking account of suggestions arising from TLA.

### The Trialogical Learning Approach (TLA)

The Trialogical Learning Approach (TLA) combines knowledge building theory (Scardamalia & Bereiter, 2006) and Engeström's concept of expansive learning (Engeström, 1999). Despite the differences among these theories, both agree that learning occurs when people collaboratively create knowledge artifacts. Paavola and Hakkarainen (2005, 2014) have proposed the term "Trialogical" to refer to those processes where people are collaboratively and systematically developing shared and real "knowledge objects." The Trialogical metaphor tries to overcome dichotomies between individual (monological) and social processes (dialogical) involved in learning (Sfard, 1998). In Trialogical learning settings, students collaboratively develop new objects of inquiry, such as knowledge artifacts, practices, ideas, models, and representations. Interaction is strongly supported when participants are committed to building Trialogical objects. People do not only dialogue with each other; rather, communication is directed toward and shaped by the shared object under construction. However, participation is not enough to achieve learning; people should have a common goal which directs their practices and actions. The work of the group is animated by the different versions of an object, and people adapt their actions to achieve the object's transformation.

The Trialogical metaphor can be understood as a continuum from dialogues to trialogues. Dialogues among people are ensured by *common ground* or what Wenger (2009) terms a *shared repertoire*, which provides a set of common concepts, language, and tools that support mutual understanding of the objects. The possibility to reshape and negotiate meanings of the shared repertoire comes very close to the idea of trialogues. The trialogic adds to the dialogic perspective an important focus on the objects built, which orient and shape both the dialogue and the processes necessary to build the objects. Paavola and Hakkarainen (2009) argue that from a Trialogical learning perspective, "people don't need to have complete agreement or shared understanding of these shared objects but these objects provide a concrete reference point which can then be collaboratively modified and clarified during the process" (p. 12).

The line between dialogue and trialogue is not clear cut because often dialogue and participation are strictly intertwined when realizing a Trialogical work. The main feature of the TLA is the focus on participation in the development of the shared object. TLA is strongly connected to the emergence of technology that can be used to transform intangible ideas into shareable digital artifacts. New technological trends, such as Cloud and Open-source, can promote collaborative work at a distance around shared objects. However, the use of technology is not enough to guarantee Trialogical processes. To transform existing pedagogical practices toward more Trialogical knowledge practices, we suggest six design principles (DPs), which characterize the general features of the TLA (Table 1).

**Table 1** The design principles (DP) defined by the TLA

| |
|---|
| DP1: Organizing activities around shared "objects." The central idea of TLA is that learning is organized around shared objects like conceptual artifacts, tangible products, and/or practices |
| DP2: Supporting interaction between personal and collective agency. The way in which people integrate their own personal and group work for developing shared objects by dividing labor and combining participants' expertise into the group's achievement |
| DP3: Fostering long-term processes of knowledge advancement. Learning and working around shared objects that do not have a specific deadline but are always considered improvable. Recognitions of the limits and indications for further improvements should be outlined |
| DP4: Emphasizing development through transformation and reflection between various forms of knowledge and practices. Knowledge could be converted from one form to another one, for instance, from a text to a map; from a list to a project; and from a draft prototype to a functioning object |
| DP5: Cross-fertilization of various knowledge practices across communities and institutions. TLA requires that learners solve complex authentic problem outside educational institutions. Hybridization among communities and practices can support these investigative learning processes |
| DP6: Providing flexible mediation tools. TLA requires appropriate technologies that help participants to create, share, and transform artifacts and practices |

TLA has been used in HE to reduce the gap between university education and the needs of a workforce in a knowledge society. Lakkala, Toom, Ilomäki, and Muukkonen (2015) compared benefits and challenges of three re-designed university course based on TLA. The results suggested that when professional working processes are used to design the courses, the shift from individual practice to collaborative outcomes supports greater success. The authors further suggest that teachers and trainers should create a meaningful, overarching object that can orient group assessment, drawing on authentic professional working processes rather than artificial collaboration activities.

The ideas and principles of the TLA are deeply embedded into the BCCP model. Techniques such as Role-Taking and Jigsaw, which were already implemented in the previous version, were redefined in the light of TLA suggestions. For instance, in M1, the DP1 of the TLA is applied by organizing the activities around the collaborative construction of a concept map. The map is conceived as a way to gather a collective answer to a question the teacher poses at the outset of the course. These questions are meant to challenge the sense of the course and to model students' thinking around critical argumentation, leading toward knowledge building.

The group activity and the interaction between individual and collective agency (DP2) are supported and structured by combining the Jigsaw technique and the RT (described in detail in 3.2 and 3.3), which allow participants to shift between individual and group dimensions. The maps developed by the groups could be reused as theoretical references to design the objects built in M2, fostering long-term processes of knowledge advancement (DP3). This is just one example of how the DPs of the TLA are implemented in M1. A full report is provided in Table 2.

In M2, corporate representatives from professional domains relevant to the course are invited to introduce their company via webinars or in person (depending on availability and preference). They describe the object they would like the students to participate in constructing it and provide the criteria they will use to assess the object and the group work. Each company nominates at least one tutor to maintain constant communication with the students throughout the M2. About halfway through M2, each group presents a first draft of the object to the whole course cohort. During this presentation, the audience provides feedback and the presenters draw on this feedback to finalize the object, which is displayed – again face-to-face – at the end of the module. This activity is designed to develop several skills such as public speaking and responsiveness to feedback, in the sense of both providing insightful comments and implementing the feedback received.

In Table 2, there is a summary of how the DPs are applied in our course, in both M1 and M2.

As already stated, the TLA opened up new ways of considering existing and familiar techniques, such as RT and Jigsaw. In the next section, we describe how these two techniques were implemented in both modules.

**Table 2** The six TLA design principles applied in M1 and M2 composing the BCCP model

| | |
|---|---|
| DP1 | M1: The teacher asks students to collaboratively design a map aimed at answering a general question about the course<br>M2: Companies introduce themselves and proposed to develop an object which is part of their core business. Students use different digital tools and interact with the companies, receiving specific feedback |
| DP2 | RT and the Jigsaw are combined to support the shift from individual to groups and vice versa<br>M1: Individually, students learn about the educational material assigned and then compare what they learned with other students who had the same material. Later, students are assigned to groups where each member has different study material<br>M2: Students are assigned to a specific company to develop the object required. During the building process, they also join groups comprised of students allocated to different companies to compare the work and provide reciprocal feedback |
| DP3 | M1: The materials created by the students are meant to be used in the M2 as theoretical bases for the construction of the objects commissioned by the companies<br>M2: Students consider how their objects could be further developed and placed into the market. Companies and students may decide to implement the changes outlined when the course is ended |
| DP4 | M1: Students are provided with educational materials in the format of chapters and papers. These materials can be transformed individually (for instance, individual reviews) or through a collaborative process (the conceptual map)<br>M2: Students use the knowledge acquired in M1, together with the instruction given by the company, into a first draft or prototype. In turn, these can be transformed into PowerPoint presentations, videos, or reports to present the objects<br>In both modules, each transformation is supported by reflective discussions via web forum |
| DP5 | M1: By studying the educational material, students enter the scientific world. To make this transition more effective, some contemporary authors of the material could be invited to discuss their articles or chapters with the students via web forums, emails, or social media platforms<br>M2: Entrepreneurs are invited (either face-to-face or remotely) to introduce their companies and the objects they would like the students to build. During the building process, students are exposed to professional practices because they are included in the professional groups made available by the company |
| DP6 | In both modules, many technological tools are used: An open-source learning management system (LMS), Google drive, LinkedIn, Padlet, WhatsApp, and doodle. In some cases, companies proposed other communication tool (e.g., Slack, Trello, Yammer) |

## Role-Taking (RT)

RT can be considered a specific type of peer collaboration (Fischer, Kollar, Stegmann, & Wecker, 2013). In education, a "role" is defined as a system of functions that students should assume when working in a group, to guide individual behaviors and regulate interactions among the group members (Cesareni et al., 2016). Covering a role implies being "associated with a position in a group with rights and duties toward one or more other group members" (Hare, 1994, p. 434). Research has shown that RT can promote individual responsibility and group cohesion, as well as positive interdependence (Strijbos & Weinberger, 2010). Taking a role facilitates the social dimension of group dynamics, such as group members' awareness of peer contributions and a group's overall performance (Strijbos, Martens, Jochems, & Broers, 2004). Role-Taking also supports collaborative knowledge building because the roles can be viewed as "multiple interpretive perspectives that conflict, stimulate, intertwine and be negotiated" in a community (Stahl, 2006, p. 4).

In the BCCP model, RT has been implemented by requiring each student to experience a series of roles, deliberately aligned with the course aims. The roles are outlined in detail at the outset of the course, including the tasks, the timing, the tools recommended, and the precise activities to be performed. Instructions are given face-to-face, and the role is initially taken up in the digital environment based on the belief that online, the screen can be a mediator to overcome shyness or embarrassment in public speaking.

Here are some examples of roles used in the course:

(i) E-tutor or leader. This student coordinates discussions and collaborative activities within the group, stimulates the participation of colleagues, and monitors deadlines. This role requires the student in charge to have a clear conception of the objectives of the group discussions and related tasks. The e-tutor is a temporary leader, using appropriate communication strategies to stimulate the group to be collaborative (Sansone, Ligorio, & Buglass, 2018).
(ii) The process supervisor. When taking on this role, students summarize the content and lead discussion in their groups. It is a metacognitive role, promoting the capacity to analyze and describe dynamics and discussion methods, acquiring and giving back to the group an overview of the discussions. The skills acquired in this role involve carefully reading the discussion, its management, and evolution, with the ultimate aim of giving directions about how to make the discussion more effective and attuned to knowledge building principles.
(iii) The researcher. This role supports the teacher's work by seeking additional educational documents and sources related to the topic under discussion. It is not uncommon, in fact, that the teaching materials provided by the teacher generate requests for clarification and/or more information. In this instance, the researcher has the specific task of satisfying the demands emerging during the discussion. Since this task is carried out mainly online, this role also promotes the capacity to identify reliable and reputable digital sources and make connections with material already provided by the instructor.

These are just a few examples of roles that can be designed and implemented online. Roles can be conceived both as a method and as a goal.

RT is also active in M2, although it is implemented in a more flexible way. The assumption is that, once the students have experienced the RT, they may internalize this strategy and take up the role autonomously. In addition to the roles already deployed in M1, companies may propose new roles taken from their actual organization charts (e.g., story-boarder, video-maker). RT in M1 gave an initial impression of how roles can support group work, which can be considered an accessible way to introduce professional roles. In M2, roles are more aligned with those in real professional contexts. Through this mechanism, students can approach professional roles gradually and with support.

As a method, roles are used to structure participation; as a goal, roles allow students to develop critical skills, teamwork, and a positive attitude toward the online experience (Edwards & La Ferle, 2003). For this reason, it is important to rotate roles, so that each student can experience the skills associated with the various roles. Furthermore, in our case, we also created a specific forum for each role where those students who have just completed a role can reflect upon their experience. Students describe their expectations of and fears about the role and how the role was activated and offer suggestions for the next student who will take on that role. This forum helps the newcomers avoid silly mistakes and advances the efficacy of the role.

## The Jigsaw Method

The term "Jigsaw" indicates a particular type of saw used for cutting pieces with rounded corners. This is a fitting metaphor to describe this educational strategy. In the original formulation proposed by Aronson (1978), Jigsaw is a group training and management technique where groups are formed, work separately, and are then broken down and re-formed. The procedure comprises the following steps:

(i) Brainstorming. The aim of the initial brainstorming is to stimulate interest in and curiosity about the topic proposed by the teacher. Post-it notes can be used in the classroom to be distributed to the participants, asking them to write down their own ideas or curiosities. If anonymity is desired, students can be asked not to sign the post-it. Anonymity is also possible online by using tools such as Padlet. This modality supports democratization of brainstorming, as all the contributions are treated equally, without being influenced by knowing who produced the notes.

(ii) Formation of the main concepts. This stage involves collective discussion – either online or face-to-face – around the topics that emerged during brainstorming, to identify the main themes. If post-it notes are used, these can be easily grouped together after placing them on a wall or a blackboard. The same is possible with Padlet or a web forum. In any case, we recommend that the teacher knows in advance how many groups to form and then identify the same number of thematic concepts. In this way, at the end of this step, a different theme can be assigned to each group.

(iii) Expert groups. After deciding which and how many thematic concepts will be addressed during the course, the expert groups are formed. At this stage, each participant chooses the topic to work on and, consequently, the group to participate in. Students could select a certain group because they recognize their own contribution to a specific theme or because they want to be part of a group formed by certain peers. In any event, letting students choose what group to join is a way to enhance motivation and interest. These groups will have to become experts on the topic assigned to them because they must teach the topic – in the next step – to a new group. This phase enhances involvement and increases responsibility-taking, as work done here will be the foundation for future collaborative work. Expert groups can produce a summary or critical text or draw up a scheme. Furthermore, because of the acquired expert knowledge, these groups elaborate on assessment tasks, which can be in the form of tests, questionnaires, games, etc., to be submitted to the whole class to verify the knowledge of the specific theme in which they are expert. Of course, elaboration on the assessment tasks is itself a learning moment and simultaneously makes students active participants in a task (the evaluation) from which they are normally excluded.

(iv) Jigsaw or learning groups. In this phase, expert groups are dissolved and new groups are formed, comprising at least one member from each of the previous groups. Participants in the Jigsaw groups must contribute by offering the "piece" on which they had worked in the expert groups. As a group product, students can create various objects: a conceptual map that captures the links between the content analyzed; a multimedia product such as blog, video, and interactive presentation; or a professional tool such as an observation grid or a questionnaire. Furthermore, these groups may collect and organize the evaluation materials elaborated on by the expert groups in the previous phase to build a unique and coherent tool.

(v) Comparison of products. If desired, this step can be added to support the creation of a collective work in which the products of each Jigsaw group are compared with a view to developing a single final product which captures and refines the various groups' work.

Within both expert and Jigsaw groups, students are required to take on the roles described in the previous paragraph.

In M1, the Jigsaw activity can be organized as follows. During the first week, the teacher divides the students into groups – called "expert" groups – of between four and 10 students. The teacher selects a range of study material corresponding to the number of students in the groups. All the material is introduced during an initial face-to-face lecture, which ends by negotiating a challenging research question to guide subsequent activities. The purpose of setting a research question is to avoid rote learning and trigger a progressive inquiry approach (Hakkarainen, 2003). Students download the learning materials from Google Drive and discuss these materials within expert groups via asynchronous environments, complemented by scheduled face-to-face discussions. For this activity, up to five days a week may be needed. Once the "expert" discussion ends, students are individually required to write a brief review, using a template provided by the teacher. In these reviews, students highlight content useful for answering to the research question. Once the reviews are ready, they are posted on Google Drive. The Jigsaw groups are then activated, and they compare and combine the various answers to the research question, gleaned through the reviews with the aim of creating a map, collaboratively designed using online tools (e.g., Google Drawing).

This activity again takes place via web forum, interspersed with scheduled face-to-face encounters.

In M2, students will replicate the same structure as M1 with a few differences. The content is different: M1 is adherent to the syllabus and covers the theoretical and practical information considered essential for understanding the course content. In M2, the content is driven by the knowledge and competencies required by the companies. Therefore, in M1, the expert groups studied the content provided by the instructor; in M2, expert groups are involved with a company. Furthermore, in M1, Jigsaw groups compared different educational content; in M2, Jigsaw groups examined and commented on the different objects commissioned by the companies. In this way, students can acquire a broad picture of educational content (M1) and of the companies' products (M2). Contrasting different cases can also support understanding of specific features that make a case distinctive (Schwendimann et al., 2015). These two processes – comparing and specifying – allow students to experiment with shifting between contextualized practice (in the expert group; working with a company) and a de-contextualized and broader integration of companies' knowledge practices (in the Jigsaw group).

Across the two modules, we also implemented informal discussions via web forum. These were intended to support a sense of belonging to a virtual community (Blanchard & Markus, 2002; Tonteri, Kosonen, Ellonen, & Tarkiainen, 2011). To this end, when groups are formed, they should give themselves a name. Searching for a name involves identifying commonalities and distinguishing features. Therefore, participants are encouraged to talk about themselves and build relationships.

A few more activities are included in the model for assessment purposes; these are described in the following section.

A synopsis of the internal structure of the two modules is reported in Fig. 1 and Fig. 2.

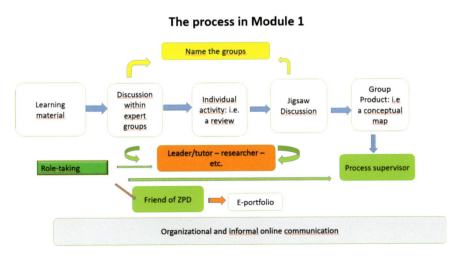

**Fig. 1** Synopsis of the internal structure of Module 1

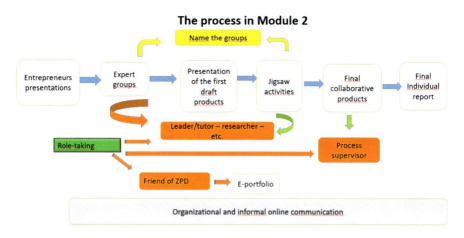

**Fig. 2** Synopsis of the internal structure of Module 2

## Evaluation: E-Portfolio and "Friend of Zone of Proximal Development" (ZPD)

In an innovative course such the one implemented using the BCCP model, assessment cannot follow the traditional format. This model encourages collaborative strategies, personal involvement, and reflexive strategies; therefore, these are the dimensions that need to be monitored and assessed. In our case, we developed a specific multidimensional assessment protocol where both the effectiveness of the group and the individual participation is assessed for each activity (Sansone & Ligorio, 2015). Learning outcomes are not necessarily useful indicators, because all the students who participated in our course received high scores based on the assessment received through the protocol and the product assessment. The way the course is structured, with so many activities and repetition of the modules' internal structure, makes failure very unlikely. Moreover, we consider the best learning outcome is that companies employ students who demonstrate potential. This means the BCCP model can actually increase professional opportunity and employability. Furthermore, we are interested in the processes activated by the BCCP model. In particular, we want to address the question of how to sustain and assess the soft skills advocated by APA (see the Introduction).

For these reasons, two tools are embedded into the BCCP model: the e-portfolio and a new role called the "friend of proximal zone of development" (ZPD).

E-portfolios are a purposeful aggregation of digital items – ideas, evidence, reflections, feedback, etc., – which "presents" evidence of learning and/or ability to a selected audience (Sutherland & Powell, 2007). This tool allows users to create a representation of the self, to gather evidence of personal development, and to describe the competencies achieved (Brown, 2015). In e-portfolios, students are required to tell a story about themselves in the form of self-narratives (Humpreys &

Brown, 2002) that include what they believe to be the most significant aspects of their history/biography as learners and aspiring professionals. E-portfolios are artifacts supporting transition to professional contexts. Akkerman and Bakker (2011) interpret the e-portfolio as a "boundary object" that supports connection and communication between different aspects of educational interaction, such as learning and professionalization.

In our case at the end of M1, students outline personal goals for M2. At the end of M2, students summarize the competencies acquired during the course, examine their initial expectations, and comment on them. The activities around the e-portfolio begin as soon the course starts. To familiarize them with the platform provided by the course, students are required to create personal e-portfolios, including anything personal they would like to share and their expectations of the course in general. At the end of M1, students select what they think best represents their performance during the module and then set their personal goals for M2. Our model suggests to initially (in M1) host the e-portfolio on a Learning Management System (LMS). Later (in M2), students are required to describe skills acquired, expectations not met or achieved, and goals for their professional life. In doing this, students are required to consider a wider audience than that of the course; they can do it by addressing the wider professional community of which they would like to be a part. In this case, LinkedIn was considered a suitable digital tool.

Furthermore, within their e-portfolio, students are required to select a peer and to nominate him/her as "friend of zone of proximal development" (ZPD), based on personal relationship and trust. The person covering this special role should monitor the activities in the e-portfolio and give suggestions for improvements. Clearly inspired by Vygotsky (1978), this role is crucial in supporting interaction and improving e-portfolio quality. Within the e-portfolio, a web forum is reserved for the dyad comprising the e-portfolio holder and her/his friend of ZPD. The implementation of this role allows animation of activities within the e-portfolio that would otherwise be independent or private activity.

Although the whole course was designed to support boundary crossing between university and professional competences, we believe that the e-portfolio is the place where such boundary crossing is made most visible. We assume that to cross-boundaries between university and workplaces, students need to renegotiate their identity positions (Hermans, 2013) by combining practical activities and self-reflectiveness.

Hermans' vision on the "self" is influenced by William James (1890) who considers the "self" not as a whole, but as consisting of multiple "selves" or "I-positions," depending on where people are or which role they assume at a particular point in time. For instance, a coach or counsellor may enter the life of a client as an external position in the self and may give, in a particular period of the client's life, a valuable contribution to his or her internal dialogues and self-reflections (Visser, 2016). In our case, we suggest that positions can be triggered by the various activities comprising the BCCP. Roles, for example, can be seen as tools that push participants to try out and, maybe, internalize positions connected to the roles.

Inspired by the polyphonic novel of Dostoevsky (1985), the self is conceived as comprising several characters who are not subordinate to the author but have their own voice, thoughts, and behavior. Each of these characters can have independent viewpoints, sometimes agreeing and at other times disagreeing with the author. They can tell their own story and are involved in dialogical relationships. The central theme in Hermans' theory (Meijers & Hermans, 2017) is that there is a dialogical relationship not only between the self and his (social) environment but also between different positions within the same person, for example, "I as student" and "I as professional." One must know the parts to understand the functioning of the self as a whole.

There is never a fixed set of positions; each person has a specific position-scenario, and this may evolve depending on experience and context. Therefore, considering the relevance of the TLA in our case, we defined three clusters of positions inhabiting the e-portfolios that developed during the course: monologic, dialogic, and trialogic. Monologic positions are internal positions (e.g., I think, I am a student, I want to...), dialogic positions concern the relationship between two or more positions (e.g., my colleague told me, the tutor said to us, our group), and trialogic positions consider the relationship between positions and a shared object.

## Core Findings and Current Trends

The applications of the BCCP model have been analyzed in many contexts. When applied to higher education, our main research interest was on the development of students' I-positions. To look at students positioning trajectories, we defined a grid of positions used to analyze positions emerging in M1 and M2. Table 3 displays the positions we defined, based on the content analysis of students' e-portfolio.

Each of these positions developed a unique pattern across the course (Amenduni & Ligorio, 2017; Ligorio, Amenduni, & McLay, 2019), and, when looking at the differences between M1 and M2 e-portfolios' positions, we found that Trialogical positions occurred more in the latter. A closer qualitative interrogation revealed that in M2, the objects were used by the students as *evidence* of their professional identity. The impact of the friend of ZPD is also significant. When comparing the first time this role was introduced with previous course iterations when this role was not assigned, we found that this role significantly promoted the emergence of professional I-positions (Impedovo, Ligorio, & McLay, 2018).

Boundary-crossing can be also studied and assessed by analyzing the features of the objects students built. These objects can be defined as boundary objects, since they support boundary crossing by fulfilling a bridging function and intersecting at least two communities – students and professionals, but also many other sub-communities involved, and several practices (Star, 1989). Boundary objects have different meanings in different social contexts but, at the same time, have a structure that is common enough to make them recognizable across these contexts (Akkerman & Bakker, 2011).

**Table 3** Grid of identity positioning categories used to analyze students' e-portfolios

| Positioning's cluster | Positioning | Description |
|---|---|---|
| Monologic positions (M) | Personal position | Personal emotions, ideas, attitude |
|  | Student position | I as student |
|  | Formal role | I as .... *[one of the roles assigned during the course]* |
|  | Professional position | I as skillful, oriented to professional role |
|  | Meta-positioning | Reflections about the current position |
|  | Past position | Positions in the past |
|  | Present position | Positions in the present |
|  | Future position | Positions in the future |
|  | Promoter position | Giving support and suggestions to another student |
| Dialogical positions (D) | Peer otherness | Explicit or implicit reference to other students |
|  | Teacher/tutors otherness | Explicit or implicit reference to professional tutors and teacher |
|  | Professionals otherness | Explicit or implicit reference to professional tutors |
|  | Shared object – Personal | Interaction between a student and the object |
| Trialogical positions (T) | Shared object – Intra-student groups | Interaction between students of the same group and the object |
|  | Shared object among student and future target | Reference to people that can re-use the shared object |

In our case, the objects proposed by companies are boundary objects creating bridges between academic and professional communities. Companies were asked to assess the final objects constructed with the participation of the students, based on their own criteria. We placed the criteria proposed by the companies into three categories: (i) criteria related to the intrinsic qualities of the object, that is, the extent to which the object is aligned with specific quality standards; (ii) criteria related to the process, or the extent to which the collaborative process of object creation was effective and efficient; and (iii) criteria related to the technical skills acquired by the students while building the object. Table 4 provides a summary of how many companies adopted these criteria in the last five years.

The criteria connected to the objects are most frequently used by the entrepreneurs. We suggest this indicates that entrepreneurs are primarily interested in the features the object can display as a product for the market. Entrepreneurs expect students to be able to consider such criteria and may also feel this is their main mission in participating to the course. The least used criteria (only one company) relate to technical skills. It is evident that companies do not consider it crucial to provide computer- or software-based skills. This type of capability changes rapidly, along with the arrival of new technologies and tools; therefore, they are considered to be self-taught skills that are always changing.

**Table 4** Criteria used by companies to assess the objects

| Criteria | Examples | Number of companies adopting the criteria |
|---|---|---|
| Related to the objects | • How engaging the object is<br>• Coherence with the target<br>• Reusability | 9 |
| Related to the process | • Internal communication within the group<br>• External communication with the company<br>• Realistic and achievable objectives | 5 |
| Related to the students' technical skills | • Video-making skills<br>• Planning<br>• Editing | 1 |

## Teaching and Learning Resources

The BCCP model requires the combined used of many digital tools. First, the course should be implemented in a Learning Management System (LMS) where the two modules can be easily visualized. Online environments supporting document sharing should be embedded into the LMS. These tools can be used not only to download and upload the educational material but also to share documents students are building collaboratively, for instance, Cloud tools (e.g., Google Drawing) that support the collaborative construction of the maps, required within M1.

Furthermore, the BCCP model creates regular opportunities for informal discussions, for instance, when groups are required to name themselves, or when students exchange impressions and recommendations about a role just completed or yet to be adopted. In these cases, students could be free to select tools for synchronous meetings (e.g., WhatsApp) or to use asynchrony tools, such as web forums. To plan the work and have a wide overview of the deadlines for the various activities, project management tools are recommended (e.g., Trello, Slack, or Yammer).

It is also suggested that teachers create an email list of students for general communication with the whole class.

Some activities may need to be preceded by brainstorming, for instance, when deciding the relevant concepts to be included into the maps. In these instances, we recommend using tools such as Padlet or Mentimeter.

Company presentations should be organized via Webinar to facilitate entrepreneurs' participation (they usually prefer not to leave the company for such commitments). Webinars could also be recorded so students can review the presentation when needed while participating in M2.

Finally, we included the use of LinkedIn as a continuation of the e-portfolio started in M1 and, consequently, as a strategy to support students in moving from the learning community of the course to the professional community.

## Challenges and Lessons Learned

When first introducing the BCCP model, students often reported difficulties in shifting from traditional study methods to practices that are typical of workplaces. Usually, in the first module, students reported anxiety about deadline pressure and time management. Moreover, some students did not feel at ease working with so many technologies at one time and did not trust that real learning could be accomplished. To overcome this aspect, we suggest that M1 should be conceived as a safe warm-up for M2, when students will meet the companies and the entrepreneurs. Other challenges faced relate to poor resources provided by the university. Before the COVID-19 emergency, no institutional LMS was available, and even during the lockdown, the platforms are not always purposely designed for education. This often means that students and teachers have to adapt or "tweak" the features of digital tools at their disposal.

Overall, the reader may have the impression that the course's architecture is complex and perhaps hard to manage. But the model we developed can be unpacked and recombined, depending on the specific contextual needs and available affordances. For instance, the number of roles introduced can be increased or decreased, as can the number of modules. In our case, e-learning companies functioned as an external community, but in other cases, the external agent can be other institutions or agents related to the objectives of the course (e.g., hospitals, clinics, private psychotherapists, etc.). However, it is crucial to have a psycho-pedagogical vision of the BCCP model of teaching and learning. Using proven and tested techniques – such as RT and Jigsaw – is a good starting point, but new theories and approaches should also be considered to address contemporary needs and demands. In our case, the TLA helped to renew "old" techniques, empowering the blended dimension and making the course more effective overall.

To this end, specific teacher training would be beneficial. University teacher training is a contested issue, rarely tackled in the literature and even less frequently in practice (Guasch, Alvarez, & Espasa, 2010). Teaching at any level needs to be constantly engaged with social change, and tertiary educators should not be exempt. In designing a training program for academics, we suggest the following:

(i) Allot adequate time for planning, testing, assessing, and monitoring. These are time-consuming activities, and it is very hard to do these important tasks well within the hours currently devoted to teaching.
(ii) Connect teaching to research. Research on the effectiveness of academic teaching is needed, and each teacher could contribute. This does not need to be completely new research but could connect with existing research in this field by contributing, for instance, reflective field notes, questionnaires, interviews, and any other form of data. Results on a large scale will support better understanding of which features of a blended or online course work better and why.
(iii) Tutor training. The amount of work needed to plan, test, and monitor a BCCP course is considerable, so having tutors supporting the teacher is a great solution. Tutors could be drawn from the previous course iterations or from

former students working in a relevant field. Some extra time should be allocated for this training, but it is worthwhile. Tutors, once trained, relieve the teachers' workload, function as a mediator between students and the professor, and can help monitor online activity and give timely feedback to the teacher about the course development.

(iv) Ask the company to provide a contact person. Companies may be very busy, and despite their best intentions, it may be difficult to answer students' requests promptly. Therefore, it is important to know exactly who is responsible for supervising the students. It is also important that the contact person is provided with the assessment criteria and interacts with the university teacher and tutor. This will reassure students that curriculum, pedagogy, and assessment are aligned when interacting with the company. It is also advisable to ask tutors to collect questions and requests and to act as a bridge between students and companies.

(v) The content needs to be re-designed. It is naive to think that a blended format can deliver the same content in the same way as it would be face-to-face. First, it is important to set at least two modules with the content of each sufficiently distinct. Second, the course should foster a learning object-like organization (Wiley, 2000), which is required by any online course. This means the content should be chunked into meaningful pieces, and connections between the pieces should also be considered as learning objects.

(vi) Prevent attrition. Online and blended courses suffer of a high attrition rate, but both internal and external factors can help reduce this. Internal factors include self-efficacy, self-determination, autonomy, and time management, while external factors include family, organizational, and technical support (Street, 2010). Furthermore, students should have enough time to familiarize themselves with the digital tools and structure, the overall management of the course should be transparent, problems with technology should be minimized, and individual learning preferences should be considered. These elements may affect motivation and, in turn, the learning outcomes (Frankola, 2001).

(vii) Care about students' interaction. We have often witnessed online courses that tend to be a close replication of face-to-face instruction. However, it is widely recognized that knowledge transfer is not enough to achieve the various goals of contemporary education. Formal and informal social interaction, collaborative building of ideas, collaborative construction of objects, teamwork, and dialogic interaction are all elements that enrich learning, both online and face-to-face. Therefore, this aspect must not be neglected. Having parallel groups working online is much easier than having them operate face-to-face; therefore, we recommend exploiting all the potentialities technology may offer and not using technology only to transmit information.

**Recommended Further Reading References**

1. Blanchard, A. L., & Markus, M. L. (2004). The experienced "sense" of a virtual community: characteristics and processes. *ACM Sigmis Database: the database for advances in information systems, 35*(1), 64–79.

This paper explaines in what consists the "sense of community" within virtual communities and how it differs comparing to physical communities. The nature of these differences is plausibly related to the differences between electronic and face-to-face communication. The authors content that even digitally is possible to create and recognize identities and to develop reciprocal trust. The implications for electronic business are also discussed.

2. Bonk, C. J., Graham, C. R., Cross, J., & Moore, M. G. (2005). *The handbook of blended learning: Global perspectives.* Local Designs, Pfeiffer & Company.

This is a fundamental book to understand the practices and trends in blended. The book provides examples of learning options that combine face-to-face instruction with online learning in the workplace, more formal academic settings, and the military. The focus is on real-world practices, and it targets trainers, consultants, professors, university staff distance-learning center directors, learning strategists general managers of learning, CEOs, chancellors, deans, and directors of global talent and organizational development. This diversity and breadth helps understanding the wide range of possibilities available when designing blended learning environments.

3. Ligorio, M. B., & César, M. (Eds.). (2013). *Interplays between dialogical learning and dialogical self.* IAP.

The Dialogical Approach, inspired by Bakhtin, has considerably contaminated education. This book is a collection of experiences and theoretical implications concerning new questions that this approach has raised, for instance: How does learning affect identity? How does participation to educational settings, scenarios, and situations impact the way we are or became? Can changes in how we perceive ourselves be considered as part of the learning process? As the blended approach touches also these issues, this book will help in framing them.

4. Loperfido, F. F., Sansone, N., Ligorio, M. B., & Fujita, N. (2014). Understanding I/We positions in a blended university course: Polyphony and chronotopes as dialogical features. *Open and Interdisciplinary Journal of Technology, Culture and Education, 9*(2), 51.

In this paper, the dialogical approach has been used to explore university students' positions before and after participating to a BCCP instantiation. The results discussed are obtained through the qualitative analysis of focus group discussions held at the beginning and at the end of the course. An increase of students' polyphony has been recorded together with We-positions, probably connected to the strong collaborative dimension of the model.

5. Mercer, N., Wegerif, R., & Major, L. (Eds.). (2019). *The Routledge international handbook of research on dialogic education.* Routledge London.

This book provides a comprehensive overview of the main ideas and themes within the framework of Dialogic Education. A few chapters refer also to the dialogical dimensions when blended education is considered. Indeed, there is a specific section devoted to Dialogic Education and digital technology and a nice chapter, authored by Wegerif, about Dialogic Theory of Education for the Internet Age.

6. Shroff, R. H., Deneen, C. C., & Ng, E. M. (2011). Analysis of the technology acceptance model in examining students' behavioural intention to use an e-portfolio system. *Australasian Journal of Educational Technology, 27*(4).

This paper analyses the Technology Acceptance Model (TAM) in order to examine students' behavioral intention to use an electronic portfolio system, meaning how students use and appropriate it within the specific framework of a course. This paper is recommended to those who want to elaborate on the use of e-portfolio.

7. Strivens, J. (2015). A Typology of ePortfolios. *The international Journal for Recording Achievements Planning and Portfolios*. (Vol 1) 3–5.

This paper helps in understanding what an e-portfolio can be. Different types of e-portfolios are described: personal portfolio, the so-called me-portfolio; professional e-portfolio, a "workbook" that learners use to learn through reflection on their experiences; and "promotional" e-portfolio that students can use to demonstrate their achievements in job application. Another type of e-portfolio is the task-portfolio. This type of e-portfolio does not contain a personal message but a description of what has been done, including processes, projects, placements, and products. These features inspired the definition of the e-portfolio in our BCCP model.

8. Tannhauser, A., C., Reynolds, S., Moretti M., Cariolato E. (2010) Trialogical Learning – A handbook for teachers. Retrieved from: https://docplayer.net/47420549-Trialogical-learning.html

This is a handbook specifically addressing teachers in higher education. It represents the first complete publication introducing the Trialogical approach. The roots and general frame within which this approach raised is explained, with particular reference to the knowledge society requirements.

9. Traetta, M. (2012) (Eds.) Dialogical Approach in Virtual Communities: Theories and Methods. *Qwerty International Journal* http://www.ckbg.org/qwerty/index.php/qwerty/issue/view/27

This is a special issue with a collection of papers useful for who is searching appropriate tools to study complex dynamics in communities with different degrees of virtuality (virtual and blended). The interconnections between methods and theoretical questions are always in the foreground. A few case studies are reported.

10. Cattaneo, A., Evi-Colombo, A., Ruberto, M. & Stanley, J. (2019). *Video Pedagogy for Vocational Education. An overview of video-based teaching and learning*. Turin: European Training Foundation.

This report aims to provide a research-grounded and, at the same time, practice-oriented overview of how video can contribute in different contexts related to learning at the boundaries between education and workplaces, as suggested in the Trialogical Learning literature, reported in this chapter. Authors explained how video can make connections between learning contexts, for example, work-based and school-based. Video can be used also to support learners to form a community or support each other through observation, trial and error, and peer coaching.

## Cross-References

▶ Educational Psychology: Learning and Instruction
▶ Formative Assessment and Feedback Strategies
▶ General Psychology Motivation
▶ Teaching of General Psychology: Problem Solving
▶ Technology-Enhanced Psychology Learning and Teaching
▶ Teaching of Work and Organizational Psychology in Higher Education

## References

Akkerman, S. F., & Bakker, A. (2011). Boundary crossing and boundary objects. *Review of Educational Research, 81*(2), 132–169.
Amenduni, F., & Ligorio, M. B. (2017). Becoming at the borders: The role of positioning in boundary-crossing between university and workplaces. *Cultural-Historical Psychology, 13*(1), 89–104.
APA (2012). https://www.apa.org/ed/graduate/benchmarks-evaluation-system
Arifin, S., & Ikhfan, H. (2018). Assessing soft skills of undergraduate students: Framework for improving competitiveness, innovation and competence of higher education graduates. *Studia Humanitatis, 1*.
Aronson, E. (1978). *The jigsaw classroom*. Sage.
Aronson, E., & Patnoe, S. (2010). *Cooperation in the classroom: The jigsaw method*. Pinter & Martin.
Avedon, M., & Grabow, K. (2010). Professional identity: Organizational psychologists as chief human resource executives. *Industrial and Organizational Psychology, 3*(3), 266–268.
Blanchard, A. L., & Markus, M. L. (2002, January). Sense of virtual community-maintaining the experience of belonging. In *Proceedings of the 35th Annual Hawaii International Conference on System Sciences* (pp. 3566–3575). IEEE.
Bliuc, A., Ellis, R. A., Goodyear, P., & Piggott, L. (2011). A blended learning approach to teaching foreign policy: Student experiences of learning through face-to-face and online discussion and their relationship to academic performance. *Computers & Education, 56*(3), 856–864.

Brown, P. (2015). Communities of practice: A heuristic for workplace reflection in higher education. *The International Journal for Recording Achievement, Planning and Portfolios., 1*(1), 31–41.

Bruno, A., & Dell'Aversana, G. (2017). Reflective practice for psychology students: The use of reflective journal feedback in higher education. *Psychology Learning & Teaching, 16*(2), 248–260.

Cesareni, D., Cacciamani, S., & Fujita, N. (2016). Role taking and knowledge building in a blended university course. *International Journal of Computer-Supported Collaborative Learning, 11*(1), 9–39.

Dostoevsky, M. (1985). *The double* (E. Harden, Trans.). Ann Arbor, MI: Ardis. (Original work published 1846).

Edwards, S. M., & La Ferle, C. (2003). Role-taking: Enhancing the online experience. *Journal of Current Issues & Research in Advertising, 25*(2), 45–56.

Egloffstein, M., & Ifenthaler, D. (2017). Employee perspectives on MOOCs for workplace learning. *TechTrends, 61*(1), 65–70.

Engeström, Y. (1999). Activity theory and individual and social transformation. *Perspectives on Activity Theory, 19*(38), 19–30.

Erbe, D., Eichert, H. C., Riper, H., & Ebert, D. D. (2017). Blending face-to-face and internet-based interventions for the treatment of mental disorders in adults: Systematic review. *Journal of Medical Internet Research, 19*(9), e306.

Fischer, F., Kollar, I., Stegmann, K., & Wecker, C. (2013). Toward a script theory of guidance in computer-supported collaborative learning. *Educational Psychologist, 48*(1), 56–66.

Frankola, K. (2001). Why online learners drop out. *Workforce-Costa Mesa, 80*(10), 52–61.

Guasch, T., Alvarez, I., & Espasa, A. (2010). University teacher competencies in a virtual teaching/learning environment: Analysis of a teacher training experience. *Teaching and Teacher Education, 26*(2), 199–206.

Hakkarainen, K. (2003). Progressive inquiry in a computer-supported biology class. *Journal of Research in Science Teaching, 40*(10), 1072–1088.

Hare, A. P. (1994). Types of roles in small groups: A bit of history and a current perspective. *Small Group Research, 25*, 443–448.

Hermans, H. J. (2013). The dialogical self in education: Introduction. *Journal of Constructivist Psychology, 26*(2), 81–89.

Humpreys, M., & Brown, A. D. (2002). Narratives of organizational identity and identification: A case study of hegemony and resistance. *Organization Studies, 23*(3), 421–447.

Impedovo, M. A., Ligorio, M. B., & McLay, K. F. (2018). The "friend of zone of proximal development" role: Empowering ePortfolios as boundary objects from student to-work I-position transaction. *Journal of Assisted Computer Learning, 34*(6), 753–761.

James, W. (1890). *The principles of psychology* (Vol. I). London: Macmillan.

Lakkala, M., Toom, A., Ilomäki, L., & Muukkonen, H. (2015). Re-designing university courses to support collaborative knowledge creation practices. *Australasian Journal of Educational Technology, 31*(5).

Lenhart, A., Purcell, K., Smith, A., & Zickuhr, K. (2010). Social Media and Mobile Internet Use among Teens and Young Adults. *Pew Internet & American Life Project*. http://www.pewinternet.org/2010/02/03/social-media-and-young-adults

Ligorio, M. B., Amenduni, F., & McLay, K. (2019). Triangulating identity, groups and objects. A university case. In N. Mercer, R. Wegerif, & L. Major (Eds.), *The Routledge international handbook of research on dialogic education* (pp. 509–5249). Routledge.

Ligorio, M. B., & Annese, S. (2010). Blended activity design approach: A method to innovate e-learning for higher education. *Psychology Research*, 165–188.

Ligorio, M. B., Loperfido, F. F., Sansone, N., & Spadaro, P. F. (2011). Blending educational models to design blended activities. In *Techniques for fostering collaboration in online learning communities: Theoretical and practical perspectives* (pp. 64–81). IGI Global.

Ligorio, M. B., & Sansone, N. (2009). Structure of a blended university course: Applying constructivist principles to blended teaching. In *Information technology and constructivism in higher education: Progressive learning frameworks* (pp. 216–230). Igi Global.

Means, B., Murphy, R., & Baki, M. (2013). The effectiveness of online and blended learning: A meta-analysis of the empirical literature. *Teachers College Record, 115*(3), 1–47.

Meijers, F., & Hermans, H. (Eds.). (2017). *The dialogical self theory in education: A multicultural perspective* (Vol. 5). Springer.

Melanthiou, Y., Pavlou, F., & Constantinou, E. (2015). The use of social network sites as an e-recruitment tool. *Journal of Transnational Management, 20*(1), 31–49.

Naufel, K. Z., Appleby, D. C., Young, J., Van Kirk, J. F., Spencer, S. M., Rudmann, J., ...Richmond, A. S. (2018). *The skillful psychology student: Prepared for success in the 21st century workplace*. Retrieved from: www.apa.org/careers/resources/guides/transferable-skills.pdf

Paavola, S., & Hakkarainen, K. (2005). The knowledge creation metaphor–an emergent epistemological approach to learning. *Science & Education, 14*(6), 535–557.

Paavola S., and Hakkarainen K. (2009). From meaning making to joint construction of knowledge practices and artefacts: a trialogical approach to CSCL. In *Proceedings of the 9th international conference on Computer supported collaborative learning – Vol. 1 (CSCL'09). International Society of the Learning Sciences* (pp. 83–92).

Paavola, S., & Hakkarainen, K. (2014). Trialogical approach for knowledge creation. In *Knowledge creation in education* (pp. 53–73). Singapore: Springer.

Pan, L., Zhong, T. T., Zhang, X. Y., & Chang, Y. C. (2020). A study of the effects of school environment, teacher identity, and students' self-efficacy and interpersonal relationship on learning outcomes of students in the universities in Hainan, China. *International Journal of Organizational Innovation (Online), 13*(1), 290–230.

Pham, A. V. (2014). Navigating social networking and social media in school psychology: Ethical and professional considerations in training programs. *Psychology in the Schools, 51*(7), 767–778.

Sansone, N., Cesareni, D., Ligorio, M. B., Bortolotti, I., & Buglass, S. L. (2020). Developing knowledge work skills in a university course. *Research Papers in Education, 35*(1), 23–42.

Sansone, N., & Ligorio, M. B. (2015). A protocol for multidimensional assessment in university online courses. *Research on Education and Media, 7*(1).

Sansone, N., Ligorio, M. B., & Buglass, S. L. (2018). Peer e-tutoring: Effects on students' participation and interaction style in online courses. *Innovations in Education and Teaching International, 55*(1), 13–22.

Scardamalia, M., & Bereiter, C. (2006). Knowledge building. *The Cambridge*.

Schwendimann, B. A., Cattaneo, A. A., Dehler Zufferey, J., Gurtner, J. L., Bétrancourt, M., & Dillenbourg, P. (2015). The 'Erfahrraum': A pedagogical model for designing educational technologies in dual vocational systems. *Journal of Vocational Education & Training, 67*(3), 367–396.

Sfard, A. (1998). On two metaphors for learning and the dangers of choosing just one. *Educational Researcher, 27*(2), 4–13.

Sharpe, R., Benfield, G., & Roberts, G. (2006). *The undergraduate experience of blended e-learning: A review of UK literature and practice*. London: Higher Education Academy.

Stahl, G. (2006). *Group cognition: Computer support for building collaborative knowledge*. Cambridge, MA: MIT Press.

Star, S. L. (1989). The structure of ill-structured solutions: Boundary objects and heterogeneous distributed problem solving. In *Distributed artificial intelligence* (pp. 37–54). Morgan Kaufmann.

Street, H. (2010). Factors influencing a learner's decision to drop-out or persist in higher education distance learning. *Online Journal of Distance Learning Administration, 13*(4).

Strijbos, J. W., Martens, R., Jochems, W. M. G., & Broers, N. J. (2004). The effect of functional roles on group efficiency: Using multilevel modeling and content analysis to investigate computer-supported collaboration in small groups. *Small Group Research, 35*(2), 195–229.

Strijbos, J. W., & Weinberger, A. (2010). Emerging and scripted roles in computer-supported collaborative learning. *Computers in Human Behavior, 26*, 491–494.

Sutherland, S., & Powell, A. 2007, July 9. CETIS Portfolio SIG mailing list discussions https://ipark.hud.ac.uk/content/e-portfolios

Thibaut, P., Curwood, J. S., Carvalho, L., & Simpson, A. (2015). Moving across physical and online spaces: A case study in a blended primary classroom. *Learning, Media and Technology, 40*(4), 458–479.

Tonteri, L., Kosonen, M., Ellonen, H. K., & Tarkiainen, A. (2011). Antecedents of an experienced sense of virtual community. *Computers in Human Behavior, 27*(6), 2215–2223.

Visser, H. (2016). Self-confrontation method: Assessment and process-promotion in career counselling. In *Assessing and stimulating a dialogical self in groups, teams, cultures, and organizations* (pp. 19–36). Cham: Springer.

Vygotsky, L. (1978). Interaction between learning and development. *Readings on the Development of Children, 23*(3), 34–41.

Wenger, E. (2009). A social theory of learning. In *Contemporary theories of learning* (pp. 217–240). Routledge.

Wiley, D. A. (2000). *Learning object design and sequencing theory* (Doctoral dissertation, Brigham Young University).

# Learning and Instruction in Higher Education Classrooms

**58**

Neil H. Schwartz and Anna N. Bartel

## Contents

| | |
|---|---|
| Introduction | 1432 |
| Section 1: Organizing and Structuring Your Course | 1433 |
|     The Value of Organization | 1433 |
|     The Value of Structure | 1435 |
| Section 2: Activities that Foster Learning | 1438 |
|     The Value of Activity as Engagement | 1438 |
|     Activities in Class | 1441 |
|     Activity Inside of Class | 1444 |
|     Activity Inside or Outside of Class | 1445 |
| Section 3: The Way to Lecture | 1448 |
|     Directing and Sustaining Attention | 1449 |
|     Using Personal Examples | 1449 |
|     Activating Positive Student Emotions | 1450 |
| Section 4: Concluding Remarks | 1451 |
| Cross-References | 1451 |
| References | 1451 |

### Abstract

This chapter inventories the essential components necessary to leverage theory and research in the deployment of effective instruction in higher education. The chapter begins with a discussion of the importance of structuring and organizing a higher education course to foster deep and enduring learning based on the evidence which supports it. The chapter then provides a rich chronology of the

---

N. H. Schwartz (✉)
Department of Psychology, California State University, Chico, CA, USA

A. N. Bartel
Department of Psychology, University of Wisconsin, Madison, WI, USA

© This is a U.S. Government work and not under copyright protection in the U.S.;
foreign copyright protection may apply 2023
J. Zumbach et al. (eds.), *International Handbook of Psychology Learning and Teaching*,
Springer International Handbooks of Education,
https://doi.org/10.1007/978-3-030-28745-0_70

seminal theoretical ideas that support the value of student cognitive and behavioural activity that gives rise to active engagement during learning. Next, the importance of activities in and out of the classroom are discussed, with evidence-based examples illustrating the diverse and effective methods that lead to deep learning. Finally, for better or for worse, higher-educational classrooms still deliver much their instruction using the method of lecture. Thus, the chapter concludes with evidence-based research that explains the way to lecture properly by directing and sustaining attention, using personal examples, and activating student emotions to build cognitive models of new knowledge and motivate students to learn.

**Keywords**

Course organization · Course structure · Higher education · Learning and Instruction · Activity as engagement · Cognitive elaboration · Effective lecturing · Activating positive emotions · Learning activity

## Introduction

Your course should be organized. However, it is not so much that it is organized, it should make sense. Many people organize a course around the table of contents of the book they use for the course—at least in the USA, since most courses in the USA are built around a required textbook. However, just because a textbook author organized content around what made sense to him or her, the course should be organized around what makes sense to you. After all, you are teaching it.

There are many ways to do this: Pick a book with a table of contents that makes sense to you; rearrange chapters in a book so that the order of assigned chapter readings conforms to the way you want to use the book; get copyright permission and assemble chapters from various books (and/or research articles) into a purchasable compendium in the order you see fit; or write the book yourself.

The organization of your course needs to build logically. This logical structure is known as an instructional hierarchy. That is, you start with the prerequisite information necessary to teach subsequent information and order the content relative to the layers of knowledge necessary for subsequent understanding. In math and statistics, for example, the instructional hierarchy is clear. In history, while it may appear that the instructional hierarchy is also clear—that is, a chronology of events and dates is most sensible for delivering content—the hierarchy is not necessarily clear at all. You may want students to develop an understanding of the social, economic, and educational factors that give rise to authoritarian leaders among developed and transitioning countries. The instructional hierarchy for this content certainly has a common core of prerequisite knowledge, but it also would be expected to be built with the unique thumbprint of the way you understand and view the topic conceptually.

Once the content of a course is logically assembled, the methods and activities need to be selected for teaching that content. There is little doubt that students need to be active when learning in order to build knowledge. Activity in learning makes concepts not only easier to understand, but it also makes the concepts more enduring in memory over time. This means that activities need to engender an engaged response from the learner. Engaged learning can be generated in activities as simple as taking notes during a lecture (Bretzing & Kulhavy, 1981; Peper & Mayer, 1978, 1986), creating a personal mind map of target information after a lecture has been completed, or, for example, building an infographic that consolidates the information into a sensible graphic display. Engaged responding can also be complex—for example, building a scale model of a timeline leading up to a historical event, writing and producing a homemade documentary, or working in the community on a social problem. What is common in these examples is that learning becomes embodied and personal so that students integrate the knowledge they already have with the knowledge that is new. The activities serve to ground that knowledge—to anchor it in substantive artifacts that have personal meaning. This engagement is essential for the new knowledge you seek to build within the learners who take your course—engagement that requires attention, reasoning, problem-solving, decision-making, and judgment, the kind of cognitive activities from which authentic learning is borne.

At the same time, most instructors do some variety of lecturing. Often those lectures make use of visual media—PowerPoint, Prezi, Canva, Google Slides, Samepage, Adobe Connect, and others—but the way you lecture and the visual media you choose has a powerful influence on your students. Lecturing also has an important affective component—the degree to which you can grab attention, keep that attention, and stir emotional arousal.

In the chapter that follows, we will examine these pedagogical features. First, we will discuss the value and necessity of structure; next, we will explore the value of activity during learning and why student engagement is so important; in the third section, we will explain the necessity and methods of directing attention and awakening emotions of students during classroom instruction; at the end, we will conclude with final remarks.

## Section 1: Organizing and Structuring Your Course

### The Value of Organization

Constructing and organizing a course for your students may sound simple enough: create student learning objectives, create the curriculum to help students meet said objectives, and prepare exams to assess how effectively you presented the course content. However, these steps are not necessarily simple to complete and should not be overlooked. While there is always new, up-and-coming research to support different instructional practices, it is important not to lose sight of the simple impact that course organization has on different student outcomes. Sometimes it does not have to be a showy solution; in fact, research throughout the decades has consistently suggested that the order and organization of course content affects student achievement (Braxton, Bray, & Berger, 2000; Bray, Pascarella, & Pierson, 2004; Feldman, 1989; Glynn & Di Vesta, 1977; Roksa, Trolian, Blaich, & Wise, 2017).

Consider Feldman (1989); he examined several different teaching practices and their relationship with student achievement (e.g., teacher availability and interest, intellectual challenge, encouragement of questions, discussion/openness to opinions of others, etc.). Among all of the different teaching practices, the **two** specific practices that emerged as having the strongest relationship with student achievement were (1) organization of course and (2) clarity.

Additionally, Wang, Pascarella, Nelson, Laird, and Ribera (2015) analyzed longitudinal survey data comprised of student data from multiple different institutions. Across four years of student data, the authors revealed that students' perceptions of receiving organized course instruction were positively associated with higher-order learning (e.g., applying theories to novel situations), integrative learning (e.g., integrating information from various sources), and reflective learning (e.g., learning something that influenced a student's perspective to understand). Additionally, organized course instruction had positive effects on students' critical thinking and need for cognition by the end of the students' fourth year.

Another benefit of effective course organization is that it is a low-cost way to increase students' academic engagement and performance (Pascarella, Salisbury, & Blaich, 2011; Pascarella, Seifert, & Whitt, 2008). Pascarella et al. (2011) expanded upon a previous study (Pascarella et al., 2008) which suggested that being exposed to organized course instruction had an influence on first year university students' intent to re-enroll in school for a second year. Pascarella et al. (2011) replicated and expanded upon the previous study by discovering that the effect of student persistence on exposure to organized course instruction held true across different types of universities (e.g., community colleges, teaching and research universities, etc.) **and** for students with different levels of college preparation.

In short, having an organized course is of considerable importance for student achievement in classroom learning. However, as Pascarella and colleagues demonstrate, creating an organized course could also have important implications from a socioeconomic perspective. That is, creating an organized course, which is essentially cost-free, could help first-generation students and students from low socioeconomic statuses stay engaged in courses, receive better grades, and, in the long run, graduate.

It is interesting to note that, for the most part, the studies above used student ratings on various scales to obtain an aggregate score of student perceptions of course organization. While statements measuring course organization and clarity may vary across authors, we present an example set of questions used by Blaich, Wise, Pascarella, and Roksa (2016) to measure student perception of course organization. To be specific, Blaich et al. (2016) asked students to rate how often they had experienced the following statements given their interactions with different faculty on a five-point scale ranging from **Never** to **Very Often.**

The statements were as follows:

- Faculty gave clear explanations.
- Faculty made good use of examples and illustrations to explain difficult points.
- Faculty effectively reviewed and summarized the material.
- Faculty interpreted abstract ideas and theories clearly.
- Faculty gave assignments that helped in learning the course material.
- The presentation of material was well-organized.
- Faculty were well prepared for class.
- Class time was used effectively.
- Course goals and requirements were clearly explained.
- Faculty had a good command of what they were teaching.

What all of this information suggests is that student perceptions of organization matter for learning. Even if you believe your course to be organized and clear, it is still important to remember that the ideas and experiences your students bring into the classroom matter. If you are ever curious, you may consider giving these items to your students to get a better understanding of their perceptions of your course before the students give their formal course evaluations.

The research examining how organized instruction is related to academic performance and beyond is based in the constructivist theory of learning (Dochy & Alexander, 1995; Neumann, 2014). The most basic principle of the constructivist approach is that new knowledge is **constructed** from a prior knowledge base. You should recognize that the experiences students bring into your classroom are fundamental to their learning, and the way you organize your course should enable them to engage and activate their existing knowledge. In the constructivist framework, creating an engaging environment between you and your students enhances your students' active role in learning. The take-home message regarding course organization in a constructivist framework is that it allows there to be an emphasis on learning in context, which will emerge as a theme throughout the following sections.

## The Value of Structure

It is not only important to discuss why it is important to have an organized course, but it is equally important to consider how you can create structure within that course. We have chosen the concept of instructional hierarchies (Haring, Lovitt, Eaton, & Hansen, 1978) to illustrate this structural concept.

While the foundations of instructional hierarchies are rooted in behaviorism, there are clear links of constructivism as an underlying theory of learning between both course organization and structure (Mayer, 1992). In the following paragraphs, we will discuss both the behavioral and constructivist elements in instructional hierarchies. The behavioral elements are the classic foundations of students' behaviors as described by Haring et al. (1978); the constructivist elements are showcased in how you can structure your assignments to enhance learning and learning environments throughout the hierarchy.

The premise of an instructional hierarchy is simple: course organization should follow how students learn new information and skills, beginning with achieving accuracy of the subject matter (Ardoin & Daly, 2007; Haring et al., 1978). However, it is not so simple as to be ignored; it is important to have an understanding of the different stages in an instructional hierarchy because there have been a number of academic interventions developed to improve students' performance at different learning stages through different instructional techniques (Ardoin & Daly, 2007; Daly, Lentz, & Boyer, 1996; Lannie & Martens, 2008; Martens & Witt, 2004; Parker & Burns, 2014). As such, when you are able to identify what learning stage your student is in, you can employ instructional techniques that match your student's learning needs—thereby increasing the likelihood of your student's mastery of the learning stages. The four stages are detailed in the paragraphs below; furthermore, examples of student behaviors and suggested teacher approaches to the learning stages are shown in Table 1.

**Table 1** Student behaviors and teacher approaches to learning stages

*Corresponding teacher approaches and student behaviors in learning stages*

| Learning stages | Example student behaviors | Suggested teacher approaches |
|---|---|---|
| Acquisition: Learning to demonstrate skill | Students cannot yet perform the task with complete accuracy | Teacher demonstrates active performance of the entire skill |
|  | Student accuracy may be highly variable | Teachers provide prompts to cue or scaffold a specific response needed for the skill |
| *Students move from acquisition to fluency when they perform skills accurately with few scaffolds* |||
| Fluency: Demonstrating skill with automaticity | Students can perform the task with greater accuracy | Teachers provide activities that afford active responses from students |
|  | Students perform slowly but with more reliable accuracy | Students are given ample problems to repeat skill |
| *Students move from fluency to generalization when the skill is learned well enough to be automatic* |||
| Generalization: Demonstrating skill on similar problems | May start trying to apply skill to new settings but do so with variable accuracy | Teachers provide assignments where the skill is used in different contexts |
|  | May confuse skill with similar skills | Teachers provide problems designed to help discriminate skills |
| *Students move from generalization to adaptation when the skill is used in different settings* |||
| Adaptation: Demonstrating novel applications of skill | Like generalization, student is accurate and fluent | Teachers provide assignments where skill can be applied to novel situations |
|  | Student applies skill to new situations without teacher prompts or scaffolds | Teacher provides scaffolds to help students find **their own ways** to adapt the skill to different situations |

Retrieved from Wright (n.d.), https://www.interventioncentral.org/academic-interventions/general-academic/instructional-hierarchy-linking-stages-learning-effective-in

The first learning stage is **acquisition** where students are learning how to perform a specific skill in a class, more specifically gaining adequate accuracy of the skill. While a student in this stage is neither fully accurate nor fluent in the skill, the ultimate goal is for the student's accuracy to be improving (Daly, Martens, Hamler, Dool, & Eckert, 1999). Teachers may consider structuring their course in a way that begins with lecture or assignments that are focused on building accuracy. Some suggestions for helping students gain skill accuracy in the acquisition phase may include, but are not limited to, demonstrating the skill, modeling the skill, and prompting use of the skill (Espin & Deno, 1989). Thus, following demonstration or modeling, sprinkling brief moments in class to have your student act out, explain, or solve a quick simple problem requiring the skill is a good use of class time to provide for acquisition.

The second learning stage is **fluency.** In this stage, students are now able to complete a skill with accuracy, but using the skill requires a concentrated effort, and the student is typically slow to complete tasks. The goal of the fluency learning stage is for students to eventually produce the skill with automaticity, that is, quickly and with little effort or heavy thinking (Poncy, Skinner, & Jaspers, 2007). Some suggestions for teachers to help students reach automaticity of a skill may include, but are not limited to, creating activities that encourage active responses from students (e.g., teachers are no longer demonstrating the entire skill), giving students ample opportunities to repeatedly practice the skill (e.g., "drilling"), and generally creating assignments to facilitate overlearning and maintenance of the skill. This stage is ultimately one of practice. During a classic university lecture course, fluency development is extremely difficult unless an entire lecture period is devoted to it, but it is very valuable in a lab setting if the course has a lab attached to the course.

In the third learning stage—**generalization**—students have achieved accuracy and fluency of a skill and are beginning to apply this skill to similar, but novel, situations. During this stage, students will have difficulty applying the learned skill in different contexts. Therefore, the goal of the generalization learning stage is for the students to be able to discriminate between the skill and other similar skills. By learning to discriminate the skill, the students are then able to use the skill in different contexts. Some suggestions for teachers to help students reach generalization of a skill may include, but are not limited to, diversifying prompts such that the same skill can be used in contexts that only initially appear to be unfamiliar (e.g., when learning to count coins, a teacher could ask both, "how much money do these coins make?" **and** "is the amount of money that these coins make more or less than x?") and providing different types of problems that help discriminate between similar skills (Poncy, Duhon, Lee, & Key, 2010). As in the acquisition stage, the generalization stage is not particularly difficult to accomplish in a college classroom. For example, you might want to take a short segment of your class to have students work in pairs applying a skill set to two different problems types or contexts.

The fourth and final stage is **adaptation** where students have achieved accuracy and fluency and are able to generalize but are learning to apply, or adapt, the skill to completely new problems. The goal of the adaptation learning stage is for students to be able to identify specific elements within the skill they previously learned that could potentially be successfully adapted and used in novel situations (Burns,

Codding, Boice, & Lukito, 2010). We believe it is during this stage that teachers, especially in higher-level courses, need to heavily use (at the appropriate time in the semester) the creation of assignments and tasks. The adaptation learning stage affords immense creativity from both instructors and students alike.

Although instructional hierarchies are rooted in behaviorism, the active constructivist influence of a teacher can have a significant impact on the ability of students to advance through the learning stages by the activities teachers use to leverage that advancement. Thus, as shown in Table 1, it is important for teachers to match the type of instruction they are giving to their students based on their students' behaviors. Certainly, we are not suggesting that you create different course organizations to tailor your instruction to each individual student's needs; however, it is valuable to consider how the average student progresses through your course, so you can structure your course with appropriate assignments and activities that maximize the likelihood of **most** of your students achieving skill adaptation over a semester.

## Section 2: Activities that Foster Learning

### The Value of Activity as Engagement

In the section above, we explained how, from a constructivist point of view, organization and structure is important in designing your course. However, it is equally important to recognize that **activity** during learning is critical as well. That is, learning is constructed, not necessarily by having your students listen to you as an expert telling them **about** a concept, but rather providing opportunities for your students to develop the concept themselves.

That means conceptual development, when it is personal, is real, authentic, and grounded in activities that give rise to meaningful experience—experience that provides for your students to interact with their environment in the context of a real problem to solve. Under this condition, your students are able to discover the way things work by interacting with them and developing a cognitive model of those machinations. The cognitive model allows your students to construct a theory of the interaction they experienced and generate hypotheses to more deeply comprehend the intricacies and complexities of the concept they are trying to grasp; in short, their cognitive model sets up a direction and plan for their subsequent interactions.

It is certainly possible for your students to build a cognitive model without activity and engagement; however, the model they build will not be particularly useful for real learning. That is, an activity-free model of a concept is what is called "inert knowledge"—knowledge your student may be able to recite verbally to someone else but cannot be used in real-world problem-solving (Whitehead, 1929). For example, your student may be able to list the elements integral to the concept of operant conditioning, but not comprehend the relationship between different types of consequences or the relationship of consequences to behavior or behavior-antecedent connections. Thus, activity and engagement not only make your students' cognitive models more utilitarian, but they also make your students' cognitive models more enduring and better available for new learning.

And yet, the idea of activity and engagement is not new. Piaget discussed it in the 1930s (Piaget, 1930), Bruner in the 1960s (Bruner, 1961). It was seen in Ernst Rothkopf's work on mathemagenic behaviors in the 1960s (Rothkopf, 1970), Merle Wittrock's generative learning theory (Wittrock, 1974) in the 1970s and 1980s, and more recently in Richard Mayer's cognitive theory of multimedia learning (Mayer, 2014) and Michelene Chi's interactive-cognitive-active-passive (ICAP) framework (Chi, 2009; Chi et al., 2018; Chi & Wylie, 2014). Indeed Rothkopf, in an interview on the subject (Rothkopf & Shaughnessy, 2005), reflected that during the early 1960s when operant conditioning was used to explain learning, **evoking a student's overt behavior was essential** in maintaining and shaping the engagement between the student and the instructional matter—that is, for authentic learning to occur, "engagement was critical in educational situations" (pg. 52). Thus, for Rothkopf, students were viewed as both a processor and **active elaborator** of information. In other words, students, in order to build a cognitive model that provided the framework for new learning, had to actively **do** something during learning to make that learning useful.

Wittrock's (1974) theory of generative learning underscored the importance of engagement and activity, as well. In his theory, Wittrock explained that learning was an active process where students needed to be engaged in connecting what they were learning with what they already knew; that active engagement during learning required attending, thinking, and doing—in other words, "generating and transferring meaning for stimuli and events from one's background, attitudes, abilities, and experiences" (Wittrock, 2010, pg. 43). Thus, for Wittrock, generating new knowledge and transferring it to problems of the real world meant that knowledge building had to be constructive, effortful, generative, and intentional.

Wittrock's theory was pioneering in that it fleshed out the utility and function of activity and engagement in developing deep comprehension during learning, but it also laid the groundwork for the theories that followed it. For example, as to the utility and function of activity, Wittrock showed in a number of studies that students who were tasked with actively generating cognitive associations between words not only remembered those words better, but the words were remembered for longer periods of time and were more easily transferred to solve new word problems (Goulet, 1970; Goulet & Wittrock, 1971; Wittrock & Carter, 1975). Wittrock also documented the value of generative learning both in and out of traditional classrooms—for example, with high school students in an economics class comprised of 15 hours of instruction (Kourilsky & Wittrock, 1992) and classes in the development of basic reading skills for Army service personnel on military bases (Wittrock, 1989).

As for the groundwork Wittrock laid for others, Mayer's (2014) select-organize-integrate (SOI) model was a part that foundation. Mayer's (2014) model explained that a student must actively first **select** the most relevant incoming information out of a cacophony of new information that may make little to no sense to the student, especially if he or she has had no previous exposure to the subject matter; next, the student must **organize** in mind the appropriately selected information into a coherent cognitive representation by building conceptual connections between the relevant elements of the information based on its internal structure so that the student understands the information without distorting or changing it; finally, the student needs to **integrate** that newly constructed cognitive representation with the relevant knowledge structures he or she already has. Thus, like Wittrock, Mayer's SOI model underscored that, for students to learn during instruction, they must be active and constructive **mentally** beyond the mere memorization of, say, the types of vocabulary definitions, lists, charts, and diagrams that might exist on a whiteboard or PowerPoint slides or merely listening passively to the orations of their teacher, a podcast, or a video clip. In short, they must be **thinking—actively.**

There are a number of investigations that have documented the constructive nature of engagement during instruction that leads to active thinking. For example, Fiorella, Stull, Shelbi, and Mayer (2019) had 196 college students learn about the human kidney by watching a video narrated by a teacher. The teacher explained with diagrams shown part by part or the teacher dynamically drew while explaining. While the dynamically drawn diagrams produced better learning, what's most important is that the students learned substantially more when they wrote personal explanations of what they viewed, rather than creating a drawing of what they watched, or rewatching the video. In another example, Fiorella and Kuhlman (2019) had college students study a scientific text about the human respiratory system and then either explain to a fictitious student what they learned while creating their own drawings of what they learned, or just explain, or create a drawing only, or just restudy what they read. Not only did explaining while drawing produce better and more enduring learning, but the researchers found that the students' oral explanations were substantially more elaborative. Elaboration revealed much deeper understanding.

Finally, the importance and value of engagement in student learning has also come from the work of Michelene Chi. Chi and her colleagues (Chi et al., 2018) explained there are essentially four different levels of engagement—**i**nteractive engagement, **c**onstructive engagement, **a**ctive engagement, and **p**assive engagement. Each level of engagement leads to different kinds of actual learning behaviors, with learning outcomes different for each. That is, students' overt learning behaviors create knowledge-change processes that can be observed in the ability of the students to store new information in memory, activate prior knowledge, link the new information with the knowledge they already have, and make substantive and effective inferences based on those linkages. **Interactive, constructive,** and **active** engagement is superior to passive engagement because passive engagement reveals that students are really not doing much behaviorally. Instead, they may, or may not, be paying close attention, other than simply looking at instructional materials—e.g., listening to a lecture or reading slides from a PowerPoint, but not really **thinking** about the content being shared with them. The other three types of engagement require students to be **doing** something during learning. Passive engagement leads to learning that is shallow and more often than not isolated and unintegrated—and, at the end of the day, rather nonutilitarian except for somewhat low-level routine tasks.

The point is that Chi's four types of engagement flow in a hierarchical arrangement of progressive levels of cognitive activity during learning, where **I** is more engaging then **C**, **C** is more engaging than **A**, and **A** is more engaging then **P**. In short, **I > C > A > P**. As Chi explained, interactive engagement may be the holy grail of learning when you are teaching because it generates the most substantive and deepest knowledge building activity of all. Indeed, you can see this type of interactive engagement when two students work together collaboratively. That is, when students work in pairs, each learner must generate inferences from their own knowledge in conjunction with the knowledge of their partner **while** they are learning. In effect, this generative exchange creates a space for the two students to infer from their own knowledge, infer from their partner's knowledge, and then activate what they already know, link the combinations, and then store it in memory.

On the other hand, simply being generative alone—as occurs when in constructive engagement only—misses the value of the inferential transaction that takes place when two minds collaboratively learn together. When learning is simply active without the interactive or constructive component, your students may activate what they already know; they may even link that new information to their prior knowledge and then store it in memory. However, there is no dynamic and transactional inferential thinking taking place. Thus, in order to reach the level of integrative engagement, your students must be generating inferences of what they are trying to learn while co-generating and mingling those inferences with another student. In either case, whether it is constructive or interactive engagement, the inferences your students generate can be metaphorically conceived of as the "glue" that builds their cognitive model—a model that is of potential utility for them in solving the real-world problems that will come to them beyond the classroom. When your students are passive during instruction, they may be directing their attention to the new information you are teaching, but they do not link that new information to what they already know—nor do they do the heavy cognitive lifting of making inferences—again, the kind of inferences that create enriched and elaborative models of knowledge.

## Activities in Class

One question that might arise as you consider Chi's ICAP model is the type of actual activities you can engage in when you teach. The levels of engagement, along with their example activities, knowledge-change processes, expected changes in knowledge, and their expected cognitive and learning outcomes, can be seen in Table 2.

What is valuable to consider in these examples is that your students are talking—either in mind to themselves or to another student. We contend that talking is a good thing during class time, as long as it is targeted, regulated, and timed. That means making space for your students to consider what you might have just presented, either by taking interpretive notes about what they were just exposed to, writing down questions or generating hypotheses in these notes, or discussing with a neighbor how what they just heard makes sense to them or applies to their personal

**Table 2** ICAP framework example activities, knowledge processes, and outcomes

| Category characteristics | *Passive* **receiving** | *Active* **manipulating** | *Constructive* **generating** | *Interactive* **dialoguing** |
|---|---|---|---|---|
| Example activities | Listening to explanations; watching a video | Taking verbatim notes; highlighting sentences | Self-explaining; comparing and contrasting | Discussing with a peer; drawing a diagram with a partner |
| Knowledge-change processes | Isolated "storing" processes in which information is stored episodically in encapsulated form without embedding it in a relevant schema, no integration | "Integrating" processes in which the selected and emphasized information activates prior knowledge and schema, and new information can be assimilated into the activated schema | "Inferring" processes include integrating new information with prior knowledge; inferring new knowledge; connecting, comparing, and contrasting different pieces of new information to infer new knowledge; analogizing, generalizing, reflecting on conditions of a procedure, explaining why something works | "Co-inferring" processes involve both partners taking turns mutually creating. This mutuality further benefits from opportunities and processes to incorporate feedback and to entertain new ideas, alternative perspectives, new directions, etc. |
| Expected changes in knowledge | New knowledge is stored but stored in an encapsulated way | Existing schema is more complete, coherent, salient, and strengthened | New inferences create new knowledge beyond what was encoded; thus existing schema may become more enriched; procedures may be elaborated with meaning, rationale, and justifications; and mental models may be accommodated; and schema may be linked with other schemas | New knowledge and perspectives can emerge from co-creating knowledge that neither partner knew |

(continued)

**Table 2** (continued)

| Category characteristics | *Passive* **receiving** | *Active* **manipulating** | *Constructive* **generating** | *Interactive* **dialoguing** |
|---|---|---|---|---|
| Expected cognitive outcomes | Recall: knowledge can be recalled verbatim in identical context (e.g., reuse the same procedure or explanation for identical problems or concepts) | Apply: knowledge can be applied to similar but nonidentical contexts (i.e., similar problems or concepts that need to be explained) | Transfer: knowledge of procedures can be applied to a novel context or distant problem; knowledge of concepts permits interpretation and explanations of new concepts | Co-create: knowledge and perspectives can allow partners to invent new products, interpretations, procedures, and ideas |
| Learning outcomes | Minimal understanding | Shallow understanding | Deep understanding, potential for transfer | Deepest understanding, potential to innovate novel ideas |

*From Chi and Wylie (2014; pg.22)*

lives. Activity like this is possible in a higher education classroom if your students are primed for it on the first day of class as an integral component of your class structure and thereupon reminded of the structure at the beginning of your class for the first couple of weeks. It also means that you punctuate your class time with these segments—albeit brief—and take moments to stop presenting so your students can write their notes and take a moment to cognitively catch up. Catching up means giving time to think; and thinking means being able to generate the inferences that potentially lead to the rich cognitive models your students will use to apply their new knowledge outside of your classroom.

Earlier we noted that, as far back as the 1960s, Rothkopf viewed students as both a processor and **active elaborator** of information, and while the work of Wittrock (1974, 1989, 2010), Mayer (2014), and Chi (Chi et al., 2018) fleshed out this view extensively, others have done so as well, approaching the concept by using the term **elaboration**. Indeed, the idea that information is better understood, processed, and retrieved if students have an opportunity to elaborate on that information has been fairly well established (Anderson & Reder, 1979; Reder, 1980); and in education there are many ways in which this condition can be fulfilled. For example, students can elaborate on information by answering questions about a text (see the instructional hierarchy learning stages fluency and generalization from this chapter; see also Anderson & Biddle, 1975), by formulating and critically examining hypotheses about a given problem (see the instructional hierarchy learning stage adaptation; see Chi's constructive and integrative engagement), by taking notes (Peper & Mayer, 1978, 1986), and by creating mind maps and other spatial displays (c.f. Eppler, 2006). These are all forms of elaboration that are discussed in this chapter. However, we believe that it is valuable to have an understanding of the benefits of providing your students opportunities to engage in elaboration: Engaging in elaboration not only provides the redundancy in memory needed to support your students' encoding and eventual retrieval of the information you are teaching them (see Chi's active engagement; Reder, 1980), but it also stimulates the generation of inferences we discussed above.

## Activity Inside of Class

One way to support student's elaborative engagement is through notetaking. Opportunities for students to take notes during a lecture should be ample; in fact, the vast majority of college students report taking notes during lectures (Morehead, Dunlosky, Rawson, Blasiman, & Hollis, 2019). Notetaking is beneficial because previous research has demonstrated that students who take notes recall more key concepts from lectures; furthermore, the students who take notes recall more conceptually relevant content in comparison to students who take no notes at all (Peper & Mayer, 1978, 1986).

In general, there has been a consensus over several decades that taking notes is effective during lectures. However, much of notetaking research was conducted before students had access to technology to take notes (Barnett, Di Vesta, & Rogozinski, 1981; Kiewra et al., 1991; Peper & Mayer, 1978, 1986). In fact, given the increase of technology use in the classroom, taking notes by hand is now considered more of a traditional form of taking notes (Lin & Bigenho, 2011).

From students' perspective, using laptops to take notes is reported as being overall beneficial (Skolnick & Puzo, 2008). However, from teachers' perspective, the use of laptops in the classroom is generally regarded as a distraction and in fact results in increased students' off-task behavior (Kay & Lauricella, 2011; Skolnick & Puzo, 2008). Specifically, Kraushaar and Novak (2010) revealed that students who use a laptop during class are off task (defined as having non-course-related applications open during class) 42% of the time, which in turn leads to lower performance in the course (Glass & Kang, 2019; Sana, Weston, & Cepeda, 2013). Therefore, one seemingly obvious reason that teachers may believe notetaking by hand is preferable to laptop notetaking is because there are fewer distractions at hand for the student to easily engage with.

And yet, it is important to note that even the most recent research on the benefits of notetaking by hand versus laptop notetaking should be interpreted cautiously. That is, there are contrasting conclusions in the literature regarding which form of notetaking is most beneficial for your students. For example, while the studies mentioned above found a benefit of notetaking by hand, research by Bui, Myerson, and Hale (2013) suggested that students who take notes on laptops outperform students who take notes by hand. Furthermore, various studies have found that students who take notes on a computer usually generate more words and ideas than students who take notes by hand. Still, whether this demonstrates that taking notes on a laptop is better than notetaking by hand is presently strongly debated (Bui et al., 2013; Mueller & Oppenheimer, 2014).

In our opinion, it makes sense that a consensus has eluded the field between by-hand and laptop notetaking. In a recent integrative review detailing the cognitive costs and benefits of taking notes (see Jansen, Lakens, & IJsselsteijn, 2017 for full review), Jansen et al. (2017) suggested that it is difficult, if not impossible, to directly compare the results of notetaking studies in order to make a definitive decision about which one is best for a classroom policy because (1) some of the studies detailing the benefits of notetaking by hand were conducted before laptops were common in classrooms; (2) studies used different lecture formats (e.g., audio, video, text); (3) lecture formats varied in difficulty and length; (4) testing across studies was not uniform (e.g., free recall, recognition, short answer, multiple choice, tapping procedural or conceptual knowledge constructs, course exam, writing an essay); and (5) different sample sizes were used.

It can be easily argued that an increase in off-task behavior, such as opening non-course-related applications, would be completely curtailed if laptops were prohibited in your classroom; however, we believe that banning laptops from a university classroom would be counterproductive. For example, students with certain learning challenges may be unable to take notes without a computer and may not want to be singled out for having to do so. Thus, in light of our position, there are several instructional techniques you can use without having to create a technology-free classroom. First, you can design a seating arrangement where your students who prefer to take laptop notes can sit in the front corners of your classroom. As a result, other students, who may be particularly distracted by screens, can choose seats out of view of laptop screens. Second, on the first day of class, during a time where the syllabus is typically being explained, you may give additional instruction and resources on how to take notes for your course. This suggestion is based on recent research by Morehead et al. (2019) who demonstrated that the majority of college students were actually not even aware that there were other notetaking techniques available to them (e.g., Cornell notes). Indeed, the researchers found that students welcomed the opportunity to have more instruction on how to take notes. Third and finally, while you may allow laptops in your classroom, it is also quite effective to intermittently direct your students to close their laptops when you are discussing key or complex topics.

In sum, while it may be unsatisfying that the notetaking research fails to lead to a specific set of recommendations, notetaking in general is still fairly well supported. It is just that the jury is out as to whether notes should be taken by hand or by laptop and whether laptop use should be directed only for the specific use of classroom learning.

## Activity Inside or Outside of Class

On the other hand, we do believe that, in order for learning to occur, it is essential that your students be given the opportunity for agency, creativity, and growth and be active during learning. Indeed, as the underlying thread of this chapter, we know that meaningful learning occurs by students **actively** integrating new concepts into prior knowledge structures. Therefore, you may consider assigning activities that afford your students active consolidation and reflection on the new knowledge they are attempting to learn—**during** class (Dhindsa & Anderson, 2011; Twardy, 2004). As a result of being assigned such activities, your students are given the opportunity to bring their personal experience, perspective, and creativity into your classroom, which is an essential component of reflecting on, and learning, new material (Plummer, 2001).

The question then becomes: What types of activities can you provide that involve your students' personal experience/perspective, reflection, and integration of old and new knowledge? Commonly, spatial visualizations have been used effectively in this endeavor (Larkin & Simon, 1987; Tufte, 1983).

Spatial visualizations, such as mind maps and concept maps, may be particularly useful because they are often constructed in some type of organizational or hierarchical concept structure. Having this type of visual structure showcases the relationships between concepts and ideas (Eppler, 2006). Since the concepts are clearly connected to each other structurally and visually, these spatial visualization formats actually become physical artifacts of students' developing knowledge structures (Nousiainen, 2012). Furthermore, the different types of spatial visualization formats enhance learning because information is presented in more than one modality—textually and visually (Schwartz, 1988).

Although the underlying learning mechanisms are similar between different forms of spatial visualization formats, there are differences in their application. Specifically, the spatial visualization formats we are referring to here are mind maps (Buzan, 2006) and concept maps (Davies, 2011). While there are many other formats (for argument maps see Davies, 2011; for conceptual diagrams see Eppler, 2006), for brevity we will only be discussing the two. Please refer to Table 3 for an adapted table from Eppler (2006) highlighting the difference between these two spatial visualization formats.

Concept maps were initially developed by Novak (1998) with the main goal of enhancing meaningful learning by having students list and connect various concepts in a relational nature. Indeed, affording students the opportunity to make relational connections between relevant concepts is, from the perspective of teachers, possibly the greatest advantage that concept maps offer (Davies, 2011). As we discussed previously, this is exactly how meaningful learning takes place—linking new concepts to existing knowledge structures—and there is a plethora of evidence that demonstrates the benefits of using concept maps in education settings for this purpose (Amundsen, Weston, & McAlpine, 2008; Kinchin, 2000; Sanchiz et al., 2019). Still, it is important to note that concept maps are not without their disadvantages. They require some expertise to learn and constructing them can be challenging and overwhelming (Kinchin, 2000).

Mind maps, by comparison, were initially developed by Buzan (2006), with the goal of creating a method of notetaking that is brief and interesting (Buzan & Buzan, 2006). According to Buzan (2006), mind mapping is a strategy to think about and organize information visually by creating nonlinear relationships between ideas and colors. Similar to concept maps, several studies have demonstrated the effectiveness

**Table 3** Comparison of two spatial visualization formats: concept maps and mind maps

| | Concept map | Mind map |
|---|---|---|
| Example visualization | (Retrieved from West, Pomeroy, Park, Gerstenberger, & Sandoval, 2000) | (Retrieved from https://sites.psu.edu/kzg128/2012/12/07/mind-maps/) |
| Definition | Top-down diagram that shows relationship between concepts, cross-connections between concepts, and examples | Image-centered, multicolored, radial diagram that represents semantic or other connections between portion of hierarchically learned material |
| Function | Shows systematic relationships among sub-concepts that relate to one main concept | Shows sub-topics of a domain in a creative and seamless manner |
| Suggested application guidelines | Use it as a learner support tool for students to summarize key course topics or clarify the elements/examples of an abstract topic | Use it for brainstorming and rapid notetaking or to structure the main contents of a course/topic hierarchically |
| Advantages | Emphasizes relationships and connections among object | Encourages creativity and self-expression |
| | Provides systematic overview | Provides concise hierarchic overview |
| | Ability to assess quality of concept map through evaluative rules | Easy to extend and add additional content |
| Disadvantages | Not easily applied by novices; requires training | Represents mostly hierarchic relationships |
| | Tend to be idiosyncratic | Tend to be idiosyncratic, hard for others to read |
| | Time-consuming to create evaluative rules | Picture can become too large and overly complex |

*From Eppler (2006; pp.203, 206)*

of mind maps in educational settings (Biktimirov & Nilson, 2006; Eriksson & Hauer, 2004; Farrand, Hussain, & Hennessy, 2002). From teachers' perspectives, possibly the greatest advantage of mind maps is the creative potential they afford their students (Davies, 2011). But again, there are also disadvantages: They are idiosyncratic to each student and can potentially become overly complex.

Finally, note that mind mapping and concept mapping are functionally distinct (Davies, 2011; Eppler, 2006). Concept maps visualize structured, relational connections between concepts; mind maps visualize spontaneous, creative, and associative connections between ideas. Therefore, mind maps are used to show **associative** connections between concepts; concept maps are used to show **relational** connections between concepts **and** sub-concepts (Davies, 2011). Still, both spatial visualizations not only align with our underlying approach to learning in that they provide an actively constructed visual form to support reflection, associations between ideas, and relations between concepts (Kinchin, Streatfield, & Hay, 2010), but they are also perceived positively by teachers and students. Keles (2012) discovered that teachers found using mind maps with their students to be enjoyable, believing that mind maps increased their students' motivation of the topic they were trying to teach. Likewise, students perceived positively the use of spatial visualizations—in all its various formats—as an effective activity from which to learn (Goodnough & Woods, 2002). In short, employing these different spatial visualizations is valuable— before class to introduce concepts from assigned readings, as a summary of what was discussed during class and in lecture presentations, and in taking notes (see Table 3 suggested applications).

## Section 3: The Way to Lecture

Throughout this chapter, we have assumed that lecturing comprises much of what goes on in most higher education classrooms, and there is evidence that this assumption is true. Consider the work of Stains et al. (2018). They observed 2,008 STEM classes within 709 courses across 25 universities—24 doctorate-granting and 1 primarily undergraduate institution. What they found was remarkable: 55% of those observations were traditional lecture formats in which teachers spent 80% or more of those lectures speaking. While roughly a quarter (27%) of those observations consisted of some sort of student-centered activity during class (e.g., some group activity or handheld clickers to answer questions), only 18% of the classes saw a heavily student-centered approach to instruction. Moreover, during each measured 2-minute interval of class time, (a) instructors lectured approximately 75% of the time, and (b) students primarily listened to their instructor lecture 81% percent of the time and asked questions only 10%. Therefore, as demonstrated by Stains et al. (2018), lecturing still consumes the lion's share of most college classrooms.

And yet, while we do not suggest that you spend most of your class time lecturing, if you do, it is essential to know that lecturing is not a one-dimensional activity.

When most teachers lecture, they tend to do so by **describing** the concepts, principles, axioms, techniques, and other categories of information that comprise the curriculum of their course. Indeed, describing—or, perhaps more commonly, reading off a PowerPoint slide and giving or asking for examples—is what is typically seen in most college classrooms (Schmidt et al., 2010; Stains et al., 2018; Wieman, 2017). However, describing **per se** is a relatively flat, uninteresting, and nonengaging method of presenting information to your students. Instead, lecturing is most effective when it is inspiring, emotionally stirring, and relatable—the type of lecturing that has the capacity to get your students to **think** *while* they are learning.

And yet, it is also important to note that when a student takes their seat in your classroom, they have to make a cognitive shift from the conditions and situations of their everyday lives. They may have rushed to your class from a previous one; they may have been thinking of their friends and the social conditions (positive or negative) that infuse their lives; or they may be worried about their finances, social engagements, or family dynamics at home. Today, it is not uncommon for students to work part or full time to meet, or at least help with, their college expenses (Lipka, 2007; Snyder, de Brey, & Dillow, 2019). Thus, they may be concerned about making it to work on time, wondering about their upcoming work schedule, or thinking about their workplace performance relative to the expectations of their boss. The point is that all of these concerns are formidable hurdles to clear in order to pull your students into the subject matter you are intending for them to learn while they are seated in front of you at the top of the hour.

So, what is important to think about when lecturing in your classroom? We believe that there are three major areas that can effectively pull your students into the subject matter of your course: directing and sustaining their attention, using personal examples, and invoking their emotional commitment.

## Directing and Sustaining Attention

One of the simplest ways to direct and sustain attention in your students is to awaken their situational interest and sense of value when you lecture. Situational interest refers to features of your lecture that highlight **real** human activity or meaningful themes of life (Ainley, Hidi, & Berndorff, 2002; Hidi, 1990), as well as an emotional response your students experience directly (Hidi & Harackiewicz, 2000). Value refers to whether your students share the merit you find in the subject matter you teach—in practical terms, whether your goals invoke in them a sense of importance to their own identity, utility in the achievement of their own goals, and activities they find interesting and/or enjoyable (Wigfield & Eccles, 2000). Students, when their interest is activated, show closer and more sustained attention, learn more, and experience enjoyment to a greater degree than students whose interest is low (Ainley et al., 2002).

## Using Personal Examples

Personal examples are valuable to use in your lectures, as well. Personal examples increase your students' interest and sense of ownership in the material you present; they activate the previous knowledge your students already have in order to build the cognitive models necessary for them to acquire still new knowledge (Abrahamson, 2005). Both the personal examples of your own experience and the examples of your students enhance their desire to actively think while you are lecturing, as well as fostering a positive interpersonal relationship between both of you (Abrahamson, 2005).

There is little doubt that students already report using self-generated examples as a learning technique while they are studying (Gurung, Widert, & Jeske, 2010). However, it is also important to point out that they organically come up with their own examples for a reason: Student-generated examples make concept learning more successful (Rawson & Dunlosky, 2016); those concepts lead to more comprehensible and more enduring knowledge structures over time (Barnett & Cici, 2002); and student-generated examples lead to better problem-solving. Indeed, Hamilton (1989) observed that learners who generated two personal examples for each definition of a psychological concept performed better on problem-solving questions than did learners who generated no personal examples at all. The point is that when you infuse personal examples into your lectures—examples that are either yours or those of your students—your students not only make better connections to what they already know, and learn more because of it, but the examples both of you generate also serve to enhance your relationship with each other.

## Activating Positive Student Emotions

Finally, we suggested above that lecturing is most effective when it is inspiring, emotionally stirring, and relatable. Thus, beyond the recognition that stimulating situational interest and using personal examples is effective in enhancing student learning, activating emotions in your students is valuable, as well. Activating emotion during lecture leads to what Cavanaugh (2016) calls "emotional contagion"—the idea that if teachers foster positive emotions in their students, both toward the material and themselves, then their students may show more engagement with the course and the material and show higher overall course achievement. Cavanaugh reasoned that, since the systems of the brain involved in learning and emotion are not separate but neurologically linked, it makes sense that positive emotional arousal should lead to enhanced learning.

While there is a trail of research going back to the 1980s suggesting that Cavanaugh may, in practice, be correct (c.f. Bower, 1981; Bower, Gilligan, & Monteiro, 1981; Isen, Daubman, & Nowicki, 1987), Pekrun and Stephens (2010a) caution that emotional influences should be carefully crafted in educational courses because their antecedents in an ecologically valid setting still have not been thoroughly well examined. Nevertheless, we suggest that evoking positive emotional arousal among your student during lecture, if incurred judiciously, is probably productive. Thus, we agree with Cavanaugh (2016) since we believe that there is sufficient evidence to support it. For example, students experiencing more positive emotions also engaged more with their classroom material, and more engagement with the material led to higher achievement (Buff, Reusser, Rakoczy, & Pauli, 2011); students' positive emotions increased their intrinsic motivation by stimulating their curiosity to explore new information, leading to better academic performance (Pekrun & Stephen, 2010b; Um, Plass, Hayward, & Homer, 2012); stimulating positive emotions in students induced the students to show greater creativity and flexibility when attempting to solve problems, as well as more efficiency in decisions they were asked to make (Isen, 2000); positive emotions helped students pay better attention to classroom content (Park & Lim, 2007); and, finally, students when learning in a negative mood performed worse than students in a positive mood on a set of logical inference problems (Jung, Wranke, Hamburger, & Knauff, 2014). The take-home message is this: Incurring your students to be activated emotionally in positive ways when you teach can lead to better learning and more productive thinking and contribute to higher achievement.

## Section 4: Concluding Remarks

The theme of this chapter is based upon the premise that, in order for students to learn in higher education classrooms, they must be engaged. And yet, in order to be engaged, it is essential to understand what is meant by engagement—that the concept has a rich history of theories and models that support it and lead to methods that foster it. The most important core to those methods centers around activity—not necessarily physical activity per se, although physical activity is important vis-à-vis the notion of embodiment, but activity that leads your students to think—while they are learning. We inventoried ways in which you can incur that active thinking but added that thinking, without the activation of emotion in your students, may not be enough to leverage the higher education classroom to its potential for meaningful student learning.

## Cross-References

▶ Assessment of Learning in Psychology
▶ Basic Principles and Procedures for Effective Teaching in Psychology
▶ First Principles of Instruction Revisited
▶ Formative Assessment and Feedback Strategies
▶ Inquiry-Based Learning in Psychology
▶ Problem-Based Learning and Case-Based Learning
▶ Small Group Learning

## References

Abrahamson, C. E. (2005). Motivating students through personal connections: Storytelling as a pedagogy in introductory psychology. *Best practices for teaching introduction to psychology* (pp. 245–258). Mahwah, NJ: Lawrence Erlbaum Associates.
Ainley, M., Hidi, S., & Berndorff, D. (2002). Interest, learning, and the psychological processes that mediate their relationship. *Journal of Educational Psychology, 94*(3), 545.

Amundsen, C., Weston, C., & McAlpine, L. (2008). Concept mapping to support university academics' analysis of course content. *Studies in Higher Education, 33*(6), 633–652.

Anderson, J. R., & Reder, L. M. (1979). An elaborative processing explanation of depth of processing. In L. S. Cermak & F. I. M. Craik (Eds.), *Levels of processing in human memory (Erlbam, 1979)* (pp. 385-404).

Anderson, R. C., & Biddle, W. B. (1975). On asking people questions about what they are reading. In *Psychology of learning and motivation* (Vol. 9, pp. 89–132). Waltham, MA: Academic Press.

Ardoin, S. P., & Daly, E. J. (2007). Introduction to the special series: Close encounters of the instructional kind—How the instructional hierarchy is shaping instructional research 30 years later. *Journal of Behavioral Education, 16*(1), 1–6.

Barnett, J. E., Di Vesta, F. J., & Rogozinski, J. T. (1981). What is learned in note taking? *Journal of Educational Psychology, 73*(2), 181.

Barnett, S. M., & Ceci, S. J. (2002). When and where do we apply what we learn? A taxonomy for far transfer. *Psychological Bulletin, 128*, 612–637.

Biktimirov, E. N., & Nilson, L. B. (2006). Show them the money: Using mind mapping in the introductory finance course. *Journal of Financial Education, 32,* 72–86.

Blaich, C., Wise, K., Pascarella, E. T., & Roksa, J. (2016). Instructional clarity and organization: It's not new or fancy, but it matters. *Change: The Magazine of Higher Learning, 48*(4), 6–13.

Bower, G. H. (1981). Mood and memory. *American Psychologist, 36*(2), 129.

Bower, G. H., Gilligan, S. G., & Monteiro, K. P. (1981). Selectivity of learning caused by affective states. *Journal of Experimental Psychology: General, 110*(4), 451.

Braxton, J. M., Bray, N. J., & Berger, J. B. (2000). Faculty teaching skills and their influence on the college student departure process. *Journal of College Student Development, 41*(2), 215.

Bray, G. B., Pascarella, E. T., & Pierson, C. T. (2004). Postsecondary education and some dimensions of literacy development: An exploration of longitudinal evidence. *Reading Research Quarterly, 39*(3), 306–330.

Bretzing, B. H., & Kulhavy, R. W. (1981). Note-taking and passage style. *Journal of Educational Psychology, 73*(2), 242.

Bruner, J. S. (1961). The act of discovery. *Harvard Educational Review, 31*, 21–32.

Buff, A., Reusser, K., Rakoczy, K., & Pauli, C. (2011). Activating positive affective experiences in the classroom: "Nice to have" or something more? *Learning and Instruction, 21*(3), 452–466.

Bui, D. C., Myerson, J., & Hale, S. (2013). Note-taking with computers: Exploring alternative strategies for improved recall. *Journal of Educational Psychology, 105*(2), 299.

Burns, M. K., Codding, R. S., Boice, C. H., & Lukito, G. (2010). Meta-analysis of acquisition and fluency math interventions with instructional and frustration level skills: Evidence for a skill-by-treatment interaction. *School Psychology Review, 39*(1), 69.

Buzan, T. (2006). *The ultimate book of mind maps: Unlock your creativity, boost your memory, change your life.* London, UK: HarperCollins.

Buzan, T., & Buzan, B. (2006). *The mind map book*. Pearson Education.

Cavanagh, S. R. (2016). *The spark of learning: Energizing the college classroom with the science of emotion.* Morgantown, WA: West Virginia University Press.

Chi, M. T. (2009). Active-constructive-interactive: A conceptual framework for differentiating learning activities. *Topics in Cognitive Science, 1*(1), 73–105.

Chi, M. T., Adams, J., Bogusch, E. B., Bruchok, C., Kang, S., Lancaster, M., et al. (2018). Translating the ICAP theory of cognitive engagement into practice. *Cognitive Science, 42*(6), 1777–1832.

Chi, M. T., & Wylie, R. (2014). The ICAP framework: Linking cognitive engagement to active learning outcomes. *Educational Psychologist, 49*(4), 219–243.

Daly, E. J., III, Lentz, F. E., Jr., & Boyer, J. (1996). The instructional hierarchy: A conceptual model for understanding the effective components of reading interventions. *School Psychology Quarterly, 11*(4), 369.

Daly, E. J., III, Martens, B. K., Hamler, K. R., Dool, E. J., & Eckert, T. L. (1999). A brief experimental analysis for identifying instructional components needed to improve oral reading fluency. *Journal of Applied Behavior Analysis, 32*(1), 83–94.

Davies, M. (2011). Concept mapping, mind mapping and argument mapping: What are the differences and do they matter? *Higher Education, 62*(3), 279–301.

Dhindsa, H. S., & Anderson, O. R. (2011). Constructivist-visual mind map teaching approach and the quality of students' cognitive structures. *Journal of Science Education and Technology, 20*(2), 186–200.

Dochy, F. J., & Alexander, P. A. (1995). Mapping prior knowledge: A framework for discussion among researchers. *European Journal of Psychology of Education, 10*(3), 225–242.

Eppler, M. J. (2006). A comparison between concept maps, mind maps, conceptual diagrams, and visual metaphors as complementary tools for knowledge construction and sharing. *Information Visualization, 5*(3), 202–210.

Eriksson, L. T., & Hauer, A. M. (2004). Mind map marketing: A creative approach in developing marketing skills. *Journal of Marketing Education, 26*(2), 174–187.

Espin, C. A., & Deno, S. L. (1989). The effects of modeling and prompting feedback strategies on sight word reading of students labeled learning disabled. *Education and Treatment of Children, 12*(3), 219–231.

Farrand, P., Hussain, F., & Hennessy, E. (2002). The efficacy of the 'mind map' study technique. *Medical Education, 36*(5), 426–431.

Feldman, K. A. (1989). The association between student ratings of specific instructional dimensions and student achievement: Refining and extending the synthesis of data from multisection validity studies. *Research in Higher Education, 30*(6), 583–645.

Fiorella, L., & Kuhlmann, S. (2019). Creating drawings enhances learning by teaching. *Journal of Educational Psychology, 112*(4), 811–822.

Fiorella, L., Stull, A. T., Kuhlmann, S., & Mayer, R. E. (2019). Instructor presence in video lectures: The role of dynamic drawings, eye contact, and instructor visibility. *Journal of Educational Psychology, 111*(7), 1162.

Glass, A. L., & Kang, M. (2019). Dividing attention in the classroom reduces exam performance. *Educational Psychology, 39*(3), 395–408.

Glynn, S. M., & Di Vesta, F. J. (1977). Outline and hierarchical organization as aids for study and retrieval. *Journal of Educational Psychology, 69*(2), 89.

Goodnough, K., & Woods, R. (2002). *Student and teacher perceptions of mind mapping: A middle school case study*.

Goulet, L. R. (1970). Training, transfer, and the development of complex behavior. *Human Development, 13*(4), 213–240.

Goulet, L. R., & Wittrock, M. C. (1971). Transfer of training models and developmental processes. In *Biennial meeting of the society for research in child development*. Minneapolis, MN.

Gurung, R. A. R., Weidert, J., & Jeske, A. (2010). Focusing on how students study. *Journal of the Scholarship of Teaching and Learning, 10*, 28–35.

Hamilton, R. (1989). The effects of learner-generated elaborations on concept learning from prose. *The Journal of Experimental Education, 57*(3), 205–217.

Haring, N. G., Lovitt, T. C., Eaton, M. D., & Hansen, C. L. (1978). *The fourth R: Research in the classroom*. Columbus, OH: Charles E. Merrill Publishing Company.

Hidi, S. (1990). Interest and its contribution as a mental resource for learning. *Review of Educational Research, 60*(4), 549–571.

Hidi, S., & Harackiewicz, J. M. (2000). Motivating the academically unmotivated: A critical issue for the 21st century. *Review of Educational Research, 70*(2), 151–179.

Isen, A. M. (2000). Positive affect and decision making. In M. Lewis & J. Haviland (Eds.), *Handbook of emotions* (pp. 720), Guilford, NY: The Guilford Press.

Isen, A. M., Daubman, K. A., & Nowicki, G. P. (1987). Positive affect facilitates creative problem solving. *Journal of Personality and Social Psychology, 52*(6), 1122.

Jansen, R. S., Lakens, D., & IJsselsteijn, W. A. (2017). An integrative review of the cognitive costs and benefits of note-taking. *Educational Research Review, 22*, 223–233.

Jung, N., Wranke, C., Hamburger, K., & Knauff, M. (2014). How emotions affect logical reasoning: Evidence from experiments with mood-manipulated participants, spider phobics, and people with exam anxiety. *Frontiers in Psychology, 5*, 570.

Kay, R. H., & Lauricella, S. (2011). Unstructured vs. structured use of laptops in higher education. *Journal of Information Technology Education, 10*(1), 33–42.

Keles, Ö. (2012). Elementary teachers' views on mind mapping. *International Journal of Education, 4*(1), 93.

Kiewra, K. A., DuBois, N. F., Christian, D., McShane, A., Meyerhoffer, M., & Roskelley, D. (1991). Note-taking functions and techniques. *Journal of Educational Psychology, 83*(2), 240.

Kinchin, I. M. (2000). Concept mapping in biology. *Journal of Biological Education, 34*(2), 6168.

Kinchin, I. M., Streatfield, D., & Hay, D. B. (2010). Using concept mapping to enhance the research interview. *International Journal of Qualitative Methods, 9*(1), 52–68.

Kourilsky, M., & Wittrock, M. C. (1992). Generative teaching: An enhancement strategy for the learning of economics in cooperative groups. *American Educational Research Journal, 29*(4), 861–876.

Kraushaar, J. M., & Novak, D. C. (2010). Examining the affects of student multitasking with laptops during the lecture. *Journal of Information Systems Education, 21*(2), 11.

Lannie, A. L., & Martens, B. K. (2008). Targeting performance dimensions in sequence according to the instructional hierarchy: Effects on children's math work within a selfmonitoring program. *Journal of Behavioral Education, 17*(4), 356.

Larkin, J. H., & Simon, H. A. (1987). Why a diagram is (sometimes) worth ten thousand words. *Cognitive Science, 11*(1), 65–100.

Lin, L., & Bigenho, C. (2011). Note-taking and memory in different media environments. *Computers in the Schools, 28*(3), 200–216.

Lipka, S. (2007). More students seek campus jobs as work-study positions dwindle. *The Chronicle of Higher Education, 53*(21), A40.

Martens, B. K., & Witt, J. C. (2004). Competence, persistence, and success: The positive psychology of behavioral skill instruction. *Psychology in the Schools, 41*(1), 19–30.

Mayer, R. E. (1992). *Thinking, problem solving, cognition*. WH Freeman/Times Books/Henry Holt & Co.

Mayer, R. E. (2014). Multimedia instruction. In *Handbook of research on educational communications and technology* (pp. 385–399). New York, NY: Springer.

Morehead, K., Dunlosky, J., Rawson, K. A., Blasiman, R., & Hollis, R. B. (2019). Note-taking habits of 21st century college students: Implications for student learning, memory, and achievement. *Memory, 27*(6), 807–819.

Mueller, P. A., & Oppenheimer, D. M. (2014). The pen is mightier than the keyboard: Advantages of longhand over laptop note taking. *Psychological Science, 25*(6), 1159–1168.

Neumann, A. (2014). Staking a claim on learning: What we should know about learning in higher education and why. *The Review of Higher Education, 37*(2), 249–267.

Nousiainen, M. (2012). Making concept maps useful for physics teacher education: Analysis of epistemic content of links. *Journal of Baltic Science Education, 11*(1), 29–42.

Novak, J. D. (1998). *Learning, creating and using knowledge: Concept maps as facilitative tools in schools and corporations*. Mahwah, NJ: Lawrence Erlbaum Associates.

Park, S., & Lim, J. (2007). Promoting positive emotion in multimedia learning using visual illustrations. *Journal of Educational Multimedia and Hypermedia, 16*(2), 141–162.

Parker, D. C., & Burns, M. K. (2014). Using the instructional level as a criterion to target reading interventions. *Reading & Writing Quarterly, 30*(1), 79–94.

Pascarella, E. T., Salisbury, M. H., & Blaich, C. (2011). Exposure to effective instruction and college student persistence: A multi-institutional replication and extension. *Journal of College Student Development, 52*(1), 4–19.

Pascarella, E. T., Seifert, T. A., & Whitt, E. J. (2008). Effective instruction and college student persistence: Some new evidence. *New Directions for Teaching and Learning, 2008*(115), 55–70.

Pekrun, R., & Stephens, E. J. (2010a). Achievement emotions in higher education. In *Higher education: Handbook of theory and research* (pp. 257–306). Dordrecht, The Netherlands: Springer.

Pekrun, R., & Stephens, E. J. (2010b). Achievement emotions: A control-value approach. *Social and Personality Psychology Compass, 4*(4), 238–255.
Peper, R. J., & Mayer, R. E. (1978). Note taking as a generative activity. *Journal of Educational Psychology, 70*(4), 514.
Peper, R. J., & Mayer, R. E. (1986). Generative effects of note-taking during science lectures. *Journal of Educational Psychology, 78*(1), 3.
Piaget, J. (1930). *The child's conception of causality.* London, UK: Kegan Paul.
Plummer, K. (2001). The call of life stories in ethnographic research. *Handbook of Ethnography* (pp. 395–406).
Poncy, B. C., Duhon, G. J., Lee, S. B., & Key, A. (2010). Evaluation of techniques to promote generalization with basic math fact skills. *Journal of Behavioral Education, 19*(1), 76–92.
Poncy, B. C., Skinner, C. H., & Jaspers, K. E. (2007). Evaluating and comparing interventions designed to enhance math fact accuracy and fluency: Cover, copy, and compare versus taped problems. *Journal of Behavioral Education, 16*(1), 27–37.
Rawson, K. A., & Dunlosky, J. (2016). How effective is example generation for learning declarative concepts? *Educational Psychology Review, 28*(3), 649–672.
Reder, L. M. (1980). The role of elaboration in the comprehension and retention of prose: A critical review. *Review of Educational Research, 50*(1), 5–53.
Roksa, J., Trolian, T. L., Blaich, C., & Wise, K. (2017). Facilitating academic performance in college: Understanding the role of clear and organized instruction. *Higher Education, 74*(2), 283–300.
Rothkopf, E., & Shaughnessy, M. F. (2005). An interview with Ernst Rothkopf: Reflections on Educational Psychology. *North American Journal of Psychology, 7*(1), 51.
Rothkopf, E. Z. (1970). The concept of mathemagenic activities. *Review of Educational Research, 40*(3), 325–336.
Sana, F., Weston, T., & Cepeda, N. J. (2013). Laptop multitasking hinders classroom learning for both users and nearby peers. *Computers & Education, 62*, 24–31.
Sanchiz, M., Lemarié, J., Chevalier, A., Cegarra, J., Paubel, P. V., Salmerón, L., & Amadieu, F. (2019). Investigating multimedia effects on concept map building: Impact on map quality, information processing and learning outcome. *Education and Information Technologies, 24*(6), 3645–3667.
Schmidt, H. G., Cohen-Schotanus, J., Van Der Molen, H. T., Splinter, T. A., Bulte, J., Holdrinet, R., & Van Rossum, H. J. (2010). Learning more by being taught less: A "time-for-self-study" theory explaining curricular effects on graduation rate and study duration. *Higher Education, 60*(3), 287–300.
Schwartz, N. H. (1988). *Cognitive processing characteristics of maps: Implications for instruction.* Educational & Psychological Research.
Skolnik, R., & Puzo, M. (2008). Utilization of laptop computers in the school of business classroom. *Academy of Educational Leadership Journal, 12*(2), 1.
Snyder, T. D., de Brey, C., & Dillow, S. A. (2019). *Digest of education statistics 2017, NCES 2018-070.* National Center for Education Statistics.
Stains, M., Harshman, J., Barker, M. K., Chasteen, S. V., Cole, R., DeChenne-Peters, S. E., et al. (2018). Anatomy of STEM teaching in North American universities. *Science, 359*(6383), 1468–1470.
Tufte, E. R. (1983). *The visual display of quantitative information* (Vol. 2). Cheshire, CT: Graphics press.
Twardy, C. (2004). Argument maps improve critical thinking. *Teaching Philosophy, 27*(2), 95–116.
Um, E., Plass, J. L., Hayward, E. O., & Homer, B. D. (2012). Emotional design in multimedia learning. *Journal of Educational Psychology, 104*(2), 485.
Wang, J. S., Pascarella, E. T., Nelson Laird, T. F., & Ribera, A. K. (2015). How clear and organized classroom instruction and deep approaches to learning affect growth in critical thinking and need for cognition. *Studies in Higher Education, 40*(10), 1786–1807.

West, D. C., Pomeroy, J. R., Park, J. K., Gerstenberger, E. A., & Sandoval, J. (2000). Critical thinking in graduate medical education: A role for concept mapping assessment? *JAMA, 284*(9), 1105–1110.

Whitehead, A. N. (1929). *The aims of education*. New York, NY: Macmillan.

Wieman, C. (2017). *Improving how universities teach science*. Cambridge, MA: Harvard University Press.

Wigfield, A., & Eccles, J. S. (2000). Expectancy–value theory of achievement motivation. *Contemporary Educational Psychology, 25*(1), 68–81.

Wittrock, M. (2010). Learning as a generative process. *Educational Psychologist, 45*(1), 40–45.

Wittrock, M. C. (1974). Learning as a generative process. *Educational Psychologist, 11*(2), 8795.

Wittrock, M. C. (1989). Generative processes of comprehension. *Educational Psychologist, 24*(4), 345–376.

Wittrock, M. C., & Carter, J. F. (1975). *Generative processing of organized information*. Unpublished manuscript.

Wright, J. (n.d.). *The instructional hierarchy: Linking stages of learning to effective instructional techniques*. Retrieved from https://www.interventioncentral.org/academic-interventions/general-academic/instructional-hierarchy-linking-stages-learning-effective-in

# Index

**A**
Abductive reasoning, 971
ABGERO specialist, 1044
Ability, 518, 521, 522, 525
Abnormal psychology, 26, 303
    case study, 70
    course, 50–60
    reasons for teaching, 50
    teaching methods, 60–66
Aboriginal healing practices, 729
Aboriginal social and emotional well-being, 728, 729
Aboriginal suicide, 728
Abstraction and categorization, 970
Academic domain, 40
Acceptance commitment therapy, 36
Acceptance from peers, 1082
Accreditation, 948, 958
Achievement motivation, 951
Acquiring competencies, 922
Acquisition, 933
Action control, 218
Action factors, 637
Action potentials, 405
Action regulation theory, 543
Action research, 316, 1362
Action teaching, 316–318
ActionTeaching.org, 332
Activation-principle, 1212
Activation-structure, 1216
Active learning, 110, 410, 413, 1215, 1236, 1249
Active lectures, 188, 192
Active teaching methodology, 876
Activist practitioner, 736
Activist scholars, 736, 737
Activities for teaching statistics and research methods, 429

Activity system in the training programs, 721
Activity theory, 718
Adaptive control of thought-(ACT-) and script theory, 929
Adaptive learning, 376, 1401
Adaptive support, 1296
Addiction, drug, 771, 776
Adulthood without experiencing the birth and development of someone else's infant, 288
Advanced statistical skills, 36
Advertising, 621
Aesthetics, 994, 1001, 1003
Affective-cognitive processes, 752
African Framework of Standards and Competences, 814–818
Age groups, 263
Agency, 203, 211, 225
Agents of socialization, educational resources, 678, 679
Aggression, 612–619, 623
Agile systems, 559
Aging, 1047, 1050, 1052, 1061, 1068–1070
Albeit functional competencies, 29
Ambulatory assessment, 515, 523
American Academy of Pediatrics, 615
American Association of Colleges and Universities, 413
American Association of Medical Colleges (AAMC, 2011), 984
American Board of geropsychology (ABGERO), 1044
American Board of Professional Psychology (ABPP), 1044
Americanization, 291
American Psychological Association, Coalition for Psychology in Schools and Education (APA-CPSE), 821

American Psychological Association (APA), 33, 36, 117, 303, 320, 331, 340, 361, 396, 611, 614, 615, 617–619, 624, 641, 701, 716, 850, 854–860, 947, 1408
  APA-accredited doctoral programs, 36
  Custom Course Books, 1176
  guidelines, 303
  internal organization, 701
  National Standards for High School Psychology Curricula, 1147, 1148
  Psychology: Major Competencies, 1149
American school psychology following the Thayer Conference, 702
Amerindian Support Network, 751
Analysis of the addressees, 1391
Analysis of variance (ANOVA), 36, 424
Analytical scoring method, 1180
Animal models, 104
Anorexia nervosa, 620
Anterior cingulate cortex, 219
Anthropologist on Mars, 598
Anti-gender campaigns in Europe, 692
Anti-poverty approach, 671
Anxiety/arousal, 515, 951
Applicability of knowledge, 168
Application principle, 1213
Applied behavior analysis (ABA), 104
Applied experience, 117
Applied psychological research, 549
Applied teaching techniques, 265–266
Arguments to authority, 618
Art appreciation, 995, 1001, 1002, 1006
Artifact analysis, 463
Artificial intelligence (AI), 137, 141, 376, 377
Artistic experience, 1001
Arts-based research, 465
Ashrama dharma, stages, 281
Ashrama theory, 280, 281
Asian parenting, 296
Ask instructional event, 1214
Assessment, 32–36, 41, 146–147, 322–324, 431, 934, 1245
  authentic, 13, 1338–1340
  align assessments with learning goals, 12–14
  in cognition, 188–190
  of cognitive control abilities, 215–216
  courses, 35, 836
  in cultural psychology, 598
  developmental psychology, 262
  embedded assessment, 12–13, 18
  in engineering psychology, 574
  formative (see Formative assessment)
  in geropsychology, 1062–1065
  in health psychology, 345
  learning, 190–192
  methods, 523
  in motivation science, 166–167
  in neuroscience, 402
  in physiological psychology, 304
  problem solving, 141–144
  resources, 121–124, 168, 196, 267, 311, 331, 380–383, 412, 1167–1169
  in sensation and perception, 84, 88
  in social psychology, 322–324
  students' learning, knowledge, and competences, 115, 190–191, 836
  summative, 115, 323, 378
  training programs, 35
  *See also* Psychological Assessment
Association for Applied Sport Psychology (AASP), 946, 947, 958
Association of European Qualitative Researchers in Psychology (EQuiP), 455
Attention deficit hyperactivity disorder (ADHD), 104, 214, 1190
Attitudes, 516, 520, 522, 814
AT triangle, 720
Attributions, 154, 321, 921, 951
Attribution theory, 366
Attrition, 1424
Auditory hallucinations, 63
Auditory process, 90
Augmented reality (AR), 1396, 1400
Australasian Society for Behavioral Health and Medicine, 349
Australian Professional Standards for Teachers, 811–812
Australian Psychological Society (APS), 349, 727, 1043
Australian standards, 811
Authentic assessments, 13, 1338–1340
Authentic evidence of learning, 1313, 1318
Authoring software, 1395, 1397
Autism, 63, 104
Autoethnography, 465
Automation, 569–570, 573, 577, 580, 581
Autonomy and proficiency, 878
Avoidance, 161

**B**

Backward course design, 9–15, 109, 322
Backyard brains, 783
Bandura's Bobo doll studies, 614, 623
Bandwidth-fidelity dilemma, 514, 526

Basic psychological knowledge, 831
Basic psychological research, 549
Behavior, 515–516, 519–522, 524
  behavior change, 956
  probability/rate, 119
Behavioral addictions, 204, 210, 214, 224
Behavioral and social sciences (BSS), 980
Behavioral cognitive theories, 922
Behavioral pharmacology, 775
Behavioral problems, 1082–1084, 1088
Behaviorism, 104, 276, 663, 1435
  cognitive psychology, 103
  dominance, 103
  mental process, 103
  professional associations and publications, 104
  tenets, 104
Behaviorists, 103
Behavior therapy, 35
Beliefs, 520, 521
  persistence, 118
Bem's Sex Role Inventory (BSRI), 666
Big data assignment, 193–194
Binary approaches of life, 669
Biological theories, 521
Biologization of conduct, 286
Biomedical research activities, 302
Biopsychology, 393, 399, 401, 403
Biopsychosocial (approach) model, 50, 54, 56, 340, 344, 649, 916
Blackboard, 330
Blackboard virtual learning environment (VLE), 1158
Black Lives Matter, 330
Blended Collaborative and Constructive Participation (BCCP), 1410, 1419, 1420, 1422, 1423
  Jigsaw method, 1415–1418
  RT, 1413–1415
  TLA, 1410–1412
Blended learning, 957, 1409
Blind angle accidents, 82
Blood oxygen level-dependent (BOLD) response, 220
Bloom, B.S., 1313
  revised taxonomy, 1181
  taxonomy, 110
Board of Educational affairs (BEA), 857, 1160
Body dissatisfaction, 620, 621
Body image, 611
Bologna process model, 681, 682
Brain-based incremental learning, 182
Brainstorming, 1415

British Association for Sport and Exercise Science (BASES), 948
British Psychological Society accreditation criteria, 31
British Psychology Society (BPS), 33, 348, 948
Bronfenbrenner's ecological perspective, 56
Buddhism, 280
Burnout, 920
Business and organizational contexts, 542

C
Caffeine, 773
Campus learning management system, 107
Canadian Psychological Association (CPA), 346
Career
  adaptability, 913
  autonomy, 918
  competence, 918
  portfolio, 1339
  resilience, 913
  satisfaction and career success, 913
  self-determination, 918
Career development learning (CDL), 893
Care practices, 296
Case-based learning (CBL), 552, 1206, 1238, 1393
  examinations, 1245
  in North-American Medical Schools, 1236
  scheduling, 1244
  self-directed, 1243–1244
  teacher-centered and student-centered, 1238
Case-based lectures, 1237
Case-based reasoning (CBR), 1239
Case-selection and implementation, 715
Categories of learning
  outcomes, 1204
  strategies, 1156
Category-domains, 370
Category-oriented methods
  grounded theory methodology, 467
  qualitative content analysis, 466–467
Certification, 946–948, 958
Certified Mental Performance Consultant (CMPC), 946, 948
Chalkboard, 1184
Change, 515, 523, 525, 526
Change blindness, 87–88
Character, 520, 954
Chernobyl disaster, 569
Child data language exchange system (CHILDES, 187

Childhood and the care of children, 279, 280
Child Protection, 287
Chinese Association for Mental Health (CAMH), 633
Chinese Psychological Society (CPS), 633
Choosing textbooks, 1176
Chronic traumatic encephalopathy (CTE), 410
4C/ID model, 1390
Citizen psychologists, 1307
Citizenship, 919
Civic internships, 1320
Civic learning, 1307, 1320
Classical test theory (CTT), 523, 532
Classification of instructional variables, 1203
Classroom
  atmosphere, 1190
  centered around social justice, 732
  environment, 1184
  incivilities, 1192
  response systems, 113
  teaching and learning, 838
Client-advocacy, 649
Client-centered practice, 643
Climate change, 1321
Clinical and educational psychology, 549
Clinical psychological communication, 41
Clinical psychologists, 28
Clinical psychology, 144, 731
  American Psychological Association, 27
  behavioral and mental health issues, 26
  challenges, 40
  core contents, 34, 35
  curriculum, 27, 28, 40
  definition, 26
  doctoral and higher education, 31, 33, 34
  experimental work, 27
  field of Psychology and Health Sciences, 37
  graduate education, 29, 31
  lessons, students, 29
  psychological assessment, 27
  regulated mental health profession, 27
  research and clinical skills, 29, 30
  substantial development, 41
  and traditional approaches to psychotherapy, 727
Clinical science model, 27
Clinical skills, 33
Clinical supervision, 966, 969, 974
  collaborative learning, 975, 976
  modalities, 968
  process, 966
  triadic model, 966
Coaching, 1213, 1216

Code of ethics, 947, 1322
Co-genetic dynamic, 967
Cognition, 365, 518
  and learning, 709
Cognitive/intellectual disabilities, 1081, 1084
Cognitive and constructivist theories of learning, 922
Cognitive apprenticeship, 361, 833
Cognitive behavior(al) therapy (CBT), 35, 36, 60, 104, 649, 731
Cognitive computing, 136
Cognitive control training, 211, 224
Cognitive development, 278
Cognitive development and learning, 709
Cognitive flexibility, 215, 226–229
Cognitive functioning, 295
Cognitive impairment, 1070
Cognitive mechanisms, 214–215
Cognitive model, 1438
Cognitive neuropsychology, 179, 186
Cognitive neuroscience, 186, 204, 219, 220, 225
Cognitive outcomes in children, 295
Cognitive psychology, 103, 104, 141, 180, 364
Cognitive revolution, 103
Cognitive science, 178
Cognitive systems, 134
Cognitive theory, 179, 186, 521
  of multimedia learning, 929
Cognitivist renaissance, 103
Cohesion, 952
Cohort effects, 256
Co-Lab project, 1274
Collaboration, 407, 1314
Collaboration script approach, 1293
Collaborative learning, 1286, 1287, 1290, 1292, 1294, 1295
Collective implementation intentions, 164
Collective uncounscious, 997
Collectivism, 289
College Board Advanced Placement (AP) program, 848
Colonialism, 747
Colonization, 742
Office of Suicide Prevention and Cactus, 677
Committee of Clinical and Counseling Psychology in the Chinese Psychological Society, 633
Committee of Counseling and Psychotherapy, 633
Common instructional sequence, 1214
Communication, 260–261
Communication and interpersonal skills, 35

Community
  benefits, 1308, 1318
  educators in the classroom, 733
  health psychology, 1155
  outcomes, 1316–1317
  partners, 1307, 1311, 1314, 1315, 1320, 1322, 1323
  psychology programs, 731
  quality, 1086
Community-based approaches, 730
  to family relationships, 730
  to psychological issues, 730
Community-based programs, 1035
Community-campus partnerships, 1318
Community-psychology
  consciousness-raising, 728
  critical national problems, 728
  direct intervention, 728
  ecological model, 727
  origins, 726, 727
  personal network of interactions, 728
  psychological reflections, 745
Comparative cognition, 104
Competence(s), 594, 809–811, 916
  acquisition, 917, 922, 924
  assessment, 640
  attribution, 921
  communication and mediation, 931
  definition, 922
  education, 917
  experience, 918
  formally acquired, 917
  framework, 811
  job-related, 924
  knowledge and skills, 924
  learning process, 924
  models, 918
  needs, 917
  personality, 920
  professional, 145–146, 924, 1057
  profiles, 913, 915, 932
  recognition, 914
  reflection and reorientation, 931
  self-organizing disposition, 921
Competence-based education, 923
Competence-based ICVT, 923
Competence level of the German education guidelines for Master's programs in W/O-Psychology, 547
Competence-orientation, 928
Competence-oriented didactics in teaching, 558
Competence-performance model, 917
Competencies, 32, 34, 922

Competencies students, 363–364
Competency-based approach, 481, 487
Competency-based assessment, 1216
Competency-based turn, 923
Competency model, 362
Competitive context, 447
Complementary learning systems (CLS) theory, 181
Complex adaptation processes, 916
Complexity, 719, 877
Component display theory, 1203, 1204, 1224
Component skills, 1208, 1218
Comprehensive assessment curricula, 35
Comprehensive psychological services to children, 701
Computational models, 223–224
Computational models of cognitive control, 205, 210, 223–224
Computer assisted/aided qualitative data analysis (CAQDAS), 470
Computer-assisted therapies (CAT), 641, 642
Computer-based collaborative learning (CSCL), 1393
Computer-based instruction system, 1203
Computer-based learning environment, 1290
Computer-delivered assessment, 146
Computer-mediated communication, 641
Computer-supported collaborative learning, 1293
Computer-supported intentional learning environment (CSILE), 1274
Concept maps, 1446–1448
Conceptual-change based learning, 156, 167
Conceptual replications, 327
Conditioned stimuli, 103
Condition(ing), 1207
  fundamentals, 117
  procedure, 112
Conference systems, 1395
Confidentiality, 37
Confidence, 952
Confirmatory factor analysis (CFA), 523
Conflict, 216
Conflict-monitoring theory, 209
Connecting information, 114
Connectionism, 179
Connectionist models, 223
Conscientiousness, 1290
Consistency, 514, 518, 526
Constricted collectivism, 289
Construct, 514, 518, 520, 521, 524, 526
Construction objects, 967
Constructive activities, 1289

Constructive alignment (CA), 560, 828
Constructivism, 1435
Construct validity, 1341
Consultation and Collaboration, 705
Consumer warming, 82
Content, 817
　elements, 1208, 1209
　structuring, 1394
　validity, 1341
Content-first approach, 1217
Content-material and activities, 822–828
Context(s), 596, 792–794, 796, 801, 804
　of practice, 1036
　sensitive help, 1213
Contextual cultural experiences, 645
Contextual dynamics, 802
Contextualization, 969
Continuing education
　challenges, 931
　competence profile, 932
　course designing, 914
　courses, 927
　individual/professional profiles, 916
　initial education, 928
　innovation, 933
　landscape, 914, 929
　learning, 916
　open studies, 917
　psychologists, 933
　psychology, 933
　response, 914
　theories, 914
Continuing professional development (CPD), 933
Continuing professional enhancement, 645
Continuous transformation, 967
Control dilemmas, 222
Controlled processes, 206, 214
Control network (central executive network), 209
Conversation analysis (CA), 468–469
Conversations of gestures, 794
Cookbook science labs, 1156
Cooperative learning, 1286
Co-participation, 1036
Copyright laws, 1176
Core Knowledge in Psychology and Education, 709
Core teaching, 362–363
Core teaching and learning objectives, 818–820
Coronavirus pandemic, 330
Corrective feedback, 1213, 1215
Correlation, 515, 518, 524

Correlational designs, 523
Co-teaching approach, 579
Council of Chief State School Officers (CCSSO), 814
Council of Europe, 1320
Council of Professional Geropsychology Training Programs (CoPGTP), 1044
Counseling, 631, 930
Counseling and psychotherapy, 630
　in Asia, 632
　in China, 632, 633
　clinical and technical skills, 638
　competence continuum, 639
　conceptualization and critical thinking, 637
　critical thinking, 638
　culturally and ethically sensitive manner, 639
　in India, 633, 634
　in Japan, 635
　legal and ethical guidelines, 638
　in South Korea, 635, 636
　therapeutic alliances, 637
Counseling competence, 637
Counselor competency, 638
Counselor training, 645
Counterargument, 1293
Counter-normative, 1321
Course-based undergraduate research experiences (CUREs), 413
Course
　concepts, 40
　design process, 482
　evaluations, 1180
　goals, 1173
　learning objectives for introductory psychology, 11–12
Course-level assessment, 1335
Course's content delivery system, 305
Covering research methods, 108
COVID pandemic, 41, 351, 721
Create-integration, 1216
Creative arts, 735, 736
Crisis management, 731
Criterion-based system, 1179
Criterion-referenced grading, 1178
Criterion validity, 1341
Critical pedagogy for privileged students, 732
Critical psychology, 1020
Critical scientists, 1020
Critical thinking, 611, 614, 616, 622–625
Critical to human-centered cognitive computing, 136
Cross-cultural research, 326
Cross-sectional research designs, 256

Cultural and dialogical psychologies, 743
Cultural canalization processes, 447, 448
Cultural contexts, 157, 280, 799, 800, 920
Cultural defamiliarization, 600–602
Cultural diversity, 79
Cultural dynamic, 800–803
Cultural historical activity theory (CHAT), 718
Cultural-historical perspective, 592, 798–800
Culturally-structured contexts, 448
Cultural nature, 801
Cultural norms, 913
Cultural practices in children's care, 287
Cultural psychology, 444, 744
    challenges and lessons, 602–603
    core contents, 596
    culture role, 591
    current trends, 593–594
    description, 590
    historical context, 591–593
    purposes and rationale, 594–596
    scientific status, 591
    teaching, learning and assessment, 598–599
Cultural regulation, 975
Cultural responsivity, 896–897
Cultural semiotic psychology, 1022
Cultural sensitivity, 1034
Cultural specificity, 297
Cultural values, 444
Culture(s), 321, 793, 797
    of assessment, 1373
    and communities, 294, 295
    and personality, 592
    and science, 293
Cumulative (final) exam, 116, 181, 1183
Curricular continuing education programs, 917
Curricular design, 367
Curriculum, 517, 529, 1237
    competencies students, 363–364
    core contents and topics, 241–242
    core teaching and learning objectives, 362–363
    design, 369, 836
    design and implementation, 40
    developmental psychology, 241
    educational psychology, 361
    psychologists, 361
    student training and mentoring, 361
    superordinate learning objectives, 364
Custodial sanctions, 1034
Customer-based approach, 580
Cybernetic control model, 164
Cybernetics and systems, 731
Cyberspace, 135

## D

Dana Foundation, 782
Data-based decision making and accountability, 705
Data-based recommendations, 562
Data box, 524
Data graphs, 76–78, 89
Data production
    documents and artifacts, 463
    fixing the data, 465–466
    group discussion, 461
    interviews, 459–461
    observation and ethnography, 462–463
    qualitative experiments, 464
    videography, 463
Data science, 135
    educational assessment, 146
    in psychology, 146
Day of Compassion, 318–319
DEAL model for critical reflection, 1313
Deception, 328
Decision-making, 874
Decision oriented instructional design (DO ID) model, 1389, 1390
Decolonizing clinical psychology, 737, 738
Deep cultural expertise combined with family therapy, 730
Deep learning (DL), 135, 141
Deep thinking, 193
Defamiliarization, 600–602
Deliberate action, 809, 838
Deliberate practice, 638, 649
Deliberate professionals, 837
DeMaes, 675
Demand characteristics, 613, 614
Democratic civic engagement, 1320
Democratization of learning, 733
Demonstration (principle), 90, 1212
Demonstrative speech, 749
Depression, 214, 224
Depth hermeneutics, 469
Depth of processing theory, 365
Design of application and case-oriented learning in W/O-Psychology, 552, 553
Desirable competencies, 368
Desirable teacher behavior, 1173
Developmental psychology, 263, 526, 921, 922
    challenges, 267
    children's developing minds and activities, 275
    culture, 276
    curriculum, 241
    developmental concerns, 275

Developmental psychology (cont.)
  experimental conditions, 277
  international interventions, 278
  intersectionality, 278
  psychology, 240
  qualitative methodologies, 276
  suggestions, 263
  teaching application, 254
Developmental theories, 253–254
Developmental trajectories, 1031
Development policy for women, 671
Dharma (righteousness), principles of, 280
Diagnoses-centered approach, 37
Diagnostic and Statistical Manual of Mental
    Disorders, 50
  competencies related to limitations of,
      56–59
  language of, 53
Diagnostic assessments, 39
Diagnostic classificatory systems, 37
Dialogical conceptualization, 975
Dialogical model, 972
Dialogical psychologies, 744
Dialogical self-system resources, 447
Dialogical skills, 601–602
Dialogicity, 972, 973
Dialogism, 746
Didactic skills, 42, 932
Differential psychology, 550
Digital media, 42
  in higher education teaching, 558
Digital teaching, 929
Digital tools, 718
Digital transformation, 1409
Digitization of the world of work, 543
Digitization of work and business processes,
    559
Diligence, 638, 639
Diminishing coaching, 1215
Dionisos Teatro Project, 675
Disciplinary differentiation, 743
Disciplinary orientation, 544
Discourse analysis, 468
Discussion board, 955
Discussion rules, 1188
Dispositions, 514, 515, 519, 522
Dissatisfaction, 916
Distributed practice, 113, 114, 324, 1182
Diversity, 320, 852, 1314, 1318,
    1320, 1323
  and complexity, 747
  in development and learning, 705
  of dialogues and aims, 973, 974

Doctoral programs
  in clinical psychology, 31
  in W/O-psychology, 545
Document analysis, 463
Do example, 1224
DO-execute (DOex), 1220
DO-identify (DOid), 1220
Domain-general competences, 917
Domains of professional competency, 1152
Domain-specific principle, 133
Dominance of individualism, 726
Dorsal anterior cingulate cortex (dACC), 221
Dot lattice stimuli, 84
Double loop learning, 928
Drives, 152, 153
Drug abuse, 1070
Dry-erase board, 1184
Dualisms, 289
Dual process theories, 522
Dual systems/dual process theories (of self-
    control), 208, 218
Dynamic nature of motivational process, 156
Dynamic system theories (DST)
  applications, 253
  existing developmental theories, 253–254
  integrative theory, 249–252
Dynamic transformations, 253
Dysexecutive syndrome, 209, 220


E
East-West divide and the failure, mutuality, 292,
    293
Eating disorder, 620, 621
Ecological assessment, 731
Ecological model, 796, 1151
Ecological momentary assessment, 221, 228
Ecological networks, 138, 139
Ecological validity, 298
Economic reforms, 634
Education, 792, 802, 804, 915
Educational achievement, 515, 535
Educational competences, 932
Educational (Instructional) Technology, 1388,
    1389
Educational policy, 1091
Educational practice, 834, 839
Educational psychology, 550, 810, 929
  approaches and strategies, 367–371
  complexities and vagaries, 360
  core topics, 364–367
  curriculum, 361–364
  deliberate action, 809

domains, 358
dynamic human-environmental transactions, 358
education community, 838
evidence-based reflection, 809
field of study, 358
precursory thinking, 359
psychology's application, 360
students' special needs, 359
supplementary discipline, 834
teacher education programs, 810
teleological point of view, 359
textbooks, 821
tracing, 359
trajectory, 360
Education and Training for Counseling and Therapy, 642
Education for Sustainable Development (ESD), 927
Education process, 878
Education system, 706
Effective, efficient and engaging ($e^3$) instruction, 1204, 1214, 1220–1222
Effectiveness, 931
Effective teaching, 371–372
  ad hoc decisions, 1195
  characteristics, 1173, 1174
  course materials, 1175, 1176
  desirable difficulties, 1182, 1183
  evaluations, 1179
  evaluations by colleagues, 1194
  evaluations by students, 1193, 1194
  first day of class, 1183–1185
  formative feedback, 1180
  grading system, 1178, 1179
  international differences, 1172
  massed vs. distributed practice, 1182
  mental health services, 1172
  post-mortem reflection, 1195
  prompt feedback, 1183
  psychology of learning, 1182
  responsibilities, 1172
  self-evaluation, 1194
  setting goals, 1173, 1175
  student behavior problems, 1192, 1193
  summative feedback, 1180
  syllabus, 1176, 1177
  teaching role, 1172
  testing effect, 1182
  test items, 1191, 1192
  tests and quizzes, 1180, 1181
  United States, 1172
  writing assignments, 1182

Efficiency, 671, 931
EFPA Standing Committee, 1044
Ego depletion, 208, 218
Elaboration theory, 822
Elaborative processing, 324
E-learning, 929
Electroencephalogram (EEG), 215
Elements of content, 1205
Elements of instructional content, 1206
Embedded assessment, 13
Embodied approach to cognition, 180
Embryonic fallacy, 286
Emotion, 518, 525
Emotional climate or atmosphere, 970
Emotional competence, 639
Emotional design, 1396
Emotional landscapes, 283
Emotional tension, 974
Emotion regulation, 53, 207, 217, 221
Emotions and stress, 397
Empathy, 317
Empirical-supported treatment, 40
Empiricism, 1120
Employability, 884–885
Empowerment
  models, 672
  of marginalized gender, 671, 672
  practices, 731
Encephalography (EEG), 255
Engineering psychology, 568, 571, 574, 583–586
  automation, 569–570
  case studies, 578–579
  Chernobyl disaster, 569
  core contents and topics, 573–574
  co-teaching approach, 579
  customer-based approach, 580
  definition, theories and models, 571
  empirical findings and practical applications, 572
  Fitts' law, 570
  involvement of practitioners, 579–580
  lectures, 574
  methods, 572
  seminar on automation, 581
  small-group practicals, 582–583
  small group teaching, 580–581
  target audience, 579
  teaching, learning and assessment resources, 585–586
English Lexicon Project (ELP), 187
Enthusiasm, 37
Entrepreneurship, 918

Entrepreneurship skills, 649
Entry point for therapist training, 643, 644
Environment, 794–798
Environmental circumstances, 640
Environmental psychology, 86
Environmental systems, 916
Episodic future thinking, 207, 217
Epistemic network analysis, 138, 140, 1295
Epistemology, 747, 834
    analytic and synthetic truth statements, 1124
    basic definition of knowledge, 1119
    behaviorism, 1136
    behaviorist psychology, 1123
    Cartesianism, 1131
    classical theory of knowledge, 1127
    communitarian epistemology, 1126
    communities, 1132, 1133
    criticism, 1129
    depth hermeneutics, 1138
    dichotomy of facts and values, 1134
    ecology of mind, 1138
    empiricism, 1134
    epistemic justice, 1138
    epistemic situation, 1119
    experiences, 1132
    explanation and understanding, 1132, 1136
    factors, 1135
    features, 1132
    feminist epistemologies, 1126
    genetic epistemology, 1135
    Habermas, 1127
    historical and cultural objects, 1135
    history, 1125
    history of psychology, 1133
    human consciousness, 1137
    human engagement, 1138
    humanism, 1129
    humanistic epistemic culture, 1120
    human kinds, 1132
    human knowledge, 1118
    individualism, 1137
    induction, 1123
    intentionality, 1137
    interpretants, 1137
    intersubjectivity, 1127
    knowledge interests, 1127
    legacy of ancient Greek, 1129
    meaning, 1125, 1136
    methodology, 1127, 1128, 1137
    methods, 1136
    microcosmos, 1119
    model of knowledge, 1128
    modernity, 1130
    modern sciences, 1129
    natural kinds, 1132
    participational, 1128
    philosophy, 1135
    physical/socio-cultural environment, 1119
    physical space, 1133
    positivism, 1120
    positivist, 1120–1122
    qualitative approaches, 1128
    quantitative methodology, 1136
    Renaissance, 1129
    scientism, 1124
    self-confident program, 1131
    sensory organs, 1128
    the sensus communis, 1132
    signification, 1133
    skepticism, 1130
    social facts, 1132
    of the South, 1020
    subjectivity, 1125
    subject-matter psychology, 1135
    symbolic forms, 1133
    teaching and learning psychology, 1134
    theory of meaning, 1124
    theory of (scientific) knowledge, 1118, 1119, 1135
    understanding, 1125, 1129
    verum ipsum factum, 1131
E-portfolio, 1339, 1418–1421
Equity approach, 671
Erikson's theory, 281
E-seminars (webinars), 1399
eService Learning (eSL), 1321
Essential elements, of service learning, 1307, 1311
Ethical codes, 650, 651
Ethical dimension of WOP teaching, 872, 873
Ethical requirements, 915
Ethics, 754, 1322
Ethnography, 462–463
Ethnopsychiatry, 744
Ethnopsychoanalysis, 744
Euro-American mainstream epistemologies, 1020
Euro-American psychological science, 278
European Agency for Development in Special Needs Education, 1081
European Federation of Psychologists' Association (EFPA), 31, 348, 706, 1043, 1146
European Health Psychology Society (EHPS), 349

European Higher Education Area (EHEA), 396, 1160
European Qualification in Psychology, 348
European Qualifications Framework (EQF), 814, 828, 1162
EuroPsy, 31, 1146
Evaluative competence, 932
Evidence-based decision making and accountability, 721
Evidence-based practice (EBP), 914, 915, 1155
Evidence-based psychological principles, 377
Evidence-based reflection, 809, 838
Evidence-based teaching, 5, 410
Evolutionary psychologists, 322
Evolutionary theory, 665
Evolution by natural selection, 107, 108
Evolved psychotherapy, 630
Exact replications, 327
Excuses, 1190
Executive functions, 203, 205, 206, 212
Exemplary domain, saliency of faces, 258
Exercise motivation, 953
Exosystem, 797
Expansive learning model, 715
Expectancies, 154
Expected utility theory, 208, 216
Expected value of control theory, 209, 222
Experiencing Researcher: Educated Intuition, 441–443
Experiential learning, 39, 556, 928, 1308
Experimental and mixed designs, 523
Expert groups, 1415
Expertise, 1247
Explaining videos, 1393, 1394
ExplanationConstructor, 1274
Explicit dispositions, 522
Exploitation-exploration dilemma, 222
Expository generality, 1224
Expository instance, 1224
Extraversion, 1290
Extrinsic motivation, 156
Eye tracking, 88, 266
Eysenck's model, 526

**F**

Face-to-face instruction, 402, 404, 411, 412
Factor analysis, 526, 532
Faculty development, 1322
Faculty–student rapport, 1190
Faculty-student relationships
 complaints, 1190, 1191
 problems, 1190, 1191
 student requests, 1190, 1191
 teacher power, 1189, 1190
Fair game, 153
Familism, 282
Family, 288
 adjustment, 1087
 life-cycle, 288
 relationships, 280
 therapists, 726
Family-centered social care, 1027
Family-centered social work, 1028, 1029
Family–School Collaboration Services, 705
Feedback, 1245, 1290
Feelings of incompetence (FOI), 640
Feminist movement, 662, 663
Feminist orientation, 663
Feminist readings on Michael Foucault's concept of biopower, 668
Feminization of development, 290
Field-specific experts, 368
Fiji study, 620, 623
Filter metaphor, 85
First Amendment, 625
First principles of instruction, 372–373, 822, 1211
 activation principle, 1211, 1212
 application principle, 1211, 1213
 demonstration principle, 1211, 1212
 $e^3$ instruction, 1220–1222
 elements of content, 1205
 formative evaluation, 1223
 historical context and rationale, 1203–1204
 implications, for learning and teaching psychology, 1224–1225
 instructional design theory, 1204
 instructional goals, 1204
 instructional interaction, 1205–1206
 instructional strategies, 1206, 1214–1216
 integration principle, 1211, 1213
 measurement of complex task/problem-solving performance, 1216–1217
 pebble-in-the-pond model, 1217–1219
 prescriptive instructional design theory, 1223–1224
 problem-centered principle, 1211, 1212
 problem-progression model, 1210–1211
 problem-solving model, 1206–1209
Fitts' law, 570
Five core propositions, 814–816
Flanker task, 207, 215
Flexibilization, 917
Flexibilization of the world of work, 544
Flexner Report, 981

Flip chart, 1184
Flipped classroom/inverted classroom, 955, 1238, 1393
Focused interview, 460
Folk psychology, 285
Formally acquired competences, 917
Formative assessment, 112, 323, 324, 379–383, 499, 504, 683, 828–830, 835–836, 957, 1331–1355
　adaptation strategy, 1368
　challenges, 1378, 1379
　characteristics, 1375
　characteristics of the learner, 1366, 1375
　codes and modes of feedback representation, 1368
　cognitive, meta-cognitive and motivational, 1367
　cognitive dispositions, 1376
　cognitive operations, 1367
　competence, 1376
　competency frameworks, 1366
　computer-based tutoring systems, 1365
　cyclical process, 1362
　design, 1368
　diagnostic, 1361
　dialogic feedback cycle, 1368, 1369
　evidence-based perspective, 1360
　exemplary approaches, 1371
　external feedback, 1363, 1364, 1367
　feedback culture, 1369
　feedback cycle, 1365
　feedback design principles, 1371
　feedback literacy, 1377
　feedback loops, 1364
　feedback scheduling, 1368
　feedback timing, 1368
　formative feedback strategies, 1360
　Higher Education, 1360, 1369
　implications, 1378, 1379
　individual and context-related factors, 1375
　information technologies, 1377
　instructional contexts, 1363, 1366
　interactive assessment, 1363
　interactive two-feedback loops model, 1364
　internal control action, 1365
　internal feedback, 1363, 1364, 1376
　internal processing, 1365
　interviews, 1366
　learning, 1379, 1380
　learning outcomes, 1367
　learning task level, 1367
　log-files, 1366
　meta-analyses, 1370
　meta-task level, 1367
　methods, 1361
　misconceptions, 1367
　monitoring, 1376
　motivational and meta-cognitive factors, 1376
　motivational task level, 1367
　multidimensional instructional approaches, 1375
　online-resources and tools, 1381, 1382
　peer-assessment, 1372
　peer feedback, 1362, 1376
　performance feedback, 1370
　purpose, 1361
　qualitative research, 1375
　questionnaires, 1366
　recommended readings, 1380
　research issues, 1373, 1374
　reviews, 1370
　self-assessment, 1372
　self-regulated learning, 1362
　strategies, 1367
　student learning, 1363
　students, 1368
　summative or formative, 1360
　teacher feedback literacy, 1377
　teachers, 1368
　teaching, 1379, 1380
　technology-enhanced assessment, 1372
　tests, 1366
Format of the instruction, 1391
Foundational competency, 1153
Foundational knowledge, 1307, 1309
Foundations of School Psychological Service Delivery, 705
Four–component instructional design model (4C/ID), 832
Framework of Indicators to Gauge Gender Sensitivity in Media Operations and Content, 684
Frameworks for Professional Standards and Competences
　Australian standards, 811
　competences, 811
　South East Asia Standards, 811
　US standards and competences for teachers, 811–814
Free speech, 617, 622, 624–625
Free will, 203, 211, 212, 225, 229
Freud's theory, 520
Friendship, 1083, 1085–1086
Functional competency, 1153
Functional connectivity, 220

Functional decomposition, 215–216
Functional dissociation, 209, 220
Functional integration, 1079
Functionality, 1150
Functional magnetic resonance imaging (fMRI), 219, 255
Functional near-infrared spectroscopy (fNIRS), 255
Functional neurology, 104
Functional prototype, 1219
Functional wellbeing, 1150–1152
Future time perspective, 206, 213

**G**

Ganzheitspsychologie, 464
Gay Affirmative Counselling Practice (GACP), 670
Gaze following, 259
GEAR Tool of the European Institute of Gender Equality, 682, 683
Gender and media, 683
Gender-based discrimination and harassment (GBDH), 687, 688
Gender-based discrimination and violence, 684
Gender-based violence, 661
Gender bias(es), 669, 682
    in fairytales, media and schools, 679, 680
Gender biased attitudes and negative stereotypes, 661
Gender Competence Centre Berlin, 680
Gender empowerment instances, 661
    Gender equality, 687
    Gender Equality and Girls' Education Initiative in Viet Nam project, 680
    Integrative Model for Gender Equality in the Workplace, 687
Gender gap, 692, 693
Gender impact assessment (GIA), 692, 693
Gender implicit association test, 667
Gender-inclusive practices in education, 680
Gender inequality index of the Human Development Report 2019, 672
Genderlessness, 663
Gender schema theory, 680
Gender segregation, 683
Gender sensitive governance and policy making, 661
Gender-sensitive interventions, 672
Gender sensitive trends in diagnosis and therapy, 669, 670
    trend of using male-based norms, 669
Gender socialization in Indian families, 690

Gender studies
    in psychological research, 666–668
    of psychological tests, 665, 666
    in psychological theories, 664, 665
    women's movements, 664
General instructional strategy, 1394
Generalizability, 326
Generalization, 969, 971
General linear model, 532
General problem solver (GPS), 141
General psychology, 550, 745
Generative process of unlimited semiosis, 967
Generic model of psychotherapy, 643
Genetic epistemology, 254
Genetics, 521
Geropsychology
    acting in everyday life, 1052
    age, aging and aged, 1052
    age-related diseases, 1053, 1054
    applied geropsychological assessment, 1058
    assessment tasks for learning outcomes, 1064, 1065
    bachelor and master programs, 1044
    basic components of geropsychological acting, 1048
    course sequences over semesters, 1062
    diversity of study programs, 1046, 1047
    domains of acting, functioning, and development, 1049, 1050
    ethical foundations, 1057
    evaluation methods, 1058
    extended abstract level of competence, 1051
    family caregivers, 1056
    general foundations, 1047, 1048
    geriatric syndromes, 1053, 1054
    Handbooks/Encyclopedias, 1068, 1069
    influence of historical events and changes, 1054
    intended learning outcomes, 1062, 1063
    intervention methods, 1059, 1060
    journals, 1071, 1072
    legal foundations, 1057
    level of competencies, 1051
    master programs, 1045
    mental disorders, 1044
    modules of study programs, 1061, 1062
    multi-directional relationships between research, teaching, and practice, 1066
    multi-structural level of competence, 1051
    multi-volume encyclopedias, 1043
    non-normative life transitions, 1055
    non-psychological bachelor, 1045

Geropsychology (*cont.*)
  non-psychological study programs, 1065, 1066
  non-university research institutes, 1043
  normative life transitions, 1054
  nursing science programs, 1045
  older people and professionals, 1056
  organizing and updating curricula, 1067
  personal resources of older people, 1055
  personal self-regulation, 1053
  physical and technological resources, 1056
  professional caregivers, 1057
  professionalization, 1043
  psychological and psychotherapeutic institutes, 1044
  psychology, 1043
  psychotherapy education, 1044
  qualification, 1045, 1046
  reference levels of geropsychological acting, 1049
  relational level of competence, 1051
  research and practical application, 1066, 1067
  research and teaching, 1067
  research methods, 1058
  research resources, 1058
  semester-by-semester schedule, 1068
  settings of geropsychological work, 1047, 1050, 1051, 1060, 1061
  social resources of older people, 1055, 1056
  social work, 1045
  target groups of geropsychological acting, 1050
  teaching, 1043
  teaching and learning activities, 1063, 1064, 1068
  teaching and practical application, 1067
  text books, 1069, 1070
  unistructural level of competence, 1051
  URL-links, 1072
*Ginkgo Biloba*, 764
Global citizen(ship), 887, 1308, 1323
Global culture, 293
Global Gender Gap Report 2018, 671
Global quality scoring, 1180
Global Standards for Quality Improvement for Medical Education, 980
Go/no-go task, 215, 229
Goal(s), 154
  based scenarios, 1393, 1399
  commitment, 162
  goal-directed behavior, 164
  orientation, 162, 366
  realization, 162
  setting, 162, 953, 955
Go-public-integration, 1216
Government/policy making models, 689, 690
Grade point average (GPA), 1342
Grading, 1245
Grading rubric, 1180
Graduate programs, 643
Graduate student (GR), 1221
Grant proposals, 776
Graphics design and layout, 1398
Grounded theory methodology (GTM), 466, 467
Group awareness tools, 1294, 1296
Group discussion, 461–462, 464, 466, 474, 1244
Group dynamics, 952
Grouping
  by proximity, 83
  by similarity, 84
Group processes, 731
Group therapy, 641
Group work/learning, 1156
Guidance process, temporality frame, 971, 972
Guidelines for Psychological Practice with Older Adults, 1044

**H**
Habits, 203, 213
Habitual response, 202, 203, 208
Haptic information, 91
Hashtag, Twitter post, 308
Hawthorne experiments of Mayo, 542
Health, 515, 535
  care, 636, 673
  and relationships, 673
  and stress, 408
Health and Care Professions Council, 948
Healthcare policies, 1025
Health psychology, 340, 342, 350, 351, 1144, 1145
  adaptive model, 1152
  administrative changes, 1163
  advising coordinator, 1162
  advising plan, 1163
  approaches and strategies, 1155–1158
  assessment, 1160
  in Australia, 349
  in Canada, 346
  in Central and South America, 346–347
  challenges, 1161–1162
  curriculum, 1146–1150

in Egypt and Lebanon, 350
eudaimonic model, 1152
in Europe, 348–349
foundational competency, 1153
functional competency, 1153
health psychologist job requirements, 1153–1155
interactive Web advising tutorial, 1163
learning outcomes, 1163
mass advising, 1163
online teaching and learning, 1158–1160
professional competency, 1152
psychology teachers, 1164–1165
purposes, rationale and content, health psychology curriculum, 343–344
role performance model, 1151
in South Africa, 349
teaching, learning and assessment, 345
in United Kingdom, 348
Health Psychology division of the APA, 1144
Health system, 1025
Healthy skepticism, 932
Heritability, 521, 525, 527
Hermeneutics, 1124, 1129, 1134, 1138
Heterosexual identity, 668
Hidden curriculum, 144
Hierarchical personality structure, 526
Higher education, 1244
　acquisition, 1436, 1437
　active engagement, 1439, 1440
　activities, knowledge processes and outcomes, 1442
　activity and engagement, 1438, 1439
　adaptation, 1436, 1437
　classroom policy, 1445
　concept maps, 1446–1448
　constructive engagement, 1441
　course organization, 1434, 1435
　directing and sustaining attention, 1449
　fluency, 1436, 1437
　generalization, 1436, 1437
　interactive engagement, 1441
　laptops, 1445
　learning challenges, 1445
　lecturing, 1448–1451
　mind maps, 1446, 1447
　notetaking, 1444, 1445
　passive engagement, 1440
　personal examples, 1449–1450
　positive student emotions, 1450–1451
　seating arrangement, 1445
　syllabus, 1445
Higher-order thinking, 115

High impact pedagogical practice, 1309
High impact practices (HIPs), 324, 411, 413–414
　collaborative assignments and projects, 325
　undergraduate research, 325
　writing intensive activities, 324–325
Hinduism, 280
Holistic and ideosyncratic level, 971
How-to component skill, 1205, 1207, 1208
Human
　action, 867
　communication, 260–261
　development, 916
　factors, 571, 572, 576, 577, 582
　mental chronometry, 185
　problem solving, 132
　resource management, 931
　service, 635
Humanism, 278
Humanistic theories, 521
Human-machine interaction, 80, 83, 573, 576, 584
Hybrid grading approaches, 1179
Hybrid pedagogies, 1320
Hybrid teaching forms, 929
Hyper-generalization, 287
Hypothesis testing, 432

I
ICAP, see Interactive-cognitive-active-passive (ICAP) framework
I-CARE model, 675
Identity, 668, 669, 920
Ideomotor principle, 92
ID framework model, 1388
Imaginations, 750, 755, 756, 999
Immense complexity of kin terminology, 290
Implementation, 1213
　intentions, 218
　strategy, 1398
Implicit
　association test, 328
　biases, 328
　dispositions, 522
Impulse control, 203, 205
Impulsive choices, 204
Impulsive response, 202
Impulsivity, 210, 217
Impulsivity-compulsivity spectrum disorders, 214, 224
Incidental informal learning, 292
In-class demonstrations, 194, 776
　of experimental designs, 189

Inclusive attitudes, 1082–1084, 1085, 1087–1090
Inclusive practice, 1090–1093
In-company training, 917
Indian cultural context, 634
Indian model of psychotherapy, 634
Indian psychology, 278
Indian sense of self, 281–282
Indicator, 518, 526
Indigenous ethos, 753
Indigenous knowledge construction, 745
Indigenous psychology, 742
    conscious *vs.* unconscious, 747
    core contents and topics, 748
    creative approximations, 756
    dialogical exchange, 757
    eclectic attitude, 748
    education, 747
    extra-verbal, 747
    fundamental human rights, 747
    knowledge construction, 747
    linguistic, 747
    listening and the participation, 755
    mind *vs.* body, 747
    nomothetic *vs.* idiographic, 747
    public health policies, 747
    rites and rituals of the communities, 751
    semiotic mediation, 757
    socio-cultural traditions, 756
    spiritualism *vs.* materialism, 747
    suspicion, 747
    teaching and learning objectives, 746
    time-space, 747
Individual centering, 928
Individual Educational Plan (IEP), 853
Individualism-collectivism paradigm, 282
Individualization, 917
Industrial and organizational psychology, 544
Industry 4.0, 914
Infant-directed speech, 262
Informal education, 920
Informal learning, 292, 916
Informally acquired competences, 917, 924
Informal writing, 776
Information-about component skill, 1205
Information and communication technologies (ICT), 682, 1378
Information networks, 137
Information Paper on Protection against Sexual Orientation, Gender Identity and Expression and Sexual Characteristics (SOGIESC) Discrimination, 687
Information processing, 132

Informed instructor, 660
Initial and Continuing Vocational Training (ICVT), 923
Initiating joint attention (IJA), 259
Innovative instructional approaches, 929
Innovative method, 41
Inquiry-based learning (IBL), 556, 928, 1256
    challenges, 1276–1277
    cognitive and guidance dimension effects, 1265–1266
    cognitive dimensions of, 1264
    computer tools, 1273–1276
    definition, 1258
    design issues and approaches, 1259
    guidance dimension of, 1265
    in higher education, 1271–1273
    implications for learning and teaching, 1266
    inquiry phases, 1259–1260
    instructional technology, 374
    learning process, 374
    objectives, 1257
    pedagogy, 374
    professional and scientific issues, 1257
    psychological literacy, 375
    research issues, 1262–1263
    scientific reasoning, 1267–1268
    synthesis of inquiry phases and cycles, 1260–1261
    teaching, learning and assessment resources, 1277–1279
    tools supporting data interpretation, 1275
    transfer advantage of, 1258
Inquisitory generality, 1224
Inquisitory instance, 1224
Institutionalization of work, 877
Institutional psychology, 1024
Institutional review board (IRB), 327, 1339
Institutional strategies, 914
Instruction
    approach, 1236
    content, 1205
    events, 1225
    faculty, 369
    goals, 1204
    guidance, 1239
    hierarchies, 1432, 1435, 1436, 1438, 1443
    interaction, 1205–1206
    practice, 817
    redesign, 561
    strategies, 1203, 1206, 1214–1216
    variables, 1203
Instructional design (ID), 831
    design decisions, 1389

digital teaching, 1388
formats, 1391
graphics design, layout, 1398
implementation, 1398
learning material, 1388
learning tasks, 1394
multimedia-based teaching, 1388
narration, 1394
psychology teaching and learning, 1389
simulations, 1399
subject matter, 1391
technical aspects, 1394, 1395
technological statements, 1388
theory, 1204, 1212, 1223–1224
time allocation, 1397
W/O-psychology, 551
Instructional systems development (ISD), 1217
Instructor's enthusiasm and knowledge, 304
Integrated development model, 643
Integrated method education, 474–475
Integrated properties from both SNA and ENA, 140
Integration, 1079
principle, 1213
Integrative papers, 1337–1338
Integrative psychotherapy, 731
Integrative theory, 249–252
Intellectual history of gender in psychology, 664
Intelligence, 521, 522, 525
in academic psychology, 282
Intention-behavior gap, 160
Intentions, 154, 205, 206, 212, 214, 229
Interaction, 521, 522, 524, 535
design, 1396, 1397
mode, 1206
Interactive activities, 1288, 1289, 1292, 1293, 1296
Interactive-cognitive-active-passive (ICAP) framework, 1287–1289, 1292, 1293, 1439
Interactive lectures
active learning, 110
advantages, 110
courses, 111
criticisms, 109
formative and summative assessments, 111
scientist-educator model, 110
Interactive tutoring feedback model, 1363
Interactive two-feedback loops model (ITFL-model), 1363
Interactive videos, 1397

Interamerican Society of Psychology (Sociedad Interamericana de Psicología; SIP), 347
Interconnectedness, 933
Interconnected systemic processes, 916
Intercultural competence, 919
Interdependence, 1287
Interest, 515, 518, 520, 527, 529
Interference, 207, 210, 222, 226
Intergenerational transmission and differentiation, 975
Intergovernmental Panel on Climate Change, 1321
Inter-individual differences, 242
Interlocking of theory and practice, 551
International associations and universities, 722
International Baccalaureate (IB) program, 848
International Classification of Functioning, Disability, and Health (ICF), 1049, 1080
International classificatory systems of mental illness, 669
International dialogue, 650
International Federation of Social Workers (IFSW), 1017
Internationalization and globalization of the economy, 543
International School Psychology Association (ISPA), 703, 709, 710
International SL, 1320
International Standard Classification of Education (ISCED), 816
International Statistical Classification of Diseases and Related Health Problems (ICD-11), 50–55
classification system, 50–51
competencies related to limitations of, 56–59
International Trade Union Confederation (ITUC) World Congress in Copenhagen, 686
Internet of Things (IoT), 136, 137
Internships, 580, 833, 1146
Interobjectivity, 286
Interpersonal skills, 712
Inter-rater reliability, 1341
Intersectionality, 668
of gender studies, 667
perspective, 668
Intersectoral policies, 1031
Interstate Teacher Assessment and Support Consortium (InTASC) model, 814
Intersubjective relations, 754
Intersubjectivity, 286, 472, 800
Intertemporal choice, 207, 217

Intervention, 33
Intervention programs, 287
Interventions and Instructional Support to Develop Academic Skills, 705
Interventions and Mental Health Services to Develop Social and Life Skills, 705
Interview
  schedules, 461
  variants of qualitative interviews, 459–461
Intervision, 924
Intra-individual changes, 242
Intramental phenomena, 286
Intrinsic motivation, 156
Introductory psychology, 394
  core contents and topics, 15–18
  evolution of, 6–9
  growth and popularity of course, 7
  importance of backwards design, 9–15
  objectives for teachers, 7
  students, 5
  teachers of, 5
Introductory Psychology Initiative (IPI), 857, 858
Introspection, 465
Invasion of Americas, 750
ISPA, see International School Psychology Association (ISPA)
Italian Association of Psychology (AIP), 706
Item analysis programs, 1180

**J**
Jaagratha Samithi, 691, 692
Jainism, 280
JAMOVI, 430
Japanese Association of Counseling Sciences, 635
Japanese government licenses medical doctors, 635
Japanese psychologists, 635
Japan Society of Certified Clinical Psychologists, 635
Jigsaw (approach) method, 66, 408, 777, 1292–1293, 1415–1418
Job success, 515, 535
Joint attention, 259
Journal clubs, 777
Juvenile justice system, 1031, 1033

**K**
Karma (actions and their consequences), principles of, 280
Key competences, 917
Kind-of component skill, 1205, 1207, 1208

Kinesiology, 958
Knowledge, 518–520, 594, 814, 924
  acquisition, 1286, 1287, 1290, 1291, 1293, 1297
  building model, 715
  construction, 756
  creating companies, 715
  development, 950
  domains, 1378
  integration principle, 133
  memorization and retaining, 876
  or truth (according to Hinduism, Buddhism and Jainism), 282
Kudumbashree model, in Kerala, 690–691

**L**
Lab course, 395
Labor and organizations, 878
Laboratory classes, 578
Language-based models, 975
Language shrinkage, 290
Leadership, 952–953
  style, 920
Learn.Genetics, 782
Learnable context-specific performance dispositions, 924
Learner
  control, 1203
  guidance, 1215
  and learning, 817
Learning, 380–382, 714, 1182
  academic repercussions, 107
  analytics, 376, 1401
  behavioral change, 107
  *vs.* cognition, 103
  curriculum, 104, 105
  disabilities, 1190
  and educational systems, 139
  environments, 832, 914
  factors, 637
  fields, 105, 106
  figures, 102
  goals, 571, 572, 574
  goal taxonomies, 559
  and knowledge, 283
  objectives, 105, 190, 191, 212, 362–363
  opportunities, 922
  outcomes, 559
  problems, 1031
  processes, 928
  as schooling, 291, 292
  of self-knowledge, 675
  Skinner, 103
  stimuli, 103

strategies, 324
tasks, 1394
and teaching dynamics, 717
ubiquitous, 107
Learning courses
    approaches (see Strategies of learning courses)
    challenges, 117
    content instructors, 105
    diversity, 105
    evolution by natural selection, 107, 108
    operant conditioning, 106
    Pavlovian conditioning, 106
    research methods, 108
    titles, 105
Learning Events Review Rubric, 1225
Learning management software, 774
Learning management system (LMS), 1395, 1419, 1422, 1423
Lecture-based cases, 1237
Lecture centered approach, 37
Lectures, 109, 574, 577
Legal, ethical, and professional practice, 706
Legal measures, 1032
Levels of instructional strategy, 1214–1216
Levels of processing theory, 184
Lewin's field theory, 795
Licensing and regulation, 647, 648
Life events, 525
Lifelong and lifewide learning, 885
Life outcomes, 515, 524, 535
Lifespan, 516, 520, 525, 530
Life transitions, 516, 525
Limitations of DSM/ICD manuals, 56–59
Linguistic anthropologists, 291
Literacy, 918, 919
Lived experience, by community leaders, 736
Lived Experience and Alcoholics Anonymous, 737
Local psychology, global consequences, 284, 285
Local science, 293
Longitudinal and cross-sectional designs, 256, 258, 523
Longitudinal studies, 1318
Long-term care (LTC) staff, 1057
Long-term retention, 1182

# M
Machine learning (ML), 107, 141, 1296
Macrochronological systems, 798
Macrosystem, 798
Magnetoencephalography (MEG), 255
Mainstream psychology, 274

Major cognitive and practical subspecialties, 1154
Maladaptive behavior, 112
Man Therapy Campaign, 677
Maori indigenous people in *Aotearoa* New Zealand, 755
Marginalization, 1087
Mariwala Health Initiative (MHI), 678
Martin Heidegger, 1001
Masculinity-femininity scale of Minnesota Multiphasic Personality Inventory (MMPI–Mf), 666
Massed practice, 114, 1182
Massive open online courses (MOOCs), 329–331, 1221, 1378
Master-seminar, 41
Master's level education, 643
Maurice Merleau-Ponty, 1001
Meaning, 792, 794, 800–803
Meaning-making processes, 591, 592
Measurement models, 523
Mechanisms
    causal, 516
    defense, 519
Media effects, 619–622
    civil debate, 623–624
    in classroom, 611–612
    free speech, 624–625
    introductory psychology textbooks, 622
    reader-friendly textbooks, 622
    replication crisis, 623
    research methods, 623
Mediating variables, 1316, 1320
Mediator, 518
Media violence, 612
    arguments to authority, 618
    Bandura's origin myth of aggression, 612–614
    in-class debates, 617
    false narratives, 621
    media psychology courses, 617
    meta-analyses, 618–619
    politics, 617
    research, 614–616
Medical College Admissions Test (MCAT), 395
Medical education
    attitudes, 988
    barriers to integrating psychology, 982
    behavioral and social variables, 980
    behavioral change, 987
    biopsychosocial approach, 985
    biopsychosocial model, 980
    cognitive functions, 987
    effective communication skills, 987
    evidence-based medicine, 981

Medical education (*cont.*)
   health, illness and disease, 985, 986
   healthcare systems, 980
   health problems, 981
   managing dependent patients, 987
   medical education in United States, 981
   medical students, 980
   organizations, 984
   overcoming barriers to teaching psychology, 982–985
   personal values, 988
   psychological/behavioral factors, 986
   psychological responses to illness, 986
   psychology, 981
   psychology contributions, 986
   psychosocial aspects of pain, 987
   psychosocial development, 986
   selfcare, 988
   stress and coping, 986
   teaching psychology, overcoming barriers to, 982
   teamwork skills, 988
   treatment adherence, 987
Meditations on First Philosophy, 1131
Megatrends, 913
Memory, 1182
   research, 186
Mental and representational uncertainty, 924
Mental contrasting, 163
Mental Health Care Act, 644
Mental health
   literacy, 634
   prevention and promotion, 731
   professionals, 1070
   treatment, 1030
Mental health services, 640–642
   in culturally diverse countries, 648
Mental models or schemes in the learning process, 714
Mental pathology, 726
Mental processing theories, 182
Mental skills, 953
Mental suffering, 630
Mental toughness, 952
Mesosystem, 796
Meta-analysis, 618, 619, 1246, 1318
Metacognition, 115, 324
Metacompetences, 916, 917
Meta-control, 222
Methodological competence, 924
Methodological purity, 285
Methodology cycle (MC), 438, 439, 444, 445, 450

MeToo movement, 672, 684
MHI's approach to training and practice, 678
Microgenetic research designs, 257
Micro-process, 968, 970
Microsystem, 796
Milgram, 613
Mind, 793–794, 800–803
Mindfulness-based stress reduction/schema therapy, 36
Mind maps, 1446, 1447
Mindset, 163
Mini lectures, 1392
Minnesota multiphasic personality inventory (MMPI), 487
Misconceptions, 118, 119
Mixed methods, 297, 458
Mixed reality (MR), 1396, 1400
Model of teaching, 1397
Moderators, 1246–1248
Moderator variables, 1320
Monolingualism and word count, 290
MOOCs, *see* Massive open online courses (MOOCs)
Mood, 954
Moodle, 330
Moral development, 954
Moral panic, 612
Mother, central role, 290
Motivation theory, 517, 951
   inner states of, 153
Motivational psychology, 161
Motivation science, 152
   approaches and strategies, 166–167
   central issues, 156–157
   challenges and lessons, 167–168
   core contents and topics, 160
   curriculum, 157–160
   historical roots, 152–155
   purposes, 157–160
   rationale, 157–160
   teaching, learning, and assessment resources, 168–170
Motives, 155
Motive theories, 520
MPsych/PhD/DPsych, 30
Multicultural practice, 649
Multidimensional anxiety theory, 951
Multidimensional nature of wellbeing, 1086
Multidisciplinary sport science, 956
Multilingualism, 290
Multimedia-assisted self-regulated learning (MASL), 1393, 1400
Multimedia classrooms, 305

Multimedia design, 1396
Multimedia learning material, 366
Multinaturalism, 745
Multiple caregiving, 279
Multiple-choice questions, 115
Multiple-choice tests, 1180
Multiple generation households, 280

**N**
Narrative analysis, 468
NASP practice model, 703
National Association of School Psychologists (NASP), 703
National Center for Cultural Competence, 736
National concern in Australia, 729
National Council for the Social Studies (NCSS), 855
National Health System, 1026
National Institute of Drug Abuse (NIDA), 783
National Institutes of Health, 1145
National Institutes of Health Office of Behavioral and Social Sciences Research (OBSSR), 980
National K12 curriculum organizations, 855
National Mental Health Program (NMHP), 634
National Science Foundation (NSF), 850
National Standards for High School Psychology Curricula, 853
Naturalistic predication, 743
Nature and nurture, 241, 243–245
N-back tasks, 215
Near-transfer principle, 133
Needs, 152, 153
Negative reinforcement and punishment, 118
Negotiation movements and strategies, 448
Neo-liberalism, 731
Nervous system, 397
Nervous system function principles, 303
Netnography, 464
Network analysis, 137, 138
Neural mechanisms, 219–223
Neuroanatomy, 397
Neurobiological framework, 302
Neuroimaging, 404
 studies, 221
 techniques, 187
Neuroliberalism, 287
Neurological disorders, 402
Neurons, 405
Neurophobia, 410

Neuropsychology, 204, 219
 research, 186
 studies, 220
Neuroscience, in psychology curriculum, 783
 action potential simulations, 405
 active learning, 410
 applications of foundational knowledge, 397
 case studies, 409
 clinical applications, 397–402
 comparative neuroanatomy, 405
 CTE, 410
 epigenetics and schizophrenia, 409
 evidence-based strategies, 413
 foundational knowledge of nervous system, 397
 high-impact practices, 413–414
 history, 393–394
 models of nervous system, 405
 neuroanatomy exploration, Whole Brain Atlas, 404
 neurotransmitters, 405
 online learning, 411
 professional development opportunities, 414
 purposes and rationale, 395–398
 research history and harm, 409
 self-regulated learning, 411
 sleep quality questionnaire, 407
 transparency and clarity, 412
 in undergraduate psychology programs, 394–395
Neurotransmitters, 405
Newborn's care in today's world, 296
News articles, 306
News media, 310
NGO stakeholders, 1016
#NiUnaMenos movement, 672
Non-custodial sanctions, 1034
Non-fiction reading, 778
Non-formally acquired competences, 917
Non-majors' experience, 367
Non-psychological discipline, 927
Non-U.S. psychology teachers, 858–860
Norm-referenced grading, 1178, 1179
Notetaking, 1444, 1445
Nuclear family model, 290

**O**
Obedience to authority, 327
Objective hermeneutics, 469
Observable behavior, 121

Observation, 462–463
Observation skills, 599–600
Office of Teaching Resources in Psychology (OTRP), 1176
Olfactory adaptation, 92
One-minute paper, 1188
Online
  assessments, 120
  instruction, 402, 404
  lectures, 1399
  learning, 411
  open-university, 377–378
  research, 464
  resources, 304, 839–842
  teaching, 329–331
  seminars and webinars, 1393
  Twitter guide, 308
Ontogenesis, 597–598
Ontological and epistemological issues, 754
Ontological issues, 742, 746
Ontological naturalism, 745
Open education, 378
Openness, 456
Operant conditioning, 106
  behaviors, 108
  central tenet, 118
  challenges, 117
  demonstration, 121
  discussion, 119
  ethics, 117
  everyday examples, 119, 120
  natural selection process, 108
  operational definitions, 121
  predictions, 111
  real-world context, 117
  reinforcement, 118, 119
  students difficulties, 118
  time grading student-generated examples, 121
Organization for Economic Cooperation and Development (OECD), 1079
Organizational ecosystems, 559
Organizational internships, 562
Organizational psychology, 541
Organization of the work process
  computer-assisted analysis of qualitative data, 470
  performative approaches, 471
  research teams, 470
  software, 470
Ostracism, 321
Outcome-centered approach
  between-class assignments, 39
  definition, 37
  didactic elements usage, 38
  experiential learning, 39
  invite special guests, 38
  lectures, 38
  multiple in-class activities, 39
  seminars, 38
  standardized patients, 38
  supervision, 40

**P**
PACE's gender-responsive model, 673, 674
Paradigmatic commonalities, 456–457
Paradigmatic science, 36
Parental attitudes, 1084, 1090
Participation, 459, 1079–1082, 1085, 1086, 1091, 1092
Participatory action research, 731, 736
Participatory community action research (PCAR), 1311, 1317
Participatory indigenous methodology, 737
Participatory research, 459
Partnerships, 1315, 1317, 1318, 1320, 1321, 1323
Part-of component skill, 1205, 1207
Pavlovian conditioning, 103, 106, 111, 112
Pebble-in-the-pond model, for instructional design
  component skills, 1218
  content-first approach, 1217
  functional prototype, 1219
  implement adequate assessment, 1219
  peer-interaction, 1219
  principle-oriented, 1217
  problem centered, 1217
  problem progression, 1218
  problem prototype, 1217
  prototyping, 1217
  structural framework, 1218
Pedagogical foundations, 934
Pedagogical practice, 195
Pedagogical strategy, 110
Peer-collaboration, 1219
Peer-critique, 1219
Peer-discussion, 1219
Peer feedback approach, 1293
Peer instruction, 14
Peer-interaction, 1219
Peer-sharing, 1219
Perceptions, 303, 750
  of peers and adults, 1082
Perezhivanie, 998

Performance(s), 1003
  appraisal, 541
  studies, 1003
  support systems, 1393
Performative approaches, 471
Performative social science, 471
Perseveration, 222
Persistence, 203, 212
Persistent engagement, 164
Personal and social reorientation, 922
Personal competences, 923, 924
Personal development, 644, 893
Personal fulfillment, 918
Personal idiosyncrasies of researchers, 743
Personality, 920, 951
  development, 920, 921, 927
  disorders, 58
Personality assessment inventory (PAI), 487
Personal therapy, 647, 693
Personal values, 444
Person and environment, 153, 795–798
Persuasion, 317, 320
P-hacking, 616
Physical, environment, task type, timing, learning, emotion, perspective (PETTLEP), 953
Physical/location inclusion, 1079, 1090
  advantages, 1081
  attitudes towards inclusion, 1082–1085, 1088–1090
  participation, 1085, 1086
  school well being, 1086, 1087, 1090
Physical and cognitive resources, 866
Physiological psychology
  brain and behavior, 302
  core contents, 303
  course titles, 302
  curriculum, 303
  historical perspective, 302
  neurobiological systems analysis, 302
  research studies, 302
  science-based news (*see* Science in the news)
  teaching and assessment approaches, 304
  teaching resources, 311
  technology integration, 304, 305
  Twitter (*see* Twitter)
  undergraduate courses, 302
Pikes Peak Model for Training in Professional Geropsychology, 1044
Pittsburgh sleep quality index (PSQI), 407
Pleromatic semiosis, 969
Pleromatization, 969

3P model, 1164
Political empowerment, 671
Polling software, 64
Pornography, 611, 621
Positive psychology, 155, 946
Positive reinforcement, 118
Positivism, 1120–1122, 1124, 1125, 1128, 1136
Positivist identification, 297
Post-actional phase, 164
Postscript, 466
Post-traumatic stress disorder (PTSD), 104
Poverty crisis, 284
Practical oriented analysis and development, 550
Practice-based theory development, 915
Pragmatism, 359
Pre-actional and actional phases, 163–164
Precommittment, 208, 213
Pre-conceptions, 167
Pre-decisional phase, 161–163
Predictions, 111–112, 518, 526
Preference reversal, 208, 216
Prefrontal cortex (PFC), 207, 209, 219, 221
Preregistration, 616
Prescriptive instructional design theory, 1223–1224
Presentations, 777
Prevention, Mental Health Promotion and Crisis Intervention, 721
Preventive and Responsive Services, 705
Primary, secondary and tertiary levels, 1024
Primary source-only pedagogy, 778
Primary theoretical orientations, 33
Principle components analysis, 426
Problem-based learning (PBL), 143–145, 1156, 1210, 1211, 1393
  approaches, 15
  case-based teaching and learning, 1236
  challenges, 1249–1250
  current trends, 1248–1249
  different settings, 1248
  efficiency and effectiveness comparison, 1246
  grading, 1245
  inquiry-based learning leverages, 374
  instructional approach, 1236
  learning and teaching psychology, 1249–1250
  lessons learned, 1249–1250
  level, 1237
  meta-review, 1248
  moderators, 1247
  pedagogical style, 373

Problem-based learning (PBL) (*cont.*)
   problems and cases, 1240–1241
   psychology programs, 373
   purposes, 1238–1240
   rationale, 1238
   scheduling, 1244
   small-group learning approach, 1237
   structure, 1241–1242
   student participation, 1238
   tutoring, 1242
Problem-centered learning (PCL), 1210, 1211
Problem-centered interview, 460
Problem-progression model, 1210–1211, 1218
Problem prototype, 1217
Problem solving (model), 132, 133, 1206, 1241
   automated analysis, 135
   challenges, 144, 145
   conditions, 1207
   consequence, 1207
   content elements, for eating disorder treatment, 1209
   content elements, for whole problem, 1208
   historical perspective, 134
   how-to component skill, 1207, 1208
   kind-of component skill, 1207, 1208
   personalized feedback to learners and instructors, 135
   problem-centered approach, 1206
   problem-solving skill, 1207
   properties, 1207
   research on unobtrusive observation, 135
   skill, 930, 1206–1208
   system, 134
   what-happens component skill, 1207, 1208
Procedural knowledge, 1391
Professional action, 915
Professional and social community, 719
Professional approaches, 704
Professional competence, 145–146, 924, 1057
Professional development, 922
Professional education, 920
Professional identity, 918, 1023
Professionalization of counseling in Japan, 635
Professional knowledge, 1307, 1309, 1310
Professional Knowledge and Skills in Assessment and Intervention, 710, 711
Professional Practice of School Psychologists, 712
Professional practitioners, 932
Professional psychology, 1146
Professional responsibility, 817
Professional socialization, 919, 920
Professional standards, 1048

Program evaluation, 731, 1335, 1348
Program for International Student Assessment (PISA), 809
Programmatic assessment, 380
Programme for the International Assessment of Adult Competencies (PIAAC), 142
Progression of tasks, 1216
Progressive relaxation, 953
Project-based learning (PBL), 413, 558, 716, 1156
Project implicit, 334
Project syllabus, 1177
Protodeclarative pointing, 261
Protoimperative pointing, 261
Prototyping, 1217
Pseudo-empiricism, 438, 440
PSI theory, 157
PsyBA-approved areas, 30
Psychoanalysis, 278, 663, 665
Psychoanalytic psychotherapy, 36
Psychoanalytic theories, 37
Psychodynamic theories, 520
Psycho-educating clients, mental health, 645
Psychological assessments, 26, 33, 278
   assessment strategies, 501–505
   challenges and lessons learned, 506–507
   description, 482–483
   formative assessments, 504
   foundational concepts and principles, 494
   historical events, 485
   key performance indicators, 505
   objectives for courses, 489–493
   organizing frameworks for courses, 493–496
   professional and scientific issues, 483–485
   sources for teaching, learning, and assessment, 507–508
   summative assessments, 504
   teaching strategies, 496–503
   techniques, 34
Psychological competences
   challenges, 934
   expertise, 932
   general promotion, 934
   professions, 925
   profile, 927
   psychologists, 927
   role, 919
   subject-specific didactics, 916
   team-based learning, 922
Psychological counseling, 930
Psychological disorders, 402
Psychological distress, 732
Psychological facts, 596–597

Psychological instruments, 1030
Psychological knowledge, 369, 370, 918
Psychological literacy
  career development learning, 893
  challenges, 899–903
  clarification, 918
  communication ability, 919
  community, society and global goals
      application, 895–897
  components of, 887
  cultural responsivity, 896–897
  curriculum renewal, 897–899
  definition, 887, 919
  in education, 896
  employability, 884–885
  evidence-based study skills, 892
  graduate literacy, 919
  impacts, 934
  international community projects, 896
  personal goals, 891–892
  professional goals, 892–895
  and psychologically-literate citizenship, 887
  research design, 891
  self-behavior-change program, 891
  specialist knowledge, 919
  work-integrated learning, 893–895
Psychologically literate citizens, 1307, 1310, 1323
Psychological misconceptions, 837
Psychological science, 29
Psychological skills, 918, 953
Psychological study, of problem solving, 138
Psychological subjects and contents, 822, 931
Psychological systems, 746
Psychological testing, *see* Psychological assessments
Psychological theories, 28, 744, 919
Psychological therapies, 631
Psychological training courses, 912
Psychologism, 286
Psychologists in Long-Term Care (PLTC) Guidelines Revision Task Force, 1071
Psychologization, 286
Psychology, 26, 77, 291, 360, 663, 954, 669
  course, 822–828
  instruction, 828
  teacher training, 802–803
Psychology and Ageing Interest Group (PAIG), 1043
Psychology Board of Australia (PsyBA), 29
Psychology intervention
  adopting, 793
  context, 798–800
  cultural theory, 792
  environment and person, 794–798
  social context, 792
  theoretical and methodological foundations, 792
Psychology of art
  artistic experience, 994
  assessment resources, 1004
  autonomous field, 1001
  classroom, 1004
  cognitive model, 1002
  curriculums, 994, 995
  epistemological and methodological orientations, 1000
  evolutionary approaches, 1002
  Gestalt theory, 999, 1000
  human experience, 994, 1001
  inquiry, 1002
  learning, 1004
  legacy, 998, 999
  methodological feature, 1001
  neuroaesthetics, 1002
  neurology, 1000
  outspreads, 995–997
  performative turn, 1002–1004
  phenomenology, 1001
  psychoanalysis, 995–997
  teaching, 1004, 1005
  theoretical perspectives, 994
  theory of evolution, 1000
  transformations, 1005
  visual/audio/literary resources, 1004, 1005
Psychology of religion and spirituality
  abnormal psychology, 1109
  behaviorism, 1101
  biological/physiological psychology, 1110
  clinical application, 1111
  clinical practice, 1104, 1105
  clinical psychology programs, 1109
  cognitive psychology, 1110
  cognitive science, 1103
  communities, 1104
  community psychology, 1109
  contexts for the course, 1105, 1106
  conversion and deconversion, 1102
  coping and meaning, 1104
  course texts, 1106, 1107
  defining, 1098, 1099
  development, 1101, 1102
  ethics, 1111
  experience, 1102
  field, 1098
  Freud's successors, 1100

Psychology of religion and spirituality (*cont.*)
  graduate curriculum, 1112
  history, 1111
  human development, 1111
  industrial/organizational psychology, 1110
  instructional strategies, 1108
  learning, 1111
  memory, 1111
  mental/physical health, 1102, 1103
  personality psychology, 1109
  phenomenological/humanistic approach, 1100
  philosophical psychology, 1111
  positive psychology, 1110
  postsecondary education, 1105
  practices, 1103
  sensation and perception, 1111
  social psychology, 1101, 1110
  statistics and research methods, 1109
  teaching PRS, 1107, 1108
  tests and measures, 1110
  traditional forms, 1101
  Western scientific psychology, 1101
Psychometric concepts, 35
Psychometric scale, 484, 665
Psychopathology, 26, 27
Psychopharmacology, 303
Psychopharmacology teaching for undergraduates
  approach and strategies, 771
  case studies, 778
  considerations in curriculum, 768–771
  course assessments and activities, 772
  drugs and drug classes, 769–770
  drug use, abuse and dependence, 770–771
  experiential learning opportunities, 779
  forced-choice items, 773–775
  history, nomenclature and research paradigms, 768–769
  learning objectives, 767, 773–780
  mechanisms of action of drug, 771
  short answer and short essay exams and quizzes, 775–778
  websites, 782–783
Psychopolitical validity, 1316, 1317
Psychosis, 730, 731
Psycho-social competences, 923
Psychosocial development, 278, 280
Psychotherapeutic techniques, 40
Psychotherapy, 28, 29, 631, 1157
PsychTeacher listserv, 1189
Public health psychology, 1155
Purposive sampling, 457

## Q

Qualitative content analysis (QCA), 466–467
Qualitative research methodology, 950
  category-oriented methods, 466–467
  computer-assisted analysis, 470
  ethical criteria, 472–473
  participatory approaches, 459
  presentation, 471
  quality criteria, 471–472
  research question, 455
  rethinking psychology, 454
  sampling, 457–458
  secondary analysis, 458
  sequence analytical procedures, 467–469
  teaching and learning, 473–475
  theoretical-methodological foundations, 456–457
  triangulation and mixed methods, 458
  working groups, 470–471
Quality of the contexts, 1086
Quantitative research methods, 255, 257–258, 297, 457, 458, 464, 467, 471, 550, 555, 686
Quasi-experimental study, 145
Queer Affirmative Counselling Practice (QACP), 678
Question, persuade, and refer (QPR), 65
Questionnaires, 523
Questions
  age and time, 243
  application in teaching, 248
  continuous *vs.* non-continuous development, 246–247
  difficulty of differentiating, 245–246
  evolutionary processes, 243
  nature *vs.* nurture, 243–245
  nomothetic *vs.* Idiographic Research Approaches, 247
  occupied philosophy and science, 242
  theories of development, 249–252

## R

Racial selectivity, 1032
Reaction time (RT) experiments, 179
Readiness potential, 215
Real-world problem, 117, 157
Recognition, 933
Recommended (text-)books, 839
Reconstructive memory, 975
Recovery-oriented systems, 933
Redesigning curricula & pedagogy, 648, 649

Reflection, 407, 1308, 1311, 1313–1316, 1319–1321, 1323
Reflection-integration, 1216
Reflectivity, 457
Regression, 518
Regulatory focus, 162
Regulatory Framework in the Health Services Sector, 1147
Reinforcement/punishment nature, 111, 118, 119
Reinforcement learning, 135
Relational pattern of the live supervision, 973
Relational processes, 743
Relational systemic model, 968
Relevant media, 1215
Religion, 631
Reorientation, 920
Replication crisis, 613, 614, 623
Replications, 327
Representative designs, 524
Reproducing techniques and procedures, 878
Research-based learning, 553, 554, 556, 914, 915
Research methods, 325, 945–954, 956–958
  and analysis, 181
  ethics, 327–328, 472
  qualitative and quantitative (*see* Qualitative research methods; Quantitative research methods)
  research designs, 255–256
Research methods and statistics, undergraduate psychology, 422
  abstract content, 425
  assessment of learning, 431
  attention to course design, 427–428
  challenges in teaching, 424–426
  making course applicable to life, 426–427
  overcoming challenges, 426–428
  rationale for learning, 423–424
  resources, 429–430
  teacher-student enthusiasm gap, 425
Research-oriented teaching, 554
Research-practice gap, 562
Research Randomizer, 334
Resilience, 913, 930
Resources, 1391
Responding joint attention (RJA), 259
Response events, 1219
Response inhibition, 205, 207, 216, 217, 221
Restorative justice, 752, 1033
Rethinking psychology, 454
Retrieval practice, 112
  and test-enhanced learning, 189

Ringelmann effect, 952
Ritual practices, 279
Role-play simulations, 552
Role-taking (RT), 1413–1415
  e-tutor/leader, 1414
  process supervisor, 1414
  researcher, 1414
Room temperature, 80
Rubicon model, 165
  of action phases, 157
Rubric, for application instructional events, 1227
Rudimentary attitudinal change, in family system, 689

**S**
Salamanca Declaration, 1080
Saliency of faces, 258
Sampling, 457–458
Sampling bias in developmental research, 275
Scaffolding, 412, 1319–1320
Scaled measurement, 1216
Scaled set of instructional strategies, 1215
Scanning of hand luggage, 82
Scene supervision, 968
Schema-therapy, 731
Schematization, 969
Schizophrenia, 34
Scholarship of Teaching and Learning (SoTL) model, 371
School
  counseling, 636
  difficulties, 1030
  learning, 292
  psychology programs, 712
  psychology training program, 715
  social workers, 1031
School inclusion, 1081, 1087–1088
  cultural perspective, 1078, 1079
  inclusive education, 1079–1081
  inclusive learning environments, 1090–1092
  school and psychological issues, 1078
  teaching practices, 1092, 1093
School psychology
  activity system, 718
  case analysis and evaluation, 715
  clinical-functionalistic field, 701
  cultural and economic events, 702
  direct help to teachers, for classroom management and group dynamics, 708
  dissemination and consolidation, 702

School psychology (*cont.*)
  domains of, 704
  EFPA recommendations, 707
  guidelines, 713, 714
  history of, 701
  learning difficulties, 708
  management of professional and
     organizational problems, 708
  problem-solving activities, 715
  professional activities, 706
  professional profile, 703
  psychological counselling, 708
  psychological wellbeing, 708
  support for educational evaluation and
     experimentation, 708
  support for school-family relationship, 708
  teacher training, 708
  theoretical knowledge, methods and
     techniques of investigation and
     evaluation, 715
  theoretical models, 715
School-wide practices to promote learning, 705
Science, technology, engineering, and
     mathematics (STEM), 683, 854
Science efficacy, 410
Science in the news
  active learning, 305
  classroom lectures, 305
  classroom presentations, 306
  course design, 306
  drawing students' attention, 305
  finding strategies, 306, 307
  framework, 305
  general public and media outlets, 305
  in-class activity, 306
  news articles, 305
  peer-driven discussion boards, 306
  public importance, 305
  social media apps, 306
Scientific reasoning, 1267–1268
Scientism, 1121
Scientist-practitioner model, 545
SCORM, 1396
Script theory, 929
Secondary analysis, 458
Second-order change, 728
Selecting and organizing topics, 822–828
Select-organize-integrate (SOI) model, 1439
Self-acceptance, 921
Self-care and burnout prevention, 649, 650
Self-concept, 514, 520, 918
Self-control, 203, 216–219
  interventive, 208, 217
  preventive, 208, 217

Self-criticism, 932
Self-determination theory, 162, 918, 930, 953
Self-development, 930
Self-directed (individual) learning, 922, 1243
Self-education, 930
Self-efficacy, 952, 1084
Self-esteem, 514, 520
Self-management, 931
Self-positions in time living, 975
Self-referential importance, 40
Self-referential thinking, 42
Self-reflected socialization process, 920
Self-reflection, 644
Self-regulated learning, 402, 410–414
Self-regulation, 161, 923
Self-report measures, 1316, 1318
Self-responsibility, 924
Semantic priming, 185
Seminars, 38, 577, 581
Semiotic construction, 970, 971
Sensation and perception, 397
Sense of belonging, 1086–1087
SENS model, 140
Sensory and physical disabilities, 1082–1084
Sensory experience, 1120
Sequence analytical procedures, 467–468
Sequential research designs, 256
Serious games, 929, 1393
Service activities, 543, 1307, 1311, 1312, 1314,
     1320, 1323
Service learning (SL), 376, 1157, 1307, 1308,
     1313, 1315
  advocacy, 1311
  assessment, 1316
  authentic evidence, 1318–1319
  child psychology course, 1319
  communication, 1315
  community outcomes, 1316–1317
  community partners, 1314
  definition, 1307
  democratic engagement, 1320–1321
  direct service, 1310
  diversity, 1314
  educational advantages, 1312
  educational goals, 1311–1312
  eSL, 1321
  essential elements, 1307, 1311
  evaluation, 1315
  faculty development, 1322
  hybrid pedagogies, 1320
  indirect service, 1310
  international SL, 1320
  longitudinal studies, 1318
  meta-analysis, 1318

motivation, 1315
organization, 1315
PCAR, 1317
as pedagogy, 1309–1310
quality and attributes of SL course, 1320
reflection, 1319
research, 1311
research design, 1316
scaffolding, 1319–1320
service activities, 1312–1313
service tasks, 1312
social psychology course, 1319
student voice, 1314
systematic formative and summative evaluation, 1314–1315
theory, 1315–1316
Set shifting, 207, 216, 217
Shared knowledge in collaborative problem-solving, 146
Shuffled reading assignments, 1183
Sigmund Freud's psychoanalysis, 103
Signification, 1133
Simulation models, 1401
Simulations, 959, 1393, 1399
Single loop learning, 928
Single parent, 290
SIOP competences, 546
Situated knowledge, 1023
Situations, 521
Skepticism, 916
Skill(s), 522, 528–529, 594, 595, 814
    acquisition, 1287, 1289, 1294, 1295
    building, 650
    development, 874
Skinner's behaviorism, 103
Small group learning, 375–376, 1238, 1286
    collaboration script approach, 1293
    group awareness approach, 1294
    group processes, 1291–1292
    individual learning prerequisites, 1290–1291
    instructional conditions, 1292
    Jigsaw approach, 1292–1293
    PBL, 1237
    peer feedback approach, 1293
    problem solving, 1249
    purposes and rationale, 1287–1289
    and self-directed individual learning, 1243
    tutors, 1237
Small group(s), 1185
    practicals, 582–583
    teaching, 580–581
Smocks to Jocks, 950
Social and emotional development, 709

Social and emotional inclusion, 1091
Social and emotional well-being, 729
Social change, 913, 932
Social cognitive theory, 366
Social competences, 922, 924, 927
Social construction, 916
    of gender, 283, 672
    of objective and subjective realities, 746
Social contact, 1089
Social desirability, 1083
Social distancing, 41
Social exclusion, 1027
Social existence of human beings, 674
Social facilitation, 315, 945
Social influence, 315
Social integration, 1079
Social interactions, 447, 792
Socialization
    agents, 683, 686
    professional, 919
Social justice, 645, 649
Social learning theory (SLT), 278, 611, 680
Social loafing, 315
Socially responsible self-determination, 921
Socially responsive knowledge, 1307–1311, 1313, 1316, 1320, 1323
Socially shared regulation, 1292
Social media, 305
Social network analysis (SNA), 139
Social networks, 297
Social participation rule, 447
Social privilege, 732
Social processes, 919
Social psychology, 322, 550
    action teaching, 316–318
    attitudes and actions, 320
    curriculum, purposes and rationale of, 319–320
    distributed practice, 324
    elaborative processing, 324
    feedback on student performance, 323
    finding/creating assessment, 322
    generalizability, 326
    HIPs, 324–325
    history, 315–316
    instructional activities, readings and course elements, 322
    learning strategies, 324
    metacognition, 324
    network, 332
    online teaching, 329–331
    persons and situations interact, 321
    psychology training, 325–326
    replications, 327

Social psychology (*cont.*)
   research ethics, 327–328
   retrieval practice/testing effect, 324
   share samples/models, social psychology classes, 323
   social behavior, 322
   social influence, 315, 321
   social reality, 321
   social relations, 315
   social thinking, 315
   theories and findings, 550
Social representations, 1032
Social risks, 1027
Social skills, 920
Social work
   applied psychology, 1016
   capitalism, 1016
   categories, 1017
   Christian philanthropy, 1014
   citizenship, 1023
   co-created projects, 1024
   community-based interventions, 1023
   community relations, 1023
   counter-hegemonic social movements, 1015
   cultural development, 1014
   educational settings, 1030–1035
   empirical knowledge, 1018
   epistemological turn, 1014
   ethics, 1014
   health care, 1024–1026
   human activity, 1015
   human rights, 1024
   industrialism, 1016
   interdisciplinary field, 1018
   international health policies, 1014
   liquid modernity, 1014
   material resources, 1018
   Modern Age, 1016
   multi-professional teams, 1024
   national contexts, 1016
   neoliberal zeitgeist, 1015
   patronage, 1017
   principles, 1024
   professionals perform, 1016
   professions, 1013
   psychological realm, 1019
   psychological theory and practice, 1015
   psychologists, 1024
   psychologization, 1019
   qualify services, 1019
   reductionism, 1019
   responsibility, 1014
   roles, 1016
   self-reflexive process, 1015
   situated professional knowledge, 1018
   social agents, 1017
   social assistants, 1016, 1018, 1019
   social care agents, 1017
   social policies, 1015, 1018
   social protagonism, 1023
   social regulation and protection, 1018
   social sciences, 1013, 1014
   social scientists, 1018
   sociocultural turn, 1020–1023
   support, 1019
   teams, 1014
Societal development goals, 913
Societal orientation, 928
Society for Health Psychology, 343
Society for Personality and Social Psychology, 334
Society for Qualitative Inquiry in Psychology, 455
Society for the Psychological Study of Social Issues, 333
Society for the Teaching of Psychology (STP), 1176, 1189
Sociobiological explanations, 665
Socio-cognitive conflicts, 1287
Socio-constructivist genetic approach, 792
Sociocultural context, 792, 803
Socio-cultural dimensions, 714
Sociocultural turn in psychology
   child labor, 1028
   community, 1012
   critical and ethical daily practice, 1013
   cultural features, 1028
   early adolescence marriage, 1028
   general psychology, 1012
   homeless people inclusion and culture, 1029, 1030
   intersectoral services, 1027
   intervention, 1028
   mental illness/disorders, 1012
   Modern age, 1027
   multi/interdisciplinary teams, 1012
   pedagogic implications, 1013
   public policies, 1012
   public policies services work, 1028
   salient transformations, 1012
   social care professionals, 1012
   social policies, 1027
   socioeconomic features, 1027
   urban and rural contexts, 1012
Socio-technical system approach, 543
Socratic teaching methods, 193, 957

South African College of Applied Psychology
    (SACAP), 1145
South East Asia Standards, 811
Spaced practice, 114
Spatial visualizations, 1446, 1448
Special educational needs (SENs), 1078
Specialist geropsychologist, 1044
Spiral progression approach in teaching, 167
Spirituality in Clinical Practice, 1101
Sport and exercise psychology
    advanced training, 945
    anxiety/arousal, 951
    assessment considerations, 957
    challenges, 958–959
    character/moral development and
        aggression, 954
    competency issues, 946
    confidence, 952
    definition and brief history, 945
    exercise motivation and well-being,
        953–954
    flipped classroom, 955
    globalization and cultural diversity, 946
    group dynamics, 952
    historical perspectives, 949–950
    individual differences, 950–952
    knowledge development, 950
    leadership, 952–953
    motivation, 951
    multidisciplinary research, 946
    personality, 950–951
    psychological skills, 953
    psychology of injury, 954
    purposes and rationale of curriculum,
        946–949
    team, 956
    UNIFORM program, 956
Spotlight metaphor, 85
Situated contexts of practice, 1025
Stability, 525, 526
Standardized patients, 1241
Standardized testing, 282
Stanford Prison Experiment, 333, 611, 613,
    614, 622
States, 514, 515, 522, 525, 526
Statistics, 518, 532
Statistics analyses, 36
Stimulus-response associations, 203
Stop Now and Plan (SNAP) Girls, 673
Strategic knowledge, 1391
Strategies of learning courses
    active engagement, 109
    backward design, 109

classroom response systems, 113
connecting information, 114
data-supported pedagogical techniques, 109
distributed practice, 113, 114
formative and summative assessment, 115
interactive lectures, 109
making prediction, 111
operant project, 117
pedagogical experience, 108
pedagogical knowledge, 109
pedagogical techniques, 109
peer instruction, 113
retrieval practice, 112
Streib's deconversion project, 1102
Strength model, 208, 218
Stroop task, 210, 216
Structural framework, 1218, 1219
Structure of observed learning outcomes
    (SOLO), 1051, 1063
Student-centered learning, 41
Student
    disabilities, 1190
    disruptive behavior, 118
    engagement, 1189
    facility, 1347
    perceptions, 1295
    professional development, 423, 424
    voice, 1314
Students' learning formative and summative
    assessment
    additional opportunities, 116
    cumulative final exam, 116
    engaging, 115
    higher-order thinking, 115
    immediate feedback, 116
    learning course, 115
    monitoring, 115
    motivation, 116
    multiple-choice questions, 115
    open-ended questions, 115
    practical considerations, 115
    practice opportunities, 115
    *See also* Assessment
Study Process Questionnaire (SPQ), 1165
Subjectivity, 457, 469, 1022
Subject matter, 1401
Substance use disorder, 211, 224
Substitution, augmentation, modification, and
    redefinition (SAMR) model, 1379
Subsumption theory, 365
Subtractive education, 291
Suicide, 621
    intervention, 65

Summative assessment, 323, 378–379, 836, 957, 1332, 1333, 1346
  authentic assessments, 1338–1340
  challenges, 1348
  integrative papers, 1337–1338
  reliability of, 1344–1345
  student performance, 1340
  traditional exams, 1336–1337
  validity of, 1341–1343
Super Prepared Asian Mother, 685
Supervised clinical practice, 644
Supervision, 646
Support factors, 637
Surfing, 920
Surveillance, 80
Sustainable development goals (SDGs), 1310, 1323
Syllabus review checklist, 1225, 1229
Symbiotic relations, 139
Synchronous/asynchronous learning, 929
Systemic therapy, 36
Systems-level services, 705

**T**

Tactile models, 775
Talking therapy, 37
Target audience, 579
Task
  classification system, 1203
  performance, 1293
  progression, 1215
  switching, 213, 216
Taste perception, 92
Taxonomies, 933, 1313
Teacher(s)
  attitudes, 1083
  behaviors, 1173
  beliefs, 1093
  competences, 811–813, 816, 822
  professionalism, 809
  training, 1084, 1088, 1089, 1092
Teacher Behaviors Checklist (TBC), 1173
Teacher education, 369
  challenges and lessons, 836–839
  competences, 811–818
  core contents, 820
  global social challenges, 810
  PISA, 810
  Professional Standards, 811–818
  teachers' choices, 809
  teaching, learning, and assessment of psychology, 828–836
  topics of psychology programs, 820

Teacher Education Standards, 820
Teachers-in-training, 367
Teachers of Psychology in Secondary Schools (TOPSS), 857, 859, 860, 1164
Teaching, 380–382
  applications, 261–262
  biopsychology, 393, 412
  in community psychology, 736
  and learning of indigenous languages and lifestyle, 752
  methodology, 450, 451
  neuroscience, 405, 410, 411
  skills, 813
  standards, 810, 812, 814, 819
  tips, 121
Teaching and learning qualitative research
  integrated method education, 474–475
  perspectives, 473
  principles, 474
Teaching clinical psychology, 37
  course contents, 42
  engaging classroom activities, 42
  knowledge/skills/expertise, 41
  reciprocal process, 42
  recommendations, 42
  student's learning activities, 41
  Zimbardo's premises, 43
Teaching Goals Inventory (TGI), 1173
Teaching style
  answering and asking questions, 1187, 1188
  class discussion, 1188
  classroom demonstrations, 1189
  effective lecturing, 1186, 1187
Team-based learning (TBL), 375, 774, 922
Team learning, 1286
TechnoGirl, 683
Technological, pedagogical and content knowledge-model (TPACK), 822
Technological skills, 1409
Technology-enhanced learning, 1388
Technology-enhanced psychology learning, 376–377
Telemental health, 640
Telephone
  counseling helplines, 641
  interventions, 641
  services for mental health, 641
Tell-ask instructional strategy, 1215, 1220
Tell instructional event, 1214
Temperament, 519, 520
Temporal discounting, 207, 216
Temporality, 745
Temptation, 203, 208, 213, 216, 217
Tension and uncertainty, 970

Testing effect, 115, 324
Test item review form, 1192
Test-retest reliability, 1341
Test theory, 523
Textbooks, 822
Text mining, 1296
Thayer Conference, 702
The Art of Neuroscience, 783
The Benchmark Evaluation Systems, 362
The creationism of psychology, 103
The Crisis of European Sciences and
 Transcendental Phenomenology, 1124
Theoretical elaboration, 602
Theoretical knowledge, 1391
Theoretical-methodological Foundations
 paradigmatic commonalities, 456–457
 reference points, 456
Theoretical sampling, 457
Theories of behaviorism, 278
Theories of development, 249–252
Theory and practice relationship, 915
Theory-based and evidence-based approaches, 368–371
Theory mapping, 266
Theory of activity, 798–800
Theory of mind, 295
Therapeutic method, 520
Therapeutic narratives, 648
Therapeutic self-efficacy, 41
Therapist characteristics and their influence on therapy, 636
Therapist education, 644
Thermal comfort, 81
The Southeast Asia Teacher Competence Framework (SEA-TCF), 811
The study of learning
 ABA, 104
 awareness, 107
 behaviorist tradition, 103
 CBT, 104
 Darwin theory, 102
 modern scientific, 103
 psychology, 102, 104, 108
 student's perspective, 105
The Varieties of Religious Experience, 1100
Thin ideal media, 611, 620
Think-pair-share, 119
Third wave feminism, 663
Three cross-national categories of SENs, 1079
Time, 597–598
Tips for teaching, 839–841
Top-down influences, 83
Touch metaphor, 86
Touch perception, 92

Traditional exams, 1336–1337
Traditional statistical techniques, 36
Training
 centers and universities, 650
 courses, 931
 for supervision, 646
 models and theories of therapist development, 643
 observation skills, 599–600
 programs for School Psychologists, 708, 709
Traits, 514–516
Trait theories, 521
Transcranial magnetic stimulation, 186, 220
Transcription, 465
Transdisciplinary collaboration, 1316
Transfer, 813, 832, 833
 appropriate processing theory, 184
 tasks, 88
Transformational learning theory, 732
Transnational/multicultural school psychology, 711
Transversal skill school psychologist, 706
Trialogical learning approach (TLA), 1410–1412
Triangulation, 458
Tufts Medical School, 981
Tutorial guided approach, 1211
Tutorial programs, 1393
Tutoring, 1242
Tutor training, 1423
Twitter, 306
 in class participation exercise, 309–310
 in the classroom, 308–309
 online guide, 308
 in physiological psychology course, 306–308, 310
 for sharing course content, 308
 in support of teaching, 306
 student feedback, 309–310
Two-way Interactive Computer Controlled Instructional Television (TICCIT), 1203
Typology of problems, 1240

**U**

U.S. high school psychology, 848
 challenges, 854–856
 course curriculum and instruction, 851–854
 dual enrollment, 852
 history, 849–851
 IEP, 853
 NCSS, 855

U.S. high school psychology (*cont.*)
  non-U.S. psychology teachers, implications for, 858–860
  quality, 850
UK's Health and Care Professions Council (HCPC), 33
Undergraduate research, 325
UnderstandingPrejudice.org, 333
UNICEF, 683
Unified theory, 156
UNIFORM program, 956
United Nation Convention on the Rights of Persons with Disabilities (UNCRPD), 1080
United Nations, 1310
1989 United Nations Convention on the Rights of the Child, 296
United Nations Development Programme (UNDP), 684
Universal Declaration of Ethical Principles for Psychologists, 1322
Universality, 750
US standards and competences for teachers, 811–814

**V**
Validity, 519, 523
Values, 154, 514, 518, 520, 527
Variance, 527, 532
Variants of qualitative interviews, 459–461
Vedas, 281
Video games, 612, 615–617, 619, 621, 622
Videography, 463
Video lesson, 1398
Videos, interactive videos, 1400
Vienna Circle, 1121
Vietnamese Education Sector, 680
Violence and Harassment Convention 2019 of the International Labor Organization (ILO), 686
Violent behavior, 615
Virtual reality (VR), 1396, 1400
Vision
  for action, 81
  for perception, 81
Visual biases, 79
Visual illusions, 90
Viten project, 1275
Vocational education course design and didactics
  evaluation, 931, 932
  experiential learning, 928
  guidance and counseling, 930
  hybrid teaching forms, 929
  inquiry-based learning, 928, 929
  learning culture, 928
  subjects and contents, 931
Vocational education curricula purpose
  learning comprehension change, 914
  learning environment change, 914
  professional world change, 913, 914
  requirements, 915
  social change, 913
Vocational education learning and assessment
  competence development, 923, 924, 927
  optimal development, 921, 922
  personality development, 920, 921
  professional socialization, 919, 920
Vocational education objectives and rationales
  efficiency *vs.* citizenship, 918, 919
  efficiency *vs.* personal growth, 918
  formal *vs.* informal, 916–917
  general *vs.* vocationally specific, 917–918
  theory-based *vs.* practice-integrated, 915–916
Vocational training, 920
Volition, 154
Voluntary actions, 206, 207, 212
Vulnerability, 1029
Vulnerability-stress model/diathesis-stress-model, 34

**W**
Wait time, 1188
Weakness of will, 211, 212, 225
Wealthy nations with migration and poverty, 289
Web-based resources, 305
Web-lectures, E-lectures, 1392
Welfare approach, 671
Well-being, 921, 949, 953, 954
Western counseling and psychotherapy, 630
Western, educated, industrialized, rich and democratic (WEIRD) societies, 743
Western education, 294
Western psychology, 277, 278, 747
What-happens component skill, 1205, 1207, 1208
Whole Brain Atlas, 404
Wholeness, 596
Wilhelm Wundt's and Edward Titchener's introspection, 103
Willpower, 212, 218, 229
Wisconsin Card Sorting task, 215

Wittrock's theory, 1439
Women in Development (WID) approaches, 671
Women's movements, 664
Word-gap' phenomenon, 291
Work 4.0, 929
Work and organizational psychology (WOP), 867, 870, 871, 879
  application orientation, 551
  case study assignment, 554
  competence model, 546
  decision-making, 870
  development of concepts and measures, 549
  diagnostic methods, 549
  discipline program, 871
  fundamental theoretical concepts, 548
  intentional action, 867
  intervention measures, 549
  material and social bases, 874
  model-based analyses, 550
  motivation, 867
  objective conditions, 868
  occupational health and safety, 541
  partial or total transformation, 868
  pedagogical double decker, 556, 558
  performance requirements, 541
  personnel management in organizations, 541
  planning of courses, 560
  project assignment for the project seminar on research-based learning, 555
  psychological and social phenomenon, 870
  psychological concepts and methods, 547
  psychological repercussions, 868
  research approaches, 549
  research methodological approaches, 550
  skills development, 875
  study programs, 548
  supervision, 560
  surrounding material and social reality, 872
  training and development and leadership, 557
  transformation, 872
  vocational training, 869
  work contexts, 869
W/O-Psychology study programs, 548
Work design, 876
Working memory, 207, 214, 215, 217, 224
Work-integrated learning, 893–895
Workplace assessment, 480
World Health Organization (WHO), 611, 782
World report on violence and health: Summary, 661
Wounded healer, 636
Writing assignments, 1182
Written quiz, 1180
Written test, 1180

## X
X-reality systems, 377

## Y
Yoga, 279, 281, 282
Youtube videos, 304, 308

## Z
Zone of proximal development (ZPD), 1287, 1418–1420